Lecture Notes in Computer Science   14008

Founding Editors

Gerhard Goos
Juris Hartmanis

The series Lecture Notes in Computer Science (LNCS), including its subseries Lecture Notes in Artificial Intelligence (LNAI) and Lecture Notes in Bioinformatics (LNBI), has established itself as a medium for the publication of new developments in computer science and information technology research, teaching, and education.

LNCS enjoys close cooperation with the computer science R & D community, the series counts many renowned academics among its volume editors and paper authors, and collaborates with prestigious societies. Its mission is to serve this international community by providing an invaluable service, mainly focused on the publication of conference and workshop proceedings and postproceedings. LNCS commenced publication in 1973.

Carmit Hazay · Martijn Stam
Editors

Advances in Cryptology – EUROCRYPT 2023

42nd Annual International Conference on the Theory
and Applications of Cryptographic Techniques
Lyon, France, April 23–27, 2023
Proceedings, Part V

 Springer

Editors
Carmit Hazay (iD)
Bar-Ilan University
Ramat Gan, Israel

Martijn Stam (iD)
Simula UiB
Bergen, Norway

ISSN 0302-9743   ISSN 1611-3349 (electronic)
Lecture Notes in Computer Science
ISBN 978-3-031-30588-7   ISBN 978-3-031-30589-4 (eBook)
https://doi.org/10.1007/978-3-031-30589-4

This Springer imprint is published by the registered company Springer Nature Switzerland AG
The registered company address is: Gewerbestrasse 11, 6330 Cham, Switzerland

Preface

The 42nd Annual International Conference on the Theory and Applications of Cryptographic Techniques, Eurocrypt 2023, was held in Lyon, France between April 23–27 under the auspices of the International Association for Cryptologic Research. The conference had a record number of 415 submissions, out of which 109 were accepted.

Preparation for the academic aspects of the conference started in earnest well over a year ago, with the selection of a program committee, consisting of 79 regular members and six area chairs. The area chairs played an important part in enabling a high-quality review process; their role was expanded considerably from last year and, for the first time, properly formalized. Each area chair was in charge of moderating the discussions of the papers assigned under their area, guiding PC members and reviewers to consensus where possible, and helping us in making final decisions. We created six areas and assigned the following area chairs: Ran Canetti for Theoretical Foundations; Rosario Gennaro for Public Key Primitives with Advanced Functionalities; Tibor Jager for Classic Public Key Cryptography; Marc Joye for Secure and Efficient Implementation, Cryptographic Engineering, and Real-World Cryptography; Gregor Leander for Symmetric Cryptology; and finally Arpita Patra for Multi-party Computation and Zero-Knowledge.

Prior to the submission deadline, PC members were introduced to the reviewing process; for this purpose we created a slide deck that explained what we expected from everyone involved in the process and how PC members could use the reviewing system (HotCRP) used by us. An important aspect of the reviewing process is the reviewing form, which we modified based on the Crypto'22 form as designed by Yevgeniy Dodis and Tom Shrimpton. As is customary for IACR general conferences, the reviewing process was two-sided anonymous.

Out of the 415 submissions, four were desk rejected due to violations of the Call for Papers (non-anonymous submission or significant deviations from the submission format). For the remaining submissions, the review process proceeded in two stages. In the first stage, every paper was reviewed by at least three reviewers. For 109 papers a clear, negative consensus emerged and an early reject decision was reached and communicated to the authors on the 8th of December 2022. This initial phase of early rejections allowed the program committee to concentrate on the delicate task of selecting a program amongst the more promising submissions, while simultaneously offering the authors of the rejected papers the opportunity to take advantage of the early, full feedback to improve their work for a future occasion.

The remaining 302 papers progressed to an interactive discussion phase, which was open for two weeks (ending slightly before the Christmas break). During this period, the authors had access to their reviews (apart from some PC only fields) and were asked to address questions and requests for clarifications explicitly formulated in the reviews. It gave authors and reviewers the opportunity to communicate directly (yet anonymously) with each other during several rounds of interaction. For some papers, the multiple rounds helped in clarifying both the reviewers' questions and the authors' responses.

For a smaller subset of papers, a second interactive discussion phase took place in the beginning of January allowing authors to respond to new, relevant insights by the PC. Eventually, 109 papers were selected for the program.

The best paper award was granted to the paper "An Efficient Key Recovery Attack on SIDH" by Wouter Castryck and Thomas Decru for presenting the first efficient key recovery attack against the Supersingular Isogeny Diffie-Hellman (SIDH) problem. Two further, related papers were invited to the Journal of Cryptology: "Breaking SIDH in Polynomial Time" by Damien Robert and "A Direct Key Recovery Attack on SIDH" by Luciano Maino, Chloe Martindale, Lorenz Panny, Giacomo Pope and Benjamin Wesolowski.

Accepted papers written exclusively by researchers who were within four years of PhD graduation at the time of submission were eligible for the Early Career Best Paper Award. There were a number of strong candidates and the paper "Worst-Case Subexponential Attacks on PRGs of Constant Degree or Constant Locality" by Akın Ünal was awarded this honor.

The program further included two invited talks: Guy Rothblum opened the program with his talk on "Indistinguishable Predictions and Multi-group Fair Learning" (an extended abstract of his talk appears in these proceedings) and later during the conference Vadim Lyubashevsky gave a talk on "Lattice Cryptography: What Happened and What's Next".

First and foremost, we would like to thank Kevin McCurley and Kay McKelly for their tireless efforts in the background, making the whole process so much smoother for us to run. Thanks also to our previous co-chairs Orr Dunkelman, Stefan Dziembowski, Yevgeniy Dodis, Thomas Shrimpton, Shweta Agrawal and Dongdai Lin for sharing the lessons they learned and allowing us to build on their foundations. We thank Guy and Vadim for accepting to give two excellent invited talks. Of course, no program can be selected without submissions, so we thank both the authors of accepted papers, as well as those whose papers did not make it (we sincerely hope that, notwithstanding the disappointing outcome, you found the reviews and interaction constructive). The reviewing was led by our PC members, who often engaged expert subreviewers to write high-quality, insightful reviews and engage directly in the discussions, and we are grateful to both our PC members and the subreviewers. As the IACR's general conferences grow from year to year, a very special thank you to our area chairs, our job would frankly not have been possible without Ran, Rosario, Tibor, Marc, Gregor, and Arpita's tireless efforts leading the individual papers' discussions. And, last but not least, we would like to thank the general chairs: Damien Stehlé, Alain Passelègue, and Benjamin Wesolowski who worked very hard to make this conference happen.

April 2023

Carmit Hazay
Martijn Stam

Organization

General Co-chairs

Damien Stehlé — ENS de Lyon and Institut Universitaire de France, France

Alain Passelègue — Inria, France

Benjamin Wesolowski — CNRS and ENS de Lyon, France

Program Co-chairs

Carmit Hazay — Bar-Ilan University, Israel

Martijn Stam — Simula UiB, Norway

Area Chairs

Ran Canetti — Boston University, USA
(for Theoretical Foundations)

Rosario Gennaro — Protocol Labs and CUNY, USA
(for Public Key Primitives with Advanced Functionalities)

Tibor Jager — University of Wuppertal, Germany
(for Classic Public Key Cryptography)

Marc Joye — Zama, France
(for Secure and Efficient Implementation, Cryptographic Engineering, and Real-World Cryptography)

Gregor Leander — Ruhr-Universität Bochum, Germany
(for Symmetric Cryptology)

Arpita Patra — Google and IISc Bangalore, India
(for Multi-party Computation and Zero-Knowledge)

Program Committee

Masayuki Abe	NTT Social Informatics Laboratories and Kyoto University, Japan
Adi Akavia	University of Haifa, Israel
Prabhanjan Ananth	UC Santa Barbara, USA
Gilad Asharov	Bar-Ilan University, Israel
Marshall Ball	New York University, USA
Christof Beierle	Ruhr University Bochum, Germany
Mihir Bellare	UC San Diego, USA
Tim Beyne	KU Leuven, Belgium
Andrej Bogdanov	Chinese University of Hong Kong, China
Xavier Bonnetain	Inria, France
Joppe Bos	NXP Semiconductors, Belgium
Chris Brzuska	Aalto University, Finland
Ignacio Cascudo	IMDEA Software Institute, Spain
Nishanth Chandran	Microsoft Research India, India
Chitchanok Chuengsatiansup	The University of Melbourne, Australia
Michele Ciampi	The University of Edinburgh, UK
Ran Cohen	Reichman University, Israel
Jean-Sébastien Coron	University of Luxembourg, Luxembourg
Bernardo David	IT University of Copenhagen, Denmark
Christoph Dobraunig	Intel Labs, Intel Corporation, Hillsboro, USA
Léo Ducas	CWI Amsterdam and Leiden University, Netherlands
Maria Eichlseder	Graz University of Technology, Austria
Pooya Farshim	IOHK and Durham University, UK
Serge Fehr	CWI Amsterdam and Leiden University, Netherlands
Dario Fiore	IMDEA Software Institute, Spain
Pierre-Alain Fouque	Université Rennes 1 and Institut Universitaire de France, France
Steven Galbraith	University of Auckland, New Zealand
Chaya Ganesh	IISc Bangalore, India
Si Gao	Huawei Technologies Co., Ltd., China
Daniel Genkin	GeorgiaTech, USA
Craig Gentry	TripleBlind, USA
Benedikt Gierlichs	KU Leuven, Belgium
Rishab Goyal	UW-Madison, USA
Vipul Goyal	NTT Research and CMU, USA
Viet Tung Hoang	Florida State University, USA
Andreas Hülsing	Eindhoven University of Technology, Netherlands

Antoine Joux	CISPA, Helmholtz Center for Cybersecurity, Germany
Karen Klein	ETH Zurich, Switzerland
Markulf Kohlweiss	University of Edinburgh and IOHK, UK
Jooyoung Lee	KAIST, Korea
Gaëtan Leurent	Inria, France
Shengli Liu	Shanghai Jiao Tong University, China
Yunwen Liu	Cryptape Technology Co., Ltd., China
Stefan Lucks	Bauhaus-Universität Weimar, Germany
Hemanta Maji	Purdue, USA
Alexander May	Ruhr University Bochum, Germany
Nele Mentens	Leiden University, Netherlands and KU Leuven, Belgium
Tal Moran	Reichman University, Israel
Michael Naehrig	Microsoft Research, USA
Ngoc Khanh Nguyen	EPFL, Switzerland
Emmanuela Orsini	Bocconi University, Italy and KU Leuven, Belgium
Jiaxin Pan	NTNU, Norway
Omkant Pandey	Stony Brook University, USA
Anat Paskin-Cherniavsky	Ariel University, Israel
Chris Peikert	University of Michigan and Algorand, Inc., USA
Léo Perrin	Inria, France
Giuseppe Persiano	Università di Salerno, Italy
Thomas Peters	UCLouvain, Belgium
Christophe Petit	Université libre de Bruxelles, Belgium and University of Birmingham, UK
Krzysztof Pietrzak	ISTA, Austria
Bertram Poettering	IBM Research Europe – Zurich, Switzerland
Bart Preneel	KU Leuven, Belgium
Divya Ravi	Aarhus University, Denmark
Christian Rechberger	TU Graz, Austria
Ron Rothblum	Technion, Israel
Carla Ràfols	Universitat Pompeu Fabra, Spain
Paul Rösler	FAU Erlangen-Nürnberg, Germany
Yu Sasaki	NTT Social Informatics Laboratories, NIST Associate, Japan
Dominique Schröder	FAU Erlangen-Nürnberg, Germany
Omri Shmueli	Tel Aviv University, Israel
Janno Siim	Simula UiB, Norway
Daniel Slamanig	AIT Austrian Institute of Technology, Austria
Yifan Song	Tsinghua University, China

Qiang Tang	The University of Sydney, Australia
Serge Vaudenay	EPFL, Switzerland
Fernando Virdia	Intel Labs, Switzerland
Meiqin Wang	Shandong University, China
Mor Weiss	Bar-Ilan University, Israel
David Wu	UT Austin, USA

Additional Reviewers

Behzad Abdolmaleki
Damiano Abram
Hamza Abusalah
Leo Ackermann
Amit Agarwal
Ghous Amjad
Benny Applebaum
Gal Arnon
Thomas Attema
Benedikt Auerbach
Lukas Aumayr
Gennaro Avitabile
Melissa Azouaoui
Saikrishna Badrinarayanan
Karim Baghery
Kunpeng Bai
Shi Bai
David Balbás
Manuel Barbosa
Khashayar Barooti
James Bartusek
Andrea Basso
Balthazar Bauer
Carsten Baum
Michiel van Beirendonck
Josh Benaloh
Fabrice Benhamouda
Ward Beullens
Amit Singh Bhati
Ritam Bhaumik
Alexander Bienstock
Alexander Block
Jonathan Bootle
Cecilia Boschini

Katharina Boudgoust
Christina Boura
Zvika Brakerski
Lennart Braun
Marek Broll
Ileana Buhan
Matteo Campanelli
Federico Canale
Anne Canteaut
Gaëtan Cassiers
Wouter Castryck
Pyrros Chaidos
André Chailloux
T.-H. Hubert Chan
Anirudh Chandramouli
Rohit Chatterjee
Hao Chen
Long Chen
Mingjie Chen
Yanbo Chen
Yanlin Chen
Yilei Chen
Yu Long Chen
Wei Cheng
Céline Chevalier
James Chiang
Wonhee Cho
Wonseok Choi
Wutichai Chongchitmate
Hien Chu
Valerio Cini
Christine Cloostermans
Andrea Coladangelo
Daniel Collins

Sandro Coretti-Drayton
Craig Costello
Elizabeth Crites
Miguel Cueto Noval
Jan-Pieter D'Anvers
Sourav Das
Alex Davidson
Gabrielle De Micheli
Cyprien Delpech de Saint Guilhem
Patrick Derbez
Lalita Devadas
Siemen Dhooghe
Jesus Diaz
Khue Do
Jelle Don
Rafael Dowsley
Avijit Dutta
Sébastien Duval
Christoph Egger
Tariq Elahi
Lynn Engelberts
Felix Engelmann
Muhammed F. Esgin
Thomas Espitau
Andre Esser
Simona Etinski
Prastudy Fauzi
Patrick Felke
Hanwen Feng
Rex Fernando
Tako Boris Fouotsa
Danilo Francati
Sapir Freizeit
Paul Frixons
Rachit Garg
Sanjam Garg
Aymeric Genêt
Marios Georgiou
Satrajit Ghosh
Niv Gilboa
Valerie Gilchrist
Emanuele Giunta
Aarushi Goel
Eli Goldin
Junqing Gong

Alonso González
Lorenzo Grassi
Jiaxin Guan
Zichen Gui
Aurore Guillevic
Aditya Gulati
Aldo Gunsing
Chun Guo
Divya Gupta
Felix Günther
Hosein Hadipour
Mohammad Hajiabadi
Shai Halevi
Peter Hall
Shuai Han
Patrick Harasser
David Heath
Lena Heimberger
Alexandra Henzinger
Julia Hesse
Minki Hhan
Dennis Hofheinz
Maya-Iggy van Hoof
Sam Hopkins
Akinori Hosoyamada
Kristina Hostáková
Martha Norberg Hovd
Yu-Hsuan Huang
Loïs Huguenin-Dumittan
Kathrin Hövelmanns
Yuval Ishai
Muhammad Ishaq
Tetsu Iwata
Michael John Jacobson, Jr.
Aayush Jain
Samuel Jaques
Jinhyuck Jeong
Corentin Jeudy
Ashwin Jha
Mingming Jiang
Zhengzhong Jin
Thomas Johansson
David Joseph
Daniel Jost
Fatih Kaleoglu

Novak Kaluderovic
Chethan Kamath
Shuichi Katsumata
Marcel Keller
John Kelsey
Erin Kenney
Hamidreza Khorasgani
Hamidreza Khoshakhlagh
Seongkwang Kim
Elena Kirshanova
Fuyuki Kitagawa
Bor de Kock
Konrad Kohbrok
Lisa Kohl
Sebastian Kolby
Dimitris Kolonelos
Ilan Komargodski
Yashvanth Kondi
Venkata Koppula
Alexis Korb
Matthias Krause
Hugo Krawczyk
Toomas Krips
Mike Kudinov
Péter Kutas
Thijs Laarhoven
Yi-Fu Lai
Baptiste Lambin
Nathalie Lang
Abel Laval
Laurens Le Jeune
Byeonghak Lee
Changmin Lee
Eysa Lee
Seunghoon Lee
Sihyun Lee
Dominik Leichtle
Jannis Leuther
Shai Levin
Chaoyun Li
Yanan Li
Yiming Li
Xiao Liang
Jyun-Jie Liao
Benoît Libert

Wei-Kai Lin
Yao-Ting Lin
Helger Lipmaa
Eik List
Fukang Liu
Jiahui Liu
Qipeng Liu
Xiangyu Liu
Chen-Da Liu-Zhang
Satya Lokam
Alex Lombardi
Patrick Longa
George Lu
Jinyu Lu
Xianhui Lu
Yuan Lu
Zhenliang Lu
Ji Luo
You Lyu
Reinhard Lüftenegger
Urmila Mahadev
Mohammad Mahmoody
Mohammad Mahzoun
Christian Majenz
Nikolaos Makriyannis
Varun Maram
Laurane Marco
Ange Martinelli
Daniel Masny
Noam Mazor
Matthias Meijers
Fredrik Meisingseth
Florian Mendel
Bart Mennink
Simon-Philipp Merz
Tony Metger
Pierre Meyer
Brice Minaud
Kazuhiko Minematsu
Victor Mollimard
Tomoyuki Morimae
Nicky Mouha
Tamer Mour
Marcel Nageler
Mridul Nandi

María Naya-Plasencia
Patrick Neumann
Hai Nguyen
Ky Nguyen
Phong Q. Nguyen
Ryo Nishimaki
Olga Nissenbaum
Anca Nitulescu
Ariel Nof
Julian Nowakowski
Adam O'Neill
Sai Lakshmi Bhavana Obbattu
Miyako Ohkubo
Eran Omri
Claudio Orlandi
Michele Orrù
Elisabeth Oswald
Omer Paneth
Guillermo Pascual-Perez
Kenneth G. Paterson
Sikhar Patranabis
Alice Pellet-Mary
Maxime Plancon
Antigoni Polychroniadou
Alexander Poremba
Bernardo Portela
Eamonn Postlethwaite
Emmanuel Prouff
Kirthivaasan Puniamurthy
Octavio Pérez Kempner
Luowen Qian
Tian Qiu
Willy Quach
Håvard Raddum
Srinivasan Raghuraman
Justin Raizes
Sebastian Ramacher
Hugues Randriambololona
Shahram Rasoolzadeh
Simon Rastikian
Joost Renes
Nicolas Resch
Alfredo Rial Duran
Doreen Riepel
Silvia Ritsch

Melissa Rossi
Mike Rosulek
Yann Rotella
Lawrence Roy
Roozbeh Sarenche
Amirreza Sarencheh
Pratik Sarkar
Arish Sateesan
Christian Schaffner
Carl Richard Theodor Schneider
Markus Schofnegger
Peter Scholl
André Schrottenloher
Gregor Seiler
Sruthi Sekar
Nicolas Sendrier
Meghna Sengupta
Jinrui Sha
Akash Shah
Siamak Shahandashti
Moni Shahar
Shahed Sharif
Laura Shea
Abhi Shelat
Yaobin Shen
Sina Shiehian
Jad Silbak
Alice Silverberg
Luisa Siniscalchi
Tomer Solomon
Karl Southern
Nicholas Spooner
Sriram Sridhar
Srivatsan Sridhar
Akshayaram Srinivasan
François-Xavier Standaert
Uri Stemmer
Lukas Stennes
Patrick Steuer
Christoph Striecks
Patrick Struck
Chao Sun
Erkan Tairi
Akira Takahashi
Abdullah Talayhan

Titouan Tanguy
Stefano Tessaro
Emmanuel Thomé
Sri AravindaKrishnan Thyagarajan
Yan Bo Ti
Mehdi Tibouchi
Tyge Tiessen
Bénédikt Tran
Andreas Trügler
Daniel Tschudi
Aleksei Udovenko
Jonathan Ullman
Dominique Unruh
Vinod Vaikuntanathan
Daniele Venturi
Michiel Verbauwhede
Javier Verbel
Gilles Villard
Mikhail Volkhov
Satyanarayana Vusirikala
Benedikt Wagner
Roman Walch
Hendrik Waldner
Alexandre Wallet
Michael Walter
Mingyuan Wang
Yuyu Wang
Florian Weber
Hoeteck Wee
Puwen Wei
Charlotte Weitkaemper

Weiqiang Wen
Benjamin Wesolowski
Daniel Wichs
Wessel van Woerden
Ke Wu
Keita Xagawa
Hanshen Xiao
Jiayu Xu
Yingfei Yan
Xiuyu Ye
Kevin Yeo
Eylon Yogev
Albert Yu
Aaram Yun
Alexandros Zacharakis
Thomas Zacharias
Michal Zajac
Greg Zaverucha
Runzhi Zeng
Cong Zhang
Lei Zhang
Ren Zhang
Xinrui Zhang
Yuqing Zhao
Yu Zhou
Dionysis Zindros
Giorgos Zirdelis
Lukas Zobernig
Arne Tobias Ødegaard
Morten Øygarden

Sponsoring Institutions

- Platinum Sponsor: Université Rennes 1 and PEPR Quantique, Zama
- Gold Sponsor: Apple, Cryptolab, ENS de Lyon, ENS PSL, Huawei, Sandbox AQ, Thales, TII
- Silver Sponsor: Algorand Foundation, ANSSI, AWS, PQShield
- Bronze Sponsor: Cosmian, CryptoExperts, CryptoNext Security, IBM, Idemia, Inria, LIP

Contents – Part V

Signature Schemes

Cryptographic Protocols

Unique-Path Identity Based Encryption with Applications to Strongly Secure Messaging

Paul Rösler[1]([✉]) [iD], Daniel Slamanig[2] [iD], and Christoph Striecks[2] [iD]

[1] FAU Erlangen-Nürnberg, Erlangen, Germany
paul.roesler@fau.de
[2] AIT Austrian Institute of Technology, Vienna, Austria
{daniel.slamanig,christoph.striecks}@ait.ac.at

Abstract. *Hierarchical Identity Based Encryption* (HIBE) is a well studied, versatile tool used in many cryptographic protocols. Yet, since the performance of all known HIBE constructions is broadly considered prohibitive, some real-world applications avoid relying on HIBE at the expense of security. A prominent example for this is secure messaging: *Strongly secure* messaging protocols are provably equivalent to *Key-Updatable Key Encapsulation Mechanisms* (KU-KEMs; Balli et al., Asiacrypt 2020); so far, all KU-KEM constructions rely on *adaptive unbounded*-depth HIBE (Poettering and Rösler, Jaeger and Stepanovs, both CRYPTO 2018). By weakening security requirements for better efficiency, many messaging protocols dispense with using HIBE.

In this work, we aim to gain *better efficiency without sacrificing security*. For this, we observe that applications like messaging only need a restricted variant of HIBE for strong security. This variant, that we call *Unique-Path* Identity Based Encryption (UPIBE), restricts HIBE by requiring that each secret key can delegate at most one subordinate secret key. However, in contrast to fixed secret key delegation in Forward-Secure Public Key Encryption, the delegation in UPIBE, as in HIBE, is uniquely determined by variable identity strings from an exponentially large space. We investigate this mild but surprisingly effective restriction and show that it offers substantial complexity and performance advantages.

More concretely, we generically build *bounded-depth* UPIBE from only *bounded-collusion IBE* in the standard model; and we generically build *adaptive unbounded*-depth UPIBE from only *selective bounded-depth* HIBE in the random oracle model. These results significantly extend the range of underlying assumptions and efficient instantiations. We conclude with a rigorous performance evaluation of our UPIBE design. Beyond solving challenging open problems by reducing complexity and improving efficiency of KU-KEM and strongly secure messaging protocols, we offer a new definitional perspective on the bounded-collusion setting.

The full version [38] of this article is available in the IACR eprint archive as article 2023/248, at https://eprint.iacr.org/2023/248.

C. Hazay and M. Stam (Eds.): EUROCRYPT 2023, LNCS 14008, pp. 3–34, 2023.
https://doi.org/10.1007/978-3-031-30589-4_1

1   Introduction

Traditionally, Hierarchical Identity Based Encryption (HIBE) [21,29] is motivated by a real-world scenario in which a sender wants to securely encrypt a message to a receiver without knowing their individual public key. Using a global main *public* key as well as a string that identifies the receiver (e.g., their email address bob@pc.2023.ec.iacr.org), the sender can encrypt the message via (H)IBE. To decrypt a ciphertext, the receiver can obtain their individual secret key by requesting delegation from the global main *secret* key. The hierarchy in HIBE provides a fine grained, leveled delegation: the secret key of bob@pc.2023.ec.iacr.org is delegated from secret key of pc.2023.ec.iacr. org which proceeds up to delegation from secret key of org. Thereby, each secret key can only delegate secret keys of subordinate identities. For the specific case of Identity Based Encryption (IBE) [7,41], only the global main secret key can delegate identity-specific secret keys, which reduces the level depth to 1.

HIBE AS A POWERFUL BUILDING BLOCK. Independent of this real-world use case, HIBE turns out to be a versatile, powerful tool in the design of larger cryptographic protocols. For example, HIBE is used as the main component in designs of Broadcast Encryption (BE) [13], Forward-Secure Public Key Encryption (FS-PKE) [8], Puncturable FS-PKE [25], 0-RTT Key Exchange with Forward Secrecy [12,27], and Key-Updatable Key Encapsulation Mechanisms (KU-KEM) for Ratcheted Key Exchange (RKE) [37]. In most of these cases, the reason for relying on HIBE is rather the strength of HIBE secret key delegation than the traditional motivation of encrypting messages to an identity whose individual public key is unknown.

Notably, not all of these constructions utilize the full power of standard HIBE. For instance, FS-PKE can be based on relaxed Binary-Tree Encryption (BTE) [8,33]. Furthermore, KU-KEM constructions [3,30,32,37] only delegate secret keys along a single path of identities.

INTRODUCING UNIQUE-PATH IBE. Motivated by such restricted delegations, we introduce the notion of *Unique-Path Identity Based Encryption* (UPIBE). As in HIBE, UPIBE allows a sender to encrypt messages to a receiver whose individual public key is unknown by using only a string that specifies the receiver's identity as well as a global main public key. On the receiver side, UPIBE assumes that a secret key in one level delegates at most one secret key of the subjacent level. In contrast to FS-PKE, unique-path delegation in UPIBE still respects identity (sub-)strings from an exponential size string space on each level. Consequently, a receiver with email address bob@pc.2023.ec.iacr.org cannot decrypt ciphertexts encrypted to identity charlie@pc.2023.ec.iacr.org. Beyond the cryptographic utility, there are real-world examples for such a unique-path delegation behavior in linear vertical or horizontal hierarchies.[1]

One perspective on UPIBE could be that it lifts the bounded-collusion setting from IBE [15] to HIBE by restricting adversaries in corrupting at most one

---

[1] E.g., the chronological succession of presidents in a particular state or a ranking list that results from a competition.

delegated secret key in the identity hierarchy. Instead, we view the characteristic of UPIBE complementary or even orthogonal to the bounded-collusion setting: While bounded collusion means that the overall number of corrupted secret keys is limited, UPIBE limits the number of delegations—and, hence, corruptions— structurally *per delegated secret key*. In the specific case of *UPIBE*, we permit one delegation per secret key, but this can be extended to two or more delegations per secret key. Indeed, one of our results motivates research on HIBE with *at most two delegations* per secret key (see Sect. 4), which we leave as a question for future work and concentrate on UPIBE here.

UPIBE AS AN ABSTRACTION OF KU-KEM. In the context of strongly secure messaging, many cryptographic protocols use a building block called Key-Updatable Key Encapsulation Mechanism (KU-KEM) [3,30,32,37]. This extended form of standard KEM provides an update mechanism with which public keys and secret keys can be updated independently with respect to arbitrary bit strings. In addition to the security guarantees of a standard KEM, updates in KU-KEM are required to achieve *forward-secrecy* and *effective divergence*. This means that an updated secret key cannot decrypt ciphertexts directed to prior versions of the secret key; and an incompatibly updated secret key cannot decrypt ciphertexts produced with a corresponding (incompatible) public key.

The only known construction of KU-KEM relies on black-box HIBE with *unbounded hierarchy depth* secure against *adaptive adversaries* [3,30,32,37]. This induces a significant performance penalty and limits the choice of underlying assumptions (e.g., no practical[2] unbounded-depth HIBE from lattices is known). Intuitively, KU-KEM secret key updates are realized via sequential HIBE delegations. Replacing black-box HIBE in this construction by black-box UPIBE is trivial. Thus, using a black-box HIBE scheme to realize UPIBE is henceforth referred to as *trivial UPIBE construction*. By introducing UPIBE as a more general notion for KU-KEM, we are the first to lift this specific tool to a suitable abstraction and reduce the power of (underlying) HIBE to the essential. As we will see, this also allows for a substantial gain in efficiency.

DEFINITIONS AND CONSTRUCTIONS OF SECURE MESSAGING. KU-KEM was developed as a building block for constructions of secure messaging protocols.Interestingly, the impractical performance of prior KU-KEM constructions even affected security definitions in the messaging literature. These definitions can be divided into two categories: (1) those that require *full security* with respect to the modeled threats and (2) those that *relax the security requirements* by limiting adversarial power. Generally, relaxed definitions allow for more efficient constructions. Specifically, the majority of fully secure messaging protocols relies on KU-KEM [3,30,32,37], whereas the main motivation for relaxing security definitions was to analyze or develop practical protocols that can dispense with employing KU-KEM for better efficiency [2,18,31]. To emphasize and sub-

---

[2] We stress that the construction of selective-secure HIBE with unbounded delegations from CDH [17] or from any fully secure IBE [16] is an impressive, yet rather theoretic result.

stantiate this partition of the literature, Balli et al. [3] proved that KU-KEM is equivalent to fully secure messaging under weak randomness. We conclude that KU-KEM and, therefore, UPIBE play a central role in (strongly) secure messaging.

EFFICIENCY OF UPIBE AND KU-KEM. The inefficiency of the trivial KU-KEM construction from black-box HIBE leads to two questions that were posed as open problems in prior work [3,30,37] and which we will address via the UPIBE approach:

(1) Can we build (KU-KEM from) UPIBE based on weaker assumptions?
(2) Can we build (KU-KEM from) UPIBE with better efficiency?

We are the first to affirm both questions in three steps.But instead of only giving answers for the specific case of KU-KEM, we generalize it to the UPIBE setting which highlights the reasons for our improvements.

First, we consider bounded-depth UPIBE, which means that the maximal number of secret-key delegation levels is bounded a priori. Our generic construction of bounded-depth UPIBE is based on *bounded-collusion IBE*, for which we have practical instantiations from standard assumptions like DDH or QR in the standard model [15,23,42].[3] In a second step, we extend the design of our bounded-depth UPIBE construction to obtain an unbounded-depth UPIBE scheme. This unbounded-depth UPIBE construction with adaptive security can be based on *bounded-depth* HIBE with only *selective* security in the random oracle model. Finally, we prove that KU-KEM can be based on UPIBE, where the number of key updates in KU-KEM is proportionate to the number of key delegations in UPIBE.

Instantiating our unbounded-depth UPIBE construction with the bounded-depth HIBE by Boneh et al. [5] reveals the strengths of our approach. We compare this instantiation to the best known instantiation of *trivial* unbounded-depth UPIBE via the unbounded-depth HIBE by Gong et al. [24]. This comparison shows that our construction is significantly more efficient by most relevant measures. In particular, it outperforms the trivial approach substantially in terms of performance, ciphertext sizes, and encryption key sizes.

A notable feature of our unbounded-depth UPIBE construction is that its efficiency can be dynamically configured via a parameter ε. Roughly, ε trades ciphertext size against secret key size. Depending on the performance priorities in a setting (bandwidth, algorithm runtime, etc.) and depending on the expected user behavior (average length of identity strings, average number of encryptions per identity, etc.), this parameter can optimize our construction for deployment under various conditions. Setting the parameter ε to infinity yields the known trivial UPIBE construction [30,37]; consequently, there always exists an ε for which our new UPIBE construction is indeed the best known one.

---

[3] An alternative approach from standard assumptions would be to rely on the fully secure IBE from CDH by Garg and Döttling [17]. Unfortunately, this will not yield a practical instantiation.

CONTRIBUTIONS. Our first contribution is to abstract the tools in KU-KEM constructions to the more general field of Identity Based Encryption by, simultaneously, reducing the power of standard HIBE to the essential: Unique-Path IBE. Our definition from Sect. 2 shows that this new perspective on structurally limited delegation and collusion is seamlessly embedded in existing (H)IBE notions.

For comprehensibility, we start with building the simpler bounded-depth UPIBE construction in Sect. 3, which is secure in the standard model (StM):

Adaptive Bounded-Collusion IBE $\implies$ StM Adaptive Bounded-Depth UPIBE

This construction shows that UPIBE can be based on significantly reduced complexity assumptions with a practically (see Footnote 2) relevant design. We also give a concrete instantiation with small ciphertexts (two group elements) and secret keys (six group elements and one symmetric key) from DDH that takes advantage of construction internals of a bounded-collusion IBE by Dodis et al. [15].

By developing two powerful extensions on top of our first generic UPIBE construction, we are ultimately able to build unbounded-depth UPIBE:

Adaptive Bounded-Depth HIBE $\implies$ StM Adaptive Unbounded-Depth UPIBE

While conceptually inheriting core ideas of our *bounded*-depth UPIBE, this second *unbounded*-depth UPIBE construction in Sect. 4 unfolds the full strength of our approach. Its efficiency is dynamically configurable for different deployment settings and, instantiated with the most suitable bounded-depth selective HIBE [5], it reaches the best performance results compared to existing work. Along the way, inspired by techniques that turn *selective* secure bounded-depth HIBEs *adaptive* secure [4,5], we develop a guessing technique which allows for a significantly broader choice of underlying assumptions and more efficient instantiations in the random oracle model (ROM):

Selective Bounded-Depth HIBE $\implies$ ROM Adaptive Unbounded-Depth UPIBE

We note that when instantiating our construction with lattice HIBEs [1,10], we obtain the first KU-KEM secure under conjectured post-quantum assumptions.

We systematically analyze the performance of our approach when being used to instantiate KU-KEM in Sect. 7. It is notable that all prior KU-KEM constructions are a trivial special case of our new techniques. This means that our new constructions always offer the best (known) performance. For clarity, we first present semantically secure constructions of UPIBE. Using techniques known from KEM combiners [22], we show in Sect. 5 that our constructions can also be made secure against chosen-ciphertext attacks if the underlying (H)IBE schemes are.

1.1 Technical Overview

To understand the core idea of our UPIBE constructions, we briefly discuss the subtle difference between the security definitions of standard HIBE and UPIBE.

Although these definitions are conceptually identical, the crucial limitation of UPIBE is that at most one delegation per secret key is permitted. This means that the large tree of delegated secret keys in HIBE is reduced to a unique delegation path in UPIBE. Consequently, adversaries will essentially expose at most one UPIBE secret key—all descendant UPIBE keys can be obtained via delegation by the adversary itself. Consider the identity string that corresponds to this exposed UPIBE secret key. In relation to this identity string, our natural security definition requires only two types of challenge ciphertexts to remain secure: (1) those that are encrypted to *true prefix* identity strings and (2) those that are encrypted to identity strings *branching off* the exposed key's identity string. All remaining challenges can be solved trivially with the exposed secret key. Our UPIBE constructions exploit this fact to turn all prefix identity strings (case 1) into branched off identity strings (case 2) by adding a special suffix at the end of every UPIBE identity string.

COMBINED HIBE EXPOSURE. Having the definitional difference in mind, we will see that multiple colluding exposures in HIBE can be significantly more damaging than the single permitted exposure in UPIBE. More concretely, HIBE constructions have to make sure that challenge ciphertexts remain secure under *any combination* of (non-trivial) secret key exposures in the delegation hierarchy. Since the unique-path delegation in UPIBE permits at most *one exposure*, UPIBE constructions have to protect challenge ciphertexts only against the single most damaging secret key exposure. We illustrate this gap by considering the effect of a specific combination of HIBE secret key exposures.

For this we let two exposed HIBE secret keys have identities $id_{ex,1} = (id_1')$ and $id_{ex,2} = (id_1, id_2')$, and a single HIBE challenge have identity $id_{ch} = (id_1, id_2)$, such that $id_1, id_1', id_2, id_2' \in \{0,1\}^\lambda$, where λ is the bit-length per delegated sub-identity string. This means, $id_{ex,2}$ and id_{ch} branch in delegation level 2 with $id_2' \neq id_2$, and $id_{ex,1}$ branches off the former two identity strings in level 1 with $id_1' \neq id_1$. Observe that the exposed key with identity $id_{ex,1}$ still contains information for delegating subordinate keys to the second level, e.g., to sub-identity id_2 which results in full identity $id^* = (id_1', id_2)$. In contrast, the exposed key with identity $id_{ex,2}$ does not (need to) contain this information anymore as it is delegated to level 2 already. However, exposed key with identity $id_{ex,2}$ may contain information about its own delegation path along the first level with sub-identity string id_1, which differs from the information contained in exposed key with identity $id_{ex,1} = (id_1')$. One major difficulty for building HIBE is to make sure that the information about delegation along id_1 from exposed key $id_{ex,2}$ cannot be combined harmfully with the secrets available for delegation to level 2 from exposed key $id_{ex,1}$. In particular, this combination should not suffice to obtain a secret key for identity $(id_1, id_2) = id_{ch}$ because this would solve the challenge. Since the single permitted exposure in UPIBE prevents such combined exposures, we can simplify the design of our UPIBE constructions, which makes them more efficient. We stress that this difference between HIBE and UPIBE is an inevitable implication of our natural definition.

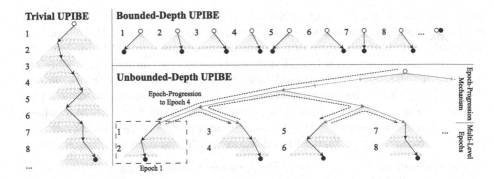

Fig. 1. Conceptual illustration of delegations in the trivial, bounded-depth, and unbounded-depth UPIBE constructions (here with $\varepsilon = 2$). The black (path of) arrows realize delegation of a UPIBE identity string with level depth 8. Light gray arrows indicate alternative and further delegations. White circles represent the (composed) main public key(s) and filled dots represent the (composed) delegated secret key(s).

BOUNDED-DEPTH UPIBE. One interpretation of the above observation is that our constructions can assume key material for lower level delegations to be per se harmless. Using this guarantee, our bounded-depth UPIBE construction implements each UPIBE delegation level with an individual IBE instance. Intuitively, this turns the vertical delegation path into a horizontal delegation sequence, as illustrated in Fig. 1. Our construction's UPIBE main public and secret key consist of all underlying IBE instances' main public and secret keys, respectively. For encryption, the UPIBE identity string is split into multiple IBE sub-strings. The UPIBE ciphertext is then obtained by executing IBE encryption for each level's sub-string and concatenating the resulting IBE ciphertexts. On UPIBE delegation, the respective level's IBE main secret key is removed after delegating an identity-specific secret key for that level. To prove security of this construction, we use the fact that every challenge identity branches off the exposed key's identity in one of it's passed delegation levels. Our reduction embeds an underlying IBE challenge in this branching level, which turns a successful UPIBE adversary into a successful IBE adversary. The above description of our scheme is highly simplified and neglects subtle enhancements that lead to better performance. Although conceptually simple in the bounded-depth case, this construction does not extend (trivially) to the unbounded-depth setting.

UNBOUNDED-DEPTH UPIBE. Therefore, we develop two crucial extensions: First, we replace each delegation level by an ε-level delegation epoch. In every such epoch, ε many sequential delegations can be processed. (See Fig. 1 where $\varepsilon = 2$.) This reduces the number of concatenated ciphertexts by a factor of $1/\varepsilon$. Then, we add an epoch-progression mechanism on top of our construction. With this mechanism, delegation from a fully-delegated epoch progresses dynamically to the next fresh epoch. This allows us to dispose of the static list of IBE instances from our bounded-depth construction. One can think of the epoch-progression mechanism as a Forward-Secure PKE scheme that generates at every step a fresh starting point for a multi-level epoch in which the actual UPIBE delegations are conducted. The security proof for our unbounded-depth UPIBE follows the same idea as the one for our bounded-depth construction, only that it reduces to bounded-depth HIBE. To rely on only *selective* bounded-depth HIBE, we develop a special guessing technique that avoids the exponential loss factor induced by known techniques [4,5] for turning selective HIBE adaptive secure. We believe that the solid design—in addition to its enhanced performance—makes our construction attractive for practical applications (such as secure messengers).

CHOSEN-CIPHERTEXT SECURITY. We investigate the options to obtain CCA security for UPIBE. Unfortunately, the well known generic BCHK (often also called CHK) compiler for HIBEs [6,9] is not applicable to UPIBE. While opting for a form of verification-by-re-encryption akin to the Fujisaki-Okamoto (FO) transform [19] is applicable, one introduces significant computational overhead as well as is bound to the ROM. Instead, we leverage chosen-ciphertext security of the underlying building blocks by effectively tying together the concatenated ciphertexts in every UPIBE ciphertext. For simplicity, we referred to UPIBE as a *Message Encryption* primitive so far, but all our results actually consider *Key Encapsulation*. Therefore, in the case of bounded-depth UPIBE we can make use of techniques developed in the context of KEM combiners [22]. These versatile techniques only change the final computation of the encapsulated UPIBE key instead of explicitly authenticating the concatenated ciphertext. A similar idea, though in the ROM, can be applied in the case of unbounded-depth UPIBE where the underlying HIBE instances can be efficiently made CCA secure via the BCHK compiler. As a result, our chosen-ciphertext secure constructions are only minimally less efficient than our semantically secure ones.

2   UPIBE Definition

For clarity, we consider Identity Based *Key Encapsulation* primitives instead of Identity Based *Message Encryption* in this work. In line with this, we call public and secret keys *encapsulation* and *decapsulation* keys, respectively. Since Unique-Path IBE is a special case of Hierarchical IBE, we introduce all relevant IBE notions modularly at once.

Syntax. All of the considered *Identity Based Encapsulation* (IBE) schemes are quadruples $IE = (IE.gen, IE.enc, IE.dec, IE.del)$ of algorithms with encapsulation and decapsulation key spaces $\mathcal{EK}$ and $\mathcal{DK}$, respectively, symmetric key space $\mathcal{K}$, and ciphertext space $\mathcal{C}$.

We specify the considered types of IBE via parameters L, λ, and D. L fixes the maximal number of *sequential* delegations (i.e., the maximal number of levels aka. The *depth*), λ fixes the bit-length of identity strings for each delegation, and D fixes the maximal number of delegations *per* decapsulation key. That means, for unbounded-depth HIBE we have $(L, D) = (\infty, 2^{\lambda})$, for bounded-depth HIBE we have $(L, D) = (L, 2^{\lambda})$ for some fixed value L, for unbounded-depth UPIBE we have $(\mathsf{L}, \mathsf{D}) = (\infty, 1)$, and for bounded-depth UPIBE we have $(\mathsf{L}, \mathsf{D}) = (L, 1)$ for some fixed value L. We treat bounded-collusion IBE as a bounded-depth HIBE with $\mathsf{L} = 1$ such that the number of colluding users is encoded as the number of maximal delegations for the main decapsulation key $\mathsf{D} = D$ for some constant D.

The four IBE algorithms' syntax is defined as follows:

- IE.gen : $\emptyset \to_\$ \mathcal{EK} \times \mathcal{DK}$
- IE.enc : $\mathcal{EK} \times \{0,1\}^{l \cdot \lambda} \to_\$ \mathcal{C} \times \mathcal{K}$, where $0 < l \le \mathsf{L}$
- IE.dec : $\mathcal{DK} \times \mathcal{C} \to \mathcal{K}$
- IE.del : $\mathcal{DK} \times \{0,1\}^\lambda \to_\$ \mathcal{DK}$

For efficiency reasons, we add derivation algorithm IE.der : $\mathcal{EK} \times \{0,1\}^\lambda \to_\$$ $\mathcal{EK}$ that computes (compact) identity-specific encapsulation keys. This allows for reducing the combined size of a main encapsulation key ek and a multi-level identity string $id = (id_1, \ldots, id_l)$, such that IE.enc$(ek, (id_1, \ldots, id_l))$ can be turned into IE.enc(IE.der($\ldots$ IE.der(ek, id_1) $\ldots, id_l$), ϵ).

Correctness. For correctness of all considered types of IBE with parameters L, λ, and D, we require for all $(ek, dk_0) \leftarrow_\$ $ IE.gen, all $id = (id_1, \ldots, id_l)$ with $id_i \in \{0,1\}^\lambda, 0 < i \le l \le \mathsf{L}$, all $dk_i \leftarrow_\$ $ IE.del(dk_{i-1}, id_i), and all $(c, k) \leftarrow_\$ $ IE.enc(ek, id), that IE.dec$(dk_l, c) = k$.

Security. We define experiment $\mathrm{IND}_{\mathrm{IE}}^b(\mathcal{A}), b \in \{0,1\}$ that models multi-instance key indistinguishability. For all considered types of IBE schemes IE, this experiment provides the following oracles to adversary $\mathcal{A}$ for which we provide a full pseudo-code specification in the full version [38] :

- Gen: **Generates** a fresh main key pair $(ek, dk) \leftarrow_\$ $ IE.gen and returns ek
- Del(i, id, id^*): **Delegates** decapsulation key $dk_{i,(id,id^*)} \leftarrow_\$ $ IE.del$(dk_{i,id}, id^*)$ from $dk_{i,id}$ with identity string $id^* \in \{0,1\}^\lambda$, unless $dk_{i,id}$ results from L sequential delegations from a main decapsulation key, or D delegations from $dk_{i,id}$ were already queried
- Chall(i, id): Issues a **challenge** encapsulation $(c, k_0) \leftarrow_\$ $ IE.enc(ek_i, id) to main encapsulation key ek_i and identity string $id \in \{0,1\}^{l \cdot \lambda}, 0 < l \le \mathsf{L}$ and returns c as well as key k_b, where $k_1 \leftarrow_\$ \mathcal{K}$, unless an exposed decapsulation key was delegated from ek_i's main decapsulation key dk_i with an identity string that equals or is a prefix of id
- Exp(i, id): **Exposes** decapsulation key $dk_{i,id}$, generated or delegated from main decapsulation key dk_i and identity string id, unless a challenge encapsulation to ek_i and identity string id' was queried, such that (ek_i, dk_i) form a main key pair and id equals or is a prefix of id'

Eventually, the adversary terminates by outputting a guess b' and wins iff $b = b'$.

If adversary $\mathcal{A}$ specifies the challenge(s) at the beginning of the game without adaptively seeing the return values of other queries, we call $\mathcal{A}$ **selective** and otherwise **adaptive**.

With the above adversarial oracles, we capture **chosen-plaintext** attacks. Selective chosen-plaintext attacks is a rather weak adversary model that helps us focusing on the core of our novel ideas when presenting our constructions. Yet, we also present adaptive **chosen-ciphertext** secure constructions. An adversary, attacking such constructions, can additionally query the following oracle:

– $\mathrm{Dec}(i, id, c)$: **Decapsulates** $k \leftarrow \mathrm{IE.dec}(dk_{i,id}, c)$ of ciphertext c under $dk_{i,id}$ and returns k, unless c was given to $\mathcal{A}$ as a challenge encapsulation to ek_i and id, $dk_{i,id}$ was (sequentially) delegated from dk_i with respect to id, and (ek_i, dk_i) form a main key pair

Definition 1. *The advantage of adversary* $\mathcal{A}$ *in winning* $\mathrm{IND}_{\mathrm{IE}}^{b}$ *is* $\mathrm{Adv}_{\mathrm{IE}}^{\mathrm{ind}}(\mathcal{A}) := \left| \Pr[\mathrm{IND}_{\mathrm{IE}}^{0}(\mathcal{A}) = 1] - \Pr[\mathrm{IND}_{\mathrm{IE}}^{1}(\mathcal{A}) = 1] \right|.$

Compared to standard (bounded-depth) (H)IBE security experiments, the only difference is our restriction to at most D delegation queries per decapsulation key. Yet, challenges can be queried without limiting the choice of identity strings, even for UPIBE.

3 Bounded-Depth UPIBE from Bounded-Collusion IBE

We present our bounded-depth UPIBE construction in Fig. 2 by explaining its components one after another, starting with decapsulation keys and ciphertexts.

Structure of Keys and Ciphertexts. The core idea behind our UPIBE constructions is that delegations along the unique 'vertical' path of identity levels are realized 'horizontally'. That means, for each delegation level in our UPIBE construction from Fig. 2 with bounded-depth L, we use a separate bounded-collusion IBE instance. Think of these IBE instances being placed horizontally next to one another from left to right as shown in Fig. 1.

To understand this idea, we describe the structure of UPIBE decapsulation keys. A *UPIBE* decapsulation key delegated to level l contains three different types of keys, two of which are *IBE* decapsulation keys: (1) One *ordinary delegated* IBE decapsulation key for *each* of the first l levels, (2) an additional *special delegated* IBE decapsulation key for *only* level l, and (3) a symmetric *forwarding* key from which (*un-delegated*) IBE main decapsulation keys for all remaining $L - l$ levels are computed. See Fig. 2 lines 02–06 for UPIBE key generation that consists of generating all IBE main encapsulation keys and sampling the initial symmetric forwarding key.

A UPIBE ciphertext, encapsulated to level l (i.e., to identity $id \in \{0,1\}^{l \cdot \lambda}$), consists of one IBE ciphertext for each of the first $l - 1$ levels encoded with suffix 1 (lines 23–25) and one additional IBE ciphertext that targets the special delegated IBE decapsulation key at level l encoded with suffix 0 (line 26). To decapsulate the former $l - 1$ ciphertexts (lines 33–34), the receiver needs to be in possession of the first $l - 1$ ordinary delegated IBE decapsulation keys. Hence, successful decapsulation shows that the receiver holds a UPIBE decapsulation key that was correctly delegated along the first $l-1$ levels of the identity path. By also being able to decapsulate the special lth IBE ciphertext (lines 35–36), the

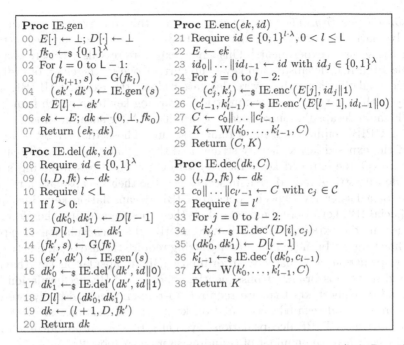

Fig. 2. Construction of bounded-depth UPIBE IE with parameters $(\mathsf{L}, \lambda, \mathsf{D} = 1)$ from PRG G and bounded-collusion IBE scheme IE′ with parameters $(\mathsf{L}', \lambda', \mathsf{D}') = (1, \lambda + 1, 2)$ and ciphertext space $\mathcal{C}$. Core function W is realized as XOR-sum $\bigoplus_{j=0}^{l-1} k'_j$ and ignores input C. In our chosen-ciphertext secure instantiation, we additionally generate a dummy ciphertext $\hat{c} \leftarrow_\$ \mathcal{C}$ and key $\hat{k} \leftarrow_\$ \mathcal{K}$ in IE.gen, which is included into ek and W to pad all unused indices $i \leq \mathsf{L}$ with $\hat{c}$ and $\hat{k}$ respectively.

receiver additionally shows that it holds the full UPIBE decapsulation key that was delegated along all l levels—and particularly not a UPIBE decapsulation key that was delegated along an *extended* identity path.

While a UPIBE ciphertext is a concatenation of all l IBE ciphertexts, the encapsulated UPIBE key is an XOR-sum of all l encapsulated IBE keys (lines 27–28). We generalize the computation of the encapsulated key via core function W to simplify the description of our chosen-ciphertext secure construction in Sect. 5.

Delegation of a UPIBE decapsulation key is in line with the above ideas by conducting four steps: (a) Removing the special IBE decapsulation key at current level l, yet keeping all ordinary IBE decapsulation keys until level l (lines 11–13), (b) computing the next forwarding key as well as a seed by evaluating a PRG on the current forwarding key (line 14), (c) generating the main IBE decapsulation key at level $l+1$ from the obtained seed (line 15), and delegating both the special delegated IBE decapsulation key for level $l + 1$ (line 16) as well as the ordinary delegated IBE decapsulation key for level $l + 1$ (line 17) from this new main IBE decapsulation key, and, lastly, (d) removing the just obtained main IBE decapsulation key at level $l + 1$ as well as the old forwarding key.

Intuition for Security. The security argument for this construction uses the fact that adversaries can expose at most one UPIBE decapsulation key per instance during the security experiment.[4] This single exposure reveals precisely one special delegated IBE decapsulation key—the current one—, the chain of ordinary IBE decapsulation keys that were delegated along the exposed UPIBE key's identity path, and the current symmetric forwarding key from which future levels' IBE main decapsulation keys can be obtained. After such an exposure, two types of UPIBE ciphertexts must remain secure: Those that target *true prefixes* of the exposed key's identity string, and those that target identity strings *branching off* the exposed key's identity string.[5] Ciphertexts targeting a true prefix identity string, indeed, remain secure because their decapsulation requires the use of a higher level special delegated IBE decapsulation key. Such prior level special IBE keys were removed before the exposure and are, therefore, not contained in the exposed UPIBE key. Similarly, the decapsulation of ciphertexts that target a branched off identity string require the use of an inaccessible IBE decapsulation key—namely, an ordinary IBE decapsulation key that was delegated along this branch. Consequently, exposed UPIBE decapsulation keys do not affect ciphertexts that are required to remain secure. Finally, we note that at most two delegated decapsulation keys per IBE instance are leaked at an exposure of a UPIBE decapsulation key. Thus, relying on bounded-collusion IBE suffices, where the number of colluding users is at most 2.

Performance. Bounded-depth UPIBE (and bounded-depth KU-KEM) actually often suffice for secure messaging protocols.[6] So far, the only known instantiation of bounded-depth UPIBE is trivially derived from bounded-depth HIBE. With our bounded-depth UPIBE construction we demonstrate a significant reduction in complexity of the underlying hardness assumption: bounded-collusion IBE instead of bounded-depth HIBE. Furthermore, we use this construction to make the reader familiar with the core ideas of our unbounded-depth UPIBE construction in Sect. 4.

Without any additional assumptions on the underlying bounded-collusion IBE, the size of UPIBE encapsulation keys in our construction is linear in the maximal level depth L, UPIBE decapsulation keys grow with the number of conducted delegations, and UPIBE ciphertexts grow in the bit-length of their corresponding identity string.

When instantiating our construction with the DDH-based bounded-collusion IBE by Dodis et al. [15], we can take advantage of the group structure to aggregate and shrink encapsulation keys, decapsulation keys, and ciphertexts. We give

---

[4] With the exposed UPIBE decapsulation key, the adversary can compute all subsequent delegations and decapsulations itself, so further exposures are meaningless.

[5] Branching here means that for two identity strings id, id^* with $\ell^* = \min(|id|, |id^*|)$, strings id and id^* differ in at least one of the first ℓ^* bits.

[6] E.g., the number of conducted key delegations in the bidirectional messaging protocol in [36, see page 22] is upper-bounded by the maximal number of ciphertexts that cross the wire during a round-trip time (i.e., at most a few dozens).

the concrete instantiation in the full version [38] in which a UPIBE decapsulation key consists of 6 exponents and 1 symmetric key, a UPIBE ciphertext consists of 2 group elements, and a UPIBE encapsulation key consists of $2 + 3(L - l)$ group elements, where l is the level for which the current encapsulation key is derived via algorithm IE.der. This is highly efficient for settings in which distribution and storage of large encapsulation keys is cheap.[7] Enhancing this construction to also obtain a compact, constant size encapsulation key remains an interesting open problem.

Security. For clarity, we first consider chosen-plaintext security IND_{IE}^b of our UPIBE construction:

Theorem 1. *Bounded-depth UPIBE protocol* IE *from Fig. 2 offers adaptive key indistinguishability in the standard model. More precisely, for every adaptive chosen-plaintext adversary $\mathcal{A}$ attacking protocol* IE *in games* IND_{IE}^b *according to Definition 1 with parameters* $(L, \lambda, D = 1)$, *there exists an adversary $\mathcal{B}_{\text{G}}$ attacking PRG* G *and an adaptive chosen-plaintext adversary $\mathcal{B}_{\text{IE}'}$ attacking bounded-collusion IBE* IE' *in games* $\text{IND}_{\text{IE}'}^b$ *according to Definition 1 with parameters* $(L', \lambda', D') = (1, \lambda + 1, 2)$ *such that* $\text{Adv}_{\text{IE}}^{\text{ind}}(\mathcal{A}) \leq q_{\text{Gen}} \cdot L^2 \cdot \text{Adv}_{\text{G}}^{\text{ind}}(\mathcal{B}_{\text{G}}) + q_{\text{Gen}} l \cdot q_{\text{Chall}} \cdot L \cdot \text{Adv}_{\text{IE}'}^{\text{ind}}(\mathcal{B}_{\text{IE}'})$, *where q_{Gen} and q_{Chall} are the number of queries to oracles* Gen *and* Chall *by adversary $\mathcal{A}$, respectively, and the running time of $\mathcal{B}_{\text{G}}$ and $\mathcal{B}_{\text{IE}'}$ is about that of $\mathcal{A}$.*

Security Proof Overview. For clarity in notation, we refer to oracles in game IND_X^b by adding the scheme's identifier X as a subscript to the oracle names (i.e., Gen_X, Chall_X, etc). Also, we first sketch our proof by focusing on a reduction from single-instance security of UPIBE to multi-instance security of IBE.

Using the PRG, we begin with a hybrid argument that replaces all unexposed symmetric forwarding keys and IBE main key pairs with independently sampled ones. Our reduction $\mathcal{B}_{\text{IE}'}$ then almost directly passes oracle queries from adversary $\mathcal{A}$ against our UPIBE construction IE in game IND_{IE} to oracles of game $\text{IND}_{\text{IE}'}$ against the underlying bounded-collusion IBE scheme IE'. The responses of oracles in game $\text{IND}_{\text{IE}'}$ can then be used almost directly to answer adversary $\mathcal{A}$'s oracle queries in game IND_{IE}. That means, $\mathcal{A}$'s queries to oracle Gen_{IE} can be answered by using responses of simple queries to oracle $\text{Gen}_{\text{IE}'}$; the same holds for queries to oracle Del_{IE}.

However, embedding challenges from game $\text{IND}_{\text{IE}'}$ in challenges of game IND_{IE} is non-trivial. To understand this, we observe that the hardness of a challenge in game IND_{IE} depends on the delegation path of the first (and w.l.o.g. only) exposed UPIBE decapsulation key in game IND_{IE}. More precisely, let id^* be the identity string that corresponds to the delegation path of the first

---

[7] Consider asymmetric communication for which ciphertexts should be small and encapsulation keys can be large: E.g., sending large encapsulation keys on hardware memory from time to time via resupply flights to the International Space Station, and sending ciphertexts over the air back to earth.

exposure via oracle $\mathrm{Exp_{IE}}$. A challenge directed to identity string id is only considered hard if id is a true prefix of id^*, or if id and id^* differ in at least one of their first ℓ^* bits, where $\ell^* = \min(|id|, |id^*|)$. On a query to oracle $\mathrm{Chall_{IE}}$ with identity string id, our reduction $\mathcal{B}_{\mathrm{IE'}}$ splits id into its λ-long sub-strings and then identifies in which of these sub-strings the first difference between id and id^* occurs. For this branching sub-string, reduction $\mathcal{B}_{\mathrm{IE'}}$ queries an IBE challenge via oracle $\mathrm{Chall_{IE'}}$. The resulting IBE challenge-ciphertext and IBE challenge-key are then embedded in the corresponding UPIBE challenge-ciphertext and UPIBE challenge-key output of oracle $\mathrm{Chall_{IE}}$. However, reduction $\mathcal{B}_{\mathrm{IE'}}$ learns string id^* only as soon as adversary $\mathcal{A}$ calls oracle $\mathrm{Exp_{IE}}$. Hence, for each challenge issued before this first exposure query, reduction $\mathcal{B}_{\mathrm{IE'}}$ has to guess in which sub-string the identities branch. Embedding this guessing step in a hybrid argument introduces a loss factor of at most $q_{\mathrm{Gen}} \cdot q_{\mathrm{Chall}} \cdot \mathsf{L}$, where q_{Gen} and q_{Chall} are the numbers of queries to oracles $\mathrm{Gen_{IE}}$ and $\mathrm{Chall_{IE}}$ by adversary $\mathcal{A}$, resp., and L is the maximal number of delegation levels for our UPIBE construction. We provide our formal proof for multi-instance security in the full version [39].

4 Unbounded-Depth UPIBE from Bounded-Depth HIBE

Our unbounded-depth UPIBE construction extends our bounded-depth construction from Sect. 3 twofold: Horizontally, it replaces each level—realized by an IBE instance in our bounded-depth construction—by a *multi-level epoch*. Each epoch can internally handle up to ε sub-identity levels/delegations. The second extension replaces the static list of IBE main keys at the top of our bounded-depth UPIBE construction by a dynamic *epoch-progression* mechanism. This mechanism realizes a dynamic progression from one epoch to another and, thereby, eliminates the a-priori bounded number of sub-identity levels/delegations; see Fig. 1 for a schematic illustration.

The only component used to build our unbounded-depth UPIBE construction is a single bounded-depth HIBE scheme. To understand how the (unbounded number of) UPIBE delegations are processed by this bounded-depth HIBE, we invite the reader to look at the tree of identities/delegations in this HIBE that is indicated by gray (dotted) lines and arrows in Fig. 1.

Epoch-Progression via Forward-Secure PKE Technique. In the top α levels of the HIBE tree, we implement the epoch-progression mechanism, where $\alpha = \lceil \log(2^\kappa/\varepsilon) \rceil$ and κ is the security parameter. Of these α top HIBE delegation levels, we only make use of a binary delegation (sub-)tree. Each path in this binary tree part of the HIBE tree is the binary-encoding of an epoch number, where first epoch 0 is encoded as the left-most path and last epoch $2^\kappa/\varepsilon - 1$ is encoded as the right-most path. The lowest nodes in this top binary tree part (i.e., nodes in level α) represent *epoch starting nodes*. The first epoch starts at the left-most node which corresponds to the identity string that binary-encodes 0 (i.e., $0^{\alpha \cdot \lambda'}$, where λ' is the bit-length of HIBE identity sub-strings per level/delegation). We defer the explanation of how UPIBE delegations are realized *within* epochs to the next paragraph. As soon as an epoch is completed, the next epoch starts at the adjacent binary-tree node to the right in level α. (That is, starting nodes of epochs 2 and 3 correspond to identity strings $0^{\alpha \cdot \lambda' - 1} \| 1$ and $0^{(\alpha-1) \cdot \lambda' - 1} \| 1 \| 0^{\lambda'}$, respectively, where each level's identity sub-string contains a $(\lambda' - 1)$-long 0-bit padding prefix.)

Progression from one epoch starting node to the next one follows the well known idea of Forward-Secure PKE from Binary Tree Encryption [8].[8] Roughly, the epoch-progression mechanism iteratively delegates HIBE decapsulation keys along the α-long path from the root to the current epoch starting node. During this path delegation, also decapsulation keys of (binary-tree) siblings along this path are delegated. After each delegation on this path, the respective parent node's key from which the two sibling keys were delegated is deleted. Only the first epoch progression starts at the root of the HIBE tree. All following epoch progressions start from the lowest level for which a delegated sibling key exists. This mechanism ensures that only starting nodes of future epochs but not of previous epochs are accessible.

Multi-level Epochs. Our UPIBE construction splits identity strings of length $l \cdot \lambda$ into $\varepsilon \cdot \lambda$-long *epoch sub-strings*. Each individual epoch sub-string is delegated in ε steps vertically in the HIBE tree under its epoch starting node (i.e., each epoch contains ε delegation levels). Hence, every epoch sub-string in the HIBE tree looks exactly the same as its UPIBE identity sub-string counterpart (see Fig. 1). However, instead of being concatenated vertically in the HIBE tree, one can think of the vertical epoch sub-strings hanging next to one another from left to right under their epoch starting nodes in level α.

Structure of Keys and Ciphertexts. Despite these two crucial extensions, the overall idea of our unbounded-depth UPIBE construction is very close to its bounded-depth counterpart from Sect. 3. This becomes evident when looking at the structure of UPIBE decapsulation keys and ciphertexts.

A *UPIBE* decapsulation key at delegation level l contains three types of delegated *HIBE* decapsulation keys: (1) up to α *epoch-progression* decapsulation keys, (2) one *ordinary* decapsulation key for each of the previous $\lceil l/\varepsilon \rceil - 1$ epochs and, potentially, one *ordinary* decapsulation key for the current epoch, and (3) a *special* decapsulation key for the current epoch. The epoch-progression decapsulation keys replace the single symmetric forwarding key from our bounded-depth construction. This allows for efficient delegation of *future* epochs' initial decapsulation keys, yet preventing access to *previous* epochs' initial decapsulation keys. Ordinary and special decapsulation keys are used for the actual decapsulation of UPIBE ciphertexts (almost) as in our bounded-depth construction.

The concrete components of a UPIBE decapsulation key are as follows. One *ordinary* HIBE decapsulation key, delegated to the lowest HIBE tree level $\alpha +$

---

[8] For clarity in our explanation, we slightly deviate from the original BTE-to-FS-PKE idea by Canetti et al. [8]: We do not use all nodes in the BTE tree as epoch starting points but only nodes in the lowest level of this BTE component.

ε, is stored for each finished epoch. All remaining HIBE decapsulation keys, ever delegated in these prior epochs, are removed from the (delegated) UPIBE decapsulation key. For the current epoch, a *special* decapsulation key delegated to HIBE level $\alpha + (l \mod \varepsilon)$ in that epoch is stored in the UPIBE decapsulation key, where l is the overall number of UPIBE delegations so far. When delegating the UPIBE decapsulation key, this *special* HIBE decapsulation key is replaced by a new one for the next level. Only in the last level $\alpha + \varepsilon$ of the current epoch where $(l = -1 \mod \varepsilon)$, the UPIBE decapsulation key contains two HIBE keys: a special *and* an ordinary HIBE decapsulation key.

A UPIBE ciphertext for level l consists of one HIBE ciphertext per existing epoch, where $\lceil l/\varepsilon \rceil$ is the number of existing epochs. Each of the first $\lceil l/\varepsilon \rceil - 1$ ciphertexts is directed to its epoch's ordinary decapsulation key, and the last ciphertext is directed to the current epoch's special decapsulation key.

All UPIBE delegations within an epoch delegate a new special HIBE decapsulation key from the previous level's special HIBE decapsulation key. After each delegation, this previous special HIBE decapsulation key is removed. In the lowest level of an epoch—in HIBE tree level $\alpha + \varepsilon$—an additional ordinary HIBE decapsulation key is delegated the from previous level's special HIBE decapsulation key. This ordinary HIBE decapsulation key is never removed from the UPIBE decapsulation key.

Intuition for Security. The intuitive security argument for this construction resembles the one from Sect. 3. Recall that, on exposure of a UPIBE decapsulation key, only those UPIBE encapsulations must remain secure whose targeted identity string either is a *true prefix* of the exposed key's identity string or *branches off* the exposed key's identity string (See Footnote 5). Encapsulations to true prefix identity strings have their last HIBE encapsulation directed to an *earlier* special HIBE decapsulation key. This special key is not stored in the exposed UPIBE decapsulation key anymore, since the latter only contains the *current* level's special HIBE decapsulation key. Encapsulations to branched off identity strings have the HIBE encapsulation of the branching epoch directed to an ordinary HIBE decapsulation key that was never stored in the exposed UPIBE decapsulation key. Finally, all exposed decapsulation keys of the epoch-progression mechanism only reveal parts of the HIBE tree from which future epochs can be delegated. Thus, UPIBE encapsulations of our unbounded-depth construction remain secure under non-trivial exposures of UPIBE decapsulation keys.

Construction. We specify our unbounded-depth UPIBE construction formally in Fig. 3. This construction uses a bounded-depth HIBE with maximal level depth $\mathsf{L} = \alpha + \varepsilon = \lceil \log(2^\kappa/\varepsilon) \rceil + \varepsilon$, where κ is the security parameter.

The UPIBE encapsulation key consists solely of the main HIBE encapsulation key. The initial UPIBE decapsulation key is generated by executing the epoch-progression mechanism with the main HIBE decapsulation key to derive the first epoch's starting decapsulation key (Fig. 3, lines 02–06). More concretely, this mechanism delegates one ephemeral and one stored decapsulation key in

```
Proc IE.gen                                        Proc IE.dec(dk, C)
00  E[·] ← ⊥; D_ep[·] ← ⊥; D_fs[·] ← ⊥            31  (l, D_fs, D_ep) ← dk
01  (ek', dk'_0) ←$ IE.gen'                        32  d ← l mod ε; e ← ⌈l/ε⌉
02  For j = 0 to α - 1:                            33  c_0‖ . . . ‖c_{e'-1} ← C with c_j ∈ C
03      dk''_0 ←$ IE.del'(dk'_0, 0^{λ+1})          34  Require e = e'
04      dk''_1 ←$ IE.del'(dk'_0, 0^λ‖1)            35  For j = 0 to e - 2
05      dk'_0 ← dk''_0; D_fs[j] ← dk''_1           36      k'_j ←$ IE.dec'(D_ep[j], c_j)
06      D_ep[0] ← dk'_0                            37  If d ≠ e - 1: dk'_1 ← D_ep[e - 1]
07  ek ← ek'; dk ← (0, D_fs, D_ep)                 38  Else: (dk'_0, dk'_1) ← D_ep[e - 1]
08  Return (ek, dk)                                39  k'_{e-1} ←$ IE.dec'(dk'_1, c_{e-1})
                                                   40  K ← W(k'_0, . . . , k'_{e-1}, C)
Proc IE.enc(ek, id)                                41  Return K
09  Require id ∈ {0,1}^{l·λ}, l ∈ ℕ^+
10  id_0‖ . . . ‖id_{l-1} ← id with id_j ∈ {0,1}^λ  Proc IE.del(dk, id)
11  d ← l mod ε; e ← ⌈l/ε⌉                         42  Require id ∈ {0,1}^λ
12  For e' = 0 to e - 2:                           43  (l, D_fs, D_ep) ← dk
13      id' ← ε                                    44  d ← l mod ε; e ← ⌊l/ε⌋
14      (e'_0, . . . , e'_{α-1}) ← e' with e'_j ∈ {0,1}  45  If d = 0 ∧ e > 0:
15      For j = 0 to α - 1:                        46      (dk'_0, dk'_1) ← D_ep[e - 1]
16          id' ←" 0^λ‖e'_j                        47      D_ep[e - 1] ← dk'_0
17      For d' = 0 to ε - 2:                       48      j ← msdb(e - 1, e)
18          id' ←" id_{e'·ε+d'}‖1                  49      dk'_0 ← D_fs[j]; D_fs[j] ← ⊥
19      id' ←" id_{e'·ε+ε-1}‖0                     50      For j to α - 1:
20      (c'_{e'}, k'_{e'}) ← IE.enc'(ek, id')      51          dk''_0 ←$ IE.del'(dk'_0, 0^{λ+1})
21      id' ← ε                                    52          dk''_1 ←$ IE.del'(dk'_0, 0^λ‖1)
22      (e'_0, . . . , e'_{α-1}) ← e - 1 with e'_j ∈ {0,1}  53          dk'_0 ← dk''_0; D_fs[j] ← dk''_1
23      For j = 0 to α - 1:                        54      D_ep[e] ← dk'_0
24          id' ←" 0^λ‖e'_i                        55      If d ≠ e - 1:
25      For d' = 0 to d - 1:                       56          D_ep[e] ←$ IE.del'(D_ep[e], id‖1)
26          id' ←" id_{(e-1)·ε+d'}‖1               57      Else:
27      (c'_{e-1}, k'_{e-1}) ← IE.enc'(ek, id')    58          dk'_0 ←$ IE.del'(D_ep[e], id‖0)
28  C ← c'_0‖ . . . ‖c'_{e-1}                      59          dk'_1 ←$ IE.del'(D_ep[e], id‖1)
29  K ← W(k'_0, . . . , k'_{e-1}, C)               60          D_ep[e] ← (dk'_0, dk'_1)
30  Return (C, K)                                  61  dk ← (l + 1, D_fs, D_ep)
                                                   62  Return dk
```

Fig. 3. Generic construction of unbounded-depth UPIBE IE from bounded-depth HIBE scheme IE' with ciphertext space $\mathcal{C}$. Function $\mathrm{msdb}(x, y)$ computes the most significant bit in which the bit-representations of x and y differ and core function W is realized as XOR-sum $\bigoplus_{j=0}^{e-1} k'_j$ and ignores input C. In our chosen-ciphertext secure instantiation we instantiate W with random oracle $\mathrm{H}^\star$.

each of the first α HIBE levels (lines 03–04). Ephemeral key dk'_0 is replaced after delegating the two decapsulation keys of the next level. Stored key dk'_1 will be used for future epoch progressions. In level α, ephemeral key dk'_0 is set as the first epoch's starting decapsulation key. We explain the specific encoding- and padding-scheme for identity strings at the end of this paragraph.

UPIBE encapsulation splits the targeted identity string id into $\varepsilon \cdot \lambda$-long *epoch sub-strings*. Our pseudo-code separates the processing of the first $e - 1$ epoch sub-strings (lines 12–20) from the last epoch's sub-string (lines 21–27). Roughly, each epoch sub-string (composed in lines 17–19 resp. 25–26) is prepended with a binary encoding of the corresponding epoch number (lines 14–16 resp. 22–

24). The binary encoding prefix represents the epoch-progression path to the epoch's starting node. For every epoch, an HIBE encapsulation directed to the concatenated string of binary-encoded *epoch number* and *epoch identity sub-string* is executed (line 20 resp. 27). The final UPIBE ciphertext is a simple concatenation of all epoch HIBE ciphertexts; the output UPIBE key is an XOR-sum of all encapsulated epoch HIBE keys.

On UPIBE decapsulation, the input ciphertext is decomposed, and each of the resulting HIBE ciphertexts is decapsulated. For all previous epochs, the stored lowest level ordinary decapsulation key is used for decapsulation (lines 35–36). In the current epoch, the special decapsulation key is used for this (line 39). Depending on whether the current epoch reached its lowest level or not, the special decapsulation key is stored solitarily (line 37) or together with the ordinary decapsulation key (line 38).

In most cases, UPIBE delegation simply uses the current epoch's special HIBE decapsulation key together with input identity string *id* to delegate a new special HIBE decapsulation key that replaces the prior one (lines 56). Only if the lowest level of the current epoch is reached, an additional ordinary HIBE decapsulation key is delegated and stored (line 58–60). A subsequent delegation starts a new epoch and, therefore, uses the epoch-progression mechanism (lines 45–54). This mechanism starts by deleting the previous epoch's special decapsulation key (lines 46–47). Then, it identifies the lowest existing decapsulation key in the underlying binary-tree structure (line 48) with which the next epoch starting node is delegated (lines 50–54). This subsequent starting node— basically the immediate neighbor node in the binary tree—is used as the new epoch's initial decapsulation key.

We elaborate on some implementation details. To realize a binary tree in the epoch-progression mechanism, the binary encoding of epoch numbers is padded with ($\lambda' - 1 = \lambda$) leading 0-bits in every level (lines 03–04, 16, 24, 51–52). For the composition of epoch sub-strings, each *level's* identity *sub-string* is appended with a 1-bit (lines 18, 26) except for the last level in any previous epoch; previous epochs' last level sub-strings have an appended 0-bit (lines 19). This corresponds to the use and delegation of special and ordinary decapsulation keys (lines 56, 58–59).

Depth of Multi-level Epochs. Our unbounded-depth UPIBE construction is parameterized by variable ε that determines the number of delegations per epoch. We note that for $\varepsilon = \infty$, our UPIBE construction reduces to the known trivial delegation design via *unbounded*-depth HIBE [3,30,37]. Thus, there is *always* an ε for which our construction is *at least as efficient* as the previous approach. Beyond that, using the flexibility of parameter ε, our construction's performance can be adapted to different use cases. For example, depending on whether ciphertexts or decapsulation keys should be small, and depending on the expected number of delegations in a setting, an optimal value ε can be configured. Our full evaluation is in Sect. 7.

2-Delegation HIBE. We want to note that each HIBE decapsulation key in our construction from Fig. 3 delegates at most two child decapsulation keys. Thus, while reducing the level depth parameter L substantially from infinity in UPIBE to a bounded value in the underlying HIBE, parameter D only grows from 1 delegation per secret key in UPIBE to 2 in the underlying HIBE. With our definition framework from Sect. 2 and our new perspective on delegation-restricted HIBE, we lay the foundation for future work that may investigate whether bounded-depth HIBE with limited delegation of D = 2 can be built more efficiently than general bounded-depth HIBE.

Security. To support comprehensibility and avoid idealized assumptions, we first reduce adaptive chosen-plaintext security IND_{IE}^b of our UPIBE construction to adaptive security of the underlying HIBE in the standard model. In Sect. 4.1, we augment our reduction with a new guessing technique that allows us to trade the strength of the underlying HIBE (only selective security instead of adaptive security) against idealized assumptions (random oracle model instead of standard model). Relying only on selective secure HIBEs for adaptive security of our UPIBE significantly extends the class of available HIBE constructions from the literature. For full security against chosen-ciphertext attacks, we consider different generic and direct techniques in Sect. 5.

Theorem 2. *Unbounded-depth UPIBE protocol IE from Fig. 3 offers adaptive key indistinguishability in the standard model. More precisely, for every adaptive chosen-plaintext adversary $\mathcal{A}$ attacking protocol IE in games IND_{IE}^b according to Definition 1 with parameters* (L = ∞, λ, D = 1), *there exists an adaptive chosen-plaintext adversary $\mathcal{B}$ attacking bounded-depth HIBE IE$'$ in games $\text{IND}_{\text{IE}'}^b$ according to Definition 1 with parameters* (L$'$, λ', D$'$) = ($\lceil \log(2^\kappa/\varepsilon) \rceil + \varepsilon$, $\lambda + 1$, 2) *such that* $\text{Adv}_{\text{IE}}^{\text{ind}}(\mathcal{A}) \leq q_{\text{Gen}} \cdot q_{\text{Chall}} \cdot \lceil l_{\text{long}}/\varepsilon \rceil \cdot \text{Adv}_{\text{IE}'}^{\text{ind}}(\mathcal{B})$, *where κ is the security parameter, ε is the construction's epoch-depth parameter, q_{Chall} and q_{Chall} are the numbers of queries to oracles Gen and Chall by adversary $\mathcal{A}$, respectively, l_{long} is the level-depth of the longest identity string queried to oracle Chall by adversary $\mathcal{A}$, and the running time of $\mathcal{B}$ is about that of $\mathcal{A}$.*

Security Proof Overview. Our security proof for Theorem 2 is very similar to the one for Theorem 1. The major technical difference is that here the security of each UPIBE instance is reduced to only one bounded-depth HIBE instance's security. Reduction $\mathcal{B}$, again, simulates all oracle queries of adversary $\mathcal{A}$ in game IND_{IE} via queries to oracles in game $\text{IND}_{\text{IE}'}$. As in our proof from Sect. 3, for certain UPIBE challenge queries to oracle Chall$_{\text{IE}}$, the reduction has to guess where to embed underlying HIBE challenges of game $\text{IND}_{\text{IE}'}$. A hybrid argument that implements theses guesses cause the loss factor in our advantage bound. The general strategy for embedding challenges is to determine where the identity string input of oracle Chall$_{\text{IE}}$ branches off the delegation path of (potentially) exposed UPIBE decapsulation keys. In contrast to our proof of Theorem 1, reduction $\mathcal{B}$ here only needs to guess the *epoch of the sub-string* in which the identity strings of challenge and exposure branch lie. We provide our formal proof in the full version [38].

4.1   Relaxing Assumptions: Adaptive UPIBE from Selective HIBE

The above outlined standard model proof for our unbounded-depth UPIBE construction from Fig. 3 relies on *adaptive* secure bounded-depth HIBE. Yet, the most suitable bounded-depth HIBEs (e.g., [5]) are only *selective* secure. Generic techniques for turning selective secure schemes adaptive secure, as done in [1,4,5,10], rely on the random oracle model and induce an exponential loss factor in the HIBE's maximal level depth L. The simple idea of these techniques is to replace each identity sub-string in the construction by the output of a random oracle evaluated on this identity sub-string (i.e., $id_0\| \ldots \|id_l$ is replaced by $H(id_0)\| \ldots \|H(id_l)$). The reduction then embeds sub-strings of the selective challenge identity in randomly chosen random-oracle-outputs. A reduction succeeds if it embeds the *selective challenge* sub-strings in those random-oracle-outputs whose input identity sub-strings form the *adaptive challenge*. This induces an exponential loss in the maximal number of identity sub-strings per adaptive challenge. This is problematic because our UPIBE construction relies on an adaptive secure bounded-depth HIBE with parameter $L = \alpha + \varepsilon = \lceil \log(2^\kappa/\varepsilon) \rceil + \varepsilon$, which is linear in the security parameter κ. Thus, the loss factor would be exponential in κ when following the generic approach of turning the underlying HIBE adaptive secure [1,4,5,10] before using this HIBE to instantiate our unbounded-depth UPIBE construction.

Solution: Guessing Essentials Only. Due to the way our construction makes use of the underlying bounded-depth HIBE, we can carefully change the generic approach from [4,5] in order to relax the assumption on the HIBE from adaptive to selective security. Our main observation is that the two (virtual) components in our UPIBE construction—*epoch-progression mechanism* and *multi-level epochs*—encode information of different density. For this, consider an HIBE identity string to which our UPIBE encapsulation internally issues an HIBE encapsulation. The first part of such an HIBE identity string encodes an integer that represents the epoch number in the upper epoch-progression mechanism. The second part encodes a sub-string of the actual UPIBE identity string (i.e., the identity sub-string for one epoch).

In order to embed a selective HIBE challenge in the adaptive UPIBE challenge, our reduction has to predict the branching epoch's full HIBE identity string in advance. In this epoch, the UPIBE challenge identity branches off the delegated identity of the corresponding (exposed) UPIBE decapsulation key. To predict this epoch's full HIBE identity string, we treat the two parts—epoch number and sub-string of UPIBE identity—differently. The branching *epoch number* can simply be guessed with high probability. The reason is that polynomially bounded users (and adversaries) only issue UPIBE identity strings of polynomial length. Thus, also the number of epochs used to represent a UPIBE identity string is polynomially bounded. To predict the second part of the HIBE identity string—the branching epoch's sub-string of the actual UPIBE identity string—we employ the generic technique [4,5] based on the random oracle model.

Since the depth of each multi-level epoch is bounded by constant parameter ε, the loss induced by this technique is only polynomial (not exponential) in κ.

Concrete Adjustments. We interpose a random oracle H in the following lines of our construction in Fig. 3: 18: $id' \xleftarrow{\text{\tiny\textquotedbl}} \text{H}(id_{e' \cdot \varepsilon + d'} \| 1)$; 19: $id' \xleftarrow{\text{\tiny\textquotedbl}} \text{H}(id_{e' \cdot \varepsilon + \varepsilon - 1} \| 0)$; 26: $id' \xleftarrow{\text{\tiny\textquotedbl}} \text{H}(id_{(e-1) \cdot \varepsilon + d'} \| 1)$; 56: $D_{ep}[e] \xleftarrow{\$} \text{IE.del}'(D_{ep}[e], \text{H}(id \| 1))$; 58: $dk'_0 \xleftarrow{\$}$ $\text{IE.del}'(D_{ep}[e], \text{H}(id \| 0))$; 59: $dk'_1 \xleftarrow{\$} \text{IE.del}'(D_{ep}[e], \text{H}(id \| 1))$. However, we leave the identity sub-strings of the upper epoch-progression mechanism untouched. Thus, lines 03–04, 16, 24, and 51–52 remain the same. A full proof of following Theorem 3 is given in the full version [39].

Theorem 3. *Adjusting unbounded-depth UPIBE protocol* IE *from Fig. 3 offers adaptive key indistinguishability in the random oracle model. More precisely, let* H *be a random oracle, then for every adaptive chosen-plaintext adversary* $\mathcal{A}$ *attacking protocol* IE *in games* IND_{IE}^b *according to Definition 1 with parameters* $(\text{L} = \infty, \lambda, \text{D} = 1)$, *there exists a selective chosen-plaintext adversary* $\mathcal{B}$ *attacking bounded-depth HIBE* IE' *in games* $\text{IND}_{\text{IE}'}^b$ *according to Definition 1 with parameters* $(\text{L}', \lambda', \text{D}') = (\lceil \log(2^\kappa / \varepsilon) \rceil + \varepsilon, \lambda + 1, 2)$ *such that* $\text{Adv}_{\text{IE}}^{\text{ind}}(\mathcal{A}) \leq q_{\text{Gen}} \cdot q_{\text{Chall}} \cdot ((l_{\text{long}})^2 \cdot (q_{\text{H}})^\varepsilon) \cdot \text{Adv}_{\text{IE}'}^{\text{ind}}(\mathcal{B})$, *where* κ *is the security parameter,* ε *is the construction's epoch-depth parameter,* $q_{\text{Gen}}, q_{\text{Chall}}$, *and* q_{H} *are the number of queries to oracles* Gen, Chall *and the random oracle by adversary* $\mathcal{A}$, *respectively,* l_{long} *is the level-depth of the longest identity string queried to oracle* Chall *by adversary* $\mathcal{A}$, *and the running time of* $\mathcal{B}$ *is about that of* $\mathcal{A}$.

5 CCA Secure UPIBE

Now we turn our focus on the task of achieving chosen-ciphertext security for bounded- and unbounded-depth UPIBE. While it might be tempting to think that similar to HIBEs one could generically convert CPA-secure UPIBE into CCA-secure ones using the BCHK (often also called CHK) compiler [6,9], this unfortunately does not work: BCHK needs one delegation *per* decapsulation from *the same* decapsulation key, but UPIBE only offers one delegation for each decapsulation key *in total*. Thus, we need to adopt different strategies for constructing CCA-secure UPIBE.

5.1 Bounded-Depth UPIBE

FO-Transform. Having in mind that we construct bounded-depth UPIBE from (bounded-collusion) IBE, a natural choice is to apply the Fujisaki-Okamoto (FO) transform [19] and in particular one of its modular variants [28]. FO typically considers single instances, but in our construction of UPIBE one has to deal with multiple parallel IBE ciphertexts and this requires some care. Recently, Cini et al. in [11] considered this issue of parallel ciphertexts in FO for reducing decryption errors as well as constructing Bloom-Filter KEMs (BFKEMs) from IBE. Though [11] relies on a single IBE instance, it is quite straightforward to adapt their approach to UPIBE.[9] Unfortunately, using FO in this way, besides being bound to the random oracle model (ROM), requires an overhead of l encryptions of the underlying IBE during decapsulation, which can be significant.

Split-Key PRF. An alternative, more efficient, and more flexible approach is made possible when we view our UPIBE construction in Sect. 3 as parallel bounded-collusion IBE and take inspiration from Giacon et al. [22]. In particular, recall that our overall ciphertext $C = c'_0 \| \dots \| c'_{l-1}$ is the concatenation of l ciphertexts of independent IBEs and the encapsulation key is computed as $K \leftarrow W(k'_0, \dots, k'_{l-1}, C)$, where W represents what is called a core function by Giacon et al. [22]. We note that [22] focuses on parallel KEM combiners, and show that if W is a split-key pseudorandom function (skPRF), it yields a CCA-secure KEM if at least one of the l KEMs is CCA secure. Various instantiations of skPRFs in the ROM and standard model with different types of trade-offs are discussed in [22]. For instance the PRF-then-XOR composition $W(k'_0, \dots, k'_{l-1}, C) := \bigoplus_{i=0}^{l-1} F_i(k'_i, C)$, where F_i's are PRFs, is a skPRF in the standard model. Our focus now is not on combiners and as the use of our instances is dynamic (i.e., the depth can vary), this does not work for UPIBE. Here we need to require that *all* instances are CCA secure. Nevertheless, as we discuss below, the use of an skPRF still gives advantages when it comes to standard model constructions.

Achieving CCA-Secure IBE. While CCA security can be easily achieved in the ROM by starting from a CPA-secure (bounded-collusion) IBE and applying the FO transform, the overall overhead due to the FO is identical when directly applying FO (as discussed above). However, we can obtain CCA-secure bounded-depth UPIBE in the standard model when relying on an IBE scheme that directly provides CCA security in the standard model (e.g., [20] or the CCA-secure version of the bounded-collusion IBE in [15]). Alternatively, if one accepts that the IBEs are replaced by CPA-secure depth 2 HIBEs, one can simply use the BCHK compiler [6,9].

Now, we will show that the bounded-depth UPIBE protocol from Fig. 2 is CCA-secure when the underlying bounded-collusion IBE IE' is CCA-secure (e.g., [15]) and the core function W is based on a split-key pseudorandom function F with $n = L$ (cf. the full version [38] for the definition). For reasons that we will discuss below, we include a special KEM key $\hat{k}$ and a special ciphertext $\hat{c}$ into ek of the UPIBE protocol IE in order to "pad" calls to W to always take L inputs (for all cases where depth $l < L$).

Theorem 4. *Bounded-depth UPIBE protocol* IE *from Fig. 2 offers adaptive key indistinguishability under chosen-ciphertext attacks in the standard model.*

---

[9] We would sample a random key k and derive $(r_0, \dots, r_{l-1}, k') = G(k)$ from a random oracle G and encapsulate k_i with randomness r_i for the i'th instance such that $K = k_0 \oplus \dots \oplus k_{l-1}$ and then use k' as the overall encapsulation key.

More precisely, for every adaptive chosen-ciphertext adversary $\mathcal{A}$ attacking protocol IE in games IND_{IE}^b according to Definition 1 with parameters $(L, \lambda, D = 1)$, there exists an adversary $\mathcal{B}_G$ attacking PRG G, an adversary $\mathcal{B}_W$ against the split-key pseudorandomness of W , and an adaptive chosen-ciphertext adversary $\mathcal{B}_{IE'}$ attacking bounded-collusion IBE IE' in games $\mathrm{IND}_{IE'}^b$ according to Definition 1 with parameters $(L', \lambda', D') = (1, \lambda + 1, 2)$ such that $\mathrm{Adv}_{IE}^{ind}(\mathcal{A}) \leq q_{Gen} L^2 \cdot \left(q_{Gen} q_{Chall} L \, \mathrm{Adv}_G^{ind}(\mathcal{B}_G) + 1 \right) + 2 q_{Gen} q_{Chall} L \cdot$ $\left(q_{Chall} \, \mathrm{Adv}_{F_i}^{pr}(\mathcal{B}_W) + \mathrm{Adv}_{IE'}^{ind}(\mathcal{B}_{IE'}) \right)$, *where q_{Chall} and q_{Gen} are the number of queries to oracle Chall and Gen by adversary $\mathcal{A}$, and the running times of $\mathcal{B}_G$, $\mathcal{B}_W$, and $\mathcal{B}_{IE'}$ is about that of $\mathcal{A}$.*

Security Proof Overview. The strategy for the proof is analogous to that of Theorem 1, but we will proceed in a sequence of Games moving from the game IND_{IE}^0 to IND_{IE}^1, which allows us to follow the strategy by Giacon et al. [22]. In contrast to their proof, in our case all instances are required to be CCA secure. This is since we require CCA security of the underlying IBE IE' at the branching positions of identities that are asked to the challenge oracle, which can be placed at any of the L positions adaptively. We need to take some care when using the pseudorandomness of the split-key pseudorandom function for W, as we use $n = L$ but the number of required inputs vary with the actual depth of the identities l. Therefore, we always use L inputs for calls to W where for the $L - l$ rightmost inputs we simply use a fixed key $\hat{k}$ and ciphertext $\hat{c}$ (we will not make this fact explicit in the proof). We provide a formal proof in the full version [38].

5.2 Unbounded-Depth UPIBE

For the same reasons as discussed in Sect. 5.1 we prefer to avoid a generic use of the FO transform for proving CCA security of our unbounded-depth UPIBE. Unfortunately, the generic skPRF approach pursued in Sect. 5.1 requires an a priori bound on the depth, which is not the case for unbounded-depth UPIBE.

Consequently, although we follow the same overall idea, as already mentioned in Fig. 3, we instantiate the core function W directly by a random oracle H^*, i.e., derive the overall key as $K \leftarrow H^*(k_1, \ldots, k_l, c_1, \ldots, c_l)$ where (k_i, c_i) are the encapsulation outputs of the chosen-ciphertext secure bounded HIBE. Since our focus is on efficiency, and the strategy to prove Theorem 3 already requires the ROM, this seems to be a meaningful choice. For CCA security of the single ciphertexts of the underlying bounded-depth HIBE, the most efficient approach is a use of the BCHK compiler [6,9]. This yields a very flexible approach as due to the choice of the required strongly secure signature scheme there are many performance and bandwidth trade-offs available (see also Sect. 7). Using this strategy we can show the following for our unbounded-depth UPIBE. The proof of Theorem 5 is provided in the full version [38].

Theorem 5. *Adjusting unbounded-depth UPIBE protocol* IE *from Fig. 3 as described in Sect. 4.1 offers adaptive key indistinguishability under chosen-ciphertext attacks in the random oracle model. More precisely, let* H *and* H* *be random oracles, then for every adaptive chosen-ciphertext adversary* $\mathcal{A}$ *attacking protocol* IE *in games* $\mathrm{IND}_{\mathrm{IE}}^{b}$ *according to Definition 1 with parameters* $(\mathsf{L} = \infty, \lambda, \mathsf{D} = 1)$*, there exists a selective chosen-ciphertext adversary* $\mathcal{B}$ *attacking bounded-depth HIBE* IE' *in games* $\mathrm{IND}_{\mathrm{IE}'}^{b}$ *according to Definition 1 with parameters* $(\mathsf{L}', \lambda', \mathsf{D}') = (\lceil \log(2^\kappa/\varepsilon) \rceil + \varepsilon, \lambda + 1, 2)$ *such that* $\mathrm{Adv}_{\mathrm{IE}}^{\mathrm{ind}}(\mathcal{A}) \leq q_{\mathrm{Gen}} \cdot q_{\mathrm{Chall}} \cdot ((l_{\mathrm{long}})^2 \cdot (q_{\mathrm{H}})^\varepsilon) \cdot \left(\mathrm{Adv}_{\mathrm{IE}'}^{\mathrm{ind}}(\mathcal{B}) + \frac{q_{\mathrm{Chall}} \cdot q_{\mathrm{H}^\star}}{|\mathcal{K}|} \right)$ *where* κ *is the security parameter,* ε *is the construction's epoch-depth parameter,* q_{Chall}*,* q_{Gen}*,* q_{H} *and* $q_{\mathrm{H}^\star}$ *are queries to oracles* Chall*,* Gen *and random oracles* H *and* H* *by adversary* $\mathcal{A}$*, respectively,* l_{long} *is the level-depth of the longest identity string queried to oracle* Chall *by adversary* $\mathcal{A}$*, and the running time of* $\mathcal{B}$ *is about that of* $\mathcal{A}$*.*

6   Key-Updatable KEM from UPIBE

A Key-Updatable Key Encapsulation Mechanism (KU-KEM) [30,37] is a KEM $\mathsf{K} = (\mathsf{K.gen}, \mathsf{K.enc}, \mathsf{K.dec}, \mathsf{K.up})$ with additional update algorithms K.up for encapsulation keys and decapsulation keys. The computation of each update $ek' \leftarrow_\$ \mathsf{K.up}(ek, ad)$ resp. $dk' \leftarrow_\$ \mathsf{K.up}(dk, ad)$ is determined by a bit string ad that is arbitrarily chosen by the user. One can think of these update bit strings as new information (aka. *associated data*) that is added to the context of the ongoing session. Updates of encapsulation keys and decapsulation keys can be conducted independently without information being transmitted between holders of encapsulation and decapsulation key. The feature of *independent* updates *with respect to bit strings* constitutes the crucial difference to significantly weaker notions like Updatable PKE [14,31] that offer more efficient instantiations. We refer the interested reader to a discussion by Balli et al. [3] who elaborate on the shortcomings of Updatable PKE in the context of *strongly* secure messaging.

As long as both components of a KU-KEM key pair are updated with respect to the same bit strings—meaning, their context is updated compatibly—, the key pair remains compatible. More precisely, a generated pair consisting of encapsulation key and decapsulation key remains compatible if the list of bit strings for updates applied on the encapsulation key equals the list of bit strings for updates applied on the decapsulation key. We follow the slightly stronger variant of KU-KEM by Balli et al. [3] that furthermore requires for compatibility of a key pair that the list of bit strings for updates together with the list of sent and received encapsulation ciphertexts equals on both sides.

For security of KU-KEM, two goals beyond pure key-indistinguishability are required: (1) *Forward-secrecy*, meaning that an updated future version of the current decapsulation key can be exposed to an adversary without harming confidentiality of ciphertexts produced with a current or previous (compatible) version of the corresponding encapsulation key—in short, old ciphertexts remain secure if future decapsulation keys are exposed; (2) *Effective divergence*, meaning that an incompatible decapsulation key can be exposed to an adversary without harming confidentiality of ciphertexts produced with the corresponding (incompatible) encapsulation key—in short, any difference in update bit strings makes encapsulation key and decapsulation key fully independent.

KU-KEM is a special form of UPIBE where KU-KEM update bit strings are implemented via UPIBE identity sub-strings, KU-KEM decapsulation key updates are realized via UPIBE delegations, and KU-KEM encapsulation key updates are realized via UPIBE derivations. The construction of KU-KEM from UPIBE is, therefore, straight forward: K.gen := IE.gen; K.up(ek, ad) := IE.der($ek, ad = id$) resp. K.up(dk, ad) := IE.del($dk, ad = id$); K.enc(ek) executes IE.enc(ek, ϵ) and updates ek via IE.der($ek, ad = c$); K.dec(dk, c) executes IE.dec(dk, c) and updates dk via IE.del($dk, ad = c$). (Pseudo-code is given in the full version [38].) This construction was first proposed by Poettering and Rösler [37] and slightly adapted in other works [3,30]. Yet, we are the first to reduce the underlying assumption from general unbounded-depth HIBE to unbounded-depth UPIBE. For space reasons, we defer the formal definition of KU-KEM by Balli et al. [3] as well as our proof of Theorem 6 to the full version [38]. This proof tightly reduces the security of the KU-KEM construction to adaptive chosen-ciphertext security of the underlying unbounded-depth UPIBE scheme.

Theorem 6. *KU-KEM protocol K offers one-wayness of encapsulated keys. More precisely, for every adaptive chosen-ciphertext adversary $\mathcal{A}$ attacking protocol K , there exists an adaptive chosen-ciphertext adversary $\mathcal{B}$ attacking unbounded-depth HIBE IE in games IND_{IE}^{b} according to Definition 1 with parameters $(\mathsf{L}', \lambda', \mathsf{D}') = (\infty, \lambda, 1)$ such that $\mathrm{Adv}_{K}^{kuow}(\mathcal{A}) \leq \mathrm{Adv}_{IE}^{ind}(\mathcal{B})$, where the running time of $\mathcal{B}$ is about that of $\mathcal{A}$.*

7   Evaluation

Our evaluation considers (asymptotic and concrete) parameter sizes of one-way CCA (formally, KUOW) secure KU-KEMs built *trivially* from unbounded-depth HIBEs on the one side and KU-KEMs based on our UPIBE construction that relies on bounded-depth HIBEs from Sect. 5.2 on the other side. Before starting the concrete analysis, we note that CCA security of (un)bounded-depth HIBEs can be generically achieved efficiently via the BCHK transform [6,9] using a strongly secure one-time-signature scheme.[10]

Since we have applicability and performance in mind for our application towards optimally secure messaging protocols, we include bounded-depth HIBE schemes that are secure in the random-oracle model (ROM). Moreover, we looked at all applicable unbounded-depth HIBEs and selected three constructions [24,34,35] that suit the application we have in mind best. Depending on

---

[10] In our concrete setting, for standard-model HIBEs, we use Groth's pairing-free signature scheme [26] while for HIBEs in the ROM, we use Schnorr signatures [40].

Table 1. Comparison of CCA secure KU-KEMs with parameter sizes and performance instantiated from the standard-model unbounded-depth HIBEs L [35], LP [34], and GCTC [24] (trivially) and the bounded-depth HIBE BBG [5] (via our KU-KEM-from-UPIBE approach from Sect. 6). Here, $\alpha + \varepsilon$ is the maximum level (and α can be considered linear in the security parameter), l is the current number of key updates, γ is the output bit length of a collision-resistant hash function, and ε is the epoch-depth in our UPIBE. $n \geq 1$ is the performance parameter of GCTC [24]. We use the type-3 pairing setting with $e : G_1 \times G_2 \to G_T$ for prime-order groups G_1, G_2, and G_T. Here, we do not consider the tightness of the reductions to the underlying assumptions.

UPIBE	Via HIBE	Encapsulation key size	Ciphertext size	Decapsulation key size	Model
Triv.	L [35]	$60|G_1| + 2|G_T| + l\lambda$	$(10l + 12)|G_1|$	$(10l + 60)|G_2|$	StM
Triv.	LP [34]	$(2\gamma + 4)|G_1| + (2\gamma + 6)|G_2| + l\lambda$	$(7l + 11)|G_1|$	$(7l + 2)|G_2|$	StM
Triv.	GCTC [24]	$(3n + 9 + \lceil l/n \rceil)|G_1| + 3|G_T|$	$(9\lceil (l+1)/n \rceil + 2)|G_1|$	$((9 + 3n)\lceil l/n \rceil + 3n + 9 - 3l)|G_2|$	StM
Ours	BBG [5]	$(1 + \lceil l/\varepsilon \rceil)|G_1| + 1|G_2|$	$(3\lceil l/\varepsilon \rceil)|G_1|$	$(\mathcal{O}(\alpha \cdot (\alpha + \varepsilon)) + \lceil l/\varepsilon \rceil + \alpha)|G_2|$	ROM

UPIBE	Via HIBE	Key generation (# exp.)	Encapsulation (# exp.)	Decapsulation (# exp., # pairings)	Ass.
Triv.	L [35]	$60 \ (G_1), 80 \ (G_2), 2 \ (G_T)$	$60l + 62 \ (G_1), 2 \ (G_T)$	$(61l \ (G_2), 10l + 1)$	DLIN
Triv.	LP [34]	$(2\gamma + 4) \ (G_1), (2\gamma + 6) \ (G_2)$	$(7l + 11) \ (G_2), 2 \ (G_T)$	$((7(l+1) + 2) \ (G_2), (7l + 2) + 1)$	SXDH
Triv.	GCTC [24]	$6(n + 3) \ (G_2), 1 \ (G_T)$	$(15\lceil l/n \rceil + 3l) \ (G_1), 3 \ (G_T)$	$(15\lceil l/n \rceil + 3l \ (G_2), 9\lceil l/n \rceil + 1)$	SXDH
Ours	BBG [5]	$1 \ (G_1), 1 \ (G_2)$	$((\lceil l/\varepsilon \rceil + 5) \ (G_1), 1 \ (G_T))$	$(\varepsilon + \alpha/\varepsilon + 2) \ (G_2), 2\lceil l/\varepsilon \rceil)$	BDHE

the concrete bounded-depth HIBE scheme, it is a common technique to reduce public parameter sizes in the ROM [5]. This, however, does not work generically. Particularly, in the HIBE scheme by Gong et al. (GCTC) [24], the underlying encapsulation key structure seemingly prevents this form of parameter compression. The same seems to be the case for Langrehr-Pan (LP) [34], while Lewko (L) [35] already has compact encapsulation keys (however, with a large constant).

For our KU-KEM construction via the UPIBE paradigm (where we only require a selectively secure HIBE with polynomially bounded depth), the strongest candidate is the Boneh-Boyen-Goh (BBG) HIBE [5]. Here, encapsulation key size is only two group elements using the ROM. However, we cannot utilize the ROM to reduce the size of BBG decapsulation keys since these keys require a certain structure. Hence, the BBG HIBE has linear-size decapsulation keys, but enjoys constant-size encapsulation keys *and* ciphertexts (all in the maximal depth).

By considering the most efficient (un)bounded-depth HIBE schemes, we conduct a fair comparison between KU-KEMs from trivial UPIBE via unbounded-depth HIBE and KU-KEMs from our novel UPIBE construction. In Table 1, we list CCA secure KU-KEMs from CCA secure (un)bounded-depth HIBEs with relevant size and performance parameters.

We see that all but one known trivial KU-KEM instantiations via [24, 34, 35] have ciphertext and decapsulation-key sizes that scale linearly in the number of delegations (which corresponds to KU-KEM key updates). Only GCTC [24] has a trade-off for ciphertext and key sizes via their performance parameter n. With our non-trivial UPIBE approach from bounded-depth HIBEs, taking the BBG scheme [5] as instantiation, we obtain ciphertext sizes that only scale linearly in the number of *epochs*, which can be adjusted by the depth-parameter ε

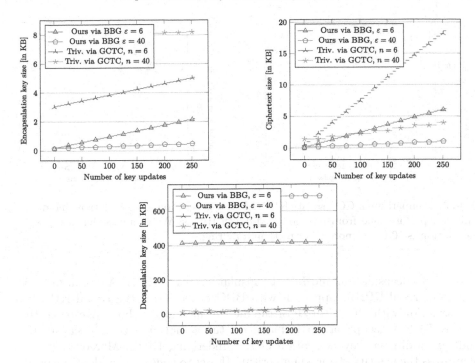

Fig. 4. Comparison of CCA secure KU-KEM encapsulation and decapsulation key as well as ciphertext sizes in kilobytes (KB) from (un)bounded-depth HIBEs. For the pairing group, we chose BLS12-381 (which gives around 128 bit security); this means per element in G_1, G_2, and G_T, we have 382, 764, 4572 bits.

as described in Sect. 4. Moreover, our KU-KEM approach via BBG enjoys very short encapsulation keys. This yields a significant reduction in encapsulation key and ciphertext sizes for KU-KEMs compared to other approaches (see Table 1).

Detailed Analysis. For our following analysis concerning parameter sizes and performance, from the three trivial standard-model KU-KEMs based on unbounded-depth HIBEs [24,34,35], we chose GCTC [24] which outperforms the other two—particularly because of their scalability parameter n that allows to trade-off ciphertext and encapsulation/decapsulation key sizes.[11] Hence, the GCTC scheme is the best suitable reference instantiation of KU-KEM via the *trivial* UPIBE construction for a concrete comparison regarding the applications we have in mind.

Application Requirements. Our focus is on short ciphertexts and encapsulations keys (for bandwidth reasons) while on the sender and the receiver sides, we

---

[11] Essentially, GCTC [24] improves Lewko [35] towards shorter ciphertext sizes and LP [34] deals with tightness of the Lewko scheme [35], at the expense of rather large encapsulation keys (see γ-factor).

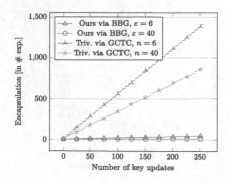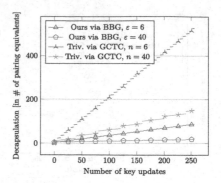

Fig. 5. Comparison of CCA secure KU-KEM key generation, encapsulation, and decapsulation performance from un-/bounded-depth HIBEs. We estimate that a G_1 exponentiation is 10 times more efficient than a pairing.

want fast encapsulation and fast decapsulation, respectively. As we argue now, our non-trivial UPIBE approach with BBG outperforms the trivial KU-KEM construction with GCTC in all of the metrics mentioned above. We recall that our KU-KEM decapsulation is based on the actual ciphertext decapsulation and an additional key delegation of the underlying HIBE. Moreover, we can compress the identity string via algorithm IE.der to compute an identity-specific encapsulation key for BBG *and* GCTC. We currently do not see how to perform this compression for [34,35].

Bandwidth Comparison. We observe that the performance parameter n in GCTC plays a similar role as our depth parameter ε in UPIBE; hence, we compare it at the same level. As illustrative examples, we choose $\varepsilon = n = 6$ and $\varepsilon = n = 40$. From the graphs in Figs. 4 and 5, we see that the encapsulation key for the BBG-based KU-KEM is very short. The ciphertext size of all KU-KEMs scales with ε and n. Our BBG-based approach has the shortest ciphertext sizes of all. For decapsulation key sizes, the GCTC approach is more efficient; however, as we argued with the application of secure messaging in mind, this is tolerable. Hence, concerning parameter sizes, we conclude that the BBG approach has shorter ciphertexts and smaller encapsulation key at the expense of slightly larger decapsulation keys compared to the trivial GCTC-based KU-KEM approach.

Computation Comparison. In terms of computation complexity (Fig. 5), we see that the BBG approach significantly outperforms the GCTC-based approach for encapsulation and decapsulation. The (initial) key generation for the BBG-based and for GCTC-based approaches are comparable efficiency-wise and constant in the number of key updates; our approach needs α many exponentiations while GCTC's number of exponentiations scales linearly in their performance parameter n. For encapsulation and decapsulation (where latter uses key delegation *and* decryption of the underlying HIBE), the BBG-based KU-KEM is more efficient; particularly, in situations when a large number of key updates is needed. See that the larger ε, the more efficient is the decapsulation of the BBG-based KU-KEM approach. The reason is that the BBG HIBE ciphertexts are of constant size and need only a constant number of pairings per ciphertext for decryption.

Summary. In conclusion, a KU-KEM via our unbounded-depth UPIBE construction, instantiated with the BBG HIBE, has shorter ciphertext and encapsulation-key sizes compared to the GCTC-based solution with analogous parameter choices (being the most efficient unbounded-depth HIBE known for trivial UPIBE) at the expense of a slightly larger decapsulation key. Additionally, the decapsulation and, particularly, the encapsulation of the BBG-based KU-KEM are significantly more efficient compared to the GCTC-based trivial KU-KEM. Hence, for our envisioned application of strongly secure messaging, we can tolerate slightly larger decapsulation keys while achieving more efficient decapsulation and encapsulation as those operations happen rather often in KU-KEMs.

Acknowledgements. This work was supported by the ECSEL Joint Undertaking (JU) under grant agreement No 826610 (COMP4DRONES) and by the Austrian Science Fund (FWF) and netidee SCIENCE under grant agreement P31621-N38 (PROFET).

References

1. Agrawal, S., Boneh, D., Boyen, X.: Efficient lattice (H)IBE in the standard model. In: Gilbert, H. (ed.) EUROCRYPT 2010. LNCS, vol. 6110, pp. 553–572. Springer, Heidelberg (2010). https://doi.org/10.1007/978-3-642-13190-5_28
2. Alwen, J., Coretti, S., Dodis, Y.: The double ratchet: security notions, proofs, and modularization for the signal protocol. In: Ishai, Y., Rijmen, V. (eds.) EUROCRYPT 2019. LNCS, vol. 11476, pp. 129–158. Springer, Cham (2019). https://doi.org/10.1007/978-3-030-17653-2_5
3. Balli, F., Rösler, P., Vaudenay, S.: Determining the core primitive for optimally secure ratcheting. In: Moriai, S., Wang, H. (eds.) ASIACRYPT 2020. LNCS, vol. 12493, pp. 621–650. Springer, Cham (2020). https://doi.org/10.1007/978-3-030-64840-4_21
4. Boneh, D., Boyen, X.: Efficient selective-ID secure identity-based encryption without random oracles. In: Cachin, C., Camenisch, J.L. (eds.) EUROCRYPT 2004. LNCS, vol. 3027, pp. 223–238. Springer, Heidelberg (2004). https://doi.org/10.1007/978-3-540-24676-3_14
5. Boneh, D., Boyen, X., Goh, E.-J.: Hierarchical identity based encryption with constant size ciphertext. In: Cramer, R. (ed.) EUROCRYPT 2005. LNCS, vol. 3494, pp. 440–456. Springer, Heidelberg (2005). https://doi.org/10.1007/11426639_26
6. Boneh, D., Canetti, R., Halevi, S., Katz, J.: Chosen-ciphertext security from identity-based encryption. SIAM J. Comput. 36(5), 1301–1328 (2007)
7. Boneh, D., Franklin, M.: Identity-based encryption from the Weil pairing. In: Kilian, J. (ed.) CRYPTO 2001. LNCS, vol. 2139, pp. 213–229. Springer, Heidelberg (2001). https://doi.org/10.1007/3-540-44647-8_13
8. Canetti, R., Halevi, S., Katz, J.: A forward-secure public-key encryption scheme. In: Biham, E. (ed.) EUROCRYPT 2003. LNCS, vol. 2656, pp. 255–271. Springer, Heidelberg (2003). https://doi.org/10.1007/3-540-39200-9_16

9. Canetti, R., Halevi, S., Katz, J.: Chosen-ciphertext security from identity-based encryption. In: Cachin, C., Camenisch, J.L. (eds.) EUROCRYPT 2004. LNCS, vol. 3027, pp. 207–222. Springer, Heidelberg (2004). https://doi.org/10.1007/978-3-540-24676-3_13
10. Cash, D., Hofheinz, D., Kiltz, E., Peikert, C.: Bonsai trees, or how to delegate a lattice basis. In: Gilbert, H. (ed.) EUROCRYPT 2010. LNCS, vol. 6110, pp. 523–552. Springer, Heidelberg (2010). https://doi.org/10.1007/978-3-642-13190-5_27
11. Cini, V., Ramacher, S., Slamanig, D., Striecks, C.: CCA-secure (Puncturable) KEMs from encryption with non-negligible decryption errors. In: Moriai, S., Wang, H. (eds.) ASIACRYPT 2020. LNCS, vol. 12491, pp. 159–190. Springer, Cham (2020). https://doi.org/10.1007/978-3-030-64837-4_6
12. Derler, D., Jager, T., Slamanig, D., Striecks, C.: Bloom filter encryption and applications to efficient forward-secret 0-RTT key exchange. In: Nielsen, J.B., Rijmen, V. (eds.) EUROCRYPT 2018. LNCS, vol. 10822, pp. 425–455. Springer, Cham (2018). https://doi.org/10.1007/978-3-319-78372-7_14
13. Dodis, Y., Fazio, N.: Public key broadcast encryption for stateless receivers. In: Feigenbaum, J. (ed.) ACM CCS-9 DRM Workshop 2002 (2002)
14. Dodis, Y., Karthikeyan, H., Wichs, D.: Updatable public key encryption in the standard model. In: Nissim, K., Waters, B. (eds.) TCC 2021. LNCS, vol. 13044, pp. 254–285. Springer, Cham (2021). https://doi.org/10.1007/978-3-030-90456-2_9
15. Dodis, Y., Katz, J., Xu, S., Yung, M.: Key-insulated public key cryptosystems. In: Knudsen, L.R. (ed.) EUROCRYPT 2002. LNCS, vol. 2332, pp. 65–82. Springer, Heidelberg (2002). https://doi.org/10.1007/3-540-46035-7_5
16. Döttling, N., Garg, S.: From selective IBE to full IBE and selective HIBE. In: Kalai, Y., Reyzin, L. (eds.) TCC 2017. LNCS, vol. 10677, pp. 372–408. Springer, Cham (2017). https://doi.org/10.1007/978-3-319-70500-2_13
17. Döttling, N., Garg, S.: Identity-based encryption from the Diffie-Hellman assumption. In: Katz, J., Shacham, H. (eds.) CRYPTO 2017. LNCS, vol. 10401, pp. 537–569. Springer, Cham (2017). https://doi.org/10.1007/978-3-319-63688-7_18
18. Durak, F.B., Vaudenay, S.: Bidirectional asynchronous ratcheted key agreement with linear complexity. In: Attrapadung, N., Yagi, T. (eds.) IWSEC 2019. LNCS, vol. 11689, pp. 343–362. Springer, Cham (2019). https://doi.org/10.1007/978-3-030-26834-3_20
19. Fujisaki, E., Okamoto, T.: Secure integration of asymmetric and symmetric encryption schemes. In: Wiener, M. (ed.) CRYPTO 1999. LNCS, vol. 1666, pp. 537–554. Springer, Heidelberg (1999). https://doi.org/10.1007/3-540-48405-1_34
20. Gentry, C.: Practical identity-based encryption without random oracles. In: Vaudenay, S. (ed.) EUROCRYPT 2006. LNCS, vol. 4004, pp. 445–464. Springer, Heidelberg (2006). https://doi.org/10.1007/11761679_27
21. Gentry, C., Silverberg, A.: Hierarchical ID-based cryptography. In: Zheng, Y. (ed.) ASIACRYPT 2002. LNCS, vol. 2501, pp. 548–566. Springer, Heidelberg (2002). https://doi.org/10.1007/3-540-36178-2_34
22. Giacon, F., Heuer, F., Poettering, B.: KEM combiners. In: Abdalla, M., Dahab, R. (eds.) PKC 2018. LNCS, vol. 10769, pp. 190–218. Springer, Cham (2018). https://doi.org/10.1007/978-3-319-76578-5_7
23. Goldwasser, S., Lewko, A., Wilson, D.A.: Bounded-collusion IBE from key homomorphism. In: Cramer, R. (ed.) TCC 2012. LNCS, vol. 7194, pp. 564–581. Springer, Heidelberg (2012). https://doi.org/10.1007/978-3-642-28914-9_32
24. Gong, J., Cao, Z., Tang, S., Chen, J.: Extended dual system group and shorter unbounded hierarchical identity based encryption. Des. Codes Cryptogr. **80**(3), 525–559 (2016)

25. Green, M.D., Miers, I.: Forward secure asynchronous messaging from puncturable encryption. In: 2015 IEEE Symposium on Security and Privacy, pp. 305–320. IEEE Computer Society Press, May 2015. https://doi.org/10.1109/SP.2015.26

26. Groth, J.: Simulation-sound NIZK proofs for a practical language and constant size group signatures. In: Lai, X., Chen, K. (eds.) ASIACRYPT 2006. LNCS, vol. 4284, pp. 444–459. Springer, Heidelberg (2006). https://doi.org/10.1007/11935230_29

27. Günther, F., Hale, B., Jager, T., Lauer, S.: 0-RTT key exchange with full forward secrecy. In: Coron, J.-S., Nielsen, J.B. (eds.) EUROCRYPT 2017. LNCS, vol. 10212, pp. 519–548. Springer, Cham (2017). https://doi.org/10.1007/978-3-319-56617-7_18

28. Hofheinz, D., Hövelmanns, K., Kiltz, E.: A modular analysis of the Fujisaki-Okamoto transformation. In: Kalai, Y., Reyzin, L. (eds.) TCC 2017. LNCS, vol. 10677, pp. 341–371. Springer, Cham (2017). https://doi.org/10.1007/978-3-319-70500-2_12

29. Horwitz, J., Lynn, B.: Toward hierarchical identity-based encryption. In: Knudsen, L.R. (ed.) EUROCRYPT 2002. LNCS, vol. 2332, pp. 466–481. Springer, Heidelberg (2002). https://doi.org/10.1007/3-540-46035-7_31

30. Jaeger, J., Stepanovs, I.: Optimal channel security against fine-grained state compromise: the safety of messaging. In: Shacham, H., Boldyreva, A. (eds.) CRYPTO 2018. LNCS, vol. 10991, pp. 33–62. Springer, Cham (2018). https://doi.org/10.1007/978-3-319-96884-1_2

31. Jost, D., Maurer, U., Mularczyk, M.: Efficient ratcheting: almost-optimal guarantees for secure messaging. In: Ishai, Y., Rijmen, V. (eds.) EUROCRYPT 2019. LNCS, vol. 11476, pp. 159–188. Springer, Cham (2019). https://doi.org/10.1007/978-3-030-17653-2_6

32. Jost, D., Maurer, U., Mularczyk, M.: A unified and composable take on ratcheting. In: Hofheinz, D., Rosen, A. (eds.) TCC 2019. LNCS, vol. 11892, pp. 180–210. Springer, Cham (2019). https://doi.org/10.1007/978-3-030-36033-7_7

33. Katz, J.: Binary tree encryption: constructions and applications. In: Lim, J.-I., Lee, D.-H. (eds.) ICISC 2003. LNCS, vol. 2971, pp. 1–11. Springer, Heidelberg (2004). https://doi.org/10.1007/978-3-540-24691-6_1

34. Langrehr, R., Pan, J.: Unbounded HIBE with tight security. In: Moriai, S., Wang, H. (eds.) ASIACRYPT 2020. LNCS, vol. 12492, pp. 129–159. Springer, Cham (2020). https://doi.org/10.1007/978-3-030-64834-3_5

35. Lewko, A.: Tools for simulating features of composite order bilinear groups in the prime order setting. In: Pointcheval, D., Johansson, T. (eds.) EUROCRYPT 2012. LNCS, vol. 7237, pp. 318–335. Springer, Heidelberg (2012). https://doi.org/10.1007/978-3-642-29011-4_20

36. Poettering, B., Rösler, P.: Asynchronous ratcheted key exchange. Cryptology ePrint Archive, Report 2018/296 (2018). eprint.iacr.org/2018/296

37. Poettering, B., Rösler, P.: Towards bidirectional ratcheted key exchange. In: Shacham, H., Boldyreva, A. (eds.) CRYPTO 2018. LNCS, vol. 10991, pp. 3–32. Springer, Cham (2018). https://doi.org/10.1007/978-3-319-96884-1_1

38. Rösler, P., Slamanig, D., Striecks, C.: Unique-path identity based encryption with applications to strongly secure messaging. Cryptology ePrint Archive, Paper 2023/248 (2023). eprint.iacr.org/2023/248

39. Rösler, P., Slamanig, D., Striecks, C.: Unique-path identity based encryption with applications to strongly secure messaging. In: Hazay, C., Stam, M. (eds.) EUROCRYPT 2023, LNCS 14008, pp. 3–34. Springer, Heidelberg (2023)

40. Schnorr, C.P.: Efficient identification and signatures for smart cards. In: Brassard, G. (ed.) CRYPTO 1989. LNCS, vol. 435, pp. 239–252. Springer, New York (1990). https://doi.org/10.1007/0-387-34805-0_22
41. Shamir, A.: Identity-based cryptosystems and signature schemes. In: Blakley, G.R., Chaum, D. (eds.) CRYPTO 1984. LNCS, vol. 196, pp. 47–53. Springer, Heidelberg (1985). https://doi.org/10.1007/3-540-39568-7_5
42. Tessaro, S., Wilson, D.A.: Bounded-collusion identity-based encryption from semantically-secure public-key encryption: generic constructions with short ciphertexts. In: Krawczyk, H. (ed.) PKC 2014. LNCS, vol. 8383, pp. 257–274. Springer, Heidelberg (2014). https://doi.org/10.1007/978-3-642-54631-0_15

End-to-End Secure Messaging
with Traceability *Only* for Illegal Content

James Bartusek[1], Sanjam Garg[1,3], Abhishek Jain[2],
and Guru-Vamsi Policharla[1(✉)]

[1] University of California, Berkeley, USA
guruvamsi.policharla@gmail.com
[2] Johns Hopkins University, Baltimore, USA
[3] NTT Research, Sunnyvale, USA

Abstract. As end-to-end encrypted messaging services become widely adopted, law enforcement agencies have increasingly expressed concern that such services interfere with their ability to maintain public safety. Indeed, there is a direct tension between preserving user privacy and enabling content moderation on these platforms. Recent research has begun to address this tension, proposing systems that purport to strike a balance between the privacy of "honest" users and traceability of "malicious" users. Unfortunately, these systems suffer from a lack of protection against malicious or coerced service providers. In this work, we address the privacy vs. content moderation question through the lens of pre-constrained cryptography [Ananth et al., ITCS 2022]. We introduce the notion of *set pre-constrained* (SPC) *group signatures* that guarantees security against *malicious key generators*. SPC group signatures offer the ability to trace users in messaging systems who originate pre-defined illegal content (such as child sexual abuse material), while providing security against malicious service providers. We construct concretely efficient protocols for SPC group signatures, and demonstrate the real-world feasibility of our approach via an implementation. The starting point for our solution is the recently introduced Apple PSI system, which we significantly modify to improve security and expand functionality.

1 Introduction

End-to-end encrypted services offer users the ability to communicate information, with the guarantee that even the service provider itself cannot access the raw information that it is storing or transmitting. Billions of people worldwide are now using end-to-end encrypted systems such as WhatsApp and Signal.

However, the strong data privacy guarantees offered by end-to-end encryption (E2EE) technology have not been universally celebrated. Law enforcement and national security agencies have argued that such services interfere with their ability to prosecute criminals and maintain public safety [19,30]. In particular, E2EE appears to directly conflict with the goals of *content moderation*, which

© International Association for Cryptologic Research 2023
C. Hazay and M. Stam (Eds.): EUROCRYPT 2023, LNCS 14008, pp. 35–66, 2023.
https://doi.org/10.1007/978-3-031-30589-4_2

refers to the ability to screen, monitor, or trace the origin of user-generated content.

One prominent example of the use of content moderation is in fighting the proliferation of child sexual abuse material, or CSAM. In the United States, the proposed EARN IT act [28] would enable legal action to be taken against internet service providers that fail to remove CSAM material from their service. It has been argued that the proposed legislation would inhibit the use of E2EE, which prevents service providers from detecting in the first place if they are hosting or transmitting CSAM [37]. In fact, a 2019 open letter to Facebook signed by then U.S. Attorney General William Barr along with international partners explicitly requested that Facebook not proceed with its planned implementation of E2EE, due to its tension with CSAM detection [29].

One can imagine that this "encryption debate" polarizes to two conceivable outcomes: a world with E2EE but without any content moderation, or a world without E2EE but with content moderation. Since neither of these outcomes seems to be truly satisfactory, it becomes vital to explore the space in between, or more fundamentally, to identify if any such space even exists. Indeed, the past few years have seen researchers paying increased attention to this very question, as covered for example by a recent report [31] released by the Center for Democracy and Technology, a technical report on the risks of client side scanning [2] and a recent talk about the question of CSAM detection vs. E2EE given at Real World Crypto 2022 [35].

In this work, we explore the viability of using cryptographic techniques to balance the need for both user privacy and illegal content moderation in messaging systems. Along the way, we also study content moderation in the context of encryption systems used by cloud service providers. This might be of independent interest.

Prior Solutions. In the setting of encrypted messaging systems, the principle goal of illegal content moderation is to identify the existence of illegal content in the system and uncover the identity of the originator of such content. The desirable privacy goals are to (i) hide the messages exchanged in the system, even from the server, and (ii) preserve the anonymity of the originator of any *harmless* content that is forwarded through the system. Note that this latter property is crucial in many real-world scenarios, e.g., whistleblowers may desire to use the protection provided by E2EE without the threat of being de-anonymized. A recent proposal [32] in this direction fails to adequately balance these goals, allowing a malicious server to de-anonymize *any* user, thereby completely violating the fundamental guarantee of E2EE.

We also note that some recent works have attempted to address the fundamentally different but related question of content moderation for *misinformation*, and we refer to Sect. 1.3 and Sect. 1.4 for discussion on this.

The Problem. The main problem with existing proposals (including the "traceback" systems for addressing misinformation that we discuss later) is that they suffer from a glaring lack of protection against a server who wishes to use the system beyond its prescribed functionality. This is a serious problem, not only because the server itself might have malicious intent, but also because of the threat of coercion from powerful actors that may want to use the technology for surveillance or censorship.

This lack of built-in protection fundamentally damages the transparency of E2EE, reducing the incentive for users to adopt the systems for their communication. While these works have indeed tried to strike a balance between privacy and content moderation, we believe that, for the deterrence of *pre-defined,*[1] *illegal* content (such as CSAM), they have over-compromised on privacy. In this work, we seek to build systems that offer similar content tracing functionality, while offering greater transparency and rigorous cryptographic guarantees about the possible scope of server behavior.

1.1   Summary of Our Contributions

We present novel definitions and efficient protocols for illegal content moderation in the setting of encrypted messaging.

Set Pre-constrained (SPC) Group Signatures. We propose a new notion of *set pre-constrained group signatures* which can be implemented in an end-to-end secure messaging application. This allows tracing users who send illegal content while ensuring privacy for everyone else.

– *Definition*: In SPC group signatures, a database D (of illegal content) can be encoded within the group's public key. The key requirement is that the signer of any message $m \in D$ can be de-anonymized by the group manager but signers of messages $m \notin D$ remain anonymous *even to the group manager*. Our definitions model *malicious* group managers and ensure that the group's public key encodes a database D that is authorized by a third-party such as the US National Center for Missing and Exploited Children (or more generally, multiple third parties). Furthermore, the public key is *publicly-verifiable*, so all clients in the system can verify for themselves (without knowing D) whether the group manager's public key encodes an acceptable D.[2]
– *Construction*: We provide a *concretely efficient* construction of SPC group signatures based on standard bilinear map assumptions, in the Random Oracle model. In this construction, we allow the group manager's public key to grow with the size of D. Crucially, however, the running time of the signing algorithm (with oracle access to the public key) as well as verification and tracing is *independent* of the size of D.

---

[1] By pre-defined, we mean any content that has been classified as "illegal", for example by a governmental body, *before* the parameters of the cloud storage or messaging system are sampled. Updating parameters to include new content classified as illegal is an interesting question in this context, which we discuss further in Sect. 1.3.

[2] In the body, we generalize our definition to consider general *functionalities* F as opposed to just the set-membership function specified by D. However, all of our constructions in this work target the special case of sets D, and we restrict our attention to such functionalities in the overview.

SPC Encryption. Along the way to constructing SPC group signatures, we define and construct efficient set pre-constrained (SPC) *encryption* schemes. Our construction builds and improves upon the recent Apple PSI protocol [10]: (1) We identify a gap in their proof of security against a malicious server and show how to efficiently build on top of their protocol in order to close this gap. (2) Further, we augment their construction to achieve a stronger notion of security that provides guarantees on the integrity of the database embedded in the public key (analogous to SPC group signatures).

Our SPC encryption scheme has public keys of size linear in the database D and constant encryption and decryption times. We demonstrate that this asymptotic efficiency trade-off is likely the "best-possible" in that further improvements would imply the elusive notion of doubly-efficient private information retrieval [11,12], which is not known to exist under standard cryptographic assumptions.

Evaluation. We implement our SPC group signature scheme and provide benchmarks in the full version [8]. We find that signing and verification take tens of milliseconds, and signature size is in the order of a few kilobytes[3]. When instantiated over the BN254 curve, the communication overhead for typical image sizes of 400 KB is under 1% and the additional computation incurs a ~15% overhead on top of message delivery time. We view these results as strong initial evidence that illegal content moderation in E2EE messaging systems – with security against malicious servers – can indeed be performed in the real world. While our current focus is on illegal content moderation, we believe that the efficiency properties of our SPC group signature and encryption schemes make them attractive tools for other applications that involve membership testing against a private "blocklist". Examples include privacy-preserving DNS blocklisting [25] where the blocklist could be proprietary, and anonymous credential systems where it is desirable to hide revocation attributes.

1.2 Our Approach

In this work, we aim to build a messaging system that satisfies, at the very least, the following set of requirements.

1. The system is end-to-end encrypted. In particular, the server cannot learn anything at all about the content transmitted in the system unless it receives some side information from a user participating in the system.
2. The originator of any piece of content remains anonymous to any user that receives the forwarded content.
3. If a user receives some illegal content, they can report it to the server, who can then determine the identity of the user who originated the content. This holds even if the content has been forwarded an arbitrary number of times before being reported.

---

[3] More precisely, for the BN254 curve, this translates to 3.5 KB per SPC group signature.

4. The originator of any *harmless* content remains anonymous, *even from the perspective of the server* who may receive a report about the content.

Naïve Approaches. To demonstrate the challenges in realizing all four properties, we first consider some existing approaches.

As a first attempt, we could try simply using end-to-end encryption. While this may satisfy the first two properties, it clearly does the support the third constraint, which we refer to as *traceability*.

A natural next attempt would be to use a *group signature* scheme [9,15] underneath E2EE in order to recover this property of traceability. In a group signature scheme, there is a group manager that generates a master public key mpk and a master secret key msk. A new client enters the system by interacting with the group manager in order to receive a client-specific secret key sk. Any client can use their sk to produce a signature σ on a message m, which can be verified by anyone that knows mpk. On the one hand, the identity of the signer remains anonymous from anyone that knows σ but not msk. On the other hand, knowing msk allows the group manager to determine which client produced σ. Thus, we can satisfy the first three goals above by having the messaging service provider additionally take on the role of the group manager. Each user in the system would then obtain a signing key sk from the server, and then attach a signature to any piece of content that they send (where the signature is also transmitted under the encryption). Unfortunately, this solution does not prevent the server from colluding with a user to identify the originator of *any* piece of content received by that user. That is, this solution appears to be fundamentally at odds with the crucial fourth requirement, or *anonymity*, stated above.

Despite some prior attempts at recovering a notion of anonymity in group signature (see Sect. 1.3 from some more discussion), we conclude that existing frameworks are insufficient for capturing the security that we demand. In order to address this issue, we must somehow *constrain* the ability of the group manager to de-anonymize anyone in the system.

SPC Group Signatures: Definitions. This motivates our first contribution, which is the definition of a *set pre-constrained group signature*, or SPC group signature. In this primitive, the group manager's master public key will be computed with respect to some set D of *illegal content* (which should remain hidden from clients even given the master public key). The novel security property we desire is that the anonymity of a client who produces a signature on some message $m \notin D$ remains intact, *even from the perspective of the group manager*.

More concretely, we ask for the following (informally stated) set of security properties.

- *Traceability*: the identity of a client who signs a message $m \in D$ should be recoverable given the signature and the master secret key.
- *Client-server anonymity*: the identity of a client who signs a message $m \notin D$ should be hidden, even given the master secret key.

- *Set-hiding:* the master public key should not reveal the set D.[4]
- *Unframeability:* no party, not even the master secret key holder, should be able to produce a signature that can be attributed to an honest client.
- *Client-client anonymity*: the identity of a client who signs any message m should be hidden from the perspective of any party who does not have the master secret key.

At this point, we must stop to consider the meaningfulness of the above security definitions as stated. In particular: who decides D? Clearly, if D is set to be the whole universe of messages, then this is no more secure than a standard group signature. And if an adversarial group manager is trying to break the client-server anonymity of the above scheme, what is preventing them from generating their master public key with respect to this "trivial" set D?

In order to constrain D in a meaningful way, we introduce a predicate $\mathcal{P}$ into the definition of client-server anonymity. The description of $\mathcal{P}$ will be fixed at setup time along with some public parameters pp known to everybody in the system and secret parameters sp known only to the group manager (we will discuss below the reason we include secret parameters). We will model client-server anonymity using an ideal functionality $\mathcal{F}_{\mathsf{anon}}$ that takes a set of items D as input from the group manager and a sequence of pairs of identities and messages $(\mathsf{pk}_1, m_1), \ldots, (\mathsf{pk}_k, m_k)$ from the client (who represents all clients in the system). If $\mathcal{P}(\mathsf{pp}, \mathsf{sp}, D) = 0$, the functionality aborts, and otherwise it delivers $\{m_i\}_{i \in [k]}, \{\mathsf{pk}_i\}_{i:m_i \in D}$ to the group manager.

This gives us a generic framework for specifying how to constrain the possible D used by the group manager. In particular, we are able to delegate the responsibility of constraining D to a *third-party* (e.g. the National Center for Missing and Exploited Children, or NCMEC), who is tasked with setting up the parameters $(\mathsf{pp}, \mathsf{sp})$ for the predicate $\mathcal{P}$. That is, we can gracefully split the responsibility of implementing/maintaining the encrypted messaging system (by e.g. WhatsApp) and the responsibility of specifying what constitutes illegal content (by e.g. NCMEC or a collection of such agencies).

Perhaps the most natural example of $\mathcal{P}$ is the "subset" predicate, which is parameterized by a set D^* of "allowed" messages (e.g. the entire database of illegal content as defined by NCMEC), and accepts only if $D \subseteq D^*$. In this case, since D^* itself represents illegal content, we do not want to make it public. Thus, we set $\mathsf{sp} = D^*$, and $\mathsf{pp} = |D^*|$. We refer to security with respect to this subset predicate as *authenticated-set security*.

In our full definition, we explicitly consider the third-party Auth as a participant in the system, who begins by setting up a pp and sp of their choice. Then, we require security against an adversary that corrupts *either* the client (and thus cannot learn anything about D), the group manager (and thus can only learn $\{\mathsf{pk}_i\}_{i:m_i \in D}$ for some "valid" D), or the third-party Auth (and thus cannot learn anything about *any* of the identities pk_i). Note that security is only vacuous if the adversary manages to corrupt both the group manager and Auth

---

[4] Note that if we want to prevent even the group manager from seeing/storing the illegal content, we can set D to be hashes of the content itself.

at the very beginning of the protocol, and thus is able to set sp and D as it wishes. While this seems like a potential limitation, our framework is general enough to support a *de-centralized* Auth. That is, we could consider many third-parties $\mathsf{Auth}_1, \ldots, \mathsf{Auth}_\ell$ who each specify a database D_i^*, and set $\mathcal{P}$ to accept D only if (for example) $D \subseteq D_1^* \cap \cdots \cap D_\ell^*$. Thus, in order to compromise the system, an adversary would have to corrupt the group manager and *all* third-party authorities *simultaneously*, while the key generation procedure is occurring.

SPC Group Signatures: Construction. We next investigate the feasibility and efficiency of constructing SPC group signatures. To do so, we abstract out the basic "pre-constraining" property we need from the group signature scheme, and re-state it in the context of an *encryption scheme*.

That is, we first define a scheme for what we call *set pre-constrained encryption*, or SPC encryption, with the following properties.

- The public key pk is generated with respect to some database D of items.
- The public key pk should not reveal D, since D may consist of sensitive or harmful content.
- Any user, given pk, can encrypt a message m with respect to an item x such that the key generator (using sk) can recover m if $x \in D$, but learns *nothing* about m if $x \notin D$.

We note that our terminology is inspired by the recent work of Ananth et al. [4] who proposed the notion of pre-constrained encryption. However, our definitions and constructions are quite different; see Sect. 1.4 for further discussion.

Our security definition for set pre-constrained encryption mirrors the anonymity definition explained above, where the key generator for the encryption scheme now plays of role of the group generator. Specifically, we can still parameterize security by a predicate $\mathcal{P}$ and parameters (pp, sp) set up by a third-party Auth.

Now, we describe a generic construction of an SPC group signature scheme from an SPC encryption scheme plus standard crytographic tools: a one-way function F, a digital signature scheme, and a zero-knowledge non-interactive argument of knowledge.

The group manager will take as input some set D and sample a public key for the SPC encryption scheme computed with respect to D. It will also include a verification key for the signature scheme in its master public key. A client can join the system by sampling a secret s, setting $\mathsf{id} = F(s)$ to be their public identity, and obtaining a signature on id from the group manager. Now, to sign a message m, the client first encrypts their identity id with respect to item m using the SPC encryption scheme, producing a ciphertext ct. Then, they produce a zero-knowledge proof π that

"I know some id, a signature on id, and s such that $\mathsf{id} = F(s)$, such that
ct is an SPC encryption of id with respect to m"

Observe that given any valid signature (ct, π) on a message $m \in D$, the group manager should be able to recover the id that produced (ct, π) by decrypting ct.

We refer to this property as *traceability*. One subtle issue that emerges here is that π can only attest that ct is in the space of valid ciphertexts encrypting id under item m, and cannot show that ct was *sampled* correctly. Thus, we will need to require that the SPC encryption is *perfectly correct*, that is, ct is perfectly binding to id when $m \in D$.

Next, we see that any signature (ct, π) on a message m hides id from any other client, which gives us the client-client anonymity property. More specific to our case, we can also show that any signature (ct, π) on a message $m \notin D$ hides id, *even from the server*, which we capture using our simulation-based security definition.

Finally, we highlight the notion of *unframeability*, which requires that a malicious server cannot produce a signature (ct, π) that can be opened to the id of any honest client. Intuitively, this follows because the server will not know the pre-image s of id, and so cannot produce a valid proof π.

SPC Encryption: Construction. With this generic compiler in hand, we provide a *concretely efficient* construction of SPC encryption, and then a *concretely efficient* instantiation of the generic compiler described above. This results in a *practical* proposal for SPC group signatures, which is our main constructive result.

Our construction of SPC encryption builds on top of the Apple PSI protocol [10]. This protocol already satisfies the basic syntax that we require, namely, the ability to embed a set D in the public key pk of an encryption scheme. However, their security notion is much weaker than the authenticated-set security we desire, and described above. Nevertheless, we can capture the security they do claim to achieve using our generic framework, and we refer to it as *bounded-set security*. In more detail, in their scheme, the key generator is completely free to choose the set D, as long as the size of D is below some public bound n. That is, $\text{pp} = n$, sp is empty, and $\mathcal{P}(n, D) = 1$ if $|D| \leq n$.

Building on their basic scheme, we provide three new contributions.

- We observe that the proof of security (for bounded-set security) given in the Apple PSI paper [10] only holds when the bound n is large enough with respect to other system parameters. This results in a large gap between correctness (the number of items that an honest server programs into its public key) and security (the number of items that a malicious server can potentially program into its public key). We show how to remedy this in a concretely efficient manner, completely closing this gap and achieving essentially no difference between the correctness and security bounds.
- We build on top of the protocol in a different manner in order to establish an efficient protocol that satisfies our novel (and much stronger) definition of *authenticated-set security*.
- We show how to tweak these schemes in order to obtain the *perfect correctness* guarantee needed to make our compiler from SPC encryption to SPC group signatures work. Interestingly, we lose an "element-hiding" property of the scheme in this process. Luckily, we don't require this property for our compiler, since elements correspond to messages in the SPC group signature

scheme, which we are not worried about leaking to the server in the event of a user report.

An in-depth overview of the Apple PSI protocol and the technical ideas involved in our improved constructions are given in Sect. 3.1.

Finally, we derive a *concretely efficient* instantiation of the SPC encryption to SPC group signature compiler, which makes use of structure-preserving signatures [1] and the Groth-Sahai proof system [24]. We provide an overview of the technical ideas involved in our constructions in Sect. 4.3. We also implement the resulting SPC group signature scheme and provide further discussion and benchmarking in the full version [8].

SPC Encryption: Limitations. As a separate contribution, we investigate generic *asymptotic* efficiency properties of SPC encryption. We identify three desirable "succinctness" properties with respect to the database size n: succinct public-key size, succinct encryption time, and succinct decryption time, where in each case, succinctness refers to poly-logarithmic complexity in n. The Apple-PSI-based protocols have non-succinct public-key size, but succinct encryption and succinct decryption. A natural question is whether it is also possible to achieve *succinct* public key. We observe the following, and provide more details in the full version.

- There are techniques in the literature [3] that can achieve succinct public key and succinct encryption with either (i) non-succinct decryption with element-hiding, or (ii) succinct decryption without element-hiding, from standard cryptographic assumptions. However, these constructions are impractical and not suitable for real-world deployment.
- An "optimal" SPC encryption scheme with succinct public key, succinct encryption, succinct decryption, and element-hiding implies the elusive notion of *doubly-efficient private-information retrieval* [11,12], which is not known to exist under any standard cryptographic assumption.

Thus, while the Apple PSI paper is not explicit about why they settled for a protocol with a non-succinct public key, our analysis validates this choice.

1.3   Discussion

CSAM Deterrence vs. Misinformation. As mentioned above, CSAM deterrence and combating misinformation are two of the most prominent applications of online content moderation. While both applications indeed fall under the umbrella of content moderation, they each introduce unique challenges from a cryptosystem perspective. The pre-constraining techniques that we make use of in this paper are designed specifically for the deterrence of illegal content, such as CSAM. On the other hand, the "traceback" systems introduced in prior works such as [34,38,43] are arguably geared more towards the application of combating misinformation.

Perhaps the biggest distinction between these applications from a cryptographic perspective is their amenability to *pre-definition*. As already discussed, illegal content must be pre-defined in some sense, for example by a governmental body. It is crucial to take advantage of this pre-definition in designing cryptosystems for illegal content deterrence. Indeed, since the description of the illegal content itself can be baked into the parameters of the system, we can hope to obtain rigorous guarantees about *which* content is being tracked and monitored by the system administrator.

On the other hand, it is not even clear in the first place how to define misinformation, or even who has the authority to define it. Plus, new content that could potentially be classified as misinformation is constantly being created and distributed. Thus, it is less clear how to obtain rigorous security guarantees against potentially malicious servers in the setting of misinformation deterrence. A potential approach could be to allow new content (such as new misinformation or abuse) to be added to the "constrained" set, so that the originators of prior messages containing this content could be traced. This feature is reminiscent of "retrospective" access to encrypted data as considered in [22] in a somewhat different context. They show that such access requires the use of powerful (and currently very inefficient) cryptographic tools, and it would be interesting to see if the same implications hold in the setting of tracing in end-to-end encrypted messaging systems.

Deniability vs. Unframeability. Another difference between illegal content and misinformation from a cryptographic perspective is reflected in the technical tension between the notions of *deniability* and *unframeability*. Deniability essentially asks that messages between users can be simulated without any user-specific secrets, where indistinguishability from real messages holds from the perspective of an entity with *full information*, including user and even server secrets. This can certainly be a desirable property of encrypted messaging systems, especially when there is a threat of coercion from powerful outside sources. However, this property conflicts with *unframeability* against malicious servers, since it enables servers to produce these simulated messages [42]. While deniability has been a sought-after feature of encrypted systems with traceback functionality [38], it actually appears to be *counter-productive* in systems that are meant to detect originators of CSAM or other illegal content. Indeed, it is important that not only can the server identify the originator, but also that the server can convince law enforcement of the identity of the content originator. On the other hand, we view unframeability against malicious servers as a crucial property of CSAM deterrence systems, since users can face dramatic consequences if framed for the generation or dissemination of illegal content. Thus, our techniques are tailored to obtain the strongest notion of unframeability and no deniability,[5] while prior work [38] that focused on combating misinformation took the opposite approach.

---

[5] Though we note that one could potentially alter our group signature scheme to obtain deniability at the cost of unframeability, by including in the zero-knowledge argument a clause along the lines of "OR I know the master secret key".

On Security Against Malicious Servers. In this work, we took steps towards ensuring privacy and anonymity against malicious (or even honest-but-curious) servers in encrypted systems with support for content moderation. As mentioned earlier in the introduction, it is absolutely vital to explore the space of solutions to the "encrytion debate" that don't give up fully on either end-to-end encryption or content moderation. There is much more work to be done in this space, and we view our techniques as one tool in an ever-expanding toolbox of techniques meant to address the broad question of privacy vs. content moderation.

In particular, while we remove the need to trust *service providers* (think, WhatsApp), the notion of authenticated-set security essentially moves this trust to a third party (think NCMEC). We consider this progress, since it splits the responsibility of providing a messaging service and defining illegal content. Moreover, as discussed earlier, our scheme would immediately extend to support *multiple* third parties that can each attest to the validity of the server's public parameters, further splitting the trust. However, we acknowledge that there is opportunity to further improve the transparency and trust in such content moderation systems.

Additional Challenges and Future Directions. We conclude our discussion with a few directions for future work. First, a desirable property of encrypted illegal content moderation systems is the ability to *update* public parameters to include new illegal content. As discussed in the Apple PSI paper [10], a simple way to handle updates is to redo setup and release the updated public key as part of system update. Achieving more efficient updates, however, is an interesting direction for future work. For example, if an update only corresponds to locations that are changed, it may start leaking the positions that correspond to database elements. This suggests the need for creative solutions, for example the use of differential privacy techniques to hide this leakage.

Next, we did not consider *thresholding* in this work, which would protect the privacy of content or anonymity of users until *multiple matches* were found in the database. While this is straightforward to incorporate into SPC encryption, it is not as immediate for SPC group signatures, at least if the goal is to maintain concrete efficiency. We leave an exploration of this to future work.

Next, we chose to use Groth-Sahai proof systems in order to demonstrate that SPC group signatures could be constructed with reasonable efficiency. However, there are other tools available, such as efficient SNARGs (succinct non-interactive arguments) that may result in better verification time at the cost of increased signer work. We leave further investigation of this to future work.

Finally, we mention broader considerations that would come with using our system in the real world. In the system, the actual database D would likely not consist of the actual CSAM images themselves, but rather *hashes* of CSAM images computed using a perceptual hash function, such as Apple's NeuralHash [5]. This introduces the possibility of adversarial use of the hash function, for example targeted collision-finding. We view this as an important attack vector to consider, especially when using these hash functions in conjunction with cryptographic protocols meant to provide privacy against malicious servers. Exploration of this topic is outside the scope of the current work, and we refer the reader to [40] and references therein for current research on the topic.

1.4   Related Work

Pre-constrained Cryptography. Our work borrows the terminology of pre-constrained cryptography from Ananth et al. [4] because of sharing a similar vision – that of putting pre-specified restrictions on the key generation authority. Our definitions and constructions, however, are different from [4]. First, we note that the notion of (set) pre-constrained group signatures is *new* to our work, while Ananth et al. [4] only focus on (pre-constrained) encryption systems. In the setting of pre-constrained encryption, the notion of malicious security in [4] is weaker than ours and allows the authority to choose *any* "constraint" from a class of constraints. This weaker notion is not meaningful in our setting, as it allows the service provider (think, WhatsApp) to use an *arbitrary set* of their choice. Ananth et al. propose constructions for different flavors of pre-constrained encryption; the one that comes closest to our setting relies on indistinguishability obfuscation [7], and is presently only of theoretical interest. In contrast, we provide concretely efficient constructions for our setting.

Traceback Systems. While our work focuses on moderation for *pre-defined illegal content*, there has also been much recent work on the adjacent question of moderation for *misinformation* or *abusive* content. Solutions for this problem typically build "traceback" mechanisms into end-to-end encrypted systems [27, 34, 38, 43], extending the reach of so-called "message franking" systems [17, 26, 42]. These solutions rely on user reporting to identify the existence of harmful content. Once a report is received by the server, the server and reporting user can work together to identify the originator of the harmful message. Unfortunately, these systems suffer from various drawbacks [21]: (1) They allow a colluding server and users to de-anonymize the originator of *any* message, even if the content is harmless. (2) Initial solutions in this space additionally require the help of users on the traceback path to identify the originator, and do not maintain their anonymity. While the latter drawback was addressed in the recent work of [38], no known solution provides security guarantees against malicious servers. Our system addresses both of these shortcomings, for our specific setting of illegal content moderation.

Group Signatures. Finally, we mention a related line of work on group signatures with *message-dependent opening* (GS-MDO) [18, 33]. Here, trust is split between the group manager and an additional entity called the "admitter". The identity of a group member that produces a signature on a message m can be revealed only if the group manager and admitter combine their private information. Unlike SPC group signatures, GS-MDO does *not* require any "commitment" to, or "pre-constraining" of, the set of messages that can be de-anonymized. This means that even after the system parameters are set up, the group manager and admitter can in principle work together to de-anonymize *every* signature while still acting "semi-honestly" w.r.t. the protocol specification. In particular, clients of the system will not have the peace of mind guaranteed by public parameters that are publicly "authenticated" to only allow de-anonymization of a particular set of illegal content specificied by some trusted (collection of) third party(ies).

2   Preliminaries

The security parameter is denoted by $\lambda \in \mathbb{N}$. A function $f : \mathbb{N} \to \mathbb{N}$ is said to be polynomial if there exists a constant c such that $f(n) \leq n^c$ for all $n \in \mathbb{N}$, and we write $\mathsf{poly}(\cdot)$ to denote such a function. A function $f : \mathbb{N} \to [0,1]$ is said to be negligible if for every $c \in \mathbb{N}$, there exists $N \in \mathbb{N}$ such that for all $n > N$, $f(n) < n^{-c}$, and we write $\mathsf{negl}(\cdot)$ to denote such a function. A probability is *noticeable* if it is not negligible, and *overwhelming* if it is equal to $1 - \mathsf{negl}(\lambda)$ for some negligible function $\mathsf{negl}(\lambda)$. For a set $\mathcal{S}$, we write $s \leftarrow \mathcal{S}$ to indicate that s is sampled uniformly at random from $\mathcal{S}$. For a random variable $\mathcal{D}$, we write $d \leftarrow \mathcal{D}$ to indicate that d is sampled according to $\mathcal{D}$. An algorithm $\mathcal{A}$ is PPT (probabilistic polynomial-time) if its running time is bounded by some polynomial in the size of its input. For two ensembles of random variables $\{\mathcal{D}_{0,\lambda}\}_{\lambda \in \mathbb{N}}$, $\{\mathcal{D}_{1,\lambda}\}_{\lambda \in \mathbb{N}}$, we write $\mathcal{D}_0 \approx_c \mathcal{D}_1$ to indicate that for all PPT $\mathcal{A}$, it holds that

$$\left| \Pr_{d \leftarrow \mathcal{D}_{0,\lambda}} [\mathcal{A}(d) = 1] - \Pr_{d \leftarrow \mathcal{D}_{1,\lambda}} [\mathcal{A}(d) = 1] \right| \leq \frac{1}{2} + \mathsf{negl}(\lambda).$$

2.1   Basic Cryptographic Primitives and Assumptions

We will use a standard symmetric-key encryption scheme $(\mathsf{Enc}, \mathsf{Dec})$ with key space $\mathcal{K}$ that satisfies *random key robustness*, which states that for any message m, $\Pr_{k,k' \leftarrow \mathcal{K}}[\mathsf{Dec}(k', \mathsf{Enc}(k, m)) = \bot] = 1 - \mathsf{negl}(\lambda)$. We will also make use of a standard digital signature scheme $(\mathsf{Gen}, \mathsf{Sign}, \mathsf{Verify})$ that is *existentially unforgeable under chosen message attacks* (EUF-CMA).

2.2   Non-interactive Arguments of Knowledge

Let $\mathcal{L}$ be an NP language and let $\mathcal{R}$ be the associated binary relation, where a statement $x \in \mathcal{L}$ if and only if there exists a witness w such that $(x, w) \in \mathcal{R}$. A non-interactive argument system for $\mathcal{R}$ consists of algorithms Setup, Prove, Verify, where $\mathsf{Setup}(1^\lambda)$ outputs a string crs, $\mathsf{Prove}(\mathsf{crs}, x, w)$ outputs a proof π, and $\mathsf{Verify}(\mathsf{crs}, x, \pi)$ outputs either 1 to indicate accept or 0 to indicate reject. We say that a non-interactive argument system for a relation $\mathcal{R}$ that satisfies the standard notions of *completeness*, *knowledge extraction*, and *zero-knowledge*, is a *zero-knowledge non-interactive argument of knowledge* (ZK-NIAoK) for $\mathcal{R}$. We will use the fact that the following relations all have highly efficient ZK-NIAoKs in the ROM. Let $\mathbb{G}$ be a group of order q with generator g.

- The relation $\mathcal{R}_{\mathsf{DLog}} = \{((g, h), \alpha) : h = g^\alpha\}$. A ZK-NIAoK for $\mathcal{R}_{\mathsf{DLog}}$ follows from applying the Fiat-Shamir heuristic [20] to Schnorr's sigma protocol [41].

- The relation $\mathcal{R}_{\mathsf{DH}} = \{((g, h_1, h_2, h_3), \alpha) : (h_1 = g^\alpha) \wedge (h_3 = h_2^\alpha)\}$. A ZK-NIAoK for $\mathcal{R}_{\mathsf{DH}}$ follows from applying the Fiat-Shamir heuristic to Chaum and Pederson's sigma protocol [14].
- For any n and $k \le n$, the relation $\mathcal{R}_{\mathsf{DLog}_n^k} = \{((g, h_1, \ldots, h_n), (S, \{\alpha_i\}_{i \in S})) : (|S| = k) \wedge (\forall i \in S, h_i = g^{\alpha_i})\}$. A ZK-NIAoK for $\mathcal{R}_{\mathsf{DLog}_n^k}$ follows from applying the Fiat-Shamir heuristic to the protocol of [16]. Moreover, an efficient *succinct* argument system for this language whose size is logarithmic in n, was shown recently by [6].

2.3   Groth-Sahai Proofs

Let $\mathcal{G}$ be a bilinear group generator that on input 1^λ returns $(p, \mathbb{G}_1, \mathbb{G}_2, \mathbb{T}, e, g_1, g_2)$, where $\mathbb{G}_1, \mathbb{G}_2, \mathbb{T}$ are groups of order p, where p is a λ-bit prime. g_1 is a generator of $\mathbb{G}_1$, g_2 is a generator of $\mathbb{G}_2$, and e is a non-degenerate bilinear map. That is, $e(g, g)$ is a generator of $\mathbb{T}$, and for all $a, b \in \mathbb{Z}_p$, it holds that $e(g_1^a, g_2^b) = e(g_1, g_2)^{ab}$. The DDH assumption is assumed to hold in each of $\mathbb{G}_1$ and $\mathbb{G}_2$. In other words, the SXDH (symmetric external Diffie-Hellman) assumption is assumed to hold.

Groth and Sahai [24] constructed efficient non-interactive zero-knowledge proof systems for statements that involve equations over bilinear maps. "GS proofs" can prove certain statements that consist of the equations over variables $X_1, \ldots, X_m \in \mathbb{G}_1, Y_1, \ldots, Y_n \in \mathbb{G}_2, x_1, \ldots,$ and $x_{m'}, y_1, \ldots, y_{n'} \in \mathbb{Z}_p$. Although, the GS proof system can handle many types of equation, we restrict our attention to two categories. The first type is *pairing product equations* – $\prod_{i=1}^n e(A_i, Y_i) \prod_{i=1}^m e(X_i, B_i) \prod_{i=1}^m \prod_{j=1}^n e(A_i, B_j)^{c_{ij}} = 1_{\mathbb{T}}$, for constants $A_i \in \mathbb{G}_1, B_i \in \mathbb{G}_2, c_{ij} \in \mathbb{Z}_p$, where $1_{\mathbb{T}}$ is the identity in $\mathbb{T}$ and b) *multi-scalar exponentiations* – $\prod_{i=1}^{n'} A_i^{y_i} \prod_{i=1}^m X_i^{b_i} \prod_{i=1}^m \prod_{j=1}^{n'} X_i^{c_{ij} y_j} = T_1$, for constants $A_i, T_1 \in \mathbb{G}_1, b_i, c_{ij} \in \mathbb{Z}_p$ and analogous statements for multi-scalar exponentiation in $\mathbb{G}_2$.

GS proofs are in the *common random string* model, and satisfy the completeness and zero-knowledge properties described in Sect. 2.2. However, they only satisfy a weaker notion of knowledge extraction which has been referred to as *partial* knowledge extraction [23]. This property states that if the witness consists of both group elements and exponents, only the group elements are extractable.

2.4   Cuckoo Hashing

A cuckoo hashing scheme consists of the algorithms (Setup, Hash), and is parameterized by a universe $\mathcal{U}$ of elements.

- Setup$(\lambda, n, \epsilon) \to (n', h_0, h_1)$: the setup algorithm takes as input an integer parameter λ, an integer bound n, and $\epsilon \ge 0$, and outputs an integer n' and two hash functions $h_0, h_1 : \mathcal{U} \to [n']$, where n' is a deterministic function of $\lambda, n,$ and ϵ.

– Hash(h_0, h_1, D) → T : the (deterministic) hashing algorithm takes hash functions $h_0, h_1 : \mathcal{U} \to [n']$ and a set $D \subseteq \mathcal{U}$, and outputs a table $T = [T_1, \ldots, T_{n'}]$, where each T_i is either an element in D or $\perp$.

For correctness, we demand that for every $x \in \mathcal{U}$, $h_0(x) \neq h_1(x)$. We will assume that this is the case for every pair of even adversarially chosen hash functions.[6] Each non-$\perp$ element of T is distinct. Finally, for any n, ϵ and set $D \subseteq \mathcal{U}$ of size n, it holds that with probability $1 - \mathsf{negl}(\lambda)$ over $(m, h_0, h_1) \leftarrow \mathsf{Setup}(\lambda, n, \epsilon)$, there exists a set $D' \subseteq D$ such that $|D'| \geq (1 - \epsilon)|D|$ and such that for any $x \in D'$, either $T_{h_0(x)} = x$ or $T_{h_1(x)} = x$, where $T := \mathsf{Hash}(h_0, h_1, D)$.

3 Set Pre-constrained Encryption

In this section, we define and construct set pre-constrained (SPC) encryption. We start by providing an overview in Sect. 3.1. We then present formal definitions of SPC encryption in Sect. 3.2, and constructions in Sect. 3.3. In the full version [8] we demonstrate that an *optimal* version of SPC encryption implies doubly-efficient private information retrieval and also prove security of our protocols.

3.1 Overview

The Basic Apple PSI Protocol. We start by recalling the basic Apple PSI protocol, viewed as an *encryption scheme*. "Basic" here refers to the protocol without the extra threshold or synthetic match functionalities, which we will not consider explicitly in this work.

A key technique used in Apple's protocol is the Naor-Reingold Diffie-Hellman random self reduction [36]. Let $\mathbb{G}$ be a cyclic group of order q with generator g, and let h_1, h_2, h_3 be three other group elements. Suppose that $\beta, \gamma \leftarrow \mathbb{Z}_q$ are sampled as uniformly random exponents, and $h'_2 :=^\beta \cdot h_2^\gamma, h'_3 := h_1^\beta \cdot h_3^\gamma$. Then it holds that (i) if (g, h_1, h_2, h_3) is a Diffie-Hellman tuple (that is, there exists α such that $g^\alpha = h_1$ and $h_2^\alpha = h_3$), then (g, h_1, h'_2, h'_3) is a Diffie-Hellman tuple, and (ii) if (g, h_1, h_2, h_3) is *not* a Diffie-Hellman tuple, then (h'_2, h'_3) are fresh uniformly random group elements.

Now, this self-reduction can be used to construct a set pre-constrained encryption scheme for a single-item set $\{x\}$ as follows. Let H be a hash function that hashes items to group elements (H will be treated as a random oracle in the security proof). The key generator, on input an item x, will sample $\alpha \leftarrow \mathbb{Z}_q$ and publish ($A = g^\alpha, B = H(x)^\alpha$) as the public key. Note that $(g, A, H(x), B)$ is a Diffie-Hellman tuple, while for any $x' \neq x$, $(g, A, H(x'), B)$ is *not* a Diffie-Hellman tuple. This suggests a natural encryption scheme. Given the public key, an item y, and a message m, the encryption algorithm will run the Naor-Reingold self-reduction on $(g, A, H(y), B)$ to produce group elements (Q, S), and then treat S as a secret key for encrypting the message m. That is, the ciphertext

---

[6] For example, h_1 can be defined to first hash x and then check if the hash is equal to $h_0(x)$ and if so add 1.

will consist of $(Q, \mathsf{SEnc}_S(m))$, where SEnc is a symmetric-key encryption scheme. If $y \neq x$, then S will be uniformly random, even from the key generator's perspective, so m remains hidden. On the other hand, if $y = x$, then (g, A, Q, S) is a Diffie-Helman tuple, and the element $S = Q^\alpha$ can be computed by the key generator and used to recover m.

This scheme can easily be extended to support larger set sizes, by having the key generator publish $(A, H(x_1)^\alpha, \ldots, H(x_n)^\alpha)$ as the public key, where $x_1, \ldots, x_n$ is its input set. However, the naive extensions of the encryption and decryption algorithms described above will have running time that grows with the size n of the set. The authors of the Apple PSI system make use of a technique called *cuckoo hashing* to significantly reduce this running time. Concretely, the key generator will hash the set $(x_1, \ldots, x_n)$ into a table T of size $n' = (1 + \epsilon)n$ for some constant ϵ, using randomly sampled hash keys h_0, h_1. The guarantee is that with high probability, for most x_i, either $T_{h_0(x_i)} = x_i$ or $T_{h_1(x_i)} = x_i$. Note that T will have $n' - n$ empty entries, which we denote with $\perp$. The key generator will then publish $(A, B_1, \ldots, B_{n'})$ as the public key, where for each $i \in [n']$, if $T_i = x$ then $B_i = H(x)^\alpha$, while if $T_i = \perp$ then $B_i = g^r$ for a random exponent r. Now, to encrypt a message m with respect to an item y, one only has to produce two pairs $(Q_0, \mathsf{SEnc}_{S_0}(m)), (Q_1, \mathsf{SEnc}_{S_1}(m))$, where (Q_b, S_b) is the result of applying the Naor-Reingold self-reduction to $(g, A, H(y), B_{h_b(y)})$.

This results in a set pre-constrained encryption scheme that can handle pre-constraining sets of size n with a public key of about $n' = (1 + \epsilon)n$ group elements, and encryption and decryption algorithms whose running times do not grow with the size of n. One can show (in the random oracle model) that this scheme already satisfies set-hiding under the DDH assumption, and can be made to satisfy element-hiding from DDH, as long as the two pairs $(Q_0, \mathsf{SEnc}_{S_0}(m))$, $(Q_1, \mathsf{SEnc}_{S_1}(m))$ that constitute the ciphertext are randomly permuted, and $B_1, \ldots, B_{n'}$ are all distinct group elements.

Achieving Bounded-Set and Authenticated-Set Security. Next, we show that augmenting the above template with *simple* and *efficient* zero-knowledge arguments suffices to achieve first bounded-set and next authenticated-set security. While the potential utility of adding zero-knowledge arguments to Apple's PSI system has previously been discussed informally [13,39], we view our formalization and efficient realization of rigorous security definitions as a necessary and important contribution in this space.

The Apple PSI paper [10] actually already claims to achieve *bounded-set* security, which guarantees that a malicious key generator can only decrypt messages that are encrypted with respect to some set of items of size at most B. However, it is left unclear what B is, and how it depends on other parameters in the system. In fact, their proof completely breaks down if $B < n'$. In particular, their proof relies on extracting the input set X of the key generator by observing random oracle queries, potentially adding one item x to X for each group element B_i in the public key. If the resulting X is such that $|X| > B$, then the ideal functionality aborts, and the malicious key generator would not receive encryptions from the client. However, this behavior does not reflect what would happen in the real world, where the client would not be able to tell how large the key generator's "effective input" actually is.

This issue in the proof occurs with good reason, since a malicious key generator can indeed publish $(A, H(x_1)^\alpha, \ldots, H(x_{n'})^\alpha)$ for n' items $x_1, \ldots, x_{n'}$ without being detected. However, correctness for honest key generators is only guaranteed to hold for up to n items (due to the cuckoo hashing). Thus, in the best case, we hope for a scheme that achieves bounded-set security with bound n.

We show how to achieve this by instructing the key generator to append to their key $(A, B_1, \ldots, B_{n'})$ a zero-knowledge non-interactive proof of knowledge that they know the discrete logarithm α of A and at least $n' - n$ discrete logarithms $\{r_i\}$ of the elements $B_1, \ldots, B_{n'}$. Highly efficient proofs supporting these languages are known [6,16]. Intuitively, the $n' - n$ group elements B_i for which the generator knows r_i such that $B_i = g^{r_i}$ are "useless" for decrypting encrypted messages. To see why, recall that, due to the Naor-Reingold self-reduction, B_i can only be used to decrypt with respect to an item x such that $(g, A, H(x), B_i)$ forms a Diffie-Hellman tuple. However, if the generator knows an x, α, and r_i such that this holds, they can break the discrete logarithm problem, since $H(x) = g^{r/\alpha}$ and $H(x)$ can be programmed by a reduction. Thus, only at most n of the elements $(B_1, \ldots, B_{n'})$ will actually be useful for decrypting messages, which we leverage to show bounded-set security with a bound of n.

Next, we consider our notion of *authenticated-set* security, which introduces a third party that chooses the set D. In our scheme, the third party first sends D to the key generator. Then, the key generator prepares a public key $(A, B_1, \ldots, B_{n'})$. In the honest case, for each i it either holds that there exists $x \in D$ such that $(g, A, H(x), B_i)$ form a Diffie-Hellman tuple, or the generator knows r_i such that $B_i = g_i^r$. Now, these are claims that the generator can prove efficiently in zero-knowledge to the third party. The third party will then checks these proofs, and if all verify, will sign the set of group elements $(A, B_1, \ldots, B_{n'})$ under its public verification key. We show in Sect. 3.3 that this is sufficient for achieving authenticated-set security.

3.2 Definitions

A set pre-constrained encryption (SPCE) scheme $\Pi_{\mathsf{SPCE}}[\mathcal{U}, \mathcal{M}, n, \epsilon]$ consists of algorithms (Gen, Enc, Dec), and is parameterized by a universe $\mathcal{U}$ of elements, a message space $\mathcal{M}$, a set size n, and a correctness parameter ϵ. $\mathcal{U}, \mathcal{M}, n, \epsilon$ may actually be infinite families parameterized by the security parameter λ, though we suppress mention of this for ease of notation.

- Gen$(1^\lambda, D) \to (\mathsf{pk}, \mathsf{sk})$: the parameter generation algorithm takes as input a security parameter 1^λ and a set $D \subseteq \mathcal{U}$ of size at most n, and outputs a public key pk and a secret key sk.
- Enc$(\mathsf{pk}, x, m) \to \mathsf{ct}$: the encryption algorithm takes as input a public key pk, an item $x \in \mathcal{U}$, and a message $m \in \mathcal{M}$, and outputs a ciphertext ct.
- Dec$(\mathsf{sk}, \mathsf{ct}) \to \{m, \bot\}$: the decryption algorithm takes as input a secret key sk and a ciphertext ct and outputs either a message $m \in \mathcal{M}$ or a symbol $\bot$.

We note that any SPC encryption scheme can be utilized for encrypted cloud storage as follows. The server initially publishes pk, and whenever the client wants to upload some content x, they would sample an (element-hiding) SPC encryption of (x, m), where m is arbitrary "associated data" (e.g. the name of the client). Then, if $x \in D$, the server would be able to use sk to recover the associated data m. Otherwise (x, m) will remain hidden from the server.

Efficiency. By default, all algorithms in an SPC encryption scheme should be polynomial-time in the size of their inputs, and $n, |x|, |m|$ should be polynomial-size in λ. However, we will want to consider a more fine-grained notion of efficiency with respect to the size n of the set D, which may be a large polynomial. We say that the scheme has *succinct public-key* if $|pk| = \mathsf{poly}(\lambda, \log n)$, *succinct encryption* if the running time of Enc is $\mathsf{poly}(\lambda, \log n)$, and *succinct decryption* if the running time of Dec is $\mathsf{poly}(\lambda, \log n)$.

Correctness. We define notions of correctness for an SPC encryption scheme. We first consider the following notion of ϵ-correctness, where the parameter ϵ essentially determines an upper bound on the fraction of the set D that is "dropped" by the Gen algorithm.[7]

Definition 1. *An* SPC *encryption scheme (*Gen, Enc, Dec*) is ϵ-correct for some $\epsilon \geq 0$ if for any $\lambda \in \mathbb{N}$ and $D \subseteq \mathcal{U}$, it holds that with probability $1 - \mathsf{negl}(\lambda)$ over $(pk, sk) \leftarrow \mathsf{Gen}(1^\lambda, D)$, there exists a $D' \subseteq D$ such that $|D'| \geq (1 - \epsilon)|D|$ and for any $x \in D'$ and $m \in \mathcal{M}$, $\Pr[\mathsf{Dec}(sk, \mathsf{Enc}(pk, x, m)) = m] = 1 - \mathsf{negl}(\lambda)$.*

Next, we define the stronger notion of *perfect ϵ-correctness* that will be useful for our application of SPC encryption to building SPC group signatures in Sect. 4.

Definition 2. *An* SPC *encryption scheme (*Gen, Enc, Dec*) is perfectly ϵ-correct for some $\epsilon \geq 0$ if the following two properties hold for any $\lambda \in \mathbb{N}$ and $D \subseteq \mathcal{U}$.*

- *With probability $1 - \mathsf{negl}(\lambda)$ over $(pk, sk) \leftarrow \mathsf{Gen}(1^\lambda, D)$, there exists a $D' \subseteq D$ such that $|D'| \geq (1 - \epsilon)|D|$ and for any m and $x \in D'$, $\Pr[\mathsf{Dec}(sk, \mathsf{Enc}(pk, x, m)) = m] = 1$.*
- *For all $(pk, sk) \in \mathsf{Gen}(1^\lambda, D)$, x, m, $\Pr[\mathsf{Dec}(sk, \mathsf{Enc}(pk, x, m)) \in \{m, \bot\}] = 1$.*

Security. We define security using the simulation framework, via an ideal functionality described in Fig. 1. The ideal functionality $\mathcal{F}^{\mathcal{P}}_{\mathsf{SPCE}}$ takes place between a *server*, who runs Gen and Dec, a *client*, who runs Enc, and a third party Auth, whose role will be described below. In full generality, the server's input is a function F, but in our applications, we will always parse F as a description of a database D of items. The client's input is a sequence of items and messages $(x_1, m_1), \ldots, (x_k, m_k)$. The client should learn nothing about D, Auth should learn nothing about the messages $m_1, \ldots, m_k$, and the server should learn only $\{m_i\}_{i:x_i \in D}$ (and potentially the elements $\{x_i\}_{i \in [k]}$).

---

[7] Traditionally, one might expect ϵ to be negligible, and thus suppressed in the definition. However, our protocols will make use of cuckoo hashing which may introduce an inverse-polynomial ϵ.

To make security against the server meaningful, we must place some restriction on D. We do this (in a modular way) by parameterizing the functionality with a predicate $\mathcal{P}$. This predicate may depend on some public parameters pp (known to both client and server) and some secret parameters sp (known only to the server). It is the job of Auth to set up these parameters. We allow a malicious adversary to corrupt either the server, the client, or Auth. We note that one could also consider collusions between any pair of parties, but in each case security becomes vacuous, so we do not consider this in our proofs of security.

Below, we describe the instantiations of $\mathcal{P}$ that we will consider in this work: one will define what we call *bounded-set security* and the other will define what we call *authenticated-set security*.

$\mathcal{F}^{\mathcal{P}}_{\mathsf{SPCE}}$

Parties: server S, client C, and authority Auth.
Parameters: universe $\mathcal{U}$, message space $\mathcal{M}$.

- Obtain input (pp, sp) from Auth. Deliver pp to both C and S, and sp to S.
- Obtain input $F = (F_S, F_{\mathsf{Auth}})$ from S and deliver F to Auth. Abort and deliver $\perp$ to all parties if $\mathcal{P}(\mathsf{pp}, \mathsf{sp}, F) = 0$.
- Obtain input $(x_1, m_1), \ldots, (x_k, m_k)$ from client, where each $x_i \in \mathcal{U}$ and each $m_i \in \mathcal{M}$.
- Deliver $F_S(\{x_i, m_i\}_{i \in [k]})$ to server and $F_{\mathsf{Auth}}(\{x_i, m_i\}_{i \in [k]})$ to Auth.

Fig. 1. Ideal functionality for SPC encryption. $\mathcal{P}$ is a predicate that takes as input some public parameters pp, secret parameters sp, and a pair of functions $F = (F_S, F_{\mathsf{Auth}})$, and outputs a bit.

Bounded-Set Security. Here, we define two predicates $\mathcal{P}[\mathsf{BS}]$ and $\mathcal{P}[\mathsf{BS\text{-}EH}]$, where BS stands for bounded-set, and EH stands for element-hiding. For each, the public parameters pp are parsed as an integer n, there are no secret parameters sp, and F is parsed as the description of a database $D \subseteq \mathcal{U}$. The predicate then outputs 1 if and only if $|D| \leq n$. For $\mathcal{P}[\mathsf{BS}]$,

$$F_S(\{x_i, m_i\}_{i \in [k]}) = \{x_i\}_{i \in [k]}, \{m_i\}_{i:x_i \in D}, \quad F_{\mathsf{Auth}}(\{x_i, m_i\}_{i \in [k]}) = \{x_i\}_{i \in [k]},$$

and for $\mathcal{P}[\mathsf{BS\text{-}EH}]$,

$$F_S(\{x_i, m_i\}_{i \in [k]}) = k, \{m_i\}_{i:x_i \in D}, \quad F_{\mathsf{Auth}}(\{x_i, m_i\}_{i \in [k]}) = k.$$

Authenticated-Set Security. Here, we define two predicates $\mathcal{P}[\mathsf{AS}]$ and $\mathcal{P}[\mathsf{AS\text{-}EH}]$, where AS stands for authenticated-set. For each, the public parameters pp are parsed as an integer n, the secret parameters are parsed as a database $D^* \subseteq \mathcal{U}$

of size n, and F is parsed as a database $D \subseteq \mathcal{U}$. The predicate then outputs 1 if and only if $D \subseteq D^*$. For $\mathcal{P}[\text{AS}]$,

$$F_S(\{x_i, m_i\}_{i \in [k]}) = \{x_i\}_{i \in [k]}, \{m_i\}_{i:x_i \in D}, \quad F_{\text{Auth}}(\{x_i, m_i\}_{i \in [k]}) = \{x_i\}_{i \in [k]},$$

and for $\mathcal{P}[\text{AS-EH}]$,

$$F_S(\{x_i, m_i\}_{i \in [k]}) = k, \{m_i\}_{i:x_i \in D}, \quad F_{\text{Auth}}(\{x_i, m_i\}_{i \in [k]}) = k.$$

One can also define a game-based notion of security against *outsiders* by extending standard notions of semantic security to capture the indistinguishability of ciphertexts corresponding to encryptions of two different messages. We defer this to the full version [8].

3.3 Construction

We begin by giving templates for SPC encryption based on Apple's PSI protocol [10]. These schemes will have succinct encryption and succinct decryption, but *non-succinct* public-key. We will first describe a scheme $\Pi_{\text{SPCE}}^{\text{Basic-EH}}$ (Protocol 2) that satisfies ϵ-correctness and security against outsiders with element-hiding. Then, we describe a related scheme $\Pi_{\text{SPCE}}^{\text{Basic-PC}}$ (Protocol 3) that satisfies *perfect* ϵ-correctness but only security against outsiders *without* element-hiding, and is tailored to support encrypting messages that are group elements. This latter scheme will be useful for our construction of set pre-constrained group signatures in Sect. 4. Following these basic templates, we will then show how to (efficiently) upgrade each to obtain bounded-set and authenticated-set security, resulting in schemes $\Pi_{\text{SPCE}}^{\text{BS-EH}}, \Pi_{\text{SPCE}}^{\text{BS-PC}}, \Pi_{\text{SPCE}}^{\text{AS-EH}}, \Pi_{\text{SPCE}}^{\text{AS-PC}}$.

Ingredients:

- A cyclic group $\mathbb{G}$ of prime order q in which the DDH problem is assumed to be hard.
- A symmetric-key encryption scheme (RobEnc, RobDec) with keyspace $\mathcal{K}$ that satisfies *random key robustness* (Sect. 2.1).
- Hash functions $H : \mathcal{U} \to \mathbb{G} \setminus \{0\}$ and $G : \mathbb{G} \to \mathcal{K}$ modeled as random oracles, where G maps the uniform distribution over $\mathbb{G}$ to (negligibly close to) the uniform distribution over $\mathcal{K}$.
- A cuckoo hashing scheme (CH.Setup, CH.Hash) (Sect. 2.4).

Achieving Bounded-Set Security. It can in fact be shown that $\Pi_{\text{SPCE}}^{\text{Basic-EH}}[\mathcal{U}, \mathcal{M}, n, \epsilon]$ (resp. $\Pi_{\text{SPCE}}^{\text{Basic-PC}}[\mathcal{U}, \mathbb{G}, n, \epsilon]$) already securely emulates $\mathcal{F}_{\text{SPCE}}^{\mathcal{P}[\text{BS-EH}]}$ (resp. $\mathcal{F}_{\text{SPCE}}^{\mathcal{P}[\text{BS}]}$) with set size $\text{pp} = n'$ where n' is such that $(n', \cdot, \cdot) \leftarrow \text{CH.Setup}(\lambda, n, \epsilon)$. However, n' may be much larger than n, which means a large gap between correctness (an honest server would be able to decrypt with respect to $(1 - \epsilon)n$ items) and security (a dishonest server would potentially be able to decrypt with respect to up to n' items).

Below, we show that an efficient tweak to the basic schemes results in schemes $\Pi_{\text{SPCE}}^{\text{BS-EH}}, \Pi_{\text{SPCE}}^{\text{BS-PC}}$ (Protocol 4) that completely close this gap. That is, for any n, the schemes $\Pi_{\text{SPCE}}^{\text{BS-EH}}, \Pi_{\text{SPCE}}^{\text{BS-PC}}$ securely emulate $\mathcal{F}_{\text{SPCE}}^{\mathcal{P}[\text{BS-EH}]}, \mathcal{F}_{\text{SPCE}}^{\mathcal{P}[\text{BS}]}$ with $\text{pp} = n$.

$$\Pi_{\text{SPCE}}^{\text{Basic}-\text{EH}}[\mathcal{U}, \mathcal{M}, n, \epsilon]$$

Parameters: universe $\mathcal{U}$, message space $\mathcal{M}$, set size n, correctness parameter ϵ, and security parameter λ.

Setup: description of the group $\mathbb{G}$ with generator g, and random oracles H, G.

Gen$(1^\lambda, D)$:

- Run $(n', h_0, h_1) \leftarrow$ CH.Setup(λ, n, ϵ) and then $T :=$ CH.Hash(h_0, h_1, D).
- Sample $\alpha \leftarrow \mathbb{Z}_q$ and set $A := g^\alpha$.
- Define $\widetilde{T}$ as follows. For each $i \in [n']$, if $T_i = \bot$ then sample $r_i \leftarrow \mathbb{Z}_q$ and set $\widetilde{T}_i := g^{r_i}$, and otherwise set $\widetilde{T}_i := H(T_i)^\alpha$.
- Output pk $:= (h_0, h_1, A, \widetilde{T})$ and sk $:= \alpha$.

Enc(pk, x, m):

- Parse pk as $(h_0, h_1, A, \widetilde{T})$ and abort if there are any duplicate entries in $\widetilde{T}$.
- For $b \in \{0, 1\}$, sample $\beta_b, \gamma_b \leftarrow \mathbb{Z}_q$, and compute $Q_b := g^{\beta_b} \cdot H(x)^{\gamma_b}, S_b := A^{\beta_b} \cdot \widetilde{T}_{h_b(x)}^{\gamma_b}, \text{ct}_b := \text{RobEnc}(G(S_b), m)$. Sample $b \leftarrow \{0, 1\}$ and output ct $:= (Q_b, \text{ct}_b, Q_{1-b}, \text{ct}_{1-b})$.

Dec(sk, ct):

- Parse sk as α and ct as $(Q_0, \text{ct}_0, Q_1, \text{ct}_1)$.
- For $b \in \{0, 1\}$ and compute $m_b := \text{RobDec}(G(Q_b^\alpha), \text{ct}_b)$. If exactly one of m_0 or m_1 is not $\bot$, then output this message, and otherwise output $\bot$.

Fig. 2. Basic SPC encryption with element-hiding

Observe that the correctness properties of $\Pi_{\text{SPCE}}^{\text{Basic}-\text{EH}}, \Pi_{\text{SPCE}}^{\text{Basic}-\text{PC}}$ are preserved by this transformation, due to the completeness of the ZK-NIAoKs, and the security against outsiders properties are also preserved, due to the zero-knowledge of the ZK-NIAoKs.

Achieving Authenticated-Set Security. Next, we describe schemes $\Pi_{\text{SPCE}}^{\text{AS}-\text{EH}}, \Pi_{\text{SPCE}}^{\text{AS}-\text{PC}}$ (Protocol 5) that satisfy authenticated set security. In order to achieve this notion, we will relax Gen to be an *interactive protocol* between the server and Auth, with the following syntax. Gen$\langle$Server, Auth$(D)\rangle(1^\lambda) \rightarrow$ (pk, sk) where the parameter generation protocol takes place between a server and Auth with input a set $D \subseteq \mathcal{U}$, and outputs to the server a public key pk and a secret key sk.

Observe that the correctness properties of $\Pi_{\text{SPCE}}^{\text{Basic}-\text{EH}}, \Pi_{\text{SPCE}}^{\text{Basic}-\text{PC}}$ are preserved by the transformation, due to the completeness of the ZK-NIAoKs and correct-

$$\Pi_{\mathsf{SPCE}}^{\mathsf{Basic-PC}}[\mathcal{U}, \mathbb{G}, n, \epsilon]$$

Parameters: same as $\Pi_{\mathsf{SPCE}}^{\mathsf{Basic-EH}}$, except that the message space is the set of group elements in $\mathbb{G}$.

Setup: Same as $\Pi_{\mathsf{SPCE}}^{\mathsf{Basic-EH}}$.

Gen($1^\lambda, D$): Same as $\Pi_{\mathsf{SPCE}}^{\mathsf{Basic-EH}}$, except that h_0, h_1, T are included in sk, and we abort if there does not exist a $D' \subseteq D$ such that $|D'| \geq (1 - \epsilon)|D|$ and such that for any $x \in D'$, either $T_{h_0(x)} = x$ or $T_{h_1(x)} = x$.

Enc(pk, x, m):

- Parse pk as $(h_0, h_1, A, \widetilde{T})$ and abort if there are any duplicate entries in $\widetilde{T}$.
- For $b \in \{0, 1\}$, sample $\beta_b, \gamma_b \leftarrow \mathbb{Z}_q$, and compute $Q_b := g^{\beta_b} \cdot H(x)^{\gamma_b}, S_b := A^{\beta_b} \cdot \widetilde{T}_{h_b(x)}^{\gamma_b}$. Output ct $:= (x, Q_0, S_0 \cdot m, Q_1, S_1 \cdot m)$.

Dec(sk, ct):

- Parse sk as (h_0, h_1, T, α) and ct as $(x, Q_0, S'_0, Q_1, S'_1)$.
- If there exists exactly one $b \in \{0, 1\}$ such that $T_{h_i(x)} = x$, then output $m = S'_b / Q_b^\alpha$. Otherwise, output $\perp$.

Fig. 3. Basic SPC encryption with perfect correctness

$$\Pi_{\mathsf{SPCE}}^{\mathsf{BS-EH}}[\mathcal{U}, \mathcal{M}, n, \epsilon], \Pi_{\mathsf{SPCE}}^{\mathsf{BS-PC}}[\mathcal{U}, \mathbb{G}, n, \epsilon]$$

Parameters: Same as $\Pi_{\mathsf{SPCE}}^{\mathsf{Basic-EH}}, \Pi_{\mathsf{SPCE}}^{\mathsf{Basic-PC}}$. Note that the parameters λ, n, and ϵ determine a maximum hash table size n', where $(n', \cdot, \cdot) \leftarrow \mathsf{Setup}(\lambda, n, \epsilon)$.

Setup: Let $(\mathsf{Prove}_{\mathsf{DLog}}, \mathsf{Verify}_{\mathsf{DLog}})$ be a ZK-NIAoK for $\mathcal{R}_{\mathsf{DLog}}$ and let $(\mathsf{Prove}_{\widetilde{\mathsf{DLog}}}, \mathsf{Verify}_{\widetilde{\mathsf{DLog}}})$ be a ZK-NIAoK for $\mathcal{R}_{\mathsf{DLog}_{n'}^{n'-n}}$ (Sect. 2.2). Both of these proof systems are in the random oracle model and have no additional setup, so there is no additional setup required for $\Pi_{\mathsf{SPCE}}^{\mathsf{BS-EH}}, \Pi_{\mathsf{SPCE}}^{\mathsf{BS-PC}}$.

Gen($1^\lambda, D$): Same as $\Pi_{\mathsf{SPCE}}^{\mathsf{Basic-EH}}, \Pi_{\mathsf{SPCE}}^{\mathsf{Basic-PC}}$, except that proofs $\pi_A \leftarrow \mathsf{Prove}_{\mathsf{DLog}}((g, A), \alpha)$ and $\pi_{\widetilde{T}} \leftarrow \mathsf{Prove}_{\widetilde{\mathsf{DLog}}}((g, \widetilde{T}), \{r_i\}_{i:T_i = \perp})$ are computed and appended to the public key pk.

Enc(pk, x, m): Same as $\Pi_{\mathsf{SPCE}}^{\mathsf{Basic-EH}}, \Pi_{\mathsf{SPCE}}^{\mathsf{Basic-PC}}$, except that the algorithm aborts if either of π_A or $\pi_{\widetilde{T}}$ fails to verify, or the number of group elements in $\widetilde{T}$ is greater than n'.

Dec(sk, ct): same as $\Pi_{\mathsf{SPCE}}^{\mathsf{Basic-EH}}, \Pi_{\mathsf{SPCE}}^{\mathsf{Basic-PC}}$.

Fig. 4. SPC encryption with bounded-set security

$$\Pi_{\mathsf{SPCE}}^{\mathsf{AS-EH}}[\mathcal{U}, \mathcal{M}, n, \epsilon], \Pi_{\mathsf{SPCE}}^{\mathsf{AS-PC}}[\mathcal{U}, \mathbb{G}, n, \epsilon]$$

Parameters: same as $\Pi_{\mathsf{SPCE}}^{\mathsf{Basic-EH}}, \Pi_{\mathsf{SPCE}}^{\mathsf{Basic-PC}}$.

Setup: let $(\mathsf{Sig.Gen}, \mathsf{Sig.Sign}, \mathsf{Sign.Verify})$ be a EUF-CMA secure signature scheme (Sect. 2.1). Before the protocol begins, Auth will sample $(\mathsf{vk_{Auth}}, \mathsf{sk_{Auth}}) \leftarrow \mathsf{Sig.Gen}(1^\lambda)$ and broadcast $\mathsf{vk_{Auth}}$ to all parties. Also, let $(\mathsf{Prove_{DLog}}, \mathsf{Verify_{DLog}})$ be a ZK-NIAoK for $\mathcal{R}_{\mathsf{DLog}}$ and $(\mathsf{Prove_{DH}}, \mathsf{Verify_{DH}})$ be a ZK-NIAoK for $\mathcal{R}_{\mathsf{DH}}$ (Sect. 2.2). Both of these proof systems are in the random oracle model, so require no additional setup beyond $\Pi_{\mathsf{SPCE}}^{\mathsf{Basic-EH}}, \Pi_{\mathsf{SPCE}}^{\mathsf{Basic-PC}}$.

$\mathsf{Gen}\langle \mathsf{Server}, \mathsf{Auth}(D)\rangle(1^\lambda)$:

- Auth sends D to Server.
- Server first runs the Gen algorithm of $\Pi_{\mathsf{SPCE}}^{\mathsf{Basic-EH}}, \Pi_{\mathsf{SPCE}}^{\mathsf{Basic-PC}}$ on input $(1^\lambda, D)$ to obtain output $(h_0, h_1, A, \widetilde{T}), \alpha$, along with table T and randomness $\{r_i\}_{i:T_i=\perp}$. Next, compute $\pi_A \leftarrow \mathsf{Prove_{DLog}}((g, A), \alpha)$. Finally, for each $i \in [n']$, where n' is the size of $T, \widetilde{T}$:
  - If $T_i = \perp$, compute $\pi_i \leftarrow \mathsf{Prove_{DLog}}((g, \widetilde{T}_i), r_i)$.
  - If $T_i \neq \perp$, compute $\pi_i \leftarrow \mathsf{Prove_{DH}}((g, A, H(T_i), \widetilde{T}_i), \alpha)$.
  Send $(A, T, \widetilde{T}, \pi_A, \{\pi_i\}_{i\in[n']})$ to Auth.
- Auth runs $\mathsf{Verify_{DLog}}((g, A), \pi_A)$ and for each $i \in [n']$: if $T_i = \perp$, runs $\mathsf{Verify_{DLog}}((g, \widetilde{T}_i), \pi_i)$ and if $T_i \neq \perp$, check that $T_i \in D$ and runs $\mathsf{Verify_{DH}}((g, A, H(T_i), \widetilde{T}_i), \pi_i)$. If all checks pass, compute $\sigma \leftarrow \mathsf{Sig.Sign}(\mathsf{sk}, (A, \widetilde{T}))$, and return σ.
- Server outputs $\mathsf{pk} := (h_0, h_1, A, \widetilde{T}, \sigma)$ and $\mathsf{sk} := \alpha$.

$\mathsf{Enc}(\mathsf{pk}, x, m)$: same as $\Pi_{\mathsf{SPCE}}^{\mathsf{Basic-EH}}, \Pi_{\mathsf{SPCE}}^{\mathsf{Basic-PC}}$, except that it first runs $\mathsf{Sig.Verify}(\mathsf{vk_{Auth}}, (A, \widetilde{T}), \sigma)^a$ and aborts if the signature fails to verify.
$\mathsf{Dec}(\mathsf{sk}, \mathsf{ct})$: same as $\Pi_{\mathsf{SPCE}}^{\mathsf{Basic-EH}}, \Pi_{\mathsf{SPCE}}^{\mathsf{Basic-PC}}$.

---

[a] Note that this verification only needs to be done once per user and not every time Enc is run, since the public key does not change.

Fig. 5. SPC encryption with authenticated-set security

ness of Sig, and the security against outsiders properties are also preserved, due to the zero-knowledge of the ZK-NIAoKs.

4 SPC Group Signatures

In this section, we define and construct SPC group signatures. We present formal definition of SPC group signatures in Sect. 4.1, and constructions in Sect. 4.2 and Sect. 4.3. We defer proofs of security to the full version [8].

4.1   Definitions

A set pre-constrained group signature (SPCGS) scheme $\Pi_{\mathsf{SPCGS}}[\mathcal{M}, \mathcal{P}, n, \epsilon]$ consists of algorithms Gen, Sign, Verify, Open, along with an interactive protocol KeyGen. We refer to the party that runs Gen as the *group manager* GM, and the KeyGen protocol is run by GM and a client C. It is parameterized by a message space $\mathcal{M}$, an identity (or public key) space $\mathcal{P}$, a set size n, and a correctness parameter ϵ.

- Gen$(1^\lambda, D) \to (\mathsf{mpk}, \mathsf{msk})$. The parameter generation algorithm takes as input a security parameter 1^λ and a set $D \subseteq \mathcal{M}$ of size at most n, and outputs a master public key mpk and a master secret key msk.
- KeyGen$\langle \mathsf{GM}(\mathsf{msk}), \mathsf{C} \rangle \to (\mathsf{pk}, \mathsf{sk})$. The KeyGen protocol is run by the group manager GM with input msk and a client C. It delivers an identity $\mathsf{pk} \in \mathcal{P}$ to both GM and C, and an identity signing key sk to C.
- Sign$(\mathsf{mpk}, \mathsf{sk}, m) \to \sigma$. The signing algorithm takes as input the master public key mpk, an identity signing key sk, and a message $m \in \mathcal{M}$, and outputs a signature σ.
- Verify$(\mathsf{mpk}, m, \sigma) \to \{\top, \bot\}$. The verification algorithm takes as input the master public key mpk, a message $m \in \mathcal{M}$, and a signature σ, and outputs either $\top$ or $\bot$, indicating accept or reject.
- Open$(\mathsf{msk}, \sigma) \to \{\mathsf{pk}, \bot\}$. The opening algorithm takes as input the master secret key msk and signature σ, and outputs either an identity $\mathsf{pk} \in \mathcal{P}$ or $\bot$.

We imagine using an SPC group signature scheme for encrypted messaging as follows. We assume that there is already a standard end-to-end encrypted messaging system in place, and the server additionally publishes mpk for the SPCGS scheme. Each client runs a KeyGen protocol with the server in order to obtain their identity pk and their secret key sk. Then, whenever they want to send a message m, they additionally compute a signature σ on m, and send the message (m, σ) *under the end-to-end encryption*. Any message received that does not have a properly verifying signature is immediately discarded by the client algorithm. Finally, if an honest client receives a pair (m, σ) for some illegal content m, they can report this to the server, who can run the Open algorithm in order to determine which identity produced the signature σ.

We now port the definitions of bounded-set and authenticated-set security against malicious servers (as previously defined for SPC encryption) to the group signature setting. Further, we follow standard definitions of *traceability*, *anonymity*, and *unframeability* for group signatures.

Definition 3 (Correctness). *An* SPC *group signature scheme* (Gen, KeyGen, Sign, Verify, Open) *is correct if for any* $\lambda \in \mathbb{N}, D \subseteq \mathcal{M}$, *and message* $m \in \mathcal{M}$, *it holds with probability* $1 - \mathsf{negl}(\lambda)$ *over* $(\mathsf{mpk}, \mathsf{msk}) \leftarrow$ Gen$(1^\lambda, D), (\mathsf{pk}, \mathsf{sk}) \leftarrow$ KeyGen$\langle \mathsf{GM}(\mathsf{msk}), \mathsf{C} \rangle$, *and* $\sigma \leftarrow$ Sign$(\mathsf{mpk}, \mathsf{sk}, m)$ *that* Verify$(\mathsf{mpk}, m, \sigma) = 1$.

Security. We formulate several notions of security for an SPC group signature scheme. First, we define a notion of *traceability*, which ensures that any signature on a message $m \in D$ that is accepted by the verification algorithm will leak the identity of the signer to the master secret key holder.

Definition 4 (Traceability). *An* SPC *group signature scheme* (Gen, KeyGen, Sign, Verify, Open) *is ϵ-traceable for some $\epsilon \geq 0$ if for any PPT adversary $\mathcal{A}$, $\lambda \in \mathbb{N}$, and $D \subseteq \mathcal{M}$, it holds that with probability $1 - \mathsf{negl}(\lambda)$ over* (mpk, msk) $\leftarrow$ Gen($1^\lambda, D$)*, there exists a $D' \subseteq D$ with $|D'| \geq (1 - \epsilon)|D|$, such that*

$$\Pr\left[\begin{array}{l} \mathsf{IsValid[mpk]}(m, \sigma, \mathsf{pk}) = 1 \\ \wedge \ (m \in D') \\ \wedge \ (\mathsf{pk} \notin \mathcal{I}_{\mathsf{Adv}}) \end{array} : \begin{array}{l} (m, \sigma) \leftarrow \mathcal{A}^{\mathcal{O}_{\mathsf{AKG}}, \mathcal{O}_{\mathsf{Open}}, \mathcal{O}_{\mathsf{HKG}}, \mathcal{O}_{\mathsf{Sign}}} \\ \mathsf{pk} \leftarrow \mathsf{Open}(\mathsf{msk}, \sigma) \end{array} \right] = \mathsf{negl}(\lambda),$$

where the oracles $\mathcal{O}_{\mathsf{AKG}}, \mathcal{O}_{\mathsf{Open}}, \mathcal{O}_{\mathsf{HKG}}, \mathcal{O}_{\mathsf{Sign}}$, set $\mathcal{I}_{\mathsf{Adv}}$ and predicate $\mathsf{IsValid[mpk]}$ are defined as follows.

- $\mathcal{O}_{\mathsf{AKG}}$ *(KeyGen initiated by the Adversary) has* msk *hard-coded and, when initialized, acts as the group manager in the* KeyGen *protocol. Define $\mathcal{I}_{\mathsf{Adv}}$ to be the set of identities obtained by* GM(msk) *as a result of the interactions between $\mathcal{A}$ and $\mathcal{O}_{\mathsf{AKG}}$.*
- $\mathcal{O}_{\mathsf{Open}}$ *has* msk *hard-coded, and on input a signature σ, outputs* Open(msk, σ).
- $\mathcal{O}_{\mathsf{HKG}}$ *(KeyGen initiated by an Honest party) has* msk *hard-coded and, when queried, runs* KeyGen$\langle$GM(msk), C$\rangle \rightarrow$ (pk, sk), *and returns* pk *(and not* sk*). Define $\mathcal{I}_{\mathsf{Hon}}$ to be the set of* pk*'s output by $\mathcal{O}_{\mathsf{HKG}}$.*
- $\mathcal{O}_{\mathsf{Sign}}$ *takes a message m and an identity* pk *as input. If* pk $\notin \mathcal{I}_{\mathsf{Hon}}$, *return nothing, and otherwise let* sk *be the secret key associated with* pk *and return* Sign(mpk, sk, m). *Define $\mathcal{J}$ to be the set of (m, pk) queried to $\mathcal{O}_{\mathsf{Sign}}$.*
- $\mathsf{IsValid[mpk]}(m, \sigma, \mathsf{pk})$ *outputs* (Verify(mpk, m, σ) = 1) $\wedge$ (($m, \mathsf{pk}) \notin \mathcal{J}$). *That is, it accepts if the adversary produced a valid message signature pair that was not a query to its signing oracle.*

Next, we define the notion of *unframeability*, which ensures that an adversary cannot produce a verifying signature with respect to some identity pk for which they do not hold the corresponding sk, even if they know the master secret key.

Definition 5 (Unframeability). *An* SPC *group signature scheme* (Gen, KeyGen, Sign, Verify, Open) *satisfies unframeability if for any PPT adversary $\mathcal{A}$ and $D \subseteq \mathcal{M}$,*

$$\Pr\left[\begin{array}{l} \mathsf{Verify}(\mathsf{mpk}, m, \sigma) = 1 \\ \wedge \ (\mathsf{mpk}, \mathsf{msk}) \in \mathsf{Gen}(1^\lambda, D) \\ \wedge \ ((m, \mathsf{pk}) \notin \mathcal{J}) \wedge (\mathsf{pk} \in \mathcal{I}_{\mathsf{Hon}}) \end{array} : \begin{array}{l} (\mathsf{mpk}, \mathsf{msk}, m, \sigma) \leftarrow \mathcal{A}^{\mathcal{O}_{\mathsf{HKG}}, \mathcal{O}_{\mathsf{Sign}}}(1^\lambda, D) \\ \mathsf{pk} \leftarrow \mathsf{Open}(\mathsf{msk}, \sigma) \end{array} \right] = \mathsf{negl}(\lambda),$$

where the oracles $\mathcal{O}_{\mathsf{HKG}}, \mathcal{O}_{\mathsf{Sign}}$ and sets $\mathcal{I}_{\mathsf{Hon}}, \mathcal{J}$ are defined as in Definition 4.

Now, we consider the notion of *anonymity*, which protects the identity of any signer who produces a signature on a message $m \notin D$, even against the group manager. Here, we will follow our simulation-based notion of security for SPC encryption. The ideal functionality $\mathcal{F}^{P}_{\mathsf{anon}}$ takes place between a *group manager*

GM who runs Gen, interacts in KeyGen, and runs Open, a *client*, who interacts in KeyGen and runs Sign, and an authority Auth, whose role will be described below. In full generality, the group manager's input is a function F, but in our applications, we will always parse F as a description of a database D of messages. The client's input is a sequence of identities and messages $(\mathsf{pk}_1, m_1), \ldots, (\mathsf{pk}_k, m_k)$. The client should learn nothing about D, Auth should learn nothing about the identities $\{\mathsf{pk}_i\}_{i \in [k]}$, and the group manager should learn nothing about the identities $\{\mathsf{pk}_i\}_{i:m_i \notin D}$, except perhaps how many "repeats" there are (if we don't require the property of *unlinkability*).

To make security against the server meaningful, we must place some restriction on D. We do this (in a modular way) by parameterizing the functionality with a predicate $\mathcal{P}$. This predicate may depend on some public parameters pp (known to both client and group manager) and some secret parameters sp (known only to the group manager). It is the job of Auth to set up these parameters.

Below, we describe the instantiations of $\mathcal{P}$ that we will consider in this work: one will define what we call *bounded-set security* and the other will define what we call *authenticated-set security*.

$$\mathcal{F}^{\mathcal{P}}_{\mathsf{anon}}$$

Parties: Group manager and client.
Parameters: message space $\mathcal{M}$, identity space $\mathcal{I}$.

- Obtain input $(\mathsf{pp}, \mathsf{sp})$ from Auth. Deliver pp to both group manager and client, and sp to group manager.
- Obtain input $F = (F_{\mathsf{GM}}, F_{\mathsf{Auth}})$ from group manager and deliver F to Auth. Abort and deliver $\bot$ to all parties if $\mathcal{P}(\mathsf{pp}, \mathsf{sp}, F) = 0$.
- Obtain input $(\mathsf{pk}_1, m_1), \ldots, (\mathsf{pk}_k, m_k)$ from client, where each $\mathsf{pk}_i \in \mathcal{I}$ and each $m_i \in \mathcal{M}$.
- Deliver $F_{\mathsf{GM}}(\{\mathsf{pk}_i, m_i\}_{i \in [k]})$ to group manager and $F_{\mathsf{Auth}}(\{\mathsf{pk}_i, m_i\}_{i \in [k]})$ to Auth.

Fig. 6. Ideal functionality for SPC group signatures with anonymity. $\mathcal{P}$ is a predicate that takes as input some public parameters pp, and a pair of functions $F = (F_S, F_{\mathsf{Auth}})$, and outputs a bit.

Bounded-Set Security. Here, we define two predicates $\mathcal{P}[\mathsf{BS}]$ and $\mathcal{P}[\mathsf{BS\text{-}link}]$, where link stands for linkability. For each, the parameters pp are parsed as an integer n, there are no secret parameters sp, and F is parsed as a description of a database $D \subseteq \mathcal{M}$. The predicate then outputs 1 if and only if $|D| \leq n$. For $\mathcal{P}[\mathsf{BS}]$,

$$F_{\mathsf{GM}}(\{\mathsf{pk}_i, m_i\}_{i \in [k]}) = \{\mathsf{pk}_i\}_{i:m_i \in D}, \{m_i\}_{i \in [k]}, \quad F_{\mathsf{Auth}}(\{\mathsf{pk}_i, m_i\}_{i \in [k]}) = \{m_i\}_{i \in [k]},$$

and for $\mathcal{P}[\mathsf{BS\text{-}link}]$,

$$F_{\mathsf{GM}}(\{\mathsf{pk}_i, m_i\}_{i \in [k]}) = \{\mathsf{pk}_i\}_{i:m_i \in D}, \mathsf{Aux}(\{\mathsf{pk}_i\}_{i:m_i \notin D}), \{m_i\}_{i \in [k]},$$

where for any multiset S, $\mathsf{Aux}(S)$ consists of the number of distinct elements in S along with how many times each appears, and

$$F_{\mathsf{Auth}}(\{\mathsf{pk}_i, m_i\}_{i \in [k]}) = \{m_i\}_{i \in [k]}.$$

Authenticated-Set Security. Here, we define two predicates $\mathcal{P}[\mathsf{AS}]$ and $\mathcal{P}[\mathsf{AS\text{-}EH}]$. For each, the public parameters pp are parsed as an integer n, the secret parameters are parsed as a database $D^* \subseteq \mathcal{M}$ of size n, and F is parsed as a database $D \subseteq \mathcal{M}$. The predicate then outputs 1 if and only if $D \subseteq D^*$. For $\mathcal{P}[\mathsf{AS}]$,

$$F_{\mathsf{GM}}(\{\mathsf{pk}_i, m_i\}_{i \in [k]}) = \{\mathsf{pk}_i\}_{i:m_i \in D}, \{m_i\}_{i \in [k]}, \quad F_{\mathsf{Auth}}(\{\mathsf{pk}_i, m_i\}_{i \in [k]}) = \{m_i\}_{i \in [k]},$$

and for $\mathcal{P}[\mathsf{AS\text{-}link}]$,

$$F_{\mathsf{GM}}(\{\mathsf{pk}_i, m_i\}_{i \in [k]}) = \{\mathsf{pk}_i\}_{i:m_i \in D}, \mathsf{Aux}(\{\mathsf{pk}_i\}_{i:m_i \notin D}), \{m_i\}_{i \in [k]},$$

where for any multiset S, $\mathsf{Aux}(S)$ consists of the number of distinct elements in S along with how many times each appears, and

$$F_{\mathsf{Auth}}(\{\mathsf{pk}_i, m_i\}_{i \in [k]}) = \{m_i\}_{i \in [k]}.$$

Finally, we consider "client-client" anonymity and unlinkability, which considers the security of signatures against other clients. Here, we can hope for stronger security properties, since clients do not hold the master secret key and thus might not be able to de-anonymize signatures even on messages $m \in D$. Thus, we give separate (game-based) definitions of anonymity and unlinkability against adversarial clients.

Definition 6 (Anonymity). *An* SPC *group signature scheme* (Gen, KeyGen, Sign, Verify, Open) *satisfies client-client anonymity if for any PPT adversary* $\mathcal{A}$, $\lambda \in \mathbb{N}$, $D \subseteq \mathcal{M}$, *and* $m \in \mathcal{M}$, *it holds that with probability* $1 - \mathsf{negl}(\lambda)$ *over* $(\mathsf{mpk}, \mathsf{msk}) \leftarrow \mathsf{Gen}(1^\lambda, D)$, $(\mathsf{pk}_0, \mathsf{sk}_0) \leftarrow \mathsf{KeyGen}\langle \mathsf{GM}(\mathsf{msk}), \mathsf{C}\rangle$, $(\mathsf{pk}_1, \mathsf{sk}_1) \leftarrow \mathsf{KeyGen}\langle \mathsf{GM}(\mathsf{msk}), \mathsf{C}\rangle$,

$$\Pr\left[\mathcal{A}^{\mathcal{O}_{\mathsf{AKG}}, \mathcal{O}_{\mathsf{HKG}}, \mathcal{O}_{\mathsf{Sign}}}\left(\begin{matrix}\mathsf{mpk}, \mathsf{pk}_0, \\ \mathsf{pk}_1, \sigma\end{matrix}\right) = b : \begin{matrix}b \leftarrow \{0,1\} \\ \sigma \leftarrow \mathsf{Sign}(\mathsf{mpk}, \mathsf{sk}_b, m)\end{matrix}\right] \leq \frac{1}{2} + \mathsf{negl}(\lambda),$$

where the oracles $\mathcal{O}_{\mathsf{AKG}}, \mathcal{O}_{\mathsf{HKG}}$, *and* $\mathcal{O}_{\mathsf{Sign}}$ *are defined as in Definition 4.*

Definition 7 (Unlinkability). *An* SPC *group signature scheme* (Gen, KeyGen, Sign, Verify, Open) *satisfies client-client unlinkability if for any PPT adversary* $\mathcal{A}$, $\lambda \in \mathbb{N}$, $D \subseteq \mathcal{M}$, *and messages* $m_0, m_1 \in \mathcal{M}$, *it holds that with probability* $1 - \mathsf{negl}(\lambda)$ *over* $(\mathsf{mpk}, \mathsf{msk}) \leftarrow \mathsf{Gen}(1^\lambda, D)$, $(\mathsf{pk}_0, \mathsf{sk}_0) \leftarrow \mathsf{KeyGen}\langle \mathsf{GM}(\mathsf{msk}), \mathsf{C}\rangle$, $(\mathsf{pk}_1, \mathsf{sk}_1) \leftarrow \mathsf{KeyGen}\langle \mathsf{GM}(\mathsf{msk}), \mathsf{C}\rangle$,

$$\Pr\left[\mathcal{A}^{\mathcal{O}_{\mathsf{AKG}}, \mathcal{O}_{\mathsf{HKG}}, \mathcal{O}_{\mathsf{Sign}}}\left(\begin{matrix}\mathsf{mpk}, \mathsf{pk}_0, \\ \mathsf{pk}_1, \sigma_0, \sigma_1\end{matrix}\right) = b : \begin{matrix}\sigma_0 \leftarrow \mathsf{Sign}(\mathsf{mpk}, \mathsf{sk}_0, m_0) \\ b \leftarrow \{0,1\} \\ \sigma_1 \leftarrow \mathsf{Sign}(\mathsf{mpk}, \mathsf{sk}_b, m_1)\end{matrix}\right] \leq \frac{1}{2} + \mathsf{negl}(\lambda),$$

where the oracles $\mathcal{O}_{\mathsf{AKG}}, \mathcal{O}_{\mathsf{HKG}}$, *and* $\mathcal{O}_{\mathsf{Sign}}$ *are defined as in Definition 4.*

4.2 Generic Construction

We show how to construct an SPC group signature scheme generically from an SPC encryption scheme that satisfies certain properties, plus a few standard cryptographic tools. Our construction is given in the random oracle model, though we note that if we were willing to assume an additional *simulation-soundness* property of the ZK-NIAoK, then we would not require a random oracle. It is presented in Protocol 7.

Ingredients:

- An SPC encryption scheme $\Pi_{\mathsf{SPCE}} = (\mathsf{SPCE.Gen}, \mathsf{SPCE.Enc}, \mathsf{SPCE.Dec})$ that satisfies *perfect ϵ-correctness*, *security against outsiders*, and either *bounded-set* security or *authenticated-set* security (Sect. 3).
- A one-way relation $(\mathcal{R}, \mathcal{R}.\mathsf{Gen}, \mathcal{R}.\mathsf{Sample})$ (Sect. 2.1). Let $\mathcal{P}$ denote the set of instances.
- An EUF-CMA secure signature scheme $\mathsf{Sig} = (\mathsf{Sig.Gen}, \mathsf{Sig.Sign}, \mathsf{Sig.Verify})$ with message space $\mathcal{P}$ (Sect. 2.1).
- A ZK-NIAoK scheme $\mathsf{ZK} = (\mathsf{ZK.Setup}, \mathsf{ZK.Prove}, \mathsf{ZK.Verify})$ in the common random string model for general NP relations (Sect. 2.2).
- A random oracle H.

4.3 An Efficient Instantiation

We now summarize our approach for a concretely efficient instantiation of the above generic template, based on constructions of SPC encryption schemes from Sect. 3. Note that we will need a concretely efficient instantiation of a zero-knowledge argument system that can be used to prove statements that involve verifying signatures and the correctness of SPC encryption. Our goal here is to avoid *non-black-box* use of the cryptography needed for signatures and SPC encryption. Thus, we use *bilinear maps*, and make use of the Groth-Sahai proof system [24], which can efficiently prove statements that involve certain operations in pairing groups.[8] We combine the GS proof system with the use of *structure-preserving signatures* [1], which support messages, verification keys, and signatures that consist solely of group elements. We provide details of the scheme, implementation and benchmarking in the full version [8].

   Our construction will make use of a bilinear map $\mathcal{G} = (p, \mathbb{G}_1, \mathbb{G}_2, \mathbb{T}, e, g_1, g_2)$ where the SXDH assumption is assumed to hold, as described in Sect. 2.3. The group signature scheme $\Pi_{\mathsf{SPCGS}}[\mathcal{M}, \mathbb{G}_1, n, \epsilon]$ will have an arbitrary message space $\mathcal{M}$ and identities consisting of group elements in $\mathbb{G}_1$. The four ingredients are instantiated as follows.

---

[8] We remark that, although GS proofs only satisfy *partial* knowledge extraction (see Sect. 2.3), this is sufficient for our construction. Indeed, the signatures extracted in order to show ϵ-traceability and unframeability only consist of group elements, and the one-way relation witness extracted during the proof of unframeability is also a group element.

$$\Pi_{\mathsf{SPCGS}}[\mathcal{M}, \mathcal{P}, n, \epsilon]$$

Parameters: message space $\mathcal{M}$, identity space $\mathcal{P}$, set size n, correctness parameter ϵ, and security parameter λ.

Setup: $\mathsf{pp} \leftarrow \mathcal{R}.\mathsf{Gen}(1^\lambda)$ and a random oracle H.

$\mathsf{Gen}(1^\lambda, D)$: run $(\mathsf{pk}_{\mathsf{SPCE}}, \mathsf{sk}_{\mathsf{SPCE}}) \leftarrow \mathsf{SPCE}.\mathsf{Gen}(1^\lambda, D)^a$ and $(\mathsf{vk}_{\mathsf{Sig}}, \mathsf{sk}_{\mathsf{Sig}}) \leftarrow \mathsf{Sig}.\mathsf{Gen}(1^\lambda)$. Set $\mathsf{mpk} := (\mathsf{pk}_{\mathsf{SPCE}}, \mathsf{vk}_{\mathsf{Sig}})$ and $\mathsf{msk} := (\mathsf{sk}_{\mathsf{SPCE}}, \mathsf{sk}_{\mathsf{Sig}})$.

$\mathsf{KeyGen}\langle\mathsf{GM}(\mathsf{msk}), \mathsf{C}\rangle$: the client C samples random coins s, computes $(\mathsf{pk}, w) := \mathcal{R}.\mathsf{Sample}(\mathsf{pp}; s)$, and sends pk to GM. GM parses msk as $(\mathsf{sk}_{\mathsf{SPCE}}, \mathsf{sk}_{\mathsf{Sig}})$ and then computes and sends $\sigma_{\mathsf{id}} \leftarrow \mathsf{Sig}.\mathsf{Sign}(\mathsf{sk}_{\mathsf{Sig}}, \mathsf{pk})$. C sets $\mathsf{sk} := (s, \sigma_{\mathsf{id}})$.

$\mathsf{Sign}(\mathsf{mpk}, \mathsf{sk}, m)$: parse mpk as $(\mathsf{pk}_{\mathsf{SPCE}}, \mathsf{vk}_{\mathsf{Sig}})$ and sk as $(s, \sigma_{\mathsf{id}})$, compute $(\mathsf{pk}, w) := \mathcal{R}.\mathsf{Sample}(\mathsf{pp}; s)$, sample random coins r, and compute $\mathsf{ct} := \mathsf{SPCE}.\mathsf{Enc}(\mathsf{pk}_{\mathsf{SPCE}}, m, \mathsf{pk}; r)$. Let $\mathsf{crs} := H(m, \mathsf{ct})$, and compute $\pi \leftarrow \mathsf{ZK}.\mathsf{Prove}(\mathsf{crs}, (\mathsf{pp}, \mathsf{pk}_{\mathsf{SPCE}}, \mathsf{vk}_{\mathsf{Sig}}, m, \mathsf{ct}), (\mathsf{pk}, s, w, \sigma_{\mathsf{id}}, r))$ for the relation that checks that

- $\mathsf{ct} = \mathsf{SPCE}.\mathsf{Enc}(\mathsf{pk}_{\mathsf{SPCE}}, m, \mathsf{pk}; r)$,
- $(\mathsf{pk}, w) = \mathcal{R}.\mathsf{Sample}(\mathsf{pp}; s)$,
- and $\mathsf{Sig}.\mathsf{Verify}(\mathsf{vk}_{\mathsf{Sig}}, \mathsf{pk}, \sigma_{\mathsf{id}})$.

Output $\sigma := (\mathsf{ct}, \mathsf{crs}, \pi)$.

$\mathsf{Verify}(\mathsf{mpk}, m, \sigma)$: parse mpk as $(\mathsf{pk}_{\mathsf{SPCE}}, \mathsf{vk}_{\mathsf{Sig}})$ and σ as $(\mathsf{ct}, \mathsf{crs}, \pi)$, check that $H(m, \mathsf{ct}) = \mathsf{crs}$ and if so output $\mathsf{ZK}.\mathsf{Verify}(\mathsf{crs}, (\mathsf{pp}, \mathsf{pk}_{\mathsf{SPCE}}, \mathsf{vk}_{\mathsf{Sig}}, m, \mathsf{ct}), \pi)$.

$\mathsf{Open}(\mathsf{msk}, \sigma)$: parse msk as $(\mathsf{sk}_{\mathsf{SPCE}}, \mathsf{sk}_{\mathsf{Sig}})$ and σ as $(\mathsf{ct}, \mathsf{crs}, \pi)$, and output $\mathsf{SPCE}.\mathsf{Dec}(\mathsf{sk}_{\mathsf{SPCE}}, \mathsf{ct})$.

---

^{a} If the SPC encryption scheme satisfies authenticated-set security, this will be an interactive procedure between GM and Auth.

Fig. 7. Generic construction of SPC group signatures.

- SPC encryption: Either the scheme $\Pi_{\mathsf{SPCE}}^{\mathsf{BS-PC}}[\mathcal{M}, \mathbb{G}_1, n, \epsilon]$ or $\Pi_{\mathsf{SPCE}}^{\mathsf{AS-PC}}[\mathcal{M}, \mathbb{G}_1, n, \epsilon]$ from Sect. 3.
- One-way relation: The Diffie-Hellman relation in $\mathbb{G}_1$, where $\mathcal{R}$ is the set of tuples $(g, g^\alpha, g^\beta, g^{\alpha \cdot \beta}) \in \mathbb{G}_1^4$. $\mathcal{R}.\mathsf{Gen}$ outputs $(g, g^\alpha) = (g, h)$, and $\mathcal{R}.\mathsf{Sample}$ chooses randomness β and outputs (g^β, h^β). This relation is one-way from the hardness of the computational Diffie-Hellman problem in $\mathbb{G}_1$.
- Signature scheme: The structure-preserving signature scheme from [1].
- ZK-NIAoK: The Groth-Sahai proof system (Sect. 2.3).

Details of our concretely efficient scheme can be found in the full version [8].

Acknowledgments. First, second and fourth authors were supported in part by DARPA under Agreement No. HR00112020026, AFOSR Award FA9550-19-1-0200, NSF CNS Award 1936826, and research grants by the Sloan Foundation, and Visa Inc. The first and the fourth author were also supported by a grant from the CLTC. The third author was supported in part by NSF CNS-1814919, NSF CAREER 1942789, Johns Hopkins University Catalyst award, AFOSR Award FA9550-19-1-0200, Office of Naval Research Grant N00014-19-1-2294, JP Morgan Faculty Award, and research gifts from Ethereum, Stellar and Cisco. Any opinions, findings and conclusions or recommendations expressed in this material are those of the authors and do not necessarily reflect the views of the United States Government or DARPA.

References

1. Abe, M., Fuchsbauer, G., Groth, J., Haralambiev, K., Ohkubo, M.: Structure-preserving signatures and commitments to group elements. In: Rabin, T. (ed.) CRYPTO 2010. LNCS, vol. 6223, pp. 209–236. Springer, Heidelberg (2010). https://doi.org/10.1007/978-3-642-14623-7_12

2. Abelson, H., et al.: Bugs in our pockets: the risks of client-side scanning (2021). https://doi.org/10.48550/ARXIV.2110.07450

3. Alamati, N., Branco, P., Döttling, N., Garg, S., Hajiabadi, M., Pu, S.: Laconic private set intersection and applications. In: Nissim, K., Waters, B. (eds.) TCC 2021. LNCS, vol. 13044, pp. 94–125. Springer, Cham (2021). https://doi.org/10.1007/978-3-030-90456-2_4

4. Ananth, P., Jain, A., Jin, Z., Malavolta, G.: Pre-constrained encryption. In: ITCS. LIPIcs, vol. 215, pp. 4:1–4:20. Schloss Dagstuhl - Leibniz-Zentrum für Informatik (2022). https://doi.org/10.4230/LIPIcs.ITCS.2022.4

5. Apple (2021) CSAM Detection Technical Summary

6. Attema, T., Cramer, R., Fehr, S.: Compressing proofs of k-Out-Of-n partial knowledge. In: Malkin, T., Peikert, C. (eds.) CRYPTO 2021. LNCS, vol. 12828, pp. 65–91. Springer, Cham (2021). https://doi.org/10.1007/978-3-030-84259-8_3

7. Barak, B., et al.: On the (Im)possibility of obfuscating programs. In: Kilian, J. (ed.) CRYPTO 2001. LNCS, vol. 2139, pp. 1–18. Springer, Heidelberg (2001). https://doi.org/10.1007/3-540-44647-8_1

8. Bartusek, J., Garg, S., Jain, A., Policharla, G.V.: End-to-end secure messaging with traceability only for illegal content. Cryptology ePrint Archive, Paper 2022/1643 (2022). https://eprint.iacr.org/2022/1643

9. Bellare, M., Micciancio, D., Warinschi, B.: Foundations of group signatures: formal definitions, simplified requirements, and a construction based on general assumptions. In: Biham, E. (ed.) EUROCRYPT 2003. LNCS, vol. 2656, pp. 614–629. Springer, Heidelberg (2003). https://doi.org/10.1007/3-540-39200-9_38

10. Bhowmick, A., Boneh, D., Myers, S., Tarbe, K., Talwar, K.: The apple PSI system (2021)

11. Boyle, E., Ishai, Y., Pass, R., Wootters, M.: Can we access a database both locally and privately? In: Kalai, Y., Reyzin, L. (eds.) TCC 2017. LNCS, vol. 10678, pp. 662–693. Springer, Cham (2017). https://doi.org/10.1007/978-3-319-70503-3_22

12. Canetti, R., Holmgren, J., Richelson, S.: Towards doubly efficient private information retrieval. In: Kalai, Y., Reyzin, L. (eds.) TCC 2017. LNCS, vol. 10678, pp. 694–726. Springer, Cham (2017). https://doi.org/10.1007/978-3-319-70503-3_23

13. Canetti, R., Kaptchuk, G.: The broken promise of apple's announced forbidden-photo reporting system - and how to fix it (2021). https://www.bu.edu/riscs/2021/08/10/apple-csam/
14. Chaum, D., Pedersen, T.P.: Wallet databases with observers. In: Brickell, E.F. (ed.) CRYPTO 1992. LNCS, vol. 740, pp. 89–105. Springer, Heidelberg (1993). https://doi.org/10.1007/3-540-48071-4_7
15. Chaum, D., van Heyst, E.: Group signatures. In: Davies, D.W. (ed.) EUROCRYPT 1991. LNCS, vol. 547, pp. 257–265. Springer, Heidelberg (1991). https://doi.org/10.1007/3-540-46416-6_22
16. Cramer, R., Damgård, I., Schoenmakers, B.: Proofs of partial knowledge and simplified design of witness hiding protocols. In: Desmedt, Y.G. (ed.) CRYPTO 1994. LNCS, vol. 839, pp. 174–187. Springer, Heidelberg (1994). https://doi.org/10.1007/3-540-48658-5_19
17. Dodis, Y., Grubbs, P., Ristenpart, T., Woodage, J.: Fast message franking: from invisible salamanders to encryptment. In: Shacham, H., Boldyreva, A. (eds.) CRYPTO 2018. LNCS, vol. 10991, pp. 155–186. Springer, Cham (2018). https://doi.org/10.1007/978-3-319-96884-1_6
18. Emura, K., et al.: Group signatures with message-dependent opening: formal definitions and constructions. Sec. Commun. Netw. **2019** (2019). https://doi.org/10.1155/2019/4872403
19. Federal Bureau of Investigation. Going Dark: Are Technology, Privacy, and Public Safety on a Collision Course? [speech] (2014)
20. Fiat, A., Shamir, A.: How to prove yourself: practical solutions to identification and signature problems. In: Odlyzko, A.M. (ed.) CRYPTO 1986. LNCS, vol. 263, pp. 186–194. Springer, Heidelberg (1987). https://doi.org/10.1007/3-540-47721-7_12
21. Green, M.: Thinking about "traceability" (2021). https://blog.cryptography engineering.com/2021/08/01/thinking-about-traceability/
22. Green, M., Kaptchuk, G., Van Laer, G.: Abuse resistant law enforcement access systems. In: Canteaut, A., Standaert, F.-X. (eds.) EUROCRYPT 2021. LNCS, vol. 12698, pp. 553–583. Springer, Cham (2021). https://doi.org/10.1007/978-3-030-77883-5_19
23. Groth, J.: Fully anonymous group signatures without random oracles. In: Kurosawa, K. (ed.) ASIACRYPT 2007. LNCS, vol. 4833, pp. 164–180. Springer, Heidelberg (2007). https://doi.org/10.1007/978-3-540-76900-2_10
24. Groth, J., Sahai, A.: Efficient non-interactive proof systems for bilinear groups. In: Smart, N. (ed.) EUROCRYPT 2008. LNCS, vol. 4965, pp. 415–432. Springer, Heidelberg (2008). https://doi.org/10.1007/978-3-540-78967-3_24
25. Grubbs, P., Arun, A., Zhang, Y., Bonneau, J., Walfish, M.: Zero-knowledge middleboxes. In: USENIX Security Symposium, pp. 4255–4272. USENIX Association (2022)
26. Grubbs, P., Lu, J., Ristenpart, T.: Message franking via committing authenticated encryption. In: Katz, J., Shacham, H. (eds.) CRYPTO 2017. LNCS, vol. 10403, pp. 66–97. Springer, Cham (2017). https://doi.org/10.1007/978-3-319-63697-9_3
27. Issa, R., Alhaddad, N., Varia, M.: Hecate: abuse reporting in secure messengers with sealed sender. In: 31st USENIX Security Symposium (USENIX Security 22), pp. 2335–2352 (2022)
28. U.S. Senate Committee on the Judiciary (2020). Graham, Blumenthal, Hawley, Feinstein Introduce EARN IT Act to Encourage Tech Industry to Take Online C hild Sexual Exploitation Seriously
29. U.S. Department of Justice (2020). International Statement: End-To-End Encrypti on and Public Safety

30. U.S. Department of Justice (2020). International Statement: End-To-End Encrypti on and Public Safety
31. Kamara, S., et al.: Outside looking in: approaches to content moderation in end-to-end encrypted systems (2021)
32. Kulshrestha, A., Mayer, J.R.: Identifying harmful media in end-to-end encrypted communication: efficient private membership computation. In: USENIX Security Symposium, pp. 893–910. USENIX Association (2021)
33. Libert, B., Joye, M.: Group signatures with message-dependent opening in the standard model. In: Benaloh, J. (ed.) CT-RSA 2014. LNCS, vol. 8366, pp. 286–306. Springer, Cham (2014). https://doi.org/10.1007/978-3-319-04852-9_15
34. Liu, L., Roche, D.S., Theriault, A., Yerukhimovich, A.: Fighting fake news in encrypted messaging with the fuzzy anonymous complaint tally system (facts). Cryptology ePrint Archive, Report 2021/1148 (2021)
35. Green, M.: An evaluation of the risks of client-side scanning (2022)
36. Naor, M., Reingold, O.: Number-theoretic constructions of efficient pseudo-random functions. J. ACM **51**, 231–262 (2004)
37. Newman, L.: The EARN IT Act Is a Sneak Attack on Encryption. Wired (2020)
38. Peale, C., Eskandarian, S., Boneh, D.: Secure complaint-enabled source-tracking for encrypted messaging. In: Proceedings of the 2021 ACM SIGSAC Conference on Computer and Communications Security, pp. 1484–1506 (2021)
39. Pinkas, B.: The private set intersection (PSI) protocol of the apple CSAM detection system (2021). https://decentralizedthoughts.github.io/2021-08-29-the-private-set-intersection-psi-protocol-of-the-apple-csam-detection-system/
40. Prokos, J., et al.: Squint hard enough: evaluating perceptual hashing with machine learning. Cryptology ePrint Archive, Report 2021/1531 (2021)
41. Schnorr, C.P.: Efficient identification and signatures for smart cards. In: Brassard, G. (ed.) CRYPTO 1989. LNCS, vol. 435, pp. 239–252. Springer, New York (1990). https://doi.org/10.1007/0-387-34805-0_22
42. Tyagi, N., Grubbs, P., Len, J., Miers, I., Ristenpart, T.: Asymmetric message franking: content moderation for metadata-private end-to-end encryption. In: Boldyreva, A., Micciancio, D. (eds.) CRYPTO 2019. LNCS, vol. 11694, pp. 222–250. Springer, Cham (2019). https://doi.org/10.1007/978-3-030-26954-8_8
43. Tyagi, N., Miers, I., Ristenpart, T.: Traceback for end-to-end encrypted messaging. In: Proceedings of the 2019 ACM SIGSAC Conference on Computer and Communications Security, pp. 413–430 (2019). https://doi.org/10.1145/3319535.3354243

Asymmetric Group Message Franking: Definitions and Constructions

Junzuo Lai[1], Gongxian Zeng[2](✉), Zhengan Huang[2](✉), Siu Ming Yiu[3],
Xin Mu[2], and Jian Weng[1](✉)

[1] College of Information Science and Technology, Jinan University,
Guangzhou, China
cryptjweng@gmail.com
[2] Peng Cheng Laboratory, Shenzhen, China
gxzeng@cs.hku.hk, zhahuang.sjtu@gmail.com, mux@pcl.ac.cn
[3] The University of Hong Kong, Hong Kong, China
smyiu@cs.hku.hk

Abstract. As online group communication scenarios become more and more common these years, malicious or unpleasant messages are much easier to spread on the internet. Message franking is a crucial cryptographic mechanism designed for content moderation in online end-to-end messaging systems, allowing the receiver of a malicious message to report the message to the moderator. Unfortunately, the existing message franking schemes only consider 1-1 communication scenarios.

In this paper, we systematically explore message franking in group communication scenarios. We introduce the notion of asymmetric group message franking (AGMF), and formalize its security requirements. Then, we provide a framework of constructing AGMF from a new primitive, called HPS-KEM$^{\Sigma}$. We also give a construction of HPS-KEM$^{\Sigma}$ based on the DDH assumption. Plugging the concrete HPS-KEM$^{\Sigma}$ scheme into our AGMF framework, we obtain a DDH-based AGMF scheme, which supports message franking in group communication scenarios.

Keywords: Message franking · Hash proof system · Key encapsulation mechanism · Signature of knowledge

1 Introduction

In recent years, secure messaging applications have become extremely popular for conversations between individuals and groups. Billions of people communicate with each other via messaging applications like Facebook Messenger, Twitter, Signal, Google Allo, etc. every day. However, these messaging applications are abused for the spread of malicious information such as harassment messages, phishing links, fake information and so on. Facebook Messenger [20,21] introduced the concept of *message franking*, which was formally studied in [24] later. Generally, (symmetric or asymmetric) message franking [21,24,36] provides *accountability*, i.e., it allows the receiver to report the malicious messages to some moderator (e.g., the platform or some trusted third party), and meanwhile guarantees

C. Hazay and M. Stam (Eds.): EUROCRYPT 2023, LNCS 14008, pp. 67–97, 2023.
https://doi.org/10.1007/978-3-031-30589-4_3

that no fake reports can be fabricated to frame an honest sender. Deniability, as also an explicit goal of Facebook's message franking based moderation system [21], is formalized for asymmetric message franking (AMF) in [36]. Informally, deniability ensures that when the receiver reports some malicious messages, only the moderator is able to validate the report. In other words, after a compromise, the sender can deny sending the messages technically, in order to avoid backlash or embarrassment (for more explanations, please refer to [36]). Now, message franking is a vital security feature for secure messaging applications, especially in government affairs, business and so on.

Compared with symmetric message franking, asymmetric message franking supports third-party moderation, decoupling the platform and the moderator, which enables cross-platform moderation of multiple messaging systems. As pointed out in [36], this property is necessary in decentralized or federated messaging systems like Matrix [2] or Mastodon [1], and is advantageous if the platform cannot adequately moderate messages, or if sub-communities want to enforce their own content policies.

However, the existing AMF [36] only considers the case of *1-1 communication*. As for another common scenarios, *group communications*, no works have ever related to this topic. Group communication plays an important role in teamwork or other multi-user scenarios, and many popular instance communication tools support it, such as WhatsApp and Signal. In addition, the IETF launched the message-layer security (MLS) working group, which aims to standardize an eponymous secure group messaging protocol. At the meanwhile, the academic researchers also paid lots of attention, such as [3,4,13,23,39].

Contributions. In this paper, we systematically explore message franking in group communication scenarios. The contributions are listed as follows.

- We introduce a new primitive called asymmetric group message franking (AGMF), and formalize its security notions.
- We present a variant of key encapsulation mechanism (KEM), called HPS-KEM$^\Sigma$, and provide a construction based on the decisional Diffie-Hellman (DDH) assumption. The construction can be extended to be built based on the k-Linear assumption.
- We provide a framework of constructing AGMF from HPS-KEM$^\Sigma$, and show that it achieves the required security properties. Actually, we also obtain a framework of constructing AMF from HPS-KEM$^\Sigma$ (i.e., when the size of the receiver set is 1).

When plugging the concrete HPS-KEM$^\Sigma$ scheme into our AGMF framework, we obtain an AGMF scheme based on the DDH assumption, which implies a

DDH-based AMF scheme. Note that the only existing AMF scheme [36][1] is constructed based on a somewhat exotic assumption, knowledge-of-exponent assumption (KEA) [5], or the Gap Diffie-Hellman (GDH) assumption [6].

AGMF Primitive. In the context of AGMF, there are three kinds of parties involved: the sender, the multiple receivers, and the moderator (or called the judge). Syntactically, similar to AMF, an AGMF consists of nine algorithms: three algorithms for generating public parameters and key pairs, three algorithms (Frank, Verify, Judge) for creating and verifying genuine signatures, and the other three algorithms (Forge, RForge, JForge) for forging signatures. In a nutshell, the sender invokes the signing algorithm Frank to generate signatures for a receiver set. Any receiver calls Verify (with his/her secret key as input) to verify the received signatures. If some receiver reports some malicious message to the moderator, the moderator verifies the report with algorithm Judge. Algorithms Forge, RForge and JForge are not intended to be run by legitimate users. Their existence guarantee deniability in particular compromise scenarios.

We consider three kinds of security requirements for AGMF: accountability, deniability, and receiver anonymity.

- *Accountability.* Accountability is formalized with two special properties: sender binding and receiver binding. Sender binding guarantees that any sender should not be able to trick receivers into accepting unreportable messages, and receiver binding guarantees that any receivers cannot deceive the judge or other honest receivers (to frame the innocent sender).
- *Deniability.* Deniability is formalized with three special properties: universal deniability, receiver compromise deniability and judge compromise deniability. Universal deniability is formalized to guarantee deniability when no receiver secret key or judge secret key is compromised. Receiver compromise deniability is formalized to guarantee deniability when the secret keys of some receivers in the receiver set are compromised. Judge compromise deniability is formalized to guarantee deniability when the judge's secret key is compromised.
- *Receiver Anonymity.* Receiver anonymity is formalized to guarantee that any one (except for the receivers in the receiver set), including the judge, cannot tell which receiver set a signature is generated for.

When formalizing the above security requirements, the existence of multiple receivers in group communication scenarios introduces new security risks, making the security models in AGMF different from that in AMF.

---

[1] Very recently, Issa et al. also consider a kind of AMF, called Hecate [28], but it is somewhat different from [36]. Firstly, [36] and this paper only focus on the intrinsic/fundamental security properties of A(G)MF, while Hecate [28] also considers others, e.g., forward/backward secrecy. Secondly, [36] only needs one round of communication and can generate the AMF signature on the fly, but Hecate [28] introduces an AMF with preprocessing model, resulting in one more preprocessing round with the moderator to get a "token" before generating the AMF signature. Hence, we follow the definition in [36], not considering Hecate [28] when talking about AMF.

First of all, due to the existence of multiple receivers, it is natural to consider that the adversary in the security models of AGMF is able to corrupt some of the receivers. These corruptions bring in the following concerns.

- Compared with receiver binding for AMF, which requires that any *single* receiver cannot deceive the judge to frame the innocent sender, receiver binding for AGMF requires that *any corrupted receivers* cannot deceive the judge or *the other honest receivers* to frame the innocent sender.
- Recall that receiver compromise deniability for AMF requires that a party with the receiver's secret key is able to create a signature, such that for other parties with access to this secret key, it is indistinguishable from honestly-generated signatures. Comparatively, receiver compromise deniability for AGMF requires that *any corrupted users in the receiver set* are able to create a signature, such that for other parties with access to *these corrupted users' secret keys*, it is indistinguishable from honestly-generated signatures.

Secondly, we also formalize a new security notion called receiver anonymity, which is not considered in AMF. Receiver anonymity requires that any one (except for the receivers in the receiver set), including the judge, cannot tell which receiver set a signature is generated for. With receiver anonymity, the receivers in group communication scenarios can report the malicious messages to the moderator with less concerns. If the AGMF scheme does not support receiver anonymity, then the judge can know some information about the identities of receivers from the report. Then the reporter may be at the risk of vengeance, especially if the judge is possible to leak the receiver's identity information to the sender. As a result, it would silence the reporters. Actually, anonymity has already been considered in many group scenarios, such as accountable anonymous group messaging system [14,35,38], and proactively accountable anonymous messaging [15].

More importantly, in all our proposed security models, the adversary is allowed to corrupt the receivers *adaptively*. In other words, how many and whose secret keys are compromised is unpredictable in practical scenarios, which is greatly different from that in AMF (i.e., only one receiver's secret key is compromised). Compared with non-adaptive corruptions (i.e., the adversary is required to announce all the corrupted users at the beginning before seeing all users' public keys), adaptive corruptions are more natural, and cryptographic schemes supporting adaptive corruptions are much more difficult to obtain, as mentioned in [3,25,26,29].

AGMF Construction. Following, we highlight the technical details of our AGMF construction.

HPS-KEM$^\Sigma$. In order to provide a framework of constructing AGMF, we introduce a new primitive. This primitive is a variant of key encapsulation mechanism (KEM) satisfying that (i) it can be interpreted from the perspective of hash proof system (HPS) [17], and (ii) for some special relations (about the public/secret keys, the encapsulated keys and ciphertexts), there exist corresponding Sigma protocols [16]. We call this primitive *HPS-based KEM supporting Sigma protocols (HPS-KEM$^\Sigma$)*.

A HPS-KEM$^\Sigma$ scheme HPS-KEM$^\Sigma$ mainly contains six algorithms: Setup, KG, encap$_c$, encap$_k$, decap and encap$_c^*$. In a nutshell, Setup outputs a public parameter, and KG outputs a pair of public/secret user keys. Taking the public parameter as input, *without user's public key*, encap$_c$ outputs a well-formed ciphertext, and encap$_c^*$ outputs a ciphertext which could be well-formed or ill-formed. The algorithm encap$_k$, sharing the same randomness space with encap$_c$, takes the public parameter and user's public key as input, and outputs an encapsulated key. With user's secret key, the algorithm decap is invoked to decapsulate the ciphertexts to get the encapsulated keys. The correctness demands that given a ciphertext output by encap$_c$ with randomness r, decap will recover an encapsulated key, which is equivalent to that generated by encap$_k$ with the same randomness r.

It is required that there are Sigma protocols to prove that some results are exactly output by KG, encap$_c$, encap$_k$ or encap$_c^*$. We also require the following properties informally.

1. Universality: when given a public key, it is difficult for any unbounded adversary without the corresponding secret key to generate an ill-formed ciphertext c, an encapsulated key k and a witness w (indicating that c is generated via encap$_c^*$), such that with the ciphertext c as input, decap outputs a key equal to k.
2. Unexplainability: it is difficult to generate a ciphertext c and a witness w (indicating that c is generated via encap$_c^*$), such that c is well-formed.
3. Indistinguishability: the ciphertext output by encap$_c^*$ is indistinguishable from the well-formed ciphertext output by encap$_c$.
4. SK-second-preimage resistance: when given a pair of public and secret keys, it is difficult to generate another valid secret key for this public key.
5. Smoothness: when given a public key, the algorithm decap, fed with a ciphertext generated via encap$_c^*$ and a user's secret key randomly sampled from the set of secret keys corresponding to the public key, will output a key uniformly distributed over the encapsulated key space.

AGMF from HPS-KEM$^\Sigma$. Taking HPS-KEM$^\Sigma$ as a building block, we construct AGMF as follows.

The public/secret key pairs of all users (including the judge) are generated by invoking the key generation algorithm KG of the HPS-KEM$^\Sigma$.

Given a pair of sender's public/secret keys (pk_s, sk_s), a receiver set $S = \{pk_{r_i}\}_{i \in [|S|]}$, the judge's public key pk_J and a message m, the sender calls Frank to generate the signature as follows:

(1) Compute $c \leftarrow$ encap$_c(pp; r)$, $k_J \leftarrow$ encap$_k(pp, pk_J; r)$ and $(k_{r_i} \leftarrow$ encap$_k(pp, pk_{r_i}; r))_{pk_{r_i} \in S}$ with the same randomness r.
(2) Consider the following relation

$$\mathcal{R} = \{ ((sk_s, r, r^*), (pp, pk_s, pk_J, c, k_J)) :$$
$$((sk_s, pk_s) \in \mathcal{R}_s \wedge (r, (c, k_J, pk_J)) \in \mathcal{R}_{c,k}) \qquad (1)$$
$$\vee ((r^*, c) \in \mathcal{R}_c^*) \}$$

where $\mathcal{R}_s$ is a relation proving that the sender's public/secret keys are valid, $\mathcal{R}_{c,k}$ is a relation proving that (c, k_J) are generated via encap$_c$ and encap$_k$

with the same randomness r, and $\mathcal{R}_c^*$ is a relation proving that c is a ciphertext output by encap_c^* with randomness r^*. As the HPS-KEM$^\Sigma$ guarantees that there are Sigma protocols for KG, encap_c, encap_k and encap_c^*, we can obtain a signature of knowledge (SoK) scheme for $\mathcal{R}$ by applying the Fiat-Shamir transform [22] and composition operations of Sigma protocols [7].

(3) Employ the SoK scheme for $\mathcal{R}$ to generate a signature proof π of statement (pp, pk_s, pk_J, c, k_J) for a message $\overline{m} = (m || \{k_{r_i}\}_{pk_{r_i} \in S})$ with a witness (sk_s, r).

(4) Return the signature $\sigma = (\pi, c, k_J, \{k_{r_i}\}_{pk_{r_i} \in S})$.

The verification algorithm Verify and the moderation algorithm Judge work similarly. When some receiver receives a message and a signature or the judge receives a report with a message and a signature, the first step of these algorithms is to verify if the proof π in the signature is valid. If not valid, Verify (resp., Judge) returns 0; otherwise, Verify (resp., Judge) returns 1 if and only if $\mathsf{decap}(pp, sk_r, c) \in \{k_{r_i}\}$ (resp., $\mathsf{decap}(pp, sk_J, c) = k_J$).

Now we turn to describe the forging algorithms Forge, RForge and JForge.

Given a sender's public keys pk_s, a receiver set $S = \{pk_{r_i}\}_{i \in [|S|]}$, the judge's public key pk_J and a message m, the universal forging algorithm Forge proceeds as follows:

(1) Compute $c \leftarrow \mathsf{encap}_c^*(pp; r^*)$ with randomness r^*, $k_J \leftarrow \mathcal{K}$, and $(k_{r_i} \leftarrow \mathcal{K})_{pk_{r_i} \in S}$.

(2) Employ the SoK scheme for $\mathcal{R}$ in Eq. (1) to generate a signature proof π of statement (pp, pk_s, pk_J, c, k_J) for a message $\overline{m} = (m || \{k_{r_i}\}_{pk_{r_i} \in S})$ with a witness r^*.

(3) Return the signature $\sigma = (\pi, c, k_J, \{k_{r_i}\}_{pk_{r_i} \in S})$.

Given a sender's public key pk_s, a receiver set $S = \{pk_{r_i}\}_{i \in [|S|]}$, the corrupted receivers' secret keys $\{sk_{r_i}\}_{pk_{r_i} \in S_{cor}}$ (where $S_{cor} \subset S$), the judge's public key pk_J and a message m, the receiver compromise forging algorithm RForge proceeds similarly to Forge, except that $(k_{r_i})_{pk_{r_i} \in S}$ are generated as follows: for each $pk_{r_i} \in S \backslash S_{cor}$, samples $k_{r_i} \leftarrow \mathcal{K}$; for each $pk_{r_i} \in S_{cor}$, computes $k_{r_i} \leftarrow \mathsf{decap}(pp, sk_{r_i}, c)$.

Given a sender's public keys pk_s, a receiver set $S = \{pk_{r_i}\}_{i \in [|S|]}$, the judge's secret key sk_J and a message m, the judge compromise forging algorithm JForge proceeds similarly to Forge, except that k_J is generated by $k_J \leftarrow \mathsf{decap}(pp, sk_J, c)$.

Security Analysis. Now we briefly show that our AGMF framework provides accountability, deniability and receiver anonymity.

Informally, sender binding requires that any malicious sender cannot generate a signature such that an honest receiver accepts it but the judge rejects it. If there exists an adversary generating such a signature $\sigma = (\pi, c, k_J, \{k_{r_i}\}_{pk_{r_i} \in S})$, then we have: (i) π is a valid proof for the relation $\mathcal{R}$; (ii) $k' = \mathsf{decap}(pp, sk_r, c) \in \{k_{r_i}\}_{pk_{r_i} \in S}$; (iii) $\mathsf{decap}(pp, sk_J, c) \neq k_J$. Observe that to generate the valid proof π for $\mathcal{R}$, the adversary needs to know witness (sk_s, r) or r^*. According to (i) and (iii), it implies that the adversary generates π using the witness r^*, which suggests that c is generated via encap_c^*. The unexplainability of HPS-KEM$^\Sigma$ implies that c is not well-formed with overwhelming probability. So according to (ii), (c, k', r^*) leads to a successful attack on universality of HPS-KEM$^\Sigma$.

Receiver binding requires that any malicious receivers cannot generate a signature such that an honest receiver or the judge accepts it.

– Supposing that there exists an adversary generating a signature $\sigma = (\pi, c, k_{\mathrm{J}},$ $\{k_{\mathrm{r}_i}\}_{pk_{\mathrm{r}_i} \in S})$ such that an honest receiver accepts it, we have: (i) π is a valid proof for the relation $\mathcal{R}$; (ii) $k' = \mathsf{decap}(pp, sk_{\mathrm{r}}, c) \in \{k_{\mathrm{r}_i}\}_{pk_{\mathrm{r}_i} \in S}$. Observe that to generate the valid proof π for $\mathcal{R}$, the adversary needs to know witness (sk_{s}, r) or r^*.
  - If the adversary knows (sk_{s}, r), it implies that sk_{s} is a valid secret key of the sender. Since the adversary is not allowed to corrupt the sender, it is contradictory to SK-second-preimage resistance of HPS-KEM$^{\Sigma}$.
  - If the adversary knows r^*, it implies that c is generated via encap_c^*. The unexplainability of HPS-KEM$^{\Sigma}$ guarantees that c is not well-formed with overwhelming probability. So according to (ii), (c, k', r^*) leads to a successful attack on universality of HPS-KEM$^{\Sigma}$.
– Supposing that there exists an adversary generating a signature $\sigma = (\pi, c, k_{\mathrm{J}},$ $\{k_{\mathrm{r}_i}\}_{pk_{\mathrm{r}_i} \in S})$ such that the judge accepts it, we have: (i) π is a valid proof for the relation $\mathcal{R}$; (ii) $\mathsf{decap}(pp, sk_{\mathrm{J}}, c) = k_{\mathrm{J}}$. With similar analysis, this leads to a successful attack on SK-second-preimage resistance or universality of HPS-KEM$^{\Sigma}$.

Next, we turn to analyze universal deniability, receiver compromise deniability, and judge compromise deniability of our AGMF framework. Due to the similarity of security analysis of these deniabilities, here we just show how universal deniability is achieved.

Universal deniability requires that the outputs of Frank and Forge are indistinguishable. For the generation of signature $\sigma = (\pi, c, k_{\mathrm{J}}, \{k_{\mathrm{r}_i}\}_{pk_{\mathrm{r}_i} \in S})$, the differences between the two algorithms are as follows.

– $(c, k_{\mathrm{J}}, \{k_{\mathrm{r}_i}\}_{pk_{\mathrm{r}_i} \in S})$: Algorithm Frank computes $c \leftarrow \mathsf{encap}_c(pp; r)$, $k_{\mathrm{J}} \leftarrow \mathsf{encap}_k$ $(pp, pk_{\mathrm{J}}; r)$ and $(k_{\mathrm{r}_i} \leftarrow \mathsf{encap}_k(pp, pk_{\mathrm{r}_i}; r))_{pk_{\mathrm{r}_i} \in S}$ with the same randomness r, while algorithm Forge computes $c \leftarrow \mathsf{encap}_c^*(pp; r^*)$ with randomness r^*, and samples $k_{\mathrm{J}} \leftarrow \mathcal{K}$ and $(k_{\mathrm{r}_i} \leftarrow \mathcal{K})_{pk_{\mathrm{r}_i} \in S}$.

The indistinguishability of HPS-KEM$^{\Sigma}$ guarantees that c output by encap_c is indistinguishable from that output by encap_c^*. When $c \leftarrow \mathsf{encap}_c(pp; r)$, we have $\mathsf{encap}_k(pp, pk_{\mathrm{r}_i}; r) = \mathsf{decap}(pp, sk_{\mathrm{r}_i}, c)$ and $\mathsf{encap}_k(pp, pk_{\mathrm{J}}; r) = \mathsf{decap}(pp, sk_{\mathrm{J}}, c)$. On the other hand, when $c \leftarrow \mathsf{encap}_c^*(pp; r^*)$, the smoothness of HPS-KEM$^{\Sigma}$ guarantees that the encapsulated keys $k_{\mathrm{r}_i} \leftarrow \mathsf{decap}(pp, sk_{\mathrm{r}_i}, c)$ and $k_{\mathrm{J}} \leftarrow \mathsf{decap}(pp, sk_{\mathrm{J}}, c)$ are indistinguishable from those random keys $k_{\mathrm{r}_i} \leftarrow \mathcal{K}$ and $k_{\mathrm{J}} \leftarrow \mathcal{K}$. Therefore, through hybrid arguments, we can show that $(c, k_{\mathrm{J}}, \{k_{\mathrm{r}_i}\}_{pk_{\mathrm{r}_i} \in S})$ output by Frank and Forge are indistinguishable.
– π: Frank generates a signature proof π for $\mathcal{R}$ with a witness (sk_{s}, r), while Forge generates π for $\mathcal{R}$ with a witness r^*. Because of zero knowledge property of the SoK scheme for $\mathcal{R}$, anyone cannot distinguish the proof output by Frank from that output by Forge.

Finally, we briefly explain why our AGMF framework achieves receiver anonymity. Informally, receiver anonymity requires that given two receiver sets S_0 and S_1 with the same size, a signature generated by Frank for S_0 is indistinguishable from that for S_1. According to the above security analysis of universal deniability, the signature output by Frank is indistinguishable from that output by Forge. Notice that, the signature generated by Forge does not contain any information about the receiver set. Thus, the signatures generated by Frank for S_0 and for S_1 are indistinguishable.

Construction of HPS-KEM$^\Sigma$. Inspired by the DDH-based HPS [17], we provide a construction of HPS-KEM$^\Sigma$, which can be extended to be built based on the k-Linear assumption. The main algorithms are constructed as follows.

KG outputs a pair of public/secret keys $(pk, sk) = (g_1^{x_1} g_2^{x_2}, (x_1, x_2))$, where g_1, g_2 are two generators of group $\mathbb{G}$ of prime order p, and x_1, x_2 are uniformly sampled from $\mathbb{Z}_p^*$.

To generate a well-formed ciphertext c, encap_c outputs $c = (u_1, u_2) = (g_1^r, g_2^r)$, where r is uniformly random sampled from $\mathbb{Z}_p^*$.

For generating a ciphertext, encap_c^* chooses randomness $r^* = (r, r') \in \mathbb{Z}_p^{*2}$ and outputs $c = (u_1, u_2) = (g_1^r, g_1^{r'})$.

Algorithm encap_k outputs an encapsulated key $k = pk^r$, where r is uniformly random sampled from $\mathbb{Z}_p^*$.

When inputting a ciphertext $c = (u_1, u_2)$ and a secret key $sk = (x_1, x_2)$, the algorithm decap outputs a key $k' = u_1^{x_1} u_2^{x_2}$.

Note that there are Sigma protocols for KG, encap_c, encap_k or encap_c^*: Okamoto's Sigma protocol [31] for KG, the Chaum-Pedersen protocol [11] for encap_c and encap_k with the same randomness, and Schnorr's Sigma protocol [33] for encap_c^*.

Now we show our HPS-KEM$^\Sigma$ construction achieves the required properties.

With similar analysis in [17], we can easily obtain universality, indistinguishability and smoothness of our construction.

For unexplainability, suppose that there exists an adversary breaking the unexplainability of our scheme. In other words, the adversary generates $c = (u_1, u_2)$ and $w = (r, r')$, such that (i) $(u_1 = g_1^r) \wedge (u_2 = g_1^{r'})$, and (ii) c is well-formed. Note that c is well-formed implies that $u_2 = g_2^r$. So we can compute $\log_{g_1} g_2 = \frac{r'}{r}$, solving the DL problem.

For SK-second-preimage resistance (SK-2PR), suppose that there exists an adversary breaking the SK-2PR of our scheme. In other words, given a public/secret key pair $(pk, sk) = (g_1^{x_1} g_2^{x_2}, (x_1, x_2))$, the adversary outputs another secret key $sk' = (x_1', x_2')$ such that $pk = g_1^{x_1'} g_2^{x_2'}$. We can compute $\log_{g_1} g_2 = (x_1 - x_1')/(x_2' - x_2)$, solving the DL problem.

Discussion I: Lower bound. Following we present a lower bound of the size of AGMF signature.

Theorem 1. *Any AGMF with receiver binding and receiver compromise deniability must have signature size $\Omega(n)$, where n is the number of the members in S.*

Proof. Suppose that there exists a distinguisher $\mathcal{D}$ who knows all receivers' secret keys. Given a signature generated by RForge with a corrupted receiver set S_{cor}, $\mathcal{D}$ can distinguish whether someone is in S_{cor} or not, by verifying validity of the signature. Note that receiver binding and receiver deniability guarantee that only the receivers in S_{cor} would accept the signature. Thus, $\mathcal{D}$ can determine the set S_{cor} when given a signature generated by RForge. Therefore, the signature must contain enough bits to indicate S_{cor}. Since $S_{cor} \subseteq S$ and it can be an arbitrary subset, there are $2^{|S|} = 2^n$ kinds of different subsets. Thus, the bit length of signature is at least $\log_2 2^{|S|} = \log_2 2^n = n$. Considering that the signature output by Frank is indistinguishable from that output by RForge, the bit length of signature output by Frank is also $\Omega(n)$. □

When plugging the concrete HPS-KEM$^\Sigma$ scheme into our AGMF framework, we obtain an AGMF scheme based on the DDH assumption. The bit length of the signature would be $9 \times |\mathbb{Z}_p^*| + (n+3) \times |\mathbb{G}|$, where n is the number of receivers and p is the order of group $\mathbb{G}$.

Theorem 1 indicates that the size of signature of AGMF is linear in n, and the coefficient of n in the size of signature of our AGMF scheme is $|cvm|$, which is almost optimal. Note that a proof with similar idea is given by Damgård et al. in [18, Theorem 1], to show the lower bound of the size of multi-designated verifier signatures with any-subset simulation and strong unforgeablity.

Discussion II: AGMF when $n = 1$. Note that our method actually provides a framework of constructing AMF from HPS-KEM$^\Sigma$ (i.e., when the size of the receiver set is 1). The AMF scheme [36] is firstly constructed based on a somewhat exotic assumption, the KEA assumption [5]. As mentioned by Tyagi et al. [36], the KEA assumption poses a challenge for interpreting the concrete security analyses since the KEA extractor is not concretely instantiated. Then, they also show a variant scheme that can be proven secure using the GDH assumption [6], at the cost of signatures with *slightly* larger size. Specifically, the bit length of the AMF signature [36] based on the GDH assumption would be $9 \times |\mathbb{Z}_p^*| + 4 \times |\mathbb{G}|$.

When plugging the concrete HPS-KEM$^\Sigma$ scheme into the AMF framework, we obtain a DDH-based AMF scheme. Although the size of the signature of our AMF scheme would be $9 \times |\mathbb{Z}_p^*| + 4 \times |\mathbb{G}|$ as well, we stress that at the same security level, the binary representation of the group element in our scheme has smaller size than that in the GDH-based AMF scheme [36].

Discussion III: AGMF from AMF [36] Directly. A trivial construction of AGMF is extended directly from the existing AMF [36], e.g., integrating AMF [36] with the "trivial" Signal group key mechanism (i.e., a set of individual links to each member of the group).

The extension has two shortcomings: i) the signature contains n NIZK proofs, and ii) it needs a non-standard assumption, which is inherited from AMF [36]. Our scheme does not have these shortcomings. We also consider another extension in the full version of this paper. The key point is that we extend the relation used in AMF [36] for one receiver to a relation for multiple receivers. However, this extension also has similar shortcomings mentioned above. Due to the space limitations, more details of the extension will be given in the full version of this paper.

Discussion IV: Integrating AGMF with Group Messaging Protocols.
For end-to-end encryption systems, there are kinds of requirements, including message franking, privacy, forward/backward security, etc. Our paper focuses on asymmetric message franking in group communication scenarios, not caring about the other intrinsic security of group messaging protocols (e.g., privacy and authenticity in the form of post-compromise forward secrecy). Discussing a unified security model capturing other security properties is out of the scope of this paper and we remain it as a future work.

A potential method to integrate AGMF with group messaging protocols (e.g., [3,13,14,23]) is similar to AMF. In other words, we treat the output of AGMF as a signature and then encrypt the message and the signature following these protocols.

Related Work. The technique of symmetric message franking (SMF) was firstly introduced by Facebook [20,21]. Grubbs et al. [24] initiated a formal study of SMF, formalizing a cryptographic primitive called compactly committing authenticated encryption with associated data (AEAD), and then showing that many in-use AEAD schemes can be used for SMF. Dodis et al. [19] pointed out that the Facebook SMF scheme is actually insecure, and proposed an efficient single-pass construction of compactly committing AEAD. Observing that in all previous SMF schemes, to make a report the receiver has to reveal the whole communication for a session, Leontiadis et al. [30] and Chen et al. [12] independently presented SMF constructions to tackle this problem. In CRYPTO 2019, Tyagi et al. [36] initiated a formal study of AMF, formalizing security notions of accountability and deniability for AMF, and showing an AMF construction via signature of knowledge [8].

Recently, some works [28,32,37] explore source-tracking, which allows the moderator to pinpoint the original source of a viral message rather than the immediate sender of the message (in the setting of message franking [24,36]). These works mainly focus on end-to-end encrypted messaging. It is an interesting direction to consider source-tracking in group settings.

Group messaging and its variants have been studied in many works [3,4,13, 14,23,39], focusing on different properties or security requirements. To the best of our knowledge, currently there are no variants of group messaging which can provide the aforementioned accountability, deniability and anonymity simultaneously.

In 2020, Damgård et al. [18] proposed the notion of *off-the-record for any subset* in the constructions of multi-designated verifier signature (MDVS) for the group Off-the-Record messaging. The notion is somewhat similar to the receiver compromise deniability defined in this paper. As designated verifier signature does not have all desired properties in the setting of AMF [36], the MDVS construction [18] does not provide all required properties (e.g., accountability) in our AGMF scenarios either.

Roadmap. We recall some preliminaries in Sect. 2. Then in Sect. 3, we present the primitive of AGMF and formalize its security notions of accountability, deniability and receiver anonymity. Next, in Sect. 4, we introduce a primitive called HPS-KEM$^\Sigma$ and present a concrete construction. Taking HPS-KEM$^\Sigma$ as a building block, we provide a framework of constructing AGMF, and show that it achieves accountability, deniability and receiver anonymity in Sect. 5.

2 Preliminaries

Notations. Throughout this paper, let λ denote the security parameter. For any $k \in \mathbb{N}$, let $[k] := \{1, 2, \cdots, k\}$. For a finite set S, we denote by $|S|$ the number of elements in S, and denote by $a \leftarrow S$ the process of uniformly sampling a from S. For a distribution X, we denote by $a \leftarrow X$ the process of sampling a from X. For any probabilistic polynomial-time (PPT) algorithm Alg, we write $\mathsf{Alg}(x; r)$ for the process of Alg on input x with inner randomness r, and use $y \leftarrow \mathsf{Alg}(x)$ to denote the process of running Alg on input x with uniformly sampled inner randomness r, and assigning y the result.

Now we recall the definitions of non-interactive zero knowledge (NIZK) proof system *in the random oracle model*, Sigma protocol, and the Fiat-Shamir heuristic [22] as follows. For convenience, the recalled NIZK is a variant integrating the notion of signature of knowledge in [9,10,36] and the notion of NIZK in [7].

NIZK Proof System. Let $\mathcal{M}$ be a message space. For a witness space $\mathcal{X}$ and a statement space $\mathcal{Y}$, let $\mathcal{R} \subseteq \mathcal{X} \times \mathcal{Y}$ be a relation. A NIZK proof scheme $\mathsf{NIZK}^\mathcal{R} = (\mathsf{prove}, \mathsf{verify})$ for witness-statement relation $\mathcal{R} \subseteq \mathcal{X} \times \mathcal{Y}$ is a pair of PPT algorithms associated with a message space $\mathcal{M}$ and a proof space Π.

- $\pi \leftarrow \mathsf{NIZK}^\mathcal{R}.\mathsf{prove}(m, x, y)$: The prove algorithm takes $(m, x, y) \in \mathcal{M} \times \mathcal{X} \times \mathcal{Y}$ as input, and outputs a proof $\pi \in \Pi$.
- $b \leftarrow \mathsf{NIZK}^\mathcal{R}.\mathsf{verify}(m, \pi, y)$: The verification algorithm takes $(m, \pi, y) \in \mathcal{M} \times \Pi \times \mathcal{Y}$ as input, and outputs a bit $b \in \{0, 1\}$.

It is required to satisfies *completeness, existential soundness, and zero-knowledge in the random oracle model*. The formal definitions are recalled as follows.

- **Completeness.** For all $m \in \mathcal{M}$ and all $(x, y) \in \mathcal{R}$, we always have $\mathsf{NIZK}^\mathcal{R}.\mathsf{verify}\,(m, \mathsf{NIZK}^\mathcal{R}.\mathsf{prove}(m, x, y), y) = 1$.
- **Existential soundness.** For any PPT adversary $\mathcal{A}$, $\mathbf{Adv}_{\mathsf{NIZK},\mathcal{A}}^{\mathrm{sound}}(\lambda)$ is negligible, where $\mathbf{Adv}_{\mathsf{NIZK},\mathcal{A}}^{\mathrm{sound}}(\lambda)$ is the probability that $\mathcal{A}$ outputs $(m, y) \in \mathcal{M} \times \mathcal{Y}$ and $\pi \in \Pi$, such that $\mathsf{NIZK}^\mathcal{R}.\mathsf{verify}(m, \pi, y) = 1$ and $(x', y) \notin \mathcal{R}$ for all $x' \in \mathcal{X}$.
- **Zero-knowledge.** There is a PPT simulator $\mathcal{S} = (\mathcal{S}_{\mathsf{prove}}, \mathcal{S}_{\mathsf{ro}})$, such that for any PPT adversary $\mathcal{A}$, the advantage

$$\mathbf{Adv}_{\mathsf{NIZK},\mathcal{A}}^{\mathrm{zk}}(\lambda) := \left| \Pr[\mathbf{G}_{\mathsf{NIZK},\mathcal{A}}^{\mathrm{real}}(\lambda) = 1] - \Pr[\mathbf{G}_{\mathsf{NIZK},\mathcal{A},\mathcal{S}}^{\mathrm{ideal}}(\lambda) = 1] \right|$$

is negligible, where $\mathbf{G}_{\mathsf{NIZK},\mathcal{A}}^{\mathrm{real}}$ and $\mathbf{G}_{\mathsf{NIZK},\mathcal{A},\mathcal{S}}^{\mathrm{ideal}}$ are both in Fig. 1. Suppose that $\mathsf{NIZK}^\mathcal{R}$ makes use of a hash function Hash, and the hash function Hash with output length *len* in Fig. 1 is modeled as a random oracle (a local array H is employed).

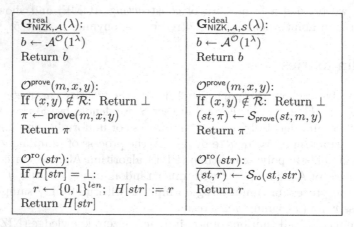

Fig. 1. Games for defining zero knowledge of $\mathsf{NIZK}^{\mathcal{R}}$

Sigma Protocol. A Sigma protocol for $\mathcal{R} \subseteq \mathcal{X} \times \mathcal{Y}$ consists of two efficient interactive protocol algorithms (P, V), where $P = (P_1, P_2)$ is the prover and $V = (V_1, V_2)$ is the verifier, associated with a challenge space $\mathcal{CL}$. Specifically, for any $(x, y) \in \mathcal{R}$, the input of the prover (resp., verifier) is (x, y) (resp., y). The prover first computes $(cm, aux) \leftarrow P_1(x, y)$ and sends the commitment cm to the verifier. The verifier (i.e., V_1) returns a challenge $cl \leftarrow \mathcal{CL}$. Then the prover replies with $z \leftarrow P_2(cm, cl, x, y, aux)$. Receiving z, the verifier (i.e., V_2) outputs $b \in \{0, 1\}$. The tuple (cm, cl, z) is called a *conversation*. We require that V does not make any random choices other than the selection of cl. For any fixed (cm, cl, z), if the final output of $V(y)$ is 1, (cm, cl, z) is called an *accepting conversation* for y. Correctness requires for all $(x, y) \in \mathcal{R}$, when $P(x, y)$ and $V(y)$ interact with each other, the final output of $V(y)$ is always 1.

The corresponding security notions are as follows.

Definition 1 (Knowledge soundness). *We say that a Sigma protocol (P, V) for $R \subseteq \mathcal{X} \times \mathcal{Y}$ provides* knowledge soundness, *if there is an efficient deterministic algorithm* Ext *such that on input $y \in \mathcal{Y}$ and two accepting conversations $(cm, cl, z), (cm, cl', z')$ where $cl \neq cl'$,* Ext *always outputs an $x \in \mathcal{X}$ satisfying $(x, y) \in \mathcal{R}$.*

Definition 2 (Special HVZK). *We say that a Sigma protocol (P, V) for $R \subseteq \mathcal{X} \times \mathcal{Y}$ with challenge space $\mathcal{CL}$ is* special honest verifier zero knowledge (special HVZK), *if there is a PPT simulator $\mathcal{S}$ which takes $(y, cl) \in \mathcal{Y} \times \mathcal{CL}$ as input and satisfies the following properties:*

(i) for all $(y, cl) \in \mathcal{Y} \times \mathcal{CL}$, $\mathcal{S}$ always outputs a pair (cm, z) such that (cm, cl, z) is an accepting conversation for y;

(ii) for all $(x, y) \in \mathcal{R}$, the tuple (cm, cl, z), generated via $cl \leftarrow \mathcal{CL}$ and $(cm, z) \leftarrow \mathcal{S}(y, cl)$, has the same distribution as that of a transcript of a conversation between $P(x, y)$ and $V(y)$.

The Fiat-Shamir heuristic. Let $\mathcal{M}$ be a message space, and $(P, V) = ((P_1, P_2), (V_1, V_2))$ be a Sigma protocol for a relation $\mathcal{R} \subseteq \mathcal{X} \times \mathcal{Y}$, where its conversations (cm, cl, z) belong to some space $\mathcal{CM} \times \mathcal{CL} \times \mathcal{Z}$. Let Hash : $\mathcal{M} \times \mathcal{CM} \rightarrow \mathcal{CL}$ be a hash function. The Fiat-Shamir non-interactive proof system $\mathsf{NIZK}_{\mathsf{FS}} = (\mathsf{prove}_{\mathsf{FS}}, \mathsf{verify}_{\mathsf{FS}})$, with proof space $\Pi = \mathcal{CM} \times \mathcal{Z}$, is as follows:

- $\mathsf{prove}_{\mathsf{FS}}(m, x, y)$: On input $(m, x, y) \in \mathcal{M} \times \mathcal{X} \times \mathcal{Y}$, this algorithm firstly generates $(cm, aux) \leftarrow P_1(x, y)$ and $cl = \mathsf{Hash}(m, cm, y)$, and then computes $z \leftarrow P_2(cm, cl, x, y, aux)$. Finally, it outputs $\pi = (cm, z)$.

- $\mathsf{verify}_{\mathsf{FS}}(m, (cm, z), y)$: On input $(m, (cm, z), y) \in \mathcal{M} \times (\mathcal{CM} \times \mathcal{Z}) \times \mathcal{Y}$, this algorithm firstly computes $cl = \mathsf{Hash}(m, cm, y)$, and then runs $V_2(y)$ to check whether (cm, cl, z) is a valid conversation for y. If so, $\mathsf{verify}_{\mathsf{FS}}$ returns 1; otherwise, it returns 0.

According to [7,22], $\mathsf{NIZK}_{\mathsf{FS}}$ is an NIZK proof system if Hash is modeled as a random oracle. To be noted, in order to reduce the size of π, we replace cm with cl (i.e., we have $\pi = (z, cl)$), following [7].

Due to the page limitations, the cryptographic assumptions (the discrete logarithm assumption and the decisional Diffie-Hellman assumption) used in our security proofs will be recalled in the full version of this paper.

3   Asymmetric Group Message Franking

In this section, we introduce a primitive called *asymmetric group message franking (AGMF)* and formalize its security notions. Generally, AGMF is a cryptographic primitive providing accountability, deniability and receiver anonymity in group communication scenarios simultaneously.

3.1   AGMF Algorithms

We will firstly present the detailed notations of AGMF, and then explain the syntax of the algorithms.

Formally, an asymmetric group message franking (AGMF) scheme AGMF = (Setup, KG$_J$, KG$_u$, Frank, Verify, Judge, Forge, RForge, JForge) is a tuple of algorithms associated with a public key space $\mathcal{PK}$, a secret key space $\mathcal{SK}$, a message space $\mathcal{M}$ and a signature space $\mathcal{SG}$. Without loss of generality, we assume that all pk inputs are in $\mathcal{PK}$, all sk inputs are in $\mathcal{SK}$, all m inputs are in $\mathcal{M}$, and all σ inputs are in $\mathcal{SG}$.

The detailed descriptions of the nine algorithms are as follows.

- $pp \leftarrow$ Setup(λ): The setup algorithm takes the security parameter as input, and outputs a global public parameters pp.
- $(pk_{\mathrm{J}}, sk_{\mathrm{J}}) \leftarrow$ KG$_{\mathrm{J}}(pp)$: The randomized key generation algorithm KG$_{\mathrm{J}}$ takes pp as input, and outputs a key pair $(pk_{\mathrm{J}}, sk_{\mathrm{J}})$ for the judge.
- $(pk, sk) \leftarrow$ KG$_{\mathrm{u}}(pp)$: The randomized key generation algorithm KG$_{\mathrm{u}}$ takes pp as input, and outputs a key pair $(pk_{\mathrm{u}}, sk_{\mathrm{u}})$ for users. Below we usually use $(pk_{\mathrm{s}}, sk_{\mathrm{s}})$ (resp., $(pk_{\mathrm{r}}, sk_{\mathrm{r}})$) to denote sender (resp., receiver) public/secret key pair.
- $\sigma \leftarrow$ Frank($pp, sk_{\mathrm{s}}, S, pk_{\mathrm{J}}, m$): The franking algorithm takes the public parameter pp, a sender's secret key sk_{s}, a polynomial-size receiver's public key set $S = \{pk_{\mathrm{r}_i}\}_{i \in [|S|]} \subset \mathcal{PK}$, the judge's public key pk_{J} and a message m as input, and outputs a signature σ.
- $b \leftarrow$ Verify($pp, pk_{\mathrm{s}}, sk_{\mathrm{r}}, pk_{\mathrm{J}}, m, \sigma$): The *deterministic* receiver verification algorithm takes $(pp, pk_{\mathrm{s}}, sk_{\mathrm{r}}, pk_{\mathrm{J}})$, a message m and a signature σ as input, and outputs a bit b, which indicates that the signature is valid or not.
- $b \leftarrow$ Judge($pp, pk_{\mathrm{s}}, sk_{\mathrm{J}}, m, \sigma$): The *deterministic* judge authentication algorithm takes $(pp, pk_{\mathrm{s}}, sk_{\mathrm{J}})$, a message m and a signature σ as input, and returns $b \in \{0, 1\}$.
- $\sigma \leftarrow$ Forge($pp, pk_{\mathrm{s}}, S, pk_{\mathrm{J}}, m$): The universal forging algorithm, on input $(pp, pk_{\mathrm{s}}, S, pk_{\mathrm{J}})$ and a message m, returns a "forged" signature σ, where $S \subset \mathcal{PK}$.
- $\sigma \leftarrow$ RForge($pp, pk_{\mathrm{s}}, (pk_{\mathrm{r}_i}, sk_{\mathrm{r}_i})_{pk_{\mathrm{r}_i} \in S_{\mathrm{cor}}}, S, pk_{\mathrm{J}}, m$): The receiver compromise forging algorithm takes $(pp, pk_{\mathrm{s}}, (pk_{\mathrm{r}_i}, sk_{\mathrm{r}_i})_{pk_{\mathrm{r}_i} \in S_{\mathrm{cor}}}, S, pk_{\mathrm{J}})$ and a message m as input, and returns a "forged" signature σ, where $S_{\mathrm{cor}} \subset S \subset \mathcal{PK}$.
- $\sigma \leftarrow$ JForge($pp, pk_{\mathrm{s}}, S, sk_{\mathrm{J}}, m$): The judge compromise forging algorithm takes $(pp, pk_{\mathrm{s}}, S, sk_{\mathrm{J}})$ and a message m as input, and outputs a "forged" signature σ, where $S \subset \mathcal{PK}$.

Correctness. For any normal signature generated by Frank, the correctness requires that (i) each receiver in the receiver set can call Verify to verify the signature successfully, and (ii) the moderator can invoke Judge to validate a report successfully once he receives a valid report. The formal requirements are shown as follows.

Given any pp generated by Setup, any key pairs $(pk_{\mathrm{s}}, sk_{\mathrm{s}})$ and $(pk_{\mathrm{r}}, sk_{\mathrm{r}})$ output by KG$_{\mathrm{u}}$, and any key pair $(pk_{\mathrm{J}}, sk_{\mathrm{J}})$ output by KG$_{\mathrm{J}}$, we require that for any $S \subset \mathcal{PK}$ satisfying $pk_{\mathrm{r}} \in S$, any message $m \in \mathcal{M}$, and any $\sigma \leftarrow$ Frank($pp, sk_{\mathrm{s}}, S, pk_{\mathrm{J}}, m$), it holds that:

(1) Verify($pp, pk_{\mathrm{s}}, sk_{\mathrm{r}}, pk_{\mathrm{J}}, m, \sigma$) = 1;
(2) Judge($pp, pk_{\mathrm{s}}, sk_{\mathrm{J}}, m, \sigma$) = 1.

3.2 Security Notions for AGMF

Now we formalize some security notions for AGMF, including the security notions for accountability, deniability and receiver anonymity of AGMF. Note that we consider the adaptive security in the following games. It means that the adversary $\mathcal{A}$ is allowed to query the corruption oracle on different public keys adaptively, obtaining corresponding secret keys.

Accountability. Analogous to the setting of end-to-end communication, one of the most important security requirements in group scenarios is to prevent malicious impersonation. In other words, AGMF needs to ensure that no one will be impersonated successfully as long as her/his secret key is not compromised. Specifically, AGMF needs to guarantee that (i) no receivers can trick the judge or any receiver in the receiver set (except the adversarial receiver herself if she is also in this set) into accepting a message that is not actually sent by the sender, and (ii) no sender can create a signature such that it is accepted by some receiver but meanwhile rejected by the judge. Following the terminology in AMF [36], we also refer to these security requirements as *receiver binding* and *sender binding*, respectively.

$G^{\text{r-bind}}_{\text{AGMF},\mathcal{A},n}(\lambda)$:	$\mathcal{O}^{\text{Cor}}(pk')$:
$pp \leftarrow \text{Setup}(\lambda); (pk_{\text{J}}, sk_{\text{J}}) \leftarrow \text{KG}_{\text{J}}(pp)$	$U_{\text{cor}} \leftarrow U_{\text{cor}} \cup \{pk'\}$
$Q_{\text{sig}} := \emptyset; U := \emptyset; U_{\text{key}} := \emptyset; U_{\text{cor}} := \emptyset$	Return sk' s.t. $(pk', sk') \in U_{\text{key}}$
For $i = 1 \ldots n$:	
$\quad (pk_i, sk_i) \leftarrow \text{KG}_{\text{u}}(pp); U \leftarrow U \cup \{pk_i\}$	$\mathcal{O}^{\text{Frank}}(pk'_{\text{s}}, S', m')$:
$\quad U_{\text{key}} \leftarrow U_{\text{key}} \cup \{(pk_i, sk_i)\}$	$Q_{\text{sig}} \leftarrow Q_{\text{sig}} \cup \{(pk'_{\text{s}}, S', m')\}$
$(pk^*_{\text{s}}, pk^*_{\text{r}}, m^*, \sigma^*) \leftarrow \mathcal{A}^{\mathcal{O}}(pp, U, pk_{\text{J}})$	Return $\text{Frank}(pp, sk'_{\text{s}}, S', pk_{\text{J}}, m')$
If $\text{Verify}(pp, pk^*_{\text{s}}, sk^*_{\text{r}}, pk_{\text{J}}, m^*, \sigma^*) = 1$:	
$\quad$ If $pk^*_{\text{s}}, pk^*_{\text{r}} \notin U_{\text{cor}}$:	$\mathcal{O}^{\text{Verify}}(pk'_{\text{s}}, pk'_{\text{r}}, m', \sigma')$:
$\quad\quad$ If $\nexists(pk^*_{\text{s}}, S', m^*) \in Q_{\text{sig}}$ s.t. $pk^*_{\text{r}} \in S'$:	Return $\text{Verify}(pp, pk'_{\text{s}}, sk'_{\text{r}}, pk_{\text{J}}, m', \sigma')$
$\quad\quad\quad$ Return 1	
If $\text{Judge}(pp, pk^*_{\text{s}}, sk_{\text{J}}, m^*, \sigma^*) = 1$:	$\mathcal{O}^{\text{Judge}}(pk'_{\text{s}}, m', \sigma')$:
$\quad$ If $(pk^*_{\text{s}} \notin U_{\text{cor}}) \wedge (\nexists(pk^*_{\text{s}}, S', m^*) \in Q_{\text{sig}})$:	Return $\text{Judge}(pp, pk'_{\text{s}}, sk_{\text{J}}, m', \sigma')$
$\quad\quad$ Return 1	
Return 0	

$G^{\text{s-bind}}_{\text{AGMF},\mathcal{A},n}(\lambda)$:	$\mathcal{O}^{\text{Cor}}(pk')$:
$pp \leftarrow \text{Setup}(\lambda); (pk_{\text{J}}, sk_{\text{J}}) \leftarrow \text{KG}_{\text{J}}(pp)$	$U_{\text{cor}} \leftarrow U_{\text{cor}} \cup \{pk'\}$
$U := \emptyset; U_{\text{key}} := \emptyset; U_{\text{cor}} := \emptyset$	Return sk' s.t. $(pk', sk') \in U_{\text{key}}$
For $i = 1 \ldots n$:	
$\quad (pk_i, sk_i) \leftarrow \text{KG}_{\text{u}}(pp); U \leftarrow U \cup \{pk_i\}$	$\mathcal{O}^{\text{Frank}}(pk'_{\text{s}}, S', m')$:
$\quad U_{\text{key}} \leftarrow U_{\text{key}} \cup \{(pk_i, sk_i)\}$	Return $\text{Frank}(pp, sk'_{\text{s}}, S', pk_{\text{J}}, m')$
$(pk^*_{\text{s}}, pk^*_{\text{r}}, m^*, \sigma^*) \leftarrow \mathcal{A}^{\mathcal{O}}(pp, U, pk_{\text{J}})$	
If $pk^*_{\text{r}} \in U_{\text{cor}}$: Return 0	$\mathcal{O}^{\text{Verify}}(pk'_{\text{s}}, pk'_{\text{r}}, m', \sigma')$:
$b_1 \leftarrow \text{Verify}(pp, pk^*_{\text{s}}, sk^*_{\text{r}}, pk_{\text{J}}, m^*, \sigma^*)$	Return $\text{Verify}(pp, pk'_{\text{s}}, sk'_{\text{r}}, pk_{\text{J}}, m', \sigma')$
$b_2 \leftarrow \text{Judge}(pp, pk^*_{\text{s}}, sk_{\text{J}}, m^*, \sigma^*)$	
Return $b_1 \wedge \neg b_2$	$\mathcal{O}^{\text{Judge}}(pk'_{\text{s}}, m', \sigma')$:
	Return $\text{Judge}(pp, pk'_{\text{s}}, sk_{\text{J}}, m', \sigma')$

Fig. 2. Games for defining receiver-binding and sender-binding of AGMF

Now, we present the formal definitions as below.

Definition 3 (r-BIND). *An AGMF scheme* AGMF *is receiver-binding, if for any PPT adversary $\mathcal{A}$, its advantage*

$$\mathbf{Adv}^{\text{r-bind}}_{\text{AGMF},\mathcal{A},n}(\lambda) := \Pr[\mathbf{G}^{\text{r-bind}}_{\text{AGMF},\mathcal{A},n}(\lambda) = 1]$$

is negligible, where $\mathbf{G}^{\text{r-bind}}_{\text{AGMF},\mathcal{A},n}(\lambda)$ *is defined in Fig. 2.*

Definition 4 (s-BIND). *An AGMF scheme* AGMF *is* sender-binding, *if for any PPT adversary* $\mathcal{A}$*, its advantage*

$$\mathbf{Adv}^{\text{s-bind}}_{\text{AGMF},\mathcal{A},n}(\lambda) := \Pr[\mathbf{G}^{\text{s-bind}}_{\text{AGMF},\mathcal{A},n}(\lambda) = 1]$$

is negligible, where $\mathbf{G}^{\text{s-bind}}_{\text{AGMF},\mathcal{A},n}(\lambda)$ *is defined in Fig. 2.*

Remark 1. The receiver binding game $\mathbf{G}^{\text{r-bind}}_{\text{AGMF},\mathcal{A},n}(\lambda)$ is much more complicated than that in AMF [36], essentially because in the setting of group scenarios, there are multiple receivers. For example, compared with the receiver binding game in AMF, here we additionally need to consider the probability that $\mathcal{A}$ tricks the other honest receivers in the same receiver set. We want to stress that this security model implies unforgeability.

Remark 2. In $\mathbf{G}^{\text{r-bind}}_{\text{AGMF},\mathcal{A},n}(\lambda)$, if $\mathcal{A}$ outputs $(pk^*_s, pk^*_r, \sigma^*, m^*)$ such that $\text{Verify}(pp, pk^*_s, sk^*_r, pk_J, m^*, \sigma^*) = 1$, then $\mathcal{A}$ wins only if

$$(pk^*_s \notin U_{\text{cor}}) \wedge (pk^*_r \notin U_{\text{cor}}) \wedge (\nexists\ (pk^*_s, S', m^*) \in Q_{\text{sig}}\ \text{s.t.}\ pk^*_r \in S').$$

That's because (i) if $pk^*_s \in U_{\text{cor}}$ or there is some $(pk^*_s, S', m^*) \in Q_{\text{sig}}$ such that $pk^*_r \in S'$, $\mathcal{A}$ can trivially win; (ii) if $pk^*_r \in U_{\text{cor}}$, $\mathcal{A}$ still can generate such a tuple to win this game by running algorithm RForge.

Remark 3. Compared with the security models of receiver-binding and sender-binding in AMF [36], here we provide the adversary $\mathcal{A}$ with more abilities. For example, in $\mathbf{G}^{\text{r-bind}}_{\text{AGMF},\mathcal{A},n}(\lambda)$ and $\mathbf{G}^{\text{r-bind}}_{\text{AGMF},\mathcal{A},n}(\lambda)$, $\mathcal{A}$ is allowed to query $\mathcal{O}^{\text{Frank}}$ on (pk'_s, S', m') and query $\mathcal{O}^{\text{Verify}}$ on $(pk'_s, pk'_r, m', \sigma')$, where pk'_s can be any users' public keys (including pk^*_s and pk^*_r), and so can pk'_r. The ability is not provided in the receiver/sender binding game of AMF in [36].

Deniability. To support deniability, we need to consider *universal deniability*, *receiver compromise deniability*, and *judge compromise deniability* for AGMF. Generally speaking, universal deniability requires that any non-participating party (i.e., no access to the secret key of the sender, the secret key of any user in the receiver set, or the secret key of the judge) can create a signature, such that for other non-participating parties, it is indistinguishable from honestly-generated signatures. Receiver compromise deniability requires that any corrupted users in the receiver set are able to create a signature, such that for other parties with access to these corrupted users' secret keys, it is indistinguishable from honestly-generated signatures. Judge compromise deniability requires that a party with the judge's secret key is able to create a signature, such that for other parties with access to the judge's secret key, it is indistinguishable from honestly-generated signatures.

The formal definitions are presented as follows.

Definition 5 (UnivDen). *An AGMF scheme* AGMF *is* universally deniable, *if for any PPT adversary* $\mathcal{A}$*, its advantage*

$$\mathbf{Adv}^{\text{UnivDen}}_{\text{AGMF},\mathcal{A},n}(\lambda) := |\Pr[\mathbf{G}^{\text{UnivDen}}_{\text{AGMF},\mathcal{A},n}(\lambda) = 1] - \frac{1}{2}|$$

is negligible, where $\mathbf{G}^{\text{UnivDen}}_{\text{AGMF},\mathcal{A},n}(\lambda)$ *is defined in Fig. 3.*

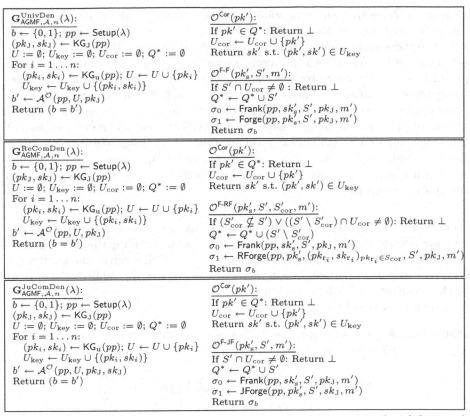

Fig. 3. Games for defining universal deniability, receiver compromise deniability, and judge compromise deniability of AGMF

Definition 6 (ReComDen). *An AGMF scheme* AGMF *is* receiver-compromise deniable, *if for any PPT adversary* $\mathcal{A}$, *its advantage*

$$\mathbf{Adv}_{\mathsf{AGMF},\mathcal{A},n}^{\mathrm{ReComDen}}(\lambda) := \mid \Pr[\mathbf{G}_{\mathsf{AGMF},\mathcal{A},n}^{\mathrm{ReComDen}}(\lambda) = 1] - \frac{1}{2} \mid$$

is negligible, where $\mathbf{G}_{\mathsf{AGMF},\mathcal{A},n}^{\mathrm{ReComDen}}(\lambda)$ *is defined in Fig. 3.*

Definition 7 (JuComDen). *An AGMF scheme* AGMF *is* judge-compromise deniable, *if for any PPT adversary* $\mathcal{A}$, *its advantage*

$$\mathbf{Adv}_{\mathsf{AGMF},\mathcal{A},n}^{\mathrm{JuComDen}}(\lambda) := \mid \Pr[\mathbf{G}_{\mathsf{AGMF},\mathcal{A},n}^{\mathrm{JuComDen}}(\lambda) = 1] - \frac{1}{2} \mid$$

is negligible, where $\mathbf{G}_{\mathsf{AGMF},\mathcal{A},n}^{\mathrm{JuComDen}}(\lambda)$ *is defined in Fig. 3.*

Remark 4. In universal deniability game (resp., judge compromise deniability game), for $\mathcal{A}$'s each $\mathcal{O}^{\mathsf{F\text{-}F}}$-oracle (resp., $\mathcal{O}^{\mathsf{F\text{-}JF}}$-oracle) query (pk_s', S', m'), $\mathcal{A}$ is not allowed to see the secret keys of the receivers in S'. In receiver compromise deniability game, for $\mathcal{A}$'s each $\mathcal{O}^{\mathsf{F\text{-}RF}}$-oracle query $(pk_s', S', S_{\mathrm{cor}}', m')$, $\mathcal{A}$ is not allowed to see the secret keys of the receivers in $S' \backslash S_{\mathrm{cor}}'$. We use Q^* to specify the receivers whose secret keys are not provided to $\mathcal{A}$.

Remark 5. Note that in these games, the adversary *is* allowed to access the sender's secret key, as long as the sender is not in the receiver set. Compared with the judge compromise deniability formally defined in AMF [36], where the adversary $\mathcal{A}$ is offered both the receiver's and the judge's keys, our judge compromise deniability only provides the judge's key to $\mathcal{A}$. We stress that the judge compromise deniability formally defined in [36] conflicts with strong authentication (i.e., as pointed out in [36], "forgeries by the moderator cannot be detected by the receiver"). Our judge compromise deniability follows one of the ideas of the judge compromise deniability formalization when considering strong authentication, which is also introduced in [36, Appendix B]. Some more discussions on definitions of deniability will be given in the full version of this paper, due to the space limitations.

Receiver Anonymity. Generally speaking, receiver anonymity requires that any one (except for the receivers in the receiver set), including the judge, cannot tell which receiver set a signature is generated for. With receiver anonymity, the receivers in group communication scenarios can report the malicious messages to the moderator with less concerns.

The formal definition is presented as follows.

Definition 8 (RecAnony). *An AGMF scheme* AGMF *is receiver anonymous, if for any PPT adversary $\mathcal{A}$, its advantage*

$$\mathbf{Adv}_{\mathsf{AGMF},\mathcal{A},n}^{\mathrm{RecAnony}}(\lambda) := |\Pr[\mathbf{G}_{\mathsf{AGMF},\mathcal{A},n}^{\mathrm{RecAnony}}(\lambda) = 1] - \frac{1}{2}|$$

is negligible, where $\mathbf{G}_{\mathsf{AGMF},\mathcal{A},n}^{\mathrm{RecAnony}}(\lambda)$ *is defined in Fig. 4.*

$\mathbf{G}_{\mathsf{AGMF},\mathcal{A},n}^{\mathrm{RecAnony}}(\lambda)$:

$b \leftarrow \{0,1\}$; $pp \leftarrow \mathsf{Setup}(\lambda)$; $(pk_\mathsf{J}, sk_\mathsf{J}) \leftarrow \mathsf{KG}_\mathsf{J}(pp)$
$U := \emptyset$; $U_{\mathrm{key}} := \emptyset$; $U_{\mathrm{cor}} := \emptyset$
$Q_{\mathrm{tpl}}^* := \emptyset$; $Q^* := \emptyset$
For $i = 1 \ldots n$:
  $(pk_i, sk_i) \leftarrow \mathsf{KG}_\mathsf{u}(pp)$; $U \leftarrow U \cup \{pk_i\}$
  $U_{\mathrm{key}} \leftarrow U_{\mathrm{key}} \cup \{(pk_i, sk_i)\}$
$(pk_\mathsf{s}^*, S_0, S_1, m^*, st) \leftarrow \mathcal{A}_1^{\mathcal{O}}(pp, U, pk_\mathsf{J}, sk_\mathsf{J})$
If $|S_0| \neq |S_1|$: Return 0
If $((S_0 \cup S_1) \cap U_{\mathrm{cor}}) \neq \emptyset$: Return 0
$Q^* \leftarrow Q^* \cup (S_0 \cup S_1)$
$\sigma^* \leftarrow \mathsf{Frank}(pp, sk_\mathsf{s}^*, S_b, pk_\mathsf{J}, m^*)$
$Q_{\mathrm{tpl}}^* \leftarrow Q_{\mathrm{tpl}}^* \cup \{(pk_\mathsf{s}^*, pk_\mathsf{r}, m^*, \sigma^*) \mid pk_\mathsf{r} \in S_0 \cup S_1\}$
$b' \leftarrow \mathcal{A}_2^{\mathcal{O}}(\sigma^*, st)$
Return $(b = b')$

$\mathcal{O}^{\mathsf{Cor}}(pk')$:

If $pk' \in Q^*$: Return $\perp$
$U_{\mathrm{cor}} \leftarrow U_{\mathrm{cor}} \cup \{pk'\}$
Return sk' s.t. $(pk', sk') \in U_{\mathrm{key}}$

$\mathcal{O}^{\mathsf{Frank}}(pk_\mathsf{s}', S', m')$:

Return $\mathsf{Frank}(pp, sk_\mathsf{s}', S', pk_\mathsf{J}, m')$

$\mathcal{O}^{\mathsf{Verify}}(pk_\mathsf{s}', pk_\mathsf{r}', m', \sigma')$:

If $pk_\mathsf{s}' \in U_{\mathrm{cor}}$: Return $\perp$
If $(pk_\mathsf{s}', pk_\mathsf{r}', m', \sigma') \in Q_{\mathrm{tpl}}^*$: Return $\perp$
Return $\mathsf{Verify}(pp, pk_\mathsf{s}', sk_\mathsf{r}', pk_\mathsf{J}, m', \sigma')$

Fig. 4. Game for defining receiver anonymity of AGMF

Discussion. In the following sections, we will present an AGMF scheme achieving the above security features. In fact, our scheme can be proved secure under stronger security models. For example, the receiver anonymity game

$G_{\mathsf{AGMF},\mathcal{A},n}^{\mathrm{RecAnony}}(\lambda)$ in Fig. 4 can be strengthened by allowing the adversary to know the secret keys of the users belonging to $S_0 \cap S_1$. Our scheme also achieves the strengthened receiver anonymity. It is an interesting direction to further strengthen these security models.

4 HPS-Based KEM Supporting Sigma Protocols

In this section, we introduce a new primitive, which we will take as a building block to construct AGMF in Sect. 5. This primitive is a variant of key encapsulation mechanism (KEM) satisfying that (i) it can be interpreted from the perspective of hash proof system (HPS) [17], and (ii) for some special relations (about the public/secret keys, the encapsulated keys and ciphertexts), there exist corresponding Sigma protocols. We call this primitive *HPS-based KEM supporting Sigma protocols (HPS-KEM$^{\Sigma}$)*. We also provide a concrete construction based on the DDH assumption. Note that our construction can be easily extended to be built based on the k-Linear assumption [27, 34].

4.1 Definition

A HPS-KEM$^{\Sigma}$ scheme HPS-KEM$^{\Sigma}$ = (KEMSetup, KG, CheckKey, encap$_{\mathrm{c}}$, encap$_{\mathrm{k}}$, encap$_{\mathrm{c}}^{*}$, decap, CheckCwel) is a tuple of algorithms associated with a secret key space $\mathcal{SK}$, an encapsulated key space $\mathcal{K}$, where encap$_{\mathrm{c}}$ and encap$_{\mathrm{k}}$ have the same randomness space $\mathcal{RS}$, and we denote by $\mathcal{RS}^{*}$ the randomness space of encap$_{\mathrm{c}}^{*}$.

- $pp \leftarrow$ KEMSetup(1^{λ}): On input a security parameter λ, it outputs a public parameter pp.
- $(pk, sk) \leftarrow$ KG(pp): On input the public parameter pp, it outputs a pair of public/secret keys (pk, sk).
- $b \leftarrow$ CheckKey(pp, sk, pk): On input the public parameter pp, a secret key sk and a public key pk, it outputs a bit b. Let $\mathcal{SK}_{pp,pk} := \{sk \in \mathcal{SK} \mid$ CheckKey(pp, sk, pk) $= 1\}$.
- $c \leftarrow$ encap$_{\mathrm{c}}$($pp; r$): On input the public parameter pp with inner randomness $r \in \mathcal{RS}$, it outputs a well-formed ciphertext c. Let $\mathcal{C}_{pp}^{\mathrm{well\text{-}f}} := \{c = $ encap$_{\mathrm{c}}$($pp; r$) $\mid r \in \mathcal{RS}\}$.
- $k \leftarrow$ encap$_{\mathrm{k}}$($pp, pk; r$): On input the public parameter pp and a public key pk with inner randomness $r \in \mathcal{RS}$, it outputs an encapsulated key $k \in \mathcal{K}$.
- $c \leftarrow$ encap$_{\mathrm{c}}^{*}$($pp; r^{*}$): On input the public parameter pp with inner randomness $r^{*} \in \mathcal{RS}^{*}$, it outputs a ciphertext c. Let $\mathcal{C}_{pp}^{*} := \{$encap$_{\mathrm{c}}^{*}$($pp; r^{*}$) $\mid r^{*} \in \mathcal{RS}^{*}\}$. We require that $\mathcal{C}_{pp}^{\mathrm{well\text{-}f}} \subset \mathcal{C}_{pp}^{*}$.
- $k' \leftarrow$ decap(pp, sk, c): On input the public parameter pp, the ciphertext c and a secret key sk, it outputs an encapsulated key $k' \in \mathcal{K}$.
- $b \leftarrow$ CheckCwel(pp, c, r^{*}): On input the public parameter pp, a ciphertext c and a random number $r^{*} \in \mathcal{RS}^{*}$, it outputs a bit b.

To generate a well-formed ciphertext and its corresponding encapsulated key, one can invoke $\mathsf{encap_c}$ and $\mathsf{encap_k}$ at the same time with the same randomness r. For simplicity, we introduce another algorithm encap, and use "$(c, k) \leftarrow \mathsf{encap}(pp, pk; r)$" to denote the procedures "$c \leftarrow \mathsf{encap_c}(pp; r), k \leftarrow \mathsf{encap_k}(pp, pk; r)$". Note that only k contains the information about the public key pk. Correctness is as follows.

(1) For any pp generated by $\mathsf{KEMSetup}(1^\lambda)$, and any (pk, sk) output by $\mathsf{KG}(pp)$, $\mathsf{CheckKey}(pp, sk, pk) = 1$.
(2) For any pp generated by $\mathsf{KEMSetup}(1^\lambda)$, any (pk, sk) satisfying $\mathsf{CheckKey}(pp, sk, pk) = 1$, and any $(c, k) \leftarrow \mathsf{encap}(pp, pk)$, it holds that $\mathsf{decap}(pp, sk, c) = k$.
(3) For any pp generated by $\mathsf{KEMSetup}(1^\lambda)$, and any c generated with $\mathsf{encap_c^*}(pp; r^*)$, $\mathsf{CheckCwel}(pp, c, r^*) = 1$ if and only if $c \in \mathcal{C}_{pp}^{\text{well-f}}$.

For any pp generated by $\mathsf{KEMSetup}(1^\lambda)$, we define some relations as follows:

$$\mathcal{R}_s = \{(sk, pk) : \mathsf{CheckKey}(pp, sk, pk) = 1\}$$
$$\mathcal{R}_{c,k} = \{(r, (c, k, pk)) : (c, k) = \mathsf{encap}(pp, pk; r)\} \quad (2)$$
$$\mathcal{R}_c^* = \{(r^*, c) : c = \mathsf{encap_c^*}(pp; r^*)\}$$

We require that for each relation in Eq. (2), there is a Sigma protocol.

We also require the properties: *universality, unexplainability, indistinguishability, SK-2PR* and *smoothness*, the definitions of which are as follows.

Definition 9 (Universality). *We say that a HPS-KEM$^\Sigma$ scheme HPS-KEM$^\Sigma$ is universal, if for any computationally unbounded adversary $\mathcal{A}$, the advantage*

$$\mathbf{Adv}_{\mathsf{HPS\text{-}KEM}^\Sigma, \mathcal{A}}^{\text{univ}}(\lambda) := \Pr[\mathbf{G}_{\mathsf{HPS\text{-}KEM}^\Sigma, \mathcal{A}}^{\text{univ}}(\lambda) = 1]$$

is negligible, where $\mathbf{G}_{\mathsf{HPS\text{-}KEM}^\Sigma, \mathcal{A}}^{\text{univ}}(\lambda)$ is defined in Fig. 5.

$\mathbf{G}_{\mathsf{HPS\text{-}KEM}^\Sigma, \mathcal{A}}^{\text{univ}}(\lambda)$:

$pp \leftarrow \mathsf{KEMSetup}(1^\lambda), (pk, sk) \leftarrow \mathsf{KG}(pp)$
$(c, k, w) \leftarrow \mathcal{A}(pp, pk)$ s.t. $((w, c) \in \mathcal{R}_c^*) \wedge (c \notin \mathcal{C}_{pp}^{\text{well-f}})$
If $k = \mathsf{decap}(pp, sk, c)$: Return 1
Else Return 0

Fig. 5. Game for defining universality of HPS-KEM$^\Sigma$

Definition 10 (Unexplainability). *We say that a HPS-KEM$^\Sigma$ scheme HPS-KEM$^\Sigma$ is unexplainable, if for any PPT adversary $\mathcal{A}$, the advantage*

$$\mathbf{Adv}_{\mathsf{HPS\text{-}KEM}^\Sigma, \mathcal{A}}^{\text{unexpl}}(\lambda) := \Pr[\mathbf{G}_{\mathsf{HPS\text{-}KEM}^\Sigma, \mathcal{A}}^{\text{unexpl}}(\lambda) = 1]$$

is negligible, where $\mathbf{G}_{\mathsf{HPS\text{-}KEM}^\Sigma, \mathcal{A}}^{\text{unexpl}}(\lambda)$ is defined in Fig. 6.

$$\mathbf{G}^{\mathrm{unexpl}}_{\mathsf{HPS\text{-}KEM}^{\Sigma},\mathcal{A}}(\lambda):$$

$pp \leftarrow \mathsf{KEMSetup}(1^{\lambda}); \quad (c, w) \leftarrow \mathcal{A}(pp) \text{ s.t. } (w, c) \in \mathcal{R}^*_c$

If $c \in \mathcal{C}^{\mathrm{well\text{-}f}}_{pp}$: Return 1

Else Return 0

Fig. 6. Game for defining unexplainability of HPS-KEM$^{\Sigma}$

Remark 6. Generally, unexplainability requires that for any PPT adversary, it is difficult to explain a well-formed ciphertext as a result generated with encap^*_c.

Definition 11 (Indistinguishability). *We say that a HPS-KEM$^{\Sigma}$ scheme* HPS-KEM$^{\Sigma}$ *is indistinguishable, if for any PPT adversary* $\mathcal{A}$*, the advantage*

$$\mathbf{Adv}^{\mathrm{ind}}_{\mathsf{HPS\text{-}KEM}^{\Sigma},\mathcal{A}}(\lambda) := |\Pr[\mathbf{G}^{\mathrm{ind}}_{\mathsf{HPS\text{-}KEM}^{\Sigma},\mathcal{A}}(\lambda) = 1] - \frac{1}{2}|$$

is negligible, where $\mathbf{G}^{\mathrm{ind}}_{\mathsf{HPS\text{-}KEM}^{\Sigma},\mathcal{A}}(\lambda)$ *is defined in Fig. 7.*

Definition 12 (SK-2PR). *We say that a* (HPS-KEM$^{\Sigma}$) *scheme* HPS-KEM$^{\Sigma}$ *is SK-second-preimage resistant, if for any PPT adversary* $\mathcal{A}$*, the advantage*

$$\mathbf{Adv}^{\mathrm{sk\text{-}2pr}}_{\mathsf{HPS\text{-}KEM}^{\Sigma},\mathcal{A}}(\lambda) := \Pr[\mathbf{G}^{\mathrm{sk\text{-}2pr}}_{\mathsf{HPS\text{-}KEM}^{\Sigma},\mathcal{A}}(\lambda) = 1]$$

is negligible, where $\mathbf{G}^{\mathrm{sk\text{-}2pr}}_{\mathsf{HPS\text{-}KEM}^{\Sigma},\mathcal{A}}(\lambda)$ *is defined in Fig. 7.*

$\mathbf{G}^{\mathrm{ind}}_{\mathsf{HPS\text{-}KEM}^{\Sigma},\mathcal{A}}(\lambda):$	$\mathbf{G}^{\mathrm{sk\text{-}2pr}}_{\mathsf{HPS\text{-}KEM}^{\Sigma},\mathcal{A}}(\lambda):$
$pp \leftarrow \mathsf{KEMSetup}(1^{\lambda})$	$pp \leftarrow \mathsf{KEMSetup}(1^{\lambda})$
$b \leftarrow \{0, 1\}$	$(pk, sk) \leftarrow \mathsf{KG}(pp)$
$c_0 \leftarrow \mathsf{encap}_c(pp)$	$sk' \leftarrow \mathcal{A}(pp, pk, sk)$
$c_1 \leftarrow \mathsf{encap}^*_c(pp)$	If $(sk' \neq sk) \wedge (\mathsf{CheckKey}(pp, sk', pk) = 1):$
$b' \leftarrow \mathcal{A}(pp, c_b)$	Return 1
Return $(b' \stackrel{?}{=} b)$	Return 0

Fig. 7. Games for defining indistinguishability and SK-second-preimage resistance of HPS-KEM$^{\Sigma}$

Definition 13 (Smoothness). *We say that a HPS-KEM$^{\Sigma}$ scheme* HPS-KEM$^{\Sigma}$ *is smooth, if for any fixed pp generated by* KEMSetup *and any fixed pk generated by* KG,

$$\Delta((c, k), (c, k')) \leq \mathsf{negl}(\lambda),$$

where $c \leftarrow \mathsf{encap}^*_c(pp)$*,* $k \leftarrow \mathcal{K}$*,* $sk \leftarrow \mathcal{SK}_{pp,pk}$ *and* $k' = \mathsf{decap}(pp, sk, c)$*.*

Remark 7. Smoothness guarantees that $\frac{1}{|\mathcal{SK}_{pp,pk}|}$ is a negligible function of λ.

4.2   Construction

Here, we present a concrete construction of HPS-KEM$^{\Sigma}$, which satisfies all the aforementioned security properties. The algorithms are described as follows.

- KEMSetup(1^{λ}): Given a security parameter λ, choose a prime-order group $\mathbb{G}$ such that the order of $\mathbb{G}$ is p and the bit-length of p is λ. Then, choose the generators g_1, g_2 of $\mathbb{G}$ uniformly at random. The public parameter is

$$pp = (\mathbb{G}, p, g_1, g_2).$$

- KG(pp): Given the public parameter $pp = (\mathbb{G}, p, g_1, g_2)$, choose two randomnesses $(x_1, x_2) \in \mathbb{Z}_p^{*2}$, set $h = g_1^{x_1} g_2^{x_2}$ and the pair of public/secret keys is set as

$$(pk = h, \ sk = (x_1, x_2)).$$

- CheckKey(pp, sk, pk): Given the public parameter $pp = (\mathbb{G}, p, g_1, g_2)$ and a pair of public/secret keys $(pk = h, \ sk = (x_1, x_2))$, check whether $g_1^{x_1} g_2^{x_2} = h$ holds. If not, output 0; otherwise output 1.
- encap$_c$($pp; r$): Given the public parameter $pp = (\mathbb{G}, p, g_1, g_2)$ and a randomness $r \in \mathbb{Z}_p^*$, output a well-formed encapsulated ciphertext

$$c = (u_1 = g_1^r, \ u_2 = g_2^r).$$

- encap$_k$($pp, pk; r$): Given the public parameter $pp = (\mathbb{G}, p, g_1, g_2)$, a public key $pk = h$ and a randomness $r \in \mathbb{Z}_p^*$, output an encapsulated key $k = h^r$.
- encap$_c^*$($pp; r^*$): Given the public parameter $pp = (\mathbb{G}, p, g_1, g_2)$ and randomness $r^* = (r, r') \in \mathbb{Z}_p^{*2}$, output a ciphertext

$$c = (u_1 = g_1^r, \ u_2 = g_1^{r'}).$$

- decap(pp, sk, c): Given the public parameter $pp = (\mathbb{G}, p, g_1, g_2)$, an encapsulated ciphertext $c = (u_1, u_2)$ and a secret key $sk = (x_1, x_2)$, output an encapsulated key $k' = u_1^{x_1} u_2^{x_2}$.
- CheckCwel(pp, c, r^*): Given the public parameter $pp = (\mathbb{G}, p, g_1, g_2)$, a ciphertext $c = (u_1, u_2)$ and a random number $r^* = (r, r') \in \mathbb{Z}_p^{*2}$, it outputs 1 if $g_2^r = u_2$; otherwise, it outputs 0.

It is clear that the above construction satisfies *correctness*. Then the relations $\mathcal{R}_s$, $\mathcal{R}_{c,k}$ and $\mathcal{R}_c^*$ are constructed as follows.

$$\mathcal{R}_s = \{((x_1, x_2), pk) : pk = g_1^{x_1} g_2^{x_2}\}$$
$$\mathcal{R}_{c,k} = \{(r, ((u_1, u_2), k, pk)) : u_1 = g_1^r \wedge u_2 = g_2^r \wedge k = pk^r\} \tag{3}$$
$$\mathcal{R}_c^* = \{((r, r'), (u_1, u_2)) : u_1 = g_1^r \wedge u_2 = g_1^{r'}\}$$

We show that there are Sigma protocols for relations $\mathcal{R}_s$, $\mathcal{R}_{c,k}$ and $\mathcal{R}_c^*$: Okamoto's Sigma protocol [31] for $\mathcal{R}_s$, the Chaum-Pedersen protocol [11] for $\mathcal{R}_{c,k}$ and Schnorr's Sigma protocol [33] for $\mathcal{R}_c^*$.

We now prove that the above construction satisfies *universality, unexplainability, indistinguishability, SK-second-preimage resistance*, and *smoothness*. Formally, we have the following theorems.

Theorem 2. *The above HPS-KEM$^\Sigma$ scheme is* universal.

Theorem 3. *If the* DL *assumption holds in* $\mathbb{G}$, *the above HPS-KEM$^\Sigma$ scheme is* unexplainable.

Theorem 4. *If the* DDH *assumption holds in* $\mathbb{G}$, *the above HPS-KEM$^\Sigma$ scheme is* indistinguishable.

Theorem 5. *If the* DL *assumption holds in* $\mathbb{G}$, *the above HPS-KEM$^\Sigma$ scheme is* SK-second-preimage resistant.

Theorem 6. *The above HPS-KEM$^\Sigma$ scheme is* smooth.

The proofs of Theorem 2–6 are as follows.

Proof (of Theorem 2). For any computationally unbounded adversary $\mathcal{A}$ attacking universality of HPS-KEM$^\Sigma$, let $(pp = (\mathbb{G}, p, g_1, g_2), pk = g_1^{x_1} g_2^{x_2})$ be $\mathcal{A}$'s input, where $(pk, sk = (x_1, x_2))$ are generated by $\mathsf{KG}(pp)$. Denote by $a := \log_{g_1} g_2$. Let $(c = (u_1, u_2), k, w = (r, r'))$ be $\mathcal{A}$'s final output satisfying $((w, c) \in \mathcal{R}_c^*) \wedge (c \notin \mathcal{C}_{pp}^{\text{well-f}})$.

Note that $(w, c) \in \mathcal{R}_c^*$ implies that $u_1 = g_1^r$ and $u_2 = g_1^{r'}$. On the other hand, since $\mathcal{C}_{pp}^{\text{well-f}} = \{(g_1^{\tilde{r}}, g_2^{\tilde{r}}) \mid \tilde{r} \in \mathbb{Z}_p^*\} = \{(g_1^{\tilde{r}}, g_1^{a\tilde{r}}) \mid \tilde{r} \in \mathbb{Z}_p^*\}$, we derive that $r' \neq ar$.
As a result,

$$\mathsf{decap}(pp, sk, c) = u_1^{x_1} u_2^{x_2} = g_1^{r x_1} g_1^{r' x_2} = g_1^{r(x_1 + a x_2) + r' x_2 - r a x_2}$$
$$= (g_1^{x_1} g_2^{x_2})^r \cdot g_1^{(r' - ra) x_2} = pk^r \cdot g_1^{(r' - ra) x_2}.$$

Notice that $sk = (x_1, x_2)$ is uniformly sampled from $\mathbb{Z}_p^{*2}$, and the only information that $\mathcal{A}$ has about sk is $\log_{g_1} pk = x_1 + a x_2$. Thus, from $\mathcal{A}$'s point of view, given (pp, pk), x_2 is still uniformly distributed, which implies that $\mathsf{decap}(pp, sk, c) = pk^r \cdot g_1^{(r' - ra) x_2}$ is also uniformly distributed.

Hence, $\mathbf{Adv}_{\text{HPS-KEM}^\Sigma, \mathcal{A}}^{\text{univ}}(\lambda) = \Pr[k = \mathsf{decap}(pp, sk, c)]$ is negligible, concluding the proof of this theorem. $\square$

Proof (of Theorem 3). Suppose that there exists a PPT adversary $\mathcal{A}$ winning the game of unexplainability with non-negligible probability. It is easy to construct a PPT algorithm $\mathcal{B}$ that makes use of $\mathcal{A}$ to solve the DL problem with non-negligible probability. Algorithm $\mathcal{B}$ is given a random tuple $(\mathbb{G}, p, g, g^a)$, and runs $\mathcal{A}$ as follows.

$\mathcal{B}$ first sets $g_1 = g$ and $g_2 = g^a$, and sends the public parameter $pp = (\mathbb{G}, p, g_1, g_2)$ to $\mathcal{A}$. Then, the adversary $\mathcal{A}$ outputs $(w, c) \in \mathcal{R}_c^*$. Parse $c = (u_1, u_2)$ and $w = (r, r')$. Note that $(w, c) \in \mathcal{R}_c^*$ guarantees that $u_1 = g_1^r$ and $u_2 = g_1^{r'}$. If $\mathcal{A}$ wins the game of unexplainability, then $c \in \mathcal{C}_{pp}^{\text{well-f}}$, which means that $u_1 = g_1^r$ and $u_2 = g_2^r$. In this case, we have $u_2 = g_2^r = g_1^{r'}$. Therefore, $\mathcal{B}$ can output $a = \frac{r'}{r}$ as the solution of the DL problem. $\square$

Proof (of Theorem 4). Suppose that there exists a PPT adversary $\mathcal{A}$ winning the game of indistinguishability with non-negligible probability. It is easy to construct a PPT algorithm $\mathcal{B}$ that makes use of $\mathcal{A}$ to solve the DDH problem with non-negligible probability. Algorithm $\mathcal{B}$ is given a random tuple $(\mathbb{G}, p, g, g^a, g^b, Z)$, where $Z = g^{ab}$ or Z is uniformly and independently sampled in $\mathbb{G}$. $\mathcal{B}$ runs $\mathcal{A}$ as follows.

$\mathcal{B}$ first sets $g_1 = g$, $g_2 = g^a$, $u_1 = g^b$, $u_2 = Z$. Then, it sends the public parameter $pp = (\mathbb{G}, p, g_1, g_2)$ and the encapsulated ciphertext $c = (u_1, u_2)$ to the adversary $\mathcal{A}$. Finally, $\mathcal{A}$ outputs a bit and $\mathcal{B}$ also outputs the bit.

Observe that, if $Z = g^{ab}$, then $u_1 = g_1^b, u_2 = g_2^b$, and from the perspective of the adversary the distribution of the ciphertext $c = (u_1, u_2)$ is identical to the distribution of the well-formed encapsulated ciphertext generated by $\mathsf{encap_c}$. If Z is a random element in $\mathbb{G}$, then u_1, u_2 are random elements in $\mathbb{G}$, and from the perspective of the adversary the distribution of the ciphertext $c = (u_1, u_2)$ is identical to the distribution of the ciphertext generated by $\mathsf{encap_c^*}$. Therefore, if $\mathcal{A}$ can win the game of indistinguishability with non-negligible probability, $\mathcal{B}$ can make use of $\mathcal{A}$ to solve the DDH problem with non-negligible probability. $\square$

Proof (of Theorem 5). Suppose that there exists a PPT adversary $\mathcal{A}$ winning the game of SK-second-preimage resistance with non-negligible probability. It is easy to construct a PPT algorithm $\mathcal{B}$ that makes use of $\mathcal{A}$ to solve the DL problem with non-negligible probability. Algorithm $\mathcal{B}$ is given a random tuple $(\mathbb{G}, p, g, g^a)$, and runs $\mathcal{A}$ as follows.

$\mathcal{B}$ first sets $g_1 = g$ and $g_2 = g^a$. Next, it chooses $x_1, x_2 \in \mathbb{Z}_p^*$ uniformly at random, and generates a pair of public/secret keys $(pk = g_1^{x_1} g_2^{x_2}, sk = (x_1, x_2))$. Then, $\mathcal{B}$ sends the public parameter $pp = (\mathbb{G}, p, g_1, g_2)$ and the pair of public/secret keys (pk, sk) to $\mathcal{A}$. The adversary $\mathcal{A}$ outputs a secret key $sk' = (x_1', x_2')$. If $\mathcal{A}$ wins the game of SK-second-preimage resistance, we have $sk' \neq sk$ and $\mathsf{CheckKey}(pp, sk', pk) = 1$. That is to say, $g_1^{x_1'} g_2^{x_2'} = g_1^{x_1} g_2^{x_2}$ and $x_1' \neq x_1, x_2' \neq x_2$. Therefore, $\mathcal{B}$ can output $a = (x_1 - x_1')/(x_2' - x_2)$ as the solution of the DL problem. $\square$

Proof (of Theorem 6). For any fixed $pp = (\mathbb{G}, p, g_1, g_2)$ and any fixed $pk = h$ generated by KG, let $a := \log_{g_1} g_2$, $b := \log_{g_1} h$. Then, $\mathcal{SK}_{pp,pk} = \{(x_1, x_2) \in \mathbb{Z}_p^{*2} \mid x_1 + ax_2 = b\}$.

Note that the ciphertext space of $\mathsf{encap_c^*}$ is $\mathcal{C}^* = (\mathbb{G} \setminus \{1_{\mathbb{G}}\})^2$, where $1_{\mathbb{G}}$ is the identity element of $\mathbb{G}$, and the encapsulated key space $\mathcal{K} = \mathbb{G}$. For all $\hat{c} \in (\mathbb{G} \setminus \{1_{\mathbb{G}}\})^2$, we parse $\hat{c} = (\hat{u}_1, \hat{u}_2)$, and write $S_1 := \{(\hat{u}_1, \hat{u}_2) \in (\mathbb{G} \setminus \{1_{\mathbb{G}}\})^2 \mid \log_{g_1} \hat{u}_2 \neq a \log_{g_1} \hat{u}_1\}$ and $S_2 := \{(\hat{u}_1, \hat{u}_2) \in (\mathbb{G} \setminus \{1_{\mathbb{G}}\})^2 \mid \log_{g_1} \hat{u}_2 = a \log_{g_1} \hat{u}_1\}$.

So,

$$\Delta((c,k),(c,k')) = \frac{1}{2} \sum_{(\hat{c},\hat{k})\in \mathcal{C}^* \times \mathcal{K}} |\Pr[(c,k)=(\hat{c},\hat{k})] - \Pr[(c,k')=(\hat{c},\hat{k})]|$$

$$= \frac{1}{2} \sum_{\hat{c}\in S_1} \sum_{\hat{k}\in \mathcal{K}} |\Pr[(c,k)=(\hat{c},\hat{k})] - \Pr[(c,k')=(\hat{c},\hat{k})]|$$

$$+ \frac{1}{2} \sum_{\hat{c}\in S_2} \sum_{\hat{k}\in \mathcal{K}} |\Pr[(c,k)=(\hat{c},\hat{k})] - \Pr[(c,k')=(\hat{c},\hat{k})]|. \quad (4)$$

We present the following two lemmas with postponed proofs.

Lemma 1. $\sum_{\hat{c}\in S_1} \sum_{\hat{k}\in \mathcal{K}} |\Pr[(c,k)=(\hat{c},\hat{k})] - \Pr[(c,k')=(\hat{c},\hat{k})]| = 0.$

Lemma 2. $\sum_{\hat{c}\in S_2} \sum_{\hat{k}\in \mathcal{K}} |\Pr[(c,k)=(\hat{c},\hat{k})] - \Pr[(c,k')=(\hat{c},\hat{k})]| = \frac{2}{p}.$

Combining Eq. (4), Lemma 1 and Lemma 2, we obtain $\Delta((c,k),(c,k')) = \frac{1}{p}$, concluding the proof of this theorem.

So what remains is to prove the above two lemmas.

Proof (of Lemma 1). For any $\hat{c} = (\hat{u}_1, \hat{u}_2) \in S_1$ and any $\hat{k} \in \mathcal{K} = \mathbb{G}$, we have $\Pr[(c,k)=(\hat{c},\hat{k})] = \frac{1}{(p-1)^2 p}$, and $\Pr[(c,k')=(\hat{c},\hat{k})] = \frac{1}{(p-1)^2} \Pr[k'=\hat{k} \mid c=\hat{c}]$.

Note that $c = (g_1^r, g_1^{r'}) = \hat{c}$ implies $r = \log_{g_1} \hat{u}_1$ and $r' = \log_{g_1} \hat{u}_2$. Since $\hat{c} \in S_1$, we obtain $r' \neq ar$. We also notice that $sk = (x_1, x_2)$ is uniformly sampled from $\mathcal{SK}$, so the distribution of sk can be seen as "uniformly sampling x_2 from $\mathbb{Z}_p^*$, and letting $x_1 = b - ax_2$". As a result, given a fixed $c = \hat{c}$ (i.e., given fixed $r = \log_{g_1} \hat{u}_1$ and $r' = \log_{g_1} \hat{u}_2$), when $sk \leftarrow \mathcal{SK}$, $k' = \mathsf{decap}(pp, sk, c) = g_1^{rx_1} g_1^{r'x_2} = g_1^{r(b-ax_2)+r'x_2} = h^r g_1^{(r'-ar)x_2}$ is uniformly distributed over $\mathcal{K}$. Hence, $\Pr[k'=\hat{k} \mid c=\hat{c}] = \frac{1}{p}$.

So we conclude that for any $\hat{c} \in S_1$ and any $\hat{k} \in \mathcal{K}$, $\Pr[(c,k')=(\hat{c},\hat{k})] = \frac{1}{(p-1)^2 p} = \Pr[(c,k)=(\hat{c},\hat{k})]$. □

Proof (of Lemma 2). For any $\hat{c} = (\hat{u}_1, \hat{u}_2) \in S_2$ and any $\hat{k} \in \mathcal{K} = \mathbb{G}$, we have $\Pr[(c,k)=(\hat{c},\hat{k})] = \frac{1}{(p-1)^2 p}$, and $\Pr[(c,k')=(\hat{c},\hat{k})] = \frac{1}{(p-1)^2} \Pr[k'=\hat{k} \mid c=\hat{c}]$.

Note that $c = (g_1^r, g_1^{r'}) = \hat{c}$ implies $r = \log_{g_1} \hat{u}_1$ and $r' = \log_{g_1} \hat{u}_2$. Since $\hat{c} \in S_2$, we obtain $r' = ar$. Thus, given a fixed $c = \hat{c}$ (i.e., given fixed $r = \log_{g_1} \hat{u}_1$ and $r' = \log_{g_1} \hat{u}_2$), we derive that $k' = \mathsf{decap}(pp, sk, c) = g_1^{rx_1} g_1^{r'x_2} = g_1^{r(b-ax_2)+r'x_2} = h^r g_1^{(r'-ar)x_2} = h^r = h^{\log_{g_1} \hat{u}_1}$, which is also fixed (since $pk = h$ and $\hat{u}_1$ are both fixed values).

Hence,

$$\sum_{\hat{c} \in S_2} \sum_{\hat{k} \in \mathcal{K}} |\Pr[(c,k) = (\hat{c},\hat{k})] - \Pr[(c,k') = (\hat{c},\hat{k})]|$$

$$= \sum_{\hat{c} \in S_2} \sum_{\hat{k} \in \mathcal{K}} |\frac{1}{(p-1)^2 p} - \frac{1}{(p-1)^2} \Pr[k' = \hat{k} \mid c = \hat{c}]|$$

$$= \sum_{\hat{c} \in S_2} (\sum_{\hat{k} \neq h^{\log_{g_1} \hat{u}_1}} |\frac{1}{(p-1)^2 p} - 0| + |\frac{1}{(p-1)^2 p} - \frac{1}{(p-1)^2} \cdot 1|)$$

$$= \sum_{\hat{c} \in S_2} ((p-1)\frac{1}{(p-1)^2 p} + \frac{1}{(p-1)p}) = \sum_{\hat{c} \in S_2} \frac{2}{(p-1)p} = \frac{2}{p}.$$

□

Thus, we complete the proof.   □

5   Generic Construction of AGMF from HPS-KEM$^\Sigma$

In this section, we provide a framework of constructing AGMF from HPS-KEM$^\Sigma$, and show that it achieves the required securities.

Let HPS-KEM$^\Sigma$ = (KEMSetup, KG, CheckKey, encap$_c$, encap$_k$, encap$_c^*$, decap, CheckCwel) be a HPS-KEM$^\Sigma$ scheme supporting universality, unexplainability, indistinguishability, SK-second-preimage resistance and smoothness, where $\mathcal{RS}$ denotes the randomness space of encap$_c$ and encap$_k$, $\mathcal{RS}^*$ denotes the randomness space of encap$_c^*$, and $\mathcal{K}$ denotes the encapsulated key space.

Our generic AGMF scheme AGMF = (Setup, KG$_J$, KG$_u$, Frank, Verify, Judge, Forge, RForge, JForge) is described as follows.

Setup, KG$_J$ and KG$_u$ are shown in Fig. 8, where Setup directly invokes the setup algorithm of HPS-KEM$^\Sigma$, and both KG$_J$ and KG$_u$ invoke the key generation algorithm of HPS-KEM$^\Sigma$.

Setup(λ): $pp \leftarrow$ KEMSetup(1^λ); Return pp

KG$_J$(pp): $(pk_J, sk_J) \leftarrow$ KG(pp); Return (pk_J, sk_J)

KG$_u$(pp): $(pk, sk) \leftarrow$ KG(pp); Return (pk, sk)

Fig. 8. Algorithm descriptions of Setup, KG$_J$ and KG$_u$

The main body of AGMF (i.e., Frank, Verify and Judge) is shown in Fig. 9. Specifically, algorithm Frank calls encap$_c$ and encap$_k$ of HPS-KEM$^\Sigma$ to generate a well-formed ciphertext and encapsulated keys respectively. Besides, it calls a NIZK proof algorithms NIZK$^\mathcal{R}$.PoK to generate a NIZK proof, where the relation $\mathcal{R}$ is defined in Eq. (5) and NIZK$^\mathcal{R}$ = (PoK, PoKVer) is a NIZK proof using the Fiat-Shamir transform from the Sigma protocols induced by HPS-KEM$^\Sigma$. The verification algorithm Verify and the moderation algorithm Judge are similar.

$\mathsf{Frank}(pp, sk_s, S, pk_J, m):$
$r \leftarrow \mathcal{RS}; c \leftarrow \mathsf{encap}_c(pp; r); k_J \leftarrow \mathsf{encap}_k(pp, pk_J; r)$
For $pk_{r_i} \in S:$
  $k_{r_i} \leftarrow \mathsf{encap}_k(pp, pk_{r_i}; r)$
$x \leftarrow (sk_s, r, \perp); y \leftarrow (pp, pk_s, pk_J, c, k_J)$
$\overline{m} \leftarrow (m\|\{k_{r_i}\}_{pk_{r_i} \in S}); \pi \leftarrow \mathsf{NIZK}^{\mathcal{R}}.\mathsf{PoK}(\overline{m}, x, y)$
Return $\sigma \leftarrow (\pi, c, k_J, \{k_{r_i}\}_{pk_{r_i} \in S})$

$\mathsf{Verify}(pp, pk_s, sk_r, pk_J, m, \sigma):$
$(\pi, c, k_J, \{k_{r_i}\}_{pk_{r_i} \in S}) \leftarrow \sigma; y \leftarrow (pp, pk_s, pk_J, c, k_J)$
$\overline{m} \leftarrow (m\|\{k_{r_i}\}_{pk_{r_i} \in S})$
If $\mathsf{NIZK}^{\mathcal{R}}.\mathsf{PoKVer}(\overline{m}, \pi, y) = 0$: Return 0
If $\mathsf{decap}(pp, sk_r, c) \in \{k_{r_i}\}_{pk_{r_i} \in S}$: Return 1
Return 0

$\mathsf{Judge}(pp, pk_s, sk_J, m, \sigma):$
$(\pi, c, k_J, \{k_{r_i}\}_{pk_{r_i} \in S}) \leftarrow \sigma; y \leftarrow (pp, pk_s, pk_J, c, k_J)$
$\overline{m} \leftarrow (m\|\{k_{r_i}\}_{pk_{r_i} \in S})$
If $\mathsf{NIZK}^{\mathcal{R}}.\mathsf{PoKVer}(\overline{m}, \pi, y) = 0$: Return 0
If $\mathsf{decap}(pp, sk_J, c) \neq k_J$: Return 0
Return 1

Fig. 9. Algorithm descriptions of Frank, Verify and Judge

They first call $\mathsf{NIZK}^{\mathcal{R}}.\mathsf{PoKVer}$ to check if the NIZK proof is valid, and then call decap with the receiver's/judge's secret key to check whether the encapsulated key and the corresponding decapsulated key are identical or not.

The three forging algorithms (i.e., Forge, RForge, JForge), focusing on different compromise scenarios, are described in Fig. 10. They firstly call encap_c^* of HPS-KEM$^{\Sigma}$ to generate an ill-formed ciphertext. Then, for each one of the receivers (and for the judge) whose secret key is not compromised, randomly samples an encapsulated key from $\mathcal{K}$; for each one of the receivers (and for the judge) whose secret key is compromised, employ decap to generate an encapsulated key. Finally, they call $\mathsf{NIZK}^{\mathcal{R}}.\mathsf{PoK}$ to generate a NIZK proof.

For the NIZK proof system $\mathsf{NIZK}^{\mathcal{R}} = (\mathsf{PoK}, \mathsf{PoKVer})$ used in Fig. 9 and Fig. 10, we obtain it as follows. The relation $\mathcal{R}$ is defined in Eq. (5).

$$\mathcal{R} = \{ ((sk_s, r, r^*), (pp, pk_s, pk_J, c, k_J)) :$$
$$((sk_s, pk_s) \in \mathcal{R}_s \wedge (r, (c, k_J, pk_J)) \in \mathcal{R}_{c,k}) \tag{5}$$
$$\vee ((r^*, c) \in \mathcal{R}_c^*) \}$$

where $\mathcal{R}_s$, $\mathcal{R}_{c,k}$ and $\mathcal{R}_c^*$ are defined in Eq. (2). Note that for every sub-relation (i.e., $\mathcal{R}_s$, $\mathcal{R}_{c,k}$, $\mathcal{R}_c^*$), the HPS-KEM$^{\Sigma}$ scheme guarantees that there is a Sigma protocol. So, with the technique of trivially combining Sigma protocols for AND/OR proofs [7, Sec. 19.7], we obtain a new Sigma protocol for relation $\mathcal{R}$. Then, using the Fiat-Shamir transform, we derive a NIZK proof system $\mathsf{NIZK}^{\mathcal{R}} = (\mathsf{PoK}, \mathsf{PoKVer})$ for $\mathcal{R}$ in the random oracle model.

Now, we provide some explanations about relation $\mathcal{R}$.

$Forge(pp, pk_s, S, pk_J, m)$:
$r^* \leftarrow \mathcal{RS}^*$; $c \leftarrow \mathsf{encap}_c^*(pp; r^*)$; $k_J \leftarrow \mathcal{K}$
For $pk_{r_i} \in S$: $k_{r_i} \leftarrow \mathcal{K}$
$x \leftarrow (\bot, \bot, r^*)$; $y \leftarrow (pp, pk_s, pk_J, c, k_J)$; $\overline{m} \leftarrow (m || \{k_{r_i}\}_{pk_{r_i} \in S})$
$\pi \leftarrow \mathsf{NIZK}^{\mathcal{R}}.\mathsf{PoK}(\overline{m}, x, y)$
Return $\sigma \leftarrow (\pi, c, k_J, \{k_{r_i}\}_{pk_{r_i} \in S})$

$RForge(pp, pk_s, \{pk_{r_i}, sk_{r_i}\}_{pk_{r_i} \in S_{cor}}, S, pk_J, m)$:
$/\!/ S_{cor}$ here is the set of corrupted receivers
$r^* \leftarrow \mathcal{RS}^*$; $c \leftarrow \mathsf{encap}_c^*(pp; r^*)$; $k_J \leftarrow \mathcal{K}$
For $pk_{r_i} \in S \backslash S_{cor}$: $k_{r_i} \leftarrow \mathcal{K}$
For $pk_{r_i} \in S_{cor}$: $k_{r_i} \leftarrow \mathsf{decap}(pp, sk_{r_i}, c)$
$x \leftarrow (\bot, \bot, r^*)$; $y \leftarrow (pp, pk_s, pk_J, c, k_J)$; $\overline{m} \leftarrow (m || \{k_{r_i}\}_{pk_{r_i} \in S})$
$\pi \leftarrow \mathsf{NIZK}^{\mathcal{R}}.\mathsf{PoK}(\overline{m}, x, y)$
Return $\sigma \leftarrow (\pi, c, k_J, \{k_{r_i}\}_{pk_{r_i} \in S})$

$JForge(pp, pk_s, S, sk_J, m)$:
$r^* \leftarrow \mathcal{RS}^*$; $c \leftarrow \mathsf{encap}_c^*(pp; r^*)$; $k_J \leftarrow \mathsf{decap}(pp, sk_J, c)$
For $pk_{r_i} \in S$: $k_{r_i} \leftarrow \mathcal{K}$
$x \leftarrow (\bot, \bot, r^*)$; $y \leftarrow (pp, pk_s, pk_J, c, k_J)$; $\overline{m} \leftarrow (m || \{k_{r_i}\}_{pk_{r_i} \in S})$
$\pi \leftarrow \mathsf{NIZK}^{\mathcal{R}}.\mathsf{PoK}(\overline{m}, x, y)$
Return $\sigma \leftarrow (\pi, c, k_J, \{k_{r_i}\}_{pk_{r_i} \in S})$

Fig. 10. Algorithm descriptions of Forge, RForge and JForge

The first part (i.e., $((sk_s, pk_s) \in \mathcal{R}_s) \wedge ((r, (c, k_J, pk_J)) \in \mathcal{R}_{c,k}))$ of the expression of $\mathcal{R}$ contains two sub-parts: (i) $((sk_s, pk_s) \in \mathcal{R}_s)$ guarantees the authentication of the sender; (ii) $((r, (c, k_J, pk_J)) \in \mathcal{R}_{c,k})$ guarantees that the ciphertext c and the corresponding encapsulated key k_J for the judge are well-formed, and further convinces the receiver that c and k_J can be verified successfully by the judge. In other words, once the receiver reports to the judge, the judge will accept the report.

The second part (i.e., $((r^*, c) \in \mathcal{R}_c^*)$) of the expression of $\mathcal{R}$ is prepared to guarantee deniability. More specifically, it is prepared for the forgers (including the universal, the receivers and the judge) to construct a valid NIZK proof, since they do not know the sender's secret key. The three forging algorithms in Fig. 10 show that the forgers generate the ill-formed ciphertext via $\mathsf{encap}_c^*(pp; r^*)$. Therefore, the forgers can always obtain the witness r^* for the second part of $\mathcal{R}$.

The relation $\mathcal{R}$ combines the two parts with an "OR" operation, so either the sender or the forgers can generate a valid NIZK proof for $\mathcal{R}$.

Remark 8. In our framework AGMF, in order to reduce the size of signature, k_J and k_{r_i} are all encapsulated in the same ciphertext c. This suggests that KG_J and KG_u are built based on the identical HPS-KEM$^{\Sigma}$. Actually, k_J can be encapsulated in another ciphertext, which can be generated with an independent HPS-KEM$^{\Sigma}$. Hence, the judge can run KG_J based on an independent HPS-KEM$^{\Sigma}$, to generate the public/secret key pair. In this case, the obtained AGMF can support third-party moderation better.

Correctness. Now we show the correctness of the above scheme AGMF here. For any signature $\sigma \leftarrow \mathsf{Frank}(pp, sk_s, S, pk_J, m)$ and any $pk_r \in S$, we parse $\sigma = (\pi, c, k_J, \{k_{r_i}\}_{pk_{r_i} \in S})$, and let $y := (pp, pk_s, pk_J, c, k_J)$ and $\overline{m} := (m \| \{k_{r_i}\}_{pk_{r_i} \in S})$.

We first analyze the output of Verify as follows: (i) the correctness of $\mathsf{NIZK}^{\mathcal{R}}$ guarantees that $\mathsf{NIZK}^{\mathcal{R}}.\mathsf{PoKVer}(\overline{m}, \pi, y) = 1$; (ii) the correctness of $\mathsf{HPS\text{-}KEM}^{\Sigma}$ guarantees that $\mathsf{decap}(pp, sk_r, c) \in \{k_{r_i}\}_{pk_{r_i} \in S}$ since $pk_r \in S$. So, Verify will return 1.

Next, we analyze the output of Judge as follows: (i) the correctness of $\mathsf{NIZK}^{\mathcal{R}}$ guarantees that $\mathsf{NIZK}^{\mathcal{R}}.\mathsf{PoKVer}(\overline{m}, \pi, y) = 1$; (ii) the correctness of $\mathsf{HPS\text{-}KEM}^{\Sigma}$ guarantees that $\mathsf{decap}(pp, sk_J, c) = k_J$. Therefore, Judge will also return 1.

Security. For security, we have the following theorem.

Theorem 7. *If a $\mathsf{HPS\text{-}KEM}^{\Sigma}$ scheme $\mathsf{HPS\text{-}KEM}^{\Sigma}$ is universal, unexplainable, indistinguishble, SK-second-preimage resistant and smooth, and $\mathsf{NIZK}^{\mathcal{R}} = (\mathsf{PoK}, \mathsf{PoKVer})$ is a Fiat-Shamir NIZK proof system for $\mathcal{R}$, then our scheme AGMF achieves the accountability (receiver binding and sender binding), deniability (universal deniability, receiver compromise deniability, and judge compromise deniability) and receiver anonymity simultaneously.*

Due to the page limitations, the proof of Theorem 7 will be provided in the full version of this paper.

Acknowledgements. We would like to express our sincere appreciation to the anonymous reviewers for their valuable comments and suggestions! Junzuo Lai was supported by National Natural Science Foundation of China under Grant No. U2001205, Guangdong Basic and Applied Basic Research Foundation (Grant No. 2023B1515040020), Industrial project No. TC20200930001. Siu Ming Yiu was supported by HKU-SCF FinTech Academy and Shenzhen-Hong Kong-Macao Science and Technology Plan Project (Category C Project: SGDX20210823103537030). Xin Mu was supported by the National Natural Science Foundation of China (62106114). Jian Weng was supported by National Natural Science Foundation of China under Grant Nos. 61825203 and U22B2028, Major Program of Guangdong Basic and Applied Research Project under Grant No. 2019B030302008, National Key Research and Development Plan of China under Grant No. 2020YFB1005600, Guangdong Provincial Science and Technology Project under Grant No. 2021A0505030033, Science and Technology Major Project of Tibetan Autonomous Region of China under Grant No. XZ202201ZD0006G, National Joint Engineering Research Center of Network Security Detection and Protection Technology, and Guangdong Key Laboratory of Data Security and Privacy Preserving.

References

1. Mastodon social network (2018). https://joinmastodon.org/
2. Matrix: an open network for secure, decentralized communication (2018). https://matrix.org/
3. Alwen, J., Coretti, S., Dodis, Y., Tselekounis, Y.: Security analysis and improvements for the IETF MLS standard for group messaging. In: Micciancio, D., Ristenpart, T. (eds.) CRYPTO 2020. LNCS, vol. 12170, pp. 248–277. Springer, Cham (2020). https://doi.org/10.1007/978-3-030-56784-2_9

4. Alwen, J., Coretti, S., Dodis, Y., Tselekounis, Y.: Modular design of secure group messaging protocols and the security of MLS. In: ACM CCS 2021, pp. 1463–1483 (2021)
5. Bellare, M., Palacio, A.: The knowledge-of-exponent assumptions and 3-round zero-knowledge protocols. In: Franklin, M. (ed.) CRYPTO 2004. LNCS, vol. 3152, pp. 273–289. Springer, Heidelberg (2004). https://doi.org/10.1007/978-3-540-28628-8_17
6. Boneh, D., Lynn, B., Shacham, H.: Short signatures from the Weil pairing. In: Boyd, C. (ed.) ASIACRYPT 2001. LNCS, vol. 2248, pp. 514–532. Springer, Heidelberg (2001). https://doi.org/10.1007/3-540-45682-1_30
7. Boneh, D., Shoup, V.: A graduate course in applied cryptography. Draft 0.5 (2020)
8. Camenisch, J.: Group signature schemes and payment systems based on the discrete logarithm problem. Ph.D. thesis, ETH Zurich (1998)
9. Camenisch, J., Stadler, M.: Efficient group signature schemes for large groups. In: Kaliski, B.S. (ed.) CRYPTO 1997. LNCS, vol. 1294, pp. 410–424. Springer, Heidelberg (1997). https://doi.org/10.1007/BFb0052252
10. Chase, M., Lysyanskaya, A.: On signatures of knowledge. In: Dwork, C. (ed.) CRYPTO 2006. LNCS, vol. 4117, pp. 78–96. Springer, Heidelberg (2006). https://doi.org/10.1007/11818175_5
11. Chaum, D., Pedersen, T.P.: Wallet databases with observers. In: Brickell, E.F. (ed.) CRYPTO 1992. LNCS, vol. 740, pp. 89–105. Springer, Heidelberg (1993). https://doi.org/10.1007/3-540-48071-4_7
12. Chen, L., Tang, Q.: People who live in glass houses should not throw stones: targeted opening message franking schemes. Cryptology ePrint Archive, Report 2018/994 (2018)
13. Cohn-Gordon, K., Cremers, C., Garratt, L., Millican, J., Milner, K.: On ends-to-ends encryption: asynchronous group messaging with strong security guarantees. In: CCS 2018, pp. 1802–1819 (2018)
14. Corrigan-Gibbs, H., Ford, B.: Dissent: accountable anonymous group messaging. In: CCS 2010, pp. 340–350 (2010)
15. Corrigan-Gibbs, H., Wolinsky, D.I., Ford, B.: Proactively accountable anonymous messaging in verdict. In: USENIX Security 2013, pp. 147–162 (2013)
16. Cramer, R.: Modular design of secure yet practical cryptographic protocols. Ph. D. thesis, CWI and University of Amsterdam (1996)
17. Cramer, R., Shoup, V.: Universal hash proofs and a paradigm for adaptive chosen ciphertext secure public-key encryption. In: Knudsen, L.R. (ed.) EUROCRYPT 2002. LNCS, vol. 2332, pp. 45–64. Springer, Heidelberg (2002). https://doi.org/10.1007/3-540-46035-7_4
18. Damgård, I., Haagh, H., Mercer, R., Nitulescu, A., Orlandi, C., Yakoubov, S.: Stronger security and constructions of multi-designated verifier signatures. In: Pass, R., Pietrzak, K. (eds.) TCC 2020. LNCS, vol. 12551, pp. 229–260. Springer, Cham (2020). https://doi.org/10.1007/978-3-030-64378-2_9
19. Dodis, Y., Grubbs, P., Ristenpart, T., Woodage, J.: Fast message franking: from invisible salamanders to encryptment. In: Shacham, H., Boldyreva, A. (eds.) CRYPTO 2018. LNCS, vol. 10991, pp. 155–186. Springer, Cham (2018). https://doi.org/10.1007/978-3-319-96884-1_6
20. Facebook: Facebook messenger app (2016). https://www.messenger.com/
21. Facebook: Messenger secret conversations technical whitepaper (2016). https://fbnewsroomus.files.wordpress.com/2016/07/secret_conversations_whitepaper-1.pdf

22. Fiat, A., Shamir, A.: How to prove yourself: practical solutions to identification and signature problems. In: Odlyzko, A.M. (ed.) CRYPTO 1986. LNCS, vol. 263, pp. 186–194. Springer, Heidelberg (1987). https://doi.org/10.1007/3-540-47721-7_12

23. Goldberg, I., Ustaoğlu, B., Van Gundy, M.D., Chen, H.: Multi-party off-the-record messaging. In: CCS 2009, pp. 358–368 (2009)

24. Grubbs, P., Lu, J., Ristenpart, T.: Message franking via committing authenticated encryption. In: Katz, J., Shacham, H. (eds.) CRYPTO 2017. LNCS, vol. 10403, pp. 66–97. Springer, Cham (2017). https://doi.org/10.1007/978-3-319-63697-9_3

25. Hofheinz, D.: Algebraic partitioning: fully compact and (almost) tightly secure cryptography. In: Kushilevitz, E., Malkin, T. (eds.) TCC 2016. LNCS, vol. 9562, pp. 251–281. Springer, Heidelberg (2016). https://doi.org/10.1007/978-3-662-49096-9_11

26. Hofheinz, D.: Adaptive partitioning. In: Coron, J.-S., Nielsen, J.B. (eds.) EURO-CRYPT 2017. LNCS, vol. 10212, pp. 489–518. Springer, Cham (2017). https://doi.org/10.1007/978-3-319-56617-7_17

27. Hofheinz, D., Kiltz, E.: Secure hybrid encryption from weakened key encapsulation. In: Menezes, A. (ed.) CRYPTO 2007. LNCS, vol. 4622, pp. 553–571. Springer, Heidelberg (2007). https://doi.org/10.1007/978-3-540-74143-5_31

28. Issa, R., AlHaddad, N., Varia, M.: Hecate: Abuse reporting in secure messengers with sealed sender. Cryptology ePrint Archive (2021)

29. Jafargholi, Z., Kamath, C., Klein, K., Komargodski, I., Pietrzak, K., Wichs, D.: Be adaptive, avoid overcommitting. In: Katz, J., Shacham, H. (eds.) CRYPTO 2017. LNCS, vol. 10401, pp. 133–163. Springer, Cham (2017). https://doi.org/10.1007/978-3-319-63688-7_5

30. Leontiadis, I., Vaudenay, S.: Private message franking with after opening privacy. Cryptology ePrint Archive, Report 2018/938 (2018). https://eprint.iacr.org/2018/938

31. Okamoto, T.: An efficient divisible electronic cash scheme. In: Coppersmith, D. (ed.) CRYPTO 1995. LNCS, vol. 963, pp. 438–451. Springer, Heidelberg (1995). https://doi.org/10.1007/3-540-44750-4_35

32. Peale, C., Eskandarian, S., Boneh, D.: Secure complaint-enabled source-tracking for encrypted messaging. In: CCS 2021, pp. 1484–1506 (2021)

33. Schnorr, C.P.: Efficient identification and signatures for smart cards. In: Brassard, G. (ed.) CRYPTO 1989. LNCS, vol. 435, pp. 239–252. Springer, New York (1990). https://doi.org/10.1007/0-387-34805-0_22

34. Shacham, H.: A Cramer-Shoup Encryption Scheme from the Linear Assumption and from Progressively Weaker Linear Variants. Cryptology ePrint Archive, Report 2007/074 (2007)

35. Syta, E., Corrigan-Gibbs, H., Weng, S.C., Wolinsky, D., Ford, B., Johnson, A.: Security analysis of accountable anonymity in dissent. TISSEC 17(1), 1–35 (2014)

36. Tyagi, N., Grubbs, P., Len, J., Miers, I., Ristenpart, T.: Asymmetric message franking: content moderation for metadata-private end-to-end encryption. In: Boldyreva, A., Micciancio, D. (eds.) CRYPTO 2019. LNCS, vol. 11694, pp. 222–250. Springer, Cham (2019). https://doi.org/10.1007/978-3-030-26954-8_8

37. Tyagi, N., Miers, I., Ristenpart, T.: Traceback for end-to-end encrypted messaging. In: CCS 2019, pp. 413–430 (2019)

38. Wolinsky, D.I., Corrigan-Gibbs, H., Ford, B., Johnson, A.: Dissent in numbers: making strong anonymity scale. In: OSDI 2012, pp. 179–182 (2012)

39. Wong, C.K., Gouda, M., Lam, S.S.: Secure group communications using key graphs. IEEE/ACM Trans. Network. 8(1), 16–30 (2000)

Password-Authenticated TLS via OPAQUE and Post-Handshake Authentication

Julia Hesse[1]([✉]), Stanislaw Jarecki[2], Hugo Krawczyk[3], and Christopher Wood[4]

[1] IBM Research Europe – Zurich, Rüschlikon, Switzerland
jhs@zurich.ibm.com
[2] UC Irvine, Irvine, USA
stanislawjarecki@gmail.com
[3] Algorand Foundation, Boston, USA
hugokraw@gmail.com
[4] Cloudflare, San Francisco, USA
caw@heapingbits.net

Abstract. OPAQUE is an Asymmetric Password-Authenticated Key Exchange (aPAKE) protocol being standardized by the IETF (Internet Engineering Task Force) as a more secure alternative to the traditional "password-over-TLS" mechanism prevalent in current practice. OPAQUE defends against a variety of vulnerabilities of password-over-TLS by dispensing with reliance on PKI and TLS security, and ensuring that the password is never visible to servers or anyone other than the client machine where the password is entered. In order to facilitate the use of OPAQUE in practice, integration of OPAQUE with TLS is needed. The main proposal for standardizing such integration uses the Exported Authenticators (TLS-EA) mechanism of TLS 1.3 that supports post-handshake authentication and allows for a smooth composition with OPAQUE. We refer to this composition as TLS-OPAQUE and present a detailed security analysis for it in the Universal Composability (UC) framework.

Our treatment is general and includes the formalization of components that are needed in the analysis of TLS-OPAQUE but are of wider applicability as they are used in many protocols in practice. Specifically, we provide formalizations in the UC model of the notions of post-handshake authentication and channel binding. The latter, in particular, has been hard to implement securely in practice, resulting in multiple protocol failures, including major attacks against prior versions of TLS. Ours is the first treatment of these notions in a computational model with composability guarantees.

We complement the theoretical work with a detailed discussion of practical considerations for the use and deployment of TLS-OPAQUE in real-world settings and applications.

Keywords: Transport Layer Security · Passwords · Authentication

J. Hesse–This work was supported by the Swiss National Science Foundation (SNSF) under the AMBIZIONE grant "Cryptographic Protocols for Human Authentication and the IoT".

C. Hazay and M. Stam (Eds.): EUROCRYPT 2023, LNCS 14008, pp. 98–127, 2023.
https://doi.org/10.1007/978-3-031-30589-4_4

1 Introduction

For a multitude of reasons, passwords remain a ubiquitous type of authenticator. Despite the existence of tools for improving passwords (password managers) and password-less authentication protocols (e.g., WebAuthn), password-based authentication remains commonplace. Legacy software and lack of support for modern alternatives, integration issues for better tooling to improve password quality, and usability problems in adopting any new form of authenticator have all contributed in one way or another to the prolonged usage of passwords for authentication onn the Internet (and beyond).

As a result, much of the security infrastructure depends to a large extent on passwords. And, yet, the prime mechanism of client-server password authentication in practice has not changed in the last decades and remains the traditional password-over-TLS (more generally, the transport of passwords over channels protected by public key encryption). Weaknesses of this mechanism include, though are not limited to: visibility of plaintext passwords to the application server and to other decrypting intermediaries, accidental storage of passwords in the clear (as several high-profile incidents have shown [1,2]), and ease of password leakage in the event of phishing attacks.

Recently, the IETF (Internet Engineering Task Force) has initiated a process of standardizing a much stronger mechanism, the so-called *Asymmetric Password-Authenticated Key Exchange (aPAKE)* that does not rely on PKI (except, optionally, at user registration time) and ensures that user passwords are never visible outside the client machine. Essentially, aPAKE protocols are as secure as possible, restricting attacks to unavoidable password guesses and offline attacks upon server compromise. The specific protocol chosen for instantiation of the aPAKE standard is OPAQUE [9,18]. In addition to enjoying the aPAKE security (including an enhancement in the form of security against pre-computation attacks), OPAQUE offers the flexibility of working with any authenticated key exchange mechanism. Hence, it is a natural candidate for integration with existing protocols such as TLS 1.3, IKEv2, etc.

Clearly, integration with TLS is desirable for improving the security of password authentication in TLS, but also because while OPAQUE provides authentication and key exchange, it does not offer the secure channels required to protect data; TLS provides such functionality via its record layer. Additionally, integration with TLS allows for protection of user account information during a login protocol.

A natural approach to such integration is to use the *post-handshake authentication (PHA)* mechanism of TLS 1.3[1] [23] that allows clients to authenticate after the TLS handshake (the key establishment component of TLS) has completed, and within the ensuing record-layer session (where data is exchanged under the protection of the keys established by the handshake). For example, a server can serve public webpages to an unauthenticated client but may require client authentication once the client requests access to restricted pages, thus

---

[1] Except if said otherwise, we use 'TLS' to refer to TLS 1.3.

triggering post-handshake authentication by the client. More general support for PHA is provided in a TLS 1.3 extension standard called *Exported Authenticators (TLS-EA)* [26] (we often shorten TLS-EA to EA). EA extends the post-handshake client authentication component of TLS 1.3 and can support multiple authentications within the same TLS session for both clients and servers. As such, EA is a natural tool for integrating OPAQUE into TLS 1.3 as a way to enable strong password authentication within TLS connections. While EA natively supports certificate-based authentication, its fields can easily be repurposed for transporting OPAQUE's signature-based authentication. This integration of OPAQUE and TLS-EA, referred to here as TLS-OPAQUE, has been proposed for standardization in the TLS Working Group of the IETF [27] (Fig. 1).

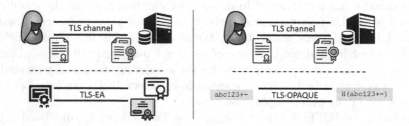

Fig. 1. (Post-)Authentication options for TLS channels. **Left:** The Exported Authenticators TLS extention (TLS-EA) allows both channel endpoints to subsequently add more public-key identities to a TLS channel. **Right:** TLS-OPAQUE allows to subsequently add (asymmetric) password identities to a TLS channel.

In this work we investigate the security of the above schemes: TLS-EA as a general post-handshake mechanism and TLS-OPAQUE for password-authenticated TLS. However, our treatment is more general and independent of any particular protocol instantiation. We formalize the notion of post-handshake authentication in the Universal Composability (UC) setting [11] with two authentication flavors: via public-key certificates as the EA protocol [26] specifies and via passwords as TLS-OPAQUE requires.

While this formalization of PHA serves the analysis of EA and TLS-OPAQUE, post-handshake authentication is a more general notion implemented in practice as extension to multiple protocols, including IPsec, SSH as well as previous versions of TLS. In general terms, the PHA main functionality is to enable multiple authentications (possibly using different credentials and identities) of a previously established channel between two endpoints; *it guarantees that in each of these authentications, the authenticating parties are the same as those that established the channel in the first place.*

Thus, a crucial ingredient in the implementation of any PHA protocol is a mechanism for *binding* the PHA authentications to the original channel. A common design, that we follow in our PHA instantiations, is to define a *channel binding* value generated at the time of the original channel establishment and passed to PHA for inclusion in all subsequent authentications. This channel binder can take the form of a handshake transcript digest, a cryptographic key, or a combination of both. While the notion itself is simple, its implementation in the real world has been remarkably challenging and has led to serious security failures against multiple protocols, including major attacks against previous versions of TLS such as the notorious renegotiation [22,24,25] and triple-handshake attacks [5]. See [6] for an account of attacks on multiple protocols based on PHA failures due to wrong channel binding designs. It is a main goal and motivation of our work to set an analytical framework and proofs to prevent this type of failures in new designs such as those presented here.

To capture the channel binding requirements, we extend the traditional formalism of secure channel functionalities [12] with a *channel binder* element that is output from the channel generation module (e.g., a key exchange) and used by parties engaging in a PHA as a way to bind their post-handshake authentication to the original channel establishment. Informally, we set two requirements on the channel binder: *being unique among all channels established by an honest party and being pseudorandom*. The latter property enables the use of the binder as a cryptographic key in the process of post-handshake authentication. The uniqueness element is crucial for defeating what is known as channel synchronization attacks [3,6], the source of many of the serious attacks against PHA mechanisms in practice. We formally prove in Theorem 1 in Sect. 4 that TLS 1.3 with its Exporter Main Secret (EMS) implements a secure channel with such binder qualities.

We frame the security of post-handshake authentication via a UC functionality that enforces that only valid credentials presented by the *original endpoints of the channel* (technically, those that know the binder's cryptographic key) are accepted. Our PHA formalism comes in two flavors: one that supports public keys as the post-handshake authentication means and one that supports password-based authentication. The first flavor captures the essence of the security requirements of TLS-EA, namely, the ability to support any number of PK-based authentications[2] by the creators of a TLS channel, and only by those. Therefore formally proving the security of the TLS-EA protocol from [26] reduces to showing that the protocol realizes the PK-based PHA functionality. This is shown in Theorem 2 in Sect. 5. In particular, the proof of this theorem validates that the channel binder defined by TLS 1.3 (called EMS, for Exporter Master Secret) has the required properties for the purpose of implementing a secure post-handshake authentication mechanism.

We now consider the TLS-OPAQUE protocol [19,27] that uses the TLS-EA mechanism to transport the OPAQUE messages for providing *password-based* post-handshake authentication to the TLS channel. To prove security of this protocol, we show it realizes our password-based PHA functionality. The latter functionality essentially ensures that any mechanism that realizes the functionality provides authentication guarantees similar to those of an aPAKE. Namely, the key established upon channel creation (even if anonymous at the time) is

---

[2] In the particular case of TLS-EA, it is signature-based authentication.

authenticated by the client and server; the only way to subvert the protocol is by an online password guessing attack or an offline dictionary attack if the server is compromised. Furthermore, not only does the password-based PHA functionality ensure the correct authentication by the endpoints of the original channel but it also guarantees that no other than these endpoints will succeed in such authentication. By proving that TLS-OPAQUE realizes the password-based PHA functionality (Theorem 3 in Sect. 6) we get that TLS-OPAQUE enjoys all these aPAKE-like security properties.

On a technical level, our analysis of TLS-OPAQUE builds on the proven guarantees of EA detailed above. In a nutshell, TLS-OPAQUE strips the key exchange part from OPAQUE, and uses only OPAQUE's password authentication mechanism to authenticate the already established TLS key material. This authentication is signature-based and can be outsourced to EA. We detail in Sect. 2 how exactly TLS-OPAQUE is combined from both EA and (parts of) OPAQUE. A main goal of our analysis is to tame the complexity of TLS-OPAQUE by modularizing the security proof: we first prove the security of EA, and then analyze the security of TLS-OPAQUE assuming that EA is already secure. We refer the reader to the technical roadmap below for a summary of all formal results in the paper, and how they combine with each other.

Altogether, our work delivers the first formal analysis of TLS-EA in the UC framework, and of TLS-OPAQUE overall. Our modular approach yields formal models for widely-used concepts such as channel binders as well as public-key and password-based post-handshake authentication. Our models deepen the understanding of these concepts, and we expect them to be useful for real-world protocol analysis beyond our work.

Finally, we would like to highlight a fundamental element in our treatment: We do not assume the original channel to be authenticated upon creation, only that no one other than the endpoints of the channel can transmit over the channel (as enforced by the encryption and authentication keys created within the channel, e.g., via a plain Diffie-Hellman exchange). Therefore, the security of TLS-OPAQUE depends on the Diffie-Hellman key exchange of TLS 1.3 but not on the server and/or client authentication of this exchange. Thus, TLS-OPAQUE is secure even if the original channel was anonymous. On the other hand, if this channel was originally authenticated, say by the server, that authentication property is additional to the password-based authentication provided by TLS-OPAQUE.

DEPLOYMENT CONSIDERATIONS. TLS-OPAQUE provides real improvements for password-based authentication systems in a variety of environments. Mobile applications, for example, can use TLS-OPAQUE for secure password authentication without any risk of disclosing the password to the server, and without any noticeable change in user experience. Use cases where TLS-OPAQUE is used without fallback to password-over-TLS also mitigate common phishing vectors: even if an attacker can intercept the underlying TLS connection, clients never reveal the plaintext password to the attacker. TLS-OPAQUE also complements modern authentication technologies such as password managers and multi-factor authentication protocols such as WebAuthn [16].

Using TLS-OPAQUE is not without tradeoffs, however, as TLS-OPAQUE requires changes to applications *and* the underlying TLS implementations. However, such changes are not insurmountable in practice. Additionally, in environments where fallback to password-over-TLS authentication must be supported for backwards compatibility purposes, such as the web, concerns such as phishing remain. Client-side user interface changes may help mitigate such risks, though additional user studies are required to demonstrate feasibility.

TECHNICAL ROADMAP. The analysis of real-world protocols in abstract complexity-theoretic formalisms like the UC framework typically requires simplifications that ignore many technical aspects of the full specifications. Yet, such analysis serves to validate the core cryptographic design at the basis of the protocols. To be concrete, in Sect. 2 (Figs. 3 and 5), we present the core cryptographic elements extracted from IETF RFCs and Internet Drafts [23, 26, 27] that we analyze and that we use as the basis for abstract representation of these protocols in subsequent sections.

Our formal treatment includes the following elements. In Sect. 4 we formalize secure channels exporting pseudorandom and unique channel binders in the UC framework (functionality $\mathcal{F}_{cbSC}$ in Fig. 6), and prove in Theorem 1 that the TLS handshake protocol implements such functionality. We then formalize in Sect. 5 secure channels with post-handshake public-key authentication (functionality $\mathcal{F}_{PHA}$ in Fig. 8), and present a modular version of TLS-EA (Π_{EA} in Fig. 9) that uses secure channels with binders (i.e., $\mathcal{F}_{cbSC}$) as an abstract building block. Theorem 2 proves that this modular version of TLS-EA implements $\mathcal{F}_{PHA}$. Invoking the UC composition theorem on Theorems 1 and 2 yields our first main result, namely that "real" EA, which corresponds to Π_{EA} with calls to the handshake part of TLS 1.3 instead of $\mathcal{F}_{cbSC}$, securely implements $\mathcal{F}_{PHA}$.

We then turn to analyze TLS-OPAQUE. First, we formalize secure channels with post-handshake password authentication (functionality $\mathcal{F}_{pwPHA}$ in Fig. 10), and present a modular version of TLS-OPAQUE ($\Pi_{TLS-OPAQUE}$ in Fig. 12) that uses secure channels with post-handshake public-key authentication (i.e., $\mathcal{F}_{PHA}$) as an abstract building block. Theorem 3 proves that this modular version of TLS-OPAQUE implements $\mathcal{F}_{pwPHA}$. Invoking again the UC composition theorem on Theorems 2 and 3 yields our second main result, namely that "real" TLS-OPAQUE, which corresponds to $\Pi_{TLS-OPAQUE}$ with calls to TLS-EA (i.e., Π_{EA}) instead of $\mathcal{F}_{PHA}$, securely implements $\mathcal{F}_{pwPHA}$.

The full version of this paper [15] provides previously known security notions for signatures and MACs, as well as details on Oblivious Pseudorandom Functions (OPRFs), a detailed walk-through of functionality $\mathcal{F}_{cbSC}$, considerations for implementing, deploying, operating, and using TLS-OPAQUE in a variety of use case, and full proofs and sketches of all our Theorems.

RELATED WORK. TLS 1.3 is perhaps one of the most carefully analyzed security protocols used on the Internet today. Our work analyzes, in the UC model, the aspects of TLS 1.3 that are directly relevant to TLS-EA and TLS-OPAQUE, yet it may set a basis for a broader UC analysis of TLS 1.3. Our study of these protocols also fits with the analysis-prior-to-deployment approach that characterized the development of TLS 1.3,

Partial study of post-handshake authentication in a game-based model appears in [21] which focused on post-handshake client authentication as a way of upgrading a unilaterally authenticated key exchange to a mutually authenticated one, but did not consider the server side or multiple authentications. In particular, it did not analyze the security of the TLS-EA mechanism.

Most relevant to the subject of our work is the analysis of channel binding and post-handshake authentication techniques (under the notion of *compound authentication*) presented in [6]. The paper analyzes these techniques in several deployed protocols (but not TLS 1.3), showing a variety of attacks due to short-comings in the channel binding design. They carry a formal analysis of these mechanisms using the protocol analyzer ProVerif [8]. Extending this work, [17] presents an automated analysis of the Exported Authenticators (TLS-EA) protocol [26] based on a symbolic model of the protocol using the Tamarin Prover. Additional papers relevant to the analysis of channel binding mechanisms in practice (particularly pointing to vulnerabilities) include [3,4,7,13,25]. Finally, we mention [10] who formalize (using game-based definitions) a notion of channel binding but with a different functionality than ours. In their case the binding is between identities and a key in a 3-party key exchange setting. Their mechanisms and formal treatment do not seem to apply to our setting.

2   TLS-OPAQUE Specification

In this section we describe the protocols we study in this work: OPAQUE, TLS 1.3 Handshake, TLS-EA, and TLS-OPAQUE. We start by recalling OPAQUE [9,18] in schematic form in Fig. 2 (more details are included in the presentation of TLS-OPAQUE in Fig. 5).

FIGURE 2 (SIMPLIFIED SCHEMATIC OPAQUE PROTOCOL). During registration, the user creates an "envelope" containing a user's private key and a server's public key. The envelope is protected (for secrecy and authentication) by a key computed jointly between user and server using an Oblivious PRF (OPRF) (to which the user inputs its password and the server inputs a secret user-specific OPRF key; neither party learns the other's input). The server stores the envelope as well as the user's public key and the server's own private key. For login, the user receives the envelope from the server and obtains the key to unlock the envelope by running the OPRF with the client using the same password as upon registration. Now, user and server have the keys to run an authenticated key exchange between them (for TLS-OPAQUE, these keys will be signature keys similar to those used in TLS).

Next, we recall the elements from the TLS 1.3 handshake that play a role in this work, and which serve as a basis for TLS-EA and TLS-OPAQUE.

SIMPLIFIED SCHEMATIC TLS HANDSHAKE (FIG. 3). The figure shows a schematic representation of a subset of the TLS 1.3 handshake, the key exchange

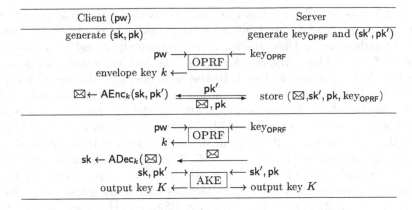

Fig. 2. OPAQUE registration (top) and key exchange (bottom).

Client C		Server S
$\mathrm{rand}_C \leftarrow \{0,1\}^\lambda, x \leftarrow \mathbb{Z}_p$	$\xrightarrow{\mathrm{rand}_C, g^x}$ $\xleftarrow{\mathrm{rand}_S, g^y}$	$\mathrm{rand}_S \leftarrow \{0,1\}^\lambda, y \leftarrow \mathbb{Z}_p$
	$m' \leftarrow (\mathsf{Cert}_S, \mathsf{Sig}_S(\mathrm{tr}_1), \mathsf{MAC}_{\mathsf{HSm}_S}(\mathrm{tr}_2))$	
$m \leftarrow ([\mathsf{Cert}_C, \mathsf{Sig}_C(\mathrm{tr}_3),] \mathsf{MAC}_{\mathsf{HSm}_C}(\mathrm{tr}_4))$		
$\mathsf{auth}_C \leftarrow \mathsf{Enc}_{\mathsf{HSe}_C}(m)$	$\xleftarrow{\mathsf{auth}_S}$ $\xrightarrow{\mathsf{auth}_C}$	$\mathsf{auth}_S \leftarrow \mathsf{Enc}_{\mathsf{HSe}_S}(m')$

Fig. 3. Schematic representation of TLS 1.3 Handshake (showing subset considered in our analysis).

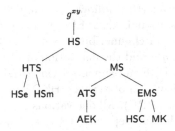

Fig. 4. Key Derivation in TLS 1.3

part of TLS. It is intended to show the components that play a role in the protocols studied here. The first two flows show the exchange of nonces (rand_C, rand_S) and an unauthenticated Diffie-Hellman run between client and server resulting in a key g^{xy} from which a key, HS (for Handshake Secret), is extracted as shown in the key derivation tree in Fig. 4. In the next message, the server authenticates to the client using TLS's sign-and-mac mechanism. The signature (called `CertificateVerify` in TLS) is applied to the handshake transcript and is verified by the client using the server's public key transported in a certificate Cert_S. The MAC part (known as the `Finish` message) uses key HSm_S derived from HS and is applied to the transcript as well. The following message shows client authentication mimicking the server's where the signature part is optional; only the MAC part is mandatory in TLS 1.3. Messages auth_S and auth_C are protected using an authenticated encryption with keys HSe_S and HSe_C also derived from HS. Our analysis in the following sections *proves security of TLS-EA and TLS-OPAQUE even if the handshake DH is unauthenticated,* hence from the point of view of this analysis these authentication messages can be omitted.[3] Each of the transcripts $\mathsf{tr}_1, ..., \mathsf{tr}_4$ cover all previous elements in the handshake until the point of use of the transcript. However, since our analysis does not require the sending of the auth messages, we can set $\mathsf{tr} \leftarrow (\mathsf{rand}_C, g^x, \mathsf{rand}_S, g^y)$.

HANDSHAKE'S KEY DERIVATION (FIG. 4). The figure shows a key derivation tree used by TLS 1.3. Some of the keys have separate server and client derivations (e.g., $\mathsf{HSC}_S, \mathsf{HSC}_C$) but for simplicity we show them as one key. The root of the tree, g^{xy}, is the product of the handshake's DH exchange. A key HS (for Handshake Secret) is extracted from g^{xy} and from it a tree of keys is derived; we explain their roles. Key HTS (for Handshake Traffic Secret) spawns two keys: HSe for encrypting messages auth_S and auth_C, and HSm used as a MAC key in server and client authentication. Key MS (for Main Secret) has two siblings ATS (Application Traffic Secret) and EMS (Exporter Main Secret). Key AEK, derived from ATS, is used to derive Authenticated Encryption keys for protecting data exchanged in the record layer (that follows the handshake) - it can be thought as the session key in a traditional AKE. EMS spawns HSC and MK which play the critical role (see below) of channel binders in TLS-EA and TLS-OPAQUE. The extraction of HS from g^{xy} and the derivation of MS use HKDF-Extract while all other derivations use a PRF implemented via HKDF-Expand (because of the particular way that the derivation of MS uses HKDF-Extract, also this derivation can be seen as produced by a PRF). All derivations use public labels and parts of the transcript to enforce domain separation and (computational) independence of the keys.

---

[3] Proving our results in the case of an unauthenticated handshake, shows that although TLS handshake is commonly authenticated by the server, TLS-EA's security does not depend on this authentication. On the other hand, when certificate-based server authentication is present during the handshake that precedes a run of TLS-OPAQUE, one gets the benefits of both certificate-based and password-based authentications.

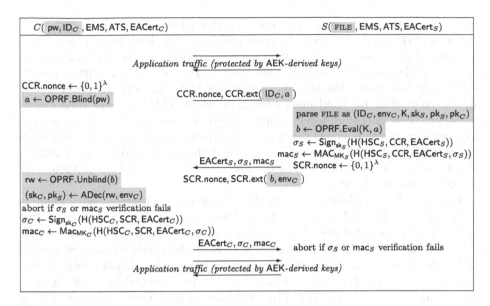

Fig. 5. The TLS-OPAQUE protocol, formed by the subset of the TLS handshake shown in Fig. 3 and the present figure. Omitting blue-colored parts (which correspond to the OPAQUE envelope decryption) one obtains two TLS-EA instances. (Color figure online)

FIGURE 5 (TLS-EA AND TLS-OPAQUE PROTOCOLS). We are now ready to explain TLS-EA and TLS-OPAQUE. We show protocol TLS-OPAQUE in Fig. 5. However, if one ignores all the blue-colored elements in Fig. 5, one obtains two instances of the TLS-EA protocol [26], the first one authenticating the server to the client, the second one vice versa. This presentation shows how TLS-OPAQUE is built as an extension of TLS-EA, because all the additional cryptography required by OPAQUE is carried using CCR and SCR extension fields of TLS-EA. Note that Fig. 5 shows only the post-handshake authentication parts of TLS-OPAQUE and TLS-EA, while the full protocols are obtained by running the TLS handshake shown in Fig. 3 followed by the post-handshake authentication shown in Fig. 5.

TLS-EA allows an application that established a TLS connection via the handshake to request its peer (client or server) to authenticate at any time after the handshake is completed. For the client to request server authentication, TLS-EA defines a message ClientCertificateRequest (abbreviated CCR) that includes a nonce called certificate_request_context and which we denote by CCR.nonce. In addition, CCR has an extensions field (we denote it CCR.ext) where an application can carry additional auxiliary information. The analogous message ServerCertificateRequest (SCR) (or simply called CertificateRequest in the case of the server) is used by the server to request client authentication. The response to such requests is an authentication message by the responder that includes a certificate, a signature and a MAC, implementing the regular sign-and-mac mechanism of TLS with elements σ and mac (i.e., TLS's `CertificateVerify` and `Finish` messages). The keys for generating and verifying σ correspond to the public keys transported in the certificates (this changes in the case of OPAQUE – see below). The goal of this authentication is not only to validate the identity of the peer but also to tie this peer to the specific connection (or handshake session) on which TLS-EA is executed and to the secure channel (record layer) established by this handshake. A party accepting a set of credentials via TLS-EA is linking these credentials to the party with whom it originally ran the handshake even if that party did not authenticate with these credentials during the handshake, and possibly did not authenticate during the handshake at all.

Linkage of an authentication to the handshake is obtained via a *channel binder* that in TLS-EA (and in our modeling in Sect. 4) is composed of two elements: a transcript digest (HSC) included under the signature σ and a MAC key (MK) used to produce the value mac. Key MK needs to have properties similar to a session key in a regular key exchange protocol. Informally, it can be seen in the derivation tree of Fig. 4 that MK is a descendant of the original key g^{xy} and is independent (via PRF derivations) from keys used elsewhere by the protocol such as ATS and HTS (exact requirements and proofs are provided in our extensive formal treatment in the following sections). What is less clear is why HSC qualifies as a handshake transcript digest. This property follows from the fact that EMS is computed as an output of a PRF computed on input the handshake's transcript tr, with the PRF instantiated by HKDF [20]. Hence EMS is the product of a chain of hashes computed on tr, and since none of these hash computations is truncated, this ensures that EMS is an output of a collision resistant function computed on tr. The digest property also applies to HSC which is derived from EMS using HKDF, hence as the output of a chain of collision resistant hashes.

The uncolored part of Fig. 5 shows the flows for the case where a client request is followed by a server response and then a server request is followed by a client response. Protocol TLS-OPAQUE adds the colored elements that transport OPAQUE messages inside the extension fields of TLS-EA. This includes OPAQUE's OPRF messages and the user's envelope transmitted from server to client. In this case, signature authentication uses the OPAQUE keys rather than the normal certificate-based keys of TLS. For the client, it uses the private key contained in the envelope and for the server it is the server's signing key stored at the server and whose corresponding public key is included in the envelope. Verification at the server uses the user's public key stored at the server.

Note on the Record Layer Protection of TLS-OPAQUE Messages. When the TLS-EA messages are transported over TLS's record layer, all the messages in Fig. 5 are protected by the record layer keys (derived from AEK). In our treatment we ignore this protection as TLS-EA does not mandate transmission within the channel[4]. Thus our results establish that TLS-EA and TLS-OPAQUE

---

[4] From [26]: "The application MAY use the existing TLS connection to transport the authenticator." The use of MAY makes this protected transport optional.

security does not depend on this protection. On the other hand, the addition of this layer of protection does not jeopardize security; this is so since AEK is derived from ATS which is (computationally) independent from any element used in TLS-EA. Indeed, the latter only uses keys derived from EMS which is a sibling of ATS in the derivation from MS, hence independent from AEK (formally, one can simulate the record layer encryption using a random independent ATS). Finally, we note that while not required for TLS-OPAQUE security, running TLS-OPAQUE over a protected record layer can provide privacy to user account information transmitted as part of the protocol.

3 Preliminaries

NOTATION. We denote by $x \leftarrow A$ the assigment of the outcome of A to variable x if A is an algorithm or a function. In case A is a set, $x \leftarrow A$ denotes that x is sampled uniformly at random from A.

OBLIVIOUS PSEUDORANDOM FUNCTIONS. An Oblivious Pseudorandom Function (OPRF) is a 2-party protocol between an evaluator and a server, where the evaluator contributes an input x and the server contributes a PRF key k. The outcome of the protocol is that the evaluator learns $\mathsf{PRF}_k(x)$ but nothing beyond, and the server learns nothing at all. OPRFs have been extensively used in password-based protocols, and they are also the main building block of the OPAQUE protocol [18]. We use a UC formalization of OPRFs by Jarecki et al. [18], modified regarding its output of transcripts which we now describe on a high level. The OPRF functionality of [18] has a (session-wise unique) "transcript prefix" prfx that the adversary contributes. If the view of both parties of this prefix match, the adversary cannot use the honest evaluation session anymore to evaluate the PRF himself (e.g., by modifying the transcript). For the purpose of analyzing TLS-OPAQUE, we introduce two changes to their functionality:

1. We add a "transcript postfix" pstfx, which is also determined by the adversary. prfx and pstfx together constitute the full transcript of the OPRF protocol. In particular, if the view of both parties on prfx and pstfx match, then the OPRF output computed by the evaluator is guaranteed to be correct.
2. We let the evaluator output prfx and require the sender to input prfx. Likewise, the sender outputs pstfx and the evaluator requires it as input to complete the evaluation. These changes are only syntactical since as outputs both prfx and pstfx are adversarially-determined, and as inputs both are leaked to the adversary. However, in TLS-OPAQUE the OPRF transcript is transported over EA messages, hence making it fully visible to the environment enables a modular usage of $\mathcal{F}_{\mathsf{OPRF}}$ in our analysis of TLS-OPAQUE.

Furthermore, our functionality $\mathcal{F}_{\mathsf{OPRF}}$ fixes an important omission in the OPRF functionality as written in [18]. Namely, if the adversary compromises server $\mathcal{P}_S$, the adversary gains the ability not only to offline evaluate the (O)PRF values, via interface Eval (as in [18]), but also to perform server-side operations in the online protocol instances, via interface SNDRCOMPLETE. Our functionality

$\mathcal{F}_{\mathsf{OPRF}}$ is shown in the full version of this paper [15], where we also present a slight modification of the 2HashDH protocol of [18] which UC-emulates our modified $\mathcal{F}_{\mathsf{OPRF}}$.

CORRUPTION MODEL. In this paper we consider two types of corruption. First, every party can be statically and maliciously corrupted by the adversary using standard "corrupt party $\mathcal{P}$" instructions that can be issued by the adversary in the UC model at the beginning of the protocol, against any party $\mathcal{P}$ [11]. This means that party $\mathcal{P}$ will be corrupted from its first activation on, and can deviate arbitrarily from the protocol code. Second, our functionalities $\mathcal{F}_{\mathsf{OPRF}}, \mathcal{F}_{\mathsf{PHA}}, \mathcal{F}_{\mathsf{pwPHA}}$ have a special type of corruption we call "compromise" (modeled, respectively, by adversarial interfaces COMPROMISE and STEALPWDFILE). If such corruption happens to a party which stores long-term protocol data, such as in our setting a server storing an OPRF key or password files, the adversary obtains the stored data. However, the server continues to follow the protocol honestly. Formally, a compromise is hence an adaptive but passive corruption.

4   Secure Channels with Binders

In this section we analyze the security of TLS 1.3 Handshake, Fig. 3 as a universally composable *unauthenticated* secure channel establishment protocol. The *Key Exchange* (KE) part of the TLS 1.3 Handshake generates a communication key which is subsequently used to implement a *secure channel*, i.e. the secure message transmission, and a *channel binder*, which can be subsequently used by TLS-EA and TLS-OPAQUE to bind post-execution authentication decisions to this secure channel.[5]

In Fig. 6 we show functionality $\mathcal{F}_{\mathsf{cbSC}}$ which models both parts, i.e. an (unauthenticated) secure channel establishment extended by outputting an (exported) channel binder, and a secure communication using this channel. The first part is implemented by interfaces NEWSESSION, ATTACK, and CONNECT, the second by interfaces SEND, DELIVER, and interface EXPIRESESSION allows any party to close the channel. Functionality $\mathcal{F}_{\mathsf{cbSC}}$ in Fig. 6 is a standard unauthenticated secure channel functionality (e.g., [12]), extended with a channel binder CB. We mark this extension with gray boxes. The channel binder CB is output to both channel endpoints. The code that determines CB is very similar to the way in which (unauthenticated) key exchange (KE) is modeled in UC [12]. Just like a session key created by KE, CB is a random bitstring if the adversary allows two parties to passively "connect" by transmitting the messages between them. However, if the adversary plays a man-in-the-middle, which is modeled by the

---

[5] TLS Handshake includes authentication, implemented by messages auth_S and auth_C in Fig. 3. However, as mentioned in footnote 3, we treat it as *unauthenticated* key exchange/secure channel establishment, because this allows us to show that the security of TLS-EA and TLS-OPAQUE is *independent* of the security of the initial authentication performed within the TLS 1.3 Handshake.

ATTACK interface, it can arbitrarily set the channel binder the attacked parties output, subject to it being unique among all channel binders output by honest parties. This is how channel binders differ from session keys: It makes no difference if $\mathcal{P}$ and $\mathcal{P}'$ use the same session key on two attacked sessions, because the adversary can anyway decrypt all messages sent by $\mathcal{P}$ and it can re-encrypt them so they are successfully received by $\mathcal{P}'$. On the contrary, any authentication action, whether via TLS-EA or TLS-OPAQUE done by $\mathcal{P}$ will pertain to its channel binder CB for that session, and because $\mathcal{F}_{cbSC}$ enforces that the channel binder output CB' of $\mathcal{P}'$ satisfies CB' $\neq$ CB, the signatures issued in protocols TLS-EA and TLS-OPAQUE protocols by $\mathcal{P}$ (cf. Fig. 5) are useless for creating signatures that can be accepted by $\mathcal{P}'$. In Fig. 5 the channel binder role is played by key EMS, and since value HSC$_C$ is derived from EMS using HKDF-Expand, which is both a PRF and a collision-resistant hash, if EMS $\neq$ EMS' then HSC$_C$ $\neq$ HSC$'_C$, and since HSC$_C$ is one of the signed fields, unforgeability of a signature implies that the signature σ_C issued by $\mathcal{P}$ is not useful in authenticating to $\mathcal{P}'$. In our analysis of TLS-HS below we will argue that it realizes functionality $\mathcal{F}_{cbSC}$ with CB implemented as EMS, see Fig. 6.

We refer the reader to the full version of this paper [15] for an explanation of $\mathcal{F}_{cbSC}$ interfaces.

4.1 TLS 1.3 as UC Secure Channel with Binder

We analyze TLS 1.3 as a realization of the ideal functionality $\mathcal{F}_{cbSC}$. In Fig. 7 we specify how TLS 1.3 implements $\mathcal{F}_{cbSC}$ commands NEWSESSION and SEND, used resp. to start a handshake, shown in Fig. 3, and to send a message on a secure channel established by it, and we show how parties form their outputs based on received network messages, resp. in FINALIZE which finalizes the handshake, and RECEIVED which stands for receiving a message on the channel.

The implementation in Fig. 7 follows the schematic protocol of Fig. 3 except for adding cid fields to the handshake messages, which model sender TCP port number. Also, in Fig. 7 for brevity we denote function HKDF-Extract used to derive the handshake secret HS from the Diffie-Hellman value g^{xy} as H, treated as a Random Oracle in the security analysis, and we shortcut the derivation of the Exporter Main Secret EMS (which is output as *channel binder*) and the traffic-encrypting keys AEK$_C$, AEK$_S$ from HS using key derivation function KDF^f(MS, tr) for flags $f \in \{0, 1, 2\}$, where KDF$^f(k, x)$ stands for KDF$(k, (x|f))$. The key derivation procedure in Fig. 3 can be rendered by setting each derived key in this way. Since function HKDF-Expand used in TLS 1.3 is implemented as HMAC, it implies that KDF is both a secure PRF and a collision-resistant hash on full input $(k, x|f)$ [20], and we use both properties in the security analysis. Finally, we emulate TLS message transport by implementing command (SEND, cid, m) of $\mathcal{P}$ as sending (cid', c) where cid' is the presumed counterparty channel identifier for session $(\mathcal{P}, \text{cid})$ and $c = $ AEnc(AEK$_\mathcal{P}$, (ctr, m)) where ctr is the current value of the counter for this traffic direction. (Note that each direction, $\mathcal{P}$-to-$\mathcal{P}'$ and $\mathcal{P}'$-to-$\mathcal{P}$, uses a separate key AEK and counter ctr.)

The security of TLS handshake and message transport is captured as follows:

The functionality talks to arbitrarily many parties $\mathfrak{P} = \{\mathcal{P}, \mathcal{P}', ...\}$ and to the adversary $\mathcal{A}$. It maintains list CBset of all created channel binders.

Channel establishment

On (NEWSESSION, cid, $\mathcal{P}'$, role) from party $\mathcal{P}$:
[N.1] If role $\in \{\text{clt}, \text{srv}\}$ and $\nexists$ record (SESSION, $\mathcal{P}$, cid, $*$) then create record (SESSION, $\mathcal{P}$, cid, role) labeled wait and send (NEWSESSION, $\mathcal{P}$, cid, $\mathcal{P}'$, role) to $\mathcal{A}$.

On (ATTACK, $\mathcal{P}$, cid, cid*, CB*) from $\mathcal{A}$:
[A.1] If $\exists$ record (SESSION, $\mathcal{P}$, cid, role) labeled wait and CB$^* \notin$ CBset then add CB* to CBset , re-label this record att, and send (FINALIZE, cid, cid*, role, CB*) to $\mathcal{P}$.

On (CONNECT, $\mathcal{P}$, cid, $\mathcal{P}'$, cid$'$, cid*, CB*) from $\mathcal{A}$, if $\exists$ record (SESSION, $\mathcal{P}$, cid, role) labeled wait:
[C.1] If $\exists$ rec. (SESSION, $\mathcal{P}'$, cid$'$, role$'$) labeled conn($\mathcal{P}$, cid) s.t. role$' \neq$ role
    [C.1.1] then set CB $\leftarrow$ CB$'$ for CB$'$ used in message (FINALIZE, cid$'$, cid, role$'$, CB$'$) sent formerly to $\mathcal{P}'$;
    [C.1.2] otherwise:
        [C.1.2.1] If $\mathcal{P}$ honest and ($\mathcal{P}'$ honest $\vee$ $\mathcal{P}' = \bot$) then CB $\leftarrow \{0,1\}^\lambda$;
        [C.1.2.2] If $\mathcal{P}$ or $\mathcal{P}'$ is corrupted and CB$^* \notin$ CBset then CB $\leftarrow$ CB* (if CB$^* \in$ CBset then drop this query);
[C.2] Initialize an empty queue QUEUE($\mathcal{P}$, cid, $\mathcal{P}'$, cid$'$), re-label record (SESSION, $\mathcal{P}$, cid, role) as conn($\mathcal{P}'$, cid$'$), add CB to CBset, and send (FINALIZE, cid, cid*, role, CB) to $\mathcal{P}$.

Using the channel

On (SEND, cid, m) from party $\mathcal{P}$, if $\exists$ record (SESSION, $\mathcal{P}$, cid, role) marked flag then:
[S.1] If flag = att send (SEND, $\mathcal{P}$, cid, m) to $\mathcal{A}$;
[S.2] If flag = conn($\mathcal{P}'$, cid$'$) add m to the back of queue QUEUE($\mathcal{P}$, cid, $\mathcal{P}'$, cid$'$) and send (SEND, $\mathcal{P}$, cid, $|m|$) to $\mathcal{A}$;
[S.3] If flag $\in \{\text{wait}, \text{exp}\}$ ignore this query.

On (DELIVER, $\mathcal{P}'$, cid$'$, m^*) from $\mathcal{A}$, if $\exists$ record (SESSION, $\mathcal{P}'$, cid$'$, role$'$) marked flag then:
[D.1] If flag = att send (RECEIVED, cid$'$, m^*) to $\mathcal{P}'$;
[D.2] If flag = conn($\mathcal{P}$, cid) remove m from the front of QUEUE($\mathcal{P}$, cid, $\mathcal{P}'$, cid$'$) (ignore this query if this queue does not exist or is empty) and send (RECEIVED, cid$'$, m) to $\mathcal{P}'$;
[D.3] If flag $\in \{\text{wait}, \text{exp}\}$ ignore this query.

On (EXPIRESESSION, cid) from $\mathcal{P}$, if $\exists$ record (SESSION, $\mathcal{P}$, cid, role):
[E.1] label it exp and send (EXPIRESESSION, $\mathcal{P}$, cid) to $\mathcal{A}$.

Fig. 6. Secure channel functionality $\mathcal{F}_{\text{cbSC}}$. Without gray parts, the functionality implements secure unauthenticated channels. The gray parts provide both ends of a channel with a high-entropy unique "channel binder" CB that can be used for, e.g., subsequent authentication.

Theorem 1 (Security of TLS as unauthenticated secure channel). *TLS 1.3 handshake and message transport protocol specified in Fig. 7 UC-emulates functionality $\mathcal{F}_{\text{cbSC}}$ in the $\mathcal{F}_{\text{RO}}$-hybrid model, with H modeled as random oracle, if function KDF is both a PRF and a CRH, AEnc is CUF-CCA secure, and the Gap CDH assumption holds on group $\langle g \rangle$, assuming static malicious corruptions.*

We refer to the full version of this work [15] for the cryptographic assumptions in this theorem, and for its full proof. Sketching it briefly, we exhibit simulator $\mathcal{S}$ which sends $Z_i = g^{z_i}$ for random z_i on behalf of each session $i = (\mathcal{P}, \text{cid})$, hence it can predict its outputs in case of active attacks, but if two honest parties are passively connected $\mathcal{S}$ picks a random key AEK (which it uses to emulate secure channel communication) while $\mathcal{F}_{\text{cbSC}}$ picks channel binder EMS independently at random. Since in the protocol AEK and EMS are derived via KDF from HS = H(K) for $K = g^{z_i * z_j}$, computing this value given passively observed values $Z_i = g^{z_i}$ and $Z_j = g^{z_j}$ is related to breaking Diffie-Hellman. By

---

parameters: group $\langle g \rangle$ of order p, sec. par. λ, hash H onto $\{0,1\}^\lambda$

Party $\mathcal{P}$ on input (NEWSESSION, $\text{cid}_C, \mathcal{P}', \text{clt}$) [here $\mathcal{P}$ is a Client]:
- Pick $\text{rand}_C \leftarrow \{0,1\}^\lambda$, $x \leftarrow \mathbb{Z}_p$, send ($\text{cid}_C, \text{rand}_C, g^x$) to $\mathcal{P}'$;
- On receiving network message ($\text{cid}'_S, \text{rand}'_S, Y'$),
  - set $K \leftarrow (Y')^x$, HS $\leftarrow$ H(K), tr $\leftarrow$ ($\text{rand}_C, g^x, \text{rand}'_S, Y'$),
  - EMS $\leftarrow$ KDF^0(HS, tr), AEK$_C \leftarrow$ KDF^1(HS, tr), AEK$_S \leftarrow$ KDF^2(HS, tr),
  - save ($\text{cid}_C, \mathcal{P}', \text{cid}'_S, \text{AEK}_C, \text{AEK}_S, 0, 0$),
  - output (FINALIZE, $\text{cid}_C, \text{cid}'_S, \text{clt}, \text{EMS}$).

Party $\mathcal{P}$ on input (NEWSESSION, $\text{cid}_S, \mathcal{P}', \text{srv}$) [here $\mathcal{P}$ is a Server]:
- On receiving network message ($\text{cid}'_C, \text{rand}'_C, X'$),
  - pick $\text{rand}_S \leftarrow \{0,1\}^\lambda$, $y \leftarrow \mathbb{Z}_p$, send ($\text{cid}_S, \text{rand}_S, g^y$) to $\mathcal{P}'$,
  - set $K \leftarrow (X')^y$, HS $\leftarrow$ H(K), tr $\leftarrow$ ($\text{rand}'_C, X', \text{rand}_S, g^y$),
  - EMS $\leftarrow$ KDF^0(HS, tr), AEK$_C \leftarrow$ KDF^1(HS, tr), AEK$_S \leftarrow$ KDF^2(HS, tr),
  - save ($\text{cid}_S, \mathcal{P}', \text{cid}'_C, \text{AEK}_S, \text{AEK}_C, 0, 0$),
  - output (FINALIZE, $\text{cid}_S, \text{cid}'_C, \text{srv}, \text{EMS}$).

Party $\mathcal{P}$ on local input (SEND, cid, m):
- Retrieve (cid, $\mathcal{P}', \text{cid}', \text{AEK}, \text{AEK}', \text{ctr}, \text{ctr}'$) (abort if it is not found),
  - send (cid$'$, AEnc(AEK, (ctr, m))) to $\mathcal{P}'$ and increment ctr.

Party $\mathcal{P}$ on network message (cid$'$, c):
- Retrieve (cid, $\mathcal{P}', \text{cid}', \text{AEK}, \text{AEK}', \text{ctr}, \text{ctr}'$) (abort if it is not found),
  - (ctr*, m) $\leftarrow$ ADec(AEK$'$, c), abort if output doesn't parse as such pair
  - if ctr* = ctr$'$ then output (RECEIVED, cid, m) and increment ctr$'$.

Party $\mathcal{P}$ on input (EXPIRESESSION, cid):
- Erase record (cid, $\mathcal{P}', \text{cid}', \text{AEK}, \text{AEK}', \text{ctr}, \text{ctr}'$).

Fig. 7. TLS 1.3 as realization of functionality $\mathcal{F}_{\text{cbSC}}$

hybridizing over all sessions, and guessing the identity of a passively connected counterparty and the H query which computes the key, it is possible that one could base security on a standard computational DH assumption, albeit with very loose security reduction. Instead, we show a tight reduction to the gap version of the Square DH assumption (which is equivalent to Gap CDH). The reduction embeds a randomization of a single SqDH challenge into all Z_i values, and uses the DDH oracle to detect hash queries H(K) for $K = \text{DH}(Z'_i, Z'_j)$ into which it can either embed a chosen key HS, if one of Z'_i, Z'_j is adversarial, or which it can map to the SqDH challenge, if both Z'_i and Z'_j come from honest parties.

5 Post-Handshake Authentication

In this Section we provide a model for post-handshake authentication (PHA), that is, a secure channel that allows for *later* public key authentication of the channel endpoints *after* already establishing the (unauthenticated) channel. As a side product, we will prove security of "real-world" TLS-EA. Namely, we demonstrate that Exported Authenticators is a secure post-handshake authentication protocol.

5.1 Post-Handshake Authentication Model

Figure 8 shows a UC model $\mathcal{F}_{\text{PHA}}$ for post-handshake authentication, which allows establishing an *unauthenticated* secure channel between any two parties,

The functionality talks to arbitrarily many parties $\mathfrak{P} = \{\mathcal{P}, \mathcal{P}', ...\}$ and to the adversary $\mathcal{A}$. It maintains lists pkReg (all registered public keys), pkComp (all compromised keys), pkey[pid] (standard public keys generated by party pid), keReg (all key envelopes) and an array tkey[aux, h] associating transportable keys with handle h and auxiliary information aux.

Channel establishment and Use

[C.1] NEWSESSION, ATTACK, CONNECT, SEND, DELIVER, and EXPIRESESSION, as in $\mathcal{F}_{cbSC}$, Figure 6, but without gray parts.

Key Generation and Corruption

On (KEYGEN, kid, ak, aux, mode) from pid $\in \mathfrak{P} \cup \{\mathcal{A}\}$:

[G.1] Send (KEYGEN, kid, pid, aux, mode) to $\mathcal{A}$ and receive back (kid, ske, pk).

[G.2] If (pid $\neq \mathcal{A} \wedge$ pk $\in$ pkReg), or if (mode = tk $\wedge$ ske $\in$ keReg) then abort;

[G.3] Else,
  - If mode = std then add pk to pkey[pid];
  - If mode = tk then set tkey[ak, ske] $\leftarrow$ (aux, pk);
  - Add pk to pkReg, and if pid = $\mathcal{A}$ then also add pk to pkComp;
  - Finally, output (KEY, kid, ak, ske, aux, pk) to party pid.

On (COMPROMISE, $\mathcal{P}$) from $\mathcal{A}$ *(requires permission from $\mathcal{Z}$)*:
  - Add pkey[$\mathcal{P}$] to pkComp.

On (GETAUXDATA, ak, ske) from pid $\in \mathfrak{P} \cup \{\mathcal{A}\}$:

[T.1] If pid = $\mathcal{A}$ then parse $(*, pk) \leftarrow$ tkey[ak, ske] and add pk to pkComp;

[T.2] Output tkey[ak, ske] to pid;

Active Attack

On (ACTIVEATTACK, $\mathcal{P}$, cid, ssid, ctx*, pk*) from $\mathcal{A}$

[A.1] If $\exists$ record (SESSION, $\mathcal{P}$, cid, role) marked att, or $\exists$ record (SESSION, $\mathcal{P}$, cid, role) marked conn($\mathcal{P}'$, cid') with $\mathcal{P}'$ corrupt, then do:
  - If pk* $\notin$ pkReg \ pkComp then record (AUTH, ε, ε, $\mathcal{P}$, cid, ssid, ctx*, pk*).

[A.2] Output (AUTHSEND, cid', ssid) to $\mathcal{P}'$.

Unilateral Public-Key Authentication

On (AUTHSEND, $\mathcal{P}'$, cid, ssid, ctx, ak, ske, pk, mode) from $\mathcal{P}$:

[S.1] If mode = tk and tkey[ak, ske] is not defined then send (ssid, ak, ske) to $\mathcal{A}$ and receive back activation;

[S.2] If $\exists$ record (SESSION, $\mathcal{P}$, cid, role) marked conn($\mathcal{P}'$, cid') then initialize $b \leftarrow 0$ and:
  - If mode = std and [S.2.1] pk $\in$ pkey[$\mathcal{P}$] then set $b \leftarrow 1$;
  - If mode = tk and tkey[ak, ske] = $(*, pk')$ then set pk $\leftarrow$ pk' and $b \leftarrow 1$.
  - If $b = 1$ then record (AUTH, $\mathcal{P}$, cid, $\mathcal{P}'$, cid', ssid, ctx, pk)

[S.3] Send (AUTHSEND, $\mathcal{P}$, $\mathcal{P}'$, cid, ssid, ctx, pk, mode, b) to $\mathcal{A}$ and receive back activation.

[S.4] Output (AUTHSEND, cid', ssid) to $\mathcal{P}'$.

On (AUTHVERIFY, cid', ssid, ctx, pk) from $\mathcal{P}'$

[V.1] Send (AUTHVERIFY, $\mathcal{P}'$, cid', ssid, ctx, pk) to $\mathcal{A}$ and receive back flag f.

[V.2] If $f = 1$ and $\exists$ record (AUTH, *, *, $\mathcal{P}'$, cid', ssid, ctx, pk) then $b \leftarrow 1$ else $b \leftarrow 0$;

[V.3] Send (AUTHVERIFY, cid', ssid, b) to $\mathcal{P}'$.

Fig. 8. $\mathcal{F}_{PHA}$ model for post-handshake authentication, which allows for public key authentication on an already existing unauthenticated channel. $\mathcal{F}_{PHA}$ offers mode = std key generation as used by, e.g., EA, as well as *transportable-key* mode tk, which makes $\mathcal{F}_{PHA}$ a useful modular building block for, e.g., TLS-OPAQUE. For brevity we omit the overall session identifier from all interfaces.

and then performing subsequent authentication of that channel with public keys. On a very high level, $\mathcal{F}_{\mathsf{PHA}}$ provides the following guarantees:

- **Unforgeability:** Eve cannot authenticate to Bob under Alice's public key;
- **Channel binding:** Eve cannot authenticate (even with her own keys) on channels that she is not an endpoint of.

AN HONEST WALK-THROUGH. We exemplarily describe channel establishment and authentication for two parties C and S, with C authenticating to S. We ask the reader to ignore fields mode, ak, ske of $\mathcal{F}_{\mathsf{PHA}}$ for the sake of this walk-through; an explanation of these special fields follows further below.

$\mathcal{F}_{\mathsf{PHA}}$ inherits [C.1] all channel interfaces of $\mathcal{F}_{\mathsf{cbSC}}$, but without channel binder CB, implementing secure but unauthenticated channels. Both C and S call NEWSESSION of $\mathcal{F}_{\mathsf{PHA}}$ to establish a channel. Let us assume that the adversary decides to connect their requests. Both parties receive a FINALIZE notification and learn the channel identifier $\mathsf{cid}_C/\mathsf{cid}_S$ under which the other endpoint knows the channel. We note however that neither C nor S learn with whom they actually got connected. The established channel can be used to send messages securely.

To tell his peer on channel cid_C who he is actually connected to, C first generates a key by querying $\mathcal{F}_{\mathsf{PHA}}$ with (KEYGEN, kid, ε, ε, std), resulting in output (KEY, kid, ε, ε, ε, pk) with [G.1] adversarially-chosen but [G.2] fresh pk. kid denotes a non-secret identifier which helps C managing her public keys. ε denotes an empty string – these fields are only used in a special mode of $\mathcal{F}_{\mathsf{PHA}}$ called *transportable key mode* (mode = tk, see explanation further below). For this walkthrough, we use standard key generation (mode = std). $\mathcal{F}_{\mathsf{PHA}}$ adds pk to [G.3] lists pkReg and pkey[C]. pkReg contains all public keys generated through $\mathcal{F}_{\mathsf{PHA}}$ (in any mode). pkey[C] is a list containing all standard public keys that C generated through $\mathcal{F}_{\mathsf{PHA}}$, and which C can use for authenticating on her channels.

Now that C has created pk, C wants to use pk to authenticate to S on channel cid_C. To do so, C queries (AUTHSEND, S, cid_C, ssid, ctx, ε, ε, pk, std). ctx denotes optional auxiliary public context information that C wants to transmit alongside the authentication request. If [S.2.1] C is allowed to authenticate under pk, $\mathcal{F}_{\mathsf{PHA}}$ records (AUTH, C, cid_C, S, cid_S, ssid, ctx, pk), representing the fact that C successfully performed authentication under pk in this channel. $\mathcal{F}_{\mathsf{PHA}}$ then informs the adversary about the authentication attempt, including all its data and whether authentication was successful (the bit b).

To receive the result of C's authentication, the receiver S has to choose a public key and a context for verification. This data is contributed by S via interface AUTHVERIFY, allowing applications to actively choose under which public key and context verification should be performed. Hence, we assume these public values to be transmitted by the application. In case the verifier wants to perform verification under the same pk and ctx that C performed the authentication with, $\mathcal{F}_{\mathsf{PHA}}$ [V.2] outputs success.

TRANSPORTABLE KEY MODE. $\mathcal{F}_{PHA}$ as described above binds usage of pk to S, the party who generated pk via interface KEYGEN. This is however not realistic in dynamic settings, where, e.g., S transfers her keys to another machine in encrypted form. A concrete example is OPAQUE, where secret keys are encrypted and the resulting envelopes are sent to the server, who then stores them. In order to enable a modular analysis of such "key-handling" protocols, we introduce the notion of *transportable keys* to the UC framework, and to our $\mathcal{F}_{PHA}$. When generating a transportable key by querying (KEYGEN, kid, ak, aux, tk), a party provides a key identifier kid, an *application key* ak and an optional label aux. $\mathcal{F}_{PHA}$ keeps the application key secret but [G.1] leaks all other values to the adversary. The requesting party then receives back [G.1] adversarially-generated *key envelope* ske and public key pk. One can think of these values as ske being an encryption of sk belonging to pk, encrypted symmetrically with key ak. $\mathcal{F}_{PHA}$ stores (aux, pk) in tkey[ak, ske]. The semantics of the tkey array are as follows: whoever provides input i, where tkey[i] = (aux, pk), can authenticate under pk (see below), and [T.2] retrieve label aux and public key pk via interface GETAUXDATA. Hence, knowledge of both application key ak and envelope ske will be sufficient to authenticate under pk. Since the requesting party outputs ske, ske can be used by applications which require secret keys to be objects that can be sent around, stored, further encrypted etc.

To authenticate with transportable keys, S calls AUTHSEND with inputs ak, ske and mode = tk. In case [S.1] ak, ske are not known to $\mathcal{F}_{PHA}$ (i.e., tkey[ak, ske] does not store any pk), no security is guaranteed and the adversary obtains ak, ske. $\mathcal{F}_{PHA}$ then [S.2] checks again whether tkey[ak, ske] stores pk, and if so, it grants authentication by creating the corresponding AUTH record including pk, and notifies the adversary about the authentication attempt, including all its data and whether authentication was successful (bit b). We note that the double check of tkey[ak, ske] is necessary since the adversary could have registered ak, ske in between both checks.

ADVERSARIAL INTERFACES. The adversary $\mathcal{A}$ can register both std and tk keys via interface KEYGEN. $\mathcal{F}_{PHA}$ adds such compromised keys to set pkComp. For transportable keys ak, ske, the adversary can also reveal which public key they "work for", by querying (GETAUXDATA, ak, ske). $\mathcal{F}_{PHA}$ returns [T.2] (aux, pk) = tkey[ak, ske] (or $\perp$ if empty) and [T.1] adds pk to pkComp, accounting for $\mathcal{A}$ now knowing transportable keys for pk. Altogether, in pkComp we find all keys generated in any mode by $\mathcal{F}_{PHA}$ that are compromised: the adversary can authenticate with these keys (as well as unknown keys $\notin$ pkReg) on his channels [A.1] using the ACTIVEATTACK interface. $\mathcal{A}$ can always make authentication fail by [V.1-2] sending $f = 0$ in its AUTHVERIFY query to $\mathcal{F}_{PHA}$. Regarding leakage, $\mathcal{A}$ learns all inputs of AUTHSEND except for uncompromised transportable keys ak, ske, as well as public verification values pk, ctx. With such a strong adversary, $\mathcal{F}_{PHA}$ guarantees that an authentication mechanism does not rely on the secrecy of messages.

ON USAGE OF PARTY IDENTIFIERS. Our modeling of PHA, just as our modeling of unauthenticated channels in Sect. 4, does not provide any initial guarantees about the identity of a peer. Hence, throughout this paper, party identifiers are interpreted only as process identifiers. For example, pid could be a unique combination of IP address and port, and we make only the minimal assumption that it is always the same process sending from this addresses' port. Consequently, party identifiers are used by functionalities only to determine which messages were generated by the same process. In protocol instructions, sending a message requires specification of an intended recipient, and hence we add the intended recipient to input AUTHSEND of $\mathcal{F}_{\mathsf{PHA}}$. However, since our modeling of unauthenticated channels is weak in the sense that parties are oblivious of which process (i.e., which pid) their channel actually got connected to, the intended recipient might not coincide with the process holding the other end of the channel. By this we capture an authentication-less setting with a network adversary who is freely rerouting/rewriting messages. Consequently, $\mathcal{F}_{\mathsf{PHA}}$ overlooks any mismatch in a party's perception and instead bases authentication decisions for a specific channel and pk solely on whether an endpoint (=pid) is eligible to authenticate under pk.

5.2   The Exported Authenticators Protocol

The EA protocol that we consider for our analysis is depicted in Fig. 9. It generalizes Exported Authenticators as specified in Sect. 2 in several aspects:

1. Π_{EA} abstracts from the channel establishment and can provide post-handshake authentication for any "handshake" protocol that securely instantiates $\mathcal{F}_{\mathsf{cbSC}}$
2. Π_{EA} works with standard signature keys and *transportable* keys (see below), which enable Π_{EA} to use key material provided by an application
3. Π_{EA} does not hash messages before signing/mac'ing
4. Π_{EA} sends messages in the clear instead of sending them over the channel-to-authenticate
5. Public key and context are verification is provided by the application instead of being sent by the authenticator
6. Fields EACert and extensions ext are subsumed in the ctx object, about which no further assumptions are made

In Π_{EA}, parties can establish channels by calling $\mathcal{F}_{\mathsf{cbSC}}$. If the channel is finalized, the endpoints share a unique channel binder EMS (cf. Sect. 4 for details). The endpoints, let's call them C and S, then derive transcript digest and MAC keys $\mathsf{MK}_C, \mathsf{MK}_S, \mathsf{HSC}_C, \mathsf{HSC}_S$ from EMS. We note that this is the only place in this paper where the roles clt, srv have an effect: these are roles that parties have in some application, such as TLS, and they help us here to derive different digest and MAC key for C and S from public labels $\mathsf{lbl}_{\mathsf{MK,clt}}, \mathsf{lbl}_{\mathsf{MK,srv}}, \mathsf{lbl}_{\mathsf{HSC,clt}}, \mathsf{lbl}_{\mathsf{HSC,srv}}$ that reflect these roles.

Π_{EA} is a multi-party protocol that allows arbitrary parties to establish channels with each other, allows unlimited generation of keys and unlimited numbers of unilateral authentication sessions per channel. We exemplarily describe such

118   J. Hesse et al.

Fig. 9. Protocol Π_{EA} is a unidirectional post-handshake authentication of channel binder EMS provided by hybrid functionality $\mathcal{F}_{cbSC}$. We depict a C-to-S authentication flow with either $\mathtt{std}$ key mode or transportable key mode $\mathtt{tk}$. For brevity we omit the functionality's identifier sid from all queries and messages.

an authentication performed by C for a channel with S as depicted in Fig. 9. We start with standard signing keys and for now ignore the gray parts of the figure. Upon input $(\text{KEYGEN}, \mathtt{kid}, \mathtt{ak}, \mathtt{aux}, \mathtt{std})$, C generates a key pair $(\mathtt{sk}, \mathtt{pk})$ by running the key generation of the signature scheme (values $\mathtt{ak}, \mathtt{aux}$ are ignored in normal mode), and outputs $\mathtt{pk}$ to the application. When C wants to authenticate on her channel $\mathtt{cid}_C$, she looks up[6] identifier $\mathtt{cid}_S$ in the FINALIZE output

---

[6] We assume C to learn this information as otherwise, when sending messages over plain connections, we would have no mean of informing S which channel the authentication is intended for. This can be avoided by instead sending messages *over* the secure channel.

of $\mathcal{F}_{cbSC}$, and signs message $(\mathsf{HSC}_C, \mathsf{ssid}, \mathsf{ctx})$ with sk, where ssid is the EA nonce and ctx is the EACert field (containing identity information such as, e.g., a certificate) that C wants to convey. Then C macs the message together with the signature under mac key MK_C. C then sends all values to S, who accepts or rejects depending on whether signature and mac verify for $\mathsf{HSC}_C, \mathsf{MK}_C$ that S computes from channel binder EMS for her channel cid_S.

INSTANTIATING TRANSPORTABLE KEYS. A transportable key is a protected secret key, also called *envelope* throughout the paper. One can think of an envelope as, e.g., an encryption of the secret key. Π_{EA} allows parties to export such envelopes to the application. Since this way envelopes can "travel" to other parties who can then attempt to extract the secret key from them, transportable keys can be used by any party who possesses both the envelope and whatever is required to unlock the secret key from it. A transportable key requires a signature key pair $(\mathsf{pk}, \mathsf{sk}) \leftarrow \mathsf{KG}(1^\lambda)$. Then, an encryption key k is generated as $k \leftarrow \mathsf{H}(\mathsf{ak}, \mathsf{nonce})$, where ak is an *application key*, and H hashes to the key space of a symmetric cipher. The envelope is then $\mathsf{ske} \leftarrow (\mathsf{nonce}, \mathsf{ae})$, where ae is an encryption of $\mathsf{aux}, \mathsf{sk}$ under k, for auxiliar information (e.g., a label) aux. Obviously, the application key ak is enough to decrypt sk from envelope ske. Hence, the authentication step in Π_{EA} can alternatively be conducted by an authenticator C running on inputs $\mathsf{ak}, \mathsf{ske}, \mathsf{pk}$ (cf. gray parts in Fig. 9): before signing and mac'ing, C first recovers sk from $\mathsf{ak}, \mathsf{ske}$.

This concludes our description of Π_{EA}, and we are ready to state its security. We refer to the full version [15] for the formal definitions of the cryptographic assumptions within the Theorem and for the full proof.

Theorem 2 (Security of Π_{EA}). *Protocol Π_{EA} depicted in Fig. 9 UC-emulates functionality $\mathcal{F}_{\mathsf{PHA}}$ in the $(\mathcal{F}_{\mathsf{RO}}, \mathcal{F}_{cbSC})$-hybrid model, PRF is both a secure PRF and a collision-resistant hash function, with H modeled as random oracle, (KG, PKGen, Sign, Vfy) a perfectly complete and EUF-CMA-secure signature scheme, MAC is perfectly complete and EUF-CMA-secure MAC, and (AEnc, ADec) a CUF-CCA- and RKR-secure encryption scheme that is equivocable, and restriction to static malicious corruptions and adaptive server compromise.*

There are 6 discrepancies described above between Π_{EA} and EA as described in Sect. 2. As already argued in Sect. 1, (4) does not void security, and neither does hashing (3). (1), (2), (5), (6) are strict generalizations of the Exported Authenticators protocol. Hence, the security of TLS-EA follows from the security of Π_{EA}, with $\mathcal{F}_{cbSC}$ instantiated with the TLS-HS through the standard UC composition theorem [11].

Corollary 1. *Protocol TLS-EA specified in Sect. 2 securely realizes $\mathcal{F}_{\mathsf{PHA}}$.*

6 Security of TLS-OPAQUE

6.1 Password-Based Post-Handshake Authentication

We give a model $\mathcal{F}_{\mathsf{pwPHA}}$ for password-based post-handshake authentication in Fig. 10. On a high level, $\mathcal{F}_{\mathsf{pwPHA}}$ guarantees the following:

- **Limitation to one guess per online attack:** Each run of the protocol reveals at most one bit of information about the opponent's password to each participant;
- **Resistance to offline attacks:** Dictionary attacks on passwords are prevented unless a server is compromised;
- **Resistance to precomputation attack:** An attacker cannot speed up dictionary attacks through computation performed prior to server compromise;
- **Enable rate limiting:** Servers can map login attempts to registered user accounts;
- **Channel binding:** One cannot authenticate (even with correct password) on channels one is not an endpoint of;

We explain how the functionality can be used by a client C and server S to first establish an unauthenticated channel, and then subsequently authenticate to each other using a password (client) and password file (server). We emphasize how $\mathcal{F}_{pwPHA}$ enforces the above guarantees alongside our explanation. To start, the client registers [F.1] with the server by storing some password-dependent information (called *password file*), under some user name uid. This results in $\mathcal{F}_{pwPHA}$ registering that a file with uid, pw was stored at S, by [C.1] installing record FILE. This process can be stopped by the adversary by not sending STOREPWDCOMPLETE, allowing analysis of protocols with interactive registration phase and without guaranteed delivery of messages.

Parties C and S can establish an unauthenticated channel by calling $\mathcal{F}_{pwPHA}$'s NEWSESSION interface. See Sect. 4 or description of $\mathcal{F}_{PHA}$ in Sect. 5.1 for more details. We note that registration and channel establishment do not rely on each other and can thus be performed in arbitrary order.

Having concluded registration and channel establishment, parties connected via a channel can now authenticate to each other using password (client) and file (server). Password authentication is always initialized by the client calling PWINIT with credential uid, pw. The client also specifies the channel to authenticate, cid_C, and intended recipient S. Similar to our modeling of EA, $\mathcal{F}_{pwPHA}$ ignores intended recipients and instead [In.4] refers to (SESSION, *, *) records to figure out who the end points of a channel are. Assuming that C's channel cid_C is with S, $\mathcal{F}_{pwPHA}$ [In.4] stores a record (PWAUTH, ssid, C, cid_C, S, cid_S, uid, pw, init, 0) and [In.5] notifies S of the authentication session, the channel and the uid, where disclosure of the uid **enables rate-limiting**. This record reflects initiator and responder roles by order of mention. Having been notified, S can now either accept or decline to participate by calling PWPROCEED for said session. An application can hence apply rate-limiting policies, such as "at most 5 authentication attempts for uid per minutes" by calling PWPROCEED in a policy-conforming way. PWPROCEED will only move authentication forward [P.3] if there is a file stored for S and uid: if the password in that file matches pw, then the state of the PWAUTH record is rewritten to `match`, otherwise it is rewritten to `fail`. It is instructive to see that $\mathcal{F}_{pwPHA}$ bases this decision on password data *held by corresponding channel endpoints* [In.4], ensuring that authentication can only be

The functionality talks to arbitrarily many parties $\mathfrak{P} = \{P, P', ...\}$ and to the adversary $\mathcal{A}$. It maintains counters ctr[P, uid] initially set to 0.

Channel establishment and Use

NewSession, Attack, Connect, Send, Deliver, and ExpireSession, *as in* $\mathcal{F}_{cbSC}$, *Figure 6, but without gray parts.*

Password Registration, Compromise, and Offline Dictionary Attack

On (StorePwdFile, ssid, P, uid, pw,) from P':
[F.1] If $\nexists$ record (Store, P, ssid, $\cdot$, $\cdot$), record (Store, P, ssid, uid, pw) and send (Store, P', ssid, P, uid) to $\mathcal{A}$.

On (StorePwdComplete, P^*, ssid) from $\mathcal{A}$:
[C.1] If $\exists$ record (Store, $*$, ssid, uid, pw) but $\nexists$ record (File, P^*, uid, $\cdot$) then record (File, P^*, uid, pw) and mark it **uncompromised**.

On (StealPwdFile, P, uid) from $\mathcal{A}$ *(requires permission from $\mathcal{Z}$)*:
[S.1] If $\nexists$ record (File, P, uid, pw), return "no file" to $\mathcal{A}$;
[S.2] Else mark this record **compromised** and return "file stolen".

On (OfflTestPwd, P, uid, pw') from $\mathcal{A}$ *(requires permission from $\mathcal{Z}$)*:
[O.1] If $\exists$ record (File, P, uid, pw) marked **compromised** then return "correct guess" if pw = pw' and "wrong guess" if pw $\neq$ pw'.

Active Attacks

On (ActiveAttack, ssid', P, cid, uid) from $\mathcal{A}$:
[A.1] If $\exists$ record (session, P, cid) marked att, or if $\exists$ record (session, P', cid') marked conn(P, cid) where P' is corrupted, then create record (pwAuth, ssid', $\mathcal{A}$, ε, P, cid, uid, ε, init, 0)
[A.2] Output (pwInit, ssid', cid, uid) to P.

On (TestPwd, P, uid, pw') from $\mathcal{A}$:
[T.1] If $\exists$ record (File, P, uid, pw) and ctr[P, uid] > 0 then do:
    [T.1.1] If pw = pw' then return "correct guess" and rewrite init to match in all records (pwAuth, $*$, $\mathcal{A}$, ε, P, $*$, uid, ε, init, 0);
    [T.1.2] If pw $\neq$ pw' then return "wrong guess";
    [T.1.2] Set ctr[P, uid] $--$.

On (Impersonate, ssid', P, uid, pw*) from $\mathcal{A}$:
[Im.1] If pw* = ε and $\exists$ record (File, P, uid, pw') marked **compromised** and record (pwAuth, $*$, $*$, $\mathcal{A}$, ε, uid, pw, init, 0), if pw = pw' overwrite init with match and reply with "correct guess", otherwise overwrite init with fail and reply with "wrong guess";
[Im.2] If pw* $\neq$ ε and $\exists$ record (pwAuth, ssid', $*$, $*$, $\mathcal{A}$, ε, uid, pw, init, 0), if pw = pw* then overwrite init with match and reply with "correct guess", otherwise overwrite init with fail and reply with "wrong guess".

Asymmetric Password Authentication

On (pwInit, P'', cid, ssid', uid, pw) from $P \in \mathfrak{P}$:
[In.1] Drop the query if it is not the first one for ssid';
[In.2] Send (pwInit, P, P'', cid, ssid', uid) to $\mathcal{A}$ and receive back (pwInit, P, P'', cid, ssid', uid, ok);
[In.3] If $\exists$ record (session, P, cid) marked att, create record (pwAuth, ssid', P, cid, $\mathcal{A}$, ε, uid, pw, init, 0), set $P'' \leftarrow \mathcal{A}$;
[In.4] If $\exists$ record (session, P, cid) marked conn(P', cid') create record (pwAuth, ssid', P, cid, P', cid', uid, pw, init, 0), set $P'' \leftarrow P'$, cid $\leftarrow$ cid';
[In.5] Output (pwInit, cid, ssid', uid) to P''

On (pwProceed, ssid') from P:
[P.1] Send (pwProceed, P, cid, ssid', uid) to $\mathcal{A}$;
[P.2] If $\exists$ record (pwAuth, ssid', $\mathcal{A}$, ε, P, $*$, uid, ε, init, 0) then set ctr[P, uid] $++$;
[P.3] If $\exists$ records (pwAuth, ssid', $*$, $*$, P, $*$, uid, pw, init, 0) with pw $\neq$ ε and (File, P, uid, pw'), then overwrite init with match if pw = pw' and with fail otherwise.

On (pwDeliver, ssid', P, b) from $\mathcal{A}$
[D.1] If $b = 0$ output (pwDecision, ssid', fail) to P.
[D.2] Find record (pwAuth, ssid', P', $*$, P'', $*$, $*$, $*$, state, ctr) with $P = P''$ or $P = P'$, otherwise drop query;
[D.3] Rewrite state from init to fail, then set result = state and ctr $++$; if ctr = 2 overwrite state with completed in the record;
[D.4] Output (pwDecision, ssid', result) to P.

Fig. 10. $\mathcal{F}_{pwPHA}$ model of *password-based* post-handshake authentication, again omitting session identifier sid.

successful for parties sharing a channel (**channel binding**). Finally, $\mathcal{F}_{\mathsf{pwPHA}}$ creates adversarially-scheduled (via interface PWDELIVER) outputs [D.4] reflecting the state of the PWAUTH record [D.2-3], namely `fail` or `match`, towards both C and S, notifying them about the outcome of authentication. As soon as two outputs are delivered, $\mathcal{F}_{\mathsf{pwPHA}}$ [D.3] marks a record as `completed`, which concludes the authentication flow.

ADVERSARIAL INTERFACES. $\mathcal{F}_{\mathsf{pwPHA}}$ has a very simple leakage pattern - all inputs are public except for passwords (see messages to $\mathcal{A}$ in [F.1],[In.2] and [P.1]). To account for interactive protocols, we let adversary $\mathcal{A}$ acknowledge all honest inputs ([C.1],[In.1] and [P.1]), modeling Denial-of-Service attacks at different stages of the execution, and we let $\mathcal{A}$ make any authentication session fail [D.1]. STEALPWDFILE, OFFLTESTPWD and IMPERSONATE model adaptive compromise of server's password files. If the attacker wants to compromise a file, say, for uid stored at server S, it informs $\mathcal{F}_{\mathsf{pwPHA}}$ by sending (STEALPWDFILE, S, uid). $\mathcal{F}_{\mathsf{pwPHA}}$ [S.2] marks the corresponding file as `compromised`, which "unlocks" interfaces OFFLTESTPWD and IMPERSONATE (**resistance to offline attacks**): $\mathcal{A}$ can now make unlimited password guesses against the file via OFFLTESTPWD [O.1], and it can use the file to actively play the role of the honest server S in authentication sessions described above, using (IMPERSONATE, ssid, S, uid, ε) [Im.1]. We capture the ability of the attacker of compute its own password files by an optional input pw to IMPERSONATE. If this input [Im.2] is set, $\mathcal{A}$ is specifying which password it wants to use for file creation. $\mathcal{A}$ can only mount such attacks *on an attacked channel*, which is enforced by $\mathcal{F}_{\mathsf{pwPHA}}$ by [In.3] checking whether the attacked client a channel that is flagged `att`. If so, $\mathcal{F}_{\mathsf{pwPHA}}$ creates [In.3] a PWAUTH record with $\mathcal{A}$ as server and follows the procedure of honest authentication, except that it expects $\mathcal{A}$ to use an IMPERSONATE query instead of PWPROCEED. This concludes already the description of active attacks that $\mathcal{F}_{\mathsf{pwPHA}}$ allows to mount against a client. We further note that $\mathcal{F}_{\mathsf{pwPHA}}$ features a strong OFFLTESTPWD interface since it enforces **resistance to precomputation attacks** [18]: $\mathcal{F}_{\mathsf{pwPHA}}$ does not allow to pre-register guesses[7] and obtain a batched reply upon file compromise. Further, as common for asymmetric password authentication models, server compromise constitutes a form of corruption, which requires permission from the environment $\mathcal{Z}$, and hence STEALPWDFILE and OFFLTESTPWD can only be queried by $\mathcal{A}$ upon being instructed by $\mathcal{Z}$.

ACTIVEATTACK and TESTPWD interfaces allow an adversary to actively attack server S, guessing which password was used to generate a file. $\mathcal{A}$ initializes such attack by calling ACTIVEATTACK, specifying S, uid. $\mathcal{F}_{\mathsf{pwPHA}}$ initializes the [A.1] corresponding PWAUTH record with $\mathcal{A}$ in client role and [A.2] notifies the server. $\mathcal{A}$ can postpone the password guess, allowing analysis of protocols such as TLS-OPAQUE, where the attacker is not committed to a password guess from the very beginning of the attack. We complement the ACTIVEATTACK

---

[7] As a real-world example of an attack that is excluded by $\mathcal{F}_{\mathsf{pwPHA}}$, imagine an adversary preparing a list of hashed password guesses and, upon compromise, searching this list for a match. See [14] for a "non-strong" aPAKE functionality allowing for such attacks.

interface with interface TESTPWD, with inputs S, uid and password guess pw. Since cracking a password file of S, uid results in the insecurity of all ongoing and future authentication session with S, uid, interface TESTPWD is not session-based but file-based, and a successful guess results in all ongoing active attacks against this file being successful (i.e., $\mathcal{F}_{pwPHA}$ [T.1.1] rewrites the corresponding PWAUTH records to match). To make sure that the number of adversarial TESTPWD queries does not exceed the number of active attacks against a specific file, i.e., to ensure **limitation to one guess per online attack**, we let $\mathcal{F}_{pwPHA}$ maintain a counter ctr$[S,$ uid$]$ for every file ([P.2],[T.1] and [T.1.2]), indicating the remaining password guesses that $\mathcal{A}$ can issue against the file for uid.

On Registration and Authentication. Typically, user registration will assume some form of authenticated channels for the user and servers to identify each other. This authentication can take many forms from PKI to physical rendezvous. However, we do not force authentication into the model so it can also support, for example, anonymous settings where no authentication, or one-way authentication, is deemed sufficient. We stress that besides optional authentication during registration, our modeling (and TLS-OPAQUE in particular) is "password-only" where the user is not assumed to carry any information other than the password.

6.2   A UC Version of **TLS-OPAQUE**

We now give a modular representation of TLS-OPAQUE in Fig. 12, called $\Pi_{TLS-OPAQUE}$, which allows for asymmetric password authentication on an unauthenticated channel. $\Pi_{TLS-OPAQUE}$ is a UC protocol where parties issue calls to one instance of each functionality $\mathcal{F}_{PHA}$ for PHA, and $\mathcal{F}_{OPRF}$ for an oblivious pseudorandom function (OPRF), (see the full version [15] for details on OPRFs).

In a nutshell, parties use the OPRF to turn their passwords into an application key rw. During registration, rw is used to generate a key pair at $\mathcal{F}_{PHA}$, of which the server stores the public key. To authenticate, a client then recomputes rw from pw, then uses rw to recover (pk, sk) from $\mathcal{F}_{PHA}$, and subsequently authenticates to the server using sk and the public-key authentication interface of $\mathcal{F}_{PHA}$. The flow is depicted in Fig. 11. It is important to note that, due to our modular modeling, the client never actually sees the key pair (pk, sk), because $\mathcal{F}_{PHA}$ never gives out actual keys. However, $\mathcal{F}_{PHA}$ has the option to bootstrap key generation from any string, in our case the PRF value rw. Since the client can recover rw from only a password, it can, during authentication, re-claim the key pair at $\mathcal{F}_{PHA}$ from only pw. This concept of *transportable keys* in $\mathcal{F}_{PHA}$ was explained in more detail in the previous section, and it is the central tool that allows us to abstract the public-key building block of TLS-OPAQUE, i.e., write TLS-OPAQUE modularly with calls to $\mathcal{F}_{PHA}$.

$\Pi_{TLS-OPAQUE}$ consists of three phases: registration, channel establishment and asymmetric password authentication.

Registration: If client C with username uid$_C$ and password pw$_C$ wants to register with server S, then C initiates by sending uid$_C$ to S. S then creates a (normal) public key pk$_S$ at $\mathcal{F}_{PHA}$ and sends it to C. Both parties engage in an OPRF protocol, where S plays the server role on random key K and C evaluates

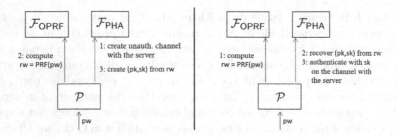

Fig. 11. Flows of TLS-OPAQUE using calls to hybrid functionalities $\mathcal{F}_{\mathsf{OPRF}}$ and $\mathcal{F}_{\mathsf{PHA}}$. **Left:** registration and channel establishment. **Right:** password authentication of the unautenticated channel. Note that the key pair $(\mathsf{pk},\mathsf{sk})$ is implicit in $\mathcal{F}_{\mathsf{PHA}}$ and is never seen by $\mathcal{P}$. It is generated and can be re-claimed from the application key rw.

$\mathsf{rw} = PRF_{K,S\|\mathsf{uid}}(\mathsf{pw}_C)$. Finally C then generates a transportable key at $\mathcal{F}_{\mathsf{PHA}}$ with application key $\mathsf{ak} = \mathsf{rw}$ and $\mathsf{aux} = \mathsf{pk}_S$, receiving back $\mathsf{ske}, \mathsf{pk}_C$, C sends $\mathsf{ske}, \mathsf{pk}_C$ to S and erases her memory, and S stores $(\mathsf{uid}_C, \mathsf{ske}, \mathsf{pk}_S, \mathsf{pk}_C)$ as the password file.

Channel Establishment: C and S establish an unauthenticated channel as in Fig. 9. If establishment goes unattacked, the channel is established between C and S, but both parties are oblivious of whether they actually got connected to the intended process. From their point of view, they might be connected to the adversary, or to a different honest process.

Password Authentication: In order to establish some knowledge about the counterparty in their channel, a party can initiate a password authentication. In our example, C initiates such authentication on his channel cid_C, with username uid_C and password pw_C. On a high level, both C and S will now each perform one public-key authentication, where S uses pk_S stored in the password file, and C uses key material contained in the envelope ske that S piggy-backs to his own authentication flow using the ctx field of $\mathcal{F}_{\mathsf{PHA}}$'s interface AUTHSEND. To authenticate with public keys, both parties invoke $\mathcal{F}_{\mathsf{PHA}}$. S, using "normal" public key pk_S to authenticate, invokes it in std mode. C, who receives ske from S, recovers application key $\mathsf{rw} = PRF_{K,S\|\mathsf{uid}}(\mathsf{pw}_C)$ by engaging with S in one PRF evaluation of $\mathcal{F}_{\mathsf{OPRF}}$ with session identifier $\mathsf{sid} = S\|\mathsf{uid}$. C then starts an authentication using transportable keys $\mathsf{rw}, \mathsf{ske}$. Both parties piggy-back the OPRF transcript values a', b' to their authentication flows using ctx fields of $\mathcal{F}_{\mathsf{PHA}}$. If C sees a successful authentication under public key pk_S, which C retrieves as auxiliary data from ske using $\mathcal{F}_{\mathsf{PHA}}$ interface GETAUXDATA, then C outputs success, else it outputs failure. If S sees a successful authentication under pk_C from the password file, C outputs success, else C outputs failure. Due to the guarantees of $\mathcal{F}_{\mathsf{PHA}}$, both parties can only output success if they are connected to each other, and if S has a password file that corresponds to pw_C entered by C.

Π_{EA} generalizes TLS-OPAQUE as specified in Sect. 2 in several aspects:

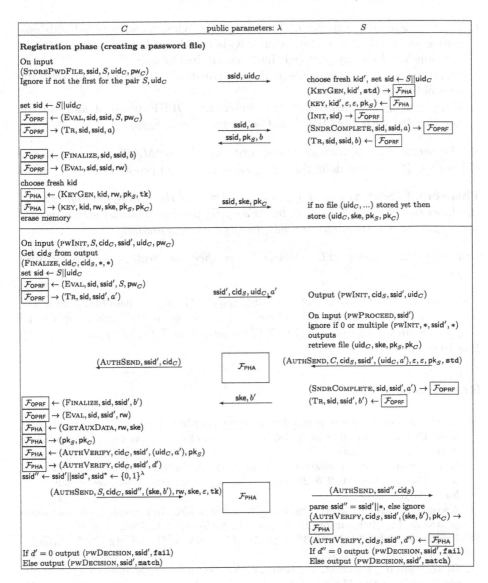

Fig. 12. Protocol $\Pi_{\text{TLS-OPAQUE}}$, using channel and public-key authentication facilities provided by $\mathcal{F}_{\text{PHA}}$. We exemplarily show C registering a password with S, and subsequent authentication of a channel between C, providing a clear-text password, and S, using the data stored at registration. ε denotes the empty string. For brevity we omit handling of NewSession, Send and ExpireSession inputs, which are simply relayed to $\mathcal{F}_{\text{PHA}}$. We also omit the identifiers with which $\mathcal{F}_{\text{PHA}}$ and $\mathcal{F}_{\text{OPRF}}$ are called. An application can simply set those to be, e.g., `tls-opaque_pha` and `tls-opaque_oprf`.

1. $\Pi_{\mathsf{TLS-OPAQUE}}$ abstracts from the exact secure channel with post-handshake public-key authentication and can provide post-handshake password authentication based on any protocol that securely instantiates $\mathcal{F}_{\mathsf{PHA}}$
2. $\Pi_{\mathsf{TLS-OPAQUE}}$ sends messages in the clear instead of sending them over the channel-to-authenticate
3. $\Pi_{\mathsf{TLS-OPAQUE}}$ abstracts from the underlying OPRF protocol and can be instantiated with any OPRF that securely realizes $\mathcal{F}_{\mathsf{OPRF}}$.

We are now ready to state the security of TLS-OPAQUE. We refer to the full version [15] for the definition of $\mathcal{F}_{\mathsf{OPRF}}$ and the full proof.

Theorem 3 (Security of $\Pi_{\mathsf{TLS-OPAQUE}}$). *Protocol $\Pi_{\mathsf{TLS-OPAQUE}}$ (Fig. 12) UC-emulates functionality $\mathcal{F}_{\mathsf{pwPHA}}$ in the $(\mathcal{F}_{\mathsf{PHA}}, \mathcal{F}_{\mathsf{OPRF}})$-hybrid model with respect to static malicious corruptions and adaptive server compromise.*

Corollary 2. *Protocol TLS-OPAQUE specified in Sect. 2 securely realizes $\mathcal{F}_{\mathsf{pwPHA}}$.*

The corollary follows from instantiating $\mathcal{F}_{\mathsf{PHA}}$ with Π_{EA} (Theorem 2) using the UC composition theorem [11], where in turn $\mathcal{F}_{\mathsf{cbSC}}$ is instantiated with the TLS 1.3 protocol snippet from Fig. 7 (Theorem 1), and $\mathcal{F}_{\mathsf{OPRF}}$ instantiated with 2HashDH [15].

References

1. Facebook stored hundreds of millions of passwords in plain text (2019). https://www.theverge.com/2019/3/21/18275837/facebook-plain-text-password-storage-hundreds-millions-users
2. Google stored some passwords in plain text for fourteen years (2019). https://www.theverge.com/2019/5/21/18634842/google-passwords-plain-text-g-suite-fourteen-years
3. Asokan, N., Niemi, V., Nyberg, K.: Man-in-the-middle in tunnelled authentication protocols. In: Christianson, B., Crispo, B., Malcolm, J.A., Roe, M. (eds.) Security Protocols 2003. LNCS, vol. 3364, pp. 28–41. Springer, Heidelberg (2005). https://doi.org/10.1007/11542322_6
4. Bhargavan, K., Blanchet, B., Kobeissi, N.: Verified models and reference implementations for the TLS 1.3 standard candidate. In: IEEE Symposium on Security and Privacy, pp. 483–502. IEEE Computer Society (2017)
5. Bhargavan, K., Delignat-Lavaud, A., Fournet, C., Pironti, A., Strub, P.-Y.: Triple handshakes and cookie cutters: breaking and fixing authentication over TLS. In: IEEE Symposium on Security and Privacy, pp. 98–113. IEEE Computer Society (2014)
6. Bhargavan, K., Delignat-Lavaud, A., Pironti, A.: Verified contributive channel bindings for compound authentication. In: NDSS (2015)
7. Bhargavan, K., Leurent, G.: Transcript collision attacks: breaking authentication in TLS, IKE and SSH. In: 23rd Annual Network and Distributed System Security Symposium, NDSS (2016)
8. Blanchet, B.: An efficient cryptographic protocol verifier based on prolog rules. In: IEEE Computer Security Foundations Workshop CSFW-14, pp. 82–96. IEEE Computer Society (2001)

9. Bourdrez, D., Krawczyk, H., Lewi, K., Wood, C.: The OPAQUE Asymmetric PAKE Protocol, draft-irtf-cfrg-opaque, July 2022. https://tools.ietf.org/id/draft-irtf-cfrg-opaque

10. Brzuska, C., Jacobsen, H.: A modular security analysis of EAP and IEEE 802.11. In: Cryptology ePrint Archive, Paper 2017/253 (PKC 2017) (2017)

11. Canetti, R., Universally composable security: a new paradigm for cryptographic protocols. In: IEEE Symposium on Foundations of Computer Science - FOCS 2001, pp. 136–145. IEEE (2001)

12. Canetti, R., Krawczyk, H.: Universally composable notions of key exchange and secure channels. In: Knudsen, L.R. (ed.) EUROCRYPT 2002. LNCS, vol. 2332, pp. 337–351. Springer, Heidelberg (2002). https://doi.org/10.1007/3-540-46035-7_22

13. Cremers, C., Horvat, M., Scott, S., van der Merwe, T.: Automated analysis and verification of TLS 1.3: 0-rtt, resumption and delayed authentication. In: IEEE Symposium on Security and Privacy, pp. 470–485. IEEE Computer Society (2016)

14. Gentry, C., MacKenzie, P., Ramzan, Z.: A method for making password-based key exchange resilient to server compromise. In: Dwork, C. (ed.) CRYPTO 2006. LNCS, vol. 4117, pp. 142–159. Springer, Heidelberg (2006). https://doi.org/10.1007/11818175_9

15. Hesse, J., Jarecki, S., Krawczyk, H.: Password-authenticated tls via opaque and post-handshake authentication. Cryptology ePrint Archive, Report 2023/220 (2023). https://ia.cr/2023/220

16. Hodges, J., Jones, J.C., Jones, M.B., Kumar, A., Lundberg, E.: Web authentication: an API for accessing public key credentials level 2, August 2021. https://www.w3.org/TR/webauthn-2/

17. Hoyland, J.: An analysis of TLS 1.3 and its use in composite protocols. Ph.D. thesis, RHUL, Egham, UK (2018)

18. Jarecki, S., Krawczyk, H., Xu, J.: OPAQUE: an asymmetric PAKE protocol secure against pre-computation attacks. In: Nielsen, J.B., Rijmen, V. (eds.) EURO-CRYPT 2018. LNCS, vol. 10822, pp. 456–486. Springer, Cham (2018). https://doi.org/10.1007/978-3-319-78372-7_15

19. Krawczyk, H.: The OPAQUE Asymmetric PAKE Protocol, draft-krawczyk-cfrg-opaque-06, June 2020. https://www.ietf.org/archive/id/draft-krawczyk-cfrg-opaque-06.txt

20. Krawczyk, H.: Cryptographic extraction and key derivation: the HKDF scheme. In: Rabin, T. (ed.) CRYPTO 2010. LNCS, vol. 6223, pp. 631–648. Springer, Heidelberg (2010). https://doi.org/10.1007/978-3-642-14623-7_34

21. Krawczyk, H.: Unilateral-to-mutual authentication compiler for key exchange (with applications to client authentication in tls 1.3). In: ACM CCS 2016 (2016)

22. Ray, M., Dispensa, S.: Authentication gap in tls renegotiation (2009)

23. Rescorla, E.: The transport layer security (TLS) protocol version 1.3, rfc 8446, August 2018. http://www.rfc-editor.org/rfc/rfc8446.txt

24. Rex, M.: Mitm attack on delayed TLS-client auth through renegotiation, November 2009

25. Salowey, J., Rescorla, E.: TLS renegotiation vulnerability (2009)

26. Sullivan, N.: Exported Authenticators in TLS, RFC 9261, July 2022. https://datatracker.ietf.org/doc/html/rfc9261

27. Sullivan, N., Krawczyk, H., Friel, O., Barnes, R.: OPAQUE with TLS 1.3, draft-sullivan-tls-opaque-01, February 2021. https://datatracker.ietf.org/doc/html/draft-sullivan-tls-opaque

Randomized Half-Ideal Cipher on Groups with Applications to UC (a)PAKE

Bruno Freitas Dos Santos📵, Yanqi Gu📵, and Stanislaw Jarecki(✉)📵

University of California, Irvine, Irvine, USA
{brunof,yanqig1,sjarecki}@uci.edu

Abstract. An Ideal Cipher (IC) is a cipher where each key defines a random permutation on the domain. Ideal Cipher on a group has many attractive applications, e.g., the *Encrypted Key Exchange* (EKE) protocol for Password Authenticated Key Exchange (PAKE) [8], or asymmetric PAKE (aPAKE) [31,33]. However, known constructions for IC on a group domain all have drawbacks, including key leakage from timing information [12], requiring 4 hash-onto-group operations if IC is an 8-round Feistel [22], and limiting the domain to half the group [9] or using variable-time encoding [39,47] if IC is implemented via (quasi-) bijections from groups to bitstrings [33].

We propose an IC relaxation called a *(Randomized) Half-Ideal Cipher* (HIC), and we show that HIC on a group can be realized by a *modified 2-round Feistel* (m2F), at a cost of 1 hash-onto-group operation, which beats existing IC constructions in versatility and computational cost. HIC weakens IC properties by letting part of the ciphertext be non-random, but we exemplify that it can be used as a drop-in replacement for IC by showing that EKE [8] and aPAKE of [33] realize respectively UC PAKE and UC aPAKE even if they use HIC instead of IC. The m2F construction can also serve as IC domain extension, because m2F constructs HIC on domain D from an RO-indifferentiable hash onto D and an IC on 2κ-bit strings, for κ a security parameter. One application of such extender is a modular lattice-based UC PAKE using EKE instantiated with HIC and anonymous lattice-based KEM.

1 Introduction

The Ideal Cipher Model (ICM) dates back to the work of Shannon [46], and it models a block cipher as an Ideal Cipher (IC) oracle, where every key, even chosen by the attacker, defines an independent random permutation. Formally, an efficient adversary who evaluates a block cipher on any key k of its choice cannot distinguish computing the cipher on that key in the forward and backward direction from an interaction with oracles $E_k(\cdot)$ and $E_k^{-1}(\cdot)$, where $\{E_i\}$ is a family of random permutations on the cipher domain. The Ideal Cipher Model has seen a variety of applications in cryptographic analysis, e.g. [13,24,28,37, 38,44,45,48], e.g. the analysis of the Davies-Meyer construction of a collision-resistant hash [13,45], of the Even-Mansour construction of a cipher from a

© International Association for Cryptologic Research 2023
C. Hazay and M. Stam (Eds.): EUROCRYPT 2023, LNCS 14008, pp. 128–156, 2023.
https://doi.org/10.1007/978-3-031-30589-4_5

public pseudorandom permutation [28], or of the DESX method for key-length extension for block ciphers [38]. A series of works [18, 19, 22, 26, 36] shows that ICM is equivalent to the Random Oracle Model (ROM) [7]. Specifically, these papers show that n-round Feistel, where each round function is a Random Oracle (RO), implements IC for some n, and the result of Dai and Steinberger [22] shows that $n = 8$ is both sufficient and necessary. Other IC constructions include iterated Even-Mansour and key alternating ciphers [4, 21, 27], wide-input (public) random permutations [10, 11, 20], and domain extension mechanisms, e.g. [17, 34], constructions based on

Ideal Ciphers on Groups: Applications. All the IC applications above consider IC on a domain of fixed-length bitstrings. However, there are also attractive applications of IC whose domain is a *group*. A prominent example is a Password Authenticated Key Exchange (PAKE) protocol called *Encrypted Key Exchange* (EKE), due to Bellovin and Meritt [8]. EKE is a compiler from plain key exchange (KE) whose messages are pseudorandom in some domain D, and it implements a secure PAKE if parties use an IC on domain D to password-encrypt KE messages.[1] The EKE solution to PAKE is attractive because it realizes UC PAKE given any key-private (a.k.a. anonymous) KEM [5], or KE with a mild "random message" property, at a cost which is the same as the underlying KE(M) *if* the cost of IC on KE(M) message domain(s) is negligible compared to the cost of KE(M) itself. However, instantiating EKE with e.g. Diffie-Hellman KE (DH-KE) [25] requires an IC on a group because DH-KE messages are random group elements.

Recently Gu et al. [33] and Freitas et al. [31] extended the EKE paradigm to cost-minimal compilers which create UC *asymmetric* PAKE (aPAKE), i.e. PAKE for the client-server setting where one party holds a one-way hash of the password instead of a password itself, from any key-hiding Authenticated Key Exchange (AKE). The AKE-to-aPAKE compilers of [31, 33] are similar to the "EKE" KE-to-PAKE compiler of [8] in that they also require IC-encryption of KE-related values, but they use IC to password-encrypt a KEM public key rather than KE protocol messages. The key-hiding AKE's exemplified in [31, 33], namely HMQV [40] and 3DH [42], are variants and generalizations of DH-KE where public keys are group elements, hence the AKE-to-aPAKE compilers of [31, 33] instantiated this way also require IC on a group.

Ideal Ciphers on Groups: Existing Constructions. The above motivates searching for efficient constructions of IC on a domain of an arbitrary group. Note first that a standard block cipher on a bitstring domain does not work. The elements of any group G can be encoded as bitstrings of some fixed length n, but unless these encodings cover almost all n-bit strings, i.e. unless $(1 - |G|/2^n)$ is negligible, encrypting G elements under a password using IC on n-bit strings

---

[1] Bellare et al. [6] showed that EKE+IC is a game-based secure PAKE, then Abdalla et al. [1] showed that EKE variant with explicit key confirmation realizes UC PAKE, and recently McQuoid et al. [43] showed that a round-minimal EKE variant realizes UC PAKE as well (however, see more on their analysis below).

exposes a scheme to an offline dictionary attack, because the adversary can decrypt a ciphertext under any password candidate and test if the decrypted plaintext encodes a G element.

Black and Rogaway [12] showed an elegant black-box solution for an IC on G given an IC on n-bit strings provided that $c = (2^n/|G|)$ is a constant: To encrypt element $x \in G$ under key k, use the underlying n-bit IC in a loop, i.e. set x_0 to the n-bit encoding of x, and $x_{i+1} = \mathsf{IC.Enc}_k(x_i)$ for each $i \geq 0$, and output as the ciphertext the first x_i for $i \geq 1$ s.t. x_i encodes an element of group G. (Decryption works the same way but using $\mathsf{IC.Dec}$.) This procedure takes expected c uses of $\mathsf{IC.Enc}$, but timing measurement of either encryption or decryption leaks roughly $\log c$ bits of information on key k per each usage, because given the ciphertext one can eliminate all keys which form decryption cycles whose length does not match the length implied by the timing data.

To the best of our knowledge there are only two other types of constructions of IC on a group. First, the work of [18,19,22,26,36] shows that n-round Feistel network implements an IC for $n \geq 8$. Although not stated explicitly, these results imply a (randomized) IC on a group, where one Feistel wire holds group elements, the xor gates on that wire are replaced by group operations, and hashes onto that wire are implemented as RO hashes onto the group. However, since $n = 8$ rounds is minimal [22], this construction incurs four RO hashes onto a group per cipher operation. Whereas there is progress regarding RO-indifferentiable hashing on Elliptic Curve (EC) groups, see e.g. [29], current implementations report an RO hash costs in the ballpark of 25% of scalar multiplication. Hence, far from being negligible, the cost of IC on group implemented in this way would roughly equal the DH-KE cost in the EKE compiler. The second construction of (randomized) IC combines any (randomized) quasi-bijective encoding of group elements as bitstrings with an IC on the resulting bitstrings [33]. However, we know of only two quasi-bijective encodings for Elliptic Curve groups, Elligator2 of Bernstein et al. [9] and Elligator^2 of Tibouchi et al. [39,47], and both have some practical disadvantages. Elligator2 works for only some elliptic curves, and it can encode only half the group elements, which means that any application has to re-generate group elements until it finds one in the domain of Elligator2. Elligator^2 works for a larger class of curves, but its encoding procedure is non-constant time and it appears to be significantly more expensive than one RO hash onto a curve. Elligator^2 also encodes each EC element as a pair of underlying field elements, effectively doubling the size of the EC element representation.

IC Alternative: Programmable-Once Public Function. An alternative path was recently charted by McQuoid et al. [43], who showed that a 2-round Feistel, with one wire holding group elements, implements a randomized cipher on a group which has some IC-like properties, which [43] captured in a notion of Programmable Once Public Function (POPF). Moreover, they argue that POPF can replace IC in several applications, exemplifying it with an argument that EKE realizes UC PAKE if password encryption is implemented with a POPF in place of IC. This would be very attractive because if 2-round Feistel can indeed function as an IC replacement in applications like the PAKE of

[8] or the aPAKE's of [31,33], this would form the most efficient and flexible implementation option for these protocols, because it works for any group which admits RO-indifferentiable hash, and it uses just one such hash-onto-group per cipher operation.

However, it seems difficult to use the POPF abstraction of [43] as a replacement for IC in the above applications because the POPF notion captures 2-round Feistel properties with game-based properties which appear not to address *non-malleability*. For that reason we doubt that it can be proven that UC PAKE is realized by EKE with IC replaced by POPF as defined in [43]. (See below for more details.) The fact that the POPF abstraction appears insufficient does not preclude that UC PAKE can be realized by EKE with encryption implemented as 2-round Feistel, but such argument would not be modular. Moreover, each application which uses 2-round Feistel in place of IC would require a separate non-modular proof. Alternatively, one could search for a "POPF+" abstraction, realized by a 2-round Feistel, which captures sufficient non-malleability properties to be useful as an IC replacement in PAKE applications, but in this work we chose a different route.

Our Results: Modified 2-Feistel as (Randomized) Half-Ideal Cipher. Instead of trying to work with 2-Feistel itself, we show that adding a block cipher BC to one wire in 2-Feistel makes this transformation non-malleable, and we capture the properties of this construction in the form of a UC notion we call a (Randomized) Half-Ideal Cipher (HIC). In Fig. 1 we show a simple pictorial comparison of 2-Feistel, denoted 2F, and our modification, denoted m2F. The modified 2-Feistel has the same efficiency and versatility as the 2-Feistel used by McQuoid et al. [43]: It works for any group with an RO-indifferentiable hash onto a group, it runs in fixed time, and it requires only one RO hash onto a group per cipher operation.

One drawback of m2F is that the ciphertext is longer than the plaintext by 2κ bits, where κ is a security parameter. However, that is less than any IC implementation above (including POPF, which does not realize IC) except for Elligator2: IC results from n-round Feistel have loose security bounds, hence they need significantly longer randomness to achieve the same provable security; Elligator2 adds κ bits for general moduli, due to encoding of field elements as random bitstrings; Elligator^2 uses an additional field element, which adds at least 2κ bits, plus another κ bits for the field-onto-bits encoding; Finally, 2-Feistel requires at least 3κ bits of randomness when used in EKE [43].

The UC HIC notion is a relaxation of an Ideal Cipher notion, but it does not prevent applicability in protocols like [8,31,33], which we exemplify by showing that the following protocols remain secure with (any realization of) IC replaced by (any realization of) HIC:

(I) UC PAKE is realized by an EKE variant with IC replaced by HIC, using round-minimal KE with a random-message property;

(II) UC PAKE is realized by an EKE variant with IC replaced by HIC, using anonymous KEM with a uniform public keys property;

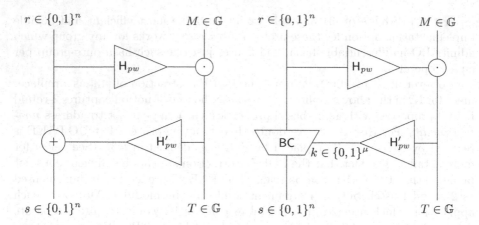

Fig. 1. Left: two-round Feistel (2F) used in McQuoid et al. [43]; Right: our circuit m2F. The change from 2F to m2F is small: If $k = H'(pw, T)$, then 2F sets $s = k \oplus r$, whereas m2F sets $s = \mathsf{BC.Enc}(k, r)$, where BC is a block cipher.

(III) UC aPAKE is realized by KHAPE [33] with IC replaced by HIC, using key-hiding AKE.

Regarding the first two proofs, we are not aware of full proofs exhibited for the corresponding statements where these EKE variants use IC instead of HIC, but the third proof follows the blueprint of the proof given in [33] for the KHAPE protocol using IC, and it exemplifies how little such proof changes if IC is replaced by HIC.

Half-Ideal Cipher. The first difference between IC on group $\mathbb{G}$ and HIC on group $\mathbb{G}$ is that the latter is a cipher on an extended domain $\mathcal{D} = \mathcal{R} \times \mathbb{G}$ where $\mathcal{R} = \{0,1\}^n$ is the randomness space, for $n \geq 2\kappa$ where κ is the security parameter. In the decryption direction, HIC acts exactly like IC on domain $\mathcal{D}$, i.e. unless ciphertext $c \in \mathcal{D}$ is already associated with some plaintext in the permutation table defined by key k, an adversarial decryption of c under key k returns a random plaintext m, chosen by the HIC functionality with uniform distribution over those elements in domain $\mathcal{D}$ which are not yet assigned to any ciphertext in the permutation table for key k. However, in the encryption direction HIC is only *half-ideal* in the following sense: If plaintext m is not yet associated with any ciphertext in the permutation table for key k then encryption of m under key k returns a ciphertext $c = (s, T) \in \mathcal{D} = \mathcal{R} \times \mathbb{G}$ s.t. the $T \in \mathbb{G}$ part of c *can be freely specified by the adversary*, and the $s \in \mathcal{R}$ part of c is then chosen by the HIC functionality at random with uniform distribution over s's s.t. $c = (s, T)$ is not yet assigned to any plaintext in the permutation table for key k. In short, HIC decryption on any (k, c) returns a random plaintext m (subject to the constraint that $\mathsf{HIC}(k, \cdot)$ is a permutation on $\mathcal{D}$), but HIC encryption on any (k, m) returns $c = (s, T)$ s.t. T can be correlated with other values in an arbitrary way, which is modeled by allowing the adversary to choose it, but s is random (subject to the constraint that $\mathsf{HIC}(k, \cdot)$ is a permutation).[2]

Intuitively, the reason the adversarial ability to manipulate part of IC ciphertext does not affect typical IC applications is that these applications typically rely on the following properties of IC: (1) that decryption of a ciphertext on any other key from the one used in encryption outputs a random plaintext, (2) that any change to a ciphertext implies that the corresponding plaintext is random and hence uncorrelated to the plaintext in the original ciphertext, and (3) that no two encryption operations can output the same ciphertext, regardless of the keys used, and moreover that the simulator can straight-line extract the unique key used in a ciphertext formed in the forward direction. Only properties (2) and (3) could be affected by the adversarial ability to choose the T part of a ciphertext in encryption, but the fact that the s part is still random, and that $|s| \geq 2\kappa$, means that just like in IC, except for negligible probability each encryption outputs a ciphertext which is different from all previously used ones. Consequently, just like in IC, a HIC ciphertext commits the adversary to (at most) a *single* key used to create that ciphertext in a forward direction, the simulator can straight-line extract that key, and the decryption of this ciphertext under any other key samples random elements in the domain.

Further Applications: IC Domain Extension, LWE-Based UC PAKE. The modified 2-Feistel construction can also be used as a *domain extender* for (randomized) IC on *bitstrings*. Given an RO hash onto $\{0,1\}^t$ and an IC on $\{0,1\}^{2\kappa}$, the m2F construction creates a HIC on $\{0,1\}^t$, for any $t = \mathsf{poly}(\kappa)$. The modified 2-Feistel is simpler than other IC domain extenders, e.g. [17,34], and it has better exact security bounds, hence it is an attractive alternative in applications where HIC can securely substitute for IC on a large bitstring domain. For example, by our result (II) above, m2F on long bitstrings can be used to implement UC PAKE from any lattice-based IND-secure and anonymous KEM. This includes several post-quantum LWE-based KEM proposals in the NIST competition, including Saber [23], Kyber [14], McEliece [2], NTRU [35], Frodo [3], and possibly others.[3] Such UC PAKE construction would add only 3κ bits in bandwidth to the underlying KEM, and its computational overhead over the underlying KEM operations would be negligible, i.e. the LWE-based UC PAKE would have essentially exactly the same cost as the LWE-based unauthenticated Key Exchange, i.e. an IND-secure KEM. We show a concrete construction of UC PAKE from Saber KEM in the full version [30].

---

[2] This describes only the *adversarial* interface to the HIC functionality. Honest parties' interface is as in IC in both directions, except that it hides encryption randomness, i.e. encryption takes only input $M \in \mathbb{G}$ and decryption outputs only the $M \in \mathbb{G}$ part of the "extended" HIC plaintext $m \in \mathcal{D}$.

[3] Two recent papers [41,49] investigate anonymity of several CCA-secure LWE-based KEMs achieved via variants of the Fujisaki-Okamoto transform [32] applied to the IND-secure versions of these KEM's. However, the underlying IND-secure KEM's are all anonymous, see e.g. [41,49] and the references therein.

Half-Ideal Cipher versus POPF. Our modified 2-Feistel construction and the UC HIC abstraction we use to capture its properties can be thought of as a "non-malleability upgrade" to the 2-Feistel, and to the game-based POPF abstraction used by McQuoid et al. [43] to capture its properties. One reason why the UC HIC notion is an improvement over the POPF notion is that a UC tool is easier to use in protocol applications than a game-based abstraction. More specifically, the danger of game-based properties is that they often fail to adequately capture non-malleability properties needed in protocol applications, e.g. in the EKE protocol, where the man-in-the-middle attacker can modify the ciphertexts exchanged between Alice and Bob.[4] Indeed, POPF properties seem not to capture ciphertext non-malleability. As defined in [43], POPF has two security properties, *honest simulation* and *uncontrollable outputs*. The first one says that if ciphertext c is output by a simulator on behalf of an honest party, then decrypting it under any key results in a random element in group $\mathbb{G}$, except for the (key,plaintext) pair, denoted (x^*, y^*) in [43], which was programmed into this ciphertext by the simulator. The second property says that any ciphertext c^* output by an adversary decrypts to random elements in group $\mathbb{G}$ for all keys except for key k^*, denoted x^* in [43], which was used by the adversary to create c^* in the forward direction, and which can be straight-line extracted by the simulator.[5] However, these properties do not say that the (key,plaintext) pairs behind the adversary's ciphertext c^* cannot bear any relation to the (key,plaintext) pairs behind the simulator's ciphertext c.

Note that non-malleability is necessary in a protocol application like EKE, and for that reason we think that it is unlikely that EKE can provably realize UC PAKE based on the POPF properties alone. Consider a cipher Enc on a multiplicative group s.t. there is an efficient algorithm A s.t. if $c = \mathsf{Enc}(k, M)$ and $c^* = A(c)$ then $M^* = \mathsf{Dec}(k, c^*)$ satisfies relation $M^* = M^2$ if $\mathsf{lsb}(k) = 0$, and $m^* = m^3$ if $\mathsf{lsb}(k) = 1$. If this cipher is used in EKE for password-encryption of DH-KE messages then the attacker would learn lsb of password pw used by Alice and Bob: If the attacker passes Alice's message $c_A = \mathsf{Enc}(pw, g^x)$ to Bob, but replaces Bob's message $c_B = \mathsf{Enc}(pw, g^y)$ by sending a modified message $c_B^* = A(c_B)$ to Alice, then $c_B^* = \mathsf{Enc}(pw, g^{y \cdot (2+b)})$ where $b = \mathsf{lsb}(pw)$, hence an attacker who sees Alice's output $k_A = g^{xy \cdot (2+b)}$ and Bob's output $k_B = g^{xy}$, can learn bit b by testing if $k_A = (k_B)^{(2+b)}$. More generally, any attack A which transforms ciphertext $c = \mathsf{Enc}(k, M)$ to ciphertext $c^* = \mathsf{Enc}(k^*, M^*)$ s.t. (k, M, k^*, M^*) are in some non-trivial relation, is a potential danger for EKE. We do not believe that 2-Feistel is subject to such attacks, but POPF properties defined in [43] do not seem to forbid them.

---

[4] A potential benefit of a game-based notion over a UC notion is that the former *could* be easier to state and use, but this does not seem to be the case for the POPF properties of [43], because they are quite involved and subtle.

[5] Technically [43] state this property as pseudorandomness of outputs of any weak-PRF on the decryptions of c^* for any $k \neq k^*$, and not the pseudorandomness of the decrypted plaintexts themselves.

If one uses 2-Feistel directly rather than the POPF abstraction then it might still be possible to prove that EKE with 2-Feistel realizes UC PAKE. We note that 2-Feistel is subject to the following restricted form of "key-dependent malleability", which appears not to have been observed in [43] and which would have to be accounted for in such proof. Namely, consider an adversary who given ciphertext $c = (s, T)$ outputs ciphertext $c^* = (s^*, T^*)$ for any T^* and s^* s.t. $s^* \oplus \mathsf{H}'(pw^*, T^*) = s \oplus \mathsf{H}'(pw^*, T)$. Note that this adversary is not performing a decryption of c under pw^*, because it is not querying $\mathsf{H}(pw^*, r)$ for $r = s \oplus \mathsf{H}'(pw^*, T)$, but plaintexts $M^* = \mathsf{Dec}(pw, c^*)$ and $M = \mathsf{Dec}(pw, c)$ satisfy a non-trivial relation $M^*/M = T^*/T$ if $pw = pw^*$ and not otherwise. On the other hand, since this adversarial behavior seems to implement just a different form of an online attack using a unique password guess pw^*, it is still possible that EKE realizes UC PAKE even when password encryption is implemented as 2-Feistel. However, rather than considering such non-modular direct proofs for each application of IC on a group, in this paper we show that a small change in the 2-Feistel circuit implies realizing a HIC relaxation of the IC model, and this HIC relaxation is as easy to use as IC in the security proofs for protocols like EKE [8] or aPAKE's of Gu et al. [31,33].

Finally, we note that an extension of the above attack shows that 2-Feistel itself, without our modification, cannot realize the HIC abstraction. Observe that if the adversary computes t hashes $Z_i = \mathsf{H}(pw, r_i)$ for some pw and $r_1, ..., r_t$ and then t hashes $k_j = \mathsf{H}'(pw, T_j)$ for some $T_1, ..., T_t$, then it can combine them to form t^2 valid (plaintext, ciphertext) pairs (M_{ij}, c_{ij}) under key pw where $M_{ij} = Z_i \cdot T_j$ and $c_{ij} = (r_i \oplus k_j, T_j)$. Note that the t^2 plaintexts are formed using just $2t$ group elements $(Z_1, T_1), ..., (Z_t, T_t)$, so they are correlated. For example, the value of quotient $M_{ij}/M_{i'j}$ is the same for every j. Creating such correlations on plaintexts is impossible in the UC HIC, hence 2-Feistel by itself, without our modification, does not realize it.

Roadmap. In Sect. 2, we recall the syntax and properties of Key Exchange (KE) and Key Encapsulation Mechanism (KEM). In Sect. 3 we define the UC notion of Half-Ideal Cipher (HIC). In Sect. 4 we present the modified 2-Feistel construction, and we show that it realizes UC HIC. In Sect. 5 we define two variants of the EKE protocol, denoted EKE and EKE-KEM, based on respectively KE and KEM, with password encryption implemented as HIC, and we show that both variants realizes UC PAKE.

Because of space constraints we defer some parts to the full version of this paper [30]. Specifically, the full version contains the details of game changes used in the security proofs of the above two results, i.e. that modified 2-Feistel realizes UC RIC, and that EKE with encryption using HIC realizes UC PAKE. It also contains the security proof of the EKE-KEM protocol, and the proof that the KHAPE protocol of [33] realizes UC aPAKE with IC encryption replaced by HIC. It also illustrates an instantiation of EKE-KEM protocol with Saber KEM [23], and compares the resulting protocol to prior lattice-based PAKEs.

2   Preliminaries

We focus our treatment of the EKE protocol to instantiations that use Key Exchange (KE) with either a single simultaneous flow or 2 flows. Since a 2-flow KE is equivalent to a key encapsulation mechanism (KEM), we will use "KE" to refer to a single-round key exchange, and "KEM" to a KEM *and* to a two-flow key exchange implied by it.

2.1   Single-Round Key Exchange (KE) Scheme

A (single-round) KE scheme is a pair of algorithms $\mathsf{KA} = (\mathsf{msg}, \mathsf{key})$, where:

- msg, on input a security parameter κ, generates message M and state x;
- key, on input state x and incoming message M', generates session key K.

The correctness requirement is that if two parties exchange honestly generated messages then they both output the same session key, i.e. if $(x_1, M_1) \leftarrow \mathsf{msg}(1^\kappa)$ and $(x_2, M_2) \leftarrow \mathsf{msg}(1^\kappa)$ then $\mathsf{key}(x_1, M_2) = \mathsf{key}(x_2, M_1)$. The KE security requirement is that a KE transcript hides the session key, but as noted by Bellare et al. [6], the EKE protocol requires an additional property of KE called a *random-message* property, namely that messages output by msg are indistinguishable from values sampled from a uniform distribution over some domain $\mathcal{M}$. (In the security analysis of EKE by [6], the EKE employs an Ideal Cipher on domain $\mathcal{M}$ for password-encryption of KE protocol messages.)

Definition 1. *KE scheme* $(\mathsf{msg}, \mathsf{key})$ *is secure if distributions* $\{(M_1, M_2, K)\}$ *and* $\{(M_1, M_2, K^*)\}$ *are computationally indistinguishable, where* $(x_1, M_1) \leftarrow \mathsf{msg}(1^\kappa)$, $(x_2, M_2) \leftarrow \mathsf{msg}(1^\kappa)$, $K \leftarrow \mathsf{key}(x_1, M_2)$, *and* $K^* \xleftarrow{r} \{0,1\}^\kappa$.

Definition 2. *KE scheme* $(\mathsf{msg}, \mathsf{key})$ *has the* random-message *property on domain* $\mathcal{M}$, *indexed by sec. par.* κ, *if the distribution* $\{M \mid (x, M) \leftarrow \mathsf{msg}(1^\kappa)\}$ *is computationally indistinguishable from uniform over set* $\mathcal{M}[\kappa]$.

2.2   Key Encapsulation Mechanism (KEM)

A KEM scheme is a tuple of efficient algorithms $\mathsf{KEM} = (\mathsf{kg}, \mathsf{enc}, \mathsf{dec})$, where:

- kg, on input secpar κ, generates public and private keys pk and sk;
- enc, on input a public key pk, generates ciphertext e and session key K;
- dec, on input a private key sk and a ciphertext e, outputs a session key K.

The correctness requirement is that if $(sk, pk) \leftarrow \mathsf{kg}(1^\kappa)$ and $(e, K) \leftarrow \mathsf{enc}(pk)$ then $\mathsf{dec}(sk, e) = K$. Note that KEM models any 2-flow key exchange scheme, where the public key pk is the initiator's message, and the ciphertext e is the responder's message. We require IND security of KEM, and two additional randomness/anonymity properties: First, public keys must be *uniform* in the sense that their distribution must be indistinguishable from a uniform distribution over some set $\mathcal{PK}$. Secondly, KEM must be anonymous [5], i.e. ciphertexts must be unlinkable to public keys. Note that these are slightly weaker properties than we asked of KA. Since a key exchange implied by KEM takes 2 flows, the EKE variant using KEM, see Fig. 10 in Sect. 5.1, can use the (randomized) ideal cipher only for the first flow, i.e. the public key, while the second flow, i.e. the KEM ciphertext, can be sent as is, as long as the responder attaches to it a key confirmation message. Consequently, the second message must be unlinkable to the first, but it does not have to be indistinguishable from a random element in a domain of an ideal cipher.

Definition 3. *KEM scheme is* IND *secure if distributions* $\{(pk, e, K)\}$ *and* $\{(pk, e, K^*)\}$ *are computationally indistinguishable, where* $(sk, pk) \xleftarrow{r} \mathsf{kg}(1^\kappa)$, $(e, K) \xleftarrow{r} \mathsf{enc}(pk)$ *and* $K^* \xleftarrow{r} \{0, 1\}^\kappa$.

Definition 4. *KEM scheme has* uniform public keys *for domain* $\mathcal{PK}$, *indexed by the security parameter* κ, *if the distribution* $\{pk \mid (sk, pk) \xleftarrow{r} \mathsf{kg}(1^\kappa)\}$ *is computationally indistinguishable from uniform over set* $\mathcal{PK}[\kappa]$

Definition 5. *KEM scheme is* anonymous *if distributions* $\{(pk_0, pk_1, e_0)\}$ *and* $\{(pk_0, pk_1, e_1)\}$ *are computationally indistinguishable, where* $(sk_0, pk_0) \xleftarrow{r} \mathsf{kg}(1^\kappa)$, $(sk_1, pk_1) \xleftarrow{r} \mathsf{kg}(1^\kappa)$, $(e_0, K_0) \xleftarrow{r} \mathsf{enc}(pk_0)$, *and* $(e_1, K_1) \xleftarrow{r} \mathsf{enc}(pk_1)$.

Note that the last two properties are trivially achieved by the Diffie-Hellman KEM, where both the public keys and ciphertexts are random group elements. However, both properties are also achieved by several lattice-based KEM's, as discussed in Sect. 1.

3   Universally Composable Half-Ideal Cipher

We define a new functionality $\mathcal{F}_{\mathsf{HIC}}$ in the UC framework ([15]), called a *(Randomized) Half-Ideal Cipher* (HIC), where the 'half' in the name refers to the fact that only half of the ciphertext is random to the adversary during encryption, as we explain below.

UC HIC is a weakening of the UC Ideal Cipher notion. Intuitively, we allow adversaries to predict or control part of the output of the cipher while the remainder is indistinguishable from random just as in the case of IC. Formally, we can interpret this as allowing the adversary to embed some tuples in the table that the functionality uses - but in a very controlled manner. We define the UC notion of Half-Ideal Cipher via functionality $\mathcal{F}_{\mathsf{HIC}}$ defined in Fig. 2.[6]

Notes on $\mathcal{F}_{\mathsf{HIC}}$ Interfaces. A half-ideal cipher functionality $\mathcal{F}_{\mathsf{HIC}}$ is parametrized by the (randomized) cipher domain $\mathcal{D} = \mathcal{R} \times \mathcal{G}$, where the first component is the randomness and the second is the plaintext. Figure 2 separates between $\mathcal{F}_{\mathsf{HIC}}$ interfaces Enc and Dec which are used by honest parties, and the adversarial interfaces AdvEnc and AdvDec. Interfaces Enc and Dec model

---

[6] In Fig. 2 we use pw to denote keys used in the HIC cipher because we use variables k and K for other keys in the later sections. Moreover, in PAKE and aPAKE applications the role of a HIC key is played by a password.

Notation: Functionality $\mathcal{F}_{\mathsf{HIC}}$ is parametrized by domain $\mathcal{D} = \mathcal{R} \times \mathcal{G}$, and it is indexed by a session identifier sid which is a global constant, hence we omit it from notation. We denote HIC keys as passwords pw to conform to the usage of $\mathcal{F}_{\mathsf{HIC}}$ in PAKE and aPAKE applications, but keys pw are arbitrary bitstrings.

Initialization: For all $pw \in \{0,1\}^*$, initialize THIC_{pw} as an empty table.

Interfaces for Honest Parties P:

on query (Enc, pw, M) from party P, for $M \in \mathcal{G}$:

$r \xleftarrow{\text{r}} \mathcal{R}$
if $\exists c$ s.t. $((r, M), c) \in \mathsf{THIC}_{pw}$ then return c to P, else do:
    $c \xleftarrow{\text{r}} \{\hat{c} \in \mathcal{D} : \nexists m \text{ s.t. } (m, \hat{c}) \in \mathsf{THIC}_{pw}\}$
    add $((r, M), c)$ to THIC_{pw} and return c to P

on query (Dec, pw, c) from party P, for $c \in \mathcal{D}$:

query $(r, M) \leftarrow \mathcal{F}_{\mathsf{HIC}}.\mathsf{AdvDec}(pw, c)$ and return M to P

Interfaces for Adversary $\mathcal{A}$ *(or corrupt parties):*

on query $(\mathsf{AdvEnc}, pw, (r, M), T)$ from adversary $\mathcal{A}$, for $(r, M) \in \mathcal{D}$ and $T \in \mathcal{G}$:

if $\exists c$ s.t. $((r, M), c) \in \mathsf{THIC}_{pw}$ then return c to $\mathcal{A}$, else do:
    $s \xleftarrow{\text{r}} \{\hat{s} \in \mathcal{R} : \nexists \hat{m} \text{ s.t. } (\hat{m}, (\hat{s}, T)) \in \mathsf{THIC}_{pw}\}$
    set $c \leftarrow (s, T)$, add $((r, M), c)$ to THIC_{pw}, and return c to $\mathcal{A}$

on query (AdvDec, pw, c) from adversary $\mathcal{A}$, for $c \in \mathcal{D}$:

if $\exists m$ s.t. $(m, c) \in \mathsf{THIC}_{pw}$ then return m to $\mathcal{A}$, else do:
    $m \xleftarrow{\text{r}} \{\hat{m} \in \mathcal{D} : \nexists \hat{c} \text{ s.t. } (\hat{m}, \hat{c}) \in \mathsf{THIC}_{pw}\}$
    add (m, c) to THIC_{pw} and return m to $\mathcal{A}$

Fig. 2. Ideal functionality $\mathcal{F}_{\mathsf{HIC}}$ for *(Randomized) Half-Ideal Cipher* on $\mathcal{D} = \mathcal{R} \times \mathcal{G}$

honest-party's usage of HIC, i.e. a real-world implementation of HIC will consists of two algorithms, Enc and Dec, where Enc on input key pw and plaintext $M \in \mathcal{G}$ outputs a ciphertext $c \in \mathcal{D}$ and Dec on input key pw and ciphertext $c \in \mathcal{D}$ outputs a plaintext $M \in \mathcal{G}$. Our target realization of these procedures is a *randomized cipher*, i.e. a family of functions Π_{pw} s.t. for each $pw \in \{0,1\}^*$, Π_{pw} is a permutation on $\mathcal{D}$, and both Π_{pw} and Π_{pw}^{-1} are efficiently evaluable given pw. Given cipher Π, algorithm $\mathsf{Enc}(pw, M)$ picks $r \xleftarrow{\text{r}} \mathcal{R}$ and outputs $c \leftarrow \Pi_{pw}(m)$ for $m = (r, M)$, while $\mathsf{Dec}(pw, c)$ computes $m \leftarrow \Pi_{pw}^{-1}(c)$ and output M for $(r, M) = m$.

Functionality Walk-Through. Functionality $\mathcal{F}_{\mathsf{HIC}}$ reflects honest user's interfaces to randomized encryption: When an honest party P encrypts a message it specifies only $M \in \mathcal{G}$ and delegates the choice of randomness $r \xleftarrow{\text{r}} \mathcal{R}$ to the functionality. Similarly, when an honest party decrypts a ciphertext, the functionality discards the randomness r and reveals only M to the application. This implies that honest parties must use fresh randomness at each encryption and must discard it (or at least not use it) at decryption. By contrast, an adversary $\mathcal{A}$ has stronger interfaces than honest parties (for notational simplicity we assume corrupt parties interact to $\mathcal{F}_{\mathsf{HIC}}$ via $\mathcal{A}$), namely: (1) When $\mathcal{A}$ encrypts it can choose randomness r at will; (2) When $\mathcal{A}$ decrypts it learns the randomness r and does not have to discard it; (3) $\mathcal{A}$ can manipulate the (plaintext, ciphertext) table of each permutation Π_{pw} in the following way: If we denote ciphertexts as $c = (s, T) \in \mathcal{R} \times \mathcal{G}$, the adversary has no control of the s component of the ciphertext at encryption, i.e. it is random in $\mathcal{R}$ (up to the fact that the map has to remain a permutation), but the adversary can freely choose the T component. Items (1) and (2) are consequences of the fact that HIC is a *randomized* cipher, but item (3) is what makes this cipher *Half-Ideal*, because the adversary can control part of the value $c = \mathsf{Enc}(pw, m)$ during encryption, namely its $\mathcal{G}$ component.

The above relaxations of Ideal Cipher (IC) properties are imposed by the modified 2-Feistel construction, which in Sect. 4 we show realizes this model. However, this relaxation is harmless for many IC applications the following reason: In a typical IC application the benefit of ciphertext randomness is that it (1) hides the plaintext, and (2) it prevents the adversary from creating the same ciphertext as an encryption of two different plaintexts under two different keys. For both purposes randomness in the $s \in \mathcal{R}$ component of the ciphertext suffices as long as $\mathcal{R}$ is large enough to prevent ever encountering collisions.

The adversarial interfaces AdvEnc and AdvDec of $\mathcal{F}_{\mathsf{HIC}}$ reflect the above, and give more powers than the honest party's interfaces Enc and Dec. In encryption query AdvEnc, the adversary is allowed to pick its own randomness r *and* the $T \in \mathcal{G}$ part of the resulting ciphertext, while its s part is chosen at random in $\mathcal{R}$. In decryption AdvDec, the adversary can decrypt any ciphertext $c = (s, T)$ and it learns the full plaintext $m = (r, M)$, but $\mathcal{F}_{\mathsf{HIC}}$ chooses the whole plaintext m at random. (This is another motivation for the moniker 'half-ideal': $\mathcal{F}_{\mathsf{HIC}}$ lets the adversary have some control over ciphertexts in encryption but it does not let the adversary have any control over plaintexts in decryption.)

Our goal when designing $\mathcal{F}_{\mathsf{HIC}}$ was to keep all IC properties which are useful in applications while allowing for efficient concrete instantiation of $\mathcal{F}_{\mathsf{HIC}}$ for a group domain $\mathcal{G}$. Most importantly, ciphertext collisions in encryption can occur only with negligible probability, which is crucial in our HIC applications: An adversarial ciphertext c commits the adversary to a single key pw on which the adversary could have computed c as an encryption of some message of its choice. Secondly, just as with an ideal cipher, the adversary cannot learn any information on encrypted plaintexts except via decryption with correct decryption key.

4   Half-Ideal Cipher Construction: Modified 2-Feistel

We modify the two-round Feistel construction of the Programmable Once Public Functions (POPF) of McQuoid et al. [43] by replacing the xor operation in the second round by an application of an ideal block cipher BC on bitstrings, with keys and plaintext block both of size 2κ where κ is the security parameter.

We call this construction a *modified 2-Feistel*, denoted m2F. This construction takes (1) an ideal cipher BC on bitstrings, i.e. an ideal cipher whose domain is $\{0,1\}^n$ and key space is $\{0,1\}^\mu$, (2) a random oracle hash H' with range $\{0,1\}^\mu$, and (3) a random oracle hash H whose range is an arbitrary *group* $\mathbb{G}$, and creates a *(Randomized) Half-Ideal Cipher* (HIC) over domain $\mathcal{D} = \mathcal{R} \times \mathbb{G}$ where $\mathcal{R} = \{0,1\}^n$. In essence, we combine a random oracle hash onto a group and a bitwise ideal cipher to create a half-ideal cipher over a group. The exact security analysis of the m2F construction shows that μ and n can both be set to 2κ for this construction to realize UC HIC.

For each key pw, function $\mathsf{m2F}_{pw}$ is pictorially shown in Fig. 1. Here we define it by the algorithms which compute $\mathsf{m2F}_{pw}$ and $\mathsf{m2F}_{pw}^{-1}$. (Throughout the paper we denote group $\mathbb{G}$ operation as a multiplication, but this is purely a notational choice, and the construction applies to additive groups as well.)

$$\mathsf{m2F}_{pw} : \{0,1\}^n \times \mathbb{G} \;\rightarrow\; \{0,1\}^n \times \mathbb{G} \tag{1}$$

where:

$\mathsf{m2F}_{pw}(r, M)$:

1. $T \leftarrow M/\mathsf{H}(pw, r)$
2. $k \leftarrow \mathsf{H}'(pw, T)$
3. $s \leftarrow \mathsf{BC.Enc}(k, r)$
4. Output (s, T)

$\mathsf{m2F}_{pw}^{-1}(s, T)$:

1. $k \leftarrow \mathsf{H}'(pw, T)$
2. $r \leftarrow \mathsf{BC.Dec}(k, s)$
3. $M \leftarrow \mathsf{H}(pw, r) \cdot T$
4. Output (r, M)

The following theorem captures the security of the m2F construction:

Theorem 1. *Construction* m2F *realizes functionality* $\mathcal{F}_{\mathsf{HIC}}$ *in the domain* $\mathcal{R} \times \mathbb{G}$ *for* $\mathcal{R} = \{0,1\}^n$ *if* $\mathsf{H} : \{0,1\}^* \times \{0,1\}^n \rightarrow \mathbb{G}$, $\mathsf{H}' : \{0,1\}^* \times \mathbb{G} \rightarrow \{0,1\}^\mu$ *are random oracles,* $\mathsf{BC} : \{0,1\}^\mu \times \{0,1\}^n \rightarrow \{0,1\}^n$ *is an ideal cipher, and* μ *and* n *are both* $\Omega(\kappa)$.

Proof. The proof for Theorem 1 must exhibit a simulator algorithm SIM, which plays a role of an ideal-world adversary interacting with functionality $\mathcal{F}_{\mathsf{HIC}}$, and then show that no efficient environment $\mathcal{Z}$ can distinguish, except for negligible probability, between (1) a *real-world game*, i.e. an interaction with (1a) honest parties who execute $\mathcal{Z}$'s encryption and decryption queries using Enc and Dec implemented with circuit m2F (see Sect. 3), and (1b) RO/IC oracles H, H', BC, BC^{-1}, and (2) an *ideal-world game*, i.e. an interaction with (2a) parties P who execute $\mathcal{Z}$'s encryption and decryption using interfaces Enc, Dec of $\mathcal{F}_{\mathsf{HIC}}$, and (2b) simulator SIM, who services $\mathcal{Z}$'s calls to H, H', BC, BC^{-1} using interfaces AdvEnc and AdvDec of $\mathcal{F}_{\mathsf{HIC}}$.

We start by describing the simulator algorithm SIM, shown in Fig. 3. Note that SIM interacts with an adversarial environment algorithm $\mathcal{Z}$ by servicing $\mathcal{Z}$'s queries to the RO and IC oracles H, H', BC, BC^{-1}. Intuitively, SIM populates input, output tables for these functions, TH, TH' and TBC, in the same way as these idealized oracles would, except when SIM detects a possible encryption or

---

Initialization

Let TH be a set of tuples in $\{0,1\}^* \times \{0,1\}^n \times \mathbb{G}$,
  TH$'$ be a set of tuples in $\{0,1\}^* \times \mathbb{G} \times \{0,1\}^\mu$,
  and TBC be a set of triples in $\{0,1\}^\mu \times \{0,1\}^n \times \{0,1\}^n$.

---

on adversary's query H(pw, r)	on adversary's query H$'$(pw, T)
if $\nexists h$ s.t. $(pw, r, h) \in$ TH: $\quad h \xleftarrow{\text{r}} \mathbb{G}$ $\quad$ add (pw, r, h) to TH return h	if $\nexists k$ s.t. $(pw, T, k) \in$ TH$'$: $\quad k \xleftarrow{\text{r}} \{0,1\}^\mu$ $\quad$ if $\exists(p\hat{w}, \hat{T})$ s.t. $(p\hat{w}, \hat{T}, k) \in$ TH$'$ then abort (col.abort) $\quad\quad$ if $\exists(\hat{r}, \hat{s})$ s.t. $(k, \hat{r}, \hat{s}) \in$ TBC then abort (bckey.abort) $\quad\quad$ add (pw, T, k) to TH$'$ $\quad\quad$ return k

---

on adversary's query BC.Enc(k, r)	on adversary's query BC.Dec(k, s)
if $\nexists s$ s.t. $(k, r, s) \in$ TBC: $\quad$ if $k = $ TH$'$(pw, T)^a: $\quad\quad M \leftarrow $ H(pw, r) $\cdot T$ $\quad\quad (s, \hat{T}) \leftarrow \mathcal{F}_{\text{HIC}}$.AdvEnc($pw, (r, M), T$) $\quad\quad$ if $\hat{T} \neq T$ then abort $\quad$ (advenc.abort) $\quad$ else: $\quad\quad s \xleftarrow{\text{r}} \{s \in \{0,1\}^n : \nexists \hat{r}$ s.t. $(k, \hat{r}, s) \in$ TBC$\}$ $\quad\quad$ add (k, r, s) to TBC return s ―――――――― ^{a} If it exists, we denote by TH$'$(pw, T) the (unique) k s.t. $(pw, T, k) \in$ TH$'$	if $\nexists r$ s.t. $(k, r, s) \in$ TBC: $\quad$ if $k = $ TH$'$(pw, T): $\quad\quad (r, M) \leftarrow \mathcal{F}_{\text{HIC}}$.AdvDec($pw, (s, T)$) $\quad\quad$ if $\exists \hat{s}$ s.t. $(k, r, \hat{s}) \in$ TBC then abort (advdec.abort) $\quad\quad$ if $\exists h$ s.t. $(pw, r, h) \in$ TH then abort (rcol.abort) $\quad\quad$ add $(pw, r, M \cdot T^{-1})$ to TH $\quad$ else: $\quad\quad r \xleftarrow{\text{r}} \{r \in \{0,1\}^n : \nexists \hat{s}$ s.t. $(k, r, \hat{s}) \in$ TBC$\}$ $\quad\quad$ add (k, r, s) to TBC return r

---

Fig. 3. Simulator SIM for the proof of Theorem 1

decryption computation of the modified 2-Feistel circuit. In case SIM decides that these queries form either computation of m2F or m2F^{-1} on new input, SIM detects that input, invokes the adversarial interfaces AdvEnc or AdvDec of $\mathcal{F}_{\text{HIC}}$ to find the corresponding output, and it embeds proper values into these tables to emulate the circuit leading to the computation of this output. The detection of m2F and m2F^{-1} evaluation is relatively straightforward: First, SIM treats every BC.Dec query (k, s) as a possible m2F^{-1} evaluation on key pw and ciphertext $c = (s, T)$ for T s.t. $k = $ H$'$(pw, T). If it is, SIM queries $\mathcal{F}_{\text{HIC}}$.AdvDec on (pw, c) to get $m = (r, M)$. Since this is a random sample from the HIC domain, with overwhelming probability H was not queried on r so SIM can set H(pw, r) to M/T. Second, SIM treats every BC.Enc query (k, r) as possible m2F evaluation on (r, M) s.t. $M = $ H(pw, r) $\cdot T$ for T s.t. $k = $ H$'$(pw, T). However, here is where the difference between IC and HIC shows up: The $\mathcal{F}_{\text{HIC}}$.AdvEnc query fixes the encryption of $m = (r, M)$ to $c = (s, T)$, and whereas s can be random (and SIM can set BC.Enc(k, r) := s for any $c = (s, T)$ returned by $\mathcal{F}_{\text{HIC}}$.AdvEnc as encryption of m under key pw), value T was fixed by H$'$ output k (except for the negligible probability of finding collisions in H$'$). This is why our $\mathcal{F}_{\text{HIC}}$ model must allow the simulator, i.e. the ideal-world adversary, to fix the T part of the ciphertext in the adversarial encryption query AdvEnc.

<u>Initialization</u>

Let TH be a set of tuples in $\{0,1\}^* \times \{0,1\}^n \times \mathbb{G}$,
    TH$'$ be a set of tuples in $\{0,1\}^* \times \mathbb{G} \times \{0,1\}^\mu$,
    and TBC be a set of triples in $\{0,1\}^\mu \times \{0,1\}^n \times \{0,1\}^n$.

For each $pw \in \{0,1\}^*$, initialize empty sets THIC_{pw} and usedR_{pw}.

---

define $\mathcal{F}_{\mathsf{HIC}}.\mathsf{AdvEnc}(pw, (r, M), T)$:

if $\nexists c$ s.t. $((r, M), c) \in \mathsf{THIC}_{pw}$:
$\quad s \xleftarrow{r} \{\hat{s} \in \{0,1\}^n : (*, (\hat{s}, T)) \notin \mathsf{THIC}_{pw}\}$
$\quad c \leftarrow (s, T)$
$\quad$add $((r, M), c)$ to THIC_{pw}
return c

define $\mathcal{F}_{\mathsf{HIC}}.\mathsf{AdvDec}(pw, (s, T))$:

if $\nexists (r, M)$ s.t. $((r, M), (s, T)) \in \mathsf{THIC}_{pw}$:
$\quad (r, M) \xleftarrow{r} \mathcal{D}$
$\quad$if $\exists \hat{c}$ s.t. $((r, M), \hat{c}) \in \mathsf{THIC}_{pw}$ then abort
$\quad$abort if $r \in \mathsf{usedR}_{pw}$ else add r with tag m2F
$\quad$add $((r, M), (s, T))$ to THIC_{pw}
return M

---

on query $\mathsf{Enc}(pw, M)$:

$r \xleftarrow{r} \{0,1\}^n$
abort if $r \in \mathsf{usedR}_{pw}$, else add r with tag m2F
if $\nexists c$ s.t. $((r, M), c) \in \mathsf{THIC}_{pw}$:
$\quad c \xleftarrow{r} \{\hat{c} : \nexists \hat{m}$ s.t. $(\hat{m}, \hat{c}) \in \mathsf{THIC}_{pw}\}$
$\quad$add $((r, M), c)$ to THIC_{pw}
return c

on query $\mathsf{Dec}(pw, c)$:

$(r, M) \leftarrow \mathcal{F}_{\mathsf{HIC}}.\mathsf{AdvDec}(pw, c)$
return M

---

on query $\mathsf{H}(pw, r)$

abort if $r \in \mathsf{usedR}_{pw}$ tagged m2F, else add r
if $\nexists h$ s.t. $(pw, r, h) \in \mathsf{TH}$:
$\quad h \xleftarrow{r} \mathbb{G}$
$\quad$add (pw, r, h) to TH
return h

on query $\mathsf{H}'(pw, T)$

if $\nexists k$ s.t. $(pw, T, k) \in \mathsf{TH}'$:
$\quad k \xleftarrow{r} \{0,1\}^\mu$
$\quad$if $\exists (\hat{pw}, \hat{T})$ s.t. $(\hat{pw}, \hat{T}, k) \in \mathsf{TH}'$ then abort
(col.abort)
$\quad$if $\exists (\hat{r}, \hat{s})$ s.t. $(k, \hat{r}, \hat{s}) \in \mathsf{TBC}$ then abort
(bckey.abort)
$\quad$add (pw, T, k) to TH'
return k

---

on query $\mathsf{BC.Enc}(k, r)$

if $k = \mathsf{TH}'(pw, T)$:
$\quad$if $r \in \mathsf{usedR}_{pw}$ is tagged m2F then abort
$\quad$else add r to usedR_{pw}
if $\nexists s$ s.t. $(k, r, s) \in \mathsf{TBC}$:
$\quad$if $k = \mathsf{TH}'(pw, T)$:
$\quad\quad M \leftarrow \mathsf{H}(pw, r) \cdot T$
$\quad\quad (s, \hat{T}) \leftarrow \mathcal{F}_{\mathsf{HIC}}.\mathsf{AdvEnc}(pw, (r, M), T)$
$\quad\quad$if $\hat{T} \neq T$ then abort $\quad\quad$ (advenc.abort)
$\quad$else:
$\quad\quad s \xleftarrow{r} \{s \in \{0,1\}^n : \nexists \hat{r}$ s.t. $(k, \hat{r}, s) \in \mathsf{TBC}\}$
$\quad$add (k, r, s) to TBC
return s

on query $\mathsf{BC.Dec}(k, s)$

if $\nexists r$ s.t. $(k, r, s) \in \mathsf{TBC}$:
$\quad$if $k = \mathsf{TH}'(pw, T)$:
$\quad\quad (r, M) \leftarrow \mathcal{F}_{\mathsf{HIC}}.\mathsf{AdvDec}(pw, (s, T))$
$\quad\quad$if $\exists \hat{s}$ s.t. $(k, r, \hat{s}) \in \mathsf{TBC}$ then abort
(advdec.abort)
$\quad\quad$if $\exists h$ s.t. $(pw, r, h) \in \mathsf{TH}$ then abort
(rcol.abort)
$\quad\quad$add $(pw, r, M \cdot T^{-1})$ to TH
$\quad$else:
$\quad\quad r \xleftarrow{r} \{r \in \{0,1\}^n : \nexists \hat{s}$ s.t. $(k, r, \hat{s}) \in \mathsf{TBC}\}$
$\quad$add (k, r, s) to TBC
if $k = \mathsf{TH}'(pw, T)$:
$\quad$remove tag m2F from record $r \in \mathsf{usedR}_{pw}$
return r

Fig. 4. The ideal-world Game 0, and its modification Game 1 (text in gray)

Game 2: replacing decryption by circuit

on query m2F.Dec$(pw, (s, T))$:

$k \leftarrow \mathsf{H}'(pw, T)$
$r \leftarrow \mathsf{BC.Dec}(k, s)$
$M \leftarrow \mathsf{H}(pw, r) \cdot T$
if m2F.Dec query was fresh, add tag m2F to $r \in$ usedR$_{pw}$
return M

Game 3: Enc calls AdvDec

on query m2F.Enc(pw, M):

$r \xleftarrow{\mathrm{r}} \{0,1\}^n$
if $r \in$ usedR$_{pw}$ abort, else add r to it with tag m2F
if $\nexists c$ s.t. $((r, M), c) \in$ THIC$_{pw}$:
$\quad T \xleftarrow{\mathrm{r}} \mathsf{G}$
$\quad c \leftarrow \mathcal{F}_{\mathsf{HIC}}.\mathsf{AdvEnc}(pw, (r, M), T)$
return c

Game 4: replacing encryption by circuit

on query m2F.Enc(pw, M):

$r \xleftarrow{\mathrm{r}} \{0,1\}^n$
if $r \in$ usedR$_{pw}$ abort
$T \leftarrow M/\mathsf{H}(pw, r)$
$k \leftarrow \mathsf{H}'(pw, T)$
$s \leftarrow \mathsf{BC.Enc}(k, r)$
assign tag m2F to r in the set usedR$_{pw}$
return (s, T)

Game 5: H is a random oracle

$\mathcal{F}_{\mathsf{HIC}}.\mathsf{AdvDec}$ not used anymore

on query BC.Dec(k, s):

if $\nexists\, r$ s.t. $(k, r, s) \in$ TBC:
$\quad$ if $k = \mathsf{TH}'(pw, T)$:
$\quad\quad r \xleftarrow{\mathrm{r}} \{0,1\}^n$
$\quad\quad$ if $r \in$ usedR$_{pw}$ abort, else add r to it
$\quad\quad h \leftarrow \mathsf{H}(pw, r)$
$\quad\quad M \leftarrow h \cdot T$
$\quad\quad$ if $\exists\hat{c}$ s.t. $((r, M), \hat{c}) \in$ THIC$_{pw}$ then abort
$\quad\quad$ add $((r, M), (s, T))$ to THIC$_{pw}$
$\quad$ else:
$\quad\quad r \xleftarrow{\mathrm{r}} \{r \in \{0,1\}^n : \nexists \hat{s}$ s.t. $(k, r, \hat{s}) \in$ TBC$\}$
$\quad\quad$ add (k, r, s) to TBC
remove tag m2F from record $r \in$ usedR$_{pw}$ if $k =$ TH$'(pw, T)$
return r

Game 6: simplifying parameters

define $\mathcal{F}_{\mathsf{HIC}}.\mathsf{AdvEnc}(pw, r, T)$:

if $\nexists s$ s.t. $(r, (s, T)) \in$ THIC$_{pw}$:
$\quad s \xleftarrow{\mathrm{r}} \{\hat{s} \in \{0,1\}^n : \nexists\hat{r}$ s.t. $(\hat{r}, (\hat{s}, T)) \in$ THIC$_{pw}\}$
$\quad$ add $(r, (s, T))$ to THIC$_{pw}$
return s

on query BC.Dec(k, s):

if $\nexists r$ s.t. $(k, r, s) \in$ TBC:
$\quad$ if $k = \mathsf{TH}'(pw, T)$:
$\quad\quad r \xleftarrow{\mathrm{r}} \{0,1\}^n$
$\quad\quad$ if $r \in$ usedR$_{pw}$ abort, else add r to it
$\quad\quad$ query $\mathsf{H}(pw, r)$ and discard the output
$\quad\quad$ if $\exists\hat{c}$ s.t. $(r, \hat{c}) \in$ THIC$_{pw}$ then abort
$\quad\quad$ add $(r, (s, T))$ to THIC$_{pw}$
$\quad$ else:
$\quad\quad r \xleftarrow{\mathrm{r}} \{r \in \{0,1\}^n : \nexists\hat{s}$ s.t. $(k, r, \hat{s}) \in$ TBC$\}$
$\quad\quad$ add (k, r, s) to TBC
remove tag m2F from record $r \in$ usedR$_{pw}$ if $k =$ TH$'(pw, T)$
return r

on query BC.Enc(k, r):

if $k = \mathsf{TH}'(pw, T)$:
$\quad$ if $r \in$ usedR$_{pw}$ is tagged m2F then abort
$\quad\quad\quad\quad\quad\quad$ else add r to usedR$_{pw}$
if $\nexists s$ s.t. $(k, r, s) \in$ TBC:
$\quad$ if $k = \mathsf{TH}'(pw, T)$:
$\quad\quad$ query $\mathsf{H}(pw, r)$ and discard the output
$\quad\quad s \leftarrow \mathcal{F}_{\mathsf{HIC}}.\mathsf{AdvEnc}(pw, r, T)$
$\quad$ else:
$\quad\quad s \xleftarrow{\mathrm{r}} \{s \in \{0,1\}^n : \nexists\hat{r}$ s.t. $(k, \hat{r}, s) \in$ TBC$\}$
$\quad\quad$ add (k, r, s) to TBC
return s

Game 7: using k

Initialization: $\forall k$ initialize empty THIC$_k$

define $\mathcal{F}_{\mathsf{HIC}}.\mathsf{AdvEnc}(k, r)$:

if $\nexists s$ s.t. $(r, s) \in$ THIC$_k$:
$\quad s \xleftarrow{\mathrm{r}} \{\hat{s} \in \{0,1\}^n : \nexists\hat{r}$ s.t. $(\hat{r}, \hat{s}) \in$ THIC$_k\}$
$\quad$ add (r, s) to THIC$_k$
return s

on query BC.Dec(k, s):

if $\nexists r$ s.t. $(k, r, s) \in$ TBC:
$\quad$ if $k = \mathsf{TH}'(pw, T)$:
$\quad\quad r \xleftarrow{\mathrm{r}} \{0,1\}^n$
$\quad\quad$ if $r \in$ usedR$_{pw}$ abort, else add r to it
$\quad\quad$ if $\exists\hat{s}$ s.t. $(r, \hat{s}) \in$ THIC$_k$ then abort
$\quad\quad$ add (r, s) to THIC$_k$
$\quad$ else:
$\quad\quad r \xleftarrow{\mathrm{r}} \{r \in \{0,1\}^n : \nexists\hat{s}$ s.t. $(k, r, \hat{s}) \in$ TBC$\}$
$\quad\quad$ add (k, r, s) to TBC
remove tag m2F from $r \in$ usedR$_{pw}$ if $k =$ TH$'(pw, T)$
return r

on query BC.Enc(k, r):

if $k = \mathsf{TH}'(pw, T)$:
$\quad$ if $r \in$ usedR$_{pw}$ is tagged m2F then abort
$\quad\quad\quad\quad\quad\quad$ else add r to usedR$_{pw}$
if $\nexists s$ s.t. $(k, r, s) \in$ TBC:
$\quad$ if $k = \mathsf{TH}'(pw, T)$:
$\quad\quad s \leftarrow \mathcal{F}_{\mathsf{HIC}}.\mathsf{AdvEnc}(k, r)$
$\quad$ else:
$\quad\quad s \xleftarrow{\mathrm{r}} \{s \in \{0,1\}^n : \nexists\hat{r}$ s.t. $(k, \hat{r}, s) \in$ TBC$\}$
$\quad\quad$ add (k, r, s) to TBC
return s

Fig. 5. Game-changes (part 1) in the proof of Theorem 1

Game 8: THIC is redundant

Initialization: Drop THIC usage.
$\mathcal{F}_{\mathsf{HIC}}$.AdvEnc not used anymore

on query BC.Enc(k, r):
if $k = \mathsf{TH}'(pw, T)$:
    if $r \in \mathsf{usedR}_{pw}$ is tagged m2F, abort, else add
$r \in \mathsf{usedR}_{pw}$
if $\nexists s$ s.t. $(k, r, s) \in \mathsf{TBC}$:
    $s \xleftarrow{r} \{s \in \{0,1\}^n : \nexists \hat{r}$ s.t. $(k, \hat{r}, s) \in \mathsf{TBC}\}$
    add (k, r, s) to TBC
return s

on query BC.Dec(k, s):
if $\nexists r$ s.t. $(k, r, s) \in \mathsf{TBC}$:
    if $\exists(pw, T)$ s.t. $(pw, T, k) \in \mathsf{TH}'$:
        $r \xleftarrow{r} \{0,1\}^n$
        if $r \in \mathsf{usedR}_{pw}$ abort, else add r to it
    else:
        $r \xleftarrow{r} \{r \in \{0,1\}^n : \nexists \hat{s}$ s.t. $(k, r, \hat{s}) \in \mathsf{TBC}\}$
    add (k, r, s) to TBC
remove tag m2F from record $r \in \mathsf{usedR}_{pw}$ if $k = \mathsf{TH}'(pw, T)$
return r

Fig. 6. Game-changes (part 2) in the proof of Theorem 1

Proof Overview. The proof must show that for any environment $\mathcal{Z}$, its view of the real-world game defined by algorithms Enc, Dec which use the randomized cipher m2F, and the ideal-world game defined by functionality $\mathcal{F}_{\mathsf{HIC}}$ and simulator SIM of Fig. 3. The proof starts from the ideal-world view, which we denote as Game 0, and via a sequence of games, each of which we show is indistinguishable from the next, it reaches the real-world view, which we denote as Game 9. For space-constraint reasons we include the details of the game changes and reductions to the full version [30], but we show the code of all successive games in Figs. 4, 5, and 6. Figure 4 describes the ideal-world Game 0 and its mild modification Game 1. All these games, starting from Game 0 in Fig. 4, interact with an adversarial environment $\mathcal{Z}$, and each game provides two types of interfaces corresponding two types of $\mathcal{Z}$'s queries: (a) the honest party's interfaces Enc, Dec, which $\mathcal{Z}$ can query via any honest party, and (b) RO/IC oracles H, H', BC, BC^{-1}, which $\mathcal{Z}$ can query via its "real-world adversary" interface. Figure 4 defines two sub-procedures, $\mathcal{F}_{\mathsf{HIC}}$.AdvEnc and $\mathcal{F}_{\mathsf{HIC}}$.AdvDec, whose code matches exactly the corresponding interfaces of $\mathcal{F}_{\mathsf{HIC}}$. These subprocedures are used internally by Game 0: They are invoked by the code that services $\mathcal{Z}$'s queries BC.Enc and BC.Dec, because Game 0 follows SIM's code on these queries, and AdvDec is also invoked by Dec, because this is how $\mathcal{F}_{\mathsf{HIC}}$ implements Dec.

Figures 5 and 6 describe the modifications created by all subsequent games, except for the last one, the real-world game denoted Game 9, which is very similar to Game 8, which is the last game shown in Fig. 6. By the arguments for indistinguishability of successive games shown in the full version [30], the total distinguishing advantage of environment $\mathcal{Z}$ between the real-world and the ideal-world interaction is upper-bounded by the following expression, which sums up the bounds given by equations shown in the proof, see [30]:

$$|P_0 - P_9| \leq q^2 \left(\frac{10}{2^n} + \frac{4}{2^n \cdot |\mathbb{G}|} + \frac{6}{2^\mu} \right) \leq q^2 \left(\frac{14}{2^n} + \frac{6}{2^\mu} \right)$$

Since this quantity is negligible, this implies Theorem 1

Notes on Exact Security. By the above equation, the distinguishability advantage implies by our proof can be upper-bounded as $O(q^2/2^n) + O(q^2/2^\mu)$. We assert that both of these factors are unavoidable for our m2F construction. First, while in the $\mathcal{F}_{\mathsf{HIC}}$ functionality we allow the T component of two AdvEnc adversarial calls to be completely independent, this is not the case in our modified two-round Feistel encryption: reuse of a (pw, r) pair implies relations between the T component of different encryption calls that are not seen in $\mathcal{F}_{\mathsf{HIC}}$. Hence we must avoid r collisions in Enc calls, irrespective of how our proof is structured, and asymptotically this gives a $q^2/2^n$ factor in the distinguishing advantage.

Secondly, we need to avoid H' collisions. Indeed, if $\mathsf{H}'(pw, T) = \mathsf{H}'(\hat{pw}, \hat{T})$ then m2F's decryptions using (pw, T) and $(\hat{pw}, \hat{T})$ create the same $s \mapsto r$ map, which would be in stark contrast to our functionality's ideal-cipher like decryption behavior. We conclude that the $q^2/2^\mu$ term also can't be avoided. Notice that these two terms dominate the probability of the environment distinguishing m2F from our functionality $\mathcal{F}_{\mathsf{HIC}}$. In particular, they do not involve $|\mathbb{G}|$, i.e., the size of the message space of our $\mathcal{F}_{\mathsf{HIC}}$.

5   Encrypted Key Exchange with Half-Ideal Cipher

We show that the Encrypted Key Exchange (EKE) protocol of Bellovin and Meritt [8] is a universally composable PAKE if the password encryption is implemented with a (Randomized) Half-Ideal Cipher on the domain of messages output by the key exchange scheme, provided that the key exchange scheme has the random-message property (see Sect. 2). As discussed in the introduction, the same statement was argued by Rosulek et al. [43] with regards to password-encryption implemented using a Programmable Once Public Function (POPF) notion defined therein, which can also be thought of as a weak form of ideal cipher. However, since as we explain in the introduction, the POPF notion is unlikely to suffice in an EKE application, so we need to verify that the notion of UC (Randomized) Half-Ideal Cipher *does* suffice in such application.

In Fig. 7 we show the Encrypted Key Exchange protocol EKE, specialized to use a Half-Ideal Cipher for the password-encryption of the message flows of the underlying Key Agreement scheme KA. In Fig. 7 we assume that KA is a *single-round* scheme. In Sect. 5.1 we extend this to the case of two-flow KA, i.e. to EKE protocol instantiated with a KEM scheme. We note that these two treatments are incomparable because in the case of single-flow KA we start from a more restricted KA scheme and we argue security of a single-flow version of EKE, whereas in the case of two-flow KA, i.e. if KA = KEM, we start from a more general KA scheme but we argue security of a two-flow version of EKE.

The EKE instantiation shown in Fig. 7 assumes that the Half-Ideal Cipher HIC works on domain $\mathcal{D} = \mathcal{R} \times \mathcal{M}$ where $\mathcal{M}$ is the message domain of the scheme KA. The "randomness" set $\mathcal{R}$ is arbitrary, but its size influences the security bound we show for such EKE instantiations. In particular we require that $\log(|\mathcal{R}|) \geq 2\kappa$. If HIC is instantiated with the modified 2-Feistel construction m2F of Sect. 4, one can set $\mathcal{R} = \{0, 1\}^{2\kappa}$, and this instantiation of EKE will send messages whose sizes match those of the underlying KA scheme extended by 2κ bits of randomness due to the Half-Ideal Cipher encryption.

In Fig. 7 for presentation clarity we assume that party identifiers P_0, P_1 are lexicographically ordered. The full protocol will use two helper functions order and bit, defined as order(sid, P, CP) = (sid, P, CP) and bit(P, CP) = 0 if P $<_{lex}$ CP, and order(sid, P, CP) = (sid, CP, P) and bit(P, CP) = 1 if CP $<_{lex}$ P[7]. Party P on input (NewSession, sid, P, CP, pw) will then set fullsid←order(sid, P, CP) and b←bit(P, CP) and it will use HIC.Enc on key $\hat{pw}_b = $ (fullsid, b, pw) to encrypt its outgoing message, and it will use HIC.Dec on key $\hat{pw}_{\neg b} = $ (fullsid, $\neg b$, pw) to decrypt its incoming message.

- Single-round Key Exchange KA = (msg, key) with message space $\mathcal{M}$
- Half-Ideal Cipher HIC on domain $\mathcal{R} \times \mathcal{M}$ for $\mathcal{R} = \{0, 1\}^{\Omega(\kappa)}$

P_0 on NewSession(sid, P_0, P_1, pw_0) P_1 on NewSession(sid, P_1, P_0, pw_1)

(Assume $P_0 <_{lex} P_1$ and let fullsid = (sid, P_0, P_1))

$(x_0, M_0) \xleftarrow{r}$ KA.msg $(x_1, M_1) \xleftarrow{r}$ KA.msg
$c_0 \leftarrow$ HIC.Enc((fullsid, 0, pw_0), M_0) $c_1 \leftarrow$ HIC.Enc((fullsid, 1, pw_1), M_1)
                                        $\xrightarrow{c_0} \quad \xleftarrow{c_1}$

$\hat{M}_1 \leftarrow$ HIC.Dec((fullsid, 1, pw_0), c_1) $\hat{M}_0 \leftarrow$ HIC.Dec((fullsid, 0, pw_1), c_0)
output $K_0 \leftarrow$ KA.key($x_0, \hat{M}_1$)   output $K_1 \leftarrow$ KA.key($x_1, \hat{M}_0$)

Fig. 7. EKE: Encrypted Key Exchange with Half-Ideal Cipher

In Theorem 2 below we show that protocol EKE realizes the (multi-session version of) the PAKE functionality of Canetti et al. [16], denoted $\mathcal{F}_{pwKE}$ (e.g., see [30]). The reason we target the multi-session version of PAKE functionality directly, rather than targeting its single-session version and then resorting to Canetti's composition theorem [15] to imply the security of an arbitrary (and concurrent) number of EKE instances, is that for the latter to work we would need the underlying UC HIC to be instantiated separately for each EKE session identifier sid. Our UC HIC notion of Sect. 3 is a "global" functionality, i.e. it does not natively support separate instances indexed by session identifiers. The modified 2-Feistel construction *could* support such independent instances of HIC by prepending sid to the inputs of all its building block functions H, H', BC, where in the last case value sid would have to be prepended to the key of the (ideal) block-cipher BC. However, this implies longer inputs for each of these blocks, which is especially problematic in case of the block cipher, so it is preferable not to rely on it and show security for a protocol variant where each EKE instance accesses a single HIC functionality, and hence can be implemented with the same instantiation of the modified 2-Feistel HIC construction.

Theorem 2. *If* KA *is a secure key-exchange scheme with the random-message property on domain* $\mathcal{M}$ *and* HIC *is a UC Half-Ideal Cipher over domain* $\mathcal{R} \times \mathcal{M}$, *then protocol* EKE, *Fig. 7, realizes the UC PAKE functionality* $\mathcal{F}_{pwKE}$.

---

[7] We assume that no honest P ever executes (NewSession, sid, P, CP, ·) for CP = P.

SIM interacts with environment $\mathcal{Z}$'s interface $\mathcal{A}$ and with functionality $\mathcal{F}_{\mathsf{pwKE}}$. W.l.o.g. we assume that $\mathcal{A}$ uses AdvDec to implement Dec queries to $\mathcal{F}_{\mathsf{HIC}}$.

Initialization: Set $\mathsf{Cset} = \{\}$, set $\mathsf{THIC}_{p\hat{w}}$ as an empty table and $\mathsf{c2pw}[c] := \bot$ for all values $p\hat{w}$ and c.

Notation (used in all security games in Figure 9)

Let $\mathsf{THIC}_{p\hat{w}}.\mathsf{s}[T]$ be a shortcut for set $\{s \in \mathcal{R} : \nexists \hat{m} \text{ s.t. } (\hat{m}, (s, T)) \in \mathsf{THIC}_{p\hat{w}}\}$.

Let $\mathsf{THIC}_{p\hat{w}}.\mathsf{c}$ be a shortcut for set $\{c \in \mathcal{D} : \nexists \hat{m} \text{ s.t. } (\hat{m}, c) \in \mathsf{THIC}_{p\hat{w}}\}$.

Let $\mathsf{THIC}_{p\hat{w}}.\mathsf{m}$ be a shortcut for set $\{m \in \mathcal{D} : \nexists \hat{c} \text{ s.t. } (m, \hat{c}) \in \mathsf{THIC}_{p\hat{w}}\}$.

On query (NewSession, sid, P, CP) from $\mathcal{F}_{\mathsf{pwKE}}$:

Set $\mathsf{fullsid} \leftarrow \mathsf{order}(\mathsf{sid}, \mathsf{P}, \mathsf{CP})$, $b \leftarrow \mathsf{bit}(\mathsf{P}, \mathsf{CP})$, $c \xleftarrow{\text{r}} \mathcal{D}$ (abort if $c \in \mathsf{Cset}$), add c to Cset, record $(\mathsf{sid}, \mathsf{P}, \mathsf{CP}, \mathsf{fullsid}, b, c)$, return c.

Emulating functionality $\mathcal{F}_{\mathsf{HIC}}$:

- On $\mathcal{A}$'s query (Enc, $p\hat{w}, M$) to $\mathcal{F}_{\mathsf{HIC}}$: Set $r \xleftarrow{\text{r}} \mathcal{R}$, $m \leftarrow (r, M)$. If $(m, c) \in \mathsf{THIC}_{p\hat{w}}$ return c; Else pick $c \xleftarrow{\text{r}} \mathsf{THIC}_{p\hat{w}}.\mathsf{c}$ (abort if $c \in \mathsf{Cset}$), set $\mathsf{c2pw}[c] \leftarrow p\hat{w}$, add c to Cset and (m, c) to $\mathsf{THIC}_{p\hat{w}}$, return c.

- On $\mathcal{A}$'s query (AdvEnc, $p\hat{w}, m, T$) to $\mathcal{F}_{\mathsf{HIC}}$: If $(m, c) \in \mathsf{THIC}_{p\hat{w}}$ return c; Else pick $s \xleftarrow{\text{r}} \mathsf{THIC}_{p\hat{w}}.\mathsf{s}[T]$, set $c \leftarrow (s, T)$ (abort if $c \in \mathsf{Cset}$), set $\mathsf{c2pw}[c] \leftarrow p\hat{w}$, add c to Cset and (m, c) to $\mathsf{THIC}_{p\hat{w}}$, return c.

- On $\mathcal{A}$'s query (AdvDec, $p\hat{w}, c$) to $\mathcal{F}_{\mathsf{HIC}}$: If $(m, c) \in \mathsf{THIC}_{p\hat{w}}$ return m; Else pick $r \xleftarrow{\text{r}} \mathcal{R}$ and $(x, M) \xleftarrow{\text{r}} \mathsf{KA.msg}$, set $m \leftarrow (r, M)$, add (m, c) to $\mathsf{THIC}_{p\hat{w}}$ (abort if $\exists \hat{c} \neq c$ s.t. $(m, \hat{c}) \in \mathsf{THIC}_{p\hat{w}}$), save (backdoor, $c, p\hat{w}, x$), return m.

On $\mathcal{A}$'s message $\hat{c}$ to session $\mathsf{P}^{\mathsf{sid}}$: (accept only the first such message)

Retrieve record $(\mathsf{sid}, \mathsf{P}, \mathsf{CP}, \mathsf{fullsid}, b, c)$ and do:

1. If there is record $(\mathsf{sid}, \mathsf{CP}, \mathsf{P}, \mathsf{fullsid}, \neg b, \hat{c})$: send (NewKey, sid, P, $\bot$) to $\mathcal{F}_{\mathsf{pwKE}}$;

2. Otherwise set $p\hat{w} \leftarrow \mathsf{c2pw}[\hat{c}]$ and do the following:
   (a) If $p\hat{w} = \bot$ or $p\hat{w} = (\mathsf{full\hat{s}id}, \hat{b}, \cdot)$ for $(\mathsf{full\hat{s}id}, \hat{b}) \neq (\mathsf{fullsid}, \neg b)$, send (TestPwd, sid, P, $\bot$) and (NewKey, sid, P, $\bot$) to $\mathcal{F}_{\mathsf{pwKE}}$;
   (b) If $p\hat{w} = (\mathsf{fullsid}, \neg b, pw^*)$ retrieve $((\hat{r}, \hat{M}), \hat{c})$ from $\mathsf{THIC}_{p\hat{w}}$ and:
      i. service $\mathcal{F}_{\mathsf{HIC}}$'s query (AdvDec, $(\mathsf{fullsid}, b, pw^*), c$), retrieve (backdoor, $c, (\mathsf{fullsid}, b, pw^*), x$);
      ii. set $K \leftarrow \mathsf{KA.key}(x, \hat{M})$, send (TestPwd, sid, P, pw^*) and (NewKey, sid, P, K) to $\mathcal{F}_{\mathsf{pwKE}}$.

Fig. 8. Simulator SIM for the proof of Theorem 2

Proof. Let $\mathcal{Z}$ be an arbitrary efficient environment. In the rest of the proof we will assume that the real-world adversary $\mathcal{A}$ is an interface of $\mathcal{Z}$. In Fig. 8 we show the construction of a simulator algorithm SIM, which together with functionality $\mathcal{F}_{\mathsf{pwKE}}$ defines the ideal-world view of $\mathcal{Z}$. As is standard, the role of SIM is to emulate actions of honest parties executing protocol EKE given the information revealed by functionality $\mathcal{F}_{\mathsf{pwKE}}$, and to convert the actions of the real-world adversary into queries to $\mathcal{F}_{\mathsf{pwKE}}$. (In Fig. 8 we use $\mathsf{P}^{\mathsf{sid}}$ to denote P's session indexed by sid which is emulated by SIM.) The proof then consists of a sequence of games, shown in Fig. 9, starting from the real-world game, Game 0, where $\mathcal{Z}$ interacts with the honest parties running protocol EKE, and ending with the ideal-world game, Game 7, where $\mathcal{Z}$ interacts via dummy honest parties with functionality $\mathcal{F}_{\mathsf{pwKE}}$ which in turn interacts with simulator SIM. (This last game is not shown in Fig. 9 because its code can be derived from the code of simulator SIM, Fig. 8, and functionality $\mathcal{F}_{\mathsf{pwKE}}$, e.g., see [30].) We note that in each game in Fig. 9 we write $\boxed{\text{output } [...]}$ for output of queries that service $\mathcal{Z}$'s interaction with EKEinstances, and we write "return [...]" for output of queries that service $\mathcal{Z}$'s interaction with $\mathcal{F}_{\mathsf{HIC}}$.

At each step we prove that the two consecutive games are indistinguishable, which implies the claim by transitivity of computational indistinguishability. Note that we argue security of EKE in the $\mathcal{F}_{\mathsf{HIC}}$-hybrid model. Specifically, algorithm SIM emulates a "global" $\mathcal{F}_{\mathsf{HIC}}$ functionality which services any number of EKE protocol instances. Note that $\mathcal{Z}$ or $\mathcal{A}$ can call $\mathcal{F}_{\mathsf{HIC}}$ on keys which correspond to all strings $\hat{pw} = (\mathsf{fullsid}, b, pw)$ including for $\mathsf{fullsid}$ corresponding to sessions which were not (yet) started by $\mathcal{Z}$. Indeed, algorithm SIM treats queries pertaining to any key $\hat{pw}$ equally, and embeds random ciphertext c in response to Enc queries, random partial ciphertext s in response to AdvEnc queries, and random KA message M in response to AdvDec and Dec queries, saving the corresponding KA local state in (backdoor, ...) records. Since Dec is a wrapper over AdvDec we assume that the adversary uses only interface AdvDec, and we implement the EKE code of $\mathsf{P}^{\mathsf{sid}}$ using AdvDec as well.

The intuition for the simulation is that it sends an outgoing EKE message on behalf of $\mathsf{P}^{\mathsf{sid}}$ at random, since this is how HIC encryptions are formed. SIM services HIC encryption queries as $\mathcal{F}_{\mathsf{HIC}}$ does except that it collects the ciphertexts created by any encryption query and the ciphertexts chosen for every honest session in set Cset, and aborts if either process regenerates a ciphertext in Cset. Here we use the fact that even though an adversary can set the T part of the ciphertext $c = (s, T)$ resulting from an adversarial encryption query AdvEnc, the s part of c is chosen at random, and this prevents ciphertext collisions (except with negligible probability) if $|\mathcal{R}| \geq 2^{2\kappa}$. Hence, assuming that $\mathcal{R}$ is big enough, we have that (1) each adversarial ciphertext can be matched to (at most) one password on which it decrypts to a non-random value in space $\mathcal{M}$, and (2) the simulator can extract this unique password and retrieve the corresponding plaintext (SIM stores the key $\hat{pw}$ which was used to create ciphertext c in the c2pw table by setting $\mathsf{c2pw}[c] \leftarrow \hat{pw}$). Moreover, since by the same collision-resistant property of $\mathcal{F}_{\mathsf{HIC}}$ ciphertexts the adversary cannot "hit" any honest session $\mathsf{P}^{\mathsf{sid}}$'s ciphertext c via an encryption query, the decryption of $\mathsf{P}^{\mathsf{sid}}$'s ciphertext on each password is also a random value in $\mathcal{M}$. By the message-randomness property of KA, simulator SIM can embed messages of fresh KA instances into each decryption query, and combining this with fact (1) above allows for a reduction of EKE instances corresponding to "wrong" password guesses to the KA's security.

Let q_{IC} be the bound on the number of queries $\mathcal{Z}$ makes to the interfaces of the (randomized) ideal cipher $\mathcal{F}_{\mathsf{HIC}}$, and let q_P be the upper-bound on the number of honest EKE sessions $\mathsf{P}^{\mathsf{sid}}$ which $\mathcal{Z}$ invokes for any identifiers P, sid.[8] Let $\varepsilon_{\mathsf{KA.sec}}$ and $\varepsilon_{\mathsf{KA.rand}}$ be the upper-bounds on the distinguishing advantage against, respectively, the security and the random-message properties of the key exchange scheme KA (see Sect. 2) of an adversary whose computational resources are roughly those of an environment $\mathcal{Z}$ extended by execution of $q_{IC} + q_P$ instances of the key exchange scheme KA.[9]

For space-constraint reasons we defer the details of the game changes and reductions to the full version [30], but we show the code of all successive games in Fig. 9. By the arguments for indistinguishability of successive games, the total distinguishing advantage of environment $\mathcal{Z}$ between the real-world and the ideal-world interaction is upper-bounded by the following expression, which sums up the bounds argued in the full proof, see [30]:

$$(q_{IC} + q_P)\left[\frac{1}{|\mathcal{R}|} \cdot \left\{2q_P + q_{IC} + 2 \cdot \frac{q_{IC} + q_P}{|\mathcal{M}|}\right\} + \varepsilon_{\mathsf{KA.rand}} + q_P \cdot \varepsilon_{\mathsf{KA.sec}}\right] \quad (2)$$

Since this quantity is negligible if $\mathcal{R} = \{0,1\}^n$ for $n = O(\kappa)$, it implies Theorem 2.

Notes on Exact Security. The dominating factors are $(q_{IC} + q_P)^2/|\mathcal{R}|$ and $(q_{IC} + q_P) \cdot (\varepsilon_{\mathsf{KA.rand}} + q_P \cdot \varepsilon_{\mathsf{KA.sec}})$. The first factor is due to possible collisions in Half-Ideal Cipher, and it is unavoidable using an arbitrary HIC realization because it is the probability of generating the same ciphertext c as an encryption of two different KA instances under two different passwords, which would also form an explicit attack on the security of EKE (the adversary would effectively make two password guesses in one on-line interaction). However, whereas the bound $(q_{IC})^2/|\mathcal{R}|$ is tight if the encryption is modeled as a Half-Ideal Cipher, we do not know if it is tight in relation to the specific modified 2-Feistel instantiation of Half-Ideal Cipher, because we do not know how to stage an explicit attack on EKE using modified 2-Feistel along these lines. This relates to the fact that whereas the modified 2-Feistel realizes functionality $\mathcal{F}_{\mathsf{HIC}}$, this functionality allows more freedom to the adversary than the modified 2-Feistel construction. Namely, whereas $\mathcal{F}_{\mathsf{HIC}}$ allows the adversary to encrypt any messages M using a ciphertext $c = (s, T)$ where T can be freely set, the same is not true about the modified 2-Feistel construction, where for any fixed M the adversary can choose T from the set of values of the form $T = M/\mathsf{H}(pw, r)$ for some r.

The second factor is due to reductions to KA security properties. Note that some KA schemes, e.g. Diffie-Hellman, have perfect message-randomness, i.e. $\varepsilon_{\mathsf{KA.rand}} = 0$. Further, if the KA scheme is *random self-reducible*, as is Diffie-Hellman, then this factor can be reduced to $\varepsilon_{\mathsf{KA.sec}}$ because a reduction to KA security for the transition between Games 4 and 5, see the proof in [30], can then be modified so that it deals with all honest sessions at once instead of staging a hybrid argument over all sessions, and it embeds randomized versions of the KA challenge into each decryption query rather than guessing a target query.

---

[8] We assume that $\mathcal{Z}$ invokes at most two sessions for any fixed identifier sid.

[9] This bound involves $q_{IC} + q_P$ instead of q_P key exchange instances because our reductions to KA security run KA.msg for each adversarial AdvDec query to $\mathcal{F}_{\mathsf{HIC}}$.

Game 0: real-world interaction

initialization

Initialize $\mathsf{Cset} = \{\}$ and $\forall \hat{pw}$ empty $\mathsf{THIC}_{\hat{pw}}$

on $(\mathsf{NewSession}, \mathsf{sid}, \mathsf{P}, \mathsf{CP}, pw)$ to P:
fullsid $\leftarrow$ order(sid, P, CP), $b \leftarrow$ bit(P, CP), $\hat{pw} \leftarrow$
(fullsid, b, pw)
$(x, M) \xleftarrow{r} \mathsf{KA.msg}$
$c \leftarrow \mathcal{F}_{\mathsf{HIC}}.\mathsf{Enc}(\hat{pw}, M)$
save (sid, P, CP, fullsid, b, pw, x, c, $\perp$), $\boxed{\text{output } c}$

on message $\hat{c}$ to session $\mathsf{P}^{\mathsf{sid}}$ (accept only one):
if $\exists$ record (sid, P, CP, fullsid, b, pw, x, $\cdot$, $\perp$):
$\quad (\hat{r}, \hat{M}) \leftarrow \mathcal{F}_{\mathsf{HIC}}.\mathsf{AdvDec}((\mathsf{fullsid}, \neg b, pw), \hat{c})$
$\quad K \leftarrow \mathsf{KA.key}(x, \hat{M})$ and $\boxed{\text{output (sid, P, } K)}$

on query $\mathcal{F}_{\mathsf{HIC}}.\mathsf{Enc}(\hat{pw}, M)$:
$r \xleftarrow{r} \mathcal{R}$, set $m \leftarrow (r, M)$
If $\exists$ c s.t. $(m, c) \in \mathsf{THIC}_{\hat{pw}}$:
$\quad$ return c
else:
$\quad$ pick $c \xleftarrow{r} \mathsf{THIC}_{\hat{pw}}.c$,
$\quad$ add c to Cset and (m, c) to $\mathsf{THIC}_{\hat{pw}}$
$\quad$ return c

on query $\mathcal{F}_{\mathsf{HIC}}.\mathsf{AdvEnc}(\hat{pw}, m, T)$:
if $\exists$ c s.t. $(m, c) \in \mathsf{THIC}_{\hat{pw}}$:
$\quad$ return c
else:
$\quad s \xleftarrow{r} \mathsf{THIC}_{\hat{pw}}.s[T]$, set $c \leftarrow (s, T)$,
$\quad$ add c to Cset and (m, c) to $\mathsf{THIC}_{\hat{pw}}$
$\quad$ return c

on query $\mathcal{F}_{\mathsf{HIC}}.\mathsf{AdvDec}(\hat{pw}, c)$:
if $\exists$ m s.t. $(m, c) \in \mathsf{THIC}_{\hat{pw}}$:
$\quad$ return m
else:
$\quad m \xleftarrow{r} \mathsf{THIC}_{\hat{pw}}.m$, add (m, c) to $\mathsf{THIC}_{\hat{pw}}$
return m

Game 1: randomizing protocol communication

on $(\mathsf{NewSession}, \mathsf{sid}, \mathsf{P}, \mathsf{CP}, pw)$ to P:
set (fullsid, b, $\hat{pw}$) as in Game 0
$(x, M) \xleftarrow{r} \mathsf{KA.msg}$, $r \xleftarrow{r} \mathcal{R}$, $c \xleftarrow{r} \mathcal{D}$
abort if $((r, M), *) \in \mathsf{THIC}_{\hat{pw}}$ or $c \in \mathsf{Cset}$
add $((r, M), c)$ to $\mathsf{THIC}_{\hat{pw}}$
save (sid, P, CP, fullsid, b, pw, x, c, $\perp$), $\boxed{\text{output } c}$

Game 2: binding adversarial ciphertexts to passwords

on $\mathcal{F}_{\mathsf{HIC}}.\mathsf{Enc}(\hat{pw}, M)$ or $\mathcal{F}_{\mathsf{HIC}}.\mathsf{AdvEnc}(\hat{pw}, m, T)$:
Before adding c to Cset, do the following:
$\quad$ abort if $c \in \mathsf{Cset}$
$\quad$ set c2pw[c] $\leftarrow \hat{pw}$

Game 3: adding trapdoors to decryption

on query $\mathcal{F}_{\mathsf{HIC}}.\mathsf{AdvDec}(\hat{pw}, c)$:
if $\exists m$ s.t. $(m, c) \in \mathsf{THIC}_{\hat{pw}}$ return m, otherwise:
$\quad (x, M) \xleftarrow{r} \mathsf{KA.msg}(1^\kappa)$, $r \xleftarrow{r} \mathcal{R}$, $m \leftarrow (r, M)$
$\quad$ abort if $(m, *) \in \mathsf{THIC}_{\hat{pw}}$
$\quad$ add (m, c) to $\mathsf{THIC}_{\hat{pw}}$
$\quad$ save (backdoor, c, $\hat{pw}$, x), return m

Game 4: KA messages via AdvDec

on $(\mathsf{NewSession}, \mathsf{sid}, \mathsf{P}, \mathsf{CP}, pw)$ to P:
set (fullsid, b, $\hat{pw}$) as in Game 0
$c \xleftarrow{r} \mathcal{D}$, abort if $c \in \mathsf{Cset}$, otherwise add c to Cset
query $\mathcal{F}_{\mathsf{HIC}}.\mathsf{AdvDec}(\hat{pw}, c)$
retrieve (backdoor, c, $\hat{pw}$, x)
save (sid, P, CP, fullsid, b, pw, x, c, $\perp$), $\boxed{\text{output } c}$

Game 5: extracting passwords

on message $\hat{c}$ to session $\mathsf{P}^{\mathsf{sid}}$:
if $\exists$ record rec $=$ (sid, P, CP, fullsid, b, pw, x, c, $\perp$):
$\quad$ if $\exists$ record (sid, CP, P, fullsid, $\neg b$, pw, $\cdot$, $\hat{c}$, $\hat{K}$)
$\quad$ s.t. $\mathcal{Z}$ sent c to $\mathsf{CP}^{\mathsf{sid}}$:
$\quad\quad K \leftarrow \hat{K}$
$\quad$ else:
$\quad\quad \hat{pw} \leftarrow$ c2pw[$\hat{c}$]
$\quad\quad$ if $\hat{pw} = $ (fullsid, $\neg b$, pw):
$\quad\quad\quad$ retrieve $((\hat{r}, \hat{M}), \hat{c})$ from $\mathsf{THIC}_{\hat{pw}}$,
$\quad\quad\quad$ set $K \leftarrow \mathsf{KA.key}(x, \hat{M})$
$\quad\quad$ else:
$\quad\quad\quad K \xleftarrow{r} \{0, 1\}^\kappa$
$\quad\quad$ reset rec $\leftarrow$ (sid, P, CP, fullsid, b, pw, x, c, K)
$\quad \boxed{\text{output (sid, P, } K)}$

Game 6: delaying password usage

on $(\mathsf{NewSession}, \mathsf{sid}, \mathsf{P}, \mathsf{CP}, pw)$ to P:
fullsid $\leftarrow$ order(sid, P, CP), $b \leftarrow$ bit(P, CP)
$c \xleftarrow{r} \mathcal{D}$, abort if $c \in \mathsf{Cset}$, otherwise add c to Cset
save (sid, P, CP, fullsid, b, pw, $\perp$, c, $\perp$), $\boxed{\text{output } c}$

on message $\hat{c}$ to session $\mathsf{P}^{\mathsf{sid}}$:
if $\exists$ record (sid, P, CP, fullsid, b, pw, $\perp$, c, $\perp$):
$\quad$ if $\exists$ record (sid, CP, P, fullsid, $\neg b$, pw, $\perp$, $\hat{c}$, $\hat{K}$):
$\quad\quad K \leftarrow \hat{K}$
$\quad$ else:
$\quad\quad \hat{pw} \leftarrow$ c2pw[$\hat{c}$]
$\quad\quad$ if $\hat{pw} = $ (fullsid, $\neg b$, pw):
$\quad\quad\quad$ query $\mathcal{F}_{\mathsf{HIC}}.\mathsf{AdvDec}((\mathsf{fullsid}, b, pw), c)$,
$\quad\quad\quad$ retrieve (backdoor, c, $\cdot$, x)
$\quad\quad\quad$ retrieve $((\hat{r}, \hat{M}), \hat{c})$ from $\mathsf{THIC}_{\hat{pw}}$,
$\quad\quad\quad$ set $K \leftarrow \mathsf{KA.key}(x, \hat{M})$
$\quad\quad$ else:
$\quad\quad\quad K \xleftarrow{r} \{0, 1\}^\kappa$
$\quad\quad$ reset rec $\leftarrow$ (sid, P, CP, fullsid, b, pw, x, c, K)
$\quad \boxed{\text{output (sid, P, } K)}$

Fig. 9. Game changes for the proof of Theorem 2 (compare Fig. 8 for notation)

5.1   EKE with Half-Ideal Cipher: The KEM Version

In Fig. 10 we show protocol EKE-KEM, which is a KEM version of the EKE protocol using a Half-Ideal Cipher. In the 1-flow protocol EKE considered in Fig. 7, the message flows are generated by a single-round KA scheme, whereas here we consider an EKE variant which is built from any two-flow key exchange, i.e. KEM, see Sect. 2.2. The drawback is that it is 2-flow instead of 1-flow, but the benefits are that the HIC can be used only for one message, so if KEM is instantiated with Diffie-Hellman and HIC is implemented using m2F, this implies a single RO hash onto a group per party instead of two such hashes. Moreover, this version of EKE can use any CPA-secure KEM as a black box, as long as the KEM satisfies the anonymity and uniform public keys properties, which implies, e.g., lattice-based UC PAKE given any lattice-based KEM with these properties.

- KEM scheme KEM = (kg, enc, dec) with public key space $\mathcal{PK}$
- Half-Ideal Cipher HIC on domain $\mathcal{R} \times \mathcal{PK}$ for $\mathcal{R} = \{0,1\}^{\Omega(\kappa)}$
- Random oracle hash H onto $\{0,1\}^\kappa$

P_0 on NewSession(sid, P_0, P_1, pw_0) P_1 on NewSession(sid, P_1, P_0, pw_1)

(Assume $P_0 \leq_{lex} P_1$ and let fullsid = (sid, P_0, P_1))

$(sk, pk) \xleftarrow{r} \text{kg}$
$c \leftarrow \text{HIC.Enc}((\text{fullsid}, pw_0), pk) \quad\xrightarrow{\ c\ }\quad pk' \leftarrow \text{HIC.Dec}((\text{fullsid}, pw_1), c)$
$\qquad\qquad\qquad\qquad\qquad\qquad\qquad\qquad\qquad (e, K) \leftarrow \text{enc}(pk'),$
$\qquad\qquad\qquad\qquad\qquad\qquad\qquad\qquad\qquad \tau \leftarrow \text{H}(K, pk')$
$K \leftarrow \text{dec}(sk, e) \qquad\qquad \xleftarrow{\ e, \tau\ } \qquad \text{output } K_1 \leftarrow \text{H}(K)$
if $\tau = \text{H}(K, pk)$ output $K_0 \leftarrow \text{H}(K)$, else $K_0 \xleftarrow{r} \{0,1\}^\kappa$

Fig. 10. EKE-KEM: Encrypted Key Exchange with Half-Ideal Cipher (KEM version)

Note that in the protocol of Fig. 10 party P_0 outputs a random session key if the key confirmation message τ fails to verify. This is done only so that the protocol conforms to the implicit-authentication functionality $\mathcal{F}_{\text{pwKE}}$. In practice P_0 could output $\bot$ in this case, and this would implement explicit authentication in the P_1-to-P_0 direction.

Theorem 3. *If* KEM *is IND secure, anonymous, and has uniform public keys in domain* $\mathcal{PK}$ *(see Sect. 2.2),* HIC *is a UC Half-Ideal Cipher in domain* $\mathcal{R} \times \mathcal{PK}$, *and* H *is an RO hash, then protocol* EKE-KEM *realizes the UC PAKE functionality* $\mathcal{F}_{\text{pwKE}}$.

The proof of Theorem 3 is deferred to the full version [30]. It follows the same blueprint as the proof of Theorem 2. The most important intuition needed for the adaptation of the proof of Theorem 2 to the proof of Theorem 3 is why it works for KEMs that satisfy the anonymity property: The key issue is that we need anonymity of the KEM ciphertext e only for honest keys pk and not for adversarial ones, and the reason for this is that the only non-random pk under which an honest party encrypts is the key pk decrypted under a unique password guess pw^* used in the adversarial ciphertext c this party receives. If pw^* equals to P_1's password pw then this session is already successfully attacked, so the non-randomness of P_1's ciphertext is not an issue. But if $pw^* \neq pw$ then KEM ciphertext e is effectively encrypted under key $pk' = \mathsf{AdvDec}(pw, c)$ which is random, and the key confirmation works as a commitment to the KEM key pk decrypted from HIC ciphertext c, hence also to the password used in that decryption. This commitment is also effectively encrypted under the KEM session key K, hence it can be verified only by a party which created pk and HIC-encrypted it under the right pw. Here we again rely on the property of HIC, which just like IC assures that decryption under any password except for the unique password committed in the ciphertext results in a random plaintext, i.e. a random KEM public key pk, which makes the KEM session key K encrypted under such pk hidden to the adversary by KEM security.

We note that the key confirmation could involve directly pw instead of pk, but pk is a commitment to pw unless the adversary creates a collision in HIC plaintext, and using pk instead of pw lets P_0 erase pw after sending its first message. This way an adaptive compromise on party P_0 during protocol execution allows for offline dictionary attack on the password, but does not leak it straight away. (Note that adaptive party compromise is not part of our security model.) We note also that RO hash H can probably be replaced by a key derivation function which is both a CRH (because it needs to commit to pk) and a PRF (because it must encrypt this commitment under K), but since HIC implies RO hash (and indeed our m2F uses it) we opt for the simpler option of RO hash to compute the authenticator.

6   Applications of Half-Ideal Cipher to aPAKE

Gu et al. [33] proposed an asymmetric PAKE protocol called KHAPE which is a generic compiler from any UC *key-hiding* Authenticated Key Exchange (AKE), using an Ideal Cipher on the domain formed by (private, public) key pairs of the AKE. We show that KHAPE realizes UC aPAKE if IC is replaced by HIC. For lack of space the proof of the following Theorem is deferred to the full version [30]. For reference, for AKE functionality $\mathcal{F}_{\mathsf{khAKE}}$ see e.g., [33], and for aPAKE functionality $\mathcal{F}_{\mathsf{aPAKE}}$ see e.g., [30].

Theorem 4. *Protocol* KHAPE *of [33] realizes the UC aPAKE functionality* $\mathcal{F}_{\mathsf{aPAKE}}$ *if the AKE protocol realizes the Key-Hiding AKE functionality* $\mathcal{F}_{\mathsf{khAKE}}$ *assuming that* kdf *is a secure PRF and* HIC *is a half-ideal cipher over message space of private and public key pairs in AKE.*

We note that Freitas et al. [31] showed a UC aPAKE which improves upon protocol KHAPE of [33] in round complexity. The aPAKE of [31] relies on IC in a similar way as protocol KHAPE, and the proof therein should also generalize to the case when IC is replaced by HIC.

References

1. Abdalla, M., Catalano, D., Chevalier, C., Pointcheval, D.: Efficient two-party password-based key exchange protocols in the UC framework. In: Malkin, T. (ed.) CT-RSA 2008. LNCS, vol. 4964, pp. 335–351. Springer, Heidelberg (2008). https://doi.org/10.1007/978-3-540-79263-5_22
2. Albrecht, M.R., et al.: Classic McEliece: NIST round 3 submission (2021). https://csrc.nist.gov/Projects/post-quantum-cryptography/round-3-submissions
3. Alkim,E., et al.: FrodoKEM: NIST round 3 submission (2021). https://csrc.nist.gov/Projects/post-quantum-cryptography/round-3-submissions
4. Andreeva, E., Bogdanov, A., Dodis, Y., Mennink, B., Steinberger, J.P.: On the indifferentiability of key-alternating ciphers. In: Canetti, R., Garay, J.A. (eds.) CRYPTO 2013. LNCS, vol. 8042, pp. 531–550. Springer, Heidelberg (2013). https://doi.org/10.1007/978-3-642-40041-4_29
5. Bellare, M., Boldyreva, A., Desai, A., Pointcheval, D.: Key-privacy in public-key encryption. In: Boyd, C. (ed.) ASIACRYPT 2001. LNCS, vol. 2248, pp. 566–582. Springer, Heidelberg (2001). https://doi.org/10.1007/3-540-45682-1_33
6. Bellare, M., Pointcheval, D., Rogaway, P.: Authenticated key exchange secure against dictionary attacks. In: Preneel, B. (ed.) EUROCRYPT 2000. LNCS, vol. 1807, pp. 139–155. Springer, Heidelberg (2000). https://doi.org/10.1007/3-540-45539-6_11
7. Bellare, M., Rogaway, P.: Random Oracles are practical: a paradigm for designing efficient protocols. In: Denning, D.E., Pyle, R., Ganesan, R., Sandhu, R.S., Ashby, V. (eds.) ACM CCS 1993, pp. 62–73. ACM Press, November 1993. https://doi.org/10.1145/168588.168596
8. Bellovin, S.M., Merritt, M.: Encrypted key exchange: password-based protocols secure against dictionary attacks. In: IEEE Computer Society Symposium on Research in Security and Privacy - S&P 1992, pp. 72–84. IEEE (1992)
9. Bernstein, D.J., Hamburg, M., Krasnova, A., Lange, T.: Elligator: elliptic-curve points indistinguishable from uniform random strings. In: Sadeghi, A.R., Gligor, V.D., Yung, M. (eds.) ACM CCS 2013, pp. 967–980. ACM Press, November 2013. https://doi.org/10.1145/2508859.2516734
10. Bernstein, D.J., et al.: GIMLI: a cross-platform permutation. In: Fischer, W., Homma, N. (eds.) CHES 2017. LNCS, vol. 10529, pp. 299–320. Springer, Cham (2017). https://doi.org/10.1007/978-3-319-66787-4_15
11. Bertoni, G., Daemen, J., Peeters, M., Van Assche, G.: Keccak. In: Johansson, T., Nguyen, P.Q. (eds.) EUROCRYPT 2013. LNCS, vol. 7881, pp. 313–314. Springer, Heidelberg (2013). https://doi.org/10.1007/978-3-642-38348-9_19
12. Black, J., Rogaway, P.: Ciphers with arbitrary finite domains. In: Preneel, B. (ed.) CT-RSA 2002. LNCS, vol. 2271, pp. 114–130. Springer, Heidelberg (2002). https://doi.org/10.1007/3-540-45760-7_9
13. Black, J., Rogaway, P., Shrimpton, T.: Black-box analysis of the block-cipher-based hash-function constructions from PGV. In: Yung, M. (ed.) CRYPTO 2002. LNCS, vol. 2442, pp. 320–335. Springer, Heidelberg (2002). https://doi.org/10.1007/3-540-45708-9_21
14. Bos, J., et al.: CRYSTALS - kyber: a CCA-secure module-lattice-based KEM. In: 2018 IEEE European Symposium on Security and Privacy (EuroS P), pp. 353–367 (2018). https://doi.org/10.1109/EuroSP.2018.00032
15. Canetti, R.: Universally composable security: a new paradigm for cryptographic protocols. In: IEEE Symposium on Foundations of Computer Science - FOCS 2001, pp. 136–145. IEEE (2001)

154   B. F. D. Santos et al.

16. Canetti, R., Halevi, S., Katz, J., Lindell, Y., MacKenzie, P.: Universally composable password-based key exchange. In: Cramer, R. (ed.) EUROCRYPT 2005. LNCS, vol. 3494, pp. 404–421. Springer, Heidelberg (2005). https://doi.org/10.1007/11426639_24
17. Coron, J.-S., Dodis, Y., Mandal, A., Seurin, Y.: A domain extender for the ideal cipher. In: Micciancio, D. (ed.) TCC 2010. LNCS, vol. 5978, pp. 273–289. Springer, Heidelberg (2010). https://doi.org/10.1007/978-3-642-11799-2_17
18. Coron, J.-S., Patarin, J., Seurin, Y.: The random oracle model and the ideal cipher model are equivalent. In: Wagner, D. (ed.) CRYPTO 2008. LNCS, vol. 5157, pp. 1–20. Springer, Heidelberg (2008). https://doi.org/10.1007/978-3-540-85174-5_1
19. Dachman-Soled, D., Katz, J., Thiruvengadam, A.: 10-round feistel is indifferentiable from an ideal cipher. In: Fischlin, M., Coron, J.-S. (eds.) EUROCRYPT 2016. LNCS, vol. 9666, pp. 649–678. Springer, Heidelberg (2016). https://doi.org/10.1007/978-3-662-49896-5_23
20. Daemen, J., Hoffert, S., Assche, G.V., Keer, R.V.: The design of Xoodoo and Xoofff. IACR Trans. Symm. Cryptol. **2018**(4), 1–38 (2018). https://doi.org/10.13154/tosc.v2018.i4.1-38
21. Dai, Y., Seurin, Y., Steinberger, J., Thiruvengadam, A.: Indifferentiability of iterated even-mansour ciphers with non-idealized key-schedules: five rounds are necessary and sufficient. In: Katz, J., Shacham, H. (eds.) CRYPTO 2017. LNCS, vol. 10403, pp. 524–555. Springer, Cham (2017). https://doi.org/10.1007/978-3-319-63697-9_18
22. Dai, Y., Steinberger, J.: Indifferentiability of 8-round feistel networks. In: Robshaw, M., Katz, J. (eds.) CRYPTO 2016. LNCS, vol. 9814, pp. 95–120. Springer, Heidelberg (2016). https://doi.org/10.1007/978-3-662-53018-4_4
23. D'Anvers, J.-P., Karmakar, A., Sinha Roy, S., Vercauteren, F.: Saber: module-LWR based key exchange, CPA-secure encryption and CCA-secure KEM. In: Joux, A., Nitaj, A., Rachidi, T. (eds.) AFRICACRYPT 2018. LNCS, vol. 10831, pp. 282–305. Springer, Cham (2018). https://doi.org/10.1007/978-3-319-89339-6_16
24. Desai, A.: The security of all-or-nothing encryption: protecting against exhaustive key search. In: Bellare, M. (ed.) CRYPTO 2000. LNCS, vol. 1880, pp. 359–375. Springer, Heidelberg (2000). https://doi.org/10.1007/3-540-44598-6_23
25. Diffie, W., Hellman, M.E.: New directions in cryptography. IEEE Trans. Inf. Theory **22**(6), 644–654 (1976)
26. Dodis, Y., Puniya, P.: Feistel networks made public, and applications. In: Naor, M. (ed.) EUROCRYPT 2007. LNCS, vol. 4515, pp. 534–554. Springer, Heidelberg (2007). https://doi.org/10.1007/978-3-540-72540-4_31
27. Dodis, Y., Stam, M., Steinberger, J., Liu, T.: Indifferentiability of confusion-diffusion networks. In: Fischlin, M., Coron, J.-S. (eds.) EUROCRYPT 2016. LNCS, vol. 9666, pp. 679–704. Springer, Heidelberg (2016). https://doi.org/10.1007/978-3-662-49896-5_24
28. Even, S., Mansour, Y.: A construction of a cipher from a single pseudorandom permutation. In: Imai, H., Rivest, R.L., Matsumoto, T. (eds.) ASIACRYPT 1991. LNCS, vol. 739, pp. 210–224. Springer, Heidelberg (1993). https://doi.org/10.1007/3-540-57332-1_17
29. Faz-Hernandez, A., Scott, S., Sullivan, N., Wahby, R., Wood, C.: Hashing to elliptic curves, irft-cfrg active draft (2022). https://datatracker.ietf.org/doc/draft-irtf-cfrg-hash-to-curve/
30. Freitas Dos Santos, B., Gu, Y., Jarecki, S.: Randomized half-ideal cipher on groups with applications to UC (a)PAKE. Cryptology ePrint Archive, Report 2023/295 (2023). http://eprint.iacr.org/2023/295

31. Dos Santos, B.F., Gu, Y., Jarecki, S., Krawczyk, H.: Asymmetric PAKE with low computation and communication. In: Dunkelman, O., Dziembowski, S. (eds) Advances in Cryptology – EUROCRYPT 2022. EUROCRYPT 2022. Lecture Notes in Computer Science, vol 13276. Springer, Cham (2022). https://doi.org/10.1007/978-3-031-07085-3_5

32. Fujisaki, E., Okamoto, T.: Secure integration of asymmetric and symmetric encryption schemes. In: Wiener, M. (ed.) CRYPTO 1999. LNCS, vol. 1666, pp. 537–554. Springer, Heidelberg (1999). https://doi.org/10.1007/3-540-48405-1_34

33. Gu, Y., Jarecki, S., Krawczyk, H.: KHAPE: asymmetric PAKE from key-hiding key exchange. In: Malkin, T., Peikert, C. (eds.) CRYPTO 2021. LNCS, vol. 12828, pp. 701–730. Springer, Cham (2021). https://doi.org/10.1007/978-3-030-84259-8_24

34. Guo, C., Lin, D.: Improved domain extender for the ideal cipher. Cryptogr. Commun. **7**(4), 509–533 (2015). https://doi.org/10.1007/s12095-015-0128-7

35. Hoffstein, J., Pipher, J., Silverman, J.H.: NTRU: a ring-based public key cryptosystem. In: Buhler, J.P. (ed.) ANTS 1998. LNCS, vol. 1423, pp. 267–288. Springer, Heidelberg (1998). https://doi.org/10.1007/BFb0054868

36. Holenstein, T., Künzler, R., Tessaro, S.: The equivalence of the random oracle model and the ideal cipher model, revisited. In: Fortnow, L., Vadhan, S.P. (eds.) 43rd ACM STOC, pp. 89–98. ACM Press, June 2011. https://doi.org/10.1145/1993636.1993650

37. Jaulmes, É., Joux, A., Valette, F.: On the security of randomized CBC-MAC beyond the birthday paradox limit a new construction. In: Daemen, J., Rijmen, V. (eds.) FSE 2002. LNCS, vol. 2365, pp. 237–251. Springer, Heidelberg (2002). https://doi.org/10.1007/3-540-45661-9_19

38. Kilian, J., Rogaway, P.: How to protect DES against exhaustive key search. In: Koblitz, N. (ed.) CRYPTO 1996. LNCS, vol. 1109, pp. 252–267. Springer, Heidelberg (1996). https://doi.org/10.1007/3-540-68697-5_20

39. Kim, T., Tibouchi, M.: Invalid curve attacks in a GLS setting. In: Tanaka, K., Suga, Y. (eds.) IWSEC 2015. LNCS, vol. 9241, pp. 41–55. Springer, Cham (2015). https://doi.org/10.1007/978-3-319-22425-1_3

40. Krawczyk, H.: HMQV: a high-performance secure Diffie-Hellman protocol. In: Shoup, V. (ed.) CRYPTO 2005. LNCS, vol. 3621, pp. 546–566. Springer, Heidelberg (2005). https://doi.org/10.1007/11535218_33

41. Grubbs, P., Maram, V., Paterson, K.G.: Anonymous, robust post-quantum public key encryption. In: Dunkelman, O., Dziembowski, S. (eds.) Advances in Cryptology – EUROCRYPT 2022. Lecture Notes in Computer Science, vol. 13277. Springer, Cham (2022). https://doi.org/10.1007/978-3-031-07082-2_15

42. Marlinspike, M., Perrin, T.: The X3DH key agreement protocol (2016). https://signal.org/docs/specifications/x3dh/

43. McQuoid, I., Rosulek, M., Roy, L.: Minimal symmetric PAKE and 1-out-of-n OT from programmable-once public functions. In: 2020 ACM SIGSAC Conference on Computer and Communications Security, CCS 2020, Virtual Event, USA, 9–13 November 2020 (2020). https://doi.org/10.1145/3372297.3417870, https://eprint.iacr.org/2020/1043

44. Merkle, R.C.: One way hash functions and DES. In: Brassard, G. (ed.) CRYPTO 1989. LNCS, vol. 435, pp. 428–446. Springer, New York (1990). https://doi.org/10.1007/0-387-34805-0_40

45. Preneel, B., Govaerts, R., Vandewalle, J.: Hash functions based on block ciphers: a synthetic approach. In: Stinson, D.R. (ed.) CRYPTO 1993. LNCS, vol. 773, pp. 368–378. Springer, Heidelberg (1994). https://doi.org/10.1007/3-540-48329-2_31

46. Shannon, C.E.: Communication theory of secrecy systems. The Bell Syst. Tech. J. **28**(4), 656–715 (1949). https://doi.org/10.1002/j.1538-7305.1949.tb00928.x
47. Tibouchi, M.: Elligator squared: uniform points on elliptic curves of prime order as uniform random strings. In: Christin, N., Safavi-Naini, R. (eds.) FC 2014. LNCS, vol. 8437, pp. 139–156. Springer, Heidelberg (2014). https://doi.org/10.1007/978-3-662-45472-5_10
48. Winternitz, R.S.: Producing a one-way hash function from DES. In: Chaum, D. (eds.) Advances in Cryptology. Springer, Boston (1984). https://doi.org/10.1007/978-1-4684-4730-9_17
49. Xagawa, K.: Anonymity of NIST PQC Round 3 KEMs. In: Dunkelman, O., Dziembowski, S. (eds) Advances in Cryptology – EUROCRYPT 2022. EUROCRYPT 2022. Lecture Notes in Computer Science, vol 13277. Springer, Cham (2022). https://doi.org/10.1007/978-3-031-07082-2_20

End-to-End Encrypted Zoom Meetings: Proving Security and Strengthening Liveness

Yevgeniy Dodis[1], Daniel Jost[1], Balachandar Kesavan[2],
and Antonio Marcedone[2]

[1] New York University, New York, USA
{dodis,daniel.jost}@cs.nyu.edu
[2] Zoom Video Communications, San Jose, USA
{balachandar.kesavan,antonio.marcedone}@zoom.us

Abstract. In May 2020, Zoom Video Communications, Inc. (Zoom) announced a multi-step plan to comprehensively support end-to-end encrypted (E2EE) group video calls and subsequently rolled out basic E2EE support to customers in October 2020. In this work we provide the first formal security analysis of Zoom's E2EE protocol, and also lay foundation to the general problem of E2EE group video communication.

We observe that the vast security literature analyzing asynchronous messaging does not translate well to synchronous video calls. Namely, while strong forms of forward secrecy and post compromise security are less important for (typically short-lived) video calls, various *liveness* properties become crucial. For example, mandating that participants quickly learn of updates to the meeting roster and key, media streams being displayed are recent, and banned participants promptly lose any access to the meeting. Our main results are as follows:

1. Propose a new notion of *leader-based continuous group key agreement with liveness*, which accurately captures the E2EE properties specific to the synchronous communication scenario.
2. Prove security of the core of Zoom's E2EE meetings protocol in the above well-defined model.
3. Propose ways to strengthen Zoom's liveness properties by simple modifications to the original protocol, which have since been deployed in production.

1 Introduction

Group video communication tools have gained immense popularity both in personal and professional settings. They were instrumental in bringing people closer together at a time when travel and in-person interaction were severely limited by the COVID-19 pandemic. Zoom Video Communications, Inc. (Zoom) is one of the leading providers of video communications with millions of active users,

---

Yevgeniy Dodis and Daniel Jost–Research conducted while contracting for Zoom.

C. Hazay and M. Stam (Eds.): EUROCRYPT 2023, LNCS 14008, pp. 157–189, 2023.
https://doi.org/10.1007/978-3-031-30589-4_6

and aims to distinguish itself not just in ease-of-use and richness of features, but also by offering strong security and privacy capabilities.

Historically, Zoom meetings have been encrypted in transit between the clients and the Zoom servers. This allows Zoom to offer features that require the server to access meeting streams, such as live transcription and the ability to join a meeting by dialing a phone number through the telephony network. In May 2020, Zoom announced a multistep plan to comprehensively support end-to-end (E2E) encrypted group video calls [46] and rolled out basic E2EE support to the public in October 2020 [32]. E2EE protects the privacy of attendees against any compromise to Zoom's infrastructure/keys.

Zoom has also published a whitepaper [11] describing its protocol, design goals, and methodology for E2EE meetings. The whitepaper explains how the protocol is run as part of a group call and provides intuition on the threat model and security. Subsequent academic work has performed an initial analysis of the protocol [29], emphasizing a number of potential attacks at the boundary of the threat model outlined in the whitepaper. However, this security analysis is far from comprehensive and does not include any formal security definitions or theorems.

Group Video Calls. E2EE group video calls have not gained any major scrutiny from the academic community. This stands in stark contrast to related fields such as secure text messaging, where the ubiquitously used Signal protocol [34] has received significant attention [2,10,17]. For secure group messaging, the Internet Engineering Task Force (IETF) has even launched the Messaging Layer Security (MLS) working group [8] with mutual support from industry and academia, resulting in a number of analyses [3–5].

A defining feature of any group video call that distinguishes it from the asynchronous nature of text messaging is that video calls happen in real-time with all participants online at the same time. This suggests that protocols could achieve strong *liveness properties* generally deemed to be intrinsically unattainable in messaging. First, an attacker should not be able to arbitrarily delay communication. For example, if Alice sends a video stream at time t, then Bob should not accept it at a time significantly later than t. Depending on the type of content, such delays may pose a significant threat; for instance, if the message is an instruction to buy or sell a certain stock, then the ability to delay it might allow an attacker to front-run the transaction. Second, if the meeting host decides on a certain management action, such as adding or removing parties, then an attacker must not be able to delay or prevent those decisions from taking effect. These liveness properties are new and not demanded in the (asynchronous) group messaging setting, in which the network attacker can simply pretend that the initiating party is offline, without any of the other parties being able to detect the attack.

Goals of This Work. In this work we aim to analyze the core of Zoom's E2EE meetings protocol[1]. We follow the approach successfully used to analyze (group) messaging protocols and single out the key agreement using the abstraction of a so-called *continuous group key agreement (CGKA)* protocol [3], albeit with weaker forward secrecy (FS) and post-compromise security (PCS) properties than for secure messaging, as explained below. The CGKA abstraction establishes a sequence of shared symmetric keys, accounting for the need to re-key when parties join or leave the meeting (even without strong FS/PCS). The current key — known exactly to the current members of the meeting — can then be used with authenticated encryption with associated data (AEAD) to achieve secure communication.

To provide the first formal security analysis of Zoom's E2EE protocol, our main objectives are, thus, to:

1. Propose a CGKA definition that takes Zoom's unique aspects into account and captures the liveness properties made possible by the online assumption.
2. Provide an analysis of the core of Zoom's E2EE protocol in the above well-defined model.

To the best of our knowledge, Zoom is the only E2EE group video protocol that aims to provide stringent liveness properties. We believe our work is the first in the realm of CGKA to formalize and analyze such assurances. As part of this process, we observed that Zoom's liveness assurances could be strengthened and thus, we set out to:

3. Propose tangible strengthenings to Zoom's liveness properties, via two simple modifications to the protocol which offer different tradeoffs between efficiency and security. Zoom has evaluated these modifications and deployed one of them in production (in version 5.13 of the Zoom meetings client).

1.1   Contributions

Definition. We formally define a *leader-based continuous group key agreement with liveness* (LL-CGKA), which encompasses all the desired security properties of Zoom's core E2EE meetings protocol in a single security game[1]. In general terms, an LL-CGKA protocol requires the following properties:

- At each stage of the meeting, the shared symmetric key is only known to the set of current participants as decided by the current meeting host.
- All participants have a consistent view of the set of current meeting participants (as displayed in the UI) as well as of the key.
- Changes to the group, decided by the meeting host, are applied within a bounded (and short) amount of time; otherwise, participants drop out of the meeting.

---

[1] We analyze the Zoom E2EE meetings protocol as deployed in the Zoom meeting client version 5.12. In this paper, we refer to this version as the *current* protocol/scheme.

Attacker Model. We consider a powerful adversary that has control over the evolution of the group, fully controls the network and Zoom's server infrastructure, and can passively corrupt any parties, thereby obtaining their current state. We remark, however, that most of our guarantees hold only when the current meeting leader and participants execute the protocol honestly, and any active attackers previously in the meeting have been removed.

FS and PCS. Due to the short-lived nature of video calls, our CGKA notion, however, differs from those in realm of secure messaging by requiring neither strong forward secrecy nor post-compromise security guarantees within a single meeting. An attacker compromising a party's state in an ongoing meeting may learn both past and future content of said meeting. We do, however, require the following properties: first, corrupting a party must not reveal any of the meeting's content before the party has been admitted or after it has been removed by the meeting host. Second, compromising a party after a meeting has ended must not compromise the meeting in any form (weak FS). Third, even if a party's long-term secret have been leaked, this party can still securely join meetings as long as the adversary does not act as an active meddler-in-the-middle.

Modularization. One of the contributions of this work is to distill out basic building blocks of Zoom's protocol, which could be instantiated differently in pursuit of improved efficiency or, e.g. to achieve post-quantum security. To this end, we consider the intermediate *continuous multi-recipient key encapsulation (cmKEM)* abstraction from which we then build the aforementioned LL-CGKA notion. Put simply, the former naturally captures that in Zoom's protocol a designated party (the meeting host) chooses the symmetric key and distributes it to all the meeting participants. The latter abstraction then models the core of Zoom's E2EE meetings protocol, including the unique liveness properties.

Finally, we discuss how Zoom's overall protocol is built on top of the LL-CGKA protocol, considering audio and video encryption. In particular, we relate the respective confidentiality, authenticity and liveness assurances to those of the LL-CGKA notion.

We remark that the above modularization follows Zoom's whitepaper [11] version 4.0, with the cmKEM notion roughly corresponding to Sects. 7.6.2 - 7.6.6, the LL-CGKA notion to Sect. 7.6.7, and video stream encryption discussed in Sects. 7.2 and 7.11, among others.

Liveness. One of the main novelties of Zoom's E2EE protocol is its focus on liveness properties. They assure that whenever the host adds or removes a participant, the action cannot be withheld by an adversary for any extended period of time. That is, if for instance the host removes a member from the group, such as when removing a candidate at the end of an interview so that the hiring panel can reach a decision, that member must no longer be able to decrypt meeting contents even if they manage to compromise Zoom's cloud infrastructure or exert significant control over the network.

In this work, we present a simple time-based model that allows us to formalize and analyze those liveness properties. Our model balances simplicity and generality by assuming that parties have access to local clocks that all run at the same speed, but are otherwise not assumed to be synchronized. We then formalize liveness as follows: whenever a participant is in a given state at time t, then the meeting host has been in the same state recently, i.e., at some time $t' \geq t - \Delta$ where Δ is some protocol-dependent liveness slack. Turned around, whenever the host moves on to a new state (e.g., by changing the group roster) then all participants must also move on within time Δ (or else drop from the meeting).

While the protocol we analyze[1] achieves good liveness properties, these assurances degrade in the number of host changes. As part of this paper we propose two potential improvements. First, we propose a modification that strictly improves on the liveness and yields bounds independent of the number of host changes. This comes at the cost of increased communication by making the protocol more interactive. As an alternative, we propose a strengthening that does not incur any communication overhead and improves on Zoom's properties if parties have well-synchronized clocks; we believe this to be the common case for modern devices. After testing, Zoom implemented the first option, which is deployed in version 5.13 of the Zoom meetings client.

1.2   Related Work

We have already commented above on the relationship of this work to the areas of secure messaging.

Group Video Calls. There are numerous solutions for group video calls. The vast majority offers transport layer encryption, with some of them [7, 11, 16, 43, 44] offering E2EE group calls, and others offering this feature only for two-party calls [27,34]. While some of the solutions do offer intuitive security descriptions in the form of a whitepaper, such as Wire [44], Cisco [16], and WhatsApp [43], to the best of our knowledge only Cisco WebEx enjoys formal security claims, as it is directly built on top of the IETF MLS draft [3–5,8].

Liveness. The terms liveness, liveliness, and aliveness are frequently used to describe various *authentication properties* of key agreement protocols, e.g., in [33] (and many subsequent works). Those properties, roughly speaking, guarantee that if one party completes a run of the protocol, then its peer at some point also has run the same protocol. (Slightly stronger variants exist.) As such most of those definitions not only have no direct relation to *physical time* but also are typically not enforced on an ongoing basis, contrary to our liveness definition. Further, in the context of E2EE group messaging, some work previously used the liveness as synonymous to correctness [39] — with no direct relation to actions having to occur in a timely manner.

However, using timing is not new in the design and analysis of cryptographic protocols. Some such works (e.g., [23,30,37]) use timing assumptions to improve efficiency (or overcome impossibility results) for problems which do not inherently require timing assumptions. Other works (e.g., [9,12,22,40]) use various forms of "moderately hard function" to achieve different cryptographic properties which critically rely on the notion of time. The type of liveness used in this work is much more closely related to more traditional distributed computing literature (e.g., [21,24]) on consensus and, more recently, blockchain protocols (e.g., [26,36]). However, the existence of a unique meeting leader, coupled with the online assumption, makes Zoom's protocol (and our security model) much more lightweight. Finally, the use of heartbeats to ensure liveness is similar to the heartbeat extension of the TLS protocols [41].

Related Notions. The cmKEM notion is an extension of multi-recipient Key Encapsulation (mKEM) [38,42,45] to the setting of dynamically changing groups. Zoom's scheme is based around the authenticated public-key encryption[2] scheme from the libsodium library [20]. It is very similar to one of the early authenticated public-key encryption schemes formally analyzed by An [6] (and simpler then the recently analyzed HPKE standard [1]).

The LL-CGKA notion is further related to Dynamic Group Key Agreement with an extensive body of literature, notable examples including [14,28,31]. Similar to CGKA, the Dynamic GKA notion supports changes to group membership during a session and, in fact, in terms of FS and PCS guarantees those notions resemble our LL-CGKA notion more closely than most prior CGKA variants. In contrast to CGKA, Dynamic GKA schemes are designed for an interactive setting, i.e., typically require all parties to contribute to any one operation via interactive rounds, and / or rely on a trusted group manager. (In contrast to LL-CGKA the group manager is, however, static and cannot be replaced mid-session.) Further, we note that while group video calls in principle can tolerate interactive protocols, such as [31], requiring several parties to contribute to each operation can be nevertheless problematic, as for example parties can unexpectedly drop out. Furthermore, we believe this simplifies extending our notion for a more advanced group video call protocol, compared to a Dynamic GKA based one. Closely related to Dynamic GKA are further Multicast Encryption, e.g., [35], and line of work on Logical Key Hierarchies, e.g., [15].

Another related notion to both cmKEM and LL-CGKAis Multi-Stage Authenticated Key Exchange [25]. Several variants, each with slightly different guarantees, have been considered and the notion has e.g., been used to analyze the Double Ratchet protocol [18]. In contrast to CGKA, Multi-Stage AKE has exclusively been applied to the two-party setting.

---

[2] Authenticated public-key encryption schemes are often also referred to as *signcryption schemes*. The latter term is however more commonly used to denote schemes satisfying insider security rather than outsider security, as achieved by libsodium's scheme.

2   Continuous Multi-Recipient KEM

Zoom's protocol works by having a designated party distribute shared symmetric key material to all the participants upon each change to the group. We abstract this as a *Continuous Multi-Recipient Key Encapsulation* (cmKEM) scheme that allows the designated party to encapsulate a stream of shared symmetric keys to a dynamically evolving set of recipients. This results in a sequence of independent and uniformly random *keys*, each only known to the authorized parties. We number the states (i.e., keys) using two counters: the *epoch* and a sub-epoch called *period*.[3]

In the following, we call the designated party *leader*.[4] We assume that the leader is told whom to add or remove, ignoring policy aspects.

The cmKEM notion distinguishes long-term identities and *ephemeral users*. Each long-term identity id is assumed to have an associated public key ipk. A party id can then create one or more ephemeral users, identified by uid, each linked to a specific *meeting*. That is, each meeting will consist of a group of ephemeral uids that just exist for the duration of that meeting. Roughly speaking, in Zoom, each long-term identity id corresponds to a device; if a user logs into multiple devices, each will have its own long-term key material. Note that a device can be part of the same meeting under different ephemeral identities over time, e.g., after leaving the meeting and then rejoining it.

To cope with the leader suddenly losing connection, leader switches are initiated by the (untrusted) server without any hand-off. As a result, a user uid can be asked at any point of time to become the new leader of a meeting, with any given set of participants, as long as they are associated with the same meeting. To simplify notation, we introduce the notion of a *session* that denotes a segment of meeting between leader changes.

2.1   Syntax

For simplicity, we define the clients' cmKEM algorithms to be non-interactive, making all the interaction explicit by having multiple algorithms. User algorithms moreover have implicit access to a PKI described in the next section. The server aids the protocol execution by performing explicit message routing.

Definition 1. *A cmKEM scheme consists of the following algorithms. For ease of presentation, the client state* ust *is assumed to expose the current key* ust.k, *epoch* ust.e, *and period* ust.p.

---

[3] Looking ahead, rotating the period instead of the full epoch during group additions is more efficient. Zoom's protocol currently does not take advantage of period rotations, but we capture and analyze this option since it is being considered as a future optimization.

[4] Typically the leader coincides with the meeting host, but if e.g. the host is on a low-bandwidth connection those concepts can be decoupled.

User management:

- (ust, uid, sig) ← CreateUser(id, meetingId) *creates an ephemeral user belonging to* id *and the meeting* meetingId. *It outputs the initial state* ust, *the user's identity* uid, *and credentials* sig *binding* uid *to* id.
- (id, ipk) ← Identity(uid) *and* meetingId ← Meeting(uid) *deterministically compute* uid*'s long-term information, and associated meeting respectively.*

Session management:

- (ust′, M) ← StartSession(ust, {(uid$_i$, ad$_i$, sig$_i$)}$_{i\in[n]}$) *instructs the user to start a new session with the given members. For each member, credentials* sig$_i$ *as well as associated data* ad$_i$ *(which need to match with the user's respective value when joining) are provided. The welcome message* M *is to be distributed to the other group members by the server.*
- ust′ ← JoinSession(ust, uid$_{lead}$, sig$_{lead}$, m, ad) *makes the user join the leader's session using their share* m *of the welcome message.*

Group and management (leader):

- (ust′, M) ← Add(ust, {(uid$_i$, ad$_i$, sig$_i$)}$_{i\in[n]}$, newEpoch) *adds the users* uid$_1$ *to* uid$_n$ *to the group. The boolean flag* newEpoch *indicates whether this action should create a new epoch or period.*
- (ust′, M) ← Remove(ust, {uid$_i$}$_{i\in[n]}$) *removes the users* uid$_1$ *to* uid$_n$ *from the group.*

Message processing (non-leaders):

- ust′ ← Process(ust, m) *lets a participant advance to the next epoch or period.*

Message passing (server):

- pub ← InitSplitState() *generates an initial public server state.*
- (pub, {(uid$_i$, m$_i$)}$_{i\in[n]}$) ← Split(pub, M) *deterministically splits* M *into shares* m$_i$ *for each recipient.*

2.2   PKI

The ephemeral user id's uid are bound to the long-term identity id via the credentials. To this end, id has a long-term signing key isk. In order to prevent meddler-in-the-middle (MITM) attacks, other parties must authenticate the respective long-term public key ipk. For the sake of our analysis, we assume a simple (long-term) public-key infrastructure (PKI). The PKI provides to each long-term identity id their respective private signing key isk while allowing all other users to verify that the respective public verification key ipk belongs to id.

Zoom currently does not have any such PKI but relies on the host reading out a *meeting leader security code* — a digest of ipk — that all participants then compare to ensure they have the host's correct key. Authentication crucially depends on the leader visually recognizing participants and vice versa. Formalizing the exact guarantees given by this process is outside the scope of this work — specifically because the authenticity is only established during and not before a meeting, and because it relies on non-cryptographic assumptions such as the host recognizing participants' faces.

In the future, Zoom plans to build a PKI based on key transparency and external identity providers, whose analysis is left for future work. We refer to the full version of this work for a more in-depth discussion on how Zoom currently verifies public keys, as well as their ongoing efforts for improving user authentication.

2.3 Security Definition

The security notion for the cmKEM primitive encompasses all the desired security properties in a single game. We next describe its the high-level workings, with the full formal definition presented in the full version of this work.

Game Overview. The attacker has full control over the evolution of the group and the network. We now sketch the various oracles the adversary may call. First, the adversary can *create a user* for a provided long-term identity id and meeting meetingId. The game ensures that the generated user id uid is unique.

The adversary can then instruct uid_{lead} to *start a session* for a provided list of participants and their respective credentials. Afterwards, they can instruct a user uid to *join* uid_{lead} *'s session* using a welcome message m of the adversary's choice. The leader can also be instructed to *add or remove members*. In the former case, it is up to the adversary to specify whether this should initiate a new epoch or period. Finally, the adversary can get a participant uid to *process an arbitrary message m*. (The protocol might of course reject such malicious messages.)

The game ensures that additions and removals only succeed if the adversary does not try to add existing members or remove nonexistent ones. Additionally, the leader must not remove themselves from the group. (This would have to be done by instructing another party to assume the role of the leader, excluding the old leader from the group.) The game keeps track of, for each leader's epoch and period, the leader's view of the session state, which consists of the meeting key and participant roster. Throughout the execution, the game then ensures consistency of the parties' view with their leader's respective view, which we discuss below.

The attacker can passively corrupt long-term identities, which reveals (a) the secret states of all still active associated ephemeral identities and (b) the long-term identity's signing key from the PKI.

Key Confidentiality. The adversary must not be able to distinguish the keys produced by the cmKEM scheme from random ones. To this end, the adversary may try to guess a bit b by challenging a state's key (identified by the leader, epoch, and period) to either receive the real key (if $b = 0$) or a uniform random one (if $b = 1$). Additionally, the game allows the adversary to instead request the actual key, irrespective of the bit b, which may be useful since it is not subject to the same restrictions on compatible corruptions described below.

The game needs to rule out trivial wins stemming from the adversary being able to compute certain keys themselves after passively corrupting parties. Since Zoom's scheme neither encompasses forward secrecy (FS) nor post-compromise security (PCS) within a session, this has to be reflected in our notion. In short, corrupting a user potentially reveals the key for all epochs and periods where he has been a member of a given session. However, keys must remain secure in the following situations:

- A user must never know keys from before being added to, or after having been removed from the group. Hence, the confidentiality of those keys must not be affected by compromising the given user.
- Corrupting a device after a session has ended, i.e., after the respective ephemeral identity has been deleted, must not affect the sessions' confidentiality.[5]
- Corrupting a long-term identity id (and thus learned isk) must not affect the security of future sessions involving an honestly generated ephemeral identity uid for id. (The adversary might of course impersonate id by creating a valid ephemeral user uid' instead, which would compromise the session's security.)

Consistency Properties. Parties must agree on the key for each epoch and period within a given session. That is, no two parties should ever output conflicting keys, unless after an active attack in which the adversary uses either the leader's or the receiving party's leaked state to tamper with the messages.[6] Consistency, moreover, takes into account at which point in time parties can reach a given state. Our notion distinguishes between epochs and periods, among other, due to those properties differing. Participants must only move to an epoch once their leader arrived there, while for periods we allow participants to run ahead and, thus, reach periods that formally are not supposed to exist. (Still, parties must agree on the keys for those spurious periods.)

Finally, consistency must hold even if the adversary tampers with, reorders, or replaces messages — as long as the involved parties are honest. Due to the leader-based nature of the cmKEM primitive, a malicious leader however could always break consistency by simply sending inconsistent messages to the respective parties. To formalize outsider security, we thus simply deem attacks enabled by corrupting one of the involved parties trivial and no longer enforce consistency properties for a user uid once either uid or their leader uid_{lead} has been corrupted.

---

[5] I.e., similar to TLS, we require FS on the granularity of sessions.
[6] This formalizes an outsider notion actually achieved by Zoom. Stronger protocols could tolerate leaking the recipient's state.

Member Authentication. For many of the operations, such as adding users to an existing session or instructing a user to join another session, the adversary is allowed to provide the respective user identifiers. Our security notion ensures that the adversary cannot impersonate long-term identities unless they have been corrupted, i.e., the adversary cannot inject an ephemeral user uid unless the associated long-term identity id has been corrupted.

2.4 Zoom's Scheme

Zoom's cmKEM scheme uses point-to-point encryption — i.e., does not leverage any efficiency gains from sending the same message to multiple recipients — to communicate fresh keys to the participants. It is based around Diffie-Hellman key exchange over a cyclic group $\mathbb{G} = \langle g \rangle$ with a fixed generator g. The identifier uid mainly consists of a Diffie-Hellman public key $\mathsf{upk} \in \mathbb{G}$, alongside the contextual data of the meeting identifier, the user's long-term identity id, and the user's long-term public key ipk, and a signature under the user's long-term signing key isk binding it all together. The respective secret key $\mathsf{usk} := \mathsf{DLog}_g(\mathsf{upk})$ is stored as part of the protocol's state. See Fig. 1 for a formal description of the scheme.

For each epoch, the leader samples a new *seed*, from which the sequence of period keys are derived by iteratively applying a PRG to derive the key and seed for the next period of that epoch[3]. (Observe that this construction is forward secure.) When removing parties, the leader initiates the next epoch and communicates the new seed to all remaining participants, as described below. They then all derive the first key and the seed for the second key using the PRG. Analogously, to add participants with newEpoch = true, the leader communicates the seed to all participants. More efficiently, however, when adding participants with newEpoch = false, the leader only sends the seed for the next key to the freshly joined parties and instructs the others to just ratchet forward.

To send a seed to a party, the scheme first derives for each recipient a shared symmetric key from a Diffie-Hellman element of its own secret key usk and the recipient's public key upk'. The scheme uses HKDF for this derivation, which for the purpose of the security analysis we model as an random oracle. For efficiency reasons, this key is cached as part of the sender's secret state and reused for future messages to or from the same party. The seed is then encrypted using nonce-based AEAD, for a random nonce that is transmitted as part of the resulting ciphertext. The associated data contains the meeting and sender identifiers, and a fixed context string.

Server Protocol. The protocol works by delivering the respective AEAD-ciphertext to each party and sending a special "ratchet period" message to parties for which no such ciphertext is specified. For simplicity, we model that the message $M = (G, C)$ sent to the server includes the current set of recipients. More concretely, each user uid' for which C contains a share obtains $m = (\text{'epoch'}, C[\text{uid}'])$, while for other users the server delivers $m = \text{'period'}$.

Protocol cmKEM Client Protocol

User management

Algorithm: CreateUser(id, meetingId)
  usk ←$ {0, 1, ..., |G| − 1}; upk ← g^{usk}
  (isk, ipk) ← PKI.get-sk(id) // id's long-term keys
  me ← (meetingId, id, ipk, upk)
  sig ← Sig.Sign(isk, 'EncryptionKeyAnnouncement', me)
  $K[\cdot]$, uid$_{\mathsf{lead}}$, G ← ⊥
  return (me, sig)

Algorithm: Meeting(uid)
  parse (meetingId, id, ipk, upk) ← uid
  return meetingId

Algorithm: Identity(uid)
  parse (meetingId, id, ipk, upk) ← uid
  return (id, ipk)

Session management

Algorithm: StartSession({(uid$_i$, ad$_i$, sig$_i$)}$_{i∈[n]}$)
  G ← {uid$_1$, ..., uid$_n$}
  req me ≠ ⊥ ∧ me ∉ G
  $AD[\cdot]$ ← ⊥
  for $i ∈ [n]$ do
    req *verify-user(uid$_i$, sig$_i$)
    AD[uid$_i$] ← ad$_i$
  uid$_{\mathsf{lead}}$ ← me
  if $e ≠ ⊥$ then $e ← e + 1$
  else $e ← 1$
  $p ← 0$; seed ← PRG.Init($1^κ$)
  C ← *encrypt-seed(G, AD)
  M ← (G, C)
  (seed, k) ← PRG.Eval(seed)
  return M

Algorithm: JoinSession(uid$'_{\mathsf{lead}}$, sig$'_{\mathsf{lead}}$, m, ad)
  req me ≠ ⊥ ∧ uid$'_{\mathsf{lead}}$ ≠ me ∧ uid$'_{\mathsf{lead}}$ ≠ uid$_{\mathsf{lead}}$
  req *verify-user(uid$'_{\mathsf{lead}}$, sig$'_{\mathsf{lead}}$)
  uid$_{\mathsf{lead}}$ ← uid$'_{\mathsf{lead}}$
  parse ('epoch', c) ← m
  (e', p, seed') ← *decrypt-seed(c, uid$'_{\mathsf{lead}}$, ad)
  if $e ≠ ⊥$ then
    req (e', p') = (e + 1, 0)
    $e ← e'$
  (seed, k) ← PRG.Eval(seed')

Group and key management (leader)

Algorithm: Add({(uid$_i$, ad$_i$, sig$_i$)}$_{i∈[n]}$, newEpoch)
  req me ≠ ⊥ ∧ uid$_{\mathsf{lead}}$ = me
  $AD[\cdot]$ ← ⊥
  for $i ∈ [n]$ do
    req uid$_i$ ≠ me ∧ uid$_i$ ∉ G ∧ *verify-user(uid$_i$, sig$_i$)
    AD[uid$_i$] ← ad$_i$
  G ← G ∪ {uid$_1$, ..., uid$_n$}
  if newEpoch then
    (e, p) ← (e + 1, 0)
    seed ← PRG.Init($1^κ$)
    G' ← G
  else
    (e, p) ← (e, p + 1)
    G' ← {uid$_1$, ..., uid$_n$}
  C ← *encrypt-seed(G', AD)
  (seed, k) ← PRG.Eval(seed)
  return M ← (G, C)

Algorithm: Remove({uid$_i$}$_{i∈[n]}$)
  req me ≠ ⊥ ∧ uid$_{\mathsf{lead}}$ = me
  for $i ∈ [n]$ do req uid$_i$ ∈ G
  G ← G \ {uid$_1$, ..., uid$_n$}
  (e, p) ← (e + 1, 0)
  seed ← PRG.Init($1^κ$)
  $AD[\cdot]$ ← ⊥
  C ← *encrypt-seed(G, AD)
  (seed, k) ← PRG.Eval(seed)
  return M ← (G, C)

Message processing (participants)

Algorithm: Process(m)
  req me ≠ ⊥ ∧ uid$_{\mathsf{lead}}$ ≠ ⊥ ∧ uid$_{\mathsf{lead}}$ ≠ me
  if m = ('epoch', c) then
    (e', p', seed') ← *decrypt-seed(c, uid$_{\mathsf{lead}}$, ⊥)
    req (e', p') = (e + 1, 0)
    (e, p) ← (e', p')
    (seed, k) ← PRG.Eval(seed')
  else if m = 'period' then
    $p ← p + 1$
    (seed, k) ← PRG.Eval(seed)

Helper: *encrypt-seed(G', AD)
  $C[\cdot]$ ← ⊥
  for uid' ∈ G' do
    parse (·, ·, ·, upk') ← uid'
    nonce ←$ AEAD.$\mathcal{N}$
    if K[uid'] = ⊥ then
      K[uid'] ← HKDF(upk'^{usk}, 'KeyMeetingSeed')
    ad' ← (meetingId, me, AD[uid'])
    ad'' ← Hash('EncryptionKeyMeetingSeed'
       ‖ Hash(ad'))
    c' ← AEAD.Enc(K[uid'], nonce, (e, p, seed), ad'')
    C[uid'] ← (c', nonce)
  return C

Helper: *decrypt-seed(c, uid$_{\mathsf{lead}}$, ad)
  parse (·, id', ·, upk') ← uid$_{\mathsf{lead}}$
  if K[uid$_{\mathsf{lead}}$] = ⊥ then
    K[uid$_{\mathsf{lead}}$] ← HKDF(upk'^{usk}, 'KeyMeetingSeed')
  ad' ← (meetingId, id', ad)
  ad'' ← Hash('EncryptionKeyMeetingSeed') ‖ Hash(ad'))
  parse (c', nonce) ← c
  parse (e', p', seed') ← AEAD.Dec(K[uid$_{\mathsf{lead}}$], nonce, c', ad'')
  return (e', p', seed')

Helper: *verify-user(uid', sig')
  parse (meetingId', id', ipk', upk') ← uid'
  return meetingId' = meetingId
    ∧ Sig.Verify(ipk', 'EncryptionKeyAnnouncement', uid', sig')
    ∧ PKI.verify-pk(id', ipk')

Fig. 1. The client protocol of Zoom's cmKEM scheme. The protocol implicitly maintains a state ust, which exposes the key ust.k, epoch ust.e, and period ust.p.

Security. The following theorem establishes the security of the scheme.

Theorem 1. *Zoom's cmKEM scheme is secure according to the outlined definition under the Gap-DH assumption, if the AEAD scheme is secure,* Hash *collision resistant, the signature scheme is EUF-CMA secure, the PRG satisfies the standard indistinguishability from random notion, and* HKDF *is modeled as a random oracle.*

A full proof is presented in the full version of this work. In short, based on the security of Gap Diffie Hellman, we can first switch to an hybrid where we use independently generated symmetric keys, as opposed to the outputs of the DH operation (between the leader and each participant), programming the random oracle to make things look consistent on corruption. Then, we can argue that each of the adversary's winning conditions in the game cannot be triggered, based on the unforgeability of the signature scheme (credentials cannot be forged), the authenticity of the AEAD (malicious keys cannot be injected), and the confidentiality of the AEAD (encrypted keys cannot be distinguished from encryptions of random messages).

According to the whitepaper [11], Zoom's scheme performs Diffie-Hellman over Curve25519.[7] We note that the Gap-DH assumption (rather than e.g. CDH) appears to be rather intrinsic to this kind of simple Diffie-Hellman based protocol and has been assumed for Curve25519 before [1,10]. Moreover, Zoom uses XChaCha20Poly1305 with 192-bit nonces as the nonce-based AEAD scheme, and HKDF for both the key-derivation as well as the PRG. (We model the latter use as a PRG to clarify the exact required security properties.) Finally, for a signature scheme, Zoom uses EdDSA over Ed25519 satisfying EUF-CMA security [13].

3   Leader-Based GCKA with Liveness

We now abstract the core of Zoom's E2EE meetings protocol[1] as a *leader-based continuous group key agreement with liveness* (LL-CGKA) scheme. On a high level, the primitive works similarly to the previously introduced cmKEM one, with the following differences: (1) participants are aware of the group roster and in particular only use keys for which they know the roster, (2) as a result participants can no longer run ahead of their leader in terms of the period, and (3) liveness is enforced.

Liveness. To achieve liveness, the LL-CGKA primitive is time based. More concretely (1) algorithms can depend on time and (2) in addition to event-based actions (e.g., reacting to an incoming packet), there are also time-driven actions. We make the following (simplifying) assumptions:

---

[7] Technically, Curve25519 breaks the abstraction of cyclic groups we, for simplicity, use for the presentation of our scheme. We refer to the analysis of the HPKE standard [1] for an extended discussion and the formalization of *nominal groups* with the respective Gap-DH assumption. Their results directly apply to our construction.

- Each party has a *local clock*, which all run at *the same speed* (constant drift).
- Local algorithms complete instantaneously, i.e., no time elapses between invocation and completion. As a consequence, the algorithms simply take the party's current time as an input argument.

We remark that the vast majority of Zoom meetings last only a couple of hours, limiting any practical clock drift significantly and, thus, justifying the former assumption.

3.1   Syntax

The algorithms of a LL-CGKA scheme closely follow the ones of a cmKEM scheme, with two major differences. First, client algorithms take the current *local time* as input. Second, there are *clock ticking* algorithms that allow to specify clock-driven actions, i.e., actions that happen at a certain time rather upon receiving a message.

As in cmKEM, the server performs message routing. Additionally, it hands out the current public[8] group state to newly joining parties, freeing the leader from maintaining additional state.

Definition 2. *A LL-CGKA scheme consists of the algorithms described in the following, where, for ease of presentation, the client state* ust *is assumed to expose the following fields:*

- *The user's current epoch* ust.e *and period* ust.p.
- *For each epoch and period a key* ust.k$[e, p]$ *(or $\perp$ if not known yet). It is assumed that operations do not change keys once they are defined.*
- *The user's current view on the group* ust.G.

User Management:

- (ust, uid, sig) $\leftarrow$ CreateUser(time, id, meetingId) *creates an ephemeral user for the given identity and meeting. Outputs the user's initial state* ust, *their identity* uid, *and credentials* sig *binding* uid *to* id.
- id $\leftarrow$ Identity(uid) *and* meetingId $\leftarrow$ Meeting(uid) *are deterministic algorithms that return the ephemeral user's long-term identity and meeting, respectively.*
- ust$'$ $\leftarrow$ CatchUp(ust, time, grpPub) *prepares the user for joining the group by processing the current public group state* grpPub *provided by the sever.*

Leader's Algorithms:

- (ust$'$, M) $\leftarrow$ Lead(ust, time, $\{(uid_i, sig_i)\}_{i \in [n]}$) *instructs the user to become the new group leader with the specified participants. Outputs a message to be split and distributed to the other group members.*

---

[8] By public, we mean known to the (untrusted) Zoom server; i.e., the current roster, but not any keys.

- $(\mathsf{ust'}, \mathsf{M}) \leftarrow \mathsf{Add}(\mathsf{ust}, \mathsf{time}, \{(\mathsf{uid}_i, \mathsf{sig}_i)\}_{i \in [n]})$ *is used to add users* uid_1 *to* uid_n *to the group.*
- $(\mathsf{ust'}, \mathsf{M}) \leftarrow \mathsf{Remove}(\mathsf{ust}, \mathsf{time}, \{\mathsf{uid}_i\}_{i \in [n]})$ *is used to remove users* uid_1 *to* uid_n *from the group.*
- $(\mathsf{ust'}, \mathsf{M}) \leftarrow \mathsf{LeaderTick}(\mathsf{ust}, \mathsf{time})$ *is executed on each clock tick by the leader. Outputs the leader's updated state and an optional messages* M.

Participants' Algorithms:

- $\mathsf{ust'} \leftarrow \mathsf{Follow}(\mathsf{ust}, \mathsf{time}, \mathsf{m}, \mathsf{uid}'_{\mathsf{lead}}, \mathsf{sig}'_{\mathsf{lead}})$ *instructs the user to treat* $\mathsf{uid}'_{\mathsf{lead}}$ *as the new leader. Expects the first message share* m *from the new leader.*
- $\mathsf{ust'} \leftarrow \mathsf{Process}(\mathsf{ust}, \mathsf{time}, \mathsf{m})$ *is used by participants to process any incoming message* m.
- $(\mathsf{alive}, \mathsf{sig'}) \leftarrow \mathsf{ParticipantTick}(\mathsf{ust}, \mathsf{time})$ *is executed by a participant on each clock tick. The flag* alive *indicates whether the participant is still in the meeting or dropped out (for a violation of liveness) and optionally updates the credentials (for the server) with* $\mathsf{sig'} = \bot$ *denoting no update.*

Server's Algorithms:

- $\mathsf{pub} \leftarrow \mathsf{Init}()$ *generates an initial server state.*
- $(\mathsf{pub'}, \{(\mathsf{uid}_i, \mathsf{m}_i)\}_{i \in [n]}) \leftarrow \mathsf{Split}(\mathsf{pub}, \mathsf{M})$ *is a deterministic algorithm that takes message* M *and splits out each user* uid*'s share* m.
- $\mathsf{grpPub} \leftarrow \mathsf{GroupState}(\mathsf{pub}, \mathsf{meetingId})$ *is a deterministic algorithm that returns the public group state.*

We discuss correctness, and in particular how it is affected by the liveness properties, in the full version of this work.

Meeting Flow. Let us briefly discuss how Zoom uses the above defined LL-CGKA abstraction to orchestrate a meeting. To start a meeting, Zoom instructs the initial host to invoke the Lead algorithm. For a participant to join the meeting, the server first hands them the most recent public group state (using GroupState) that the participant processes using CatchUp. Afterwards, the participant is instructed of the leader (using Follow) where alongside it is given their respective message share from the message the leader generated in the respective Add invocation. Observe that at this point the participant might not have a usable symmetric key yet. Instead, it might take up to the next message generated by LeaderTick for the participant to fully join the meeting.

To switch leaders, the new one is instructed to invoke Lead and all other participants are instructed to invoke Follow. Note that it is not required for the new leader to have joined the meeting beforehand — the CatchUp algorithm can directly be followed by Lead (instead of Follow) to immediately start as the new leader.

3.2   Security Definition

Overall, the game follows closely the one of the cmKEM primitive outlined in Sect. 2.3. In the following we discuss the key aspects and highlight the differences to the cmKEM game. We refer to the full version of this work for a formal definition.

Clocks. The security game maintains a global clock time. Each honestly created user uid maintains a local clock that is specified as an offset to the global one; that is, all local clocks run at the same speed. (For our analysis, we do not make use of the fact that two users uid and uid' belonging to the same long-term identity id, i.e. a device, typically would have the same local clock. Obviously our results also hold for this special case.)

The adversary chooses each user's offset and drives the global clock, i.e., decides whenever the clock is supposed to advance by a tick. Those ticks model an abstract discrete unit of time, which can be thought of as milliseconds or nanoseconds, roughly corresponding to the precision of clocks used by the various parties. Whenever the adversary ticks the global clock, each party's local clock thus also advances, and their respective procedures LeaderTick or ParticipantTick are invoked, depending on whether the party is currently a leader or not.

Liveness. An important objective of the LL-CGKA primitive is to ensure liveness: all participants must either keep up with the current meeting's state or drop out of the meeting. This is formalized as follows: whenever ParticipantTick indicates that uid is still alive, then the participant's state must not be too outdated, which in turn is defined as that the participant's current leader *must have been in the same state recently*. How recently exactly is a parameter of our security definition we call the *liveness slack*; we introduce the concrete slack achieved by Zoom's protocol as part of its description below.

Observe that this formalization essentially means that whenever the leader makes a change to the group by either adding or removing parties — resulting in an epoch or period change — then this change cannot be withheld by a malicious server. We thus call this property *key liveness* and briefly discuss *content liveness* in Sect. 5.

Confidentiality. Group key confidentiality is formalized analogously to the one of a cmKEM scheme. That is, upon a challenge, the security game outputs, depending on a bit b, either the real or an independent uniform random key. We remark that the game only allows to challenge keys for epochs and periods that are to be used in the higher-level application, omitting those that are skipped by the LPL mechanism and hence never output. This simplifies the notion as, in contrast to the cmKEM security notion, each challengeable key has a well-defined group roster associated.

Consistency, Authenticity, and No-Merging. The game ensures both *key consistency* and *group consistency*, meaning that for a given honest (and uncompromised) leader, epoch, and period, all (uncompromised) participants agree on a key and group roster. A malicious server can cause the group to split by assigning different leaders to different partitions of the group, in which case those partitions will no longer agree on the key. Furthermore, two parties, say Alice and Bob, in different partitions might both believe to have a third party Charlie in their group, or even believe to be in the same group with the other party. (That is, the group rosters output by different partitions are not guaranteed to be disjoint.) However, the game ensures that after such an aforementioned (inherent) splitting attack, the various partitions cannot be re-merged into a consistent state, which makes the attack easier to detect.

Remark 1 (Insider security). This work focuses on outsider security, and only formalizes limited insider security guarantees. For instance, whenever the adversary performs a trivial injection, enabled by e.g. a corruption of the leader, most security properties are (temporarily) disabled. On the other hand, we do formalize that confidentiality and authenticity recover after switching from a malicious leader to an honest one. While Zoom's protocol does not aim to provide strong guarantees in the presence of malicious insiders (as full insider security would e.g. require asymmetric authentication for video data), a more comprehensive analysis of the properties it does achieve would nevertheless be interesting.

3.3 Zoom's Scheme

We now describe Zoom's LL-CGKA scheme. On a high-level, the protocol enhances the cmKEM scheme by having the leader broadcasting the group membership to the participants and regularly broadcast so-called heartbeat messages for liveness. A formal description is presented in Figs. 2 and 3. Additional details can be found in the full version of this work.

Leader Participant List. For the participants to learn the group roster, the session leader broadcasts the so-called *leader participant list (LPL)* tabulating the members. The LPL is, for bandwidth efficiency, represented as a linked list of differential updates containing the set of added and removed participants since the last LPL. Each message also references the leader's current epoch e and period p. For efficiency reasons, an LPL message is not sent on every single change to the group roster, but on regular intervals instead. (It is skipped if no change to the group roster has been done in the meantime.) To ensure that parties know to whom they speak to, the scheme only proceeds to epochs and periods for has been certified by an LPL message. (Re-keying is nevertheless done eagerly, potentially leading to unused keys.)

The protocol furthermore relies on the LPL to communicate the group to newly joining parties. To avoid having new parties process the entire history of LPL messages, thus increasing the server's storage requirement, the leader

---

Protocol Zoom's Client LL-CGKA

User management

Algorithm: CreateUser(time, id, meetingId)
  (st, me, sig) ← cmKEM.CreateUser(id, meetingId)
  (isk, ·) ← PKI.get-sk(id)
  lastHb ← time
  uid_{lead} ← ⊥
  G ← ∅
  $e, p, e_{next}, p_{next}, v, t$ ← 0
  $k[\cdot, \cdot]$ ← ⊥
  $\delta[\cdot]$ ← ∞
  lplHash, hbHash ← ⊥
  return (me, sig)

Algorithm: Identity(uid)
  return cmKEM.Identity(uid)

Algorithm: Meeting(uid)
  return cmKEM.Meeting(uid)

Algorithm: CatchUp(ust, time, grpPub)
  req uid_{lead} = ⊥
  parse (lpls′, hb′) ← grpPub
  // Process LPLs
  while lpls ≠ ⟨⟩ **do**
    lpl′ ← lpls′.deq()
    try *receive-LPL(lpl′)
  // Store Heartbeat (no verification)
  hbHash ← Hash(hb′)

Participants' algorithms

Algorithm: Follow(time, m′, uid'_{lead}, sig'_{lead})
  req uid_{lead} ≠ ⊥ ∧ uid_{lead} ≠ me
  parse (m′$_K$, lpl′, hb′) ← m′
  try st ← cmKEM.JoinSession(st, uid'_{lead}, sig'_{lead}, m′$_K$, ⊥)
  Key[st.e, st.p] ← st.k
  if lpl′ ≠ ⊥ **then**
    try *receive-LPL(lpl′)
  if hb′ ≠ ⊥ **then**
    try *receive-heartbeat(hb′)

Algorithm: Process(time, m′)
  req uid_{lead} ≠ ⊥ ∧ uid_{lead} ≠ me
  parse (m′$_K$, lpl′, hb′) ← m′
  if m′$_K$ ≠ ⊥ **then**
    try st ← cmKEM.Process(st, m′$_K$)
    Key[st.e, st.p] ← st.k
  if lpl′ ≠ ⊥ **then**
    try *receive-LPL(lpl′)
  if hb′ ≠ ⊥ **then**
    try *receive-heartbeat(hb′)

Leader's algorithms

Algorithm: Lead(time, $\{(uid_i, sig_i)\}_{i \in [n]}$)
  uid_{lead} ← me
  try (st, M$_K$)
    ← cmKEM.StartSession(st, $\{(uid_i, \bot, sig_i)\}_{i \in [n]}$)
  G ← $\{uid_1, \ldots, uid_n\}$ ∪ {me}
  Added, Removed ← ∅
  numLplLinks ← max-links
  lpl ← *send-LPL()
  hb ← *send-heartbeat()
  M ← (me, M$_K$, lpl, hb)
  return M

Algorithm: Add(time, $\{(uid_i, sig_i)\}_{i \in [n]}$)
  req uid_{lead} = me
  for $i \in [n]$ **do**
    req $uid_i \notin G$
  G ← G ∪ $\{uid_1, \ldots, uid_n\}$
  Added ← Added ∪ $\{uid_1, \ldots, uid_n\}$
  if p ≥ p_{MAX} **then**
    try (st, M$_K$) ←
        cmKEM.Add(st, $\{(uid_i, \bot, sig_i)\}_{i \in [n]}$, true)
    (e, p) ← (st.e, st.p)
  else
    try (st, M$_K$) ←
        cmKEM.Add(st, $\{(uid_i, \bot, sig_i)\}_{i \in [n]}$, false)
  return (me, M$_K$, ⊥, ⊥)

Algorithm: Remove(time, $\{uid_i\}_{i \in [n]}$)
  req uid_{lead} = me
  for $i \in [n]$ **do**
    req $uid_i \in G$ ∧ uid_i ≠ me
  G ← G \ $\{uid_1, \ldots, uid_n\}$
  Removed ← Removed ∪ $\{uid_1, \ldots, uid_n\}$
  Added ← Added \ $\{uid_1, \ldots, uid_n\}$
  try (st, M$_K$) ← cmKEM.Remove(st, $\{uid_i\}_{i \in [n]}$)
  (e, p) ← (st.e, st.p)
  return (me, M$_K$, ⊥, ⊥)

Time driven

Algorithm: LeaderTick(time)
  req uid_{lead} = me
  lpl, hb ← ⊥
  if time − lastHb ≥ Δ_{LPL} **then**
    if Added ≠ ∅ ∨ Removed ≠ ∅ **then**
      lpl ← *send-LPL()
      hb ← *send-heartbeat()
    else if time − lastHb ≥ $\Delta_{heartbeat}$ **then**
      hb ← *send-heartbeat()
  return (me, ⊥, lpl, hb)

Algorithm: ParticipantTick(time)
  req uid_{lead} ≠ ⊥ ∧ uid_{lead} ≠ me
  alive ← (time − lastHb ≤ Δ_{live})
  return (alive, ⊥) // no updated credentials

Fig. 2. The client part of Zoom's overall LL-CGKA scheme. The description implicitly keeps the state ust.

Protocol Zoom's Client LL-CGKA Helpers

Helper: *send-LPL()
  $v \leftarrow v + 1$
  if numLplLinks $\geq$ max-links then
    $lpl \leftarrow (me, v, true, \bot, G, \bot, e, p)$
    numLplLinks $\leftarrow 1$
  else
    $lpl \leftarrow (me, v, false, lplHash, Added, Removed, e, p)$
    numLplLinks $\leftarrow$ numLplLinks $+ 1$
  lplHash $\leftarrow$ Hash(lpl)
  (Added, Removed) $\leftarrow \varnothing$
  return lpl

Helper: *receive-LPL(lpl')
  parse $(uid'_{lead}, v', coalesced', lplHash',$
              $Added', Removed', e', p') \leftarrow lpl'$
  req $v = \bot \lor v' = v + 1$
  $v \leftarrow v'$
  if $\neg coalesced$ then
    req lplHash' = lplHash $\land$ lplHash $\neq \bot$
    req (Removed' $\setminus G$) = $\varnothing$
    $G \leftarrow G \setminus$ Removed'
    req (Added $\cap G$) = $\varnothing$
    $G \leftarrow G \cup$ Added'
  else
    $G \leftarrow$ Added'
  lplHash $\leftarrow$ Hash(lpl')
  $(e_{next}, p_{next}) \leftarrow (e', p')$

Helper: *send-heartbeat()
  $t \leftarrow t + 1$
  $sig_{hb} \leftarrow$ Sig.Sign(isk, 'LeaderParticipantList',
              (me, t, hbHash, time, v, lplHash, e, p))
  $hb \leftarrow (t, time, sig_{hb})$
  hbHash $\leftarrow$ Hash(hb), lastHb $\leftarrow$ time
  return hb

Helper: *receive-heartbeat(hb)
  parse $(t', time', sig'_{hb}) \leftarrow hb$
  req $t = \bot \lor t' = t + 1$
  $t \leftarrow t'$
  $(\cdot, ipk') \leftarrow$ cmKEM.Identity(uid_{lead})
  req Sig.Verify(ipk', 'LeaderParticipantList', (uid_{lead}, t,
              hbHash, time, v, lplHash, e_{next}, p_{next}), sig'_{hb})
  req Key[e_{next}, p_{next}] $\neq \bot$
  $(e, p) \leftarrow (e_{next}, p_{next})$
  *update-drift(time')
  *update-liveness(time')
  hbHash $\leftarrow$ Hash(hb)
  $t \leftarrow t'$

Helper: *update-drift(time')
  $\delta[uid_{lead}] \leftarrow \min(\delta[uid_{lead}], time - time')$

Helper: *update-liveness(time')
  lastHb $\leftarrow$ time' $+ \delta[uid_{lead}]$

Fig. 3. Helper algorithms for the client part of Zoom's overall LL-CGKA scheme.

will from time to time use a special *coalesced* LPL message encoding the entire group.[9] A joining party therefore needs all the links up to and including the latest coalesced message only. The frequency of coalesced messages is determined by the parameter max-links.

Heartbeats. The LPL messages are unauthenticated. To authenticate them, the leader broadcasts a signature (of a hash) thereof under the leader's long-term identity key. Those signatures moreover form another hash chain, with each signature including the hash of the previous one, to ensures the continuity of the meeting. That is, while certain splitting attacks — where a malicious server might tell subgroups to accept different leaders — are unavoidable, those diverging meetings cannot be rejoined later.

The leader broadcasts one such signature at least at a fixed interval $\Delta_{heartbeat}$, even when no LPL has been sent for lack of any change to the group membership. Since they are regularly sent, these signatures are called *heartbeat messages* and double as a mechanism to ensure liveness. To this end, the signature additionally includes the latest epoch e, and period p. Hence, if an attacker attempts to withhold either key rotations or updates to the membership, causing a participant to

---

[9] In the deployed version of the protocol, the coalesced LPL also includes a list of all participants who were in the meeting at some point in the past but have since left. This additional information is displayed in the client's user interface, but is not modeled in this work.

be stuck in an old state, they would need to withhold the heartbeat message as well, for this to go unnoticed. As a countermeasure, participants drop out from the meeting if they do not receive a heartbeat message for too long.

For this mechanism to not abruptly end meetings (despite potential network hiccups), participants do not expect to receive the heartbeats in perfectly regular intervals. Rather, each heartbeat itself contains a timestamp time' (the sending time) whose state it certifies. Receiving this heartbeat then prolongs the liveness of the receiver until time $\mathsf{time}' + \delta + \Delta_{\mathsf{live}}$, when the party will drop out if no further heartbeat has been received. Here, δ denotes an estimate on the clock drift (between the participant and their respective leader) and Δ_{live} denotes a protocol parameter. In a best effort to prevent this from happening, the server will elect a new leader whenever the current one struggles to upload heartbeats.

The protocol estimates the clock drift δ as follows: Upon receiving the first heartbeat with timestamp t' at local time t from a given leader, the protocol simply assumes that $t - t'$ is the drift, i.e., that the heartbeat has been delivered instantaneously. Clearly, $t' + \delta = t$ is an upper bound on the effective sending time. Upon receiving a subsequent heartbeat, the party corrects the drift to $t - t'$ whenever this is smaller, and otherwise keeps it unchanged. Hence, if the network delay, and thus the interval between received heartbeat, increases (e.g., due to a network attacker) then each subsequently received heartbeat extends liveness by a smaller amount, until the party eventually drops out. Conversely, if the network delay decreases, the drift estimates and, hence, the liveness assurances improve.

Evolving the Group. The protocol uses the cmKEM scheme to rotate keys whenever the group membership changes. The participants, however, do not immediately transition to the new epoch or period upon receiving such a cmKEM message. Rather, they just store the new key. Only once the group membership is known via receiving a corresponding LPL message and heartbeat, they transition to the new epoch and period and advertise the respective key for content encryption to the higher-level protocol. For membership changes containing only additions, the protocol avoids overly frequent epoch changes by rotating the period instead, however, limiting the number of consecutive periods to a fixed number $\mathsf{p_{MAX}}$.

Joining a Meeting. To join a meeting, a party needs to learn the latest key and group roster in an authenticated manner. The former is communicated via a cmKEM message and the latter via the sequence of LPL messages starting with the latest coalesced one. Authentication of the LPL is achieved by verifying the latest heartbeat message that certifies the final LPL message, as well as epoch and period numbers. (The previous links are implicitly authenticated due to the links forming a hash chain.)

Leader Changes. A newly elected leader continues the meeting by starting a new cmKEM session and generating a coalesced LPL message and a heartbeat,

which the server then distributes to the other participants. The new leader will
continue the relevant counters (i.e., e, p, and t) and hash chains where the old
leader left off, such that they uniquely identify a meeting state. The server is
responsible to ensure that the party has the latest state the moment it becomes
the new leader.

Note that the new leader obtains the group roster from the server, rather
than deducing it from the previous LPL messages. Otherwise, they might inad-
vertently revert some of the previous leader's final changes to the group, if for
instance the previous leader added or removed a party on the cmKEM level but
did not manage to broadcast a corresponding LPL message before dropping out.
Users are shown a warning on every leader change, and are advised to manually
check whether the group roster displayed in their client matches the expected
one.

The Server Scheme. The messages the leader uploads consist of up to three
components, a cmKEM message, a LPL and a heartbeat message. If the message contains a cmKEM message, then the server splits this using the respective
cmKEM algorithm and forwards the respective share alongside the LPL and
heartbeat (if present) to the users. Otherwise, the server forwards the LPL and
heartbeat messages to the last known roster, as derived from the cmKEM messages. See the full version of this work for details.

Security. Security is summarized in our main result below, with a more detailed
proof given in the full version of this work.

Theorem 2. *Zoom's LL-CGKA scheme is secure with the liveness slack of P
being at most*

$$\min(n \cdot \Delta_{\mathsf{live}}, t_{\mathsf{now}} - t_{\mathsf{joined}}) + \Delta_{\mathsf{live}},$$

*where t_{now} denotes the current time, t_{joined} the time P joined the meeting, and
n denotes the number of distinct leaders P encountered so far. Liveness holds
if all those leaders have followed the protocol, while all other properties hold as
long as the current leader is honest.*

Proof (Sketch). Confidentiality and key consistency follow directly from the
underlying cmKEM scheme which is used to distribute the group keys. While
the LL-CGKA notion mandates slightly stronger properties, those additional
assurances relate directly to members only transitioning to subsequent periods
if their leader initiated this. This is ensured by parties only transitioning to a new
state once a heartbeat certified it, leveraging the unforgeability of the employed
signature scheme. Similarly, group consistency — i.e., authenticity of each participant's view on the group roster — is ensured by the combined LPL and
heartbeat mechanism, with the LPL distributing the group and the heartbeat
authenticating the LPL. Additionally, the hash links of the heartbeat messages
yields the no-merging property after a group-splitting attack.

Finally, observe that liveness slack is directly linked to the accuracy of each party's estimate on the clock drift with their respective leader: If the estimate were precise, then each party would have a liveness slack of at most Δ_{live} since they would know exactly when the last heartbeat they received has been sent allowing them to drop out Δ_{live} after. Further, the estimate only degrades by at most Δ_{live} with each leader change — the maximum interval between receiving the old leader's last heartbeat and the new leader's first one.

The above theorem relies on the underlying cmKEM scheme being secure according to the respective definition, the signature scheme being EUF-CMA secure, and the hash function being collision resistant. According to the whitepaper [11], Zoom's instantiation uses SHA256 and EdDSA (as provided by libsodium) for the hash function and signature algorithm, respectively, satisfying those requirements [13,19].

Concrete Parameters. At the time of writing, Zoom uses $\Delta_{\text{live}} = 100s$, $\Delta_{\text{heartbeat}} = 10s$, $\Delta_{\text{LPL}} = 2s$, and max-links $= 20$, respectively. Moreover, $p_{\text{MAX}} = 0$, i.e., Zoom always ratchets the full epoch instead of the period[3].

4   Improved Liveness

4.1   Limitations of Zoom's Protocol

For a typical meeting with a single (honest) host that stays online for the duration of the entire meeting — and thus is the leader for the entire meeting — Zoom's current scheme[1] provides strong liveness properties. Indeed, to the best of our knowledge, Zoom is the only E2EE group video protocol that provides any such liveness assurance. As highlighted by Theorem 2, however, there two distinct aspects with respect to which the assurances could be further improved:

1. Zoom's current liveness assurance degrade in the number of meeting leaders encountered. This is sub-optimal for a protocol such as Zoom where the (untrusted) server can initiate leader changes.[10]
2. While all other security properties, such as key confidentiality and authenticity, recover after removing a malicious party from the meeting, liveness does not.[11]

We particularly stress that both aspects are not merely deficiencies of our analysis. Concrete but contrived attacks exist, even if they could be mitigated by countermeasures relying on the end user, such as user-interface warnings.

---

[10] This is currently remedied by the client showing a warning upon each leader change, since the leader-authentication codes anyway require to repeat the authentication process in this event. With the introduction of the advanced PKI replacing the leader-authentication codes, Zoom might however consider dropping those warnings.

[11] Note that Zoom does not aim to provide strong guarantees *while* a malicious insider is part of the meeting. Yet, removing a malicious party should ideally reestablish security without the need to restart the entire meeting.

Lemma 1. *Even with all honest participants, the liveness properties of Zoom's LL-CGKA scheme degrade in the number of leader changes, assuming an all powerful malicious server carefully orchestrating the meeting.*

Proof. Consider a meeting with parties $P_1, P_2, \ldots, P_n$, as well as a designated party P^*. All parties, unbeknownst to each other, have precisely synchronized clocks. The party P_1 is the one to start the meeting and act as its initial leader. When adding the parties $P_2, \ldots, P_n$ to the meeting, the network adversary delivers the respective messages immediately. That is, the moment those parties create their ephemeral user identities $\mathsf{uid}_2, \ldots, \mathsf{uid}_n$, party P_1 is immediately instructed to add them to the meeting using Add producing M, and the respective shared obtained by split are handed to the parties to execute Follow without any delay. (To this end, assume that the heartbeat interval perfectly aligns with the moment all those parties join.) This results in each of those parties estimating their drift to be 0, i.e., $\delta_{\mathsf{uid}_j}[\mathsf{uid}_1] = 0$ for $j \in \{2, \ldots, n\}$.

In contrast, when party P^* joins the meeting their respective ephemeral identity uid^* is still handed immediately to P_1, but the respective response delayed by Δ_{live}. Assuming P^* created their identity at time t and got the LL-CGKA message at time $t + \Delta_{\mathsf{live}}$, but with timestamp t, then P^* assumes that their clock runs ahead by Δ_{live}, i.e., $\delta_{\mathsf{uid}^*}[\mathsf{uid}_1] = \Delta_{\mathsf{live}}$. All subsequent heartbeats from P_1 are then delivered to P^* with a delay of Δ_{live}. As a result, if P_1 sends a further heartbeat at time t', P^* will set $\mathsf{lastHb} \leftarrow t' + \Delta_{\mathsf{live}}$ and therefore extend the time until they drop out until $t' + 2\Delta_{\mathsf{live}}$ (instead of the optimal $t' + \Delta_{\mathsf{live}}$).

Next, consider P_1 sending their last heartbeat at time $t_2 \geq t + \Delta_{\mathsf{live}}$ (which is delivered to all parties as previously described) and immediately afterwards the party P_2 becoming the leader, still at time t_2. Again, the messages derived from the output of Lead are distributed to $P_3, \ldots, P_n$ without delay, again resulting in $\delta_{\mathsf{uid}_j}[\mathsf{uid}_2] = 0$. For P^*, on the other hand, P_1's last heartbeat is delivered at time $t_2 + \Delta_{\mathsf{live}}$, extending liveness until $t_2 + 2\Delta_{\mathsf{live}}$. The adversary now takes advantage of the fact by delaying the first message from P_2 as well as all subsequent ones by $2\Delta_{\mathsf{live}}$. This process can then be repeated with sequentially switching leaders to $P_3, P_4, \ldots, P_n$, leading to a liveness slack of $(n+1)\Delta_{\mathsf{live}}$.   □

Lemma 2. *If parties join a meeting that currently has a malicious leader colluding with a party with extensive control over Zoom's server infrastructure, then the liveness assurance can be arbitrarily broken even after all malicious parties have been removed from the meeting (and a honest leader has taken over).*

Proof. Consider a malicious insider attacker P_M starting a meeting. Moreover, assume that there are two honest parties P_A and P_B, where first P_A wants to join and at a later point P_B wants to join. Assume that all have perfectly synchronized clocks. In the meeting, attacker first adds P_A to the group, without any delay, i.e., such that $\delta_{\mathsf{uid}_A}[\mathsf{uid}_M] = 0$. At time t, right when P_B is about to join (e.g., once P_B advertised their ephemeral uid_B) the malicious insider does the following:

1. P_M creates k heartbeat messages $\mathsf{t}+1, \mathsf{t}+2, \ldots, \mathsf{t}+k$ (when t denotes the number of heartbeats created so far) for which they pretend to be normally spaced out by $\Delta_{\mathsf{heartbeat}}$ with respect to the included timestamps.
2. P_M then adds P_B to the meeting in state $\mathsf{t}+k$, i.e., the first heartbeat signing over the LPL containing uid_B is with counter $\mathsf{t}+k+1$.

The attacker controlling Zoom's server infrastructure now delivers those messages as follows:

1. Immediately deliver the welcoming message, including the $(\mathsf{t}+k+1)$-th heartbeat, at time t to P_B. As a result P_B will set $\delta_{\mathsf{uid}_B}[\mathsf{uid}_M] = -k \cdot \Delta_{\mathsf{heartbeat}}$, since to P_B it looks like the clock of P_M simply runs ahead.
2. Immediately make P_B the new leader at time t.
3. Deliver all the k intermediate heartbeats to P_A at the regular interval $\Delta_{\mathsf{heartbeat}}$. At time $t + k \cdot \Delta_{\mathsf{heartbeat}}$ first deliver the messages corresponding to P_B joining and then, immediately afterwards, the first message from the new leader P_B.

It is easy to see that P_A does not drop out as they get heartbeats exactly as if the meeting would progress normally. More concretely, to P_A it looks like a perfectly normal meeting in which P_B joins at time $t + k \cdot \Delta_{\mathsf{heartbeat}}$. At the end, P_A will still accept the message from P_A, thinking that the clock of P_A must run ahead.

As a result, we now propose two alternative strengthened liveness protocols.

4.2   Additional Interaction

As a first proposal we suggest adding additional interaction in the form of sporadic messages of each participant. This proposal has been implemented in the Zoom meeting client since version 5.13.

The Protocol. Concretely, our enhancement to Zoom's protocol is as follows: First, each party generates an unpredictable nonce nonce (from some nonce space $\mathcal{N}$, e.g., 192-bit strings) at regular intervals. These nonces are seen as part of a party's credential and hence ParticipantTick outputs new credentials whenever the nonce is update. (In practice one would of course only upload the nonce, not the entire credentials, each time.) For simplicity, we choose the same parameter Δ_{live} as for the overall liveness slack.

Whenever a new leader is elected, they get each participants latest nonce from the server. We encode this as part of the credentials sig for the Lead algorithm, which can now be thought as some sort of time-based credentials. The new leader then uses those nonces as associated data for the cmKEM primitive (which for Zoom's instantiation means it is used as associated data for the authenticated PKE). The same mechanism is used for adding new members to the group.

Each party as part of the Follow algorithm provides their current nonce as associated data to JoinSession, thus verifying that the new leader used the correct

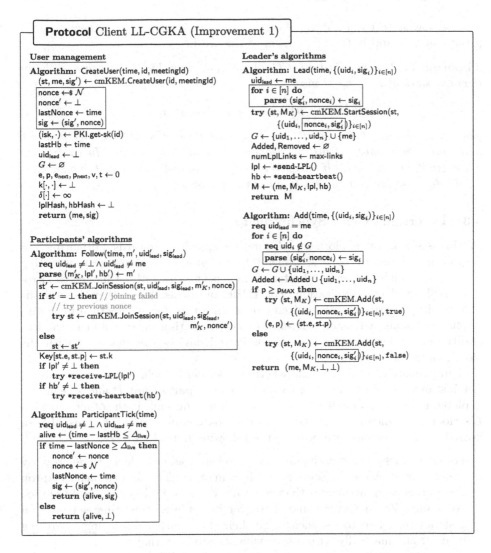

Fig. 4. The proposed changes with respect to Zoom's scheme from Fig. 2.

one. To prevent race conditions, parties moreover stores their second latest nonce $nonce'$ and try with that one if JoinSession initially fails. See Fig. 4 for a formal description of the changes with respect to Zoom's current scheme from Fig. 2.

Security. Our proposal improves the liveness properties twofold. First, the liveness slack no longer degrades in the number of leader changes. Second, liveness now holds even if a *past leader* has been corrupted as long as the current leader is honest.

We now state the resulting theorem. A more formal version thereof and a proof can be found in the full version of this work.

Theorem 3. *The modified LL-CGKA scheme from Fig. 4 is secure with the liveness slack of P being at most*

$$\min\{\min(3, n) \cdot \Delta_{\text{live}}, t_{\text{now}} - t_{\text{joined}}\} + \Delta_{\text{live}},$$

where t_{now} denotes the current time, t_{joined} the time P joined the meeting, and n denotes the number of distinct leaders P encountered so far. In contrast to Theorem 2, liveness holds if the current leader is honest (as apposed to all leaders encountered so far), analogous to all other properties.

4.3   Leveraging Clock Synchronicity

In this section, we explore an alternative approach towards mitigating the degrading liveness properties. Concretely, we propose to leverage pre-existing clock synchronicity to achieve better liveness properties without having to introduce additional communication. For E2EE protocols, however, it is undesirable to simply assume synchronized clocks since this, for all practical purposes, implies assuming a trusted reference clock (some time server) and introduces additional friction for users on misconfigured devices (for example, with the wrong timezone settings.).

Unfortunately, even detecting whether clocks are synchronized is non-trivial. For instance, consider the interaction between a participant P and a leader L depicted in Fig. 5: in one situation, L's clock is in sync while in the other situation L's clock runs ahead — yet the scenarios look completely indistinguishable to both P and L. As such, we propose the following hybrid strategy:

- For correctness, i.e., functionality of the scheme, assume clocks to be properly synchronized. After all, Zoom is usually run on modern devices such as laptop computers or smartphones that generally do have well synchronized clocks. An honest Zoom server could moreover detect erroneous time setting and instruct the client to re-synchronize their clock (either displaying a warning or do it automatically with a somewhat trusted external server).
- For security, well synchronized clocks should yield tight liveness assurances, while worst case liveness should degrade to the current[1] protocol's properties.

The Protocol. We now discuss our proposed mechanism. In a nutshell, our proposed improvement works by each party P not maintaining a single (best-effort) estimate $\delta_P[L]$ to their current leader L, but strict lower and upper bounds $\delta_P^{\min}[L] \leq \text{offset}_{L \to P} \leq \delta_P^{\max}[L]$ on their respective drift $\text{offset}_{L \to P}$ gradually improved over the course of the protocol execution. Analogous to the current estimate, those bounds are derived from simple causality observations and in turn used to adjust the timestamp indicated as part of the heartbeat messages. See Fig. 6 for a formal description of the proposed modifications with respect to Zoom's current scheme.

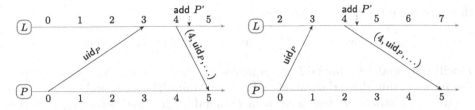

Fig. 5. The leader L's clock running ahead (right) negatively affects liveness as the addition of P' can be withheld longer from P.

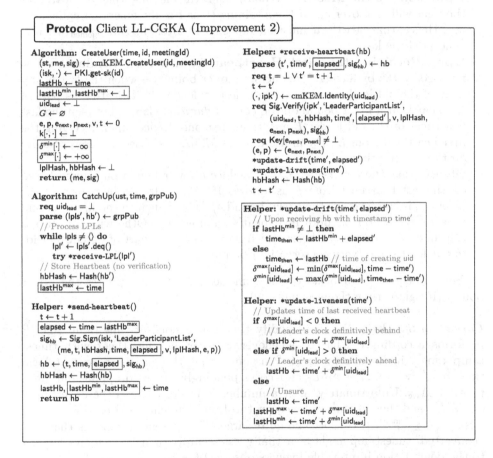

Fig. 6. The proposed changes with respect to Zoom's scheme from Fig. 2.

Deriving Bounds. To this end, consider the case that P receives a heartbeat with timestamp time_L (according to L's clock) at time t_{now} (according to P's clock). Clearly, P knows that the heartbeat has not been sent after t_{now}, i.e. $\text{time}_L + \text{offset}_{L \to P} \leq t_{\text{now}}$. Furthermore, assume that (for whatever reason) P knows that this heartbeat has been sent definitely not before t_{then}. P can use this to deduce the following bounds:

$$t_{\text{then}} - \text{time}_L \leq \delta_P^{\max}[L] \qquad \text{and} \qquad \delta_P^{\min}[L] \leq t_{\text{now}} - \text{time}_L.$$

P will only update a bound if it improves the current one. (At the beginning, the protocol initializes them to $\delta_P^{\max}[L] = +\infty$ and $\delta_P^{\min}[L] = -\infty$.)

In our protocol, P will have a meaningful such lower bound t_{then} in the following two situations:

- **Upon Joining the Meeting:** When P joins the meeting, the first heartbeat they get will sign over an LPL containing their freshly generated ephemeral key. Hence, that heartbeat must have been sent after the time t_{joined} when P generated the key.
- **Upon Receiving the First Heartbeat from a New Leader L':** The protocol works by having P deducing a lower bound on when the last heartbeat of the old leader was sent, and the new leader L' indicating as part of the heartbeat a lower bound on the *elapsed duration* elapsed between the last heartbeat of the old leader L and their first one. Hence, upon receiving the first heartbeat from L', P can use $\text{time}_L + \delta_P^{\min}[L] + \text{elapsed}$ as a lower bound on the sending time.

  Observe that the new leader L' can deduce a lower bound on elapsed based on the last heartbeat from L as follows: If L' has already been part of the meeting, it can leverage their own bound $\delta_{L'}^{\max}[L]$ to deduce the upper bound $\text{time}_L + \delta_{L'}^{\max}[L]$ on the prior heartbeat's sending time. Otherwise, L' can use the time they got the last heartbeat from the server as part of CatchUp yielding at least some (very conservative) bound.

For subsequent heartbeats of the same leader, P only updates the upper bound (if tighter than the previous one).

Correcting the Drift. We then modify the "conversion" of timestamp that P performs accordingly. That is, whenever P receives a heartbeat with timestamp time'_L, in Zoom's protocol P assumes that this has been sent at local time $\text{time}'_P := \text{time}'_L + \delta_P[L]$ and correspondingly delays dropping out until $\text{time}'_P + \Delta_{\text{live}}$. Unfortunately, after a number of leader changes the uncertainty on $\delta_P[L]$ (and thus in our improved protocol the difference between $\delta_P^{\min}[L]$ and $\text{offset}_{L \to P} \leq \delta_P^{\max}[L]$) can become quite large. This potentially means that this "converted" timestamp might be actually less accurate than the sent one, leading to the degradation in provable liveness observed for Zoom's protocol.

We, thus, want to be careful not to destroy the assurances in case the clocks are well synchronized. Hence, the protocol conservatively adjusts the received timestamp if and only if the leader's clock is surely behind or ahead, respectively:

$$\text{time}'_P := \begin{cases} \text{time}'_L + \delta_P^{\min}[L] & \text{if } \delta_P^{\min}[L] > 0, \\ \text{time}'_L + \delta_P^{\max}[L] & \text{if } \delta_P^{\max}[L] < 0, \\ \text{time}'_L & \text{otherwise.} \end{cases}$$

Security. We now state the respective security statement. A more formal version thereof and a proof is given in the full version of this work.

Theorem 4. *The modified LL-CGKA scheme from Fig. 6 is secure with the following improved liveness slack*

$$\min\{|\text{offset}_{L \to P}|, \; n \cdot \Delta_{\text{live}}, \; t_{\text{now}} - t_{\text{joined}}\} + \Delta_{\text{live}},$$

where $\text{offset}_{L \to P}$ *denotes the clock drift between* P *and their respective leader* L, t_{now} *denotes the current time,* t_{joined} *the time* P *joined the meeting, and* n *denotes the number of distinct leaders* P *encountered so far. Liveness holds if all those leaders have followed the protocol, while all other properties hold as long as the current leader is honest.*

5 Meeting Stream Security

The notion of LL-CGKA formalizes the key agreement portion of Zoom's E2EE meeting protocol. While our formal analysis stops at the level of the key agreement, we now comment on how these guarantees extend to the full protocol.

The symmetric meeting key that participants agree upon is leveraged in a straightforward way to provide security guarantees for the whole meeting, by composing it with AEAD. Concretely, given the meeting key, Zoom clients derive a specific per-stream subkey by using HKDF and mixing in a specific stream identifier which depends on the stream type as well as the participant identifier. This subkey is used by each participant to encrypt their streams using AES-GCM. Incrementing nonces provide protection against replay and out of order delivery.

Confidentiality and Authenticity. Informally, confidentiality of the meeting key (as formalized in the LL-CGKA abstraction) implies confidentiality of the streams, as distinguishing encrypted meeting streams from encryptions of random noise would require breaking the AEAD scheme. Similarly, AEAD provides integrity protection against external attackers who do not have access to the meeting key, guaranteeing that any received ciphertexts was produced by someone with knowledge of the meeting (sub)key. As pointed out in the whitepaper [11], it is possible for attendees with privileged network access to tamper with each other's streams.

Liveness. The liveness properties proven for the LL-CGKA directly guarantee that group operations in an E2EE meeting cannot be withheld, and extend analogously to the encrypted meeting streams, but with different parameters. Indeed, as of version 5.13 of the Zoom meetings client, meeting participants stop decryption using old meeting keys shortly after a newer one is advertised from the key agreement, i.e., the LL-CGKA scheme (with a tolerance $\Delta_{\text{stream}} = 10$ seconds to account for network latency). In addition, meeting leaders rotate these keys at least once every $t = 5$ minutes even when there is no change in the participant list. Assuming the above, the protocol guarantees that each packet sent by an honest participant and successfully decrypted was sent within $t + \Delta_{\text{stream}} + \Delta$ of its decryption, where Δ is the liveness slack from the key agreement protocol. Alternatively, the protocol could include the heartbeat counter from the key agreement as associated data in the video encryption, yielding liveness $\Delta + \Delta_{\text{stream}} + \Delta_{\text{heartbeat}}$ without the need to frequently re-key.[12]

6   Conclusions

In this work, we provided the first formal security analysis of Zoom's E2EE meetings protocol, which is one of the most popular group video communication tools in the world. Our work lead to a deployed improvement of the Zoom E2EE meetings protocol, which strengthens its security properties. Of independent interest, our work is also the first that defines and studies *liveness* in the context of end-to-end encryption, which we hope should find other applications beyond Zoom meetings.

References

1. Alwen, J., Blanchet, B., Hauck, E., Kiltz, E., Lipp, B., Riepel, D.: Analysing the HPKE standard. In: Canteaut, A., Standaert, F.-X. (eds.) EUROCRYPT 2021. LNCS, vol. 12696, pp. 87–116. Springer, Cham (2021). https://doi.org/10.1007/978-3-030-77870-5_4
2. Alwen, J., Coretti, S., Dodis, Y.: The double ratchet: security notions, proofs, and modularization for the signal protocol. In: Ishai, Y., Rijmen, V. (eds.) EUROCRYPT 2019. LNCS, vol. 11476, pp. 129–158. Springer, Cham (2019). https://doi.org/10.1007/978-3-030-17653-2_5
3. Alwen, J., Coretti, S., Dodis, Y., Tselekounis, Y.: Security analysis and improvements for the ietf mls standard for group messaging. In: Micciancio, D., Ristenpart, T. (eds.) CRYPTO 2020. LNCS, vol. 12170, pp. 248–277. Springer, Cham (2020). https://doi.org/10.1007/978-3-030-56784-2_9
4. Alwen, J., Coretti, S., Dodis, Y., Tselekounis, Y.: Modular design of secure group messaging protocols and the security of MLS. In: Vigna, G., Shi, E. (eds.) ACM CCS 2021. pp. 1463–1483. ACM Press (Nov 2021). https://doi.org/10.1145/3460120.3484820
5. Alwen, J., Coretti, S., Jost, D., Mularczyk, M.: Continuous group key agreement with active security. In: Pass, R., Pietrzak, K. (eds.) TCC 2020. LNCS, vol. 12551, pp. 261–290. Springer, Cham (2020). https://doi.org/10.1007/978-3-030-64378-2_10
6. An, J.H.: Authenticated encryption in the public-key setting: Security notions and analyses. Cryptology ePrint Archive, Report 2001/079 (2001), https://eprint.iacr.org/2001/079
7. Apple: Facetime & privacy. https://www.apple.com/legal/privacy/data/en/facetime/

---

[12] This is, however, non-trivial to achieve in a backwards compatible way.

8. Barnes, R., Beurdouche, B., Millican, J., Omara, E., Cohn-Gordon, K., Robert, R.: The messaging layer security (mls) protocol (draft-ietf-mls-protocol-latest). Tech. rep., IETF (Oct 2020), https://messaginglayersecurity.rocks/mls-protocol/draft-ietf-mls-protocol.html

9. Bellare, M., Goldwasser, S.: Verifiable partial key escrow. In: Graveman, R., Janson, P.A., Neuman, C., Gong, L. (eds.) ACM CCS 97. pp. 78–91. ACM Press (Apr 1997). https://doi.org/10.1145/266420.266439

10. Bienstock, A., Fairoze, J., Garg, S., Mukherjee, P., Raghuraman, S.: What is the exact security of the signal protocol? Preprint (2021), https://cs.nyu.edu/afb383/publication/uc_signal/uc_signal.pdf

11. Blum, J., et al.: Zoom cryptography whitepaper - v4.0. https://github.com/zoom/zoom-e2e-whitepaper/raw/master/archive/zoom_e2e_v4.pdf (2022)

12. Boneh, D., Naor, M.: Timed commitments. In: Bellare, M. (ed.) CRYPTO 2000. LNCS, vol. 1880, pp. 236–254. Springer, Heidelberg (2000). https://doi.org/10.1007/3-540-44598-6_15

13. Brendel, J., Cremers, C., Jackson, D., Zhao, M.: The provable security of ed25519: Theory and practice. In: 2021 IEEE Symposium on Security and Privacy (SP). pp. 1659–1676 (2021). https://doi.org/10.1109/SP40001.2021.00042

14. Bresson, E., Chevassut, O., Pointcheval, D.: Dynamic group diffie-hellman key exchange under standard assumptions. In: Knudsen, L.R. (ed.) EUROCRYPT 2002. LNCS, vol. 2332, pp. 321–336. Springer, Heidelberg (2002). https://doi.org/10.1007/3-540-46035-7_21

15. Canetti, R., Garay, J., Itkis, G., Micciancio, D., Naor, M., Pinkas, B.: Multicast security: a taxonomy and some efficient constructions. In: IEEE INFOCOM '99. Conference on Computer Communications. Proceedings. Eighteenth Annual Joint Conference of the IEEE Computer and Communications Societies. The Future is Now (Cat. No.99CH36320). vol. 2, pp. 708–716 (1999)

16. Cisco: Zero-trust security for webex - white paper. https://www.cisco.com/c/en/us/solutions/collateral/collaboration/white-paper-c11-744553.html (2021)

17. Cohn-Gordon, K., Cremers, C., Dowling, B., Garratt, L., Stebila, D.: A formal security analysis of the signal messaging protocol. J. Cryptol. 33(4), 1914–1983 (2020). https://doi.org/10.1007/s00145-020-09360-1

18. Cohn-Gordon, K., Cremers, C.J.F., Dowling, B., Garratt, L., Stebila, D.: A formal security analysis of the signal messaging protocol. In: 2017 IEEE European Symposium on Security and Privacy, EuroS&P 2017, pp. 451–466. IEEE (2017). https://doi.org/10.1109/EuroSP.2017.27, https://doi.org/10.1109/EuroSP.2017.27

19. Coron, J.-S., Dodis, Y., Malinaud, C., Puniya, P.: Merkle-Damgård Revisited: how to construct a hash function. In: Shoup, V. (ed.) CRYPTO 2005. LNCS, vol. 3621, pp. 430–448. Springer, Heidelberg (2005). https://doi.org/10.1007/11535218_26

20. Denis, F.: The sodium cryptography library. https://download.libsodium.org/doc/ (Jun 2013)

21. Dolev, D., Strong, H.R.: Polynomial algorithms for multiple processor agreement. In: 14th ACM STOC. pp. 401–407. ACM Press (May 1982). https://doi.org/10.1145/800070.802215

22. Dwork, C., Naor, M.: Pricing via processing or combatting junk mail. In: Brickell, E.F. (ed.) CRYPTO 1992. LNCS, vol. 740, pp. 139–147. Springer, Heidelberg (1993). https://doi.org/10.1007/3-540-48071-4_10

23. Dwork, C., Naor, M., Sahai, A.: Concurrent zero-knowledge. In: 30th ACM STOC. pp. 409–418. ACM Press (May 1998). https://doi.org/10.1145/276698.276853

24. Feldman, P., Micali, S.: Optimal algorithms for byzantine agreement. In: 20th ACM STOC, pp. 148–161. ACM Press (May 1988). https://doi.org/10.1145/62212.62225]

25. Fischlin, M., Günther, F.: Multi-stage key exchange and the case of Google's QUIC protocol. In: Ahn, G.J., Yung, M., Li, N. (eds.) ACM CCS 2014, pp. 1193–1204. ACM Press (Nov 2014). https://doi.org/10.1145/2660267.2660308

26. Garay, J., Kiayias, A., Leonardos, N.: The bitcoin backbone protocol with chains of variable difficulty. In: Katz, J., Shacham, H. (eds.) CRYPTO 2017. LNCS, vol. 10401, pp. 291–323. Springer, Cham (2017). https://doi.org/10.1007/978-3-319-63688-7_10

27. Gruszczyk, J.: End-to-end encryption for one-to-one microsoft teams calls now generally available. Microsoft Teams Blog - December 14, 2021. https://techcommunity.microsoft.com/t5/microsoft-teams-blog/end-to-end-encryption-for-one-to-one-microsoft-teams-calls-now/ba-p/3037697 (12 2021)

28. Harder, E.J., Wallner, D.M.: Key Management for Multicast: Issues and Architectures. RFC 2627 (Jun 1999). 10.17487/RFC2627, https://www.rfc-editor.org/info/rfc2627

29. Isobe, T., Ito, R.: Security analysis of end-to-end encryption for zoom meetings. In: Baek, J., Ruj, S. (eds.) Information Security and Privacy, pp. 234–253. Springer International Publishing, Cham (2021)

30. Katz, J.: Efficient and non-malleable proofs of plaintext knowledge and applications. In: Biham, E. (ed.) EUROCRYPT 2003. LNCS, vol. 2656, pp. 211–228. Springer, Heidelberg (2003). https://doi.org/10.1007/3-540-39200-9_13

31. Kim, Y., Perrig, A., Tsudik, G.: Tree-based group key agreement. Cryptology ePrint Archive, Report 2002/009 (2002), https://eprint.iacr.org/2002/009

32. Krohn, M.: Zoom rolling out end-to-end encryption offering. Zoom Blog - October 14, 2020. https://blog.zoom.us/zoom-rolling-out-end-to-end-encryption-offering/ (10 2020)

33. Lowe, G.: A hierarchy of authentication specifications. In: Proceedings 10th Computer Security Foundations Workshop, pp. 31–43 (1997). https://doi.org/10.1109/CSFW.1997.596782

34. Marlinspike, M., Perrin, T.: The double ratchet algorithm (11 2016), https://whispersystems.org/docs/specifications/doubleratchet/doubleratchet.pdf

35. Panjwani, S.: Tackling adaptive corruptions in multicast encryption protocols. In: Vadhan, S.P. (ed.) TCC 2007. LNCS, vol. 4392, pp. 21–40. Springer, Heidelberg (2007). https://doi.org/10.1007/978-3-540-70936-7_2

36. Pass, R., Seeman, L., shelat, a.: Analysis of the blockchain protocol in asynchronous networks. In: Coron, J.S., Nielsen, J.B. (eds.) EUROCRYPT 2017, Part II. LNCS, vol. 10211, pp. 643–673. Springer, Heidelberg (Apr / May 2017). https://doi.org/10.1007/978-3-319-56614-6_22

37. Perrig, A., Song, D., Canetti, R., Tygar, J.D., Briscoe, B.: Timed Efficient Stream Loss-Tolerant Authentication (TESLA): Multicast Source Authentication Transform Introduction. IETF RFC 4082 (Informational) (2005)

38. Pinto, A., Poettering, B., Schuldt, J.C.: Multi-recipient encryption, revisited. p. 229–238. ASIA CCS '14, Association for Computing Machinery, New York, NY, USA (2014). https://doi.org/10.1145/2590296.2590329, https://doi.org/10.1145/2590296.2590329

39. Poettering, B., Rösler, P., Schwenk, J., Stebila, D.: SoK: game-based security models for group key exchange. In: Paterson, K.G. (ed.) CT-RSA 2021. LNCS, vol. 12704, pp. 148–176. Springer, Cham (2021). https://doi.org/10.1007/978-3-030-75539-3_7

40. Rivest, R.L., Shamir, A., Wagner, D.A.: Time-lock puzzles and timed-release crypto (1996)
41. Seggelmann, R., Tuexen, M., Williams, M.: Transport layer security (tls) and datagram transport layer security (dtls) heartbeat extension. IETF RFC 6520 (Standards Track) (2012)
42. Smart, N.P.: Efficient key encapsulation to multiple parties. In: Blundo, C., Cimato, S. (eds.) SCN 2004. LNCS, vol. 3352, pp. 208–219. Springer, Heidelberg (2005). https://doi.org/10.1007/978-3-540-30598-9_15
43. WhatsApp: Whatsapp encryption overview (2017), retrieved 05/2020 from https://www.whatsapp.com/security/WhatsApp-Security-Whitepaper.pdf
44. Wire Swiss GmbH: Wire security whitepaper. https://wire-docs.wire.com/download/Wire+Security+Whitepaper.pdf (2021)
45. Yang, Z.: On constructing practical multi-recipient key-encapsulation with short ciphertext and public key. Sec. and Commun. Netw. 8(18), 4191–4202 (dec 2015). https://doi.org/10.1002/sec.1334, https://doi.org/10.1002/sec.1334
46. Yuan, E.S.: Zoom acquires keybase and announces goal of developing the most broadly used enterprise end-to-end encryption offering. Zoom Blog - May 7, 2020. https://blog.zoom.us/zoom-acquires-keybase-and-announces-goal-of-developing-the-most-broadly-used-enterprise-end-to-end-encryption-offering/ (5 2020)

Caveat Implementor! Key Recovery Attacks on MEGA

Martin R. Albrecht[1], Miro Haller[2], Lenka Mareková[3(✉)],
and Kenneth G. Paterson[2]

[1] King's College London, London, UK
martin.albrecht@kcl.ac.uk
[2] Applied Cryptography Group, ETH Zurich, Zurich, Switzerland
miro.haller@ethz.ch, kenny.paterson@inf.ethz.ch
[3] Information Security Group, Royal Holloway, University of London, London, UK
lenka.marekova.2018@rhul.ac.uk

Abstract. MEGA is a large-scale cloud storage and communication platform that aims to provide end-to-end encryption for stored data. A recent analysis by Backendal, Haller and Paterson (IEEE S&P 2023) invalidated these security claims by presenting practical attacks against MEGA that could be mounted by the MEGA service provider. In response, the MEGA developers added lightweight sanity checks on the user RSA private keys used in MEGA, sufficient to prevent the previous attacks.

We analyse these new sanity checks and show how they themselves can be exploited to mount novel attacks on MEGA that recover a target user's RSA private key with only slightly higher attack complexity than the original attacks. We identify the presence of an ECB encryption oracle under a target user's master key in the MEGA system; this oracle provides our adversary with the ability to partially overwrite a target user's RSA private key with chosen data, a powerful capability that we use in our attacks. We then present two distinct types of attack, each type exploiting different error conditions arising in the sanity checks and in subsequent cryptographic processing during MEGA's user authentication procedure. The first type appears to be novel and exploits the manner in which the MEGA code handles modular inversion when recomputing $u = q^{-1} \bmod p$. The second can be viewed as a small subgroup attack (van Oorschot and Wiener, EUROCRYPT 1996, Lim and Lee, CRYPTO 1998). We prototype the attacks and show that they work in practice.

As a side contribution, we show how to improve the RSA key recovery attack of Backendal-Haller-Paterson against the unpatched version of MEGA to require only 2 logins instead of the original 512.

We conclude by discussing wider lessons about secure implementation of cryptography that our work surfaces.

© International Association for Cryptologic Research 2023
C. Hazay and M. Stam (Eds.): EUROCRYPT 2023, LNCS 14008, pp. 190–218, 2023.
https://doi.org/10.1007/978-3-031-30589-4_7

1 Introduction

MEGA is a cloud storage and communication platform with over 265 million user accounts and more than 10 million daily users [14], advertising itself as secure and private by design. The platform distinguishes itself from other major providers by offering end-to-end encryption for stored data. On MEGA, user files should remain confidential even if the storage provider is malicious or has been compromised through a breach, implying security in a strong threat model. The security of MEGA in this setting was recently analysed in detail by [2], which describes five attacks on the cryptographic protocol used by MEGA to authenticate users and encrypt user data. The first two of these attacks completely broke the confidentiality of user files. Shortly after, [29] significantly improved the first attack in [2], reducing its requirement of 512 user logins to just 6.

At their heart, the attacks in [2] exploit the lack of both key separation and integrity protection for stored keys in the MEGA design: a single user master key is used to encrypt both the user's RSA private key (used during user authentication) and the user's file encryption keys themselves; meanwhile AES in ECB mode is used for the encryption. This allowed the authors of [2] to corrupt the RSA private key in certain ways that leaked useful information during the authentication protocol, as well as to "cut and paste" AES-ECB blocks from file encryption keys into the RSA private key.

The authors of [2] proposed an immediate and non-invasive mitigation step in the form of adding a MAC to the existing construction.[1] In response, MEGA chose to not implement this or any of the other originally suggested countermeasures. Instead, MEGA added extra sanity checks in the client software to do more validation of payloads during or after decryption [17]. These checks were sufficient to prevent the specific attacks of [2,29].

Shortly after MEGA released their patch addressing the attacks of [2], they made one other change which (as we will show below) further increased the attack surface of their code: they added detailed error reporting during the decryption and sanity checking processes done by the client as part of the authentication protocol [18]. The errors produced during these steps are mostly distinguishable from one another and the error messages are sent to the server in place of the usual authentication response. A malicious storage provider can exploit this verbose behaviour, triggering the errors by supplying specially crafted inputs in an attempt to learn something about the decrypted data.

1.1 Contributions

In the MEGA infrastructure, each user has a master key k_M that is used with AES-ECB mode to encrypt multiple items, including the user's RSA private

---

[1] This by itself does not suffice for authenticated encryption security, but presents the "immediate" level of countermeasures, i.e. the most easily achievable solution in the short term. [2] outlines further levels of countermeasures termed "minimal" and "recommended", which provide better guarantees but require more fundamental changes to the MEGA platform.

key and individual file encryption keys (in a special obfuscated format). In this work we describe two new attacks on the patched MEGA infrastructure in the malicious server setting which achieve an AES-ECB *decryption* capability under k_M. These attacks can be used to recover individual 128-bit blocks of a target user's RSA private key. Combining this with lattice techniques, we can efficiently recover the entirety of the target user's RSA private key after recovering four specific blocks. Once this private key is recovered, the adversary can trivially decrypt the RSA ciphertexts appearing in file sharing messages to recover the keys needed to decrypt any files shared with the target user. The attacks can also be used to recover individual file encryption keys directly. As with [2], these attacks exploit the lack of key separation and integrity protection in the MEGA design, showing that the patch and further changes made by MEGA in response to [2] were not only insufficient but actively harmful.

Both attacks make use of an ECB *encryption* oracle that is present in the MEGAdrop feature, a part of the MEGA system that is supposed to be independent of the authentication protocol, yet uses the same master key k_M. This feature enables the receiving of shared files from unregistered users. In short, MEGAdrop encrypts a newly shared file's encryption key to a user's public RSA key, but the user's client then silently re-encrypts that file encryption key under k_M using AES-ECB whenever the user is logged in. Since a malicious server can arbitrarily choose the file encryption key when sharing files with the user and then observe the resulting AES-ECB ciphertext, this provides the ECB encryption oracle that we need. For technical reasons explained later, we obtain two AES-ECB encrypted 128-bit blocks for each use of the oracle. Notably, the ECB encryption oracle can be realised without any user interaction. Details can be found in Sect. 2.

The attacks also exploit the distinguishable errors arising during user authentication. We describe the individual errors in detail in Sect. 2. Both attacks can be seen as *key overwriting* attacks, since they rely on manipulating the values that are interpreted as the RSA private key by the client, and on including the target AES-ECB ciphertext block in a particular position in the encoded and encrypted RSA private key. This causes the errors that are triggered during client-side cryptographic processing to depend on the target plaintext block. User interaction is formally required for these attacks, which is why we measure their cost in terms of the number of login attempts they need (they are otherwise computationally inexpensive). As a secondary measure of attack complexity, we account for the number of ECB encryption oracle calls needed.

The first attack, described in Sect. 3, exploits an implicit error in the computation of modular inverses when sanity checking the RSA private key. It is an (un)fortunate consequence of an otherwise harmless bug in the code (not checking whether an inverse exists) which is caught by the client and reported to the server. The malicious server can use this oracle repeatedly to learn the value of the target AES-ECB plaintext block modulo a number of small primes, which enables recovery of the full block using the CRT. The attack requires on average $2^{9.29}$ login attempts per recovered AES-ECB plaintext block and 66 ECB encryption oracle queries per attacked user.

The second attack, described in Sect. 4, relies on how RSA decryption is carried out by the client during user authentication. It exploits a legacy artefact in the code that changes the resulting RSA plaintext length if a certain byte condition on the plaintext does not hold, in combination with an explicit error arising from a plaintext length check that is again reported to the server. The core idea is as follows. Because the user's RSA private key is encrypted as a sequence of AES-ECB blocks, we can use the ECB encryption oracle to overwrite parts of that key – including p, q, and d – on the granularity of 128-bit blocks. The attack exploits this capability to mount a small order subgroup attack [12, 34] by overwriting the RSA primes p, q with values such that $(p-1)(q-1)$ has known small prime factors. The attack also overwrites d with a value that is completely known except in the target plaintext block. By also choosing the RSA ciphertext, the server can force the client's RSA decryption to take place in any one of the small subgroups corresponding to each of the small prime factors of $(p-1)(q-1)$. Then, the malicious server can use the length check oracle repeatedly to learn the overwritten value of d, and hence the target plaintext block, modulo each of the small primes. The final step again combines these values using the CRT to recover the target block.

We present two main versions of the second attack: one that is simpler but which requires a large amount of precomputation and one that is more complex but only requires negligible precomputation. On average, these versions require $2^{11.24}$ and $2^{11.63}$ login attempts per block, respectively. In both versions, this second attack requires a smaller number (up to 15) of ECB encryption oracle queries per attacked user than our first attack does. Further, this second attack exploits different errors from the first one and also relies on behaviours resulting from the "legacy" check on the second byte of plaintext. We include this attack to showcase that the existence of such checks and differentiated error reporting increases the attack surface.

Since the two attacks work on a per-block basis, we discuss how best to recover the entire RSA private key of the target user with the help of lattice techniques in Sect. 5. This reduces the number of blocks that need to be recovered using either of the two attacks to 4 instead of the 9 that would be required if the attacks were used directly to e.g. recover all of p. The attack complexity of recovering the full RSA private key using our first attack is then $2^{11.29}$ login attempts on average.

As a side contribution, we show in Sect. 6 how to combine the ECB encryption oracle obtained from the MEGAdrop feature with the second attack in [2] to recover a target user's RSA private key from an *unpatched* MEGA client using only 2 logins (compared to the 512 logins needed in [2] and the 6 needed in [29]). This shows that the original, unpatched MEGA system was even weaker than previously thought.

We conclude by briefly discussing attack mitigation in Sect. 7, noting the problematic nature of relying on easy-to-implement countermeasures that do not properly address the core security vulnerabilities. In that section, we also draw wider lessons from our work.

1.2 Related Work

The work of [2] provided a detailed overview of the MEGA infrastructure as well as attacks on confidentiality and integrity of user data stored on the platform. The follow-up work [29] significantly reduced the amount of user interaction required by the first attack of [2] but was already prevented by MEGA's patches. The attacks in this work draw inspiration from the small-order subgroup attacks on DH [12,34] and the key overwriting attacks on OpenPGP [5,10]. The use of a plaintext checking oracle is reminiscent of Bleichenbacher's attack on RSA with PKCS#1 v1.5 encoding [4] but we target private key recovery rather than plaintext recovery.

1.3 Validation

We have verified the presence of the ECB encryption oracle, implemented the attacks and verified them in practice on test account data, using a TLS-MitM setup with mitmproxy [33] to minimise interaction with the real MEGA servers and a locally-run MEGA web client (version 4.21.4) [15]. We made a single modification to the web client to automatically simulate repeated client login attempts after one initial manual login. The attacks were able to recover arbitrary AES-ECB-encrypted blocks of the test user's RSA private key with query costs consistent with our analysis (averaging $2^{9.30}$ login attempts for the first attack). We also implemented a proof of concept for recovering the entire RSA private key given four known blocks using lattice techniques. The code is available as supplementary material.

1.4 Disclosure

We contacted MEGA to inform them of the vulnerabilities in their system on 29.09.2022. We suggested a 90-day disclosure period. We also suggested mitigations, stressing the importance of providing proper cryptographic integrity for data stored under users' master keys. MEGA acknowledged receipt of our disclosure on 30.09.2022. They said they would begin working on fixes and liaise with us before deploying them. On 28.11.2022, MEGA informed us that they were working on hardening their client software, which would include changing how private keys are stored, removing the ECB encryption oracle as well as replacing the asmcrypto.js library. We provided high-level feedback on the proposed changes. The upgrade should mitigate against our specific attacks as well as potential future attacks, though we have not reviewed the changes in detail. Given the scale of the changes, we agreed to move the disclosure to 06.03.2023 to coincide with the rolling-out of the upgraded client software and the publication of this paper. MEGA awarded a bug bounty.

2   Oracles

2.1   Notation

We begin by establishing some notation that we use throughout. Concatenation is denoted by $\parallel$. $[m]_k$ denotes an encryption of m under the key k, where the algorithm is determined by the context. B denotes bytes, and for x, $|x|_B$ denotes the length of x in bytes and $|x|_b$ denotes the length of x in bits.[2] For a tuple $X = (x_0, \ldots, x_{n-1})$, $|X| = n$ denotes its size. For a byte string $m = b_0 \parallel b_1 \parallel \ldots \parallel b_{n-1}$ of length n and $s, t \in \mathbb{N}$, we define $m[s] := b_s$, and $m[s : t] := b_s \parallel \ldots \parallel b_{t-1}$ for $s < t$. An empty object is denoted by null, and a zero byte by 00. $\mathsf{ZeroPad}(m, n) := 00 \parallel 00 \parallel \ldots \parallel m$ such that $|m|_B = n$, i.e. left-pad m with zero bytes. If it is necessary to distinguish between a byte representation and other types, m (as opposed to m) denotes a byte string. Conversion between byte strings and integers remains implicit, so we may write $m \leftarrow m$ and vice-versa. $(\mathbb{Z}/n\mathbb{Z})^\times$ denotes the multiplicative group of integers modulo n. By $x \leftarrow_\$ S$ we denote x sampled uniformly at random from S. In our attacks, B denotes a target plaintext block, which is a byte string with $|B|_b = 128$. To differentiate it from a value computed while attempting to recover this block (which could be different if the attack is not correct), we denote the computed value by B^*.

2.2   ECB Encryption Oracle

MEGA's webclient exposes an ECB encryption oracle under a user's master key k_M. This oracle allows MEGA, or anyone controlling their infrastructure, to encrypt 32 bytes of chosen plaintext in AES-ECB mode under the target user's master key k_M in a single query. Since AES-ECB without any additional measures does not provide any integrity protection, ciphertexts containing blocks that the adversary queried to the oracle cannot be distinguished without additional tests on the expected structure of the plaintext.

The oracle stems from code related to the MEGAdrop feature as shown in Fig. 1. MEGAdrop enables anyone to upload files to a folder in the cloud storage of the recipient without needing an account on MEGA. The recipient activates MEGAdrop for one of their folders and obtains a link that they can share with others. Unlike shared folders, senders do not see any file stored in the MEGAdrop upload folder.

---

[2] For $x \in \mathbb{Z}$, the value of $|x|_b$ as understood by the MEGA client implementations is not always exact. In the big integer representation used by the web client, $|x|_b$ is normally rounded up to the closest multiple of 8 or 32.

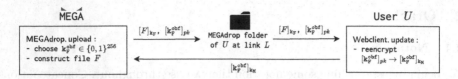

Fig. 1. Overview of the ECB encryption oracle under a user's master key k_M.

The left algorithm of Fig. 2 describes the upload feature of MEGAdrop. The adversary can pick some file key k_F, nonce N_F, and file F during the upload process for the MEGAdrop folder at the link L. The upload feature locally encrypts the file with AES-CCM using k_F and some nonce N_F picked by the client. Backendal et al. describe MEGA's encryption in more detail[3] on lines 2–11 of Fig. 2 in [2].

MEGAdrop.upload(k_F, N_F, F, L)	Webclient.update()
1 : $[F]_{k_F}, T_{cond} \leftarrow$ File.enc(k_F, N_F, F)	1 : **while true do**
2 : $k_F^{obf} \leftarrow$ ObfKey(k_F, N_F, T_{cond})	2 : $\tau \leftarrow$ Server.fetch_update(k_M, sk)
3 : $pk \leftarrow$ Server.lookup(L)	3 : **if** $\tau \neq \perp$ **then**
4 : $\left[k_F^{obf}\right]_{pk} \leftarrow$ RSA.Enc(pk, k_F^{obf})	4 : $[F]_{k_F}, \left[k_F^{obf}\right]_{pk} \leftarrow \tau$
5 : Server.upload($[F]_{k_F}, \left[k_F^{obf}\right]_{pk}$)	5 : $k_F^{obf} \leftarrow$ RSA.Dec($sk, \left[k_F^{obf}\right]_{pk}$)
	6 : $\left[k_F^{obf}\right]_{k_M} \leftarrow$ AES-ECB.Enc(k_M, k_F^{obf})
	7 : Server.upload($\left[k_F^{obf}\right]_{k_M}$)
	8 : **endif**
	9 : **endwhile**

Fig. 2. MEGAdrop pseudocode. MEGAdrop.upload encrypts a file F with key k_F and nonce N_F, uploaded to the MEGAdrop folder with link L. Webclient.update shows how active clients regularly poll for updates and re-encrypt node keys immediately.

To instantiate an ECB encryption oracle, the adversary sets k_F^{obf} to 32 bytes of its choosing. Since $k_F^{obf} = (k_F \oplus x) \parallel x$ for $x = N_F \parallel T_{cond}$, the obfuscated key defines the values for k_F, N_F, and T_{cond} used in the file encryption (cf. Fig. 4 in [2]). The adversary can use the file reconstruction part of the framing attack described in [2] to obtain a file F that, when encrypted with k_F and N_F, produces the MAC tag value T_{cond}. Consequently, the adversary can run MEGAdrop.upload(k_F, N_F, F, L) to upload k_F^{obf}, encrypted under the receiver's public RSA key, to the server.

Section 9.12 of MEGA's security white paper [16] states that to "conserve CPU cycles, RSA-encrypted keys are transformed into AES-encrypted keys when

---

[3] For instance, we omit the file attributes in our description for simplicity.

encountered". Indeed, the webclient regularly polls for new files in the background and, when encountering an RSA-encrypted key $[k_F^{obf}]_{pk}$, re-encrypts k_F^{obf} with k_M and AES-ECB to produce an AES-ECB ciphertext that we denote by $[k_F^{obf}]_{k_M}$. It then uploads this updated key to the server (cf. [24]) as shown in the right half of Fig. 2. Therefore, the malicious server can learn the AES-ECB plaintext-ciphertext pair $(k_F^{obf}, [k_F^{obf}]_{k_M})$.

While testing this oracle in mitmproxy [33], we noticed that the server can pretend that a new file was uploaded to a MEGAdrop folder. The webclient re-encrypts the key as described in Fig. 2 even if the recipient does not use MEGAdrop and the file has an invalid path. Thus, we have an efficient ECB encryption oracle that does not require any user interaction and leaves no persistent traces in the user's cloud storage. It encrypts 32 B per query and can be accessed repeatedly.

2.3   Oracles from Decoding and Decryption Error Reports

Consider the authentication and session ID exchange that takes place every time a user logs into their account, summarized in Fig. 3 and described in more detail in [2]. Let k_e be the user's 128-bit symmetric encryption key derived from their password, k_M the user's 128-bit symmetric master key and (pk, sk) the user's 2048-bit RSA keypair.

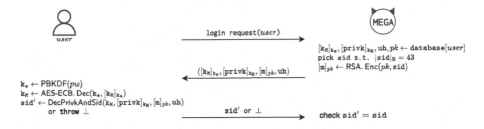

Fig. 3. Simplified overview of the MEGA login procedure.

Here, we focus on one part of this exchange, namely when the server responds to the user's request with the tuple $([k_M]_{k_e}, [privk]_{k_M}, [m]_{pk}, uh)$, where $[k_M]_{k_e}$ and $[privk]_{k_M}$ are AES-ECB-encrypted, $[m]_{pk}$ is RSA-encrypted and uh is in plaintext. Then, privk encodes the secret key sk for RSA-CRT as shown in Fig. 4, m encodes the session ID sid and uh is an 11-byte user handle string. The exact alignments of the fields in privk with respect to the AES-ECB block boundaries will be important in our attacks. The processing done by the client after it decrypts $[k_M]_{k_e}$ is shown in Fig. 5. This is the updated behaviour resulting from the patches described in Sect. 1 and converted into pseudocode as faithfully as possible, i.e. in some cases surfacing lower-level processing if it is relevant.

In Fig. 5, we adopt the notation "**require** *condition* **else** *error*" to mean that the client checks the *condition* and if it is not satisfied, it aborts and outputs

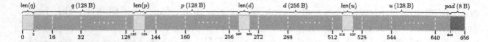

Fig. 4. Encoding of the RSA secret key together with the block boundaries marking the start of different 16-byte AES-ECB blocks. Each length encoding field consists of 2 bytes, meaning that data fields start progressively further into AES-ECB blocks.

the *error* to the server. Decoding between base64-strings, bytes and integers is left implicit unless relevant to some error. Computation of a^{-1} mod b should be understood to return `null` if $\gcd(a, b) \neq 1$.

In DecodePrivk(privk), the function Parse(privk) sequentially reads through the bytes of privk whose expected form, shown in Fig. 4, is len(q) ∥ q ∥ len(p) ∥ p ∥ len(d) ∥ d ∥ len(u) ∥ u ∥ pad where len(x) denotes the two-byte big-endian length encoding of the byte-length of x and pad is padding, and returns the tuple of integers $P = (q, p, d, u)$. If DecPrivkAndSid(·) returns successfully, then sid is sent to the server in the requests that follow. Notice that in addition to DecPrivkAndSid(·) returning a range of different error messages depending on the processing of secret values, it also modifies the resulting plaintext depending on whether the second byte of the RSA-decrypted value is 00 or not (line 9 of DecryptSid(·, ·)), a quirk that is explained in the original code only with the comment "Old bogus padding workaround" [23].

DecPrivkAndSid(k_M, $[\texttt{privk}]_{k_M}$, $[\texttt{m}]_{pk}$, uh):	DecryptSid(sk, $[\texttt{m}]_{pk}$):
1 : **require** $|\texttt{uh}|_B = 11$ **else** $\perp_1$	1 : $N, e, d, p, q, d_p, d_q, u \leftarrow sk$
2 : $\texttt{privk} \leftarrow$ AES-ECB.Dec(k_M, $[\texttt{privk}]_{k_M}$)	2 : $c \leftarrow [\texttt{m}]_{pk}$
3 : $sk \leftarrow$ DecodePrivk($\texttt{privk}$)	3 : **require** $c < N$ **else** $\perp_7$
4 : $\texttt{m} \leftarrow$ DecryptSid(sk, $[\texttt{m}]_{pk}$)	4 : $x \leftarrow c^{d_p} \bmod p$; $y \leftarrow c^{d_q} \bmod q$
5 : **require** $|\texttt{m}|_B = 255$ **else** $(\perp_2, |\texttt{m}|_B)$	5 : $t \leftarrow x - y \bmod p$
6 : **require** $\texttt{m}[16:27] = \texttt{uh}$ **else** $\perp_3$	6 : $h \leftarrow u \cdot t \bmod p$
7 : $\texttt{sid} \leftarrow \texttt{m}[0:43]$	7 : $m \leftarrow h \cdot q + y \bmod 2^{|N|_b}$
8 : **return sid**	8 : $\texttt{m} \leftarrow$ ZeroPad($\texttt{m}, |N|_B$)
	9 : **if** $\texttt{m}[1] \neq 00$ **then**
	10 : $\texttt{m}' \leftarrow 00 \parallel \texttt{m}$
	11 : **else**
	12 : $\texttt{m}' \leftarrow \texttt{m}$
	13 : **return** $\texttt{m}'[2 : |\texttt{m}'|_B]$

DecodePrivk($\texttt{privk}$):

1 : $P, \mathsf{pad} \leftarrow$ Parse($\texttt{privk}$)

2 : **require** $|P| = 4 \wedge |\mathsf{pad}|_B < 16$ **else** $\perp_4$

3 : $q, p, d, u \leftarrow P$

4 : $N \leftarrow p \cdot q$

5 : $e \leftarrow d^{-1} \bmod (p-1)(q-1)$

6 : $d_p \leftarrow d \bmod p$; $d_q \leftarrow d \bmod q$

7 : $u' \leftarrow q^{-1} \bmod p$

8 : **require** $u' \neq \texttt{null}$ **else** $\perp_5$

9 : $cond \leftarrow |p|_b, |q|_b, |u|_b > 1000 \wedge |d|_b > 2000$

10 : **require** $cond \wedge (u' = u)$ **else** $\perp_4$

11 : $sk \leftarrow N, e, d, p, q, d_p, d_q, u$

12 : **require** $e \neq \texttt{null}$ **else** $\perp_6$

13 : **return** sk

Fig. 5. Client decoding and decryption to process the session ID, derived from [23, 25–27].

Caught and Uncaught Exceptions. Some of the errors shown in Fig. 5 are implicit, i.e. they are a result of lower-level exceptions caught at a higher level (the ones corresponding to $\perp_5$ and $\perp_6$). In all cases, they are shown at the exact place where the code aborts.

Further, due to some lower-level bugs in asmcrypto.js [19], the bigint and crypto library used by the web client, there are cases where the implementation never terminates:

- In DecodePrivk(privk) during Parse(privk), if one of q, p, d, u is 0.
- In DecodePrivk(privk) during the computation of $q^{-1} \bmod p$ [21], if $q \bmod p = 0$. We observed that this is because the implementation of $gcd(0, p)$ never terminates. The same issue arises during the computation of $d^{-1} \bmod (p - 1)(q - 1)$ if $d \bmod (p - 1)(q - 1) = 0$.

Similarly, there are cases when the implementation returns incorrect output:

- In DecryptSid(sk, c) during the computation of $x \leftarrow c^{d_p} \bmod p$ (and likewise $y \leftarrow c^{d_q} \bmod q$), there are several issues.
  - If p is even, the code computes $x = 0$ regardless of the other input values, because modular power computations were not implemented for even moduli [20].
  - If $|p|_{\mathsf{b}} > 1024$, the implementation of Montgomery reduction [22] does not return correct values, and so the output x is also incorrect.

We were forced to work around some of these implementation errors in our attacks.

3   Attack Based on Modular Inverse Computation

Our first attack enables block-by-block plaintext recovery of AES-ECB blocks encrypted under k_M. In particular, this enables RSA private key recovery, i.e. the recovery of privk. Let $[B]_{k_M}$ be such a target ciphertext block with unknown target plaintext block B, for example corresponding to an unknown block of q from privk.

This attack is in the malicious server setting, or equivalently the TLS-MitM setting, and makes use of the ECB encryption oracle described in Sect. 2.2. It exploits the error type $\perp_5$, which arises on line 7 and line 8 of DecodePrivk(privk) in Fig. 5 when $gcd(p, q) \neq 1$. To get to this point, the server must submit inputs such that none of the previous error types are triggered. The server will only replace the $[privk]_{k_M}$ value and expect to abort before executing DecryptSid$(\cdot, \cdot)$, so the only condition that must be satisfied is the one on line 2, which requires that the decrypted privk parses into 4 values without too much extra padding. Then, error $\perp_5$ can be distinguished from any of the errors that could follow, though with overwhelming probability this will be error $\perp_4$ from line 10 due to the server overwriting parts of privk.

The main idea behind this attack rests in the observation that if the server can construct $[privk^*]_{k_M}$ such that the decrypted and decoded p is divisible by a small prime r, and the decrypted and decoded q contains the target block B in its least-significant position, then the outputting of error $\perp_5$ leaks that $gcd(p, q) \neq 1$ and thus (if some further conditions are satisfied), that $q \bmod r = 0$. From this, the server can learn the value of $B \bmod r$. Repeating this for a sufficient number of different primes r_i and combining the values using the Chinese Remainder Theorem (CRT), the server can learn the value of $B \bmod r_0 \cdot \ldots \cdot r_{n-1}$. If $|r_0 \cdot \ldots \cdot r_{n-1}|_{\mathsf{b}} \geq 128$, the server recovers B.

In the following subsections, we describe two versions of the attack in more detail, starting with the simple, block-aligned version and then describing an attack that is more general and resistant to simple fixes. Both versions have been implemented and verified using our TLS-MitM setup described in Sect. 1.3.

3.1 Block-Aligned, Small-Length Version

The attack proceeds in two distinct phases. The first phase calls the ECB encryption oracle to obtain a set of chosen-plaintext blocks, which are then combined with a target block to form the ciphertexts submitted to the client as part of the second phase. The second phase relies on the client making a number of online login attempts. The ECB encryption oracle calls are shown as $[\mathbf{x}]_{k_M} \leftarrow \mathsf{OECB}_{k_M}(\mathbf{x})$ (if $\mathbf{x}$ consists of 2ℓ blocks, this call will involve ℓ uses of the actual oracle described in Sect. 2.2). The content of the modified ciphertexts that will be submitted to the client is shown in Fig. 6. Note that we aim to reduce the number of $\mathsf{OECB}_{k_M}()$ calls by ensuring most of the content consists of all-zero blocks (or blocks containing the value 1), which only need to be queried once.

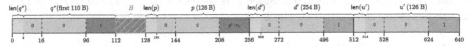

Fig. 6. The plaintext content of $\mathsf{ct}_{i,t}$, where the all-zero blocks are light green, the blocks containing 1 are dark green and the placement of the target block B is in red. (Color figure online)

Precomputation Using the ECB Encryption Oracle. Take $\{r_0, \ldots, r_{n-1}\} = \{7, 11, \ldots, 103\}$, $n = 24$ small odd primes such that their product $R = \prod_{i=0}^{n-1} r_i$ has $|R|_b \geq 128$. Let $[B]_{k_M}$ be the target ciphertext block and denote by B^* the plaintext block computed as part of this attack.

1. Generate a random prime p' such that $|p'|_b = 256$.
2. Let $d' \leftarrow 1$, $u' \leftarrow 1$ and encode them as byte strings $\mathbf{d}', \mathbf{u}'$ such that $|\mathbf{d}'|_B = 254$, $|\mathbf{u}'|_B = 126$.
3. Let $\mathtt{rest} \leftarrow \mathsf{len}(\mathbf{d}') \parallel \mathbf{d}' \parallel \mathsf{len}(\mathbf{u}') \parallel \mathbf{u}'$ and obtain $[\mathtt{rest}]_{k_M} \leftarrow \mathsf{OECB}_{k_M}(\mathtt{rest})$.
4. For $i \in \{0, \ldots, n-1\}$, do the following:
   (a) Compute $p \leftarrow p' \cdot r_i$ and encode it as a byte string $\mathbf{p}$ such that $|\mathbf{p}|_B = 126$.[4]
   (b) Let $\mathtt{ptp}_i \leftarrow \mathsf{len}(\mathbf{p}) \parallel \mathbf{p}$ and obtain $[\mathtt{ptp}_i]_{k_M} \leftarrow \mathsf{OECB}_{k_M}(\mathtt{ptp}_i)$.
5. For $t \in \{0, \ldots, r_{n-1} - 1\}$, do the following:
   (a) Compute $q^* \leftarrow 2^{128} \cdot t$ and encode it as a byte string q^* such that $|q^*|_B = 126$.
   (b) Let $\mathtt{ptq}_t \leftarrow \mathsf{len}(q^*) \parallel q^*[0:110]$, which skips the last block of q^* to make space for the target. Obtain $[\mathtt{ptq}_t]_{k_M} \leftarrow \mathsf{OECB}_{k_M}(\mathtt{ptq}_t)$.
6. For $i \in \{0, \ldots, n-1\}$, do the following:
   (a) For $t \in \{0, \ldots, r_i - 1\}$, do the following:
       Store $\mathtt{ct}_{i,t} \leftarrow [\mathtt{ptq}_t]_{k_M} \parallel [B]_{k_M} \parallel [\mathtt{ptp}_i]_{k_M} \parallel [\mathtt{rest}]_{k_M}$.

---

[4] We include the prime p' for several reasons. First, because of one of the uncaught errors, we must make sure that $q \bmod p \neq 0$. Further, to avoid false positives from error $\perp_5$, we need the $\gcd(p, q) \neq 1$ signal to be equivalent to $\gcd(p, q) = r_i$.

Online Attack. Suppose we have a set of $\mathsf{ct}_{i,t}$ as described above.

1. For $i \in \{0, \ldots, n-1\}$, do the following:
   (a) For $t \in \{0, \ldots, r_i - 1\}$, do the following:
      i. When the client initiates a login, respond to the client's request with
         $([\mathsf{k_M}]_{\mathsf{k_e}}, \mathsf{ct}_{i,t}, [\mathsf{m}]_{pk}, \mathsf{uh})$, where everything but $\mathsf{ct}_{i,t}$ is as it would be
         in an honest response.
      ii. If the client returns $\bot_5$, save the value of t and break out of this loop.
   (b) Save $B_i^* \leftarrow -2^{128} \cdot t \bmod r_i$.
2. Then, compute $B^* \bmod R$ by solving the system $B^* \equiv B_i^* \pmod{r_i}$ for $i \in \{0, \ldots, n-1\}$ using CRT.

Correctness. Notice that for each decrypted $\mathsf{ct}_{i,t}$, $\mathsf{DecodePrivk}(\cdot)$ results in $p \leftarrow p' \cdot r_i$ and $q \leftarrow 2^{128} \cdot t + B$. The error $\bot_5$ will be triggered if and only if $\gcd(p, q) \neq 1$, which is equivalent to $\gcd(p, q) = r_i$, since p' is a prime larger than q. Hence $\bot_5$ is triggered if and only if $q \bmod r_i = 0$, and so if and only if $B \equiv -2^{128} \cdot t \pmod{r_i}$. This means that for the computed value B_i^* we have $B_i^* \equiv B \pmod{r_i}$. It follows that $B^* \equiv B \pmod{R}$. Since R is such that $|R|_{\mathsf{b}} \geq 128$ and $|B|_{\mathsf{b}} = 128$, we deduce that $B^* = B$ (over the integers).

Cost. First, we count the cost of recovering the target in terms of ECB encryption oracle calls, assuming that each repeated value (such as an all-zero block) is only queried once. As can be seen in Fig. 6, the encoding of q^*, p, d' and u' is block-aligned. The value rest consists of four non-zero blocks: two blocks that include a length encoding, and two identical blocks containing the value 1. Next, ptp_i also has four non-zero blocks: one length-encoding block and three blocks for $p' \cdot r_i$ since $|p' \cdot r_i|_{\mathsf{b}} < 263 < 3 \cdot 128$; similarly, ptq_t has two non-zero blocks: one length-encoding block and one block for t since $|t|_{\mathsf{b}} \leq |r_{n-1}|_{\mathsf{b}} < 128$. Finally, notice that $\mathsf{ptp}_i[0:16]$ is the same for all i, and similarly $\mathsf{ptq}_t[0:16]$ is the same for all t, so the length-encoding blocks can be reused. Recalling that each use of the oracle returns two blocks of ciphertext, together the attack requires $\lceil \frac{1}{2} \cdot (1 + 3 + 2 + n \cdot 3 + r_{n-1}) \rceil = 91 \approx 2^{6.5}$ queries. Further, the result of these queries can be reused when recovering multiple blocks for a given target user.

   Second, we count the number of online login attempts. On average, the attack requires $\frac{1}{2} \cdot \sum_{i=0}^{n-1} r_i = 627 \approx 2^{9.29}$ logins ($2^{10.29}$ in the worst case).[5]

3.2   Full-Length Version

The attack in Sect. 3.1 could technically be prevented by a number of simple checks, e.g. by moving the check on bit lengths before the client computes $q^{-1} \bmod p$ (and so possibly triggers $\bot_5$), by ensuring that $|p|_{\mathsf{b}}, |q|_{\mathsf{b}} = 1024$ or that $d, u \neq 1$. However, none of these changes would prevent this type of attack:

---

[5] Note that the attack can be easily modified to use one less login for each r_i. This is because, in the online phase, if the server does not get a positive answer from the oracle for any of the values $t \in \{0, \ldots, r_i - 2\}$, it means that the value $r_i - 1$ is the correct one and so does not need to be submitted explicitly.

here we provide a more general version that would still work if these changes were made. The content of the modified ciphertexts that will be submitted to the client is shown in Fig. 7.

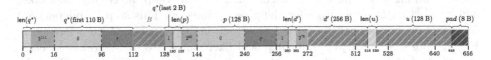

Fig. 7. The plaintext content of $ct_{i,t}$, where the all-zero blocks are light green, the parts containing fixed values are dark green, the placement of the target block B is in red and the placement of the unmodified values from ct is in yellow. (Color figure online)

Precomputation Using the ECB Encryption Oracle. As before, take $\{r_0, \ldots, r_{n-1}\} = \{7, 11, \ldots, 103\}$, $n = 24$ small odd primes such that their product $R = \prod_{i=0}^{n-1} r_i$ has $|R|_b \geq 128$. Let $[B]_{k_M}$ be the target ciphertext block and denote by B^* the plaintext block computed as part of this attack. Let $ct \leftarrow [privk]_{k_M}$ be the original ciphertext encrypting the user's private RSA key.

1. Let $d' \leftarrow 2^{2047}$ and encode it as a byte string d' such that $|d'|_B = 256$.
2. Let $ptd \leftarrow$ 00 00 00 01 $\|$ len(d') $\|$ $d'[0:10]$ and get $[ptd]_{k_M} \leftarrow OECB_{k_M}(ptd)$.
3. Let $[rest]_{k_M} \leftarrow ct[272 : |ct|_B]$. The slice begins with the ciphertext block that encrypts the most-significant full block of the original d.
4. For $i \in \{0, \ldots, n-1\}$, do the following:
   (a) Compute $p \leftarrow 2^{1023} + 2^{32} \cdot \varrho + 1$ for ϱ such that $p \equiv 0 \pmod{r_i}$ and p/r_i is prime. Encode it as a byte string p such that $|p|_B = 128$.
   (b) Let $ptp_i \leftarrow$ 00 01 $\|$ len(p) $\|$ $p[0:124]$ and get $[ptp_i]_{k_M} \leftarrow OECB_{k_M}(ptp_i)$.
5. For $t \in \{0, \ldots, r_{n-1} - 1\}$, do the following:
   (a) Compute $q^* \leftarrow 2^{1023} + 2^{128+16} \cdot t + 1$ and encode it as a byte string q^* such that $|q^*|_B = 128$.
   (b) Let $ptq_t \leftarrow$ len(q^*) $\|$ $q^*[0:110]$ and obtain $[ptq_t]_{k_M} \leftarrow OECB_{k_M}(ptq_t)$.
6. For $i \in \{0, \ldots, n-1\}$, do the following:
   (a) For $t \in \{0, \ldots, r_i - 1\}$, do the following:
       Store $ct_{i,t} \leftarrow [ptq_t]_{k_M} \| [B]_{k_M} \| [ptp_i]_{k_M} \| [ptd]_{k_M} \| [rest]_{k_M}$.

Correctness. In this version, the precomputation must construct a modified ciphertext such that all values q, p, d, u are of the expected bit length. Recall that the plaintext encoding has the form: len(q) $\|$ q $\|$ len(p) $\|$ p $\|$ len(d) $\|$ d $\|$ len(u) $\|$ u $\|$ pad. Since each value is encoded by prefixing a two-byte length field and the original lengths are either 1024 bits or 2048, the values in the resulting plaintext are not block-aligned. This is why we construct the "partial" block ptd in Step 2. separately: it is composed of the final 4 bytes of p, len(d') and the first 10 bytes of d'. Similarly, the block-aligned plaintext ptp in Step 4b begins with another partial block which consists of the final 2 bytes of q^*, len(p) and the first 12 bytes of p.[6] Finally, the modified blocks are "stitched" together in Step 6a as in the simple version of the attack, ensuring that the target B is interpreted as the last "full" block of q.

Cost. Finding p of the correct form for each i in Step 4a is easy and takes $326 \approx 2^{8.35}$ trials on average for the given primes r_i. This step is independent of user data and so can be reused to attack multiple users. With reference to Fig. 7, note that both $\mathtt{ptp}_i$ and $\mathtt{ptq}_t$ will likely have two non-zero blocks each. We assume the reuse of the length-encoding blocks as in Sect. 3.1. Thus the attack requires $\lceil \frac{1}{2} \cdot (1 + 1 + 2 + n + r_{n-1}) \rceil = 66 \approx 2^{6.04}$ queries.

Online Attack. Suppose we have a set of $\mathtt{ct}_{i,t}$ as described above.

1. For $i \in \{0, \dots, n-1\}$, do the following:
   (a) For $t \in \{0, \dots, r_i - 1\}$, do the following:
       i. When the client initiates a login, respond to the client's request with $([\mathtt{k_M}]_{\mathtt{k_e}}, \mathtt{ct}_{i,t}, [\mathtt{m}]_{pk}, \mathtt{uh})$, where everything but $\mathtt{ct}_{i,t}$ is as it would be in an honest response.
       ii. If the client returns $\perp_5$, save the value of t and break out of this loop.
   (b) Save $B_i^* \leftarrow (2^{16})^{-1} \cdot (-2^{1023} - 2^{128+16} \cdot t - 1) \bmod r_i$.
2. Then, compute $B^* \bmod R$ by solving the system $B^* \equiv B_i^* \pmod{r_i}$ for $i \in \{0, \dots, n-1\}$ using CRT.

Correctness. Recall that for each decrypted $\mathtt{ct}_{i,t}$, $\mathsf{DecodePrivk}(\cdot)$ gets $p \leftarrow 2^{1023} + 2^{32} \cdot \varrho + 1$ and $q \leftarrow 2^{1023} + 2^{128+16} \cdot t + 2^{16} \cdot B + 1$. The overwritten values are encoded so that the parsing succeeds, and there are no other explicit errors that could be triggered before the error we are using for the attack.[7] The error $\perp_5$ will be triggered if and only if $\gcd(p, q) \neq 1$, which is equivalent to $\gcd(p, q) = r_i$ with high probability, since p/r_i is a large prime and the probability that $q \equiv 0 \pmod{(p/r_i)}$ is $\approx 1/(p/r_i) \leq 2^{-1016}$. Hence $\perp_5$ is triggered if and only if $q \bmod r_i = 0$, and hence if and only if $B = (2^{16})^{-1} \cdot (-2^{1023} - 2^{128+16} \cdot t - 1) \bmod r_i$. Thus we have $B_i^* \equiv B \pmod{r_i}$. The rest of the analysis follows as for the simpler version of the attack.

Cost. The attack requires the same number of online login attempts as the simpler version in Sect. 3.1. We confirmed this in our implementation: in 500 runs of the attack recovering random ECB-encrypted blocks, the average number of login attempts required by the full version of the attack was $632 \approx 2^{9.30}$. The histogram is shown in Fig. 8.

---

[6] That is, $\mathtt{ptd}[0:4] = \mathtt{p}[124:128]$ for all $\mathtt{p}$, and $\mathtt{ptp}_i[0:2] = \mathtt{q}^*[126:128]$ for all $\mathtt{q}^*$.
[7] There is a possibility that $d^* \bmod (p-1)(q-1) = 0$ where $d^* \leftarrow d' + (d \bmod 2^{1968})$ and d is the original value encrypted in $\mathtt{ct}$. Because of the uncaught non-termination bug arising during the computation of $(d^*)^{-1} \bmod (p-1)(q-1)$, in this case the attack would fail, but this is highly unlikely to happen in practice.

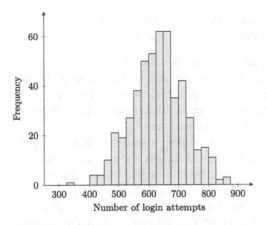

Fig. 8. Number of login attempts used by the attack over 500 runs.

4   Attack Based on Small Subgroups

Here, we present our second AES-ECB decryption attack. In terms of login attempts it is less efficient than the attack in Sect. 3. However it requires fewer uses of the ECB encryption oracle. Further, it exploits a number of additional errors and also behaviours resulting from the "legacy" check on the second byte of the RSA plaintext.

The attack is also in the malicious server/TLS-MitM setting and uses the ECB encryption oracle from Sect. 2.2 with the aim of recovering blocks of d from the original privk (or any other AES-ECB-encrypted blocks that can be placed in their position). It exploits the errors $\perp_2$ and $\perp_3$ arising on line 5 and line 6 of DecPrivkAndSid(k_M, [privk*]$_{k_M}$, c*, uh*) in Fig. 5 for an adversarially supplied privk* (created with the help of the ECB encryption oracle), c* and uh*. It also requires working around some of the uncaught exceptions described in Sect. 2.3. To reach the needed error, the checks that trigger the earlier errors $\perp_1, \perp_4, \perp_5, \perp_6$ and $\perp_7$ must all be satisfied: uh* must be a UTF-8 string of size 11, privk* must encode q^*, p^*, d^*, u^* of sufficient length such that $\gcd(q^*, p^*) = 1$ and $\gcd(d^*, (p^* - 1)(q^* - 1)) = 1$ so that the corresponding inverses exist, $u^* = (q^*)^{-1} \bmod p^*$ and $c^* < N^*$ where $N^* = p^* \cdot q^*$.

Under these constraints, observe that DecryptSid(sk, c*) behaves differently depending on whether the second byte of the decrypted value $m^* \leftarrow (c^*)^{d^*} \bmod N^*$ is 00, where m^* is first zero-padded to the length of N^* to form m*. Suppose the server supplied p^*, q^* such that $|N^*|_B = 256$. Let m $\leftarrow$ DecryptSid(sk, c*) and m′ be the intermediate value such that m $=$ m′$[2 : |m′|_B]$. Then, based on the error returned by the client, the server can distinguish the following two cases:

- Case ($\perp_2$, 254): This means that $|m|_B = 254$, so $|m′|_B = 256 = |N^*|_B = |m^*|_B$, so the condition on line 9 was not satisfied, i.e. m*$[1] = $ 00.[8]

---

[8] Note that the server does not know whether this is because prior to zero-padding, we have $|m^*|_B \leq |N^*|_B - 2$ and therefore trivially m*$[1] = $ 00 or because $|m^*|_B = |N^*|_B$ and m*$[1] = $ 00. However, the root cause is immaterial to our attack.

– Case $\perp_3$: This means that $|\mathtt{m}|_B = 255$, so $|\mathtt{m}'|_B = 257 = |N^*|_B + 1 = |\mathtt{m}^*|_B + 1$, which can only arise if $\mathtt{m}' = \mathtt{00} \parallel \mathtt{m}^*$ and so $\mathtt{m}^*[1] \neq \mathtt{00}$.

A similar case analysis can be done for arbitrary values of $|N^*|_B$; then the errors may be swapped. However due to the bugs in the modular power implementation in MEGA code, the attack actually only works for $|N^*|_B \leq 256$.

We explain next how to exploit this behavioural difference to leak information about a target user's RSA private key.

The server constructs $[\mathtt{privk}^*]_{k_M}$ using the ECB encryption oracle such that in the "d" field it knows the plaintext for all blocks except the least-significant full block. That block will be the target of the attack; it can be an arbitrary AES-ECB-encrypted block $[B]_{k_M}$. Let d^* denote the "d" component constructed in this way. The server must also precompute p^*, q^* of a special form and a number of values $\mathtt{m}^*$ with $\mathtt{m}^*[1] = \mathtt{00}$ such that it can interpret one of the errors arising on decryption of a corresponding ciphertext as confirmation of a correct "guess".

At a high level, the primes p^* and q^* are constructed so that $(p^* - 1)(q^* - 1)$ contains small prime factors r_i of a given bit length such that their product is at least 128 bits.[9] Let $\mathbb{G} = (\mathbb{Z}/N^*\mathbb{Z})^\times$ so that $|\mathbb{G}| = (p^* - 1)(q^* - 1)$. For each factor r_i, the server computes $g_i \in \mathbb{G}$ such that g_i has order r_i and such that a value $t_i \in \{1, \ldots, r_i - 1\}$ (or a set of such values $\mathcal{T}_i$) exists with the property that $g_i{}^{t_i} \bmod N^*$ has second byte $\mathtt{00}$ after zero-padding to the length of N^*. The value of u^* is then set to $(q^*)^{-1} \bmod p^*$.

Then, in the online phase of the attack, the server submits $\mathtt{privk}^*$ constructed using the ECB encryption oracle to contain q^*, p^*, d^*, u^*. For each r_i, it sets $x_i = 1, 2, \ldots, r_i - 1$ and submits $c_{i,t}^* \leftarrow g_i{}^{x_i} \bmod N^*$ until the client returns the error that confirms the second byte of the decrypted value was $\mathtt{00}$ (which is $(\perp_2, 254)$ in the case that $|N^*|_B = 256$ which we will use in the attack). Then, based on the precomputed values it learns that, for the specific value x_i triggering the error, $x_i \cdot d^* \equiv t_i \pmod{r_i}$. Here d^* is a value that is known except for its least significant full block, where it contains B. From this equation, the value of $B \pmod{r_i}$ can be recovered. Finally, using CRT and taking some care with non-block-aligned inputs, allows recovery of the block B.

The attack is described in more detail in the following subsections, first a simpler but less-efficient version and then the full version. The ECB encryption oracle calls are shown as $[\mathtt{x}]_{k_M} \leftarrow \mathrm{OECB}_{k_M}(\mathtt{x})$ as before. Since both versions of the attack must "stitch" AES-ECB blocks together to create the final ciphertext, we provide the algorithm in Fig. 9 to avoid repetition. This algorithm combines the chosen values $\mathtt{q}^*, \mathtt{p}^*, \mathtt{d}', \mathtt{u}^*$ so that they parse as expected, with the target block B being placed in the position of the least-significant full block of $\mathtt{d}^*$ and overwriting the corresponding block of $\mathtt{d}'$. This is visualised in Fig. 10.

---

[9] The factors do not need to be common between $(p^* - 1)$ and $(q^* - 1)$, and can be freely distributed between the two.

Stitch($\mathsf{q}^*, \mathsf{p}^*, \mathsf{d}', \mathsf{u}^*, [B]_{k_M}$)
1 : $\quad \mathsf{pt}_0 \leftarrow \mathsf{len}(\mathsf{q}^*) \,\|\, \mathsf{q}^* \,\|\, \mathsf{len}(\mathsf{p}^*) \,\|\, \mathsf{p}^* \,\|\, \mathsf{len}(\mathsf{d}') \,\|\, \mathsf{d}'[0 : 234]$
2 : $\quad \mathsf{pad} \leftarrow_\$ (\{0, 1\}^8)^8 \quad /\!/ \text{ random padding, could also be 00s}$
3 : $\quad \mathsf{pt}_1 \leftarrow \mathsf{d}'[250 : 256] \,\|\, \mathsf{len}(\mathsf{u}^*) \,\|\, \mathsf{u}^* \,\|\, \mathsf{pad}$
4 : $\quad [\mathsf{pt}_0]_{k_M} \leftarrow \mathsf{OECB}_{k_M}(\mathsf{pt}_0)$
5 : $\quad [\mathsf{pt}_1]_{k_M} \leftarrow \mathsf{OECB}_{k_M}(\mathsf{pt}_1)$
6 : $\quad \mathsf{ct}^* \leftarrow [\mathsf{pt}_0]_{k_M} \,\|\, [B]_{k_M} \,\|\, [\mathsf{pt}_1]_{k_M}$
7 : $\quad \mathbf{return} \ \mathsf{ct}^*$

Fig. 9. Combining modified values produced using the ECB encryption oracle with the target ciphertext block in the correct format, reusing known AES-ECB blocks where possible. This assumes that $|\mathsf{q}^*|_B = |\mathsf{p}^*|_B = |\mathsf{u}^*|_B = 128$ and $|\mathsf{d}'|_B = 256$, as is the case for legitimate MEGA keys.

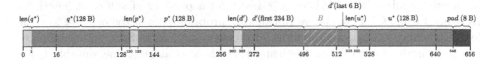

Fig. 10. The plaintext content of ct^*, with the placement of the target block B in red. (Color figure online)

4.1 Simplified Version

This version of the attack assumes a single t_i value per factor, which simplifies the presentation but imposes a high cost at the precomputation stage. Further, there is a non-negligible probability of the attack aborting and thus failing to complete. We will remove this restriction in the full version of the attack below.

Precomputation. Take $\{r_0, \ldots, r_{n-1}\}$ where each r_i is a prime such that $|r_i|_b = 8$, and n is such that $|\prod_{i=0}^{n-1} r_i|_b \geq 128$. This imposes the constraint $16 \leq n \leq 19$. Let $[B]_{k_M}$ be the target ciphertext block.

1. Find primes p^*, q^* such that $|p^*|_b = |q^*|_b = 1024$ and

$$p^* = 2 \cdot \left(\prod_{i=0}^{\lceil n/2 \rceil - 1} r_i \right) \cdot p' + 1, \quad q^* = 2 \cdot \left(\prod_{i=\lceil n/2 \rceil}^{n-1} r_i \right) \cdot q' + 1$$

where p', q' is each a product of 2-4 large primes.[10] Encode p^*, q^* as byte strings $\mathsf{p}^*, \mathsf{q}^*$.
2. Set $N^* \leftarrow p^* \cdot q^*$ and $\mathbb{G} \leftarrow (\mathbb{Z}/N^*\mathbb{Z})^\times$.

---

[10] These primes could repeat, the goal here is to avoid $(p^* - 1)(q^* - 1)$ having any other small factors except for $r_0, \ldots, r_{n-1}$.

3. For $i \in \{0, \ldots, n-1\}$:
   (a) Find $g_i \in \mathbb{G}$ of order r_i, e.g. by sampling $h \leftarrow_\$ \mathbb{G}$ and computing $g_i \leftarrow h^{(p^*-1)(q^*-1)/r_i} \bmod N^*$ until $g_i \neq 1$.
   (b) Find a value $t_i \in \{1, \ldots, r_i - 1\}$ such that for $m \leftarrow g_i^{t_i} \bmod N^*$; $\mathtt{m} \leftarrow \mathsf{ZeroPad}(m, N^*)$, we have $\mathtt{m}[1] = \mathtt{00}$. If no such t_i is found or there are multiple possible values, restart the precomputation.
4. Compute $u^* \leftarrow (q^*)^{-1} \bmod p^*$ and encode it as a byte string $\mathtt{u}^*$ with $|\mathtt{u}^*|_\mathsf{b} = 1024$.
5. Let $d' \leftarrow 2^{2047} + 1$ and encode it as a byte string $\mathtt{d}'$ with $|\mathtt{d}'|_\mathsf{b} = 2048$.
6. Obtain $\mathtt{ct}^* \leftarrow \mathsf{Stitch}(\mathtt{q}^*, \mathtt{p}^*, \mathtt{d}', \mathtt{u}^*, [B]_{\mathtt{k_M}})$. Let $d^* \leftarrow d' + 2^{48} \cdot B$ (where B is the unknown target block) denote the unknown value in the "d" field that will arise on decrypting $\mathtt{ct}^*$.[11]

Success Probability. For random $m \in \mathbb{G}$ we have $\Pr[\mathtt{m}[1] = \mathtt{00}] = 2^{-8}$. For each factor r_i the probability that Step 3b finds exactly one suitable t_i is $(r_i - 1) \cdot 2^{-8} \cdot (1 - 2^{-8})^{r_i - 2}$, which is greater than 0.18 for $2^7 < r_i < 2^8$. However, this needs to occur for all n factors where $n \geq 16$ to get a product of sufficient length to recover B using CRT, so the overall success probability is of the order $\approx 2^{-39}$ or less. To reduce the required amount of precomputation, in Sect. 4.2 we increase the bit length of each factor to ensure that there is at least one suitable t_i for each r_i and provide a strategy to disambiguate between multiple fitting t_i values.

Online Attack. Let $R = \prod_{i=0}^{n-1} r_i$ and $\mathtt{ct}^*, \{g_i\}_{i \in \mathcal{I}}, \{t_i\}_{i \in \mathcal{I}}$ be as computed before, for $\mathcal{I} = \{0, \ldots, n-1\}$.

1. When the client initiates a login, respond to the client's request with $([\mathtt{k_M}]_{\mathtt{k_e}}, \mathtt{ct}^*, [\mathtt{m}]_{pk}, \mathtt{uh})$, where everything but $\mathtt{ct}^*$ is as it would be in an honest response. If the client returns $\perp_6$, abort.
2. For $i \in \{0, \ldots, n-1\}$, do the following:
   (a) For $x \in \{1, \ldots, r_i - 1\}$, do the following:
       i. Compute $c_{i,x}^* \leftarrow (g_i)^x \bmod N^*$.
       ii. When the client initiates a login, respond to the client's request with $([\mathtt{k_M}]_{\mathtt{k_e}}, \mathtt{ct}^*, c_{i,x}^*, \mathtt{uh})$, where everything but $\mathtt{ct}^*$ and $c_{i,x}^*$ is as it would be in an honest response.[12]
       iii. If the client returns $(\perp_2, 254)$, save the value of x and break out of this loop.
   (b) If there is a saved value x, then we have $d^* \equiv x^{-1} \cdot t_i \pmod{r_i}$ for unknown d^*.
3. Then, use CRT to compute $d^* \bmod R$ from the values collected in Step 2b. Recall that by construction $d^* = d' + 2^{48} \cdot B$, so $d^* = 2^{2047} + 2^{48} \cdot B + 1$. Hence compute

---

[11] Note that by the choice of d', overwriting the least significant full block of d' with B is equivalent to adding $2^{48} \cdot B$ to d'.
[12] An honest response refers to the data that an honest server would have sent. Note that in this case, the "honest" $\mathtt{uh}$ will not match the value recovered from $c_{i,x}^*$, but this check only comes after the errors triggered by the attack. The attacker could equally replace the $\mathtt{uh}$ value with an arbitrary 11-byte UTF-8 string.

$$B \equiv \left(2^{48}\right)^{-1} \cdot \left(d^* - 2^{2047} - 1\right) \pmod{R},$$

to recover the target plaintext block since $|R|_b \geq 128$.

Cost. In the worst case, the main cost of the online attack is $\sum_{i \in \mathcal{I}}(r_i - 1)$ login attempts. This is bounded from above by $n \cdot (2^8 - 1) \approx 2^{12.24}$ for $n \leq 19$. In the average case, for each i we expect Step 2a to conclude after approximately $\frac{1}{2} \cdot 2^8$ trials, so the overall bound becomes $n \cdot 2^7 \approx 2^{11.24}$ for $n \leq 19$.

Probability of Abort. Note that the attack aborts if it receives error $\perp_6$. This error is returned whenever the decrypted $d^* = d' + 2^{48} \cdot B$ is such that $\gcd(d^*, (p^* - 1)(q^* - 1)) \neq 1$. Since d^* is odd by construction,[13] the error can only be caused if at least one of the following is true:

- $d^* \equiv 0 \pmod{r_i}$ for at least one r_i,
- $d^* \equiv 0 \pmod{p'_j}$ for at least one $p'_j \mid p'$, or
- $d^* \equiv 0 \pmod{q'_k}$ for at least one $q'_k \mid q'$.

The values p'_j, q'_k are large primes by construction, so the probability of an abort being caused by those cases is negligible. However, each factor r_i is only 8 bits in size, which means that assuming a random B the probability that the attack aborts because $d^* \equiv 0 \pmod{r_i}$ for at least one r_i is bounded by $n \cdot 2^{-7} \approx 0.15$ with $n \leq 19$. In Sect. 4.2, we discuss strategies for avoiding the abort.

Correctness. Now, assume the attack does not abort. By construction, the values of q^*, p^*, d', u^* pass the check on bit length, we have $\gcd(q^*, p^*) = 1$, $u^* = (q^*)^{-1} \bmod p^*$ and all $c^*_{i,x} < N^*$. During $\mathsf{DecryptSid}(sk, c^*_{i,x})$, the client will compute $m = \left(c^*_{i,x}\right)^{d^*} \bmod N^* = (g_i)^{x \cdot d^*} \bmod N^*$. If it is the case that $m = (g_i)^{t_i} \bmod N^*$ and therefore $x \cdot d^* \equiv t_i \pmod{r_i}$, the second byte of zero-padded m will be 00 and so the client will return $(\perp_2, 254)$ to the server. Otherwise, it will proceed with the computation and with very high probability return $\perp_3$, since the uh value will not match the relevant substring of m. Hence the attack recovers the target plaintext block.

4.2   Full Version

Here, we provide strategies to improve the running time and the success probability of our second attack. First, we discuss the use of multiple t_i values per factor r_i, incorporate this into the attack and show the effect of this strategy. For practical purposes, this strategy is already sufficient to reduce the precomputation cost and the likelihood of aborts.

---

[13] This is also why we cannot make the block-aligned simplification for this attack, because if we aligned it such that the least-significant block of d^* is full and therefore placed our target block B there, then if $B \equiv 0 \pmod 2$ the client would output error $\perp_6$ on all queries.

In this version of the attack, we increase the bit length of the factors r_i. As a result, the probability of finding a suitable t_i value during precomputation is increased. However this also implies that there will be more than one such value. We therefore have to also amend the online part of the attack to provide a way of determining which $t \in \mathcal{T}_i$ value has caused the expected error for a given x. There are multiple ways in which this could be achieved, and here we describe one option.

Take r_i, $\mathcal{T}_i$ and assume that we got the $(\perp_2, 254)$ error for some $x \in \{1, \ldots, r_i - 1\}$. We can test each potential value $t_j \in \mathcal{T}_i$ by submitting another query $c^*_{i,x_j} \leftarrow (g_i)^{x_j} \bmod N^*$ where $x_j \leftarrow x \cdot t_j^{-1} \bmod r_i$. If the guess for t_j is correct, we have $x \cdot d^* \equiv t_j \pmod{r_i}$, and so decryption of c^*_{i,x_j} will produce $(g_i)^{x_j \cdot d^*} \bmod N^* = (g_i)^{x \cdot t_j^{-1} \cdot d^*} \bmod N^* = g_i$ as the plaintext. Then, as long as g_i is such that its second byte is not 00, which we can ensure in the precomputation phase, the check that produces $\perp_2$ will pass. Since the server knows g_i and is able to set uh to arbitrary 11-byte values, it can also make sure to pass the check that produces $\perp_3$, and therefore get 43 bytes of g_i from the client via the returned sid value when the guess is correct. However, if the guess is not correct, it is very unlikely that the server-modified uh would match the resulting plaintext, leading to $\perp_3$. So the server can distinguish between the two cases.

Precomputation. Take $\{r_0, \ldots, r_{n-1}\}$ where each r_i is a prime such that $|r_i|_b = 12$, and n is such that for $R \leftarrow \prod_{i=0}^{n-1} r_i$ we have $|R|_b \geq 128$, so $11 \leq n \leq 12$. Let $[B]_{k_M}$ be the target ciphertext block.

1. Find primes p^*, q^* such that $|p^*|_b = |q^*|_b = 1024$ and

$$p^* = 2 \cdot \left(\prod_{i=0}^{\lceil n/2 \rceil - 1} r_i \right) \cdot p' + 1, \quad q^* = 2 \cdot \left(\prod_{i=\lceil n/2 \rceil}^{n-1} r_i \right) \cdot q' + 1$$

where p', q' is each a product of 2-4 large primes. Encode p^*, q^* as byte strings p*, q*.
2. Set $N^* \leftarrow p^* \cdot q^*$ and $\mathbb{G} \leftarrow (\mathbb{Z}/N^*\mathbb{Z})^\times$.
3. For $i \in \{0, \ldots, n-1\}$:
   (a) Find $g \in \mathbb{G}$ of order r_i, e.g. by sampling $h \leftarrow_\$ \mathbb{G}$ and computing $g \leftarrow h^{(p^*-1)(q^*-1)/r_i} \bmod N^*$ until $g \neq 1$.
   (b) Initialise $\mathcal{T}_i = \emptyset$.
   (c) For $t \in \{1, \ldots, r_i - 1\}$, do the following:
      i. Let $\mathbf{g}' \leftarrow \mathsf{ZeroPad}(g', N^*)$ for $g' \leftarrow g^t \bmod N^*$.
      ii. If $\mathbf{g}'[1] = 00$, add t to $\mathcal{T}_i$. Else if $\mathbf{g}'[17 : \alpha]$ for some $\alpha \geq 28$ is a valid UTF-8 string of size 11[14], save $g_i \leftarrow g'$, $a \leftarrow t$ and $\mathsf{uh}^*_i \leftarrow \mathbf{g}'[17 : \alpha]$.
   (d) If $\mathcal{T}_i = \emptyset$ or a is undefined, restart the precomputation.

---

[14] Note that an 11 B byte string interpreted as a valid UTF-8 string will likely not be a string of size 11, i.e. a string consisting of 11 characters, since not all byte values are interpreted as text and non-ASCII characters require multiple bytes to encode [36].

(e) Shift $\mathcal{T}_i$ by replacing each $t \in \mathcal{T}_i$ by $t \cdot a^{-1}$ mod r_i. This ensures that the values in $\mathcal{T}_i$ are with respect to the new generator g_i instead of g.

4. Compute $u^* \leftarrow (q^*)^{-1}$ mod p^* and encode it as a byte string u^* with $|u^*|_b = 1024$.

5. Compute $d' \leftarrow 2^{2047} + 2^{48+128} \cdot \delta + 1$ for $\delta < R$ such that $d' \equiv 0 \pmod{R}$. Encode it as a byte string d' with $|d'|_b = 2048$.

6. Obtain $ct^* \leftarrow \text{Stitch}(q^*, p^*, d', u^*, [B]_{k_M})$.

Success Probability. Increasing the bit length of the factors means that now for each factor r_i the probability that Step 3(c)ii finds at least one suitable t is $1 - (1 - 2^{-8})^{r_i - 1}$, which is greater than 0.9996 for $2^{11} < r_i < 2^{12}$. Across all n factors for $n \leq 12$, it is still greater than 0.99. Next, the probability that a random 11-byte string is a valid UTF-8 string is ≈ 0.001634. Hence for each factor r_i the probability that at least one such string will be found is $1 - (1 - 0.001634)^{r_i - 1} > 0.9648$, and across all factors it is at least 0.65. In practice, if the precomputation fails at this point, it can simply be re-run again with different r_i values.

Cost. This version tests all possible values of t for every r_i, so overall it must check at most $n \cdot 2^{12} \approx 2^{15}$ values of g^t (these can however be cycled through for each r_i). The prime generation is a one-time cost in the sense that the values can be reused in attacks on multiple users. Finally, since d' will be composed mostly of zero-blocks, building the ciphertext ct^* requires up to 15 uses of the ECB encryption oracle (which, recall, produces 2 blocks at a time).

Online Attack. Let $ct^*, \{g_i\}_{i \in \mathcal{I}}, \{\mathcal{T}_i\}_{i \in \mathcal{I}}$ be the values computed before where $\mathcal{I} = \{0, \ldots, n-1\}$.

1. When the client initiates a login, respond to the client's request with $([k_M]_{k_e}, ct^*, [m]_{pk}, uh)$, where everything but ct^* is as it would be in an honest response. If the client returns $\perp_6$, abort.

2. For $i \in \mathcal{I}$, do the following:
   (a) For $x \in \{2, \ldots, r_i - 1\}$, do the following:
      i. Compute $c^*_{i,x} \leftarrow (g_i)^x$ mod N^*.
      ii. When the client initiates a login, respond to the client's request with $([k_M]_{k_e}, ct^*, c^*_{i,x}, uh)$, where everything but ct^* and $c^*_{i,x}$ is as it would be in an honest response.
      iii. If the client returns $(\perp_2, 254)$, save the value of x and break out of this loop.
   (b) If $\mathcal{T}_i = \{t_i\}$ has a single element, skip this step. Otherwise, for $t \in \mathcal{T}_i$, do the following:
      i. Let $x' \leftarrow x \cdot t^{-1}$ mod r_i.
      ii. Compute $c^*_{i,x'} \leftarrow (g_i)^{x'}$ mod N^*.
      iii. When the client initiates a login, respond to the client's request with $([k_M]_{k_e}, ct^*, c^*_{i,x'}, uh^*_i)$, where only $[k_M]_{k_e}$ is as it would be in an honest response.

      iv. If the client returns $\texttt{sid} = g_i[1:44]$, save the value $t_i \leftarrow t$ and break out of this loop.

  (c) We have that $d^* = d' + 2^{48} \cdot B \equiv x^{-1} \cdot t_i \pmod{r_i}$, and so $B \equiv \left(2^{48}\right)^{-1} \cdot x^{-1} \cdot t_i \pmod{r_i}$.

3. Then, use CRT to compute $B \bmod R$ from the values collected in Step 2c, which in turn recovers the target plaintext block since $|R|_{\mathsf{b}} \geq 128$.

Success Probability. As in the attack in Sect. 4.1, this attack aborts if it receives error $\perp_6$. However, the probability that this happens becomes smaller with the increased bit length of the factors r_i. Assuming a random B, for 12-bit factors the probability of an abort is bounded by $n \cdot 2^{-11} \approx 0.006$ with $n \leq 12$. In the full version of this work we give a more complex attack strategy that avoids the abort altogether.

In practice, the attack's success probability may be impacted by another factor, namely differing implementations of UTF-8 validation. Suppose that the values g produced in Step 3(c)ii of the precomputation in Sect. 4.2 have valid UTF-8 substrings of size 11 in Python: this does not guarantee that they will be interpreted as such by the Javascript webclient. This requires implementing additional strategies for disambiguation in case the UTF-8-based one never yields the expected $\texttt{sid}$ request.[15]

Cost. In the worst case, the main cost of the online phase of the attack is the $\sum_{i \in \mathcal{I}}(r_i - 1)$ login attempts needed. This is bounded by $n \cdot (2^{12} - 1) \approx 2^{15.58}$ for $n \leq 12$. In the average case, for each i we expect Step 2a to conclude after at most 2^8 trials and Step 2b to finish after around $\frac{1}{2} \cdot |\mathcal{T}_i| \approx \frac{1}{2} \cdot r_i \cdot 2^{-8}$ trials. Added together, the number of login attempts needed in the average case is bounded by $n \cdot (2^8 + \frac{1}{2} \cdot 2^{12} \cdot 2^{-8}) \approx 2^{11.63}$ for $n \leq 12$. Performing the experimental analysis over a large number of runs as in Sect. 3.2 would be more difficult due to the interaction between the disambiguation strategies and the web client with automated logins, which causes the web client to freeze or begin sending requests in large batches. This can impact the success rate (in particular, the attack may produce one x or t value that is slightly off) and hinders automating the attack. We stress that this is purely an artefact of our proof-of-concept implementation.

Note that to keep the presentation of the attacks simpler, we have assumed specific values of $|r_i|_{\mathsf{b}}$ and thus constrained the value of n. In reality, using different values would allow making a different tradeoff between the precomputation cost and the number of login attempts needed in the online phase. For instance, using 10-bit primes would lower the (online) worst-case bound to $n \cdot (2^{10} - 1) \approx 2^{13.91}$ for $n \leq 15$, but slightly increase the (online) average-case bound to $n \cdot (2^8 + \frac{1}{2} \cdot 2^{10} \cdot 2^{-8}) \approx 2^{11.92}$ login attempts. It would also make the

---

[15] One alternative is to instead for all $t \in \mathcal{T}_i$ submit $x' \leftarrow x \cdot t^{-1} \cdot t_j \bmod r_i$ for some $t_j \in \mathcal{T}_i, t_j \neq t$, and use the original error $(\perp_2, 254)$ as the confirmation signal. This still has a potential for false positives and false negatives, however. A final, and most expensive, failover strategy is then to cycle through all values of x, saving the ones for which the client returns $(\perp_2, 254)$ and then running an offline computation to determine which x values are matched to which t values.

precomputation phase much less likely to succeed in a single run: the probability of finding suitable t values for all r_i would fall to around 0.11, while the probability of finding generators with suitable UTF-8 substrings for all r_i would only be around 0.0002.

5   Recovering the RSA Private Key

Our attacks in Sects. 3 and 4 can be seen as building generic AES-ECB decryption oracles. In this section, we turn this capability into an RSA private key recovery attack. Naively we would expect to call our costly AES-ECB decryption oracle up to nine times: each factor p, q of N has 1024 bits, but these are not perfectly aligned with AES block boundaries, necessitating to cover (partial) plaintexts from nine different 128-bit blocks. However, using a post-processing stage, we can reduce this number to four.

In particular, as illustrated in Fig. 4, the block alignments of p and q differ. For reasons that will become apparent below we will need to recover at least 512 bits. Based on the specific alignments, we will aim to recover the 512+16 least significant bits of q: 512 bits (i.e. four 128-bit blocks) are recovered using the attacks from Sects. 3 and 4 and the least significant 16 bits are "recovered" using exhaustive search (which avoids the query cost of recovering a fifth block). If instead we targeted p, we would need to recover 32 bits using exhaustive search, which would have prohibitive cost. Thus, next, we discuss how to recover the remaining bits of q given the $\ell = 512 + 16$ least significant bits of q. In particular, we will solve the following computational problem.

Definition 1. *Let $N = p \cdot q$ be a 2048-bit RSA modulus with p, q having 1024 bits each. Given ℓ consecutive least significant bits of q, recover q.*

Our approach is a simple combination of exhaustive search, lattice reduction and root finding over $\mathbb{Z}$ following Coppersmith's method [6]. In particular, we use the Howgrave-Graham variant [8,9,13,28] of this algorithm. Let $\lceil \log_2 q \rceil - \ell < 1024$, $q = 2^{\lceil \log_2 q \rceil - \ell} \cdot r + q_0'$, where r are the bits we are trying to recover and $|q_0'| \le 2^\ell$ are the known bits of q. Then r satisfies $f'(x) \equiv 0 \bmod q$ for $f'(x) := q_0' + 2^{\lceil \log_2 q \rceil - \ell} \cdot x \bmod q$. Given this we can consider

$$q_0 := 2^{-\lceil \log_2 q \rceil + \ell} \cdot q_0' \quad \text{and} \quad f(x) := q_0 + x \bmod q$$

and note that r still satisfies $f(x) \equiv 0 \bmod q$. That is, we translate our problem into one where the most significant bits are known rather than the least significant ones, cf. [28].

From this, the algorithm proceeds by constructing several polynomials that evaluate to zero modulo q or a multiple thereof, such as (powers of) N. In more detail, Let $h \ge 2 \in \mathbb{N}$ and $u < h \in \mathbb{N}$, for $0 \le i < h$ we let

$$f_i(x) := \begin{cases} N^{u-i} \cdot (q_0 + x)^i & \text{for } 0 \le i < u, \\ x^{i-u} \cdot (q_0 + x)^u & \text{for } u \le i < h. \end{cases}$$

For example, picking $h = 4$ and $u = 2$ we get

$$N^2, \quad N \cdot q_0 + N \cdot x, \quad q_0^2 + 2\,q_0 \cdot x + x^2 \quad \text{and} \quad q_0^2 \cdot x + 2\,q_0 \cdot x^2 + x^3.$$

First, note that all $f_i(x)$ evaluate to zero modulo q^u at the correct r. Second, note the maximal degree of the $f_i(x)$ is $h-1$, i.e. $\max_{0 \le i < h}(\deg(f_i(x))) = h-1$ and thus each polynomial has at most h coefficients.

Now, letting $X = 2^{\lceil \log_2 q \rceil - \ell}$ and $f_i^{(j)}$ denote the coefficient of x^j in $f_i(x)$, we construct a matrix $\mathbf{A}$ where the entry $A_{i,j} := f_i^{(j)} \cdot X^j$. Continuing with our example, we would have

$$\mathbf{A} := \begin{pmatrix} N^2 & 0 & 0 & 0 \\ N \cdot q_0 & N \cdot X & 0 & 0 \\ q_0^2 & 2\,q_0 \cdot X & X^2 & 0 \\ 0 & q_0^2 \cdot X & 2\,q_0 \cdot X^2 & X^3 \end{pmatrix}.$$

Since the matrix is triangular we can read off the determinant $\det(\mathbf{A}) = N^{u \cdot (u+1)/2} \cdot X^{h \cdot (h-1)/2}$. The rows of this matrix $\mathbf{A}$ span a lattice which contains a vector $\mathbf{v}$ of Euclidean norm $\|\mathbf{v}\| \le \sqrt{h} \cdot \left(N^{u \cdot (u+1)/2} \cdot X^{h \cdot (h-1)/2}\right)^{1/h}$ by Minkowski's theorem. In other words, there exists an integer-linear combination of the rows of $\mathbf{A}$ that produces a vector with at most this Euclidean norm. Using lattice reduction we can find this shortest vector.[16] Now, given a vector of Euclidean norm $\|\mathbf{v}\|$ we know that its ℓ_1 norm, i.e. the sum of the absolute values of its entries, is bounded by $|\mathbf{v}|_1 \le \sqrt{h} \cdot \|\mathbf{v}\|$. Finally, if $\mathbf{v} \ne 0$ and $|\mathbf{v}|_1 \le q^u$, we can extract a polynomial that evaluates to zero modulo q^u on r but which evaluated at r is strictly smaller than q^u.[17] In other words, this polynomial evaluates to zero at r over $\mathbb{Z}$. The algorithm concludes by finding the roots of this polynomial, which can be accomplished in polynomial time (and efficiently in practice).

To select h and u, by abuse of notation let h also be a formal variable and set $u := 1/2 \cdot h - 1$. As in [8, p. 102], we then find a root > 0 of

$$\frac{1024 - \ell}{2048} \cdot h \cdot (h-1) - u \cdot h + u \cdot (u+1).$$

This succeeds for $\ell > 512$ and the solution grows as ℓ approaches 512 from above.

As mentioned above, in our setting we consider $\ell = 512 + 16$: We run the attack from Sect. 3 on four blocks to recover 512 bits and run an exhaustive search over the remaining 16 bits (which are contained in a non-aligned block). In this setting, we picked $h = 36$ and $u = 18$. In our experiments, using LLL, finding a sufficiently short vector takes about 26 s on a Intel(R) Xeon(R) Gold 6252 CPU @ 2.10 GHz using SageMath/FPLLL [31,32]. In 1024 experiments,

---

[16] The traditional presentation of this algorithm invokes the LLL algorithm which gives a short vector that is at most an exponential factor away from the shortest vector. However, the lattice dimensions involved here are in the range where the shortest vector problem (SVP) can be solved efficiently in practice – say, up to dimension 150 [7] – and we may thus simply assume we solve SVP. In any case, the exponential factor is $\approx 1.0219^h$ which is < 3 for $h \le 50$.

[17] We extract $g(x)$ as $g^{(j)} := v_j / X^j \in \mathbb{Z}$.

we obtained a success rate of 100%. Thus, we expect to be able to recover q in time $2^{16} \cdot 26$ seconds, or about 20 core days.[18]

The overall cost of the RSA private key recovery attack is $4 \cdot 2^{9.29} = 2^{11.29} \approx$ 2500 login attempts, 66 ECB encryption oracle calls, and about 20 core days of computation (using the attack of Sect. 3 in combination with the attack in this section).

6   Attacking Unpatched Clients

We briefly revisit the attacks of [2] against unpatched MEGA clients in the light of our discovery of the ECB encryption oracle described in Sect. 2.2.

Attack 1 in [2] uses an estimated 512 logins to recover a target user's RSA private key. The number of logins required was subsequently reduced to 6 in [29] by using more sophisticated lattice techniques.

Attack 2 in [2] then exploits knowledge of that private key to recover two blocks of AES-ECB plaintext per login. This is done by overwriting two blocks of the encrypted version of u with the target AES-ECB ciphertext blocks and selecting a carefully crafted RSA ciphertext in the authentication protocol; the session ID returned by the client in that protocol then leaks the two AES-ECB plaintext blocks. This approach is used to build an efficient procedure for recovering file encryption keys in [2].

Interestingly, however, the RSA private key used in Attack 2 in [2] does not need to be the target user's true key – it only needs to be a key known to the adversary and any valid RSA private key (in the appropriate format) will do. Hence, an adversary can use the ECB encryption oracle to create a suitably encrypted, known RSA private key. By carefully reusing all-zero blocks for most of q, p and d, the number of ECB encryption oracle calls needed can be made as small as 7. The adversary then applies Attack 2 from [2] with the target AES-ECB ciphertext blocks being selected from those encrypting the least significant bits of q (from the actual private key). With two applications of the attack, the adversary recovers 4 plaintext blocks, or 512 bits of q. Applying the lattice attack from Sect. 5, the adversary recovers the full RSA private key.

The cost of the attack is 2 login attempts and a small number of ECB encryption oracle calls.

Note that Attack 2 of [2] is prevented by patched MEGA client code because of the requirement that the client-selected 11-byte string uh appear in m at a specific location and because overwriting u with a target ciphertext would make the check at line 10 in DecodePrivk(privk) fail.

---

[18] We note that this computation is "proudly parallel" or "embarrassingly parallel". This is because for each of our 2^{16} guesses we can run an independent lattice reduction. We also note that the running time is independent of whether the input instance corresponds to a correct or incorrect guess. Moreover, incorrect solutions resulting from incorrect guesses can be filtered out using the known public key.

7   Discussion and Future Work

On the one hand, the conclusion to be drawn from this work for practitioners and designers is no different from the one derived from [2]. The root causes at play here were already identified in [2], whose suggestion of protecting the integrity of encrypted keys using a MAC would have prevented the attacks in this work as well. Further, the existence of the ECB encryption oracle in a feature completely separate from the attacked protocol highlights the continued fragility of the MEGA infrastructure, made possible also by the lack of key separation.

However, our attacks also highlight issues going beyond the ones exposed in previous works. First, some of the errors that our attacks exploit as oracles are not explicit, but derive from bugs in the big integer arithmetic provided by asmcrypto.js. This presents a challenge already mentioned in [3] which called for a verified big integer library that could serve as a common core for different projects. In the case considered here, such a library would need to be cross-compilable to JavaScript or WebAssembly. We consider this a pressing area for future work.

There are also further lessons to be drawn for a cryptanalytic audience. First, our attacks serve as an additional example of key overwriting attacks [2,5,10], a class of attacks that appears to deserve more exploration in terms of targets (deployed in practice) and attack refinement. Moreover, our attacks make use of the detailed and verbose error reporting by MEGA clients. This enables powerful side-channel attacks that can be observed remotely,[19] highlighting the practical significance of these classes of attacks. Finally, our work, along with other recent works attacking widely deployed protocols such as [1,5,11,30,35], underlines that while it might seem that the "golden age" of cryptographic attacks against deployed protocols is over – given the level of academic involvement and formal rigour that went into the design of TLS 1.3 – the target has simply moved up the stack. As cryptographic applications move beyond "simple" protection of data in transit or at rest, more complex cryptographic solutions are deployed at scale, often without significant input from the cryptographic community. This suggests a broad and impactful field for cryptanalysis of targets "in the wild". It is well known that attacks are typically required to convince practitioners to adopt cryptographic recommendations. This in turn suggests that to achieve the adoption of more secure and formally analysed cryptographic solutions in practice, further cryptanalytical work on the "current generation" of deployed solutions is needed.

Finally, the two attacks presented in this work require a large number of login attempts. This was also the case for the first attack of [2] and used as an argument by MEGA that the attack was not practical. However, later work by [29] reduced the number of login attempts to six, and we have further reduced it to just two. Beyond reinforcing the truism that attacks only get better, this poses the open problem to improve the attacks presented in this work in terms of login attempt complexity.

---

[19] In contrast to timing-based side-channel attacks, generally considered less practical in the remote, as opposed to local, setting.

Acknowledgements. The research of Mareková was carried out in part during a visit to the Applied Cryptography Group at ETH Zürich. She was also supported by the EPSRC and the UK Government as part of the Centre for Doctoral Training in Cyber Security at Royal Holloway, University of London (EP/P009301/1). The work of Paterson was supported in part by a gift from VMware. The work of Albrecht was done while Albrecht was at Royal Holloway.

References

1. Albrecht, M.R., Mareková, L., Paterson, K.G., Stepanovs, I.: Four attacks and a proof for Telegram. In: 43rd IEEE Symposium on Security and Privacy, SP 2022, San Francisco, CA, USA, 22–26 May 2022, pp. 87–106. IEEE (2022). https://doi.org/10.1109/SP46214.2022.9833666

2. Backendal, M., Haller, M., Paterson, K.G.: MEGA: malleable encryption goes awry. In: 44th IEEE Symposium on Security and Privacy (2023, to appear). https://eprint.iacr.org/2022/959

3. Barbosa, M., et al.: SoK: computer-aided cryptography. In: 2021 IEEE Symposium on Security and Privacy, pp. 777–795. IEEE Computer Society Press, May 2021. https://doi.org/10.1109/SP40001.2021.00008

4. Bleichenbacher, D.: Chosen ciphertext attacks against protocols based on the RSA encryption standard PKCS #1. In: Krawczyk, H. (ed.) CRYPTO 1998. LNCS, vol. 1462, pp. 1–12. Springer, Heidelberg (1998). https://doi.org/10.1007/BFb0055716

5. Bruseghini, L., Paterson, K.G., Huigens, D.: Victory by KO: attacking OpenPGP using key overwriting. In: ACM Conference on Computer and Communications Security (ACM CCS) (2022, to appear). https://doi.org/10.3929/ethz-b-000545839

6. Coppersmith, D.: Finding a small root of a bivariate integer equation; factoring with high bits known. In: Maurer, U. (ed.) EUROCRYPT 1996. LNCS, vol. 1070, pp. 178–189. Springer, Heidelberg (1996). https://doi.org/10.1007/3-540-68339-9_16

7. Ducas, L., Stevens, M., van Woerden, W.: Advanced lattice sieving on GPUs, with tensor cores. In: Canteaut, A., Standaert, F.-X. (eds.) EUROCRYPT 2021. LNCS, vol. 12697, pp. 249–279. Springer, Cham (2021). https://doi.org/10.1007/978-3-030-77886-6_9

8. Howgrave-Graham, N.A.: Computational Mathematics Inspired by RSA. Ph.D. thesis, University of Bath (1998). https://researchportal.bath.ac.uk/en/studentTheses/computational-mathematics-inspired-by-rsa

9. Howgrave-Graham, N.: Finding small roots of univariate modular equations revisited. In: Darnell, M. (ed.) Cryptography and Coding 1997. LNCS, vol. 1355, pp. 131–142. Springer, Heidelberg (1997). https://doi.org/10.1007/BFb0024458

10. Klima, V., Rosa, T.: Attack on private signature keys of the OpenPGP format, PGP(TM) programs and other applications compatible with OpenPGP. Cryptology ePrint Archive, Report 2002/076 (2002). https://eprint.iacr.org/2002/076

11. Len, J., Grubbs, P., Ristenpart, T.: Partitioning oracle attacks. In: Bailey, M., Greenstadt, R. (eds.) USENIX Security 2021, pp. 195–212. USENIX Association, August 2021

12. Lim, C.H., Lee, P.J.: A key recovery attack on discrete log-based schemes using a prime order subgroup. In: Kaliski, B.S. (ed.) CRYPTO 1997. LNCS, vol. 1294, pp. 249–263. Springer, Heidelberg (1997). https://doi.org/10.1007/BFb0052240

13. May, A.: Using LLL-reduction for solving RSA and factorization problems. In: Nguyen, P., Vallée, B. (eds.) The LLL Algorithm. Information Security and Cryptography. Springer, Heidelberg (2009). https://doi.org/10.1007/978-3-642-02295-1_10

14. MEGA: About Us, September 2022. https://mega.io/about
15. MEGA: Mega.nz web client (2022). https://github.com/meganz/webclient
16. MEGA: Security White Paper, June 2022. https://mega.nz/SecurityWhitepaper. pdf
17. MEGA: webclient - #15273: Patch for ETH Zurich exploit, June 2022. https://github.com/meganz/webclient/commit/d2a0d054d4dbb90f035b3b4b421f 780adafaa78e
18. MEGA: webclient - #15295: Output detailed information about RSA decoding failures, June 2022. https://github.com/meganz/webclient/commit/ cd4ab89b2cd0e388b0ea55753b86c8808f810138
19. MEGA: webclient - asmcrypto.js, August 2022. https://github.com/meganz/ webclient/blob/v4.21.4/js/vendor/asmcrypto.js
20. MEGA: webclient - asmcrypto.js: Modulus, August 2022. https://github.com/ meganz/webclient/blob/v4.21.4/js/vendor/asmcrypto.js#L10325
21. MEGA: webclient - asmcrypto.js: Modulus_inverse. https://github.com/meganz/ webclient/blob/v4.21.4/js/vendor/asmcrypto.js#L10382 (August 2022)
22. MEGA: webclient - asmcrypto.js: mredc, August 2022. https://github.com/ meganz/webclient/blob/v4.21.4/js/vendor/asmcrypto.js#L9706
23. MEGA: webclient - asmcrypto.js: RSA_decrypt, August 2022. https://github.com/ meganz/webclient/blob/v4.21.4/js/vendor/asmcrypto.js#L10746
24. MEGA: webclient - crypto.js: api_updfkeysync, September 2022. https://github. com/meganz/webclient/blob/v4.21.4/js/crypto.js#L3050
25. MEGA: webclient - crypto.js: crypto_decodeprivkey, August 2022. https://github. com/meganz/webclient/blob/v4.21.4/js/crypto.js/#L2047
26. MEGA: webclient - nodedec.js: crypto_rsadecrypt, August 2022. https://github. com/meganz/webclient/blob/v4.21.4/nodedec.js/#L550
27. MEGA: webclient - security.js: decryptRsaKeyAndSessionId, August 2022. https://github.com/meganz/webclient/blob/v4.21.4/js/security.js#L1231
28. Micheli, G.D., Heninger, N.: Recovering cryptographic keys from partial information, by example. Cryptology ePrint Archive, Report 2020/1506 (2020). https:// eprint.iacr.org/2020/1506
29. Ryan, K., Heninger, N.: Cryptanalyzing MEGA in six queries. Cryptology ePrint Archive, Report 2022/914 (2022). https://eprint.iacr.org/2022/914
30. Shakevsky, A., Ronen, E., Wool, A.: Trust dies in darkness: shedding light on samsung's TrustZone keymaster design. Cryptology ePrint Archive, Report 2022/208 (2022). https://eprint.iacr.org/2022/208
31. Stein, W., et al.: Sage Mathematics Software Version 9.5. The Sage Development Team (2022). http://www.sagemath.org
32. The FPLLL development team: FPLLL, a lattice reduction library (2021). https:// github.com/fplll/fplll
33. The mitmproxy development team: mitmproxy - an interactive HTTPS proxy (2022). https://mitmproxy.org/
34. van Oorschot, P.C., Wiener, M.J.: On Diffie-Hellman key agreement with short exponents. In: Maurer, U. (ed.) EUROCRYPT 1996. LNCS, vol. 1070, pp. 332–343. Springer, Heidelberg (1996). https://doi.org/10.1007/3-540-68339-9_29
35. Vanhoef, M., Ronen, E.: Dragonblood: analyzing the dragonfly handshake of WPA3 and EAP-pwd. In: 2020 IEEE Symposium on Security and Privacy, pp. 517–533. IEEE Computer Society Press, May 2020. https://doi.org/10.1109/SP40000.2020. 00031
36. Wikipedia: UTF-8 (2022). https://en.wikipedia.org/wiki/UTF-8

Public-Key Cryptanalysis

Publisher / Explanation

Finding Many Collisions via Reusable Quantum Walks
Application to Lattice Sieving

Xavier Bonnetain[1], André Chailloux[2], André Schrottenloher[3]([✉]) [iD],
and Yixin Shen[4] [iD]

[1] Université de Lorraine, CNRS, Inria, Nancy, France
[2] Inria, Paris, France
[3] Inria, Univ. Rennes, IRISA, Rennes, France
andre.schrottenloher@m4x.org
[4] Royal Holloway, University of London, Egham, UK

Abstract. Given a random function f with domain $[2^n]$ and codomain $[2^m]$, with $m \geq n$, a collision of f is a pair of distinct inputs with the same image. Collision finding is an ubiquitous problem in cryptanalysis, and it has been well studied using both classical and quantum algorithms. Indeed, the quantum query complexity of the problem is well known to be $\Theta(2^{m/3})$, and matching algorithms are known for any value of m.

The situation becomes different when one is looking for *multiple* collision pairs. Here, for 2^k collisions, a query lower bound of $\Theta(2^{(2k+m)/3})$ was shown by Liu and Zhandry (EUROCRYPT 2019). A matching algorithm is known, but only for relatively small values of m, when many collisions exist. In this paper, we improve the algorithms for this problem and, in particular, extend the range of admissible parameters where the lower bound is met.

Our new method relies on a *chained quantum walk* algorithm, which might be of independent interest. It allows to extract multiple solutions of an MNRS-style quantum walk, without having to recompute it entirely: after finding and outputting a solution, the current state is reused as the initial state of another walk.

As an application, we improve the quantum sieving algorithms for the shortest vector problem (SVP), with a complexity of $2^{0.2563d+o(d)}$ instead of the previous $2^{0.2570d+o(d)}$.

Keywords: Quantum algorithms · quantum walks · collision search · lattice sieving

1 Introduction

Quantum walks are a powerful algorithmic tool which has been used to provide state-of-the-art algorithms for various important problems in post-quantum

Part of this work was done while André Schrottenloher was at CWI, Amsterdam, The Netherlands.

C. Hazay and M. Stam (Eds.): EUROCRYPT 2023, LNCS 14008, pp. 221–251, 2023.
https://doi.org/10.1007/978-3-031-30589-4_8

cryptography, such as the shortest vector problem (SVP) via lattice sieving [9], the subset sum problem [4], information set decoding [22], etc.

These applications are all established under a particular quantum walk framework called the MNRS framework [26], and the quantum walks look for marked nodes in a so-called Johnson graph [22] (or a product of Johnson graphs). When walking on this particular graph, the MNRS framework is somewhat rigid. First, it requires to setup the uniform superposition of all nodes along with their attached data structure, then it applies multiple times reflection operators which move this quantum state close to the uniform superposition of all marked nodes.

Due to this rigidity, previously, the best way to find k different marked nodes was to run the whole quantum walk (including the setup) k times. In [9] the authors noticed that a way to output *multiple* solutions instead of a single one with quantum walks would improve the quantum time complexity of their algorithm for solving the SVP.

A natural observation which guides us throughout this paper is that in certain cases, after obtaining the uniform superposition of all marked nodes via the MNRS quantum walk, it is possible to retrieve part of the solution and start another MNRS quantum walk using the remaining part of the quantum state as the new starting state. By doing so, we avoid repeating the setup cost for each new quantum walk, and we now benefit from a trade-off.

In particular, using this observation, we tackle the following problem:

Problem 1 (Multiple collision search). Let $f : \{0,1\}^n \rightarrow \{0,1\}^m$, $n \leq m \leq 2n$ be a random function. Let $k \leq 2n - m$. Find 2^k *collision pairs*, that is, pairs of distinct x, y such that $f(x) = f(y)$.

The constraints on the input and output domain are such that a significant $(\Theta\left(2^{2n-m}\right))$ number of collisions pairs exist in the random case. This problem has several applications both in asymmetric and symmetric cryptography. For example, the problem of finding multiple vectors close to a target vector, which appears in lattice sieving (as mentioned above) can be seen as a special case. The limited-birthday problem in symmetric cryptanalysis (e.g., impossible differential attacks and rebound distinguishers [16]) is another example.

Lower Bounds. While quantum query lower bounds for the collision problem (with a single solution) had been known for a longer time, Liu and Zhandry proved more recently in [25] a query lower bound in $\Omega\left(2^{2k/3+m/3}\right)$ to find 2^k solutions, which holds for all values of $m \geq n$.

For relatively small values of k and m (precisely, $k \leq 3n - 2m$, as we explain in Sect. 6), the BHT collision search algorithm [8] allows to reach this bound. Besides this algorithm, Ambainis' algorithm [2] uses a quantum walk to find one collision in time $\widetilde{\mathcal{O}}\left(2^{m/3}\right)$. However, no matching algorithm was known for other values, neither in time nor in queries.

Contributions. Our main contribution in this paper is a *chained quantum walk* algorithm to solve the multiple collision search problem. We formalize the intuitive idea that the output state of a quantum walk can be *reused*, to some extent, as the starting state of another. For any admissible values of k, n, m such that $k \leq \frac{m}{4}$, our algorithm requires $\mathcal{O}\left(2^{\frac{2}{3}k+\frac{m}{3}}\right)$ queries, and also $\widetilde{\mathcal{O}}\left(2^{\frac{2}{3}k+\frac{m}{3}}\right)$ quantum gates (i.e., time) and space in the qRAM model.

Theorem 4 (Sect. 4). Let $f : \{0,1\}^n \to \{0,1\}^m$, $n \leq m \leq 2n$ be a random function. Let $k \leq \min(2n - m, m/4)$. There exists a quantum algorithm making $\mathcal{O}\left(2^{2k/3+m/3}\right)$ quantum queries to f and with a gate count $\widetilde{\mathcal{O}}\left(2^{2k/3+m/3}\right)$, that outputs 2^k collision pairs of f.

By combining our algorithm with the BHT approach, we can now meet the lower bound over all values of k, n, m, except a range of (k, m) contained in $\left[\frac{n}{3}, n\right] \times [n, 1.6n]$, as summarized in Fig. 1. Nevertheless, our approach also improves the known complexities in this range.

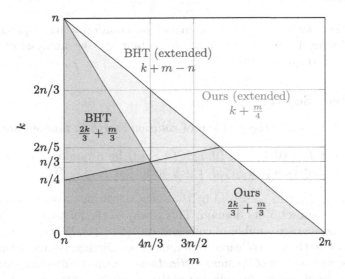

Fig. 1. Gate count exponent in the algorithm depending on the relative values of k, m and n. Both our algorithm and the BHT approach can be extended to the whole triangle, but we show only the one achieving the best complexity. In the purple region (bottom left), both approaches reach the same complexity exponent $\frac{2k}{3} + \frac{m}{3}$.

Using our new algorithm, we improve the state-of-the-art time complexity of quantum sieving to solve the SVP in [9] from $2^{0.2570d+o(d)}$ to $2^{0.2563d+o(d)}$ quantum gates. We also provide time-memory trade-offs that are conjectured to be tight [15]:

Theorem 7 (Sect. 4). Let $f : \{0,1\}^n \to \{0,1\}^m$, $n \leq m \leq 2n$ be a random function. For all $k \leq \ell \leq \max(2n-m, m/2)$, there exists an algorithm that computes 2^k collisions using $\widetilde{\mathcal{O}}\left(2^\ell\right)$ qubits and $\widetilde{\mathcal{O}}\left(2^{k+m/2-\ell/2}\right)$ quantum gates and quantum queries to f.

Organization. In Sect. 2 we provide several technical preliminaries on quantum algorithms, especially Grover's quantum search algorithm. Indeed, an MNRS quantum walk actually emulates a quantum search, and these results are helpful in analyzing the behavior of such a walk. In Sect. 3, we give important details on the MNRS framework, and in particular, the *vertex-coin encoding*, which is a subtlety often omitted from depictions of the framework in the previous literature. In Sect. 4 we detail our algorithm assuming a suitable quantum data structure is given, and in Sect. 5 we detail the *quantum radix trees*. While they were already proposed in [21], we give new (or previously omitted) details relative to the radix tree operations, memory allocation, and how we can efficiently and robustly extract collisions. We give a general summary of the multiple collision search problem in Sect. 6 and our applications in Sect. 7.

2   Preliminaries

In this section, we give some preliminaries on collision search, quantum algorithms and Grover search, which are important for the analysis of quantum walks and their data structures.

2.1   Collision Search

In this paper, we study the problem of *collision search* in random functions.

Problem 2. Let $f : \{0,1\}^n \to \{0,1\}^m$ $(n \le m)$ be a random function. Find a collision of f, that is, a pair $(x, y), x \ne y$ such that $f(x) = f(y)$.

The case $m < n$ can be solved by the same algorithms as the case $m = n$ by reducing f to a subset of its domain. This is why in the following, we focus only on $m \ge n$. The average number of collisions is $\mathcal{O}\left(2^{2n-m}\right)$. When $m \ge 2n$, we can assume that exactly one collision exists, or none. Distinguishing between these two cases is the problem of *element distinctness*, which is solved by searching for the collision. In all cases, the collision problem can be solved in:

- $\Theta(2^{m/2})$ classical time (and queries to f). When $m = n$, the problem is the easiest, as it requires only $\mathcal{O}\left(2^{n/2}\right)$ time and $\mathsf{poly}(n)$ memory using Pollard's rho method. When $m = 2n$, the problem is harder since the best algorithm also uses $\Theta(2^n)$ memory.
- $\Theta(2^{m/3})$ quantum time (and quantum queries to f). A first algorithm was given by Brassard, Høyer and Tapp to reach this for $m = n$ [8], then the lower bound was proven to be $\Omega(2^{m/3})$ [1], and afterwards, Ambainis solved the *element distinctness* problem (the case $m = 2n$) by a quantum walk algorithm [2] which can be adapted for any value of m.

In our case, we want to solve the problem of *multiple collision search*: as there will be expectedly many collisions in the outputs of f, we want to find a significant (exponential in n) number of them.

Problem 3. Let $f : \{0,1\}^n \to \{0,1\}^m$, $n \leq m \leq 2n$, $k \leq 2n - m$. Find 2^k distinct collisions of f.

Here the state of the art differ classically and quantumly:

- Classically, it is well known that the problem can be solved for any m and k in $\Theta(2^{(k+m)/2})$ queries (as long as 2^k does not exceed the average number of collisions of f).
- Quantumly, Liu and Zhandry [25] gave a query lower bound $\Omega(2^{2k/3+m/3})$. However, a matching algorithm is only known for small m. For example, this lower bound is matched for $m = n$ by adapting the BHT algorithm [17,25].

Note that we assume that the collision pairs are fully distinct. In the case $m < n$, $k \geq m$, there are not enough distinct images, and we only obtain multicollision tuples. The lower bound of [25] does not apply here. If $m < n$ and $k \leq m$, we restrict the inputs of the function to a set of size $\{0, 1\}^m$, and this case is covered by a variant of the BHT algorithm. Thus, like in the case of a single collision, we will only consider $n \leq m$.

On the Memory Complexity. For $m = n$, the best known classical algorithm for multiple collision-finding is the parallel collision search (PCS) algorithm by van Oorschot and Wiener [28]. It generalizes Pollard's rho method which finds a single collision in $\mathcal{O}\left(2^{n/2}\right)$ time and $\mathsf{poly}(n)$ memory. Dinur [12] showed that in this regime, the time-space trade-off of the PCS algorithm is optimal. Using a restricted model of computation, it can also be shown optimal for larger values of m.

Quantumly, a time-space lower bound of $T^3 S \geq \Omega\left(2^{3k+m}\right)$ has been shown [15]. However, the authors conjecture this bound can be improved to $T^2 S \geq \Omega\left(2^{2k+m}\right)$. All known quantum algorithms for collisions, including our new algorithms, match this conjectured lower bound.

2.2   Quantum Algorithms

We refer to [27] for an introduction to quantum computation. We write our quantum algorithms in the standard *quantum circuit model*, where algorithms are written as a sequence of standard *quantum gates*. We are interested in the minimal achievable gate count. This means that we do not consider any parallelization trade-offs, even though there is some literature on the topic for SVP algorithms [24]. By default, we use the (universal) Clifford+T gate set, although our complexity analysis remains asymptotic, and we do not detail our algorithms at the gate level.

Memory Models. Many memory-intensive quantum algorithms require some kind of *quantum random-access model* (qRAM), which can be stronger than the standard quantum circuit model. One can encounter two types of qRAM:

- Classical memory with quantum random access (QRACM): a classical memory of size M can be addressed *in quantum superposition* in polylog(M) operations.
- Quantum memory with quantum random access (QRAQM): M *qubits* can be addressed *in quantum superposition* in polylog(M) operations.

The QRAQM model is required by most quantum walk based algorithms for cryptographic problems, e.g., subset-sum [3,4], information set decoding [22] and the most recent quantum algorithm for lattice sieving [9]. It requires to augment the set of gates available with a "qRAM" gate addressing all M memory cells (e.g., individual bits) in superposition. In this paper, we use a definition taken from [2]:

$$|y_1, \ldots, y_M\rangle |x\rangle |i\rangle \xrightarrow{\text{qRAM}} |y_1, \ldots, y_{i-1}, x, y_{i+1}, \ldots y_M\rangle |y_i\rangle |i\rangle . \qquad (1)$$

This operation implies the ability to *read* in superposition by querying the cell at index i, but also to *write*. This is necessary for efficient data structures such as the ones studied in [2] or the *quantum radix trees* from the literature (see Sect. 5).

While the qRAM gate can be simulated with $\widetilde{O}(M)$ Clifford+T gates, in the following, the gate count of our algorithms is given asymptotically on the "Clifford + T + qRAM" gate set, so we assume the qRAM has unit cost, as is required by previous works.

Collision Finding Without qRAM. To date, the best quantum algorithms for collision finding, and the ones that reach the query lower bound, require the qRAM model: the BHT algorithm [8] uses QRACM and Ambainis' quantum walk uses QRAQM [2] to define gate-efficient quantum data structures. Initially Ambainis used a *skip list*. We will focus on the more recent *quantum radix tree*, but the QRAQM requirement remains the same.

To some extent, it is possible to get rid of qRAM. For $m = n$, the complexity rises from $O\left(2^{m/3}\right)$ to $O\left(2^{2m/5}\right)$ gates [10]. For $m = 2n$, the complexity rises to $O\left(2^{3m/7}\right)$ [20]. These algorithms can also be adapted for multiple collision finding, where they will outperform the classical ones for some parameter ranges (but not all).

2.3   Grover's Algorithm

In this section, we recall Grover's quantum search algorithm [14] and give a few necessary results for the rest of our analysis. Indeed, as shown in [26], an MNRS quantum walk actually emulates a quantum search, up to some error. If we manage to put this error aside, the analysis of the walk follows from the following lemmas.

Original Quantum Search. In the original setting of Grover's search, we have a function $g : \{0,1\}^n \to \{0,1\}$ and the goal is to find x st. $g(x) = 1$ using queries to g. In the quantum setting, we have access to the unitary $O_g : |x\rangle |b\rangle \to |x\rangle |b \oplus g(x)\rangle$, which is an efficient quantum unitary if g is efficiently computable. In particular we can compute $|\psi_U\rangle = \frac{1}{\sqrt{2^n}} \sum_{x \in \{0,1\}^n} |x\rangle |g(x)\rangle$ with a single call to O_g. Let $\varepsilon = \frac{|\{x : g(x) = 1\}|}{2^n}$. We also define the normalized states

$$|\psi_B\rangle = \frac{1}{\sqrt{(1 - \varepsilon)2^n}} \sum_{x:g(x)=0} |x\rangle |g(x)\rangle, \quad |\psi_G\rangle = \frac{1}{\sqrt{\varepsilon 2^n}} \sum_{x:g(x)=1} |x\rangle |g(x)\rangle$$

and $|\psi_U\rangle = \sqrt{1 - \varepsilon} |\psi_B\rangle + \sqrt{\varepsilon} |\psi_G\rangle$. Let $\mathcal{H} = \mathrm{span}(\{|\psi_B\rangle, |\psi_G\rangle\})$. Let Rot_θ be the θ-rotation unitary in $\mathcal{H}$:

$$\mathrm{Rot}_\theta(\cos(\alpha) |\phi_B\rangle + \sin(\alpha) |\psi_G\rangle) = \cos(\alpha + \theta) |\psi_B\rangle + \sin(\alpha + \theta) |\psi_G\rangle \ .$$

For a fixed ε, let $\alpha = \arcsin(\sqrt{\varepsilon})$ so that

$$|\phi_U\rangle = \sqrt{1 - \varepsilon} |\psi_B\rangle + \sqrt{\varepsilon} |\psi_G\rangle = \cos(\alpha) |\psi_B\rangle + \sin(\alpha) |\psi_G\rangle,$$

For a state $|\psi\rangle \in \mathcal{H}$, let $\mathrm{Ref}_{|\psi\rangle}$ be the reflection over $|\psi\rangle$ in $\mathcal{H}$:

$$Ref_{|\psi\rangle} |\psi\rangle = |\psi\rangle \quad \text{and} \quad Ref_{|\psi\rangle} |\psi^\perp\rangle = - |\psi^\perp\rangle$$

where $|\psi^\perp\rangle$ is any state in $\mathcal{H}$ orthogonal to $|\psi\rangle$[1] We have

$$\mathrm{Ref}_{|\psi_U\rangle} \mathrm{Ref}_{|\psi_B\rangle} = \mathrm{Rot}_{2\alpha} \ .$$

Assume that we have access to a *checking oracle* O_{check} which performs:

$$\begin{cases} O_{\mathrm{check}} |\psi_B\rangle |0\rangle = |\psi_B\rangle |0\rangle \\ O_{\mathrm{check}} |\psi_G\rangle |0\rangle = |\psi_G\rangle |1\rangle \end{cases}$$

In the standard setting described above, this is just copying the last register. Starting from an "initial state" $|\psi_U\rangle$, we apply repeatedly an iterate consisting of a reflection over $|\psi_U\rangle$, and a reflection over $|\psi_B\rangle$. This progressively transforms the current state into the "good state" $|\psi_G\rangle$. Typically $\mathrm{Ref}_{|\psi_U\rangle}$ is constructed from a circuit that computes $|\psi_U\rangle$ and $\mathrm{Ref}_{|\psi_B\rangle}$ is implemented using the checking oracle above: in that case, we are actually performing an *amplitude amplification* [7].

Proposition 1 (Grover's algorithm, known α). *Consider the following algorithm, with $\alpha \leq \pi/4$:*

1. *Start from $|\psi_U\rangle$.*
2. *Apply $\mathrm{Rot}_{2\alpha} = \mathrm{Ref}_{|\psi_U\rangle} \mathrm{Ref}_{|\psi_B\rangle}$ N times on $|\psi_U\rangle$ with $N = \lfloor \frac{\pi/2 - \alpha}{2\alpha} \rfloor$.*
3. *Apply O_{check} and measure the last qubit.*

---

[1] For a fixed $|\psi\rangle$, $|\psi^\perp\rangle$ is actually unique up to a global phase.

This procedure measures 1 wp. at least $1 - 4\alpha^2$ and the resulting state is $|\psi_G\rangle$.

Proof. Let us define $\gamma = \alpha + 2N\alpha$. We have

$$(Rot_{2\alpha})^n |\psi_U\rangle = \cos(\alpha + 2N\alpha)|\psi_B\rangle + \sin(\alpha + 2N\alpha)|\psi_G\rangle = \cos(\gamma)|\psi_B\rangle + \sin(\gamma)|\psi_G\rangle.$$

Notice that we chose N st. $\gamma \leq \frac{\pi}{2} < \gamma + 2\alpha$ so $\frac{\pi}{2} - \gamma \in [0, 2\alpha)$. After applying the checking oracle, we obtain the state

$$\cos(\gamma)|\psi_B\rangle|0\rangle + \sin(\gamma)|\psi_G\rangle|1\rangle.$$

Measuring the last qubit gives outcome 1 with probability $\sin^2(\gamma)$ and the resulting state in the first register is $|\psi_G\rangle$. In order to conclude, we compute

$$\sin^2(\gamma) = \cos^2(\pi/2 - \gamma) \geq \cos^2(2\alpha) \geq 1 - 4\alpha^2. \qquad \square$$

In our algorithms, we will start not from the uniform superposition $|\psi_U\rangle$, but from the *bad subspace* $|\psi_B\rangle$. We show that this makes little difference.

Proposition 2. (Starting from $|\psi_B\rangle$, known α). *Consider the following algorithm, with $\alpha \leq \pi/4$:*

1. *Start from $|\psi_B\rangle$.*
2. *Apply $Rot_{2\alpha} = \text{Ref}_{|\psi_U\rangle}\text{Ref}_{|\psi_B\rangle}$ N' times on $|\psi_B\rangle$ with $N' = \lfloor \frac{\pi/2}{2\alpha} \rfloor$.*
3. *Apply the checking oracle and measure the last qubit.*

This procedure measures 1 with probability at least $1 - 4\alpha^2$ and the resulting state is $|\psi_G\rangle$.

Proof. The proof is essentially the same as the previous one. Let $\gamma' = 2N'\alpha$. We have

$$(Rot_{2\alpha})^{N'}|\psi_B\rangle = \cos(2N'\alpha)|\psi_B\rangle + \sin(2N'\alpha)|\psi_G\rangle = \cos(\gamma')|\psi_B\rangle + \sin(\gamma')|\psi_G\rangle.$$

Notice that we chose N' st. $\gamma' \leq \frac{\pi}{2} < \gamma' + 2\alpha$ so $\frac{\pi}{2} - \gamma' \in [0, 2\alpha)$. After applying the checking oracle, we obtain the state

$$\cos(\gamma')|\psi_B\rangle|0\rangle + \sin(\gamma')|\psi_G\rangle|1\rangle.$$

Measuring the last qubit gives 1 wp. $\sin^2(\gamma')$ and the resulting state in the first register is $|\phi_G\rangle$. In order to conclude, we compute

$$\sin^2(\gamma') = \cos^2(\pi/2 - \gamma') \geq \cos^2(2\alpha) \geq 1 - 4\alpha^2. \qquad \square$$

After applying the check and measuring, if we don't succeed, we obtain the state $|\psi_B\rangle$ again. So we can run the quantum search again.

In Grover's algorithm, we have a procedure to construct $|\psi_U\rangle$ and we use this procedure to initialize the algorithm and to perform the operation $\text{Ref}_{|\psi_U\rangle}$. A quantum walk will have the same general structure as Grover's algorithm, but we will manipulate very large states $|\psi_U\rangle$. Though $|\psi_U\rangle$ is long to construct (the *setup* operation), performing $\text{Ref}_{|\psi_U\rangle}$ will be less costly.

In the MNRS framework, $|\psi_U\rangle$ is chosen as the unique eigenvector of eigenvalue 1 of an operator related to a random walk in a graph. To perform $\text{Ref}_{|\psi_U\rangle}$ efficiently, we use phase estimation on this operator.

3   Quantum Walks for Collision Finding

In this section, we present MNRS quantum walks, which underlie most cryptographic applications of quantum walks to date, and give important details on their actual implementation using a *vertex-coin encoding*.

3.1   Definition and Example

We consider a regular, undirected graph $G = (V, E)$, which in cryptographic applications (e.g., collision search), is usually a Johnson graph (as in this paper) or a product of Johnson graphs (a case detailed e.g. in [22]).

Definition 1 (Johnson graph). *The Johnson graph $J(N, R)$ is a regular, undirected graph whose vertices are the subsets of $[N]$ containing R elements, with an edge between two vertices v and v' iff $|v \cap v'| = R - 1$. In other words, v is adjacent to v' if v' can be obtained from v by removing an element and adding an element from $[N] \backslash v$ in its place.*

In collision search, a vertex in the graph specifies a set of R inputs to the function f under study, where its domain $\{0, 1\}^n$ is identified with $[2^n]$. Let $M \subseteq V$ be a set of *marked* vertices, e.g., all the subsets $S \subseteq \{0, 1\}^n$ which contain a collision of f: $\exists x, y \in S, x \neq y, f(x) = f(y)$. A classical *random walk* on G finds a marked vertex using Algorithm 1.

Algorithm 1: Classical random walk on G

Setup an arbitrary vertex $x \in V$
repeat
  repeat
    Update: move to a random adjacent vertex
  until *the current vertex is uniformly random*
  Check if the current vertex is marked
until *the current vertex is marked*

The quantum walk is analogous to this process. Let $\varepsilon = \frac{|M|}{|V|}$ be the proportion of marked vertices and δ be the spectral gap of G. Starting from any vertex, after $\mathcal{O}\left(\frac{1}{\delta}\right)$ updates, we sample a vertex of the graph uniformly at random. For a Johnson graph $J(N, R)$, $\delta = \frac{N}{R(N-R)} \simeq \frac{1}{R}$. Let S be the time to **Setup**, U the time to **Update**, C the time to **Check** a given vertex. Then Algorithm 1 finds a marked vertex in time: $\mathcal{O}\left(S + \frac{1}{\varepsilon}\left(\frac{1}{\delta}U + C\right)\right)$. Magniez *et al.* [26] show how to translate this generically in the quantum setting, provided that quantum analogs of these operations (SETUP, UPDATE, CHECK) can be implemented.

Theorem 1 (From [26]). *Assume that quantum algorithms SETUP, UPDATE and CHECK are given. Then there exists a quantum algorithm that* finds a marked vertex with gate count: $\widetilde{\mathcal{O}}\left(\mathsf{S} + \frac{1}{\sqrt{\varepsilon}}\left(\frac{1}{\sqrt{\delta}}\mathsf{U} + \mathsf{C}\right)\right)$ instead of $\mathcal{O}\left(\frac{1}{\sqrt{\varepsilon}}\left(\mathsf{S} + \mathsf{C}\right)\right)$ with a naive search.

Using this framework generically, we can recover the complexity of Ambainis' algorithm for collision search: $\widetilde{\mathcal{O}}\left(2^{m/3}\right)$ for any codomain bit-size m. We use the Johnson graph $J(2^n, 2^{m/3})$. Its spectral gap is approximately $2^{-m/3}$. A vertex is marked if and only if it contains a collision, so the probability of being marked is approximately $2^{2m/3-m} = 2^{-m/3}$. Using a quantum data structure for unordered sets, we can implement SETUP in gate count $\widetilde{\mathcal{O}}\left(2^{m/3}\right)$, UPDATE and CHECK in $\mathsf{poly}(n)$. The formula of Theorem 1 gives the complexity $\widetilde{\mathcal{O}}\left(2^{m/3}\right)$.

3.2   Details of the MNRS Framework

In the d-regular graph $G = (V, E)$, for each $x \in V$, let N_x be the set of neighbors of x, of size d. In the case $G = J(N, R)$, we have $d = R(N - R)$. For a vertex x, let $|x\rangle$ be an arbitrary encoding of x as a quantum state, let $D(x)$ be a *data structure* associated to x, and let $|\widehat{x}\rangle = |x\rangle\,|D(x)\rangle$.

Remark 1. The encoding of x is commonly thought of as the set itself, and the data structure as the images of the set by f. But whenever we look at quantum walks from the perspective of gate count (and not query complexity), an efficient quantum data structure is already required for x itself, i.e., an unordered set data structure in the case of a Johnson graph, and one cannot really separate x from $D(x)$. This is why we will favor the notation $|\widehat{x}\rangle$.

For a vertex x, let $|p_x\rangle$ be the uniform superposition over its neighbors: $|p_x\rangle = \frac{1}{\sqrt{d}}\sum_{y \in N_x}|y\rangle$, and: $|\widehat{p_x}\rangle = \frac{1}{\sqrt{d}}\sum_{y \in N_x}|\widehat{y}\rangle$. From now on, we consider a walk on *edges* rather than vertices in the graph, and introduce:

$$\begin{cases} |\psi_U\rangle = \frac{1}{\sqrt{|V|}}\sum_{x \in V}|\widehat{x}\rangle\,|p_x\rangle & \text{the superposition of vertices (and neighbors)} \\ |\psi_M\rangle = \frac{1}{\sqrt{|M|}}\sum_{x \in M}|\widehat{x}\rangle\,|p_x\rangle & \text{the superposition of marked vertices} \\ A = \mathrm{span}\{|\widehat{x}\rangle\,|p_x\rangle\}_{x \in V} \\ B = \mathrm{span}\{|\widehat{p_y}\rangle\,|y\rangle\}_{y \in V} \end{cases}$$

Let Ref_A and Ref_B be respectively the reflection over the space A and the space B. The core of the MNRS framework is to use these operations to emulate a reflection over $|\psi_U\rangle$. By alternating such reflections with reflections over $|\psi_M\rangle$ (using the checking procedure), the quantum walk behaves exactly as a quantum search, and the analysis of Sect. 2.3 applies.

Proposition 3 (From [26]). *Let $W = \mathrm{Ref}_B\mathrm{Ref}_A$. We have $\langle\psi_U|\,W\,|\psi_U\rangle = 1$. For any other eigenvector $|\psi\rangle$ of W, we have $\langle\psi|\,W\,|\psi\rangle = e^{i\theta}$ with $\theta \in [2\sqrt{\delta}, \pi/2]$.*

To reflect over $|\psi_U\rangle$, we perform a *phase estimation* of the unitary W, which allows to separate the part with eigenvalue 1, from the part with eigenvalue $e^{i\theta}$

with $\theta \in [2\sqrt{\delta}, \pi/2]$. The phase estimation circuit needs to call W a total of $\mathcal{O}\left(\frac{1}{\sqrt{\delta}}\right)$ times to estimate θ up to sufficient precision. It has some error, which can be made insignificant with a polynomial increase in complexity; thus in the following, we will consider the reflection Ref_U to be exact.

To construct W, we need to implement Ref_A and Ref_B. We first remark that:

$$\text{Ref}_B = \text{SWUP} \circ \text{Ref}_A \circ \text{SWUP} \ , \tag{2}$$

where $\text{SWUP} |\widehat{x}\rangle |y\rangle = |\widehat{y}\rangle |x\rangle$. This SWUP (Swap-Update) operation can furthermore be decomposed into an update of the database (UP_D) followed by a register swap:

$$|\widehat{x}\rangle |y\rangle = |x\rangle |D(x)\rangle |y\rangle \xrightarrow{\text{UP}_D} |x\rangle |D(y)\rangle |y\rangle \xrightarrow{\text{Swap}} |y\rangle |D(y)\rangle |x\rangle = |\widehat{y}\rangle |x\rangle \ , \tag{3}$$

so $\text{SWUP} = \text{Swap} \circ \text{UP}_D$.

We would then implement Ref_A using an update unitary that, from a vertex x, constructs the uniform superposition of neighbors. However this would require us to write $\log_2(|V|)$ data, and in practice, $|V|$ is doubly exponential (the vertex is represented by an exponential number of bits). Thankfully, in d-regular graphs, and in particular in Johnson graphs, we can avoid this loophole by making the encoding of edges more compact. Instead of storing a pair of vertices (x, y), which will eventually result in having to rewrite entire vertices, we can store a single vertex and a *direction*, or *coin*.

3.3 Vertex-Coin Encoding

The encoding is a reversible operation: $O_{\text{Enc}} |\widehat{x}\rangle |y\rangle = |\widehat{x}\rangle |c_{x \to y}\rangle$, which compresses an edge (x, y) by replacing y by a much smaller register of size $\lceil \log_2(d) \rceil$. Note that we only need the *existence* of such a circuit. We never use it during the algorithms; all operations are directly performed using the compact encoding.

Let $|\psi_{\text{Unif}}^{coin}\rangle = \frac{1}{\sqrt{d}} \sum_c |c\rangle$ be the uniform superposition of coins. In the vertex-coin encoding, Ref_A corresponds to $I \otimes Ref_{|\psi_{\text{Unif}}^{coin}\rangle}$:

$$\text{Ref}_A = O_{\text{Enc}}^{-1} \circ \left(I \otimes \text{Ref}_{|\psi_{\text{Unif}}^{coin}\rangle}\right) \circ O_{\text{Enc}}.$$

Now, for the SWUP operation, we have to decompose again UP_D and Swap in the encoded space. First, we define UP_D' such that:

$$|x\rangle |D(x)\rangle |c_{x \to y}\rangle \xrightarrow{UP_D'} |x\rangle |D(y)\rangle |c_{x \to y}\rangle .$$

Moreover, we define Swap′ such that:

$$|x\rangle |c_{x \to y}\rangle \xrightarrow{\text{Swap}'} |y\rangle |c_{y \to x}\rangle .$$

and we define $\text{SWUP}' = \text{Swap}' \circ \text{UP}_D'$ (we abuse notation here, by extending Swap′ where we apply the identity to the middle register), so:

$$\text{SWUP}' |\widehat{x}\rangle |c_{x \to y}\rangle = |\widehat{y}\rangle |c_{y \to x}\rangle \ ,$$

and $\text{SWUP}' = O_{\text{Enc}} \circ \text{SWUP} \circ O_{\text{Enc}}^{-1}$. So we define

$$\begin{cases} \text{Ref}'_A = I \otimes \text{Ref}_{|\psi^{coin}_{\text{Unif}}\rangle} = O_{\text{Enc}} \circ Ref_A \circ O_{\text{Enc}}^{-1} \\ \text{Ref}'_B = \text{SWUP}' \circ \text{Ref}'_A \circ \text{SWUP}' = O_{\text{Enc}} \circ \text{Ref}_B \circ O_{\text{Enc}}^{-1} \\ W' = \text{Ref}'_B \circ \text{Ref}'_A \end{cases} \qquad (4)$$

By putting everything together, we have $W' = O_{\text{Enc}} \circ W \circ O_{\text{Enc}}^{-1}$. Since O_{Enc} is a unitary operator, W and W' are unitarily equivalent, i.e., they have the same eigenvalues. Thus, Proposition 3 applies to W' the same as it does to W, and gives its spectral properties. We can perform phase estimation on W', and combine afterwards with Proposition 1. Since constructing the uniform superposition of coins is trivial, all relies on the unitary SWUP'.

Theorem 2 (MNRS, adapted). *Let $|\widehat{x}\rangle$ be an encoding of the vertex x (incl. data structure) and assume that a vertex-coin encoding is given. Let $\alpha = \arcsin\sqrt{\varepsilon}$. Starting from the state: $\frac{1}{\sqrt{|V|}}\sum_{x\in V}|\widehat{x}\rangle\,|\psi^{coin}_{\text{Unif}}\rangle$, apply $\left\lfloor \frac{\pi/2-\alpha}{2\alpha} \right\rfloor$ iterates of: • a checking procedure which flips the phase of marked vertices; • a phase estimation of W'; then apply the checking again and measure. With probability at least $1 - 4\alpha^2$, we measure 1 and collapse on the uniform superposition of marked vertices.*

Finally, we can adapt this analysis by starting from the bad vertices, with a proof that is the same as Proposition 2. This will be the main building block of our new algorithm.

Theorem 3 (MNRS, starting from bad vertices). *Starting from the state: $\frac{1}{\sqrt{|V|-|M|}}\sum_{x\in V\backslash M}|\widehat{x}\rangle\,|\psi^{coin}_{\text{Unif}}\rangle$ (the superposition of unmarked vertices), apply $\left\lfloor \frac{\pi/2}{2\alpha} \right\rfloor$ iterates of: • a checking procedure which flips the phase of marked vertices; • a phase estimation of W'; then apply the checking again and measure. With probability at least $1 - 4\alpha^2$, we measure 1 and collapse on the uniform superposition of marked vertices. Otherwise, we collapse on the uniform superposition of unmarked vertices.*

Coins for a Johnson Graph. In a Johnson graph $J(N, R)$, a coin $c = (j, z)$ is a pair where:

- $j \in [R]$ is the index of the element that will be removed from the current vertex (given an arbitrary ordering, e.g. the lexicographic ordering of bitstrings).
- $z \in [N - R]$ is the index of an element that does not belong to the current vertex, and will be added as a replacement.

4   A Chained Quantum Walk to Find Many Collisions

In this section, we prove our main result.

Theorem 4. *Let $f : \{0,1\}^n \to \{0,1\}^m$, $n \leq m \leq 2n$ be a random function. Let $k \leq \min(2n - m, m/4)$. There exists a quantum algorithm making $\mathcal{O}\left(2^{2k/3+m/3}\right)$ quantum queries to f and using $\tilde{\mathcal{O}}\left(2^{2k/3+m/3}\right)$ Clifford+T+qRAM gates, that outputs 2^k collision pairs of f.*

Our new algorithm, which is detailed in Sect. 4.1 and Sect. 4.2, solves the case $k \leq \frac{m}{4}$. The case $k \leq 2n - m$ was already solved by adapting the BHT algorithm, as detailed in Sect. 6.

Note that if we are only interested in the query complexity, our technique is still necessary to improve over previous results, but the radix tree data structure that we detail in Sect. 5 can be replaced by a simple ordered list with expensive update operations (see [19]).

4.1   New Algorithm

We detail here our *chained quantum walk* algorithm. Recall that the Johnson graph $J(N, R)$ is the regular, undirected graph whose vertices are subsets of size R of $[N]$, and edges connect each pair of vertices which differ in exactly one element. We identify $[N]$ with $\{0,1\}^n$, the domain of f.

We assume that an efficient quantum unordered set data structure is given, which makes vertices in the Johnson graph correspond to quantum states, while allowing to implement efficiently the operations required for the MNRS quantum walks. It will be detailed in Sect. 5. In the following we write $|S\rangle$ for the quantum state corresponding to a set S.

Idea of Our Algorithm. After running a quantum walk on a Johnson graph, we obtain a superposition of vertices which contain a collision. We remove the collision from the vertex, and we measure the elements that form this collision: we still obtain a superposition of sets, which might be exploited for the next walk. The sets in this superposition have a very important property: because we just removed the collision (more generally, we will remove all collisions that the vertex contains), they actually *do not* contain one with certainty. Thus, we do not have the uniform superposition of vertices of our next MNRS walk, but the uniform superposition of *unmarked* vertices. However, we have seen that this made little difference, and we can continue using Theorem 3. When we measure the result of a walk step, it will succeed with at least constant probability. In the case of failure, we collapse on the superposition of unmarked vertices again, which means we simply have to restart the walk. The extraction of collisions modifies the walk parameters (vertex size, graph, marked vertices) in a way that we track throughout the algorithm, and is detailed below.

Technical Details. Let C be a table in classical memory of all the multi-collisions found so far. This table contains entries of the form: $u : (x_1, \ldots, x_r)$ where $f(x_1) = \ldots = f(x_r) = u$ forms a multicollision of f, indexed by the image. We define the *size* of C, its set of *preimages* and its set of *images*:

$$\begin{cases} \mathsf{Preim}(C) := \bigcup_{u:(x_1,\ldots,x_r) \in C} \{x_1, \ldots, x_r\} \\ \mathsf{Im}(C) := \bigcup_{u:(x_1,\ldots,x_r) \in C} \{u\} \end{cases} \tag{5}$$

Given the table C, given a size parameter R, we define the two sets of sets:

$$\begin{cases} V_R^C := \{S \subseteq (\{0,1\}^n \backslash \mathsf{Preim}(C)), |S| = R\} \\ M_R^C := \{S \subseteq (\{0,1\}^n \backslash \mathsf{Preim}(C)), |S| = R, \\ \qquad (\exists x \neq y \in S, f(x) = f(y) \vee \exists z \in S, f(z) \in \mathsf{Im}(C))\} \end{cases} \tag{6}$$

The first one will be the set of vertices for the current walk, and the second one its set of *marked* vertices. As we can see, the current walk excludes a set of previously measured inputs, and a vertex is marked if it leads to a new collision, *or* to a preimage of one of the previously measured images. The second case simply extends one of the currently known multicollision tuples. The probability for a vertex to be marked can be easily computed, and we just need to bound it as follows:

$$\max\left(\frac{R|\mathsf{Im}(C)|}{2^m}, \frac{R(R-1)}{2^{m+1}}\right) \leq \varepsilon_{R,C} \leq \frac{R|\mathsf{Im}(C)|}{2^m} + \frac{R(R-1)}{2^{m+1}},$$

since any vertex containing a collision, or a preimage from the table C, is marked.

In Sect. 5, we will show that with an appropriate data structure, there exists an *extraction* algorithm EXTRACT which does the following:

$$\text{EXTRACT} : C, R, \frac{1}{\sqrt{|M_R^C|}} \sum_{S \in M_R^C} |S\rangle \mapsto C', R', \frac{1}{\sqrt{|V_{R'}^{C'} \backslash M_{R'}^{C'}|}} \sum_{S \in V_{R'}^{C'} \backslash M_{R'}^{C'}} |S\rangle ,$$

where $R' = R - r$ for some value r, and C' contains exactly r new elements (collisions adding new entries, or preimages going into previous entries). Thus, EXTRACT transforms the output of a successful walk into the set of *unmarked vertices* for the next walk.

We can now give Algorithm 2, depending on a tunable parameter ℓ.

4.2   Complexity Analysis

Theorem 5 (Time-memory tradeoff). *For all* $k \leq \ell \leq \min(2k/3 + m/3, m/2)$, *Algorithm 2 computes* 2^k *collisions using* $\tilde{O}\left(2^\ell\right)$ *qubits and* $\tilde{O}\left(2^{k+m/2-\ell/2}\right)$ *Clifford+T+qRAM gates.*

Proof. We start by noticing that although Algorithm 2 outputs a set of multicollisions rather than collisions, the number of collisions and multicollisions

---

Algorithm 2: Chained quantum walk algorithm for multiple collisions.

Input: quantum access to $f : \{0,1\}^n \to \{0,1\}^m$, parameter k
Output: a table of multicollisions C such that $|\mathsf{Im}(C)| \geq 2^k$
$C \leftarrow \emptyset$, $R \leftarrow 2^\ell$ /* Initialize an empty table   */
$|\psi\rangle \leftarrow \sum_{S \in V^C_{2^\ell}} |S\rangle$ /* SETUP   */

while $|\mathsf{Im}(C)| < 2^k$ **do**

> Run the quantum walk:
> - Starting state: $|\psi\rangle = \sum_{S \in V^C_R \setminus M^C_R} |S\rangle$
> - Graph: $J(\{0,1\}^n \setminus \mathsf{Preim}(C), R)$ (Johnson graph with vertices of size R, excluding the preimages of C)
> - Marked vertices: M^C_R
> - Iterates: $\lfloor (\pi/2)/(2\alpha) \rfloor$, where $\alpha = \arcsin \sqrt{\varepsilon_{R,C}}$
> - Spectral gap: $\delta \simeq \frac{1}{R}$
>
> Apply CHECK and measure the result: let flag be the output
> **if** *flag is true* **then**
>> /* The state collapses on: $\sum_{S \in M^C_R} |S\rangle$ */
>> Apply EXTRACT (contains measurements)
>>
>> - Update the table C
>> - Update the current width R
>> - Update the state: $|\psi\rangle = \sum_{S \in V^C_R \setminus M^C_R} |S\rangle$
>
> /* Otherwise, the state collapses on: $\sum_{S \in V^C_R \setminus M^C_R} |S\rangle$ for the previous R and C. There is nothing to extract from it, C and R remain unchanged.   */

return C

---

that are actually obtained are closely related. Indeed, for a function from $[2^n]$ to $[2^n]$, there is a polynomial (in n) limit to the width of multicollisions that can appear for a non-negligible fraction of the functions. Indeed, by Theorem 4 in [13], the average number of r-collisions in such a random function is $\frac{2^n e^{-1}}{r!}$. Thus, there exists a universal constant c such that with probability $1 - o(2^{-n})$, such a random function does not have any r-collision with $r \geq cn$.

This means that regardless of the state of the current table C, we have:

$$|\mathsf{Im}(C)| \leq |\mathsf{Preim}(C)| \leq cn|\mathsf{Im}(C)| \ .$$

In particular, by taking 2^ℓ greater than $cn2^{k+1}$, we ensure that during the algorithm, $R > 2^{\ell-1}$. This means that we never run out of elements.

Secondly, we can bound $\varepsilon_{R,C} \geq \frac{R(R-1)}{2^{m+1}}$. This allows to upper bound easily the time complexity of any of the walks: if the current vertex size is R then it runs for $\mathcal{O}\left(2^{m/2}/R\right)$ iterates, and each iterate contains $\widetilde{\mathcal{O}}\left(\sqrt{R}\right)$ operations. The constants in the $\mathcal{O}$ are the same throughout the algorithm. This means that we can upper bound the complexity of each walk by $\widetilde{\mathcal{O}}\left(2^{m/2}/\sqrt{R}\right) \leq \widetilde{\mathcal{O}}\left(2^{m/2-\ell/2}\right)$.

By Theorem 3, the success probability of this walk is bigger than $1 - 4\varepsilon_{R,C}$. If we do not succeed, the CHECK followed by a measurement make the current state collapse again on the superposition of unmarked vertices, and we run the exact same walk again. Note that for this algorithm to work, we must have $\varepsilon_{R,C} < 0.5$. This corresponds to the probability that the list contains a collision, or a new preimage of $\mathsf{Im}(C)$, which is $\tilde{\mathcal{O}}\left(2^{2\ell-m}\right)$. Hence, we must have $\ell \leq m/2$.

Then, as $\ell \leq 2k/3 + m/3$, the final complexity of the algorithm is

$$\tilde{\mathcal{O}}\left(2^{\ell} + 2^{k}2^{m/2-\ell/2}\right) = \tilde{\mathcal{O}}\left(2^{k+m/2-\ell/2}\right),$$

where 2^{ℓ} is the cost of the SETUP, and the second term accounts for all the walk steps.   □

5   Quantum Radix Trees and Extractions

In this section, we detail the *quantum radix tree* data structure, a history-independent unordered set data structure introduced in [21]. We show that it allows to perform, exactly and in a polynomial number of Clifford+T+qRAM gates, the two main operations required for our walk: SWUP′ and EXTRACT. We describe these operations in pseudocode, while ensuring that they are reversible and polynomial.

5.1   Logical Level

Following [21], the *quantum radix tree* is an implementation of a radix tree storing an unordered set S of n-bit strings. It has one additional property: its concrete memory layout is history-independent. Indeed, there are many ways to encode a radix tree in memory, and as elements are inserted and removed, we cannot have a unique bit-string $T(S)$ representing a set S. We use instead a uniform superposition of all memory layouts of the tree, which makes the *quantum state* $|T(S)\rangle$ unique, and independent of the order in which the elements were inserted or removed. Only the entry point (the root) has a fixed position.

We separate the encoding of S into $|T(S)\rangle$ in two levels: first, a *logical level*, in which S is encoded as a unique radix tree $R(S)$; second, a *physical level*, in which $R(S)$ is encoded into a quantum state $|T(S)\rangle$. The logical mapping $S \to R(S)$ is standard.

Definition 2 (From [21]). *Let S be a set of n-bit strings. The radix tree $R(S)$ is a binary tree in which each leaf is labeled with an element of S, and each edge with a substring, so that the concatenation of all substrings on the path from the root to the leaf yields the corresponding element. Furthermore, the labels of two children of any non-leaf node start with different bits.*

By convention, we put the "0" bit on the left, and "1" on the right. In addition to the n-bit strings stored by the tree, we append to each node the value of an ℓ-bit *invariant* which can be computed from its children, and depends only on the logical structure of the radix tree, not its physical structure. Typically the invariant can count the number of elements in the tree.

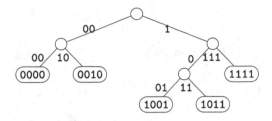

Fig. 2. Tree $R(S)$ representing the set $S = \{0000, 0010, 1001, 1011, 1111\}$ (the example is taken from [21]).

5.2 Memory Representation

We now detail the correspondence from $R(S)$ to $|T(S)\rangle$. We suppose that a quantum *bit-string data structure* is given, that handles bit-strings of length between 0 and n and performs operations such as concatenation, computing shared prefixes, testing if the bit-string has a given prefix, in time poly(n).

State of the Memory. We suppose that $\mathcal{O}(Mn)$ qubits of memory are given, where $M \geq R$ will be set later on. We divide these qubits into M *cells* of $\mathcal{O}(n)$ qubits each, which we index from 0 to $M - 1$. We encode cell addresses on $m = \lceil \log_2 M \rceil + 1$ bits, and we also define an "empty" address $\perp$. Each cell will be either empty, or contain a node of the radix tree, encoded as a tuple $(i, a_l, a_r, \ell_l, \ell_r)$ where:

- i is the value of the invariant
- a_l and a_r (m-bit strings) are respectively the memory addresses of the cells holding the left and right children, either valid indices or $\perp$. A node with $a_l = a_r = \perp$ is a leaf.
- ℓ_l and ℓ_r are the labels of the left and right edges. (ε if the node is a leaf, where ε is the empty string).

In other words, we have added to the tree $R(S)$ a choice of memory locations for the nodes, which we name informally the *memory layout* of the tree. The structure of $R(S)$ itself remains independent on its memory layout.

The root of the tree is stored in cell number 0. In Fig. 3, we give an example of a memory representation of the tree $R(S)$ of Fig. 2. We take as invariant the number of leaves which, at the root, gives the number of elements in the set. It is important to note that memory cells have an "empty" default state, which allows the radix tree to support size changes. Whether a cell is empty or not depends on the memory layout.

A radix tree encoding a set of size R contains $2R - 1$ nodes (including the root), which means that we need (a priori) no more than $M = 2R - 1$ cells in our memory. In addition to the bit-strings x, we could add any data d_x to which x serves as a unique index. (This means adding another register which is non-empty for leaf nodes only). Finally, it is possible to account for multiplicity of elements in the tree by adding multiplicity counters, but since this is unnecessary for our applications, we will stick to the case of unique indices.

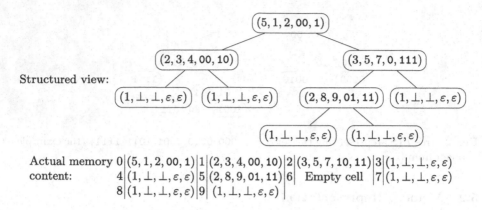

Structured view:

Actual memory content:

$0|(5,1,2,00,1)|1|(2,3,4,00,10)|2|(3,5,7,10,11)|3|(1,\perp,\perp,\varepsilon,\varepsilon)$
$4|(1,\perp,\perp,\varepsilon,\varepsilon)|5|(2,8,9,01,11)|6|$ Empty cell $|7|(1,\perp,\perp,\varepsilon,\varepsilon)$
$8|(1,\perp,\perp,\varepsilon,\varepsilon)|9|(1,\perp,\perp,\varepsilon,\varepsilon)|$

Fig. 3. Example of memory layout for the tree of Fig. 2, holding the set $S = \{0000, 0010, 1001, 1011, 1111\}$.

Definition. Let S be a set of size R, encoded in a radix tree with $2R-1$ nodes. We can always take an arbitrary ordering of the nodes in the tree, for example the lexicographic ordering of the paths to the root (left $= 0$, right $= 1$). This means that, for any sequence of non-repeating cell addresses I, of length $2R-1$, we can define a mapping: $S, I \mapsto T_I(S)$ which specifies the writing of the tree in memory, by choosing the addresses $I = (i_1 = 0, \dots, i_{2R-1})$ for the elements. For example, the tree of Fig. 3 would correspond to the sequence $(0, 1, 3, 4, 2, 5, 8, 9, 7)$. We can then define the *quantum radix tree encoding* S as the quantum state:

$$|T(S)\rangle = \sum_{\text{valid sequences } I} |T_I(S)\rangle \ , \tag{7}$$

where we take a uniform superposition over all valid memory layouts.

For two different sets S and S', and for any pair I, I' (even if $I' = I$), we have $T_{I'}(S) \neq T_I(S')$: the encodings always differ. This means that, as expected, we have $\langle T(S)|T(S')\rangle = 0$.

Memory Allocator. In order to maintain this uniform superposition over all possible memory layouts, we need an implementation of a *memory allocator*. This unitary ALLOC takes as input the current state of the memory, and returns a uniform superposition over the indices of all currently unoccupied cells. Possible implementations of ALLOC are detailed in Sect. 5.4.

5.3   Basic Operations

We show how to operate on the quantum radix trees in poly(n) Clifford+T +qRAM gates. We start with the basics: lookup, insertion and deletion.

Lookup. We define a unitary LOOKUP which, given S and a new element x, returns whether x belongs to S:

$$\text{LOOKUP} : |x\rangle |T(S)\rangle |0\rangle \mapsto |x\rangle |T(S)\rangle |x \in S\rangle \ . \tag{8}$$

Algorithm 3: LOOKUP as a classical algorithm.

Input: element x, quantum radix tree $T(S)$
Output: whether $x \in S$
$(i, a_l, a_r, \ell_l, \ell_r) \leftarrow$ root
$y \leftarrow \varepsilon$ (empty string)
while $a_l \neq \bot$ *(node is not a leaf)* **do**
    if $y||\ell_l$ *is a prefix of* x **then**
        $y \leftarrow y||a_l$
        $(i, a_l, a_r, \ell_l, \ell_r) \leftarrow$ node at address a_l
    else if $y||\ell_r$ *is a prefix of* x **then**
        $y \leftarrow y||a_l$
        $(i, a_l, a_r, \ell_l, \ell_r) \leftarrow$ node at address a_r
    else
        Break (not a solution)
return *true if* $y = x$

We implement LOOKUP by descending in the radix tree $R(S)$; the pseudocode is given in Algorithm 3. Since the "while" loop contains at most n iterates, quantumly these n iterates are performed controlled on a flag that says whether the computation already ended. After obtaining the result, they are recomputed to erase the intermediate registers.

Insertion. We define a unitary INSERT, which, given a new element x, inserts x in the set S. If x already belongs to S, its behavior is unspecified.

$$\text{INSERT} \; : |x\rangle \, |T(S)\rangle \mapsto |x\rangle \, |T(S \cup \{x\})\rangle \; . \tag{9}$$

The implementation of INSERT is more complex, but the operation is still reversible. The pseudocode is given in Algorithm 4. At first, we find the point of insertion in the tree, then we call ALLOC twice to obtain new memory addresses for two new nodes. We modify locally the layout to insert these new nodes, including a new leaf for the new element x. Then, we update the invariant on the path to the new leaf. Finally, we uncompute the path to the new leaf (all the addresses of the nodes on this path). To do so, we perform a loop similar to LOOKUP, given the knowledge of the newly inserted element x.

Deletion. The deletion can be implemented by uncomputing INSERT, since it is a reversible operation. It performs:

$$\text{INSERT}^\dagger \; : |x\rangle \, |T(S \cup \{x\})\rangle \mapsto |x\rangle \, |T(S)\rangle \; . \tag{10}$$

Algorithm 4: INSERT as a classical algorithm.

Input: element x, quantum radix tree $T(S)$
Output: element x, quantum radix tree $T(S \cup \{x\})$
Find the first node $j_1 : (i, a_l, a_r, \ell_l, \ell_r)$ such that y is a prefix of x, $y||\ell_l$ is not a prefix of x and $y||\ell_r$ is not a prefix of x either. Write all the addresses of the nodes on the path from the root to j_1

```
/* If at this point we have found that the element belongs to S
   instead, then the rest of the computation is meaningless.      */
/* By construction ℓ_l starts with 0 and ℓ_r starts with 1. One of them
   shares a non-empty prefix z with the remaining part of x. Without
   loss of generality, we assume that it is ℓ_l.                  */
```

Let $\ell_l = z||t$ and $x = y||z||x'$
Call ALLOC to obtain an address j_2
Replace a_l with j_2 in the node $j_1 : (i, a_l, a_r, \ell_l, \ell_r)$ (move a_l to a temporary register)
Call ALLOC to obtain an address j_3
Write at address j_3: $(*, \perp, \perp, \varepsilon, \varepsilon)$

```
/* Information at this point: x, a_l, j_2, j_3, the path to j_1 and the tree
   */
```

if t *starts with 0* **then**

> Move a_l and cut ℓ_l to modify the two nodes in positions j_1 and j_2 as follows: $j_1 : (i, j_2, a_r, z, \ell_r)$ and $j_2 : (*, a_l, j_3, t, x')$.

else

> Move a_l and cut ℓ_l to modify the two nodes in positions j_1 and j_2 as follows: $j_1 : (i, j_2, a_r, z, \ell_r)$ and $j_2 : (*, j_3, a_l, t, x')$.

```
/* We make this choice so that the left edge is always labeled
   starting with a 0 and the right edge with a 1                  */
/* Since we have moved j_3 and a_l, the remaining information is: x,
   the modified tree, j_2 and the path to j_1 (actually the path to x
   in the new tree)                                               */
```

Recompute the invariants on the path to x, in reverse order (starting from the address j_2).

```
/* The recomputation of the invariants is reversible (but we still
   know the path to x)                                            */
```

Do a lookup of x to uncompute the path to x.

```
/* Now the only information that remains is x, T(S ∪ {x}).         */
```

The deletion of an element that is not in S is unspecified.

Quantum Lookup. We can implement a "quantum lookup" unitary QLOOKUP which produces a uniform superposition of elements in S having a specific property P. The only requirement is that the invariant of nodes has to store the number of nodes in the subtree having this property (and so, leaf nodes will indicate if the given x satisfies $P(x)$ or not).

$$\text{QLOOKUP} : |T(S)\rangle |0\rangle \mapsto |T(S)\rangle \sum_{x \in S | P(x)} |x\rangle \ . \tag{11}$$

This unitary is implemented by descending in the tree coherently (i.e., in superposition over the left and right paths) with a weight that depends on the number of solutions in the left and right subtrees. First, we initialize an address register $|a\rangle$ to the root. Then, for n times (the maximal depth of the tree), we update the current address register as follows:

- We count the number of solutions in the left and right subtrees of the node at address $|a\rangle$ (say, t_l and t_r).
- We map $|a\rangle$ to $|a\rangle \left(\sqrt{\frac{t_l}{t_l+t_r}} \,|\text{left child of } a\rangle + \sqrt{\frac{t_r}{t_l+t_r}} \,|\text{right child of } a\rangle \right)$. (We do nothing if $|a\rangle$ is a leaf).

In the end, we obtain a uniform superposition of the paths to all elements satisfying P. We can query these elements, then uncompute the paths using an inverse LOOKUP. Likewise, we can also perform a quantum lookup of pairs satisfying a given property, e.g., retrieve a uniform superposition of all collision pairs in S.

5.4   Quantum Memory Allocators

We now define the unitary ALLOC, which given the current state of the memory, creates the uniform superposition of unallocated cells:

$$\text{ALLOC} : |\text{current memory}\rangle \,|0\rangle \mapsto |\text{current memory}\rangle \sum_{i \text{ unoccupied}} |i\rangle \ . \tag{12}$$

We do not need to define a different unitary for un-allocation; we only have to recompute ALLOC to erase the addresses of cells that we are currently cleaning. To implement ALLOC, we add to each memory cell a flag indicating if it is allocated. We propose two approaches.

Quantum Search Allocation. Classically, we can allocate new cells by simply choosing addresses at random and checking if they are already allocated or not. Quantumly, we can follow this approach using a *quantum search* over all the cells for unallocated ones. Obviously, for this approach to be efficient, we need the proportion of unallocated cells to be always constant. Besides, if we keep a counter of the number of allocated cells (which does not vary during our quantum walk steps anyway), we can make this operation exact using Amplitude Amplification (Theorem 4 in [7]). Indeed, this counter gives the proportion of allocated cells, so we know exactly the probability of success of the amplified algorithm.

We can implement this procedure with a single iteration of quantum search as long as we have a 33% overhead on the maximal number of allocated cells (similarly to the case of searching with a single query studied in [11]).

Quantum Tree Allocation. A more standard, but less time-efficient approach to implement ALLOC is to organize the memory cells in a complete binary tree (a heap), so that each node of the tree stores the number of unallocated cells in its children. This tree is not a quantum radix tree, since its size never changes, and no elements are inserted or removed. In order to obtain the uniform superposition of free cell addresses, we mimic the approach of QLOOKUP.

5.5   Higher-Level Operations for Collision Walks

We now implement efficiently the higher-level operations required by our algorithms: setting up the initial vertex (SETUP), performing a quantum walk update (SWUP'), looking for collisions (CHECK) and extracting them (EXTRACT).

Representation. We consider the case of (multi-)collision search. Here the set S is a subset of $[N] = \{0,1\}^n$, but we also need to store the images of these elements by the function $f : \{0,1\}^n \to \{0,1\}^m$. Let $F = \{f(x)||x, x \in S\}$. A collision of f is a pair $(f(x)||x), (f(y)||y)$ such that $f(x) = f(y)$, i.e., the bit-strings have the same value on the first m bits.

  Since our goal is to retrieve efficiently the collision pairs, we will store both a radix tree $T(S)$ to keep track of the elements, and $T(F)$ to keep track of the collisions. One should note that the sets F and S have the same size. When inserting or deleting elements, we insert and delete both in $T(S)$ and $T(F)$. These trees are stored in two separate chunks of memory cells.

SETUP. The unitary SETUP starts from an empty state $|0\rangle$ and initializes the tree to a uniform superposition of subsets of a given set. As long as sampling uniformly at random from this set is efficient, we can implement SETUP using a sequence of insertions in a tree that starts empty.

SWUP'. We show an efficient implementation of the unitary SWUP':

$$\text{SWUP}' |T(S)\rangle |T(F)\rangle |c_{S\to S'}\rangle = |T(S')\rangle |T(F')\rangle |c_{S'\to S}\rangle \tag{13}$$

where $c_{S\to S'}$ is the *coin register* which contains information on the transition of a set S to a set S'. As we have detailed before, the coin is encoded as a pair (j, z) where $j \in [R]$ is the index of an element in S, which has to be removed, and $z \in [N - R]$ is the index of an element in $\{0,1\}^n \backslash S$, which has to be inserted. We implement SWUP' as follows:

1. First, we convert the coin register to a pair x, y where: • y is the z-th element of $\{0,1\}^n$ which is not in S and • x is the j-th element of S (according to the lexicographic ordering of bit-strings). For the first, we need a specific algorithm detailed in the full version of the paper [5], which accesses the tree $T(S)$. The second can be done easily if the invariant of each node stores the number of leaves in its subtree. Note that both the mapping from z to y, and from j to x, are reversible. At this point the state is $|T(S)\rangle |T(F)\rangle |x, y\rangle$.

2. We use INSERT† to delete x from $T(S)$, and delete $f(x)\|x$ from $T(F)$.
3. We use INSERT to insert y in $T(S)$ and $f(y)\|y$ in $T(F)$. At this point the state is: $|T(S')\rangle\,|T(F')\rangle\,|x,y\rangle$ where $S' = (S\backslash\{x\}) \cup \{y\}$ and F' is the set of corresponding images.
4. Finally, we convert the pair x, y back to a coin register.

Remark 2 (Walking in a reduced set). In our walk, we actually reduce the set of possible elements, due to the previously measured collisions. So the coin does not encode an element of $\{0,1\}^n\backslash S$, but of $\{0,1\}^n\backslash S\backslash\mathsf{Preim}(C)$, where C is our current table of multicollisions. An adapted algorithm is also given in the full version of the paper [5] for this case.

Checking. We make the CHECK operation trivial, by defining an appropriate invariant of the tree $T(F)$. For each node in the tree, we count the number of multicollisions and preimages of $\mathsf{Im}(C)$ that the subtree rooted at this node contains. Then, the unitary CHECK simply tests whether the invariant at the root is zero.

During the operations of insertion and deletion in the tree, the invariant can be updated appropriately. Besides checking if the inserted element creates a new collision (resp., the deleted element removes one), we also need to check whether the image belongs to the set $\mathsf{Im}(C)$. During the run of the algorithm, $\mathsf{Im}(C)$ is classical, and can be stored in quantum-accessible classical memory.

Extracting. The most important property for our chained quantum walk is the capacity to *extract* multicollisions from the radix tree, in a way that preserves the rest of the state, and allows to reuse a superposition of *marked* vertices for the current walk, as a superposition of *unmarked* vertices for the next one. Recall from Sect. 4.1 that we have defined a table of multicollisions C, a set V_R^C of sets of size R in $\{0,1\}^n\backslash\mathsf{Preim}(C)$, and a set $M_R^C \subseteq V_R^C$ of *marked vertices*, which contain either a new element mapping to $\mathsf{Im}(C)$, or a new collision. Recall also from the proof of Theorem 5 that a random function, with probability $1-o(2^{-n})$, does not admit an r-collision $(x_1,\ldots,x_r)$ with $r = \mathcal{O}(n)$ for some appropriate constant. This limit on the size of multicollisions ensures that the extraction does not reduce too much the size of the current vertex.

The operation EXTRACT does:

$$\text{EXTRACT} : C, R, \frac{1}{\sqrt{|M_R^C|}} \sum_{S\in M_R^C} |S\rangle \mapsto C', R', \frac{1}{\sqrt{|V_{R'}^{C'}\backslash M_{R'}^{C'}|}} \sum_{S\in V_{R'}^{C'}\backslash M_{R'}^{C'}} |S\rangle \ ,$$

i.e., it updates the current vertex state, but also reduces R to a smaller value R', and updates the table C into a bigger table C'. It is implemented as Algorithm 5. Although it is not strictly necessary, we have separated the subroutine CHECK into: CHECKP, which finds whether the set contains a new preimage of C, and CHECKC, which finds whether there is a new collision.

We now prove the correctness of Algorithm 5. We start with the uniform superposition of marked vertices, i.e., sets $S \subseteq \{0,1\}^n\backslash\mathsf{Preim}(C)$ of size R, which

---

Algorithm 5: Multicollision extraction: EXTRACT.

Input: C, R, uniform superposition over M_R^C
Output: C' R', uniform superposition over $V_{R'}^{C'} \backslash M_{R'}^{C'}$

flag $\leftarrow$ true
$C' \leftarrow C$, $R' \leftarrow R$
Apply CHECKP and measure the result: let flag be the output
while *flag is true* **do**

> Perform a "quantum lookup" of the solution (new preimage)
> Select one uniformly at random, denote it x
> Copy x outside the tree; apply INSERT† to remove it; measure x
> $R' \leftarrow R - 1$
> Insert x in C', at the index of its image $f(x)$
> Apply CHECKP and measure the result: let flag be the output

Apply CHECKC and measure the result: let flag be the output
while *flag is true* **do**

> Perform a "quantum lookup" of the solution (new collision)
> Select one uniformly at random, denote it $(x_1, \ldots, x_r)$
> Write r in a new register
> Copy $(x_1, \ldots, x_r)$ outside the tree
> Apply INSERT† a total of $\mathcal{O}(n)$ times, in a controlled way depending on
>   the exact value of r, to remove $x_1, \ldots, x_r$
> Measure r and $x_1, \ldots, x_r$
> $R' \leftarrow R - r$
> Insert a new entry $(x_1, \ldots, x_r)$ in C'
> Apply CHECKC and measure the result: let flag be the output

---

contain *at least* a solution tuple $x_1, \ldots, x_r$ which is either a (multi)-collision, or a new preimage.

The first loop removes all new preimages. Each time we measure an element, we collapse on the superposition of sets which contained it. After CHECKP returns 0 for the first time, the state collapses on the uniform superposition of all sets S such that:

$$S \subseteq (\{0,1\}^n \backslash \mathsf{Preim}(C')), |S| = R' = R - t, \left(\forall z \in S, f(z) \notin \mathsf{Im}(C') \right) ,$$

where t is the number of iterates of the loop that we had to perform. There is a variable number of such iterates but we expect only one to occur on average, since the typical case is for vertices to contain only one solution.

The second loop will run until there are no collisions anymore. New preimages cannot appear since we extract entire multicollision tuples. At the first loop iterate, assuming that CHECKC returns 1, we collapse on the uniform superposition of sets:

$$S \subseteq (\{0,1\}^n \backslash \mathsf{Preim}(C')), |S| = R',$$
$$\left(\forall z \in S, f(z) \notin \mathsf{Im}(C') \land \exists x, y \in S, x \neq y, f(x) = f(y) \right) .$$

We select one of the solutions $(x_1, \ldots, x_r)$ at random, remove it, and measure the tuple $x_1, \ldots, x_r$. Let $u = h(x_1)$. After measurement, the state collapses on *all sets that do not contain* $x_1, \ldots, x_r$, *and contain no preimage of* u.

Since we update R' and C' accordingly, we obtain the sets:

$$S \subseteq (\{0,1\}^n \backslash \mathsf{Preim}(C')), |S| = R', \left(\forall z \in S, f(z) \notin \mathsf{Im}(C') \right) .$$

After repeatedly calling CHECKC and measuring, we will continue extracting collisions until CHECKC returns 0, i.e., we have collapsed on the sets which *do not* contain a collision. At this point, we have a uniform superposition of:

$$S \subseteq (\{0,1\}^n \backslash \mathsf{Preim}(C')), |S| = R',$$

$$\left(\forall z \in S, f(z) \notin \mathsf{Im}(C') \wedge \forall x, y \in S, f(x) \neq f(y) \right) .$$

This is, by definition, the set of unmarked vertices (see Equation (6)).

Note that for this algorithm to work, we need to maintain invariants of the number of solutions (new preimages and multicollisions) that any subtree contains. These invariants only decrease during the loop iterates, and they are updated accordingly when we remove the solutions from the tree.

6 Searching for Many Collisions, in General

As we have seen, our new algorithm is valid (and tight) for all values of n, m and $k \leq 2n - m$ such that $k \leq \frac{m}{4}$. Two approaches can be used for higher k.

BHT. A standard approach to find multiple collisions, which works when m is small, is to extend the BHT algorithm [8]. We select a parameter ℓ, then make 2^ℓ queries, and look for 2^k collisions on this list of queries. This is done by a quantum search on $\{0,1\}^n$ for an input colliding with the list.

There are on average 2^{2n-m} collision pairs in the function, so a random element of $\{0,1\}^n$ has a probability $\mathcal{O}(2^{n-m})$ to be in a collision pair. This gives $\mathcal{O}(2^{\ell-m+n})$ collision pairs for the initial list.

Thus, a search for a collision with the list has $\mathcal{O}(2^{\ell-m+n})$ solutions in a search space of size 2^n, and it requires $\sqrt{\frac{2^n}{2^{\ell+m-n}}} = 2^{(m-\ell)/2}$ iterates.

If this procedure is to output 2^k collisions, we need ℓ such that $2^{\ell-m+n} \geq 2^k$ i.e. $\ell - m + n \geq k$. By trying to equalize the complexity of the two steps, we obtain: $\ell = k + \frac{m-\ell}{2} \implies \ell = \frac{2k}{3} + \frac{m}{3}$ which is only valid for $k \leq 3n - 2m$. For a bigger k, we can repeat this. We find 2^{3n-2m} collisions in time (and memory) 2^{2n-m}, and we do this $2^{k-(3n-2m)}$ times, for a total time $\widetilde{\mathcal{O}}(2^{k+m-n})$. If we want to restrict the memory then we obtain the tradeoff of $\widetilde{\mathcal{O}}(2^{k+m/2-\ell/2})$ time using $\mathcal{O}(2^\ell)$ memory.

Using Our Method. If $k > m/4$, then the memory limitation in Theorem 5 on ℓ becomes relevant. In that case, as we are restricted to $\ell \leq m/2$, the minimal achievable time is $\widetilde{\mathcal{O}}(2^{k+m/2-\ell/2}) = \widetilde{\mathcal{O}}(2^{k+m/4})$.

Conclusion. The time and memory complexities of the problem are the following (in $\log_2$ and without polynomial factors):

- If $k \leq 3n - 2m$: $\frac{2k}{3} + \frac{m}{3}$ time and memory using BHT
- Otherwise, if $k \leq \frac{m}{4}$: $\frac{2k}{3} + \frac{m}{3}$ time and memory using our algorithm
- Otherwise, if $m \leq \frac{4}{3}n$: $k + m - n$ time and $2n - m$ memory using BHT
- Otherwise, if $m \geq \frac{3}{4}n$: $k + \frac{m}{4}$ time and $\frac{m}{2}$ memory using our algorithm

This situation is summarized in Fig. 1, and it allows us to conclude:

Theorem 6. *Let $f : \{0,1\}^n \to \{0,1\}^m$, $n \leq m \leq 2n$ be a random function. Let $k \leq 2n - m$. There exists an algorithm finding 2^k collisions in $\tilde{O}\left(2^{C(k,m,n)}\right)$ Clifford+T+qRAM gates, and using $\tilde{O}\left(2^{C(k,m,n)}\right)$ quantum queries to f, where:*

$$C(k,m,n) = \max\left(\frac{2k}{3} + \frac{m}{3}, k + \min\left(m - n, \frac{m}{4}\right)\right). \tag{14}$$

Proof. We check that: $k \leq 3n - 2m \iff \frac{2k}{3} + \frac{m}{3} \geq k + m - n$ and $k \leq \frac{m}{4} \iff \frac{2k}{3} + \frac{m}{3} \geq k + \frac{m}{4}$. □

We conjecture that the best achievable complexity is, in fact, $C(k,m,n) = \frac{2k}{3} + \frac{m}{3}$ for any admissible values of k, m and n. It would however require a non-trivial extension of our algorithm, capable of outputting collisions at a higher rate than what we currently achieve.

In terms of time-memory trade-offs, we can summarize the results as:

Theorem 7 (General Time-memory tradeoff). *For all $k \leq \ell \leq \min(2k/3 + m/3, \max(2n - m, m/2))$, there exists an algorithm that computes 2^k collisions using $\tilde{O}\left(2^\ell\right)$ qubits and $\tilde{O}\left(2^{k+m/2-\ell/2}\right)$ Clifford+T+qRAM gates and quantum queries to f.*

Similarly, as in [15], we conjecture that the trade-off should be achievable for all $\ell \leq 2k/3 + m/3$.

7 Applications

In this section, we show how our algorithm can be used as a building block for lattice sieving and to solve the limited birthday problem. We also discuss the problem of multicollision search.

7.1 Improvements in Quantum Sieving for Solving the Shortest Vector Problem

In this section, we present the improvement of our reusable quantum walks to lattice sieving algorithms. A lattice $\mathcal{L} = \mathcal{L}(\mathbf{b}_1, \ldots, \mathbf{b}_d) := \{\sum_{i=1}^d z_i \mathbf{b}_i : z_i \in \mathbb{Z}\}$ is the set of all integer combinations of linearly independent vectors $\mathbf{b}_1, \ldots, \mathbf{b}_d \in \mathbb{R}^d$. We call d the *rank* of the lattice and $(\mathbf{b}_1, \ldots, \mathbf{b}_d)$ a *basis* of the lattice.

The most important computational problem on lattices is the Shortest Vector Problem (SVP). Given a basis for a lattice $\mathcal{L} \subseteq \mathbb{R}^d$, SVP asks to compute a non-zero vector in $\mathcal{L}$ with the smallest Euclidean norm. The main lattice reduction algorithm used for lattice-based cryptanalysis is the famous BKZ algorithm [29]. It internally uses an algorithm for solving (near) exact SVP in lower-dimensional lattices. Therefore, finding faster algorithms to solve exact SVP is critical to choosing security parameters of cryptographic primitives.

Previously, the fastest quantum algorithm solved SVP under heuristic assumptions in $2^{0.2570d+o(d)}$ time [9]. It applies the MNRS quantum walk technique to the state-of-the-art classical algorithm called lattice sieving, where we combine close vectors together to obtain shorter vectors at each step. It was noted in [9] that the algorithm could be slightly improved if we could find many marked vertices in a quantum walk without repaying the setup each time, which is exactly what we showed in Sect. 4. We redid the analysis of [9] with this improvement and show the following

Proposition 4. *There exists a quantum algorithm that solves SVP under heuristic assumptions in* $2^{0.2563d+o(d)}$

Proving this statement requires to restate the whole framework and analysis of [9]. We briefly present here the main calculation to achieve our result but we refer to the full version of the paper [5] for a more comprehensive analysis. Let $V_d(\alpha)$ be the ratio of the volume of a spherical cap of angle α to the volume of the d-dimensional sphere. We have $V_d(\alpha) = \text{poly}(d)\sin^d(\alpha)$.

Proposition 5. *The algorithms of [9] has the following asymptotic running time:*

$$T = \max\{1, N^{c-\varsigma}\} \cdot (N + N^{1-c}FAS_1). \tag{15}$$

where $N = \frac{1}{V_d(\pi/3)}$, α *st.* $V_d(\alpha) = N^{-(1-c)}$, $\theta_\alpha^* = 2\arcsin(\frac{1}{2\sin(\alpha)})$, ς *st.* $N^\varsigma = N^{2c}V_d(\theta_\alpha^*)$, *and* FAS_1 *is the running time of the* FAS_1 *subroutine.*

The authors of [9] use a quantum walk in order to solve the FAS_1 problem.

Proposition 6 ([9]). *For a parameter* c_1, *let* β *st.* $V_d(\beta) = \frac{1}{N^{c_1}}$, ρ_0 *st.* $N^{\rho_0} = \frac{V_d(\beta)}{W_d(\beta,\theta_\alpha^*)}$, *where* $W_d(\beta,\theta_\alpha^*) = \text{poly}(d) \cdot \left(1 - \frac{2\cos^2(\beta)}{1+\cos(\theta_\alpha^*)}\right)^{d/2}$. *In order to solve* FAS_1 *with parameter* c_1, *it is enough to repeat* N^{ρ_0} *times a quantum walk on a graph where we each time need to find* $N^{\varsigma-\rho_0}$ *marked elements with the following properties*

$$\mathsf{S} = N^{c_1}, \ \delta = N^{-c_1}, \ \varepsilon = N^{2c_1-\rho_0}V_{d-1}(\theta_\alpha^*), \ \mathsf{U} = 1, \ \mathsf{C} = 1.$$

Using Theorem 4, we obtain $FAS_1 = N^{\rho_0} \cdot \left(\mathsf{S} + \frac{N^{\varsigma-\rho_0}}{\sqrt{\varepsilon}}\left(\frac{1}{\sqrt{\delta}}\mathsf{U} + \mathsf{C}\right)\right)$. We take the following set of parameters: $c \approx 0.3875, c_1 \approx 0.27$ which gives $\varsigma \approx 0.1568$ and $\rho_0 \approx 0.1214$. Notice that with these parameters, we are indeed in the range of Theorem 4 since the number of solutions we extract is $2^k = N^{\varsigma-\rho_0} \approx N^{0.0354}$

and the range of the function f on which we collision is $2^m = 2^{c_1} \approx N^{0.27}$ (the number of points in the code), so we indeed have $k \le \frac{m}{4}$. The parameters of the quantum walk become:

$$S \approx N^{0.27}, \ \varepsilon \approx N^{-0.2}, \ \delta \approx N^{-0.27}, \ U = C = 1 \ .$$

This gives $FAS_1 \approx N^{0.27}$. Plugging this into Equation (15), we get a total running time of $T = N^{1.2347}$ which is equal to $T = 2^{0.2563d+o(d)}$ improving slightly the previous running time of $2^{0.2570d+o(d)}$.

7.2   Solving the Limited Birthday Problem

The following problem is very common in symmetric cryptanalysis. It appears for example in impossible differential attacks [6], but also in rebound distinguishers [16]. In the former case we use generic algorithms to solve the problem for a black-box E, and in the latter, a valid distinguisher for E is defined as an algorithm outputting the pairs faster than the generic one.

Problem 4 (Limited Birthday). Given access to a black-box permutation $E :$ $\{0,1\}^n \to \{0,1\}^n$ and possibly its inverse E^{-1}, given two vector spaces $\mathcal{D}_{\mathrm{in}}$ and $\mathcal{D}_{\mathrm{out}}$ of sizes $2^{\Delta_{\mathrm{in}}}$ and $2^{\Delta_{\mathrm{out}}}$ respectively, find 2^k pairs x, x' such that $x \ne x', x \oplus x' \in \mathcal{D}_{\mathrm{in}}, E(x) \oplus E(x') \in \mathcal{D}_{\mathrm{out}}$.

For simplicity, we will focus only on the time complexity of the problem, although some parameter choices require a large memory as well. Classically the best known time complexity is given in [6]:

$$\max\left(\min_{\Delta \in \{\Delta_{\mathrm{in}}, \Delta_{\mathrm{out}}\}} \left(\sqrt{2^{k+n+1-\Delta}}\right), 2^{k+n+1-\Delta_{\mathrm{in}}-\Delta_{\mathrm{out}}}\right) \ . \tag{16}$$

This complexity is known to be tight for $2^k = 1$ [16].

In the quantum setting, we need to consider superposition access to E and possibly E^{-1} to have a speedup on this problem. Previously the methods used [23] involved only individual calls to Ambainis' algorithm (when there are few solutions) or an adaptation of the BHT algorithm (when there are many solutions).

The quantum algorithm, as the classical one, relies on the definition of *structures* of size $2^{\Delta_{\mathrm{in}}}$, which are subsets of the inputs of the form $T_x = \{x \oplus v, v \in \mathcal{D}_{\mathrm{in}}\}$ for a fixed x. For a given structure T_x, we can define a function $h_x : \{0,1\}^{\Delta_{\mathrm{in}}} \to \{0,1\}^{n-\Delta_{\mathrm{out}}}$ such that any collision of h_x yields a pair solution to the limited birthday problem. The expected number of collisions of a single h_x is $C := 2^{2\Delta_{\mathrm{in}}+\Delta_{\mathrm{out}}-n}$, and there are three cases:

1. $C < 1$: we follow the approach of [23], which is to repeat 2^k times a Grover search among structures, to find one that contains a pair (this is done with Ambainis' algorithm). The time exponent is $k + \frac{n-\Delta_{\mathrm{out}}}{2} - \frac{\Delta_{\mathrm{in}}}{3}$.
2. $1 < C < 2^k$: we need to consider several structures and to extract all of their collision pairs. Using Theorem 6 this gives a time exponent:

$$\max\left(k + \frac{2}{3}(n - \Delta_{\mathrm{in}} - \Delta_{\mathrm{out}}), k + \min\left(n - \Delta_{\mathrm{out}} - \Delta_{\mathrm{in}}, \frac{n - \Delta_{\mathrm{out}}}{4}\right)\right)$$

3. $2^k < C$: we need only one structure. To recover 2^k pairs, we need a time exponent (by Theorem 6):

$$\max\left(\frac{2k}{3} + \frac{n - \Delta_{\text{out}}}{3}, k + \min\left(n - \Delta_{\text{out}} - \Delta_{\text{in}}, \frac{n - \Delta_{\text{out}}}{4}\right)\right)$$

Finally, we can swap the roles of Δ_{in} and Δ_{out} and take the minimum. Unfortunately this does not lead to an equation as simple as Equation (16).

7.3   On Multicollision-Finding

A natural extension of this work would be to look for multicollisions.

Problem 5 (r-collision search). Let $f : \{0,1\}^n \to \{0,1\}^m$ be a random function. Find an r-collision of f, that is, a tuple $(x_1, \ldots, x_r)$ of distinct elements such that $f(x_1) = \ldots = f(x_r)$.

As with collisions, the lower bound by Liu and Zhandry [25] is known to be tight when $m \leq n$. The corresponding algorithm is an extension of the BHT algorithm which constructs increasingly smaller lists of i-collisions, starting with 1-collisions (evaluations of the function f on arbitrary points) and ending with a list of r-collisions.

This algorithm, given in [17,18], finds 2^k r-collisions in time and memory:

$$\widetilde{O}\left(2^{k\frac{2^{(r-1)}}{2^r - 1}} 2^{m\frac{2^{(r-1)} - 1}{2^r - 1}}\right).$$

As with 2-collisions, it is possible to extend it when $m > n$. Of course, there's a constraint: the list i must contain more tuples that are part of an $i+1$-collision than the size of the list $i + 1$.

The size of each i-collision list is $N_i = 2^{k\frac{2^r - 2^{r-i}}{2^r - 1}} 2^{m\frac{2^{r-i} - 1}{2^r - 1}}$. The probability that an i-collision extends to an $i + 1$-collision is of order 2^{n-m}. Hence, for the algorithm to work, we must have, for all i, $N_{i+1}/N_i \leq 2^{n-m}$. This means:

$$k\frac{2^{r-i-1}}{2^r - 1} - m\frac{2^{r-i-1}}{2^r - 1} \leq n - m .$$

This constraint is the most restrictive for the largest possible i, $r - 1$. We obtain the following constraint, which subsumes the others:

$$k\frac{1}{2^r - 1} + m\left(1 - \frac{1}{2^r - 1}\right) \leq n .$$

This gives the point up to which this algorithm meets the lower bound. We could use our new algorithm as a subroutine in this one, to find 2-collisions, and this would allow to relax the constraint over N_2/N_1. Unfortunately, this cannot help to find multicollisions, as the other constraints are more restrictive. More generally, these constraints show that it is not possible to increase the range of the BHT-like r-collision algorithm solely by using an $r - i$-collision algorithm with an increased range.

Acknowledgments. A.S. wants to thank Nicolas David and María Naya-Plasencia for discussions on the limited birthday problem. A.S. has been supported by ERC-ADG-ALGSTRONGCRYPTO (project 740972). Y.S. is supported by EPSRC grant EP/S02087X/1 and EP/W02778X/1. This work received funding from the France 2030 program managed by the French National Research Agency under grant agreement No. ANR-22-PETQ-0007 EPiQ and ANR-22-PETQ-0008 PQ-TLS. All authors would like to thank Schloss Dagstuhl and the organizers of the Dagstuhl Seminar 21421 "Quantum Cryptanalysis" where this work was initiated, and the reviewers of EUROCRYPT 2023 for helpful comments.

References

1. Aaronson, S., Shi, Y.: Quantum lower bounds for the collision and the element distinctness problems. J. ACM **51**(4), 595–605 (2004)
2. Ambainis, A.: Quantum walk algorithm for element distinctness. SIAM J. Comput. **37**(1), 210–239 (2007)
3. Bernstein, D.J., Jeffery, S., Lange, T., Meurer, A.: Quantum algorithms for the subset-sum problem. In: Gaborit, P. (ed.) PQCrypto 2013. LNCS, vol. 7932, pp. 16–33. Springer, Heidelberg (2013). https://doi.org/10.1007/978-3-642-38616-9_2
4. Bonnetain, X., Bricout, R., Schrottenloher, A., Shen, Y.: Improved classical and quantum algorithms for subset-sum. In: Moriai, S., Wang, H. (eds.) ASIACRYPT 2020. LNCS, vol. 12492, pp. 633–666. Springer, Cham (2020). https://doi.org/10.1007/978-3-030-64834-3_22
5. Bonnetain, X., Chailloux, A., Schrottenloher, A., Shen, Y.: Finding many collisions via reusable quantum walks. IACR Cryptol. ePrint Arch, p. 676 (2022)
6. Boura, C., Naya-Plasencia, M., Suder, V.: Scrutinizing and improving impossible differential attacks: applications to CLEFIA, Camellia, LBlock and SIMON. In: Sarkar, P., Iwata, T. (eds.) ASIACRYPT 2014. LNCS, vol. 8873, pp. 179–199. Springer, Heidelberg (2014). https://doi.org/10.1007/978-3-662-45611-8_10
7. Brassard, G., Hoyer, P., Mosca, M., Tapp, A.: Quantum amplitude amplification and estimation. Contemp. Math. **305**, 53–74 (2002)
8. Brassard, G., HØyer, P., Tapp, A.: Quantum cryptanalysis of hash and claw-free functions. In: Lucchesi, C.L., Moura, A.V. (eds.) LATIN 1998. LNCS, vol. 1380, pp. 163–169. Springer, Heidelberg (1998). https://doi.org/10.1007/BFb0054319
9. Chailloux, A., Loyer, J.: Lattice sieving via quantum random walks. In: Tibouchi, M., Wang, H. (eds.) ASIACRYPT 2021. LNCS, vol. 13093, pp. 63–91. Springer, Cham (2021). https://doi.org/10.1007/978-3-030-92068-5_3
10. Chailloux, A., Naya-Plasencia, M., Schrottenloher, A.: An efficient quantum collision search algorithm and implications on symmetric cryptography. In: Takagi, T., Peyrin, T. (eds.) ASIACRYPT 2017. LNCS, vol. 10625, pp. 211–240. Springer, Cham (2017). https://doi.org/10.1007/978-3-319-70697-9_8
11. Chi, D.P., Kim, J.: Quantum database search by a single query. In: Williams, C.P. (ed.) QCQC 1998. LNCS, vol. 1509, pp. 148–151. Springer, Heidelberg (1999). https://doi.org/10.1007/3-540-49208-9_11
12. Dinur, I.: Tight time-space lower bounds for finding multiple collision pairs and their applications. In: Canteaut, A., Ishai, Y. (eds.) EUROCRYPT 2020. LNCS, vol. 12105, pp. 405–434. Springer, Cham (2020). https://doi.org/10.1007/978-3-030-45721-1_15

13. Flajolet, P., Odlyzko, A.M.: Random mapping statistics. In: Quisquater, J.-J., Vandewalle, J. (eds.) EUROCRYPT 1989. LNCS, vol. 434, pp. 329–354. Springer, Heidelberg (1990). https://doi.org/10.1007/3-540-46885-4_34

14. Grover, L.K.: A fast quantum mechanical algorithm for database search. In: Proceedings of the Twenty-Eighth Annual ACM Symposium on the Theory of Computing 1996, pp. 212–219. ACM (1996)

15. Hamoudi, Y., Magniez, F.: Quantum time-space tradeoff for finding multiple collision pairs. In: TQC. LIPIcs, vol. 197, pp. 1:1–1:21. Schloss Dagstuhl - Leibniz-Zentrum für Informatik (2021)

16. Hosoyamada, A., Naya-Plasencia, M., Sasaki, Y.: Improved attacks on sliscp permutation and tight bound of limited birthday distinguishers. IACR Trans. Symm. Cryptol. **2020**(4), 147–172 (2020)

17. Hosoyamada, A., Sasaki, Yu., Tani, S., Xagawa, K.: Improved quantum multicollision-finding algorithm. In: Ding, J., Steinwandt, R. (eds.) PQCrypto 2019. LNCS, vol. 11505, pp. 350–367. Springer, Cham (2019). https://doi.org/10.1007/978-3-030-25510-7_19

18. Hosoyamada, A., Sasaki, Y., Tani, S., Xagawa, K.: Quantum algorithm for the multicollision problem. Theor. Comput. Sci. **842**, 100–117 (2020)

19. Jaques, S., Schanck, J.M.: Quantum cryptanalysis in the RAM model: claw-finding attacks on SIKE. In: Boldyreva, A., Micciancio, D. (eds.) CRYPTO 2019. LNCS, vol. 11692, pp. 32–61. Springer, Cham (2019). https://doi.org/10.1007/978-3-030-26948-7_2

20. Jaques, S., Schrottenloher, A.: Low-gate quantum golden collision finding. In: Dunkelman, O., Jacobson, Jr., M.J., O'Flynn, C. (eds.) SAC 2020. LNCS, vol. 12804, pp. 329–359. Springer, Cham (2021). https://doi.org/10.1007/978-3-030-81652-0_13

21. Jeffery, S.: Frameworks for Quantum Algorithms. Ph.D. thesis, University of Waterloo, Ontario, Canada (2014). http://hdl.handle.net/10012/8710

22. Kachigar, G., Tillich, J.-P.: Quantum information set decoding algorithms. In: Lange, T., Takagi, T. (eds.) PQCrypto 2017. LNCS, vol. 10346, pp. 69–89. Springer, Cham (2017). https://doi.org/10.1007/978-3-319-59879-6_5

23. Kaplan, M., Leurent, G., Leverrier, A., Naya-Plasencia, M.: Quantum differential and linear cryptanalysis. IACR Trans. Symm. Cryptol. **2016**(1), 71–94 (2016)

24. Kirshanova, E., Mårtensson, E., Postlethwaite, E.W., Moulik, S.R.: Quantum algorithms for the approximate k-list problem and their application to lattice sieving. In: Galbraith, S.D., Moriai, S. (eds.) ASIACRYPT 2019. LNCS, vol. 11921, pp. 521–551. Springer, Cham (2019). https://doi.org/10.1007/978-3-030-34578-5_19

25. Liu, Q., Zhandry, M.: On finding quantum multi-collisions. In: Ishai, Y., Rijmen, V. (eds.) EUROCRYPT 2019. LNCS, vol. 11478, pp. 189–218. Springer, Cham (2019). https://doi.org/10.1007/978-3-030-17659-4_7

26. Magniez, F., Nayak, A., Roland, J., Santha, M.: Search via quantum walk. SIAM J. Comput. **40**(1), 142–164 (2011)

27. Nielsen, M.A., Chuang, I.: Quantum computation and quantum information (2002)

28. van Oorschot, P.C., Wiener, M.J.: Parallel collision search with cryptanalytic applications. J. Cryptol. **12**(1), 1–28 (1999)

29. Schnorr, C.: A hierarchy of polynomial time lattice basis reduction algorithms. Theor. Comput. Sci. **53**, 201–224 (1987). https://doi.org/10.1016/0304-3975(87)90064-8

Just How Hard Are Rotations of $\mathbb{Z}^n$? Algorithms and Cryptography with the Simplest Lattice

Huck Bennett[2], Atul Ganju[1], Pura Peetathawatchai[3], and Noah Stephens-Davidowitz[1(✉)]

[1] Cornell University, Ithaca, USA
noahsd@gmail.com
[2] Oregon State University, Corvallis, USA
[3] Stanford University, Stanford, USA

Abstract. We study the computational problem of finding a shortest non-zero vector in a rotation of $\mathbb{Z}^n$, which we call $\mathbb{Z}$SVP. It has been a long-standing open problem to determine if a polynomial-time algorithm for $\mathbb{Z}$SVP exists, and there is by now a beautiful line of work showing how to solve it efficiently in certain very special cases. However, despite all of this work, the fastest known algorithm that is proven to solve $\mathbb{Z}$SVP is still simply the fastest known algorithm for solving SVP (i.e., the problem of finding shortest non-zero vectors in *arbitrary* lattices), which runs in $2^{n+o(n)}$ time.

We therefore set aside the (perhaps impossible) goal of finding an efficient algorithm for $\mathbb{Z}$SVP and instead ask what else we can say about the problem. E.g., can we find *any* non-trivial speedup over the best known SVP algorithm? And, if $\mathbb{Z}$SVP actually *is* hard, then what consequences would follow? Our results are as follows.

1. We show that $\mathbb{Z}$SVP is in a certain sense strictly easier than SVP on arbitrary lattices. In particular, we show how to reduce $\mathbb{Z}$SVP to an *approximate* version of SVP in the same dimension (in fact, even to approximate *unique* SVP, for any constant approximation factor). Such a reduction seems very unlikely to work for SVP itself, so we view this as a qualitative separation of $\mathbb{Z}$SVP from SVP. As a consequence of this reduction, we obtain a $2^{n/2+o(n)}$-time algorithm for $\mathbb{Z}$SVP, i.e., the first non-trivial speedup over the best known algorithm for SVP on general lattices. (In fact, this reduction works for a more general class of lattices—semi-stable lattices with not-too-large λ_1.)

Due to space constraints, we have omitted some discussion, proofs, and figures from this version of the paper. We strongly encourage the reader to look at the full version, which is available at [7].

Part of this work was while H.B. was at the University of Michigan and supported by the National Science Foundation under Grant No. CCF-2006857. N.S. was supported in part by the National Science Foundation under Grant No. CCF-2122230. The views expressed are those of the authors and do not necessarily reflect the official policy or position of the National Science Foundation.

C. Hazay and M. Stam (Eds.): EUROCRYPT 2023, LNCS 14008, pp. 252–281, 2023.
https://doi.org/10.1007/978-3-031-30589-4_9

2. We show a simple public-key encryption scheme that is secure if (an appropriate variant of) ZSVP is actually hard. Specifically, our scheme is secure if it is difficult to distinguish (in the worst case) a rotation of $\mathbb{Z}^n$ from *either* a lattice with all non-zero vectors longer than $\sqrt{n/\log n}$ *or* a lattice with smoothing parameter significantly smaller than the smoothing parameter of $\mathbb{Z}^n$. The latter result has an interesting qualitative connection with reverse Minkowski theorems, which in some sense say that "$\mathbb{Z}^n$ has the largest smoothing parameter."

3. We show a distribution of bases **B** for rotations of $\mathbb{Z}^n$ such that, if ZSVP is hard for *any* input basis, then ZSVP is hard on input **B**. This gives a satisfying theoretical resolution to the problem of sampling hard bases for $\mathbb{Z}^n$, which was studied by Blanks and Miller [9]. This worst-case to average-case reduction is also crucially used in the analysis of our encryption scheme. (In recent independent work that appeared as a preprint before this work, Ducas and van Woerden showed essentially the same thing for general lattices [15], and they also used this to analyze the security of a public-key encryption scheme. Similar ideas also appeared in [5,11,20] in different contexts.)

4. We perform experiments to determine how practical basis reduction performs on bases of $\mathbb{Z}^n$ that are generated in different ways and how heuristic sieving algorithms perform on $\mathbb{Z}^n$. Our basis reduction experiments complement and add to those performed by Blanks and Miller, as we work with a larger class of algorithms (i.e., larger block sizes) and study the "provably hard" distribution of bases described above. Our sieving experiments confirm that heuristic sieving algorithms perform as expected on $\mathbb{Z}^n$.

1   Introduction

A lattice $\mathcal{L} \subset \mathbb{R}^n$ is the set of all integer linear combinations of linearly independent basis vectors $\mathbf{B} := (\boldsymbol{b}_1, \ldots, \boldsymbol{b}_n) \in \mathbb{R}^{n \times n}$, i.e.,

$$\mathcal{L} = \mathcal{L}(\mathbf{B}) = \{z_1 \boldsymbol{b}_1 + \cdots + z_n \boldsymbol{b}_n \ : \ z_i \in \mathbb{Z}\}.$$

Lattices have recently played a central role in cryptography, as many powerful cryptographic schemes have been constructed using lattices. (See [32] and the references therein.) These schemes' security rests on the hardness of (worst-case) computational problems related to lattices, such as the Shortest Vector Problem (SVP), in which the goal is to find a non-zero lattice vector whose ℓ_2 norm is minimal, given a basis **B** for the lattice.

Perhaps the simplest example of a lattice is the *integer lattice* $\mathbb{Z}^n$, which has the identity matrix as a basis. Of course, the shortest non-zero vectors in $\mathbb{Z}^n$ are simply the standard basis vectors and their negations $\pm\boldsymbol{e}_1, \ldots, \pm\boldsymbol{e}_n$, which have length one. So, it is trivially easy to find a shortest non-zero vector in $\mathbb{Z}^n$ by simply outputting one of these vectors. Other computational lattice problems are also easy when the relevant lattice is $\mathbb{Z}^n$.

However, suppose that we are given some basis $\mathbf{B}$ for a *rotation* of $\mathbb{Z}^n$, i.e., a basis $\mathbf{B}$ such that the lattice $\mathcal{L}(\mathbf{B})$ generated by this basis is $R\mathbb{Z}^n$ for some orthogonal matrix $R \in O_n(\mathbb{R})$. Of course, if the basis $\mathbf{B}$ is simply R itself, then it is still easy to find a shortest vector in this lattice. (Any column of R will do.) But, it does not need to be so easy. For example, the lovely matrix

$$
\mathbf{B} := \begin{pmatrix}
3\sqrt{3898} & -5382\sqrt{\frac{2}{1949}} & \frac{31195}{\sqrt{3898}} & \frac{15857}{3} \cdot \sqrt{\frac{2}{1949}} \\
0 & \sqrt{\frac{682378}{1949}} & -110727\sqrt{\frac{2}{664977361}} & \frac{676011}{\sqrt{1329954722}} \\
0 & 0 & \sqrt{\frac{64221}{682378}} & \frac{67240}{3} \cdot \sqrt{\frac{2}{21911498769}} \\
0 & 0 & 0 & \frac{1}{3\sqrt{128442}}
\end{pmatrix}
$$

is a basis for a rotation of $\mathbb{Z}^4$, but it is not immediately clear how to find a vector of length one in the lattice generated by $\mathbf{B}$.[1] We write $\mathbb{Z}$SVP for the problem of finding vectors of length one in a rotation $\mathcal{L}$ of $\mathbb{Z}^n$, given a basis for $\mathcal{L}$.

Indeed, this is a well known problem, and it has been a long-standing open problem to settle the complexity of $\mathbb{Z}$SVP, leading to a beautiful line of work [12,17,19,22,24,25,38]. Frustratingly, despite all of this wonderful work, the fastest known algorithm that is proven to solve $\mathbb{Z}$SVP is still simply the fastest known algorithm that is proven to solve SVP on arbitrary lattices, a $2^{n+o(n)}$-time algorithm [2]. So, we do not even know whether $\mathbb{Z}$SVP is *any* easier at all than SVP on arbitrary lattices, let alone whether there exists a polynomial-time algorithm!

1.1 Our Results

In this paper, we set aside the (apparently difficult) question of whether a polynomial-time algorithm for $\mathbb{Z}$SVP exists and instead ask what else we can say about $\mathbb{Z}$SVP. Specifically, we study the following questions.

1. Can we at least solve $\mathbb{Z}$SVP in time better than $2^{n+o(n)}$? (In other words, can we at least do better than just plugging in an algorithm that solves SVP on all lattices?)
2. If it is hard to solve $\mathbb{Z}$SVP (or variants of it), does this imply any interesting cryptography?
3. In particular, is there some (efficiently sampleable) distribution of instances of $\mathbb{Z}$SVP such that these instances are provably hard if $\mathbb{Z}$SVP is hard in the worst case? I.e., is there a "hardest possible" distribution of bases suitable for use in cryptography?
4. Do known algorithms perform any differently on rotations of $\mathbb{Z}^n$ empirically?

We essentially give positive answers to all of these questions, giving a richer perspective on $\mathbb{Z}$SVP and related problems, as we detail below.

---

[1] Of course, this is not actually a hard problem, since it is only four-dimensional and SVP can be solved efficiently when the dimension n is constant. Indeed, one example of a unit length vector in this lattice is $\mathbf{B}z$, where $z := (59, 396, 225, -326)^T$.

Provably Faster Algorithms for $\mathbb{Z}^n$. Our first main result, presented in Sect. 5, is an exponential-time algorithm for $\mathbb{Z}$SVP that is faster than the fastest known algorithm for SVP over arbitrary lattices. In fact, we show something significantly stronger: an efficient dimension-preserving reduction from $\mathbb{Z}$SVP to γ-approximate GapSVP over general lattices for any constant $\gamma = O(1)$ (where GapSVP is the decision version of SVP in which the goal is simply to determine whether there exists a short vector, rather than to actually find one). In other words, we show that in order to find an exact shortest non-zero vector in a rotation of $\mathbb{Z}^n$, it suffices to simply approximate the length of a shortest non-zero vector in an arbitrary lattice. (In fact, we reduce to the γ-*unique* Shortest Vector Problem, which is SVP in which the shortest vector is guaranteed to be a factor of γ shorter than "the second shortest vector," appropriately defined.)

Theorem 1 (Informal. See Corolloary 2). *There is an efficient reduction from $\mathbb{Z}$SVP to γ-approximate GapSVP (in fact, to γ-unique SVP, a potentially easier problem) in the same dimension for any constant $\gamma = O(1)$.*

If we plug in the fastest known algorithm for $O(1)$-GapSVP, we immediately obtain a $2^{n/2+o(n)}$-time provably correct algorithm for $\mathbb{Z}$SVP [2]. (And, under a purely geometric conjecture, we obtain a running time of $(4/3)^{n+o(n)} \approx 2^{0.415n}$ [37].) See the full version [7] for a discussion of a more general class of lattices to which these results apply.

However, the specific running times are perhaps less interesting than the high-level message: solving exact SVP on rotations of $\mathbb{Z}^n$ is no harder than solving *approximate* (or even *unique*) SVP on arbitrary lattices in the same dimension. We certainly do not expect such a reduction to work for arbitrary lattices, so this shows that there is in fact something inherently "easier" about $\mathbb{Z}^n$.

A Public-Key Encryption Scheme. Our next main result, presented in Sect. 4, is a public-key encryption scheme whose security can be based on the (worst-case) hardness of variants of $\mathbb{Z}$SVP.

To be clear, we feel that it is premature to base the security of real-world cryptography on the hardness of $\mathbb{Z}$SVP and related problems. Indeed, although $\mathbb{Z}$SVP is fairly well-studied, it is not nearly as well-studied as, e.g., (plain) SVP or factoring, and should therefore be treated with more skepticism. Furthermore, there is currently no consensus about whether $\mathbb{Z}$SVP is actually hard among those who study it.

With that said, we show an encryption scheme that is secure if it is difficult to distinguish a rotation of $\mathbb{Z}^n$ *either* from (1) a lattice with no non-zero vectors with length less than roughly γ for $\gamma \approx \sqrt{n/\log n}$; or (2) from a lattice with smoothing parameter $\eta_\varepsilon(\mathcal{L})$ smaller than $\eta_\varepsilon(\mathbb{Z}^n)/\alpha$ for any $\alpha > \omega(1)$. (See Sect. 2.1 for the definition of the smoothing parameter.) We call these problems γ-$\mathbb{Z}$GapSVP and α-$\mathbb{Z}$GapSPP, respectively.

Theorem 2 (Informal, see Theorem 12). *There is a public-key encryption scheme that is secure if either γ-$\mathbb{Z}GapSVP$ or α-$\mathbb{Z}GapSPP$ is hard, for $\gamma \approx \sqrt{n/\log n}$ and any $\alpha > \omega(1)$.*

We stress that both $\mathbb{Z}$GapSVP and $\mathbb{Z}$GapSPP are *worst-case* (promise) problems. In particular, our encryption scheme is secure unless there is a polynomial-time algorithm that correctly distinguishes *all* bases of rotations of $\mathbb{Z}^n$ from *all* lattices that either have no short vectors or have small smoothing parameter. (A critical step in our proof is a worst-case to average-case reduction showing how to sample a basis for a rotation of $\mathbb{Z}^n$ that is provably as secure as *any* basis. We discuss this more below.)

We note that the approximation factor $\gamma \approx \sqrt{n/\log n}$ might look quite impressive at first. Specifically, prior work shows public-key encryption schemes that are secure if γ'-GapSVP (as opposed to γ-$\mathbb{Z}$GapSVP) is hard for $\gamma' \approx n^{3/2}$, where γ'-GapSVP asks us to distinguish a lattice with a non-zero vector with length at most one from a lattice with no non-zero vectors with length less than γ'. So, our approximation factor $\gamma \approx \sqrt{n/\log n}$ seems much better. (And, perhaps it is. In particular, we do not know algorithms that solve γ-$\mathbb{Z}$GapSVP faster than γ'-GapSVP or even γ-GapSVP.)

Of course, our reduction only works for γ-$\mathbb{Z}$GapSVP, which is potentially a much easier problem than γ-GapSVP, or even than γ'-GapSVP. (Indeed, we are not even willing to conjecture that $\mathbb{Z}$SVP is hard, let alone γ-$\mathbb{Z}$GapSVP.) And, from another perspective, the approximation factor of $\gamma \approx \sqrt{n/\log n}$ seems rather weak. Specifically, since $\mathbb{Z}^n$ (and any rotation of $\mathbb{Z}^n$) has determinant one, it is trivial by Minkowski's theorem to distinguish a rotation of $\mathbb{Z}^n$ from a lattice with no non-zero vectors with length less than roughly $\sqrt{n}$. So, from this point of view, our approximation factor γ is just a factor of $\sqrt{\log n}$ smaller than trivial.

The approximation factor α for $\mathbb{Z}$GapSPP is harder to interpret, but in the full version [7] we include some discussion.

Sampling Provably Secure Bases. Our next main result, presented in Sect. 3, is a way to sample a "hardest possible" basis $\mathbf{B}$ for a rotation of $\mathbb{Z}^n$. For example, we show an explicit (efficiently sampleable) distribution of bases $\mathbf{B}$ for rotations of $\mathbb{Z}^n$ such that, if it is hard to solve $\mathbb{Z}$SVP in the worst case, then it is hard to solve $\mathbb{Z}$SVP on input $\mathbf{B}$. The basic idea is to use the discrete Gaussian sampling algorithm of [18] to use any basis of a rotation $\mathcal{L}$ of $\mathbb{Z}^n$ to obtain many discrete Gaussian samples from $\mathcal{L}$—sufficiently many that we have a generating set of $\mathcal{L}$. We can then apply any suitable algorithm that converts a generating set into a basis. (Similar ideas have previously appeared in somewhat different contexts [5, 11,20]. In particular, [11] introduced the idea of sampling a "discrete Gaussian basis" from an arbitrary basis. More recently, in independent work that was published on ePrint before this work, [15] used similar ideas in a context very similar to ours. See Sect. 1.2.)

This gives a theoretically rigorous answer to the question studied by Blanks and Miller [9], who considered the relative hardness of solving $\mathbb{Z}$SVP for different input bases and asked whether there was a clear choice for a how to generate "hardest possible" bases. We show that there is in fact a relatively simple input distribution that is provably as hard as any other. Indeed, we have already implicitly mentioned this result, as it is crucially used in the security reductions for our encryption scheme.

Experimental Results for $\mathbb{Z}$SVP. Our final contribution, presented in Sect. 6, consists of a number of experimental results showing how practical heuristic lattice algorithms perform on $\mathbb{Z}^n$.

Our first such set of experiments ran state-of-the-art basis reduction algorithms on bases of $\mathbb{Z}^n$ that were generated in different ways and compared their effectiveness.[2] These experiments complement similar experiments performed by Blanks and Miller [9]. Our experiments differ from those of Blanks and Miller in that we used the BKZ algorithm with larger block sizes; performed more trials; and performed experiments on the distribution of bases resulting from our worst-case to average-case reduction.

Here, our results were broadly comparable to those of [9]. See Sect. 6.1 for the details. However, we note that our new experiments on the distribution of bases resulting from worst-case to average-case reductions suggest that these bases achieve comparable security to the bases studied in [9] with *much* shorter vectors (which corresponds to a more efficient encryption scheme).

Our second set of experiments document a *threshold* phenomenon that is evident in these basis reduction experiments with $\mathbb{Z}^n$. Specifically, the output of basis reduction algorithms run on bases of $\mathbb{Z}^n$ is almost always an *exact* shortest non-zero vector or a vector much longer than this. I.e., once basis reduction finds a vector in $\mathbb{Z}^n$ whose length is below some threshold, it nearly always simply finds a shortest vector. We document this phenomenon in our context. (After a preliminary version of this paper was released, we learned of a body of work studying this phenomenon in a larger context and providing compelling heuristic explanations of it, such as in [4,13]. See [14, Sect. 4.2] for more recent experiments, discussion of this phenomenon in the specific context of $\mathbb{Z}^n$, and additional references.)

Our third and final set of experiments studies the performance of a *heuristic sieving algorithm* on $\mathbb{Z}^n$. Specifically, we ran the Gauss sieve, due to Micciancio and Voulgaris [30], on $\mathbb{Z}^n$. In fact, $\mathbb{Z}^n$ is a particularly interesting lattice for heuristic sieving algorithms because $\mathbb{Z}^n$ is known to grossly violate the heuristics that are used to design and analyze these algorithms. (See Sect. 6.3.) Nevertheless, we confirm that the Gauss sieve performs more-or-less exactly the same on $\mathbb{Z}^n$ as it does on other lattices—in spite of the fact that some of the heuristic justification for the Gauss sieve does not extend to $\mathbb{Z}^n$. To our knowledge, such experiments had not been published before.

1.2   Related Work

As we mentioned above, there is by now a beautiful sequence of works showing polynomial-time algorithms for certain special cases of $\mathbb{Z}$SVP [12,17,19,24,25]. A summary of their results is beyond the scope of this work, but we note that their techniques are very different from those in this work with the exception of Szydlo's heuristic algorithm [38]. In particular, Szydlo presented a heuristic

---

[2] Note that we ran these experiments directly on bases of $\mathbb{Z}^n$, rather than on rotations of bases of $\mathbb{Z}^n$ because the algorithms themselves are rotation invariant.

algorithm that solves $\mathbb{Z}$SVP by finding many vectors of length roughly $c\sqrt{n}$ (where the constant $c > 0$ is unspecified), which can be viewed as a heuristic reduction from $\mathbb{Z}$SVP to $c\sqrt{n}$-SVP. In contrast, we give an efficient reduction with a proof of correctness from $\mathbb{Z}$SVP to γ-uSVP for any constant γ (and, more generally, a roughly $(n/\gamma^2)^{\gamma^2}$-time reduction for $\gamma \leq \sqrt{n}/2$).

Our public-key encryption scheme is quite similar to a scheme recently proposed by Ducas and van Woerden [15], in a beautiful independent work that appeared as a preprint before the present work was finished. On one hand, Ducas and van Woerden's construction is more general than ours—it works with any "remarkable" lattice, of which $\mathbb{Z}^n$ is an example. (We do note in passing that our constructions also make sense for a more general class of lattices, but we do not attempt to make this precise.) On the other hand, because we specialize to $\mathbb{Z}^n$, our scheme is arguably simpler, and the hardness assumptions that we require for security, while formally incomparable, are arguably weaker.

Perhaps the biggest difference is that in [15], the ciphertext is a target point that is very close to the lattice, effectively within the unique decoding radius of $\mathbb{Z}^n$, i.e., $1/2$ (or for more general lattices, within whatever radius one can efficiently decode, uniquely). And, the [15] decryption algorithm recovers the unique lattice vector within this distance of the target point. In this context, $\mathbb{Z}^n$ is not a particularly good lattice because its unique decoding radius is rather small (relative to, e.g., its determinant). (Of course, Ducas and van Woerden list many "remarkable" lattices, many of which are better suited to their construction.) In contrast, our ciphertext is a target point that is quite far away from the lattice, at distance $\Theta(\sqrt{n})$ (well above the radius at which unique decoding is possible), and our decryption algorithm simply determines whether the target is closer or farther than a certain threshold value. Indeed, our scheme is particularly well suited to $\mathbb{Z}^n$ (as we discuss more in the full version [7]). Because of this difference, our scheme achieves security under arguably weaker hardness assumptions. The assumptions are not directly comparable, however, as [15]'s hardness assumptions concern the lattice $\mathbb{Z}^n \oplus \alpha \mathbb{Z}^n$ for a cleverly chosen scaling factor α, whereas our hardness assumptions work with $\mathbb{Z}^n$ directly. Ducas and van Woerden also show a signature scheme and a zero-knowledge proof, while we do not.

Ducas and van Woerden's work also contains more-or-less the same worst-case to average-case reduction that we describe in Sect. 3, and therefore also more-or-less the same distribution of bases that we propose. Indeed, in this case their work is essentially strictly more general than ours. (Similar ideas also appeared in [5,11,20], though in different contexts.)

Blanks and Miller introduced two of the basis-generating procedures that we study, and performed experiments on them to determine if basis reduction algorithms could break them [9]. Our empirical work on different bases for $\mathbb{Z}^n$ is best viewed as follow-up work to [9]. In particular, we perform more trials and run BKZ with larger block sizes. Additionally, we perform experiments on the discrete Gaussian bases described above, which were not considered in [9].

Finally, we note that recent follow-up work to this paper [8] has continued the study of the cryptosystem that we propose.

2 Preliminaries

We write I_n for the identity matrix. We write $\mathsf{O}_n(\mathbb{R})$ for the set of all orthogonal linear transformations. That is $\mathsf{O}_n(\mathbb{R})$ is the set of matrices $R \in \mathbb{R}^{n \times n}$ with the property that $R^T R = I_n$. We often informally refer to orthogonal transformations as "rotations." We refer to integer-valued matrices with determinant ± 1 (i.e., matrices in $\mathrm{GL}_n(\mathbb{Z})$) as *unimodular*. By default logarithms are base e.

We refer the reader to the full version [7] for basic definitions of lattices, the successive minima λ_i, the lattice determinant, the Gram matrix, SVP, GapSVP, and unique SVP.

2.1 The Continuous and Discrete Gaussian Distributions and the Smoothing Parameter

For a vector $\boldsymbol{y} \in \mathbb{R}^n$ and parameter $s > 0$, we write

$$\rho_s(\boldsymbol{y}) := \exp(-\pi \|\boldsymbol{y}\|^2 / s^2)$$

for the Gaussian mass of $\boldsymbol{y}$ with parameter s. We write D_s^n for the symmetric continuous Gaussian distribution on $\mathbb{R}^n$, that is, the distribution with probability density function given by

$$\Pr_{\boldsymbol{X} \sim D_s^n}[\boldsymbol{X} \in S] = \frac{1}{s^n} \cdot \int_S \rho_s(\boldsymbol{y}) \mathrm{d}\boldsymbol{y}$$

for any (measurable) subset $S \subseteq \mathbb{R}^n$. We simply write D_s for D_s^1.

We prove the following lemma in the full version [7]. It shows that when $\boldsymbol{X}$ is sampled from D_s^n, $\mathrm{dist}(\boldsymbol{X}, \mathbb{Z}^n)$ is highly concentrated.

Lemma 1. *For any $s > 0$, positive integer n, and $\varepsilon > \varepsilon_0$*

$$\Pr_{\boldsymbol{X} \sim D_s^n}[|\mathrm{dist}(\boldsymbol{X}, \mathbb{Z}^n)^2 - \nu| > \varepsilon n] \leq 2 \exp(-(\varepsilon - \varepsilon_0)^2 n / 10) \,,$$

where $\nu := \frac{n}{12} - \frac{\exp(-\pi s^2)}{\pi^2} \cdot n$, and $\varepsilon_0 := \frac{\exp(-4\pi s^2)}{6} \cdot (1 + 1/s^2)$.

The Gaussian mass of a lattice $\mathcal{L} \subset \mathbb{R}^n$ with parameter $s > 0$ is

$$\rho_s(\mathcal{L}) := \sum_{y \in \mathcal{L}} \rho_s(\boldsymbol{y}) \,.$$

The *discrete Gaussian distribution* $D_{\mathcal{L},s}$ is the distribution over $\mathcal{L}$ induced by this measure, i.e., for any $\boldsymbol{y} \in \mathcal{L}$,

$$\Pr_{\boldsymbol{X} \sim D_{\mathcal{L},s}}[\boldsymbol{X} = \boldsymbol{y}] = \rho_s(\boldsymbol{y}) / \rho_s(\mathcal{L}) \,.$$

We will need the following theorem from [10], which is a slight strengthening of a result in [18].

Theorem 3. *There is an efficient algorithm that takes as input a basis* $\mathbf{B} = (\boldsymbol{b}_1, \ldots, \boldsymbol{b}_n) \in \mathbb{R}^{n \times n}$ *for a lattice* $\mathcal{L} \subset \mathbb{R}^n$ *and a parameter* $s \geq \sqrt{\log(2n+4)/\pi} \cdot \max_i \|\boldsymbol{b}_i\|$ *and outputs a sample from* $D_{\mathcal{L},s}$.[3]

For $\varepsilon > 0$, the *smoothing parameter* of a lattice $\mathcal{L} \subset \mathbb{R}^n$ is the unique parameter $\eta_\varepsilon(\mathcal{L}) > 0$ such that

$$\rho_{1/\eta_\varepsilon(\mathcal{L})}(\mathcal{L}^*) = 1 + \varepsilon .$$

Lemma 2 ([29, **Lemma 4.1**]). *For any lattice* $\mathcal{L} \subset \mathbb{R}^n$ *and parameter* $s > \eta_\varepsilon(\mathcal{L})$ *for some* $\varepsilon \in (0,1)$, *if* $\boldsymbol{X} \sim D_s^n$, *then* $\boldsymbol{X}$ mod $\mathcal{L}$ *is within statistical distance* $\varepsilon/2$ *of the uniform distribution modulo* $\mathcal{L}$.

Lemma 3 ([29, **Lemma 3.2**]). *For any lattice* $\mathcal{L} \subset \mathbb{R}^n$ *and any* $\varepsilon > 2^{-n}$

$$\eta_\varepsilon(\mathcal{L}) \leq \sqrt{n}/\lambda_1(\mathcal{L}^*) .$$

Lemma 4 ([20, **Lemma 5.4**]). *For any* $s \geq 1$ *and* $m \geq n^2 + n\log(s\sqrt{n})(n + 20\log\log(s\sqrt{n}))$, *if* $\boldsymbol{y}_1, \ldots, \boldsymbol{y}_m \sim D_{\mathbb{Z}^n,s}$ *are sampled independently from* $D_{\mathbb{Z}^n,s}$, *then* $\boldsymbol{y}_1, \ldots, \boldsymbol{y}_m$ *is a generating set of* $\mathbb{Z}^n$ *except with probability* $2^{-\Omega(n)}$.

2.2 Lattice Problems

We will use a result of Lyubashevsky and Micciancio that gives an efficient, dimension-preserving reduction from γ-uSVP to γ-GapSVP for polynomially bounded $\gamma = \gamma(n)$.

Theorem 4 ([28, **Theorem 3**]). *For any* $1 \leq \gamma \leq \text{poly}(n)$, *there is a dimension-preserving Cook reduction from* γ-uSVP *to* γ-GapSVP.

We will also make use of the following algorithm.

Theorem 5 ([2, **Corollary 6.6**]). *There is a* $2^{n/2+o(n)}$-*time algorithm that solves* γ-GapSVP *with* $\gamma = 1.93 + o(1)$.

Lattice problems on rotations of $\mathbb{Z}^n$. We say that two lattices $\mathcal{L}_1, \mathcal{L}_2$ of dimension n are *isomorphic*, which we denote by $\mathcal{L}_1 \cong \mathcal{L}_2$, if there exists $R \in O_n(\mathbb{R})$ such that $R(\mathcal{L}_1) = \mathcal{L}_2$. We call lattices $\mathcal{L}$ satisfying $\mathcal{L} \cong \mathbb{Z}^n$ "rotations of $\mathbb{Z}^n$." We define γ-$\mathbb{Z}$SVP to be γ-SVP with the additional requirement that the input basis $\mathbf{B}$ satisfy $\mathcal{L}(\mathbf{B}) \cong \mathbb{Z}^n$.

Definition 1. *For* $\gamma = \gamma(n) \geq 1$, *the* γ-*approximate Shortest Vector Problem on rotations of* $\mathbb{Z}^n$ (γ-$\mathbb{Z}$SVP) *is the search problem defined as follows. Given a basis* $\mathbf{B} \in \mathbb{R}^{n \times n}$ *of a lattice* $\mathcal{L}$ *satisfying* $\mathcal{L} \cong \mathbb{Z}^n$ *as input, output a non-zero vector* $\boldsymbol{v} \in \mathcal{L}$ *with* $\|\boldsymbol{v}\| \leq \gamma \cdot \lambda_1(\mathcal{L})$.

When $\gamma = 1$, we simply write γ-$\mathbb{Z}$SVP as $\mathbb{Z}$SVP.

---

[3] In fact, the algorithm even works for any parameter $s \geq \sqrt{\log(2n+4)/\pi} \cdot \max_i \|\widetilde{\boldsymbol{b}}_i\|$, where $\widetilde{\boldsymbol{b}}_i$ is the ith Gram-Schmidt vector of the basis $\mathbf{B}$.

2.3 Primitive Vectors and Vector Counting

Given a lattice $\mathcal{L}$, a vector $\boldsymbol{x} \in \mathcal{L}$ is called *primitive* if $\boldsymbol{x} \notin a\mathcal{L}$ for any integer $a >$ 1. Note that $\boldsymbol{0}$ is not primitive regardless of $\mathcal{L}$. Let $\mathcal{L}_{\mathrm{prim}}$ denote the set of primitive vectors in $\mathcal{L}$. For a lattice $\mathcal{L}$ and $r > 0$, let $N(\mathcal{L}, r) := |\{\boldsymbol{x} \in \mathcal{L} : \|\boldsymbol{x}\| \leq r\}|$ and let $N_{\mathrm{prim}}(\mathcal{L}, r) := |\{\boldsymbol{x} \in \mathcal{L}_{\mathrm{prim}} : \|\boldsymbol{x}\| \leq r\}| / 2$, where in the latter expression we divide by two so that we effectively count $\pm\boldsymbol{x} \in \mathcal{L}$ as a single vector.

We will use the following bound from [34] on the number of integer points in a ball $r\mathcal{B}_2^n$ for various radii r, where $\mathcal{B}_2^n$ denotes the closed Euclidean unit ball.

Proposition 1 ([34, Claim 8.2]). *For any $n \geq 1$ and any radius $1 \leq r \leq \sqrt{n}$ with $r^2 \in \mathbb{Z}$,*

$$(2n/r^2)^{r^2} \leq |\mathbb{Z}^n \cap r\mathcal{B}_2^n| \leq (2e^3 n/r^2)^{r^2} .$$

A lattice $\mathcal{L} \subseteq \mathbb{R}^n$ satisfying $\det(\mathcal{L}') \geq 1$ for all sublattices $\mathcal{L}' \subseteq \mathcal{L}$ is called *semi-stable*. We will also use the following bound from [34] on $|\mathcal{L} \cap r\mathcal{B}_2^n|$ where $\mathcal{L}$ is a semi-stable lattice.

Proposition 2 ([34, Corollary 1.4, Item 1]). *Let $t := 10(\log n + 2)$ and let $\mathcal{L}$ be a semi-stable lattice. Then for any $r \geq 1$, $|\mathcal{L} \cap r\mathcal{B}_2^n| \leq 3e^{\pi t^2 r^2}/2$.*

2.4 Probability

Lemma 5 (Chernoff-Hoeffding bound [21]). *Let $X_1, \ldots, X_M \in [0,1]$ be independent and identically distributed random variables. Then, for $s > 0$,*

$$\Pr\left[\left|M\mathbb{E}[X_i] - \sum X_i\right| \geq sM\right] \leq 2e^{-Ms^2/10} .$$

3 How to Sample a Provably Secure Basis

In this section, we show how to sample a basis $\mathbf{B}$ for a rotation of $\mathbb{Z}^n$ that is "provably at least as secure as any other basis." In particular, we show a distribution of bases $\mathbf{B}$ of rotations of $\mathbb{Z}^n$ that can be sampled efficiently given any basis of a rotation of $\mathbb{Z}^n$ together with the orthogonal transformation R mapping the original lattice to the new lattice. This implies that "if a computational problem can be solved efficiently given a basis from this distribution, then it can be solved efficiently given any basis." (We do not try to make this very general statement formal. In particular, we do not try to classify the set of computational problems for which this result applies. Instead, we simply provide an example.) Similar ideas appeared in [5,11,15,20].

We say that an algorithm $\mathcal{A}$ that takes as input vectors $\boldsymbol{y}_1, \ldots, \boldsymbol{y}_N \in \mathcal{L}$ that form a generating set of a lattice $\mathcal{L}$ and outputs a basis $\mathbf{B}$ of $\mathcal{L}$ is *rotation-invariant* if for any orthogonal transformation $R \in \mathsf{O}_n(\mathbb{R})$, $\mathcal{A}(R\boldsymbol{y}_1, \ldots, R\boldsymbol{y}_N) = R(\mathcal{A}(\boldsymbol{y}_1, \ldots, \boldsymbol{y}_N))$. For example, the LLL algorithm yields an efficient rotation-invariant algorithm that converts a generating set to a basis, and in Sect. 3.1 we give a more efficient algorithm that also does this. Given such an $\mathcal{A}$, our distribution is then the following.

Definition 2. *For any efficient rotation-invariant algorithm $\mathcal{A}$ that converts a generating set to a basis and parameter $s = s(n) \geq 1$ the distribution $(\mathcal{A}, s)$-$\mathbb{Z}DGS$ is sampled as follows. For $i = 1, 2, 3, \ldots$, sample $\boldsymbol{z}_i \sim D_{\mathbb{Z}^n, s}$. Let $\mathbf{B} := \mathcal{A}(\boldsymbol{z}_1, \ldots, \boldsymbol{z}_i)$. If $\mathbf{B} \in \mathbb{Z}^{n \times n}$ is full rank and $|\det(\mathbf{B})| = 1$, then sample a uniformly random orthogonal matrix $R \sim O_n(\mathbb{R})$ and output $\mathbf{B}' := R\mathbf{B}$. Otherwise, continue the loop.*

Notice that the resulting basis is in fact a basis of a rotation of $\mathbb{Z}^n$, specifically, $R\mathbb{Z}^n$. By Lemma 4, the above procedure terminates in polynomial time except with negligible probability.

Theorem 6. *For any efficient rotation-invariant algorithm $\mathcal{A}$ that converts a generating set into a basis, there is an efficient randomized algorithm that takes as input a basis $\mathbf{B} = (\boldsymbol{b}_1, \ldots, \boldsymbol{b}_n) \in \mathbb{R}^{n \times n}$ for a rotation $\mathcal{L}$ of $\mathbb{Z}^n$ and a parameter $s \geq \sqrt{\log(2n+4)/\pi} \cdot \max \|\boldsymbol{b}_i\|$ and outputs a basis $\mathbf{B}' \in \mathbb{R}^{n \times n}$ generating $\mathcal{L}'$ that is distributed exactly as $(\mathcal{A}, s)$-$\mathbb{Z}DGS$ together with an orthogonal transformation $R \in O_n(\mathbb{R})$ such that $R\mathcal{L} = \mathcal{L}'$.*

Proof. The algorithm behaves as follows. For $i = 1, 2, 3, \ldots$, the algorithm uses the procedure from Theorem 3 to sample $\boldsymbol{y}_i \sim D_{\mathcal{L}, s}$, where $\mathcal{L}$ is the lattice generated by $\mathbf{B}$. It then computes $\mathbf{B}^\dagger := \mathcal{A}(\boldsymbol{y}_1, \ldots, \boldsymbol{y}_i)$. If the lattice generated by $\mathbf{B}^\dagger$ has full rank and determinant one, then the algorithm outputs $\mathbf{B}' := R\mathbf{B}^\dagger$ and R, where $R \sim O_n(\mathbb{R})$ is a uniformly random rotation. Otherwise, it continues.

To see why this is correct, let $R' \in O_n(\mathbb{R})$ be an orthogonal transformation such that $\mathbb{Z}^n = R'\mathcal{L}$. Let $\boldsymbol{y}'_i := R'\boldsymbol{y}_i$, and notice that the $\boldsymbol{y}'_i$ are distributed as independent samples from $D_{\mathbb{Z}^n, s}$. It follows from the fact that $\mathcal{A}$ is rotation invariant that $R'\mathbf{B}^\dagger = \mathcal{A}(\boldsymbol{y}'_1, \ldots, \boldsymbol{y}'_i)$. Clearly $\mathbf{B}^\dagger$ is full rank and has determinant one if and only if $R'\mathbf{B}^\dagger$ has this same property. Therefore, $\mathbf{B}'$ is distributed exactly as $R(R')^{-1}\mathcal{A}(\boldsymbol{y}'_1, \ldots, \boldsymbol{y}'_i)$ (conditioned on the rank and determinant conditions being satisfied). Since R is a uniformly random orthogonal transformation, this is distributed identically to $R''\mathcal{A}(\boldsymbol{y}'_1, \ldots, \boldsymbol{y}'_i)$ for $R'' \sim O_n(\mathbb{R})$. Notice that this is exactly the $\mathbb{Z}DGS$ distribution.

Finally, as we observed above, Lemma 4 implies that after $\mathrm{poly}(n, \log s)$ samples, $\boldsymbol{y}'_1, \ldots, \boldsymbol{y}'_i$ will generate $\mathbb{Z}^n$ with high probability, in which case $\boldsymbol{y}_1, \ldots, \boldsymbol{y}_i$ will generate $\mathcal{L}$. Therefore, the algorithm terminates in polynomial time (with high probability).

The following corollary shows that we can achieve the same result for a fixed parameter s (regardless of the length of the input basis).

Corollary 1. *For any efficient rotation-invariant algorithm $\mathcal{A}$ that converts a generating set into a basis, there is an efficient randomized algorithm that takes as input any basis $\mathbf{B} \in \mathbb{R}^{n \times n}$ for a rotation $\mathcal{L}$ of $\mathbb{Z}^n$ and outputs a basis $\mathbf{B}' \in \mathbb{R}^{n \times n}$ generating $\mathcal{L}'$ and rotation R such that $\mathbf{B}'$ is distributed as $(\mathcal{A}, s)$-$\mathbb{Z}DGS$ and $R\mathcal{L} = \mathcal{L}'$, where $s = 2^n$.*

Proof. The algorithm simply runs the LLL algorithm on $\mathbf{B}$, receiving as output some basis $\mathbf{B}^\dagger = (\boldsymbol{b}_1^\dagger, \ldots, \boldsymbol{b}_n^\dagger)$ for $\mathcal{L}$ with $\|\boldsymbol{b}_i^\dagger\| \leq 2^{n/2}$. It then runs the procedure from Theorem 6 and outputs the result.

Using Corollary 1, we can easily reduce worst-case variants of lattice problems on rotations of $\mathbb{Z}^n$ to variants in which the input basis is sampled from $\mathbb{Z}$DGS. As an example, we show a random self-reduction for SVP over rotations of $\mathbb{Z}^n$ below. (We also use this idea in Sect. 4.)

Definition 3. *For any $\gamma = \gamma(n) \geq 1$ and any efficient rotation-invariant algorithm $\mathcal{A}$, the $(\mathcal{A}, \gamma)$-acZSVP problem is defined as follows. The input is a basis $\mathbf{B} \in \mathbb{R}^{n \times n}$ sampled from $(\mathcal{A}, 2^n)$-ZDGS generating a rotation $\mathcal{L}$ of $\mathbb{Z}^n$. The goal is to output $\boldsymbol{y} \in \mathcal{L}$ with $0 < \|\boldsymbol{y}\| \leq \gamma$.*

Theorem 7. *For any efficient rotation-invariant algorithm $\mathcal{A}$ and any $\gamma \geq 1$, there is an efficient reduction from γ-ZSVP to $(\mathcal{A}, \gamma)$-acZSVP.*

Proof. The reduction takes as input a basis $\mathbf{B} \in \mathbb{R}^{n \times n}$ for a rotation $\mathcal{L}$ of $\mathbb{Z}^n$ and simply runs the procedure from Corollary 1, receiving as output a basis $\mathbf{B}'$ sampled from $(\mathcal{A}, 2^n)$-ZDGS generating $\mathcal{L}'$ together with a rotation R such that $R\mathcal{L} = \mathcal{L}'$. It then calls its $(\mathcal{A}, \gamma)$-acZSVP oracle on input $\mathbf{B}'$, receiving as output some vector $\boldsymbol{y}' \in \mathcal{L}'$. Finally, it outputs $\boldsymbol{y} := R^{-1}\boldsymbol{y}'$.

3.1 A Rotation-Invariant Generating Set to Basis Conversion Algorithm

For completeness, we now specify and analyze a rotation-invariant algorithm (Algorithm 1) for converting a generating set $Y = (\boldsymbol{y}_1, \ldots, \boldsymbol{y}_N)$ to a basis. After we published a preliminary version of this work, we learned that Li and Nguyen developed a very similar algorithm in [26, Algorithm B.1], and showed an optimized variant in [27, Section 4].

The algorithm $\mathcal{A}$ itself is perhaps best viewed as a "lazy" variant of the LLL algorithm. In particular, unlike LLL, $\mathcal{A}$ simply works to find *some* basis of the lattice generated by Y, and makes no attempt to further reduce the basis. More quantitatively, in Theorem 8, we upper bound the number of swaps performed by Algorithm 1 for (rotations of) integer lattices by $n \log_2 \beta$, where n is the rank of the input lattice and β is the maximum norm of a vector in the input generating set Y. (It is common in the literature to state the running time of basis reduction algorithms in this form.) For comparison, standard analysis of the LLL algorithm (see, e.g., [33]) upper bounds the number of swaps it performs by $O(n^2 \log \beta)$.

Define the (generalized) Gram-Schmidt vectors corresponding to a sequence $\boldsymbol{y}_1, \ldots, \boldsymbol{y}_N$ of (not necessarily linearly independent) vectors as follows:

$$\widetilde{\boldsymbol{y}}_1 := \boldsymbol{y}_1 \,,$$

$$\widetilde{\boldsymbol{y}}_i := \boldsymbol{y}_i - \sum_{\substack{j < i, \\ \widetilde{\boldsymbol{y}}_j \neq 0}} \frac{\langle \boldsymbol{y}_i, \widetilde{\boldsymbol{y}}_j \rangle}{\langle \widetilde{\boldsymbol{y}}_j, \widetilde{\boldsymbol{y}}_j \rangle} \widetilde{\boldsymbol{y}}_j \qquad \text{for } i = 2, \ldots, N.$$

We next prove that Algorithm 1 is correct, rotation invariant, and in fact quite efficient. Recall that a generating-set-to-basis conversion algorithm $\mathcal{A}$ being

---

Algorithm 1: Rotation-Invariant Generating Set to Basis Conversion

---

Input: A generating set $Y = (\boldsymbol{y}_1, \ldots, \boldsymbol{y}_N) \in \mathbb{R}^{m \times N}$ of a lattice $\mathcal{L}$ of rank $1 \leq n \leq N$.
Output: A basis of $\mathcal{L}$.

// Size-reduction step.
Compute the Gram-Schmidt vectors $\widetilde{\boldsymbol{y}}_1, \ldots, \widetilde{\boldsymbol{y}}_N$ corresponding to $\boldsymbol{y}_1, \ldots, \boldsymbol{y}_N$.
for $i = 2, \ldots, N$ **do**
    for $j = i - 1, \ldots, 1$ with $\widetilde{\boldsymbol{y}}_j \neq \boldsymbol{0}$ **do**
        $\boldsymbol{y}_i \leftarrow \boldsymbol{y}_i - \lfloor \mu_{i,j} \rceil \cdot \boldsymbol{y}_j$ // $\mu_{i,j} := \langle \boldsymbol{y}_i, \widetilde{\boldsymbol{y}}_j \rangle / \langle \widetilde{\boldsymbol{y}}_j, \widetilde{\boldsymbol{y}}_j \rangle$.
    end
end
Delete any identically zero columns from Y, and update N to be the new number of columns in Y.

// Swap step.
if *there exists* $i \in \{2, \ldots, N\}$ *such that* $\widetilde{\boldsymbol{y}}_i = \boldsymbol{0}$ **then**
    Swap $\boldsymbol{y}_j$ and $\boldsymbol{y}_i$, where $j < i$ is the minimum index such that
    $\boldsymbol{y}_i \in \text{span}(\boldsymbol{y}_1, \ldots, \boldsymbol{y}_j)$.
    goto size-reduction step.
end

return Y.

---

rotation invariant means that for all input generating sets $Y \in \mathbb{R}^{m \times N}$ and $R \in \text{O}_m(\mathbb{R})$, $R\mathcal{A}(Y) = \mathcal{A}(RY)$.

Theorem 8. *On input a generating set* $Y = (\boldsymbol{y}_1, \ldots, \boldsymbol{y}_N) \in \mathbb{R}^{m \times N}$ *of a lattice* $\mathcal{L}$ *of rank* $n \geq 1$, *Algorithm 1 outputs a basis of* $\mathcal{L}$. *Furthermore, Algorithm 1 is rotation invariant and performs at most* $n \log_2 \beta - \log \det(\mathcal{L})$ *swap operations, where* $\beta := \max_{i \in \{1, \ldots, N\}} \|\boldsymbol{y}_i\|$. *In particular, if* $\mathcal{L}$ *is (a rotation of an) integer lattice then* $\det(\mathcal{L}) \geq 1$ *and so Algorithm 1 performs at most* $n \log_2 \beta$ *swaps.*

Proof. In the full version [7], we include a (straightforward) proof that Algorithm 1 does in fact output a basis and is in fact rotation invariant.

It remains to upper bound the number of swaps performed by Algorithm 1. Define the potential function

$$P(Y) := \prod_{\substack{i \in \{1, \ldots, N\}, \\ \widetilde{\boldsymbol{y}}_i \neq \boldsymbol{0}}} \|\widetilde{\boldsymbol{y}}_i\| \, ,$$

and note that $P(Y)$ is equal to the determinant of the sublattice of $\mathcal{L}$ spanned by vectors $\boldsymbol{y}_i$ with $\widetilde{\boldsymbol{y}}_i \neq \boldsymbol{0}$. Therefore, because the algorithm maintains the invariant that Y is a generating set of $\mathcal{L}$, we have that $P(Y) \geq \det(\mathcal{L})$. Using the same invariant, we also have that at each iteration there are exactly n vectors with non-zero Gram-Schmidt vectors. So, by definition of β, the input generating set

$Y_0 = (\boldsymbol{y}_1, \ldots, \boldsymbol{y}_N)$ satisfies

$$P(Y_0) = \prod_{\substack{i \in \{1,\ldots,N\}, \\ \widetilde{\boldsymbol{y}}_i \neq \boldsymbol{0}}} \|\widetilde{\boldsymbol{y}}_i\| \leq \prod_{\substack{i \in \{1,\ldots,N\}, \\ \widetilde{\boldsymbol{y}}_i \neq \boldsymbol{0}}} \|\boldsymbol{y}_i\| \leq \beta^n . \tag{1}$$

Finally, we show that $P(Y)$ decreases by a multiplicative factor of at least 2 after each swap operation. Let $Y = (\boldsymbol{y}_1, \ldots, \boldsymbol{y}_N)$ and $Y' = (\boldsymbol{y}_1', \ldots, \boldsymbol{y}_N')$ denote the respective generating sets in Algorithm 1 before and after performing a given swap operation on $\boldsymbol{y}_j$ and $\boldsymbol{y}_i$ for $j < i$.

We claim that $\widetilde{\boldsymbol{y}}_k' = \widetilde{\boldsymbol{y}}_k$ for all $k \neq j$. This is immediate for $k < j$ because $\boldsymbol{y}_k' = \boldsymbol{y}_k$ for such k. For $k > j$, it follows by noting that $\mathrm{span}(\boldsymbol{y}_1', \ldots, \boldsymbol{y}_j') = \mathrm{span}(\boldsymbol{y}_1, \ldots, \boldsymbol{y}_j)$, which in turn follows by noting that, by the algorithm's choice of i and j, $\boldsymbol{y}_j' = \boldsymbol{y}_i$ and $\boldsymbol{y}_i \in \mathrm{span}(\boldsymbol{y}_1, \ldots, \boldsymbol{y}_j) \setminus \mathrm{span}(\boldsymbol{y}_1, \ldots, \boldsymbol{y}_{j-1})$. Furthermore, $\boldsymbol{y}_i \in \mathrm{span}(\boldsymbol{y}_1, \ldots, \boldsymbol{y}_j) \setminus \mathrm{span}(\boldsymbol{y}_1, \ldots, \boldsymbol{y}_{j-1})$ implies that $\widetilde{\boldsymbol{y}}_j$ is non-zero.

Let π_k denote projection onto $\mathrm{span}(\boldsymbol{y}_1, \ldots, \boldsymbol{y}_k)^\perp$. We then have that

$$\frac{P(Y')}{P(Y)} = \prod_{\substack{k \in \{1,\ldots,N\}, \\ \widetilde{\boldsymbol{y}}_k \neq \boldsymbol{0}}} \frac{\|\widetilde{\boldsymbol{y}}_k'\|}{\|\widetilde{\boldsymbol{y}}_k\|} = \frac{\|\widetilde{\boldsymbol{y}}_j'\|}{\|\widetilde{\boldsymbol{y}}_j\|} = \frac{\|\pi_{j-1}(\boldsymbol{y}_i)\|}{\|\widetilde{\boldsymbol{y}}_j\|} = \frac{|\mu_{i,j}| \cdot \|\widetilde{\boldsymbol{y}}_j\|}{\|\widetilde{\boldsymbol{y}}_j\|} \leq 1/2 .$$

The final equality again uses the fact that $\boldsymbol{y}_i \in \mathrm{span}(\boldsymbol{y}_1, \ldots, \boldsymbol{y}_j)$, and the inequality holds because $\mu_{i,j} := \langle \boldsymbol{y}_i, \widetilde{\boldsymbol{y}}_j \rangle / \langle \widetilde{\boldsymbol{y}}_j, \widetilde{\boldsymbol{y}}_j \rangle$ has magnitude at most $1/2$ after the size-reduction step.

Therefore, by Eq. (1), Algorithm 1 performs at most

$$\log_2(P(Y_0)/\det(\mathcal{L})) \leq n \log_2 \beta - \log \det(\mathcal{L})$$

swap operations, as needed.

4 We Have an Encryption Scheme to Sell You

We now consider the possibility that it actually is "hard to recognize $\mathbb{Z}^n$" (where we must formalize what this means rather carefully), and we show that this implies the existence of a relatively simple public-key encryption scheme. (See also [8] for follow-up work implementing the scheme and studying its security.)

The encryption scheme itself is described below. There are public parameters $s > 0$ and $r > 0$, which are functions of the security parameter n (i.e., $s = s(n)$ and $r = r(n)$). In particular, the parameter s will control the length of the basis used as the public key, and the parameter r is a noise parameter. In the full version [7], we provide more discussion of these parameters.

- Gen(1^n): Sample vectors $\boldsymbol{z}_1, \boldsymbol{z}_2, \boldsymbol{z}_3, \ldots$ independently from $D_{\mathbb{Z}^n,s}$ until $\boldsymbol{z}_1, \ldots, \boldsymbol{z}_k$ generate $\mathbb{Z}^n$. Run Algorithm 1[4] on input $\boldsymbol{z}_1, \ldots, \boldsymbol{z}_k$ to obtain a basis $\mathbf{B}$ of $\mathbb{Z}^n$ and let $\boldsymbol{G} := \mathbf{B}^T \mathbf{B}$. Output $sk := \mathbf{B}$ and $pk := \boldsymbol{G}$.

---

[4] One can instead run any rotation-invariant algorithm that converts generating sets into bases, as defined in Sect. 3. We simply suggest Algorithm 1 for concreteness.

- Enc($pk, b \in \{0,1\}$):
  - If $b = 0$, sample $\boldsymbol{X} \in \mathbb{R}^n$ from a continuous Gaussian distribution with probability density function

$$\frac{\det(\boldsymbol{G})^{1/2}}{r^n} \cdot \exp(-\pi \boldsymbol{X}^T \boldsymbol{G} \boldsymbol{X}/r^2) = \frac{\det(\mathbf{B})}{r^n} \cdot \exp(-\pi \boldsymbol{X}^T \boldsymbol{G} \boldsymbol{X}/r^2) ,$$

    and output $\boldsymbol{c} := \boldsymbol{X} \bmod 1$ (i.e., the coordinates of $\boldsymbol{c}$ are the fractional parts of the coordinates of $\boldsymbol{X}$).
  - If $b = 1$, output uniformly random $\boldsymbol{c} \sim [0,1)^n$.
- Dec($sk, \boldsymbol{c}$): Set $\boldsymbol{t} = (t_1, \ldots, t_n)^T := \mathbf{B}\boldsymbol{c}$. Output 1 if $\sum(t_i - \lfloor t_i \rceil)^2 > d$ and 0 otherwise, where

$$d := \frac{n}{12} - \frac{\exp(-\pi r^2)}{2\pi^2} \cdot n .$$

We first concern ourselves with the correctness of this scheme. In particular, the following lemma tells us that the decryption algorithm will answer correctly except with probability roughly $\exp(-e^{-\pi r^2} n)$. In order to be conservative, we will want to take r to be as big as possible, so we will take r to be slightly smaller than $\sqrt{\log n / \pi}$. E.g., we can take $r = \sqrt{\log n/(10\pi)}$. This is the maximal choice for r up to a constant, since if we took, e.g., $r \geq \sqrt{\log n}$, then ciphertexts of zero would be statistically close to ciphertexts of one, making decryption failures unreasonably common.

Lemma 6. *For* $r \geq 1$, *let* $\delta := \exp(-\pi r^2)$. *Then, the decryption algorithm described above outputs the correct bit* b *except with probability at most* $2\exp(-c\delta^2 n)$ *for some constant* $c > 0$.

Proof. For the case $b = 1$, we simply notice that $\boldsymbol{t}$ is uniformly random in a fundamental domain of $\mathbb{Z}^n$. It follows that $t_i - \lfloor t_i \rceil$ is uniformly random in the interval $[-1/2, 1/2)$ and independent of the other coordinates. In particular $\mathbb{E}[(t_i - \lfloor t_i \rceil)^2] = 1/12$. It then follows from the Chernoff-Hoeffding bound (Lemma 5) that

$$\Pr\left[\sum(t_i - \lfloor t_i \rceil)^2 \leq d\right] \leq \exp(-\delta^2 n/1000) .$$

We now consider the case $b = 0$. Write $\boldsymbol{c} = \boldsymbol{X} + \boldsymbol{z}$ for $\boldsymbol{z} \in \mathbb{Z}^n$. Then, $\boldsymbol{t} = \mathbf{B}\boldsymbol{c} = \mathbf{B}\boldsymbol{X} + \mathbf{B}\boldsymbol{z} = \mathbf{B}\boldsymbol{X} \bmod 1$. (Here, we crucially rely on the fact that $\mathbf{B}$ is an integer matrix.) Notice that $\mathbf{B}\boldsymbol{X}$ is distributed exactly as a continuous Gaussian with covariance $\mathbf{B}(r^2 \boldsymbol{G}^{-1})\mathbf{B}^T = r^2$, i.e., as D_r^n. Therefore, $\sum(t_i - \lfloor t_i \rceil)^2$ is distributed identically to $\mathrm{dist}(\boldsymbol{Y}, \mathbb{Z}^n)^2$, where $\boldsymbol{Y} \sim D_r^n$. By Lemma 1,

$$\Pr[\mathrm{dist}(\boldsymbol{Y}, \mathbb{Z}^n)^2 > d] \leq 2\exp(-(d - \nu - \varepsilon n)^2/10) ,$$

where $\nu := \frac{n}{12} - \frac{\delta}{\pi^2} \cdot n$, and $\varepsilon := \delta^4/3$. Notice that $\frac{d - \nu - \varepsilon n}{n} = \frac{\delta}{2\pi^2} - \delta^4/3 > \delta/100$. The result follows.

4.1   Basic Security

We now observe that the above scheme is semantically secure if (and only if)
the following problem is hard. The only distinction between this problem and
the problem of breaking the semantic security of the encryption scheme is that
in the problem below the underlying lattice is specified by a worst-case basis
B instead of an average-case Gram matrix **G**. We will reduce between the two
problems using the ideas from Sect. 3.

Here and below, we have an additional parameter ρ, which is a bound on the
lengths of the input basis vectors. If we set $s = 2^n$ in our encryption scheme,
then we could remove ρ by using the LLL algorithm, as we did in Sect. 3.

Definition 4. *For parameters $\rho = \rho(n) > 0$ and $r = r(n) > 0$, the (ρ, r)-$\mathbb{Z}GvU$
problem (Gaussian versus Uniform mod $\mathbb{Z}^n$) is the promise problem defined as
follows. The input is a basis $\mathbf{B} = (\boldsymbol{b}_1, \ldots, \boldsymbol{b}_n) \in \mathbb{R}^{n \times n}$ such that $\|\boldsymbol{b}_i\| \leq \rho$
that generates a rotation of $\mathbb{Z}^n$, and a vector $\boldsymbol{y} \in [0, 1)^n$, where $\boldsymbol{y}$ is sampled
as follows. A bit $b \sim \{0, 1\}$ is sampled uniformly at random. If $b = 0$, $\boldsymbol{y} =
\mathbf{B}^{-1}\boldsymbol{X} \bmod 1$ for $\boldsymbol{X} \sim D_r$, and if $b = 1$, $\boldsymbol{y} \sim [0, 1)^n$. The goal is to output b.*

*We say that (ρ, r)-$\mathbb{Z}GvU$ is hard if no probabilistic polynomial-time algorithm
$\mathcal{A}$ can solve this problem with probability better than $1/2 + \mathrm{negl}(n)$.*

Theorem 9. *If (ρ, r)-$\mathbb{Z}GvU$ is hard for some ρ, r, then the above encryption
scheme is semantically secure with parameters $s := \sqrt{\log(2n + 4)/\pi} \cdot \rho$ and r.*

Proof. Suppose that there is a probabilistic polynomial-time adversary $\mathcal{B}$ that
has non-negligible advantage in breaking the semantic security of the encryption
scheme. We construct an efficient algorithm $\mathcal{E}$ that solves $\mathbb{Z}GvU$ with probability
non-negligibly larger than $1/2$.

The algorithm $\mathcal{E}$ takes as input a basis $\mathbf{B} \in \mathbb{R}^{n \times n}$ generating a lattice $\mathcal{L}$,
and $\boldsymbol{y} \in [0, 1)^n$. It then uses the procedure from Theorem 6 with Algorithm 1 to
convert this into a basis $\mathbf{B}'$ for a rotation of $\mathcal{L}$ and sets $\boldsymbol{G} := (\mathbf{B}')^T \mathbf{B}'$. It then
sets $\boldsymbol{c} := (\mathbf{B}')^{-1} \mathbf{B} \boldsymbol{y} \bmod 1$. Finally, $\mathcal{E}$ calls $\mathcal{B}$ on input $\boldsymbol{G}$ and $\boldsymbol{c}$ and outputs
whatever $\mathcal{B}$ outputs.

It is clear that $\mathcal{E}$ is efficient. Furthermore, if $\boldsymbol{y}$ is uniformly random modulo
1, then clearly $\boldsymbol{c}$ is also uniformly random modulo 1. On the other hand, if
$\boldsymbol{y} = \mathbf{B}^{-1}\boldsymbol{X} \bmod 1$ for $\boldsymbol{X} \sim D_r$, then

$$\boldsymbol{c} = (\mathbf{B}')^{-1} \mathbf{B} \boldsymbol{y} \bmod 1 = (\mathbf{B}')^{-1} \boldsymbol{X} \bmod 1 .$$

Notice that $(\mathbf{B}')^{-1}\boldsymbol{X}$ is distributed exactly as a Gaussian with covariance $r^2 \boldsymbol{G}^{-1}$.
Therefore, when $b = 0$, $\boldsymbol{c}$ is distributed exactly like an encryption of zero, and
when $b = 1$, $\boldsymbol{c}$ is distributed exactly like an encryption of one. □

4.2   A Worst-Case to Average-Case Reduction (of a Sort)

Of course, $\mathbb{Z}GvU$ is a rather artificial problem. Below, we show reductions to
it from worst-case problems that ask us to distinguish $\mathbb{Z}^n$ from a lattice that is

different from $\mathbb{Z}^n$ in a specific way. These can be thought of as "$\mathbb{Z}^n$ versions" of the traditional worst-case lattice problems GapSPP and GapSVP.

Recall that $\eta_\varepsilon(\mathbb{Z}^n) \approx \sqrt{\log(2n/\varepsilon)/\pi}$ for small ε.

Definition 5. *For any approximation factor $\alpha = \alpha(n) \geq 1$, $\varepsilon \in (0,1/2)$, and a length bound $\rho = \rho(n) > 0$, the problem $(\alpha, \varepsilon, \rho)$-$\mathbb{Z}$GapSPP is defined as follows. The input is a basis $\mathbf{B} = (\boldsymbol{b}_1, \ldots, \boldsymbol{b}_n) \in \mathbb{R}^{n \times n}$ for a lattice $\mathcal{L}$ satisfying $\|\boldsymbol{b}_i\| \leq \rho$. The goal is to output YES if $\mathcal{L} \cong \mathbb{Z}^n$ and to output NO if $\eta_\varepsilon(\mathcal{L}) < \eta_\varepsilon(\mathbb{Z}^n)/\alpha$.*

The below reduction shows that if $(\alpha, \varepsilon, \rho)$-$\mathbb{Z}$GapSPP is hard, then our encryption scheme with $r := \sqrt{\log n/(10\pi)}$ is secure for any $\varepsilon < n^{-\omega(1)}$ and $\alpha \leq \eta_\varepsilon(\mathbb{Z}^n)/r \approx \sqrt{10\log(n/\varepsilon)/\log n} \approx \sqrt{\log(1/\varepsilon)/\log n}$.

Theorem 10. *For any efficiently computable $\varepsilon = \varepsilon(n) \in (0,1/2)$ and integer $\ell = \ell(n) \geq 100n/(\delta - \varepsilon)^2$, there is a reduction from $(\alpha, \varepsilon, \rho)$-$\mathbb{Z}$GapSPP to (ρ, r)-$\mathbb{Z}GvU$ that runs in time $\mathrm{poly}(n) \cdot \ell$ and answers correctly except with probability at most 2^{-n}, where $\alpha := \eta_\varepsilon(\mathbb{Z}^n)/r$ and the success probability of the $\mathbb{Z}GvU$ oracle is $1/2 + \delta$, provided that $\delta > \varepsilon$.*

In particular, if $(\alpha, \varepsilon, \rho)$-$\mathbb{Z}GapSPP$ is hard for any negligible $\varepsilon = \varepsilon(n) < n^{-\omega(1)}$, then (ρ, r)-$\mathbb{Z}GvU$ is hard.

Proof. The reduction takes as input a basis $\mathbf{B}$ for a lattice $\mathcal{L} \subset \mathbb{R}^n$ and behaves as follows. For $i = 1, \ldots, \ell$, it samples a uniformly random bit $b_i \sim \{0,1\}$. If $b_i = 0$, it samples $\boldsymbol{X}_i \sim D_r^n$ and sets $\boldsymbol{y}_i := \mathbf{B}^{-1}\boldsymbol{X}_i \bmod 1$, and if $b_i = 1$, it samples $\boldsymbol{y}_i \sim [0,1)^n$. It then calls the $\mathbb{Z}GvU$ oracle on input $\mathbf{B}$ and $\boldsymbol{y}_i$, receiving as output some bit $b_i^* \in \{0,1\}$.

Let p be the fraction of indices i such that $b_i = b_i^*$. The algorithm outputs YES if $p \geq 1/2 + \varepsilon + \sqrt{20n/\ell}$. Otherwise, it outputs NO.

The running time is clear. To prove correctness, we first notice that in the YES case, the input to the $\mathbb{Z}GvU$ oracle is distributed identically to the $\mathbb{Z}GvU$ input. It follows that for each i, $\Pr[b_i^* = b_i] = 1/2 + \delta$. Furthermore, these events are independent. Therefore, by the Chernoff-Hoeffding bound (Lemma 5),

$$\Pr[p < 1/2 + \varepsilon + \sqrt{20n/\ell}] \leq 2\exp(-\ell(\delta - \varepsilon - \sqrt{20n/\ell})^2/10) \leq 2^{-n} ,$$

as needed.

On the other hand, in the NO case, by Lemma 2, $\boldsymbol{y}_i$ is within statistical distance ε of a uniformly random element in $[0,1)^n$. It follows that, regardless of the behavior of the oracle, for each i, $\Pr[b_i^* = b_i] \leq 1/2 + \varepsilon$, and again these events are independent. Therefore, by the Chernoff-Hoeffding bound again,

$$\Pr[p \geq 1/2 + \varepsilon + \sqrt{20n/\ell}] \leq 2\exp(-2n) \leq 2^{-n} ,$$

as needed.

(Note that the following definition is not simply the restriction of GapSVP to rotations $\mathcal{L}$ of $\mathbb{Z}^n$—which would be a meaningless problem since all such $\mathcal{L}$ have $\lambda_1(\mathcal{L}) = 1$. Instead, it is the problem of distinguishing $\mathbb{Z}^n$ from a lattice $\mathcal{L}$ with significantly larger $\lambda_1(\mathcal{L}^*)$. Of course, since $\mathbb{Z}^n$ is self dual, and since one can efficiently test whether a lattice is self dual, we could without loss of generality restrict our attention to self-dual lattices and then equivalently work with $\lambda_1(\mathcal{L})$ instead of $\lambda_1(\mathcal{L}^*)$.)

Definition 6. *For parameters $\rho = \rho(n) > 0$ and $\gamma = \gamma(n) \geq 1$, the problem (ρ, γ)-$\mathbb{Z}\mathsf{GapSVP}$ is defined as follows. The input is a basis $\mathbf{B} = (\boldsymbol{b}_1, \ldots, \boldsymbol{b}_n) \in \mathbb{R}^{n \times n}$ for a lattice $\mathcal{L}$ satisfying $\|\boldsymbol{b}_i\| \leq \rho$. The goal is to output YES if $\mathcal{L} \cong \mathbb{Z}^n$ and to output NO if $\lambda_1(\mathcal{L}^*) > \gamma$.*

Theorem 11. *For any $\varepsilon = \varepsilon(n)$ with $2^{-n} < \varepsilon < 1/2$, $\rho = \rho(n) > 0$, and $\gamma = \gamma(n) \geq 10\sqrt{n/\log(n/\varepsilon)}$, there is an efficient reduction from (ρ, γ)-$\mathbb{Z}\mathsf{GapSVP}$ to $(\alpha, \varepsilon, \rho)$-$\mathbb{Z}\mathsf{GapSPP}$ for $\alpha := \gamma\sqrt{\log(n/\varepsilon)/n}/10$.*

Proof. The reduction simply calls its $\mathbb{Z}\mathsf{GapSPP}$ oracle on its input, and outputs whatever the oracle outputs. To see that this reduction is correct, it suffices to consider the NO case. Indeed, by Lemma 3 if $\lambda_1(\mathcal{L}^*) > \gamma$, then $\eta_\varepsilon(\mathcal{L}) < \sqrt{n}/\gamma \leq 10\sqrt{n/\log(n/\varepsilon)} \cdot \eta_\varepsilon(\mathbb{Z}^n)/\gamma = \eta_\varepsilon(\mathbb{Z}^n)/\alpha$, so that the oracle must output NO.

4.3 Putting Everything Together

Finally, we put the reductions above together to obtain a correct public-key encryption scheme that is secure assuming that $\mathbb{Z}\mathsf{GapSVP}$ (or even $\mathbb{Z}\mathsf{GapSPP}$) is hard.

Theorem 12. *Let $r := \sqrt{\log n/(10\pi)}$, and let d be as in Lemma 6. Then, the above encryption scheme is correct, and for any $s = s(n) > 0$ and any $2^{-n} < \varepsilon < n^{-\omega(1)}$ the scheme is secure either if $(\alpha, \varepsilon, \rho)$-$\mathbb{Z}\mathsf{GapSPP}$ is hard for $\alpha := \eta_\varepsilon(\mathbb{Z}^n)/r \approx \sqrt{10\log(n/\varepsilon)/\log n}$ and $\rho := s/\sqrt{(\log 2n + 4)/\pi}$ or if (ρ, γ)-$\mathbb{Z}\mathsf{GapSVP}$ is hard for $\gamma := 10\sqrt{n/\log(n/\varepsilon)} \cdot \alpha \approx \sqrt{10n/\log n}$.*

5 Reductions and Provable Algorithms

In this section, we give a reduction from $\mathbb{Z}\mathsf{SVP}$ to *approximate* (unique-)SVP. In particular, our main result yields a randomized polynomial-time reduction from $\mathbb{Z}\mathsf{SVP}$ to γ-uSVP for any constant $\gamma \geq 1$. By combining this reduction with a known approximation algorithm for uSVP, we show that for any constant $\varepsilon > 0$ there is a $2^{n/2+o(n)}$-time algorithm for $\mathbb{Z}\mathsf{SVP}$.[5] This improves exponentially over the fastest known algorithm for SVP on general lattices [2], which runs in $2^{n+o(n)}$ time and was previously the fastest known algorithm even for the special case of $\mathbb{Z}\mathsf{SVP}$. In fact, our $2^{n/2+o(n)}$-time algorithm works more generally for semi-stable lattices whose minimum distance is not too large.

We note that our reduction is similar to the reduction from SVP to uSVP in [36] though it works in a very different regime (we solve *exact* $\mathbb{Z}\mathsf{SVP}$ using

---

[5] We note again in passing that under a purely geometric conjecture we would in fact obtain a running time of $(4/3)^{n+o(n)} \approx 2^{0.415n}$ [37].

a γ-uSVP oracle for any constant γ, while [36] solves *approximate* SVP using a γ-uSVP oracle for $\gamma \leq 1 + O(\log n/n))$.

Interpreted differently, our reduction also shows conditional *hardness* of uSVP. Namely, if one were to hypothesize that there is no (possibly randomized) polynomial-time algorithm for $\mathbb{Z}$SVP, then it implies that there is no randomized polynomial-time algorithm for solving γ-uSVP for any constant $\gamma \geq 1$. This is notable because uSVP is not known to be NP-hard for any constant factor greater than 1. We also note that our main reduction generalizes to arbitrary lattices with few short vectors and may be of independent interest.

5.1   The Main Reduction and Algorithms

We next present our main reduction, from which we get our main algorithms.

Sampling using a γ-uSVP oracle Our reduction crucially uses the following theorem, which shows how to use a γ-uSVP oracle to sample short primitive vectors. It is very similar to results in [1,35], but those results are in a slightly different form from what we need. See the full version of the paper [7] for a proof.

Theorem 13. *For any $\gamma = \gamma(n) \geq 1$ and $r > 0$, there is a polynomial-time randomized algorithm with access to a γ-uSVP oracle that takes as input (a basis of a) lattice $\mathcal{L}$ and an integer $A' \geq A := N_{prim}(\mathcal{L}, \gamma r)$ and outputs a vector $\boldsymbol{y} \in \mathcal{L}$ such that if $\boldsymbol{x} \in \mathcal{L}$ is a primitive vector with $\|\boldsymbol{x}\| \leq r$ then*

$$\Pr[\boldsymbol{y} = \boldsymbol{x}] \geq \frac{1}{200\, A' \log(100\, A')} \ .$$

Furthermore, the algorithm makes a single query to its γ-uSVP oracle on a full-rank sublattice of $\mathcal{L}$.

We emphasize that Theorem 13 holds for any $r > 0$, but that r need not be provided as input.

The Main Reduction. We now present our main reduction. Intuitively, it says that exact SVP is not much harder than approximate uSVP on lattices with few short vectors. Namely, it says that there is an algorithm for solving exact SVP by making roughly A/G queries to a γ-uSVP oracle (and which uses roughly A/G time overall), where $A := N_{\mathrm{prim}}(\mathcal{L}, \gamma \cdot \lambda_1(\mathcal{L}))$ and $G := N_{\mathrm{prim}}(\mathcal{L}, \lambda_1(\mathcal{L})).$[6]

Theorem 14. *Let $\gamma = \gamma(n) \geq 1$ and let $\mathcal{L}$ be a lattice of dimension n. Let $G := N_{prim}(\mathcal{L}, \lambda_1(\mathcal{L}))$ and let $A := N_{prim}(\mathcal{L}, \gamma \cdot \lambda_1(\mathcal{L}))$. Then there is a randomized Turing reduction from (exact) SVP on $\mathcal{L}$ to γ-uSVP that makes $(A/G) \cdot \mathrm{poly}(n)$ queries to its γ-uSVP oracle, runs in $(A/G) \cdot \mathrm{poly}(n)$ time overall, and makes all oracle queries on full-rank sublattices of $\mathcal{L}$. In particular, the reduction is dimension-preserving.*

---

[6] We have used the standard mnemonic of G representing "good" vectors and A representing "annoying" vectors, although here A representing "all" primitive vectors shorter than $\gamma \cdot \lambda_1(\mathcal{L})$, including the good vectors, is more appropriate. We note in passing that $2G$ is the so-called kissing number of $\mathcal{L}$.

Proof. It suffices to prove the claim for $\gamma \leq 2^{n/2}$. Indeed, suppose that the claim is true for $\gamma = 2^{n/2}$. Then we can solve SVP on $\mathcal{L}$ using $N_{\mathrm{prim}}(\mathcal{L}, 2^{n/2} \cdot \lambda_1(\mathcal{L}))$ · poly(n) queries to a $2^{n/2}$-uSVP oracle and in $N_{\mathrm{prim}}(\mathcal{L}, 2^{n/2} \cdot \lambda_1(\mathcal{L})) \cdot$poly($n$) time overall. But, because the $2^{n/2}$-uSVP oracle can be instantiated with a poly(n)-time algorithm (the LLL algorithm [23]), this implies that there is an algorithm that solves SVP on $\mathcal{L}$ and runs in $N_{\mathrm{prim}}(\mathcal{L}, 2^{n/2} \cdot \lambda_1(\mathcal{L})) \cdot$ poly(n) time (without using any oracles), and therefore an algorithm that runs in $N_{\mathrm{prim}}(\mathcal{L}, \gamma \cdot \lambda_1(\mathcal{L})) \cdot$ poly(n) time and has access to a γ-uSVP oracle for any $\gamma > 2^{n/2}$.

The reduction from SVP on $\mathcal{L}$ to γ-uSVP for $\gamma \leq 2^{n/2}$ works as follows:

1. Guess G' satisfying $G/2 \leq G' \leq G$, and guess A' satisfying $A \leq A' \leq 2A$.
2. Sample $K := \lceil 200A' \log(100A')/G' \rceil \cdot n$ vectors $\boldsymbol{y}_1, \ldots, \boldsymbol{y}_K$ using the algorithm in Theorem 13 with (a basis of) $\mathcal{L}$ and A' as input.
3. Return a shortest vector among the vectors $\boldsymbol{y}_1, \ldots, \boldsymbol{y}_K$.

Due to space constraints, we defer proving correctness and performing runtime analysis to the full versionof the paper [7]. □

Algorithms from Theorem. 14 Let $T_{\mathrm{uSVP}}(\gamma, n)$ denote the fastest runtime of a (possibly randomized) algorithm for γ-uSVP on lattices of dimension n. By combining the reduction in Theorem 14, the point counting bound for $\mathbb{Z}^n$ in Proposition 1, the reduction from approximate uSVP to approximate GapSVP from Theorem 4, and the algorithm for $(1.93 + o(1))$-uSVP from Theorem 5 we get the following algorithmic result for $\mathbb{Z}$SVP.

Corollary 2. *For $1 \leq \gamma \leq \sqrt{n}$, there is a randomized algorithm that solves $\mathbb{Z}$SVP on lattices of dimension n in $(2e^3 n/\gamma^2)^{\gamma^2} \cdot T_{\mathrm{uSVP}}(\gamma, n) \cdot$ poly(n) time. In particular, there is a randomized algorithm that solves $\mathbb{Z}$SVP on lattices $\mathcal{L}$ of dimension n in $2^{n/2+o(n)}$ time.*

Proof. By the rotational invariance of the ℓ_2 norm and Proposition 1,

$$A := N_{\mathrm{prim}}(\mathcal{L}, \gamma \cdot \lambda_1(\mathcal{L})) = N_{\mathrm{prim}}(\mathbb{Z}^n, \gamma \cdot \lambda_1(\mathbb{Z}^n)) \leq N(\mathbb{Z}^n, \gamma) \leq (2e^3 n/\gamma^2)^{\gamma^2} .$$

The main result then follows immediately from Theorem 14.

The $2^{n/2+o(n)}$-time algorithm for $\mathbb{Z}$SVP follows by instantiating the main result with $T_{\mathrm{uSVP}}(1.93 + o(1), n) \leq 2^{n/2+o(n)}$, which follows by combining the fast algorithm for $(1.93 + o(1))$-GapSVP from Theorem 5 with the efficient dimension-preserving reduction from uSVP to GapSVP in Thoerem 4. □

We again emphasize that the $2^{n/2+o(n)}$-time algorithm in Corollary 2 substantially improves over the $2^{n+o(n)}$-time SVP algorithm for general lattices from [2], which was also the previous fastest known algorithm for $\mathbb{Z}$SVP.

In fact, Theorem 14 leads to a $2^{n/2+o(n)}$-time algorithm for SVP on a much larger class lattices than rotations of $\mathbb{Z}^n$, namely, on *semi-stable* lattices $\mathcal{L}$ with $\lambda_1(\mathcal{L})$ not too large. (Recall that a semi-stable lattice $\mathcal{L}$ is one with $\det(\mathcal{L}') \geq 1$ for all sublattices $\mathcal{L}' \subseteq \mathcal{L}$.) Namely, combining Theorem 14 with the point-counting bound for semi-stable lattices in Proposition 2 gives such an algorithm.

Corollary 3. *Let $\gamma = \gamma(n) \geq 1$ and let $t := 10(\log n + 2)$. There is a randomized algorithm that solves* SVP *on semi-stable lattices $\mathcal{L}$ of dimension n in $(3e^{\pi t^2 (\gamma \cdot \lambda_1(\mathcal{L}))^2}/2) \cdot T_{\mathrm{uSVP}}(\gamma, n) \cdot \mathrm{poly}(n)$ time. In particular, there is a randomized algorithm that solves* SVP *on semi-stable lattices of dimension n with $\lambda_1(\mathcal{L}) \leq o(\sqrt{n}/\log n)$ in $2^{n/2+o(n)}$ time.*

Proof. The main result follows by plugging $r := \gamma \cdot \lambda_1(\mathcal{L})$ into Proposition 2 to upper bound $A := N_{\mathrm{prim}}(\mathcal{L}, \gamma \cdot \lambda_1(\mathcal{L}))$ and then invoking Theorem 14. The $2^{n/2+o(n)}$-time algorithm for semi-stable lattices of dimension n with $\lambda_1(\mathcal{L}) \leq o(\sqrt{n}/\log n)$ follows by noting that, if $\gamma = O(1)$ (in particular, if $\gamma = 1.93+o(1)$), then $e^{\pi t^2 (\gamma \cdot \lambda_1(\mathcal{L}))^2}/2 = 2^{o(n)}$. Indeed, the claim then follows by again using the fact that $T_{\mathrm{uSVP}}(1.93 + o(1), n) \leq 2^{n/2+o(n)}$.

We note that Theorem 14 and Corollaries 2 and 3 answer a special case of an interesting question of Ducas and van Woerden [15], which asks whether there is a reduction from exact SVP on "f-unusual" lattices—essentially lattices for which Minkowski's Theorem (or, more-or-less equivalently, the Gaussian heuristic) is loose by a factor of at least f—to (approximate) uSVP. Semi-stable lattices $\mathcal{L}$ are $\Omega(\sqrt{n}/\lambda_1(\mathcal{L}))$-unusual in this sense (in particular, rotations of $\mathbb{Z}^n$ are $\Theta(\sqrt{n})$-unusual), and so we answer a special case of this question. Our results *do not* hold for f-unusual lattices more generally, essentially because a lattice that is loose with Minkowski's Theorem may nevertheless have a dense sublattice (i.e., may not be semi-stable).

Hardness from Thoerem. 14 Corollaries 2 and 3 combine the reduction in Theorem 14 with algorithms for γ-uSVP to get algorithms for SVP on rotations of $\mathbb{Z}^n$ and certain semi-sstable lattices. However, interpreting the reduction in the other direction—assuming that SVP on rotations of $\mathbb{Z}^n$ and certain semi-stable lattices is hard—leads to new *hardness results* for approximate uSVP. Namely, if one assumes that there is no randomized polynomial-time algorithm for $\mathbb{Z}$SVP then there is also no randomized polynomial-time algorithm for solving γ-uSVP for any constant $\gamma \geq 1$. This is notable because γ-uSVP is not known to be NP-hard (or to the best of our knowledge, known to be hard under any other generic complexity-theoretic assumption) for any constant $\gamma > 1$. Indeed, it is only known to be NP-hard (under randomized reductions) for $\gamma = 1+1/\mathrm{poly}(n)$; see [3,36]. Similarly, if one assumes that there is no randomized quasipolynomial-time algorithm for SVP on stable lattices with sufficiently small minimum distance then there is also no randomized quasipolynomial-time algorithm for solving γ-uSVP for any quasipolynomial γ.

We also get similar hardness for the α-Bounded Distance Decoding Problem (α-BDD), the problem in which, given a (basis of a) lattice $\mathcal{L}$ and a target point t satisfying $\mathrm{dist}(t, \mathcal{L}) \leq \alpha \cdot \lambda_1(\mathcal{L})$ as input, the goal is to output a closest lattice point to t (i.e., $x \in \mathcal{L}$ satisfying $\|t - x\| = \mathrm{dist}(t, \mathcal{L})$).

Corollary 4. *The following hardness results hold for γ-uSVP and α-BDD:*

1. *If there is no randomized* $\mathrm{poly}(n)$-*time algorithm for* $\mathbb{Z}$SVP, *then there is no randomized* $\mathrm{poly}(n)$-*time algorithm for* γ-uSVP *for any constant $\gamma \geq 1$ or for* α-BDD *for any constant $\alpha > 0$.*

2. *If there is no randomized $2^{\mathrm{poly}(\log n)}$-time algorithm for SVP on stable lattices $\mathcal{L}$ with $\lambda_1(\mathcal{L}) \leq \mathrm{poly}(\log n)$, then there is no randomized $2^{\mathrm{poly}(\log n)}$-time algorithm for γ-uSVP for any $\gamma \leq 2^{\mathrm{poly}(\log n)}$ or for α-BDD for any α with $(1/\alpha) \leq 2^{\mathrm{poly}(\log n)}$.*

Proof. The contrapositive of the claims for uSVP follow immediately from Corollaries 2 and 3. The claims for BDD follow from this by additionally noting that [28] gives an efficient reduction from γ-uSVP to $(1/\gamma)$-BDD for any $\gamma = \gamma(n) \leq \mathrm{poly}(n)$.

6 Experiments

The code and raw data for our experiments can be found at [6].

6.1 Experiments on Different Procedures for Generating Bases

In this section, we present experimental results examining the effectiveness of standard basis reduction algorithms for solving $\mathbb{Z}$SVP. Specifically, we generate bases of $\mathbb{Z}^n$ (which we then treat as instances of $\mathbb{Z}$SVP) using three procedures: discrete-Gaussian-based sampling, unimodular-matrix-product-based sampling, and Bézout-coefficient-based sampling. Using each of these procedures, we generate bases in dimensions $n = 128$, 256, and 512 with a variety of settings for procedure-specific parameters.[7] These results extend those in [9], which included experiments on bases generated using the second two procedures.

For each basis generating procedure (and corresponding set of parameters), we run the LLL algorithm and BKZ reduction algorithm (as implemented in fplll [16]) with different block sizes. For BKZ, we use block sizes 3, 4, 5, 10, and 20—though in dimension 512, we left out block size 20 for most of our experiments due to computational constraints. We often treat LLL as "BKZ with block size 2" (though this is not strictly true). We run these algorithms sequentially. That is, we run BKZ with block size 3 on the matrix returned by the LLL algorithm, we run BKZ with block size 4 on the matrix returned by BKZ with block size 3, and so forth.

For each parameter set of each basis generation procedure, we performed this experiment twenty times, and we report below on the smallest block size that found a shortest non-zero vector in the lattice (where, again, we think of LLL as BKZ with block size 2), if one was found. More data can be found in the associated repository [6].

At a high level, the data tell a relatively simple story. We were able to find a shortest vector in all cases in dimension 128 (often with block size 10). In dimensions 256 and 512, we were generally unable to find shortest vectors when the basis was generated with "reasonable parameters," where the definition of which parameters settings are reasonable of course depends on the procedure used to generate the basis.

---

[7] We note that these experiments were actually performed on bases of $\mathbb{Z}^n$ itself—not rotations of $\mathbb{Z}^n$—because this allows us to work with bases with integer entries. This does not affect our results because all of our algorithms are invariant under rotation.

Discrete Gaussian-Based Sampling. We start by presenting the results of experiments performed on bases generated essentially as described in Sect. 3 (which is also what we use for our encryption scheme in Sect. 4). However, we make three minor modifications. First, instead of sampling vectors one at a time until we find a generating set of $\mathbb{Z}^n$, we simply sample $n+10$ vectors. Empirically, we found that this yielded a generating set with high probability. Notice that this is much better than what is proven in Lemma 4. See also [31].

Second, recall that the basis sampling procedure in Sect. 3 requires an algorithm $\mathcal{A}$ that converts such a generating set into a basis (and is rotation invariant), as does our description of the sampling technique below. Since LLL is such an algorithm, and since we intend to run LLL anyway, we simply skip this step and run LLL directly on the generating set. Third, we do not bother to apply a rotation to the basis, because the algorithms that we are running are invariant under rotation (as noted in Footnote 7).

Table 1. Experimental results for basis reduction performed on bases generated using the discrete-Gaussian-based construction described in Sect. 6.1. The entries under each block size represent the number of times (out of a total of twenty experiments) that a shortest non-zero vector was found with a given block size (but no smaller block size), and the entries in the "unbroken" column represent the number of times that we failed to find a shortest non-zero vector. Non-zero entries are highlighted.

n	s	2	3	4	5	10	20	unbroken
128	1	20	0	0	0	0	0	0
128	10	0	0	1	1	18	0	0
128	1000	0	0	0	3	17	0	0
256	1	2	2	1	0	3	3	9
256	10	0	0	0	0	0	0	20
256	1000	0	0	0	0	0	0	20
512	1	0	0	0	0	0	0	20
512	10	0	0	0	0	0	0	20
512	1000	0	0	0	0	0	0	20

In our experiments, we took $s \in \{1, 10, 1000\}$. See Table 1. Setting $s = 1$ is not a "reasonable" parameter choice, as the resulting vectors are unreasonably sparse. (Each coordinate of each vector in the generating set is zero with probability roughly 0.92.) In particular, we would certainly *not* recommend using parameter $s = 1$ for cryptography. Nevertheless, interestingly, in all twenty runs, we were actually unable to find a shortest vector even for $s = 1$ in dimension $n = 512$.

For $s = 10$ and $s = 1000$, we found shortest vectors in dimension $n = 128$ (as we did in all experiments in $n = 128$ dimensions) and failed to find shortest vectors in dimensions $n = 256$ and $n = 512$. The data suggest that there was not too much difference between parameter $s = 10$ and parameter $s = 1000$. E.g., in dimension $n = 128$, there is no obvious difference between the block size needed to break the $s = 10$ case and the block size needed to break the $s = 1000$ case. (In contrast, LLL was able to break the $s = 1$ case.)

Unimodular Matrix Product Sampling. The second basis sampling technique that we analyze was proposed in [9], where it is called Algorithm 3. To introduce it, we start by discussing a family of embedding maps $\phi_{k_1,\dots,k_d}$: $\mathbb{R}^{d \times d} \to \mathbb{R}^{n \times n}$ for size d subsets of indices $\{k_1, \dots, k_d\} \subseteq \{1, \dots, n\}$ that embed a smaller $d \times d$ matrix H into a larger $n \times n$ matrix $\phi(H)$:

$$(\phi_{k_1,\dots,k_d}(H))_{i',j'} = \begin{cases} H_{i,j} & \text{if } i' = k_i \text{ and } j' = k_j \text{ for some } i, j \leq d; \\ 1_{i'=j'} & \text{otherwise,} \end{cases}$$

where $H = (H_{i,j}) \in \mathbb{R}^{d \times d}$ and $\phi_{k_1,\dots,k_d}(H) = H' = (H'_{i',j'}) \in \mathbb{R}^{n \times n}$. With this, we can define the next basis sampling technique, which we call "unimodular matrix product" sampling.

The algorithm takes as input a dimension n, a block size $2 \leq d \leq n$, an entry magnitude size bound $B \geq 1$, and a word length $L \geq 1$. It then samples L uniformly random matrices $\mathbf{M}_1, \dots, \mathbf{M}_L$ from $\mathrm{GL}_d(\mathbb{Z}) \cap [-B, B]^{d \times d}$. I.e., each $\mathbf{M}_i$ is sampled from the set of all integer matrices with entries of magnitude at most B and determinant ± 1. Additionally, it samples L uniformly random subsets $K_1, \dots, K_L \subseteq \{1, \dots, n\}$ of d indices with $K_i = \{k_1^{(i)}, \dots, k_d^{(i)}\}$. Finally, it outputs the basis $\mathbf{A} := \prod_{i=1}^{L} \phi_{k_1^{(i)},\dots,k_d^{(i)}}(\mathbf{M}_i)$. (We also refer the reader to the description of this algorithm in [9, Algorithm 3].)

In our experiments, we considered all combinations of parameters $d \in \{2, 3, 4\}$, $B = 1$, and $L \in \{10n, 20n, 30n, 40n, 50n\}$, except that we did not perform experiments with some of the larger parameter choices when $n = 512$ when our experiments failed to find short vectors with smaller parameters. See Table 2. (These parameter settings are roughly in line with those studied in in [9].)

We refer the reader to the full version [7] for discussion of our results and a comparison with those in [9].

Bézout-Coefficient-Based Sampling. We next describe our third basis-sampling algorithm, which was suggested by Joseph Silverman and studied as Algorithm 4 in [9]. The algorithm is based on the following observation. Given the matrix $\mathbf{M} = (m_1, \dots, m_{n-1}) \in \mathbb{Z}^{n \times (n-1)}$, if (and only if) all the minors in $\mathbf{M}$ of size $n - 1$ have no non-trivial common factor, then there exists a vector a for which the matrix $\mathbf{M}' := (m_1, \dots, m_{n-1}, a)$ is unimodular. Moreover, if this is the case, then we can find such a vector a efficiently using the extended Euclidean algorithm.

Indeed, with these observations, this Bézout-coefficient-based sampling algorithm is straightforward to describe. It takes as input a dimension n and an entry magnitude size bound $B \geq 1$. It repeatedly samples a uniformly random matrix $\mathbf{M} = (m_1, \dots, m_{n-1}) \in \{-B, -(B-1), \dots, B-1, B\}^{n \times (n-1)}$ until the minors of $\mathbf{M}$ of size $n-1$ have no non-trivial common factors. It then uses the extended

Table 2. Experimental results for basis reduction performed on bases generated using the product of sparse unimodular matrices method described in Sect. 6.1. The entries under each block size represent the number of times (out of a total of twenty trials) that a shortest non-zero vector was found with a given block size (but no smaller block size), and the entries in the "unbroken" column represent the number of times that we failed to find a shortest non-zero vector. Non-zero entries are highlighted. Cells that are grayed out represent block sizes that were not tested.

n	B	L	d	2	3	4	5	10	20	unbroken
128	1	1280	2	20	0	0	0	0	0	0
128	1	2560	2	0	0	1	3	16	0	0
128	1	3840	2	0	0	1	5	14	0	0
128	1	5120	2	0	0	1	3	16	0	0
128	1	6400	2	0	0	0	2	18	0	0
128	1	1280	3	0	0	2	5	13	0	0
128	1	2560	3	0	0	0	4	16	0	0
128	1	3840	3	0	0	1	5	14	0	0
128	1	5120	3	0	0	1	4	15	0	0
128	1	6400	3	0	0	1	4	15	0	0
128	1	1280	4	0	0	1	5	14	0	0
128	1	2560	4	0	0	3	5	12	0	0
128	1	3840	4	0	0	2	4	14	0	0
128	1	5120	4	0	1	3	2	14	0	0
128	1	6400	4	0	0	0	4	16	0	0

n	B	L	d	2	3	4	5	10	20	unbroken
256	1	2560	2	20	0	0	0	0	0	0
256	1	5120	2	0	0	0	0	0	0	20
256	1	7680	2	0	0	0	0	0	0	20
256	1	10240	2	0	0	0	0	0	0	20
256	1	12800	2	0	0	0	0	0	0	20
256	1	2560	3	0	0	0	0	0	0	20
256	1	5120	3	0	0	0	0	0	0	20
256	1	7680	3	0	0	0	0	0	0	20
256	1	10240	3	0	0	0	0	0	0	20
256	1	12800	3	0	0	0	0	0	0	20
256	1	2560	4	0	0	0	0	0	0	20
256	1	5120	4	0	0	0	0	0	0	20
256	1	7680	4	0	0	0	0	0	0	20
256	1	10240	4	0	0	0	0	0	0	20
256	1	12800	4	0	0	0	0	0	0	20

n	B	L	d	2	3	4	5	10	20	unbroken
512	1	5120	2	20	0	0	0	0		0
512	1	10240	2	20	0	0	0	0		0
512	1	15360	2	0	0	0	0	0		20
512	1	20480	2	0	0	0	0	0		20
512	1	25600	2	0	0	0	0	0		20
512	1	5120	3	0	0	0	0	0		20
512	1	10240	3	0	0	0	0	0		20
512	1	15360	3	0	0	0	0	0		20
512	1	5120	4	0	0	0	0	0		20

Euclidean algorithm to compute a such that $M' := (m_1, \ldots, m_{n-1}, a)$ is unimodular, and outputs M'. (We also refer the reader to the description of this algorithm in [9, Algorithm 4].) In our experiments, we took $B \in \{1, 10, 100\}$. See Table 3.

We refer the reader to the full version [7] for discussion of minor differences between our implmentation and the implementation in [9].

Our experiments showed that the effect of the parameter B was not discernible in our experiments. Indeed, for dimensions 256 and 512, our algorithms failed to find a shortest vector for all choices of B, including $B = 1$. And, in dimension 128, we found a shortest vector in all cases (as we always did), but the block size needed shows no obvious dependence on B. These results are quite similar to those in [9].

Table 3. Experimental results for basis reduction performed on bases generated using the Bézout-coefficient-based construction described in Sect. 6.1. The entries under each block size represent the number of times (out of a total of twenty experiments) that a shortest non-zero vector was found with a given block size (but no smaller block size), and the entries in the "unbroken" column represent the number of times that we failed to find a shortest non-zero vector. Non-zero entries are highlighted. Cells that are grayed out represent block sizes that were not tested.

		block size						
n	B	2	3	4	5	10	20	unbroken
128	1	0	0	0	3	17	0	0
128	10	0	0	1	2	17	0	0
128	100	0	0	1	6	13	0	0
256	1	0	0	0	0	0	0	20
256	10	0	0	0	0	0	0	20
256	100	0	0	0	0	0	0	20
512	1	0	0	0	0	0		20
512	10	0	0	0	0	0		20
512	100	0	0	0	0	0		20

6.2 A Threshold Phenomenon

In our data, we noticed a phenomenon. We found that the shortest vector in the bases returned by our basis reduction algorithms almost always had either length one or had length larger than some threshold τ. After a preliminary version of this work was published, we learned about a body of work studying such phenomena and providing compelling heuristic explanations for it. And, Ducas, Postlethwaite, Pulles, and van Woerden did additional experiments shedding much more light on this phenomenon [14].

In an earlier version of this work, we speculated more about the causes of this phenomenon and guessed that the threshold was roughly $\tau \approx \sqrt{n}/2$, but [14] give strong evidence that it actually happens at $\tau \approx \Theta(n)$. We now simply include the results of our experiments in Fig. 1 and refer the reader to [14] for more information and additional references.

6.3 Sieving Experiments

Finally, we ran experiments with heuristic sieving on $\mathbb{Z}^n$. In some sense, $\mathbb{Z}^n$ is a particularly interesting lattice for heuristic sieving algorithms because $\mathbb{Z}^n$ violates the *Gaussian heuristic*, which says that the number of non-zero lattice vectors of length at most r (in a determinant-one lattice) should be approximately equal to the volume of a ball with radius r, which is roughly $(2\pi e r^2/n)^{n/2}$ in large dimensions. Of course, $\mathbb{Z}^n$ completely violates this for small radii. E.g., $\mathbb{Z}^n$ has $2n$ non-zero lattice vectors with length at most 1, while the ball of radius 1 has volume roughly $(2\pi e/n)^{n/2}$, which is much less than one. More generally, for small radii $r \ll \sqrt{n}$, $\mathbb{Z}^n$ has roughly $(Cn/r^2)^{r^2}$ points in a ball of radius r

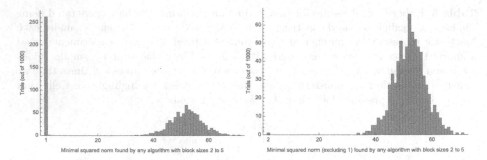

Fig. 1. On the left is a histogram of the squared norm of the shortest vector found by BKZ with block size ≤ 5 for discrete Guassian bases with $n = 128$ and $s = 1000$. On the right is the same histogram without the trials where this norm was 1.

(as in Proposition 1), which is of course much larger than the volume of such a ball.

One might not expect this to cause actual problems for sieving algorithms, but it is worth testing. So, we ran experiments using the Gauss sieve, due to Micciancio and Voulgaris [30], running trials in dimensions $20 \leq n \leq 50$ with Gaussian parameters $s \in \{10, 100, 1000\}$. We ran twenty trials with each pair of values (n, s) (for a total of $20 \cdot 31 \cdot 3 = 1680$ trials). We found that the behavior of this sieving procedure on $\mathbb{Z}^n$ was quite similar to its predicted behavior on lattices that do satisfy the Gaussian heuristic.

Of course, the most important metric of a sieving algorithm is whether it actually finds a shortest non-zero vector. We adopted the common heuristic of running the algorithm until it finds the zero vector (i.e., until there is a collision),

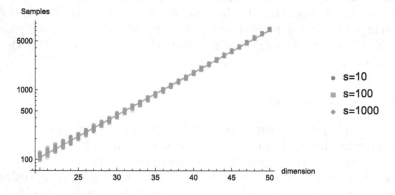

Fig. 2. Scatter plot of the number of vectors sampled by the sieving algorithm in different dimensions with different parameters s, together with the fitted line $6.4 \cdot 1.15^n$. (The fact that the three different parameter values are not distinguishable in the plot reflects the fact that the number of sampled vectors was essentially independent of the parameter size, which is to be expected.)

and we studied how often the algorithm found a shortest *non-zero* vector before this happened. It would be natural to guess that this should happen in all but a $1/(2n+1)$ fraction of the trials—i.e., we assume that the first vector found with length either 0 or 1 is chosen uniformly at random from the $2n+1$ such vectors. This heuristic matches the data reasonably well.

Next, the number of vectors N sampled by the algorithm (a measure of its space complexity) was well approximated by $N \approx 6.4 \cdot 1.15^n$, as shown in Fig. 2. This is completely in line with the predicted behavior of roughly $N = O^*((4/3)^{n/2}) \approx 1.15^n$ (even though this prediction is partially based on a heuristic that does not directly apply to $\mathbb{Z}^n$), and in line with the numbers reported by Micciancio and Voulgaris and others for sieving experiments on other lattices. So, if sieving algorithms perform differently on $\mathbb{Z}^n$, the difference is rather small. This result did not noticeably depend on the parameter s—i.e. on the lengths of the vectors sampled—which is also what one would expect from a basic heuristic model.

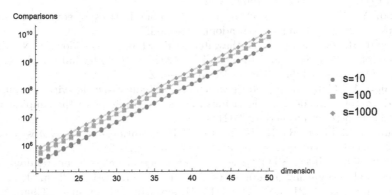

Fig. 3. The number of comparisons made by Micciancio and Voulgaris's Gauss sieve algorithm on $\mathbb{Z}^n$ with different Gaussian parameters s. The trend lines are (roughly) $500 \cdot 1.37^n$, $1000 \cdot 1.37^n$, and $1500 \cdot 1.37^n$ respectively.

The running time of the algorithm is also well within what we would expect. For example, for parameter $s = 10$, our running times were well approximated by $1.40^n/43000$ seconds (we did not attempt to optimize our code for speed), compared to the expected running time of $O^*((4/3)^n) \approx 1.33^n$, and the running time appears to be proportional to the logarithm of the parameter s, which is again what would be expected. Of course, this running time is subject to many minor implementation details. A less fickle measure is the number of *comparisons* made by the algorithm (i.e., the number of times that the algorithm tests whether subtracting one vector from another will make the latter vector shorter). For this data the simple exponential fit is quite tight and relatively close to what we expect. E.g., for $s = 10$, the number of comparisons is well approximated by $500 \cdot 1.37^n$; for $s = 100$, the fit was $1000 \cdot 1.37^n$; and for $s = 1000$, the fit was

$1500 \cdot 1.37^n$. See Fig. 3. The slightly larger base of the exponent can likely be explained by lower-order effects, which would require data from a wider range of dimensions to fully explore.

References

1. Aggarwal, D., Chen, Y., Kumar, R., Li, Z., Stephens-Davidowitz, N.: Dimension-preserving reductions between SVP and CVP in different p-norms. In: SODA (2021)
2. Aggarwal, D., Dadush, D., Regev, O., Stephens-Davidowitz, N.: Solving the shortest vector problem in 2^n time using discrete Gaussian sampling. In: STOC (2015)
3. Aggarwal, D., Dubey, C.K.: Improved hardness results for unique shortest vector problem. Inf. Process. Lett. **116**(10), 631–637 (2016)
4. Albrecht, M.R., Göpfert, F., Virdia, F., Wunderer, T.: Revisiting the expected cost of solving uSVP and applications to LWE. In: Takagi, T., Peyrin, T. (eds.) ASIACRYPT 2017. LNCS, vol. 10624, pp. 297–322. Springer, Cham (2017). https://doi.org/10.1007/978-3-319-70694-8_11
5. Aono, Y., Espitau, T., Nguyen, P.Q.: Random lattices: theory and practice. https://espitau.github.io/bin/random_lattice.pdf
6. Bennett, H., Ganju, A., Peetathawatchai, P., Stephens-Davidowitz, N.: Experiments on solving SVP on rotations of $\mathbb{Z}^n$ (2021). https://github.com/poonpura/Experiments-on-Solving-SVP-on-Rotations-of-Z-n
7. Bennett, H., Ganju, A., Peetathawatchai, P., Stephens-Davidowitz, N.: Just how hard are rotations of $\mathbb{Z}^n$? Algorithms and cryptography with the simplest lattice (2021). https://eprint.iacr.org/2021/1548
8. Bennett, H., Little, R.: Revisiting the BGPS rotations-of-$\mathbb{Z}^n$ cryptosystem: An implementation, challenges, and attacks. Preprint (2023)
9. Blanks, T.L., Miller, S.D.: Generating cryptographically-strong random lattice bases and recognizing rotations of $\mathbb{Z}^n$. In: Cheon, J.H., Tillich, J.-P. (eds.) PQCrypto 2021 2021. LNCS, vol. 12841, pp. 319–338. Springer, Cham (2021). https://doi.org/10.1007/978-3-030-81293-5_17
10. Brakerski, Z., Langlois, A., Peikert, C., Regev, O., Stehlé, D.: Classical hardness of Learning with Errors. In: STOC (2013)
11. Cash, D., Hofheinz, D., Kiltz, E., Peikert, C.: Bonsai trees, or how to delegate a lattice basis. J. Cryptol. **25**(4), 601–639 (2012), preliminary version in EUROCRYPT 2010. https://doi.org/10.1007/978-3-642-13190-5_27
12. Chandrasekaran, K., Gandikota, V., Grigorescu, E.: Deciding orthogonality in Construction-A lattices. SIAM J. Discret. Math. **31**(2), 1244–1262 (2017)
13. Dachman-Soled, D., Ducas, L., Gong, H., Rossi, M.: LWE with side information: attacks and concrete security estimation. In: Micciancio, D., Ristenpart, T. (eds.) CRYPTO 2020. LNCS, vol. 12171, pp. 329–358. Springer, Cham (2020). https://doi.org/10.1007/978-3-030-56880-1_12
14. Ducas, L., Postlethwaite, E.W., Pulles, L.N., van Woerden, W.: Hawk: Module LIP makes lattice signatures fast, compact and simple. In: Asiacrypt (2023). https://doi.org/10.1007/978-3-031-22972-5_3
15. Ducas, L., van Woerden, W.: On the lattice isomorphism problem, quadratic forms, remarkable lattices, and cryptography. In: EUROCRYPT (2022). https://doi.org/10.1007/978-3-031-07082-2_23

16. FPLLL development team: fplll, a lattice reduction library, Version: 5.4.1. https://github.com/fplll/fplll,
17. Geißler, K., Smart, N.P.: Computing the $M = U^T U$ integer matrix decomposition. In: Cryptography and Coding (2003)
18. Gentry, C., Peikert, C., Vaikuntanathan, V.: Trapdoors for hard lattices and new cryptographic constructions. In: STOC (2008)
19. Gentry, C., Szydlo, M.: Cryptanalysis of the revised NTRU signature scheme. In: Knudsen, L.R. (ed.) EUROCRYPT 2002. LNCS, vol. 2332, pp. 299–320. Springer, Heidelberg (2002). https://doi.org/10.1007/3-540-46035-7_20
20. Haviv, I., Regev, O.: On the lattice isomorphism problem. In: SODA (2014)
21. Hoeffding, W.: Probability inequalities for sums of bounded random variables. J. Am. Stat. Assoc. **58**, 13–30 (1963)
22. Hunkenschröder, C.: Deciding whether a lattice has an orthonormal basis is in co-NP (2019)
23. Lenstra, A.K., Lenstra, H.W., Jr., Lovász, L.: Factoring polynomials with rational coefficients. Math. Ann. **261**(4), 515–534 (1982)
24. Lenstra, H.W., Silverberg, A.: Revisiting the gentry-Szydlo algorithm. In: Garay, J.A., Gennaro, R. (eds.) CRYPTO 2014. LNCS, vol. 8616, pp. 280–296. Springer, Heidelberg (2014). https://doi.org/10.1007/978-3-662-44371-2_16
25. Lenstra, H.W., Silverberg, A.: Lattices with symmetry. J. Cryptol. **30**(3), 760–804 (2017)
26. Li, J., Nguyen, P.Q.: Approximating the densest sublattice from Rankin's inequality. LMS J. Comput. Math. **17**(A), 92–111 (2014)
27. Li, J., Nguyen, P.Q.: Computing a lattice basis revisited. In: ISAAC (2019)
28. Lyubashevsky, V., Micciancio, D.: On bounded distance decoding, unique shortest vectors, and the minimum distance problem. In: Halevi, S. (ed.) CRYPTO 2009. LNCS, vol. 5677, pp. 577–594. Springer, Heidelberg (2009). https://doi.org/10.1007/978-3-642-03356-8_34
29. Micciancio, D., Regev, O.: Worst-case to average-case reductions based on Gaussian measures. SIAM J. Comput. **37**(1), 267–302 (2007)
30. Micciancio, D., Voulgaris, P.: Faster exponential time algorithms for the Shortest Vector Problem. In: SODA (2010)
31. Nguyen, P.Q., Pujet, L.: The probability of primitive sets and generators in lattices (2022)
32. Peikert, C.: A decade of lattice cryptography. Foundations Trends Theoret. Comput. Sci. **10**(4), 283–424 (2016)
33. Regev, O.: LLL algorithm (2004). https://cims.nyu.edu/regev/teaching/lattices_fall_2004/ln/lll.pdf
34. Regev, O., Stephens-Davidowitz, N.: A reverse Minkowski theorem. In: STOC (2017)
35. Stephens-Davidowitz, N.: Discrete Gaussian sampling reduces to CVP and SVP. In: SODA (2016)
36. Stephens-Davidowitz, N.: Search-to-decision reductions for lattice problems with approximation factors (slightly) greater than one. In: APPROX (2016)
37. Stephens-Davidowitz, N.: Lattice algorithms (2020). https://www.youtube.com/watch?v=o4Pl-0Q5-q0, talk as part of the Simons Institute's semester on lattices
38. Szydlo, M.: Hypercubic lattice reduction and analysis of GGH and NTRU signatures. In: Biham, E. (ed.) EUROCRYPT 2003. LNCS, vol. 2656, pp. 433–448. Springer, Heidelberg (2003). https://doi.org/10.1007/3-540-39200-9_27

M-SIDH and MD-SIDH: Countering SIDH Attacks by Masking Information

Tako Boris Fouotsa[1]([⊠])(iD), Tomoki Moriya[2](iD), and Christophe Petit[3,4](iD)

[1] LASEC-EPFL, Lausanne, Switzerland
tako.fouotsa@epfl.ch
[2] The University of Tokyo, Tokyo, Japan
tomoki_moriya@mist.i.u-tokyo.ac.jp
[3] Université Libre de Bruxelles, Brussels, Belgium
Christophe.Petit@ulb.be
[4] University of Birmingham, Birmingham, UK

Abstract. The SIDH protocol is an isogeny-based key exchange protocol using supersingular isogenies, designed by Jao and De Feo in 2011. The protocol underlies the SIKE algorithm which advanced to the fourth round of NIST's post-quantum standardization project in May 2022. The algorithm was considered very promising: indeed the most significant attacks against SIDH were meet-in-the-middle variants with exponential complexity, and torsion point attacks which only applied to unbalanced parameters (and in particular, not to SIKE).

This security picture dramatically changed in August 2022 with new attacks by Castryck-Decru, Maino-Martindale and Robert. Like prior attacks on unbalanced versions, these new attacks exploit torsion point information provided in the SIDH protocol. Crucially however, the new attacks embed the isogeny problem into a similar isogeny problem in a higher dimension to also affect the balanced parameters. As a result of these works, the SIKE algorithm is now fully broken both in theory and in practice.

Given the considerable interest attracted by SIKE and related protocols in recent years, it is natural to seek countermeasures to the new attacks. In this paper, we introduce two such countermeasures based on partially hiding the isogeny degrees and torsion point information in the SIDH protocol. We present a preliminary analysis of the resulting schemes including non-trivial generalizations of prior attacks. Based on this analysis we suggest parameters for our M-SIDH variant with public key sizes of 4434, 7037 and 9750 bytes respectively for NIST security levels 1, 3, 5.

Keywords: Isogenies · SIDH attacks · Countermeasures · M-SIDH · MD-SIDH

1 Introduction

In 1994, Peter Shor [35] described a polynomial quantum algorithm to solve the integer factorization problem and the discrete logarithm problem. This implies

© International Association for Cryptologic Research 2023
C. Hazay and M. Stam (Eds.): EUROCRYPT 2023, LNCS 14008, pp. 282–309, 2023.
https://doi.org/10.1007/978-3-031-30589-4_10

that the widely deployed cryptographic protocols we use today would become vulnerable in presence of a large-scale quantum computer. To mitigate this threat, research on *post-quantum cryptography*, namely cryptographic protocols that will hopefully remain secure against both classical and quantum computers, has considerably developed in the last two decades. Several standardization competitions were initiated, among which the NIST PQC [29]. Many new candidates for post-quantum hard problems have been suggested to date based on lattices, codes, *isogenies*, multivariate systems of equations, and other problems.

Isogenies are maps between elliptic curves. For cryptographic applications, we restrict ourselves to curves defined over finite fields $\mathbb{F}_q$. When there exists an isogeny $\phi : E \to E'$, we say the elliptic curves E and E' are *isogenous*. There are infinitely many isogenies connecting two isogenous elliptic curves. The *pure isogeny problem* is stated as follows.

Problem 1. Given two isogenous elliptic curves E and E', compute an isogeny from E to E'.

An isogeny from a curve E to itself is called an *endomorphism of E*, and the set of all the endomorphisms of E (together with the 0 map) is called the *endomorphism ring of E*.

Over finite fields, there are two categories of elliptic curves, namely *ordinary elliptic curves* and *supersingular elliptic curves*. The endomorphism ring of any ordinary curve is an order in a quadratic imaginary field (hence is commutative), whereas the endomorphism ring of a supersingular curve is a maximal order in a quaternion algebra (hence is non-commutative). Isogenies connect ordinary curves between themselves and supersingular curves between themselves.

There is a straightforward adaptation of the well-known Diffie-Hellman key exchange protocol to isogenies in the ordinary/commutative case. This is in fact what is done in isogeny based schemes like CRS [14,34], CSIDH [8], OSIDH [10] and derivatives. The high level idea is as follows: there is a starting curve E_0. Alice selects a secret isogeny $\phi_A : E_0 \to E_A$, and Bob selects a secret isogeny $\phi_B : E_0 \to E_B$. Both parties exchange E_A and E_B. Each party recomputes their secret isogeny from the other party's public curve. Since the isogenies "are commutative", they get the same end curve E_{AB} (up to isomorphism) whose j-invariant is used as the shared secret. Note that the isogeny $E_A \to E_{AB}$ computed by Alice is not exactly the isogeny ϕ_A since they do not have the same domain and codomain. This isogeny is in general denoted by ϕ'_A. Similarly, Bob's isogeny is also denoted by ϕ'_B. This is illustrated in Fig. 1 where we have $\phi'_A \circ \phi_B = \phi'_B \circ \phi_A$.

When it comes to using supersingular curves, designing a Diffie-Hellman type key exchange is less straightforward because their endomorphism rings are non-commutative. In 2011, Jao and De Feo [24] had a brilliant idea on how to obtain a commutative diagram in the supersingular case. To achieve this goal:

1. One fixes the respective degrees A and B of the isogenies ϕ_A and ϕ_B, with A and B coprime;
2. Alice reveals the images of a basis of the B-torsion of E_0 (that is $E_0[B]$), and Bob reveals the image of a basis of the A-torsion of E_0 (that is $E_0[A]$).

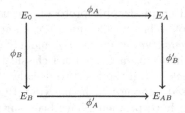

Fig. 1. Generic commutative isogeny key exchange.

This idea led to the Supersingular Isogeny Diffie-Hellman protocol (SIDH), which has received a lot of attention in the last decade. This protocol and other isogeny-based schemes are attractive for their very compact secret and public keys. This has been one of the most valuable advantages of SIKE, a Key Encapsulation Mechanism (KEM) derived from SIDH, compared to other post-quantum KEMs. SIKE became widely regarded as a promising post-quantum candidate for standardization, and in particular the algorithm made it to the 4th round of the NIST competition.

With the exception of the CGL hash function [9] and GPS signatures [21], most isogeny-based protocols in the literature do not directly rely on the pure isogeny problem, but on some variants of this problem. In the case of SIDH/SIKE, an attacker is provided with additional non-trivial information: the degree of the isogeny and the images of torsion points. More precisely, the security of SIDH relies on the following problem.

Problem 2. Let E_0 be a supersingular curve defined over $\mathbb{F}_{p^2}$ with $p = AB-1$. Set $E_0[A] = \langle P, Q \rangle$. Let $\phi : E_0 \to E'$ be an isogeny of degree B and let $P' = \phi(P)$, $Q' = \phi(Q)$. Given E_0, P, Q, E', P' and Q', compute the isogeny ϕ.

Furthermore, in SIDH/SIKE, the starting curve E_0 is special: its endomorphism ring is publicly available. In 2017, Petit [31] exploited the knowledge of the endomorphism ring of E_0 and the torsion point information to design attacks that recover the secret isogeny in polynomial time assuming that $A \ll B$. After a recent improvement [32], the attack still required imbalanced A and B, hence it does not apply to SIDH where $A \approx B$.

In July 2022, Castryck and Decru [7] described devastating attacks on SIDH that recovered the secret key in SIDH and SIKE, instantiated with the NIST parameters, in a few hours. The attacks were also developed in a concurrent work by Maino and Martindale [26]. Various follow-up works by other authors quickly improved the practical runtime time to minutes and seconds, and clarified the asymptotic complexities. The best attacks on balanced SIDH parameters had suddenly gone from exponential time to subexponential time, with a further reduction to polynomial time complexity when the endomorphism ring of the starting curve is available (as was the case in SIKE). Things could only get worse for SIDH, and a few days later they did, when Robert described an improved attack with polynomial time complexity working for arbitrary starting curves [33].

We note that like Petit's attacks before them, the Castryck-Decru-Maino-Martindale-Robert attacks exploit knowledge of both torsion point information and the degree of the secret isogeny.

While the Castryck-Decru-Maino-Martindale-Robert attacks constitute a clear cryptanalysis breakthrough on a flagship isogeny-based cryptographic protocol, they do not apply to other isogeny-based schemes in which no torsion point information is revealed: CRS [14,34], CSIDH [8] and CSIDH-based signatures (SeaSign [15], SCI-FiSh [3], ...), CGL [9], GPS [21], SQISign [17], and many more. The new attacks do not imply that the whole of isogeny-based cryptography is insecure, but only that the field is getting mature! In particular, a natural question now is whether one can find countermeasures against the Castryck-Decru-Maino-Martindale-Robert attacks and repair the SIDH protocol.

Contributions[1]. In this paper, we propose and analyze two countermeasure candidates to the Castryck-Decru attack: Masked-Degree SIDH (MD-SIDH) and Masked torsion points SIDH (M-SIDH).

The main idea in MD-SIDH is to mask the degree of the secret isogeny: the degrees A and B of the secret isogenies in SIDH are no longer fixed, but uniformly random divisors of A and B respectively. To prevent the degree from being recovered by a pairing computation and some discrete logarithms in a group of smooth order, the images of the torsion points are scaled by a random integer.

The main idea in M-SIDH is to keep the degrees of the secret isogenies fixed as in SIDH, and mask only the torsion point information: the images of the torsion points are scaled by a random integer. To prevent an efficient recovery of the secret scalar used in M-SIDH (using pairings and discrete logarithms), we set the isogeny degrees A and B to have $t \geq 2\lambda$ distinct prime divisors, so that the scalar cannot be recovered despite the fact that its square modulo A or B is known.

We perform a thorough security analysis of the two countermeasures, including non-trivial extensions of prior attacks. In particular, we give an expected polynomial time attack on the M-SIDH variant when the starting curve has a known small endomorphism, and a reduction from any MD-SIDH instance to an M-SIDH instance. We also show that isogeny degrees in the M-SIDH variant must have at least 2λ distinct factors, where λ is the security parameter. Finally, we provide non-trivial variants of adaptive attacks on SIDH, including the GPST attack and the Fouotsa-Petit attack.

Based on our analysis, the M-SIDH variant is the most promising one as it features smaller keys at identical security levels. The variant must be used with a randomly generated starting curve to avert the attack mentioned above (note that this is not an issue in a key encapsulation mechanism as the starting curve may be constructed by the key generation algorithm). Our analysis suggests

---

[1] This paper is an extended merge of the preprints [18] and [27].

that public key sizes of 4434, 7037 and 9750 bytes are sufficient to reach AES-128, AES-192 and AES-256 security levels (NIST security levels 1, 3, 5), and asymptotically public keys should be a factor $O(\log \lambda)$ larger than in SIDH.

1.1   Outline

In Sect. 2 we briefly present the SIDH protocol and discuss attacks on SIDH. In Sect. 3 we describe our two constructions Masked-degree SIDH and Masked SIDH (M-SIDH). In Sects. 4, 5 and 6, we do a security analysis of both schemes and in Sect. 7 we suggest parameters. We conclude the paper in Sect. 8.

2   The SIDH Protocol and Attacks

The Supersingular Isogeny Diffie-Hellman protocol (SIDH) is a key exchange protocol designed by Jao and De Feo [24], which underlies the SIKE submission to NIST post-quantum cryptography project [23]. Interest in the SIDH protocol grew steadily since 2011, but passive cryptanalytic success remained limited until new attacks fully broke it in August 2022.

2.1   The SIDH Protocol

The SIDH protocol is a Diffie-Hellman-like key exchange scheme that uses torsion point information to complete a (pseudo) commutative diagram:

$$
\begin{array}{ccc}
(E_0, P_A, Q_A, P_B, Q_B) & \longrightarrow & (E_A, \phi_A(P_B), \phi_A(Q_B)) \\
\downarrow & & \downarrow \\
(E_B, \phi_B(P_A), \phi_B(Q_A)) & \longrightarrow & E_{AB} \cong E_{BA}
\end{array}
$$

The precise scheme is as follows:

Public parameter: Let E_0 be the elliptic curve of j-invariant 1728. Set a prime p as $p = 2^{e_A} 3^{e_B} - 1$. Let P_A and Q_A (resp. P_B and Q_B) be points generating $E_0[2^{e_A}] \cong (\mathbb{Z}/2^{e_A}\mathbb{Z})^2$ (resp. $E_0[3^{e_B}] \cong (\mathbb{Z}/3^{e_B}\mathbb{Z})^2$).

Public key (Alice): Alice first generates a random value $k_A \in (\mathbb{Z}/2^{e_A}\mathbb{Z})^\times$ as her secret key. Let $R_A = P_A + k_A Q_A$. Alice computes an isogeny $\phi_A \colon E_0 \to E_A := E_0/\langle R_A \rangle$ and image points $\phi_A(P_B), \phi_A(Q_B)$. Alice sends to Bob E_A and these image points as a public key.

Public key (Bob): Bob first generates a random value $k_B \in (\mathbb{Z}/3^{e_B}\mathbb{Z})^\times$ as his secret key. Let $R_B = P_B + k_B Q_B$. Bob computes an isogeny $\phi_B \colon E_0 \to E_B := E_0/\langle R_B \rangle$ and image points $\phi_A(P_B), \phi_A(Q_B)$. Bob sends to Alice E_B and these image points as a public key. Let k_B be his secret key.

Shared key: Let $R'_A = \phi_B(P_A) + k_A \phi_B(Q_A)$, and let $R'_B = \phi_A(P_B) + k_B \phi_A(Q_B)$. Alice computes $E_{AB} := E_B/\langle R'_A \rangle$, and Bob computes an isogeny $E_{BA} := E_A/\langle R'_B \rangle$. The value $j(E_{AB}) = j(E_{BA})$ is the shared key.

The SIDH protocol is the basis of the SIKE algorithm, which was selected for Round 4 of NIST post-quantum standardization project in June 2022.

2.2 Cryptanalysis Attempts and Successes

A natural problem to consider in the cryptanalysis of SIDH is the isogeny with torsion problem: Problem 2 with $A = 2^{e_A}$ and $B = 3^{e_B}$. One approach to solve this problem is to entirely ignore the torsion point information, and recover the isogeny with some advanced brute force strategy such as a meet-in-the-middle algorithm or Van Oorschot-Wiener's algorithm [36]. These approaches have guided the parameter selection of SIKE submission to NIST [23].

The first passive attacks exploiting torsion point information[2] were introduced by Petit [31]. The key idea in his attack is to consider an endomorphism Ψ of E' of the form

$$\psi = d + \phi \circ \theta \circ \hat{\phi}$$

where $d \in \mathbb{Z}$ and θ is a trace 0 non scalar endomorphism of E_0 such that

$$\deg \psi = d^2 + B^2 \deg \theta$$

divides A. Provided such parameters, one can use torsion point information on ϕ to deduce torsion point information on ψ, then use this information to recover $\ker \psi$ via a (smooth order hence efficient) discrete logarithm computation, and finally deduce ϕ. Note that this strategy requires at least partial knowledge of the endomorphism ring of E_0 (for θ) and moreover it only works if A is large enough compared to B. (In particular, it does not work when $A \approx B$ as in SIKE.) Improvements in later work increased the range of parameters vulnerable to these attacks but they did not fundamentally change these limitations [5,32].

In August 2022, Castryck and Decru [7] (and independently Maino and Martindale [26]) introduced new powerful attacks against SIDH, with polynomial time complexity when the endomorphism ring of E_0 is known and subexponential complexity in general. Extensions by Robert [33] further reduced the complexity to polynomial time in the general case. In a sense, these attacks can be seen as generalizations of previous torsion point attacks[3], but with a key additional insight: they crucially embed the SIDH isogeny problem into a higher dimensional isogeny problem, where more endomorphisms are readily available. In a nutshell, Robert's attack considers the genus 8 Abelian variety $E_0^4 \times E'^4$, and its endomorphism

$$\Psi = \begin{pmatrix} \alpha_0 & \hat{\Phi} \\ -\Phi & \hat{\alpha'} \end{pmatrix},$$

---

[2] Torsion point information was previously used in active attacks against SIDH [20] and prompted the inclusion of a CCA transform (a variant of Fujisaki-Okamoto transform) within SIKE.

[3] The original Castryck-Decru's paper did not initially make a connection with prior torsion point attacks, but this connection then rapidly emerged and is clearly described in [26,33].

where Φ is the natural extension of ϕ on E_0^4, $\hat{\Phi}$ is its dual, and α_0 and α' are the endomorphisms on E_0^4 and E'^4 with action given by the matrix

$$M = \begin{pmatrix} a_0 & a_1 & a_2 & a_3 \\ -a_1 & a_0 & -a_4 & a_3 \\ -a_3 & a_4 & -a_1 & a_2 \\ -a_4 & -a_3 & a_2 & a_1 \end{pmatrix}$$

with a_0, a_1, a_2, a_3 such that $a := a_0^2 + a_1^2 + a_2^2 + a_3^2 = A - B$. We then have

$$\Psi\hat{\Psi} = AI_8$$

where $\hat{\Psi} = \begin{pmatrix} \hat{\alpha}_0 & -\hat{\Phi} \\ \Phi & \alpha' \end{pmatrix}$ is the dual of Ψ, i.e., Ψ is an endomorphism of degree A.

As in previous torsion point attacks, one can evaluate Ψ on the A torsion using torsion point information provided in the SIDH problem. One can then compute Ψ and finally deduce ϕ.

From now on we will refer to these attacks as "the CD-MM-R attacks". Compared to previous torsion point attacks, these new attacks do not require any knowledge on the endomorphism ring of the starting curve, and work whenever $A \geq B$. One can further improve this to $A \geq \sqrt{B}$ as in the "dual isogeny variant" of [32]: let $a := A^2 - B$; recover the first halves of the endomorphisms Ψ and $\hat{\Psi}$ using torsion point information; and finally deduce the whole of Ψ and ϕ [33].

While they do not require any knowledge of $\mathrm{End}(E_0)$, the new attacks still use torsion point information and general SIDH parameters, including the isogeny degrees. In the following section, we describe two countermeasures: the first one consists in making the torsion point images while the second one consists in masking the isogeny degrees.

3 Masked SIDH Variants

Recall that the CD-MM-R attack requires two main ingredients:

1. the degree A of the secret supersingular isogeny $\phi : E_0 \to E$;
2. the images $\phi(P), \phi(Q)$ of a torsion basis (P, Q) of the B-torsion $E_0[B]$ where B is an integer coprime to A such that $B > A$.

The countermeasures we suggest here consist in masking each of the above. Firstly, we suggest Masked torsion points SIDH or M-SIDH for short, in which one masks the torsion point images by scaling them with a random scalar. Secondly, we suggest Masked-degree SIDH or MD-SIDH for short, in which the isogenies computed do not have a fixed degree.

In the rest of this paper, we will often use the following lemma.

Lemma 3. *Let $\phi : E \longrightarrow E'$ be an isogeny of unknown degree d and let B be a smooth integer coprime to d such that $E[B] \subset E(\mathbb{F}_{p^2})$. Set $E[B] = \langle P, Q \rangle$. Then given P, Q, $\phi(P)$ and $\phi(Q)$, there exists a polynomial time algorithm to recover $d \bmod B$.*

Proof. One computes the Weil pairing values $e_B(P, Q)$ and $e_B(\phi(P), \phi(Q)) = e_B(P, Q)^{\deg \phi}$, then one solves a discrete logarithm instance between both quantities to recover $d \bmod B$. Since $E[B] \subset E(\mathbb{F}_{p^2})$, the pairing computations run in polynomial time. Since B is smooth, then using the Pohlig-Hellman algorithm the discrete logarithm computation runs in polynomial time as well.   □

3.1 Masked Torsion Points Variant

The aim here is to instantiate SIDH such that the direct images $\phi(P)$, $\phi(Q)$ of P and Q are not available to adversaries, but the key exchange still succeeds: this means that when given a point $R \in E_0[B]$, one should be able to compute a generator of the group $\phi(\langle R \rangle)$.

To achieve this goal, the images $\phi(P)$, $\phi(Q)$ of P and Q are scaled by a random integer $\alpha \in \mathbb{Z}/B\mathbb{Z}^\times$. That is instead of revealing $\phi(P)$, $\phi(Q)$, one reveals $[\alpha]\phi(P)$, $[\alpha]\phi(Q)$. Note that since the degree of the secret isogeny ϕ is fixed, one can recover $\alpha^2 \deg \phi$ by applying Lemma 3, from which one derives $\alpha^2 \bmod B$. Taking a square root α_0 of α^2, one recovers $[\alpha\alpha_0^{-1}]\phi(P)$ and $[\alpha\alpha_0^{-1}]\phi(Q)$ where $(\alpha\alpha_0^{-1})^2 = 1 \mod B$. Hence one can sample α directly from $\mu_2(B)$ where

$$\mu_2(N) = \{x \in \mathbb{Z}/N\mathbb{Z} \mid x^2 = 1 \bmod N\}.$$

Note that for the scheme to be secure against the CD-MM-R attack, it is necessary that an attacker should not be able to recover the scalar α. The isogeny degrees are chosen such that there is an exponential number of square roots of 1 modulo B. This leads to the following variant of SIDH: M-SIDH.

Public parameter: Let λ be the security parameter and let $t = t(\lambda) \in \mathbb{N}$ be an integer depending on λ. Let $p = ABf - 1$ be a prime such that $A = \prod_{i=1}^{t} \ell_i$ and $B = \prod_{i=1}^{t} q_i$ are coprime integers, ℓ_i, q_i are distinct small primes, $A \approx B \approx \sqrt{p}$ and f is a small cofactor. Let E_0 be a supersingular curve defined over $\mathbb{F}_{p^2}$. Set $E_0[A] = \langle P_A, Q_A \rangle$ and $E_0[B] = \langle P_B, Q_B \rangle$. The public parameters are $E_0, p, A, B, P_A, Q_A, P_B, Q_B$.

Public key (Alice): Alice samples uniformly at random two integers α and a from $\mu_2(B)$ and $\mathbb{Z}/A\mathbb{Z}$ respectively. She computes the cyclic isogeny $\phi_A : E_0 \to E_A = E_0/\langle P_A + [a]Q_A \rangle$. Her public key is the tuple $\mathsf{pk}_A = (E_A, [\alpha]\phi_A(P_B), [\alpha]\phi_A(Q_B))$ and her secret key is $\mathsf{sk}_A = a$. The integer α is deleted.

Public key (Bob): Analogously, Bob samples uniformly at random two integers β and b from $\mu(A)$ and $\mathbb{Z}/B\mathbb{Z}$ respectively. His public key is $\mathsf{pk}_B = (E_B, [\beta]\phi_B(P_A), [\beta]\phi_B(Q_A))$ where $\phi_B : E_0 \to E_B = E_0/\langle P_B + [b]Q_B \rangle$ and his secret key is $\mathsf{sk}_B = b$. The integer β is deleted.

Shared key: Upon receiving Bob's public key (E_B, R_a, S_a), Alice checks that $e_A(R_a, S_a) = e_A(P_A, Q_A)^B$, if not she aborts. She computes the isogeny $\phi'_A : E_B \to E_{BA} = E_B/\langle R_a + [a]S_a \rangle$. Her shared key is $j(E_{BA})$. Similarly, upon receiving (E_A, R_b, S_b), Bob checks that $e_B(R_b, S_b) = e_B(P_B, Q_B)^A$, if not he aborts. He computes the isogeny $\phi'_B : E_A \to E_{AB} = E_A/\langle R_b + [b]S_b\rangle$. His shared key is $j(E_{AB})$.

The problem underlying the security of M-SIDH is stated as follows.

Problem 4. Let $A = \ell_1 \cdots \ell_t$ and let $B = q_1 \cdots q_t$ be two smooth coprime integers, let f be a small cofactor such that $p = ABf - 1$ is a prime, with $A \approx B$. Let $E_0/\mathbb{F}_{p^2}$ be a supersingular elliptic curve such that $\#E_0(\mathbb{F}_{p^2}) = (p+1)^2 = (ABf)^2$, set $E_0[B] = \langle P, Q\rangle$. Let $\phi : E_0 \to E$ be a uniformly random A-isogeny and let α be a uniformly random element of $\mu_2(B)$.
Given $E_0, P, Q, E_A, P' = [\alpha]\phi(P), Q' = [\alpha]\phi(Q)$, compute ϕ.

It is immediate that Problem 4 is not hard for too small values of t. Recall that we want 1 to have an exponential number of square roots modulo A and modulo B. At first, one may be tempted to set $t = \lambda$ so that there are about 2^λ square roots of 1 modulo A and modulo B. But, as we will see in Sect. 4, this is not secure and t needs to be larger.

The main difference between Problem 4 and Problem 2 is that in Problem 4 torsion point images are only provided up to a scalar multiple (more precisely, a square root of unity). When trying to apply Robert's attack, the endomorphism Ψ appearing in this attack can no longer be evaluated exactly and its kernel can no longer be computed directly. The same holds for the attacks described in Castryck-Decru and Maino-Martindale papers.

3.2   Masked-Degree Variant

Rather than masking the torsion points as described in the previous section, we suggest a second countermeasure where one masks the degree of the secret isogeny.

Set the prime p to be of the form $p = ABf - 1$ where A and B are two smooth coprime integers, and f is a small cofactor. Alice will use cyclic isogenies of degree A' dividing A and Bob will use cyclic isogenies of degree B' dividing B. In an SIDH prime $A = \ell_A^{e_A}$ and $B = \ell_B^{e_B}$, hence A and B have only $e_A + 1$ and $e_B + 1$ divisors respectively. For this reason, one needs to move away from SIDH primes and use CSIDH-style primes with $A = \ell_1^{a_1} \cdots \ell_t^{a_t}$ and $B = q_1^{b_1} \cdots q_t^{b_t}$ where t, as well as the a_is and the b_is, depend on the security parameter λ.

To generate her public key, Alice samples a random degree A' (divisor of A) for her secret isogeny, samples a random point $R_A \in E_0[A']$, computes the A'-isogeny $\phi_A : E_0 \to E_A := E_0/\langle R_A\rangle$ and $\phi_A(P_B), \phi_A(Q_B)$ where $E_0[B] = \langle P_B, Q_B\rangle$. But, by Lemma 3, any adversary can recover $A' = \deg \phi_A$. In order to avoid this, Alice also generates a uniformly random integer $\alpha \in \mathbb{Z}/B\mathbb{Z}^\times$ and outputs $(E_A, [\alpha]\phi_A(P_B), [\alpha]\phi_A(Q_B))$ as her public key. More precisely, Masked-degree SIDH (MD-SIDH) is as follows:

Public parameter: Let E_0 be a supersingular elliptic curve. Let $t = t(\lambda) \in \mathbb{N}$ be an integer depending[4] on λ. Let $A = \ell_1^{a_1} \cdots \ell_t^{a_t}$ and $B = q_1^{b_1} \cdots q_t^{b_t}$ be

---

[4] Note that we use the same notation $t = t(\lambda)$ for M-SIDH and MD-SIDH. It will always be clear from the context whether we are referring to M-SIDH or MD-SIDH.

two smooth coprime integers such that $p = ABf - 1$ is a prime (where f is a small cofactor). Set P_A and Q_A (resp. P_B and Q_B) be points generating $E_0[A] = \langle P_A, Q_A \rangle$ and $E_0[B] = \langle P_B, Q_B \rangle$.

Public key (Alice): Alice samples a uniformly random divisor A' of A and a random point $R_A \in E_0[A']$. Her secret key is $\mathsf{sk}_A = R_A$. She computes the isogeny $\phi_A : E_0 \to E_A := E_0/\langle R_A \rangle$ together with $\phi_A(P_B)$ and $\phi_A(Q_B)$. She samples a uniformly random integer[5] $\alpha \in \mathbb{Z}/B\mathbb{Z}^\times$ and her public key is $\mathsf{pk}_A = ([\alpha]\phi_A(P_B), [\alpha]\phi_A(Q_B))$.

Public key (Bob): Bob samples a uniformly random divisor B' of B and a random point $R_B \in E_0[B']$. His secret key is $\mathsf{sk}_B = R_B$. He computes the isogeny $\phi_B : E_0 \to E_B := E_0/\langle R_B \rangle$ together with $\phi_B(P_A)$ and $\phi_B(Q_A)$. He samples a uniformly random integer $\beta \in \mathbb{Z}/A\mathbb{Z}^\times$ and his public key is $\mathsf{pk}_B = ([\beta]\phi_B(P_A), [\beta]\phi_B(Q_A))$.

Shared key: From $[\beta]\phi_B(P_A)$ and $[\beta]\phi_B(Q_A)$, Alice recovers $\langle R'_A \rangle = \langle \phi_B(R_A) \rangle$. From $[\alpha]\phi_A(P_B), [\alpha]\phi_A(Q_B)$, Bob recovers $\langle R'_B \rangle = \langle \phi_A(R_B) \rangle$. Alice computes $E_{AB} := E_B/\langle R'_A \rangle$, and Bob computes $E_{BA} := E_A/\langle R'_B \rangle$. The value $j(E_{AB}) = j(E_{BA})$ is the shared key.

The problem underlying the security of MD-SIDH is stated as follows.

Problem 5. Let $A = \ell_1^{a_1} \cdots \ell_t^{a_t}$ and let $B = q_1^{b_1} \cdots q_t^{b_t}$ be two smooth coprime integers, let f be a small cofactor such that $p = ABf - 1$ is a prime, with $A \approx B$. Let $E_0/\mathbb{F}_{p^2}$ be a supersingular elliptic curve such that $\#E_0(\mathbb{F}_{p^2}) = (p+1)^2 = (ABf)^2$, set $E_0[B] = \langle P, Q \rangle$. Let $A' = \ell_1^{a'_1} \cdots \ell_t^{a'_t}$ be a uniformly random divisor of A and and let α be a uniformly random element of $\mathbb{Z}/B\mathbb{Z}^\times$. Let $\phi : E_0 \to E_A$ be a uniformly random isogeny of degree A'. Given $E_0, P, Q, E_A, P' = [\alpha]\phi(P), Q' = [\alpha]\phi(Q)$, compute ϕ.

The MD-SIDH protocol can be seen as a generalization of the M-SIDH protocol, where the degree is no longer fixed and the torsion point hidden scalars α and β are no longer restricted to square roots of unity. From a security point of view, hiding the isogeny degrees might present the attacker with an additional obstacle in running the CD-MM-R attacks, since these degrees are explicitly used to construct attack parameters.

3.3 On the Effectiveness of the Countermeasures

We provide some arguments on why we believe the CD-MM-R attacks do not extend to the countermeasures.

The attacks embed the secret isogeny ϕ of degree B into a higher genus isogeny Ψ of degree $A = B + a$ where $a = A - B$ and A is the order of the torsion points. In M-SIDH, the degree of the secret isogeny is $\beta^2 B$ where β is a secret

---

[5] The integers α (for Alice) and β (for Bob) can be deleted immediately after key generation.

scalar and $\beta^2 \pmod{A} = 1$. Embedding this isogeny into a higher genus isogeny the same way would lead to an isogeny of degree

$$\beta^2 B + a = \beta^2 B + A - B = A + B(\beta^2 - 1) = A\left(1 + B\frac{\beta^2 - 1}{A}\right).$$

This degree is unknown to the attacker, because he does not know β. Now, since the degree of Ψ is $A(1 + B\frac{\beta^2-1}{A})$, then $\Psi = \Psi_2 \circ \Psi_1$ where Ψ_1 has degree A and Ψ_2 has degree $1 + B\frac{\beta^2-1}{A}$. Evaluating Ψ on the A torsion (using the masked torsion point information available) gives you Ψ_1. The isogeny Ψ_2 whose unknown degree $1 + B\frac{\beta^2-1}{A}$ is larger than B and probably non smooth remains unknown. Hence, one cannot recover Ψ. Clearly, if $\beta = \pm 1$ then $\beta^2 = 1$ and Ψ_2 has degree 1 and Ψ is fully recovered.

A similar argument applies for MD-SIDH as well. In MD-SIDH, the degree of the secret isogeny is $\beta^2 B'$ where β is a secret scalar and B' is a random divisor of B (say $B = B'B_1$). Embedding this isogeny into a higher genus isogeny the same way would lead to an isogeny of degree

$$\beta^2 B' + a = \beta^2 B' + A - B'B_1 = A + B'(\beta^2 - B_1).$$

This degree is unknown to the attacker, because he does not know neither β nor B' (or B_1). Let $d = gcd(A, \beta^2 - B_1)$, then $\Psi = \Psi_2 \circ \Psi_1$ where Ψ_1 has degree d and Ψ_2 has degree $\frac{A}{d} + B'\frac{\beta^2-B_1}{d}$. Evaluating Ψ on the A torsion (using the masked torsion point information available) gives you Ψ_1. The isogeny Ψ_2 whose unknown degree $\frac{A}{d} + B'\frac{\beta^2-B_1}{d}$ is larger than B and probably non smooth remains unknown. Hence, one cannot recover Ψ.

Remark 6. One could try to use a different value a' instead of $a = A - B$ when embedding the secret isogeny into a higher genus isogeny. This would only make things more complicated. In fact the unknown degree of Ψ is $\beta^2 B + a'$ for M-SIDH and $\beta^2 B' + a'$ for MD-SIDH. As before, setting d to be the greatest common divisor of this degree and A, then $\Psi = \Psi_2 \circ \Psi_1$ where Ψ_1 has degree d. The isogeny Ψ_1, can be recovered, but Ψ_2 whose unknown degree is larger than A and B, and is probably non smooth cannot be efficiently recovered.

4   Security Analysis of the Masked Torsion Points Variant

Recall that the M-SIDH variant differs from SIDH in that parties send torsion point images only up to a constant α, which is a square root of unity.

We first describe a general attack that simply consists of guessing enough exact torsion point information to run the CD-MM-R attacks. This attack has exponential complexity in the number of prime divisors of A and B, and it works for any starting curve, even when the endomorphism ring is unknown.

We then describe a *polynomial time* attack when the initial curve is $j = 1728$, and we generalize it to starting curves with (known) small degree endomorphisms. We argue that it appears hard to extend this attack to the case where the endomorphism ring of the starting curve is unknown.

We end this section with a suggestion of parameters with respect to our analysis. In what follows we consider an isogeny of degree B, with images of torsion points of order A revealed up to a scalar α.

4.1   Guessing Enough Exact Torsion Point Information

Since Bob's isogeny has degree $B \approx A$, then we only need the exact images of the $\sqrt{B} \approx \sqrt{A}$ torsion points to run the CD-MM-R attacks. We are provided with the images of the A-torsion points where $A = \ell_1 \cdots \ell_t$.

Let $n \geq 1$ be the largest index such that $\sqrt{B} \leq \ell_n \cdots \ell_t$. Set $N = \ell_n \cdots \ell_t$. Then Bob's secret isogeny ϕ_B can be recovered from its action on the N-torsion points. From the action of $[\alpha] \circ \phi_B$ on the A-torsion points, one deduces the action of $[\alpha] \circ \phi_B$ on the N-torsion points. The only thing preventing us from applying the CD-MM-R attack is the unknown square root of unity α. Since N has $t - n + 1$ prime factors, then there are at most 2^{t-n+1} square roots of unity modulo N. One can hence try all these square roots of unity till one gets one for which the CD-MM-R attack is successful.

The overall complexity of this attack is $\tilde{O}(2^{t-n+1})$ using a classical computer. Since $N \approx \sqrt{A}$ and N is made up of the largest prime factors of A, then we must have $t/2 < n$, which implies $t - n + 1 \leq t/2$. This attack is summarized in Algorithm 1. We deduce Theorem 7.

Algorithm 1. Attack by using less torsion point information

Require: E_0, P_A, Q_A, E_B, $P' = [\beta]\phi_B(P_A)$, $Q' = [\beta]\phi_B(Q_A)$ from an M-SIDH instance.

Ensure: ϕ_B.

1: Set $N = \ell_n \cdots \ell_t$ where $n \geq 1$ be the largest index such that $\sqrt{B} \leq \ell_n \cdots \ell_t$;
2: Compute $P_1 = [\frac{A}{N}]P'$ and $Q_1 = [\frac{A}{N}]Q'$;
3: **for** each square root γ of unity modulo N **do**
4:     try to run the CD-MM-R attack to recover ϕ_B from E_0, P_A, Q_A, E_B, $[\gamma^{-1}]P_1$,
5:     $Q' = [\gamma^{-1}]Q_1$;
6:     **if** The CD-MM-R attack is successful **then**
7:         **return** ϕ_B.

Theorem 7. *Algorithm 1 is correct and runs in time $\tilde{O}(2^{t-n+1})$ using a classical computer with $t - n + 1 \leq t/2$.*

The above discussion only considers classical security. When we use a quantum computer, the complexity of the attack can be improved because Grover algorithm [22] allows us to find the correct γ in Algorithm 1 in time $\tilde{O}(2^{(t-n+1)/2})$. We deduce Theorem 8.

Theorem 8. *Algorithm 1 is correct and runs in time $\tilde{O}(2^{(t-n+1)/2})$ using a quantum computer with $t - n + 1 \leq t/2$.*

Remark 9. From Theorem 7 and 8, the value t should be greater than or equal to 2λ for AES-λ security (i.e. λ bits of classical security and $\lambda/2$ bits of quantum security).

4.2   Polynomial Time Attack When E_0 Has j-invariant $= 1728$

Castryck-Decru, Maino-Martindale and Robert's new SIDH attacks seem to require exact knowledge of torsion point images, motivating the M-SIDH variant. On the other hand, older torsion point attacks only required these images up to a constant [2,19], though of course they also required A much larger than B. This suggests looking for an improved attack combining the best of both worlds.

Let $\iota \in \mathrm{End}(E_0) : (x,y) \to (-x,iy)$ be a non-trivial automorphism of E_0 and let

$$\psi := \phi \circ \iota \circ \hat{\phi}$$

be the "lollipop endomorphism" constructed in Petit's attack and variants (see Sect. 2.2). As the images of torsion points through ϕ are provided up to a scalar α where $\alpha^2 = 1 \mod A$, then we have that

$$[\alpha]\phi \circ \iota \circ \widehat{[\alpha]\phi} = [\alpha^2] \circ \phi \circ \iota \circ \hat{\phi} = [\alpha^2] \circ \psi.$$

Hence, from the action of $[\alpha]\phi$ on the A-torsion, one can recover the action of $[\alpha^2] \circ \psi$ on the A-torsion. Since $\alpha^2 = 1 \mod A$, then the images of $A-$torsion points through ψ are exact. Moreover as ψ has degree $B^2 \approx A^2$ and images of torsion points of order A are known, we can apply Robert's attack to ψ instead of ϕ! After recovering ψ, one can recover φ efficiently.

Remark 10. One can recover ψ from ϕ as in [31]: compute $G := \ker \phi \cap E'[B]$ and extract the largest cyclic subgroup in G. Generically this is a large subgroup of $\ker \phi$, and the remaining part of $\ker \phi$ is simply guessed. Note that the powersmooth case (as in M-SIDH) is considered a worst case in [31], but even in this "worst case situation" the cost is shown to be polynomial time in expectation (for randomly chosen ϕ).

4.3   Generalization to Other Starting Curves

More generally, given the endomorphism ring of the starting curve, one can apply the LLL algorithm to compute a short non scalar endomorphism in it. One can then replace the endomorphism ι of degree 1 in the previous attack by another higher degree endomorphism θ.

As $\deg \psi = B^2 \deg \theta$ and Robert's attack requires $\deg \psi \leq A^2$, this strategy would require to first guess the action of ϕ on a torsion A' subgroup with $A' \geq \sqrt{\deg \theta}$, up to a scalar. This involves guessing the images of two cyclic A'-torsion subgroups, hence it requires $O(A'^2) \approx \deg \theta$ attempts.

The attack will be relevant for any starting curve with a small non-trivial endomorphism. For generic curves, we will have $\deg \theta \approx \sqrt{p}$, so the attack will not provide any improvement over a trivial guessing strategy.

4.4   Generalization Attempt to Unknown Endomorphism Rings

When the endomorphism ring of the starting curve is unknown to the attacker, one may hope to generalize the previous attack in the same way as previous torsion point attacks were generalized by the Castryck-Decru's, Maino-Martindale's and Robert's attacks: by embedding the isogeny problem into an isogeny problem of higher dimension.

In particular, one could try to achieve this is by considering the genus 3 product $A := E_0 \times E_0 \times E'$, and an endomorphism

$$\psi : (P_1, P_2, P_3) \to (P_1, P_2, \phi_2\theta_{12}\hat{\phi}_1(P_3))$$

where $\phi_i : E_0^{(i)} \to E'$ for $i = 1, 2$ are two copies of the secret isogeny ϕ, and $\theta_{12} : E_0^{(1)} \to E_0^{(2)}$ is a small degree isogeny from one copy of E_0 to the other one. However, a closer look at this attempt reveals that $\phi_2\theta_{12}\hat{\phi}_1$ is just a scalar multiplication on E', and it can therefore not help to recover ϕ. Other similar strategies we tried led to the same issue.

5   Security Analysis of the Masked Degree Variant

In this section, we discuss the security of our second countermeasure MD-SIDH. First, we prove that the square-free part of the degree of the secret isogeny can be recovered efficiently; this is done in Subsect. 5.1 below (together with 5.2 for a technical lemma). In Subsect. 5.3 we show how to reduce any instance of Masked-degree SIDH into an instance of Masked torsion points SIDH when the square-free part of the secret isogeny is known. The latter implies that all the attacks presented in Sect. 4 can be extended to MD-SIDH through this reduction. Taking this into account, we suggest parameters for MD-SIDH in Subsect. 7.3.

Recall that in the MD-SIDH setting, $A = \ell_1^{a_1} \cdots \ell_t^{a_t}$, $B = q_1^{b_1} \cdots q_t^{b_t}$ and $p = ABf - 1$ where f is a small cofactor. We are targeting Bob's secret isogeny $\phi : E_0 \to E_B$ whose degree $B' = q_1^{b'_1} \cdots q_t^{b'_t}$ is an unknown divisor of B, and we are provided with $E_0, P, Q, E_B, P' = [\beta]\phi(P), Q' = [\beta]\phi(Q)$ where $E_0[A] = \langle P, Q \rangle$ and $\beta \in \mathbb{Z}/A\mathbb{Z}^\times$ is unknown.

5.1   Recovering the Degree up to Squares

From Lemma 3, one can assume that $\beta^2 B' \mod A$ is known. In this section we show how to deduce a small set of candidates for the square-free part of B'.

Let $\mathcal{D}(B)$ be the set of positive divisors of B. Given $\underline{b}' = (b'_1, \cdots, b'_t) \in \mathbb{Z}^t$, we write $B(\underline{b}') = q_1^{b'_1} \cdots q_t^{b'_t}$, and similarly if $B' = B(\underline{b}')$, we write $\underline{b}' = b(B')$. These maps restrict to a one-to-one correspondence between $\prod_{i=1}^t \mathbb{Z}/(b_i + 1)\mathbb{Z}$ and $\mathcal{D}(B)$. For simplicity, we suppose that the ℓ_is and the q_is are odd primes[6].

---

[6] The case where $\ell_i = 2$ in general does not fit our definition of χ since there are more than two square roots of 1 modulo 2^r for $r > 2$. Nevertheless, if the power of 2 diving A or B is at least 4, then the security of the scheme is not affected.

Let $\chi_{\ell_i^{a_i}}$ be the natural surjection $\chi_{\ell_i^{a_i}} \colon (\mathbb{Z}/\ell_i^{a_i}\mathbb{Z})^\times \rightarrow (\mathbb{Z}/\ell_i^{a_i}\mathbb{Z})^\times /$ $((\mathbb{Z}/\ell_i^{a_i}\mathbb{Z})^\times)^2 \cong \{-1, 1\}$. Consider the map

$$\Phi \colon \mathbb{Z}^t \longrightarrow \{-1, 1\}^t$$
$$\underline{b}' \longmapsto \left(\chi_{\ell_1^{a_1}}(B(\underline{b}')), \dots, \chi_{\ell_t^{a_t}}(B(\underline{b}'))\right),$$

where we regard $B(\underline{b}')$ as an element in $(\mathbb{Z}/\ell_i^{b_i}\mathbb{Z})^\times$. Clearly, Φ is a group morphism and $(2\mathbb{Z})^t \subset \ker \Phi$. This implies that the following group homomorphism is well-defined:

$$\overline{\Phi} \colon (\mathbb{Z}/2\mathbb{Z})^t \longrightarrow \mathrm{Im}(\Phi) \subset \{-1, 1\}^t$$
$$\underline{b}' \longmapsto \Phi(\underline{b}').$$

Since the cardinality of the domain of the group morphism $\overline{\Phi}$ is 2^t, then $\# \ker \overline{\Phi} = 2^{t_\Phi}$ for some $0 \le t_\Phi \le t$. This implies that when given $\Phi(b(B'))$, we have $\#\overline{\Phi}^{-1}(\Phi(b(B'))) = 2^{t_\Phi}$. In other words, giving $\Phi(b(B'))$ is the same as giving $t - t_\Phi$ bits of information about $b(B') \bmod 2$. Furthermore, when $t_\Phi = 0$, that is when $\overline{\Phi}$ is an isomorphism, then $\Phi(\underline{b}')$ uniquely determines $b(B') \bmod 2$. Note that for any representative $\underline{b}'$ in the class $b(B') + 2\mathbb{Z}^t$, the integers $B(\underline{b}')$ and B' have the same square-free factor.

Lemma 11. *Consider the notations above. Let B_1' be the square-free part of B'. Then given E_0, P, Q, E_B, P' and Q', there exists a probabilistic polynomial time algorithm that reduces the search space for B_1' to a set of order 2^{t_Φ} where $2^{t_\Phi} = \# \ker \overline{\Phi}$.*

Proof. From P, Q, E_B, P', and Q', use Lemma 3 to recover $d = \beta^2 B' \bmod A$. Compute

$$\Phi(b(d)) = \left(\chi_{\ell_1^{a_1}}(\beta^2 B'), \cdots, \chi_{\ell_t^{a_t}}(\beta^2 B')\right) = \left(\chi_{\ell_1^{a_1}}(B'), \cdots, \chi_{\ell_t^{a_t}}(B')\right) = \Phi(b(B')).$$

Compute $\ker \overline{\Phi}$ and a preimage $\underline{b_0}$ of $\Phi(b(d))$ with respect to $\overline{\Phi}$. Return the set $\{B(\underline{b}) \mid \underline{b} \in \underline{b_0} + \ker \overline{\Phi}\}$ of square-free integers.

Clearly, all the computational steps described above run in polynomial time. The correctness follows from the properties of the morphism Φ and $\overline{\Phi}$ discussed before the lemma. □

In the next subsection, we show that t_Φ is expected to be small for most parameters, and the squarefree part of B' can therefore be guessed with a high probability.

5.2   On the Value of t_Φ

In this section we estimate t_Φ. We start by observing the following.

Lemma 12. *Let t be an integer and let M be a random $t \times t$ matrix over $\mathbb{F}_2$. Then as t tends towards ∞, we have have $t - 2 \le \mathrm{rank}(M)$ with probability 0.9947145498.*

Proof. Let $p_t(k)$ be the probability that a uniformly random $t \times t$-matrix over $\mathbb{F}_2$ has rank $t - k$. Then, from [25, p.33] and [11, Theorem 1], it holds that

$$
\pi(k) := \lim_{t \to \infty} p_t(k) = \begin{cases} \prod_{i=1}^{\infty} \left(1 - \dfrac{1}{2^i}\right), & (k = 0) \\[2ex] \dfrac{\prod_{i=k+1}^{\infty}(1 - (1/2^i))}{\prod_{i=1}^{k}(1 - (1/2^i))} \dfrac{1}{2^{k^2}}, & (k \geq 1). \end{cases}
$$

From [11, Table 1], we have $\pi(0)$ is about 0.2887880951, $\pi(1)$ is about 0.5775761902, $\pi(2)$ is about 0.1283502645, and $\pi(k)$'s for $k \geq 3$ are less than 0.0052387863. Therefore,

$$
\Pr(k \leq 2) = \pi(0) + \pi(1) + \pi(2) \approx 0.9947145498.
$$

$\square$

Consider the matrix M^* of the morphism $(1 - \bar{\Phi})/2$ (operations are done component wise). Lemma 12 applies to random matrices and t needs to be somehow large. In practice, t is relatively small, $t \approx O(\lambda)$ where λ is the security parameter, and, A and B are system parameters, which could in theory be chosen to maximize t_ϕ. However, for the sake of the scheme's practicality, the integers A and B need to be as small as possible. Also, in order to not weaken one of the participants, A and B need to satisfy $A \approx B$. With these constraints, we do not expect to have $2 < t_\phi$. Intuitively, if $2 < t_\phi$, then there are t_ϕ square-free integers that are all quadratic residues modulo all the t prime power divisors of A. Given a random square-free integer N, N is a quadratic residue modulo a given prime power with probability $\frac{1}{2}$, hence it is a quadratic residue modulo t "independent" distinct prime powers with probability roughly $\frac{1}{2^t}$. Since $t \approx O(\lambda)$, then $\frac{1}{2^t}$ is negligible. Hence the probability that there exists many such integers N rapidly decreases below $\frac{1}{2^\lambda}$. For example, given t, let $\ell_1, q_1, \ell_2, q_2, \ldots, \ell_t, q_t$ be the smallest $2t$ odd primes. For $t = 64, 96, 128, 192, 286, 420, 426, 566, 637, 856$, we obtained $t_\phi = 1, 0, 1, 2, 0, 0, 1, 0, 1, 0$ respectively.

In conclusion, we believe that it is computationally hard in practice to come up with integers A and B such that $2 \ll t_\phi$. Also, if ever such integers were computed, A and B would be too large, which would lead to an impractical scheme.

5.3 Reduction to the M-SIDH Variant

We now show how to reduce a MD-SIDH instance to an M-SIDH instance.

Recall that in the MD-SIDH case (Problem 5), we are given E_0, P, Q, $E_B, P' = [\beta]\phi(P), Q' = [\beta]\phi(Q)$, where $E_0[A] = \langle P, Q \rangle$, ϕ is a random isogeny of degree B' with B' being a random divisor of B, and β is a random integer coprime to A; and we are asked to recover ϕ.

Following Subsects. 5.1 and 5.2, we assume that the square-free part of the degree of the secret isogeny is known. Let B_1' be the square-free part of B'. Let

B_0 be the largest divisor of B which is equal to B' up to squares, and let β_0 be the divisor of B such that $B_0 = \beta_0^2 B'$. Since B is a smooth integer and we know B_1', we can compute B_0.

Let $\phi_0 = [\beta_0] \circ \phi$. We then know $\deg \phi_0 = \beta_0^2 \deg \phi = \beta_0^2 B' = B_0 \leq B$. Moreover, we have

$$\begin{cases} P' = [\beta]\phi(P) = [(\beta\beta_0^{-1}) \cdot \beta_0]\phi(P) = [\beta\beta_0^{-1}]\phi_0(P) \\ Q' = [\beta]\phi(Q) = [(\beta\beta_0^{-1}) \cdot \beta_0]\phi(Q) = [\beta\beta_0^{-1}]\phi_0(Q) \end{cases}$$

From Lemma 3, we can recover $\beta^2 B' \bmod A$, and compute

$$\beta_1^2 = \beta_0^2 B' \cdot (\beta^2 B')^{-1} \bmod A = (\beta_0 \cdot \beta^{-1})^2 \bmod A.$$

We sample a random square root β_1' of $\beta_1^2 \bmod A$, namely $\beta_1' = \mu\beta_1$ where μ is some square root of unity modulo A. We compute

$$\begin{cases} [\beta_1']P' = [\mu \cdot \beta_1]P' = [\mu \cdot \beta_0 \cdot \beta^{-1} \cdot \beta]\phi(P) = [\mu \cdot \beta_0]\phi(P) = [\mu]\phi_0(P) \\ [\beta_1']Q' = [\mu \cdot \beta_1]P' = [\mu \cdot \beta_0 \cdot \beta^{-1} \cdot \beta]\phi(Q) = [\mu \cdot \beta_0]\phi(Q) = [\mu]\phi_0(Q) \end{cases}$$

From here, one solves for ϕ_0 where E_0, P, Q, E_B, $[\mu]\phi_0(P)$, $[\mu]\phi_0(Q)$ and $\deg \phi_0 = \beta_0^2 B'$ are provided. This is in fact an M-SIDH instance, with the only difference that the secret isogeny is not cyclic. This is not a problem since the higher genus torsion points attack has no restriction on the type of isogeny (cyclic or not) in play.

5.4   Reduction Impact: Porting M-SIDH Attacks to MD-SIDH

In this section we revisit the attacks of Sect. 4 and check that they still apply when the secret isogeny is not cyclic. Recall that the isogeny to recover here is $\phi_0 = [\beta_0] \circ \phi$ where β_0 is an unknown integer such that the degree $B_0 = \beta_0^2 B'$ of ϕ_0 divides B. We are provided with the $B_0 = \deg \phi_0$ and the action of ϕ_0 on the A torsion group up to a scalar (a root of unity modulo A).

We start with Robert's attack (see Sect. 2.2), and observe that neither the definition of the isogeny Ψ nor the way ϕ is deduced from this isogeny rely on ϕ being a cyclic isogeny. The attack of Sect. 4.1 simply guesses the exact torsion point images on the minimal amount of torsion point information needed for Robert's attack. As before, allowing for non cyclic isogenies does not affect Robert's attack.

Regarding the attack of Sect. 4.2, one first applies Robert's attack on $\psi = \phi_0 \circ \iota \circ \hat{\phi_0} = [\beta_0^2] \circ \phi \circ \iota \circ \phi$, then one deduces the isogeny ϕ_0 using [31, §4.3]. The first part is again an application of Robert's attack to a non cyclic isogeny. The second part requires some clarification.

When $\phi_0 = \phi$ is cyclic ($\beta_0 = 1$), in [31, §4.3], the attacker computes $G := \ker \psi \cap E_B[B_0]$, which clearly contains $\ker \phi$, and is in general isomorphic to $\mathbb{Z}/N\mathbb{Z} \times \mathbb{Z}/N'\mathbb{Z}$ for some $N'|N|B_0$ such that $NN' = B_0$. When $N' = 1$ we have $G = \ker \phi$. For a cyclic isogeny ϕ, we have $N' > 1$ exactly when ι leaves either $\ker \phi \cap E_0[N']$ or $\ker \hat{\phi} \cap E_B[N']$ invariant: this leaves at most 2^r candidates for

$\ker \phi$, where r is the number of prime factors in N'. But, since ϕ is uniformly random (because it is the secret isogeny), then N' is relatively small and hence has very few prime factors.

Let us return to the case where $\phi_0 = [\beta_0] \circ \phi$ with ϕ being cyclic and $\beta_0 > 1$ is unknown, and let us assume that $\psi = \phi_0 \circ \iota \circ \hat{\phi}_0 = [\beta_0^2] \circ \phi \circ \iota \circ \phi$ has been recovered. After evaluating ψ on the B_0 torsion, we will get a group isomorphic to $\mathbb{Z}/C\mathbb{Z} \times \mathbb{Z}/C'\mathbb{Z}$ where $C'|C|B_0$. Since ψ is divisible by β_0^2, the β_0^2-torsion is killed by ψ and the group $\mathbb{Z}/C\mathbb{Z} \times \mathbb{Z}/C'\mathbb{Z}$ is the group one would have got if one was evaluating $\phi \circ \iota \circ \phi$ on the $B' = B_0/\beta_0^2$ torsion. Hence $CC' = B' = \deg \phi$ as discussed in the previous paragraph and $\beta_0 = \sqrt{B_0/B'}$. One then recovers ϕ as in the previous paragraph.

6 Adaptive Attacks

In this section, we show that M-SIDH and MD-SIDH, as SIDH, are vulnerable to adaptive attacks. We also discuss the use of B-SIDH primes in M-SIDH and future work. We first discuss the Fouotsa-Petit attack, then the GPST attack.

6.1 Fouotsa-Petit Adaptive Attack

Fouotsa-Petit [19] adaptive attack consists in actively transforming a balanced SIDH instance ($A \approx B$) into an imbalanced one ($B < A^* = NA$ where $N \approx p$), then running Petit's torsion point attacks [31,32] on the imbalanced SIDH (where the secret isogeny has degree B and the torsion points have order $A^* = NA$) to recover the secret isogeny.

In [19, Section 3.2], the authors show that Petit's torsion point attacks can be run even when the torsion point images are scaled with an unknown scalar. Petit's attacks also apply to non cyclic isogenies. In fact, to recover an isogeny $\phi : E \longrightarrow E'$ from its action on large enough torsion points, Petit's attack (see Sect. 2.2) uses the torsion point information and a suitable endomorphism θ of E to compute the endomorphism $\psi = \phi \circ \theta \circ \phi$ of E'; then the techniques of [31, §4.3] (also see Sect. 5.4) are used to recover ϕ. As before, ϕ not being cyclic does not impact the first step where one recovers ψ. There are some subtleties when trying to recover ϕ from ψ when ϕ is non cyclic, but they were already covered in Sect. 5.4. However, Petit's attacks do require knowledge of the degree of the secret isogeny.

The generalization of the Fouotsa-Petit [19] adaptive attack to M-SIDH is therefore straightforward. For MD-SIDH, one can use the techniques from Sect. 5 to reduce the MD-SIDH instance to an M-SIDH instance, and then run the Fouotsa-Petit attack on the M-SIDH instance.

6.2 GPST Adaptive Attack

Recall that in the GPST attack on SIDH, Bob (the honest party) has a static secret key/public key pair $(b, (E_B, \phi_B(P_A), \phi_B(Q_A))$. Alice (the dishonest party) maliciously generates public keys (E_A, R, S) with modified torsion points images, and repeatedly runs the key exchange with Alice using these malicious public keys. The attack assumes that Alice is provided with an oracle $O(E_A, R, S, E')$ that outputs 1 if E' is the shared secret computed by the honest Bob when using (E_A, R, S) as Alice's public key, and 0 otherwise. Then the GPST adaptive attack recovers the secret b with only $\log b$ queries to the oracle O. The attack provides the points (R_i, S_i) to be used at each query. We refer to [20] for details about the GPST adaptive attack.

One thing to notice here is that

$$O(E_A, R, S, E') = 1 \iff E_A/\langle R + [b]S \rangle = E_A/\langle \phi_A(P_B) + [b]\phi_A(Q_B) \rangle$$
$$\iff \langle R + [b]S \rangle = \langle \phi_A(P_B) + [b]\phi_A(Q_B) \rangle$$

where the second equivalence holds except with neglible probability. Hence, assuming E_A is fixed, we can see O as an oracle that when given R, S, outputs 1 if $\langle R + [b]S \rangle = \langle \phi_A(P_B) + [b]\phi_A(Q_B) \rangle$, and 0 if not. Note that the malicious points R and S are obtained by doing a linear combination of $\phi_A(P_B)$ and $\phi_A(Q_B)$, say $R = [e_1]\phi_A(P_B) + [e_2]\phi_A(Q_B)$ and $S = [f_1]\phi_A(P_B) + [f_2]\phi_A(Q_B)$.

When it comes to M-SIDH, the image points are scaled with a secret invertible scalar β. But, as the scalar is invertible and everything is linear, the attack can proceed in the same way.

For MD-SIDH, the degree B' of Bob's secret isogeny is an unknown divisor of B. The torsion points R and S are first scaled by the secret integer $B_1 = \frac{B}{B'}$ before being used by Bob; that is Bob computes the isogeny $E_A \to E_A/\langle [B_1](R + [b]S) \rangle$. Hence our new oracle here acts as follows: when given R and S, it outputs 1 if $\langle [B_1](R + [b]S) \rangle = \langle [B_1](\phi_A(P_B) + [b]\phi_A(Q_B)) \rangle$, and 0 otherwise.

Here, blindly applying the GPST adaptive attack would not work, as the attacker first needs to recover the degree B' of the secret isogeny or equivalently the integer $B_1 = \frac{B}{B'}$. Moreover unlike for the Fouotsa-Petit attack, one cannot simply apply our reduction from Sect. 4 to recover the degree and then apply GPST attack, because the GPST attack assumes a cyclic secret isogeny.

To recover the integer B_1, we instead use the above oracle. Let q^e be a prime power divisor of B. We would like to recover the largest integer $e' \le e$ such that $q^{e'}$ divides B'. We repeatedly query the oracle with the points

$$R_i = \phi_A(P_B) + \left[\frac{B}{q^i}\right]\phi_A(Q_B), \quad S_i = \phi_A(Q_B), \quad 1 \le i \le e.$$

We have the following lemma.

Lemma 13. *With the notations as above, we have*

$$O\left(\phi_B(P_A) + \left[\frac{B}{q^i}\right]\phi_A(Q_B), \phi_A(Q_B)\right) = 1$$

if and only if q^i divides B_1.

Proof. Set $R_i = \phi_A(P_B) + \left[\frac{B}{q^i}\right]\phi_A(Q_B)$ and $S_i = \phi_A(Q_B)$. We have

$$\langle [B_1](R_i + [b]S_i)\rangle = \langle [B_1](\phi_A(P_B) + \left[\frac{B}{q^i}\right]\phi_A(Q_B) + [b]\phi_A(Q_B))\rangle$$
$$= \langle [B_1]\left(\phi_A(P_B) + [b]\phi_A(Q_B)\right) + [\frac{B}{q^i}][B_1]\phi_A(Q_B)\rangle.$$

Clearly, the points $[B_1](\phi_A(P_B) + [b]\phi_A(Q_B))$ and $[B_1]\phi_A(Q_B)$ have order B' and are linearly independent. Hence

$$\langle [B_1]\left(\phi_A(P_B) + [b]\phi_A(Q_B)\right)\rangle = \langle [B_1]\left(\phi_A(P_B) + [b]\phi_A(Q_B)\right) + \left[\frac{B}{q^i}\right][B_1]\phi_A(Q_B)\rangle$$

if and only if $\frac{B}{q^i} = 0 \mod B'$, that is if and only if q^i divides B_1. The Lemma then follows from the definition of the oracle O. □

Using Lemma 13, one recovers each prime power divisor $q_i^{e_i'}$ of $B_1 = \frac{B}{B'}$ with at most e_i queries, where $B = q_1^{e_1} \cdots q_t^{e_t}$, $i = 1, \ldots, t$. The total maximum number of queries to recover the secret degree B' is $\sum_{i=1}^{t} e_i$. Once the degree is recovered, one then runs the usual GPST attack.

7   Parameter Selection and Efficiency

In this section, we discuss the choice of the starting curve E_0, and we use the analysis from the previous sections to infer parameter selections for both M-SIDH and MD-SIDH. We conclude that the M-SIDH variant is always more secure than the MD-SIDH variant at comparable parameter sizes, and discuss its efficiency.

7.1   Choosing the Starting Curve E_0

From the attack in Sect. 4.2 and its generalization to MD-SIDH in Sect. 5.4, an elliptic curve with a short-degree endomorphism (e.g., the curve of j-invariant 1728) should not be used for a starting curve in either scheme. Therefore the setup algorithm needs to generate E_0 as a curve with no short-degree endomorphism. There are three possibilities here:

1. the endomorphism ring of the curve is public,
2. the endomorphism ring of the curve is not public, but known by one party (either Alice or Bob);
3. the endomorphism ring is unknown to everyone.

The advantage of the first possibility is that since the endomorphism ring of E_0 is public, everyone can verify that E_0 does not have small endomorphisms by determining the norm of the shortest element $\text{End}(E_0)$ (this is a dimension 4 lattice, so computing the shortest element is easy). One can use Bröker's algorithm [6] to generate E_0, or obtain E_0 by performing a random walk from a supersingular curve computed using Bröker's algorithm. The first option is not secure since the supersingular curves generated using Bröker's algorithm have small endomorphisms. In the second option, the party that generates the curve could backdoor it. In fact, they could generate a weak curve in the sense of [32]. Weak curves are curves for which Petit's torsion point attack has the best efficiency for a given set of parameters.

In the second scenario, one of the participants generates the curve and does not reveal its endomorphism ring. This party could hence potentially cheat and use a curve with small endomorphisms or a weak curve, then use it to attack the other party. This is not acceptable for a key exchange protocol. Nevertheless, in the setting of a SIKE-type key encapsulation mechanism or public key encryption scheme, we can let the key generation algorithm generate the starting curve and publish it together with their public key: indeed using a weak curve here would only make their own secret key weaker.

Regarding the third scenario, one should note that generating a supersingular curve with unknown endomorphism ring is a hard problem [4,28]. Instead, one can rely on a trusted third party (possibly simulated by a multiparty protocol [1]) to generate a truly random supersingular E_0 curve by performing a long random walk for a known supersingular curve, and forgets (deletes) the walk they used. Then the obtained curve could be used as starting curve for the schemes suggested in this scheme.

In conclusion, restricting E_0 to curves which do not have small endomorphisms is sufficient when instantiating M-SIDH and MD-SIDH. Nevertheless, one would need to trust the party generating the curve since they could backdoor it (we could not find a method to generate curves with no small endomorphisms in the literature). Since we would need to trust them anyway, it is better to just ask this party to generate a curve with unknown endomorphism ring. This can also be done using the MPC techniques described in [1].

7.2 Parameter Selection for M-SIDH

Recall that the M-SIDH primes are of the form $p = ABf - 1$ where $A = \ell_1 \cdots \ell_t$ and $B = q_1 \cdots q_t$ are coprime integedoℓ_i, q_i are distinct small primes, $A \approx B \approx \sqrt{p}$ and f is a small cofactor. Let λ be the security parameter. From Subsect. 4.1, we need $t - n + 1 \geq \lambda$ for classical security and $t - n + 1 \geq 2\lambda$ for quantum security, where n is the largest integer satisfying $\sqrt{B} \leq \ell_n \cdots \ell_t$, where λ is a security parameter.

We now explain how to generate the public parameters of M-SIDH for AES-λ security (i.e., classical λ bits security and quantum $\lambda/2$ bits security). Given λ, we sample the $2t$ smallest primes for $t \geq 2\lambda$, we partition them into two sets of equal size, we use the first set to get A and we use the second to get B, such that $A \approx B$. We then check the value $t - n + 1$ described in Subsect. 4.1. If $\lambda < t - n + 1$, we restart with a larger t. If $\lambda \geq t - n + 1$, find a cofactor f such that $p = ABf - 1$ is prime.

For AES-128 (NIST level 1), AES-192 (NIST level 3) and AES-256 (NIST level 5) security levels, Table 1 presents the key sizes, including secret key, public key and compressed public key. The suggested primes for M-SIDH are

$$p_{128} = 2^2 \cdot \ell_1 \cdots \ell_{571} \cdot 10 - 1,$$

$$p_{192} = 2^2 \cdot \ell_1 \cdots \ell_{851} \cdot 207 - 1$$

and

$$p_{256} = 2^2 \cdot \ell_1 \cdots \ell_{1131} \cdot 13 - 1$$

respectively; where ℓ_i is the ith odd prime. Alice uses $A = 2^2 \cdot \ell_2 \cdot \ell_4 \cdots \ell_{t-2}$ and Bob uses $B = \ell_1 \cdot \ell_3 \cdots \ell_{t-1}$.

Table 1. Suggested parameters for 128, 192 and 256 bits of security.

AES	NIST	p (in bits)	secret key	public key	compressed pk
128	level 1	5911	$\approx$ 369 bytes	4434 bytes	$\approx$ 2585 bytes
192	level 3	9382	$\approx$ 586 bytes	7037 bytes	$\approx$ 4103 bytes
256	level 5	13000	$\approx$ 812 bytes	9750 bytes	$\approx$ 5687 bytes

7.3   Parameter Selection for MD-SIDH

We showed in previous sections that MD-SIDH can be broken by the same attacks as M-SIDH. Therefore, $t - n + 1$ must be greater than or equal to λ for AES-λ security, where n is the largest integer such that there is a subset $S \subset \{1, \ldots, t\}$ satisfying $\sqrt{B} \leq \prod_{i \in S} \ell_i^{a_i}$ and $n = t + 1 - \#S$. Moreover, to mask the degree of the secret isogeny, the size of the space of degrees needs to be $2^{\lambda+t}$ since the Weil pairing will reduce it by a factor 2^t.

Given λ, we sample the $2t$ smallest primes for $t \geq \lambda$, we set $a_1 = \cdots = a_\lambda = b_1 = \cdots = b_\lambda = 3$ and the other exponents are 1, and we partition them into two sets of equal size. We use the first set to get A and the second to get B, such that $A \approx B$. We check the value $t - n + 1$ described above. If $\lambda < t - n + 1$, we restart with a larger t. If $\lambda \geq t - n + 1$, we find a cofactor f such that $p = ABf - 1$ is prime.

For AES-128 (NIST level 1), AES-192 (NIST level 3) and AES-256 (NIST level 5) security levels, Table 2 presents the key sizes: secret key, public key and compressed public key. The suggested primes for M-SIDH are

$$p_{128} = 2^3 \cdot \ell_1^3 \cdots \ell_{255}^3 \ell_{256} \cdots \ell_{839} \cdot 537 - 1,$$

$$p_{192} = 2^3 \cdot \ell_1^3 \cdots \ell_{383}^3 \ell_{384} \cdots \ell_{1273} \cdot 131 - 1$$

and

$$p_{256} = 2^3 \cdot \ell_1^3 \cdots \ell_{511}^3 \ell_{512} \cdots \ell_{1711} \cdot 1485 - 1$$

respectively; where ℓ_i is the ith odd prime. Alice uses $A = 2^3 \cdot \ell_2^3 \cdots \ell_{\lambda-2}^3 \ell_\lambda \cdots \ell_{t-2}$ and Bob uses $B = \ell_1^3 \cdots \ell_{\lambda-1}^3 \ell_{\lambda+1} \cdots \ell_{t-1}$.

Table 2. Suggested parameters for 128, 192 and 256 bits of security.

AES	NIST	p (in bits)	secret key	public key	compressed pk
128	level 1	13810	≈ 863 bytes	10358 bytes	≈ 6040 bytes
192	level 3	22291	≈ 1393 bytes	16719 bytes	≈ 9751 bytes
256	level 5	31226	≈ 1951 bytes	23420 bytes	≈ 13660 bytes

7.4   Preliminary Efficiency Analysis

From the two subsections above, it is clear that the M-SIDH variant is more secure than the MD-SIDH variant for comparable parameter sizes.

Compressed public key sizes for M-SIDH have 2585, 4103 and 5687 bytes at security levels 128, 192 and 256. This is roughly 6.8, 7.3 and 7.8 bigger than previously suggested SIKE keys for the same security levels. Asymptotically, Keys scale quasi-linearly in the security parameter, whereas SIKE keys scaled linearly.

Computations required in M-SIDH are similar to those required in SIDH, with additional (comparably negligible) scalar multiplications to mask torsion points, individual isogeny steps of degrees $O(\lambda \log \lambda)$ instead of 2 and 3, and larger parameter sizes. In SIDH, we have $O(\lambda \log \lambda)$ isogeny steps with optimal strategies [16], with each step costing $O(1)$ field operations. Field sizes are $O(\lambda)$ so each field operation costs $O(\lambda \log \lambda)$ bit operations asymptotically, neglecting $\log \log$ factors. This leads to a total asymptotic bit complexity of $O(\lambda^2 \log^2 \lambda)$ bit operations. In M-SIDH, we use $O(\lambda)$ primes each of size $O(\log \lambda)$, so the total prime size is $O(\lambda \log \lambda)$. There are still $O(\lambda \log \lambda)$ steps involved with optimal strategies. Each step requires $O(\sqrt{\lambda \log \lambda})$ field operations using square root Vélu formulae. Field operations cost $O(\lambda \log^2 \lambda)$ bit operations asymptotically, again neglecting $\log \log$ factors. This gives a total of $O(\lambda^{2.5} \log^{7/2} \lambda)$ bit operations. Concrete efficiency should be determined in future work, but a slowdown compared to SIDH should be expected, with a factor in the order of $O(\sqrt{\lambda} \log^{3/2} \lambda)$.

Most efficiency and implementation tricks developed for SIDH should also be available for M-SIDH, and potentially more, but we argue in Appendix B that the B-SIDH approach will not be applicable.

8   Conclusion and Perspectives

We introduced two variants of the SIDH protocols aimed at defeating the Castryck-Decru-Maino-Martindale-Robert recent attacks. The two variants respectively hide the secret isogeny degree and the torsion point information to the attacker (more precisely they only reveal an integer multiple of the degree, and they reveal torsion point images only up to a scalar).

Our thorough security analysis of both variants suggests that the M-SIDH variant offers the best security-efficiency tradeoff. Public key sizes are 4434, 7037 and 9750 bytes respectively for AES-128 (NIST level 1), AES-192 (NIST level 3) and AES-256 (NIST level 5) security, and efficiency is expected to asymptotically be a factor in the order of $O(\sqrt{\lambda} \log^{3/2} \lambda)$ slower compared to SIDH.

Our work suggests that it may be possible to repair the SIDH protocol, although at a non negligible efficiency cost, and it similarly offers a way forward to the numerous cryptographic schemes based on SIDH that were developed in recent years. Further work should aim at developing additional countermeasures and at improving the efficiency and security analysis of our schemes.

Acknowledgements. We thank Castryck and Onuki for their valuable feedback on a preliminary version of the results in this paper, as well as those of the participants at ANTS 2022 that also gave us some feedback. The first author thanks Andrea Basso and Luca De Feo for several discussions regarding this work. We thank anonymous reviewers for their valuable feedback. This research was in part conducted under a contract of "Research and development on new generation cryptography for secure wireless communication services" among "Research and Development for Expansion of Radio Wave Resources (JPJ000254)", which was supported by the Ministry of Internal Affairs and Communications, Japan. Christophe Petit's work is in part supported by an EPSRC fellowship grant (EP/V011324/1).

A   On the claims of ePrint 2022/1667

The ePrint 2022/1667 vaguely claims attacks on M-SIDH. Reading through it, it clearly does not contain any attack against M-SIDH; it is easy to see that the "experimental evidence" provided there only applies to SIDH parameters and does not generalize to the parameters we recommend.

This ePrint paper runs the Castryck-Decru attack on Masked SIDH instantiated with SIDH primes, that is $A = 2^a$ and $B = 3^b$. Note that using SIDH primes in Masked SIDH is totally insecure at the first place. Nevertheless, when the 2^a torsion points are masked, intuitively, one expects the Castryck-Decru attack to succeed 50% of the time. In fact, there are 4 roots of unity modulo 2^a, these are $1, -1, 2^{a-1} - 1$ and $2^{a-1} + 1$. As precised earlier in Sect. 3.3, the attack succeeds when $\beta = 1, -1$, hence one expects the Castryck-Decru attack to succeed when the masking scalar β is 1 or -1, and fail when β is $2^{a-1} - 1$ or $2^{a-1} + 1$. The ePrint 2022/1667 ran the attack and noticed that the attack always succeeds, then claimed that this would be the case even when the correct parameters are used. We have already explained why we do not expect the attack to work on Masked degree instantiated with the correct parameters (see Sect. 3.3). Now, why does the Castryck-Decru attack works 100% of the time (instead of 50%) when instantiated with SIDH parameters? Well, it turns out it is because the Castryck-Decru attack does not fully use the torsion points provided in the public key, but scales them by a small power of 2 first. This is because the implementation of the attack needs a' and b' such that $c = 2^{a'} - 3^{b'}$ is smooth and its prime factors are congruent to 1 mod 4 (this is required for the attack to be efficient, see [7]). This implies that the order of the torsion points actually used in the attack divides 2^{a-1}. Therefore, the masking scalar β which lies in $\{1, -1, 2^{a-1}-1, 2^{a-1}+1\}$ becomes $\beta \mod 2^{a-1} = 1, -1 \pmod{2^{a-1}}$. This justifies why the Castryck-Decru attack always succeeds when SIDH primes are used.

The attack clearly does not succeed when the torsion point images having order $2^{a'}$ are masked with a scalar which is neither 1 nor -1 modulo $2^{a'}$. This can be verified using the sage implementation of the attack provided in [30]. One goes to the line where the torsion point images of order $2^{a'}$ are computed (for example, in line 57 of the file *castryck_decru_shortcut.sage* in https://github. com/jack4818/Castryck-Decru-SageMath), and replaces the torsion points $2^{alp} * P_B$ and $2^{alp} * Q_B$ by $(2^{a_i-1}-1) * 2^{alp} * P_B$ and $(2^{a_i-1}-1) * 2^{alp} * Q_B$ respectively.

Note. The non-applicability of the attacks claimed in the ePrint 2022/1667 to M-SIDH was also pointed out on Twitter by Luca De Feo, Steven Galbraith, Péter Kutas, Benjamin Wesolowski and other isogenists, and we thank them for that.

B   Using B-SIDH primes in M-SIDH

B-SIDH is one variant of SIDH proposed by Costello [12]. The main characteristic of B-SIDH is the use of quadratic twists. This allows us to use the torsion points in $E[p-1]$ and $E[p+1]$ without extending the base field, while in the original SIDH, points which we can use must be in $E[p+1]$. Thus, the size of the prime for B-SIDH is at most half that for SIDH.

If we can adapt this technique to our scheme, then the size of the prime may be at most halved. Since the MD-SIDH primes are larger than twice the M-SIDH primes, we only consider the case of M-SIDH.

In the setting of SIDH, the size of A needs to be large enough for its security; however, in the setting of M-SIDH, the number of primes dividing A needs to large enough. Therefore, the restriction of smoothness is harder in M-SIDH than in SIDH.

To use the B-SIDH method for M-SIDH, we need to find a prime p satisfying the following property:

$$p+1 = \ell_1 \cdots \ell_t \cdot f,$$
$$p-1 = q_1 \cdots q_t \cdot f',$$

where $t \geq 2\lambda$, and $\ell_1, \ldots, \ell_t$ and $q_1, \ldots, q_t$ are distinct primes, respectively.

The basic approach to find the B-SIDH prime is to construct an integer m such that both m and $m+1$ are smooth. If $2m+1$ is prime, we set $p = 2m+1$. In [12] and [13], some methods to find such m's are proposed. The current most useful method is the method proposed in [13]. The main idea of this method is to use already known solutions of the Prouhet-Tarry-Escott (PTE) problem, which provide pairs of integer coefficient polynomials $a(x) = (x-a_1) \cdots (x-a_s)$

and $b(x) = (x - b_1) \cdots (x - b_s)$ whose difference is a constant value c. If we find an integer ℓ such that all $\ell - a_i$'s and $\ell - b_i$'s are smooth, and $a(\ell)/c$ and $b(\ell)/c$ are integers, then $b(\ell)/c$ can be taken as m.

The main issue with this approach is that such ℓ's have a very small probability to exist. For a polynomial $a \in \mathbb{Z}[x]$, define

$$\Psi_a(N, M) = \#\{1 \le m \le N \mid a(m) \text{ is } M\text{-smooth}\}.$$

Then, heuristically it holds that $\Psi_a(N, N^{1/u})/N \sim \rho(d_1 u) \cdots \rho(d_k u)$ as $N \to \infty$, where $d_1, \ldots, d_k$ are degrees of distinct irreducible factors of a, and ρ is the Dickman–de Bruijn function.

Since $t \ge 2\lambda$, both m and $m + 1$ are divided by at least 2λ distinct primes. Then, we heuristically assume that the target value m is $m^{1/\lambda}$-smooth. Since $\ell \approx m^{1/s}$, the probability of target ℓ's is

$$\frac{\Psi_a(m^{1/s}, m^{1/\lambda})}{m^{1/s}} \sim \rho(\lambda/s)^s.$$

Note that s is less than or equal to 12 for an already known solution of the PTE problem. With $\lambda = 128$, we have $\rho(\lambda/s)^s < 2^{-463}$; with $\lambda = 192$, we have $\rho(\lambda/s)^s < 2^{-835}$; and with $\lambda = 256$, we have $\rho(\lambda/s)^s < 2^{-1246}$.

References

1. Basso, A., et al.: Supersingular curves you can trust. Cryptology ePrint Archive, Report 2022/1469 (2022). https://eprint.iacr.org/2022/1469

2. Basso, A., Kutas, P., Merz, S.-P., Petit, C., Sanso, A.: Cryptanalysis of an oblivious PRF from supersingular isogenies. In: Tibouchi, M., Wang, H. (eds.) ASIACRYPT 2021. LNCS, vol. 13090, pp. 160–184. Springer, Cham (2021). https://doi.org/10.1007/978-3-030-92062-3_6

3. Beullens, W., Kleinjung, T., Vercauteren, F.: CSI-FiSh: efficient isogeny based signatures through class group computations. In: Galbraith, S.D., Moriai, S. (eds.) ASIACRYPT 2019. LNCS, vol. 11921, pp. 227–247. Springer, Cham (2019). https://doi.org/10.1007/978-3-030-34578-5_9

4. Booher, J., et al.: Failing to hash into supersingular isogeny graphs. Cryptology ePrint Archive, Report 2022/518 (2022). https://eprint.iacr.org/2022/518

5. Bottinelli, P., de Quehen, V., Leonardi, C., Mosunov, A., Pawlega, F., Sheth, M.: The dark SIDH of isogenies. Cryptology ePrint Archive, Report 2019/1333 (2019). https://eprint.iacr.org/2019/1333

6. Bröker, R.: Constructing supersingular elliptic curves. J. Comb. Numb. Theory 1(3), 269–273 (2009)

7. Castryck, W., Decru, T.: An efficient key recovery attack on SIDH (preliminary version). Cryptology ePrint Archive, Report 2022/975 (2022). https://eprint.iacr.org/2022/975

8. Castryck, W., Lange, T., Martindale, C., Panny, L., Renes, J.: CSIDH: an efficient post-quantum commutative group action. In: Peyrin, T., Galbraith, S. (eds.) ASIACRYPT 2018. LNCS, vol. 11274, pp. 395–427. Springer, Cham (2018). https://doi.org/10.1007/978-3-030-03332-3_15

9. Charles, D.X., Lauter, K.E., Goren, E.Z.: Cryptographic hash functions from expander graphs. J. Cryptol. **22**(1), 93–113 (2007). https://doi.org/10.1007/s00145-007-9002-x

10. Colò, L., Kohel, D.: Orienting supersingular isogeny graphs. Cryptology ePrint Archive, Report 2020/985 (2020). https://eprint.iacr.org/2020/985

11. Cooper, C.: On the rank of random matrices. Rand. Struct. Algor. **16**(2), 209–232 (2000). https://doi.org/10.1002/(SICI)1098-2418(200003)16:2⟨209::AID-RSA6⟩3.0.CO;2-1

12. Costello, C.: B-SIDH: supersingular isogeny Diffie-Hellman using twisted torsion. In: Moriai, S., Wang, H. (eds.) ASIACRYPT 2020. LNCS, vol. 12492, pp. 440–463. Springer, Cham (2020). https://doi.org/10.1007/978-3-030-64834-3_15

13. Costello, C., Meyer, M., Naehrig, M.: Sieving for twin smooth integers with solutions to the prouhet-tarry-escott problem. In: Canteaut, A., Standaert, F.-X. (eds.) EUROCRYPT 2021. LNCS, vol. 12696, pp. 272–301. Springer, Cham (2021). https://doi.org/10.1007/978-3-030-77870-5_10

14. Couveignes, J.M.: Hard homogeneous spaces. Cryptology ePrint Archive, Report 2006/291 (2006). https://eprint.iacr.org/2006/291

15. De Feo, L., Galbraith, S.D.: SeaSign: compact isogeny signatures from class group actions. In: Ishai, Y., Rijmen, V. (eds.) EUROCRYPT 2019. LNCS, vol. 11478, pp. 759–789. Springer, Cham (2019). https://doi.org/10.1007/978-3-030-17659-4_26

16. De Feo, L., Jao, D., Plût, J.: Towards quantum-resistant cryptosystems from supersingular elliptic curve isogenies. J. Math. Cryptol. **8**(3), 209–247 (2014). https://doi.org/10.1515/jmc-2012-0015

17. De Feo, L., Kohel, D., Leroux, A., Petit, C., Wesolowski, B.: SQISign: compact post-quantum signatures from quaternions and isogenies. In: Moriai, S., Wang, H. (eds.) ASIACRYPT 2020. LNCS, vol. 12491, pp. 64–93. Springer, Cham (2020). https://doi.org/10.1007/978-3-030-64837-4_3

18. Fouotsa, T.B.: SIDH with masked torsion point images. Cryptology ePrint Archive, Report 2022/1054 (2022). https://eprint.iacr.org/2022/1054

19. Fouotsa, T.B., Petit, C.: A new adaptive attack on SIDH. In: Galbraith, S.D. (ed.) CT-RSA 2022. LNCS, vol. 13161, pp. 322–344. Springer, Cham (2022). https://doi.org/10.1007/978-3-030-95312-6_14

20. Galbraith, S.D., Petit, C., Shani, B., Ti, Y.B.: On the security of supersingular isogeny cryptosystems. In: Cheon, J.H., Takagi, T. (eds.) ASIACRYPT 2016. LNCS, vol. 10031, pp. 63–91. Springer, Heidelberg (2016). https://doi.org/10.1007/978-3-662-53887-6_3

21. Galbraith, S.D., Petit, C., Silva, J.: Identification protocols and signature schemes based on supersingular isogeny problems. J. Cryptol. **33**(1), 130–175 (2019). https://doi.org/10.1007/s00145-019-09316-0

22. Grover, L.K.: A fast quantum mechanical algorithm for database search. In: 28th Annual ACM Symposium on Theory of Computing, pp. 212–219. ACM Press, Philadephia (1996). https://doi.org/10.1145/237814.237866

23. Jao, D., et al.: SIKE. Technical report, National Institute of Standards and Technology (2020). https://csrc.nist.gov/projects/post-quantum-cryptography/post-quantum-cryptography-standardization/round-3-submissions

24. Jao, D., De Feo, L.: Towards quantum-resistant cryptosystems from supersingular elliptic curve isogenies. In: Yang, B.-Y. (ed.) PQCrypto 2011. LNCS, vol. 7071, pp. 19–34. Springer, Heidelberg (2011). https://doi.org/10.1007/978-3-642-25405-5_2

25. Kovalenko, I., Levitskaya, A., Savchuk, M.: Selected Problems in Probabilistic Combinatorics. Naukova Dumka, Kiev (1986)

26. Maino, L., Martindale, C.: An attack on SIDH with arbitrary starting curve. Cryptology ePrint Archive, Report 2022/1026 (2022). https://eprint.iacr.org/2022/1026
27. Moriya, T.: Masked-degree SIDH. Cryptology ePrint Archive, Report 2022/1019 (2022). https://eprint.iacr.org/2022/1019
28. Mula, M., Murru, N., Pintore, F.: Random sampling of supersingular elliptic curves. Cryptology ePrint Archive, Report 2022/528 (2022). https://eprint.iacr.org/2022/528
29. National Institute of Standards and Technology: Post-quantum cryptography standardization (2016). https://csrc.nist.gov/Projects/Post-Quantum-Cryptography/Post-Quantum-Cryptography-Standardization
30. Oudompheng, R., Pope, G.: A note on reimplementing the castryck-decru attack and lessons learned for SageMath. Cryptology ePrint Archive, Report 2022/1283 (2022). https://eprint.iacr.org/2022/1283
31. Petit, C.: Faster algorithms for isogeny problems using torsion point images. In: Takagi, T., Peyrin, T. (eds.) ASIACRYPT 2017. LNCS, vol. 10625, pp. 330–353. Springer, Cham (2017). https://doi.org/10.1007/978-3-319-70697-9_12
32. de Quehen, V., et al.: Improved torsion-point attacks on SIDH variants. In: Malkin, T., Peikert, C. (eds.) CRYPTO 2021. LNCS, vol. 12827, pp. 432–470. Springer, Cham (2021). https://doi.org/10.1007/978-3-030-84252-9_15
33. Robert, D.: Breaking SIDH in polynomial time. Cryptology ePrint Archive, Report 2022/1038 (2022). https://eprint.iacr.org/2022/1038
34. Rostovtsev, A., Stolbunov, A.: Public-Key Cryptosystem Based On Isogenies. Cryptology ePrint Archive, Report 2006/145 (2006). https://eprint.iacr.org/2006/145
35. Shor, P.W.: Algorithms for quantum computation: discrete logarithms and factoring. In: 35th Annual Symposium on Foundations of Computer Science, pp. 124–134. IEEE Computer Society Press, Santa Fe (1994). https://doi.org/10.1109/SFCS.1994.365700
36. van Oorschot, P.C., Wiener, M.J.: Parallel collision search with cryptanalytic applications. J. Cryptol. **12**(1), 1–28 (1999). https://doi.org/10.1007/PL00003816

Disorientation Faults in CSIDH

Gustavo Banegas[1(✉)], Juliane Krämer[2(✉)], Tanja Lange[3,4(✉)],
Michael Meyer[2(✉)], Lorenz Panny[4(✉)], Krijn Reijnders[5(✉)],
Jana Sotáková[6(✉)], and Monika Trimoska[5(✉)]

[1] Inria and Laboratoire d'Informatique de l'Ecole polytechnique,
Institut Polytechnique de Paris, Palaiseau, France
gustavo@cryptme.in
[2] University of Regensburg, Regensburg, Germany
juliane.kraemer@ur.de, michael@random-oracles.org
[3] Eindhoven University of Technology, Eindhoven, The Netherlands
tanja@hyperelliptic.org
[4] Academia Sinica, Taipei, Taiwan
lorenz@yx7.cc
[5] Radboud University, Nijmegen, The Netherlands
krijn@cs.ru.nl, monika.trimoska@ru.nl
[6] University of Amsterdam and QuSoft, Amsterdam, The Netherlands
j.s.sotakova@uva.nl

Abstract. We investigate a new class of fault-injection attacks against
the CSIDH family of cryptographic group actions. Our *disorientation
attacks* effectively flip the direction of some isogeny steps. We achieve
this by faulting a specific subroutine, connected to the Legendre symbol
or Elligator computations performed during the evaluation of the group
action. These subroutines are present in almost all known CSIDH implementations. Post-processing a set of faulty samples allows us to infer
constraints on the secret key. The details are implementation specific,
but we show that in many cases, it is possible to recover the full secret
key with only a modest number of successful fault injections and modest
computational resources. We provide full details for attacking the original CSIDH proof-of-concept software as well as the CTIDH constant-time

The full version with additional material can be found at https://ia.cr/2022/1202.
Author list in alphabetical order; see https://ams.org/profession/leaders/
CultureStatement04.pdf. This work began at the online Lorentz Center workshop
"Post-Quantum Cryptography for Embedded Systems" held in February 2022. This
research was funded in part by the European Commission through H2020 SPARTA,
the Deutsche Forschungsgemeinschaft (DFG, German Research Foundation) under
SFB 1119 – 236615297 and under Germany's Excellence Strategy—EXC 2092 CASA—
390781972 "Cyber Security in the Age of Large-Scale Adversaries", the Taiwan's
Executive Yuan Data Safety and Talent Cultivation Project (AS-KPQ-109-DSTCP),
the German Federal Ministry of Education and Research (BMBF) under the project
QuantumRISC (ID 16KIS1039), the Academia Sinica Investigator Award AS-IA-
109-M01, the Dutch Research Council (NWO) through Gravitation-grant Quantum
Software Consortium – 024.003.037, and a gender balance subsidy of the Faculty of
Science, Radboud University, project number 6201362. This work was done in part
while Tanja Lange was visiting the Simons Institute for the Theory of Computing.
Date of this document: 2023-02-23.

C. Hazay and M. Stam (Eds.): EUROCRYPT 2023, LNCS 14008, pp. 310–342, 2023.
https://doi.org/10.1007/978-3-031-30589-4_11

implementation. Finally, we present a set of lightweight countermeasures against the attack and discuss their security.

Keywords: Fault-injection attack · isogenies of elliptic curves · post-quantum cryptography

1 Introduction

Isogeny-based cryptography is a contender in the ongoing quest for post-quantum cryptography. Perhaps the most attractive feature is small key size, but there are other reasons in favor of isogenies: Some functionalities appear difficult to construct from other paradigms. For instance, the *CSIDH* [15] scheme gives rise to non-interactive key exchange. CSIDH uses the action of an ideal-class group on a set of elliptic curves to mimic (some) classical constructions based on discrete logarithms, most notably the Diffie–Hellman key exchange. Recently, more advanced cryptographic protocols have been proposed based on the CSIDH group action: the signature schemes SeaSign [22] and CSI-FiSh [8], threshold schemes [23], oblivious transfer [27], and more.

The group action in CSIDH and related schemes is evaluated by computing a sequence of small-degree *isogeny steps*; the choice of degrees and "directions" is the private key. Thus, the control flow of a straightforward implementation is directly related to the secret key, which complicates side-channel resistant implementations [3,7,12,26,30,31].

In a side-channel attack, passive observations of physical leakage (such as timing differences, electromagnetic emissions, or power consumption) during the execution of sensitive computations help an attacker infer secret information. A more intrusive class of physical attacks are *fault-injection attacks* or *fault attacks*: By actively manipulating the execution environment of a device (for instance, by altering the characteristics of the power supply, or by exposing the device to electromagnetic radiation), the attacker aims to trigger an error during the execution of sensitive computations and later infer secret information from the outputs, which are now potentially incorrect, i.e., *faulty*.

Two major classes of faults are *instruction skips* and *variable modifications*. Well-timed skips of processor instructions can have far-reaching consequences, e.g., omitting a security check entirely, or failing to erase secrets which subsequently leak into the output. Variable modifications may reach from simply randomized CPU registers to precisely targeted single-bit flips. They cause the software to operate on unexpected values, which (especially in a cryptographic context) may lead to exploitable behavior. In practice, the difficulty of injecting a particular kind of fault (or a combination of multiple faults) depends on various parameters; generally speaking, less targeted faults are easier.

Our Contributions. We analyze the behavior of existing CSIDH implementations under a new class of attacks that we call *disorientation faults*. These faults occur when the attacker confuses the algorithm about the *orientation* of a point used during the computation: The effect of such an error is that a subset of the secret-dependent isogeny steps will be performed in the opposite direction, resulting in an incorrect output curve.

The placement of the disorientation fault during the algorithm influences the distribution of the output curve in a key-dependent manner. We explain how an attacker can post-process a set of faulty outputs to fully recover the private key. This attack works against almost all existing CSIDH implementations.

To simplify exposition we first assume access to a device that applies a secret key to a given public key (i.e., computing the shared key in CSIDH) and returns the result (e.g., an HSM providing a CSIDH accelerator). We also discuss variants of the attack with weaker access; this includes a *hashed* version where faulty outputs are not revealed as-is, but passed through a key-derivation function first, as is commonly done for a Diffie–Hellman-style key exchange, and made available to the attacker only indirectly, e.g., as a MAC under the derived key.

Part of the tooling for the post-processing stage of our attack is a somewhat optimized meet-in-the-middle *path-finding* program for the CSIDH isogeny graph, dubbed `pubcrawl`. This software is intentionally kept fully generic with no restrictions specific to the fault-attack scenario we are considering, so that it may hopefully be usable out of the box for other applications requiring "small" neighborhood searches in CSIDH in the future. Applying expensive but feasible precomputation can speed up post-processing for all attack variants and is particularly beneficial to the hashed version of the attack.

To defend against disorientation faults, we provide a set of *countermeasures*. We show different forms of protecting an implementation and discuss the pros and cons of each of the methods. In the end, we detail two of the protections that we believe give the best security. Both of them are lightweight, and they do not significantly add to the complexity of the implementation.

Note on Security. We emphasize that CSIDH, its variants, and the protocols based on the CSIDH group action are not affected by the recent attacks that break the isogeny-based scheme SIDH [14,29,34]. These attacks exploit specific auxiliary information which is revealed in SIDH.

CSIDH is a relatively young cryptosystem, being introduced only in 2018, but it is based on older systems due to Couveignes [21] and Rostovtsev and Stolbunov [35] which have received attention since 2006. The best non-quantum attack is a meet-in-the-middle attack running in $O(\sqrt[4]{p})$; a low-memory version was developed in [24]. On a large quantum computer Kuperberg's attack can be mounted as shown in [19]. This attack runs in $L_{\sqrt{p}}(1/2)$ calls to a quantum oracle. The number of oracle calls was further analyzed in [9] and [33] for concrete parameters, while [7] analyzes the costs per oracle call in number of quantum operations. Combining these results shows that breaking CSIDH-512 requires around 2^{60} qubit operations on logical qubits, i.e., not taking into account the overhead for quantum error correction. Implementation papers such as CTIDH [3] use the CSIDH-512 prime for comparison purposes and also offer larger parameters. Likewise, we use the CSIDH-512 and CTIDH-512 parameters for concrete examples.

Related Work. *Loop-abort* faults on the SIDH cryptosystem [25], discussed for CSIDH in [10], lead to leakage of an intermediate value of the computation rather than the final result. Replacing torsion points with other points in SIDH [36, 37] can be used to recover the secret keys; faulting intermediate curves in SIDH [2] to learn if secret isogeny paths lead over subfield curves can also leak information on secret keys. But the two latter attacks cannot be mounted against CSIDH due to the structural and mathematical differences between SIDH and CSIDH.

Recently, several CSIDH-specific fault attacks were published. One can modify memory locations and observe if this changes the resulting shared secret [11]. A different attack avenue is to target fault injections against dummy computations in CSIDH [10,28]. We emphasize that these are attacks against specific implementations and variants of CSIDH. Our work, in contrast, features a generic approach to fault attacks, exploiting an operation and data flow present in almost all current implementations of CSIDH.

2   Background

CSIDH is based on a group action on a certain set of elliptic curves. We assume some familiarity with elliptic curves and isogenies, see [15] for details.

2.1   CSIDH

We fix a prime p of the form $p = 4 \cdot \ell_1 \cdots \ell_n - 1$ with distinct odd primes ℓ_i. We define $\mathcal{E}$ to be the set of supersingular elliptic curves over $\mathbb{F}_p$ in Montgomery form, up to $\mathbb{F}_p$-isomorphism. All such curves admit an equation of the form $E_A : y^2 = x^3 + Ax^2 + x$ with a unique $A \in \mathbb{F}_p$. For $E_A \in \mathcal{E}$, the group of rational points $E_A(\mathbb{F}_p)$ is cyclic of order $p+1$. The quadratic twist of $E_A \in \mathcal{E}$ is $E_{-A} \in \mathcal{E}$.

Isogeny Steps. For any ℓ_i and any $E_A \in \mathcal{E}$ there are two ℓ_i-isogenies, each leading to another curve in $\mathcal{E}$. One has kernel generated by any point P_+ of order ℓ_i with both coordinates in $\mathbb{F}_p$. We say this ℓ_i-isogeny is in the *positive direction* and the point P_+ has *positive orientation*. The other ℓ_i-isogeny has kernel generated by any point P_- of order ℓ_i with x-coordinate in $\mathbb{F}_p$ but y-coordinate in $\mathbb{F}_{p^2} \setminus \mathbb{F}_p$. We say this isogeny is in the *negative direction* and the point P_- has *negative orientation*. Replacing E_A by the codomain of a positive and negative ℓ_i-isogeny from E_A is a *positive and negative ℓ_i-isogeny step*, respectively. As the name suggests, a positive and a negative ℓ_i-isogeny step cancel.

Fix $i \in \mathbb{F}_{p^2} \setminus \mathbb{F}_p$ with $i^2 = -1 \in \mathbb{F}_p$ and note that a negatively oriented point is necessarily of the form (x, iy) with $x, y \in \mathbb{F}_p$. Moreover, $x \in \mathbb{F}_p^*$ defines a positively oriented point on E_A whenever $x^3 + Ax^2 + x$ is a square in $\mathbb{F}_p$, and a negatively oriented point otherwise.

The Group Action. It is a non-obvious, but very useful fact that the isogeny steps defined above *commute*: Any sequence of them can be rearranged arbitrarily without changing the final codomain curve [15]. Thus, taking a combination of various isogeny steps defines a group action of the abelian group $(\mathbb{Z}^n, +)$ on $\mathcal{E}$: The vector $(e_1, \ldots, e_n) \in \mathbb{Z}^n$ represents $|e_i|$ individual ℓ_i-isogeny steps, with the sign of e_i specifying the orientation: if $\mathfrak{l}_i$ denotes a single positive ℓ_i-isogeny step, the action of $(e_1, \ldots, e_n) \in \mathbb{Z}^n$ on a curve E denotes the sequence of steps $(\mathfrak{l}_1^{e_1} \cdots \mathfrak{l}_n^{e_n}) * E$. We refer to $(e_1, \ldots, e_n)$ as an *exponent vector*.

2.2   Algorithmic Aspects

Every step is an oriented isogeny, so applying a single $\mathfrak{l}_i^{\pm 1}$ step requires a point P with two properties: P has order ℓ_i and the right orientation. The codomain of $E \to E/\langle P \rangle$ is computed using either the Vélu [39] or $\sqrt{\text{é}}$lu [5] formulas.

Determining Orientations. All state-of-the-art implementations of CSIDH use x-only arithmetic and completely disregard y-coordinates. So, we sample a point P by sampling an x-coordinate in $\mathbb{F}_p$. To determine the orientation of P, we then find the field of definition of the y-coordinate, e.g., through a Legendre symbol computation. An alternative method is the "Elligator 2" map [6] which generates a point of the desired orientation.

Sampling Order-ℓ Points. There are several methods to compute points of given order ℓ. The following Las Vegas algorithm is popular for its simplicity and efficiency: As above, sample a uniformly random point P of either positive or negative orientation, and compute $Q := [(p + 1)/\ell]P$. Since P is uniformly random in a cyclic group of order $p+1$, the point Q has order ℓ with probability $1 - 1/\ell$. With probability $1/\ell$, we get $Q = \infty$. Retry until $Q \neq \infty$. Filtering for points of a given orientation is straightforward.

Multiple Isogenies from a Single Point. To amortize the cost of sampling points and determining orientations, implementations usually pick some set S of indices of exponents of the same sign, and attempt to compute one isogeny per degree ℓ_i with $i \in S$ from one point. If $d = \prod_{i \in S} \ell_i$ and P a random point, then the point $Q = [\frac{p+1}{d}]P$ has order dividing d. If $[d/\ell_i]Q \neq \infty$ we can use it to construct an isogeny step for $\ell_i \in S$. The image of Q under that isogeny has the same orientation as P and Q and order dividing d/ℓ_i.

  In CSIDH and its variants, the set S of isogeny degrees depends on the secret key and the orientation s of P. For example in Algorithm 1 (from [15]), for the first point that is sampled with positive orientation, the set S is $\{i \mid e_i > 0\}$.

  The order of a random point P is not divisible by ℓ_i with probability $1/\ell_i$. This means that in many cases, we will not be able to perform an isogeny for *every* $i \in S$, but only for some (large) subset $S' \subset S$ due to P lacking factors ℓ_i in its order for those remaining $i \in S \setminus S'$. In short, a point P performs the action $\prod_{i \in S'} \mathfrak{l}_i^s$ for some $S' \subset S$, with s the orientation of P (interpreted as

---

Algorithm 1. Evaluation of CSIDH group action

Input: $A \in \mathbb{F}_p$ and a list of integers $(e_1, \ldots, e_n)$.
Output: $B \in \mathbb{F}_p$ such that $\prod [l_i]^{e_i} * E_A = E_B$
1: **while** some $e_i \neq 0$ **do**
2:     Sample a random $x \in \mathbb{F}_p$, defining a point P.
3:     Set $s \leftarrow \texttt{IsSquare}(x^3 + Ax^2 + x)$.
4:     Let $S = \{i \mid e_i \neq 0, \text{sign}(e_i) = s\}$. **Restart** with new x if S is empty.
5:     Let $k \leftarrow \prod_{i \in S} \ell_i$ and compute $Q \leftarrow [\frac{p+1}{k}]P$.
6:     **for each** $i \in S$ **do**
7:         Set $k \leftarrow k/\ell_i$ and compute $R \leftarrow [k]Q$. If $R = \infty$, **skip** this i.
8:         Compute $\phi : E_A \to E_B$ with kernel $\langle R \rangle$.
9:         Set $A \leftarrow B$, $Q \leftarrow \phi(Q)$, and $e_i \leftarrow e_i - s$.
10: **return** A.

± 1). Sampling a point and computing the action $\prod_{i \in S'} l_i^s$ is called a *round*; we perform rounds for different sets S until we compute the full action $\mathfrak{a} = \prod l_i^{e_i}$.

Strategies. There are several ways of computing the group action as efficiently as possible, usually referred to as *strategies*. The strategy in Algorithm 1 is called *multiplicative strategy* [7,15,31]. Other notable strategies from the literature are the *SIMBA strategy* [30], *point-pushing strategies* [18], and *atomic blocks* [3].

1-Point and 2-Point Approaches. The above samples a single point, computes some isogenies with the same orientation, and repeats this until all steps $l_i^{\pm 1}$ are processed. This approach, introduced in [15], is called *1-point approach*. In contrast, one can sample two points per round, one with positive and one with negative orientation, and attempt to compute isogenies for each degree ℓ_i per round, independent of the sign of the e_i [32]. Constant-time algorithms require choosing S independent of the secret key, and all state-of-the-art constant-time implementations use the *2-point approach*, e.g., [3,17].

Keyspace. In both CSIDH and CTIDH, each party's private key is an integer vector $(e_1, \ldots, e_n)$ sampled from a bounded subset $\mathcal{K} \subset \mathbb{Z}^n$, the *keyspace*. Different choices of $\mathcal{K}$ have different performance and security properties. The original scheme [15] uses $\mathcal{K}_m = \{-m, \ldots, m\}^n \subset \mathbb{Z}^n$, e.g. $m = 5$ for CSIDH-512. As suggested in [15, Rmk. 14] and shown in [30], using different bounds m_i for each i can improve speed. The shifted keyspace $\mathcal{K}_m^+ = \{0, \ldots, 2m_i\}^n$ was used in [30]. Other choices of $\mathcal{K}$ were made in [16,17,32], and CTIDH [3] (see Sect. 5.2).

3   Attack Scenario and Fault Model

Throughout this work, we assume physical access to some hardware device containing an unknown CSIDH private key $\mathfrak{a}$. In the basic version of the attack, we suppose that the device provides an interface to pass in a CSIDH public-key curve E and receive back the result $\mathfrak{a} * E$ of applying $\mathfrak{a}$ to the public key E as in the second step of the key exchange.

We assume that the attacker is able to trigger an error during the computation of the orientation of a point in a specific round of the CSIDH algorithm: whenever a point P with orientation $s \in \{-1, 1\}$ is sampled during the algorithm, we can flip the orientation $s \mapsto -s$ as shown below. This leads to some isogenies being computed in the opposite direction throughout the round. The effect of this flip will be explored in Sect. 4.

Diffie–Hellman key agreement typically *hashes* the shared secret to derive symmetric key material, instead of directly outputting curves. Our attacks are still applicable in this *hashed version*, although the complexity for post-processing steps from Sect. 4 will increase. We postpone this discussion to Sect. 7.

Square Check. In CSIDH, cf. Algorithm 1, the point P is generated in Step 2 and its orientation s is determined in Step 3. The function IsSquare determines s by taking as input the non-zero value $z = x^3 + Ax^2 + x$, and computing the Legendre symbol of z. Hence, $s = 1$ when z is a square and $s = -1$ when z is not a square. Many implementations simply compute $s \leftarrow z^{\frac{p-1}{2}}$.

A successful fault injection in the computation $z \leftarrow x^3 + Ax^2 + x$, by skipping an instruction or changing the value randomly, ensures random input to IsSquare and so in about half of the cases the output will be flipped by $s \mapsto -s$. In the other half of the cases, the output of IsSquare remains s. The attacker knows the outcome of the non-faulty computation and can thus discard those outputs and continue with those where the orientation has been flipped.

There are other ways to flip the orientation s. For example, one can also inject a random fault into x after s has been computed, which has a similar effect. The analysis and attack of Sects. 4 and 5 apply to all possible ways to flip s, independent of the actual fault injection. The countermeasures introduced in Sect. 9 prevent all possible ways to flip s that we know of.

Faulting the Legendre symbol computation in IsSquare, in general, leads to a random $\mathbb{F}_p$-value as output instead of ± 1. The interpretation of this result is heavily dependent on the respective implementation. For instance, the CSIDH implementation from [15] interprets the output as boolean value by setting $s = 1$ if the result is $+1$, and -1 otherwise. In this case, faults mostly flip in one direction: from positive to negative orientation. Thus, faulting the computation of z is superior in our attack setting.

Elligator. Implementations using a 2-point strategy often use Elligator 2 [6]. On input of a random value, Elligator computes two points P and P' of opposite orientations. An IsSquare check is used to determine the orientation of P. If P has positive orientation, we set $P_+ \leftarrow P$ and $P_- \leftarrow P'$. Otherwise, set $P_+ \leftarrow P'$ and $P_- \leftarrow P$. Again, we can fault the input to this IsSquare check, which flips the assignments to P_+ and P_-; hence, the orientation of *both* points is flipped.

As before, this means that all isogenies computed using either of these points are pointing in the wrong direction. A notable exception is CTIDH, where two independent calls to Elligator are used to produce points for the 2-point strategy.

This is due to security considerations, and the algorithmic and attack implications are detailed in Sect. 5.2.

4 Exploiting Orientation Flips

In Sect. 3, we defined an attack scenario that allows us to flip the orientation s in Line 3. If this happens, the net effect is that we will select an incorrect set S' with opposite orientation, and hence perform an isogeny walk in the *opposite* direction for all the indices in S'. Equivalently, the set S selected in Line 3 has opposite orientation to the point P. For simplicity, we will always fix the set S first and talk about the point P being flipped. We assume that we can successfully flip the orientation in any round r, and that we get the result of the faulty evaluation, which is some *faulty curve* $E_t \neq \mathfrak{a} * E$.

4.1 Implications of Flipping the Orientation of a Point

In this section, all points will have full order, so Line 7 never skips an i.

Suppose we want to evaluate the group action $\prod_{i \in S} \mathfrak{l}_i * E_A$ for some set of steps S. Suppose we generate a negatively oriented point P, but flipped its orientation. This does not change the point (still negatively oriented), but if we use P to evaluate the steps in what we believe is the *positive* direction, we will in fact compute the steps in the negative direction: $E_f = \prod_{i \in S} \mathfrak{l}_i^{-1} * E_A$. More generally, if we want to take steps in direction s and use a point of opposite orientation, we actually compute the curve $E_f = \prod_{i \in S} \mathfrak{l}_i^{-s} * E_A$.

Suppose we flip the orientation of a point in one round of the isogeny computation $E_B = \mathfrak{a} * E_A$ and the rest of the computation is performed correctly. The resulting curve E_t is called a *faulty curve*. If the round was computing steps for isogenies in S with direction s, the resulting curve satisfies $E_B = \prod_{i \in S} \mathfrak{l}_i^{2s} * E_t$, that is, the faulty curve differs from the correct curve by an isogeny whose degree is given by the (squares of) primes ℓ_i for $i \in S$, the set S in the round we faulted. We call S the *missing set* of E_t.

Distance Between Curves. We define the *distance* d between two curves E and E' as the lowest number of different degrees for isogenies $\phi : E \to E'$. Note that the distance only tells us how many primes we need to connect two curves, without keeping track of the individual primes ℓ_i or their multiplicity. Specifically for a faulty curve with $E_B = \prod_{i \in S} \mathfrak{l}_i^{2s} * E_t$, we define the distance to E_B as the number of flipped steps $|S|$. Note that each $\mathfrak{l}_i$ appears as a square; this gets counted *once* in the distance.

Positive and Negative Primes. Suppose the secret key $\mathfrak{a}$ is given by the exponent vector (e_i). Then every ℓ_i is used to take e_i steps in direction $\text{sign}(e_i)$. Define the set of *positive* primes $L_+ := \{i \mid e_i > 0\}$, *negative* primes $L_- := \{i \mid e_i < 0\}$, and *neutral* primes $L_0 := \{i \mid e_i = 0\}$. For 1-point strategies and any faulty curve E_t with missing set S, we always have $S \subset L_+$ or $S \subset L_-$.

However, using 2-point strategies, the sets S may contain positive and negative primes. We use the terminology 'flipping a batch' when we refer to the effect of an orientation flip to the primes being performed: when we flip the orientation s of a negative point from negative to positive, the final result has performed a batch of positive primes in the negative direction.

Example 1. Take CSIDH-512. Assume we flip the orientation $s \mapsto -s$ of the first point P. From Algorithm 1, we see the elements of S are exactly those i such that $|e_i| \geq 1$ and $\mathrm{sign}(e_i) = -s$. Therefore, we have $S = L_{-s}$.

4.2   Faulty Curves and Full-Order Points

We continue to assume that all points have full order, so Line 7 never skips an i, and analyze which faulty curves we obtain by flipping the orientation in round r. We treat the general case in Sect. 4.3 and Sect. 4.4.

Effective Curves. For any strategy (cf. Sect. 2.2), the computation in round r depends on what happened in previous rounds. In a 2-point strategy, we sample both a negative and a positive point and use them to perform the isogenies in both directions. So assuming points of full order, the round-r computation and the set S do not depend on the previous round but only the secret key.

In a 1-point strategy, we sample 1 point per round, and only perform isogenies in the direction of that point. So the set S in round r depends additionally on what was computed in previous rounds. However, the computation in round r only depends on previous rounds with *the same orientation*. The orientation of a round refers to which primes were used. Hence, a *positive* round means that the steps were performed for the positive primes, in the positive or negative direction.

Notation. Let $+$ and $-$ denote the positive and negative orientation, respectively. For a 1-point strategy, we encode the choices of orientations by a sequence of $\pm$. We denote the round r in which we flip the orientation of a point by parentheses $(\cdot)$. We truncate the sequence at the moment of the fault because the rest of the computation is computed correctly. Hence, $++(-)$ means a computation starting with the following three rounds: the first two rounds were positive, the third one was a negative round with a flipped orientation, so the steps were computed for the negative primes, but in the positive direction.

Consider a flip of orientation in the second round. There are four possible scenarios:

$+(+)$. Two positive rounds, but the second positive batch of primes was flipped and we took the steps in negative direction instead.

$+(-)$. One positive round, one negative batch flipped to the positive direction.

$-(+)$. One negative round, one positive batch flipped to the negative direction.

$-(-)$. Two negative rounds, the second negative batch flipped to positive.

All four cases are equally likely to appear for 1-point strategies, but result in different faulty curves. Since the computation only depends on previous rounds with the same orientation, the case $+(-)$ is easily seen to be the same as $(-)$ and $++(-)$: all three are cases where the orientation of the point was flipped the first time a negative round occurred. However, the cases $+(+)$ and $-(+)$ are different: the latter is equivalent to $(+)$. For example, in CSIDH, the set S for $(+)$ is $\{i \mid e_i \geq 1\}$, and the set S' for $+(+)$ is $\{i \mid e_i \geq 2\}$, differing exactly at the primes for which $e_i = 1$.

Example 2 (CSIDH). For a secret key $(1, -2, -1, 3)$ in CSIDH with primes $L = \{3, 5, 7, 11\}$, the case $+(-)$ takes us to a faulty curve that is two $\{5, 7\}$-isogenies away from the desired curve, whereas the case $-(-)$ results in a curve two 5-isogenies away.

Effective Round. Let $E^{r,+}$ be the faulty curve produced by the sequence $+\cdots+(+)$ of length r, and $E^{r,-}$ the curve produced by sequence $-\cdots-(-)$. We call the curves $E^{r,\pm}$ *effective round-r curves*. For a 2-point strategy, all faulty curves from round r are effective round-r curves. For 1-point strategies, effective round-r curves can be produced from other sequences as well, e.g. $+(-)$ produces the effective round 1 curve $E^{1,-}$ and $++-+(-)$ produces an effective round-3 curve $E^{3,-}$. To get an effective round-r sample $E^{r,+}$ from a round n, the last sign in the sequence must be $(+)$, and the sequence must contain a total of r pluses.

Lemma 4.1. *Assume we use a 1-point strategy. The probability to get any effective round-r sample if we successfully flip in round n is equal to $\binom{n-1}{r-1} \cdot \frac{1}{2^{n-1}}$.*

Torsion Sets $S^{r,+}$ and $S^{r,-}$. Define the set $S^{r,s}$ as the missing set of the effective round-r curve with orientation s, i.e., $E_B = \prod_{i \in S^{r,s}} l_i^{2s} * E^{r,s}$. For example in CSIDH, the sets $S^{1,\pm}$ were already discussed in Example 1 and in general, $S^{r,+} = \{i \mid e_i \geq r\}$ and $S^{r,-} = \{i \mid e_i \leq -r\}$.

4.3 Missing Torsion: Faulty Curves and Points of Non-full Order

In Sect. 4.2, we worked under the unrealistic assumption that all points we encounter have full order. In this section, we relax this condition somewhat: we assume that every point had full order (and hence all isogenies were computed) up until round r, but the point P generated in round r potentially has smaller order. We call this the *missing torsion* case. The remaining relaxation of non-full order points in earlier rounds will be concluded in Sect. 4.4.

If the point P used to compute isogenies in round r does not have full order, the faulty curve E_t will differ from the effective round-r curve $E^{r,s}$ by the primes ℓ_i with $i \in S^{r,s}$ which are missing in the order of P.

Round-r Faulty Curves. For simplicity, assume that we are in round r, in the case $+\cdots+(+)$, and that none of the isogenies in the previous rounds failed. In round r, a negative point P is sampled, but we flip its orientation, so the batch of positive primes will be computed in the negative direction.

If the point P has full order, we obtain the curve $E^{r,+}$ at the end of the computation, which differs from E_B exactly at primes contained in $S^{r,+}$. If, however, the point P does not have full order, a subset $S \subset S^{r,+}$ of steps will be computed, leading to a different faulty curve E_t. By construction, the curve E_t is related to E_B via $E_B = \prod_{i \in S} \ell_i^2 * E_t$.

Assume we repeat this fault in T runs, leading to different faulty curves E_t. Let $n(E_t)$ be the number of times the curve E_t occurs among the T samples. For each such E_t, we know $E_B = \prod_{i \in S_t} \ell_i^{2s} * E_t$, where $S_t \subset S^{r,+}$ is determined by the order of P_t. As P_t is a randomly sampled point, it has probability $\frac{\ell_i - 1}{\ell_i}$ that its order is divisible by ℓ_i, and so probability $\frac{1}{\ell_i}$ that its order is not divisible by ℓ_i. This gives us directly the probability to end up at E_t: the order of the point P_t should be divisible by all ℓ_i for $i \in S_t$, but not by those ℓ_i for $i \in S^{r,+} \setminus S_t$. This is captured in the following result.

Proposition 4.2. *Let P_t be a random negative point, where we flip the orientation s to positive. The probability that we compute the faulty curve $E_t = \prod_{i \in S_t} \ell_i^{-2} * E_B$ is exactly $p_t = \prod_{i \in S_t} \frac{\ell_i - 1}{\ell_i} \cdot \prod_{i \in S^{r,+} \setminus S_t} \frac{1}{\ell_i}$.*

In CTIDH, the success probability of each point to match that of the smallest prime in the batch to hide which prime is handled. But for fixed batches, an analogous results to Proposition 4.2 can be given.

The expected number of appearances $n(E_t)$ of a curve E_t is $n(E_t) \approx p_t \cdot T$ for T runs. As $\frac{\ell_i - 1}{\ell_i} \geq \frac{1}{\ell_i}$ for all ℓ_i, the probability p_t is maximal when $S_t = S^{r,+}$. We denote this probability by $p^{r,+}$. Hence, the curve that is likely to appear the most in this scenario over enough samples, is the curve $E^{r,+}$ which we defined as precisely that curve with missing set $S^{r,+}$. For now, we focused solely on the positive curves. Taking into account the negative curves too, we get:

Corollary 4.3. *Let $E^{r,+} = \prod_{i \in S^{r,+}} \ell_i^{-2} * E_B$ and let $E^{r,-} = \prod_{i \in S^{r,-}} \ell_i^2 * E_B$. Then $E^{r,+}$ and $E^{r,-}$ have the highest probability to appear among the effective round-r faulty curves. As a consequence, the largest two values $n(E)$ of all effective round-r curves are most likely $n(E^{r,+})$ and $n(E^{r,-})$*

Example 3 (CSIDH). We have $S^{1,+} = \{i \mid e_i \geq 1\}$ and so $p^{1,+}$ is the probability that a random point P has order divisible by all primes ℓ_i with $e_i \geq 1$. This probability depends on the secret key $\mathfrak{a}$ and we can estimate $p^{1,+}$ if we collect enough faulty curves. Moreover, if $e_1 \neq 0$, then $\ell_1 = 3$ dominates either $p^{1,+}$ or $p^{1,-}$ through the relatively small probability of $2/3$ that P has order divisible by 3. Thus, if $n(E^{1,-})$ is larger than $n(E^{1,+})$, then we assume $p^{1,-}$ is larger than $p^{1,+}$ and so we expect $e_1 \geq 0$. In such a case, we expect to see another faulty curve E_t with $n(E_t)$ half the size of $n(E^{1,+})$; this curve E_t has *almost* full missing set $S^{1,+}$, but does not miss the 3-isogeny. That is, $S_t = S^{1,+} \setminus \{1\}$, with probability $p_t := \frac{1}{\ell_1} \cdot \frac{\ell_1}{\ell_1 - 1} \cdot p^{1,+} = \frac{1}{2} \cdot p^{1,+}$. This curve E_t is very "close" to $E^{1,+}$; they are distance 1 apart, precisely by ℓ_1^2.

The precise probabilities $p^{r,+}$ and $p^{r,-}$ depend highly on the specific implementation we target. Given an implementation, the values of $p^{r,+}$ and $p^{r,-}$ allow for a concrete estimate on the size of $n(E)$ for a specific curve E. Because ℓ_i that are missing in the order of P_t skip the misoriented steps, the curves in the neighborhood of $E^{r,+}$ differ by two ℓ_i-isogenies for $i \in S^{r,+} \setminus S_t$ in positive direction while those around $E^{r,-}$ differ by two ℓ_i-isogenies for $i \in S^{r,-} \setminus S_t$ in negative direction.

Distance Between Samples. We can generalize Example 3 for any two faulty curves E_t and $E_{t'}$ that are effective round-r samples of the same orientation, using Proposition 4.2.

Corollary 4.4. *Let E_t and $E_{t'}$ both be effective round-r samples with the same orientation s and missing torsion sets S_t and $S_{t'}$. Let S_Δ denote the difference in sets S_t and $S_{t'}$, i.e., $S_\Delta = (S_t \setminus S_{t'}) \cup (S_{t'} \setminus S_t)$. Then E_t and $E_{t'}$ are distance $|S_\Delta|$ apart, by $E_t = \left(\prod_{i \in S_{t'} \setminus S_t} \mathfrak{l}_i^{2s} \cdot \prod_{i \in S_t \setminus S_{t'}} \mathfrak{l}_i^{-2s} \right) * E_{t'}$. In particular, any effective round-r curve E_t with orientation s is close to $E^{r,s}$: since $S_t \subset S^{r,s}$, S_Δ is small.*

Corollary 4.4 will be essential to recover information on $S^{r,+}$ out of the samples E_t: Recovering small isogenies between samples allows us to deduce which i are in $S^{r,+}$ or $S^{r,-}$, and so leaks information about e_i.

4.4   Torsion Noise

Orthogonally to Sect. 4.3, we now examine the case that missing torsion occurred in an earlier round than the round we are faulting.

Example 4 (CSIDH). Suppose that $e_1 = 1$ and that in the first positive round, the point generated in Line 2 of Algorithm 1 had order not divisible by ℓ_1, but all other points have full order. Thus, the ℓ_1-isogeny attempt fails in the first positive step. Consider now the second positive round. From Sect. 4.2, we would expect to be computing steps in $S^{2,+} = \{i \mid e_i \geq 2\}$. But no ℓ_1-isogeny has been computed in the first round, so it will be attempted in this second positive round. If we now fault the second positive point, we obtain a faulty curve that is *also missing ℓ_1*, that is, $E_t = \mathfrak{l}_1^{-2} * E^{2,+}$. Unlike the faulty curves from Sect. 4.3, the positively oriented isogeny goes from E_t *towards* $E^{2,+}$. Also, note that in this scenario if $e_1 = 2$, a fault in round 2 would still result in the curve $E^{2,+}$, because the set $S^{2,+}$ contains ℓ_1 already, and so the missed ℓ_1-isogeny from round 1 will be computed in later rounds.

We refer to the phenomenon observed in Example 4 as *torsion noise*. More concretely, torsion noise happens when we fault the computation in round r for a run which is computing an ℓ_i-isogeny in round r for $|e_i| < r$ because it was skipped in a previous round.

Torsion noise is rarer than missing torsion but can still happen: the isogeny computation needs to fail and the fault must come when we are "catching up" with the computation. For CSIDH, torsion noise can only happen if $r > |e_i|$ and the computation of the ℓ_i-isogeny failed in at least $r - |e_i|$ rounds. Torsion noise is unlikely for large ℓ_i because the probability that an isogeny fails is about $1/\ell_i$.

For small primes, such as $\ell_i \in \{3, 5, 7\}$, we observe a lot of torsion noise. This can slightly affect the results as described in Sect. 4.3, but has no major impact on the results in general. Concretely, torsion noise may make it impossible to determine the correct e_i for the small primes given only a few faulted curves. Nevertheless, their exact values can be brute-forced at the end of the attack.

Remark 1 (Orientation of torsion noise). Faulty curves affected by torsion noise require contrarily oriented isogenies to the curves $E^{r,s}$ than the remaining faulty curves. Therefore, if torsion noise happens and we find a path from such a curve $E_t \to E^{r,s}$, then we can infer not just the orientation of the primes in this path, but often also bound the corresponding exponents e_i.

4.5   Connecting Curves from the Same Round

Suppose we have a set of (effective) round-r faulty curves with the same orientation s, and suppose r and s are fixed. In Corollary 4.4, we show that such curves are close to each other. In particular, the path from E_t to $E^{r,s}$ uses only degrees contained in the set $S^{r,s}$. Finding short paths among faulty curves gives us information about $S^{r,s}$, and hence about the secret key.

Component Graphs. Starting from a set $\{E_t\}$ of round-r faulty curves with orientation s, we can use them to define the graph $G^{r,s}$ as follows: The vertices of $G^{r,s}$ are given by $\{E_t\}$, and the edges are steps between the curves, labeled by i if the curves are connected by two ℓ_i-isogenies. For convenience, we sparsify the graph $G^{r,s}$ and regard it as a tree with the curve $E^{r,s}$ as the root.

Edges. Starting from a set of faulty curves, it is easy to build the graphs $G^{r,s}$. We can identify the *roots* of these graphs $E^{r,s}$ using Corollary 4.3. Then the distance from the root to any round-r faulty curve with the same orientation is small (cf. Corollary 4.4). Therefore, we can find the edges by applying short walks in the isogeny graph. Note that edges of $G^{r,s}$ give information on $S^{r,s}$.

Missing Vertices. If we do not have enough faulty curves $\{E_t\}$, it may not be possible to connect all the curves with single steps, i.e. isogenies of square degree (see Corollary 4.4). For convenience, we assume that we have enough curves. In practice, we include in the graph $G^{r,s}$ any curve on the path between E_t to $E^{r,s}$.

Components. We imagine the graphs $G^{r,s}$ as subgraphs of the *isogeny graph* of supersingular elliptic curves with edges given by isogenies. Computing short paths from $E^{r,s}$ will give us enough edges so that we can consider the graphs $G^{r,s}$ to be connected. Hence we call them *components*.

Secret Information. An effective round-r faulty curve E_t with torsion set $S_t \subset S^{r,+}$ can easily be connected by a path with labels $S^{r,+} \setminus S_t$. Moreover, the orientation $E^{r,+} \to E_t$ is positive. Therefore, we can identify which components are positive, and all the labels of the edges are necessarily in $S^{r,+}$, that is, the prime ℓ_i is positive. Torsion noise can be recognized from the opposite direction of the edges (see Remark 1). In either case, the components $G^{r,s}$ give us the orientation of all the primes occurring as labels of the edges.

Sorting Round-r Samples. Suppose we are given a set of round-r faulty curves $\{E_t\}$, but we do not have information about the orientation yet. We can again use Corollary 4.3 to find the root of the graph; then we take small isogeny steps until we have two connected components G_1, G_2. It is easy to determine the direction of the edges given enough samples; ignoring torsion noise, the positively oriented root will have outgoing edges.

In summary, we try to move curves E_t from a pile of unconnected samples to one of the two graphs by finding collisions with one of the nodes in $G^{r,+}$ resp. $G^{r,-}$. The degrees of such edges reveal information on $S^{r,+}$ and $S^{r,-}$: An edge with label i in $G^{r,+}$ implies $i \in S^{r,+}$, and analogously for $G^{r,-}$ and $S^{r,-}$. Figure 1 summarizes the process, where, e.g., $E^{r,+} \to E_7$ shows missing torsion and $E_8 \to E^{r,+}$ is an example of torsion noise.

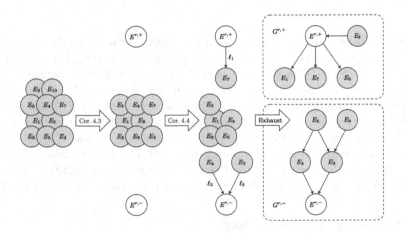

Fig. 1. Building up the component graphs of faulty curves.

4.6   Connecting the Components $G^{r,s}$

Now, we explain how to connect the components $G^{r,s}$ for different rounds r. The distance of these components is related to the sets $S^{r,+}$ and $S^{r,-}$. We then show that it is computationally feasible to connect the components via a meet-in-the-middle attack. Connecting two components gives us significantly more knowledge on the sets $S^{r,+}$ and $S^{r,-}$, such that connecting all components is enough to reveal the secret $\mathfrak{a}$ in Sect. 4.7.

Information from Two Connected Components. We take CSIDH as an example. Recall that we have $S^{r,+} = \{i \mid e_i \geq r\}$, and so $E^{r,+} = \prod_{i \in S^{r,+}} \mathfrak{l}_i^{-2} * E_B$. This means that, e.g., we have $S^{3,+} \subset S^{2,+}$, and $E^{2,+}$ has a larger distance from E_B than $E^{3,+}$. The path between $E^{3,+}$ and $E^{2,+}$ then only contains steps of degrees $\mathfrak{l}_i$ such that $i \in S^{2,+} \backslash S^{3,+}$, so $e_i = 2$. In general, it is easy to see that finding a single isogeny that connects a node E_{t_3} from $G^{3,+}$ and a node E_{t_2} in $G^{2,+}$ immediately gives the connection from $E^{3,+}$ to $E^{2,+}$. Hence, we learn all $\mathfrak{l}_i$ with $e_i = 2$ from the components $G^{3,+}$ and $G^{2,+}$.

In the general case, if we find an isogeny between two such graphs, say $G^{r,+}$ and $G^{r',+}$, we can compute the isogeny between the two roots $E^{r,+}$ and $E^{r',+}$ of these graphs. The degree of this isogeny $E^{r,+} \to E^{r',+}$ describes precisely the *difference* between the sets $S^{r,+}$ and $S^{r',+}$. The example above is the special case $r' = r + 1$, and in CSIDH we always have $S^{(r+1),+} \subset S^{r,+}$, so that the difference between $S^{r,+}$ and $S^{(r+1),+}$ is the set of $\mathfrak{l}_i$ such that $e_i = r$. In other CSIDH-variants, such sets are not necessarily nested, but connecting all components still reveals e_i as Sect. 4.7 will show. In general, we connect two subgraphs by a distributed meet-in-the-middle search which finds the shortest connection first.

Distance Between Connected Components. As we have shown, connecting two components $G^{r,+}$ and $G^{r',+}$ is equivalent to finding the difference in sets $S^{r,+}$ and $S^{r',+}$. The distance between these sets heavily depends on the implementation, as these sets are determined by the key $\mathfrak{a}$ and the evaluation of this key. For example, in CSIDH-512, the difference between $S^{r,+}$ and $S^{(r+1),+}$ are the $e_i = r$, which on average is of size $\frac{74}{11} \approx 6.7$. In practice, this distance roughly varies between 0 and 15. For an implementation such as CTIDH-512, the sets $S^{r,+}$ are smaller in general, on average of size 7, and the difference between such sets is small enough to admit a feasible meet-in-the-middle connection. See Sect. 6 for more details on how we connect these components in practice.

4.7   Revealing the Private Key

So far, we showed how connecting different components $G^{r,+}$ and $G^{r',+}$ reveals information on the difference between the sets $S^{r,+}$ and $S^{r',+}$. In this section, we show that when all components are connected, we can derive the secret $\mathfrak{a}$. This wraps up Sect. 4: Starting with disorientations in certain rounds r, we derive the secret $\mathfrak{a}$ from the resulting graph structure, assuming enough samples.

From Differences of Sets to Recoveries of Keys. By connecting the graphs of all rounds, including the one-node-graph consisting of just the correct curve E_B, we learn the difference between the sets $S^{r,+}$ and $S^{(r+1),+}$ for all rounds r (as well as for $S^{r,-}$ and $S^{(r+1),-}$). A single isogeny from some $G^{r,+}$ to $E_B = \mathfrak{a} * E_A$ then recovers $S^{r,+}$ for this round r: Such an isogeny gives us an isogeny from $E^{r,+} = \prod_{i \in S^{r,+}} \mathfrak{l}_i^{-2} * E_B$ to E_B, whose degree shows us exactly those

$\ell_i \in S^{r,+}$. From a connection between the components $G^{r,+}$ and $G^{r',+}$, we learn the difference in sets $S^{r,+}$ and $S^{r',+}$. From $S^{r,+}$, we can then deduce $S^{r',+}$. Therefore, if all graphs $G^{r,+}$ for different r are connected, and we have at least one isogeny from a node to E_B, we learn the sets $S^{r,+}$ for all rounds r (and equivalently for $S^{r,-}$). From the knowledge of all sets $S^{r,+}$ and $S^{r,-}$ we then learn $\mathfrak{a} = (e_i)$: the sign of e_i follows from observing in which of the sets $S^{r,+}$ or $S^{r,-}$ the respective ℓ_i appears, and $|e_i|$ equals the number of times of these appearances.

In practice however, due to missing torsion and torsion noise, connecting all components may not give us the *correct* sets $S^{r,+}$ resp. $S^{r,-}$. In such a case, one can either gather more samples to gain more information, or try to brute-force the difference. In practice, we find that the actual set $S^{r,+}$ as derived from $\mathfrak{a}$ and the set $\tilde{S}^{r,+}$ derived from our attack (leading to some $\mathfrak{a}'$) always have a small distance. A simple meet-in-the-middle search between $\mathfrak{a}' * E_A$ and $\mathfrak{a} * E_A$ then quickly reveals the errors caused by missing torsion and torsion noise.

4.8 Complexity of Recovering the Secret $\mathfrak{a}$

The full approach of this section can be summarized as follows:

1. Gather enough effective round-r samples E_t per round r, using Lemma 4.1.
2. Build up the components $G^{r,+}$ and $G^{r,-}$ using Corollaries 4.3 and 4.4.
3. Connect components to learn the difference in sets $S^{r,+}$ and $S^{r',+}$.
4. Compute the sets $S^{r,+}$ and $S^{r,-}$ for every round and recover $\mathfrak{a}$.

The overall complexity depends on the number of samples per round, but is in general dominated by Step 3. For Step 2, nodes are in most cases relatively close to the root $E^{r,+}$ or to an already connected node E_t, as shown in Corollary 4.4.

For Step 3, components are usually further apart than nodes from Step 2. In general, the distance between components $G^{r,+}$ and $G^{r',+}$ depends heavily on the specific design choices of an implementation. In a usual meet-in-the-middle approach, where n is the number of ℓ_i over which we need to search and d is the distance between $G^{r,+}$ and $G^{r',+}$, the complexity of finding a connection is $\mathcal{O}(\binom{n}{d/2})$. Note that we can use previous knowledge from building components or finding small-distance connections between other components to reduce the search space and thus minimize n for subsequent connections. We analyze this in detail for specific implementations in Sect. 5.

5 Case Studies: CSIDH and CTIDH

The previous steps are dependent on the actual implementation. Concretely, we select two main implementations: CSIDH-512 and CTIDH-512. We discuss CSIDH-512 in Sect. 5.1, CTIDH-512 in Sect. 5.2, and we analyze other implementations in Sect. 5.3.

5.1   Breaking CSIDH-512

The primes used in CSIDH-512 [15] are $L = \{3, 5, \ldots, 377, 587\}$, and exponent vectors are sampled as $(e_i) \in \{-5, \ldots, 5\}^{74}$ uniformly at random. For any $k \in \{-5, \ldots, 5\}$ we expect about $\frac{1}{11} \cdot 74$ primes ℓ_i with $e_i = k$; this count obeys a binomial distribution with parameters $(74, 1/11)$. We expect to see about $\frac{5}{11} \cdot 74 \approx 33.6$ positive and negative primes each, and about $\frac{1}{11} \cdot 74 \approx 6.7$ neutral primes.

In CSIDH-512, the group action is evaluated as displayed in Algorithm 1, using a 1-point strategy. In particular, after generating a point with orientation s, we set $S = \{i \mid e_i \neq 0, \ \text{sign}(e_i) = s\}$. If the value of s is flipped, we set $S = \{i \mid e_i \neq 0, \ \text{sign}(e_i) = -s\}$, but we perform the steps in direction s.

Now, we specialize the four steps to secret-key recover defined in Sect. 4.8.

Building Components $G^{r,+}$ and $G^{r,-}$. Step 2 of the attack on CSIDH-512 works exactly as described in Sect. 4.5. If E_t and $E_{t'}$ are effective samples from the same round with the same orientation, their distance is small (Corollary 4.4). We can thus perform a neighborhood search on all of the sampled curves until we have 10 connected components $G^{r,\pm}$ for $r \in \{1, \ldots, 5\}$, as in Fig. 1. This step is almost effortless: most curves will be distance 1 or 2 away from the root $E^{r,s}$. In practice, using round information and number of occurrences, we identify the 10 curves $E^{r,\pm}$ for $r = 1, \ldots, 5$, and explore all paths of small length from those 10 curves, or connect them via a meet-in-the-middle approach (e.g., using pubcrawl, see Sect. 6). The degrees of the isogenies corresponding to the new edges in $G^{r,\pm}$ reveal information on the sets $S^{r,\pm}$, which can be used to reduce the search space when connecting the components $G^{r,\pm}$.

Filter-and-Break It, Until You Make It. Step 3 is the most computationally intensive step, as it connects 11 components ($G^{r,\pm}$ and E_B) into a single large connected component. We argue that it is practical for CSIDH-512.

More specifically, we want to find connections between $G^{r,\pm}$ and $G^{(r+1),\pm}$, as well as connections from $G^{5,\pm}$ to E_B. This gives us 10 connections, corresponding to the gaps $\{i \mid e_i = k\}$ for $k \in [-5, 5] \setminus \{0\}$. Figure 2 shows an abstraction of this large connected component.

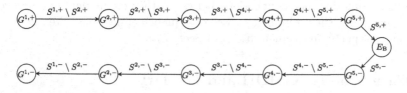

Fig. 2. Large connected component associated to an attack on CSIDH-512.

Since there are 74 primes in total, and only 10 gaps, at least one of these gaps is at most 7 primes. If we assume that at least 5 of the exponents are 0 (we expect ≈ 7 to be 0), then the smallest distance is at most 6 steps, easily found using a meet-in-the-middle search, see Sect. 6.

Let us call *support* the set of isogeny degrees used in a meet-in-the-middle neighborhood search. We can connect all components by a meet-in-the-middle search with support $\{\ell_1, \ldots, \ell_{74}\}$. This becomes infeasible for large distances, so instead, we adaptively change the support. We start by finding short connections, and use the labels we find to pick a smaller support for searching between certain components, i.e., *filter* some of the ℓ_i out of the support.

First, we learn the orientation of the components by identifying $G^{1,\pm}$ and considering the direction of the edges. Effective round-1 samples do not have torsion noise, so the root $E^{1,+}$ has only outgoing edges, whereas the root $E^{1,-}$ has only incoming edges. The labels of the edges of $G^{1,+}$ must be positive primes, and all components with a matching label are also positive. Next, all the labels that appear as degrees of edges in $G^{r,+}$ for any r are necessarily positive. Finally, positively oriented components can only be connected by positive primes, so we can remove from the support all the primes that we know are negative. Similarly for negative orientations.

After finding the first connection we restrict the support even more: we know that any label i appears in at most *one* connection. Hence, whenever we find a connection, we get more information about orientation and can reduce the support for further searches, allowing us to find larger connections. Each repetition gives more restrictions on the support until we find the full connected component.

Recovering the Secret Key. From the connected components, we recover all of the sets $S^{r,\pm}$ and we compute the secret key as described in Sect. 4.7.

Example 5 (Toy CSIDH-103). Figure 3 shows the resulting connected graph for a toy version of CSIDH using Algorithm 1 with the first $n = 21$ odd primes and private keys in $\{-3, \ldots, +3\}^n$. Each round was faulted 10 times.

The distances between the components are very small and hence connecting paths are readily found. We sparsify the graph to plot it as a spanning tree; the edges correspond to positive steps of the degree indicated by the label. This graph comes from the secret key

$$(-1, +1, +2, +3, -2, +3, +2, +3, +1, +2, -3, -3, +2, +3, -2, -3, -2, +2, +1, -3, \ 0).$$

Required Number of Samples. Recovering the full secret exponent vector in CSIDH-512 equates to computing the sets $S^{r,+}$ and $S^{r,-}$ for $r \in \{1, \ldots, 5\}$. Recall that to compute these sets we need to build a connected component including subcomponents $G^{r,+}$ and $G^{r,-}$ for $r \in \{1, \ldots, 5\}$, and E_B (the one-node-graph consisting of just the public key). We build the components $G^{r,+}$ and $G^{r,-}$ by acquiring enough effective round-r samples. More effective round-r samples may give more vertices in $G^{r,\pm}$, and more information about $S^{r,\pm}$.

Let T_r be the number of effective round-r samples and let $T = \sum T_r$. A first approach is to inject in round r until the probability is high enough that we have

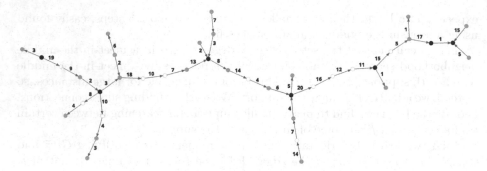

Fig. 3. Example isogeny graph of faulty curves obtained from attacking the fictitious CSIDH-103 implementation from Example 5. An edge labeled i denotes the isogeny step $\mathfrak{l}_i$. The E_B curve and the root faulty curves $E^{r,s}$ are rendered in black (from left to right: $E^{1,+}$, $E^{2,+}$, $E^{3,+}$, E_B, $E^{3,-}$, $E^{2,-}$, $E^{1,-}$), other faulty curves appearing in the dataset are gray, and white circles are "intermediate" curves discovered while connecting the components. The primes appearing on the connecting path between $E^{i,\pm}$ and $E^{i+1,\pm}$ are exactly the primes appearing i times with orientation $\pm$. For example, the primes indexed by 2, 9, 19 appearing between $E^{1,+}$ and $E^{2,+}$ have exponent $+1$ in the secret key.

enough effective round-r samples. For CSIDH-512, we take $T_1 = 16$, $T_2 = 16$, $T_3 = 32$, $T_4 = 64$ and $T_5 = 128$, so that $T = 256$. From Lemma 4.1, we then expect 8 round-5 samples (4 per orientation) and the probability that we do not get any of the elements of $G^{5,+}$ or $G^{5,-}$ is about 1.7%.

This strategy can be improved upon. Notice that we need round-5 samples, and so in any case we need T_5 rather large (in comparison to T_i with $i < 5$) to ensure we get such samples. But gathering samples from round 5 already gives us many samples from rounds before. Using Lemma 4.1 with $T_5 = 128$, we get on average 8 effective round-1 samples, 32 effective round-2 samples, 48 effective round-3 samples, 32 effective round-4 samples and 8 effective round-5 samples. In general, attacking different rounds offers different tradeoffs: attacking round 9 maximizes getting effective round-5 samples, but getting a round-1 sample in round 9 is unlikely. Faulting round 1 has the benefits that all faulty curves are effective round-1 curves; that no torsion noise appears; and that missing torsion quickly allows to determine the orientation of the small primes. Finally, note that gathering T faulty samples requires approximately $2T$ fault injections, since, on average, half of the faults are expected to will flip the orientation.

5.2   Breaking CTIDH-512

CTIDH [3] partitions the set of primes ℓ_j into b batches, and bounds the number of isogenies per batch. For a list $N \in \mathbb{Z}^b_{>0}$ with $\sum N_k = n$ and a list of non-negative bounds $m \in \mathbb{Z}^b_{\geq 0}$ define the keyspace as

$$\mathcal{K}_{N,m} := \left\{ (e_1, \ldots, e_n) \in \mathbb{Z}^n \ \middle|\ \sum_{j=1}^{N_i} |e_{i,j}| \leq m_i \text{ for } 1 \leq i \leq b \right\},$$

where $(e_{i,j})$ is a reindexed view of (e_i) given by the partition into batches.

CTIDH-512 uses 14 batches with bounds $m_i \leq 18$, requiring at least 18 rounds. In every round, we compute one isogeny per batch; using a 2-point strategy, we compute isogenies in both positive and negative direction. So, all round-r samples are effective round-r samples.

Injecting Faults. To sample oriented points, CTIDH uses the Elligator-2 map twice. First, Elligator is used to sample two points P_+ and P_- on the starting curve E_A. A direction s is picked to compute an isogeny, the point P_s is used to take a step in that direction to a curve $E_{A'}$, and the point P_s is mapped through the isogeny. Then another point P'_{-s} is sampled on $E_{A'}$ using Elligator.

We will always assume that we inject a fault into only one of these two Elligator calls (as in Sect. 3). Hence, as for CSIDH and 1-point strategies, we again always obtain either positively or negatively oriented samples.

Different Rounds for CTIDH-512. Per round, CTIDH performs one $\ell_{i,j}$ per batch $\mathcal{B}_i$. Within a batch, the primes $\ell_{i,j}$ are ordered in ascending order: if the first batch is $\mathcal{B}_1 = \{3,5\}$ and the exponents are $(2,-4)$, then we first compute 2 rounds of 3-isogenies in the positive direction, followed by 4 rounds of 5-isogenies in the negative direction. We can visualize this as a queue $[3+,3+,5-,5-,5-,5-]$ (padded on the right with dummy isogenies for the remaining rounds up to m_1). CTIDH inflates the failure of each isogeny to that of the smallest prime in the batch to hide how often each prime is used; in our example, the failure probability is $1/3$.

This implies that the sets $S^{r\pm}$ contain precisely the r-th prime in the queue for the batch $\mathcal{B}_i$. With 14 batches and an equal chance for either orientation, we expect that each $S^{r\pm}$ will contain about 7 primes. Furthermore, each set $S^{r\pm}$ can contain only one prime per batch $\mathcal{B}_i$.

The small number of batches and the ordering of primes within the batches make CTIDH especially easy to break using our disorientation attack.

Components for CTIDH-512. Given enough samples, we construct the graphs $G^{r,s}$; the slightly higher failure probability of each isogeny (because of inflating) somewhat increases the chances of missing torsion and torsion noise. The distance of the root curves $E^{r,s}$ to the non-faulted curve E_B is bounded by the number of batches. Per round r, the sum of the distances of $E^{r,\pm}$ to E_B is at most 14, so we expect the distance to be about 7.

The distance between two graphs $G^{r,s}$ and $G^{(r+1),s}$ is often much smaller. We focus on positive orientation (the negative case is analogous). The distance between $G^{r,+}$ to $G^{(r+1),+}$ is given by the set difference of $S^{r,+}$ and $S^{(r+1),+}$. If these sets are disjoint and all primes in round r and $r+1$ are positive, the distance is 28, but we expect significant overlap: The set difference contains the indices i such that either the last ℓ_i-isogeny is computed in round r or the first ℓ_i-isogeny is computed in round $r+1$. Note that these replacements need not come in pairs. In the first case, the prime ℓ_i is replaced by the next isogeny ℓ_j from the same batch only if ℓ_j is also positive. In the second case, the prime ℓ_i might have followed a negative prime that preceded it in the batch.

Therefore, given $S^{r,+}$, one can very quickly determine $S^{(r+1),+}$ by leaving out some ℓ_i's or including subsequent primes from the same batch. In practice, this step is very easy. Finding one connection $E_B \to E^{r,+}$ determines some set $S^{r,+}$, which can be used to quickly find other sets $S^{r',+}$. This approach naturally also works going backwards, to the set $S^{(r-1),+}$.

Directed Meet-in-the-Middle. Using a meet-in-the-middle approach, we compute the neighborhood of E_B and all the roots $E^{r,\pm}$ (or components $G^{r,\pm}$) of distance 4. This connects E_B to all the curves at distance at most 8. Disregarding orientation and information on batches, if we have N curves that we want to connect, the naive search will require about $2 \cdot \binom{74}{4} \cdot N \approx 2^{21} \cdot N$ isogenies. The actual search space is even smaller as we can exclude all paths requiring two isogenies from the same batch.

Moreover, isogenies in batches are in ascending order. So, if in round r we see that the 3rd prime from batch $\mathcal{B}_i$ was used, none of the rounds $r' > r$ involves the first two prime, and none of the rounds $r' < r$ can use the fourth and later primes from the batch for that direction.

Late rounds typically contain many dummy isogenies and the corresponding faulty curves are especially close to the public key. We expect to rapidly recover $S^{r,\pm}$ for the late round curves, and work backwards to handle earlier rounds.

Required Number of Samples. In CTIDH, we can choose to inject a fault into the first call of Elligator or the second one. We do not see a clear benefit of prioritizing either call. Unlike for CSIDH and 1-point strategies, there is no clear benefit from targeting a specific round. Assume we perform c successful faults per round per Elligator call, expecting to get samples for both orientations per round. As CTIDH-512 performs 18 rounds (in practice typically up to 22 because of isogeny steps failing), we require $T = 18 \cdot 2 \cdot c$ successful flips. It seems possible to take $c = 1$ and hence $T = 36$ (or up to $T = 44$) samples.

With just one sample per round r (and per orientation s), the torsion effects will be significant and we will often not be able to recover $S^{r,s}$ precisely. Let $\tilde{S}^{r,s}$ denote the index set recovered for round r and sign s. We can correct for some of these errors, looking at $\tilde{S}^{r',\pm}$ for rounds r' close to r. Consider only primes from the same batch $\mathcal{B}$, then the following can happen:

- *No* prime from $\mathcal{B}$ is contained in either $\tilde{S}^{r,+}$ or $\tilde{S}^{r,-}$: all primes from $\mathcal{B}$ are done or *missing torsion* must have happened. We can examine the primes from the batch $\mathcal{B}$ which occur in neighboring rounds $\tilde{S}^{(r\pm1),\pm}$ and use the ordering in the batch to obtain guesses on which steps should have been computed if any.
- *One* prime from $\mathcal{B}$ is contained in $\tilde{S}^{r,+} \cup \tilde{S}^{r,-}$: we fix no errors.
- *Two* primes from $\mathcal{B}$ are contained in $\tilde{S}^{r,+} \cup \tilde{S}^{r,-}$: the smaller one must have come from torsion noise in a previous round and can be removed.

Remark 2. It is possible to skip certain rounds to reduce the number of samples, and recover the missing sets $S^{r,s}$ using information from the neighboring rounds. We did not perform the analysis as to which rounds can be skipped, we feel that already two successful faults per round are low enough.

Even a partial attack (obtaining information only from a few rounds) reveals a lot about the secret key thanks to the batches being ordered, and can reduce the search space for the secret key significantly. One may also select the rounds to attack adaptively, based on the information recovered from $S^{r,s}$.

Recovering the Secret Key. Once we recover all the sets $S^{r,s}$, the secret key can be found as $\mathfrak{a} = \prod_r \left(\prod_{i \in S^{r,+}} \mathfrak{l}_i \cdot \prod_{j \in S^{r,-}} \mathfrak{l}_j^{-1} \right)$. If we misidentify $S^{r,s}$ due to torsion effects, we have to perform a small search to finish.

5.3 Other Variants of CSIDH

SIMBA. Implementations using SIMBA [30] can be attacked similarly to CSIDH (cf. Sect. 5.1). SIMBA divides the n primes ℓ_i into m *prides* (batches), and each round only computes ℓ_i-isogenies from the same pride. That is, each round only involves up to $\lceil n/m \rceil$ isogenies, and the setup of the prides is publicly known. In each round, fewer isogenies are computed, the sets $S^{r,s}$ are smaller and the distances between the components $G^{r,s}$ are shorter. It is therefore easier to find isogenies connecting the components, and recover the secret key.

Dummy-Free CSIDH. Dummy-free implementations [1,16,18] replace pairs of dummy ℓ_i-isogenies by pairs of isogenies that effectively cancel each other [16]. This is due to the fact that $\mathfrak{l}_i * (\mathfrak{l}_i^{-1} * E) = \mathfrak{l}_i^{-1} * (\mathfrak{l}_i * E) = E$. Thus, computing one ℓ_i-isogeny in positive direction and one ℓ_i-isogeny in negative direction has the same effect as computing two dummy ℓ_i-isogenies. However, this approach requires fixing the parity of each entry of the private key e_i, e.g., by sampling only even numbers from $[-10, 10]$ to reach the same key space size as before. The implementation of [16] therefore suffers a slowdown of factor 2. Nevertheless, such dummy-free implementations mitigate certain fault attacks, such as skipping isogenies, which in a dummy-based implementation would directly reveal if the skipped isogeny was a dummy computation and give respective information on the private key. Dummy-free CSIDH [1] computes $|e_i|$ ℓ_i-isogenies per i in the appropriate direction, and then computes equally many ℓ_i isogenies in both directions which cancel out, until all required isogenies have been computed. For instance, for an even e_i sampled from $[-10, 10]$, choosing $e_i = 4$ would be performed by applying $\mathfrak{l}_i^1$ in the first 5 rounds, applying $\mathfrak{l}_i^{-1}$ in round 6 and 7, applying $\mathfrak{l}_i^1$ again in round 8 and 9, and finishing with $\mathfrak{l}_i^{-1}$ in round 10.

Notice that all isogenies start in the correct direction, and that we learn $|e_i|$ from disorientation faults if we know in which round the first $\mathfrak{l}_i$ is applied in the opposite direction. Therefore, if we apply the attack of Sect. 4 and learn all sets $S^{r,+}$ and $S^{r,-}$, we can determine e_i precisely. Even better, it suffices to only attack every second round: It is clear that each prime will have the same orientation in the third round as in the second round, in the fifth and fourth, et cetera. Due to the bounds used in [1], large degree ℓ_i do not show up in later rounds, which decreases the meet-in-the-middle complexity of connecting the components $G^{r,+}$ and $G^{(r+1),+}$ for later rounds r.

SQALE. SQALE [17] only uses exponent bounds $e_i \in \{-1, 1\}$. To get a large enough key space, more primes ℓ_i are needed; the smallest instance uses 221 ℓ_i. SQALE uses a 2-point strategy and only requires one round (keeping in mind the isogeny computation may fail and require further rounds).

Set $S^+ = S^{1,+} = \{i \mid e_i = 1\}$ and $S^- = S^{1,-} = \{i \mid e_i = -1\}$. If the sampled points in round 1 have full order, the round 1 faulty curves are either:

- the 'twist' of E_B: all the directions will be flipped (if both points are flipped),
- or the curve $E^+ = (\prod_{S^+} \mathfrak{l}_i^{-2}) * E_B$, if the positive point was flipped,
- or the curve $E^- = (\prod_{S^-} \mathfrak{l}_i^2) * E_B$, if the negative point was flipped.

As $|S^+| \approx |S^-| \approx n/2 \gg 110$, we will not be able to find an isogeny to either of these curves using a brute-force or a meet-in-the-middle approach.

However, SQALE samples points randomly, and some of the isogeny computation will fail, producing faulty curves close to $E^\pm$ (and curves with the same orientation will be close to each other, as in Sect. 4.5). Getting enough faulty curves allows the attacker to get the orientation of all the primes ℓ_i, and the orientation of the primes is exactly the secret key in SQALE. We note that [18] in another context proposes to include points of full order into the system parameters and public keys such that missing torsion and torsion noise do not occur. If this is used for SQALE, our attack would not apply.

6   The pubcrawl Tool

The post-processing stage of our attack requires reconstructing the graph of connecting isogenies between the faulty CSIDH outputs. We solve this problem by a meet-in-the-middle neighborhood search in the isogeny graph, which is sufficiently practical for the cases we considered. In this section, we report on implementation details and performance results for our pubcrawl software.

We emphasize that the software is *not* overly specialized to the fault-attack setting and may therefore prove useful for other "small" CSIDH isogeny searches appearing in unrelated contexts.

Algorithm. pubcrawl implements a straightforward meet-in-the-middle graph search: Grow isogeny trees from each input node simultaneously and check for collisions; repeat until there is only one connected component left. The set of admissible isogeny degrees ("support") is configurable, as are the directions of the isogeny steps ("sign", cf. CSIDH exponent vectors), the maximum number of isogeny steps to take from each target curve before giving up ("distance"), and the number of prime-degree isogenies done per graph-search step ("multiplicity"), to allow for restricting the search to square-degree isogenies.

Size of Search Space. The number of vectors in $\mathbb{Z}^n$ of 1-norm $\leq m$ is [20, § 3]

$$G_n(m) = \sum_{k=0}^{m} \binom{n}{k}\binom{m-k+n}{n}.$$

Similarly, the number of vectors in $\mathbb{Z}_{\geq 0}^n$ of 1-norm $\leq m$ equals

$$H_n(m) = \sum_{k=0}^{m} \binom{k+n-1}{n-1}.$$

Implementation. The tool is written in C++ using modern standard library features, most importantly hashmaps and threading. It incorporates the latest version of the original CSIDH software as a library to provide the low-level isogeny computations. Public-key validation is skipped to save time. The shared data structures (work queue and lookup table) are protected by a simple mutex; more advanced techniques were not necessary in our experiments.

We refrain from providing detailed benchmark results for the simple reason that the overwhelming majority of the cost comes from computing isogeny steps in a breadth-first manner, which parallelizes perfectly. Hence, both time and memory consumption scale almost exactly linearly with the number of nodes visited by the algorithm.

Concretely, on a server with two Intel Xeon Gold 6136 processors (offering a total of 24 hyperthreaded Skylake cores) using GCC 11.2.0, we found that each isogeny step took between 0.6 and 0.8 core ms, depending on the degree. Memory consumption grew at a rate of ≈ 250 bytes per node visited, although this quantity depends on data structure internals and can vary significantly. Example estimates based on these observations are given in Table 1.

Table 1. Example cost estimates per target curve for various `pubcrawl` instances, assuming each isogeny step takes 0.7 ms and consumes 250 bytes.

sign	|support|	distance	cardinality of search space	core time	memory
both	74	≤ 4	$20, 549, 801 \approx 2^{24.29}$	4.0 h	5.1 GB
both	74	≤ 5	$612, 825, 229 \approx 2^{29.19}$	5.0 d	153.2 GB
both	74	≤ 6	$15, 235, 618, 021 \approx 2^{33.83}$	123.4 d	3.8 TB
both	74	≤ 7	$324, 826, 290, 929 \approx 2^{38.24}$	7.2 y	81.2 TB
both	74	≤ 8	$6, 063, 220, 834, 321 \approx 2^{42.46}$	134.6 y	1.5 PB
both	74	≤ 9	$100, 668, 723, 849, 029 \approx 2^{46.52}$	2234.5 y	25.2 PB
one	74	≤ 4	$1, 426, 425 \approx 2^{20.44}$	16.6 min	356.6 MB
one	74	≤ 5	$22, 537, 515 \approx 2^{24.43}$	4.4 h	5.6 GB
one	74	≤ 6	$300, 500, 200 \approx 2^{28.16}$	2.4 d	75.1 GB
one	74	≤ 7	$3, 477, 216, 600 \approx 2^{31.70}$	28.2 d	869.3 GB

There is no doubt that `pubcrawl` could be sped up if desired, for instance by computing various outgoing isogeny steps at once instead of calling the CSIDH library as a black box for each individually.

7   Hashed Version

The attacker-observable output in Diffie–Hellman-style key agreements is not the shared elliptic curve, but a certain derived value. Typically, the shared elliptic curve is used to compute a key k using a key derivation function, which is further used for symmetric key cryptography. So we cannot expect to obtain (the Montgomery coefficient of) a faulty curve E_t but only a derived value such as $k = \text{SHA-256}(E_t)$ or $\text{MAC}_k(\text{str})$ for some known fixed string `str`.

The attack strategies from Sect. 4 and Sect. 5 exploit the connections between the various faulty curves, but when we are only given a derived value, we are unable to apply isogenies. We argue that our attack, however, still extends to this more realistic setting as long as the observable value is computed deterministically from E_t and collisions do not occur. For simplicity, we refer to the observable values as *hashes* $H(E)$ of the faulty curves E. We assume that we can derive $H(E)$ for a given E, but that we cannot recover E given only $H(E)$.

As we lack the possibility to apply isogenies to the hashes, we must adapt the strategy from Sect. 4. Given a set of faulty curves, we can no longer generate the neighborhood graphs, nor find connecting paths between these graphs, and it is harder to learn the orientation of primes, which helped to reduce the possible degrees of the isogenies when applying `pubcrawl`. If we only see hashes of the faulty curves, we cannot immediately form the neighborhood graphs and determine orientations. But from the frequency analysis (Corollary 4.3), we can still identify the two most frequent new hashes h_1, h_2 per round as the probable hashes of $H(E^{r,\pm})$. For example, when faulting CSIDH in the first point, the two most common hashed values are our best guesses for the hashes of $E^{1,\pm}$, and when we consider faults in the second point, we guess $H(E^{2,\pm})$ to be the most common hashes that have not appeared in round 1.

To recover E given a hash $H(E)$, we run a one-sided `pubcrawl` search starting from E_B, where we hash all the curves we reach along the way, until we find a curve that hashes to $H(E)$. In practice, we run `pubcrawl` with one orientation (or both, in parallel) until we recognize $H(E^{r,\pm})$. Having identified $E^{r,\pm}$, we can then run a small neighborhood search around $E^{r,\pm}$ to identify the hashes of the faulty curves E_t close to $E^{r,\pm}$. In contrast to the unhashed version, in the hashed version we can only recover the faulty curves E_t by a one-sided search from a known curve E, instead of a meet-in-the-middle attack. In particular, the only known curve at the beginning of the attack is E_B.

Example 6 (CTIDH-512). In CTIDH, in the worst case the distance from E_B to any $E^{r,\pm}$ is 14 (one prime per batch, all with the same orientation) and the average distance is 7 (Sect. 5.2). Thus, in a hashed variant, if we launch `pubcrawl` in both directions up to a distance 7, we are likely to already identify many hashes

$H(E_t)$ and can recover E_t. We then crawl around these E_t to identify the other faulty curves. When we recover all E_t, we proceed as in Sect. 5.2.

Summarizing, in the hashed version, the main difference compared to the approach in Sect. 5 is that we can no longer mount meet-in-the-middle attacks between faulty curves, but we must always perform a one-way search from a given curve to a hash. Hence, we do not get the square-root speedup from meeting in the middle. Despite this increase in cost, this does not mean we cannot attack a hashed version. Although the brute-force search required to recover $E^{r,\pm}$ given only $H(E^{r,\pm})$ can get very expensive, especially for CSIDH over large fields $\mathbb{F}_p$, such a search always remains cheaper than the security level, as we only need to cover the gaps beteen all $E^{r,\pm}$ and E_B.

8   Exploiting the Twist to Allow Precomputation

In this section, we use quadratic twists and precomputation to significantly speed up obtaining the private key $\mathfrak{a}$ given enough samples E_t, especially for the "hashed" version described in Sect. 7.

Using the Twist. The attack target is a public key $E_B = \mathfrak{a} * E_0$. Previously (Sect. 3), we attacked the computation of $\mathfrak{a} * E_0$ with disorientation faults. In this section, we will use E_{-B} as the input curve instead: Negating B is related to inverting $\mathfrak{a}$ because $E_{-B} = \mathfrak{a}^{-1} * E_0$. Moreover, applying $\mathfrak{a}$ to E_{-B} gives us back the curve E_0 and faulting this computation then produces faulty curves close to the fixed curve E_0. As E_{-B} is the *quadratic twist* of E_B, we will refer to this attack variant as *using the twist*.

The main trick is that twisting induces a symmetry around the curve E_0. This can be used to speed up `pubcrawl`: the opposite orientation of E_t (starting from E_0) reaches E_{-t}, so we can check two curves at once. By precomputing a set $\mathcal{C}$ of curves of distance at most d to E_0, a faulty curve E_t at distance $d' \leq d$ is in $\mathcal{C}$ and can immediately be identified via a table lookup. Note that $\mathcal{C}$ can be precomputed once and for all, independent of the target instance, as for any secret key $\mathfrak{a}'$ the faulty curves end up close to E_0. The symmetry of E_{-t} and E_t also reduces storage by half.

Finally, this twisting attack cannot be prevented by simply recognizing that E_{-B} is the twist of E_B and refusing to apply the secret $\mathfrak{a}$ to such a curve: An attacker can just as easily pick a random masking value $\mathfrak{z}$ and feed $\mathfrak{z} * E_{-B}$ to the target device. The faulty curves E_t can then be moved to the neighborhood of E_0 by computing $\mathfrak{z}^{-1} * E_t$ at some cost per E_t, or the attacker can precompute curves around $\mathfrak{z} * E_0$. The latter breaks the symmetry of E_t and E_{-t} and does not achieve the full speedup or storage reduction, but retains the main benefits.

Twisting CTIDH. The twisting attack is at its most powerful for CTIDH. As noted before, the sets $S^{r,\pm}$ are small in every round for CTIDH. The crucial observation is that in each round and for each orientation, we use at most one prime per batch (ignoring torsion noise, see Sect. 4.4). For a faulty curve E_t, the path $E_t \to E_0$ includes only steps with the same orientation and uses at most one prime per batch. With batches of size N_i, the total number of possible paths per orientation is $\prod_i (N_i + 1)$, which is about $2^{35.5}$ for CTIDH-512. Hence, it is possible to precompute *all* possible faulty curves that can appear from orientation flips from *any* possible secret key $\mathfrak{a}$.

Extrapolating the performance of `pubcrawl` (Sect. 6), this precomputation should take no more than a few core years. The resulting lookup table occupies $\approx 3.4\,\text{TB}$ when encoded naively, but can be compressed to less than $250\,\text{GB}$ using techniques similar to [38, §4.3].

Twisting CSIDH. For this speed-up to be effective, the distance d we use to compute $\mathcal{C}$ must be at least as large as the smallest $|S^{r,\pm}|$. Otherwise, no faulty curves end up within $\mathcal{C}$. For CSIDH, the smallest such sets are $S^{r_{\max},\pm}$, where $r_{\max}$ is the maximal exponent permitted by the parameter; e.g., for CSIDH-512 $r_{\max} = 5$ and $S^{5,\pm}$ have an expected size ≈ 7. Precomputing $\mathcal{C}$ for $d \leq 7$ creates a set containing $\sum_{i=0}^{7} \binom{74}{i} \approx 2^{31}$ curves. Such a precomputation will either identify $S^{5,\pm}$ immediately, or allow us to find these sets quickly by considering a small neighborhood of the curves $E^{5,\pm}$.

Note that for all the earlier rounds $r < r_{\max}$, the sets $S^{r,s}$ include $S^{r_{\max},s}$. Therefore, if we have the orientation s and the set $S^{r_{\max},s}$, we can shift all the faulty curves by two steps for every degree in $S^{r_{\max},s}$. If we have misidentified the orientation, this shift moves the faulty curves in the wrong direction, away from E_0. This trick is particularly useful for larger r as eventually many isogenies need to be applied in the shifts and we will have identified the orientation of enough primes so that the search space for `pubcrawl` becomes small enough to be faster.

Twisting in the Hashed Version. Precomputation extends to the hashed version from Sect. 7: we simply precompute $\mathcal{C}'$ which instead of E_t includes $H(E_t)$ for all E_t in the neighborhood of E_0. Again, this works directly for attacking a hashed version of CTIDH and the effective round-$r_{\max}$ curves in CSIDH. To use precomputation for different rounds, one can replace the starting curve E_{-B} that is fed to the target device by the shift given exactly by the primes in $S^{r_{\max},s}$ (or, adaptively, by the part of the secret key that is known). This has the same effect as above: shifting all the curves E_t with the same orientation *closer* towards E_0, hopefully so that the $H(E_t)$ are already in our database. If they are not then likely the opposite orientation appeared when we faulted the computation.

Summary. The benefit of using the twist with precomputation is largest for the hashed versions: we need a brute force search from E_0 in any case, and so we would use on average as many steps per round as the precomputation takes. For the non-hashed versions, the expensive precomputation competes with meet-in-the-middle attacks running in square root time. This means that in the hashed version we do not need to amortize the precomputation cost over many targets and have a clear tradeoff between memory and having to recompute the same neighborhood searches all over again and again.

9   Countermeasures

We present our countermeasures and estimate their costs. A comparison with countermeasures to other attacks is provided in the full version.

9.1   Protecting Square Checks Against Fault Attacks

The attack described in Sect. 3 can be applied to all implementations of CSIDH that use a call to IsSquare to determine the orientations of the involved point(s). The main weakness is that the output of IsSquare is always interpreted as $s = 1$ or $s = -1$, and there is no obvious way of reusing parts of the computation to verify that the output is indeed related to the x-coordinate of the respective point. For instance, faulting the computation of the Legendre-input $z = x^3 + Ax^2 + x$ results in a square check for a point unrelated to the actual x-coordinate in use, and yields a fault success probability of 50%.

Two possible countermeasures rely on redundant computation, namely, repeating the execution of IsSquare and computing with y-coordinates. Both of these countermeasures incur significant performance loss. Moreover, for repeated computation, an attacker may be able to skip these instructions entirely.

Using Pseudo y-Coordinates. We propose a more efficient countermeasure: compute *pseudo* y-coordinates after sampling points. We sample a random x-coordinate and set $z = x^3 + Ax^2 + x$. If z is a square in $\mathbb{F}_p$, we can compute the corresponding y-coordinate $\tilde{y} \in \mathbb{F}_p$ through the exponentiation $\tilde{y} = \sqrt{z} = z^{(p+1)/4}$, and hence $\tilde{y}^2 = z$. Conversely, if z is a non-square in $\mathbb{F}_p$, the same exponentiation outputs $\tilde{y} \in \mathbb{F}_p$ such that $\tilde{y}^2 = -z$. Thus, as an alternative to IsSquare, we can determine the orientation of the sampled point by computing $z = x^3 + Ax^2 + x$, and the pseudo y-coordinate $\tilde{y} = z^{(p+1)/4}$. If $\tilde{y}^2 = z$, the point has positive orientation, if $\tilde{y}^2 = -z$ it has negative orientation. If neither of these cases applies, i.e., $\tilde{y}^2 \neq \pm z$, a fault must have occurred during the exponentiation, and we reject the point.

This method may seem equivalent to computing the sign s using IsSquare as it does not verify that z has been computed correctly from x. But having an output $\tilde{y} \in \mathbb{F}_p$ instead of the IsSquare output -1 or 1 allows for a stronger verification step later. Algorithm 2 shows the addition of this countermeasure.

In order to verify the correctness of the countermeasure, we add a verification step. First, we recompute z via $z' = x^3 + Ax^2 + x$, and in case of a correct execution, we have $z = z'$. Thus, we have $s \cdot z' = \tilde{y}^2$, which we can use as verification of the correctness of the computations of s, z, z', and $\tilde{y}$. If this were implemented through a simple check, an attacker might be able to skip this check.

Algorithm 2. Evaluation of CSIDH group action with countermeasure

---

Input: $A \in \mathbb{F}_p$ and a list of integers $(e_1, \ldots, e_n)$.
Output: $B \in \mathbb{F}_p$ such that $\prod [l_i]^{e_i} * E_A = E_B$
1: **while** some $e_i \neq 0$ **do**
2:     Sample a random $x \in \mathbb{F}_p$, defining a point P.
3:     Set $z \leftarrow x^3 + Ax^2 + x$, $\tilde{y} \leftarrow z^{(p+1)/4}$.
4:     Set $s \leftarrow 1$ if $\tilde{y}^2 = z$, $s \leftarrow -1$ if $\tilde{y}^2 = -z$, $s \leftarrow 0$ otherwise.
5:     Let $S = \{i \mid e_i \neq 0, \text{sign}(e_i) = s\}$. **Restart** with new x if S is empty.
6:     Let $k \leftarrow \prod_{i \in S} \ell_i$ and compute $Q' = (X_{Q'} : Z_{Q'}) \leftarrow [\frac{p+1}{k}]P$.
7:     Compute $z' \leftarrow x^3 + Ax^2 + x$.
8:     Set $X_Q \leftarrow s \cdot z' \cdot X_{Q'}$, $Z_Q \leftarrow \tilde{y}^2 \cdot Z_{Q'}$.
9:     Set $Q = (X_Q : Z_Q)$.
10:    **for each** $i \in S$ **do**
11:        Set $k \leftarrow k/\ell_i$ and compute $R \leftarrow [k]Q$. If $R = \infty$, **skip** this i.
12:        Compute $\phi : E_A \rightarrow E_B$ with kernel $\langle R \rangle$.
13:        Set $A \leftarrow B$, $Q \leftarrow \phi(Q)$, and $e_i \leftarrow e_i - s$.
14: **return** A.

Hence, we perform the equality check through the multiplications $X_Q = s \cdot z' \cdot X_{Q'}$ and $Z_Q = \tilde{y}^2 \cdot Z_{Q'}$, and initialize $Q = (X_Q : Z_Q)$ only afterwards, in order to prevent an attacker from skipping Step 8. If $s \cdot z' = \tilde{y}^2$ holds as expected, this is merely a change of the projective representation of Q', and thus leaves the point and its order unchanged. However, if $s \cdot z' \neq \tilde{y}^2$, this changes the x-coordinate X_Q/Z_Q of Q to a random value corresponding to a point of different order. If Q does not have the required order the isogeny computation will produce random outputs in $\mathbb{F}_p$ that do not represent supersingular elliptic curves with overwhelming probability. We can either output this random $\mathbb{F}_p$-value, or detect it through a supersingularity check (see [4,15]) at the end of the algorithm and abort. The attacker gains no information in both cases. The supersingularity check can be replaced by a cheaper procedure [10]: Sampling a random point P and checking if $[p+1]P = \infty$ is cheaper and has a very low probability of false positives, which is negligible in this case.

There are several ways in which an attacker may try to circumvent this countermeasure. A simple way to outmaneuver the verification is to perform the *same* fault in the computation of z and z', such that $z = z'$, but $z \neq x^3 + Ax^2 + x$. To mitigate this, we recommend computing z' using a different algorithm and a different sequence of operations, so that there are no simple faults that can be repeated in both computations of z and z' that result in $z = z'$. Faults in the computation of both z and z' then lead to random $\mathbb{F}_p$-values, where the probability of $z = z'$ is $1/p$.

The attacker may still fault the computation of s in Step 4 of Algorithm 2. However, this will now also flip the x-coordinate of Q to $-x$, which in general results in a point of random order, leading to invalid outputs. The only known exception is the curve $E_0: y^2 = x^3 + x$: In this case, flipping the x-coordinate corresponds to a distortion map taking Q to a point of the same order on the quadratic twist. Thus, for E_0, flipping the sign s additionally results in *actually* changing the orientation of Q, so these two errors effectively cancel each other in Algorithm 2 and the resulting curve is the correct output curve after all.

Protecting Elligator. Recall from Sect. 3 that two-point variants of CSIDH, including CTIDH, use the Elligator map for two points simultaneously, which requires an execution of IsSquare in order to correctly allocate the sampled points to P_+ and P_-.

We can adapt the pseudo y-coordinate technique from Sect. 9.1: we determine orientations and verify their correctness by applying this countermeasure for both P_+ and P_- separately. We dub this protected version of the Elligator sampling Elligreator. An additional benefit is that faulting the computations of the x-coordinates of the two points within Elligator (see [16, Algorithm 3]) is prevented by Elligreator.

In CTIDH, each round performs two Elligator samplings, and throws away one point respectively. Nevertheless, it is not known a priori which of the two points has the required orientation, so Elligreator needs to check *both* points anyway in order to find the point of correct orientation.

On the one hand, adding dummy computations, in this case sampling points but directly discarding some of them, might lead to different vulnerabilities such as safe-error attacks. On the other hand, sampling both points directly with Elligreator at the beginning of each round (at the cost of one additional isogeny evaluation) may lead to correlations between the sampled points, as argued in [3]. It is unclear which approach should be favored.

9.2 Implementation Costs

Implementing this countermeasure is straightforward. While IsSquare requires an exponentiation by $(p-1)/2$, our pseudo y-coordinate approach replaces this exponent by $(p+1)/4$, which leads to roughly the same cost. (Note that neither has particularly low Hamming weight.) Furthermore, we require a handful of extra operations for computing z', X_Q, and Z_Q in Steps 7 and 8 of Algorithm 2. For the computation of z' we used a different algorithm than is used for the computation of z, incurring a small additional cost. Therefore, using this countermeasure in a 1-point variant of CSIDH will essentially not be noticeable in terms of performance, since the extra operations are negligible in comparison to the overall cost of the CSIDH action.

In 2-point variants, we use Elligreator, which requires two exponentiations instead of one as Elligator does. Thus, the countermeasure is expected to add a more significant, yet relatively small overhead in 2-point variants as in CTIDH. CTIDH uses two calls to Elligreator per round, and both executions contain two pseudo-y checks respectively. We estimate the cost of our countermeasure in CTIDH-512. The software of [3] reports an exponentiation by $(p-1)/2$ to cost 602 multiplications (including squarings). Since CTIDH-512 requires roughly 20 rounds per run, we add two additional exponentiations by $(p+1)/4$ per round, and these have almost the same cost of 602 multiplications, the overhead is approximately $2 \cdot 20 \cdot 602 = 24080$ multiplications. Ignoring the negligible amount of further multiplications we introduce, this comes on top of a CTIDH-512 group action, which takes 438006 multiplications on average. Thus, we expect the total overhead of our countermeasure to be roughly 5.5% in CTIDH-512.

References

1. Adj, G., Chi-Domínguez, J., Rodríguez-Henríquez, F.: Karatsuba-based square-root Vélu's formulas applied to two isogeny-based protocols. J. Cryptogr. Eng. (2022). https://doi.org/10.1007/s13389-022-00293-y, https://ia.cr/2020/1109
2. Adj, G., Chi-Domínguez, J.J., Mateu, V., Rodríguez-Henríquez, F.: Faulty isogenies: a new kind of leakage. Cryptology ePrint Archive, Paper 2022/153 (2022). https://ia.cr/2022/153
3. Banegas, G., et al.: CTIDH: faster constant-time CSIDH. IACR Trans. Cryptogr. Hardw. Embed. Syst. **2021**(4), 351–387 (2021). https://doi.org/10.46586/tches. v2021.i4.351-387
4. Banegas, G., Gilchrist, V., Smith, B.: Efficient supersingularity testing over GF(p) and CSIDH key validation. Math. Cryptol. **2**(1), 21–35 (2022). https://journals. flvc.org/mathcryptology/article/view/132125
5. Bernstein, D.J., De Feo, L., Leroux, A., Smith, B.: Faster computation of isogenies of large prime degree. In: Galbraith, S.D. (ed.) Proceedings of the Fourteenth Algorithmic Number Theory Symposium, pp. 39–55. Mathematics Sciences Publishers (2020). https://doi.org/10.2140/obs.2020.4.39, https://ia.cr/2020/341
6. Bernstein, D.J., Hamburg, M., Krasnova, A., Lange, T.: Elligator: elliptic-curve points indistinguishable from uniform random strings. In: Sadeghi, A., Gligor, V.D., Yung, M. (eds.) 2013 ACM SIGSAC Conference on Computer and Communications Security, CCS 2013, Berlin, Germany, 4–8 November 2013, pp. 967–980. ACM (2013). https://doi.org/10.1145/2508859.2516734, https://ia.cr/2013/325
7. Bernstein, D.J., Lange, T., Martindale, C., Panny, L.: Quantum circuits for the CSIDH: optimizing quantum evaluation of isogenies. In: Ishai, Y., Rijmen, V. (eds.) EUROCRYPT 2019. LNCS, vol. 11477, pp. 409–441. Springer, Cham (2019). https://doi.org/10.1007/978-3-030-17656-3_15, https://ia.cr/2018/1059
8. Beullens, W., Kleinjung, T., Vercauteren, F.: CSI-FiSh: efficient isogeny based signatures through class group computations. In: Galbraith, S.D., Moriai, S. (eds.) Advances in Cryptology - ASIACRYPT 2019–25th International Conference on the Theory and Application of Cryptology and Information Security, Kobe, Japan, 8–12 December 2019, Proceedings, Part I. Lecture Notes in Computer Science, vol. 11921, pp. 227–247. Springer, Heidelberg (2019). https://doi.org/10.1007/978-3-030-34578-5_9, https://ia.cr/2019/498
9. Bonnetain, X., Schrottenloher, A.: Quantum security analysis of CSIDH. In: Canteaut and Ishai [13], pp. 493–522. https://doi.org/10.1007/978-3-030-45724-2_17, https://ia.cr/2018/537
10. Campos, F., Kannwischer, M.J., Meyer, M., Onuki, H., Stöttinger, M.: Trouble at the CSIDH: protecting CSIDH with dummy-operations against fault injection attacks. In: 17th Workshop on Fault Detection and Tolerance in Cryptography, FDTC 2020, Milan, Italy, 13 September 2020, pp. 57–65. IEEE (2020). https:// doi.org/10.1109/FDTC51366.2020.00015, https://ia.cr/2020/1005

11. Campos, F., Krämer, J., Müller, M.: Safe-error attacks on SIKE and CSIDH. In: Batina, L., Picek, S., Mondal, M. (eds.) SPACE 2021. LNCS, vol. 13162, pp. 104–125. Springer, Cham (2022). https://doi.org/10.1007/978-3-030-95085-9_6

12. Campos, F., Meyer, M., Reijnders, K., Stöttinger, M.: Patient zero and patient six: zero-value and correlation attacks on CSIDH and SIKE. Cryptology ePrint Archive, Paper 2022/904 (2022). https://ia.cr/2022/904

13. Canteaut, A., Ishai, Y. (eds.): LNCS, vol. 12106. Springer, Cham (2020). https://doi.org/10.1007/978-3-030-45724-2

14. Castryck, W., Decru, T.: An efficient key recovery attack on SIDH (preliminary version). Cryptology ePrint Archive, Paper 2022/975 (2022). https://ia.cr/2022/975

15. Castryck, W., Lange, T., Martindale, C., Panny, L., Renes, J.: CSIDH: an efficient post-quantum commutative group action. In: Peyrin, T., Galbraith, S.D. (eds.) Advances in Cryptology - ASIACRYPT 2018-24th International Conference on the Theory and Application of Cryptology and Information Security, Brisbane, QLD, Australia, 2–6 December 2018, Proceedings, Part III. Lecture Notes in Computer Science, vol. 11274, pp. 395–427. Springer, Heidelberg (2018). https://doi.org/10.1007/978-3-030-03332-3_15, https://ia.cr/2018/383

16. Cervantes-Vázquez, D., Chenu, M., Chi-Domínguez, J.-J., De Feo, L., Rodríguez-Henríquez, F., Smith, B.: Stronger and faster side-channel protections for CSIDH. In: Schwabe, P., Thériault, N. (eds.) LATINCRYPT 2019. LNCS, vol. 11774, pp. 173–193. Springer, Cham (2019). https://doi.org/10.1007/978-3-030-30530-7_9, https://ia.cr/2019/837

17. Chávez-Saab, J., Chi-Domínguez, J., Jaques, S., Rodríguez-Henríquez, F.: The SQALE of CSIDH: sublinear Vélu quantum-resistant isogeny action with low exponents. J. Cryptogr. Eng. **12**(3), 349–368 (2022). https://doi.org/10.1007/s13389-021-00271-w, https://ia.cr/2020/1520

18. Chi-Domínguez, J., Rodríguez-Henríquez, F.: Optimal strategies for CSIDH. Adv. Math. Commun. **16**(2), 383–411 (2022). https://doi.org/10.3934/amc.2020116, https://ia.cr/2020/417

19. Childs, A.M., Jao, D., Soukharev, V.: Constructing elliptic curve isogenies in quantum subexponential time. J. Math. Cryptol. **8**(1), 1–29 (2014). https://doi.org/10.1515/jmc-2012-0016, https://arxiv.org/abs/1012.4019

20. Conway, J.H., Sloane, N.J.A.: Low dimensional lattices vii: coordination sequences. Proc. Roy. Soc. Lond. Ser. A **453**, 2369–2389 (1997)

21. Couveignes, J.M.: Hard Homogeneous Spaces. IACR Cryptology ePrint Archive 2006/291 (2006). https://ia.cr/2006/291

22. De Feo, L., Galbraith, S.D.: SeaSign: compact isogeny signatures from class group actions. In: Ishai, Y., Rijmen, V. (eds.) EUROCRYPT 2019. LNCS, vol. 11478, pp. 759–789. Springer, Cham (2019). https://doi.org/10.1007/978-3-030-17659-4_26, https://ia.cr/2018/824

23. De Feo, L., Meyer, M.: Threshold Schemes from Isogeny Assumptions. In: Kiayias, A., Kohlweiss, M., Wallden, P., Zikas, V. (eds.) PKC 2020. LNCS, vol. 12111, pp. 187–212. Springer, Cham (2020). https://doi.org/10.1007/978-3-030-45388-6_7, https://ia.cr/2019/1288

24. Delfs, C., Galbraith, S.D.: Computing isogenies between supersingular elliptic curves over $\mathbb{F}_p$. Des. Codes Cryptogr. **78**(2), 425–440 (2016). https://doi.org/10.1007/s10623-014-0010-1, https://arxiv.org/abs/1310.7789

25. Gélin, A., Wesolowski, B.: Loop-abort faults on supersingular isogeny cryptosystems. In: Lange, T., Takagi, T. (eds.) PQCrypto 2017. LNCS, vol. 10346,

pp. 93–106. Springer, Cham (2017). https://doi.org/10.1007/978-3-319-59879-6_6, https://ia.cr/2017/374

26. Hutchinson, A., LeGrow, J., Koziel, B., Azarderakhsh, R.: Further optimizations of CSIDH: a systematic approach to efficient strategies, permutations, and bound vectors. In: Conti, M., Zhou, J., Casalicchio, E., Spognardi, A. (eds.) ACNS 2020. LNCS, vol. 12146, pp. 481–501. Springer, Cham (2020). https://doi.org/10.1007/978-3-030-57808-4_24, https://ia.cr/2019/1121

27. Lai, Y.-F., Galbraith, S.D., Delpech de Saint Guilhem, C.: Compact, efficient and UC-secure isogeny-based oblivious transfer. In: Canteaut, A., Standaert, F.-X. (eds.) EUROCRYPT 2021. LNCS, vol. 12696, pp. 213–241. Springer, Cham (2021). https://doi.org/10.1007/978-3-030-77870-5_8, https://ia.cr/2020/1012

28. LeGrow, J.T., Hutchinson, A.: (Short Paper) Analysis of a strong fault attack on static/ephemeral CSIDH. In: Nakanishi, T., Nojima, R. (eds.) IWSEC 2021. LNCS, vol. 12835, pp. 216–226. Springer, Cham (2021). https://doi.org/10.1007/978-3-030-85987-9_12, https://ia.cr/2020/1006

29. Maino, L., Martindale, C.: An attack on SIDH with arbitrary starting curve. Cryptology ePrint Archive, Paper 2022/1026 (2022). https://ia.cr/2022/1026

30. Meyer, M., Campos, F., Reith, S.: On lions and elligators: an efficient constant-time implementation of CSIDH. In: Ding, J., Steinwandt, R. (eds.) PQCrypto 2019. LNCS, vol. 11505, pp. 307–325. Springer, Cham (2019). https://doi.org/10.1007/978-3-030-25510-7_17, https://ia.cr/2018/1198

31. Meyer, Michael, Reith, Steffen: A faster way to the CSIDH. In: Chakraborty, Debrup, Iwata, Tetsu (eds.) INDOCRYPT 2018. LNCS, vol. 11356, pp. 137–152. Springer, Cham (2018). https://doi.org/10.1007/978-3-030-05378-9_8, https://ia.cr/2018/782

32. Onuki, H., Aikawa, Y., Yamazaki, T., Takagi, T.: (Short paper) A faster constant-time algorithm of CSIDH keeping two points. In: Attrapadung, N., Yagi, T. (eds.) Advances in Information and Computer Security - 14th International Workshop on Security, IWSEC 2019, Tokyo, Japan, August 28–30, 2019, Proceedings. Lecture Notes in Computer Science, vol. 11689, pp. 23–33. Springer (2019). https://doi.org/10.1007/978-3-030-26834-3_2, https://ia.cr/2019/353

33. Peikert, C.: He gives C-sieves on the CSIDH. In: Canteaut and Ishai [13], pp. 463–492. https://doi.org/10.1007/978-3-030-45724-2_16, https://ia.cr/2019/725

34. Robert, D.: Breaking SIDH in polynomial time. Cryptology ePrint Archive, Paper 2022/1038 (2022). https://ia.cr/2022/1038

35. Rostovtsev, A., Stolbunov, A.: Public-key cryptosystem based on isogenies. IACR Cryptology ePrint Archive 2006/145 (2006), https://ia.cr/2006/145

36. Tasso, É., De Feo, L., El Mrabet, N., Pontié, S.: Resistance of isogeny-based cryptographic implementations to a fault attack. In: Bhasin, S., De Santis, F. (eds.) COSADE 2021. LNCS, vol. 12910, pp. 255–276. Springer, Cham (2021). https://doi.org/10.1007/978-3-030-89915-8_12, https://ia.cr/2021/850

37. Ti, Y.B.: Fault attack on supersingular isogeny cryptosystems. In: Lange, T., Takagi, T. (eds.) PQCrypto 2017. LNCS, vol. 10346, pp. 107–122. Springer, Cham (2017). https://doi.org/10.1007/978-3-319-59879-6_7, https://ia.cr/2017/379

38. Udovenko, A., Vitto, G.: Breaking the $IKEp182 challenge. IACR Cryptology ePrint Archive 2021/1421 (2021). https://ia.cr/2021/1421

39. Vélu, J.: Isogénies entre courbes elliptiques. Comptes Rendus de l'Académie des Sciences de Paris **273**, 238–241 (1971). https://gallica.bnf.fr/ark:/12148/cb34416987n/date

On the Hardness of the Finite Field Isomorphism Problem

Dipayan Das[✉][iD] and Antoine Joux[iD]

CISPA Helmholtz Center for Information Security, Saarbrücken, Germany
dipayan.das@cispa.de, joux@cispa.de

Abstract. The finite field isomorphism (FFI) problem was introduced in PKC'18, as an alternative to average-case lattice problems (like LWE, SIS, or NTRU). As an application, the same paper used the FFI problem to construct a fully homomorphic encryption scheme. In this work, we prove that the decision variant of the FFI problem can be solved in polynomial time for any field characteristics $q = \Omega(\beta n^2)$, where q, β, n parametrize the FFI problem. Then we use our result from the FFI distinguisher to propose polynomial-time attacks on the semantic security of the fully homomorphic encryption scheme. Furthermore, for completeness, we also study the search variant of the FFI problem and show how to state it as a q-ary lattice problem, which was previously unknown. As a result, we can solve the search problem for some previously intractable parameters using a simple lattice reduction approach.

1 Introduction

The Finite Field Isomorphism (FFI) problem has been introduced in [4] as a new hard problem to study post-quantum cryptography. Informally, it states the following.

For a hidden element x (with sparse minimal polynomial) in the finite field $\mathbb{F}_{q^n}$, if small β-bounded linear combinations of powers of x are given, in terms of powers of a uniform generator y, it is hard to recover x.

The decisional version of the problem states the following.

Given the y-basis representation of finite field elements, it is hard to decide whether they are picked from the FFI distribution or the uniform distribution, with a non-negligible advantage over random guessing.

The FFI assumption is based on the fact that the basis transformation converts "good" representations to "bad" representations of $\mathbb{F}_{q^n}$. At a high level of abstraction, the heuristics of the FFI problem is comparable to many lattice problems, which involve recovering a "good" secret basis from a "bad" public basis (example [7,8]). However, despite this high-level similarity, the details are quite different and a dedicated security analysis is required.

In the papers [4,9], the authors thoroughly analyzed the generic hardness of the FFI problem. From their analysis, the best known attack for the decisional problem has $2^{O(n)}$ time complexity, whereas the best known attack for the search

C. Hazay and M. Stam (Eds.): EUROCRYPT 2023, LNCS 14008, pp. 343–359, 2023.
https://doi.org/10.1007/978-3-031-30589-4_12

problem has $O(n!)$ time complexity. Based on their analysis, they proceed to propose a fully homomorphic encryption scheme [4] and a signature scheme [9] as applications of the FFI problem.

1.1 Our Contribution

This paper re-examines the hardness of the FFI problem in both its decisional and computational versions. We use basic finite field theory to study the hardness of the FFI problem.

In Sect. 4, we prove the values of the trace of the hidden polynomial x-basis are bounded in absolute value by n. The proof is based on combinatorial techniques. Thus, by a linearity argument, the trace of FFI samples can be bounded in absolute value by βn^2. This observation provides a polynomial-time distinguisher to solve the decisional version of the FFI problem for any field with characteristic $q \geq 4\beta n^2$.

In Sect. 5, we complement the attack on the decisional FFI problem by breaking the semantic security of the fully homomorphic encryption scheme from [4]. First, we give a simple semantic attack by using the bound on the trace of the ciphertext. Then we provide an additional semantic attack that offers a slight improvement on the lower bound on the field characteristic q, using the distribution of the trace of the inverse of the finite field elements. Both attacks apply to the proposed parameter of the scheme.

In Sect. 6, we exploit the notion of dual basis of a finite field basis to solve the computational FFI problem. By definition, the trace of any basis element with respect to its dual basis can be expressed as the Kronecker delta function. Consequently, the traces of FFI samples with respect to the dual x-basis are bounded by β. Using this observation, we recover the dual x-basis from the given FFI samples A_i. This is done by reducing an adequate lattice built from traces of well-chosen finite field elements. We also show that a partial recovery of the dual x-basis can be leverage into a full cryptanalysis with good probability.

Finally, we provide some experiments on lattice reduction to find the shortest vectors in this lattice.

2 Preliminaries

2.1 Notations

The parameter q denotes a (moderately large) prime integer throughout the paper.

The finite field with q elements is denoted by $\mathbb{F}_q$. All vectors are in columns and are denoted with bold letters. We identify polynomials and vectors as being the same data type using the coefficient embedding. For any vector v, we write $\|v\|$ for the ℓ_∞ norm of v, and $\|v\|_2$ for the ℓ_2 norm of v. Representatives of the elements of $\mathbb{F}_q$ are centered around zero, i.e. chosen in the interval $\left[-\frac{q-1}{2}, \frac{q-1}{2}\right]$. The rationale for using this representation is that it is much better adapted to the goal of obtaining vectors with short norms.

2.2   Reminders from Finite Field Theory

For every prime q and every positive integer n, there exists a unique finite field with q^n elements. It is denoted by $\mathbb{F}_{q^n}$. The prime q and the integer n are respectively called the characteristic and degree of the finite field.

Let $f(x)$ and $F(y)$ be two irreducible polynomials of degree n over $\mathbb{F}_q$. We can construct two isomorphic representations of the finite field $\mathbb{F}_{q^n}$ as $\mathbb{X} := \mathbb{F}_q[x]/(f(x))$ and $\mathbb{Y} := \mathbb{F}_q[y]/(F(y))$. Every element of $\mathbb{F}_{q^n}$ can be uniquely represented by a polynomial in x with coefficients in $\mathbb{F}_q$ and degree less than n. Similarly, there is a representation in terms of y. In other words, the set

$$\{1, x, \dots, x^{n-1}\}$$

is a basis of $\mathbb{F}_{q^n}$, viewed as a vector space over $\mathbb{F}_q$. This basis is called the x-polynomial-basis or x-basis for short. For ease of reading, we denote finite field elements known in the x-basis by small letters and elements known in the y-basis by capital letters.

To explicit an isomorphism between these two representations of $\mathbb{F}_{q^n}$, it suffices to know the representation in the x-basis of a root of $F(y)$ or conversely the y-representation of a root of $f(x)$. Note that each of the two polynomials has n distinct roots, which are images of each other by the q-th power Frobenius map.

For every element $\alpha \in \mathbb{F}_{q^n}$, its conjugates are obtained by repeatedly applying the Frobenius map, i.e. they are $\alpha, \alpha^q, \dots, \alpha^{q^{(n-1)}}$. They are distinct if and only if the minimal polynomial of α has degree n. The trace of an element in $\mathbb{F}_{q^n}$ is defined as the sum of all its conjugates:

$$\mathsf{Tr}(\alpha) := \alpha + \alpha^q + \dots + \alpha^{q^{(n-1)}} \in \mathbb{F}_q$$

The trace function is linear, i.e.

$$\mathsf{Tr}(\alpha + c\beta) = \mathsf{Tr}(\alpha) + c\mathsf{Tr}(\beta)$$

for any $\alpha, \beta \in \mathbb{F}_{q^n}$ and $c \in \mathbb{F}_q$.

Moreover, for every linear map L from $\mathbb{F}_{q^n}$ to $\mathbb{F}_q$, there exists a unique element β in $\mathbb{F}_{q^n}$ such that:

$$\forall \alpha \in \mathbb{F}_{q^n} : L(\alpha) = \mathsf{Tr}(\beta \cdot \alpha).$$

We denote this linear function by L_β.

To every basis $\omega_1, \omega_2, \dots, \omega_n$ of $\mathbb{F}_{q^n}$ we associate a dual basis[1] $\widehat{\omega}_1, \widehat{\omega}_2, \dots, \widehat{\omega}_n \in \mathbb{F}_{q^n}$, defined as the unique one which satisfies:

$$\mathsf{Tr}(\omega_i \widehat{\omega}_j) = \delta_i^j$$

where δ_i^j is the *Kronecker delta* function. From this definition, it is clear that the bidual of a basis, i.e. the dual of its dual, is the basis itself.

---

[1] Note that this notion of the dual basis of a finite field does not correspond to the idea of the dual basis of a lattice. This paper only uses the term dual basis to refer to the former notion.

2.3   Lattice Reduction

Given a (full rank) matrix $B \in \mathbb{Z}^{d \times d}$, the lattice $\mathcal{L}$ generated by the basis B is the set $\mathcal{L}(B) := \{Bz : z \in \mathbb{Z}^d\}$, d is the lattice dimension. A lattice is called q-ary if it contains $q\mathbb{Z}^d$ as a sublattice. The volume of a lattice $\mathcal{L}(B)$ is defined as $\mathbf{Vol}(\mathcal{L}) := |\det(B)|$. Any lattice of dimension $d \geq 2$ has infinitely many bases that generate the same lattice, and any two bases B, B' are related by a unimodular matrix U such that $B = B'U$. Note that the unimodular matrix stands on the right because we use the convention of having vectors in columns. The volume of a lattice is independent of the choice of lattice basis.

For a random lattice $\mathcal{L}$, the Gaussian heuristic estimates the Euclidean norm of the shortest non-zero vector in the lattice, which is approximately $\sqrt{\frac{d}{2\pi e}}\mathbf{Vol}(\mathcal{L})^{1/d}$ [5].

For any basis B, we write B^* to represent the Gram-Schmidt orthogonalization (GSO) of B, where the i-th vector of B^* is given by $b_i^* := \pi_i(b_i)$. Here, the notation π_i denotes the projection of a vector orthogonally to the vector subspace spanned by $b_1, b_2, \ldots, b_{i-1}$.

A central problem in the algorithmics of lattices is to find shortest non-zero vectors (SVP) from a lattice basis B. This can be a handy tool in cryptanalysis. The most widely used lattice reduction algorithm is LLL [11] which is polynomial-time but only yields an approximation of SVP within an exponential factor. Since this can be insufficient for cryptanalysis, it is standard practice to use slower algorithms that produce better approximations.

For our needs, we use the implementation of the blockwise Korkine-Zolotarev (BKZ) algorithm provided with the fplll software [13].

2.4   Semantic Attack of an Encryption Scheme

An encryption scheme (KeyGen, Enc, Dec) **that only encrypts bits** (i.e. with message space $\{0, 1\}$) has (t, δ) attack against the semantic security if there exists an adversary $\mathcal{A}$ winning the following game against a challenger $\mathcal{C}$.

- $\mathcal{C}$ samples $m \hookleftarrow \{0, 1\}$, (pk, sk) $\hookleftarrow$ KeyGen(1^λ).

- $\mathcal{C}$ gives pk, $c := $ Enc(pk, m) to $\mathcal{A}$.

- $\mathcal{A}$ outputs $m' \in \{0, 1\}$.

$\mathcal{A}$ wins the game if $\mathcal{A}$ has running time t and advantage δ, where the advantage is defined by

$$|\Pr[m' = m] - \Pr[m' \neq m]|$$

3   Finite Field Isomorphism Problem

This section formally describes the FFI problem in both its computational and decisional forms.

Let $\mathbb{X}, \mathbb{Y}$ be two representations of the finite field $\mathbb{F}_{q^n}$ as before. In the rest of the paper, we assume $n \geq 50$ to be out of range of easy exhaustive search attacks. The defining polynomial of $\mathbb{X}$ is sampled uniformly from the set of all sparse irreducible polynomials of the form $x^n + g(x)$ with $\deg g(x) \leq \lfloor n/2 \rfloor$ and $\|g(x)\| \leq 1$, i.e. $g(x)$ has ternary coefficients. The defining polynomial of $\mathbb{Y}$ is sampled uniformly from the set of arbitrary monic irreducible polynomials. Let $\phi(y)$ be an isomorphism from $\mathbb{X}$ to $\mathbb{Y}$. Note that there is an efficient algorithm to compute an isomorphism between the two representations [2].[2] Let χ_β be a distribution over $\mathbb{X}$ that samples polynomials $a_i(x)$ with $\|a_i(x)\| \leq \beta$. Let $A_i(y)$ be the corresponding image of $a_i(x)$ under the isomorphism ϕ.

Definition 1 (Computational Finite Field Isomorphism Problem (CFFI$_{q,k,n,\beta}$)). *Given $\mathbb{Y}$ by $F(y)$ and k samples $A_1(y), \ldots, A_k(y)$ recover $f(x)$.*

Definition 2 (Decisional Finite Field Isomorphism Problem (DFFI$_{q,k,n,\beta}$)). *Given $\mathbb{Y}$ by $F(y)$ and k samples $B_1(y), B_2(y), \ldots, B_k(y)$ that are either sampled from FFI distribution (having pre-images bounded by β) or sampled uniformly at random in $\mathbb{Y}$, DFFI$_{q,k,n,\beta}$ problem is to distinguish, with some non-negligible advantage, the correct source distribution of the samples $B_i(y)$.*

Note that the sparsity constraint on the defining polynomial of $\mathbb{X}$ is not directly included in the definition of the FFI problem given in [4,9]. However, the noise growth analysis of [4, Appendix B] explicitly rewrites[3] $f(x)$ as $x^n + f'(x)$ and proceeds to bound the noise-growth during multiplication in $\mathbb{X}$ under the assumption that the degree d of f' satisfies $d < n/2$. For clarity, we instead chose to directly include this low-degree constraint as part of the definition.

3.1 Previous Attacks

In this section, we briefly describe all the attacks that have been considered for both decisional and computational FFI problem in [4,9].

Decisional Finite Field Isomorphism Problem

Lattice Attack

The decisional FFI problem could be solved by predicting if there is any good representation of the given samples, which is very unlikely for uniform samples. To achieve this, the authors of [4,9] suggested lattice reduction on the q-ary lattice

$$\mathcal{L}_{A,q} := \{a_i \in \mathbb{Z}^k : A\Psi_i = a_i \bmod q \text{ for some } \Psi_i \in \mathbb{Z}^n\}$$

---

[2] In practice, SAGEMATH provides the `FiniteFieldHomomorphism_generic(Hom(.))` function available under `sage.rings.finite_rings.hom_finite_field` package for this task.

[3] In the rewriting, $f'(x)$ does not denote the derivative of f but an auxiliary polynomial. In our definition, we use the notation $g(x)$ to avoid any possible confusion with the derivative.

with each row of the matrix A generated from the given y-basis representations of samples. For FFI samples, there are unusually short vectors in the
lattice that corresponds to the x-basis (or small linear combination of x-basis)
representation. For uniform samples, it is highly unlikely to have such short
vectors in the lattice.

Computational Finite Field Isomorphism Problem

Hybrid Attack
The authors of [4,9] propose to find the shortest vectors in the lattice $\mathcal{L}_{A,q}$,
in the hope that they correspond to the coefficients of some powers of x.
Since the shortest vectors appear in a somewhat random-looking order, the
authors suggested adding a combinatorial algorithm to resolve the ordering
issue and recover the x-basis representations of the FFI samples. This gives
an attack to the computational FFI problem. They estimate the cost of the
combinatorial step to be $O(n!)$, thus infeasible. One might argue that this
could possibly be improved by some form of meet-in-the-middle to $O(\sqrt{n!})$.
We do not examine this direction since we show in Sect. 6 that we can get rid
of the combinatorial step altogether.

Non-linear Attack
The non-linear attack involves solving the non-linear system of equations
to recover the hidden isomorphism ϕ using Gröbner basis computation. An
adversary can solve for $2n - 2$ unknowns of $(\phi, (a_i(x))$ from the equation
$\phi(a_i(x)) = A_i(y)$. Solving such an equation is believed to be hard.

4 Proposed Attack on the Decisional FFI Problem

This section proposes a new polynomial-time attack on the DFFI problem. We
show that when a sample $A_i(y)$ comes from the FFI distribution, the underlying
trace of $A_i(y)$ is bounded by a small multiple of n^2. We use this fact to mount
a distinguishing attack on the DFFI problem.

Lemma 1. *Let $f(x) := x^n + \sigma_1 x^{n-1} + \sigma_2 x^{n-2} + \cdots + \sigma_n$ be the defining polynomial of* $\mathbb{X}$, *where $\sigma_i \in \{-1, 0, 1\}$ for $\lceil n/2 \rceil \le i \le n$, 0 otherwise[4].*
  Then

$$
\mathsf{Tr}(x^i) \equiv \begin{cases} n \pmod{q}, & \text{if } i = 0 \\ 0 \pmod{q}, & \text{if } 1 \le i \le \lceil n/2 \rceil - 1 \\ \pm i \pmod{q}, & \text{if } \sigma_i \ne 0 \text{ and } \lceil n/2 \rceil \le i \le n - 1 \\ 0 \pmod{q}, & \text{if } \sigma_i = 0 \text{ and } \lceil n/2 \rceil \le i \le n - 1 \end{cases}
$$

---

[4] Indeed, the smallest i with $\sigma_i \ne 0$ satisfies $i + \deg g = n$. Since $\deg g = \lfloor n/2 \rfloor$ this
corresponds to $i = \lceil n/2 \rceil$.

Proof. The definition of trace function gives $\mathsf{Tr}(\boldsymbol{x}^i) = n$ when $i = 0$. To prove the Lemma for $i > 0$, let us first recall the Girard-Newton identities relating the sum of powers to symmetric polynomials. Given n arbitrary numbers $w_0, \ldots, w_{n-1}$ in an arbitrary ring, define their symmetric polynomials as usual by: $\sigma_1 = \sum_{i=0}^{n-1} w_i$, $\sigma_2 = \sum_{0 \leq i < j < n} w_i w_j$, $\sigma_3 = \sum_{0 \leq i < j < k < n} w_i w_j w_k$, $\ldots$, $\sigma_n = \prod_{i=0}^{n-1} w_i$. Then, for any $1 \leq \bar{d} < n$, we have:

$$\sum_{i=0}^{n-1} w_i^d = (-1)^d \sum_{\substack{r_1 + 2r_2 + \cdots + dr_d = d \\ r_i \in \mathbb{N}}} d \cdot \frac{(r_1 + r_2 + \cdots + r_d - 1)!}{r_1! r_2! \ldots r_d!} \prod_{j=1}^{d} (-\sigma_j)^{r_j} \quad (1)$$

Note that the coefficients in this equation, while written as fractions for notational purposes are, in fact, integers. As a consequence, the identity holds in every ring. In particular, when working modulo q as we are. However, to avoid any potential division by 0, the coefficients should first be computed as exact integers and only reduced modulo q afterwards.

The set of all the roots of $\boldsymbol{f}(\boldsymbol{x})$ are given by

$$\{\alpha_0 := \boldsymbol{x}, \alpha_1 := \boldsymbol{x}^q, \ldots, \alpha_{n-1} := \boldsymbol{x}^{q^{n-1}}\}$$

Let now the $(\sigma_j)_{1 \leq j \leq n}$ denote the n symmetric polynomials in these roots. We know that we can write

$$\boldsymbol{f}(\boldsymbol{x}) = \boldsymbol{x}^n - \sigma_1 \boldsymbol{x}^{n-1} + \sigma_2 \boldsymbol{x}^{n-2} - \ldots (-1)^n \sigma_n.$$

Thus, $\sigma_1 = \sigma_2 = \cdots = \sigma_{\lceil n/2 \rceil - 1} = 0$.

Since, $\mathsf{Tr}(\boldsymbol{x}^i)$ is a sum of i-th power of α_js, we can use the above identity to express it in terms of the σ_js. Depending on the value of i, two cases arise:

Case 1 $(1 \leq i \leq \lceil n/2 \rceil - 1)$. Since all contributions include a σ_j for $j \leq i$ with value zero, there is no non-zero term in the sum of the right-hand side of Eq. (1), we have

$$\mathsf{Tr}(\boldsymbol{x}^i) = 0$$

Case 2 $(\lceil n/2 \rceil \leq i \leq n - 1)$. Again, since $\sigma_j = 0$ for $1 \leq j \leq \lceil n/2 \rceil - 1$, there is exactly one element in the set $\{(r_1, r_2, \ldots, r_i) : \sum_{l=1}^{i} l r_l = i\}$ that contributes in the sum of the right-hand side of Eq. (1), namely $(r_1 = 0, r_2 = 0, \ldots, r_i = 1)$. Indeed, the sum of two contributions above $\lceil n/2 \rceil$ is always greater than i. This gives

$$\mathsf{Tr}(\boldsymbol{x}^i) = \begin{cases} \pm i \text{ for non-zero } \sigma_i, \\ 0 \text{ for } \sigma_i = 0 \end{cases}$$

Lemma 2. *Let $A_i(\boldsymbol{y})$ be an $\mathsf{FFI}_{q,k,n,\beta}$ sample. Then $|\mathsf{Tr}(A_i(\boldsymbol{y}))| \leq 0.39\beta n^2$.*

Proof. Let $\boldsymbol{a}_i(\boldsymbol{x})$ be the representation of $A_i(\boldsymbol{y})$ in the $\boldsymbol{x}$-basis. Since the trace of a finite field element is invariant to the basis representation, both $\boldsymbol{a}_i(\boldsymbol{x})$ and

$A_i(y)$ must have the same trace. So in order to bound the trace of $A_i(y)$, it is sufficient to bound the trace of $a_i(x)$. By the linearity of the trace and by the previous Lemma, we have

$$|\text{Tr}(A_i(y))| \leq \beta \sum_{j=\lceil n/2 \rceil}^{n} j$$

$$\leq 0.39\beta n^2 \text{ for } n \geq 50.$$

Theorem 1. *Let $q \geq 1.56\beta n^2$, then there exists a polynomial-time algorithm with advantage $1 - \Omega(1/2^k)$ to distinguish the $\text{DFFI}_{q,k,n,\beta}$ problem.*

Proof. Let $B_1(y), B_2(y), \ldots, B_k(y)$ be the given k samples to distinguish between FFI distribution and uniform distribution. The distinguisher finds the correct distribution of the samples by computing the trace of the samples. In a finite field, the trace function is uniformly distributed. Thus for a uniform sample $B_i(y)$, $\text{Tr}(B_i(y))$ is uniformly distributed over $\mathbb{F}_q$. For an FFI sample $B_i(y)$, by the previous Lemma, $|\text{Tr}(B_i(y))| \leq 0.39\beta n^2$. Combining the number of samples and condition on q, the distinguisher outputs 1 when the samples come from FFI distribution with probability 1, and outputs 1 when the samples come from uniform distribution with probability at most $1/2^k$.

It is only left to show that the distinguisher is indeed polynomial-time. The running time of the attack is dominated by trace computation of finite field elements. Since the trace of a finite field element can be computed efficiently in time $n^{1+o(1)} \log^{2+o(1)} q$ using iterated Frobenius [10,12], this is polynomial-time.

5   Proposed Semantic Attack on the Fully Homomorphic Encryption Scheme

In this section, we propose a polynomial-time attack on the semantic security of the fully homomorphic encryption scheme $\mathcal{E} := (\text{KeyGen}, \text{Enc}, \text{Dec}, \text{Eval})$ from [4]. The working principle of the scheme is given below.

- $\text{KeyGen}(1^\lambda)$: Generate the FFI parameters $\Xi := (n, q, \beta)$ as a function of λ, and two representations of the finite field by sampling $f(x), F(y)$ with an isomorphism ϕ like before. Choose two integers (S, s) satisfying $\binom{S}{s} \geq 2^\lambda$. Sample S many $c_i(x)$ from the distribution χ_β and construct $C_i(y) := p\phi(c_i(x))$ for fixed constant $p := 2$. In the rest of the section, we assume p is equal to 2 as in [4].

  The secret key is $\text{sk} := (\Xi, \phi, f(x))$.

  The public key is $\text{pk} := (\Xi, C_1(y), C_2(y), \ldots, C_S(y), F(y), s, p)$.

- $\text{Enc}(m, \text{pk})$: The encryption of a message $m \in \{0, 1\}$ is

$$C := \sum_{i \in [s]} C_i(y) + m$$

  for uniformly random s samples $C_i(y)$.

- Dec(C, sk) : The decryption recovers m by computing

$$m' := p \sum_{i \in [s]} c_i(x) + m \bmod p$$

using the inverse of the secret isomorphism ϕ.

- Eval($C, C^{(1)}, C^{(2)}, \ldots, C^{(l)}$) : The homomorphic evaluation of ciphertexts of a circuit C with gates $(+, \times)$ are done using homomorphic addition and multiplication (with noise management) on $C^{(i)}$s. It is shown that for $q = 2^{n^\epsilon}$ with $\epsilon \in (0,1)$, the above encryption scheme $\mathcal{E}$ is fully homomorphic using circular security and bootstrapping techniques (Theorem 3 of [4]).

The result of Theorem 1 invalidates the semantic security of the fully homomorphic encryption scheme $\mathcal{E}$ (Theorem 1 of [4]). The next Theorem gives a polynomial-time algorithm to break the semantic security of $\mathcal{E}$.[5]

Theorem 2. *Let $q > 0.44s\beta^2 n^5 + 0.78\beta n^2$, then there exists a deterministic polynomial time attack against the semantic security of the fully homomorphic encryption scheme $\mathcal{E}$ defined as above.*

Proof. Let the challenger $\mathcal{C}$ give the public key pk $\hookleftarrow$ KeyGen(1^λ) and an encryption C of a message $m \hookleftarrow \{0,1\}$ to the adversary $\mathcal{A}$. Then

$$C = p \sum_{i \in [s]} \phi(c_i(x)) + m \tag{2}$$

$\mathcal{A}$ wins the semantic game by the following analysis.

We consider the following two cases for the choice of n.

1. When $p = 2$ is not a divisor of n.

Note that $\sum_{i \in [s]} \phi(c_i(x))$ is an $\mathsf{FFI}_{q,1,n,s\beta}$ sample. So the trace of the summation is small. By the linearity of trace and from Eq. (2),

$$\mathsf{Tr}(C) = p\mathsf{Tr}(\sum_{i \in [s]} \phi(c_i(x))) + \mathsf{Tr}(m)$$

Since $\mathsf{Tr}(1) = n$ and p is not a divisor of n, $\mathcal{A}$ breaks the semantic game for the encryption C as below.

$$\mathsf{Tr}(C) \bmod p = 0, \text{ Return } C \text{ is an encryption of } 0$$
$$= n \bmod p = 1, \text{ Return } C \text{ is an encryption of } 1$$

---

[5] Note that the attack does not use the homomorphic property of the encryption scheme, just regular encryptions of bits.

2. When $p = 2$ is a divisor of n.

In this case, $\text{Tr}(C) \bmod p$ will be 0 for both encryptions of 0 and 1. To get a semantic attack, $\mathcal{A}$ needs to do a small modification here.

$\mathcal{A}$ picks an $\text{FFI}_{q,1,n,\beta}$ sample C^* (with pre-image c^*) such that $|\text{Tr}(C^*)|$ is not a multiple of p. As any field isomorphism map elements in $\mathbb{F}_q$ to itself, this happens with probability $1/p$ for each $p^{-1}C_i(y)$, where $C_i(y)$ for $1 \leq i \leq S$ are the public key samples, so $\mathcal{A}$ almost surely knows such a sample. Multiplying both sides of Eq. (2) by C^*, we get

$$CC^* = p \, \phi \left(\left(\sum_{i \in [s]} c_i(x) \right) c^* \right) + mC^* \qquad (3)$$

By the ternary sparse choice of the minimal polynomial of x, the noise of polynomial multiplication in $\mathbb{X}$ grows at most by a factor of n^3 (Eq. 5 of [4]). So, the product of $\phi(\sum_{i \in [s]} c_i(x))$ and $\phi(c^*)$ is an $\text{FFI}_{q,1,n,0.28s\beta^2 n^3}$ sample, and hence, by Lemma 2, the absolute value of the trace is bounded by $0.11s\beta^2 n^5$. By the linearity of trace, we have from Eq. (3)

$$\text{Tr}(CC^*) = p \, \text{Tr} \left(\phi \left(\left(\sum_{i \in [s]} c_i(x) \right) c^* \right) \right) + m\text{Tr}(C^*)$$

Since $\text{Tr}(C^*)$ is not a multiple of p, $\mathcal{A}$ breaks the semantic game for the encryption C as below.

$$\text{Tr}(CC^*) \bmod p = 0, \quad \text{Return } C \text{ is an encryption of } 0$$
$$= 1, \quad \text{Return } C \text{ is an encryption of } 1$$

If the q is chosen as in the Theorem to avoid modular reduction, $\mathcal{A}$ returns $m' \in \{0, 1\}$ with advantage $\delta = 1$. The adversary $\mathcal{A}$ runs in polynomial time by the argument given in Theorem 1.

Below we also provide an alternative approach to break the semantic security of the homomorphic encryption scheme that gives a tighter lower bound on q. The main ingredient of this approach is to break the semantic security of the scheme by the distribution of the trace of the inverse of p.

Theorem 3. *Let $q > 0.44s\beta^2 n^5 + 0.39\beta n^2$, then there exists a deterministic polynomial time attack against the semantic security of the fully homomorphic encryption scheme $\mathcal{E}$ defined as above.*

Proof. Let the challenger $\mathcal{C}$ give the public key $\text{pk} \hookleftarrow \text{KeyGen}(1^\lambda)$ and an encryption C of a message $m \hookleftarrow \{0, 1\}$ to the adversary $\mathcal{A}$. $\mathcal{A}$ computes

$$Cp^{-1} = \sum_{i \in [s]} \phi(c_i(x)) + mp^{-1} \qquad (4)$$

$\mathcal{A}$ wins the semantic game by the following analysis.

We consider the following two cases for the choice of n.

1. When $p = 2$ is not a divisor of n.

   Since any field isomorphism ϕ map elements in $\mathbb{F}_q$ to itself, $\sum_{i\in[s]} \phi(c_i(x))$ is an $\mathsf{FFI}_{q,1,n,s\beta}$ sample. As a consequence, from Eq. (4), Cp^{-1} is an $\mathsf{FFI}_{q,1,n,s\beta}$ sample for an encryption of 0, thus have small trace. But for an encryption of 1, by linearity, trace of Cp^{-1} is dominated by the trace of $1/p$. We now claim the absolute value of $\mathsf{Tr}(1/p)$ is close to the boundary point $(q - 1)/2$ of the $\mathbb{F}_q$ representation, thus trace of Cp^{-1} is large.

   By the definition of trace,

   $$\mathsf{Tr}(1/p) = n/p \bmod q$$
   $$= n(q+1)/p \bmod q \qquad (5)$$
   $$= (n+q)/p \bmod q \text{ since } p \text{ is not a divisor of } n$$

   To see the validity of the last line of the above equation, writing $n = pi + 1$, we have

   $$n(q+1)/p \bmod q = (pi+1)(q+1)/p \bmod q$$
   $$= i + (q+1)/p \bmod q$$
   $$= (n+q)/p \bmod q$$

   Finally, we have $|\mathsf{Tr}(1/p)| = (q-n)/p$ in the representation of $\mathbb{F}_q$. Thus $\mathcal{A}$ breaks the semantic game for the encryption C from Lemma 2 as below.

   $$|\mathsf{Tr}(Cp^{-1})| \leq 0.39s\beta n^2, \text{ Return } C \text{ is an encryption of } 0$$
   $$\text{Otherwise, Return } C \text{ is an encryption of } 1$$

2. When $p = 2$ is a divisor of n.

   In this case, from the first line of Eq. (5), the trace of Cp^{-1} will be small for both encryptions of 0 and 1. To get a semantic attack, $\mathcal{A}$ needs to do a small modification here as in the previous Theorem.

   $\mathcal{A}$ picks an $\mathsf{FFI}_{q,1,n,\beta}$ sample C^* such that $|\mathsf{Tr}(C^*)|$ is not a multiple of p. Multiplying both sides of Eq. (4) by C^*, we get

   $$C^* C p^{-1} = C^* \sum_{i\in[s]} \phi(c_i(x)) + m C^* p^{-1} \qquad (6)$$

   Again, by the choice of the minimal polynomial of x, the noise of polynomial multiplication in $\mathbb{X}$ grows at most by a factor of n^3 (Eq. 5 of [4]). For an encryption of 0, since C^* and Cp^{-1} are $\mathsf{FFI}_{q,1,n,\beta}$ and $\mathsf{FFI}_{q,1,n,s\beta}$ samples, respectively, C^*Cp^{-1} is an $\mathsf{FFI}_{q,1,n,0.28s\beta^2 n^3}$ sample. Thus the trace of the product C^*Cp^{-1} is still small. But for an encryption of 1, by Eq. (6), the trace of C^*Cp^{-1} is dominated by the trace of second summand C^*p^{-1}. Since the absolute value of $\mathsf{Tr}(C^*p^{-1})$ is close to the boundary point $(q-1)/2$, the trace of CC^*p^{-1} is large in this case.

   To see the above claim, let $\mathsf{Tr}(C^*) = t$, where $|t| \leq 0.39\beta n^2$ and $|t|$ is not a divisor of p. By the linearity of trace and from the previous analysis,

   $$\mathsf{Tr}(C^*p^{-1}) = 1/p\,\mathsf{Tr}(C^*)$$
   $$= (t+q)/p \bmod q$$

Finally, we have $|\mathsf{Tr}(\boldsymbol{C}^* p^{-1})| = (q - t)/p$ in the representation of $\mathbb{F}_q$. By the Eq. 5 of [4] and Lemma 2, $\mathcal{A}$ breaks the semantic game for the encryption C as below.

$$|\mathsf{Tr}(\boldsymbol{C}\boldsymbol{C}^* p^{-1})| \leq 0.11\, s\beta^2 n^5, \text{ Return } C \text{ is an encryption of } 0$$
$$\text{Otherwise, Return } C \text{ is an encryption of } 1$$

The condition on q in the Theorem ensures $\mathcal{A}$ returns $m' \in \{0, 1\}$ with advantage $\delta = 1$. The adversary $\mathcal{A}$ runs in polynomial time by the argument given in Theorem 1.

Effect of the Attacks on the Recommended Parameters: The recommended parameters of [4] (Appendix C, Table 1) for the different level of the (somewhat) fully homomorphic encryption scheme falls within the range of our semantic attacks, except the first level (which has a small q and tolerates very little noise).

6 Proposed Attack on the Computational **FFI** Problem

In this section, we first express the CFFI problem as a lattice problem. The improvement over the previous attack is that here we can avoid the additional combinatorial step (see Subsect. 3.1) to solve the CFFI problem. Furthermore, we show how to solve the problem from a small number of shortest lattice vectors. We rely on the dual of the $\boldsymbol{x}$-basis recovered from the shortest vectors of a q-ary lattice generated from FFI samples.

We first define a q-ary lattice for the given FFI samples.

Definition 3 (Trace lattice). *Let $\boldsymbol{A}_1(\boldsymbol{y}), \boldsymbol{A}_2(\boldsymbol{y}), \ldots, \boldsymbol{A}_k(\boldsymbol{y})$ be the* FFI$_{q,k,n,\beta}$ *samples for $k > n$. We define a generating matrix $\boldsymbol{T}$ of order $k \times n$ with coefficients in $\mathbb{F}_q$ and ij-th element defined by $\mathsf{Tr}(\boldsymbol{A}_i(\boldsymbol{y})\boldsymbol{y}^{j-1})$. The q-ary trace lattice is defined as*

$$\mathcal{L}_{T,q} = \{\boldsymbol{\alpha} \in \mathbb{Z}^k : \boldsymbol{T}\boldsymbol{C} = \boldsymbol{\alpha} \bmod q \text{ for some } \boldsymbol{C} \in \mathbb{Z}^n\}$$

By linearity of trace, the lattice $\mathcal{L}_{T,q}$ contains traces of every finite field element (represented in $\boldsymbol{y}$-basis) with respect to FFI samples $\boldsymbol{A}_i(\boldsymbol{y})$.

Lemma 3. *The q-ary lattice $\mathcal{L}_{T,q}$ has the following properties.*

1. *Its dimension is k.*
2. *Its volume is q^{k-n}.*
3. *It contains n linearly independent vectors $\boldsymbol{\alpha}_i$ such that $\|\boldsymbol{\alpha}_i\| \leq \beta$ for $1 \leq i \leq n$.*

Proof. The first two properties of the Lemma are true for any q-ary lattice of this form. We prove the third point.

For $1 \leq i \leq n$, let C_{i-1} be the dual x-basis in the finite field $\mathbb{F}_{q^n}$. Then, recalling the definition of the dual basis,

$$\mathsf{Tr}(x^{j-1}C_{i-1}) = \delta_{i-1}^{j-1}$$

It follows from the linearity of the trace function that any FFI sample A_j has

$$|\mathsf{Tr}(A_j C_{i-1})| \leq \beta$$

Thus the trace lattice contains n linearly independent vectors α_i (corresponding to each C_{i-1}), such that

$$\|\alpha_i\| = \|\mathsf{Tr}(A_j C_{i-1})\| \leq \beta, \ 1 \leq j \leq k$$

This concludes the proof.

Since β is reasonably smaller than $(q-1)/2$, the n vectors α_i are very likely the shortest vectors in the lattice $\mathcal{L}_{T,q}$. The lattice vectors α_i have Euclidean norm bounded above by $\beta\sqrt{k}$, which is much smaller than that of the Gaussian heuristics.

Note that the shortest vectors of the trace lattice correspond to the dual x-basis, given in the y-basis representation. By recomputing the dual of this dual basis, we obtain the x-basis in the form of its y-basis representation, thus recovering the hidden isomorphism ϕ. This approach eliminate the $O(n!)$ cost associated with the combinatorial step of the previously mentioned hybrid attack.

In practice, it is generally too costly to find the n shortest vectors in a lattice and thus get the complete C_i-basis by just using lattice reduction. When applying BKZ reductions with high block size using aborting techniques [3], which is often seen in cryptanalysis, it is more reasonable to only expect getting a small number of shortest lattice vectors. To account for this, we give a probabilistic approach to recover ϕ from a subset of two or more elements of the C_i-basis. This is based on the observation that each lattice vector associated with the C_i-basis has the same expected norm and is all as likely to appear as a shortest vector while reducing the lattice $\mathcal{L}_{T,q}$. We can thus assume that we are getting random elements from the C_i-basis.

Lemma 4. *In a set of $m > 1$ elements, sampled uniformly at random from the set of all the dual x-basis, there is, with probability $\Omega(m^2/n)$, at least a pair of dual x-basis elements (C_i, C_j) whose quotient gives ϕ.*

Proof. For the uniform choice of the dual x-basis elements, there exists at least a pair of consecutive elements (C_i, C_j) with probability $O(m^2/n)$, i.e. a pair with $j = i + 1$.

In the good case for us, this pair with $j = i + 1$ is going to satisfy $C_i = xC_j$ which allows us to compute x as C_i/C_j.

To see why, recall that by definition, C_i is the unique element such that, for all $0 \leq k < n$, $\mathsf{Tr}(x^k C_i) = \delta_i^k$. Similarly, C_j satisfies $\mathsf{Tr}(x^k C_j) = \delta_j^k$.

Rewriting $\mathsf{Tr}(x^{k-1}(xC_j))$ for $\mathsf{Tr}(x^k C_j)$, we can check that xC_j already satisfy all necessary conditions needed for C_i, except the final one with $k = n$.

However, we now prove that even this final equation is often satisfied. When, it is, we indeed have $C_i = xC_j$. We can compute the missing condition as follows:

$$\mathsf{Tr}(x^{n-1}(xC_j)) = \mathsf{Tr}(x^n C_j) = \mathsf{Tr}(-g(x)C_j),$$

the last equality holds because $x^n = -g(x) \pmod{f(x)}$. Since g has degree $< n$, $\mathsf{Tr}(-g(x)C_j)$ is simply the coefficient of x^j in $-g$. When g is chosen as in Sect. 3, as a uniform ternary polynomial of degree $\leq \lfloor n/2 \rfloor$, this coefficient is always zero when $j > \lfloor n/2 \rfloor$ and it is zero with probability at least $1/3$ otherwise.

6.1   Lattice Reduction on Trace Lattice

In this section, we discuss the experimental results of lattice reduction to find the shortest non-zero vectors in the trace lattice. The parameter $(n, q) = (256, 32771)$ appeared in the level 1 fully homomorphic encryption scheme of [4]. We consider (n, q) close to it for our experiments.

The sample size k, which is the lattice dimension, is the parameter that dominates the running time of lattice reduction. If k is too small, for instance, too close to n, the lattice reduction technique could not extract any meaningful vectors. If k is too large, then the running time of the lattice reduction algorithm is too slow. In our experiments, we choose $k = 2n$.

For small n, it is convenient to recover the shortest vectors with a small block size BKZ algorithm, as expected[6]. But as n increases, the larger block size makes the attack inadequate. To circumvent this, we reduce the lattice dimension by applying a pre-processing lattice reduction step with a smaller block size, whose cost is negligible in the context of the attack.

The choice of the parameters (n, q) in our experiments allow to find "somewhat" short vectors in the trace lattice during the pre-processing step. These short vectors do not correspond to the dual x-basis, as expected, but have meaningful properties.

Let $\bar{C}_i$ be the recovered finite field basis corresponding to the short lattice vectors. Heuristically, the $\bar{C}_i$-basis act as a *pseudo* dual x-basis in $\mathbb{F}_{q^n}$, i.e.

$$|\mathsf{Tr}(\bar{C}_i x^j)| \lesssim \beta$$

As a result, for any FFI sample A_j

$$|\mathsf{Tr}(\bar{C}_i A_j)| \lesssim n\beta^2 \tag{7}$$

The recovered $\bar{C}_i$-basis contains information about x. To exploit this additional information of x, we generate a new integer trace lattice $\mathcal{L}_{\bar{T}} \subset \mathbb{Z}^k$ of dimension

---

[6] For example, we recover the complete dual x-basis for the parameter $(n = 100, q = 10007)$ using BKZ block size 5.

Table 1. Experimental results

n	q	Pre-Processing	$\bar{C}_i$-basis	Final	Status
200	32771	BKZ 12	✓	BKZ 60	Solved
240	32771	BKZ 20	✓	–	Unsolved
256	32771	BKZ 21	✓	–	Unsolved

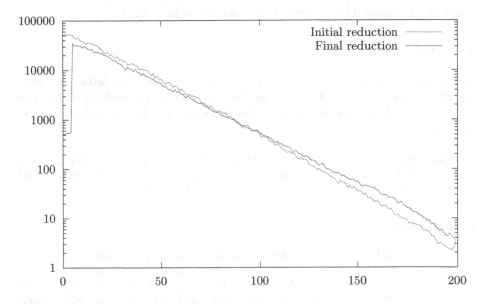

Fig. 1. Gram-Schmidt norms in log scale

n from the lattice basis $\bar{T}$ computed using the $\bar{C}_i$-basis (instead of y-basis in Definition 3).[7] The observation from Eq. (7) ensures the basis vectors are unusually small in a (relatively) low dimensional lattice, which allows using stronger lattice reduction algorithms effectively to recover the shortest vectors. The details of our experiments are given in Table 1.

In general, the running time of a BKZ lattice reduction algorithm is exponential on the blocksize. The authors of [3] successfully perform high blocksize BKZ reductions (with extreme pruning originated in [6]) on different lattices for a small number of rounds under the heuristics that most of the progress of BKZ algorithm is made in the early rounds. In the experiments, we also use a similar approach.

We apply a high block size BKZ algorithm (with extreme pruning) on the lattice basis $\bar{T}$, aborting regularly to check if some shortest lattice vectors are achieved, continuing otherwise. For $(n = 200, q = 32771)$, we could able to find five

---

[7] It is to be noted that we can always generate arbitrary many samples by doing simple arithmetic from the given FFI samples.

shortest vectors within 7 days of running BKZ 60 (aborting regularly) in an Intel Xeon CPU E5-2683 v4 @ 2.10 GHz with 1200 MHz MHz processor. The Gram-Schmidt norms of the reduced bases are given in Fig. 1. For other parameters, we couldn't find the shortest vectors running the (high block size) aborted BKZ reduction in the fplll software for a couple of months. The application of a more sophisticated lattice reduction approach is beyond the scope of the current paper. We, therefore, invite the cryptanalytic efforts on the other set of parameters, possibly using more advanced lattice reduction tools (example, G6K [1]).

7 Conclusion

In this paper, we illustrate on the FFI problem that having a lattice-reduction approach that fails to solve a problem does not necessarily imply that the problem itself is difficult. Indeed, lattice reduction might not be the optimal strategy to approach it.

Acknowledgements. We thank Anand Kumar Narayanan for helpful discussions on the finite field computation. This work has been supported by the European Union's H2020 Programme under grant agreement number ERC-669891.

References

1. Albrecht, M.R., Ducas, L., Herold, G., Kirshanova, E., Postlethwaite, E.W., Stevens, M.: The general Sieve Kernel and new records in lattice reduction. In: Ishai, Y., Rijmen, V. (eds.) Advances in Cryptology - EUROCRYPT 2019–38th Annual International Conference on the Theory and Applications of Cryptographic Techniques, Darmstadt, Germany, 19–23 May 2019, Proceedings, Part II. LNCS, vol. 11477, pp. 717–746. Springer, Cham (2019). https://doi.org/10.1007/978-3-030-17656-3_25
2. Bosma, W., Cannon, J.J., Steel, A.K.: Lattices of compatibly embedded finite fields. J. Symb. Comput. **24**(3/4), 351–369 (1997). https://doi.org/10.1006/jsco.1997.0138
3. Chen, Y., Nguyen, P.Q.: BKZ 2.0: better lattice security estimates. In: Lee, D.H., Wang, X. (eds.) Advances in Cryptology - ASIACRYPT 2011–17th International Conference on the Theory and Application of Cryptology and Information Security, Seoul, South Korea, 4–8 December 2011. Proceedings. LNCS, vol. 7073, pp. 1–20. Springer, Cham (2011). https://doi.org/10.1007/978-3-642-25385-0_1
4. Doröz, Y., et al.: Fully homomorphic encryption from the finite field isomorphism problem. In: Abdalla, M., Dahab, R. (eds.) Public-Key Cryptography - PKC 2018–21st IACR International Conference on Practice and Theory of Public-Key Cryptography, Rio de Janeiro, Brazil, 25–29 March 2018, Proceedings, Part I. LNCS, vol. 10769, pp. 125–155. Springer, Cham (2018). https://doi.org/10.1007/978-3-319-76578-5_5
5. Gama, N., Nguyen, P.Q.: Predicting lattice reduction. In: Smart, N.P. (ed.) Advances in Cryptology - EUROCRYPT 2008, 27th Annual International Conference on the Theory and Applications of Cryptographic Techniques, Istanbul, Turkey, 13–17 April 2008. Proceedings. LNCS, vol. 4965, pp. 31–51. Springer, Cham (2008). https://doi.org/10.1007/978-3-540-78967-3_3

6. Gama, N., Nguyen, P.Q., Regev, O.: Lattice enumeration using extreme pruning. In: Gilbert, H. (ed.) Advances in Cryptology - EUROCRYPT 2010, 29th Annual International Conference on the Theory and Applications of Cryptographic Techniques, Monaco/French Riviera, 30 May–3 June 2010. Proceedings. LNCS, vol. 6110, pp. 257–278. Springer, Cham (2010). https://doi.org/10.1007/978-3-642-13190-5_13
7. Goldreich, O., Goldwasser, S., Halevi, S.: Public-key cryptosystems from lattice reduction problems. In: Kaliski, B.S. (ed.) CRYPTO 1997. LNCS, vol. 1294, pp. 112–131. Springer, Cham (1997). https://doi.org/10.1007/BFb0052231
8. Hoffstein, J., Pipher, J., Silverman, J.H.: NTRU: a ring-based public key cryptosystem. In: Buhler, J.P. (ed.) ANTS 1998. LNCS, vol. 1423, pp. 267–288. Springer, Cham (1998). https://doi.org/10.1007/BFb0054868
9. Hoffstein, J., Silverman, J.H., Whyte, W., Zhang, Z.: A signature scheme from the finite field isomorphism problem. J. Math. Cryptol. 14(1), 39–54 (2020). https://doi.org/10.1515/jmc-2015-0050
10. Kedlaya, K.S., Umans, C.: Fast modular composition in any characteristic. In: 49th Annual IEEE Symposium on Foundations of Computer Science, FOCS 2008, 25–28 October 2008, Philadelphia, PA, USA, pp. 146–155. IEEE Computer Society (2008). https://doi.org/10.1109/FOCS.2008.13
11. Lenstra, A.K., Lenstra, H.W., Lovász, L.: Factoring polynomials with rational coefficients. Mathematische Annalen 261(ARTICLE), 515–534 (1982). https://doi.org/10.1007/BF01457454
12. Narayanan, A.K.: Fast computation of isomorphisms between finite fields using elliptic curves. In: Budaghyan, L., Rodríguez-Henríquez, F. (eds.) Arithmetic of Finite Fields - 7th International Workshop, WAIFI 2018, Bergen, Norway, 14–16 June 2018, Revised Selected Papers. LNCS, vol. 11321, pp. 74–91. Springer, Cham (2018). https://doi.org/10.1007/978-3-030-05153-2_4
13. The FPLLL Development Team: FPLLL, a lattice reduction library, Version: 5.4.2 (2022). https://github.com/fplll/fplll

New Time-Memory Trade-Offs for Subset Sum – Improving ISD in Theory and Practice

Andre Esser[1]($\boxtimes$)(iD) and Floyd Zweydinger[2]

[1] Technology Innovation Institute, Abu Dhabi, UAE
`andre.esser@tii.ae`
[2] Ruhr University Bochum, Bochum, Germany
`floyd.zweydinger@rub.de`

Abstract. We propose new time-memory trade-offs for the random subset sum problem defined on $(a_1, \ldots, a_n, t)$ over $\mathbb{Z}_{2^n}$. Our trade-offs yield significant running time improvements for every fixed memory limit $M \geq 2^{0.091n}$. Furthermore, we interpolate to the running times of the fastest known algorithms when memory is not limited. Technically, our design introduces a pruning strategy to the construction by Becker-Coron-Joux (BCJ) that allows for an exponentially small success probability. We compensate for this reduced probability by multiple randomized executions. Our main improvement stems from the clever reuse of parts of the computation in subsequent executions to reduce the time complexity per iteration.

As an application of our construction, we derive the first non-trivial time-memory trade-offs for Information Set Decoding (ISD) algorithms. Our new algorithms improve on previous (implicit) trade-offs asymptotically as well as practically. Moreover, our optimized implementation also improves on *running time*, due to reduced memory access costs. We demonstrate this by obtaining a new record computation in decoding quasi-cyclic codes (QC-3138). Using our newly obtained data points we then extrapolate the hardness of suggested parameter sets for the NIST PQC fourth round candidates McEliece, BIKE and HQC, lowering previous estimates by up to 6 bits and further increasing their reliability.

Keywords: representation technique · information set decoding ·
code-based cryptography · record computation · security estimates ·
NIST PQC

1 Introduction

For the ongoing NIST PQC standardisation process to be successful, large cryptanalytic efforts analysing the involved primitives are required. This includes theoretical studies of the asymptotically best attacks as well as experiments

Funded by BMBF under Industrial Blockchain-iBlockchain.

C. Hazay and M. Stam (Eds.): EUROCRYPT 2023, LNCS 14008, pp. 360–390, 2023.
https://doi.org/10.1007/978-3-031-30589-4_13

on a meaningful scale to safely extrapolate the hardness of cryptographic-sized instances. This methodology, combining theory and practice, is well established for conventional (number-theoretic) cryptographic systems and has found its adaptation to post-quantum secure schemes in recent years [1, 20, 25, 28, 41].

The best attacks on post-quantum schemes often suffer from high memory demands [6, 8, 9, 11, 18]. This either leads to an immense slowdown of the algorithm due to physical access times or, in the worst case, prevents its application entirely. In practice, both cases usually lead to a fallback to more memory-efficient but asymptotically inferior procedures. In these cases *time-memory trade-offs* for the best algorithms are needed which allow to tailor their memory consumption to any given amount while (only slightly) increasing their running time.

For post-quantum secure candidates, especially from code- and lattice-families, several of the known attacks are built on techniques initially introduced in the context of the (random) subset sum problem [8, 15, 32, 33]. This is because the underlying problems can usually be formulated as (vectorial) variants of subset sum, as it is the case for LPN/LWE, SIS or the syndrome decoding problem.

The subset sum problem defined on $(a_1, \ldots, a_n, t) \in \mathbb{Z}_{2^n}$ asks to find a subset $S \subseteq \{1, \ldots, n\}$ such that $\sum_{i \in S} a_i = t \mod 2^n$. For this problem time-memory trade-offs are actually well studied [4, 17, 19, 30]. However, the translations of those trade-offs to the aforementioned applications are mostly missing. The reason is the very diverse landscape of optimal trade-offs for subset sum, i.e., for different memory limitations there exist different optimal trade-offs. Furthermore, these trade-offs often do not match the design of the fastest subset sum algorithm used in the original application, which implies a separate translation effort for each algorithm.

In this work we construct new improved time-memory trade-offs for the subset sum problem. In contrast to previous works, our constructions follow the design by Becker-Coron-Joux (BCJ) [7], which is the basis for the fastest known algorithms. This allows for an easy adaptation of our trade-off to known applications of the BCJ algorithm. Further, our trade-offs reduce the running time of previous approaches for any fixed memory significantly. Only for very small available memory a trade-off based on a memory-less algorithm by Esser and May [27] becomes favourable. In total this reduces the trade-off landscape to only two algorithms.

We illustrate the potential of our trade-off by formalizing its application to the syndrome decoding problem, whose hardness forms the basis of code-based cryptography. Informally, the problem asks to find a low Hamming weight solution $\mathbf{e} \in \mathbb{F}_2^n$ to the matrix-vector equation $\mathbf{H} \mathbf{e} = \mathbf{s}$, where $\mathbf{H} \in \mathbb{F}_2^{r \times n}$ and $\mathbf{s} \in \mathbb{F}_2^r$. Moreover, it allows for a direct translation to a vectorial subset sum variant. Denote by $\mathbf{h}_i$ the columns of $\mathbf{H}$, then $(\mathbf{h}_1, \ldots, \mathbf{h}_n, \mathbf{s})$ defines a subset sum instance over $\mathbb{F}_2^n$, i.e., we are looking for a small subset of the $\mathbf{h}_i$ that sums to $\mathbf{s}$ over $\mathbb{F}_2^n$.

Information Set Decoding (ISD) algorithms now solve this problem by first applying a dimension reduction technique, which yields an instance with decreased n, r and smaller solution weight. Then an adaptation of the BCJ subset sum algorithm over $\mathbb{F}_2$ is applied to solve this reduced instance. Since the dimension reduction technique, in contrast to the subset sum algorithm, does not require any memory, every ISD algorithm inherits a naive time-memory trade-off. That is, reduce the instance size sufficiently so that the latter applied BCJ algorithm does not exceed the given memory. So far this simple interpolation to a full dimension-reduction based ISD algorithm proposed by Prange in 1962 [37], was the best known trade-off strategy. Our adaptation now yields the first time-memory trade-offs for advanced ISD algorithms improving their performance asymptotically as well as in practice.

1.1 Related Work

Subset Sum. Any subset sum instance can be solved in time and memory $\text{poly}(n) \cdot 2^{\frac{n}{2}}$ via a meet-in-the-middle algorithm [29]. Schroeppel and Shamir [38] then showed how to reduce the memory complexity to $\text{poly}(n) \cdot 2^{\frac{n}{4}}$. Later, their technique formed the basis for a series of advanced time-memory trade-offs [16,17,19].

The second key-ingredient for most subset sum trade-offs [7,16,27,30] is the so-called *representation technique* introduced by Howgrave-Graham and Joux (HGJ) in [30]. In their work they constructed the first algorithm breaking the $2^{\frac{n}{2}}$ time bound for *random* subset sum instances by achieving running time $2^{0.337n}$. In the cryptographic setting we usually encounter random instances, i.e., the vector $\mathbf{a} := (a_1, \ldots, a_n)$ is chosen uniformly at random and the target is set to $t = \langle \mathbf{a}, \mathbf{e} \rangle$ for a randomly chosen solution vector $\mathbf{e} \in \{0,1\}^n$ of Hamming weight $\frac{n}{2}$. Howgrave-Graham and Joux then split the solution $\mathbf{e} = \mathbf{e}_1 + \mathbf{e}_2$ with $\mathbf{e}_i \in \{0,1\}^n$ of weight $n/4$. Now, there exist multiple, namely $\binom{n/2}{n/4}$, such *representations* of $\mathbf{e}$, i.e., different combinations $\mathbf{e}_1, \mathbf{e}_2$ that sum to $\mathbf{e}$. The core observation is that it suffices to find a single of these representations to recover the solution. This representation is then constructed using a search-tree imposing restrictions on the exact form of the solution (similar to Wagners k-tree algorithm [43]) so that in expectation one representation satisfies all restrictions. Becker, Coron and Joux (BCJ) [7] improved the running time to $2^{0.291n}$ by choosing $\mathbf{e}_i \in \{-1,0,1\}^n$ to increase the amount of representations. Later Bonnetain, Bricout, Schrottenloher and Shen (BBSS) [12] further extended the digit set to $\mathbf{e}_i \in \{-1,0,1,2\}^n$ yielding a time and memory complexity of $2^{0.283n}$.

As mentioned, the time-memory trade-off landscape for subset sum is diverse [7,16,19,22,27,30]. Additionally, there are several techniques [17,19,36] improving the time-memory behaviour of the k-tree algorithm, which forms the foundation of the fastest known subset sum algorithms. However, since these techniques usually introduce asymmetries in the matching algorithm, which are inherently difficult to combine with the representation technique, they did not find a broad adaptation in trade-offs for the subset sum problem yet.

Information Set Decoding. ISD algorithms are the fastest known algorithms to solve general instances of the syndrome decoding problem and form the basis in assessing the security of code-based schemes. Introduced originally by Prange [37], the class was extended by several improved algorithms over the years [9,

21, 33, 34, 39]. All these works improve the running time by using more advanced subset sum techniques to solve the reduced instance after dimension reduction, which simultaneously increases the memory requirements. Surprisingly, there has been very limited work on time-memory trade-offs for ISD algorithms. Karpman and Lefevre [31] recently constructed advanced time-memory trade-offs for the special case of decoding ternary codes based on a subset sum trade-off strategy known as Dissection [19]. Further, a work by Wang et al. [44] extends an early ISD algorithm from Stern [39] by the Dissection approach. However, this trade-off is entirely outperformed by the previously mentioned implicit trade-offs of more advanced ISD procedures.

1.2   Our Contribution

Subset Sum. As a first contribution we give a generalized description of the BCJ algorithm, that combines previous interpretations from [12, 26]. This description then forms the basis for one of our main contributions which are new time-memory trade-offs for the random subset sum problem. Our constructions yield significantly improved running times for every fixed memory $M \geq 2^{0.091n}$, which corresponds to more than two-thirds of the meaningful memory parameters. Recall that $M = 2^{0.283n}$ memory is sufficient to instantiate the fastest known algorithm with time complexity $T = M$. In Fig. 1 we illustrate the performance of our new trade-offs in comparison to previous works. For example, if the memory is limited to $2^{0.17n}$, we improve the running time from $2^{0.51n}$ down to $2^{0.4n}$, corresponding to an improvement by a factor of $2^{0.11n}$.

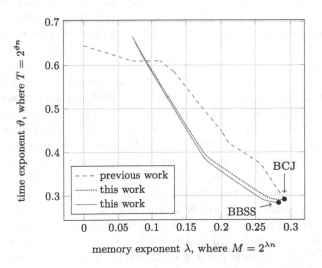

Fig. 1. Our new subset sum trade-offs in comparison to the previously best known time-memory trade-offs. The dashed line illustrates the minimum running time over the algorithms given in [7, 16, 19, 22, 27, 30]. The dotted and solid lines are obtained via our trade-off Algorithm 2 (see Sect. 4). For a memory larger than $2^{0.091n}$ ($2^{0.093n}$ resp.) our new trade-offs are superior to previous approaches.

From a technical side we allow the BCJ and BBSS construction to impose larger restrictions on the representation-space, yielding an exponentially small success probability. We then perform multiple randomized executions to compensate for the reduced probability. In this context we introduce a novel strategy of reusing lower levels of the search-tree in subsequent randomized executions to reduce the time complexity per iteration. Note that while Dinur in [17] also reuses the first level of his list construction in later repetitions, this is motivated by the use of different algorithms to construct the first and later levels. An asymmetry that makes the incorporation of representations even more difficult. In contrast our technique is symmetric, allows for easy incorporation of representations and, moreover, precisely exploits this embedding of representations when reusing lists in later stages. Also our technique extends well to every level of the construction.

Furthermore, to obtain instantiations for small memory parameters and to further reduce the time complexity, we then integrate the Dissection framework [19] in our construction, inspired by the combination of Wagners k-tree and Dissection in [17].

Information Set Decoding. We give the first non-trivial time-memory trade-offs for advanced ISD algorithms by combining our trade-offs with the ISD algorithms by May-Meuer-Thomae (MMT) [33] and Becker-Joux-May-Meurer (BJMM) [9]. Overall this yields asymptotic improved running times for every fixed memory. Moreover, for the MMT algorithm we are able to improve the memory, while maintaining its running time.

On the practical side, we extend the fastest implementation of the MMT/BJMM algorithm from [28] by our trade-off strategy observing memory and *time* improvements. Using our optimized implementation we obtain a new record computation in decoding quasi-cyclic codes (QC-3138) [3]. Further we re-break several old records, consuming less resources, i.e., time and memory. Hence, our trade-off is the first asymptotic improvement of the MMT algorithm that transfers to the implementation level. Eventually, using our newly obtained data-points in combination with an estimation script we extrapolate the hardness of suggested parameter sets for code-based NIST PQC fourth round candidates McEliece, BIKE and HQC, resulting in reduced security estimates by up to 6 bits compared to previous works. This improvement is even more significant considering that the bit-complexity estimates of code-based schemes have essentially been stable over the past decades, which is especially true for quasi-cyclic schemes. In this context, we provide estimates following two different methodologies, a conventional approximation of the bit complexity and an extrapolation method based on our practical experiments, recently suggested in [28]. Overall we find that both methods paint a comparable picture regarding the security claims of proposed parameter sets, invalidating claims that the latter method would lead to drastically decreased estimates [42].

All our used estimation and optimization scripts are available at https://
github.com/FloydZ/Improving-ISD-in-Theory-and-Practice.[1]   Our   adapted
implementation of the BJMM algorithm can be found at https://github.com/
FloydZ/Decoding.

Outline. In Sect. 2 we set up necessary notation and cover some basics on the
Dissection technique. Subsequently, in Sect. 3 we give the generalized description
of the BCJ algorithm, which is then used as a basis to build our new trade-offs in
Sect. 4. Eventually, in Sect. 5 we give the asymptotic and practical results of our
decoding application including security estimates for all NIST PQC candidates
of the ongoing forth round.

2 Preliminaries

All logarithms are base 2. We define $H(x) := -x \log(x) - (1 - x) \log(1 - x)$
to be the binary entropy function with H^{-1} its inverse on $[0, \frac{1}{2}]$. Extending
this definition, we also use the 2-way entropy function defined as $g(x, y) :=
-x \log(x) - y \log(y) - (1 - x - y) \log(1 - x - y)$. We simplify binomial and
multinomial coefficients via Sterling's formula as

$$\binom{n}{\alpha n} \simeq 2^{nH(\alpha)} \text{ and } \binom{n}{\alpha n, \beta n, \cdot} \simeq 2^{ng(\alpha,\beta)},$$

where $\binom{n}{\alpha n, \beta n, \cdot} := \binom{n}{\alpha n, \beta n, (1-\alpha-\beta)n}$. We use standard landau notation, with $\tilde{\mathcal{O}}$-
notation suppressing poly-logarithmic factors and write $A = \tilde{\mathcal{O}}(B)$ as $A \simeq B$.
Our asymptotic complexity statements are all to be understood up to poly-
logarithmic factors, even though we sometimes drop the $\tilde{\mathcal{O}}$ for convenience.

For a vector $\mathbf{x} \in \mathbb{F}_2^n$ we denote by $\text{wt}(\mathbf{x})$ its Hamming weight. Additionally
we denote by $\langle \mathbf{x}, \mathbf{y} \rangle$ the inner product of two vectors $\mathbf{x}, \mathbf{y}$.

All our algorithms target the random subset sum problem defined as follows,
even if we might omit the term *random* sometimes.

Definition 2.1 (Random Subset Sum Problem). *Let* $\mathbf{a} := (a_1, \ldots, a_n) \in
\mathbb{Z}_{2^n}^n$ *be drawn uniformly at random. For a random* $\mathbf{e} \in \{0,1\}^n$ *with* $\text{wt}(\mathbf{e}) = \frac{n}{2}$, *let*
$t := \langle \mathbf{a}, \mathbf{e} \rangle$. *The* random subset sum problem *is given* $(\mathbf{a}, t)$ *find any* $\mathbf{e}' \in \{0,1\}^n$
satisfying $\langle \mathbf{a}, \mathbf{e}' \rangle = t$. *We call any such* $\mathbf{e}'$ *a* solution *and* $(\mathbf{a}, t)$ *an* instance.

Our definition of the subset sum problem asks for a solution in $\{0, 1\}^n$. However, algorithms like the BCJ algorithm approach the problem in a divide-and-
conquer manner, which requires solving sub-instances with solutions in a different domain D. These sub-instances are usually solved via a meet-in-the-middle
strategy, which we later exchange by a more memory efficient strategy known as
Dissection.

---

[1] Our numerical optimization scripts are based on a code by Bonnetain et al. [12]
accessible at https://github.com/xbonnetain/optimization-subset-sum.

Schroeppel-Shamir and Dissection. A standard meet-in-the-middle solves a subset sum instance with solution in a set D in time and memory $|D|^{\frac{1}{2}}$ [29]. Therefore it first splits $D = D_1 \times D_2$, with $|D_i| = |D|^{\frac{1}{2}}$, enumerates all possible elements of D_1 and D_2 separately in lists L_1 and L_2 and then searches for a solution in D by combining elements from L_1 and L_2. The algorithm by Schroeppel and Shamir [38] now achieves the same time complexity of $|D|^{\frac{1}{2}}$ while improving the memory complexity to $|D|^{\frac{1}{4}}$. It works similarly by first splitting $D = D_1 \times D_2 \times D_3 \times D_4$ with $|D_i| = |D|^{\frac{1}{4}}$ and then enumerating all elements of D_i in lists L_i. Next an artificial constraint is introduced restricting the search to solutions which lie in a specific subset $(D_{12} \times D_{34}) \subseteq D$. This constraint is used to combine elements from L_1 and L_2 to obtain only elements from D_{12} in a new list L_{12} and analogously elements from D_{34} in a new list L_{34} by combining L_3 and L_4. From there the two lists L_{12} and L_{34} are combined as in the usual meet-in-the-middle case to search for a solution in D. As a priori it is not known in which subset the solution is located the algorithm partitions D in multiple subsets and re-applies the procedure for each of them. The Dissection framework introduced in [19] offers instantiations with less memory in form of a continues time-memory trade-off starting from the Schroeppel-Shamir algorithm. Besides the Schroeppel-Shamir algorithm our constructions make use of another instantiation of this framework, a so-called 7-Dissection. A 7-Dissection runs in time $|D|^{4/7}$ and uses memory $|D|^{1/7}$. Moreover, with more memory its time complexity can be gradually decreased until it reaches the complexity of the Schroeppel-Shamir algorithm. Technically a 7-Dissection works similar to the Schroeppel-Shamir technique by initially splitting $D = D_1 \times \ldots \times D_7$ and creating seven corresponding lists. Then multiple times artificial constraints are introduced to combine the lists most effectively, while, eventually, the algorithms is iterated for each possible choice of the constraints.

We summarize the time and memory complexity of the 7-Dissection in the following lemma. For more details on the dissection framework the reader is referred to [19].

Lemma 2.1 (7-Dissection, [19]). *Let $\frac{1}{7} \leq \lambda \leq \frac{1}{4}$. The 7-Dissection algorithm finds all solutions $\mathbf{e} \in D$ to a random subset sum instance in expected time $|D|^{\frac{2(1-\lambda)}{3}}$ and expected memory $|D|^{\lambda}$.*

3   The Generalized BCJ Algorithm

In this section we give a general description of the BCJ Algorithm [7] for solving the random subset sum problem. This description forms the basis for our new trade-offs presented in the following section. We advise the reader to follow Fig. 2. In our exposition we assume a certain familiarity of the reader with the representation technique, otherwise we refer to [7,30] for an introduction.

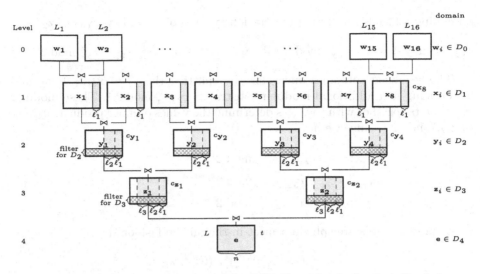

Fig. 2. Generalized tree construction of the BCJ Algorithm in depth 4. Shaded areas on the right of a list L indicate that for all elements $\mathbf{v} \in L$ the inner product $\langle \mathbf{a}, \mathbf{v} \rangle$ matches a predefined value $c_\mathbf{v}$ (resp. t) on those bits.

Basic Idea. To construct a solution $\mathbf{e}$ of the subset sum problem the BCJ algorithm splits $\mathbf{e}$ in the sum of two addends, i.e.,

$$\mathbf{e} = \mathbf{z}_1 + \mathbf{z}_2 .$$

Here the $\mathbf{z}_i$ are chosen from a set, such that there exist multiple different *representations* of the solution, i.e., different tuples that sum to $\mathbf{e}$. The goal is then to examine a respective fraction of the space of the $\mathbf{z}_1, \mathbf{z}_2$ to find one of these representations.

From $\langle \mathbf{a}, \mathbf{e} \rangle = \langle \mathbf{a}, \mathbf{z}_1 + \mathbf{z}_2 \rangle = t \mod 2^n$ we have by linearity

$$\langle \mathbf{a}, \mathbf{z}_1 \rangle = t - \langle \mathbf{a}, \mathbf{z}_2 \rangle \mod 2^n. \tag{1}$$

Note that the value of $\langle \mathbf{a}, \mathbf{z}_1 \rangle$ is not known. However, by considering only those $\mathbf{z}_1$ which fulfill $\langle \mathbf{a}, \mathbf{z}_1 \rangle = c_{\mathbf{z}_1} \mod 2^\ell$ for some fixed integer $c_{\mathbf{z}_1}$ we are able to impose a constraint on the search space. Here $\ell := \ell_1 + \ell_2 + \ell_3$ is an optimization parameter of the algorithm, with the ℓ_i's being positive integers. Moreover, since each representation of $\mathbf{e}$ fulfills Eq. (1) the value of $c_{\mathbf{z}_2} := \langle \mathbf{a}, \mathbf{z}_2 \rangle = t - c_{\mathbf{z}_1}$ mod 2^ℓ is fully determined once $c_{\mathbf{z}_1}$ is fixed.

The construction of the $\mathbf{z}_1$ and $\mathbf{z}_2$ then works recursively. Therefore, they are split again in the sum of two addends

$$\mathbf{z}_1 = \mathbf{y}_1 + \mathbf{y}_2 \text{ and } \mathbf{z}_2 = \mathbf{y}_3 + \mathbf{y}_4 ,$$

and we fix the values $\langle \mathbf{a}, \mathbf{y}_1 \rangle$ and $\langle \mathbf{a}, \mathbf{y}_3 \rangle$ to some constraints $c_{\mathbf{y}_1}$ mod $2^{\ell_1+\ell_2}$ and $c_{\mathbf{y}_3}$ mod $2^{\ell_1+\ell_2}$. Note that this again determines the inner product of the remaining addends for any representation $(\mathbf{y_1}, \mathbf{y_2})$ of $\mathbf{z_1}$ and $(\mathbf{y_3}, \mathbf{y_4})$ of $\mathbf{z_2}$ as

$$c_{\mathbf{y_2}} := \langle \mathbf{a}, \mathbf{y_2} \rangle = c_{\mathbf{z_1}} - c_{\mathbf{y_1}} \bmod 2^{\ell_1 + \ell_2} \text{ and } c_{\mathbf{y_4}} := \langle \mathbf{a}, \mathbf{y_4} \rangle = c_{\mathbf{z_2}} - c_{\mathbf{y_3}} \bmod 2^{\ell_1 + \ell_2}$$

The recursion continues once more by splitting the $\mathbf{y}_i = \mathbf{x}_{2i-1} + \mathbf{x}_{2i}$ and introducing four additional modular constraints $c_{\mathbf{x}_{2i-1}} \bmod 2^{\ell_1}$. These modular constraints together with the $c_{\mathbf{y}_i}$'s determine the values of inner products $c_{\mathbf{x}_{2i}} := \langle \mathbf{a}, \mathbf{x}_{2i} \rangle \bmod 2^{\ell_1}$, since we have

$$
\begin{aligned}
c_{\mathbf{z_2}} &:= t - c_{\mathbf{z_1}} && \bmod 2^{\ell} \\
c_{\mathbf{y}_{2i}} &:= c_{\mathbf{z}_i} - c_{\mathbf{y}_{2i-1}} && \bmod 2^{\ell_1 + \ell_2} \quad , i = 1, 2 \\
c_{\mathbf{x}_{2i}} &:= c_{\mathbf{y}_i} - c_{\mathbf{x}_{2i-1}} && \bmod 2^{\ell_1} \quad , i = 1, 2, 3, 4
\end{aligned}
\tag{2}
$$

Eventually, the $\mathbf{x}_i$'s are split in a meet-in-the-middle fashion, i.e.,

$$\mathbf{x}_i = (\mathbf{w}_{2i-1}, 0^{n/2}) + (0^{n/2}, \mathbf{w}_{2i}),$$

giving only a single representation of each $\mathbf{x}_i$.

The algorithm now starts by enumerating all possible values for the $\mathbf{w}_i$ in the base lists L_i. Then two lists are merged at a time in a new list by only considering those elements which fulfill the current constraint modulo 2^{ℓ_1}, $2^{\ell_1 + \ell_2}$, 2^{ℓ} or 2^n respectively (compare to Fig. 2). After the level-i list construction only those elements are kept whose coordinates follow a predefined distribution D_i, while all others are discarded. The choice of these distributions mainly determines the existing amount of representations and ultimately the performance of the algorithm. We give the pseudocode of the procedure in Algorithm 1.

Complexity. Let the expected list sizes *before* filtering on level i be $\mathcal{L}_i$ and let the probability of any element of a level-i list surviving the filter be q_i. Since the level-1 lists are constructed from the Cartesian product of the level-0 lists by enforcing a modular constrained on ℓ_1 bits we have

$$\mathcal{L}_1 = \frac{(\mathcal{L}_0)^2}{2^{\ell_1}}.$$

Analogously the level-2 lists are constructed from the *filtered* level-1 lists by enforcing a modular constrained on $\ell_1 + \ell_2$ bits. However, since the last ℓ_1 bits are already fixed to some value in the previous step we only enforce a new constraint on ℓ_2 bits, which results in

$$\mathcal{L}_2 = \frac{(q_1 \cdot \mathcal{L}_1)^2}{2^{\ell_2}}.$$

Analogously we obtain

$$\mathcal{L}_3 = \frac{(q_2 \cdot \mathcal{L}_2)^2}{2^{\ell_3}} \text{ and } \mathcal{L}_4 = \frac{(q_3 \cdot \mathcal{L}_3)^2}{2^{n-\ell}}.$$

Algorithm 1: BCJ ALGORITHM

Input : $\mathbf{a} \in (\mathbb{Z}_{2^n})^n, t \in \mathbb{Z}_{2^n}$
Output: $\mathbf{e} \in \mathbb{F}_2^n$ with $\langle \mathbf{a}, \mathbf{e} \rangle = t \bmod 2^n$

1 Choose optimal ℓ_1, ℓ_2, ℓ_3 and D_i, $i = 0, 1, 2, 3$
2 Enumerate

$$L_{2i-1} = \{\mathbf{w}_{2i-1} \mid \mathbf{w}_{2i-1} \in D_0 \times 0^{n/2}\}$$

$$L_{2i} = \{\mathbf{w}_{2i} \mid \mathbf{w}_{2i} \in 0^{n/2} \times D_0\}, i = 1, \ldots, 8$$

3 Choose random $c_{\mathbf{z}_1} \in \mathbb{F}_2^{\ell}, c_{\mathbf{y}_1}, c_{\mathbf{y}_3} \in \mathbb{F}_2^{\ell_1 + \ell_2}, c_{\mathbf{x}_1}, c_{\mathbf{x}_3}, c_{\mathbf{x}_5}, c_{\mathbf{x}_7} \in \mathbb{F}_2^{\ell_1}$
4 Set remaining constraints according to Eq. (2)
5 Compute (and filter)

$$L_i^{(1)} = \{\mathbf{x}_i \mid \langle \mathbf{a}, \mathbf{x}_i \rangle = c_{\mathbf{x}_i} \bmod 2^{\ell_1}, \mathbf{x}_i = \mathbf{w}_{2i-1} + \mathbf{w}_{2i}\}$$

from $L_{2i-1}, L_{2i}, \; i = 1, \ldots, 8$, then filter such that $L_i^{(1)} \subseteq D_1$

$$L_i^{(2)} = \{\mathbf{y}_i \mid \langle \mathbf{a}, \mathbf{y}_i \rangle = c_{\mathbf{y}_i} \bmod 2^{\ell_1 + \ell_2}, \mathbf{y}_i = \mathbf{x}_{2i-1} + \mathbf{x}_{2i}\},$$

from $L_{2i-1}^{(1)}, L_{2i}^{(1)}, \; i = 1, \ldots, 4$, then filter such that $L_i^{(2)} \subseteq D_2$

$$L_i^{(3)} = \{\mathbf{z}_i \mid \langle \mathbf{a}, \mathbf{z}_i \rangle = c_{\mathbf{z}_i} \bmod 2^{\ell}, \mathbf{z}_i = \mathbf{y}_{2i-1} + \mathbf{y}_{2i}\},$$

from $L_{2i-1}^{(2)}, L_{2i}^{(2)}, \; i = 1, 2$, then filter such that $L_i^{(3)} \subseteq D_3$

$$L \;\; = \{\mathbf{e} \mid \langle \mathbf{a}, \mathbf{e} \rangle = t \bmod 2^n, \mathbf{e} = \mathbf{z}_{2i-1} + \mathbf{z}_{2i}\}$$

from $L_1^{(3)}, L_2^{(3)}$, then filter such that $L \subseteq \{0, 1\}^n$

return $\mathbf{e} \in L$

The construction of each unfiltered list can be performed via hashing in time linear in the list's sizes giving an expected time complexity of

$$T = \max_i(\mathcal{L}_i) \; .$$

Since we need to store only filtered lists and the filtering can be performed on-the-fly the memory complexity becomes $M = \max_i(q_i \cdot \mathcal{L}_i)$.

Correctness. Obviously the constraint's sizes ℓ_1, ℓ_2 and ℓ_3 cannot be chosen arbitrarily large if one representation of the solution should survive all imposed constraints. On the other hand we need to ensure that multiple representations do not lead to the construction of duplicate elements in intermediate lists to ensure a proper list distribution. This leads to further restrictions on the size of ℓ_1, ℓ_2 and ℓ_3, called *saturation constraints* in [12] or simply lower bounds in [26].

In [12] this is formalized by ensuring that each list after filtering at every level is not larger than the size of the set filtered for, reduced by the total enforced constraint. Since by the randomness of the instance the elements distribute uniformly, it follows that the lists will not contain duplicate elements with high probability. The sets for which we filter on level i are D_i, $i = 1, 2, 3, 4$. Note that the choice of the sets D_i, $i \neq 4$ can be optimized, while the set D_4 has to describe the valid set of solutions, which is the set of binary vectors of length n.

Hence, to guarantee that there are no duplicates present in the level-1, level-2 and level-3 lists we need to ensure that

$$q_1 \cdot \mathcal{L}_1 \leq \frac{|D_1|}{2^{\ell_1}} \text{ and } q_2 \cdot \mathcal{L}_2 \leq \frac{|D_2|}{2^{\ell_1+\ell_2}} \text{ and } q_3 \cdot \mathcal{L}_3 \leq \frac{|D_3|}{2^{\ell}} \tag{3}$$

Next let us write the probabilities q_i in terms of the D_i and the corresponding representations. Therefore, let 2^{r_i} denote the amount of different representations of any element from D_{i+1} as the sum of two elements from D_i. Then we have

$$q_{i+1} = \frac{|D_{i+1}| \cdot 2^{r_i}}{|D_i|^2}, \tag{4}$$

describing the probability that a random sum of two elements from D_i forms a representation of any element from D_{i+1}.

Recall that we construct level-1 elements $\mathbf{x}_i = (\mathbf{w}_{2i-1}, \mathbf{w}_{2i}) \in D_0 \times D_0 = D_1$ in a meet-in-the-middle fashion from level-0 elements $\mathbf{w}_j$, which implies $\mathcal{L}_0 = \sqrt{|D_1|}$. As this gives only a single representation of any level-1 element, we have $r_0 = 0$, which leads to $q_1 = 1$, i.e., for this choice of D_0 there is no filtering on level one. It follows that the first saturation constraint from Eq. (3) is always fulfilled since

$$q_1 \cdot \mathcal{L}_1 = \frac{(\mathcal{L}_0)^2}{2^{\ell_1}} = \frac{|D_1|}{2^{\ell_1}}.$$

The second constraint of Eq. (3) gives

$$q_2 \cdot \mathcal{L}_2 = \frac{|D_2| \cdot 2^{r_1}}{|D_1|^2} \cdot \frac{(\mathcal{L}_0)^4}{2^{2\ell_1+\ell_2}} \overset{!}{\leq} \frac{|D_2|}{2^{\ell_1+\ell_2}} \Leftrightarrow r_1 \leq \ell_1.$$

Analogously we get from the last saturation constraint

$$q_3 \cdot \mathcal{L}_3 = q_3 \cdot \frac{(q_2)^2 \cdot (\mathcal{L}_1)^4}{2^{4\ell_1+2\ell_2+\ell_3}} = \frac{2^{2r_1+r_2} \cdot |D_3|}{2^{4\ell_1+2\ell_2+\ell_3}} \overset{!}{\leq} \frac{|D_3|}{2^{\ell}} \Leftrightarrow 2r_1 + r_2 \leq 3\ell_1 + \ell_2.$$

Eventually, to find exactly one representation of the solution in the final list we need to ensure that $q_4 \cdot \mathcal{L}_4 = 1$, which yields

$$q_4 \cdot \mathcal{L}_4 = \frac{q_4 \cdot (q_3)^2 \cdot (q_2)^4 (\mathcal{L}_1)^8}{2^{n+7\ell_1+3\ell_2+\ell_3}} = \frac{2^{4r_1+2r_2+r_3} \cdot |D_4|}{2^{n+7\ell_1+3\ell_2+\ell_3}} \overset{!}{=} 1$$
$$\Leftrightarrow 4r_1 + 2r_2 + r_3 = 7\ell_1 + 3\ell_2 + \ell_3, \tag{5}$$

since we have $|D_4| = 2^n$, as D_4 is the set of binary vectors of length n.

Instantiation. The description of the general BCJ algorithm gives several degrees of freedom, including the choice of sets D_i, $i = 1, 2, 3$ and the size of the constraints ℓ_1, ℓ_2, ℓ_3. The original BCJ algorithm restricts all D_i's to include only vectors with coordinates in $\{0, \pm 1\}$. The purpose of including -1's is simply to increase the number of representations. Since the final goal is to construct a binary vector, minus one entries are supposed to cancel out with one entries in the addition. Thus, the distribution D_3 is chosen as vectors of length n with exactly $\omega_3 := n/4 + \alpha_3$ one entries and $m_3 := \alpha_3$ minus one entries for some small α_3, which has to be optimized. The distribution D_2 is then composed similarly as vectors of length n with $\omega_2 := \omega_3/2 + \alpha_2$ one entries and $m_2 := m_3/2 + \alpha_2$ minus one entries, where again α_2 minus ones are supposed to cancel out. Analogously the level-1 distribution is chosen as vectors of length n with $\omega_1 := \omega_2/2 + \alpha_1$ one entries and $m_1 := m_2/2 + \alpha_1$ minus one entries, expecting α_1 cancellations. An overview of this choice of distributions is given in Table 1. The size of these sets is

$$|D_i| = \binom{n}{\omega_i, m_i, \cdot} \simeq 2^{g\left(\frac{\omega_i}{n}, \frac{m_i}{n}\right)n},$$

while the number of representations is given as

$$2^{r_{i-1}} = \binom{\omega_i}{\omega_i/2}\binom{m_i}{m_i/2}\binom{n - \omega_i - m_i}{\alpha_{i-1}, \alpha_{i-1}, \cdot} \simeq 2^{\omega_i + m_i + \rho_i},$$

where $\rho_i := g\left(\frac{\alpha_i}{n - \omega_i - m_i}, \frac{\alpha_i}{n - \omega_i - m_i}\right)(n - \omega_i - m_i)$.

Table 1. Choices of D_i made by BCJ and BBSS algorithm. The table states the proportion of coordinates equal to 1 (ω_i), -1 (m_i) and 2 (c_i). The proportion of zeros is $1 - \omega_i - m_i - c_i$. Set D_0 has half the proportions of D_1.

		D_4	D_3	D_2	D_1
BCJ	ω_i	$\frac{1}{2}$	$\frac{1}{4} + \alpha_3$	$\frac{1}{8} + \frac{\alpha_3}{2} + \alpha_2$	$\frac{1}{16} + \frac{\alpha_3}{4} + \frac{\alpha_2}{2} + \alpha_1$
	m_i	0	α_3	$\frac{\alpha_3}{2} + \alpha_2$	$\frac{\alpha_3}{4} + \frac{\alpha_2}{2} + \alpha_1$
BBSS	ω_i	$\frac{1}{2}$	$\frac{1}{4} + \alpha_3 - \gamma_3$	$\frac{1}{8} + \frac{\alpha_3 - \gamma_3}{2} + \alpha_2 - \gamma_2$	$\frac{1}{16} + \frac{\alpha_3 - \gamma_3}{4} + \frac{\alpha_2 - \gamma_2}{2} + \alpha_1 - \gamma_1$
	m_i	0	α_3	$\frac{\alpha_3}{2} + \alpha_2$	$\frac{\alpha_3}{4} + \frac{\alpha_2}{2} + \alpha_1$
	c_i	0	γ_3	$\frac{\gamma_3}{2} + \gamma_2$	$\frac{\gamma_3}{4} + \frac{\gamma_2}{2} + \gamma_1$

Here the two binomial coefficients count the number of possibilities how to distribute the one and minus one entries of an element from D_i equally over a sum of two elements. The multinomial coefficient then counts the number of possibilities how the remaining minus one and one entries can cancel out.

Note that the algorithm splits D_1 into $D_0 \times D_0$, where D_0 is the set of vectors of length $n/2$ containing exactly $\omega_1/2$ ones and $m_1/2$ minus ones. This leads to all D_i only including balanced elements, i.e., elements which contain an equal amount of ones (resp. minus ones) on their first and second half of the coordinates. However, this affects the sizes of the D_i and the amount of representations only by a polynomial factor, which is subsumed in the Landau notation.

Eventually, the BCJ algorithm chooses $\ell_1 = r_1$ and $\ell_2 = r_2 - r_1$, which yields $\ell_3 = r_3 - r_2$. A numerical optimization of the α_i results in a time complexity of $2^{0.291n}$ for the BCJ configuration.

Bonnetain et al. [12] then showed that a more flexible choice of ℓ_1 and ℓ_2 and correspondingly adapted ℓ_3 allows to decrease the time complexity to $2^{0.289n}$. They also showed that extending the digit set of the D_i to $\{0, \pm 1, 2\}$ allows to further decrease the time complexity to $2^{0.283n}$, yielding the best known time complexity for the random subset sum problem.

The BCJ algorithm achieves optimal time complexity for a depth of the search-tree of four. However, in general the optimal depth varies with the application. We therefore give for completeness and later reference the complexity and saturation constraints for variable depth in Appendix A.

4   New Subset Sum Trade-Off

The (generalized) BCJ algorithm from the previous section already inherits some time-memory trade-off potential. That is, one can try to optimize the choice of the ℓ_i with respect to the memory usage, since the larger the ℓ_i the smaller the list's sizes. However, the overall size of the ℓ_i's is bounded by the restriction that the last list should contain a representation of the solution.

On a high level our new trade-off works by relaxing this restriction, i.e. we do not require the last list to contain a solution. This allows to balance the lists more memory-friendly. We then perform multiple randomized executions of the algorithm to ensure that we find a solution overall. However, let alone this is not sufficient to obtain our improvements. The main runtime advantage of our improved trade-off comes from our observation that we can reuse parts of the tree in subsequent randomized executions, reducing the cost per iteration. A second improvement stems from our use of the Dissection framework [19] for the construction of the level-1 lists.

Note that if we change some bit-constraints in the tree (the values of c_v in Fig. 2) not necessarily all levels are affected. That means we do not need to re-compute all lists of the tree, but only those which depend on the changed constraints. Now, if the computation of each list had the same complexity, this strategy would only yield a constant factor improvement since at least one list needs to be recomputed. However, by adapting parameters accordingly and exploiting the involved filtering, we can guarantee that the creation of frequently reconstructed lists (from already existing lists) is much cheaper than a reconstruction of the whole tree. This partial reconstruction strategy in combination with relaxing the correctness constraint from Eq. (5) allows us to obtain significant improvements for rather high memory parameters $M \geq 2^{0.169n}$.

From there on the base lists, which are so far a meet-in-the-middle split of the first level domains start dominating the memory. The only possibility for the algorithm to decrease the size of those lists is to choose a set D_1 with smaller size on level 1. For the BCJ algorithm this means including less -1 entries, until ultimately no -1 entries are included in the enumeration. In this case the base lists require a memory of $\binom{n/2}{n/32} \simeq 2^{0.169n}$. From there the list sizes are as small as possible and we can not obtain instantiations for less memory. We circumvent this problem by exchanging the meet-in-the-middle strategy for exhaustive examination of the level-1 domain by the 7-Dissection algorithm. We find that apart from offering instantiations for memory parameters $M < 2^{0.169n}$, this gives also (slight) time improvements in the high memory regime $M \geq 2^{0.169n}$ as the optimization can choose a more optimal, usually larger set D_1 (implying larger D_0) without exceeding the memory limit.

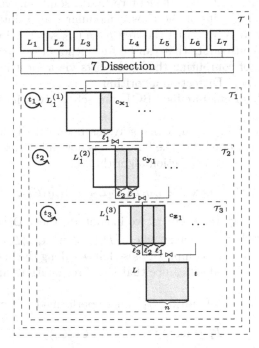

Fig. 3. Our new trade-off in depth 4. Dashed boxes frame different subtrees $\mathcal{T}_i$, which are rebuild 2^{t_i} times. The level-1 lists are constructed using the 7-Dissection algorithm.

Note that the 7-Dissection in our setting requires a memory of at least $\binom{n}{n/16}^{1/7} \simeq 2^{0.049n}$. To obtain instantiations for every $M > 0$ we could exchange the 7-Dissection by a c-Dissection for $c > 7$. However, since for a memory of $M \leq 2^{0.091n}$ a trade-off based on an algorithm by Esser-May offers a better time complexity anyway, we stick with a 7-Dissection for simplicity.

Adaptation of the BCJ Algorithm. We advise the reader to follow Fig. 3. Let $\mathcal{T}$ be the full tree and $\mathcal{T}_i, i = 1, 2, 3$ the subtrees only including the lists from level i onwards. We denote by 2^{t_i} the number of times we rebuild the subtree $\mathcal{T}_i$ from the (already existing) lists of the previous level.

We start by changing only the upper ℓ_3 bits of the modular constraint $c_{\mathbf{z}_1}$ which requires recomputing only the subtree $\mathcal{T}_3$, since the level-i lists for $i \leq 2$ do not depend on these bits. Since there are only 2^{ℓ_3} choices for those bits we have $t_3 \leq \ell_3$. If 2^{ℓ_3} iterations are not sufficient to find the solution we start modifying the upper ℓ_2 bits of the modular constraints $c_{\mathbf{y}_1}, c_{\mathbf{y}_2}, c_{\mathbf{z}_1} \bmod 2^{\ell_2}$. This implies again that $t_2 \leq 3\ell_2$. Still, for every different choice of those bits we recompute the subtree $\mathcal{T}_3$ another 2^{t_3} times for different choices of the upper ℓ_3 bits. If $2^{3\ell_2+\ell_3}$ iterations are still not sufficient to find a solution, we eventually start modifying the lower ℓ_1 bits of the chosen modular constraints. Again for each choice of lower bits we reconstruct the tree $\mathcal{T}_2$ and $\mathcal{T}_3$ several times. Furthermore, as there are seven constraints that can be freely chosen we have $t_1 \leq 7\ell_1$

Finally, instead of computing the level-1 lists via a meet-in-the-middle algorithm we now use the 7-Dissection algorithm.

The pseudocode of our modified BCJ trade-off is given in Algorithm 2.

Complexity. The memory complexity stays as before with the only difference that the memory requirement of the base lists is now substituted by the memory requirement M_{7D} of the 7-Dissection algorithm, i.e.,

$$M = \max(M_{7D}, q_1\mathcal{L}_1, q_2\mathcal{L}_2, q_3\mathcal{L}_3, q_4\mathcal{L}_4).$$

To balance the memory requirement we instantiate the 7-Dissection algorithm with $M_{7D} = |D_1|^{\max\left(\frac{1}{7}, \lambda'\right)}$ memory where $|D_1|^{\lambda'} = \max_i(q_iL_i)$.

The analysis of the time complexity also follows along the lines of the previous analysis, with the essential difference that the three subtrees are now computed differently many times.

A single construction of subtree $\mathcal{T}_1$ can be performed in time

$$T_1 = \max(T_{7D}, \mathcal{L}_1, \mathcal{L}_2, \mathcal{L}_3, \mathcal{L}_4),$$

where T_{7D} is the time it takes to compute the level-1 lists via the 7-Dissection algorithm. Recall that instantiated with $|D_1|^\delta$ memory, the 7-Dissection runs in time $T_{7D} = |D_1|^{\max\left(\frac{2(1-\delta)}{3}, \frac{1}{2}\right)}$ (compare to Lemma 2.1). The subtrees $\mathcal{T}_2$ and $\mathcal{T}_3$ can then be computed in time

$$T_2 = \max(q_1 \cdot \mathcal{L}_1, \mathcal{L}_2, \mathcal{L}_3, \mathcal{L}_4) \text{ and } T_3 = \max(q_2 \cdot \mathcal{L}_2, \mathcal{L}_3, \mathcal{L}_4),$$

as they can be computed from the stored and already filtered level-1 respectively level-2 lists. Now the total time complexity becomes

$$T = \max(2^{t_1} \cdot T_1, 2^{t_1+t_2} \cdot T_2, 2^{t_1+t_2+t_3} \cdot T_3),$$

as subtree $\mathcal{T}_i$ is rebuild $2^{t_1+\cdots+t_i}$ many times.

Algorithm 2: BCJ TRADE-OFF

   Input   : $\mathbf{a} \in (\mathbb{Z}_{2^n})^n, t \in \mathbb{Z}_{2^n}$

   Output: $\mathbf{e} \in \{0,1\}^n$ with $\langle \mathbf{a}, \mathbf{e} \rangle = t \bmod 2^n$

1 Choose optimal ℓ_1, ℓ_2, ℓ_3 and $D_i, i = 1, 2, 3$, let $r := r_3 + 2r_2 + 4r_1$

2 **repeat** $2^{t_1} := 2^{\max(7\ell_1 - r, 0)}$ **times**

3 | Choose random $c_{\mathbf{z}_1} \in \mathbb{F}_2^{\ell}, c_{\mathbf{y}_1}, c_{\mathbf{y}_3} \in \mathbb{F}_2^{\ell_1 + \ell_2}, c_{\mathbf{x}_1}, c_{\mathbf{x}_3}, c_{\mathbf{x}_5}, c_{\mathbf{x}_7} \in \mathbb{F}_2^{\ell_1}$

4 | Set remaining constraints according to Eq. (2)

5 | Compute

$$L_i^{(1)} = \{\mathbf{x}_i \mid \langle \mathbf{a}, \mathbf{x}_i \rangle = c_{\mathbf{x}_i} \bmod 2^{\ell_1}, \mathbf{x}_i \in D_1, \},$$

$$\text{via 7-Dissection,} \quad i = 1, \ldots, 8$$

6 | **repeat** $2^{t_2} := 2^{\max(7\ell_1 + 3\ell_2 - r, 0) - t_1}$ **times**

7 | | Choose randomly the upper ℓ_2 bits of $c_{\mathbf{z}_1}, c_{\mathbf{y}_1}, c_{\mathbf{y}_3} \bmod 2^{\ell_1 + \ell_2}$

8 | | Update $c_{\mathbf{z}_2}, c_{\mathbf{y}_2}, c_{\mathbf{y}_4}$ according to Eq. (2)

9 | | Compute

$$L_i^{(2)} = \{\mathbf{y}_i \mid \langle \mathbf{a}, \mathbf{y}_i \rangle = c_{\mathbf{y}_i} \bmod 2^{\ell_1 + \ell_2}, \mathbf{y}_i \in D_2, \mathbf{y}_i = \mathbf{x}_{2i-1} + \mathbf{x}_{2i}\},$$

$$\text{from } L_{2i-1}^{(1)}, L_{2i}^{(1)}, \quad i = 1, \ldots, 4$$

10 | | **repeat** $2^{t_3} := 2^{\max(7\ell_1 + 3\ell_2 + \ell_3 - r, 0) - t_1 - t_2}$ **times**

11 | | | Choose randomly the upper ℓ_3 bits of $c_{\mathbf{z}_1}$

12 | | | Update $c_{\mathbf{z}_2}$ according to Eq. (2)

13 | | | Compute

$$L_i^{(3)} = \{\mathbf{z}_i \mid \langle \mathbf{a}, \mathbf{z}_i \rangle = c_{\mathbf{z}_i} \bmod 2^{\ell}, \mathbf{z}_i \in D_3, \mathbf{z}_i = \mathbf{y}_{2i-1} + \mathbf{y}_{2i}\},$$

$$\text{from } L_{2i-1}^{(2)}, L_{2i}^{(2)}, \quad i = 1, 2$$

$$L = \{\mathbf{e} \mid \langle \mathbf{a}, \mathbf{e} \rangle = t \bmod 2^n, \mathbf{e} \in D_4, \mathbf{e} = \mathbf{z}_{2i-1} + \mathbf{z}_{2i}\},$$

$$\text{from } L_1^{(3)}, L_2^{(3)}$$

    | | | **if** $|L| > 0$ **then**

14 | | | |— **return** $\mathbf{e} \in L$

Correctness. Most of the correctness follows from the correctness of the BCJ algorithm and the 7-dissection algorithm. Note that we instantiate the 7-Dissection with at least $|D_1|^{\frac{1}{7}}$ memory, which is the minimum requirement given by Lemma 2.1.

The main difference to before is that we relaxed the restriction given in Eq. (5), such that the last list is not guaranteed to contain a solution anymore. However, we compensate for this by multiple randomized constructions of the final list. In contrast to completely independent executions of the algorithm, which would select all constraints uniformly at random, we only randomize the constraints affecting certain subtrees. However, note that under the standard assumption that the representations distribute independently and uniformly over all constraints, any set of constraints has the same independent probability of leading to a representation of the solution. Now, since we change at least one constraint for every reconstruction of the final list, we can treat the iterations as independent.

In order to ensure that over all iterations we find at least one representation, the final list's size accumulated over all its reconstructions must be at least one, which leads to (compare to Eq. (5))

$$q_4 \cdot \mathcal{L}_4 \cdot 2^{t_1+t_2+t_3} \geq 1$$
$$\Leftrightarrow \quad 4r_1 + 2r_2 + r_3 + t_1 + t_2 + t_3 \geq 7\ell_1 + 3\ell_2 + \ell_3.$$

Note that this constraint is fulfilled for our choice of

$$t_1 = \max(7\ell_1 - r, 0)$$
$$t_2 = \max(7\ell_1 + 3\ell_2 - r, 0) - t_1$$
$$t_3 = \max(7\ell_1 + 3\ell_2 + \ell_3 - r, 0) - t_1 - t_2,$$

where $r := r_3 + 2r_2 + 4r_1$ and the maximum is needed since we need to build each subtree at least once.

Configuration of Our Trade-Off. In terms of distributions we adopt the choice of the original BCJ algorithm, specified in Table 1. We then optimize the parameters $\alpha_i, \ell_i, i = 1, 2, 3$ numerically. We optimize such that the time is minimized, while simultaneously ensuring that the saturation constraints are satisfied and a given memory limit of $M = 2^{\lambda n}$ is not exceeded.

The resulting trade-off curve is depicted in Fig. 1. We observe that our trade-off outperforms all existing approaches for $M \geq 2^{0.093n}$. Prior to our work, this interval was covered by a diverse landscape of different trade-offs including [7,16,19,22,27,30]. For $M < 2^{0.093n}$ a trade-off given in [22] based on a memory-free algorithm by Esser-May [27] becomes superior to our procedure.

Extending the Digit Set. We also adopted the choice of distributions made by the BBSS algorithm [12] (see Table 1). We find that the refined choice of the D_i gives an overall slight improvement, interpolating smoothly to their $2^{0.283n}$ algorithm. The resulting trade-off curve is depicted in Fig. 1 as well, which remains superior to [22,27] as long as $M \geq 2^{0.091n}$.

Increasing the Tree-Depth. We also performed a numerical optimization of our trade-off with increased tree-depth of five. However, we were not able to obtain better instantiations, i.e., instantiations with lower time complexity for a given memory.

Linear Approximations. Observe that both our trade-offs split in three almost linear segments (compare to Fig. 1). To ease the comparison of further results to our trade-offs, we provide a linear approximation $T = -a \cdot M + b$ of these segments in Table 2. This allows to easily compare to the (approximate) running time of our trade-off, without rerunning the optimization of parameters.

Table 2. Slope a and y-intercept b of the linear approximations $T = -a \cdot M + b$ of the three different segments, each denoted by the maximal memory available in the segment. Left columns refer to the trade-off using BCJ-like representations, while right columns use BBSS-syle representations.

$\leq M$	0.18		0.27		0.28	
a	2.54	2.65	1.06	1.13	0.27	0.36
b	0.84	0.85	0.58	0.58	0.37	0.39

Translation of Provable Variant from Previous Works. In the original works of Howgrave-Graham-Joux [30] and Becker-Coron-Joux [7] the constraints on each level i are modelled as $c_{\mathbf{v}} \mod \prod_{j=1}^{i} M_i$ for M_i a prime close to 2^{ℓ_i}. This allows to apply a result for the distribution of random modular sums from [35]. In turn the authors are able to analyze the distribution of the list sizes throughout the algorithm as well as the probability that a representation of the solution survives a certain set of constraints. The algorithm in its provable variant is then adapted to repeat the construction of each level for $N \cdot 2^{\varepsilon n}$ random set of constraints, for an arbitrarily small constant $\varepsilon > 0$, and to abort constructions that exceed the expected memory complexity. It is then shown that this variant succeeds with a maximum overhead factor of $N^3 \cdot 2^{3\varepsilon n}$ in time using its expected memory complexity with probability $1 - c^{-N}$ for some constant c.

In spirit this re-randomization technique translates to our new trade-offs. Therefore first note, that we choose $M_i = 2^{\ell_i}$ as modulus just for ease of exposition, instead we could analogous to [7,30] choose primes close to 2^{ℓ_i}. Now, whenever we have to exchange a set of constraints on any level, i.e., in lines 3,7 and 11 of Algorithm 2, we have to repeat this exchange $N \cdot 2^{\varepsilon n}$ times to make sure the algorithm is successful and not aborted for at least one of those repetitions. Clearly, the running time is at most increased by a factor of $N^3 \cdot 2^{3\varepsilon n}$ while the success probability becomes $(1 - c^{-N})^R$, where $R = 2^{t_1+t_2+t_3}$ is the maximum number of times a constraint is exchanged. Note that this probability for large enough $N = \text{poly}(n)$ is still overwhelming.

To ensure that there are enough "unused" constraints available for the re-randomization approach, we have to restrict the values of t_1, t_2, t_3 to a maximum of $7\ell_1 - \delta$, $3\ell_2 - \delta$ and $\ell_3 - \delta$, respectively, where $\delta := \varepsilon n + \log N$. Technically, this leads to a slightly worse trade-off, but since ε is an arbitrarily small constant this performance gap becomes arbitrarily small.

5   Application to Decoding Binary Linear Codes

A linear code $\mathcal{C} \subset \mathbb{F}_2^n$ is a k-dimensional subspace of $\mathbb{F}_2^n$ and can efficiently be described via a parity-check matrix $\mathbf{H} \in \mathbb{F}_2^{(n-k) \times n}$, such that $\mathcal{C} = \{ \mathbf{c} \in \mathbb{F}_2^n \mid \mathbf{Hc} = \mathbf{0} \}$. Decoding an error-prone codeword $\mathbf{y} := \mathbf{c} + \mathbf{e}$ to $\mathbf{c}$ is polynomial-time equivalent to recovering $\mathbf{e}$ from the so-called *syndrome* $\mathbf{s} := \mathbf{Hy} = \mathbf{H}(\mathbf{c}+\mathbf{e}) = \mathbf{He}$. This leads to the following definition of the syndrome decoding problem.

Definition 5.1 (Syndrome Decoding Problem). *Let* $\mathbf{H} \in \mathbb{F}_2^{(n-k) \times n}$ *be the parity-check matrix of a code of length n and dimension k, with constant code-rate* $R := \frac{k}{n}$. *Given a syndrome* $\mathbf{s} \in \mathbb{F}_2^{n-k}$ *and an integer* ω *the syndrome decoding problem asks to find a vector* $\mathbf{e} \in \mathbb{F}_2^n$ *of Hamming weight* $\mathrm{wt}(\mathbf{e}) = \omega$ *satisfying* $\mathbf{H}\mathbf{e} = \mathbf{s}$.

Note that the problem admits a unique solution as long as $\omega \leq \lfloor \frac{d-1}{2} \rfloor$, where d is the minimum distance of the code, i.e., the minimum Hamming distance between two codewords. We call the setting with unique solution *half distance decoding*, while for $\omega \leq d$ we refer to *full distance decoding*. In those regimes, the time complexity generally increases with ω, such that we only consider the cases where ω is equal to those upper bounds. Further, random linear codes are known to achieve a minimum distance that is equal to the Gilbert-Varshamov bound of $d \approx H^{-1}(1 - \frac{k}{n})n$, i.e., the minimum distance is a function of the rate $R := \frac{k}{n}$ and the code-length n. In our asymptotic analysis we maximize the complexity over all constant rates R to obtain a runtime formula which only depends on n.

The best known algorithms to solve the syndrome decoding problem are Information Set Decoding (ISD) algorithms. In the full and half distance setting these algorithms have exponential time and memory complexity of the form $\tilde{\mathcal{O}}(2^{cn})$ for some constant c depending on the algorithm. On the other hand, cryptographic applications usually use a a sublinear weight, i.e., $\omega = o(n)$. In these cases the running time of ISD algorithms is subexponential of the form $\tilde{\mathcal{O}}(2^{c\omega})$ for some constant c. Moreover, it was shown [40] that in this case all known ISD algorithms converge to the same running time, i.e., they obtain the same constant c. However, in practical experiments advanced ISD algorithms were shown to provide significant speedups [10,28].

We therefore first analyse our trade-offs in the full and half distance decoding setting, which allow to easily verify their superiority since they obtain improved constants c. We then study the practical effect of our trade-offs by providing an optimized implementation. Finally, we extrapolate the hardness of cryptographic schemes using our obtained data points.

Information Set Decoding. Information Set Decoding algorithms first apply a permutation matrix $\mathbf{P}$ to the columns of the parity-check matrix. This allows to redistribute the weight of the error since the permuted instance $\mathbf{H}' := \mathbf{H}\mathbf{P}$ has as valid solution $\mathbf{e}' := \mathbf{P}^{-1}\mathbf{e}$, since $\mathbf{H}\mathbf{P}(\mathbf{P}^{-1}\mathbf{e}) = \mathbf{s}$. Then $\mathbf{H}'$ is transformed into semi-systematic form via Gaussian elimination modelled via the multiplication with an invertible matrix $\mathbf{Q}$

$$\mathbf{Q}\mathbf{H}'(\mathbf{P}^{-1}\mathbf{e}) = \begin{pmatrix} \mathbf{I}_{n-k-\ell} & \mathbf{H}_1 \\ \mathbf{0} & \mathbf{H}_2 \end{pmatrix}(\mathbf{e}_1, \mathbf{e}_2) = (\mathbf{e}_1 + \mathbf{H}_1\mathbf{e}_2, \mathbf{H}_2\mathbf{e}_2) = \mathbf{Q}\mathbf{s} = (\mathbf{s}_1, \mathbf{s}_2),$$

$$(6)$$

where we write $\mathbf{e}' := \mathbf{P}^{-1}\mathbf{e} = (\mathbf{e}_1, \mathbf{e}_2) \in \mathbb{F}_2^{n-k-\ell} \times \mathbb{F}_2^{k+\ell}$ with ℓ an optimization parameter of the algorithm. Let us further assume that the permutation distributes the weight on $\mathbf{e}'$ such that $\mathrm{wt}(\mathbf{e}_1) = \omega - p$ and $\mathrm{wt}(\mathbf{e}_2) = p$, for some p that has to be optimized, too.

Now Eq. (6) yields a (dimension) reduced syndrome decoding instance in form of the equation $\mathbf{H}_2\mathbf{e}_2 = \mathbf{s}_2$ with weight-p solution $\mathbf{e}_2 \in \mathbb{F}_2^{k+\ell}$. Usually, $\mathbf{e}_2$ is not a unique solution to this reduced instance. The algorithm therefore computes all solutions $\mathbf{x}$ to this smaller instance and checks if the corresponding $\mathbf{e}_1 = \mathbf{s}_1 + \mathbf{H}_1\mathbf{x}$ has weight $\omega - p$. In this case $\mathbf{P}(\mathbf{e}_1, \mathbf{x})$ forms a solution to the original syndrome decoding instance. If no solution is found, the algorithm is repeated for another random permutation.

Complexity. Let us briefly argue about the complexity of such a procedure. The probability of distributing the weight on $\mathbf{e}'$ as desired is

$$q := \frac{\binom{n-k-\ell}{\omega-p}\binom{k+\ell}{p}}{\binom{n}{\omega}}. \tag{7}$$

Hence, we expect that after q^{-1} random permutations one of them distributes the weight as desired. If now the cost to retrieve all weight-p solutions to the reduced instance for any of those permutations is T_S, the total complexity becomes

$$T = \tilde{\mathcal{O}}\left(q^{-1} \cdot T_\mathrm{S}\right).$$

In a nutshell different ISD algorithms differentiate in how they retrieve the solutions to the reduced instance. Usually they consider the reduced instance as a vectorial subset sum instance, where the solution encodes a size-p subset of the columns of $\mathbf{H}_2$ that sums to $\mathbf{s}_2$. Then they make use of advanced algorithms for subset sum, such as the BCJ algorithm, to retrieve the solutions to that instance. It is not hard to see, that instead of working over $\mathbb{Z}_{2^n}$, the generalized BCJ algorithm outlined in Sect. 3 and, hence, also our improved trade-off from Sect. 4, work analogously over $\mathbb{F}_2^n$.

5.1   Improved ISD Trade-Offs

The May-Meurer-Thomae (MMT) ISD algorithm [33] originally uses the BCJ construction in depth-2 to retrieve the solutions to the reduced instance. In the following we give an improved version of the MMT algorithm based on our new subset sum trade-off from Sect. 4. Our version improves the overall memory complexity and yields a better trade-off curve, i.e., we achieve runtime improvements for every fixed memory.

To make use of our generalized trade-off description (in depth 2) we need to define appropriate sets D_0, D_1 and D_2. Then, to retrieve the running time we calculate the amount of existing representations and optimize the parameter ℓ_1. The pseudocode of our improved MMT algorithm is given in Algorithm 3.

Note that in our ISD application we find that already using the Schroeppel-Shamir technique for level-1 list construction, rather than the 7-Dissection, offers optimal instantiations for all memory parameters $M > 0$. We therefore stick with the Schroeppel-Shamir technique in our description for simplicity.

Algorithm 3: NEW MMT TRADE-OFF

    Input : $\mathbf{H} \in \mathbb{F}_2^{(n-k)\times n}, \mathbf{s} \in \mathbb{F}_2^{n-k}, w \in \mathbb{N}$

    Output: $\mathbf{e} \in \mathbb{F}_2^n, \mathbf{He} = \mathbf{s}$

1 Choose optimal ℓ, ℓ_1, p

2 let $r_1 = \log \binom{p}{p/2}$

3 $\pi_{\ell_1} : \mathbb{F}_2^\ell \to \mathbb{F}_2^{\ell_1}, \pi_{\ell_1}(x_1, \ldots, x_\ell) = (x_1, \ldots, x_{\ell_1})$

4 repeat

5   choose random permutation matrix $\mathbf{P}$

6 $\bar{\mathbf{H}} = \begin{pmatrix} \mathbf{I}_{n-k-\ell} & \mathbf{H}_1 \\ 0 & \mathbf{H}_2 \end{pmatrix} = \mathbf{QHP}, \mathbf{Qs} = (\mathbf{s}_1, \mathbf{s}_2)$

7   **repeat** $2^{\ell_1 - r_1}$ **times**

8   Choose random $\mathbf{t} \in \mathbb{F}_2^{\ell_1}$

9   Compute

             $L_1^{(1)} = \{\mathbf{z}_1 \mid \pi_{\ell_1}(\mathbf{H}_2\mathbf{z}_1) = \mathbf{t}, \mathbf{z}_1 \in D_1\}$, via Schroeppel-Shamir

             $L_2^{(1)} = \{\mathbf{z}_2 \mid \pi_{\ell_1}(\mathbf{H}_2\mathbf{z}_2 + \mathbf{s}_2) = \mathbf{t}, \mathbf{z}_2 \in D_1\}$, via Schroeppel-Shamir

10   Compute $L = \{\mathbf{e}_2 \mid \mathbf{H}_2\mathbf{e}_2 = \mathbf{s}_2, \mathbf{e}_2 = \mathbf{z}_1 + \mathbf{z}_2\}$ from $L_1^{(1)}, L_2^{(2)}$

11   **for** $\mathbf{e}_2 \in L$ **do**

12 $\mathbf{e}_1 = \mathbf{H}_1\mathbf{e}_2 + \mathbf{s}_1$

13   **if** $\mathrm{wt}(\mathbf{e}_1) \leq \omega - p$ **then**

14   **return** $P(\mathbf{e}_1, \mathbf{e}_2)$

Complexity. We let D_2 be the set of vectors from $\mathbb{F}_2^{k+\ell}$ with weight p, as it defines our solution set. The MMT algorithm now chooses D_1 as vectors from $\mathbb{F}_2^{k+\ell}$ with weight $p/2$. Finally D_0 is the set of vectors from $\mathbb{F}_2^{\frac{k+\ell}{2}}$ and weight $p/4$, i.e., a meet-in-the-middle split of D_1, hence $|D_0| = \sqrt{|D_1|}$. The size of D_1 is

$$|D_1| = \binom{k+\ell}{p/2},$$

while the amount of representations of one element from D_2 as sum of two elements from D_1 is

$$2^{r_1} = \binom{p}{p/2} \simeq 2^p.$$

Observe that the binomial coefficient counts the possibilities to distribute half of the ones of the target vector over the first addend, while the other half must then be covered by the second addend. Now, to find one representation of each solution to the reduced instance in the final list we need to ensure (compare to Eq. (8))

$$\ell_1 \overset{!}{=} r_1.$$

Our trade-off from Sect. 4 now allows for $\ell_1 > r_1$ and compensates by repeating the procedure. Note that in depth-2 we have no further saturation constraints, nor can we make use of reconstructing different levels differently many times. The time complexity for finding all solutions to the vectorial subset sum problem then becomes

$$T_S = 2^{\ell_1 - r_1} \cdot \max(\sqrt{|D_1|}, |D_1|/2^{\ell_1}, |D_1|^2/2^{\ell+\ell_1})$$

The memory complexity is equal to the level-0 and level-1 lists, since elements of the final list can be checked on the fly for being a solution. Moreover, by using the Schroeppel-Shamir algorithm for the construction of the level-1 lists we can reduce the memory required for storing the level-0 lists from $|D_0| = \sqrt{|D_1|}$ to $\sqrt{|D_0|} = |D_1|^{1/4}$ (see Sect. 2), which yields

$$M = \max(|D_1|^{1/4}, |D_1|/2^{\ell_1}).$$

5.2   Asymptotic Behavior of New Trade-Offs'

For the asymptotic classification of our algorithmic improvement let us first consider the half distance setting, i.e., $\omega := H(1 - \frac{k}{n}) \cdot \frac{n}{2}$. Here our MMT variant improves the memory complexity by almost a square-root down to $2^{0.0135n}$ from $2^{0.0213n}$ of standard MMT, while maintaining the same time complexity of $T = 2^{0.05364n}$. The optimal parameters for our MMT variant in this case are

$$\ell = 0.0278n, \ \ell_1 = 0.0091n \text{ and } p = 0.0064n,$$

where the found worst case rate is $k = 0.45n$ as for standard MMT. We now further optimized the time complexity of our trade-off under a memory limitation of $M \le 2^{\lambda n}$ for decreasing λ. Figure 4 shows the complete trade-off curves for both MMT variants – the original and our improved version. We observe that our trade-off outperforms the original trade-off for all memory parameters.

In the full distance setting we obtain a similar improvement. Here our improved MMT algorithm improves the memory complexity down to $2^{0.0375n}$ from previously $2^{0.053n}$, while achieving the same time complexity of $2^{0.112n}$. Again we obtain runtime improvements over standard MMT for any fixed memory.

Even though, the MMT algorithm is not the asymptotically fastest ISD algorithm, so far none of its known asymptotic improvements [9,13,14,23,34] did transfer to the implementation level. This makes the MMT algorithm the preferred choice for record computations [3] as well as security estimates [28].

BJMM Algorithm. However, we also analyzed the algorithm by Becker-Joux-May-Meurer (BJMM) [9], which in contrast to the MMT algorithm uses slightly different sets D_i. That is, the vectors on each level have a slightly increased weight. Then, in the $\mathbb{F}_2$-addition of those vectors some weight is assumed to cancel to still obtain a vector of weight p. The different possibilities, how the weight can cancel, increase the amount of representations and lead to an increased optimal tree-depth of three. This increased tree-depth allows us to make use of our subtree reconstruction technique yielding an improved trade-off curve also shown

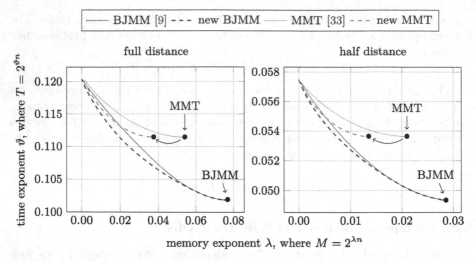

Fig. 4. Comparison between the implicit (solid) and our new trade-off (dashed) for the MMT and BJMM algorithm. Complexity uses known worst case rates of the algorithm in the full distance (left) and half distance setting (right).

in Fig. 4. We observe that the refined choice of the D_i gives the algorithm a possibility to balance the list sizes if memory is not limited. For that reason our strategy yields improvements only for limited memory in the case of the BJMM algorithm.

5.3   Practical Results and Security Estimates

We adapted the MMT/BJMM implementation from [28] to our new trade-off strategy. Interestingly, besides reducing the memory requirements we also obtain practical *running time* improvements, which stem from less, usually costly memory accesses.

We were able to solve several instances provided at https://decodingchallenge. org [3], which were either unsolved or broken using more time and memory. Most notably, we obtained a new record computation in the quasi-cyclic setting, which follows the parameter selection of NIST fourth round candidates BIKE and HQC.

New Record Computation. Precisely, we solved the QC-3138 instance with code parameters $(n, k, \omega) = (3138, 1569, 56)$ with an estimated bit complexity of 66.7 (respectively 60.7 if counted in 64-bit register operations) in only 2.23 CPU years. We estimated the expected time to solve this instance on our cluster, based on the processed permutations per second, to about 9.47 CPU years. The previous best implementation from [28] would need an expected amount of 30.31 CPU years, i.e., our implementation is about 3.2 times faster on this instance.

We also analysed the performance of our implementation on the next instance QC-3366 with parameters $(n, k, \omega) = (3366, 1683, 58)$, which has an estimated bit security of 68.7. We obtain an expected running time of 30.2 CPU years, which corresponds to an improvement by a factor of 5.7.

Furthermore we re-broke the previous QC-2918 record instance with parameters $(n, k, \omega) = (2918, 1459, 54)$ two times in just 224 CPU days, almost precisely hitting its expectation, which is about 6.9 times faster than the previous best implementation.

On McEliece like medium-sized instances we obtain a speedup by a factor of about 2.5. For the current record instance McEliece-1284 using parameters $(n, k, \omega) = (1284, 1028, 24)$ we estimated a running time of 11.06 CPU years, where the initial record computation expected 26.28 CPU years, corresponding to a speedup of about 2.4. Considering the next (unsolved) McEliece record instance with parameters $(n, k, \omega) = (1347, 1078, 25)$, we estimate a running time of about 59.74 CPU years, improving from the previous estimate of 156.6 CPU years by a factor of 2.6.

Security Estimates. Next we investigate the impact of our improvement on the security of cryptographic sized instances. Therefore, we first adapted the estimation scripts from [24] to incorporate our trade-off strategy, which allows us to precisely estimate the bit-complexity of given instances. Following previous works [5, 24, 28] we consider different memory access cost models. A memory access cost tries to model the practically faced memory access timings, by penalizing the algorithm for a high memory usage. Precisely, an algorithm with time complexity T and memory complexity M is assumed to have cost $T \cdot f(M)$, where f determines the penalty. We consider the established models of constant, logarithmic and cube-root access costs, which correspond to $f(M) = 1, f(M) = \log M$ and $f(M) = \sqrt[3]{M}$.

From here we follow two different estimation methodologies. First, we use our estimation script to obtain bit complexity estimates, which we compare directly against similar estimates obtained in [24]. For the second methodology we then extrapolate the time it would take to solve an instance of proposed parameters from our obtained record computations, comparing our results against a similar estimation performed in [28].

Let us start with the bit complexity estimation using our script.

Bit Complexity Estimation. The commonly addressed security categories 1, 3 and 5 defined by NIST relate their security to the security of AES-128, –192 and –256. NIST specifies the bit complexity to break those AES instantiations as 143, 207 and 272 respectively.

BIKE/HQC. In Table 3 we state the security margin in bits the corresponding parameter set has over breaking AES with corresponding key-size. Precisely the table states $T_{\text{Scheme}} - T_{\text{AES}}$, where T_{Scheme} is the bit complexity estimate obtained from our script and T_{AES} the bit complexity of breaking AES, i.e., 143, 207 or 272 respectively. The number in parenthesis states the improvement over the estimation performed in [24], i.e., one obtains their result as the sum of both numbers.

Table 3. Bit-difference in security of BIKE/HQC and AES with respective key-length considering different memory access cost.

Quasi-Cyclic		Category 1	Category 3	Category 5
constant:				
BIKE	message	2.90 (0.00)	4.13 (0.00)	4.22 (0.12)
	key	4.31 (0.04)	3.68 (0.08)	6.08 (0.63)
HQC		1.71 (0.00)	5.91 (0.00)	3.08 (0.00)
logarithmic:				
BIKE	message	7.04 (0.46)	8.36 (0.48)	8.62 (0.50)
	key	8.65 (0.42)	8.46 (0.45)	11.29 (0.47)
HQC		5.89 (0.48)	10.18 (0.50)	7.40 (0.52)
cube-root:				
BIKE	message	8.40 (2.57)	9.97 (2.89)	10.41 (3.14)
	key	9.92 (2.34)	9.99 (2.66)	13.01 (2.90)
HQC		7.37 (2.75)	11.91 (3.08)	9.32 (3.30)

As expected, we obtain essentially the same security margin as [24] if no memory access cost is imposed. However, for logarithmic and, especially, for cube-root memory access costs, our time-memory trade-offs yield reduced security estimates. Furthermore, note that the improvement in the cube-root case is even higher than the improvement of representation-based ISD algorithms like MMT over early algorithms like Stern and Dumer on these instances [24].

Table 4. Bit-difference in security of McEliece and AES with respective key-length considering different memory access cost.

McEliece	Category 1 $n = 3488$	Category 3 $n = 4608$	Category 5a $n = 6688$	Category 5b $n = 6960$	Category 5c $n = 8192$
constant:					
unlimited	−0.98 (0.23)	−25.09 (0.55)	−23.82 (0.17)	−24.51 (0.25)	5.37 (0.27)
$M \leq 80$	0.14 (0.56)	−22.94 (1.74)	−13.42 (1.29)	−13.13 (1.80)	21.40 (1.51)
$M \leq 60$	2.47 (1.49)	−18.84 (0.04)	−8.84 (4.52)	−8.36 (4.10)	26.65 (5.59)
logarithmic:					
unlimited	5.44 (0.22)	−18.39 (0.33)	−16.62 (0.18)	−17.28 (0.25)	12.83 (0.27)
$M \leq 80$	6.14 (0.61)	−16.88 (1.52)	−7.42 (1.23)	−7.13 (1.77)	27.45 (1.45)
$M \leq 60$	8.06 (1.37)	−13.41 (0.13)	−3.34 (4.15)	−2.83 (3.69)	32.19 (5.23)
cube-root:					
	14.25 (1.68)	−7.31 (1.76)	4.13 (2.63)	4.97 (2.35)	41.12 (3.05)

In the case of BIKE we distinguish message and key security as both settings allow for slightly different speedups [2].

McEliece. For the round 4 parameter sets of McEliece we performed a similar estimation shown in Table 4.

Since in the McEliece setting ISD algorithms tend to use very high amounts of memory we also consider memory-limited settings. In those we restrict the memory consumption of the algorithm to not exceed 2^{80} or 2^{60} bits respectively. We reduce the security estimates for McEliece by up to 6 bits and obtain the best results in memory-limited settings, where our new time-memory trade-offs can play its strength. Again the number in brackets indicates by how much we reduced the previous estimate from [24].

Note that under cube-root memory access cost none of the optimal algorithmic configurations exceeds 2^{60} bits of memory.

Table 5. Bit-difference in security of BIKE/HQC and AES with respective key-length considering different memory access cost obtained via extrapolation methodology.

Quasi-Cyclic		Category 1	Category 3	Category 5
constant:				
BIKE	message	−0.65 (3.09)	−0.59 (3.09)	0.26 (3.23)
	key	0.73 (3.15)	−1.07 (3.20)	2.13 (3.74)
HQC		−1.84 (3.08)	1.19 (3.09)	−0.86 (3.09)
logarithmic:				
BIKE	message	−0.36 (3.22)	−0.21 (3.25)	0.84 (3.26)
	key	1.24 (3.18)	−0.10 (3.21)	3.50 (3.24)
HQC		−1.51 (3.23)	1.61 (3.26)	−0.38 (3.28)
cube-root:				
BIKE	message	0.37 (4.10)	0.77 (4.43)	1.99 (4.69)
	key	1.89 (3.88)	0.79 (4.21)	4.60 (4.43)
HQC		−0.67 (4.29)	2.71 (4.63)	0.90 (4.85)

Extrapolation Methodology. Now, let us provide a security estimation, where we extrapolate the time to solve an instance of suggested parameters from our obtained record computations, as recently proposed in [28]. This methodology scales the time of the largest experiment in the respective setting by the difference in the bit-complexity of our experiment and the suggested parameters.

Methodology Example. Let us give a brief example of that methodology. Take the HQC category 1 parameter set $(n, k, \omega) = (35338, 17669, 132)$, in the constant memory access setting. This instance achieves a bit complexity of 144.7 according to our estimator, while our QC-3138 record has a bit complexity of 66.7 and took us about 2.24 CPU years to compute. We, therefore, extrapolate the time for breaking the HQC 128-bit parameters to $2.24 \cdot 2^{144.7-66.7} \approx 2^{79.16}$ CPU years.

To then set this time into context to the security categories 1, 3 and 5 that relate their security to the security of AES-128, -192 and -256, the time complexity of breaking AES on the used cluster is estimated. Therefore, one benchmarks the number of AES encryptions the cluster is able to perform per second from which the expected time to break AES with respective key size is obtained. While this methodology introduces platform dependencies, it allows for direct comparison between (scaled) practical experiments for both settings.

BIKE/HQC. Table 5 states the security margin (in bits) the corresponding parameter set has over breaking AES. Precisely the table states $\log \frac{T_{\text{Scheme}}}{T_{\text{AES}}}$. Here, T_{Scheme} is the estimated time to break the schemes parameters and T_{AES} the estimated time to break the corresponding AES instantiation on our cluster. The number in parentheses states the improvement over the analysis performed in [28].

We now observe already improvements in the constant memory access setting, which reflects our obtained speedup on the mid-sized instance used for the extrapolation. Still we obtain higher gains towards higher memory access costs, due to the reduced memory usage. Overall the margins are slightly lower using the extrapolation methodology compared to the bit complexity estimate, with larger differences towards higher memory access costs. This is because some of the memory access costs are accounted to the mid-sized instance, which is subtracted from the overall estimate in the extrapolation.

Table 6. Bit-difference in security of Classic McEliece and AES with respective key-length considering different memory access cost obtained via extrapolation methodology.

McEliece	Category 1 $n = 3488$	Category 3 $n = 4608$	Category 5a $n = 6688$	Category 5b $n = 6960$	Category 5c $n = 8192$
constant:					
unlimited	−0.65 (0.74)	−25.93 (1.07)	−23.86 (0.68)	−24.55 (0.75)	5.32 (0.78)
$M \leq 80$	0.47 (1.07)	−23.77 (2.25)	−13.47 (1.80)	−13.18 (2.31)	21.35 (2.02)
$M \leq 60$	2.80 (2.00)	−19.67 (0.55)	− 8.89 (5.03)	− 8.41 (4.61)	26.60 (6.10)
logarithmic:					
unlimited	0.84 (0.93)	−24.16 (1.05)	−21.60 (0.90)	−22.27 (0.98)	7.84 (1.00)
$M \leq 80$	1.53 (1.33)	−22.66 (2.25)	−12.41 (1.95)	−12.12 (2.49)	22.47 (2.17)
$M \leq 60$	3.45 (2.10)	−19.19 (0.86)	− 8.32 (4.86)	− 7.81 (4.41)	27.20 (5.96)
cube-root:					
	8.92 (1.45)	−13.81 (1.54)	− 1.59 (2.41)	− 0.75 (2.13)	35.40 (2.82)

McEliece. For the round 4 parameter sets of McEliece we performed a similar extrapolation shown in Table 6. For this extrapolation we used the expected time complexity of 59.74 CPU years for the McEliece-1347 instance.

While reducing the estimate in all settings, the overall picture stays the same under both estimation methods: Essentially all but the category 3 parameter set reach their security claims if cube-root memory access costs are imposed.

Acknowledgement. This work was funded by the Deutsche Forschungsgemeinschaft (DFG, German Research Foundation) - Project-ID MA 2536/12 and by BMBF under Industrial Blockchain – iBlockchain.

A   Generalization to Arbitrary Depth d

Note that in general we have

$$\mathcal{L}_{i+1} = \frac{(q_i \cdot \mathcal{L}_i)^2}{2^{\ell_i}},$$

where ℓ_i is the additional bitwise constraint introduced on level i. The time and memory complexity are then given as before. The saturation constraints extend to

$$q_i \cdot \mathcal{L}_i \leq \frac{|D_i|}{2^{\ell_1 + \ldots + \ell_i}} \text{ for } i = 2, \ldots, d-1,$$

where d is the depth of the tree. Together with the definition of the filtering probability given in Eq. (4), we can rewrite the saturation constraints for each level i as

$$\sum_{j=1}^{i} (2^{i-j} - 1)\ell_j \geq \sum_{j=1}^{i} 2^{i-j} \cdot r_j \text{ for } i = 1, \ldots d-2,$$

where there exist 2^{r_j} different representations of any element from D_{j+1} as a sum of two elements from D_j. Finally, the requirement of finding one representation of the solution in the final list is expressed via the condition

$$q_d \cdot \mathcal{L}_d = 1,$$

which similar to the saturation constraints rewrites to

$$\sum_{j=1}^{d-1} (2^{d-j} - 1)\ell_j = \sum_{j=1}^{d-1} 2^{d-j-1} \cdot r_j. \tag{8}$$

References

1. Albrecht, M.R., Ducas, L., Herold, G., Kirshanova, E., Postlethwaite, E.W., Stevens, M.: The general sieve kernel and new records in lattice reduction. In: Ishai, Y., Rijmen, V. (eds.) EUROCRYPT 2019. LNCS, vol. 11477, pp. 717–746. Springer, Cham (2019). https://doi.org/10.1007/978-3-030-17656-3_25

2. Aragon, N., et al.: BIKE: bit flipping key encapsulation (2020)
3. Aragon, N., Lavauzelle, J., Lequesne, M.: decodingchallenge.org (2019). https:// decodingchallenge.org
4. Austrin, P., Kaski, P., Koivisto, M., Määttä, J.: Space–time tradeoffs for sub-set sum: an improved worst case algorithm. In: Fomin, F.V., Freivalds, R., Kwiatkowska, M., Peleg, D. (eds.) ICALP 2013. LNCS, vol. 7965, pp. 45–56. Springer, Heidelberg (2013). https://doi.org/10.1007/978-3-642-39206-1_5
5. Baldi, M., Barenghi, A., Chiaraluce, F., Pelosi, G., Santini, P.: A finite regime analysis of information set decoding algorithms. Algorithms 12(10), 209 (2019)
6. Bardet, M., et al.: Improvements of algebraic attacks for solving the rank decoding and MinRank problems. In: Moriai, S., Wang, H. (eds.) ASIACRYPT 2020. LNCS, vol. 12491, pp. 507–536. Springer, Cham (2020). https://doi.org/10.1007/978-3-030-64837-4_17
7. Becker, A., Coron, J.-S., Joux, A.: Improved generic algorithms for hard knap-sacks. In: Paterson, K.G. (ed.) EUROCRYPT 2011. LNCS, vol. 6632, pp. 364–385. Springer, Heidelberg (2011). https://doi.org/10.1007/978-3-642-20465-4_21
8. Becker, A., Ducas, L., Gama, N., Laarhoven, T.: New directions in nearest neighbor searching with applications to lattice sieving. In: Krauthgamer, R. (ed.) 27th SODA, pp. 10–24. ACM-SIAM (Jan 2016). https://doi.org/10.1137/1.9781611974331.ch2
9. Becker, A., Joux, A., May, A., Meurer, A.: Decoding random binary linear codes in $2^{n/20}$: How 1+1= 0 improves information set decoding. In: Pointcheval, D., Johansson, T. (eds.) EUROCRYPT 2012. LNCS, vol. 7237, pp. 520–536. Springer, Heidelberg (2012). https://doi.org/10.1007/978-3-642-29011-4_31
10. Bernstein, D.J., Lange, T., Peters, C.: Attacking and defending the McEliece cryp-tosystem. In: Buchmann, J., Ding, J. (eds.) PQCrypto 2008. LNCS, vol. 5299, pp. 31–46. Springer, Heidelberg (2008). https://doi.org/10.1007/978-3-540-88403-3_3
11. Blum, A., Kalai, A., Wasserman, H.: Noise-tolerant learning, the parity problem, and the statistical query model. In: 32nd ACM STOC, pp. 435–440. ACM Press (May 2000). https://doi.org/10.1145/335305.335355
12. Bonnetain, X., Bricout, R., Schrottenloher, A., Shen, Y.: Improved classical and quantum algorithms for subset-sum. In: Moriai, S., Wang, H. (eds.) ASIACRYPT 2020. LNCS, vol. 12492, pp. 633–666. Springer, Cham (2020). https://doi.org/10.1007/978-3-030-64834-3_22
13. Both, L., May, A.: Optimizing bjmm with nearest neighbors: full decoding in 22/21n and mceliece security. In: WCC Workshop on Coding and Cryptography, vol. 214 (2017)
14. Both, L., May, A.: Decoding linear codes with high error rate and its impact for LPN security. In: Lange, T., Steinwandt, R. (eds.) PQCrypto 2018. LNCS, vol. 10786, pp. 25–46. Springer, Cham (2018). https://doi.org/10.1007/978-3-319-79063-3_2
15. Bricout, R., Chailloux, A., Debris-Alazard, T., Lequesne, M.: Ternary syndrome decoding with large weight. In: Paterson, K.G., Stebila, D. (eds.) SAC 2019. LNCS, vol. 11959, pp. 437–466. Springer, Cham (2020). https://doi.org/10.1007/978-3-030-38471-5_18
16. Delaplace, C., Esser, A., May, A.: Improved low-memory subset sum and LPN algorithms via multiple collisions. In: Albrecht, M. (ed.) IMACC 2019. LNCS, vol. 11929, pp. 178–199. Springer, Cham (2019). https://doi.org/10.1007/978-3-030-35199-1_9
17. Dinur, I.: An algorithmic framework for the generalized birthday problem. Designs, Codes Cryptogr. 1–30 (2018)

18. Dinur, I.: Cryptanalytic applications of the polynomial method for solving multivariate equation systems over GF(2). In: Canteaut, A., Standaert, F.-X. (eds.) EUROCRYPT 2021. LNCS, vol. 12696, pp. 374–403. Springer, Cham (2021). https://doi.org/10.1007/978-3-030-77870-5_14

19. Dinur, I., Dunkelman, O., Keller, N., Shamir, A.: Efficient dissection of composite problems, with applications to cryptanalysis, knapsacks, and combinatorial search problems. In: Safavi-Naini, R., Canetti, R. (eds.) CRYPTO 2012. LNCS, vol. 7417, pp. 719–740. Springer, Heidelberg (2012). https://doi.org/10.1007/978-3-642-32009-5_42

20. Ducas, L., Stevens, M., van Woerden, W.: Advanced lattice sieving on gpus, with tensor cores. In: Canteaut, A., Standaert, F.-X. (eds.) EUROCRYPT 2021. LNCS, vol. 12697, pp. 249–279. Springer, Cham (2021). https://doi.org/10.1007/978-3-030-77886-6_9

21. Dumer, I.: On minimum distance decoding of linear codes. In: Proceedings 5th Joint Soviet-Swedish International Workshop on Information Theory, pp. 50–52 (1991)

22. Esser, A.: Memory-efficient algorithms for solving subset sum and related problems with cryptanalytic applications. Ph.D. thesis, Ruhr University Bochum, Germany (2020)

23. Esser, A.: Revisiting nearest-neighbor-based information set decoding. Cryptology ePrint Archive (2022)

24. Esser, A., Bellini, E.: Syndrome decoding estimator. In: PKC 2022. LNCS, vol. 13177, pp. 112–141. Springer, Cham (2022). https://doi.org/10.1007/978-3-030-97121-2_5

25. Esser, A., Kübler, R., May, A.: LPN decoded. In: Katz, J., Shacham, H. (eds.) CRYPTO 2017. LNCS, vol. 10402, pp. 486–514. Springer, Cham (2017). https://doi.org/10.1007/978-3-319-63715-0_17

26. Esser, A., May, A.: Better sample-random subset sum in $2^{0.255n}$ and its impact on decoding random linear codes. arXiv preprint arXiv:1907.04295, withdrawn (2019)

27. Esser, A., May, A.: Low weight discrete logarithm and subset Sum in $2^{0.65n}$ with polynomial memory. In: Canteaut, A., Ishai, Y. (eds.) EUROCRYPT 2020. LNCS, vol. 12107, pp. 94–122. Springer, Cham (2020). https://doi.org/10.1007/978-3-030-45727-3_4

28. Esser, A., May, A., Zweydinger, F.: McEliece needs a break - solving McEliece-1284 and quasi-cyclic-2918 with modern ISD. In: Dunkelman, O., Dziembowski, S. (eds.) EUROCRYPT 2022, Part III. LNCS, vol. 13277, pp. 433–457. Springer, Heidelberg (2022). https://doi.org/10.1007/978-3-031-07082-2_16

29. Horowitz, E., Sahni, S.: Computing partitions with applications to the knapsack problem. J. ACM (JACM) **21**(2), 277–292 (1974)

30. Howgrave-Graham, N., Joux, A.: New generic algorithms for hard knapsacks. In: Gilbert, H. (ed.) EUROCRYPT 2010. LNCS, vol. 6110, pp. 235–256. Springer, Heidelberg (2010). https://doi.org/10.1007/978-3-642-13190-5_12

31. Karpman, P., Lefevre, C.: Time-memory tradeoffs for large-weight syndrome decoding in ternary codes. In: Public-Key Cryptography - PKC 2022–25th IACR International Conference on Practice and Theory of Public-Key Cryptography. LNCS, vol. 13177, pp. 82–111. Springer (2022). https://doi.org/10.1007/978-3-030-97121-2_4

32. May, A.: How to meet ternary LWE keys. In: Malkin, T., Peikert, C. (eds.) CRYPTO 2021. LNCS, vol. 12826, pp. 701–731. Springer, Cham (2021). https://doi.org/10.1007/978-3-030-84245-1_24

33. May, A., Meurer, A., Thomae, E.: Decoding random linear codes in $\tilde{\mathcal{O}}(2^{0.054n})$. In: Lee, D.H., Wang, X. (eds.) ASIACRYPT 2011. LNCS, vol. 7073, pp. 107–124. Springer, Heidelberg (2011). https://doi.org/10.1007/978-3-642-25385-0_6

34. May, A., Ozerov, I.: On computing nearest neighbors with applications to decoding of binary linear codes. In: Oswald, E., Fischlin, M. (eds.) EUROCRYPT 2015. LNCS, vol. 9056, pp. 203–228. Springer, Heidelberg (2015). https://doi.org/10.1007/978-3-662-46800-5_9

35. Nguyen, P.Q., Shparlinski, I.E., Stern, J.: Distribution of modular sums and the security of the server aided exponentiation. In: Cryptography and Computational Number Theory, pp. 331–342. Springer (2001). https://doi.org/10.1007/978-3-0348-8295-8_24

36. Nikolić, I., Sasaki, Yu.: Refinements of the k-tree algorithm for the generalized birthday problem. In: Iwata, T., Cheon, J.H. (eds.) ASIACRYPT 2015. LNCS, vol. 9453, pp. 683–703. Springer, Heidelberg (2015). https://doi.org/10.1007/978-3-662-48800-3_28

37. Prange, E.: The use of information sets in decoding cyclic codes. IRE Trans. Inf. Theory **8**(5), 5–9 (1962)

38. Schroeppel, R., Shamir, A.: A $T = O(2^{n/2})$, $S = O(2^{n/4})$ algorithm for certain NP-complete problems. SIAM J. Comput. **10**(3), 456–464 (1981)

39. Stern, J.: A method for finding codewords of small weight. In: Cohen, G., Wolfmann, J. (eds.) Coding Theory 1988. LNCS, vol. 388, pp. 106–113. Springer, Heidelberg (1989). https://doi.org/10.1007/BFb0019850

40. Canto Torres, R., Sendrier, N.: Analysis of information set decoding for a sub-linear error weight. In: Takagi, T. (ed.) PQCrypto 2016. LNCS, vol. 9606, pp. 144–161. Springer, Cham (2016). https://doi.org/10.1007/978-3-319-29360-8_10

41. Udovenko, A., Vitto, G.: Breaking the $ikep182 challenge. Cryptology ePrint Archive, Report 2021/1421 (2021). https://eprint.iacr.org/2021/1421

42. Various: Round 3 official comment: Classic McEliece (2021). https://groups.google.com/a/list.nist.gov/g/pqc-forum/c/ldAzu9PeaIM/m/VhLBcydEAAAJ

43. Wagner, D.: A generalized birthday problem. In: Yung, M. (ed.) CRYPTO 2002. LNCS, vol. 2442, pp. 288–304. Springer, Heidelberg (2002). https://doi.org/10.1007/3-540-45708-9_19

44. Wang, M., Liu, M.: Improved information set decoding for code-based cryptosystems with constrained memory. In: Wang, J., Yap, C. (eds.) FAW 2015. LNCS, vol. 9130, pp. 241–258. Springer, Cham (2015). https://doi.org/10.1007/978-3-319-19647-3_23

A New Algebraic Approach to the Regular Syndrome Decoding Problem and Implications for PCG Constructions

Pierre Briaud[1,2(✉)] [iD] and Morten Øygarden[3] [iD]

[1] Sorbonne Universités, UPMC Univ Paris 06, Paris, France
[2] Inria, Team COSMIQ, Paris, France
`pierre.briaud@inria.fr`
[3] Simula UiB, Bergen, Norway
`morten.oygarden@simula.no`

Abstract. The Regular Syndrome Decoding (RSD) problem, a variant of the Syndrome Decoding problem with a particular error distribution, was introduced almost 20 years ago by Augot *et al.*. In this problem, the error vector is divided into equally sized blocks, each containing a single noisy coordinate. More recently, the last five years have seen increased interest in this assumption due to its use in MPC and ZK applications. Generally referred to as "LPN with regular noise" in this context, the assumption allows to achieve better efficiency when compared to plain LPN. In all previous works of cryptanalysis, it has not been shown how to exploit the special feature of this problem in an attack.

We present the first algebraic attack on RSD. Based on a careful theoretical analysis of the underlying polynomial system, we propose concrete attacks that are able to take advantage of the regular noise distribution. In particular, we can identify several examples of concrete parameters where our techniques outperform other algorithms.

1 Introduction

The Regular Syndrome Decoding (RSD) problem is a variant of the well-known Syndrome Decoding (SD) problem, which is the standard assumption in code-based cryptography.

Definition 1 (Computational Syndrome Decoding (SD)). *Let* $(n, k, h) \in \mathbb{N}^3$ *with* $k \leq n$ *and* $h \leq n$. *Sample* $\boldsymbol{H} \leftarrow \mathbb{F}^{(n-k) \times n}$ *a full-rank matrix over a finite field* $\mathbb{F}$ *and* $\boldsymbol{e} \leftarrow \mathbb{F}^n$ *such that* $\boldsymbol{e}$ *is of Hamming weight* $|\boldsymbol{e}| = h$. *Given* $(\boldsymbol{H}, \boldsymbol{s}^\mathsf{T} := \boldsymbol{H}\boldsymbol{e}^\mathsf{T})$, *the goal is to recover the error vector* $\boldsymbol{e}$.

In the following, we will denote by $R := k/n$ (resp. $\rho := h/n$) the rate of the associated linear code (resp. error rate). RSD was introduced by Augot, Finiasz and Sendrier [6] as the underlying assumption for the Fast Syndrome-Based hash function. The only difference with SD lies in the choice of a particular error distribution:

C. Hazay and M. Stam (Eds.): EUROCRYPT 2023, LNCS 14008, pp. 391–422, 2023.
https://doi.org/10.1007/978-3-031-30589-4_14

Definition 2 (Computational Regular Syndrome Decoding (RSD)).
Let $(h, k, \beta) \in \mathbb{N}^3$ and $n = h\beta$. Sample $\boldsymbol{H} \leftarrow \mathbb{F}^{(n-k) \times n}$ a full-rank matrix over
a finite field $\mathbb{F}$ and $\boldsymbol{e} := (\boldsymbol{e}_1 || \ldots || \boldsymbol{e}_h) \leftarrow \mathbb{F}^n$ such that $\boldsymbol{e}_i \in \mathbb{F}^{\beta}$ is of Hamming
weight $|\boldsymbol{e}_i| = 1$ for $1 \leq i \leq h$. Given $(\boldsymbol{H}, \boldsymbol{s}^{\mathsf{T}} := \boldsymbol{H}\boldsymbol{e}^{\mathsf{T}})$, recover the error $\boldsymbol{e}$.

More recently, this problem has gained a renewed interest since its introduction
in secure computation. Its first use in this context is due to Hazai, Orsini, Scholl
and Soria-Vazques in their *TinyKeys* approach to design MPC-protocols with
improved efficiency [31]. Later, Boyle *et al.* suggested to rely on this assumption to build efficient Pseudo Random Correlation Generators (PCGs). These
primitives enable the generation of long sources of correlated randomness for
more advanced MPC and ZK applications [18]. This latter idea has been further
considered in a series of works [19, 20, 42, 44], where RSD is often referred to as
"LPN with regular noise".

LPN-Based Cryptography. In these more recent constructions, the LPN
problem is instantiated either with the *primal* or the *dual* formulation. The
search version of dual LPN is the computational SD problem stated in Definition 1 while primal LPN is the standard decoding problem for linear codes. Even
though these formulations are clearly equivalent in theory, choosing one instead
of the other has an impact in terms of efficiency. This can be seen when trying
to design a simple PRG relying on LPN. Given a seed $(\boldsymbol{m}, \boldsymbol{e}) \in \mathbb{F}^k \times \mathbb{F}^n$ and a
public matrix $\boldsymbol{G} \in \mathbb{F}^{k \times n}$ with $|\boldsymbol{e}| = h$, the output of the naive primal LPN-based
PRG is $\boldsymbol{m}\boldsymbol{G} + \boldsymbol{e} \in \mathbb{F}^n$. In particular, it is generally acknowledged by the community that this construction can only achieve quadratic stretch [18, Section 1.2
page 4][11, Section 2.5 page 9]. This is due to the fact that the length n cannot
be chosen too large compared to k and h, otherwise there will be k error-free
positions with non-negligible probability. On the contrary, the dual construction
$\boldsymbol{e} \mapsto \boldsymbol{e}\boldsymbol{H}^{\mathsf{T}} \in \mathbb{F}^{n-k}$ whose seed is just the low weight vector $\boldsymbol{e}$ does not exhibit the
same constraint. By fixing the weight and increasing n, one can indeed get an
output size mostly independent of the seed size. Other advantages of the dual
formulation is that the product $\boldsymbol{e}\boldsymbol{H}^{\mathsf{T}}$ is cheap to compute and the matrix $\boldsymbol{H}$
can be seen as a compression mapping $\mathbb{F}^n \to \mathbb{F}^{n-k}$. This may represent a useful
property for practical applications.

To improve computational efficiency without affecting security, it was proposed to choose d-local codes in the primal formulation, *i.e.*, matrices $\boldsymbol{G}$ such
that the Hamming weight of each column is a small integer d [4]. Such codes are
not suitable in the dual construction, see for instance [11, 18]. Therefore, other
code families such as quasi-cyclic codes [1] or MDPC codes [37] have be chosen
in this case. More importantly for us, and for the same purpose of efficiency,
various constructions have adopted a regular distribution for $\boldsymbol{e}$ [18–20, 42, 44].

Parameter Range. LPN instances used in the context of [18–20, 42, 44] typically have a higher size for the secret k, as well as a lower noise, than parameters
encountered in code-based cryptography. Echoing the above remark on primal

and dual LPN, the few proposed parameter sets may be divided into two categories depending on the application:

- instances used in the primal formulation have a rather small code rate R (non-constant) and noise rate ρ slightly larger than $\mathcal{O}(n^{-1/2})$.
- instances used in the dual formulation have constant code rate (often $1/2$ or $3/4$) and a weight h mostly independent from n.

Finally, the standard LPN problem is usually stated over the binary field $\mathbb{F}_2$, but some constructions require an LPN assumption over a larger field $\mathbb{F}$ of size typically $|\mathbb{F}| \geq 256$, for example [18,19,42], or even over more general integer rings [10,11] or polynomial rings [21].

Exploiting the Regular Distribution. A first security analysis of this type of LPN instances (over $\mathbb{F}_{2^{128}}$) was performed by Boyle et al. in [18, §5.1]. Later constructions also use it as a black box to derive their parameters [42,44]. In this particular regime, the best attacks are the folklore Gaussian attack and the Pooled Gauss variant [27], ISD algorithms [12,14,28,35,36,39] which may all be seen as refinements of the original Prange algorithm [38] and finally Statistical Decoding [23,32]. More recently, [34] studied the assumption for the same parameter range, but in a more general setting (larger fields or integer rings, not only Bernoulli distribution). Notably, they claim that some of the estimates of [18] are too conservative over large fields: ISD algorithms are still the best attack in this case, but the advantage of advanced ISD variants compared to Pooled Gauss (*e.g.*, Prange) quickly deteriorates when $|\mathbb{F}|$ increases. Finally, they show that the cost of Statistical Decoding is much higher than claimed in [18]. In particular, this is no longer the best attack even by taking into account the most recent development of [23] since the latter does not seem to perform well in this regime.

We remark that the use of a regular distribution is not seen as a clear weakness by the community [18,19,31,34,42,44], meaning that RSD is not believed to be particularly easier than SD in this PCG-relevant parameter zone. Thus, regular LPN instances are treated as random LPN instances to derive parameters. The only extensive survey about the cryptanalysis of RSD in all weight regimes was given in [31, Appendix B]. They conclude that ISD algorithms are the best attack on both SD and RSD when there is a unique solution. They also try to adapt the ISD algorithms to the regular structure [31, Appendix B.3] but the improvement does not seem apparent[1]. Finally, we have not found similar attempts to enhance LPN or SD attacks by exploiting the regular distribution and there does not seem to be any RSD-specific attack described in the literature.

---

[1] "ISD is always the most efficient attack and has roughly the same cost when considering SD and RSD" [31, p. 49].

Contribution. In this paper, we show that the regular noise distribution used in LPN may indeed be exploited by an attacker by presenting a new algebraic attack on the Regular Syndrome Decoding Problem. Contrary to known attacks, it is not an adaptation of SD techniques to solve RSD as it crucially benefits from the regular structure. It also differs in nature from the previous attacks (Gaussian Elimination, ISD and Statistical Decoding) which all boil down to exploiting a set of linear equations. More importantly, this allows us to identify a parameter range (relevant to cryptography) where algebraic attacks are not only competitive, but also outperform these algorithms.

Our attack is based on solving a polynomial system in the coordinates of the error e by combining the set of $n - k$ parity-check equations $He^{\mathsf{T}} = 0$ with another quadratic system which encodes the regular structure and which does not depend on the particular RSD instance. More precisely, for each block $e_i := (e_{i,1}, \ldots, e_{i,\beta}) \in \mathbb{F}^{\beta}$ for $1 \leq i \leq h$, we consider all equations of the form $e_{i,j_1} e_{i,j_2} = 0$ for $j_1 < j_2$. Over $\mathbb{F}_2$, we consider a variant of this combined system by adding extra structural equations of the same type. We then apply standard algorithms, e.g. XL/Gröbner bases, but a first theoretical contribution lies in the complexity analysis to estimate the degree at which the system is solved and which is always a challenge in algebraic cryptanalysis. For that purpose, we proceed by isolating the structural part of the system that we analyze on its own. Then, we formalize the assumption that the parity-check equations behave nicely in the quotient ring formed by the structural part, mimicking Bardet's definitions of semi-regularity [7]. In cases when the predicted solving degree is too large, we also propose a hybrid approach to decrease the complexity by fixing zero coordinates in the error e in the style of the regular version of Prange's algorithm given in [31, Appendix B.3].

In the same way as the Arora-Gê attack [5] takes advantage of a large number of LWE samples, our attack performs best on RSD instances where there are many parity-check equations (*i.e.* with smaller code rate R). This is typically the case for the parameter sets used to instantiate the primal LPN formulation. Under similar assumptions on our specialized systems, this hybrid technique allows us to obtain very competitive complexities for several parameters of this kind, see Table 1. Note that these various assumptions have been extensively tested.

In Table 1, we also notice that the attack seems to suffer less than linear algebra-based techniques – Gaussian elimination or ISD algorithms – when the field size is increased. Indeed, for all but the last parameter set, the increase in complexity when going from $\mathbb{F}_2$ to $\mathbb{F}_{2^{128}}$ is smaller for our attack than for the previously best known algorithms. Our method also seems to perform better in some regimes compared to others. In particular, we try to strengthen these initial intuitions by providing a sketch of asymptotic analysis of the complexity of solving our plain systems.

Table 1. Time complexity over $\mathbb{F}_2$ and $\mathbb{F}_{2^{128}}$ on parameter sets from [18,34]

n	k	h	Best $\mathbb{F}_2$ [34]	This work $\mathbb{F}_2$	Best $\mathbb{F}_{2^{128}}$ [34]	This work $\mathbb{F}_{2^{128}}$
2^{22}	64770	4788	147	103	156	111
2^{20}	32771	2467	143	126	155	131
2^{18}	15336	1312	139	123	153	133
2^{16}	7391	667	135	141	151	151
2^{14}	3482	338	132	140	150	152
2^{12}	1589	172	131	136	155	152
2^{10}	652	106	176	146	194	180

2 Preliminaries

2.1 Algebraic Background

Let A denote a polynomial ring over a field $\mathbb{F}$ in n variables. A polynomial $f \in A$ is *homogeneous* if all its monomials have the same degree and *affine* otherwise. There are two standard methods for turning an affine polynomial into a homogeneous polynomial that we will use in our analysis. For an affine polynomial f, the first one considers the polynomial $f^{(h)}$ which only consists of the terms in f of degree $\deg(f)$ (i.e., discarding all lower degree terms). The second method is to *homogenize* f by expanding the polynomial ring with a homogenization variable y and by defining $f^{(y)}(x_1, \ldots, x_n, y) := (1/y)^{\deg(f)} f(x_1/y, \ldots, x_n/y)$.

An ideal is homogeneous if there exists a set of homogeneous generators. We will turn an affine ideal $I \subset A$ into a homogeneous ideal $I^{(h)}$ (resp. $I^{(y)}$) by applying $f^{(h)}$ (resp. $f^{(y)}$) to each of its generators. When I is homogeneous, the set $I_d := \{f \in I, \deg(f) = d\} = I \cap A_d$ is a subspace of A_d the vector space of homogeneous polynomials of total degree d.

Hilbert Function and Hilbert Series. For a homogeneous ideal $I \subset A$, we consider the *Hilbert function*:

$$\mathcal{HF}_{A/I} : \mathbb{N} \longrightarrow \mathbb{N}$$
$$d \longmapsto \dim_{\mathbb{F}}(A_d/I_d).$$

The Hilbert series is a convenient tool to study the combinatorial structure of homogeneous ideals.

Definition 3 (Hilbert series). *Let $I \subset A$ be a homogeneous ideal. The Hilbert series of the quotient ring A/I is defined by*

$$\mathcal{H}_{A/I}(z) := \sum_{d=0}^{\infty} \mathcal{HF}_{A/I}(d) \cdot z^d. \tag{1}$$

Over a finite field $\mathbb{F}$, we implicitly add all the *field equations* of the form $x_i^{|\mathbb{F}|} - x_i = 0$ for $1 \leq i \leq n$. Therefore, we will study zero-dimensional ideals, *i.e.*, ideals I such that the quotient A/I is a finite dimensional vector space. For such ideals, we call *degree of regularity* d_{reg} the smallest integer d such that $I_d = A_d$. In this particular case, the Hilbert series is a polynomial.

Regular and Semi-regular Sequences. Unfortunately, Hilbert series are difficult to compute in general. Still, there is a known expression for the series of a subclass of systems whose definition is related to the notion of zero-divisor. When $m \leq n$, we say that a homogeneous system $\mathcal{F} := \{f_1, \ldots, f_m\}$ is *regular* if f_i is not a zero divisor in $A/\langle f_1, \ldots, f_{i-1} \rangle$ for any $1 \leq i \leq m$. The Hilbert series of such a system is given by

Proposition 1. *Let $\mathcal{F} := \{f_1, \ldots, f_m\}$ be a homogeneous regular system such that $\deg(f_i) = d_i$ for $1 \leq i \leq m$. We have*

$$\mathcal{H}_{A/\langle \mathcal{F} \rangle}(z) = \frac{\prod_{i=1}^{m}(1 - z^{d_i})}{(1 - z)^n}.$$

This definition has been extended to the overdetermined case, $m > n$, with the notion of *semi-regular* sequences introduced by Bardet.

Definition 4 (Semi-regular sequence, [7]). *Consider $\mathcal{F} := \{f_1, \ldots, f_m\}$ a homogeneous sequence such that $I := \langle \mathcal{F} \rangle$ is zero-dimensional with degree of regularity d_{reg}. The sequence $\mathcal{F}$ is said to be semi-regular if $I \neq A$ and if for $1 \leq i \leq m$, $g_i f_i = 0$ in $A/\langle f_1, \ldots, f_{i-1} \rangle$ with $\deg(g_i f_i) < d_{reg}$ implies $g_i = 0$ in $A/\langle f_1, \ldots, f_{i-1} \rangle$.*

Over $\mathbb{F}_2$, there is a similar definition but which needs to take the Frobenius morphism into account:

Definition 5 (Semi-regular sequence over $\mathbb{F}_2$, [7]). *Let S denote the quotient ring $\mathbb{F}_2[\boldsymbol{x}]/\langle x_1^2, \ldots, x_n^2 \rangle$. A homogeneous sequence $\mathcal{F} := \{f_1, \ldots, f_m\}$ with degree of regularity d_{reg} is semi regular over $\mathbb{F}_2$ if $I \neq S$ and if for $1 \leq i \leq m$, $g_i f_i = 0$ in $S/\langle f_1, \ldots, f_{i-1} \rangle$ with $\deg(g_i f_i) < d_{reg}$ implies $g_i = 0$ in $S/\langle f_1, \ldots, f_i \rangle$.*

The Hilbert series is also known for such systems. In particular, it is a polynomial since the corresponding ideal is zero-dimensional.

Proposition 2 ([7]). *Let $\mathcal{F} := \{f_1, \ldots, f_m\}$ be a homogeneous semi-regular system where $\deg(f_i) = d_i$ for $1 \leq i \leq m$ and let $S_{m,n,d}(z) = \frac{\prod_{i=1}^{m}(1-z^{d_i})}{(1-z)^n}$. We have*

$$\mathcal{H}_{A/\langle \mathcal{F} \rangle}(z) = [S_{m,n,\boldsymbol{d}}(z)]^+,$$

where $[\cdot]^+$ means truncation after the first non-positive coefficient.

Proposition 3 ([7]). *Let* $\mathcal{F} := \{f_1, \ldots, f_m\}$ *be a homogeneous semi-regular system over* $\mathbb{F}_2$ *where* $\deg(f_i) = d_i$ *for* $1 \leq i \leq m$ *and let* $T_{m,n,d}(z) = \frac{(1+z)^n}{\prod_{i=1}^{m}(1+z^{d_i})}$. *We have*

$$\mathcal{H}_{A/\langle \mathcal{F} \rangle}(z) = [T_{m,n,d}(z)]^{+}.$$

Finally, an affine sequence $\mathcal{F} := \{f_1, \ldots, f_m\}$ is said to be semi-regular in [7, Def. 3.5.1] if the homogeneous sequence $\mathcal{F}^{(h)} := \{f_1^{(h)}, \ldots, f_m^{(h)}\}$ is semi-regular in the sense of Definition 4. Interestingly, it turns out that this subclass of systems is somehow large since it is conjectured that most systems behave as such (this is related to the Fröberg conjecture [30]). In simpler terms, we may say that randomly chosen polynomial systems with $m \leq n$ (resp. $m > n$) have an overwhelming probability of being regular (resp. semi-regular).

Unfortunately, we will see that the polynomial systems considered in this work cannot be directly analyzed by these tools. This issue is uniquely related to structural equations inherent in the systems. It is then possible to split the polynomial system in two: the first part can be treated in a prior analysis, and the second part can be assumed to be *generic*. At this stage, we will be able to rely on the same algebraic tools as used in proofs of Proposition 2 and Proposition 3 to derive our final Hilbert series, up to minor technical amendments.

2.2 Solving Polynomial Systems

Gröbner basis techniques are generally used to solve cryptographically relevant polynomial systems, keeping in mind that this approach is closely related to the XL algorithm [26]. Both approaches typically depend on the notion of *Macaulay matrix*. If $\mathcal{F}$ is homogeneous, the (homogenous) Macaulay matrix $M_d(\mathcal{F})$ is defined as the coefficient matrix of $(\mu_{i,j} \cdot f_j)_{i,\ 1 \leq j \leq m}$ where $\mu_{i,j}$ is any monomial of degree $d - \deg(f_i)$. If $\mathcal{F}$ is affine, we prefer to consider $M_{\leq d}(\mathcal{F})$ where now $\deg(\mu_{i,j}) \leq d - \deg(f_i)$ and where the columns are indexed by all monomials of degree $\leq d$.

XL Wiedemann. The main idea of XL is to solve by linearization an augmented system in degree $\leq d$ obtained from $\mathcal{F}$ by multiplying the initial polynomials by all monomials of the suitable degree. The value of d is chosen such that there are enough linearly independent equations compared to the number of monomials and the matrix of the linearized system is simply the Macaulay matrix $M_{\leq d}(\mathcal{F})$. In the particular case when the linear system in degree d has a unique solution and is sparse enough, this approach may greatly benefit from the use of the Wiedemann algorithm [43] or its further improvements [25,41]. The application of the Wiedemann algorithm to solve Macaulay matrices has been implemented and studied in [24]. In our setting, we can estimate the cost of this approach to find the solution of the linear system to be

$$3 \cdot n_\mu \cdot \mathcal{M}_{\leq d}^2, \tag{2}$$

where n_μ is the number of terms in the polynomials of $\mathcal{F}$ (*i.e.* the row weight of $M_{\leq d}(\mathcal{F})$), where $\mathcal{M}_{\leq d}$ is the number of columns in $M_{\leq d}(\mathcal{F})$ and where the choice of a hidden constant equal to 3 is very standard in the literature on multivariate cryptography, see for example [13, Prop 3 p. 219], [17].

Witness Degree. While the degree of regularity d_{reg} is usually employed as the main parameter to estimate the complexity of Gröbner basis algorithms on homogeneous systems, we will require a related, though slightly different notion in the case of XL Wiedemann. A first reason is that we have just defined d_{reg} for homogeneous systems whereas we will typically apply this algorithm on *affine* equations. To this end, let us recall the *witness degree* d_{wit}, originally introduced in [8, Definition 2] for the binary case. For an ideal I, the notation $\mathrm{LM}(I)$ denotes the monomial ideal generated by the leading monomials of all polynomials in I for an arbitrary graded ordering.

Definition 6 (Witness degree). *Let $\mathcal{F} := \{f_1, \dots f_m\}$ be an affine polynomial system over $\mathbb{F}_q$, and $I := \langle \mathcal{F} \rangle$ its associated ideal. Define the $\mathbb{F}_q$-vector spaces*

$$I_{\leq d} := \{p \in I \mid \deg(p) \leq d\},$$

$$J_{\leq d} := \left\{ p \in I \mid p = \sum_{i=1}^{m} g_i f_i, \text{ and } \deg(g_i) \leq d - \deg(f_i) \text{ for } 1 \leq i \leq m \right\}.$$

The witness degree d_{wit} *of $\mathcal{F}$ is defined as the smallest integer d_0 such that $I_{\leq d_0} = J_{\leq d_0}$ and $LM(I_{\leq d_0}) = LM(I)$.*

We will be interested in cases where $\mathcal{F}$ contains fewer than n affine polynomials, whereas its Gröbner basis is either $\{1\}$, or a set of n affine polynomials. Thus there are non-trivial polynomials $\sum g_i f_i \in I$ where the coefficients of the higher degree terms sum to zero. It follows that if $\mathcal{F}$ is also semi-regular, then d_{reg} is a lower bound on the degree d such that $J_{\leq d} = I_{\leq d}$. This ensures $d_{\mathrm{wit}} \geq d_{\mathrm{reg}}$. Even under these assumptions, we remark that d_{reg} is only attached to $\mathcal{F}^{(h)}$, whereas the purpose of d_{wit} is precisely to analyze the lower degree parts of $\mathcal{F}$ as well.

   We will later see examples where d_{wit} is strictly larger than d_{reg}, so we need a more accurate estimate of the former than this lower bound. If the input polynomial system admits no solutions (i.e., $\langle \mathcal{F} \rangle = \langle 1 \rangle$), its witness degree can be upper bounded by the degree of regularity of the corresponding homogenized system by adding an extra homogenization variable y (see beginning of Sect. 2.1). In other words, we have

Proposition 4. *Let $\mathcal{F} = \{f_1, \dots, f_m, x_1^q - x_1, \dots, x_n^q - x_n\}$ be a sequence of polynomials in $\mathbb{F}_q[x_1, \dots, x_n]$ that admits no solutions, and let $I^{(y)}$ be its associated homogenized ideal. Then $d_{wit}(\mathcal{F}) \leq d_{reg}\left(I^{(y)}\right)$.*

This statement is shown[2] in [8, Proposition 5].

Note that the requirement of $\mathcal{F}$ being non-consistent makes sense since the BooleanSolve algorithm presented in [8] is a hybrid algorithm, and the majority of calls to a polynomial system solver is made for systems without any solutions. We will indeed follow the same strategy for the hybrid systems considered in Sect. 4. However, on the plain system, Proposition 4 cannot be applied readily to bound d_{wit}. Instead, we will propose a more direct approach of inspecting affine Macaulay matrices in Sect. 3.2.

3   Algebraic Modeling of the RSD Problem

In this section, we introduce the polynomial systems that we consider for the RSD problem. We will work over a polynomial ring $A = \mathbb{F}[e]$, where each error vector entry $e_{i,j}$ is treated as an indeterminate to be solved for. The equations of the polynomial systems are obtained from the $n - k$ parity-check equations $s^{\mathsf{T}} = He^{\mathsf{T}}$ to which we add constraints coming from the regular structure. Modeling 1 is used to solve RSD over an arbitrary (large) field $\mathbb{F}$ while Modeling 2 is specific to the binary case.

Modeling 1 (Over a large field). *For a given RSD instance (H, s^{T}) over $\mathbb{F}$, Modeling 1 is the sequence of polynomials $\mathcal{F} := \mathcal{P} \cup \mathcal{B}$, where*

i) $\mathcal{P}$ *is the set of the $n - k$ linear polynomials given by the parity-check equations $s^{\mathsf{T}} = He^{\mathsf{T}}$;*

ii) $\mathcal{B}$ *is the set of quadratic polynomials that describe the regular form of the error vector e, namely $e_{i,j_1} e_{i,j_2} = 0$ for $1 \leq i \leq h$ and $1 \leq j_1 < j_2 \leq \beta$.*

We also include the so-called field equations $e_{i,j}^{|\mathbb{F}|} - e_{i,j} = 0$, so that the ideal generated by Modeling 1 is zero-dimensional. However, these equations will not be useful for the computation due to their large degree and thus the situation is completely different over $\mathbb{F}_2$ in that respect. Also, note that Modeling 1 only captures the fact that the Hamming weight in each block is at most 1 since we have no information on the non-zero coordinate. Over $\mathbb{F}_2$ however, we know that this non-zero component is equal to 1.

Modeling 2 (Over $\mathbb{F}_2$). *For a given binary RSD instance (H, s^{T}), Modeling 2 is the sequence of polynomials $\mathcal{F}_{\mathbb{F}_2} = \mathcal{P} \cup \mathcal{B} \cup \mathcal{Q}_{\mathbb{F}_2} \cup \mathcal{L}_{\mathbb{F}_2}$, where $\mathcal{P}$ and $\mathcal{B}$ are as in Modeling 1 and where:*

i) $\mathcal{Q}_{\mathbb{F}_2}$ *is the set of field equations $e_{i,j}^2 - e_{i,j} = 0$ for $1 \leq i \leq h$ and $1 \leq j \leq \beta$;*

ii) $\mathcal{L}_{\mathbb{F}_2}$ *is the set of h linear equations $1 - \sum_{j=1}^{\beta} e_{i,j} = 0$ for $1 \leq i \leq h$ which express the fact that each block has a unique non-zero coordinate.*

---

[2] The statement in [8, Proposition 5] is only for $\mathbb{F}_2$, but we note that the same proof also works for the case of $\mathbb{F}_q$.

In both cases, the main contribution is the set $\mathcal{P}$ containing $n - k = n(1 - R)$ parity-check equations. Therefore, this approach is expected to be relevant for instances with non-constant rate. This is the case of the parameter sets used to instantiate primal LPN, see [18,34,42,44]. From the public generator matrix G, we trivially construct the equivalent dual LPN instance and we then use Modeling 1 or 2 on this dual problem. Finally, we see that the unknowns are merely the coordinates of the error vector e. In particular, we expect as many solutions as the initial RSD instance, *i.e.* 1, for the range of parameters of interest[3]. This will be needed to justify the use of the XL algorithm later.

3.1   Deriving Hilbert Series

The goal of this section is to compute the Hilbert series (Definition 3) of the homogeneous ideals $I := \langle \mathcal{F}^{(h)} \rangle$ and $I_{\mathbb{F}_2} := \langle \mathcal{F}_{\mathbb{F}_2}^{(h)} \rangle$ associated to Modeling 1 and Modeling 2 respectively. We start by observing that these sequences cannot be analyzed as semi-regular systems. Indeed, consider the equations $f_1 := e_{1,1}e_{1,2}$ and $f_2 := e_{1,2}e_{1,3}$. Since $e_{1,1}f_2 = 0$ in $A/\langle f_1 \rangle$, the polynomial f_2 is a non-trivial zero divisor in $A/\langle f_1 \rangle$. Note that this type of cancellation does not depend on the particular RSD instance, but rather comes from the regular structure of e. Thus, it still makes sense to compute Hilbert series that will be valid for generic instances of the RSD problem.

Hilbert Series for Modeling 1. Recall that Modeling 1 is the sequence $\mathcal{F} = \mathcal{P} \cup \mathcal{B}$, where $\mathcal{P}$ are the parity-check equations and where $\mathcal{B}$ describes the regular structure of the error vector. The first step will be to compute the Hilbert series $\mathcal{H}_S(z)$ by monomial counting, for $S := A/\langle \mathcal{B}^{(h)} \rangle$. Since S is not a polynomial ring, we will not formally speak about (semi-)regular sequences over S. Yet, we still want to capture the core idea of the remaining parity-check equations behaving nicely, by introducing the following assumption for Modeling 1.

Assumption 1. *Consider an instance $\mathcal{F}$ of Modeling 1 and let d_{reg} be the degree of regularity of $I := \langle \mathcal{F}^{(h)} \rangle$. Define the quotient ring $S := A/\langle \mathcal{B}^{(h)} \rangle$ and let $\mathcal{P}^{(h)} = \{ p_1^{(h)}, \ldots, p_{n-k}^{(h)} \}$ denote the set of linear parity-check equations. We assume that for $1 \leq i \leq n - k$, $g_i p_i = 0$ in $S/\langle p_1, \ldots, p_{i-1} \rangle$ with $\deg(g_i p_i) < d_{reg}$ implies $g_i = 0$ in $S/\langle p_1, \ldots, p_{i-1} \rangle$.*

Relying on this assumption, we can obtain the final Hilbert series for $I := \langle \mathcal{F}^{(h)} \rangle$:

Theorem 1. *Under Assumption 1, the Hilbert series of the homogeneous ideal $I := \langle \mathcal{F}^{(h)} \rangle$ associated with Modeling 1 is given by*

$$\mathcal{H}_{A/I}(z) = \left[(1 - z)^{n-k} \cdot \left(1 + \beta \cdot \tfrac{z}{1-z} \right)^h \right]_+ , \tag{3}$$

---

[3] Even though the weight h is slightly larger than the Gilbert-Varshamov distance, the regular structure is a much stronger requirement.

where $[.]_+$ *means truncation after the first non-positive coefficient, and where we call* $(1-z)^{n-k} \cdot \left(1 + \beta \cdot \frac{z}{1-z}\right)^h$ *the generating series of* I.

Proof. The proof can be found in Appendix A.1.   □

Hilbert Series for Modeling 2. Modeling 2 contains extra structural equations, starting from the field equations in $\mathcal{Q}_{\mathbb{F}_2}$. A difficulty arises when adding the last set of equations $\mathcal{L}_{\mathbb{F}_2}$ since it yields another type of cancellation. For $1 \le i \le h$ and $1 \le j_0 \le \beta$, we indeed have:

$$e_{i,j_0} \cdot \left(-\sum_{j=1}^{\beta} e_{i,j}\right) = 0 \bmod \{e_{i,j_0}^2, \{e_{i,j_1}e_{i,j_2}\}_{j_1<j_2}\}. \tag{4}$$

In other words, any polynomial in $\mathcal{L}_{\mathbb{F}_2}^{(h)}$ is a zero divisor in $A/\langle \mathcal{B}^{(h)} \cup \mathcal{Q}_{\mathbb{F}_2}^{(h)} \rangle$. To keep the same type of analysis as with Modeling 1, we may use $\mathcal{L}_{\mathbb{F}_2}$ to remove h variables. More formally, we define the graded ring homomorphism

$$\mathcal{L} : \mathbb{F}_2[e] \longrightarrow \mathbb{F}_2[x]$$
$$e_{i,j} \longmapsto x_{i,j}, \text{ for } 1 \le i \le h \text{ and } 1 \le j < \beta$$
$$e_{i,\beta} \longmapsto \sum_{j=1}^{\beta-1} x_{i,j} \text{ for } 1 \le i \le h.$$

Definition 7. *Consider an instance of Modeling 2, and* $\mathcal{L}$ *be as detailed above. We then define* $A' := \mathcal{L}(A)$, $I' := \mathcal{L}(I^{(h)})$, $\mathcal{B}' := \mathcal{L}(\mathcal{B}^{(h)})$, $\mathcal{Q}' := \mathcal{L}(\mathcal{Q}_{\mathbb{F}_2}^{(h)})$ *and* $S' := A'/\langle \mathcal{B}' \cup \mathcal{Q}' \rangle$.

The following lemma shows that A' is a polynomial ring and describes the structure of S'.

Lemma 1. A' *is isomorphic to* $\mathbb{F}_2[x_1, \ldots, x_{h(\beta-1)}]$. *Moreover, the ideal* $\langle \mathcal{B}' \cup \mathcal{Q}' \rangle$ *is generated by* $\mathcal{G} = \{x_{i,j}x_{i,l} \mid 1 \le i \le h \text{ and } 1 \le j, l < \beta\}$.

Proof. The first statement is immediate from the definition of $\mathcal{L}$. For the second statement, we note that $\mathcal{G}$ is exactly the image of generators of $\mathcal{B}^{(h)} \cup \mathcal{Q}_{\mathbb{F}_2}^{(h)}$ that does not contain an element $e_{i,\beta}$. To see that the image of the remaining generators of $\mathcal{Q}_{\mathbb{F}_2}^{(h)}$ does not add anything new, we get

$$\mathcal{L}(e_{i,\beta}^2) = \left(\sum_{j=1}^{\beta-1} x_{i,j}^2\right) = 0 \bmod \mathcal{G}.$$

The cancellations of the remaining generators of $\mathcal{B}^{(h)}$ were already pointed out by (4).   □

We can furthermore use Lemma 1 to count the number of monomials in S'. Indeed, the possible monomials are squarefree and contain only one variable per block due to the shape of $\mathcal{G}$. In particular, a degree d monomial defines a set of d blocks. Then, each block contains $\beta - 1$ relevant variables instead of β since we reduce modulo $\mathcal{L}_{\mathbb{F}_2}$. This shows that there are $\binom{h}{d}(\beta - 1)^d$ degree d monomials in S'.

We now need to adopt a similar assumption as with Modeling 1. Note the strong similarity between Definition 5 and the following Assumption 2:

Assumption 2. *Consider an instance of Modeling 2 with degree of regularity d_{reg}, and let S' be as defined in Definition 7. For every parity-check equation, p_i, write $p_i' = \mathcal{L}(p_i^{(h)})$. We assume that for $1 \leq i \leq n - k$, $g_i p_i' = 0$ in $S'/\langle p_1', \ldots, p_{i-1}'\rangle$ with $\deg(g_i) + \deg(p_i') < d_{reg}$ implies $g_i = 0$ in $S'/\langle p_1', \ldots, p_i'\rangle$.*

Theorem 2. *Under Assumption 2, the Hilbert series of the homogeneous ideal $I_{\mathbb{F}_2} := \langle \mathcal{F}_{\mathbb{F}_2}^{(h)}\rangle$ associated to Modeling 2 is given by*

$$\mathcal{H}_{A/I_{\mathbb{F}_2}}(z) = \left[\frac{(1+(\beta-1)\cdot z)^h}{(1+z)^{n-k}}\right]_+ . \tag{5}$$

Proof. The proof can be found in Appendix A.2.   □

3.2   Estimating the Witness Degree

As explained at the end of Sect. 2, we will use the witness degree d_{wit} of the input polynomial system (see Definition 6) to estimate the cost of the XL Wiedemann approach.

By definition, the system $\mathcal{F}$ of Modeling 1 (resp. Modeling 2) admits at least one solution and we will assume that it is unique for the range of parameters of interest. Note that a polynomial system that includes field equations[4] and admits a unique solution $(a_1, \ldots, a_n)$ has reduced Gröbner basis $\{x_1 - a_1, \ldots, x_n - a_n\}$. Recalling the conditions in Definition 6 and if $I := \langle \mathcal{F}\rangle$, we have $\mathrm{LM}(I_{\leq 1}) = \mathrm{LM}(I)$ and $\dim(I_{\leq d}) = \dim(A_{\leq d}) - 1$. In particular, we can say that $d_{\text{wit}}(\mathcal{F})$ is the smallest degree such that the rank of the associated affine Macaulay matrix is equal to the number of columns minus one.

We will use this observation to provide an estimate of the witness degree. Note that semi-regularity can be seen as the assumption that the *homogeneous* Macaulay matrices have maximal rank; we now adopt the assumption that the *affine* Macaulay matrices achieve maximal rank. With this assumption, we can reuse the Hilbert Series machinery we have developed in this section. Consider the untruncated version of the series in Eqs. (3) and (5). The coefficient in a term of degree $d < d_{\text{reg}}$ is positive and it coincides with the number of columns

---

[4] The field equations ensure that the ideal is radical, and the result follows from Hilbert's Nullstellensatz. In practice, the reliance on field equations can typically be eased for sufficiently overdetermined systems. Thus we will assume that this also holds for Modeling 1, even when the field equations are not explicitly included in $\mathcal{F}$.

that cannot be reduced in the homogeneous Macaulay matrix of degree d. When $d \geq d_{\mathrm{reg}}$, the coefficient is non-positive and measures the number of "excess" rows after full reduction of this matrix. When these rows are considered in their full affine form they will, in general, not sum to zero. Coming back to the polynomial representation, they yield what we typically call *degree falls* or *degree fall polynomials* in the literature.

Finally, we arrive at the following estimate for the witness degree by summing these coefficients.

Estimate (Plain witness degree). *Let $\mathcal{F}$ be the polynomial system of Modeling 1 (resp. Modeling 2) and let $\mathcal{H}$ denote the untruncated series of Eq. (3) (resp. Eq. (5)). Then we estimate $d_{wit}(\mathcal{F})$ to be*

$$
d_{wit,(0,0)} := \min\left\{ d \in \mathbb{Z}_{\geq 1} \;\middle|\; \sum_{j=0}^{d}[z^j]\,(\mathcal{H}(z)) \leq 0 \right\},
\tag{6}
$$

where $[z^j]\,(\mathcal{H}(z))$ denotes the coefficient of the monomial z^j in $\mathcal{H}$.

We have found this estimate to be accurate in all our experiments, which are further reported in Appendix C.

4   Hybrid Approach

As is standard in algebraic cryptanalysis, the complexity of our approach essentially depends on the value of d_{reg} or d_{wit}. However, for most of the parameter sets that we have studied, these degrees seem too high for straightforward algebraic techniques to be competitive with other types of attacks.

To decrease these degrees and possibly improve the overall complexity, we propose to add new equations in the same e variables which may hold with probability $0 < \mathcal{P} < 1$. The idea is the same as in a standard hybrid approach [16]: we hope that the complexity gain in solving the resulting system may supersede the loss coming from adding these equations since we have to repeat the process $\mathcal{O}(\mathcal{P}^{-1})$ times on average to find a solution. Due to the nature of the RSD problem, a natural idea is to fix linear constraints of the form $e_{i',j'} = 0$. Note that this is exactly what the Prange algorithm does by picking an information set I and then assuming that $e_I = \mathbf{0}$. In our case, these constraints reduce the number of non-zero monomials in degree $d \geq 1$ (even though the number of equations at hand also decreases) and thus we hope that the specialized system with these constraints will be solved at a smaller degree. In the following, we develop this hybrid approach for Modeling 1, noting that the case of Modeling 2 works in the same way.

4.1   Guessing Error-Free Positions in All Blocks

A first idea is to guess the same number of error-free positions in all blocks. A similar approach was followed in [31, B.3] to adapt ISD algorithms to a regular error distribution. Each block in the RSD problem can be seen as a random vector of length β and weight 1. The success probability of guessing u error-free positions is $\binom{\beta-1}{u}/\binom{\beta}{u}$. By exploiting the regular structure, one may guess the same number of positions in each block with probability

$$\mathcal{P}_{(u)} := \left(\frac{\binom{\beta-1}{u}}{\binom{\beta}{u}} \right)^h = (1 - u/\beta)^h. \tag{7}$$

The improvement by using Eq. (7) instead of the naive probability in the Prange algorithm (or even in more involved ISD variants) was not really apparent in [31] ("ISD is always the most efficient attack and has roughly the same cost when considering SD and RSD" [31, p. 49]). Still, we can try to adopt the same technique for Modeling 1. We start by guessing that the top part of size $0 \leq u \leq \beta$ is error-free in each block, which holds with probability $(1 - u/\beta)^h$. The main difference with [31, B.3] is that we will have $uh \ll k$. Indeed, we need to guess much fewer error-free positions to decrease the solving degree of Modeling 1 while the Prange linear system "stays" in degree 1 and needs more equations. In case of failure, we consider a permutation matrix $\boldsymbol{P}_\pi \in \mathbb{F}^{n \times n}$ which permutes the coordinates in each block (so that the regular structure is maintained) and we try again on the RSD instance $(\boldsymbol{H}\boldsymbol{P}_\pi^{-1}, \boldsymbol{s})$ which has error $\boldsymbol{\varepsilon}^\mathsf{T} = \boldsymbol{P}_\pi \boldsymbol{e}^\mathsf{T}$. By fixing the $e_{i,j}$ variables to zero for $1 \leq i \leq h$ and $1 \leq j \leq u$, the number of possible non-zero monomials in degree d is now given by the coefficient of z^d in

$$\left(1 + (\beta - u) \cdot \tfrac{z}{1-z}\right)^h.$$

To derive the Hilbert series of the specialized system, we need to adapt Assumption 1 (see Assumption 3 in Appendix B.1) to ensure that fixing variables does not introduce unexpected cancellations at higher degree among the system of $n - k$ parity-check equations $\{p_1, \ldots, p_{n-k}\}$. Under this new assumption, the Hilbert series of the hybrid system is obtained by applying Theorem 1 to an RSD instance with block size $\beta - u$:

$$\mathcal{H}_{A/I,\text{hyb1},u}(z) = \left[(1-z)^{n-k} \cdot \left(1 + (\beta - u) \cdot \tfrac{z}{1-z}\right)^h \right]_+ \tag{8}$$

Hence, while both the number of equations and monomials of degree $d \geq 1$ are affected by adding the zero constraints, they are still on a form that is captured by the Hilbert series studied in Sect. 3. In practice, we typically require a weaker form of Assumption 3. Indeed, the optimal choice of u is rather small for the parameters that we will study in Sect. 5. Heuristically, we have more confidence in our assumption with a smaller u as it implies less specialization of the polynomial system. Finally, we note that a similar statement for specialized systems is also present in the standard hybrid approach for semi-regular systems, see [16, Hypothesis 3.3]. Starting from a semi-regular system $\{f_1, \ldots, f_m\}$, they assume that all the specialized versions

$$\{f_1(x_1, \ldots, x_{n-k}, \boldsymbol{v}), \ldots, f_m(x_1, \ldots, x_{n-k}, \boldsymbol{v})\}, \ \forall \boldsymbol{v} \in \mathbb{F}^k, \ \forall 0 \leq k \leq n$$

are semi-regular.

4.2 Restricting to $f \leq h$ Blocks

A slightly more general approach is to guess $0 \leq u \leq \beta$ error-free positions in only $0 \leq f \leq h$ blocks so that the success probability becomes $\mathcal{P}_{(f,u)} := (1 - u/\beta)^f$. Under a similar assumption (see Assumption 3 in Appendix B.1 which encompasses both strategies), we can obtain the Hilbert series

$$\mathcal{H}_{A/I,\text{hyb2},f,u}(z) = \left[(1-z)^{n-k} \cdot \underbrace{\left(1 + (\beta - u) \cdot \frac{z}{1-z} \right)^f}_{\text{constraint}} \cdot \underbrace{\left(1 + \beta \cdot \frac{z}{1-z} \right)^{h-f}}_{\text{no constraint}} \right]_+ \quad (9)$$

4.3 Witness Degree for the Hybrid Approach

Similary to what we did in Sect. 3.2 for the plain system, we now derive an estimate of d_{wit} for the specialized system. Since the plain system is expected to have a unique solution, the majority of guesses will be wrong, *i.e.*, resulting in polynomial systems without any solutions. In that respect, the situation is similar to that of the original BooleanSolve algorithm of [8]. We can in this case use Proposition 4 to upper bound the witness degree by the degree of regularity of the homogenized system.

We will assume that the hybrid systems form semi-regular systems with the extra variable y. Under this assumption, it is straightforward to adapt the Hilbert series given by Eq. (8) and Eq. (9) to the homogenized versions in the following manner:

$$\mathcal{H}_{A/I,\text{hybi},f,u}(z)/(1 - z), \quad (10)$$

for $i \in \{1, 2\}$. For the hybrid approach on Modeling 2, we similarly divide by $(1-z)$ the series in Eq. (21) Appendix B.2. The degree of regularity of the homogenized systems is then obtained in the usual manner, i.e., by computing the first non-positive coefficient in the associated series. We note that this adaptation on the Hilbert series is in line with the earlier literature (c.f. [8, Proposition 6]) and it has been accurate in our experiments (see Appendix C).

4.4 Complexity with XL Wiedemann

The cost of the hybrid approach of Sect. 4.2 can now be computed as follows. For each pair (f, u) where $0 \leq f \leq h$ and $0 \leq u \leq \beta$, we proceed as explained in Sect. 4.3 to obtain an upper-bound on the witness degree which we denote by $d_{\text{wit},(f,u)}$ and that we use as our estimate of the real witness degree. To apply Eq. (2), we then need the value $\mathcal{M}^{(f,u)}_{\leq d_{\text{wit},(f,u)}}$ which is the number of monomials of degree $\leq d_{\text{wit},(f,u)}$ in the specialized system. It depends on both f, u and $d_{\text{wit},(f,u)}$. Indeed, let $\mathcal{H}_{(S,f,u)}(z) = \left(1 + (\beta - u) \cdot \frac{z}{1-z} \right)^f \cdot \left(1 + \beta \cdot \frac{z}{1-z} \right)^{h-f}$. We have

$$\mathcal{M}^{(f,u)}_{\leq d_{\text{wit},(f,u)}} = \sum_{j=0}^{d_{\text{wit},(f,u)}} [z^j] \left(\mathcal{H}_{(S,f,u)}(z) \right), \quad (11)$$

where we recall that $[z^j]\,(\mathcal{H}(z))$ is the coefficient of the monomial z^j in the series $\mathcal{H}$. Finally, we need to estimate the quantity n_μ which is the number of non-zero terms in one row of the Macaulay matrix. This is directly related to the monomial content of the initial parity-check equations. We can assume that the matrix H is given in systematic form, so that $n_\mu \leq k+1 = \mathcal{O}(k)$. For the specialized system, we can actually choose to fix the f bottom blocks of the error[5] to obtain the better factor $n_{\mu,(f,u)} \leq k+1-f\cdot u$. This allows to possibly gain a few bits in the final complexity.

Proposition 5. *Under Assumption 3 and the assumptions described in Sect. 4.3, the time complexity in $\mathbb{F}$-operations of the hybrid approach of Sect. 4.2 on Modeling 1 is estimated by*

$$\mathcal{O}\left(\min_{\substack{0\leq f\leq h \\ 0\leq u\leq\beta}}\left(\mathcal{P}_{(f,u)}^{-1}\cdot 3\cdot n_{\mu,(f,u)}\cdot\left(\mathcal{M}_{\leq d_{\mathrm{wit},(f,u)}}^{(f,u)}\right)^2\right)\right),$$

where

$\mathcal{P}_{(f,u)} := (1-u/\beta)^f,$
$n_{\mu,(f,u)} := k+1-f\cdot u,$
$\mathcal{M}_{\leq d_{\mathrm{wit},(f,u)}}^{(f,u)}$ *is defined in Eq. (11),*

and where $d_{\mathrm{wit},(f,u)}$ is the index of the first non-positive coefficient in the generating series given in Eq. (10).

We can obtain a similar statement for Modeling 2 (see Proposition 7 in Appendix B.2). Finally, we want to stress the fact that the specializations proposed in Sects. 4.1 and 4.2 are possibly the most naive ways to fix variables in the system. Even though they seem to lead the best success probability since we take advantage of the regular structure, other approaches might allow to decrease the solving degree faster.

4.5   Rationale and Experimental Verification

The assumptions that we use can be seen as very similar to those generally encountered in algebraic cryptanalysis. More specifically, in our systems these genericity assumptions concern the linear parts of the parity-check equations, and these polynomials simply depend on the matrix H. Even though the underlying code $\mathcal{C}$ is typically chosen d-local in the primal formulation, the parity-check matrix obtained from the public matrix G has no reason to be special in a certain sense. Otherwise, such a particular property may probably be exploited by attacks or indicate that this instantiation is weaker than standard LPN.

In a very similar context, the well-known Arora-Gê system [5] to solve LWE is generally assumed to be semi-regular [2,40]. In [3], some practical experiments

---

[5] There is no loss of generality: this can be seen as choosing a monomial ordering which favors the upper variables and then fixing somehow small variables.

have been performed to confirm this hypothesis ([3, §7.1]) and we also note that they try to prove (a weaker form of) it in some particular cases ([3, A.2]). Their experiments verify that the solving degree of Arora-Gê coincides with that of a random system of the same size.

We have experimentally tested the assumptions made throughout Sects. 3 and 4, the details of which are available in Appendix C. More specifically, we have tested Assumptions 1, 2 and their hybrid counterparts; the hybrid d_{wit} estimate for Modeling 1 and 2; and finally the plain d_{wit} estimate for Modeling 1. Assumptions 1 and 2 have been correct in all our experiments, and we have only been able to observe discrepancies for a few hybrid cases of Modeling 2 (see Appendix C.1 for further discussion). Finally, the estimates on the witness degree have been correct in all the tested cases.

5   Application to Some Parameters

We now estimate the complexity of the attack using the hybrid technique of Sect. 4.2 on some LPN parameter sets with non-constant rate taken from primal LPN instantiations. For each parameter set, we compute the optimal complexity using Proposition 5 for Modeling 1 (resp. Proposition 7 from Appendix B.2 for Modeling 2). We report the pair (f, u) that leads to the best complexity and the associated estimate on the witness degree $d_{conj} := d_{wit,(f,u)}$. When f and u are positive, we use the upper bound from Sect. 4.3 for $d_{wit,(f,u)}$, and when $f = u = 0$, we use the estimate in Eq. (6). The sparsity factor is $k + 1 - f \cdot u$ over large fields or $\min(k + 1 - f \cdot u, k/2 + 1)$ over $\mathbb{F}_2$. The constant from Wiedemann's algorithm is taken equal to 3 as presented in Eq. (2). For illustration, we also give the complexity of the attack without fixing any variables.

The parameters we will consider were first proposed by [18, Table 1]. Their security over $\mathbb{F}_2$ has been re-evaluated in the recent paper [34], where the same parameters are also analyzed over the larger field $\mathbb{F} = \mathbb{F}_{2^{128}}$ (see [34, Table 3]). They are presented in Table 2 and Table 3, respectively. Finally, [34, Table 1] also gives parameters whose initial security target was 128 using the analysis of [18] but which are thought to be much harder according to [34]. These parameters are presented in Tables 4 and 5. When n/h is not an integer, we set $\beta = \lfloor n/h \rfloor$ and fix the last $n - h\beta$ coordinates to zero. Note that the number of parity-check equations at hand is still $n - k$.

Small Scale. In Table 2 and Table 3, "Best" refers to the best attack according to the analysis of [34]. In the binary case, the best attack according to [34] are advanced ISD algorithms. For a field size $\log_2(|\mathbb{F}|) = 128$, they note that the Pooled Gauss attack and ISD perform equally. As Gauss can be considered as a special case of ISD, this is quite reminiscent of the result of Canto-Torres [22] which states that all ISD variants converge to the same cost when $|\mathbb{F}|$ tends to infinity and which is basically the cost of Prange's algorithm.

Larger Scale. The parameters of [34, Table 1] are obtained simply by increasing the weight h and keeping the same triples (n, k, β) as in the original parameters from [18]. In order words, the noise rate increases but the code rate remains the same. They were chosen so that they just achieve 128 bit security according to the analysis of [18] but [34] considers them to be much harder, see Column "Best" in Tables 4 and 5.

Table 2. Hybrid approach of Sect. 4.2 over $\mathbb{F}_2$ (Modeling 2).

n	k	h	Best [34]	d_{conj} plain	(f, u)	d_{conj}	XL hybrid Sect. 4.2
2^{22}	64770	2735	104	2	$(0, 0)$	2	<u>103</u>
2^{20}	32771	1419	99	3	$(1159, 2)$	2	<u>98</u>
2^{18}	15336	760	95	3	$(657, 7)$	2	104
2^{16}	7391	389	91	4	$(373, 10)$	2	108
2^{14}	3482	198	86	6	$(197, 11)$	2	106
2^{12}	1589	98	83	8	$(88, 13)$	2	103
2^{10}	652	57	94	12	$(54, 9)$	2	101

Table 3. Hybrid approach of Sect. 4.2 over $\mathbb{F}_{2^{128}}$ (Modeling 1).

n	k	h	Best [34]	d_{conj} plain	(f, u)	d_{conj}	XL hybrid Sect. 4.2
2^{22}	64770	2735	108	2	$(0, 0)$	2	<u>104</u>
2^{20}	32771	1419	107	3	$(1246, 3)$	2	<u>102</u>
2^{18}	15336	760	105	3	$(670, 8)$	2	107
2^{16}	7391	389	103	4	$(374, 11)$	2	111
2^{14}	3482	198	101	6	$(197, 12)$	2	110
2^{12}	1589	98	100	8	$(96, 13)$	2	107
2^{10}	652	57	111	14	$(55, 10)$	2	111

Ferret and Wolverine. We have also tested our methods on the parameters from [44] and [42]. While most of them seem resistant to the attack, a notable exception is the one-time parameter set with $|\mathbb{F}| = 2^{61} - 1$, $n = 642048$, $k = 19870$ and $h = 2508$ from [42, Table 2]. The authors of [42] claim to achieve 128 bits of security whereas the more recent methods of [34] would suggest that this is too conservative. More precisely, [34, Provided script] estimates 154 bit security. Four our part, we estimate that plain Modeling 1 solves the problem with 126 bit complexity in degree $d = 3$.

Table 4. Hybrid approach of Sect. 4.2 over $\mathbb{F}_2$ (Modeling 2).

n	k	h	Best [34]	d_{conj} plain	(f, u)	d_{conj}	XL hybrid Sect. 4.2
2^{22}	64770	4788	147	2	$(0, 0)$	2	<u>103</u>
2^{20}	32771	2467	143	3	$(2340, 4)$	2	<u>125</u>
2^{18}	15336	1312	139	4	$(676, 1)$	3	<u>122</u>
2^{16}	7391	667	135	5	$(604, 7)$	2	139
2^{14}	3482	338	132	7	$(322, 7)$	2	138
2^{12}	1589	172	131	11	$(154, 7)$	2	135
2^{10}	652	106	176	19	$(104, 4)$	3	<u>145</u>

Table 5. Hybrid approach of Sect. 4.2 over large field $\mathbb{F}_{2^{128}}$ (Modeling 1).

n	k	h	Best [34]	d_{conj} plain	(f, u)	d_{conj}	XL hybrid Sect. 4.2
2^{22}	64770	4788	156	3	$(4237, 1)$	2	<u>110</u>
2^{20}	32771	2467	155	3	$(0, 0)$	3	<u>131</u>
2^{18}	15336	1312	153	4	$(995, 2)$	3	<u>133</u>
2^{16}	7391	667	151	6	$(613, 8)$	2	<u>150</u>
2^{14}	3482	338	150	8	$(324, 8)$	2	150
2^{12}	1589	172	155	12	$(157, 8)$	2	<u>150</u>
2^{10}	652	106	194	24	$(105, 5)$	3	<u>179</u>

5.1   Comments on the Results

Overall, we see the complexity of our attack is rather close to the best attack even if clearly a bit above this value for most instances in Tables 2 and 3. In a way, the high witness degree for the plain system is circumvented by the hybrid component of our attack which can be seen as an analogue of Prange's algorithm. Therefore, we should not expect a big gap between the complexities in this case because our attack is not a pure algebraic attack. Also, this difference is much reduced in the parameters from Tables 4 and 5 (Larger Scale) compared to those of Tables 2 and 3 (Smaller Scale). We also observe that our attack is extremely efficient compared to ISD when we can solve at degree 2, 3 without fixing a lot of variables (see for instance the first three rows in Tables 4 and 5). This may suggest a weak zone of parameters which is not encompassed by former ISD algorithms.

Secondly, the algebraic attack seems to compare better to known techniques for larger fields. As mentioned earlier, the main reason may be that the advantage of ISD algorithms over Prange/Pooled Gauss worsens when $|\mathbb{F}| \to +\infty$. In our case, even though the witness degree for plain Modeling 1 is slightly higher than the one of Modeling 2, the difference is not enough (at most 1 for all parameter sets except the last row in Tables 4 and 5) to expect a similar increase in the cost as we observe for ISD.

6 Asymptotic Analysis

This section aims to illustrate the concrete results shown in Sect. 5 by providing a sketch of asymptotic analysis. Note that a study of convergence speed is out of the scope of this work, so the results presented here should be viewed as a purely theoretical contribution. Recall that our motivation for introducing the witness degree was to analyze the Wiedemann algorithm, which is likely to be the best tool for linear algebra for the parameters we have discussed so far. Since there are other linear algebra algorithms that may perform asymptotically better than the Wiedemann algorithm (see, e.g., [33]), we choose to focus on the degree of regularity for the remainder of this section. We start by exploring a potentially weak range of parameters where the RSD problem can be solved at degree 2. Then we go on to obtain an asymptotic equivalent of the degree of regularity in Sect. 6.2 for the plain system. All cases are considered over $\mathbb{F}_2$ using Modeling 2.

From this partial analysis, the next natural question would be to perform a broader comparison to known attacks, in particular to ISD algorithms. There is also the question of analyzing and comparing the hybrid versions of our attack. We leave both questions for future work.

6.1 Solving at Low Degree

First, note that the number of monomials in degree $\leq d$ in Modeling 2 can be well approximated by $\binom{h}{d}(\beta - 1)^d$ which is the number of exact degree d monomials (see the discussion right after Lemma 1). Using Proposition 7 Appendix B.2, we see that the complexity is polynomial in the degree of regularity d_{reg}. In particular, having a constant d_{reg} is a sufficient condition for the algorithm to run in polynomial time. Moreover, we noted in Sect. 5.1 that our techniques proved especially effective when plain RSD was close to being solved at a small degree. Thus, we start our analysis by exploring the potentially weak zone of parameters where Modeling 2 meets the strong condition being solved at degree 2. This will happen whenever the coefficient in front of z^2 in the series $\mathcal{H}_{A/I_{\mathbb{F}_2}}(z)$ given in Eq. (5) is non-positive. This coefficient reads

$$\kappa_2 := \binom{n-k+1}{2} + (\beta - 1)^2 \binom{h}{2} - (n-k)h(\beta - 1).$$

In all generality, we can view this coefficient as a function of the length n, the code rate R and the error rate ρ and study the behaviour when $n \to +\infty$. More precisely, we get

$$\kappa_2 = \frac{n \cdot \left(\rho^3 n - 2nR\rho^2 + R^2\rho n - 1 + 3\rho - R\rho - \rho^2\right)}{2\rho}.$$

Note that if the code rate R dominates over ρ, the possibly dominant term in the numerator is either $R^2\rho n$ or -1. If the term $R^2\rho n$ tends to zero, the main contribution in the numerator comes from the -1 term and κ_2 is asymptotically negative. Note also that we can find such a zone which is non-trivial in a cryptographic sense. Indeed, recall that the standard adaptation of Prange's algorithm to the regular case would be to guess k/h error-free coordinates per block. The success probability of this approach is then $(1 - k/h/n/h)^h = (1 - R)^h$. This gives a complexity of $e^{-h \cdot \ln(1-R)}$, and assuming that $R = o(1)$ the main term in the exponent $-h \cdot \ln(1 - R)$ is $hR = n\rho R$. If for instance $hR = n\rho R \sim n^\alpha$ for $0 < \alpha < 1$, it may give a subexponential algorithm. On the contrary, we can clearly find code rates for which $R^2 \rho n \to 0$ under this condition.

To simplify the analysis even further, we consider particular functions $R = \phi(n)$ and $\rho = \psi(n)$ and view $\kappa_2 := \kappa(n)$ as a function of n. Upon inspection of Table 6, it seems relevant to study a regime of the form $\rho := n^{-a}$ and $R := \log(n) \cdot n^{-a}$ for some $0 < a < 1$ even if we extrapolate from a very small number of values. With this particular choice, we obtain

$$\kappa_2(n) = -\frac{n^{a+1}}{2} + \frac{(\log(n)-1)^2 n^{2-2a}}{2} + \frac{3n}{2} - \frac{(\log(n)+1)n^{1-a}}{2}. \tag{12}$$

Lemma 2. *Under Assumption 2, the degree of regularity of plain Modeling 2 for an RSD instance with $\rho := n^{-a}$ and $R := \log(n) \cdot n^{-a}$ is asymptotically equal to 2 when $a > 1/3$.* □

Proof. In Eq. (12), the term $-\frac{n^{1+a}}{2}$ dominates when $a+1 > 2-2a$, hence $a > 1/3$. □

Recall that the Prange exponent is $nR\rho = n^{1-2a} \log(n)$ in this case, which leaves a possibly relevant zone for our attack when $1/3 < a < 1/2$.

Another choice of interest from Table 6 is $\rho := n^{-a}$ and $R := n^{-b}$ for some $0 < b < a$. In this case, we have

$$\kappa := \frac{n^{2-2a}}{2} + \frac{n^{2-2b}}{2} - n^{2-a-b} - \frac{n^{1+a}}{2} + \frac{3n}{2} - \frac{n^{1-a}}{2} - \frac{n^{1-b}}{2}. \tag{13}$$

Lemma 3. *Under Assumption 2, the degree of regularity of plain Modeling 2 for an RSD instance with $\rho := n^{-a}$ and $R := n^{-b}$ for some $0 < b < a$ is asymptotically equal to 2 when $a + 2b > 1$.*

Proof. In Eq. (13), the dominant term is either $\frac{n^{2-2b}}{2}$ or $-\frac{n^{1+a}}{2}$. The second dominates when $1 + a > 2 - 2b$, that is, $a + 2b > 1$. □

In this case the Prange exponent is $nR\rho = n^{1-a-b}$, and there is a possibly relevant zone for our attack when $1 - b < a + b < 1$.

6.2 Asymptotic Analysis of d_{reg}

A more accurate complexity analysis requires to estimate the degree of regularity d_{reg}, which is done in the following Proposition 6:

Proposition 6. *When $n \to +\infty$, the degree of regularity d_{reg} of Modeling 2 behaves asymptotically as follows:*

1. *For constant code rate R and noise rate $\rho = o(1)$, let $\kappa_R := 2-R-2\sqrt{1-R} > 0$. We have*

$$d_{reg} \sim \kappa_R h.$$

Table 6. General trends for the parameters of Sect. 5

n	k	h	$b := 1 - \frac{\log(k)}{\log(n)}$	$a := 1 - \frac{\log(h)}{\log(n)}$	$R/(\log_2(n)\rho)$
2^{22}	64770	2735	0.27	0.48	1.08
2^{20}	32771	1419	0.25	0.48	1.15
2^{18}	15336	760	0.23	0.47	1.12
2^{16}	7391	389	0.20	0.46	1.19
2^{14}	3482	198	0.16	0.46	1.26
2^{12}	1589	98	0.11	0.45	1.35
2^{10}	652	57	0.07	0.42	1.14
2^{22}	64770	4788	0.27	0.44	0.61
2^{20}	32771	2467	0.25	0.44	0.66
2^{18}	15336	1312	0.23	0.42	0.65
2^{16}	7391	667	0.20	0.41	0.69
2^{14}	3482	338	0.16	0.40	0.74
2^{12}	1589	172	0.11	0.38	0.77
2^{10}	652	106	0.07	0.33	0.62

2. *For $R = o(1)$ and $\rho = o(1)$ such that $\rho = o(R)$, we have*

$$d_{reg} + 1 \sim \frac{R^2}{4} h.$$

3. *Finally, for $R = o(1)$ and $\rho = o(1)$ such that $\rho = \lambda R$ is linear in R with $\lambda < 1$, we have*

$$d_{reg} + 1 \sim \frac{(1-\lambda)^2 R^2}{4} h. \qquad (14)$$

The main tool for the proof is the so-called saddle-point method. A detailed account of this approach in the context of Hilbert series can be found in [7, Chap. 4]. Each coefficient in the series can be obtained as a Cauchy integral, namely

$$[z^d]\mathcal{H}_{A/I_{\mathbb{F}_2}}(z) = \frac{1}{2i\pi} \oint \frac{1}{z^{d+1}} \mathcal{H}_{A/I_{\mathbb{F}_2}}(z)dz.$$

The saddle-point method allows to study the asymptotic behaviour of this integral for fixed d. Since we are interested in the value of d such that the integral vanishes when $n \to +\infty$, we then cancel the main term in the resulting development in order to obtain the first term in the development of d_{reg}. The full proof can be found in Appendix D.

Asymptotics with Hybrid Approach. It is possible to carry out the same analysis for the system obtained after hybrid approach but this is more technical. We leave this problem as a future work. In this case, the relevant question would be to find the best asymptotic trade-off between the cost coming from the fixed variables and the one of the solving step. This has already been studied in the case of quadratic semi-regular systems, see for instance [15, §4.3].

Acknowledgments. We express our warm gratitude to the Eurocrypt23' reviewers for their suggestion to analyze the witness degree. We also thank Geoffroy Couteau for motivating the study of this problem and for insightful discussions.

A   Proof of Theorems 1 and 2

This section contains the proofs of Theorem 1 and Theorem 2. Our main contribution is the strategy of splitting the system into two parts as described above. The structural part requires to compute some Hilbert series $\mathcal{H}_S(z)$ (resp. $\mathcal{H}_{S'}(z)$). On the rest of the equations, most of the technical work as explained in the main text was to state Assumption 1 (resp. Assumption 2) in order to mimick Bardet's definitions of semi-regularity (resp. semi-regularity over $\mathbb{F}_2$). From there, this structure of the proof is exactly the same as in [7, §3.3.2,§3.3.3].

A.1   Proof of Theorem 1

The theorem easily follows from the following lemmata.

Lemma 4. *Let S denote the quotient ring $A/\langle \mathcal{B}^{(h)}\rangle$, where $\mathcal{B}^{(h)}$ consists of the quadratic parts of the structural equations from Modeling 1. We have*

$$\mathcal{H}_S(z) = \left(1 + \beta \cdot \tfrac{z}{1-z}\right)^h. \tag{15}$$

Proof. The quotient S can be seen as the set of polynomials whose monomials involve at most one $e_{i,j}$ variable in each block $1 \leq i \leq h$. For a given block, admissible monomials have only one variable but their degree can be arbitrary. Therefore, the Hilbert series "for one block" will be $1 + \beta \cdot \tfrac{z}{1-z}$. Finally, a general d monomial is a product of such monomials for distinct blocks and such that the sum of their degrees is equal to d. Relying on the same symbolic argument as presented in [29] which gives the generating series of a Cartesian product, we finally obtain the series in (15).   □

Lemma 5. *Let I denote the homogeneous ideal associated to Modeling 1. Under Assumption 1, we have*

$$\mathcal{H}_{A/I}(z) = \left[(1-z)^{n-k} \cdot \mathcal{H}_S(z)\right]^+.$$

Proof. This may be seen as a particular case of [7, §3.3.2]. We give the proof here for the sake of completeness. To simplify notation, we write $\{f_1, \ldots, f_{n-k}\}$ for the set of homogeneous parity-check equations $\mathcal{P}^{(h)}$. For $1 \leq j \leq n-k$, we denote by $I(j)$ the ideal $\langle \mathcal{B}^{(h)}, f_1, \ldots, f_j\rangle$ in A and $I(0) = \langle \mathcal{B}^{(h)}\rangle$. For $1 \leq j \leq n-k$ and up to the degree of regularity of I, Assumption 1 states that we have the exact sequence of vector spaces when $d < d_{\text{reg}}$:

$$0 \to (A/I(j-1))_{d-1} \to (A/I(j-1))_d \to (A/I(j))_d \to 0$$

This gives the following equality between Hilbert functions

$$\mathcal{HF}_{A/I(j-1)}(d-1) - \mathcal{HF}_{A/I(j-1)}(d) + \mathcal{HF}_{A/I(j)}(d) = 0. \tag{16}$$

Consider now the abstract sequence $h_{d,j}$ defined by $h_{d,j} = \dim_{\mathbb{F}}(S_d)$ if $j = 0$ or $d = 0$ and the induction relation

$$h_{d,j} = h_{d,j-1} - h_{d-1,j-1}. \tag{17}$$

Let $\mathcal{G}_j$ denote the generating series for $(h_{d,j})_{d\geq 0}$. From Eq. (17) and by multiplying by z we easily obtain $\mathcal{G}_j(z) = (1 - z)\mathcal{G}_{j-1}(z)$. The generating series for $(h_{d,0})_{d\geq 0}$ being $\mathcal{G}_0(z) := \mathcal{H}_S(z)$ we get $\mathcal{G}_{n-k}(z) = (1 - z)^{n-k}\mathcal{H}_S(z)$. As long as the involved quantities are positive, Eq. (16) and Eq. (17) may be seen as the same relation. Therefore, the final Hilbert series is

$$\mathcal{H}_{A/I}(z) = \left[(1 - z)^{n-k} \cdot \mathcal{H}_S(z)\right]_+.$$

$\square$

A.2 Proof of Theorem 2

Recall A' and S' from Definition 7. Theorem 2 easily follows from the following lemmata.

Lemma 6. *We have*

$$\mathcal{H}_{S'}(z) = (1 + (\beta - 1) \cdot z)^h. \tag{18}$$

Proof. From the set of generators $\mathcal{G}$ described in Lemma 1, we observe that the admissible monomials of S' involve at most one variable from each block, with degree at most 1. The result follows by reasoning in a similar way as in the proof of Lemma 4. $\square$

Lemma 7. *Let I denote the homogeneous ideal associated to Modeling 2. Under Assumption 2, we have*

$$\mathcal{H}_{A/I}(z) = \left[\mathcal{H}_{S'}(z)/(1 + z)^{n-k}\right]_+.$$

Proof (sketch). By construction, we clearly have $\mathcal{H}_{A/I}(z) = \mathcal{H}_{A'/I'}(z)$, for the ideal I' introduced in Definition 7. As in the proof of Lemma 5, we simplify notation by writing $\{f_1, \ldots, f_{n-k}\}$ for the set of homogeneous parity-check equations $\mathcal{L}(\mathcal{P}^{(h)})$, and for $1 \leq j \leq n - k$, we denote by $I'(j)$ the ideal $\langle \mathcal{B}', \mathcal{Q}', f_1, \ldots, f_j \rangle$ in A' and $I'(0) = \langle \mathcal{B}', \mathcal{Q}' \rangle$. Assumption 2 ensures that the following sequence is exact for $d < d_{\text{reg}}$.

$$0 \to (A'/I'(j))_{d-1} \xrightarrow{\times f_j} (A'/I'(j-1))_d \xrightarrow{\pi} (A'/I'(j))_d \to 0.$$

The rest of the proof now proceeds in the same way as [9, proof of Proposition 9], starting from the equality between Hilbert functions

$$\mathcal{HF}_{A'/I'(j)}(d-1) - \mathcal{HF}_{A'/I'(j-1)}(d) + \mathcal{HF}_{A'/I'(j)}(d) = 0. \tag{19}$$

Similarly, we consider the sequence $c_{d,j}$ defined by $c_{d,j} = \dim_{\mathbb{F}}(S_d')$ if $j = 0$ or $d = 0$ and the recurrent formula

$$c_{d,j} = c_{d,j-1} - c_{d-1,j}. \tag{20}$$

Let $\mathcal{C}_j$ denote the generating series for $(c_{d,j})_{d \geq 0}$. Multiplying by z in Eq. (20) yields $(1 + z)\mathcal{C}_j(z) = \mathcal{C}_{j-1}(z)$ and we have the border condition $\mathcal{C}_0(z) = \mathcal{H}_{A'/I'(0)}(z) = \mathcal{H}_{S'}(z)$. This finally gives

$$\mathcal{H}_{A/I}(z) = \mathcal{H}_{A'/I'}(z) = \left[\frac{\mathcal{H}_{S'}(z)}{(1 + z)^{n-k}} \right]_+.$$

$\square$

B   Missing Details in Section 4

B.1   Regularity Assumption for Specialized Modeling 1

For any invertible matrix P, for $0 \leq f \leq h$ and for $0 \leq u \leq \beta$, let $\overline{\mathbf{P}_{u,f}^{-1}}$ denote the map that applies $\mathbf{P}^{-1}$ and then fixes the initial u variables to 0 in the last f blocks of the error.

Assumption 3. *Let $\mathcal{P}$ be the set of parity-check equations from an instance of Modeling 1. For every permutation matrix $\mathbf{P}$ which stabilizes each block of the error, for $0 \leq f \leq h$ and for $0 \leq u \leq \beta$, we assume $\mathcal{P}^{(h)} \circ \overline{\mathbf{P}_{u,f}^{-1}}$ satisfies Assumption 1 with ring $A \circ \overline{\mathbf{P}_{u,f}^{-1}}$ and quotient ring $S \circ \overline{\mathbf{P}_{u,f}^{-1}}$.*

We need the full version of this assumption for the approach of Sect. 4.2 while only the particular case $f = h$ is required for Sect. 4.1.

B.2   XL Wiedemann Complexity for Modeling 2

The success probability $\mathcal{P}_{(f,u)} := (1 - u/\beta)^f$ is independent of the algebraic system. Over $\mathbb{F}_2$, we may consider that $n_\mu \approx \frac{k}{2} + 1$ in general instead of simply $n_\mu \leq k + 1$ for the number of non-zero terms per equation. We leave it to the reader to state the equivalent of Assumption 3 for Modeling 2. All the following results are under this assumption, as well as the assumptions noted in Sect. 4.3. We now give the complexity of the hybrid approach of Sect. 4.2 on Modeling 2. The degree of regularity $d_{\mathrm{reg},(f,u)}$ is obtained as the index of the first non-positive coefficient in the series

$$\frac{(1 + (\beta - 1 - u) \cdot z)^f \cdot (1 + (\beta - 1) \cdot z)^{h-f}}{(1 + z)^{n-k}} \tag{21}$$

As noted in Sect. 4.3, this series is divided by $(1 - z)$, to derive an upper bound, $d_{\mathrm{wit},(f,u)}$, on the witness degree. Finally, the analogue of Eq. (11) is

$$\mathcal{M}_{\leq d_{\mathrm{wit},(f,u)}}^{(f,u)} = \sum_{j=0}^{d_{\mathrm{wit},(f,u)}} [z^j] \left(\mathcal{H}_{(S',f,u)}(z) \right),$$

where $\mathcal{H}_{(S',f,u)}(z) := (1 + (\beta - 1 - u) \cdot z)^f \cdot (1 + (\beta - 1) \cdot z)^{h-f}$.

Proposition 7. *The time complexity in $\mathbb{F}_2$ operations of the hybrid approach of Sect. 4.2 on Modeling 2 is estimated by*

$$\mathcal{O}\left(\min_{\substack{0 \leq f \leq h \\ 0 \leq u \leq \beta}} \left(\mathcal{P}_{(f,u)}^{-1} \cdot 3 \cdot n_{\mu,(f,u)} \cdot \left(\mathcal{M}_{\leq d_{\text{wit},(f,u)}}^{(f,u)} \right)^2 \right) \right).$$

C   Experiments

In this section, we present experiments that we have run on randomly generated instances of the RSD problem in order to check the validity of the assumptions from Sect. 3 and 4.

C.1   Hilbert Series

We give the parameter sets as $(h, \beta, k, f, u)_t$, where h, β and k describe the RSD problem, where f, u are the parameters for the hybrid approach of Sect. 4.2 and where t is the number of times that we have repeated the experiment. For an affine ideal I, we compute the Hilbert series of the ideal $I^{(h)}$ associated with the homogeneous upper part of I. For some of the hybrid systems, we have also computed the Hilbert series of the *homogenized* ideal $I^{(y)}$ (see Sect. 2.1 for the difference between these two notions). The tests have been run using the computer algebra system Magma V2.27-1 and the built-in command `HilbertSeries(·)`.

Experiments for Modeling 1. The systems we have tested for Modeling 1 are listed in Table 7, where we also give the associated degree of regularity d_{reg}. In all tests, the experimentally found Hilbert series is equal to the Hilbert series of Eq. (9), meaning, in particular, that Assumption 1 and 3 have been true in all our experiments. For most of the hybrid systems, we have also computed the Hilbert series of the homogenized ideals $I^{(y)}$ and given the associated degree of regularity $d_{\text{reg}}^{(y)}$. The Hilbert series in all of these tests have been equal to (the truncation of) those predicted by Eq. (10).

Table 7. Tested Hilbert Series from Hybrid Modeling 1 systems over $\mathbb{F}_{101}$.

System	d_{reg}	$d_{\text{reg}}^{(y)}$	System	d_{reg}	$d_{\text{reg}}^{(y)}$	System	d_{reg}	$d_{\text{reg}}^{(y)}$
$(5,6,15,0,0)_5$	3	-	$(5,6,20,0,0)_5$	4	-	$(5,8,20,0,0)_5$	3	-
$(5,8,30,0,0)_5$	4	-	$(7,7,30,0,0)_5$	4	-	$(8,6,30,0,0)_5$	5	-
$(10,4,25,0,0)_5$	6	-	$(12,7,50,3,2)_1$	5	-	$(7,8,30,2,3)_{10}$	3	3
$(7,8,30,6,3)_{10}$	2	3	$(10,7,40,5,2)_{10}$	4	4	$(10,7,40,5,3)_{10}$	3	4

Experiments for Modeling 2. Table 8 contains tests for Hilbert series on Modeling 2. The experimental Hilbert series of the plain cases ($f = u = 0$) are all described by our theory. While the majority of *hybrid* cases we have tested are accurately described by (21), we have been able to find a few discrepancy with the theoretical values. The systems marked by † both included a single case where the experimental Hilbert series deviated slightly from (21) in one of its terms. The system marked by ‡ was another type of outlier, where the quotient A/I contained a few cubic elements in half of the tested cases. We note that for the system marked by ‡, the corresponding (untruncated) series (21) is exactly zero at term z^2. Thus the homogeneous Macaulay matrix of degree 2 will be a square matrix over $\mathbb{F}_2$ (after removing trivial syzygies), and the quotient A/I will contain cubic terms whenever this matrix fails to be of full rank. For the other tested cases, the series have a *negative* coefficient at the term corresponding to the degree of regularity, indicating that the homogeneous Macaulay matrices will be rectangular. We believe that this difference explains the peculiar behaviour observed for case ‡. Finally, we have performed the same experiments as in Modeling 1 for the ideals $I^{(y)}$ and we obtained the same conclusive results regarding Eq. (10).

Table 8. Tested Hilbert Series from Hybrid Modeling 2 systems over $\mathbb{F}_2$.

System	d_{reg}	$d_{\mathrm{reg}}^{(y)}$	System	d_{reg}	$d_{\mathrm{reg}}^{(y)}$	System	d_{reg}	$d_{\mathrm{reg}}^{(y)}$
$(10,6,30,0,0)_{10}$	3	–	$(10,6,30,3,3)_{10}$	2	2	$(10,6,40,0,0)_{10}$	4	–
$(10,6,40,6,2)_{10}^{\dagger}$	3	–	$(14,7,50,0,0)_{10}$	4	–	$(14,7,50,2,2)_{10}$	3	4
$(14,7,50,10,2)_{10}$	$2^{\ddagger}$	3	$(15,6,70,10,3)_{10}^{\dagger}$	5	–	$(20,6,70,5,3)_{10}$	4	4
$(20,6,70,10,3)_{10}$	3	3	$(15,6,60,2,1)_{1}$	5	–	$(20,20,150,0,0)_{1}$	3	–
$(20,20,150,15,4)_{10}$	2	3	$(20,20,100,0,0)_{10}$	2	–			

C.2   Witness Degree for Plain Systems

We have also tested the witness degree for (non-hybrid) systems of Modeling 1. In these tests, we have created the affine Macaulay matrix of degree 2 or 3 and then computed its rank to check if it has a unique solution. The witness degree in all these tests was the same as the value estimated by Eq. (6) in Sect. 3.2. Details are given in Table 9, where the systems are denoted (h, β, k).

Table 9. Witness degree for Modeling 1 systems over $\mathbb{F}_{101}$.

System	d_{wit}	System	d_{wit}	System	d_{wit}	System	d_{wit}
$(8,8,18)$	2	$(4,12,21)$	2	$(15,8,27)$	2	$(12,7,20)$	2
$(7,5,16)$	3	$(8,4,13)$	3	$(4,8,20)$	3	$(8,5,18)$	3

D   Proof of Proposition 6

Proof. The starting point is the Cauchy integral

$$\mathcal{I}_d(n) := \frac{1}{2i\pi} \int \underbrace{\frac{1}{z^{d+1}} \frac{(1+(\beta-1)\cdot z)^h}{(1+z)^{n-k}}}_{=e^{n\cdot f(z)}} dz,$$

where we set $f(z) := -\frac{d+1}{n}\cdot\log(z) - (1-R)\cdot\log(1+z) + \rho\cdot\log(1+(\rho^{-1}-1)\cdot z)$.

We study the behaviour of this integral when n grows. Using Cauchy's integral theorem, we can make the path of integration to meet the saddle points so that the integral concentrates in the neighborhood of these saddle points when n tends to $+\infty$. These saddle points are solutions to the equation

$$zf'(z) = -\frac{d+1}{n} - (1-R)\cdot\frac{z}{1+z} + (1-\rho)\frac{z}{1+(\rho^{-1}-1)\cdot z} = 0.$$

It may be be rewritten as a quadratic equation $P(z) = p_2\cdot z^2 + p_1\cdot z + p_0 = 0$, where

$$p_2 := (\rho-1)\cdot(d+1+(1-R-\rho)n),$$
$$p_1 := \rho R n - n\rho^2 - d - 1,$$
$$p_0 := -\rho\cdot(d+1).$$

Then, the standard argument is that P must have a double root, *i.e.* the saddle points have to *coalesce* (otherwise the integral is exponential, see for example [7, p. 94], [3, A.1.] for details). Writing that the discriminant $\Delta(P)$ is equal to zero yields a quadratic equation $A\cdot d^2 + B\cdot d + C = 0$, where

$A := (2\rho-1)^2,$
$B := -4R\rho^2 n - 4\rho^3 n + 2R\rho n + 10n\rho^2 - 4\rho n + 8\rho^2 - 8\rho + 2,$
$C := R^2\rho^2 n^2 + \rho^4 n^2 - 2R\rho^3 n^2 - 4R\rho^2 n - 4\rho^3 n + 2R\rho n + 10n\rho^2 - 4n\rho + (2\rho-1)^2.$

Solving for d gives

$$d = \frac{-R\rho n - \rho^2 n + 2n\rho - 2\rho + 1 \pm \sqrt{\delta}}{1-2\rho}$$
$$= -1 + \frac{\rho n\left(\pm 2\sqrt{1-R}\sqrt{1-\rho}+2-\rho-R\right)}{1-2\rho}, \qquad (22)$$

where $\sqrt{\delta} := 2n\sqrt{R\rho^3 - R\rho^2 - \rho^3 + \rho^2} = 2n\rho\sqrt{1-R}\sqrt{1-\rho}$. We want the smallest positive root which is given by the minus case of $\pm\sqrt{\delta}$, in the equation above. The end of the proof then consists in studying Eq. (22) in the different regimes:

- For constant code rate R and $\rho = o(1)$, we obtain

$$-2\sqrt{1-R}\sqrt{1-\rho} + 2 - \rho - R = (2-R) - 2\sqrt{1-R} + o(1),$$

hence $d_{\mathrm{reg}} \sim \kappa_R h$, where $\kappa_R := (2-R) - 2\sqrt{1-R} > 0$.
- For $R = o(1)$ and $\rho = o(1)$ we have

$$-2\sqrt{1-R}\sqrt{1-\rho} = -2\left(1 - \frac{R}{2} - \frac{R^2}{8} + o(R^2)\right)\left(1 - \frac{\rho}{2} - \frac{\rho^2}{8} + o(\rho^2)\right)$$

$$= -2 + R + \rho + \frac{R^2}{4} + \frac{\rho^2}{4} - \frac{R\rho}{2} + o(R\rho),$$

hence $-2\sqrt{1-R}\sqrt{1-\rho} + 2 - \rho - R = \frac{R^2}{4} + \frac{\rho^2}{4} - \frac{R\rho}{2} + o(R\rho)$. This gives us $d_{\mathrm{reg}} + 1 \sim \frac{R^2}{4} h$ if $r = o(R)$ and $d_{\mathrm{reg}} + 1 \sim \frac{R^2}{4}(1-\lambda)^2 h$ if $\rho = \lambda R$ is linear in R with $\lambda < 1$.

□

References

1. Aguilar-Melchor, C., Blazy, O., Deneuville, J.C., Gaborit, P., Zémor, G.: Efficient encryption from random quasi-cyclic codes. IEEE Trans. Inf. Theory **64**(5), 3927–3943 (2018). https://doi.org/10.1109/TIT.2018.2804444
2. Albrecht, M., Cid, C., Faugère, J.C., Fitzpatrick, R., Perret, L.: On the complexity of the arora-ge algorithm against LWE. In: SCC 2012 - Third International Conference on Symbolic Computation and Cryptography, Castro Urdiales, Spain, pp. 93–99 (2012). https://hal.inria.fr/hal-00776434
3. Albrecht, M.R., Cid, C., Faugère, J.C., Perret, L.: Algebraic Algorithms for LWE. Cryptology ePrint Archive, Paper 2014/1018 (2014). https://eprint.iacr.org/2014/1018
4. Applebaum, B., Damgård, I., Ishai, Y., Nielsen, M., Zichron, L.: Secure arithmetic computation with constant computational overhead. In: Katz, J., Shacham, H. (eds.) CRYPTO 2017. LNCS, vol. 10401, pp. 223–254. Springer, Cham (2017). https://doi.org/10.1007/978-3-319-63688-7_8
5. Arora, S., Ge, R.: New algorithms for learning in presence of errors. In: Aceto, L., Henzinger, M., Sgall, J. (eds.) ICALP 2011. LNCS, vol. 6755, pp. 403–415. Springer, Heidelberg (2011). https://doi.org/10.1007/978-3-642-22006-7_34
6. Augot, D., Finiasz, M., Sendrier, N.: A family of fast syndrome based cryptographic hash functions. In: Dwason, E., Vaudenay, S. (eds.) MYCRYPT 2005: First International Conference on Cryptology in Malaysia. Lecture Notes in Computer Science, vol. 3715, pp. 64–83. Springer, Kuala Lumpur (2005). https://doi.org/10.1007/11554868_6, https://hal.inria.fr/inria-00509188
7. Bardet, M.: Étude des systèmes algébriques surdéterminés. Applications aux codes correcteurs et à la cryptographie. Theses, Université Pierre et Marie Curie - Paris VI (2004). https://tel.archives-ouvertes.fr/tel-00449609
8. Bardet, M., Faugère, J.C., Salvy, B., Spaenlehauer, P.J.: On the complexity of solving quadratic Boolean systems. J. Complex. **29**(1), 53–75 (2013). https://doi.org/10.1016/j.jco.2012.07.001

9. Bardet, M., Faugère, J.C., Salvy, B., Yang, B.Y.: Asymptotic behaviour of the index of regularity of quadratic semi-regular polynomial systems. In: Gianni, P. (ed.) The Effective Methods in Algebraic Geometry Conference (MEGA 2005), pp. 1–14 (2005)

10. Baum, C., Braun, L., Munch-Hansen, A., Razet, B., Scholl, P.: Appenzeller to brie: efficient zero-knowledge proofs for mixed-mode arithmetic and Z2k. In: Proceedings of the 2021 ACM SIGSAC Conference on Computer and Communications Security, CCS 2021, pp. 192–211. Association for Computing Machinery, New York (2021). https://doi.org/10.1145/3460120.3484812

11. Baum, C., Braun, L., Munch-Hansen, A., Scholl, P.: Mozz2karella: efficient vector-ole and zero-knowledge proofs over z2k. In: Advances in Cryptology - CRYPTO 2022: 42nd Annual International Cryptology Conference, CRYPTO 2022, Santa Barbara, CA, USA, 15–18 August 2022, Proceedings, Part IV, p. 329–358. Springer, Heidelberg (2022). https://doi.org/10.1007/978-3-031-15985-5_12

12. Becker, A., Joux, A., May, A., Meurer, A.: Decoding random binary linear codes in $2^{n/20}$: how $1 + 1 = 0$ improves information set decoding. In: Pointcheval, D., Johansson, T. (eds.) EUROCRYPT 2012. LNCS, vol. 7237, pp. 520–536. Springer, Heidelberg (2012). https://doi.org/10.1007/978-3-642-29011-4_31

13. Bernstein, D.J., Buchmann, J., Dahmen, E.: Post-Quantum Cryptography. Springer, Dordrecht (2008). https://doi.org/10.1007/978-3-540-88702-7, https://cds.cern.ch/record/1253241

14. Bernstein, D.J., Lange, T., Peters, C.: Smaller decoding exponents: ball-collision decoding. In: Rogaway, P. (ed.) CRYPTO 2011. LNCS, vol. 6841, pp. 743–760. Springer, Heidelberg (2011). https://doi.org/10.1007/978-3-642-22792-9_42

15. Bettale, L.: Cryptanalyse algébrique : outils et applications. Ph.D. thesis, Université Pierre et Marie Curie - Paris 6 (2012)

16. Bettale, L., Faugère, J.C., Perret, L.: Hybrid approach for solving multivariate systems over finite fields. J. Math. Cryptol. **3**(3), 177–197 (2010). https://doi.org/10.1515/jmc.2009.009, https://hal.archives-ouvertes.fr/hal-01148127

17. Beullens, W.: Improved cryptanalysis of UOV and rainbow. In: Canteaut, A., Standaert, F.-X. (eds.) EUROCRYPT 2021. LNCS, vol. 12696, pp. 348–373. Springer, Cham (2021). https://doi.org/10.1007/978-3-030-77870-5_13

18. Boyle, E., Couteau, G., Gilboa, N., Ishai, Y.: Compressing vector OLE. In: Proceedings of the 2018 ACM SIGSAC Conference on Computer and Communications Security, CCS 2018, pp. 896–912. Association for Computing Machinery, New York (2018). https://doi.org/10.1145/3243734.3243868

19. Boyle, E., et al.: Efficient two-round OT extension and silent non-interactive secure computation. In: Proceedings of the 2019 ACM SIGSAC Conference on Computer and Communications Security, CCS 2019, pp. 291–308. Association for Computing Machinery, New York (2019). https://doi.org/10.1145/3319535.3354255

20. Boyle, E., Couteau, G., Gilboa, N., Ishai, Y., Kohl, L., Scholl, P.: Efficient pseudorandom correlation generators: silent OT extension and more. In: Boldyreva, A., Micciancio, D. (eds.) CRYPTO 2019. LNCS, vol. 11694, pp. 489–518. Springer, Cham (2019). https://doi.org/10.1007/978-3-030-26954-8_16

21. Boyle, E., Couteau, G., Gilboa, N., Ishai, Y., Kohl, L., Scholl, P.: Efficient pseudorandom correlation generators from ring-LPN. In: Micciancio, D., Ristenpart, T. (eds.) CRYPTO 2020. LNCS, vol. 12171, pp. 387–416. Springer, Cham (2020). https://doi.org/10.1007/978-3-030-56880-1_14

22. Canto Torres, R.: Asymptotic analysis of ISD algorithms for the $q-$ary case. In: Proceedings of the Tenth International Workshop on Coding and Cryptography WCC 2017 (2017). http://wcc2017.suai.ru/Proceedings_WCC2017.zip

23. Carrier, K., Debris-Alazard, T., Meyer-Hilfiger, C., Tillich, J.P.: Statistical decoding 2.0: reducing decoding to LPN. In: Advances in Cryptology-ASIACRYPT 2022: 28th International Conference on the Theory and Application of Cryptology and Information Security, Taipei, Taiwan, 5–9 December 2022, Proceedings, Part IV, pp. 477–507. Springer, Heidelberg (2022). https://doi.org/10.1007/978-3-031-22972-5_17

24. Cheng, C.-M., Chou, T., Niederhagen, R., Yang, B.-Y.: Solving quadratic equations with XL on parallel architectures. In: Prouff, E., Schaumont, P. (eds.) CHES 2012. LNCS, vol. 7428, pp. 356–373. Springer, Heidelberg (2012). https://doi.org/10.1007/978-3-642-33027-8_21

25. Coppersmith, D.: Solving homogeneous linear equations over GF(2) via block wiedemann algorithm. Math. Comput. **62**(205), 333–350 (1994). https://doi.org/10.2307/2153413

26. Courtois, N., Klimov, A., Patarin, J., Shamir, A.: Efficient algorithms for solving overdefined systems of multivariate polynomial equations. In: Preneel, B. (ed.) EUROCRYPT 2000. LNCS, vol. 1807, pp. 392–407. Springer, Heidelberg (2000). https://doi.org/10.1007/3-540-45539-6_27

27. Esser, A., Kübler, R., May, A.: LPN decoded. In: Katz, J., Shacham, H. (eds.) CRYPTO 2017. LNCS, vol. 10402, pp. 486–514. Springer, Cham (2017). https://doi.org/10.1007/978-3-319-63715-0_17

28. Finiasz, M., Sendrier, N.: Security bounds for the design of code-based cryptosystems. In: Advances in Cryptology - ASIACRYPT 2009, 15th International Conference on the Theory and Application of Cryptology and Information Security, Tokyo, Japan, 6–10 December 2009. Proceedings. Lecture Notes in Computer Science, vol. 5912, pp. 88–105. Springer, Heidelberg (2009). https://doi.org/10.1007/978-3-642-10366-7_6. https://www.iacr.org/archive/asiacrypt2009/59120082/59120082.pdf

29. Flajolet, P., Sedgewick, R.: Analytic Combinatorics. Cambridge University Press, Cambridge (2009). https://doi.org/10.1017/CBO9780511801655. http://www.cambridge.org/uk/catalogue/catalogue.asp?isbn=9780521898065

30. Fröberg, R.: An inequality for Hilbert series of graded algebras. Mathematica Scandinavica **56**, 117–144 (1985). https://doi.org/10.7146/math.scand.a-12092. https://www.mscand.dk/article/view/12092

31. Hazay, C., Orsini, E., Scholl, P., Soria-Vazquez, E.: TinyKeys: a new approach to efficient multi-party computation. In: Advances in Cryptology - CRYPTO 2018. Lecture Notes in Computer Science, vol. 10993, pp. 3–33. Springer, Heidelberg (2018). https://doi.org/10.1007/s00145-022-09423-5

32. Jabri, A.A.: A statistical decoding algorithm for general linear block codes. In: Honary, B. (ed.) Cryptography and Coding 2001. LNCS, vol. 2260, pp. 1–8. Springer, Heidelberg (2001). https://doi.org/10.1007/3-540-45325-3_1

33. Le Gall, F.: Powers of tensors and fast matrix multiplication. In: Proceedings of the 39th International Symposium on Symbolic and Algebraic Computation, pp. 296–303 (2014). https://doi.org/10.1145/2608628.2608664

34. Liu, H., Wang, X., Yang, K., Yu, Y.: The hardness of LPN over any integer ring and field for PCG applications. Cryptology ePrint Archive, Paper 2022/712 (2022). https://eprint.iacr.org/2022/712

35. May, A., Meurer, A., Thomae, E.: Decoding random linear codes in $\tilde{\mathcal{O}}(2^{0.054n})$. In: Lee, D.H., Wang, X. (eds.) ASIACRYPT 2011. LNCS, vol. 7073, pp. 107–124. Springer, Heidelberg (2011). https://doi.org/10.1007/978-3-642-25385-0_6

36. May, A., Ozerov, I.: On computing nearest neighbors with applications to decoding of binary linear codes. In: Oswald, E., Fischlin, M. (eds.) EUROCRYPT 2015. LNCS, vol. 9056, pp. 203–228. Springer, Heidelberg (2015). https://doi.org/10.1007/978-3-662-46800-5_9

37. Misoczki, R., Tillich, J.P., Sendrier, N., Barreto, P.S.L.M.: MDPC-McEliece: new McEliece variants from moderate density parity-check codes. In: 2013 IEEE International Symposium on Information Theory, pp. 2069–2073 (2013). https://doi.org/10.1109/ISIT.2013.6620590

38. Prange, E.: The use of information sets in decoding cyclic codes. IRE Trans. Inf. Theory **8**(5), 5–9 (1962). https://doi.org/10.1109/TIT.1962.1057777

39. Stern, J.: A method for finding codewords of small weight. In: Cohen, G., Wolfmann, J. (eds.) Coding Theory 1988. LNCS, vol. 388, pp. 106–113. Springer, Heidelberg (1989). https://doi.org/10.1007/BFb0019850

40. Sun, C., Tibouchi, M., Abe, M.: Revisiting the hardness of binary error LWE. In: Liu, J.K., Cui, H. (eds.) ACISP 2020. LNCS, vol. 12248, pp. 425–444. Springer, Cham (2020). https://doi.org/10.1007/978-3-030-55304-3_22

41. Thomé, E.: Subquadratic computation of vector generating polynomials and improvement of the block wiedemann algorithm. J. Symb. Comput. **33**(5), 757–775 (2002). https://doi.org/10.1006/jsco.2002.0533

42. Weng, C., Yang, K., Katz, J., Wang, X.: Wolverine: fast, scalable, and communication-efficient zero-knowledge proofs for boolean and arithmetic circuits. In: 42nd IEEE Symposium on Security and Privacy, SP 2021, San Francisco, CA, USA, 24–27 May 2021, pp. 1074–1091. IEEE (2021). https://doi.org/10.1109/SP40001.2021.00056

43. Wiedemann, D.: Solving sparse linear equations over finite fields. IEEE Trans. Inf. Theory **32**(1), 54–62 (1986). https://doi.org/10.1109/TIT.1986.1057137

44. Yang, K., Weng, C., Lan, X., Zhang, J., Wang, X.: Ferret: fast extension for Correlated OT with Small Communication. In: Proceedings of the 2020 ACM SIGSAC Conference on Computer and Communications Security, CCS 2020, pp. 1607–1626. Association for Computing Machinery, New York (2020). https://doi.org/10.1145/3372297.3417276

An Efficient Key Recovery Attack
on SIDH

Wouter Castryck[1,2]($\boxtimes$) and Thomas Decru[1]

[1] imec-COSIC, KU Leuven, Leuven, Belgium
wouter.castryck@esat.kuleuven.be
[2] Vakgroep Wiskunde: Algebra en Meetkunde, Universiteit Gent, Ghent, Belgium
thomas.decru@esat.kuleuven.be

Abstract. We present an efficient key recovery attack on the Supersingular Isogeny Diffie–Hellman protocol (SIDH). The attack is based on Kani's "reducibility criterion" for isogenies from products of elliptic curves and strongly relies on the torsion point images that Alice and Bob exchange during the protocol. If we assume knowledge of the endomorphism ring of the starting curve then the classical running time is polynomial in the input size (heuristically), apart from the factorization of a small number of integers that only depend on the system parameters. The attack is particularly fast and easy to implement if one of the parties uses 2-isogenies and the starting curve comes equipped with a non-scalar endomorphism of very small degree; this is the case for SIKE, the instantiation of SIDH that recently advanced to the fourth round of NIST's standardization effort for post-quantum cryptography. Our Magma implementation breaks `SIKEp434`, which aims at security level 1, in about ten minutes on a single core.

Keywords: isogeny-based cryptography · SIDH · elliptic curves · genus 2 curves

1 Introduction

We present a new and powerful key recovery attack on the Supersingular Isogeny Diffie–Hellman key exchange protocol (SIDH), proposed in 2011 by Jao and De Feo [25] and considered the flagship of isogeny-based cryptography. Its instantiation SIKE [24] recently advanced to the fourth round of the post-quantum cryptography standardization process, currently run by NIST [33].

The attack is based on a "reducibility criterion" from 1997 due to Kani [26, Theorem 2.6] for determining whether an isogeny emanating from a product of two elliptic curves takes us again to a product of elliptic curves, rather than

This work was supported in part by the European Research Council (ERC) under the European Union's Horizon 2020 research and innovation programme (grant agreement ISOCRYPT - No. 101020788) and by CyberSecurity Research Flanders with reference number VR20192203.

© International Association for Cryptologic Research 2023
C. Hazay and M. Stam (Eds.): EUROCRYPT 2023, LNCS 14008, pp. 423–447, 2023.
https://doi.org/10.1007/978-3-031-30589-4_15

to the Jacobian of a genus 2 curve as one would expect. This heavily outperforms previous attack strategies, such as the ones discussed in [11,31,36,37, Sect. 5], both in theory and in practice. Run on a single core, the appended Magma code [2] breaks the Microsoft SIKE challenges $IKEp182 and $IKEp217 from [32] in about 55 s and 85 s, respectively. A run on the SIKEp434 parameters, previously believed to meet NIST's quantum security level 1, took roughly 10 m, again on a single core. We also ran the code on random instances of SIKEp503 (level 2), SIKEp610 (level 3) and SIKEp751 (level 5), which on average took about 20 m, 55 m and 3 h 15 m, respectively.

For the sake of exposition, we concentrate on the concrete set-up of SIKE and comment on more general parameter choices as we see fit. Our attack targets Bob's private key, which is a secret 3^b-isogeny $\varphi : E_{\text{start}} \to E$ between two supersingular elliptic curves E_{start}, E. The starting curve E_{start} is a system parameter and is endowed with two independent points $P_0, Q_0 \in E_{\text{start}}$ of order 2^a; the exponents a, b are system parameters too. Bob's public key consists of the codomain E and the image points $\varphi(P_0), \varphi(Q_0)$. As explained in Sect. 4, it follows from Kani's criterion that for any isogeny $\gamma : E_{\text{start}} \to C$ of degree $2^a - 3^b$ (assume for now that this is positive) the $(2^a, 2^a)$-isogeny from $C \times E$ with kernel generated by $(\gamma(P_0), \varphi(P_0)), (\gamma(Q_0), \varphi(Q_0))$ must again land on a product of elliptic curves. The idea behind our attack is that landing on a product is extremely unlikely if $E, \varphi(P_0), \varphi(Q_0)$ do *not* constitute a valid public key triple. In other words, we can use Kani's criterion as a decision tool. An easy search-to-decision reduction then allows to recover φ. The details of this reduction can be found in Sect. 6.

The main bottleneck is finding and evaluating the auxiliary isogeny γ; once this is done, the decision algorithm amounts to computing a length-a chain of $(2, 2)$-isogenies, which is very efficient (Richelot isogenies). Our focus lies on the cases where E_{start} is one of

$$y^2 = x^3 + x, \qquad\qquad y^2 = x^3 + 6x^2 + x, \qquad\qquad (1)$$

which are supersingular in characteristic $p \equiv 3 \bmod 4$. The former was the starting curve of SIKE when it was submitted to the first round of the NIST standardization effort. The use of the latter curve was proposed from the second round onwards. Both curves come equipped with an explicit endomorphism 2i satisfying 2i ∘ 2i = [−4]. As discussed in Sect. 5, this feature often lends itself to a very simple construction of γ, apart from the cost of factoring $2^a - 3^b$ (precomputable). In practice, the success probability is high enough for setting our search-to-decision reduction in motion, where now polynomially many integers of size $O(2^a)$ must be factored; concretely, these integers are all of the form $2^{a-j} - 3^{b-i}$. As the reader can tell from the above timings, the resulting attack on SIKE is devastating.

While the endomorphism 2i is sufficient for a practical break of SIKE in all security levels, the asymptotic time complexity is only sub-exponential; more precisely, modulo the said factorizations, we expect it to run in time $L_p(1/4)$, see Sect. 10. In order to reach a polynomial runtime (heuristically and again modulo factorization), one must also resort to non-scalar endomorphisms of other very small degrees. Such endomorphisms may not exist on E_{start}, but in view of the work of Love and Boneh [29] one can easily find explicit isogenies to curves on which they do occur. The KLPT algorithm from [27] then allows to transform a degree $2^a - 3^b$ isogeny emanating from such a curve into the desired instance of $\gamma : E_{\text{start}} \to C$. In fact, for this approach, it is not required that E_{start} is among (1): any starting curve whose endomorphism ring is known will do.

Remark 1. If the endomorphism ring of E_{start} is unknown, then one can still construct γ efficiently in case $2^a - 3^b$ happens to be smooth. This event is highly unlikely, but as explained in Sect. 11 one can create more leeway by extending φ and by guessing how it acts on small-order torsion; as was pointed out to us by De Feo and Wesolowski (independently), the resulting attack runs heuristically in time $L_p(1/2 + \epsilon)$.

We finally note that our attack also breaks instantiations of SIDH that make other torsion choices for Alice and Bob. Indeed, the strategy can be used for the recovery of a secret ℓ_B^b-isogeny from ℓ_A^a-torsion point information for any small primes ℓ_A, ℓ_B, as long as $\ell_B^b = O(\ell_A^a)$; in particular, when applied to SIKE this also allows to find Alice's private key. It can even handle non-prime-power torsion, as used in for example B-SIDH [9]. Our claims on the asymptotic runtime still apply, but away from $\ell_A = 2$ implementing the attack is more cumbersome because one can no longer rely on fast Richelot isogenies; see Sect. 11 for a more elaborate discussion.

Follow-Up Work

After a first version of this paper was posted online, several improvements and extensions have made an appearance; for the sake of chronology, the remainder of this paper is free of references to these follow-up works, but let us give a quick overview. It was observed by Maino and Martindale [30],[1] Oudompheng [34], Petit (personal communication) and Wesolowski [45] that Kani's machinery also allows for a direct key recovery, which is considerably faster than our decisional approach. Various other speed-ups were found in an effort led by Oudompheng and Pope to reimplement the attack in SageMath [35,40], and in a parallel effort by Steel to fine-tune our Magma implementation. Notably, the Magma kernel was updated with improved $\mathbb{F}_{p^2}$-arithmetic, resulting in a faster execution of our code (the initial timings were slower by factors 4 to 8, roughly). In the case of a starting curve with known endomorphism ring, Wesolowski rigorously proved, assuming the generalized Riemann hypothesis, that the auxiliary isogeny γ can be constructed in polynomial time, without any need for factorizations [45]. The most remarkable follow-up work is due to Robert [38], who showed how to get rid, unconditionally, of all endomorphism ring assumptions by working with abelian eightfolds rather than surfaces (using an idea that is reminiscent of the Zarhin

---

[1] Right before posting our paper online, we learned that the authors of [30] had started pursuing related ideas.

trick). He also crushed the hope for secure higher-dimensional variants of SIDH. Fouotsa, Moriya and Petit have proposed an interesting (yet impractical) variant of SIDH that aims at thwarting the current attacks [18].

2 Impact and Non-impact on Isogeny-Based Cryptosystems

Our attack also impacts various cryptographic schemes that build on SIDH, or make use of similar hardness assumptions, such as B-SIDH [9], SHealS [19] and k-SIDH [1]. As discussed in Sect. 11, even in the case of a starting curve with unknown endomorphism ring, our attack lowers the security of all these schemes. Here, an interesting target is Séta [13], which allows much leeway for an attacker, coming from largely imbalanced torsion levels.[2] On the other hand, we stress that the attack relies crucially on the torsion point images exchanged by Alice and Bob, as well as on the knowledge of the degree of the secret isogeny. In particular, it cannot be adjusted in an obvious way to attack primitives that do not reveal this information, such as CRS/CSIDH [7,10,39] and SQISign [12], and the general supersingular isogeny path problem remains unaffected [44]. We forward the reader to an online project, initiated by De Feo, which attempts at organizing the most popular isogeny-based cryptographic protocols and their best classical and quantum attacks [14].

3 Concrete Set-Up

Concretely, we will describe an algorithm which, upon input of

  (i) an SIDH prime p, i.e., $p = 2^a 3^b f - 1$ for integers $a \geq 2, b, f \geq 1$ with $2^a \approx 3^b$,
 (ii) an elliptic curve $E_0/\mathbb{F}_{p^2}$ with $\#E_0(\mathbb{F}_{p^2}) = (p+1)^2$,
(iii) generators P_0, Q_0 of $E_0[2^a]$,
 (iv) a 3^β-isogeny $\tau : E_0 \to E_{\text{start}}$ for some $\beta \geq 0$, where E_{start} is one of the two curves (1) that have served as starting curves in SIKE,
  (v) the codomain $E/\mathbb{F}_{p^2}$ of a secret cyclic 3^b-isogeny $\varphi : E_0 \to E$,
 (vi) the generators $P = \varphi(P_0)$ and $Q = \varphi(Q_0)$ of $E[2^a]$,

returns the isogeny φ. For simplicity we assume that φ is uniquely determined, which is true with overwhelming probability. If $2^{a-1} > 3^{b/2}$ then this is guaranteed by [43, Lemma 3.1]. A note on input (iv): when attacking SIKE, at the initial stage we will have $\beta = 0$ and $E_0 = E_{\text{start}}$, so the reader can keep this setting in mind for now. But our search-to-decision reduction will involve a recursion during which the value of β will grow, whence this more general formulation. Moreover, we also want to cope with larger values of β when discussing other starting curves with a known endomorphism ring.

---

[2] Séta is now fully broken in view of Robert's work [38].

4   Decision via Kani's Reducibility Criterion

We first study the following decision variant: we assume to be given (i), (ii), (iii) and an elliptic curve $E/\mathbb{F}_{p^2}$ satisfying $\#E(\mathbb{F}_{p^2}) = (p+1)^2$, along with generators P, Q of $E[2^a]$. The goal is to decide whether or not

(D)   there is a 3^b-isogeny $\varphi : E_0 \to E$ such that $\varphi(P_0) = P$ and $\varphi(Q_0) = Q$.

We impose two technical conditions that will be discussed in more detail later on:

- We suppose that $2^a > 3^b$.
- Let $c = 2^a - 3^b$. We assume that we can compute the images $P_c = \gamma(P_0)$ and $Q_c = \gamma(Q_0)$ under an arbitrary c-isogeny $\gamma : E_0 \to C$ to some codomain curve C.

We let $x \in \mathbb{Z}$ denote a multiplicative inverse of 3^b modulo 2^a. Note that $-x$ is then a multiplicative inverse of c modulo 2^a.

4.1 $(2^a, 2^a)$-Subgroups Built from Torsion Point Information

If (D) holds then we can consider the isogeny

$$\psi = [-1] \circ \varphi \circ \hat{\gamma} : C \to E,$$

where we note that $\psi(P_c) = -cP$ and $\psi(Q_c) = -cQ$. For all $R, S \in C[2^a]$ we have that

$$e_{2^a}(x\psi(R), x\psi(S)) = e_{2^a}(R, S)^{x^2 c 3^b} = e_{2^a}(R, S)^{-1}$$

or in other words the group homomorphism

$$[x] \circ \psi|_{C[2^a]} : C[2^a] \to E[2^a]$$

is a so-called "anti-isometry" with respect to the 2^a-Weil pairing. This implies that the group

$$\langle (P_c, x\psi(P_c)), (Q_c, x\psi(Q_c)) \rangle = \langle (P_c, P), (Q_c, Q) \rangle \qquad (2)$$

is maximally isotropic with respect to the 2^a-Weil pairing on the product $C \times E$ (equipped with the product polarization). Indeed,

$$e_{2^a}((P_c, x\psi(P_c)), (Q_c, x\psi(Q_c))) = e_{2^a}(P_c, Q_c) e_{2^a}(x\psi(P_c), x\psi(Q_c)) = 1$$

because the Weil pairing on $C \times E$ is just the product of the Weil pairings of the corresponding components.

Therefore it concerns the kernel of a $(2^a, 2^a)$-isogeny of principally polarized abelian surfaces. By writing this isogeny as a composition of $(2, 2)$-isogenies, it can be viewed as a walk of length a in the $(2, 2)$-isogeny graph of superspecial principally polarized abelian surfaces over $\overline{\mathbb{F}}_p$, all of whose vertices are defined over $\mathbb{F}_{p^2}$. These vertices come in two types: about $p^2/288$ products of supersingular elliptic curves and about $p^3/2880$ Jacobians of superspecial genus 2 curves, see e.g. [3]. Therefore it is to be expected that most isogenies in the chain are between Jacobians of genus 2 curves, and such isogenies can be computed efficiently using "classical" formulae due to Richelot [42]. But the first step is clearly an exception to this: with overwhelming probability, this is a "gluing" step, mapping the product $C \times E$ to a Jacobian (more precisely, by Theorem 1 below this can only fail if $C \cong E$). Formulae for this gluing step were derived in [23] and are recalled in Sect. 8.

4.2   Kani's Theorem

What is the role of the isogeny γ in all this? Its aim is to force us into the exceptional situation where the *last* step of the chain is split, i.e., the codomain of our $(2^a, 2^a)$-isogeny is again a product of elliptic curves. In that case the anti-isometry $x\psi|_{C[2^a]}$ and the group (2) are called "reducible". This event is characterized by the theorem of Kani [26, Theorem 2.6]:

Definition 1. *Let C, E be two elliptic curves and $N \geq 2$ an integer. Let $\psi : C \to E$ be a separable isogeny and let $H_1, H_2 \subset \ker \psi$ be subgroups such that $H_1 \cap H_2 = \{0\}$, $\#H_1 \cdot \#H_2 = \deg \psi$ and $\#H_1 + \#H_2 = N$. Then the triplet (ψ, H_1, H_2) is called an* isogeny diamond configuration of order N *between C and E.*

Theorem 1. *Let (ψ, H_1, H_2) be an isogeny diamond configuration of order $N \geq 2$ between two elliptic curves C and E. Let $d = \gcd(\#H_1, \#H_2)$, let $n = N/d$ and let $k_i = \#H_i/d$ for $i = 1, 2$. Then ψ factors uniquely over $[d]$, i.e. $\psi = \psi' \circ [d]$ and there is a unique reducible anti-isometry $\iota : C[N] \to E[N]$ such that*

$$\iota(k_1 R_1 + k_2 R_2) = \psi'(R_2 - R_1) \text{ for all } R_i \in [n]^{-1}H_i \ (i = 1, 2) . \qquad (3)$$

Moreover, if $N \leq p$ then every reducible anti-isometry $C[N] \to E[N]$ is of this form.

Remark 2. Kani allows for inseparable isogenies in Definition 1, in which case $\#H_i$ should be interpreted as the *degree* of the corresponding subgroup scheme. When doing so, the condition $N \leq p$ in Theorem 1 can be discarded; this was merely added to ensure that ψ is separable.

In our case, the kernel of ψ is a group of order $c3^b$, so it admits two (unique) subgroups H_1, H_2 of respective orders c and 3^b. We clearly have that $H_1 \cap H_2 = \{0\}$ and
$$\#H_1 + \#H_2 = 2^a, \quad \#H_1 \cdot \#H_2 = \deg \psi,$$
so the triplet (ψ, H_1, H_2) is an isogeny diamond configuration of order 2^a. Then Kani's theorem implies that our anti-isometry $x\psi|_{C[2^a]}$ is reducible. Indeed, let us check condition (3) explicitly: we need to verify that

$$x\psi(cR_1 + 3^b R_2) = \psi(R_2 - R_1)$$

for all points R_1, R_2 such that $2^a R_1 \in H_1$ and $2^a R_2 \in H_2$ (note that $d = 1$ in our case). But this is easy: since $\psi(R_1)$ and $\psi(R_2)$ are 2^a-torsion points, we can rewrite the left hand side as

$$x c \psi(R_1) + x 3^b \psi(R_2) = 3^{-b}(2^a - 3^b)\psi(R_1) + 3^{-b}3^b \psi(R_2)$$
$$= \psi(R_2) - \psi(R_1)$$
$$= \psi(R_2 - R_1)$$

as wanted (recall that $x 3^b \equiv -x c \equiv 1 \bmod 2^a$).

4.3 Decision Strategy

Our decision strategy amounts to testing whether or not quotienting out $C \times E$ by (2) takes us to a product of elliptic curves, as depicted in Fig. 1. As we have just argued, if (D) holds, then we pass the test.

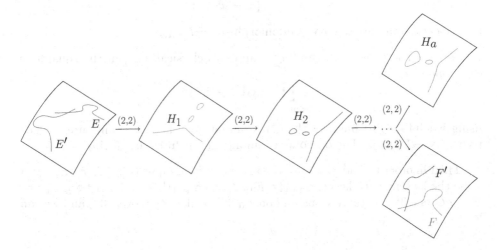

Fig. 1. Decision strategy based on Kani's reducibility criterion.

For now, we content ourselves with the loose heuristic that if (D) does not hold, then the test should fail with overwhelming probability because the proportion of products of elliptic curves among all vertices in the graph is only about $10/p$. We can actually be a bit more precise about this heuristic in the cases that are relevant for our attack, namely the "wrong guesses" in our search-to-decision reduction: see Remark 4.

5 Constructing and Evaluating the Auxiliary Isogeny γ

The assumption that we can (efficiently) compute the image points P_c and Q_c under a degree-c isogeny is non-trivial, and this is where we need the factorization of $c = 2^a - 3^b$. It is also here that we rely on the special nature of E_{start}: both options come with an endomorphism $2\mathbf{i}$ satisfying $2\mathbf{i} \circ 2\mathbf{i} = [-4]$. Indeed, on $E_{\text{start}} : y^2 = x^3 + x$ we have the automorphism $\mathbf{i} : (x, y) \mapsto (-x, \sqrt{-1}y)$ and we simply let $2\mathbf{i} = [2] \circ \mathbf{i}$. For $E_{\text{start}} : y^2 = x^3 + 6x^2 + x$ we can obtain $2\mathbf{i}$ as the composition of its outgoing 2-isogeny to $y^2 = x^3 + x$, the automorphism $\mathbf{i}$ on the latter curve, and the dual of the said 2-isogeny.

5.1   Construction

There is a reasonable chance that the prime factorization of c only involves prime factors that are congruent to 1 mod 4; this chance is inversely proportional to $\sqrt{a}$ by a theorem of Landau (see Sect. 10 for a more detailed discussion). As far as we are aware, the only known way to find out is by factoring c explicitly. Once this factorization is done and all prime factors are indeed congruent to 1 mod 4, we can efficiently write $c = u^2 + 4v^2 = (u + 2iv)(u - 2iv)$. Then

$$\gamma_{\text{start}} = [u] + [v] \circ 2\mathbf{i}$$

is an easy-to-evaluate degree-c endomorphism of E_{start}.

Remark 3. The method for finding u and v is classical: e.g., in the squarefree case, one computes

$$\prod_{\text{primes } \ell | c} \gcd(z_\ell + \mathbf{i}, \ell)$$

using Euclid's algorithm over the Gaussian integers; here z_ℓ is any integer such that $z_\ell^2 \equiv -1 \bmod \ell$. The outcome is among $\pm(u + 2iv), \pm\mathbf{i}(u + 2iv)$.

Then in order to find γ, we use the isogeny τ from input (iv). Let $\tilde{\tau} : E_{\text{start}} \to C$ be the isogeny with kernel $\gamma_{\text{start}}(\tau(E_0[3^\beta])) = \gamma_{\text{start}}(\ker \hat{\tau})$. Then $\tilde{\tau} \circ \gamma_{\text{start}} \circ \tau : E_0 \to C$ is a $3^{2\beta}c$-isogeny vanishing on $E_0[3^\beta]$, so it factors over $[3^\beta]$ and we can let

$$\gamma = \frac{\tilde{\tau} \circ \gamma_{\text{start}} \circ \tau}{3^\beta}.$$

It remains to see that γ is easy to evaluate on our 2^a-torsion points P_0 and Q_0. For this, we first discuss a special case.

5.2   Evaluation: Case $\beta \leq b$

This is the only relevant case when attacking SIDH with base curve $E_0 = E_{\text{start}}$, as in the case of SIKE: while β will grow during our search-to-decision reduction, it will never grow beyond b. But then we always have that $\ker \hat{\tau} \subset E_{\text{start}}[3^b] \subset E_{\text{start}}(\mathbb{F}_{p^2})$. So we can explicitly write down a generator $T \in E_{\text{start}}(\mathbb{F}_{p^2})$ of $\ker \hat{\tau}$ and compute the isogeny $\tilde{\tau}$ with kernel $\langle \gamma_{\text{start}}(T) \rangle$. Evaluating γ in our 2^a-torsion points P_0 and Q_0 is then simply done by feeding them to $\tilde{\tau} \circ \gamma_{\text{start}} \circ \tau$ and scalar-multiplying the outcome with a multiplicative inverse of 3^β modulo 2^a. (In fact, this evaluation will naturally simplify in the context of our search-to-decision reduction.)

5.3 Evaluation: General Case

If $\beta > b$ then we cannot simply evaluate γ_{start} in a generator of ker $\hat{\tau}$, unless we base-change to a potentially very large and costly extension of $\mathbb{F}_{p^2}$. But note that the isogeny $\tilde{\tau}$ is precisely the pushforward isogeny $[\gamma_{\text{start}}]_* \hat{\tau}$ that was studied in [12, Sect. 4]. This suggests the following alternative method for computing $\tilde{\tau}$. Note that the specific choice of E_{start} comes with an explicit isomorphism

$$\iota : \text{End}(E_{\text{start}}) \to \mathcal{O}_{\text{start}}$$

where $\mathcal{O}_{\text{start}}$ is a maximal order in the quaternion algebra $B_{p,\infty} = \langle 1, \mathbf{i}, \mathbf{j}, \mathbf{ij} \rangle_{\mathbb{Q}}$ with $\mathbf{i}^2 = -1$ and $\mathbf{j}^2 = -p$. Then:

1. First, one converts the isogeny $\hat{\tau} : E_{\text{start}} \to E_0$ into a left ideal $I_{\hat{\tau}} \subset \mathcal{O}_{\text{start}}$ of norm 3^β, e.g. following [20, Algorithm 3]. In fact, in the main use cases of this general method, a large component of the isogeny $\hat{\tau}$ will arise *from* its corresponding left $\mathcal{O}_{\text{start}}$-ideal; so in those cases this step can be simplified.
2. Next, one computes the left ideal $I_{\tilde{\tau}} = [(\iota(\gamma_{\text{start}}))]_* I_{\hat{\tau}}$ using the formula from [12, Lemma 3]; this ideal again has norm 3^β.
3. Finally, one converts the ideal $I_{\tilde{\tau}}$ into a length-β chain of 3-isogenies emanating from E_{start}, e.g. using [20, Algorithm 2]. Then $\tilde{\tau}$ is the composition of these 3-isogenies.

Then, here too, evaluating γ in P_0 and Q_0 is done by applying $\tilde{\tau} \circ \gamma_{\text{start}} \circ \tau$ and scalar-multiplying with an inverse of 3^β modulo 2^a.

5.4 Away from the Endomorphism 2i

We conclude by remarking that there are many other candidate-ways for constructing the isogeny γ. Just to give one similar example, decompositions of the form $c = u^2 + 3v^2$ are useful as soon as one knows an explicit path to $y^2 = x^3 + 1$, because this curve comes equipped with an endomorphism ω such that $\omega^2 = -3$. This type of examples will reappear in Sect. 10. A different kind of example is the case where c is very smooth: in that case one can construct the desired c-isogeny $\gamma : E_0 \to C$ as a composition of small degree isogenies *without* knowing a path to some special-featured curve. Even though this event is highly unlikely, there are tricks to create more leeway; see Sect. 11 for a more elaborate discussion.

6 Key Recovery Algorithm: Basic Version

We resume with the set-up from Sect. 3. The previous sections suggest the following iterative approach to full key recovery. We assume for simplicity that $\beta = 0$, so that the base curve E_0 coincides with E_{start}. Recall that this is the case in SIKE. In the general case, one should just replace the maps $\hat{\kappa}_1 : E_1 \to E_0$, $\widehat{\kappa_2\kappa_1} : E_2 \to E_0, \ldots$ below with their compositions with τ.

6.1   Iteration

For the first iteration, choose $\beta_1 \geq 1$ minimal such that there exists some $\alpha_1 \geq 0$ for which

$$c_1 = 2^{a-\alpha_1} - 3^{b-\beta_1}$$

is of the form $u_1^2 + 4v_1^2$. Write $\varphi = \varphi_1 \circ \kappa_1$ with κ_1 a 3^{β_1}-isogeny. To an attacker, there are a priori 3^{β_1} options for κ_1 (this assumes knowledge of an "incoming isogeny", otherwise there are $4 \cdot 3^{\beta_1-1}$ options). For each of these options, we can run our decision algorithm on

(ii) the curve $E_1 = \kappa_1(E_0)$,
(iii) the generators $P_1 = \kappa_1(2^{\alpha_1} P_0)$ and $Q_1 = \kappa_1(2^{\alpha_1} Q_0)$ of $E_1[2^{a-\alpha_1}]$,
(iv) the 3^{β_1}-isogeny $\hat{\kappa}_1 : E_1 \to E_0$,
(v) the codomain E; if the guess is correct then it is connected to E_1 via the unknown isogeny φ_1 of degree $3^{b-\beta_1}$,
(vi) the generators $2^{\alpha_1} P, 2^{\alpha_1} Q$ of $E[2^{a-\alpha_1}]$

where the numbering (ii)–(vi) is chosen to be consistent with our set-up from Sect. 3. According to our heuristic assumption discussed in Sect. 4.3, we expect that only the correct guess for κ_1 will pass the test; see also Remark 4 below.

Let us discuss in more detail what "running the test" amounts to in this case. First, one must compute the images P_{c_1}, Q_{c_1} of P_1, Q_1 under the isogeny

$$\gamma_1 = \frac{\tilde{\hat{\kappa}}_1 \circ \gamma_{\text{start}} \circ \hat{\kappa}_1}{3^{\beta_1}} \tag{4}$$

where $\tilde{\hat{\kappa}}_1 : E_{\text{start}} \to C_1$ is the isogeny with kernel $\gamma_{\text{start}}(\ker \kappa_1)$, with $\gamma_{\text{start}} = [u_1] + 2\mathbf{i} \circ [v_1]$. Observe that this simplifies: all one should do is compute

$$P_{c_1} = 2^{\alpha_1} \tilde{\hat{\kappa}}_1 \gamma_{\text{start}}(P_0), \quad Q_{c_1} = 2^{\alpha_1} \tilde{\hat{\kappa}}_1 \gamma_{\text{start}}(Q_0). \tag{5}$$

Once these points have been computed, one checks whether the quotient of $C_1 \times E$ by the $(2^{a-\alpha_1}, 2^{a-\alpha_1})$-subgroup

$$\langle (P_{c_1}, 2^{\alpha_1} P), (Q_{c_1}, 2^{\alpha_1} Q) \rangle \tag{6}$$

is again a product of elliptic curves. This is done by computing the corresponding chain of $(2,2)$-isogenies. With overwhelming probability, the first $a - \alpha_1 - 1$ steps in this chain amount to one gluing step followed by $a - \alpha_1 - 2$ Richelot isogenies between Jacobians of genus 2 curves. An easy "$\delta = 0$ test" then checks whether or not the last step splits (see Sect. 8 for algorithmic details).

If the test fails, then we try again with a different guess for κ_1. We remark that, even in the case of a wrong guess, the subgroup (6) is always maximally isotropic with respect to the Weil pairing, so this is *not* the way in which one can detect having taken the wrong direction: one really has to perform the gluing and its successive Richelot walk. (The failure of detecting wrong steps using the Weil pairing is well-known, see e.g. [21, Sect. 7.2]; with some imagination, our attack can be viewed as a refinement of this approach.) If the test passes, then very likely we have found the correct instance of κ_1.

Remark 4. If a wrong guess for κ_1 passes the test, then in view of Kani's theorem the points P_{c_1}, Q_{c_1} must be connected to $2^{\alpha_1} P, 2^{\alpha_1} Q$ via an anti-isometry coming from an isogeny $\psi : C_1 \to E$ fitting in an isogeny diamond configuration of order $2^{a-\alpha_1}$. It is easy to see that the natural candidate for ψ, namely the degree $3^{b+\beta_1}(2^{a-\alpha_1} - 3^{b-\beta_1})$-isogeny

$$\varphi \circ \hat{\kappa}_1 \circ \hat{\gamma}_1 : C_1 \to E,$$

does *not* fit in such an isogeny diamond. Indeed, if it would, then we would have

$$3^{b+\beta_1}(2^{a-\alpha_1} - 3^{b-\beta_1}) = k(2^{a-\alpha_1} - k) \tag{7}$$

for some natural number

$$k \in [1, 2^{a-\alpha_1} - 1]. \tag{8}$$

Modulo $2^{a-\alpha_1}$ the Eq. (7) implies $3^{2b} \equiv k^2$, so that k is congruent to one of

$$3^b, \quad -3^b, \quad 3^b + 2^{a-\alpha_1-1}, \quad -3^b + 2^{a-\alpha_1-1}.$$

In particular, k and $2^{a-\alpha_1} - k$ must be of the form $\pm 3^b + \lambda 2^{a-\alpha_1-1}$. On the other hand, (7) implies that either k or $2^{a-\alpha_1} - k$ is divisible by $3^{b+\beta_1}$. This can only happen if the corresponding λ is non-zero and divisible by 3^b, but then (unless we are in the trivial boundary case $\alpha_1 = a, \beta_1 = b$) we necessarily fall outside the interval (8): a contradiction.

Remark 5. We did not manage to fully rule out the existence of instances of ψ other than $\varphi \circ \hat{\kappa}_1 \circ \hat{\gamma}_1$. However, at least heuristically, the odds are strongly against this. Indeed, loosely speaking, these instances would need to act on $C_1[2^{a-\alpha_1}]$ in essentially the same way as $\varphi \circ \hat{\kappa}_1 \circ \hat{\gamma}_1$ does, and a variation on [43, Lemma 3.1] shows that there is typically no room for another such isogeny.

Once we have found the correct κ_1 we continue from E_1. That is, we let $\beta_2 > \beta_1$ be minimal such that there is some $\alpha_2 \geq 0$ for which $c_2 = 2^{a-\alpha_2} - 3^{b-\beta_2}$ is of the form $u_2^2 + 4v_2^2$. Now one tries to recover the $3^{\beta_2-\beta_1}$-component $\kappa_2 : E_1 \to E_2$ such that $\varphi_1 = \varphi_2 \circ \kappa_2$. In this case, for each guess for κ_2 one computes

$$P_{c_2} = 2^{\alpha_2} \widetilde{\kappa_2 \kappa_1} \gamma_{\text{start}}(P_0), \quad Q_{c_2} = 2^{\alpha_2} \widetilde{\kappa_2 \kappa_1} \gamma_{\text{start}}(Q_0)$$

with $\widetilde{\kappa_2 \kappa_1} : E_{\text{start}} \to C_2$ the isogeny with kernel $\gamma_{\text{start}}(\ker \kappa_2 \kappa_1)$ and $\gamma_{\text{start}} = [u_2] + 2\mathbf{i} \circ [v_2]$. One then checks whether

$$\langle (P_{c_2}, 2^{\alpha_2} P), (Q_{c_2}, 2^{\alpha_2} Q) \rangle \subset C_2 \times E$$

is reducible or not. By continuing in this way, one eventually retrieves all of φ.

6.2 Step Sizes

The gaps between the consecutive integers $0, \beta_1, \beta_2, \beta_3, \ldots, \beta_r = b$ should be as small as possible, because this reduces the number of possible guesses in each iteration. More concretely, the expected number of $(2,2)$-chains that need to be computed is

$$\frac{1}{2}\left(3^{\beta_1} + 3^{\beta_2 - \beta_1} + 3^{\beta_3 - \beta_2} + \ldots + 3^{b - \beta_{r-1}}\right). \tag{9}$$

A necessary condition on each β_i is that $b - \beta_i$ is odd, except in the last iteration where we have $\beta_r = b$. Indeed, if $b - \beta_i > 0$ is even then

$$c_i = 2^{a - \alpha_i} - 3^{b - \beta_i} \equiv 3 \bmod 4$$

cannot be of the form $u_i^2 + 4v_i^2$. Therefore the best we can hope is that the sequence grows by steps of two, in which case the estimate (9) becomes about $9b/4$. Asymptotically, this hope is too good to be true, but for the concrete SIKE parameters experiment shows that this optimal estimate lies close to reality, with the only exceptions corresponding to small β_i. This makes sense: as β_i grows, the amount of leeway (i.e., the number of candidate α_i's) grows as well, and moreover the probability of success increases as c_i is allowed to get smaller. Example: for the parameters of SIKEp434 where we have $a = 216$ and $b = 137$, one quickly finds suitable α_i for every even β_i in $\{0, 1, \ldots, b\} \setminus \{4\}$.

6.3 Rephrasing in Terms of Bob's Secret Key

In practice, SIDH comes with public generators $P_{\text{Bob}}, Q_{\text{Bob}}$ of $E_0[3^b]$ and Bob's secret isogeny φ is encoded as the integer

$$\text{sk}_{\text{Bob}} \in [0, 3^b)$$

for which $\ker \varphi = \langle P_{\text{Bob}} + \text{sk}_{\text{Bob}} Q_{\text{Bob}} \rangle$. Upon expanding

$$\text{sk}_{\text{Bob}} = k_1 + k_2 3^{\beta_1} + \ldots + k_r 3^{\beta_{r-1}}, \qquad k_i \in [0, 3^{\beta_i - \beta_{i-1}} - 1)$$

(where we let $\beta_0 = 0$), we observe that

$$\ker \kappa_1 = \langle 3^{b - \beta_1} P_{\text{Bob}} + k_1 3^{b - \beta_1} Q_{\text{Bob}} \rangle. \tag{10}$$

So the first iteration amounts to

- guessing k_1,
- determining the 3^{β_1}-isogeny $\tilde{\kappa}_1 : E_{\text{start}} \to C_1$ with kernel $\gamma_{\text{start}}(\ker \kappa_1)$, with $\ker \kappa_1$ as in (10),
- computing the points $P_{c_1}, Q_{c_1} \in C_1$ as in (5),
- checking whether or not the subgroup (6) is reducible.

After finding k_1, we proceed with

$$\ker \kappa_2 = \langle 3^{b - \beta_2} P_{\text{Bob}} + (k_1 + k_2 3^{\beta_1}) 3^{b - \beta_2} Q_{\text{Bob}} \rangle$$

in order to determine k_2 via trial-and-error, and so on. So the attack determines sk_{Bob} digit by digit. If all the gaps are of size two, then this amounts to determining one base-9 digit of sk_{Bob} at a time.

6.4 Walking Backwards

As was pointed out to us by De Feo, it may be simpler to reconstruct Bob's secret isogeny φ starting from its tail. That is: using the same $c_1 = 2^{a-\alpha_1} - 3^{b-\beta_1}$, one instead writes $\varphi = \kappa_1 \circ \varphi_1$ and one makes a guess for $\hat{\kappa}_1$. Now writing

$$E_1 = \hat{\kappa}_1(E), \ P_1 = \hat{\kappa}_1(2^{\alpha_1}P), \ Q_1 = \hat{\kappa}_1(2^{\alpha_1}Q),$$

letting γ_{start} be our degree-c_1 endomorphism on $E_0 = E_{\text{start}}$, and writing

$$P_{c_1} = 2^{\alpha_1}\gamma_{\text{start}}(P_0), \ Q_{c_1} = 2^{\alpha_1}\gamma_{\text{start}}(Q_0),$$

one now should check whether the subgroup

$$\langle(P_{c_1}, yP_1), (Q_{c_1}, yQ_1)\rangle \subset E_0 \times E_1$$

is reducible, with y a multiplicative inverse of 3^{β_1} modulo $2^{a-\alpha_1}$. The advantage of this approach is that one can work (and keep working throughout the iteration) with γ_{start} directly, i.e., one avoids the need for transformations of the kind (4).

7 Speed-Ups

We can speed up key recovery as follows:

7.1 Take α_i as Large as Possible

If for a given β_i there indeed exists some $\alpha_i \geq 0$ such that $c_i = 2^{a-\alpha_i} - 3^{b-\beta_i}$ is positive and free of prime factors congruent to 3 mod 4, then usually α_i is not the unique integer with that property, so there is some freedom. The larger we choose α_i, the smaller will be the length $a - \alpha_i$ of our chain of $(2,2)$-isogenies. Therefore, it is more efficient to take larger α_i's.

7.2 Use a Precomputed Table

We have precomputed a table which for all $s \in \{1, 3, 5, \ldots, 239\}$ stores the smallest integer $t(s)$ such that $2^{t(s)} - 3^s$ is a product of primes congruent to 1 modulo 4. It also stores corresponding values for u and v. The table is available as uvtable.m and can be used as follows: for every candidate-β_i such that $b - \beta_i$ is odd, one checks whether or not $t(b - \beta_i) \leq a$. If not, then we proceed to the next candidate. If yes, then we can use this instance of β_i, and we choose $a - t(b - \beta_i)$ as a corresponding value for α_i. This makes sure that α_i is as large as possible, and moreover we have u_i, v_i readily available, without the need for factoring. Our table is sufficiently large to be used for each of the proposed parameter sets for SIKE, up to SIKEp751 targeting NIST's security level 5.

7.3   Extend Bob's Secret Isogeny Where Useful

Imagine that some candidate-β_i does not admit an integer $\alpha_i \geq 0$ such that $2^{a-\alpha_i} - 3^{b-\beta_i}$ is a product of primes congruent to 1 mod 4 (e.g., because $b - \beta_i > 0$ is even). But imagine that $\beta_i - 1$ does. Then one can prolong Bob's secret isogeny with an arbitrary 3-isogeny φ' and let $P' = \varphi'(P)$ and $Q' = \varphi'(Q)$. Treating $\varphi' \circ \varphi$ as the new secret isogeny, the relevant expression now becomes $2^{a-\alpha_i} - 3^{b+1-\beta_i}$, and we know that there exists some $\alpha_i \geq 0$ for which this *is* a product of primes congruent to 1 mod 4. We can now use our attack to determine Bob's secret key modulo 3^{β_i} and proceed.

In practice, this means that most step sizes drop from 2 to 1, or in other words that we are determining one base-3 digit of $\mathrm{sk_{Bob}}$ at a time. The only possibly larger step occurs at the beginning of the iteration. For instance, in the case of SIKEp751, the smallest β_1 such that $2^a - 3^{b-\beta_1} > 0$ is $\beta_1 = 6$, so we cannot hope for a smaller first gap. This implies a rather costly start of the algorithm: of the 3 h15 m that we spent on breaking SIKEp751, almost 2 h were needed for determining the first 6 out of 239 ternary digits of $\mathrm{sk_{Bob}}$.

Remark 6. If 2^a is considerably smaller than 3^b, then it probably makes more sense to attack Alice's private key instead of Bob's, using chains of $(3,3)$-isogenies; see Sect. 11. Of course, if 2^a gets much smaller than 3^b, then one enters the regime of the torsion-point attacks from [36,37].

Remark 7. There is a $1/4$ probability that the random isogeny φ' matches with the dual of the last degree-3 component of φ. In this case, the wrong guesses are also at distance $3^{b-\beta_i}$ from E, so this creates false positives, leaving us clueless about which is the correct guess. However, this is easy to fix: if multiple guesses pass the test, then all one needs to do is change φ', and then we have identified the dual direction once and for all. If this happens, then it will be discovered when trying to determine the ternary digit at position $\beta_2 = \beta_1 + 1$ (and this does not affect the correctness of the first β_1 digits, as these were determined without the use of φ').

8   Computing Chains of (2, 2)-isogenies

In this section we explain how to determine whether or not a $(2^a, 2^a)$-subgroup $\langle (P_c, P), (Q_c, Q) \rangle$ of a product of elliptic curves $C \times E$ is reducible. Throughout, we avoid dealing with certain exceptional cases, e.g. every genus 2 curve H : $y^2 = h(x) = c_6 x^6 + c_5 x^5 + \ldots + c_0$ encountered is assumed to satisfy $c_6 \neq 0$, so that it has two places ∞_1, ∞_2 at infinity, and all points on its Jacobian J_H that we deal with are assumed to be representable as $(\alpha_1, \beta_1) + (\alpha_2, \beta_2) - \infty_1 - \infty_2$ with $\alpha_1 \neq \alpha_2$, so that they have a Mumford representation of the form $[x^2 + u_1 x + u_0, v_1 x + v_0]$. Moreover, all our chains of $(2,2)$-isogenies are assumed to start off by gluing $C \times E$ into a Jacobian, after which we never run into a product of elliptic curves again, except possibly at the a-th and last step. The exceptions to these assumptions are expected to occur with probability $O(p^{-1})$, so we see no need to discuss nor implement them.

8.1   Gluing Elliptic Curves into a Jacobian

In the first step we want to glue the curves C and E into the Jacobian of a genus 2 curve H via the $(2,2)$-subgroup $\langle (2^{a-1}P_c, 2^{a-1}P), (2^{a-1}Q_c, 2^{a-1}Q) \rangle$. We also need to push the points (P_c, P), (Q_c, Q) through the corresponding isogeny. The relevant equations are as follows. We refer to [23, Proposition 4] and its proof for further details.

Proposition 1. *Let* $C/K : y^2 = (x - \alpha_1)(x - \alpha_2)(x - \alpha_3)$ *and* $E : y^2 = (x - \beta_1)(x - \beta_2)(x - \beta_3)$ *be elliptic curves over a field* K *of characteristic different from two. Write* Δ_α *for the discriminant of* $(x - \alpha_1)(x - \alpha_2)(x - \alpha_3)$ *and* Δ_β *for the discriminant of* $(x - \beta_1)(x - \beta_2)(x - \beta_3)$. *Furthermore, define*

$$a_1 = (\alpha_3 - \alpha_2)^2/(\beta_3 - \beta_2) + (\alpha_2 - \alpha_1)^2/(\beta_2 - \beta_1) + (\alpha_1 - \alpha_3)^2/(\beta_1 - \beta_3),$$
$$b_1 = (\beta_3 - \beta_2)^2/(\alpha_3 - \alpha_2) + (\beta_2 - \beta_1)^2/(\alpha_2 - \alpha_1) + (\beta_1 - \beta_3)^2/(\alpha_1 - \alpha_3),$$
$$a_2 = \alpha_1(\beta_3 - \beta_2) + \alpha_2(\beta_1 - \beta_3) + \alpha_3(\beta_2 - \beta_1),$$
$$b_2 = \beta_1(\alpha_3 - \alpha_2) + \beta_2(\alpha_1 - \alpha_3) + \beta_3(\alpha_2 - \alpha_1),$$
$$A = \Delta_\beta a_1/a_2, \quad B = \Delta_\alpha b_1/b_2,$$
$$\begin{aligned} h(x) = -&\big(A(\alpha_2 - \alpha_1)(\alpha_1 - \alpha_3)x^2 + B(\beta_2 - \beta_1)(\beta_1 - \beta_3)\big) \\ \cdot&\big(A(\alpha_3 - \alpha_2)(\alpha_2 - \alpha_1)x^2 + B(\beta_3 - \beta_2)(\beta_2 - \beta_1)\big) \\ \cdot&\big(A(\alpha_1 - \alpha_3)(\alpha_3 - \alpha_2)x^2 + B(\beta_1 - \beta_3)(\beta_3 - \beta_2)\big). \end{aligned}$$

Then the $(2,2)$-*isogeny with domain* $C \times E$ *and kernel*

$$\langle ((\alpha_1, 0), (\beta_1, 0)), ((\alpha_2, 0), (\beta_2, 0)) \rangle$$

has as codomain the Jacobian of a genus 2 curve H *defined by* $y^2 = h(x)$. *The degree-2 morphisms of the dual isogeny are given by*

$$\varphi_1 : H \to C$$
$$(x, y) \mapsto (s_1/x^2 + s_2, (\Delta_\beta/A^3)(y/x^3)),$$
$$\varphi_2 : H \to E$$
$$(x, y) \mapsto (t_1 x^2 + t_2, (\Delta_\alpha/B^3)y),$$

where

$$s_1 = -(B/A)(a_2/a_1),$$
$$s_2 = \frac{1}{a_1}\left(\frac{\alpha_1(\alpha_3 - \alpha_2)^2}{\beta_3 - \beta_2} + \frac{\alpha_2(\alpha_1 - \alpha_3)^2}{\beta_1 - \beta_3} + \frac{\alpha_3(\alpha_2 - \alpha_1)^2}{\beta_2 - \beta_1}\right),$$
$$t_1 = -(A/B)(b_2/b_1),$$
$$t_2 = \frac{1}{b_1}\left(\frac{\beta_1(\beta_3 - \beta_2)^2}{\alpha_3 - \alpha_2} + \frac{\beta_2(\beta_1 - \beta_3)^2}{\alpha_1 - \alpha_3} + \frac{\beta_3(\beta_2 - \beta_1)^2}{\alpha_2 - \alpha_1}\right).$$

The morphisms φ_i extend to the Jacobian J_H by mapping

$$\left[\sum_j P_j\right] \to \sum_j \varphi(P_j)$$

and they combine into a $(2,2)$-isogeny $\Phi : J_H \to C \times E$, the dual of which is our isogeny of interest. To compute the image of a point $(P_c, P) \in C \times E$ under this dual isogeny, it suffices to compute some $[D] \in \Phi^{-1}\{(P_c, P)\} \subset J_H$ and then double it. Indeed, then we have

$$2[D] = \hat{\Phi}\Phi([D]) = \hat{\Phi}(P_c, P)$$

as wanted.

Let $D = P_H + Q_H - \infty_1 - \infty_2$ represent a point on J_H. As mentioned, we assume that its Mumford representation is of the form $[x^2 + u_1 x + u_0, v_1 x + v_0]$. To avoid the need for field extensions, let us express $\varphi_i(P_H + Q_H)$ for $i = 1, 2$ directly in terms of u_0, u_1, v_0, v_1. Note that the divisor $\infty_1 + \infty_2$ maps to ∞, both under φ_1 and under φ_2, so it suffices to concentrate on $P_H + Q_H$.

The calculation is easiest for φ_2, where the line connecting $\varphi_2(P_H)$ and $\varphi_2(Q_H)$ has slope

$$\lambda_2 = -\frac{(\Delta_\alpha/B^3)v_1}{t_1 u_1}$$

and then $\varphi_2(P_H + Q_H)$ is

$$\left(\lambda_2^2 + \sum_{i=1}^3 \beta_i - t_1(u_1^2 - 2u_0) - 2t_2 \,,\, -\lambda_2 \left(\cdots - t_2 + (u_0 v_1 - u_1 v_0)\frac{t_1}{v_1} \right) \right) \quad (11)$$

with $\cdots$ denoting a copy of the first coordinate. To derive formulae for φ_1, note that this map is of a very similar kind, except for the transformation

$$\tilde{\cdot} : (x, y) \mapsto (1/x, y/x^3)$$

by which it is preceded. Let $\tilde{u}_0, \tilde{u}_1, \tilde{v}_0, \tilde{v}_1$ be the Mumford coordinates of $\tilde{P}_H + \tilde{Q}_H$, then an easy calculation shows:

$$\tilde{u}_0 = \frac{1}{u_0}, \quad \tilde{u}_1 = \frac{u_1}{u_0}, \quad \tilde{v}_0 = \frac{u_1 v_0 - u_0 v_1}{u_0^2}, \quad \tilde{v}_1 = \frac{u_1^2 v_0 - u_0 v_0 - u_0 u_1 v_1}{u_0^2}.$$

Thus the formulae for the coordinates of $\varphi_1(P_H + Q_H)$ are the same as in (11), except for swapping the α_i's and the β_i's and for substituting $\tilde{u}_0, \tilde{u}_1, \tilde{v}_0, \tilde{v}_1$ for u_0, u_1, v_0, v_1.

This gives us 4 equations in the unknowns u_0, u_1, v_0, v_1:

$$\begin{cases} x(\varphi_1(P_H + Q_H)) = x(P_c), \\ y(\varphi_1(P_H + Q_H)) = y(P_c), \\ x(\varphi_2(P_H + Q_H)) = x(P), \\ y(\varphi_2(P_H + Q_H)) = y(P). \end{cases} \quad (12)$$

Together with the equation

$$2v_0^2 - 2v_0v_1u_1 + v_1^2(u_1^2 - 2u_0) = 2c_0 + (-u_1)c_1 + (u_1^2 - 2u_0)c_2$$
$$+ (-u_1^3 + 3u_0u_1)c_3 + (u_1^4 - 4u_1^2u_0 + 2u_0^2)c_4$$
$$+ (-u_1^5 + 5u_1^3u_0 - 5u_1u_0^2)c_5$$
$$+ (u_1^6 - 6u_1^4u_0 + 9u_1^2u_0^2 - 2u_0^3)c_6,$$

expressing that $[D] \in J_H$, this system is expected to have 4 solutions, all of which are defined over $\mathbb{F}_{p^2}$. (In practice, we found these solutions by clearing denominators in (12), running a Gröbner basis computation, and discarding solutions having zeroes among their coordinates, because they are most likely parasite solutions that were created when clearing denominators.) Taking any of these solutions and doubling the corresponding point on J_H produces the desired image of (P_c, P).

8.2   Richelot Isogenies

By assumption, the next $a - 2$ steps are $(2,2)$-isogenies between Jacobians of genus 2 curves. Such maps are called Richelot isogenies and they are classical; for a contemporary exposition, including explicit formulae, we refer to Smith's thesis [42, Chapter 8]. Starting from a hyperelliptic curve $H : y^2 = h(x)$ and a $(2,2)$-subgroup

$$\langle [g_1(x), 0], [g_2(x), 0] \rangle, \quad g_1(x) = x^2 + g_{11}x + g_{10}, \quad g_2(x) = x^2 + g_{21}x + g_{20}$$

of its Jacobian, one lets $g_3(x) = h(x)/(g_1(x)g_2(x)) = g_{32}x^2 + g_{31}x + g_{30}$. One then computes

$$\delta = \det \begin{pmatrix} g_{10} & g_{11} & 1 \\ g_{20} & g_{21} & 1 \\ g_{30} & g_{31} & g_{32} \end{pmatrix}$$

and $h'(x) = g_1'(x)g_2'(x)g_3'(x)$ where

$$g_i'(x) = \delta^{-1} \left(\frac{dg_j}{dx}g_k - g_j\frac{dg_k}{dx} \right) \text{ for } (i,j,k) = (1,2,3), (2,3,1), (3,1,2).$$

Then the codomain of our Richelot isogeny is the Jacobian of $H' : \mathbf{y}^2 = h'(\mathbf{x})$. We use different notation for the coordinates because pushing a point through this isogeny is done via the "Richelot correspondence", which is the curve $X \subset H \times H'$ defined by

$$X : g_1(x)g_1'(\mathbf{x}) + g_2(x)g_2'(\mathbf{x}) = y\mathbf{y} - g_1(x)g_1'(\mathbf{x})(x - \mathbf{x}) = 0.$$

It naturally comes equipped with two projection maps $\pi : X \to H$, $\pi' : X \to H'$. The isogeny is then

$$J_H \to J_{H'} : [D] \mapsto [\pi_*'\pi^* D] \quad \text{(pullback along } \pi \text{ and pushforward along } \pi').$$

This means that in order to compute the image of a point $[x^2 + u_1 x + u_0, v_1 x + v_0] \in J_H$, one should eliminate the variables x, y from the system

$$\begin{cases} x^2 + u_1 x + u_0 = 0, \\ y = v_1 x + v_0, \\ y^2 = h(x), \\ g_1(x)g_1'(\mathbf{x}) + g_2(x)g_2'(\mathbf{x}) = 0, \\ y\mathbf{y} = g_1(x)g_1'(\mathbf{x})(x - \mathbf{x}). \end{cases}$$

We expect the last two equations of its reduced Gröbner basis (with respect to the lexicographic order with $\mathbf{x} \prec \mathbf{y} \prec y \prec x$) to be of the form

$$\mathbf{y} = v_3'\mathbf{x}^3 + v_2'\mathbf{x}^2 + v_1'\mathbf{x} + v_0', \quad \mathbf{x}^4 + u_3'\mathbf{x}^3 + u_2'\mathbf{x}^2 + u_1'\mathbf{x} + u_0' = 0$$

and then $[\mathbf{x}^4 + u_3'\mathbf{x}^3 + u_2'\mathbf{x}^2 + u_1'\mathbf{x} + u_0', v_3'\mathbf{x}^3 + v_2'\mathbf{x}^2 + v_1'\mathbf{x} + v_0']$ are non-reduced Mumford coordinates for the image on $J_{H'}$.

8.3   Split or Not?

We now want to check whether or not the a-th $(2,2)$-isogeny takes us back to a product of elliptic curves. This is easy: we proceed as if we are dealing with a Richelot isogeny (just the codomain computation, no points need be pushed through anymore). It can be shown that the determinant δ vanishes if and only if the codomain is a product of elliptic curves instead of the Jacobian of a genus 2 curve. Therefore the final and deciding step in our computation simply amounts to verifying whether or not $\delta = 0$.

9   Magma Code

This paper comes with the following auxiliary Magma files, which are available at https://homes.esat.kuleuven.be/~wcastryc/.

- `richelot_aux.m` contains auxiliary functions, mainly for computing chains of $(2,2)$-isogenies, where the functions `FromProdtoJac` and `FromJactoJac` are implementations of the methods described in Sect. 8,
- `uvtable.m` contains precomputed values of u and v as described in Sect. 7.2,
- runs of `SIKE_challenge1.m`, resp. `SIKE_challenge2.m`, load the first two files and break $IKEp182, resp. $IKEp217, by running the algorithm from Sect. 6, incorporating the speed-ups from Sect. 7,
- a run of `SIKEp434.m` generates random input for the `SIKEp434` parameters and runs the algorithm from Sect. 6, again incorporating the speed-ups from Sect. 7; to attack `SIKEp503`, `SIKEp610` and `SIKEp751` one simply replaces the line `a := 216; b := 137;` by

  `a := 250; b := 159;`, `a := 305; b := 192;`, `a := 372; b := 239;`,

  respectively.

The reader can execute these files in order to confirm the approximate timings mentioned in Sect. 1. We ran them in Magma V2.27-5 on an Intel Xeon CPU E5-2630v2 at 2.60 GHz.

10   Achieving (heuristic) Polynomial Runtime

As $x \to \infty$, the number of integers c in the interval $[0, x]$ that admit a decomposition of the form $c = u^2 + 4v^2$ is asymptotic to

$$\frac{0.5731...}{\sqrt{\ln x}} x,$$

by (a variation on) a theorem of Landau, see [41]. We can use this to estimate the probability that our strategy from Sect. 5 succeeds in constructing an isogeny $\gamma : E_0 \to C$ of degree $c = 2^a - 3^b$: it is about $0.5731/\sqrt{a \ln 2} \approx 0.6884/\sqrt{a}$.

Let us now revisit the first iteration of our key recovery algorithm from Sect. 6, where we choose $\beta_1 \geq 1$ such that there exists an $\alpha_1 \geq 0$ for which $c_1 = 2^{a - \alpha_1} - 3^{b - \beta_1}$ is of the form $u_1^2 + 4v_1^2$. In view of Landau's theorem, we expect that we should try in the order of $\sqrt{a}$ pairs (α_1, β_1) before we succeed. So the smallest β_1 is expected to be of magnitude $\sqrt[4]{a}$. While this is good enough for breaking the concrete parameter sets of SIKE, the asymptotic runtime is $L_p(1/4)$ rather than polynomial: indeed, there are 3^{β_1} options for κ_1 to guess from.

Remark 8. The first iteration dominates the overall runtime. Indeed, once suitable α_1, β_1 are found, the expression $2^{a - \alpha_1} - 3^{b - \beta_1}$ can be recycled in the remaining iterations by extending Bob's secret isogeny, as explained in Sect. 7.3.

To achieve a polynomial time complexity, we extend the attack from sums of squares to more general quadratic forms and hope that there is a prime number $n \leq a$ such that c_1 can be written as $u_1^2 + nv_1^2$. Heuristically, this happens with overwhelming probability. We can loosely argue this as follows. Based on a generalization of Landau's theorem, see again [41], for every n the success probability remains inversely proportional to $\sqrt{a}$. If the events of being of the form $u_1^2 + nv_1^2$ are "sufficiently independent" as n varies, and if the implicit constants do not decay too quickly, then the probability of failure overall is in the order of

$$\left(1 - \frac{1}{\sqrt{a}}\right)^{\pi(a)} \approx \left(1 - \frac{1}{\sqrt{a}}\right)^{a/\ln a},$$

which decreases as $e^{-\sqrt{a}/\ln a}$ (here π is the prime-counting function). In particular, we expect that we can simply take $\beta_1 = 1$ in this case.

Once such a decomposition $u_1^2 + nv_1^2$ is found, we proceed as follows. The techniques from Love and Boneh [29] allow for the polynomial-time construction of an isogeny $\nu : E_{\text{start}} \to N_{\text{start}}$, where N_{start} is an elliptic curve possessing an endomorphism $\sqrt{n}\mathbf{i}$ satisfying $\sqrt{n}\mathbf{i} \circ \sqrt{n}\mathbf{i} = [-n]$. Thus we can consider the degree-c endomorphism $\gamma_{\text{start}} = [u_1] + \sqrt{n}\mathbf{i} \circ [v_1]$ on N_{start}. This endomorphism can be transformed into the desired degree-c isogeny $\gamma : E_0 \to C$ along $\nu \circ \tau :$ $E_0 \to N_{\text{start}}$, as outlined in Sect. 5.

Remark 9. In general, when compared to the method from Remark 3, it becomes more cumbersome to test whether or not an integer of the form $c = 2^a - 3^b$ admits a decomposition $u^2 + nv^2$ (and find corresponding u, v). Again we need to factor

$$c = \ell_1 \ell_2 \cdots \ell_s,$$

where for simplicity we assume that c is squarefree, i.e., the ℓ_i are pairwise distinct primes. Then a necessary condition is that $-n$ is a quadratic residue modulo each ℓ_i. In this case we can decompose $\ell_i \mathbb{Z}[\sqrt{-n}] = \mathfrak{l}_i \bar{\mathfrak{l}}_i$ into a product of two prime ideals of norm ℓ_i. We then look for a relation of the form

$$1 = \prod_{i=1}^{s} [\mathfrak{l}_i]^{\sigma_i}, \qquad \sigma_i \in \{\pm 1\} \tag{13}$$

in the ideal-class group of $\mathbb{Z}[\sqrt{-n}]$. If we succeed, then the ideal

$$\prod_{i=1}^{s} \mathfrak{l}_i^{\delta_{\sigma_i,1}} \bar{\mathfrak{l}}_i^{\delta_{\sigma_i,-1}}$$

(with $\delta_{\cdot,\cdot}$ the Kronecker delta) is a principal ideal of norm c, hence generated by $u + \sqrt{-n}v$ for integers u, v of the desired form. All ideal-class group arithmetic can be done in polynomial time, see e.g. [22], because $n \leq a$. The identity (13) is of knapsack type, but we nevertheless expect being able to decide if it exists (and find it) in polynomial time, because the expected value of s is $\log \log c \approx \log a$ by the Hardy–Ramanujan theorem.

11 Generalizations

In this final section, we move away from the SIKE set-up and discuss how to attack more general instantiations of SIDH.

11.1 Arbitrary Torsion

There is no theoretical obstruction to attacking Alice's public key instead of Bob's. In this case one will end up computing a chain of $(3, 3)$-isogenies, which is more convoluted, but still doable using the machinery from [4]; see also [17]. The formulae are still practical and recovering Alice's private key can then be done bit by bit (except possibly for some offset of the kind discussed in Sect. 7.3). Altogether, we expect having to compute approximately a chains of $(3, 3)$-isogenies of length at most b in order to retrieve Alice's private key. The expression Δ in the formulae from [4] plays a similar role as δ in the Richelot isogeny formulae, in the sense that $\Delta = 0$ occurs if and only if the codomain of the $(3, 3)$-isogeny is the product of two elliptic curves, see [6]. Therefore, verifying whether the final $(3, 3)$-isogeny splits is just as easy.

More generally, one can attack SIDH when set up using arbitrary small primes ℓ_A, ℓ_B instead of just $2, 3$, or even more general smooth torsion as in B-SIDH.

Inherently, this changes nothing to our attack, except that now one must compute (ℓ, ℓ)-isogenies for primes $\ell \geq 5$. For isogenies between Jacobians of genus 2 curves, we refer to the work of Cosset and Robert [8], whose formulae are a lot more involved than those to compute $(2, 2)$- and $(3, 3)$-isogenies, but they are polynomial in ℓ and likely practical enough to complete the attack. The gluing of elliptic curves and splitting of Jacobians is succinctly explained by Kuhn in [28]; for a more elaborate and practical exposition, see also [15, Sect. 1.4]. Away from $\ell = 2, 3$ we are not aware of a straightforward decision algorithm to verify whether an (ℓ, ℓ)-subgroup of a given Jacobian of a genus 2 curve results in a product of elliptic curves: the easiest way seems to try and compute an (ℓ, ℓ)-isogeny to a Jacobian as in [8] and see if the theta constants fail to create a genus 2 curve. Alternatively, one can write down a system of equations expressing that our Jacobian is "(ℓ, ℓ)-split" (i.e., (ℓ, ℓ)-isogenous to a product of elliptic curves) via our given subgroup, and verify whether this system is consistent, see [15].

11.2   Other Starting Curves with a Known Endomorphism Ring

Setting up SIDH with another starting curve E_0 with known endomorphism ring does not prevent the attack. Indeed, in view of [16,44], such a curve can always be assumed to come equipped with an explicit 3^β-isogeny $\tau : E_0 \to E_{\text{start}}$ for some $\beta \geq 0$, where E_{start} is any of the curves from (1). Therefore we fall under the set-up from Sect. 3.

11.3   Base Curves Whose Endomorphism Ring is Unknown

We now discuss the scenario of a base curve E_0 without known endomorphism ring. In particular, no path to E_{start} is known. As indicated in Sect. 5.4, if $c = 2^a - 3^b$ is smooth then it remains possible to construct the auxiliary isogeny γ. In fact, if we no longer exploit special features of E_0, then it makes more sense to let γ emanate from E rather than E_0, leading us to considering $\gamma \circ \varphi : E_0 \to C$. This isogeny has degree $c3^b$ and can again be used to decide whether or not (D) is true: this should be the case if and only if the subgroup $\langle (P_0, x\gamma(P)), (Q_0, x\gamma(Q)) \rangle \subset E_0 \times C$ is reducible, with x a multiplicative inverse of 3^b modulo 2^a.

Remark 10. Computing γ works as follows. Write c as a product of small primes $\ell_1 \ell_2 \cdots \ell_s$ and for each $i = 1, \ldots, s$ let r_i denote the multiplicative order of $-p$ modulo ℓ_i. Because p^2-Frobenius acts as $[-p]$, we can find a non-trivial point in $E_0[\ell_1] \subset E_0(\mathbb{F}_{p^{2r_1}})$ and the subgroup it generates is defined over $\mathbb{F}_{p^2}$. So this is the kernel of an $\mathbb{F}_{p^2}$-rational degree-ℓ_1 isogeny $\gamma_1 : E_0 \to C_1$ that can be computed and evaluated using formulae of Vélu type. By repeating this construction, we eventually obtain γ as a composition $\gamma_s \circ \gamma_{s-1} \circ \ldots \circ \gamma_1$ where each γ_i is an $\mathbb{F}_{p^2}$-rational ℓ_i-isogeny.

Turning this decision method into a key recovery algorithm works along the lines of Sect. 6. First, we look for the smallest $\beta \geq 1$ for which there exists an integer $\alpha \geq 0$ such that

$$c = 2^{a-\alpha} - 3^{b-\beta} \tag{14}$$

is smooth (this is an optimistic goal!). Then, for each guess for the first degree-3^β-component κ_1 of φ, we run our test to see whether or not there exists a degree-$3^{b-\beta}$-isogeny $\kappa_1(E_0) \to E$ mapping $2^\alpha\kappa_1(P_0)$ to $2^\alpha P$ and $2^\alpha\kappa_1(Q_0)$ to $2^\alpha Q$. There are 3^β possible guesses, so clearly β should be small enough for this to be feasible.

Once κ_1 is found, we can proceed by steps of degree 3 as in Sect. 7.3. Since smoothness is such a rare event, it actually makes sense to recycle the expression (14) all along. Then we can also recycle our auxiliary isogeny γ, i.e., it only has to be computed once, including pushing through torsion points. Concretely: when guessing κ_2, we extend γ with an extra degree-3 isogeny $\varphi' : C \to E'$ and we test if we took the right direction by checking whether or not there is a degree $c3^{b-\beta}$-isogeny mapping $2^\alpha\kappa_2\kappa_1(P_0)$ to $2^\alpha\varphi'\gamma(P)$ and $2^\alpha\kappa_2\kappa_1(Q_0)$ to $2^\alpha\varphi'\gamma(Q)$. Iterating this process will recreate the entire isogeny chain.

In summary: as soon as we can find a small $\beta \geq 1$ with a corresponding $\alpha \geq 0$ such that (14) is smooth, then our attack applies. The likelihood of finding a smooth c of this form is very small, but there are at least two methods for creating more leeway for an attacker:

- We can extend Bob's secret isogeny $\varphi : E_0 \to E$ by an arbitrary isogeny $\varepsilon : E \to F$ of some smooth degree e and work with $\varepsilon \circ \varphi$ instead of φ. This allows us to look for a smooth integer of the form $c = 2^{a-\alpha} - e3^{b-\beta}$ and construct a corresponding degree-c isogeny $\gamma : F \to C$.
- A second tweak can be obtained by any algorithm that can efficiently solve the following problem for a fixed d:
  - Let $H/\mathbb{F}_{p^2}$ be a genus 2 curve with superspecial Jacobian J, and $d > 1$ an integer. Is there a (d, d)-isogeny $\Psi : J \to A$ such that A is a product of elliptic curves?
  Indeed, this allows us to work with expressions of the form $c = d2^{a-\alpha} - e3^{b-\beta}$. Each test then amounts to computing a $(2^{a-\alpha}, 2^{a-\alpha})$-isogeny, using the torsion point data as before, and then checking if the resulting Jacobian is (d, d)-split. Verifying whether a given Jacobian is (d, d)-split is likely to be most efficient by means of a computation similar to those in [15], [28]. Alternatively, one can exhaust over all $O(d^3)$ outgoing (d, d)-isogenies.

E.g., consider $a = 110$ and $b = 67$ as in $IKEp217, along with the identity

$$59 \cdot 67 \cdot 107 \cdot 443^2 \cdot 487 \cdot 1049 \cdot 2711 \cdot 8297 = 109 \cdot 2^{110-35} - 119 \cdot 3^{67-20}.$$

Assuming that we do not know a path from E_0 to E_{start}, we could still try to recover Bob's key by computing

- one-time isogenies $E \xrightarrow{\varepsilon} F \xrightarrow{\gamma} C$, dominated in cost by a 2711-isogeny and a 8297-isogeny over extension fields of respective degrees 2710 and 2074,
- computing all 3^{20}-isogenous neighbours of the base curve, gluing them together by means of a $(2^{75}, 2^{75})$-isogeny and checking which one of the resulting Jacobians is $(109, 109)$-split.

The second step immediately reveals the first 20 ternary digits of Bob's secret key and we can then easily find the remaining digits as explained above.

Remark 11. It was pointed out to us by De Feo and Wesolowski that the above considerations lead to an algorithm which, heuristically, runs in time $L_p(1/2+\epsilon)$. To see this, it suffices to pick α, β in the order of $\sqrt{a}$. Then, by letting d, e range over random integers in $[1, 2^{\sqrt{a}}]$, we can think of c as a random integer of size roughly 2^a. Following well-known heuristics [5], after about

$$\sqrt{a}^{\sqrt{a}} = L_p(1/2 + \epsilon)$$

tries we expect to find an instance of c that is $2^{\sqrt{a}}$-smooth. Using these values of c, d, e, the remainder of the attack is expected to run in time $L_p(1/2)$.

Acknowledgements. We thank Craig Costello, Luca De Feo, Luciano Maino, Frederik Vercauteren, Benjamin Wesolowski, Yifan Zheng and the anonymous reviewers for helpful discussions, questions and suggestions.

References

1. Azarderakhsh, R., Jao, D., Leonardi, C.: Post-quantum static-static key agreement using multiple protocol instances. In: Adams, C., Camenisch, J. (eds.) Selected Areas in Cryptography - SAC 2017, pp. 45–63. Springer, Cham (2018). https://doi.org/10.1007/978-3-319-72565-9_3

2. Bosma, W., Cannon, J., Playoust, C.: The Magma algebra system. I. The user language. J. Symbolic Comput. **24**(3–4), 235–265 (1997). https://doi.org/10.1006/jsco.1996.0125

3. Brock, B.: Superspecial curves of genera two and three. Ph.D. thesis, Princeton University (1994)

4. Bruin, N., Flynn, E.V., Testa, D.: Descent via (3,3)-isogeny on Jacobians of genus 2 curves. Acta Arithmetica **165**(3), 201–223 (2014). http://eudml.org/doc/279018

5. Canfield, E.R., Erdős, P., Pomerance, C.: On a problem of Oppenheim concerning "factorisatio numerorum." J. Number Theory **17**(1), 1–28 (1983). https://doi.org/10.1016/0022-314X(83)90002-1

6. Castryck, W., Decru, T.: Multiradical isogenies. In: Anni, S., Karemaker, V., Lorenzo García, E. (eds.) 18th International Conference Arithmetic, Geometry, Cryptography, and Coding Theory, Contemporary Mathematics, vol. 779, pp. 57–89. American Mathematical Society (2022). https://doi.org/10.1090/conm/779

7. Castryck, W., Lange, T., Martindale, C., Panny, L., Renes, J.: CSIDH: an efficient post-quantum commutative group action. In: Peyrin, T., Galbraith, S. (eds.) Advances in Cryptology - ASIACRYPT 2018, vol. 3, pp. 395–427. Springer, Cham (2018). https://doi.org/10.1007/978-3-030-03332-3_15

8. Cosset, R., Robert, D.: Computing (ℓ, ℓ)–isogenies in polynomial time on Jacobians of genus 2 curves. Math. Comput. **84**(294), 1953–1975 (2015). https://www.ams.org/journals/mcom/2015-84-294/S0025-5718-2014-02899-8/

9. Costello, C.: B-SIDH: supersingular isogeny Diffie-Hellman using twisted torsion. In: Moriai, S., Wang, H. (eds.) Advances in Cryptology - ASIACRYPT 2020, vol. 2, pp. 440–463. Springer, Cham (2020). https://doi.org/10.1007/978-3-030-64834-3_15

10. Couveignes, J.M.: Hard homogeneous spaces. Cryptology ePrint Archive, Paper 2006/291 (2006). https://eprint.iacr.org/2006/291

11. De Feo, L., Jao, D., Plût, J.: Towards quantum-resistant cryptosystems from super-singular elliptic curve isogenies. J. Math. Cryptol. **8**(3), 209–247 (2014). https://doi.org/10.1515/jmc-2012-0015

12. De Feo, L., Kohel, D., Leroux, A., Petit, C., Wesolowski, B.: SQISign: compact post-quantum signatures from quaternions and isogenies. In: Moriai, S., Wang, H. (eds.) Advances in Cryptology - ASIACRYPT 2020, vol. 1, pp. 64–93. Springer, Cham (2020). https://doi.org/10.1007/978-3-030-64837-4_3

13. De Feo, L., et al.: Séta: supersingular encryption from torsion attacks. In: Tibouchi, M., Wang, H. (eds.) Advances in Cryptology - ASIACRYPT 2021, vol. 4, pp. 249–278. Springer, Cham (2021). https://doi.org/10.1007/978-3-030-92068-5_9

14. De Feo, L., et al.: (open project): Is SIKE broken yet? (2022). https://issikebrokenyet.github.io/

15. Djukanovic, M.: Split Jacobians and lower bounds on heights. Ph.D. thesis, Université de Bordeaux (2017)

16. Eisenträger, K., Hallgren, S., Lauter, K., Morrison, T., Petit, C.: Supersingular isogeny graphs and endomorphism rings: Reductions and solutions. In: Nielsen, J.B., Rijmen, V. (eds.) Advances in Cryptology - EUROCRYPT 2018, vol. 3, pp. 329–368. Springer, Cham (2018). https://doi.org/10.1007/978-3-319-78372-7_11

17. Flynn, E.V., Ti, Y.B.: Genus two isogeny cryptography. In: Ding, J., Steinwandt, R. (eds.) Post-quantum Cryptography, pp. 286–306. Springer, Cham (2019). https://doi.org/10.1007/978-3-030-25510-7_16

18. Fouotsa, T.B., Moriya, T., Petit, C.: M-SIDH and MD-SIDH: countering SIDH attacks by masking information. Cryptology ePrint Archive, Paper 2023/013 (2023). https://eprint.iacr.org/2023/013

19. Fouotsa, T.B., Petit, C.: SHealS and HealS: isogeny-based PKEs from a key validation method for SIDH. In: Tibouchi, M., Wang, H. (eds.) Advances in Cryptology - ASIACRYPT 2021, vol. 4, pp. 279–307. Springer, Cham (2021). https://doi.org/10.1007/978-3-030-92068-5_10

20. Galbraith, S.D., Petit, C., Silva, J.: Identification protocols and signature schemes based on supersingular isogeny problems. In: Takagi, T., Peyrin, T. (eds.) Advances in Cryptology - ASIACRYPT 2017, vol. 1, pp. 3–33. Springer, Cham (2017). https://doi.org/10.1007/978-3-319-70694-8_1

21. Galbraith, S.D., Vercauteren, F.: Computational problems in supersingular elliptic curve isogenies. Quantum Inf. Process. **17**(10), 1–22 (2018). https://doi.org/10.1007/s11128-018-2023-6

22. Hafner, J.L., McCurley, K.S.: A rigorous subexponential algorithm for computation of class groups. J. Am. Math. Soc. **2**(4), 837–850 (1989). https://doi.org/10.1090/S0894-0347-1989-1002631-0

23. Howe, E.W., Leprévost, F., Poonen, B.: Large torsion subgroups of split Jacobians of curves of genus two or three. Forum Math. **12**(3), 315–364 (2000). https://doi.org/10.1515/form.2000.008

24. Jao, D., et al.: Supersingular Isogeny Key Encapsulation. https://csrc.nist.gov/Projects/post-quantum-cryptography/round-4-submissions

25. Jao, D., De Feo, L.: Towards quantum-resistant cryptosystems from supersingular elliptic curve isogenies. In: Yang, B.Y. (ed.) Post-Quantum Cryptography, pp. 19–34. Springer, Heidelberg (2011). https://doi.org/10.1007/978-3-642-25405-5_2

26. Kani, E.: The number of curves of genus two with elliptic differentials. J. für die reine und angewandte Mathematik **1997**(485), 93–122 (1997). https://doi.org/10.1515/crll.1997.485.93

27. Kohel, D., Lauter, K., Petit, C., Tignol, J.P.: On the quaternion ℓ-isogeny path problem. LMS J. Comput. Math. **17**(A), 418–432 (2014). https://doi.org/10.1112/S1461157014000151
28. Kuhn, R.M.: Curves of genus 2 with split Jacobian. Trans. Am. Math. Soc. **307**(1), 41–49 (1988). https://doi.org/10.2307/2000749
29. Love, J., Boneh, D.: Supersingular curves with small non-integer endomorphisms. In: Algorithmic Number Theory Symposium (ANTS-XIV), MSP Open Book Series, vol. 4, pp. 7–22 (2020). https://doi.org/10.2140/obs.2020.4.7
30. Maino, L., Martindale, C.: An attack on SIDH with arbitrary starting curve. Cryptology ePrint Archive, Paper 2022/1026 (2022). https://eprint.iacr.org/2022/1026
31. Martindale, C., Panny, L.: How to not break SIDH. Cryptology ePrint Archive, Paper 2019/558 (2019). https://eprint.iacr.org/2019/558, Presented at CFAIL 2019, Columbia University
32. Microsoft: SIKE cryptographic challenge. https://www.microsoft.com/en-us/msrc/sike-cryptographic-challenge
33. National Institute of Standards and Technology (NIST): Post-quantum cryptography standardization process. https://csrc.nist.gov/projects/post-quantum-cryptography
34. Oudompheng, R.: A note on implementing direct isogeny determination in the Castryck–Decru attack. https://www.normalesup.org/~oudomphe/textes/202208-castryck-decru-shortcut.pdf
35. Oudompheng, R., Pope, G.: A note on reimplementing the Castryck–Decru attack and lessons learned for SageMath. Cryptology ePrint Archive, Paper 2022/1283 (2022). https://eprint.iacr.org/2022/1283
36. Petit, C.: Faster algorithms for isogeny problems using torsion point images. In: Takagi, T., Peyrin, T. (eds.) Advances in Cryptology - ASIACRYPT 2017, vol. 2, pp. 330–353. Springer, Cham (2017). https://doi.org/10.1007/978-3-319-70697-9_12
37. de Quehen, V., et al.: Improved torsion-point attacks on SIDH variants. In: Malkin, T., Peikert, C. (eds.) Advances in Cryptology - CRYPTO 2021, vol. 3, pp. 432–470. Springer, Cham (2021). https://doi.org/10.1007/978-3-030-84252-9_15
38. Robert, D.: Breaking SIDH in polynomial time. Cryptology ePrint Archive, Paper 2022/1038 (2022). https://eprint.iacr.org/2022/1038
39. Rostovtsev, A., Stolbunov, A.: Public-key cryptosystem based on isogenies. Cryptology ePrint Archive, Paper 2006/145 (2006). https://eprint.iacr.org/2006/145
40. SageMath: The Sage Mathematics Software System. https://www.sagemath.org
41. Shanks, D., Schmid, L.P.: Variations on a theorem of Landau. Part I. Math. Comput. **20**(96), 551–569 (1966). https://doi.org/10.2307/2003544
42. Smith, B.: Explicit endomorphisms and correspondences. Ph.D. thesis, University of Sydney (2006)
43. Urbanik, D., Jao, D.: SoK: the problem landscape of SIDH. In: Emura, K., Seo, J.H., Watanabe, Y. (eds.) Proceedings of the 5th ACM on ASIA Public-Key Cryptography Workshop, APKC@AsiaCCS, Incheon, Republic of Korea, 4 June 2018, pp. 53–60. ACM (2018). https://doi.org/10.1145/3197507.3197516
44. Wesolowski, B.: The supersingular isogeny path and endomorphism ring problems are equivalent. In: 2021 IEEE 62nd Annual Symposium on Foundations of Computer Science (FOCS), pp. 1100–1111 (2022). https://doi.org/10.1109/FOCS52979.2021.00109
45. Wesolowski, B.: Understanding and improving the Castryck–Decru attack on SIDH (2022). https://www.bweso.com/papers.php

A Direct Key Recovery Attack on SIDH

Luciano Maino[1]([✉]), Chloe Martindale[1], Lorenz Panny[2], Giacomo Pope[1,3],
and Benjamin Wesolowski[4,5,6]

[1] University of Bristol, Bristol, UK
{luciano.maino,chloe.martindale}@bristol.ac.uk, giacomo.pope@nccgroup.com
[2] Academia Sinica, Taipei, Taiwan
lorenz@yx7.cc
[3] NCC Group, Cheltenham, UK
[4] Univ. Bordeaux, CNRS, Bordeaux INP, IMB, UMR 5251, 33400 Talence, France
benjamin.wesolowski@math.u-bordeaux.fr
[5] INRIA, IMB, UMR 5251, 33400 Talence, France
[6] ENS de Lyon, CNRS, UMPA, UMR 5669, Lyon, France

Abstract. We present an attack on SIDH utilising isogenies between polarized products of two supersingular elliptic curves. In the case of arbitrary starting curve, our attack (discovered independently from [8]) has subexponential complexity, thus significantly reducing the security of SIDH and SIKE. When the endomorphism ring of the starting curve is known, our attack (here derived from [8]) has polynomial-time complexity assuming the generalised Riemann hypothesis. Our attack applies to any isogeny-based cryptosystem that publishes the images of points under the secret isogeny, for example Séta [13] and B-SIDH [11]. It does not apply to CSIDH [9], CSI-FiSh [3], or SQISign [14].

Keywords: SIDH · Elliptic curve · Isogeny · Cryptanalysis

1 Introduction

Supersingular Isogeny Diffie-Hellman (SIDH) [19] is a key exchange proposed in 2011 by Jao and De Feo. It has since become an archetype of *isogeny-based*

Author list in alphabetical order; see https://ams.org/profession/leaders/CultureStatement04.pdf. This paper is a merge of [24] by Maino and Martindale, which gives an attack on SIDH, and [39] by Wesolowski, which constitutes the proof of the main result in this paper. The implementation and algorithmic details of the implementation were contributed by Panny and Pope. This research was funded in part by the UK Engineering and Physical Sciences Research Council (EPSRC) Centre for Doctoral Training (CDT) in Trust, Identity, Privacy and Security in Large-scale Infrastructures (TIPS-at-Scale) at the Universities of Bristol and Bath, the Academia Sinica Investigator Award AS-IA-109-M01, the Agence Nationale de la Recherche under grant ANR MELODIA (ANR-20-CE40-0013), and the France 2030 program under grant agreement No. ANR-22-PETQ-0008 PQ-TLS.

C. Hazay and M. Stam (Eds.): EUROCRYPT 2023, LNCS 14008, pp. 448–471, 2023.
https://doi.org/10.1007/978-3-031-30589-4_16

cryptography, a branch of cryptography whose security relates to the presumed hardness of computing isogenies: given two (supersingular) elliptic curves over a finite field, find an isogeny between them. Many other such cryptosystems have been developed [3,9,11,13,14], fuelled by the presumed *quantum* hardness of the isogeny problem, thereby providing security against quantum adversaries. The influence of SIDH is notably illustrated by its incarnation "Supersingular Isogeny Key Encapsulation" (SIKE) [18], a primitive submitted to the NIST standardisation effort to find a new quantum-safe cryptographic standard [27].

Yet, the security of SIDH (hence, SIKE) is not guaranteed by the hardness of the 'pure' isogeny problem. It in fact relies on a variant, where the image of some torsion points under a hidden isogeny are also revealed. This is the *supersingular isogeny with torsion* (SSI-T) problem.

Supersingular Isogeny with Torsion (SSI-T):
Given coprime integers A and B, two supersingular elliptic curves $E_0/\mathbb{F}_{p^2}$ and $E_A/\mathbb{F}_{p^2}$ connected by an unknown degree-A isogeny $\varphi_A : E_0 \to E_A$, and given the restriction of φ_A to the B-torsion of E_0, recover an isogeny φ matching these constraints.

This variant has been shown to be weaker than the pure isogeny problem in a line of work pioneered by Petit [30] in 2017 and expanded in multiple papers in the last 5 years [5,16,31]. However, the SIKE parameters had not been affected by these attacks, which all applied only to variants of SIDH.

In this paper, we present an algorithm that solves SSI-T for parameters that were believed to be secure, including SIKE as well as a few other similar protocols such as B-SIDH [11] and Séta [13]. The first such polynomial-time algorithm was described (and demonstrated against SIKE) by Castryck and Decru [8]: they show that when the endomorphism ring $\text{End}(E_0)$ is known (as is the case in SIKE, B-SIDH or Séta), then SSI-T can be solved in polynomial time, under plausible heuristic assumptions. The idea of the algorithm of [8] is the following. First, they guess a small part of the isogeny φ_A. Based on this guess, they construct some isogeny $\Phi : E_A \times E \to X$, where E is a carefully crafted elliptic curve, and X is some abelian surface. They prove that the guess is correct if X is itself a product of elliptic curves, which can be efficiently detected. This guessing approach allows one to reconstruct φ_A one ternary-bit at a time, at a cost dominated by the many 2-dimensional isogenies Φ that must be computed.

The present work is semi-independent: it is the merge of a mostly independently discovered[1] attack against SIDH [24], with another work [39] subsequent to [8]. In addition to the independent discovery to [8] of such an attack, our main contributions reside in:

Practicality: We develop methods fast enough to possibly find constructive applications. Similarly to [8], we solve SSI-T via isogenies between elliptic products like $E_A \times E$, but we avoid using the iterative 'decision strategy'.

---

[1] Maino had been working together with Castryck and Decru on a tangentially related project using similar underlying ideas.

Instead, we recover the isogeny φ_A directly from a component of the matrix form of a (B, B)-isogeny, for some integer $B > 0$. As a result, in favourable settings, only one 2-dimensional isogeny computation is required,[2] instead of one per ternary-bit of the secret.

Provability: When $\mathrm{End}(E_0)$ is known, we prove that our method runs in provable polynomial time, assuming the generalised Riemann hypothesis (GRH). When $\mathrm{End}(E_0)$ is unknown, we prove that there is a subexponential attack.

The attack is further supported by a SageMath [36] proof-of-concept implementation available at:

$$\text{https://github.com/Breaking-SIDH/direct-attack}$$

In the case where $\mathrm{End}(E_0)$ is unknown, Robert [32] proved, following the first version of this work, that there also is a polynomial-time attack. This is asymptotically the fastest known attack in this setting. However, it involves the computation of a special 8-dimensional endomorphism of $E_0^4 \times E_A^4$ (or 4-dimensional, under plausible heuristics), which may limit its practicality.

Finally, note that as in [8] and [32], our attack makes full use of the public torsion points, and as such, it has no effect on isogeny-based cryptosystems that do not publish images of points under a secret isogeny, such as CSIDH [9], CSI-FiSh [3], and SQISign [14].

Outline

The success of our attack on the SSI-T problem relies on Theorem 1, which is proved in Sect. 2. This section additionally includes background material on polarized abelian surfaces. Section 3 describes a subexponential algorithm to solve the SSI-T problem without using knowledge of the endomorphism ring of the starting curve. In Sect. 4, we then show how knowledge of the endomorphism ring improves the performance of the attack, resulting in a provable polynomial time algorithm to solve the SSI-T problem. The paper concludes with Sect. 5 which we use to discuss future work.

Acknowledgements

We would like to thank Christophe Petit for useful comments regarding methods to compute isogenies with irrational kernel points and Eda Kirimli, for useful discussions. We are also extremely grateful to Luca De Feo, who shared with us a better method to find attack parameters during ANTS-XV, which in particular led to the argument in this paper that our algorithm has subexponential complexity. We would also like to thank COSIC and KU Leuven, especially Wouter Castryck and Thomas Decru, for hosting Luciano Maino as an intern, sparking his collaboration that led to this paper.

---

[2] Together with the computation of the image of one point under said isogeny.

2   The Core of the Attack

Let all notation be as in the SSI-T problem statement above. The core of the
attack is the following. First suppose that $B > A$, and that we have access to
some isogeny $\varphi_f : E \to E_0$ of degree $f = B - A$, given in any form that allows to
evaluate it on the B-torsion. We postpone the discussion on finding such a φ_f,
as the method may depend on the context. Assuming φ_f is provided, we give
an algorithm (Algorithm 1) that recovers a generator of $\ker(\varphi_A)$ (i.e., solves
SSI-T), at a cost dominated by one evaluation of a (B, B)-isogeny with known
kernel (with an A-torsion point as input), and two evaluations of $\widehat{\varphi_f}$ (with two
B-torsion points as input). In this section, we focus on the design and analysis
of Algorithm 1 for this core task.

The idea is the following. Write $g_A : E \to F$ for the isogeny of kernel
$\hat{\varphi}_f(\ker(\varphi_A))$, and $g_f : F \to E_A$ for the isogeny of kernel $g_A(\ker(\varphi_f))$, so that the
following diagram commutes:

$$
\begin{array}{ccc}
E_0 & \xrightarrow{\ \varphi_A\ } & E_A \\
\uparrow{\scriptstyle \varphi_f} & & \uparrow{\scriptstyle g_f} \\
E & \xrightarrow[\ g_A\ ]{} & F.
\end{array}
\tag{1}
$$

Now, consider the 2-dimensional isogeny

$$
\begin{aligned}
\Phi : E \times E_A &\longrightarrow E_0 \times F \\
(P, Q) &\longmapsto (\varphi_f(P) - \widehat{\varphi_A}(Q), g_A(P) + \hat{g}_f(Q)).
\end{aligned}
$$

Observe that $-\widehat{\varphi_A}$ is equal to the composition

$$
E_A \xrightarrow{\ 0 \times \mathrm{id}_{E_A}\ } E \times E_A \xrightarrow{\ \Phi\ } E_0 \times F \xrightarrow{\ \mathrm{pr}_1\ } E_0,
$$

where the first map is the inclusion map with image $\{0\} \times E_A$, the middle
map is Φ, and the last is the natural projection map. Assuming that each map
in this composition is efficiently computable, then we can evaluate $\widehat{\varphi_A}$ on any
input. That directly leads to a recovery of $\ker(\varphi_A)$, hence to a solution of SSI-
T. The difficulty is in proving that each step is indeed efficiently computable.
The computation of the first inclusion is trivial. The step Φ requires a delicate
analysis of this 2-dimensional isogeny, to prove that its kernel can be computed,
and that this kernel permits an efficient evaluation of Φ. The last step—the
projection—may seem clear, but in fact hides a subtlety. The decomposition
$E_0 \times F$ is only available if Φ is of a certain kind: it must behave well with respect
to the implicit *product polarizations* of the domain and codomain.

2.1   Isogenies Between Abelian Surfaces

Abelian surfaces can come equipped with a *polarization*. A polarization of X is an isogeny $\lambda_X : X \to X^\vee$ to the dual variety $X^\vee$. For a primer on the theory of polarizations, we refer the reader to [26]; for the purpose at hand, we recall in this section the relevant useful facts as a black-box.

Computationally, a polarization is essentially the data of an equation of the abelian surface. A relevant example: given two elliptic curves E_1 and E_2, the surface $E_1 \times E_2$ comes naturally equipped with a product polarization λ_{E_1,E_2}, which is computationally represented by the data of the equations of E_1 and E_2.

The importance of this notion becomes clear in the context of supersingular curves. If $E_1/\mathbb{F}_{p^2}$ and $E_2/\mathbb{F}_{p^2}$ are supersingular, the abelian surface $E_1 \times E_2$ is called *superspecial*. There is a unique isomorphism class of superspecial abelian surfaces over $\mathbb{F}_{p^2}$. In particular, if E_3 and E_4 are any other supersingular curves defined over $\mathbb{F}_{p^2}$, then $E_1 \times E_2$ and $E_3 \times E_4$ are isomorphic *as abelian surfaces*. However, they can be distinguished by their implicit product polarizations: the polarized surfaces $(E_1 \times E_2, \lambda_{E_1,E_2})$ and $(E_3 \times E_4, \lambda_{E_3,E_4})$ are isomorphic if and only if $E_1 \cong E_i$ and $E_2 \cong E_j$ for $\{i,j\} = \{3,4\}$.

Given a positive integer B, a B-isogeny $\Phi : (X, \lambda_X) \to (Y, \lambda_Y)$ is an isogeny such that $[B] \circ \lambda_X = \Phi^\vee \circ \lambda_Y \circ \Phi$, where $\Phi^\vee : Y^\vee \to X^\vee$ is the dual isogeny. A (B,B)-isogeny is a B-isogeny between abelian surfaces whose kernel is isomorphic to $(\mathbb{Z}/B\mathbb{Z})^2$. As we shall mention in Sect. 3.1, there are algorithms which, given a source (X, λ_X), and the kernel of a (B,B)-isogeny $\Phi : (X, \lambda_X) \to (Y, \lambda_Y)$, compute the target (Y, λ_Y) and can evaluate Φ at points, in time polynomial in $\log(B)$ and in the largest prime factor of B. In particular, if

$$\Phi : E_1 \times E_2 \longrightarrow E_3 \times E_4$$

is a (B,B)-isogeny with respect to the product polarizations, the algorithm is given as input equations of E_1 and E_2, and generators of $\ker(\Phi)$, and recovers equations for E_3 and E_4. It can also take as input two points $P_1 \in E_1$ and $P_2 \in E_2$, and output P_3 and P_4 such that $\Phi(P_1, P_2) = (P_3, P_4)$.

Finally, as products of elliptic curves will be of particular interest, let us introduce some convenient notation. Given four elliptic curves E_1, E_2, E_1', and E_2', and four isogenies $\varphi_{ij} : E_i \to E_j'$ for $i, j \in \{1, 2\}$, the matrix

$$M = \begin{pmatrix} \varphi_{11} & \varphi_{12} \\ \varphi_{21} & \varphi_{22} \end{pmatrix},$$

represents the isogeny

$$\Phi : E_1 \times E_2 \longrightarrow E_1' \times E_2'$$
$$(P_1, P_2) \longmapsto (\varphi_{11}(P_1) + \varphi_{12}(P_2), \varphi_{21}(P_1) + \varphi_{22}(P_2)).$$

We call M a matrix form of Φ.

2.2   The Algorithm

Our attack is a consequence of the following theorem, which is based on a criterion due to Kani [20]. This criterion determines whether a polarized isogeny originating from an elliptic product admits an elliptic product as codomain.

Theorem 1. *Let f, A, and B be pairwise coprime integers such that $B = f + A$, and let E, E_A, E_0, and F be elliptic curves connected by the following commutative diagram of isogenies:*

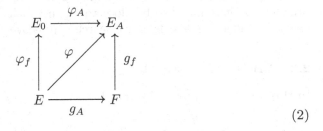

$$(2)$$

where $\deg(\varphi_f) = \deg(g_f) = f$ and $\deg(\varphi_A) = \deg(g_A) = A$.
The isogeny

$$\Phi = \begin{pmatrix} \varphi_f & -\widehat{\varphi_A} \\ g_A & \widehat{g_f} \end{pmatrix} \in \mathrm{Hom}(E \times E_A, E_0 \times F),$$

is a (B,B)-isogeny with respect to the natural product polarizations on $E \times E_A$ and $E_0 \times F$, and has kernel $\ker(\Phi) = \{([A]P, \varphi(P)) \mid P \in E[B]\}$.

This theorem allows us to compute the isogeny Φ efficiently (as long as B is smooth—preferably a power of 2 for good practical performance). Furthermore, it implies that this computation leads to the product polarization on the codomain. It leads to the following result.

Corollary 1. *Algorithm 1 is correct and costs two evaluations of $\widehat{\varphi_f}$ on B-torsion input points, at most two evaluations of a (B,B)-isogeny (given by its kernel) on A-torsion input points, and one inversion modulo B.*

Algorithm 1: Solving SSI-T, provided an isogeny of degree $B - A$.

Input: Coprime integers A and B, two supersingular elliptic curves $E_0/\mathbb{F}_{p^2}$ and $E_A/\mathbb{F}_{p^2}$ connected by an unknown degree-A isogeny $\varphi_A : E_0 \to E_A$ of cyclic kernel, a basis $\{P_B, Q_B\}$ of $E_0[B]$, a basis $\{P_A, Q_A\}$ of $E_A[A]$, the image points $P_B' = \varphi_A(P_B)$, $Q_B' = \varphi_A(Q_B)$, an isogeny $\varphi_f : E \to E_0$ of degree $f = B - A$.
Output: A generator of $\ker(\varphi_A)$.

---

1 Let $c \in \mathbb{Z}$ such that $cf \equiv 1 \bmod B$.
2 Let $P_B'' = [c] \circ \widehat{\varphi_f}(P_B)$ and $Q_B'' = [c] \circ \widehat{\varphi_f}(Q_B)$. We have $\varphi_A \circ \varphi_f(P_B'') = P_B'$, and $\varphi_A \circ \varphi_f(Q_B'') = Q_B'$.
3 Let $\Phi : E \times E_A \to E_0 \times F$ be the (B,B)-isogeny with kernel $\langle([A]P_B'', P_B'), ([A]Q_B'', Q_B')\rangle\rangle$.
4 Compute $\Phi(0, P_A) = (P_A', x)$. We have $P_A' = \widehat{\varphi_A}(P_A)$.
5 Return P_A' if it has order A.
6 Else, compute $\Phi(0, Q_A) = (Q_A', y)$ (satisfying $Q_A' = \widehat{\varphi_A}(Q_A)$), and return Q_A'.

Remark 1. Note that while the algorithm necessitates *at most* two evaluations of the (B, B)-isogeny, a single one is often sufficient. Indeed, suppose the basis $\{P_A, Q_A\}$ is uniformly random. If, for instance, $A = 2^a$, then $[2^{a-1}]P_A \notin \ker \widehat{\varphi_A}$ (i.e., P'_A has order A) with probability $2/3$. Even if P'_A does not have order precisely A, it is likely to be close to A, in which case P'_A generates most of $\ker(\varphi_A)$, and a simple exhaustive search can recover the missing information.

2.3   Proof of Theorem 1

In this section, we prove Theorem 1.

Prelude on the Adjoint. Consider an isogeny $\Phi : E_1 \times E_2 \to E'_1 \times E'_2$ represented by the matrix $M = \begin{pmatrix} \varphi_{11} & \varphi_{12} \\ \varphi_{21} & \varphi_{22} \end{pmatrix}$, where $\varphi_{ij} : E_i \to E'_j$. The adjoint of Φ is the isogeny $\tilde{\Phi} : E'_1 \times E'_2 \to E_1 \times E_2$ represented by the matrix

$$\tilde{M} = \begin{pmatrix} \hat{\varphi}_{11} & \hat{\varphi}_{21} \\ \hat{\varphi}_{12} & \hat{\varphi}_{22} \end{pmatrix}.$$

Our interest in this notion is that it offers a practical characterisation of isogenies that preserve the product polarizations: the isogeny Φ is a B-isogeny with respect to the product polarizations if and only if $\tilde{M}M = B\mathrm{Id}_2$, where Id_2 is the identity. While this property seems standard, let us provide a proof that only relies on well-documented properties of pairings. First, we show that the adjoint is closely related to the dual.

Lemma 1. *We have* $\tilde{\Phi} = \lambda_{E_1,E_2}^{-1} \circ \Phi^\vee \circ \lambda_{E'_1,E'_2}$, *where*

$$\Phi^\vee : (E'_1 \times E'_2)^\vee \to (E_1 \times E_2)^\vee,$$

is the dual.

Proof. The dual $\Phi^\vee$ is the unique isogeny that satisfies

$$e_{E'_1 \times E'_2, n}(\Phi(P), Q) = e_{E_1 \times E_2, n}(P, \Phi^\vee(Q)),$$

for any positive integer n, any $P \in (E_1 \times E_2)[n]$, and any $Q \in (E'_1 \times E'_2)^\vee[n]$, where $e_{-\times-,n}$ denotes the (unpolarized) Weil pairings. Let us show that $\Psi = \lambda_{E_1,E_2} \circ \tilde{\Phi} \circ \lambda_{E'_1,E'_2}^{-1}$ satisfies this property (hence $\Psi = \Phi^\vee$, proving the lemma). Recall that the polarized Weil pairing $e_n^{\lambda_{E_1,E_2}}$ (for the product polarization $\lambda_{E_1,E_2} : E_1 \times E_2 \to (E_1 \times E_2)^\vee$) satisfies

$$e_n^{\lambda_{E_1,E_2}}(P, Q) = e_{E_1 \times E_2, n}(P, \lambda_{E_1,E_2}(Q)) = e_{E_1,n}(P_1, Q_1)e_{E_2,n}(P_2, Q_2),$$

where $P = (P_1, P_2)$ and $Q = (Q_1, Q_2)$ are in $(E_1 \times E_2)[n]$, and $e_{E_i,n}$ are the Weil pairings on elliptic curves. We deduce that

$$e_n^{\lambda_{E_1', E_2'}}(\Phi(P), Q) = \prod_j \prod_i e_{E_j', n}(\varphi_{ij}(P_i), Q_j)$$

$$= \prod_j \prod_i e_{E_i, n}(P_i, \hat{\varphi}_{ij}(Q_j))$$

$$= e_n^{\lambda_{E_1, E_2}}(P, \tilde{\Phi}(Q)).$$

It follows that

$$e_{E_1' \times E_2', n}(\Phi(P), Q) = e_n^{\lambda_{E_1', E_2'}}(\Phi(P), \lambda_{E_1', E_2'}^{-1}(Q))$$

$$= e_n^{\lambda_{E_1, E_2}}(P, \tilde{\Phi} \circ \lambda_{E_1', E_2'}^{-1}(Q))$$

$$= e_{E_1 \times E_2, n}(P, \lambda_{E_1, E_2} \circ \tilde{\Phi} \circ \lambda_{E_1', E_2'}^{-1}(Q)),$$

hence $\Psi = \Phi^\vee$ as desired. $\qquad\square$

Lemma 2. *Let B be a positive integer. An isogeny $\Phi : E_1 \times E_2 \to E_1' \times E_2'$ is a B-isogeny with respect to the product polarizations if and only if $\tilde{\Phi} \circ \Phi = [B]$.*

Proof. Recall that Φ is a B-isogeny with respect to the product polarizations if and only if $[B] \circ \lambda_{E_1, E_2} = \Phi^\vee \circ \lambda_{E_1', E_2'} \circ \Phi$. The result thus immediately follows from Lemma 1. $\qquad\square$

For the rest of this section, assume the notation from Theorem 1.

Lemma 3. *We have that Φ is a B-isogeny with respect to the product polarizations.*

Proof. The isogeny Φ has matrix form $\begin{pmatrix} \varphi_f & -\widehat{\varphi_A} \\ g_A & \hat{g}_f \end{pmatrix}$, so its adjoint has matrix form $\begin{pmatrix} \widehat{\varphi_f} & \widehat{g_A} \\ -\varphi_A & g_f \end{pmatrix}$. We have

$$\begin{pmatrix} \widehat{\varphi_f} & \widehat{g_A} \\ -\varphi_A & g_f \end{pmatrix} \begin{pmatrix} \varphi_f & -\widehat{\varphi_A} \\ g_A & \hat{g}_f \end{pmatrix} = \begin{pmatrix} [\deg(\varphi_f) + \deg(g_A)] & 0 \\ 0 & [\deg(\varphi_A) + \deg(g_f)] \end{pmatrix}$$

$$= \begin{pmatrix} [B] & 0 \\ 0 & [B] \end{pmatrix}.$$

The result follows from Lemma 2. $\qquad\square$

Lemma 4. *We have* $\ker(\Phi) = \{([A]P, \varphi(P)) \mid P \in E[B]\}$.

Proof. Let $K = \{([A]P, \varphi(P)) \mid P \in E[B]\}$, and let us show that $\ker(\Phi) = K$. The inclusion $K \subseteq \ker(\Phi)$ follows from

$$\Phi([A]P, \varphi(P)) = (\varphi_f([A]P) - \widehat{\varphi_A} \circ \varphi(P), g_A([A]P) + \widehat{g_f} \circ \varphi(P))$$
$$= ([A] \circ \varphi_f(P) - \widehat{\varphi_A} \circ \varphi_A \circ \varphi_f(P), [A] \circ g_A(P) + \widehat{g_f} \circ g_f \circ g_A(P))$$
$$= ([A - A] \circ \varphi_f(P), [A + f] \circ g_A(P))$$
$$= (0, [B] \circ g_A(P)) = (0, 0).$$

To show that $\ker(\Phi) \subseteq K$, let $([A]P, Q) \in \ker(\Phi)$. Then, $\varphi_f([A]P) = \widehat{\varphi_A}(Q)$, hence

$$[A] \circ \varphi(P) = \varphi_A \circ \varphi_f([A]P) = \varphi_A \circ \widehat{\varphi_A}(Q) = [A]Q.$$

Since $P \in E[B]$, and A and B are coprime, we deduce $Q = \varphi(P)$, hence $([A]P, Q) \in K$. $\qquad\square$

Theorem 1 now follows from Lemma 3 and Lemma 4: the isogeny Φ is a B-isogeny with respect to the product polarizations, with kernel $\ker(\Phi) = \{([A]P, \varphi(P)) \mid P \in E[B]\}$ isomorphic to $(\mathbb{Z}/B\mathbb{Z})^2$, hence it is a (B, B)-isogeny.

3   The Case of Unknown Endomorphism Ring

To use Theorem 1 to solve the SSI-T problem, any f-isogeny $\varphi_f : E \to E_0$ suffices. When $\mathrm{End}(E_0)$ is unknown, for example in the case of a trusted setup, the problem faced by the attacker is that the computation of φ_f is not necessarily easy as there is no reason to expect $B - A$ to be smooth. To mitigate this, we increase our pool of available cofactors f by brute-forcing the last few steps of φ_A and/or by brute-forcing some extra torsion-point images; this amounts to multiplying A and B respectively by small (fractions of) integers. For ease of notation, in all that follows we will assume that $A = \ell_A^a$ and $B = \ell_B^b$, where ℓ_A and ℓ_B are coprime integers.

The picture that we should keep in mind when reading through the attack below is the following commutative diagram, where:

- $\varphi_A : E_0 \to E_A$ is the secret isogeny,
- $\varphi_f : E \to E_0$ is a f-isogeny chosen by the attacker,[3]
- $\varphi_{\ell_A^i} : E' \to E_A$ is a guess of the (dual of the) last i steps of φ_A,
- $\varphi' : E_0 \to E'$ is the corresponding first $a - i$ steps of φ_A such that $\varphi_A = \varphi_{\ell_A^i} \circ \varphi'$, and
- $\varphi : E \to E'$ is the $f\ell_A^{a-i}$-isogeny to which we apply Theorem 1.

[3] In practice, the attacker computes $\widehat{\varphi}_f$ and deduces φ_f from this.

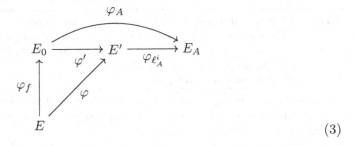

$$(3)$$

The attack is described in Algorithm 2, which is a natural generalisation of Algorithm 1. The parameters e, i, j are introduced to make $f = eB\ell_B^{-j} - A\ell_A^{-i} > 0$ smooth enough and apply Theorem 1 on the parameters $A \rightsquigarrow A\ell_A^{-i}$, $B \rightsquigarrow eB\ell_B^{-j}$, and $f \rightsquigarrow eB\ell_B^{-j} - A\ell_A^{-i}$. Once a f-isogeny $\varphi_f \colon E \to E_0$ is computed, the attacker reconstructs an $eB\ell_B^{-j}$-basis on E matching the B-basis on E_0 defined in the setup stage in SIDH. Then, the attacker guesses the last i steps of the secret isogeny φ_A computing an isogeny $\varphi_{\ell_A^i} \colon E' \to E_A$ of degree ℓ^i. For each guess, it is necessary to check all the $eB\ell_B^{-j}$-torsion points matching the B-torsion points on E_A defined by the public key. For each pair of the $eB\ell_B^{-j}$-torsion points found, the attacker tries to compute a $(eB\ell_B^{-j}, eB\ell_B^{-j})$-isogeny Φ as in Theorem 1. If the codomain of Φ consists of an elliptic product, the first $a - i$ steps of the secret isogeny are revealed in one of the components of the matrix form of Φ. This high-level overview is made clear in Algorithm 2.

Remark 2. Step 5 in Algorithm 2 has a small chance of causing the overall algorithm to fail, as a split Jacobian may accidentally be the codomain for an incorrect guess. However it is easy to check whether or not E_0 is a factor, and furthermore the chance of failure is very small.

To discuss the complexity of this attack we should split it into three parts:

1. The precomputation step (Step 1); this can be done once and for all for each parameter set A, B.
2. The cofactor isogeny computation (Step 2); if SIDH is set up with a fixed (arbitrary) E_0, this can be done once and for all for this E_0.
3. The online steps (Steps 3 to 7); these steps need to be performed for every new public key.

The Cost of the Cofactor Isogeny Computation. The cofactor isogeny remains fixed and is chosen by the attacker. As such, it does not need to be recomputed at any point due to a wrong guess when brute-forcing. We compute the isogeny φ_f via a chain of isogenies φ_{q_f} of prime degree q_f. It is worth noting that if a square factor appears in the factorization of f, we can simply perform a scalar multiplication $[q_f]$ rather than computing two q_f-isogenies. The cost of computing φ_{q_f} for the larger factors q_f is discussed in detail in Sect. 3.2; an estimate (in terms of $\mathbb{F}_p$-multiplications) can be given as $\tilde{O}(q_f^2)$.

Algorithm 2: Solving SSI-T, general approach.

Input: Coprime integers $A = \ell_A^a$ and $B = \ell_B^b$, two supersingular elliptic curves
$E_0/\mathbb{F}_{p^2}$ and $E_A/\mathbb{F}_{p^2}$ connected by an unknown degree-A isogeny
$\varphi_A : E_0 \to E_A$, a basis $\{P_B, Q_B\}$ of $E_0[B]$, a basis $\{P_A, Q_A\}$ of $E_0[A]$, the
image points $\varphi_A(P_B)$, $\varphi_A(Q_B)$.

Output: A generator of $\ker(\varphi_A)$.

---

1 Compute integers e, j, f, and i such that the overall cost according to the
  estimates in Sect. 3.1 is minimised, and $eB\ell_B^{-j} = f + A\ell_A^{-i}$. For ease of notation,
  we set $A' = A\ell_A^{-i}$ and $B' = B\ell_B^{-j}$.

2 Compute a curve that is f-isogenous to E_0, define the dual of the computed
  isogeny to be $\varphi_f : E \to E_0$, and compute $\widehat{\varphi}_f(P_B), \widehat{\varphi}_f(Q_B)$. For more details, see
  Sect. 3.2.

3 Compute a basis $\{P_{eB'}, Q_{eB'}\}$ of $E[eB']$ such that $[e]P_{eB'} = [\ell_B^j]\widehat{\varphi}_f(P_B)$ and
  $[e]Q_{eB'} = [\ell_B^j]\widehat{\varphi}_f(Q_B)$.

4 Choose a guess $\varphi_{\ell_A^i} : E' \to E_A$ for the last i steps of φ_A, recall the definition of the
  corresponding $\varphi : E \to E'$ from diagram (3), and choose $R, S \in E'[eB']$ such that

$$[e]R = [\ell_A^{-i}f\ell_B^j]\widehat{\varphi}_{\ell_A^i} \circ \varphi_A(P_B)$$

and

$$[e]S = [\ell_A^{-i}f\ell_B^j]\widehat{\varphi}_{\ell_A^i} \circ \varphi_A(Q_B),$$

  i.e. R, S are a guess for the images $\varphi(P_{eB'}), \varphi(Q_{eB'})$ respectively.

5 Compute a (eB', eB')-isogeny with domain $E \times E'$ and kernel

$$\ker(\Phi_{\text{guess}}) = \langle([A']P_{eB'}, R), ([A']Q_{eB'}, S)\rangle.$$

  If the codomain splits, continue (see Remark 2). Else, return to Step 4 and take a
  new guess $(\varphi_{\ell_A^i}, R, S)$. For more details see Sect. 3.3.

6 Choose a basis $\{P, Q\}$ of $E'[A']$; compute $\widehat{\varphi}'(P)$ and $\widehat{\varphi}'(Q)$ via

$$\Phi(0_E, P) = (-\widehat{\varphi}'(P), \widehat{g}_f(P))) \text{ and } \Phi(0_E, Q) = (-\widehat{\varphi}'(Q), \widehat{g}_f(Q))).$$

7 Compute $\ker(\varphi') = \langle\widehat{\varphi}'(P), \widehat{\varphi}'(Q)\rangle$ and return a generator of $\ker(\varphi_{\ell_A^i} \circ \varphi')$.

The Cost of the Online Steps. The discussion in Sect. 3.1 approximates the cost
of Steps 3 to 7 by $\approx C \cdot e^4\ell_A^i q_e^4 \log q_e$, where q_e is the largest prime dividing e
and C is polynomial in $\log(p)$. We allow i and e to grow to increase the pool of
options for f in order to get a smaller q_f, where q_f is the largest prime dividing f.

The Precomputation. If SIDH is set up to start every key exchange with a new
E_0, the optimal choice of (e, i, j, f) for the attacker ensures that the cost of
Step 2 is approximately the same as the cost of Steps 3 to 5. One could perform
a brute force search over all parameters (e, i, j, f) such that $q_f^2 \leq e^4\ell_A^i q_e^4 \log q_e$
and $0 \leq j \leq b$, which would be costly.

Even though this exhaustive search should be done once and for all, the search space for SIKE parameters is too big to be bruteforced. However, since sharing the first version of this paper [25], Luca De Feo shared with us a heuristic subexponential algorithm for the precomputation leading both to a subexponential cofactor isogeny computation and to subexponential online steps. His argument is as follows: suppose that we wish to target $A \approx B \approx 2^b$. To achieve subexponential complexity $L_{2^b}(c, 1/2)$, one can see from the complexity discussion of the online and cofactor steps above that it is sufficient to find parameters (e, i, j, f) such that $e, \ell_A^i \approx 2^{\sqrt{b}}$, and f is $\sqrt{b}^{\sqrt{b}}$-smooth.

To achieve this, we search for solutions to the equation

$$x A \ell_A^{-i} + y B \ell_B^{-j} = z, \tag{4}$$

where $x, y \leq 2^{\sqrt{b}}$, z is $\sqrt{b}^{\sqrt{b}}$-smooth, and i and j are fixed at some chosen values such that $\ell_A^i \approx \ell_B^j \approx 2^{\sqrt{b}}$. This corresponds to $e = -y$ (not necessarily coprime to B) and $f = -xz$; if $xz, y > 0$ then we switch the roles of A and B and this will correspond to $e = -x$ and $f = -yz$. Writing $f = -xz$ corresponds to decomposing $\varphi_f : E_f \to E_0$ into a degree-$(-z)$ isogeny $\varphi_{-z} : E_f \to E_0'$ and a degree-x isogeny $\varphi_x : E_0' \to E_0$, and recovering $\varphi_A \circ \varphi_x$ by applying Algorithm 2 with $A = xA$, $E_0 = E_0'$, and $\varphi_A = \varphi_A \circ \varphi_x$. Pictorially, this situation can be summarised by the following diagram.

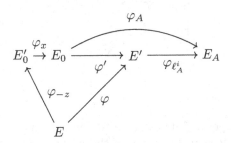

To find such (x, y, z) for a given (i, j), we run Euclid's xgcd algorithm on $(A\ell_A^{-i}, B\ell_B^{-j})$ until we find (x_0, y_0, z_0) and (x_1, y_1, z_1) such that $x_i, y_i \approx 2^{\sqrt{b}/2}$; this should correspond to $z_i \approx 2^{b-\sqrt{b}/2}$. Then, we search through all linear combinations $u z_0 + v z_1$ with $u, v \leq 2^{\sqrt{b}/2}$ and save the smoothest result; call this z. An integer (such as z) of size 2^b is $\sqrt{b}^{\sqrt{b}}$-smooth with probability $\rho(\beta)$, where $2^{b/\beta} = \sqrt{b}^{\sqrt{b}}$ and ρ is the Dickman-ρ function which can be approximated by $\rho(\beta) \approx \beta^{-\beta}$. Therefore, we are likely to find a $\sqrt{b}^{\sqrt{b}}$-smooth choice z if the number of choices for (u, v), that is $2^{\sqrt{b}}$, is $\approx \beta^\beta$. A short calculation shows that

$$\log_2(\beta^\beta) = \sqrt{b}\left(1 + \frac{2 - 2\log_2 \log_2 b}{\log_2 b}\right) \approx \log_2(2^{\sqrt{b}}).$$

We give some examples for concrete parameters in Sect. 3.1.

3.1 Heuristic Complexity of Algorithm 2

Here, we give some details on and study the complexity of the first four steps of Algorithm 2 in the case relevant to SIKE, namely $A = 3^a$ and $B = 2^b$, with a focus on the Microsoft challenge parameters $A = 3^{67}$ and $B = 2^{110}$ and the parameters $A = 3^{137}$ and $B = 2^{216}$ that were proposed for NIST Level I.

Choosing Parameters. To understand Step 1, we recall the commutative diagram that we keep in mind during this attack, where:

- $\varphi_A : E_0 \to E_A$ is the secret isogeny,
- $\varphi_f : E \to E_0$ is a f-isogeny chosen by the attacker,
- $\varphi_{\ell_A^i} : E' \to E_A$ is a guess of the last i steps of φ_A,
- $\varphi' : E_0 \to E'$ is the corresponding first $a - i$ steps of φ_A such that $\varphi_A = \varphi_{\ell_A^i} \circ \varphi'$, and
- $\varphi : E \to E'$ is the $f\ell_A^{a-i}$-isogeny to which we apply Theorem 1.

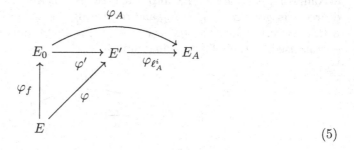

$$(5)$$

Choosing f. The shape of f determines the complexity of computing φ_f. The cofactor f does not need to be small as the isogeny can be precomputed once and for all, but it does need to be smooth: considering the extreme case that f is a prime $\approx A$, computing φ_f directly will be harder than computing φ_A directly (because of the extension field arithmetic). Exactly how smooth we require f to be depends on what we hope we can achieve in complexity for the attack. If q_f is the largest prime divisor (of odd multiplicity) of f, the complexity of Step 2 will be dominated by the cost of the computation of a q_f-isogeny, which involves operations in the field of definition of a generator of the kernel of the isogeny. The field of definition is unfortunately hard to control, and large field extensions can have a very serious performance impact. However, note that the required degree depends on arithmetic properties of the pair (p, q_f), rather than just the size of q_f: for some values of q_f the minimal k for which $E(\mathbb{F}_{p^k})$ contains a q_f-torsion point will be much smaller than q_f, but the typical case in our setting is $k \approx q_f$. Based on this preliminary discussion, we will see in more detail in Sect. 3.2 that the cost of computing φ_{q_f}, and therefore φ_f, can be approximated as $\tilde{O}(q_f^2)$.

Choosing i and e. The cost coming from i is the cost of brute-forcing all the cyclic $3^i = \ell_A^i$-isogenies from E_A, which costs $\approx 3^i$ multiplications in $\mathbb{F}_{p^2}$. This is however multiplied by the brute-force cost of guessing the images of the e-torsion points in Step 4 and by the cost of computing Φ. Guessing the images of the e-torsion points amounts to checking all the pairs of points of order e on E', which is $\approx e^4$. As a result, we have to run Steps 3 to 5 of Algorithm 2 $\approx e^4 3^i$ times.

Additionally, the isogeny Φ (which we will attempt to compute $\approx e^4 3^i$ times) is an (eB', eB')-isogeny; in particular it factors via an (e, e)-isogeny. So, in addition we require e to be q_e-smooth, where q_e is the largest prime for which it is feasible to compute (q_e, q_e)-isogenies (potentially over an extension field, which again will add a non-negligible cost). The need for the computation of the (e, e)-isogeny is the main barrier to implementing our algorithm for the proposed NIST parameters, as to do so requires a working implementation of (q_e, q_e)-isogenies, which while should theoretically be possible and reasonably fast, requires some research to achieve. There exists literature on this topic [4, 6, 22, 23], from which we have made a baseline assumption that computations of (q_e, q_e)-isogenies over $\mathbb{F}_{p^k}$ can be performed in $O(q_e^3)$ multiplications in $\mathbb{F}_{p^k}$. However, there is very little existing work in the way of practical implementation of supersingular Jacobians and products of elliptic curves. We do note here that it would be possible to avoid implementing the factors of the (e, e)-isogenies to also map to and from products of elliptic curves, as we can ensure to start and finish the computation of Φ with a (2,2)-isogeny, which may make the practical implementation of (e, e)-isogenies with regards to this attack a more achievable goal.

Working with our baseline assumption that a (q_e, q_e)-isogeny can be computed in approximately q_e^3 multiplications over the base field of its kernel, we expect the cost of computing Φ as a (eB, eB)-isogeny to be dominated by the cost of computing a (q_e, q_e)-isogeny where q_e is the largest prime factor of e. We leave a careful analysis of the sizes of the field extensions for genus 2 to later work that includes a practical implementation of (q_e, q_e)-isogenies for prime $q_e \neq 2$, but let us assume for the sake of argument that the slow down for the extension field arithmetic scales with q_e similarly to the elliptic curve case. Then, assuming that the field extensions required are large enough that it is best to use the Fast Fourier Transform for multiplication, we approximate the cost of computing the (q_e, q_e)-isogeny by $O(q_e^3 \cdot q_e \log q_e)$. This is probably an overestimate: more research is needed into the existence of $\sqrt{}$élu-style-algorithms in the case of abelian surfaces. However, if the attack costs 2^λ, note that e is already forced to be relatively small compared to this by the fact that we have to search through $\approx e^4$ pairs of possible images of e-torsion points. Because of this, we can expect e to be fairly smooth compared to f, for example, so q_e (and the corresponding field extension) need not be particularly large.

In our choice of parameters for our toy example, we have chosen to demonstrate the use of e without the need to delve into (q_e, q_e)-isogenies for $q_e > 2$ by choosing $e = 2$. In this case we need a field extension of degree 4 for the 2^{b+1}-torsion points. This is not special to this instance but a consequence of the fact that the pull-back of the multiplication-by-2 map contains a square root (and no other rational but not integral powers), and so each lift of a point of order 2^i to a point of order 2^{i+1} will either double the degree of the field extension or keep it the same.

Choosing j. The choice of j only potentially effects the precomputation step, Step 1 of Algorithm 1, as we achieve $B' = 2^{-j}B$-torsion points by multiplying the known B-torsion by 2^j; for this reason we have no restrictions on non-negative j. Notice that we do not require e to be coprime to B, so e may contain powers of two, accounting also for the possibility of negative j.

Concrete Attack Parameters. We present here some choices of attack parameters in three cases of interest: two toy examples to test our algorithm, the Microsoft challenge parameters, and the parameters of SIKEp434 that were proposed for NIST Level I.

Toy Parameters: First, we construct a small example to test our algorithm using the 34-bit prime $p = 2^{19} \cdot 3^9 - 1$, with attack parameters $e = 2$, $i = 1$, $j = 0$ and $f = 5 \cdot 13 \cdot 17 \cdot 23 \cdot 41$. The largest field extension that we need for the computation of φ_f is $\mathbb{F}_{p^{20}}$, for the 41-isogeny. The largest field extension for $e = 2$ is $\mathbb{F}_{p^4}$, for the pullbacks of the order-2^{19} points to order-2^{20} points. This runs in less than 10 s on a single core on a standard laptop; see our code linked below.

We additionally demonstrate our attack on the 64-bit prime $p = 2^{33} \cdot 3^{19} - 1$, which was introduced in [29] as a small example instance for the Castryck–Decru attack, using the attack parameters $(e, i, j, f) = (1, 3, 5, 5 \cdot 11 \cdot 13 \cdot 19 \cdot 47 \cdot 353)$. The largest field extension involved in computing φ_f is $\mathbb{F}_{p^{176}}$, for the 353-isogeny. As $e = 1$, no extension is required to perform point division. This runs in less than 1 min on a single core on a standard laptop.

Our code for attacking both of the above parameter sets is available at:

https://github.com/Breaking-SIDH/direct-attack

Challenge Parameters: We consider one of the sets of challenge parameters put forward by Microsoft [12]: $A = 3^{67}$, $B = 2^{110}$, $i = 7$, $e = 1$, $j = 2$,

$$f = 5 \cdot 7 \cdot 13^3 \cdot 43^2 \cdot 73 \cdot 151 \cdot 241 \cdot 269 \cdot 577 \cdot 613 \cdot 28111 \cdot 321193.$$

The largest field extension we would need for the computation of φ_{321193} using $\sqrt{\text{élu}}$ is of degree 642384; in this case it might be faster to use a variant of Kohel's algorithm to avoid the extension field arithmetic (see Sect. 3.2). The extension field degrees for all the factors of f are given by

$$[k, q_f] = [8, 5], [12, 7], [24, 13], [28, 43], [144, 73], [75, 151], [480, 241],$$
$$[67, 269], [1152, 577], [1224, 613], [56220, 28111], [642384, 321193].$$

The choice of $i = 7$ also means that we need to run Steps 3 to 5 of Algorithm 2 up to $3^7 \approx 2^{11}$ times. In particular, if the SIDH instantiation uses a fixed (arbitrary) starting curve, the computation of φ_f can be performed as a precomputation and the attack on an individual public key is relatively fast, just the computation of some $(2,2)$-isogenies and 3-isogenies of elliptic curves, repeated potentially 3^7 times.

We have thus far restricted ourselves to e and B being a powers of two, as we want to demonstrate our attack and do not yet have adequate resources at our disposal to compute (ℓ,ℓ)-isogenies for $\ell > 2$. However, looking at the Microsoft challenge parameters can already illustrate the freedom that being able to compute efficiently (ℓ,ℓ)-isogenies for $\ell \neq 2$ can provide: we open up more options for attack parameters, including in this case in which one requires very little brute-force (only repeating Steps 4 to Step 5 up to 4 times): $A = 2^{110}$, $B = 3^{67}$, $A' = 2^{a-j} = 2^{108}$, $B' = 3^{b-i} = 3^{48}$, $e = 1$, and

$$f = 5 \cdot 7 \cdot 13 \cdot 61 \cdot 73 \cdot 431 \cdot 593 \cdot 607 \cdot 881 \cdot 36997 \cdot 139393 \cdot 227233.$$

The extension field degrees for all the factors of f are given by

$$[k, q_f] = [8, 5], [12, 7], [24, 13], [60, 61], [144, 73],$$
$$[860, 431], [1184, 593], [303, 607], [220, 881],$$
$$[73992, 36997], [34848, 139393], [56808, 227233].$$

NIST Level I Parameters: To select attack parameters for SIKEp434, that is, with $A = 3^{137}$ and $B = 2^{216}$, we rely on the algorithm for parameter selection outlined in the 'precomputation step' complexity analysis of Sect. 3. Table 1 shows some outputs of the algorithm for SIKEp434 parameters; these represent (i, j, x, y, z) such that

$$x3^{137-i} + y2^{216-j} = z.$$

We leave the details on the best parameter choice to further study, as all these parameters require a working implementation of (ℓ,ℓ)-isogenies for $\ell > 2$. Note that the last entry in the table only requires the computation of $(3,3)$-isogenies, at the expense of some smoothness of $f = -yz$; the largest degree of elliptic-curve isogeny required in this choice is 11144321.

3.2   Computing the Cofactor Isogeny

First, notice that any finite subgroup of an elliptic curve appearing in the SIDH setting defines an $\mathbb{F}_{p^2}$-rational isogeny: this is simply because Frobenius equals a scalar multiplication for the supersingular elliptic curves employed by SIDH, hence stabilizes any subgroup by definition. Thus, when computing isogeny factors $\varphi_q : E_n \rightarrow E_{n+1}$ of φ_f, the rationality of E_{n+1} or of the images of rational points on E_n is no concern. Moreover, if Kohel's algorithm or the 'irrational' variant of the $\sqrt{\text{élu}}$ algorithm [1, Sect. 4.14] is used, evaluating the isogeny at points in some $E(\mathbb{F}_{p^r})$ can be done using arithmetic in $\mathbb{F}_{p^r}$ rather than (as is the case for Vélu and $\sqrt{\text{élu}}$) the potentially much bigger composite of the fields of definition of the kernel points and the evaluation point.

In order to make an approximation of the complexity of computing φ_f on which we can base our search for good parameters for our attack, we ran some

Table 1. Some possible attack parameters for SIKEp434

i	j	x	y	z
19	27	$41 \cdot 2333$	$-101 \cdot 241$	$-5^4 \cdot 19 \cdot 47 \cdot 61 \cdot 857 \cdot 2903 \cdot 60889 \cdot 216617$ $\cdot 342497 \cdot 2309969 \cdot 2945407 \cdot 3951767 \cdot 4037069$
16	24	1823581	$-239 \cdot 6553$	$-11 \cdot 13 \cdot 19 \cdot 29 \cdot 631 \cdot 6043 \cdot 16451 \cdot 29759 \cdot 139987$ $\cdot 364513 \cdot 1850837 \cdot 3464849 \cdot 6344729 \cdot 26440207$
15	27	123551	-2546657	$-5^2 \cdot 29 \cdot 103 \cdot 1549 \cdot 28201 \cdot 55933 \cdot 243431$ $\cdot 1874903 \cdot 4421117 \cdot 6553021 \cdot 14183149 \cdot 39691591$
16	29	$5 \cdot 7^2 \cdot 1171$	-7884713	$-173 \cdot 853 \cdot 883 \cdot 8627 \cdot 26759 \cdot 692929 \cdot 3500557$ $\cdot 5202137 \cdot 6065333 \cdot 15108221 \cdot 28512793$
16	25	$79 \cdot 139 \cdot 499$	$-197 \cdot 47777$	$-5 \cdot 11 \cdot 17 \cdot 571 \cdot 35099 \cdot 40639 \cdot 48889 \cdot 81281$ $\cdot 138899 \cdot 1285429 \cdot 8464307 \cdot 13664309 \cdot 17314859$
16	24	$-467 \cdot 5419$	$5 \cdot 434689$	$-7 \cdot 103 \cdot 109 \cdot 2791 \cdot 3643 \cdot 36191 \cdot 47581 \cdot 99817$ $\cdot 401119 \cdot 749467 \cdot 2690497 \cdot 2863607 \cdot 3014203$
16	25	$-197 \cdot 9391$	$11 \cdot 307 \cdot 941$	$-5 \cdot 233 \cdot 431 \cdot 659 \cdot 4219 \cdot 237277 \cdot 371341 \cdot 820643$ $\cdot 2362589 \cdot 3896323 \cdot 14204429 \cdot 55510211$
17	26	-1	1	$-11 \cdot 23 \cdot 31 \cdot 131 \cdot 281 \cdot 311 \cdot 601 \cdot 3331 \cdot 8059 \cdot 8761$ $\cdot 163411 \cdot 1164091 \cdot 2101681 \cdot 4027511 \cdot 11144321$

experiments to investigate the behaviour of extension degrees for different values of p. As an illustration we consider $E_{1728}/\mathbb{F}_p$ with $p = 2^{216}3^{137} - 1$ as in the proposed NIST Level I parameters for SIKE. Only the even-degree fields are relevant as we are working with extensions of $\mathbb{F}_{p^2}$. Figures 1(a), (b), and (c) show the q_f for which there exists an even $k \leq 1000$ such that there is an $\mathbb{F}_{p^k}$-rational point of order q_f (only the minimal even k is depicted). In total, we find 72% of the primes $< 10^2$ (cf. Fig. 1(a)), 62.5% of the primes $< 10^3$ (cf. Fig. 1(b)), and 22% of the primes $< 10^4$ (cf. Fig. 1(c)). Based on these experiments, to guide our parameter selection for our attack we crudely estimate that the minimal field extension degree k for the maximal q_f dividing f is close to degree q_f over $\mathbb{F}_{p^2}$. Below, we will often use the fact $k \leq q_f$.

To compute with elements in an extension field of degree k, one requires an irreducible polynomial of that degree over the ground field (here, $\mathbb{F}_{p^2}$). There are many algorithms for this task. We specifically mention one approach due to Shoup [33], which has a complexity of $\tilde{O}(k^2 + k \log p)$ operations in $\mathbb{F}_p$.

To find a point of order q_f, we may then sample a random point $P \in E(\mathbb{F}_{p^k})$ and multiply it by a cofactor on the order of p^k. Using square-and-multiply, this amounts to $O(k \log p)$ multiplications in $\mathbb{F}_{p^k}$. Thus, finding a point of order q_f in this way costs $\tilde{O}(k^2 \log p)$ when using FFT-based multiplication for $\mathbb{F}_{p^k}$. Under the assumption that $\log p \in (\log q_f)^{O(1)}$, which would for instance follow from the heuristic estimates on f given above, this gives us a rough estimate of $\tilde{O}(q_f^2)$ for the complexity of computing the kernel of a φ_q-isogeny. Note that if the largest factor of the smoothest possible choice of f only admits very large extension fields, it will be worthwhile to opt for a slightly less smooth f, i.e., a slightly bigger q_f, for which the field extensions are smaller.

To compute a large-degree isogeny from an explicit kernel point over $\mathbb{F}_{p^k}$, we can either apply $\sqrt{\text{élu}}$ directly over $\mathbb{F}_{p^k}$ or first recover the kernel polynomial using [15, Algorithm 4] and then run Kohel's algorithm. The cost for the first method is $\tilde{O}(q_f^{1/2})$ arithmetic operations in $\mathbb{F}_{p^k}$, or $\tilde{O}(q_f^{3/2})$ operations in $\mathbb{F}_p$ using FFT-based multiplication in $\mathbb{F}_{p^k}$. The cost for the second method is $O(q_f^2)$. (Note that the first method will require working in composite extension fields to evaluate the isogeny at points, whereas the second gives an expression for the isogeny with coefficients in $\mathbb{F}_{p^2}$.)

Overall, the dominating part of the algorithm is the large scalar multiplication to find the kernel of a q_f-isogeny. Therefore, to guide our choice of attack parameters, we take the complexity of computing and evaluating large-degree isogenies to be $\tilde{O}(q_f^2)$.

We mention in passing that the field extension degree can be halved whenever it is even, by using x-only elliptic-curve arithmetic.

An Alternative Approach. Instead of finding an irreducible polynomial for $\mathbb{F}_{p^k}$ and computing a large scalar multiplication, it is also possible to extract an isogeny kernel from the q_f-division polynomial directly, as follows.

The q_f-division polynomial for $E/\mathbb{F}_{p^2}$ is the unique monic squarefree polynomial with coefficients in $\mathbb{F}_{p^2}$ whose roots are precisely the x-coordinates of nonzero q_f-torsion points on E. It can either be precomputed for a generic curve E with symbolic coefficients (e.g., a single Montgomery coefficient A) or computed directly for a given E using a recursive expression [34, Exercise 3.7]. A careful analysis of both approaches to computing division polynomials is given in [2, Sect. 9]: Evaluation of a precomputed polynomial can be faster if q_f is fairly small, but once q_f is large enough that multiplying polynomials of degree q_f^2 benefits from FFT-based multiplication, it becomes faster to compute the polynomials instantiate for a given E directly. For these large q_f, the cost of computing the division polynomial is $O(q_f^2 \log q_f)$ base-ring operations.

Let $\mathbb{F}_{p^{2k}}$ be the smallest extension of $\mathbb{F}_{p^2}$ where the q_f-torsion is defined, and define $k' = k/2$ if k is even and $k' = k$ otherwise. All irreducible divisors of the division polynomial have degree k': for the curves used in SIDH, the p^2-Frobenius π equals $[-p]$, hence for any point $P = (x, y)$ of order q_f we have $\pi^k(P) = [(-p)^k]P = P$. Dropping the y-coordinate corresponds to quotienting the elliptic-curve group by negation, which shows $x^{k'} = x$, and k' is minimal with this property since k was minimal. Thus, the irreducible divisor of ψ_{q_f} which vanishes at x has degree k' as claimed. We may thus apply 'equal-degree splitting'—see e.g. [17, Algorithm 14.8])— recursively to find a single irreducible divisor h of ψ_{q_f}. This involves $O(d \log p + \log q_f)$ operations on polynomials of degree $O(q_f^2)$; assuming the use of FFT-based multiplication the cost in $\mathbb{F}_p$-operations is $\tilde{O}(q_f^3) \log p$. By construction h is then a minimal polynomial for a q_f-isogeny in the sense of [15, Definition 15]. We may compute the isogeny in time $O(k'q_f) + \tilde{O}(q_f)$ by running [15, Algorithm 3] and applying Kohel's algorithm. Overall, the cost for

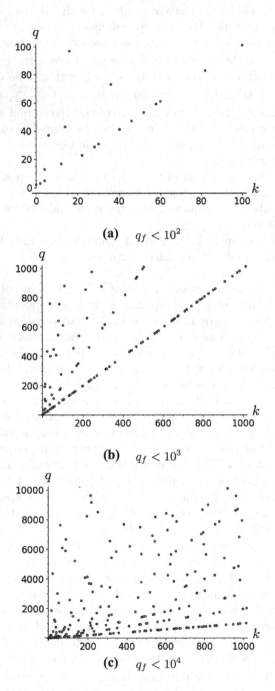

(a) $q_f < 10^2$

(b) $q_f < 10^3$

(c) $q_f < 10^4$

Fig. 1. Extension field degrees < 1000 needed for $\mathbb{F}_{p^k}$-rational q_f-torsion

this is $\tilde{O}(q_f^3) \log p$, which is worse than finding an irreducible polynomial first and then running the multiplication-based method above.

3.3 Computing (ℓ, ℓ)-isogenies

In order for our algorithm to reach its full potential, it is necessary to consider integers e in Step 1 of Algorithm 2 that do not divide B, and in particular are not necessarily powers of two. It may also be that there is a nice parameter choice (e, i, j, f) with A a power of 2 and B a power of 3 (cf. the attack parameter suggestions in Sect. 3.1), or one may want to consider more general setups. In all of these cases, in Step 5 of Algorithm 2 it will be necessary to compute (ℓ, ℓ)-isogenies for $\ell \neq 2$, which as observed above requires more research to achieve practically (for $\ell = 3$ there is however already some interesting work on this topic [6]). For this reason, we leave all instantiations of the attack that use e not dividing B to future work and focus on the case of $(2,2)$-isogenies, that is, $B = 2^b$ and $e \mid B$. Recall that we set $B' = B2^{-j}$, where $0 \leq j \leq b$.

In order to compute the chain of $(2,2)$-isogenies whose composition is the (eB', eB')-isogeny Φ, we need to able to compute three different flavours of $(2,2)$-isogenies between principally polarized abelian surfaces:

- A (2,2)-isogeny from a Jacobian of a genus 2 curve to a Jacobian of a genus 2 curve, for which we refer to reader to [37, Sect. 2.3.1].
- A (2,2)-isogeny from a product of elliptic curves to the Jacobian of a genus 2 curve, for which we refer the reader to [8] for more details. (This is required for the first step of Φ).
- A (2,2)-isogeny from a Jacobian of a genus 2 curve to a product of elliptic curves, for which we refer the reader to [35, Proposition 8.3.1]. (This is required for the last step of Φ).

Our proof-of-concept implementation uses Rémy Oudompheng and collaborators' SageMath implementation [28,29] for these steps.

4   The Case of Known Endomorphism Ring

Algorithm 1 solves SSI-T, assuming that $B > A$, and an isogeny $\varphi_f : E \to E_0$ of degree $B - A$ is known, in a way that allows efficient evaluation of $\widehat{\varphi_f}$ on the B-torsion. In this section, we describe how to find such an isogeny in polynomial time, provided E_0 and a description of the endomorphism ring $\text{End}(E_0)$.

More precisely, we prove the following theorem. An *efficient representation* of an isogeny φ is an encoding of the isogeny, together with an algorithm that can evaluate it on points in time polynomial in the length of the input.

Theorem 2. *Assume the generalised Riemann hypothesis. There is an algorithm that solves the following task in polynomial time (in the length of the input): given a supersingular curve E_0, four endomorphisms of E_0 in efficient representation, and a positive integer f, finds an isogeny $\varphi : E_0 \to E$ of degree f in efficient representation.*

Together with Corollary 1, this theorem immediately implies a polynomial time algorithm for SSI-T, when the endomorphism ring of E_0 is known, and assuming the generalised Riemann hypothesis (GRH).

Algorithm 3: Finding an ideal of prescribed norm.

Input: A basis $(\alpha_i)_{i=1}^4$ of $\mathrm{End}(E_0)$ in efficient representation, and an integer f coprime to 2 and p.

Output: A left ideal I of norm f in $\mathrm{End}(E_0)$

---

1 Find a solution of $\deg(\alpha_0) = z_0^2 f$ with $\alpha_0 \in \mathrm{End}(E_0)$ and $z_0 \in \mathbb{Z}$. It is a homogenous quadratic equations of dimension 5, so can be solved in polynomial time by [7].

2 Deduce another solution (α, z) for which z is coprime with f, using the technique of [38, Algorithm 7, Step 3].

3 Return $I = \mathrm{End}(E_0)\alpha + \mathrm{End}(E_0)f$.

Proof of Theorem 2. The idea is the following: first, find an ideal I in $\mathrm{End}(E_0)$ of norm f. Then, assuming GRH, one can find the codomain of $\varphi = \varphi_I : E_0 \to E$ and evaluate φ on any input using [16, Lemma 3.3].

Finding the ideal I requires more explanation. First observe that the problem reduces to the case where f is coprime to $2p$: write $f = 2^i p^j f'$ with $(f', 2p) = 1$, solve the problem for f', and then compose the resulting isogeny with i isogenies of degree 2 and j Frobenius isogenies. The steps to find I are then given in Algorithm 3. Let us explain Step (2). Finding the desired solution heuristically is simple, so the motivation of the following discussion is mostly to get a provable method. Write the solutions (α, z) in the form $(x, z) \in \mathbb{Z}^4 \times \mathbb{Z}$, where x represents the coefficients of α in the provided basis of $\mathrm{End}(E_0)$. The equation can then be written as $x^t G x = z^2 f$, or $x^t Q x = 0$, where G is the Gram matrix of the basis, and $Q = G \oplus \langle -f \rangle$ (the 5×5 matrix with G in the upper-left corner, $-f$ in the lower-right corner, and zeros elsewhere). Note that we can assume that x_0 (the vector of coordinates of α_0) is primitive (i.e., the greatest common divisor of its coefficients is 1) and $z_0 \in \mathbb{Z}_{>0}$. We are looking for another solution where x is coprime with f. The rest of the proof reproduces *mutatis mutandi* the technique of [38, Algorithm 7, Step 3]. From [10, Proposition 6.3.2], the general solution $X = (x, z)$ is given by

$$X = d((R^t Q R)X_0 - 2(R^t Q X_0)R),$$

for arbitrary $R \in \mathbb{Q}^5$ and $d \in \mathbb{Q}^*$, where $X_0 = (x_0, z_0)$ is our initial solution. Fix $d = 1$. Write $R = (r_x, r_z)$ with $r_x \in \mathbb{Z}^4$ and $r_z \in \mathbb{Z}$. The last coordinate of X is given by the integral quadratic form

$$r_x^t G r_x z_0 - 2 r_x^t G x_0 r_z + f z_0 r_z^2 = \frac{(r_x z_0 - x_0 r_z)^t G (r_x z_0 - x_0 r_z)}{z_0}.$$

It is of rank 4, so let $M \in M_{4 \times 4}(\mathbb{Z})$ be a matrix whose columns generate $\Lambda = z_0\mathbb{Z}^4 + x_0\mathbb{Z}$, and

$$g(v) = \frac{v^t(M^tGM)v}{z_0}.$$

It is positive definite, since G is and $z_0 > 0$. Let us show that g is (almost) primitive. If s is a prime that does not divide z_0, both M and z_0 are invertible modulo s, so g is primitive at s because G is. Now suppose $s \mid z_0$. Then, writing $Mv = r_xz_0 - x_0r_z$, we have

$$g(v) \equiv -2r_x^tGx_0r_z \bmod s.$$

Therefore, if $s \neq 2$ and $Gx_0 \not\equiv 0 \bmod s$, then g is primitive at s. If $Gx_0 \equiv 0 \bmod s$, since x_0 is primitive, s must divide $\mathrm{disc}(G)$, so s is 2 or p. This proves that the only primes where g might not be primitive are 2 and p. We can then write $g = g'/a$ where g' is primitive and a may only be divisible by the primes 2 and p. Applying [38, Proposition 3.6], we can find in polynomial time a v such that $z' = g'(v)$ is a prime larger than f. With $z = az'$, we obtain a solution of $x^tGx = fz^2$. Since f is coprime to $2p$, it is also coprime to z.

5   Future Work

We have provided an implementation of a toy example, but with a practical implementation of (ℓ, ℓ)-isogenies for $\ell > 2$ it should be possible to provide a practical implementation of larger interesting instances. Additionally, our implementation does not yet incorporate the fast $(2,2)$-isogeny formulas of Kunzweiler [21], which especially when working over field extensions will have a positive impact on performance.

Finally, given the speed of recovering the secret isogeny using our algorithm, especially in the case of known endomorphism ring, we also hope that it will be possible to use these methods for constructive purposes.

References

1. Bernstein, D.J., De Feo, L., Leroux, A., Smith, B.: Faster computation of isogenies of large prime degree. In: Galbraith, S. (ed.) ANTS XIV: Proceedings of the Fourteenth Algorithmic Number Theory Symposium, pp. 39–55. Mathematical Sciences Publishers (2020). https://iac.r/2020/341
2. Bernstein, D.J., Lange, T., Martindale, C., Panny, L.: Quantum circuits for the CSIDH: optimizing quantum evaluation of isogenies. In: Ishai, Y., Rijmen, V. (eds.) EUROCRYPT 2019. LNCS, vol. 11477, pp. 409–441. Springer, Cham (2019). https://doi.org/10.1007/978-3-030-17656-3_15
3. Beullens, W., Kleinjung, T., Vercauteren, F.: CSI-FiSh: efficient isogeny based signatures through class group computations. In: Galbraith, S.D., Moriai, S. (eds.) ASIACRYPT 2019. LNCS, vol. 11921, pp. 227–247. Springer, Cham (2019). https://doi.org/10.1007/978-3-030-34578-5_9

4. Bisson, G., Cosset, R., Robert, D.: AVIsogenies (abelian varieties and isogenies). MAGMA package. https://gitlab.inria.fr/roberdam/avisogenies

5. Bottinelli, P., de Quehen, V., Leonardi, C., Mosunov, A., Pawlega, F., Sheth, M.: The Dark SIDH of Isogenies. Preprint (2019). https://ia.cr/2019/1333

6. Bröker, R., Howe, E.W., Lauter, K.E., Stevenhagen, P.: Genus-2 curves and Jacobians with a given number of points. LMS J. Comput. Math. **18**(1), 170–197 (2015). https://doi.org/10.1112/S1461157014000461

7. Castel, P.: Solving quadratic equations in dimension 5 or more without factoring. Open Book Ser. **1**(1), 213–233 (2013)

8. Castryck, W., Decru, T.: An efficient key recovery attack on SIDH (preliminary version). Preprint (2022). https://ia.cr/2022/975

9. Castryck, W., Lange, T., Martindale, C., Panny, L., Renes, J.: CSIDH: an efficient post-quantum commutative group action. In: Peyrin, T., Galbraith, S. (eds.) ASIACRYPT 2018. LNCS, vol. 11274, pp. 395–427. Springer, Cham (2018). https://doi.org/10.1007/978-3-030-03332-3_15

10. Cohen, H.: Number Theory: Volume I: Tools and Diophantine Equations, vol. 239. Springer, New York (2008). https://doi.org/10.1007/978-0-387-49923-9

11. Costello, C.: B-SIDH: supersingular isogeny Diffie-Hellman using twisted torsion. In: Moriai, S., Wang, H. (eds.) ASIACRYPT 2020. LNCS, vol. 12492, pp. 440–463. Springer, Cham (2020). https://doi.org/10.1007/978-3-030-64834-3_15

12. Costello, C.: The case for SIKE: a decade of the supersingular isogeny problem. In: The NIST 3rd Post-Quantum Cryptography Standardization Conference (2021). https://ia.cr/2021/543

13. De Feo, L., et al.: Séta: supersingular encryption from torsion attacks. In: ASIACRYPT (4). LNCS, vol. 13093, pp. 249–278. Springer, Cham (2021). https://doi.org/10.1007/978-3-030-92068-5_9

14. De Feo, L., Kohel, D., Leroux, A., Petit, C., Wesolowski, B.: SQISign: compact post-quantum signatures from quaternions and isogenies. In: Moriai, S., Wang, H. (eds.) ASIACRYPT 2020. LNCS, vol. 12491, pp. 64–93. Springer, Cham (2020). https://doi.org/10.1007/978-3-030-64837-4_3

15. Eriksen, J.K., Panny, L., Sotáková, J., Veroni, M.: Deuring for the People: Supersingular Elliptic Curves with Prescribed Endomorphism Ring in General Characteristic. Preprint (2023). https://ia.cr/2023/106

16. Fouotsa, T.B., Kutas, P., Merz, S., Ti, Y.B.: On the isogeny problem with torsion point information. In: Hanaoka, G., Shikata, J., Watanabe, Y. (eds.) Public Key Cryptography (1). LNCS, vol. 13177, pp. 142–161. Springer, Cham (2022). https://doi.org/10.1007/978-3-030-97121-2_6

17. von zur Gathen, J., Gerhard, J.: Modern Computer Algebra, 3rd edn. Cambridge University Press, Cambridge (2013)

18. Jao, D., et al.: Supersingular Isogeny Key Encapsulation. Submission to [27] (2017, 2019, 2020). https://sike.org

19. Jao, D., De Feo, L.: Towards quantum-resistant cryptosystems from supersingular elliptic curve isogenies. In: Yang, B.-Y. (ed.) PQCrypto 2011. LNCS, vol. 7071, pp. 19–34. Springer, Heidelberg (2011). https://doi.org/10.1007/978-3-642-25405-5_2

20. Kani, E.: The number of curves of genus two with elliptic differentials (1997). https://doi.org/10.1515/crll.1997.485.93

21. Kunzweiler, S.: Efficient Computation of $(2^n, 2^n)$-Isogenies. Preprint (2022). https://ia.cr/2022/990

22. Lubicz, D., Robert, D.: Fast change of level and applications to isogenies. In: ANTS XV: Proceedings of the Fifteenth Algorithmic Number Theory Symposium (2022). https://doi.org/10.1007/s40993-022-00407-9

23. Lubicz, D., Somoza, A.: AVIsogenies SageMath package. https://gitlab.inria.fr/roberdam/avisogenies/-/tree/sage
24. Maino, L., Martindale, C.: An attack on SIDH with arbitrary starting curve. Preprint (2022). Version 2: https://eprint.iacr.org/archive/2022/1026/20220825:192029
25. Maino, L., Martindale, C.: An attack on SIDH with arbitrary starting curve. Preprint (2022). Version 1: https://eprint.iacr.org/archive/2022/1026/20220808:211318
26. Milne, J.S.: Abelian varieties. In: Cornell, G., Silverman, J.H. (eds.) Arithmetic Geometry, pp. 103–150. Springer, New York (1986). https://doi.org/10.1007/978-1-4613-8655-1_5
27. National Institute of Standards and Technology: Post-Quantum Cryptography Standardization, December 2016. https://csrc.nist.gov/Projects/Post-Quantum-Cryptography/Post-Quantum-Cryptography-Standardization
28. Oudompheng, R., Panny, L., Pope, G., et al.: SageMath Reimplementation of the SIDH key recovery attack (2022). https://github.com/jack4818/Castryck-Decru-SageMath
29. Oudompheng, R., Pope, G.: A note on Reimplementing the Castryck-Decru attack and lessons learned for SageMath. Preprint (2022). https://ia.cr/2022/1283
30. Petit, C.: Faster algorithms for isogeny problems using torsion point images. In: Takagi, T., Peyrin, T. (eds.) ASIACRYPT 2017. LNCS, vol. 10625, pp. 330–353. Springer, Cham (2017). https://doi.org/10.1007/978-3-319-70697-9_12
31. de Quehen, V., et al.: Improved torsion-point attacks on SIDH variants. In: Malkin, T., Peikert, C. (eds.) CRYPTO 2021. LNCS, vol. 12827, pp. 432–470. Springer, Cham (2021). https://doi.org/10.1007/978-3-030-84252-9_15
32. Robert, D.: Breaking SIDH in polynomial time. Preprint (2022). https://ia.cr/2022/1038
33. Shoup, V.: Fast construction of irreducible polynomials over finite fields. J. Symb. Comput. **17**(5), 371–391 (1994). https://doi.org/10.1006/jsco.1994.1025
34. Silverman, J.H.: The Arithmetic of Elliptic Curves, vol. 106. Springer, New York (2009). https://doi.org/10.1007/978-0-387-09494-6
35. Smith, B.: Explicit endomorphisms and correspondences. Ph.D. thesis, University of Sydney (2005)
36. The Sage Developers: SageMath, the Sage Mathematics Software System (Version 9.6) (2022). https://sagemath.org
37. Ti, Y.B.: Isogenies of Abelian Varieties in Cryptography. Ph.D. thesis, University of Auckland (2019)
38. Wesolowski, B.: The supersingular isogeny path and endomorphism ring problems are equivalent. In: 62nd IEEE Annual Symposium on Foundations of Computer Science, FOCS 2021, Denver, CO, USA, 7–10 February 2022, pp. 1100–1111. IEEE (2021). https://doi.org/10.1109/FOCS52979.2021.00109
39. Wesolowski, B.: Understanding and improving the Castryck-Decru attack on SIDH. Preprint (2022)

Breaking SIDH in Polynomial Time

Damien Robert[1,2(✉)]

[1] INRIA Bordeaux-Sud-Ouest, 200 Avenue de la Vieille Tour,
33405 Talence Cedex, France
damien.robert@inria.fr
[2] Institut de Mathématiques de Bordeaux, 351 cours de la liberation,
33405 Talence Cedex, France

Abstract. We show that we can break SIDH in (classical) polynomial time, even with a random starting curve E_0.

1 Introduction

1.1 Result

We extend the recent attacks by [CD22, MM22] and prove that there exists a proven polynomial time attack on SIDH [JD11, DJP14]/SIKE [JAC+17], even with a random starting curve E_0.

Both papers had the independent beautiful idea to use isogenies between abelian surfaces (using [Kan97, Sect. 2]) to break a large class of parameters for SIDH. Namely, on a random starting curve E_0, if the degree of the secret isogenies are $N_A > N_B$, their attack essentially applies whenever $a := N_A - N_B$ is smooth. This is highly unlikely, however they use the fact that it is possible to tweak the parameters N_A and N_B to augment the probability of success (or reduce the smoothness bound on a), see Sect. 6. In the case where $\mathrm{End}(E_0)$ is known, [CD22] also have a (heuristic) polynomial time attack, essentially because one can use the endomorphism ring to compute an a-isogeny on E_0 even if a is not smooth, see Sect. 5.

A natural idea is to work in higher dimensions to extend the range of parameters for which an attack is possible, even on a random curve E_0. We show in Sect. 2 that by going to dimension 8, it is possible to break in polynomial time all parameters for SIDH. The algorithm is deterministic, except for a randomized polynomial time precomputation (which does not depend on E_0) to decompose $N_A - N_B$ as a sum of four integer squares (see Remark 1).

From now and for the rest of this paper, we let $N_A > N_B$ be two coprime integers, and we assume that we are given their factorisations. We denote by ℓ_N the largest prime divisor of an integer N, and by ℓ_A the largest prime divisor of N_A, and ℓ_B the largest prime divisor of N_B.

Theorem 1. *Assume that we are given a decomposition $N_A - N_B = a_1^2 + a_2^2 + a_3^2 + a_4^2$ as a sum of four integer squares. Let $\phi_B : E_0 \to E_B$ be a N_B-isogeny*

C. Hazay and M. Stam (Eds.): EUROCRYPT 2023, LNCS 14008, pp. 472–503, 2023.
https://doi.org/10.1007/978-3-031-30589-4_17

defined over a finite field $\mathbb{F}_q$. *Assume that* $E_0[N_A] \subset E_0(\mathbb{F}_q)$ *and that we are given a basis* (P_1, P_2) *of* $E_0[N_A]$ *and the image of* ϕ_B *on this basis.*

Then there is an algorithm $\mathtt{Eval}(E_0, E_B, P_1, P_2, \phi_B(P_1), \phi_B(P_2), P)$ *which returns* $\phi_B(P)$ *for any point* P *of* $E_0(\mathbb{F}_q)$ *in* $\widetilde{O}(\ell_A^8 \log N_A)$ *arithmetic operations over* $\mathbb{F}_q$.

In particular, if $\mathrm{Ker}\,\phi_B \subset E_0[N_B](\mathbb{F}_q)$ *and we are given a basis* R_1, R_2 *of* $E_0[N_B](\mathbb{F}_q)$, *there is an algorithm*

$$\mathtt{ComputeKernel}(E_0, E_B, P_1, P_2, R_1, R_2, \phi_B(P_1), \phi_B(P_2))$$

which returns a generator for the kernel of ϕ_B *in* $\widetilde{O}(\ell_A^8 \log N_A + \ell_B^{1/2} \log N_B)$ *arithmetic operations over* $\mathbb{F}_q$.

Proof (Outline) The full proof will be given in Sect. 2.

Notably, we will build in Sect. 2, Lemma 1 an explicit N_A-endomorphism[1] $F : E_0^4 \times E_B^4$ in dimension $g = 8$ (given by an 8×8 matrix) such that evaluating F at (P, P, P, P, Q, Q, Q, Q), for any $P \in E_0(\mathbb{F}_q), Q \in E_B(\mathbb{F}_q)$ allows to recover $\phi_B(P)$ and $\widetilde{\phi}_B(Q)$, where $\widetilde{\phi}_B$ is the dual (more precisely contragredient) isogeny. Furthermore the kernel of F is described by 8 explicit rational generators which can be computed in time $O(\log N_A)$ by Lemma 2.

This reduces evaluating ϕ_B to evaluating the isogeny F in dimension 8 on a point given generators of its kernel. As explained in Sect. 2, using the algorithm of [LR23], such an isogeny can be evaluated, via the naive algorithm to compute smooth isogenies, in time $O(\ell_A^8 \log N_A + \log^2 N_A)$. This cost can even be reduced to $\widetilde{O}(\ell_A^8 \log N_A)$ using the optimised computation of smooth isogenies of [DJP14, Sect. 4.2.2].

In particular, if $\mathrm{Ker}\,\phi_B \subset E_0[N_B](\mathbb{F}_q)$, and we are given a basis of $E_0[N_B](\mathbb{F}_q)$, we can evaluate ϕ_B on this basis by two calls to $\mathtt{Eval}$, and then solve a DLP in a cyclic group of order N_B for a cost of $\widetilde{O}(\log N_B \ell_B^{1/2})$ by Pohlig-Hellman's algorithm to recover a generator of $\mathrm{Ker}\,\phi_B$. We refer to Sect. 2 for more details and an alternative strategy to recover the kernel. $\square$

Remark 1. – The decomposition of a as a sum of four squares is a precomputation step that only depends on N_A and N_B. It can be done in random polynomial time $O(\log^2 a)$ binary operations by [RS86, PT18]. This is the only step of the algorithm which is not deterministic, we refer to [PT18, Sect. 5] for conjectural deterministic polynomial time algorithms.

– In the context of SIDH, E_0 and E_B will be supersingular curves defined over $\mathbb{F}_q = \mathbb{F}_{p^2}$, the factorisations of N_B and N_A are known and we are given a basis of $E_0[N_A]$, $E_0[N_B]$ over $\mathbb{F}_q$, along with the evaluation of a N_A-isogeny ϕ_A on the basis of $E_0[N_B]$ and of a N_B-isogeny ϕ_B on the basis of $E_0[N_A]$, see Sect. 1.3. So we can apply Theorem 1 if $N_A > N_B$. Otherwise, if $N_B > N_A$ we will simply try to recover Alice's secret isogeny ϕ_A instead.

---

[1] We refer to Definition 1 for the definition of a N-isogeny $F : A \to B$ in higher dimension, if A and B are elliptic curves this simply means that F is of degree N.

By considering the dual isogeny $\widetilde{F}$, we will also see in Sect. 6.4 that as in [QKL+21], in Theorem 1 it is also possible to directly reconstruct ϕ_B (with the same complexity) as long as $N_A^2 > N_B$.

- When $\ell_A = O(1)$, or even $\ell_A = O(\log \log N_A)$, the attack is thus "quasi-linear", i.e., in $\widetilde{O}(\log N_A)$ arithmetic operations in $\mathbb{F}_q$. So it is as efficient asymptotically as the key exchange itself (with a higher constant of course).
- The attack also breaks the TCSSI-security assumption of [DDF+21, Problem 3.2].
- Another contribution of this paper is to give a precise (but heuristic, see Heuristic 1) complexity bound for a dimension 4 attack: $\widetilde{O}(\log N_A \ell_A^4)$ arithmetic operations (after a precomputation), see Sect. 4. This precise complexity bound uses the fact mentioned above that we can also explicitly build a N_A^2-isogeny F rather than just a N_A-isogeny. This gives more freedom for the tweaking of parameters needed for the dimension 4 attack.
- The method of Sects. 2 and 3 shows that the following powerful embedding lemma holds: for any N-isogeny $f : A \to B$ between abelian varieties of dimension g, and any $N' > N$, it is possible to efficiently embed f as a matrix coefficient of a N'-isogeny F in dimension $8g$ (or $4g$ or $2g$ in certain cases). This provides considerable flexibility at the cost of going up in dimension, and was used in [Rob22b] to show that an isogeny over a finite field always admits an efficient representation.

In this paper, if not specified our complexities should be understood as arithmetic complexities over the base field.

1.2   Outline

We prove Theorem 1 in Sect. 2. This Section is written to be short and self-contained, and since it applies in all cases, without requiring any parameter tweaks, the complexity analysis is straightforward. We recommend the reader, unless interested in the gory details of the dimension 2 and 4 attacks, to skip directly to this section.

For reasons stated in Remark 3, for practical attacks it would be more convenient to stay in lower dimension. We first describe a common framework encapsulating possible dimension $2g$ attacks in Sect. 3, before describing our dimension 4 attack in Sect. 4. We explain how the dimension 2 attacks of [CD22, MM22] fit into this common framework in Sect. 5. Parameter tweaks, needed for the dimensions 2 attack and the dimension 4 attack, are described in Sect. 6.

For this introduction, we give more context in Sect. 1.3 to explain how our attacks fit into the broad class of "torsion point attacks" in Sect. 1.4, and summarize in Sect. 1.5 the different complexities of the different dim 2, 4 and 8 attacks of [CD22, MM22, Rob22a].

1.3   Context

Supersingular Isogeny Diffie-Hellman (SIDH) is a post-quantum key exchange protocol initially proposed in [JD11] with further ameliorations (among many other papers) in [DJP14, CLN16]. A standard transform gives a key encapsulation method SIKE (supersingular isogeny key encapsulation) [JAC+17], which was submitted to the NIST post-quantum competition and recently selected as an alternative candidate in the fourth round of the competition.

The key hardness problem of many isogeny based protocols is based on the difficulty of recovering a large degree isogeny $f : E \to E'$ between two ordinary or supersingular elliptic curves, the so-called *isogeny path problem*. To the best of our knowledge, without more information on E and E' (like an explicit representation of part of their endomorphism rings) this problem still has *exponential quantum security for supersingular curves*.

However, for the SIDH key exchange, Bob will reveal not only the codomain E_B of his secret N_B-isogeny $\phi_B : E_0 \to E_B$ (N_B a large smooth number) but also the action of ϕ_B on the N_A-*torsion* $E_0[N_A]$ for an integer N_A prime to N_B, typically by revealing the image $Q_1 = \phi_B(P_1), Q_2 = \phi_B(P_2)$ of a basis (P_1, P_2) of $E_0[N_A]$. This added information then allows Alice to pushforward her secret N_A isogeny $\phi_A : E_0 \to E_A$ to $\phi'_A : E_B \to E_{AB}$, via $\operatorname{Ker} \phi'_A = \phi_B(\operatorname{Ker} \phi_A)$. Alice also reveals the action of her secret isogeny ϕ_A on $E_0[N_B]$, and then Bob can pushforward his secret N_B isogeny to $\phi'_B : E_A \to E_{AB}$ via $\operatorname{Ker} \phi'_B = \phi_A(\operatorname{Ker} \phi_B)$. The codomain is the same since the maps $\phi'_B \circ \phi_A : E_0 \to E_A \to E_{AB}$ and $\phi'_A \circ \phi_B : E_0 \to E_B \to E_{AB}$ have the same kernel $\operatorname{Ker} \phi_A + \operatorname{Ker} \phi_B$:

$$
\begin{array}{ccc}
E_0 & \xrightarrow{\phi_B} & E_B \\
\downarrow{\phi_A} & & \downarrow{\phi'_A} \\
E_A & \xrightarrow{\phi'_B} & E_{AB}
\end{array}
$$

The supersingular curve E_{AB} is then the common secret of Alice and Bob.

But as we will see, this is a *key weakness* that allows one to break the SIDH key exchange. This is worth emphasising: the work of [CD22, MM22, Rob22a] only breaks *SSI-T*, the supersingular isogeny with torsion problem, not the more general supersingular isogeny path problem. In particular, it does not apply to protocols like [CLM+18, DKL+20].

1.4 Torsion Points Attacks

Let us recall the setup. Eve wants to recover the secret N_B-isogeny ϕ_B, and she knows the image of ϕ_B on a basis of $E_0[N_A]$. It has been well known that the publication of these so called torsion points could, for some parameters, reduce the security of the supersingular isogeny problem.

Petit in [Pet17] had the first key idea of the following "torsion points" attack: assume that the attacker Eve could somehow combine Bob's secret N_B-isogeny ϕ_B and/or its dual $\tilde{\phi}_B$ with an isogeny α she controls into a N_A-isogeny $F : E_0 \to E'$. Eve knows the action of ϕ_B on $E_0[N_A]$ because Bob published it, and she also knows the action of the dual isogeny $\tilde{\phi}_B : E_B \to E_0$ on $E_B[N_A]$. Indeed, if (P_1, P_2) is a basis of $E_0[N_A]$, and $Q_1 = \phi_B(P_1), Q_2 = \phi_B(P_2)$, then

$\widetilde{\phi}_B(Q_1) = N_B P_1, \widetilde{\phi}_B(Q_2) = N_B P_2$. Notice that Q_1, Q_2 is a basis of $E_B[N_A]$ since N_A is prime to N_B.

Since she knows the action of α too because she controls it, she can recover the action of F on (a basis of) $E_0[N_A]$. It is then easy for Eve to compute the kernel of F using some linear algebra and discrete logarithms, see Lemma 4. These discrete logarithms are inexpensive because N_A is assumed to be smooth.

From this kernel $\operatorname{Ker} F$, she can then evaluate F on any point of E_0 via an isogeny algorithm, from which she can try to recover ϕ_B if extracting ϕ_B from F is possible.

In his attack, Petit considers for F an endomorphism of E_0 of the form $F = \widehat{\phi}_B \circ \gamma \circ \phi_B + [d]$, where γ is a trace 0 endomorphism (meaning that $\widetilde{\gamma} = -\gamma$) of degree e. Then it is easy to check that F is a $(N_B^2 e + d^2)$-isogeny, so it remains to find parameters such that $N_B^2 e + d^2 = N_A$, and to construct a γ of degree e. From the knowledge of F, it is not too hard to extract ϕ_B.

Remark 2. A variant is to "tweak" the parameters, in order to increase the range of susceptible parameters. For instance if we can find parameters such that $N_B^2 e + d^2 = u N_A$ with u smooth, then F will be a $u N_A$-isogeny. We only know its action on $E_0[N_A]$, so we cannot recover it directly. However F is a composition $F_2 \circ F_1$ of a N_A-isogeny F_1 followed by an u-isogeny F_2, so we can at least recover F_1 and then try to brute force F_2. A similar strategy holds for higher dimensional attacks, we will describe more possible tweaks in Sect. 6.

This attack, while powerful, can only apply to unbalanced parameters (here $N_A > N_B^2$); and requires the knowledge of a non-trivial endomorphism of E_0. Further work, like [QKL+21], improves the range of parameters susceptible to these attacks, but still requires a non-trivial endomorphism.

For SIKE's NIST submission, such an endomorphism is easy to find because the starting curve $E_0 = E_{\mathrm{NIST}}$ is defined over $\mathbb{F}_p$. So in [Cos21], Costello argues that if this line of "torsion points" attacks is improved to reach the SIKE parameters submitted to NIST, a preventive measure would be to switch the starting elliptic curve E_0 to a "random" one, so that Eve has no prior information on its endomorphism ring. (This was not considered for SIKE's submission because it would involve either a trusted multipartite setup to build E_0 or for Alice to first walk a random path and publish a "random" E_0, hence adding some complexity to the key exchange.)

The second key breakthrough was in the recent attacks by [CD22, MM22] by Castryck–Decru and Maino–Martindale respectively (we refer to Sects. 1.5 and 5 for more details on these two articles). They both, independently, had the beautiful idea that it is possible to extend the range of parameters susceptible to "torsion points" attack by constructing a N_A-isogeny F in dimension 2, on a product of two supersingular curves. Indeed, going up in dimension largely opens up the range of isogeny we can construct explicitly.

They exploit the following lemma, due to Kani in [Kan97] as part of his deep work on classifying covers $C \to E$ of elliptic curves by genus 2 curves: given a N_B-isogeny $\phi_B : E_0 \to E_B$ and an a-isogeny $\alpha : E_0 \to E'$, with a prime to N_B, it is possible to build an explicit $(a + N_B)$-isogeny $F : E_0 \times E'' \to E_B \times E'$

in dimension 2 (see Lemma 6 for a generalisation to dimension g). This means, assuming $N_A > N_B$, that Eve can break SIDH as long as she can find an isogeny from E_0 of degree $a = N_A - N_B$.

This is in particular the case whenever a is smooth, and is the focus of Maino and Martindale's article (Castryck and Decru also consider this case briefly). While the probability to get a smooth a is small, tweaking the parameters can increase it, and subsequent analysis by De Feo showed that this gives a (heuristic) subexponential $L(1/2)$ attack. In particular, torsion points attacks can apply even to "random curves"!

Castryck and Decru furthermore exploit the fact that for the NIST submission, the curve $E_0 = E_{\text{NIST}}$ is either $y^2 = x^3 + x$ or $y^2 = x^3 + 6x^2 + x$. It has an explicit endomorphism $2i$, hence it is easy to construct an a-isogeny α (which can be evaluated efficiently) whenever $a = a_1^2 + 4a_2^2$. In particular, they obtain a (heuristic) polynomial time attack for this specific E_0 (assuming the factorisation of a is precomputed).

Our current work stems from the fact that it is easy to extend Kani's lemma to dimension g abelian varieties (see Sect. 3). Namely, from an a-isogeny and a N_B-isogeny in dimension g (with a prime to N_B), we can build an explicit $(a + N_B)$-isogeny in dimension $2g$. We will apply this to the diagonal embedding of ϕ_B to $E_0^g \to E_B^g$, this is still an N_B-isogeny, so it remains to find an a-isogeny on E_0^g, where $a = N_A - N_B$. We then exploit that even if we do not know End(E_0), on E_0^2 we can always build endomorphisms of the form $\alpha = \begin{pmatrix} a_1 & a_2 \\ -a_2 & a_1 \end{pmatrix}$, which give $(a_1^2 + a_2^2)$-endomorphisms. Hence we get a dimension $2g$ attack, $g = 2$, whenever $a = a_1^2 + a_2^2$ (eventually after parameter tweaks).

The general case stems from the fact that an integer is always a sum of four squares: $a = a_1^2 + a_2^2 + a_3^2 + a_4^2$, from which we can then build an a-endomorphism α on E_0^4 in dimension $g = 4$, hence get a dimension $2g = 8$ attack. The fact that there always exist a-endomorphisms on A^4 for any abelian variety A and any integer a was first used by Zarhin in [Zar74] to show that $A^4 \times \widehat{A}^4$ always has a principal polarisation, and is known as "Zarhin's trick" or the "quaternion trick".

We remark also that unlike the decomposition of a as a sum of two squares, which requires its factorisation, the decomposition as a sum of four squares can be done in (random) polynomial time, see Remark 1. It is then easy to build by hand a $(N_B + a)$-endomorphism on $E_0^4 \times E_B^4$, we will see in Sect. 2 that

$$F = \begin{pmatrix} \alpha & \widetilde{\phi}_B \\ -\phi_B & \widetilde{\alpha} \end{pmatrix} \text{ fits.}$$

As mentioned above, this endomorphism F can be seen as a special case of the dimension g generalisation in Sect. 3 of Kani's lemma to build isogenies on product of abelian varieties. But it can also be seen as a variant of Petit's endomorphism to higher dimension. Indeed, if F_1 is a d_1-endomorphism and F_2 is a d_2-endomorphism, then $F_1 + F_2$ is a $(d_1 + d_2)$-endomorphism whenever $\widetilde{F_1}F_2 = -\widetilde{F_2}F_1$. Our dimension 8 endomorphism is the case $F = F_1 + F_2$ with

$F_1 = \begin{pmatrix} \alpha & 0 \\ 0 & \widetilde{\alpha} \end{pmatrix}$ an a-endomorphism and $F_2 = \begin{pmatrix} 0 & \widetilde{\phi}_B \\ -\phi_B & 0 \end{pmatrix}$, a N_B-endomorphism.
Petit's endomorphism $F = \widetilde{\phi}_B \circ \gamma \circ \phi_B + [d]$ is the case where $F_1 = \widetilde{\phi}_B \circ \gamma \circ \phi_B$ is antisymmetric (i.e., of trace 0, i.e., $\widetilde{F_1} = -F_1$) and $F_2 = [d]$ is symmetric (i.e., $\widetilde{F_2} = F_2$), with $F_1 F_2 = F_2 F_1$.

1.5   Complexities of the Different Attacks

The article by Castryck and Decru was first posted on 2022-07-30, with only minor revisions since. As mentioned above, this article mainly focuses on the dimension 2 attack when $E_0 = E_{\text{NIST}}$ is NIST's starting curve, i.e., contains the endomorphism $2i$. In this case they obtain a heuristic polynomial time algorithm (with no explicit bound).

The heuristic is due to two reasons. First in [CD22], Castryck and Decru guess a starting path for ϕ_B and use F as an oracle to know if the guess was correct or not, then they iterate the process. The heuristic is then that if a wrong path is guessed, the codomain of F will be a Jacobian of a superspecial curve rather than a product of two supersingular elliptic curves. Assuming heuristically that the codomain of F for a wrong guess is uniform among all superspecial surfaces, the probability of a mistake is $\approx 1/p$, hence negligible. But, as first noticed by Maino and Martindale in [MM22], and also independently by Oudompheng [Oud22], Petit, and Wesolowski [Wes22b], the isogeny F allows one to directly recover ϕ_B. This gives a more direct attack (no need to guess many isogenies), and removes the first heuristic.

The second reason is that for their attack to work on the starting curve $E_0 = E_{\text{NIST}}$, they need $a = N_A - N_B$ to be of the form $a = a_1^2 + 4a_2^2$. In this case they can build an a-isogeny α which can be evaluated in $O(\log a)$ arithmetic operations. For a uniform integer less than x, the probability to be decomposed in this form is roughly $1/\sqrt{\log x}$ (see Remark 9), so assuming that parameter tweaks behave like uniform integers, we may assume that we can tweak the parameters without increasing their size too much in such a way that the attack can apply. Also this decomposition (which is a precomputation) supposes access to a factorisation oracle; hence is in polynomial time only in the quantum model.

This second heuristic (and the need for factorisation) can be removed (under GRH) using work by Wesolowski [Wes22b] explaining how to directly build a $N_A - N_B$-isogeny α when $\text{End}(E_0)$ is known. More precisely, Wesolowski builds an ideal I_α of norm a which represents α, and evaluating α on a point is done by using [FKM+22, Lemma 3.3]. Constructing this isogeny and then evaluating it on a point can be done in polynomial time, but there is no clear complexity bound as of yet. But the evaluation of α on a basis of $E_0[N_A]$ can be seen as a polynomial time precomputation, depending on E_0. Via this precomputation, the attack then reduces to evaluating a N_A-isogeny F in dimension 2.

We mention also that Castryck and Decru implemented their attack in Magma (so far this is the only publicly available implemented attack), which showed that it was practical, breaking Microsoft's and the NIST submission parameters. The timings were then considerably improved in an open source reimplementation in Sage [POP+22], where Oudompheng implemented the direct isogeny recovery of [MM22] and the extended parameter tweaks of [Rob22a] (see Sect. 5).

The article by Maino and Martindale was posted on 2022-08-08, with a second major revision on 2022-08-25, fixing an error where their initial endomorphism candidate did not respect the product polarisations. The second version uses the correct matrix from [Rob22a, Oud22, Wes22b]. They focus on the case where $\text{End}(E_0)$ is not known, which was also briefly investigated by Castryck and Decru. The first version does not contain a complexity estimate, but in the second version they use an analysis due to De Feo which shows that, using slightly more general parameter tweaks, they have a heuristic subexponential $L(1/2)$ attack. They then incorporated work by Panny, Pope and Wesolowski in their submission to eurocrypt [MMP+23].

This current article [Rob22a] was first posted on 2022-08-11 focusing mainly on the polynomial time dimension 8 attack (and explaining very briefly the dimension 4 attack). It was followed by revisions expanding on the dimension 4 attack and its complexity, and on giving a general dimension $2g$ framework.

At the time of its posting, [Rob22a] was the only one containing a precise complexity estimate, and the only available polynomial time attack (with or without random starting curve) with no heuristics. Due to the work of Wesolowski and De Feo mentioned above, and the improved parameters tweaks of Sect. 6, the current situation (as far as I am aware) is now as follows:

- When $E_0 = E_{\text{NIST}}$ is NIST's starting curve, the attack of Castryck-Decru using the endomorphism $2i$ (as implemented in [POP+22]) is in heuristic polynomial time. We refer to Proposition 3 for a complexity analysis: We can find a decomposition $N_A = (b_1 + 4b_2^2)N_B/D + (a_1 + 4a_2^2)$ where D is a divisor of N_B heuristically of magnitude $\Theta(\log N_B)$ in $O(\log^3 N_A)$ binary operations for this precomputation step. The attack is then in $\widetilde{O}(D \log N_A \ell_A^2) = \widetilde{O}(\log^2 N_A \ell_A^2)$ arithmetic operations. We can reduce the magnitude of D to $\Theta(\sqrt{\log N_B})$ (heuristically) at the price of doing $O(\sqrt{\log N_B})$ factorisation calls in the precomputation. The attack is then in $\widetilde{O}(\log^{1.5} N_A \ell_A^2)$ arithmetic operations.
  (In their version updated for the submission to eurocrypt, Castryck and Decru argue in [CD22, Sect. 10] that their attack is in heuristic subexponential time $L(1/4)$ when using only the endomorphism $2i$, and that they need to consider more general endomorphisms to obtain an heuristic polynomial time attack. This discrepancy with our analysis above comes from the fact that we use more general parameter tweaks.)
  Using [Wes22b], the dimension 2 attack can also apply to any elliptic curve with known endomorphism ring in proven polynomial time under GRH (but the exact degree has not been bounded yet). More precisely, after a polynomial time precomputation to construct the a-isogeny α and its action on a basis of $E_0[N_A]$, the attack is the same as in Theorem 1 except that F is computed in dimension 2, hence its evaluation costs $\widetilde{O}(\log N_A \ell_A^2)$ arithmetic operations in $\mathbb{F}_q$, see Proposition 4.

- When E_0 is a "random" curve, the dimension 2 attack of Maino and Martindale (and also Castryck and Decru) is in (heuristic) subexponential time $L(1/2)$ [MM22].

  The dimension 4 attack of Sect. 4 is in heuristic polynomial time (because it needs parameter tweaks). The precomputation is very similar to the precomputation done for Castryck-Decru using the endomorphism $2i$ (because both attacks rely on decomposing an integer as a sum of two squares), except that in this case we can also build a N_A^2-isogeny with no added (asymptotic) cost by Sect. 6.4. Under Heuristic 1, the precomputation costs $O(\log^3 N_A)$ binary operations to find a decomposition $N_A^2 = (b_1^2 + 2b_2)^2 N_B + (a_1^2 + a_2^2)$, and then the attack is in $\widetilde{O}(\log N_A \ell_A^4)$ arithmetic operations by Proposition 2. We stress that for the dimension 4 attack the heuristic only concerns the average complexity of finding this decomposition of N_A^2 (provided it exists), not the attack itself.

  The dimension 8 attack of Sect. 2 is in proven polynomial time, and is in $\widetilde{O}(\log N_A \ell_A^8)$ arithmetic operations by Theorem 1. The precomputation step is the decomposition of $N_A - N_B$ as a sum of four squares and can be done in randomized $O(\log^2 N_A)$ binary operations.

  The dimension 8 (resp., 4) attack remains the only proven (resp., heuristic) polynomial time attack for a random curve E_0.

- When $\ell_A = O(1)$ (or even $O(\log \log N_A)$), the dimension 8, dimension 4, and if $\mathrm{End}(E)$ is known, the dimension 2 attacks, all have quasi-linear complexity of $\widetilde{O}(\log N_A)$ arithmetic operations.

  The constants involved will be larger for the higher dimensional attack, however the precomputation of the dimension 8 attack is faster than the precomputation of the dimension 2 attack. Furthermore, in dimension 2, when E has known endomorphisms but is not E_{NIST}, the precomputation step also depends on the starting curve E_0. An implementation is ongoing to compare timings.

1.6 Thanks

Many thanks are due to the persons who commented on the prior versions. Special thanks to Benjamin Wesolowski and Marco Streng. Thanks to the anonymous referees for numerous suggestions to improve the exposition of this paper.

This work was supported by the ANR ANR-19-CE48-0008 project Ciao.

2 Dimension 8 Attack

Since $N_A > N_B$, write $N_A = N_B + a$ for a positive integer $a > 0$. It is harmless to suppose that N_A is prime to N_B, otherwise if $d = \gcd(N_A, N_B)$, we could recover the kernel of a d-isogeny through which ϕ_B factors (since we know its action on $E_0[d] \subset E_0[N_A]$), so we could reduce to solving the problem with new coprime parameters $N_A' = N_A/d$, $N_B' = N_B/d$.

As N_A is prime to N_B, $\gcd(N_A, a) = 1$. Let $M \in M_4(\mathbb{Z})$ be a 4×4 matrix such that $M^T M = a\,\mathrm{Id}$. Explicitly we write $a = a_1^2 + a_2^2 + a_3^2 + a_4^2$ and take

$$M = \begin{pmatrix} a_1 & -a_2 & -a_3 & -a_4 \\ a_2 & a_1 & a_4 & -a_3 \\ a_3 & -a_4 & a_1 & a_2 \\ a_4 & a_3 & -a_2 & a_1 \end{pmatrix},$$

the matrix of the multiplication of $a_1 + a_2 i + a_3 j + a_4 k$ in the standard quaternion algebra $\mathbb{Z}[i,j,k]$ $i^2 = j^2 = k^2 = -1, ij = k$. Let α_0 be the endomorphism on E_0^4 represented by the matrix M. The dual (with respect to the product principal polarisation) $\widetilde{\alpha}_0$ of α_0 is represented by the matrix M^T (since integer multiplications are their own dual), so $\widetilde{\alpha}_0 \alpha_0 = a\,\mathrm{Id}$, hence α_0 is an a-isogeny, which can be evaluated in $O(\log a)$ arithmetic operations. We let α_B be the endomorphism of E_B^4 given by the same matrix M, and by abuse of notation we denote by $\phi_B\,\mathrm{Id} : E_0^4 \to E_B^4$ the diagonal embedding of $\phi_B : E_0 \to E_B$. We remark that since α_0 is given by an integral matrix, it commutes with ϕ_B in the sense that we have the equation: $\phi_B \alpha_0 = \alpha_B \phi_B$:

$$\begin{array}{ccc} E_0^4 & \xrightarrow{\phi_B\,\mathrm{Id}} & E_B^4 \\ \downarrow{\scriptstyle\alpha_0} & & \downarrow{\scriptstyle\alpha_B} \\ E_0^4 & \xrightarrow{\phi_B\,\mathrm{Id}} & E_B^4 \end{array}$$

Lemma 1. *With the notations above, let* $F = \begin{pmatrix} \alpha_0 & \widetilde{\phi}_B\,\mathrm{Id} \\ -\phi_B\,\mathrm{Id} & \widetilde{\alpha}_B \end{pmatrix}$, *where* $\widetilde{\phi}_B$ *is the dual isogeny* $E_B \to E_0$ *of* ϕ_B. *Then* F *is a* N_A-*endomorphism on the 8-dimensional abelian variety* $X = E_0^4 \times E_B^4$.

Proof. This is a special case of Lemma 6 in Sect. 3.2 below. We give a direct proof: since the dual $\widetilde{F}$ of F is given by $\widetilde{F} = \begin{pmatrix} \widetilde{\alpha}_0 & -\widetilde{\phi}_B\,\mathrm{Id} \\ \phi_B\,\mathrm{Id} & \alpha_B \end{pmatrix}$ by Lemma 3 in Sect. 3.1 below, we compute

$$\widetilde{F}F = F\widetilde{F} = \begin{pmatrix} N_B + a & 0 \\ 0 & N_B + a \end{pmatrix} = N_A\,\mathrm{Id}.$$

Hence F is a N_A-isogeny on X (with respect to the product polarisations). □

As in Sect. 1.4, since Bob reveals the action of ϕ_B on a basis of the N_A-torsion, the action of F on the N_A-torsion is explicit, hence we can recover its kernel. We can also directly recover $\mathrm{Ker}\,F$ as follows:

Lemma 2. *Let* (P_1, P_2) *be a basis of* $E_0[N_A]$. *The kernel of* F *is given by the 8 generators* $(g_1, \ldots, g_8) = \{(\widetilde{\alpha}_0(P), (\phi_B\,\mathrm{Id})(P))\}$ *for* $P = (P_1, 0, 0, 0)$, $(P_2, 0, 0, 0)$, $(0, P_1, 0, 0)$, $(0, P_2, 0, 0)$, $(0, 0, P_1, 0)$, $(0, 0, P_2, 0)$, $(0, 0, 0, P_1)$, $(0, 0, 0, P_2)$. *These generators can be computed in* $O(\log a)$ *arithmetic operations in* $E_0(\mathbb{F}_q)$.

Proof. The kernel is given by the image of $\widetilde{F}$ on $X[N_A]$. Since a is prime to N_A, by Lemma 6 in Sect. 3.2 below, Ker F is exactly the image of $\widetilde{F}$ on $E_0^4[N_A] \times 0$:
$$\text{Ker } F = \{(\widetilde{\alpha}_0(P), (\phi_B \text{ Id})(P)) \mid P \in E_0^4[N_A]\}. \qquad \square$$

We can now prove Theorem 1.

Proof (of Theorem 1). Since we have generators of the kernel of F, we can compute F (on any point $P \in X(\mathbb{F}_q)$) using an isogeny algorithm in dimension 8. We decompose the N_A-endomorphism F as a chain of ℓ-isogenies for ℓ the prime factors of N_A. If ℓ_A is the largest prime divisor of N_A, the complexity of the first ℓ_A-isogeny computation will first be $\widetilde{O}(\log N_A)$ arithmetic operations in $A(\mathbb{F}_q)$ to compute the multiples $\frac{N_A}{\ell_A} g_i$, followed by the individual ℓ_A-isogeny computations on P and the g_i. These isogeny computations cost $O(\ell_A^8)$ operations over $\mathbb{F}_q$ using [LR23]. Since we compute a composition of at most $O(\log N_A)$ isogenies, the total cost of evaluating F on P is $O(\log^2 N_A + \log N_A \ell_A^8 \log \ell_A)$. This naive method uses $O(\log N_A)$ ℓ-isogeny calls where $\ell \mid N_A$, and multiplications which cost $O(\log^2 N_A)$ in total. The optimised method of [DJP14, Sect. 4.2.2] shows that by increasing the number of isogeny calls to $\widetilde{O}(\log N_A)$, the multiplication cost can be reduced to $\widetilde{O}(\log N_A)$ multiplications by $\ell \mid N_A$. This optimised version thus costs $\widetilde{O}(\ell_A^8 \log N_A + \ell_A \log N_A) = \widetilde{O}(\ell_A^8 \log N_A)$. (Note that since a ℓ-isogeny in dimension 8 is going to be much more expensive than a multiplication by ℓ, for practical attacks it will be important to apply the optimised *weighted* strategy of [DJP14, Sect. 4.2.2] rather than their *balanced* strategy.)

Thus we can evaluate F on any point of X, so we can evaluate ϕ_B or $\widetilde{\phi}_B$ on any point of E_0 (resp., E_B). This is enough to recover the kernel of ϕ_B on E_0, this is a special case of Lemma 5 and Remark 5 in Sect. 3.1 below. We can give a direct proof: if Ker $\phi_B \subset E_0[N_B](\mathbb{F}_q)$ and we are given a basis (R_1, R_2) of $E_0[N_B](\mathbb{F}_q)$ (we allow the possibility for R_2 to be 0 if $E_0[N_B](\mathbb{F}_q)$ is cyclic), we can compute $\phi_B(R_1), \phi_B(R_2)$ in two calls to the evaluation of F. We can then solve a DLP to recover a minimal linear relation between $\phi_B(R_1)$ and $\phi_B(R_2)$ from which we obtain a generator for the kernel of ϕ_B. The DLP costs $\widetilde{O}(\ell_B^{1/2} \log N_B)$ arithmetic operations by Lemma 4 below.

We also remark that if $E_B[N_B]$ is rational, we have an alternative strategy to recover Ker ϕ_B. Indeed it is the image of $\widetilde{\phi}_B$ on $E_B[N_B]$. So if (Q_1, Q_2) is a basis of $E_B[N_B]$, we compute $Q_i' = \widetilde{\phi}_B(Q_i)$ by evaluating F on the point $(0, 0, 0, 0, Q_i, 0, 0, 0)$, and the kernel of ϕ_B is generated by whichever Q_i' has order N_B. Checking the order costs $O(\log N_B \log \log N_B)$ operations in $E_0(\mathbb{F}_q)$ using a binary tree.

This concludes the complexity analysis of Theorem 1. $\qquad \square$

Remark 3. The isogeny computations in [LR23, BCR10, Som21] use a (level $m = 4$ or $m = 2$) theta model of X, which we can compute as the (fourfold) product theta structure of the theta models of E_0 and E_B. It is also well known how to switch between the theta model and the Weierstrass model on an elliptic curve, and it is not hard to extend the conversion to the product of elliptic curves, since the product theta structure is given by the Segre embedding. The arithmetic on the theta models can be done in $O(1)$ arithmetic operations in a $O(1)$-extension of $\mathbb{F}_q$ (if $8 \mid N_A N_B$ the theta model will already be rational). However the big $O()$ notation hides an exponential complexity in the dimension g. In dimension 8 and level $m = 4$, the theta model uses 2^{16} coordinates, so we would need in practice to switch to the *Kummer* model by working in level $m = 2$ which "only" requires 2^8 coordinates. This is another reason why we would prefer to compute an endomorphism in dimension $g = 4$ rather than $g = 8$: in dimension 4 we would only need 2^8 coordinates in level $m = 4$, or 2^4 coordinates in level $m = 2$.

Finally, there is one technical difficulty when working with the theta model in level m: it involves choosing a level m symmetric theta structure. Even if we start with a product theta structure on $E_0^4 \times E_B^4$, when computing F we will not generally end with a product theta structure. So we need to correct the level m structure we end up with by a symplectic action to get a product structure: this is important to project back to E_0. We can either try all of them (this is a $O(1)$ operation, but with a very big constant since we are in dimension 8). A much better strategy, if N_A is prime to m, is to guess the image of $E_0[m]$ by ϕ_B. Since we know the image of α, if our guess is correct, this directly gives us the symplectic matrix we need to correct our theta structure with. So this greatly lowers the number of matrices we need to test. If m is not prime to N_A, we need to guess the image of $E_0[mN_A]$ under ϕ_B instead; recall that we already know the image of $E_0[N_A]$, so we also have few guesses to make. In fact, if $m \mid N_A$ we can also use Sect. 6.4 to write F as a (N_A/m)-isogeny followed by an m-isogeny, and in this case we have enough information to directly know how to glue the theta structures together in the middle.

Remark 4. It is immediate to generalise Theorem 1 to recover a N_B-isogeny ϕ_B between abelian varieties E_0, E_B of dimension g. The attack reduces to computing one N_A-isogeny in dimension $8g$ (or eventually $4g$ or even $2g$ if the parameters allow for it).

The same proof as above holds; the complexity of evaluating the dimension $8g$ N_A-isogeny will be $\widetilde{O}(\log N_A \ell^{8g})$ arithmetic operations using [LR23] and the fast smooth isogeny computation of [DJP14, Sect. 4.2.2]. We can then recover $\operatorname{Ker} \phi_B$ using Lemma 5 below.

3   Description of the Dimension $2g$ Attack

In this section we generalize the construction of Sect. 2, which will be used in Sects. 4 and 5 to mount an attack in dimensions 4 and 2.

3.1 N-isogenies

Definition 1. *A N-isogeny $f : (A, \lambda_A) \to (B, \lambda_B)$ of principally polarised abelian varieties is an isogeny such that $f^* \lambda_B := \hat{f} \circ \lambda_B \circ f = N \lambda_A$, where $\hat{f} : \hat{B} \to \hat{A}$ is the dual isogeny. Letting $\tilde{f} = \lambda_A^{-1} \hat{f} \lambda_B$ be the dual isogeny $\tilde{f} : B \to A$ of f with respect to the principal polarisations, this condition is equivalent to $\tilde{f}f = N$.*

If Θ_B is a divisor associated to λ_B, then since $\lambda_B : P \mapsto t_P^* \Theta_B - \Theta_B \in \text{Pic}^0(B) = \widehat{B}$ (where t_P is the translation by P), we see that $f^* \lambda_B$ is the polarisation associated to $f^* \Theta_B$, so f is a N-isogeny exactly when this polarisation is equal to $N \lambda_A$.

If Θ_A is a divisor associated to λ_A, sections of $m\Theta_A$ give coordinates on A (if $m \geq 3$ we get a projective embedding by Lefschetz' theorem). Given a suitable model of $(A, m\Theta_A)$, a representation of the kernel $K = \text{Ker } f$ of a N-isogeny f (for instance coordinates for its generators), and the coordinates of a point $P \in A$, a N-isogeny algorithm will output a suitable model of $(B, m\Theta_B)$ and the coordinates of the image $f(P)$ in this model. For instance, the N-isogeny algorithm from [LR23] uses a theta model of level $m = 2$ or $m = 4$, and in dimension g can compute the image of an N-isogeny in $O(N^g)$ arithmetic operations over the base field (where the theta model is defined).

Note that in general, for a N-isogeny algorithm, we only have the kernel K and the source polarised abelian variety (A, Θ_A). We first need to check that the divisor $N\Theta_A$ descends through the isogeny $f : A \to B = A/K$. This implies that K must be a subgroup of the kernel of the polarisation $N\lambda_A : A \to \widehat{A}$ associated to $N\Theta_A$. And by descent theory [Mum66, Proposition 1 p. 291]; [Mum70, Theorem 2 p. 231], the descents of $N\Theta_A$ correspond exactly to level subgroups $\widetilde{K}$ of K in Mumford's theta group $G(N\Theta_A)$. Hence $N\Theta_A$ descends if and only if K is isotropic for the commutator pairing of $G(N\Theta_A)$ (and the descent Θ_B will be of degree one if and only if K is maximal isotropic by a standard degree computation). Mumford proves in [Mum70, (5) p. 229] that this commutator pairing is yet another incarnation of the Weil pairing. So the descent condition is thus equivalent to K being maximal isotropic for e_{N,Θ_A} in $A[N]$, as is well known (see e.g., [Kan97, Proposition 1.1]). Such a K is usually the entry point of a N-isogeny algorithm.

Our current situation is different: we already have a target codomain B with a polarisation λ_B, and we want $N\Theta_A$ to descend to λ_B, not just any other principal polarisation λ_B' (of which there will be many, see Remark 7). So it does not suffice to check that $\text{Ker } f$ is maximal isotropic for the Weil pairing, we want $f^* \Theta_B \simeq N\Theta_A$ (isomorphism up to algebraic equivalence), i.e., $\widetilde{f} \circ f = N$.

If this condition is satisfied, we know that $N\Theta_A$ descend, hence by the above discussion we automatically know that $\text{Ker } f$ is maximal isotropic. Another way to see that without invoking descent theory is to use the fact that $\text{Ker } f = \text{Im } \widehat{f} \mid B[N]$, and that since $\widehat{f}$ is the dual of f for the Weil pairings $e_{A,N}$ on $(A \times \widehat{A})[N]$ and $e_{B,N}$ on $(B \times \widehat{B})[N]$, then $\widetilde{f}$ is the dual of f for the Weil pairings $e_{\lambda_A,N}$ on $(A \times A)[N]$ and $e_{\lambda_B,N}$ on $(B \times B)[N]$. In particular, if $x, y \in \text{Ker } f$, $x = \widetilde{f}(x'), y = \widetilde{f}(y')$ for $x', y' \in B[N]$, so $e_{\lambda_A,N}(x,y) = e_{\lambda_A,N}(\widetilde{f}(x'), \widetilde{f}(y')) = e_{\lambda_B,N}(x', f \circ \widetilde{f}(y')) = e_{\lambda_B,N}(x', Ny') = 1$.

We need the following standard Lemma:

Lemma 3. *If* $F = \begin{pmatrix} a & b \\ c & d \end{pmatrix} : (A, \lambda_A) \times (B, \lambda_B) \rightarrow (C, \lambda_C) \times (D, \lambda_D)$, *then for the product polarisations on* $A \times B$ *and* $C \times D$, $\widetilde{F} = \begin{pmatrix} \widetilde{a} & \widetilde{c} \\ \widetilde{b} & \widetilde{d} \end{pmatrix}$.

Proof. Recall that we have a canonical isomorphism $\hat{A} \simeq \mathrm{Pic}^0(A)$, and that under this isomorphism the dual of f is given by $\hat{f} = f^*$. This shows that $\hat{F} : \hat{C} \times \hat{D} \rightarrow \hat{A} \times \hat{B}$ is given by $\hat{F} = \begin{pmatrix} \hat{a} & \hat{c} \\ \hat{b} & \hat{d} \end{pmatrix}$ (see e.g., [EGM12, Proposition 11.28]). Since the product polarisations act component by component by definition (see e.g., the proof of [BL04, Corollary 5.3.6] or the proof of [Kan16, Proposition 61]), we then get that $\widetilde{F} = \begin{pmatrix} \widetilde{a} & \widetilde{c} \\ \widetilde{b} & \widetilde{d} \end{pmatrix}$. $\qquad\square$

We will also use the fact that once we have evaluated an isogeny on a basis of the N-torsion it is easy to evaluate it on any other N-torsion point:

Lemma 4. *Let* $f : A \rightarrow B$ *be an isogeny between abelian varieties. Assume that the N-torsion of A is rational and that we are given a basis* $(P_1, \ldots P_{2g})$ *of it. Then given the evaluation $f(P_i)$ of all P_i, it is possible to evaluate f on a point $P \in A[N]$ in time $\widetilde{O}(\log N \ell_N^{1/2})$ arithmetic operations, where ℓ_N denotes the largest prime divisor of N.*

Proof. Given a point $P \in A[N]$, we can evaluate the Weil pairing $e_N(P, P_i)$ in $O(\log N)$ arithmetic operations (this assumes we work over a model which can compute the Weil pairing; this will be the case in the theta model by [LR10, LR15]).

From the Weil pairing matrix of the $e_N(P_i, P_j)$, we can first do $O(g^2)$ discrete logarithm computations from a N-th root of unity ζ to get a matrix with coefficients in $\mathbb{Z}/N\mathbb{Z}$. By linear algebra over $\mathbb{Z}/N\mathbb{Z}$, it is easy to compute a symplectic basis $(a_1, \ldots, a_g, a'_1, \ldots a'_{2g})$ of the N-torsion, along with the values of f on this basis. Using a naive linear algebra algorithm, this can be done in $O(g^3 \log N)$. The dominant cost will be the discrete logarithms.

The Pohlig-Hellman algorithm [PH78] has complexity $O(E \log N \ell_N^{1/2})$ operations in A, where if $N = \prod \ell_i^{e_i}$, $E = \sum e_i$. The iterative version of Pohlig-Hellman's algorithm which increases the current exponent e in the ℓ_i-discrete logarithm by 1 at each step, can be replaced by a Newton like version which double the precision. This faster variant, described in [Sho09, Sect. 11.2.3], has complexity[2] $\widetilde{O}(\log N \ell_N^{1/2})$.

Given the symplectic basis, one can decompose a point P in this basis by $O(g)$ calls to the Weil pairing and discrete logarithms. Evaluating $f(P)$ can thus be done in $\widetilde{O}(\log N \ell_N^{1/2})$. If $P = \sum_{i=1}^g \lambda_i a_i + \lambda'_i a'_i$, then $f(P) = \sum_{i=1}^g (\lambda_i f(a_i) + \lambda'_i f(a'_i))$. $\qquad\square$

---

[2] Since we use the Weil pairing to reduce to DLPs over $\mathbb{F}_q^*$, the index calculus method gives an algorithm subexponential in ℓ_N rather than in $\widetilde{O}(\ell_N^{1/2})$. But in our applications ℓ_N will be small, so the generic algorithm will be faster in our case.

We can use Lemma 4 to recover the kernel of a N-isogeny given its evaluation on a basis of the N-torsion.

Lemma 5. *Let g be a fixed integer, and $f : A \to B$ be a N-isogeny in dimension g and $\tilde{f} : B \to A$ the contragredient isogeny. Assume that we are given a rational basis $P_1, \dots, P_{2g}$ and $Q_1, \dots, Q_{2g}$ of $A[N]$ and $B[N]$ respectively, and either the images of the basis P_i by f or the images of the basis Q_i by $\tilde{f}$. Then it is possible to recover a basis of $\operatorname{Ker} f$ in $\widetilde{O}(\log N \ell_N^{1/2})$ arithmetic operations.*

If $\operatorname{Ker} f$ is of rank g and we are given the image of the basis Q_i by $\tilde{f}$, it is also possible to recover a basis of $\operatorname{Ker} f$ in $\widetilde{O}(\log N)$ arithmetic operations.

Proof. Assume first we are given the images $f(P_i)$. Since f is an isogeny, $\operatorname{Ker} f \subset A[N]$. Since we are given a rational basis of $B[N]$, we can first transform this into a symplectic basis $(b_1, \dots, b_g, b_1', \dots b_g')$ as in the proof of Lemma 4. We can express $f(P_i)$ in this basis using the Weil pairing and discrete logarithms, and solve a linear system over $\mathbb{Z}/N\mathbb{Z}$. The discrete logarithms will dominate the complexity analysis and cost $\widetilde{O}(\log N \ell_N^{1/2})$. We remark that in this situation, we do not require a full rational basis of $A[N]$, we just need that $\operatorname{Ker} f \subset A[N](\mathbb{F}_q)$ and to have a basis of $A[N](\mathbb{F}_q)$.

If we are given the images $\tilde{f}(Q_i)$, then since f is a N-isogeny, $\operatorname{Ker} f = \operatorname{Im} \tilde{f} \mid B[N]$, so the $\tilde{f}(Q_i)$ generate $\operatorname{Ker} f$. Like above, using discrete logarithms (via the Weil pairing), we can then extract a basis of $\operatorname{Ker} f$ by linear algebra.

If $\operatorname{Ker} f$ is of rank g, we can also find a basis of $\operatorname{Ker} f$ by finding a subset of g points of the basis Q_i such that the $\tilde{f}(Q_i)$ generate the full kernel. We write the $2g \times 2g$ Weil pairing matrix of the P_i with the $\tilde{f}(Q_i)$, and we look for a $2g \times g$ submatrix that generates the full image. This reduces to finding a $g \times g$ submatrix whose determinant δ is of primitive order N.

If $\omega(N)$ is the number of distinct prime divisors of N, checking if $\delta^{N/\ell} \neq 1$ for each prime $\ell \mid N$ costs $O(\omega(N) \log N)$ arithmetic operations. This can be improved to $O(\log N \log \log N)$ using a binary tree. Note however that this last method has a complexity exponential in g.   □

Remark 5. Let $f : A \to B$ be a N-isogeny between abelian varieties in dimension g whose kernel if of rank g. If $\operatorname{Ker} f \subset A(\mathbb{F}_q)$ and we are given the image of f on a basis of $A[N](\mathbb{F}_q)$, but we are not given a basis of $B[N]$, we can no longer reduce to DLPs over $\mathbb{F}_q^*$ via the Weil pairing so we need to use a multidimensional DLP. By [Sut11], we can recover a basis of $\operatorname{Ker} f$ in $\widetilde{O}(\log N \ell_N^{g/2})$.

Likewise, if $\operatorname{Ker} f = \tilde{f}(B[N](\mathbb{F}_q))$ (this holds if $B[N] \subset B(\mathbb{F}_q)$ or more generally if the N-Tate pairing is trivial on $\operatorname{Ker} f \times \operatorname{Ker} f$), and we are given the image of $\tilde{f}$ on a basis of $B[N](\mathbb{F}_q)$, we obtain generators of $\operatorname{Ker} f$ from which we can extract a basis in $\widetilde{O}(\log N \ell_N^{g/2})$ by [Sut11].

3.2   Isogeny Diamonds

The endomorphism F of Sect. 2 is a particular case of a construction due to Kani for $g = 1$ [Kan97, Sect. 2, Proof of Theorem 2.3], which generalises immediately to $g > 1$.

We define a (d_1, d_2)-isogeny diamond as a decomposition of a $d_1 d_2$-isogeny $f : A \to B$ between principally polarised abelian varieties of dimension g into two different decompositions $f = f_1' \circ f_1 = f_2' \circ f_2$ where f_1 is a d_1-isogeny and f_2 is a d_2-isogeny. Then f_1' will be a d_2-isogeny and f_2' a d_1-isogeny:

$$
\begin{array}{ccc}
A & \xrightarrow{f_1} & A_1 \\
\downarrow{\scriptstyle f_2} & & \downarrow{\scriptstyle f_1'} \\
A_2 & \xrightarrow{f_2'} & B
\end{array}
$$

Lemma 6 (Kani). *Let $f = f_1' \circ f_1 = f_2' \circ f_2$ be a (d_1, d_2)-isogeny diamond as above. Then $F = \begin{pmatrix} f_1 & \widetilde{f_1'} \\ -f_2 & \widetilde{f_2'} \end{pmatrix}$ is a d-isogeny $F : A \times B \to A_1 \times A_2$ where $d = d_1 + d_2$.*

Its kernel is given by the image of $\widetilde{F} = \begin{pmatrix} \widetilde{f_1} & -\widetilde{f_2} \\ f_1' & f_2' \end{pmatrix}$ on $(A_1 \times A_2)[d]$. If d_1 is prime to d_2, we also have $\mathrm{Ker}\, F = \{(\widetilde{f_1}(P), f_1'(P)) \mid P \in A_1[d]\}$, the kernel is thus of rank $2g$.

Proof. We check, using Lemma 3, that $\widetilde{F}F = d\,\mathrm{Id}$. Furthermore if d_1 is prime to d_2, then the restriction of $\widetilde{F}$ to $A_1[d] \times \{0\}$ is injective, hence its image spans the full kernel since $\#A_1[d] = d^{2g}$. $\qquad\square$

The matrix F from Sect. 2 is a special case of Lemma 6 where $A = E_0^4$, $B = E_B^4$ and F is actually an endomorphism.

3.3   Description of the Attack

Write $N_A = N_B + a$, $a > 0$. Suppose that we can find an explicit a-isogeny $\alpha_0 : E_0^g \to X_0$. Then we can consider the following pushout:

$$
\begin{array}{ccc}
E_0^g & \xrightarrow{\phi_B} & E_B^g \\
\downarrow{\scriptstyle \alpha_0} & & \downarrow{\scriptstyle \alpha_B} \\
X_0 & \xrightarrow{\phi_B'} & X_B
\end{array}
$$

Hence we have the following isogeny diamond

$$
\begin{array}{ccc}
X_0 & \xrightarrow{\widetilde{\alpha_0}} & E_0^g \\
\downarrow{\scriptstyle \phi_B'} & & \downarrow{\scriptstyle \phi_B} \\
X_B & \xrightarrow{\widetilde{\alpha_B}} & E_B^g
\end{array}
$$

so by Lemma 6, $F = \begin{pmatrix} \widetilde{\alpha_0} & \widetilde{\phi_B} \\ -\phi'_B & \alpha_B \end{pmatrix}$ is a N_A-isogeny $F : X_0 \times E_B^g \to E_0^g \times X_B$. In particular, $\operatorname{Ker} F$ is the image of $\widetilde{F}$ on $(E_0^g \times X_B)[N_A]$. Since a is prime to N_B, it is also the image of $\widetilde{F}$ on $E_0^g[N_A] \times 0$: $\operatorname{Ker} F = \{(\alpha_0(P), \phi_B(P)) \mid P \in E_0^g[N_A]\}$. In particular, we don't need to build X_B, we will recover it when evaluating F. Evaluating F gives the evaluation of ϕ_B which we can use to recover the kernel of ϕ_B.

Notice that if $\alpha_0 : E_0 \to E'$ is an a-isogeny, then $\operatorname{diag}(\alpha_0) : E_0^g \to X_0 := E'^g$ is also an a-isogeny. So on our product of elliptic curves, we can always compose or precompose with smooth isogenies, see Sect. 6.2.

To increase the parameters susceptible to this attack, we can also postcompose and precompose $\phi_B : E_0^g \to E_B^g$ by isogenies β_1, β_2. Write $N_A = bN_B + a$, $a, b > 0$; eventually applying the parameter tweaks of Sect. 6. Note that since N_A is coprime to N_B, then dividing by $\gcd(N_A, a, b)$ if necessary, we may assume that N_A, a, b are coprime. Write $b = b_1 b_2$, and suppose that we can find an explicit b_1-isogeny $\beta_1 : E_0^g \to Y_0$, a b_2-isogeny $\beta_2 : E_B^g \to Y_B$, and an a-isogeny $\alpha_0 : E_0^g \to X_0$. Let $\gamma = \beta_2 \circ \phi_B \circ \widetilde{\beta_1} : Y_0 \to Y_B$, it is a bN_B-isogeny. Consider the following pushouts,

$$
\begin{array}{ccccccc}
Y_0 & \xleftarrow{\ \beta_1\ } & E_0^g & \xrightarrow{\ \phi_B\ } & E_B^g & \xrightarrow{\ \beta_2\ } & Y_B \\
\downarrow{\scriptstyle \alpha_0'} & & \downarrow{\scriptstyle \alpha_0} & & \downarrow{\scriptstyle \alpha_B} & & \downarrow{\scriptstyle \alpha_B'} \\
Z_0 & \xleftarrow{\ \beta_1'\ } & X_0 & \xrightarrow{\ \phi_B'\ } & X_B & \xrightarrow{\ \beta_2'\ } & Z_B
\end{array}
$$

since a is prime to bN_B, $\gamma' = \beta_2' \circ \phi_B' \circ \widetilde{\beta_1'} : Z_0 \to Z_B$ is a $N_B b$-isogeny and α_0', α_B' are a-isogenies.

We thus have the following isogeny diamond

$$
\begin{array}{ccc}
Z_0 & \xrightarrow{\ \widetilde{\alpha_0'}\ } & Y_0 \\
\downarrow{\scriptstyle \gamma'} & & \downarrow{\scriptstyle \gamma} \\
Z_B & \xrightarrow{\ \widetilde{\alpha_B'}\ } & Y_B
\end{array}
$$

so by Lemma 6, $F = \begin{pmatrix} \widetilde{\alpha_0'} & \widetilde{\gamma} \\ -\gamma' & \alpha_B' \end{pmatrix}$ is a N_A-isogeny $F : Z_0 \times Y_B \to Y_0 \times Z_B$. In particular, $\operatorname{Ker} F$ is the image of $\widetilde{F}$ on $(Y_0 \times Z_B)[N_A]$. Since a is prime to bN_B, it is also the image of $\widetilde{F}$ on $Y_0[N_A] \times 0$: $\operatorname{Ker} F = \{(\alpha_0'(P), \gamma(P)) \mid P \in Y_0[N_A]\}$. Note that as before, this means that we don't need to construct Z_B explicitly, however in this case we need to construct the pushout Z_0.

This allows one to compute F as a smooth N_A-isogeny of dimension $2g$ in time $O(\log^2 N_A + \log N_A \ell_A^{2g})$ by [LR23] or even $\widetilde{O}(\log N_A \ell_A^{2g})$ via the fast isogeny decomposition of [DJP14, Sect. 4.2.2]. We can hence evaluate F on the N_A-torsion to recover the kernel of $\widetilde{F}$, which allows us to evaluate $\widetilde{F}$ too. In particular, we can compute $\gamma = \beta_2 \circ \phi_B \circ \widetilde{\beta_1}$ on any point of Y_0. It remains to recover ϕ_B from γ. Applying $\widetilde{\beta_2}$ and β_1, we can always recover $b\phi_B$, hence we may recover ϕ_B whenever b is prime to N_B. Otherwise, we at least recover a $(N_B/\gcd(b, N_B))$-isogeny through which ϕ_B factors, and we iterate, which is possible as long as $\gcd(b, N_B) < N_B$. Alternatively, since F gives us the evaluation of $\widetilde{\gamma}$, we can recover $b\widetilde{\phi}_B$ by the same method, which is also enough to give the kernel of ϕ_B as long as b is prime to N_B.

In summary we have reduced recovering ϕ_B to evaluating the isogeny F in dimension $2g$:

Theorem 2. *Let $\phi_B : E_0 \to E_B$ be a N_B-isogeny defined over a finite field $\mathbb{F}_q$. Assume that $E_0[N_A] \subset E_0(\mathbb{F}_q)$ and that we are given a basis (P_1, P_2) of $E_0[N_A]$ and the image of ϕ_B on this basis.*

Suppose that we can find $a, b > 0$ such that $N_A = bN_B + a$, with a, b, N_a coprime, $b = b_1 b_2$, and an b_1-isogeny $\beta_1 : E_0^g \to Y_0$, a b_2-isogeny $\beta_2 : E_B^g \to Y_B$, and an a-isogeny $\alpha_0 : E_0^g \to X_0$. Assume furthermore for simplicity that $\gcd(b, N_B) = 1$ (or is small). Let T be a bound on the arithmetic operations required to evaluate β_1, β_2 (and their duals) and the pushout α' of α and β_1 on a basis of the N_A-torsion of E_0^g, E_B^g, Y_0 respectively. Then, there is an algorithm to evaluate ϕ_B on any point $P \in E_0(\mathbb{F}_q)$(resp. $\widetilde{\phi}_B$ on any point in $E_B(\mathbb{F}_q)$) in $O(\ell_A^{2g} \log N_A + \log^2 N_A + T)$ arithmetic operations in $\mathbb{F}_q$, or even in $\widetilde{O}(\ell_A^{2g} \log N_A + T)$.

Remark 6. In the situation of Theorem 2, we will see in Sect. 6 ways to tweak the parameters N_A, N_B to improve our range of parameters which can be decomposed as in the Theorem. Since we can evaluate ϕ_B and $\widetilde{\phi}_B$, we can use Lemma 5 and Remark 5 to recover a generator of its kernel.

We leave to the reader the case where we have an isogeny $\alpha_B : E_B^g \to X_B$ constructed from E_B instead of the isogeny α_0. Note that, using discrete logarithms if needed, we only need to evaluate $\alpha_0, \beta_1, \beta_2$ on a basis of the N_A-torsion of their respective domains. It is thus better to build the isogenies from E_0^g rather than from E_B^g, indeed for α' and β_1 these evaluations can then be seen as a precomputation (involving the parameters and E_0).

Remark 7. In dimension 8, the domain (and codomain) of F is a product of supersingular elliptic curves, so is a superspecial abelian variety. The same is true for the isogeny F in dimension $2g$: since F is a N_A-isogeny with N_A prime to the characteristic of the base field, F, or its decomposition into a product of ℓ-isogenies, preserves the a-number of the intermediate abelian varieties. Hence they have a-number equal to $2g$, so they are still superspecial. By a theorem due to Deligne, Ogus and Shioda [Shi79, Theorem 3.5], they are all isomorphic (without the polarisation!) to E_0^{2g}. So in the decomposition of F we always stay on the same abelian variety E_0^{2g}, except that we gradually change its polarisation. For instance in the dimension 2 attack, we start with a product polarisation but the intermediate polarisations will generically be indecomposable, hence correspond to Jacobians of genus 2 hyperelliptic superspecial curves.

4   Dimension 4 Attack

In dimension 2, we can always write an a-endomorphism on E_0^2 whenever $a = a_1^2 + a_2^2$. So using Sect. 3, we can do a dimension 4 attack whenever we can find $a, b > 0$ such that $N_A = bN_B + a$ and both a and b are a sum of two squares. Note that unlike the decomposition of a as a sum of four squares from Sect. 2, these decompositions into a sum of two squares requires the factorisation of a, b. To increase our probability of success, we can also tweak the parameters N_A and N_B as explained in Sect. 6.

Remark 8. Since we can always prolong α and β by isogenies of smooth degree using Sect. 6.2, we can consider the more general decompositions: $N_A = (b_1^2 + b_2^2)eN_B + (a_1^2 + a_2^2)f$ with e, f sufficiently smooth. But smooth integers are of negligible density compared to sum of two squares, so for simplicity we focus only on the case $e = f = 1$ here.

Theorem 3. *Let $\phi_B : E_0 \to E_B$ be a N_B-isogeny defined over a finite field $\mathbb{F}_q$. Assume that $E_0[N_A] \subset E_0(\mathbb{F}_q)$ and that we are given a basis (P_1, P_2) of $E_0[N_A]$ and the image of ϕ_B on this basis.*

Suppose that we can find $a, b > 0$ such that $N_A = bN_B + a$ with N_A, a, b coprime and a, b can be written as a sum of two squares: $a = a_1^2 + a_2^2$, $b = b_1^2 + b_2^2$. Assume furthermore for simplicity that $\gcd(b, N_B)$ has its odd prime divisors congruent to 1 modulo 4, and if $2 \mid \gcd(b, N_B)$ then $4 \nmid b$.

Then, given the decomposition of a and b as these sums of two squares (e.g., given their factorisations), we can evaluate ϕ_B on any point $P \in E_0(\mathbb{F}_q)$ in time $O(\ell_A^4 \log \ell_A \log N_A + \log^2 N_A)$ arithmetic operations in $\mathbb{F}_q$, or even $\widetilde{O}(\log N_A \ell_A^4)$ with the fast variant of smooth isogeny computation.

As in Remark 6, we can use Lemma 5 and Remark 5 to recover a generator of $\operatorname{Ker}\phi_B$.

Proof. Write $\alpha = \begin{pmatrix} a_1 & -a_2 \\ a_2 & a_1 \end{pmatrix}$, $\beta = \begin{pmatrix} b_1 & -b_2 \\ b_2 & b_1 \end{pmatrix}$. These matrices can be interpreted as endomorphisms α_0 of E_0^2 or α_B of E_B^2 and commute with $\phi_B \operatorname{Id}$: $\beta_B \phi_B \operatorname{Id} = \phi_B \operatorname{Id} \beta_0$, $\alpha_B \phi_B \operatorname{Id} = \phi_B \operatorname{Id} \alpha_0$. Furthermore, $\widetilde{\alpha}\alpha = (a_1^2 + a_2^2) \operatorname{Id}$, so α is an a-endomorphism, and similarly β is a b-endomorphism:

$$
\begin{array}{ccc}
E_0^2 & \xrightarrow{\ \alpha_0\ } & E_0^2 \\
{\scriptstyle \phi_B\beta}\downarrow & & \downarrow{\scriptstyle \phi_B\beta} \\
E_B^2 & \xrightarrow{\ \alpha_B\ } & E_B^2
\end{array}
$$

We can now apply Theorem 2. We can also check directly using Lemma 6 or a direct computation, that $F = \begin{pmatrix} \alpha_0 & \widetilde{\phi_B \operatorname{Id}\beta_B} \\ -\beta_B\phi_B \operatorname{Id} & \widetilde{\alpha_B} \end{pmatrix}$ is a N_A-endomorphism of $E_0^2 \times E_B^2$ with $N_A = a + bN_B$. Its kernel is given by $\operatorname{Ker} F =$

$\{(\widetilde{\alpha_0}(P), \beta_B \phi_B \operatorname{Id}(P)) \mid P \in E_0^2[N_A]\}$. We can thus evaluate F, hence evaluate $\beta_B \phi_B \operatorname{Id} = \phi_B \operatorname{Id} \beta_0$ on any point in $E_0^2(\mathbb{F}_q)$ in $O(\log^2 N_A + \log N_A \ell_A^4)$ arithmetic operations over $\mathbb{F}_q$ by [LR23].

In this situation we can recover more than just $b\phi_B$. Indeed from the matrix $\beta_B \phi_B \operatorname{Id}$ we can directly recover $b_1 \phi_B$ and $b_2 \phi_B$; so if $b' = \gcd(b_1, b_2)$, we can recover $b' \phi_B$ in $O(\log b)$ arithmetic operations on E_B. This means that we can recover the kernel of a $N_B / \gcd(N_B, b')$-isogeny $E_0 \to E'_B$ through which ϕ_B factors. If $\gcd(N_B, b') = 1$ we have directly recovered ϕ_B, otherwise we iterate the process, which is possible as long as $\gcd(N_B, b') < N_B$.

Under the hypothesis of Theorem 3, we have $\gcd(N_B, b') = 1$ by Remark 9 below, so we can directly recover ϕ_B. $\qquad\qquad\qquad\qquad\qquad\qquad\square$

Remark 9 (Sum of two squares). To decompose a number b as a sum of two squares $b = b_1^2 + b_2^2$ is the same as finding a factorisation $b = (b_1 + i b_2)(b_1 - i b_2) = \beta\bar{\beta}$ in the Gaussian integers $\mathbb{Z}[i]$. The order $\mathbb{Z}[i] \subset \mathbb{Q}(i)$ is of discriminant -4, so it is the maximal order, and it is euclidean, hence is principal. The prime $(2) = ((1+i)(1-i)) = ((1+i)^2)$ is ramified, and the other integer primes are unramified. By the quadratic reciprocity law, when p is an odd prime, -1 is a square modulo p if and only if $p \equiv 1 \pmod 4$. Hence when $p \equiv 1 \pmod 4$ it splits in $\mathbb{Z}[i]$, otherwise when $p \equiv 3 \pmod 4$ it stays inert. In particular, p is a sum of two squares if and only if $p = 2$ or $p \equiv 1 \pmod 4$.

We deduce that b is a sum of two squares if and only if all odd primes $p \equiv 3 \pmod 4$ dividing b have even exponent $v_p(b)$. Also, $\gcd(b_1, b_2) \mid \gcd(\beta, \bar{\beta}) \mid 2\gcd(b_1, b_2)$. Therefore, if $b = b_1^2 + b_2^2$, $\gcd(b_1, b_2) = 2^{\lfloor v_2(b)/2 \rfloor} \times \prod_{p \mid b, p \equiv 3 \pmod 4} p^{v_p(b)/2}$. In particular, b admits a primitive representation as a sum of two squares if and only if the odd prime divisors of b are all congruent to 1 modulo 4 and $4 \nmid b$. We will call such a sum $b = b_1^2 + b_2^2$ with $\gcd(b_1, b_2) = 1$ a primitive sum of two squares. More generally, if the odd prime divisors of $\gcd(b, N_B)$ are congruent to 1 modulo 4, and either $2 \nmid N_B$ or $4 \nmid b$, we can find a decomposition $b = b_1^2 + b_2^2$ such that $\gcd(b_1, b_2, N_B) = 1$.

In Sect. 5, we will need decompositions of the form $b = b_1^2 + 4b_2^2$. Such a decomposition exists if $\beta \in \mathbb{Z}[2i]$, which is a suborder of $\mathbb{Z}[i]$ of index 2. So b admits such a decomposition if and only if it can be written a sum of two squares and $v_2(b)$ is even.

Furthermore, the number of integers less than x that can be written as a sum of two squares is given by the asymptotic behaviour of the L-function $L(s) = (1 - \frac{1}{2^s})^{-1} \prod_{p \equiv 1 \pmod 4} (1 - \frac{1}{p^s})^{-1} \prod_{p \equiv 3 \pmod 4} (1 - \frac{1}{p^{2s}})^{-1}$ at $s = 1$. By Perron's formula, it is equivalent to $Cx/\sqrt{\log x}$ [LeV12, Volume 2, pp. 260–263], where $C \approx 0.7642$ is the Landau-Ramanujan constant. Adapting the proof, the same asymptotic bound holds for the number of integers that are a primitive sum of two squares (resp., of the form $b_1^2 + 4b_2^2$) via the L-function $L(s) = (1 + \frac{1}{2^s}) \prod_{p \equiv 1 \pmod 4} (1 - \frac{1}{p^s})^{-1}$ (resp., $L(s) = (1 - \frac{1}{2^{2s}})^{-1} \prod_{p \equiv 1 \pmod 4} (1 - \frac{1}{p^s})^{-1} \prod_{p \equiv 3 \pmod 4} (1 - \frac{1}{p^{2s}})^{-1}$), except with a different constant $C \approx 0.49$ (resp., $C \approx 0.57$).

4.1 Parameter Selection

In order to find parameters such that we may apply Theorem 3, a first idea is the following. We search, using Sect. 6, for parameters a, b such that $eN_A = bN_B/D + a$, where e is an integer, D is some divisor of N_B (that we will want as small as possible), and a, b primitive sum of two squares. Since $N_A > N_B$, there are $O(eD)$ possible choices for b, among which $\Omega(eD/\sqrt{\log eD})$ will be a primitive sum of two squares by Remark 9. We thus have $\Omega(eD/\sqrt{\log eD})$ candidates for a. If we make the *heuristic assumption* that these a behave like a random integer between 0 and N_A, the probability to find an a that is a sum of two squares is $\Omega(1/\sqrt{\log N_A})$ by Remark 9. Hence we need to take $eD = \widetilde{O}(\sqrt{\log N_A})$. There are $O(D)$ candidate D-isogenies through which ϕ_B may factor, and we need to apply Theorem 3 to each of these candidates. Likewise, there are $O(e^3)$ possibilities to guess the image of ϕ_B on the $N_A e$-torsion (and this does not even take into account the cost of finding the eN_A-torsion which possibly lives in an extension of $\mathbb{F}_q$). Thus it appears that for the tweaking of parameters, it is preferable to use $e = 1$, $D = \widetilde{O}(\sqrt{\log N_A})$. So these parameter tweaks will lose a factor $O(D)$ in the final arithmetic complexity of the attack.

However, for the dimension 4 attack, we will see that by using Sect. 6.4 we can actually set $e = N_A$ without extra cost (asymptotically).

The question remains of the cost of the precomputation of the parameters a, b. We can directly iterate through sums of two squares for b, but checking if a is a sum of two squares requires its factorisation. Here we can use a trick from [Wes22a]: we restrict to the case a is a prime congruent to 1 modulo 4. This only requires a primality test, hence is much less expensive. However the probability that a is a prime (congruent to 1 modulo 4) will only be (heuristically) $\Omega(1/\log N_A)$, so this strategy will require larger parameters eD. Luckily, for the dimension 4 attack we can take $e = N_A$ as we have seen, which is more than large enough.

Reframing the above discussion, we need the following heuristic:

Heuristic 1. – *Let $N_1 > N_2$ be two coprime integers, with N_2 and N_1/N_2 sufficiently large. Then if b is uniform amongst the numbers $x < N_1/N_2$ that are sum of two squares (resp., a primitive sum of two squares, resp., of the form $u^2 + 4v^2$), the probability that $a = N_1 - bN_2$ is a sum of two squares (resp., a primitive sum of two squares, resp., of the form $u^2 + 4v^2$) is $\Omega(1/\sqrt{\log N_1})$.*

– *Under the same assumptions, if b is uniform amongst the numbers $x < N_1/N_2$ that are sum of two squares (resp., a primitive sum of two squares, resp., of the form $u^2 + 4v^2$), the probability that $a = N_1 - bN_2$ is prime and a sum of two squares is $\Omega(1/\log N_1)$.*

Motivation. The motivation behind this heuristic is that the a we get will behave like a uniform integer between 1 and N_1. The density of sum of two squares (resp., a primitive sum of two squares, resp., of the form $u^2 + 4v^2$) less than N_1 is equal asymptotically to $C/\sqrt{\log N_1}$, where C depends on the exact form we want. Likewise, the density of primes congruent to 1 less than N_1 is equivalent asymptotically to $C/\log N_1$ by the prime number theorem and Dirichlet's theorem on arithmetic progressions. □

This heuristic allows us to derive the following complexity cost of the precomputation step.

Proposition 1. *Assume Heuristic 1 is true. Let $N_1 > N_2$ be two coprime integers, with N_2 sufficiently large. If $\epsilon > 0$, then there is a constant C_ϵ such that if $N_1/N_2 > C_\epsilon \log^{1/2} N_1$, we can find with probability $> 1 - \epsilon$ a decomposition $N_1 = bN_2 + a$ where a, b are sum of two squares (resp., a primitive sum of two squares, resp., of the form $u^2 + 4v^2$). This decomposition requires on average $O(\sqrt{\log N_1})$ factorisation calls and $O(\log^{2.5} N_A)$ binary operations.*

If $N_1/N_2 > C_\epsilon \log N_1$, we can find such a decomposition on average $O(\log N_1)$ tests of primality. It will cost on average $O(\log^3 N_1)$ binary operations.

Proof. By Heuristic 1, we need to sample $\Omega(\log^{1/2} N_1)$ b of the form $b_1^2 + b_2^2$ to find an a which is also a sum of two squares, or $\Omega(\log N_1)$ if we also want a prime. The same also holds for the other decomposition, only the constant in the Ω changes.

We first look at the complexity analysis of the second case. Testing the primality of a via the Miller-Rabin pseudo-primality test [Mil76, Rab80] costs $O(\log^2 a)$, and we have the same average complexity to find an integer z such that $z^2 = -1$ (mod a) (this is more or less equivalent to the Miller-Rabin pseudo-primality test). From z and a, a continued fraction expansion allows one to decompose a as a sum of two squares, so given z, the decomposition $a = a_1^2 + a_2^2$ can be done in time $O(\log^2 a)$ by the Euclidean algorithm (it is well known that the complexity can be improved to $\widetilde{O}(\log a)$, see e.g., [BCG+17, Sect. 6.3]) for a total complexity of $O(\log^2 a)$ on average to test the primality of a and write it as a sum of two squares.

For the first case, we need to factor a to see if it can be written as a sum of two squares. Given the prime factors of a, we can use the method above to find the decomposition of a into irreducible factors in the Gaussian integers $\mathbb{Z}[i]$, so we can also decompose a as a sum of two squares in time $O(\log^2 a)$. □

Proposition 2. *Assume Heuristic 1 is true. The precomputation step of the dimension 4 attack takes average time $O(\log^3 N_A)$ binary operations to find a decomposition $N_A^2 = (b_1^2 + b_2^2)N_B + a_1^2 + a_2^2$. Once this decomposition is found, the dimension 4 attack can be done in $\widetilde{O}(\log N_A \ell_A^4)$ arithmetic operations.*

Proof. By Heuristic 1, we can find $e \mid N_A$ such that $eN_A = (b_1^2 + b_2^2)N_B + (a_1^2 + a_2^2)$ with b_1, b_2 coprime. This precomputation costs $\widetilde{O}(\log^3 N_A)$ by Proposition 1. We can now construct an eN_A-endomorphism $F : X \to X$ where $X = E_0^2 \times E_B^2$ as in Theorem 3. We only know its action on $X[N_A]$, but by considering $\widetilde{F}$, we can explicitly decompose F as $F = F_2 \circ F_1$ where F_1 is a N_A-isogeny and F_2 an e-isogeny, see Sect. 6.4. This decomposition costs $\widetilde{O}(\log N_A + \log e\ell_A^4)$ to compute (more precisely: to recover the domain of F_2 and its kernel), and evaluating F via this decomposition costs $\widetilde{O}(\log N_A \ell_A^4)$. □

5   Dimension 2 Attack

We briefly describe how the dimension 2 attacks, due to [CD22, MM22], fit into the general framework of Sect. 3.

Write $N_A = bN_B + a$. To apply Sect. 3 for $g = 1$, we need to construct an a-isogeny $\alpha = \alpha_0 : E_0 \to X_0$ and a b-isogeny $\beta : E_0 \to Y_0$ (or $\beta : E_B \to Y_B$) to get the push-out square:

$$
\begin{array}{ccccc}
Y_0 & \xleftarrow{\ \beta\ } & E_0 & \xrightarrow{\ \phi_B\ } & E_B \\
\downarrow{\scriptstyle\alpha_0'} & & \downarrow{\scriptstyle\alpha_0} & & \downarrow{\scriptstyle\alpha_B} \\
Z_0 & \xleftarrow{\ \beta'\ } & X_0 & \xrightarrow{\ \phi_B'\ } & X_B
\end{array}
$$

The corresponding isogeny diamond

$$
\begin{array}{ccc}
Z_0 & \xrightarrow{\ \widetilde{\alpha_0'}\ } & Y_0 \\
\downarrow{\scriptstyle\phi_B' \circ \widetilde{\beta'}} & & \downarrow{\scriptstyle\phi_B \circ \widetilde{\beta}} \\
X_B & \xrightarrow{\ \widetilde{\alpha_B}\ } & E_B
\end{array}
$$

shows that $F = \begin{pmatrix} \widetilde{\alpha_0'} & \beta \circ \widetilde{\phi_B} \\ -\widetilde{\phi_B'} \circ \widetilde{\beta'} & \widetilde{\alpha_B} \end{pmatrix}$ is a N_A-isogeny $F : Z_0 \times E_B \to Y_0 \times X_B$ by Lemma 6.

If we don't assume that $\mathrm{End}(E_0)$ is known, we can only construct an a-endomorphism whenever a is a square: if $a = a_1^2$ we take the a-endomorphism $[a_1]$. More generally, since it is also easy to construct isogenies of smooth degree starting from E_0 or E_B (see Sect. 6.2), the framework of Sect. 3 shows that the attack applies whenever $N_A = b_1^2 e N_B + a_1^2 f$ where e, f are sufficiently smooth. This is essentially the attack of [MM22]; in the first version they only looked at $N_A - N_B$ smooth (and tweaking of parameters), but to get a subexponential complexity they needed to look at the more general $N_A = e N_B + f$ case, which was already considered in [CD22] (squares are of negligible density compared to smooth numbers, so we can forget about them).

As mentioned in Sect. 1.5, in [CD22] the authors use the matrix F as an oracle attack, which requires many isogeny guesses compared to the direct isogeny recovery of [MM22]. However, they also use the fact that for the parameters of SIKE submitted to NIST (or the Microsoft challenge [Cos21]), E_0 has a known endomorphism $\gamma = 2i$, so $\mathrm{End}(E_0) \supset \mathbb{Z}[2i]$. Hence we can construct an explicit a-endomorphism α on E_0 whenever $a = a_1^2 + 4a_2^2$, which is possible whenever all primes p such that $p \equiv 3 \mod 4$ or $p = 2$ are of even exponent in a by Remark 9. By Sect. 3, prolonging by isogenies of smooth degrees if necessary, for this starting curve E_0 the attack holds whenever $N_A = (b_1^2 + 4b_2^2)e N_B + (a_1^2 + 4a_2^2)f$. Otherwise, one needs to do some guesses, as in Sect. 6. In [CD22], the authors only look at $N_A = N_B + (a_1^2 + 4a_2^2)f$, but in [POP+22], Oudompheng, inspired by an earlier version of this paper describing the dimension 4 attack, implemented the more general formula above. This bumped down the time to solve the SIKEp217 challenge from 9 to 2 s and SIKEp964 instances from more than one hour to thirty seconds.

The discussion of Sect. 4.1 shows:

Proposition 3. *Assume Heuristic 1 is true and assume that E_0 has known endomorphism $\gamma = 2i$. The dimension 2 attack has, after a precomputation step involving $O(\sqrt{\log N_A})$ factorisations and $O(1)$ calls to γ, complexity $\widetilde{O}(\log^{1.5} N_A \ell_A^2)$ arithmetic operations.*

Alternatively, we can dispense with factorisations in the precomputation step at the cost of increasing the complexity of the attack: still under Heuristic 1, after a precomputation step costing $O(\log^3 N_A)$ binary operations and $O(1)$ calls to γ, the dimension 2 attack has complexity $\widetilde{O}(\log^2 N_A \ell_A^2)$ arithmetic operations.

Proof. We proceed as in the proof of Proposition 2. In Proposition 1, we require a, b to decompose as $a = a_1^2 + 4a_2^2$ and $b = b_1^2 + 4b_2^2$. To find such a and b, we look for relations $N_A = bN_B/D + a$ where D is a divisor of N_B. When we look for a a sum of two squares in Proposition 1, we can take $D = \Theta(\sqrt{\log N_A})$, if we require furthermore that a is prime to decrease the precomputation cost, then we need $D = \Theta(\log N_A)$. We assume implicitly that it is possible to find a divisor D of N_B of this magnitude, this will be the case if N_B is sufficiently smooth.

Also, since the endomorphisms α and β are built from γ, the evaluation cost of these endomorphisms will depend on the cost of evaluating γ. But we only need to evaluate α, β on N_A-torsion points, so we may consider the computation of γ on a basis of $E_0[N_A]$ to be a precomputation (depending on E_0). Evaluating α and β then takes $\widetilde{O}(\log N_A \ell_A^{1/2})$ by Lemma 4. When $E_0 = E_{\mathrm{NIST}}$, the evaluation of γ is done in $O(1)$, so evaluating α and β can be done directly in $O(\log N_A)$.

Once these precomputations are done, the evaluation of F takes time $\widetilde{O}(\log N_A \ell_A^2)$ arithmetic operations. We need to multiply this complexity by $O(D)$, the number of isogenies we need to guess. $\qquad\square$

When $E_0 \neq E_{\mathrm{NIST}}$ has known endomorphisms, Castryck and Decru use [KLP+14, LB20] to build a path from E_{NIST} to E_0. This allows them to pushforward the a-isogeny α_{NIST} from E_{NIST} to an a-isogeny α on E_0 using the methods of [GPS17, GPS20, DKL+20]. This time, evaluating α on rational points can only be done in polynomial time. But since the attack only needs the action of α on the N_A-torsion, it is sufficient to evaluate α on a basis of $E_0[N_A]$. This can be seen as a precomputation, which in this case involves not only the parameters N_A, N_B but also the starting curve E_0. The remaining evaluations on points of N_A-torsion can then be done in $\widetilde{O}(\log N_A \ell_A^{1/2})$ by Lemma 4.

Recall also from Sect. 1.5 that [Wes22b] gives a method to construct an a-isogeny in proven polynomial time on any supersingular elliptic curve with known endomorphism ring. This isogeny can also be evaluated in polynomial time. Applying this to $a = N_A - N_B$, computing this a-endomorphism α and its evaluation on a basis $E_0[N_A]$ can be seen as a precomputation, and then we have a direct isogeny recovery without parameter tweaks as in Sect. 2, except we only need to compute isogenies in dimension 2 rather than 8.

Proposition 4 (Wesolowski). *If* $\text{End}(E_0)$ *is known, after a polynomial time precomputation to compute an* a*-isogeny* α *and its action on the* N_A*-torsion, the dimension 2 attack has complexity* $O(\log N_A \ell_A^2)$ *arithmetic operations.*

Unfortunately, it is not clear what is the exact bound on the precomputation step of Wesolowski's approach.

Finally, we mention that for the isogeny computations in dimension 2, since any principally polarised surface is either a Jacobian or a product of two elliptic curves, one can also use the Jacobian model of [CE14] (which can be extended to the case of product of elliptic curves), rather than the theta model of [LR23].

6 Parameter Tweaks

We recall the decomposition of the parameters we need for the different attacks from the generic framework of Sect. 3:

- In dimension 8, or in dimension 2 when $\text{End}(E_0)$ has known endomorphism ring (using [Wes22b]), no tweaks!
- In dimension 4, we need a decomposition $N_A = e(b_1^2 + b_2^2)N_B + f(a_1^2 + a_2^2)$, e, f sufficiently smooth. For the dimension 2 attack of [CD22] where $\text{End}(E_0)$ has endomorphism $2i$, we need the very similar decomposition $N_A = (b_1^2 + 4b_2^2)eN_B + (a_1^2 + 4a_2^2)f$.
- For [MM22], in dimension 2 when $\text{End}(E_0)$ is not known, we need $N_A = eN_B + f$ with e, f sufficiently smooth.

These decompositions rely on the fact that we can build isogenies of smooth degree on E_0 and E_B; we detail that complexity in Sect. 6.2.

We can furthermore tweak the parameters N_A and N_B as follows, as in the strategies of [CD22, MM22]. In the following, we assume that we are in the context of SIDH, so E_0, E_B are supersingular elliptic curves defined over $\mathbb{F}_q$ with $q = p^2$.

1. We can replace N_A by $N_A' = N_A/d_A$ where d_A any divisor of N_A.
2. We can replace N_B by N_B/d_B, where d_B is a small divisor of N_B. This requires guessing the first d_B-isogeny step of ϕ_B, and we have $O(d_B)$ guesses.
3. We can replace N_A by $N_A' = eN_A$ where e is a small integer prime to N_B. This means that we will construct F a $(N_A' = eN_A)$-isogeny in dimension $2g$, but we only know its action on the N_A-torsion. To evaluate F (e.g., to recover its kernel), we need to know its action on the N_A'-torsion. For a general e, we explain possible strategies in Sect. 6.3, strategies which can be much improved when $e \mid N_A$, see Sect. 6.4.

The rest of this section is devoted to determining the complexity of these tweaks.

6.1   Constructing a Basis of the e-torsion of E

We look at the complexity of building a basis of the e-torsion on E.

Lemma 7. *Let $E/\mathbb{F}_q$ be a supersingular elliptic curve, and k the degree of the smallest extension where $E[\ell] \subset E(\mathbb{F}_{q^k})$. We can find a basis of the e-torsion in randomized time $\widetilde{O}(k^2 \log^2 q) = O(e^2 \log^2 q)$ operations.*

Proof. By the group structure theorem of supersingular elliptic curves, since $\pi_{q^k} = (-p)^k$ where π_{q^k} is the Frobenius of $E/\mathbb{F}_{q^k}$, $E(\mathbb{F}_{q^k}) \simeq \mathbb{Z}/((-p)^k - 1) \oplus \mathbb{Z}/((-p)^k - 1)$. Hence the smallest extension of $\mathbb{F}_q$ where the e-torsion points of E live is of degree k, the order of $-p$ modulo e, so $k = O(e)$. Sampling a basis of the e-torsion of E can be done by constructing the field $\mathbb{F}_{q^k}$, sampling random points in $E(\mathbb{F}_{q^k})$, multiplying by the cofactor $\frac{(-p)^k - 1}{e}$ and then checking if we have a basis using the Weil pairing. The construction of $\mathbb{F}_{q^k}$ costs $\widetilde{O}(k^2 \log q + k \log^2 q)$ using [Sho94] or $\widetilde{O}(k \log^5 q)$ using [CL13]. The dominant cost will be the sampling phase, which costs $O(k \log q)$ arithmetic operations in $\mathbb{F}_{q^k}$. In total we get $\widetilde{O}(k^2 \log^2 q) = O(e^2 \log^2 q)$ operations.   □

6.2   Building a Smooth Isogeny on a Supersingular Elliptic Curve $E/\mathbb{F}_{p^2}$

We want to build a smooth isogeny of degree e. We can build it as a composition of $O(\log e)$ ℓ-isogenies, for primes $\ell \mid e$. If $\ell \mid N_A N_B$, since we have access to a rational N_A and N_B torsion basis, we can simply use it to sample an element of order ℓ in time $O(\min(\log N_A, \log N_B))$ arithmetic operations, and the isogeny can then be computed in time $\widetilde{O}(\sqrt{\ell})$ arithmetic operations using sqrtVelu [BDL+20].

We now detail the general case.

Lemma 8. *Let $E/\mathbb{F}_q$ be a supersingular elliptic curve. We can recover the kernel of a ℓ-isogeny with domain E in $\widetilde{O}(\ell^2 \log q + \ell \log^2 q)$ arithmetic operations.*

Proof. Since $\pi_q = [-p]$, all cyclic kernels of order ℓ of E are rational, and their generators live in an extension of degree at most $k = O(\ell)$, the order of $-p$ modulo ℓ. We can construct $\mathbb{F}_{q^k}$ then sample a generator (any non zero point P of ℓ-torsion) in $O(k^2 \log^2 q)$ operations as in Sect. 6.1, then compute the isogeny using Vélu's formula [Vél71] or the sqrtVelu algorithm [BDL+20] in time $O(\ell k \log q)$ (resp., $\widetilde{O}(\ell^{1/2} k \log q)$) for a total cost of $\widetilde{O}(k^2 \log^2 q + \ell^{1/2} k \log q) = \widetilde{O}(\ell^2 \log^2 q)$.

An alternative is to compute and factor the ℓ-division polynomial ψ_ℓ. It is of degree $O(\ell^2)$ and can be computed in time $\widetilde{O}(\ell^2 \log q)$ via the recurrence formula. Furthermore, all points of ℓ-torsion live in the same extension of degree k. If ℓ is odd and $P \in E[\ell]$, x_P will live in the same extension as P unless k is even, in which case $\pi_q^{k/2} P = -P$ so x_P lives in an extension of degree $k/2$. This shows that the factors of ψ_ℓ are all of the same degree k if k is odd or $k/2$ if k is even. We can then skip the distinct degree factorisation phase, hence compute a factorisation of ψ_ℓ in time $\widetilde{O}(\ell^2 \log^2 q)$ by [VS92]. Any factor Q of ψ_f then gives us a construction of $\mathbb{F}_{q^k}$ and of a point of ℓ-torsion P in $E(\mathbb{F}_{q^k})$ via, if $E : y^2 = h(x)$, $P = \big(x \mod Q(x), y \mod (y^2 - h(x), Q(x))\big)$. Note that the polynomial $y^2 - h(x)$ splits in $\mathbb{F}_q[x]/Q(x)$ if $\deg Q = k$, otherwise it is irreducible, $\deg Q = k/2$ and it allows one to construct $\mathbb{F}_{q^k}$ as a degree 2 tower over $\mathbb{F}_{q^{k/2}} = \mathbb{F}_q[x]/Q(x)$. We can then apply Vélu or $\texttt{sqrtVelu}$ to P as above, for a total cost of $\widetilde{O}(\ell^2 \log^2 q)$.

A third method is to construct a ℓ-isogeny using the ℓ-modular polynomial ϕ_ℓ (and its derivative), as in the SEA algorithm [Sch95]. We can evaluate this modular polynomial in time $\widetilde{O}(\ell^2 \log q)$ by an easy adaptation of [Kie20] (see [Rob21, Remark 5.3.9]), then recover a root in time $\widetilde{O}(\ell \log^2 q)$. Recovering the isogeny can then be done in quasi-linear time by solving a differential equation [BMS+08, Rob21, Sect. 4.7.1]. This reduces the complexity to $\widetilde{O}(\ell^2 \log q + \ell \log^2 q)$ operations. □

6.3   Recovering a $N_A e$-isogeny from Its Action on the N_A-torsion

We have a $N_A e$-isogeny F in dimension $2g$, that Eve built from the secret isogeny $\phi_B : E_0 \to E_B$ and some auxiliary isogeny she controls. She wants to recover F in order to retrieve ϕ_B from it.

One way to do that is to guess the action of ϕ_B on the eN_A-torsion of E_0. This requires one to compute a basis of the eN_A-torsion on E_0, as described in Sect. 6.1, possibly taking an extension of degree k, and then guessing the images of ϕ_B on the $N_A e$-torsion. Note that since the N_A-torsion is rational by assumption, we have $k = O(e)$. Guessing the image of ϕ_B on this basis involves $O(e^3)$-tries, using the compatibility of ϕ_B with the Weil pairing and the known image of the N_A-torsion.

An alternative strategy, when the codomain Y of $F : X \to Y$ is known, is as follows: since F is a $(N_A' = eN_A)$-isogeny, and we know the action of ϕ_B on the N_A-torsion, we can still recover $\operatorname{Ker} F \cap X[N_A]$. So taking a maximal isotropic subgroup of $\operatorname{Ker} F \cap X[N_A]$ for the Weil pairing e_{N_A} (for the F we build in Sect. 3, this intersection is already maximal isotropic), we can thus recover F_1 in a decomposition $F = F_2 \circ F_1$, with F_1 a N_A-isogeny and F_2 an e-isogeny. Then we can try to bruteforce F_2 by an e-isogeny search in dimension $2g$.

6.4   Recovering a N_A^2-isogeny from Its Action on the N_A-torsion

When $F : X \to Y$ is a $N_A e$-isogeny with $e \mid N_A$, and the action of F on $X[N_A]$ is known, then by using the dual $\widetilde{F}$ there is a much better strategy to recover F than in Sect. 6.3. This is the same strategy used in [QKL+21] when F is an endomorphism of elliptic curves.

Lemma 9. *Let $F : X \to Y$ be a Ne-isogeny between principally polarised abelian varieties in dimension g, whose kernel has rank g. Assume that we are given a basis of $X[N]$, $Y[N]$ over $\mathbb{F}_q$ along with the image of F on this basis of*

$X[N]$, and that $e \mid N$. Then we can decompose $F = F_2 \circ F_1$ with $F_1 : X \to X_1$ a N-isogeny and $F_2 : X_1 \to Y$ an e-isogeny. Furthermore, we can compute a basis of the kernels of F, $\widetilde{F}$, F_1 and $\widetilde{F_2}$ in $\widetilde{O}(\log N\ell_N^{1/2})$; and a basis of the kernel of F_2 in $\widetilde{O}(\log N\ell_N^{1/2})$ along with $2g$ evaluations of $\widetilde{F_2}$. Once the kernels of F_1 and F_2 are computed, we can evaluate F on any point in $\widetilde{O}(\log N\ell_N^g)$ arithmetic operations.

Proof. Since $K = \mathrm{Ker}\, F$ is of rank g, it admits a symplectic complement K': $X[eN_A] = K \oplus K'$, and $\mathrm{Ker}\, \widetilde{F} = F(X[eN_A]) = F(K')$. Decompose $F = F_2 \circ F_1$, $F_1 : X \to X_1$, $F_2 : X_1 \to Y$, with $\mathrm{Ker}\, F_1 = \mathrm{Ker}\, F \cap X[N_A] = K[N_A]$. Then we have $\mathrm{Ker}\, \widetilde{F_2} = \mathrm{Im}\, F_2 \mid X_1[e] = \mathrm{Im}\, F \mid X[e] = \mathrm{Ker}\, \widetilde{F} \cap Y[e] = F(K')[e] = F(K'[e])$ (indeed $\mathrm{Im}\, F \mid X[e] \subset \mathrm{Im}\, F_2 \mid X_1[e]$ but they have the same cardinality e^{2g} since the kernel is of rank $2g$, so we have equality). So we can build F_1 from X through its kernel $\mathrm{Ker}\, F \cap X[N_A]$ (which is maximal isotropic of rank $2g$ in $X[N_A]$), build $\widetilde{F_2}$ from Y through its kernel $\mathrm{Im}\, F \mid X[e]$, then compute $\mathrm{Ker}\, F_2 = \mathrm{Im}\, \widetilde{F_2} \mid Y[e]$ to recover F_2, hence $F = F_2 \circ F_1$. We can recover these kernels via DLPs as in Lemma 4. We also notice that evaluating $\widetilde{F_2}$ takes $\widetilde{O}(\log e\ell_e^g)$ arithmetic operations.

Once we have the kernels of F_1 and F_2 evaluate F by an isogeny algorithm. $\qquad\square$

Example 1. Note that the isogeny F in dimension $2g$ constructed in Sect. 3 has its kernel of rank $2g$. In particular this strategy applies for the attacks in dimension 4 of Sect. 4 and in dimension 8 of Sect. 2.

Let us detail this case: in these examples, the endomorphism F of $E_0^g \times E_B^g$ is always of the form $F = \begin{pmatrix} \alpha_0 & \widetilde{\beta}\widetilde{\phi_B}\,\mathrm{Id} \\ -\phi_B\beta & \widetilde{\alpha_B} \end{pmatrix}$ with α_0 an a-endomorphism of E_0^g, β a b-endomorphism of E_0^g, and α_B the a-endomorphism of E_B^g making the diagram commute:

$$
\begin{array}{ccc}
E_0^g & \xrightarrow{\phi_B\beta} & E_B^g \\
\downarrow{\scriptstyle\alpha_0} & & \downarrow{\scriptstyle\alpha_B} \\
E_0^g & \xrightarrow{\phi_B\beta} & E_B^g
\end{array}
$$

We also have a, b, N_A coprime to each other. In particular, $\mathrm{Ker}\, F = \{(\widetilde{\alpha_0}(P), (\phi_B\beta)(P)) \mid P \in E_0^g[eN_A]\}$, and $\mathrm{Ker}\, \widetilde{F} = \{(\alpha_0(P), (-\phi_B\beta)(P)) \mid P \in E_0^g[eN_A]\}$ are of rank g. We decompose $F = F_2 \circ F_1$, where $\mathrm{Ker}\, F_1 = \mathrm{Ker}\, F[N_A] = \{(\widetilde{\alpha_0}(P), (\phi_B\beta)(P)) \mid P \in E_0^g[N_A]\}$, and $\mathrm{Ker}\, \widetilde{F_2} = \mathrm{Ker}\, \widetilde{F}[e] = \{(\alpha_0(P), (-\phi_B\beta)(P)) \mid P \in E_0^g[e]\}$. Since we know the image of ϕ_B on a basis of $E_0[N_A]$, we know the image of ϕ_B on a basis of $E_0[e]$ via $O(\log(N_A/e))$ arithmetic operations. So we can recover the image of $\phi_B\beta$ on this basis in $\widetilde{O}(\log N_A\ell_A^{1/2})$ and $O(1)$ evaluations of β by Lemma 4. We also need $O(1)$ calls to α_0.

In these examples, the endomorphisms β and α_0 can be evaluated in time $O(\log N_A)$, so the kernel of F_1 and of $\widetilde{F_2}$ can be computed in time $\widetilde{O}(\log N_A\ell_A^{1/2})$. A linear complement of $\mathrm{Ker}\, \widetilde{F_2}$ is given by $0 \times E_B^g[e]$. Indeed it is of rank g and cardinality q^{2g}, and if $x = (0, Q) \in \operatorname{Ker} \widetilde{F_2}$, then $Q = -\phi_B \beta(P)$ for a $P \in E_0^g[e]$ such that $\alpha_0 P = 0$. But this implies $aP = 0$, hence $P = 0$ since a is prime to $e \mid N_A$, so $Q = 0$. So $\operatorname{Ker} F_2 = \widetilde{F_2}(0 \times E_B^g[e])$ can be recovered in $2g$ calls to the evaluation of the e-isogeny $\widetilde{F_2}$.

The total cost to recover the domain of F_2 and a basis of its kernel is thus $\widetilde{O}(\log N_A \ell_A^{1/2} + \log e\ell_e^{2g}) = \widetilde{O}(\log N_A \ell_A^{2g})$.

Unfortunately, this strategy does not work for the dimension 2 attack of Sect. 5, because (with the notations of this Section), X_B is constructed as a pushout, and we only obtain it when we compute the codomain of F. But this means that if F is a N_A^2-isogeny, there is no easy way to obtain $\operatorname{Ker} \widetilde{F}[N_A]$, hence split F as a product of two N_A-isogenies, without first computing F fully.

7   Open Problem

By Theorem 1 and Remark 1, we have a new toolbox for recovering an N_B-isogeny $f : A \to B$ given its action on the N_A-torsion as long as $N_A^2 \geq N_B$ and N_A is sufficiently smooth. This tool allows one to break SIDH efficiently in all cases. Can it also be used to build new isogeny based cryptosystems?

References

[BDL+20] Bernstein, D., De Feo, L., Leroux, A., Smith, B.: Faster computation of isogenies of large prime degree. In: Algorithmic Number Theory Symposium (ANTS XIV), vol. 4.1, pp. 39–55. Mathematical Sciences Publishers (2020). arXiv:2003.10118. https://msp.org/obs/2020/4/p04.xhtml

[BL04] Birkenhake, C., Lange, H.: Complex Abelian Varieties, vol. 302. Grundlehren der Mathematischen Wissenschaften [Fundamental Principles of Mathematical Sciences], pp. xii+635. Springer, Cham (2004). ISBN: 3-540-20488-1, https://doi.org/10.1007/978-3-662-06307-1

[BCR10] Bisson, G., Cosset, R., Robert, D.: AVIsogenies. Magma package devoted to the computation of isogenies between abelian varieties (2010). https://www.math.u-bordeaux.fr/damienrobert/avisogenies/. Free software (LGPLv2+), Registered to APP (Reference IDDN.FR.001.440011. 000.R.P.2010.000.10000). Latest version 0.7, Released on 13 Mar 2021

[BMS+08] Bostan, A., Morain, F., Salvy, B., Schost, E.: Fast algorithms for computing isogenies between elliptic curves. Math. Comput. **77**(263), 1755–1778 (2008)

[BCG+17] Bostan, A., et al.: Algorithmes efficaces en calcul formel (2017). https://hal.inria.fr/hal-01431717/document

[CD22] Castryck, W., Decru, T.: An efficient key recovery attack on SIDH (preliminary version). Cryptology ePrint Archive, Paper 2022/975 (2022). https://eprint.iacr.org/2022/975

[CLM+18] Castryck, W., Lange, T., Martindale, C., Panny, L., Renes, J.: CSIDH: an efficient post-quantum commutative group action. In: Peyrin, T., Galbraith, S. (eds.) ASIACRYPT 2018. LNCS, vol. 11274, pp. 395–427. Springer, Cham (2018). https://doi.org/10.1007/978-3-030-03332-3_15

[Cos21] Costello, C.: The case for SIKE: a decade of the supersingular isogeny problem. In: Cryptology ePrint Archive (2021)

[CLN16] Costello, C., Longa, P., Naehrig, M.: Efficient algorithms for supersingular isogeny Diffie-Hellman. In: Robshaw, M., Katz, J. (eds.) CRYPTO 2016. LNCS, vol. 9814, pp. 572–601. Springer, Heidelberg (2016). https://doi.org/10.1007/978-3-662-53018-4_21, https://ecc2017.cs.ru.nl/slides/ecc2017-costello.pdf

[CE14] Couveignes, J.-M., Ezome, T.: Computing functions on Jacobians and their quotients. LMS J. Comput. Math. 18(1), 555–577 (2014). arXiv:1409.0481

[CL13] Couveignes, J.-M., Lercier, R.: Fast construction of irreducible polynomials over finite fields. Israel J. Math. 194(1), 77–105 (2013)

[DDF+21] De Feo, L., et al.: Séta: supersingular encryption from Torsion attacks. In: Tibouchi, M., Wang, H. (eds.) ASIACRYPT 2021. LNCS, vol. 13093, pp. 249–278. Springer, Cham (2021). https://doi.org/10.1007/978-3-030-92068-5_9

[DJP14] De Feo, L., Jao, D., Plût, J.: Towards quantum-resistant cryptosystems from supersingular elliptic curve isogenies. J. Math. Cryptol. 8(3), 209–247 (2014)

[DKL+20] De Feo, L., Kohel, D., Leroux, A., Petit, C., Wesolowski, B.: SQISign: compact post-quantum signatures from quaternions and isogenies. In: Moriai, S., Wang, H. (eds.) ASIACRYPT 2020. LNCS, vol. 12491, pp. 64–93. Springer, Cham (2020). https://doi.org/10.1007/978-3-030-64837-4_3

[EGM12] Edixhoven, B., van der Geer, G., Moonen, B.: Abelian Varieties. Book Project (2012). http://van-der-geer.nl/gerard/AV.pdf

[FKM+22] Fouotsa, T.B., Kutas, P., Merz, S.P., Ti, Y.B.: On the isogeny problem with torsion point information. In: Hanaoka, G., Shikata, J., Watanabe, Y. (eds.) Public-Key Cryptography, PKC 2022. LNCS, vol. 13177, pp. 142–161. Springer, Cham (2022). https://doi.org/10.1007/978-3-030-97121-2_6

[GPS17] Galbraith, S.D., Petit, C., Silva, J.: Identification protocols and signature schemes based on supersingular isogeny problems. In: Takagi, T., Peyrin, T. (eds.) ASIACRYPT 2017. LNCS, vol. 10624, pp. 3–33. Springer, Cham (2017). https://doi.org/10.1007/978-3-319-70694-8_1

[GPS20] Galbraith, S.D., Petit, C., Silva, J.: Identification protocols and signature schemes based on supersingular isogeny problems. J. Cryptol. 33(1), 130–175 (2020)

[JAC+17] Jao, D., et al.: SIKE: supersingular isogeny key encapsulation (2017). https://sike.org/

[JD11] Jao, D., De Feo, L.: Towards quantum-resistant cryptosystems from supersingular elliptic curve isogenies. In: Yang, B.-Y. (ed.) PQCrypto 2011. LNCS, vol. 7071, pp. 19–34. Springer, Heidelberg (2011). https://doi.org/10.1007/978-3-642-25405-5_2

[Kan97] Kani, E.: The number of curves of genus two with elliptic differentials. J. für die reine und angewandte Mathematik 485, 93–122 (1997)

[Kan16] Kani, E.: The moduli spaces of Jacobians isomorphic to a product of two elliptic curves. Collectanea mathematica 67(1), 21–54 (2016)

[Kie20] Kieffer, J.: Evaluating modular polynomials in genus 2 (2020). arXiv: 2010.10094 [math.NT]. HAL: hal-02971326

[KLP+14] Kohel, D., Lauter, K., Petit, C., Tignol, J.-P.: On the quaternion isogeny path problem. LMS J. Comput. Math. 17(A), 418–432 (2014)

[LeV12] LeVeque, W.J.: Topics in Number Theory, vol. I and II. Courier Corporation, New York (2012)

502   D. Robert

[LB20]   Love, J., Boneh, D.: Supersingular curves with small noninteger endomorphisms. In: Open Book Series (ANTS XIV), vol. 4(1), pp. 7–22 (2020). https://msp.org/obs/2020/4/p02.xhtml

[LR10]   Lubicz, D., Robert, D.: Efficient pairing computation with theta functions. In: Hanrot, G., Morain, F., Thomé, E. (eds.) ANTS 2010. LNCS, vol. 6197, pp. 251–269. Springer, Heidelberg (2010). https://doi.org/10.1007/978-3-642-14518-6_21

[LR15]   Lubicz, D., Robert, D.: A generalisation of Miller's algorithm and applications to pairing computations on abelian varieties. J. Symb. Comput. **67**, 68–92 (2015). https://doi.org/10.1016/j.jsc.2014.08.001

[LR23]   Lubicz, D., Robert, D.:. Fast change of level and applications to isogenies. Res. Number Theory (ANTS XV Conf.) **9**(1), 7 (2023). https://doi.org/10.1007/s40993-022-00407-9

[MM22]   Maino, L., Martindale, C.: An attack on SIDH with arbitrary starting curve. Cryptology ePrint Archive, Paper 2022/1026 (2022). https://eprint.iacr.org/2022/1026

[MMP+23] Maino, L., Martindale, C., Panny, L., Pope, G., Wesolowski, B.: A direct key recovery on SIDH. In: Eurocrypt. Springer, Cham (2023)

[Mil76] Miller, G.L.: Riemann's hypothesis and tests for primality. J. Comput. Syst. Sci. **13**(3), 300–317 (1976)

[Mum66] Mumford, D.: On the equations defining abelian varieties. I. Invent. Math. **1**, 287–354 (1966)

[Mum70] Mumford, D.: Abelian Varieties. Tata Institute of Fundamental Research Studies in Mathematics, vol. 5, pp. viii+242. Published for the Tata Institute of Fundamental Research, Bombay (1970)

[Oud22] Oudompheng, R.: A note on implementing direct isogeny determination in the Castryck-Decru SIKE attack, August 2022. http://www.normalesup.org/oudomphe/textes/202208-castryckdecru-shortcut.pdf

[Pet17] Petit, C.: Faster algorithms for isogeny problems using torsion point images. In: Takagi, T., Peyrin, T. (eds.) ASIACRYPT 2017. LNCS, vol. 10625, pp. 330–353. Springer, Cham (2017). https://doi.org/10.1007/978-3-319-70697-9_12

[PH78]   Pohlig, S., Hellman, M.: An improved algorithm for computing logarithms over GF(p) and its cryptographic significance (Corresp.). IEEE Trans. Inf. Theory **24**(1), 106–110 (1978)

[PT18]   Pollack, P., Treviño, E.: Finding the four squares in Lagrange's theorem. Integers **18**, A15 (2018)

[POP+22] Pope, G., Oudompheng, R., Panny, L., et al.: Castryck-Decru Key Recovery Attack on SIDH, August 2022. https://github.com/jack4818/Castryck-Decru-SageMath

[QKL+21] de Quehen, V., et al.: Improved torsion-point attacks on SIDH variants. In: Malkin, T., Peikert, C. (eds.) CRYPTO 2021. LNCS, vol. 12827, pp. 432–470. Springer, Cham (2021). https://doi.org/10.1007/978-3-030-84252-9_15

[Rab80] Rabin, M.O.: Probabilistic algorithm for testing primality. J. Number Theory **12**(1), 128–138 (1980)

[RS86]   Rabin, M.O., Shallit, J.O.: Randomized algorithms in number theory. Commun. Pure Appl. Math. **39**(S1), S239–S256 (1986)

[Rob21] Robert, D.: Efficient algorithms for abelian varieties and their moduli spaces. HDR thesis. Université Bordeaux, June 2021. http://www.normalesup.org/robert/pro/publications/academic/hdr.pdf. Slides: 2021-06-HDR-Bordeaux.pdf (1h, Bordeaux)

[Rob22a] Robert, D.: Breaking SIDH in polynomial time, August 2022

[Rob22b] Robert, D.: Evaluating isogenies in polylogarithmic time, August 2022

[Sch95] Schoof, R.: Counting points on elliptic curves over finite fields. J. Théor. Nombres Bordeaux **7**(1), 219–254 (1995)

[Shi79] Shioda, T.: Supersingular K3 surfaces. In: Lønsted, K. (ed.) Algebraic Geometry. LNM, vol. 732, pp. 564–591. Springer, Heidelberg (1979). https://doi.org/10.1007/BFb0066664

[Sho94] Shoup, V.: Fast construction of irreducible polynomials over finite fields. J. Symb. Comput. **17**(5), 371–391 (1994)

[Sho09] Shoup, V.: A Computational Introduction to Number Theory and Algebra. Cambridge University Press, Cambridge (2009)

[Som21] Somoza, A.: thetAV. Sage package devoted to the computation with abelian varieties with theta functions, rewrite of the AVIsogenies magma package (2021). https://gitlab.inria.fr/roberdam/avisogenies/-/tree/sage

[Sut11] Sutherland, A.: Structure computation and discrete logarithms in finite abelian p-groups. Math. Comput. **80**(273), 477–500 (2011)

[Vél71] Vélu, J.: Isogénies entre courbes elliptiques. Compte Rendu Académie Sciences Paris Série A-B **273**, A238–A241 (1971)

[VS92] Von Zur Gathen, J., Shoup, V.: Computing Frobenius maps and factoring polynomials. Comput. Complexity **2**(3), 187–224 (1992)

[Wes22a] Wesolowski, B.: The supersingular isogeny path and endomorphism ring problems are equivalent. In: 2021 IEEE 62nd Annual Symposium on Foundations of Computer Science (FOCS), pp. 1100–1111. IEEE (2022)

[Wes22b] Wesolowski, B.: Understanding and improving the Castryck-Decru attack on SIDH, August 2022. https://www.dropbox.com/s/pmv3lrsg1gayl13/attacksidh.pdf?dl=0

[Zar74] Zarhin, J.G.: A remark on endomorphisms of abelian varieties over function fields of finite characteristic. Math. USSR-Izvestiya **8**(3), 477 (1974)

Signature Schemes

A Lower Bound on the Length of Signatures Based on Group Actions and Generic Isogenies

Dan Boneh[1], Jiaxin Guan[2(✉)] ⓘ, and Mark Zhandry[2,3] ⓘ

[1] Stanford University, Stanford, USA
[2] Princeton University, Princeton, USA
jiaxin@guan.io
[3] NTT Research, Inc., Sunnyvale, USA

Abstract. We give the first black box lower bound for signature protocols that can be described as group actions, which include many based on isogenies. We show that, for a large class of signature schemes making black box use of a (potentially non-abelian) group action, the signature length must be $\Omega(\lambda^2/\log\lambda)$. Our class of signatures generalizes all known signatures that derive security exclusively from the group action, and our lower bound matches the state of the art, showing that the signature length cannot be improved without deviating from the group action framework.

1 Introduction

Post-quantum cryptography aims to develop classical cryptosystems that remain secure against an adversary who has access to a large-scale quantum computer. One approach to post-quantum cryptography relies on the observation that Shor's discrete log algorithm [35] does not apply in an algebraic structure called a *group action*. This gives rise to group-action-based cryptography for post-quantum public key encryption, key exchange, digital signatures, and more [1,4,21]. The resulting cryptosystems look somewhat similar to classical systems that rely on the difficulty of discrete log in a finite cyclic group.

Informally, a group action is a mapping of the form $* : G \times X \to X$, where G is a finite group and X is a set, such that for any $g_1, g_2 \in G$ and any $x \in X$, we have $g_1 * (g_2 * x) = (g_1 g_2) * x$. Moreover, if $e \in G$ is the identity of G then $e * x = x$ for all $x \in X$. The discrete log problem for such a group action is to find a $g \in G$, if one exists, such that $x_0 = g * x_1$, given only $x_0, x_1 \in X$ as input. Note that Shor's algorithm fails to solve this problem precisely because there is no efficiently computable group operation on the set X. The best known quantum algorithms for group action discrete log run in sub-exponential time in the security parameter [22,23,29,31].

Currently the most widely studied cryptographic group action is derived from isogeny graphs of elliptic curves [7,33]. To avoid the sub-exponential quantum algorithm mentioned above, some constructions use *supersingular* isogeny

© International Association for Cryptologic Research 2023
C. Hazay and M. Stam (Eds.): EUROCRYPT 2023, LNCS 14008, pp. 507–531, 2023.
https://doi.org/10.1007/978-3-031-30589-4_18

graphs [17,20], which present less structure than a group action. However, a recent attack by Castryck and Decru [5] and Maino and Martindale [25] shows that certain key exchange protocols that rely on supersingular isogeny graphs (in particular, rely on the SIDH assumption) are insecure. The attack does not appear to affect various isogeny-based signature schemes such as SeaSign [9,12], CSI-FiSh [3,8,16], and SQISign [10,11].

Short Signatures. An important open problem in post-quantum cryptography is to construct a signature scheme for which the combined length of a public key and a signature is comparable to that of the Schnorr scheme, namely $32 + 64 = 96$ bytes (for 128-bit security). The four post-quantum NIST signature finalists [6] have the following combined public-key/signature lengths: 3740 bytes for Dilithium2, 1563 bytes for Falcon512, and over 50 KB for both Rainbow variants. These numbers are an order of magnitude higher than the combined length for the Schnorr scheme. We note that the combined public-key/signature length for SQISign is only 268 bytes—better than the NIST candidates, but still worse than Schnorr. SQISign uses specific properties of supersingular isogenies, and is not a generic group-action signature scheme.

Can we do better? One might expect that due to the similarity between group-action-based systems and systems using a finite cyclic group, one should be able to design a post-quantum Schnorr-like signature scheme using a generic group action. However, this remains an open problem. For example, the signature scheme SeaSign [9], which can be described as a generic group-action signature scheme (as in Sect. 1.3), has a combined public-key/signature length of about 3 KB (see column 3 of Table 2 from [9]). In this paper we show that this is no accident.

1.1   Our Results

Let λ be a security parameter. Our main result is a lower bound of $\Omega(\lambda^2/\log \lambda)$ for a wide class of group-action-based signatures. This lower bound matches the signature length of state-of-the-art constructions such as SeaSign. Concretely, we prove the following theorem about *identification* (ID) protocols:

Theorem 1.1 (Informal). *For any public-coin identification protocol secure against eavesdropping in a black box (potentially non-abelian) group action model, the sender must send at least $(\lambda - 1)/\log_2 \lambda$ set elements in order to achieve soundness $2^{-\lambda}$.*

Here, public coin means that the verifier generates its messages by simply sampling uniform bit strings. Note that Theorem 1.1 works for any such group action; in particular we do not assume any regularity or transitivity. Also note that by handling *non-abelian* group actions, our model easily incorporates features like twists, as twists can be seen as action by a slightly larger group arising from a semi-direct product.

Since set elements need to be at a minimum λ bits to prevent solving discrete logarithms, we thus obtain a lower bound of $(\lambda - 1)^2 / \log_2 \lambda$ bits for the communication from prover to verifier.

All known efficient group-action-based signature schemes are built by transforming a public coin ID protocol into a signature, typically via Fiat-Shamir [18], but other transforms are also possible [37]. Thus, our lower bound yields a lower bound on the length of signatures in such protocols.

Our Model of Black Box Group Actions. We formalize black box group actions by adapting Maurer's [26] generic group model to the black box group action setting. In this model, instead of getting set elements "in the clear", all parties are only given handles to the set elements, and then operate on these handles via an oracle. This reflects how current group-action based signature and ID protocols are constructed. Below, we discuss why we choose to adapt Maurer's model instead of Shoup's [36] model.

Extensions. We also discuss several extensions to structures that generalize group actions. In particular, many isogenies cannot be framed straightforwardly as group actions. We therefore formalize a *graph action* model, which generalizes group actions to these more general structures, and observe that our impossibility readily applies in this more general setting as well.

1.2 Discussion

Schnorr identification requires sending only a single group element, and security can be proven under the discrete logarithm assumption in plain groups. Theorem 1.1 shows that the situation is quite different in the group action setting. In the language of [32], our result shows there is no semi-black box construction of an efficient ID protocol from hard discrete logarithms over group actions. Even more, "discrete logarithm" can be replaced by *any* problem that is (classically) unconditionally hard in generic group actions, including CDH and even more exotic assumptions such as the linear hidden shift assumption [1]. Thus, to sidestep our lower bound, one must design signatures that are *not* based on ID protocols, rely on non-generic use of the group action, or rely on cryptographic hardness assumptions beyond what a group action alone provides.

On Our Black Box Model. A natural question is whether our lower bound also applies to an analog of Shoup's generic group model tailored to group actions, replacing handles with random labels. Unfortunately, lower bounding signatures in Shoup's model appears to be very challenging. In particular, a lower bound in such a model would imply as a special case a lower bound in the *random oracle model* (ROM)[1]. Even through the best-known (many-time) random oracle signatures have signature size $\Omega(\lambda^3)$ [27][2], it is a long-standing open problem to

---

[1] Shoup's generic groups imply random oracles [39], and the proof readily adapts to group actions with random labels.

[2] If the number of messages is a priori bounded, it is possible to have signatures of length $O(\lambda^2)$ [28].

510   D. Boneh et al.

obtain *any* non-trivial bound. We cannot even rule out that optimal $O(\lambda)$-length signatures from random oracles exist. We sidestep this major barrier by instead utilizing Maurer's model.

Our model of group actions using handles captures all known techniques for efficient ID protocols from group actions. However, it is known that such a model fails to capture a number of standard generic techniques [38]. These standard generic techniques are typically used in symmetric key settings, as they involve operations like breaking strings into individual bits or XORs. Such operations break algebraic structure, seemingly negating the purpose of introducing algebraic tools in the first place. Nevertheless, such techniques could perhaps be employed in combination with algebraic tools to achieve more efficient signatures. As such, our impossibility does not fully rule out short signatures from group actions, but still represents a significant barrier.

On ID Protocols. At a technical level, our lower bound is for ID protocols. This is because it is known that signatures are *impossible* in Maurer's generic group model [15], and the impossibility readily extends to our formalization of the black box group action model using handles. As such, any direct lower bound for signatures in our group action model would be completely meaningless.

Thus, any attempt at proving a lower bound for signatures is presented with a conundrum: work in Shoup's version of group actions, where the long-standing open problem of signature length from random oracles presents a major barrier. *Or* work in Maurer's model, where signatures are simply impossible.

While signatures do not exist in Maurer's version of black box groups/group actions, ID protocols *do* exist. The transformation from ID protocol to signature, say via Fiat-Shamir, is then the only part of the signature that doesn't work in Maurer's model. This is because applying Fiat-Shamir requires hashing a group element/set element into a bit string. Such hashing is of course allowed in the standard model, but it is forbidden in Maurer's since only the group (action) operation is allowed to be applied to elements. Fortunately, the most efficient signature schemes from groups and group actions are obtained by transforming ID protocols.

The Fiat-Shamir transformation is well-understood, both classically [2,30] and quantumly [14,24], and adds zero signature-length overhead over the underlying ID protocol[3]. But the length of any signature based on ID protocols is always lower-bounded by the ID protocol itself. Thus, our lower bound immediately applies to signatures based on ID protocols, which captures all-known practical group-action based signatures. Thus, our lower bound shows that a $\Omega(\lambda^2/\log_2 \lambda)$ signature length is inherent with current techniques.

Note that our lower bound is only for public coin protocols. This is inherent, as group actions give public key encryption, and any public key encryption scheme can be turned into an ID protocol, as follows [13]: the verifier encrypts a random message and sends the ciphertext, and the prover simply decrypts the ciphertext and sends the resulting message. The number of set elements in the

---

[3] Other transforms such as Unruh's [37] do require overhead.

protocol is just the number of set elements in a ciphertext, which in the case of group-action-based public key encryption, is just a constant. This protocol, however, is secret coin, as the verifier's message is a ciphertext that hides both the message and the encryption randomness. Such secret coin ID protocols are not amenable to Fiat-Shamir or related transformations, and there is no known direct way to turn them into signatures. Thus, our restriction to public coin protocols is justified by the ultimate goal of lower-bounding signatures.

1.3 Technical Overview

Existing Group Action-Based Signatures. The main group-action-based signatures are built from a public coin identification (ID) protocol, and then by converting the ID protocol into a signature. This conversion is typically Fiat-Shamir [18], but other transforms are possible [37]. For reasons explained above, we focus on analyzing the underlying ID protocol.

Throughout, we will focus on the number of set elements sent by the prover, which is a proxy for the total communication of the ID protocol. Note that when converting into a signature scheme, usually not all the terms of the ID protocol need to be sent explicitly, since they can be computed from the other terms for a valid signature. Nevertheless, the number of set elements remains linear in the total signature size.

The usual way to build an ID protocol from group actions, is the following adaptation of Schnorr's identification protocol [34] for plain groups:

- The public key contains two set elements x_0, x_1 such that $x_0 = g * x_1$. The secret key is a random $g \in G$.
- The prover first chooses a random $h \in G$, and sends $a = h * x_1$.
- The verifier replies with a random bit b.
- The prover then outputs $r = hg^{b-1}$.
- The verifier checks that $a = r * x_b$

The ID protocol is easily seen to be zero knowledge. The protocol has (classical) soundness error $1/2$: if an adversary can break security with probability non-negligibly greater than $1/2$, then a standard rewinding argument shows that it can compute hg^{b-1} for both $b = 0$ and $b = 1$; dividing gives g, the discrete log between x_0 and x_1, which is presumably hard to compute. On the other hand, it is trivial to break security with probability $1/2$: the prover simply guesses the bit b, and computes $a = r * x_b$ for a random r. Conditioned on the guess for b being correct, the transcript seen by the verifier will have the correct distribution.

To achieve better soundness, one can run the protocol many times, either sequentially or in parallel. To get soundness error $2^{-\lambda}$, one would need λ trials, requiring λ set elements to be sent from the prover.

One can do slightly better, at the cost of a somewhat larger public key. Abstracting an optimization of De Feo and Galbraith [9] (See [9], Sect. 4) to the setting of group actions, consider the following protocol:

- The public key contains P set elements $x_1, \ldots, x_P$. The secret key is $g_2, \ldots, g_P$ such that $x_i = g_i * x_1$ for $i > 1$.

- The prover chooses a random $h \in G$, and sends $a = h * x_1$.
- The verifier replies with a random $c \in [P]$
- The prover then outputs $r = hg_c^{-1}$, where $g_1 = 1$.
- The verifier checks that $a = r * x_c$

The above protocol achieves soundness error $1/P$, without any additional set elements in the protocol, but at the cost of expanding the public key to P set elements. To achieve soundness error $2^{-\lambda}$, we can set $P = \lambda/\log \lambda$, and repeat the protocol P times. The result is public keys and protocol transcripts containing P set elements.

Generalizing both protocols, if we let P, N be the number of set elements in the public key and protocol transcript, and S the soundness error, both protocols above have $S = P^{-N}$.

We note that if one relaxes zero knowledge, then smaller soundness error is possible. For example, for security against direct attacks, the prover can just reveal g, and now soundness matches the hardness of computing discrete logarithms. For eavesdropping security where the attacker sees t transcripts, one can modify the large public key protocol above to have the prover simply reveal a discrete logarithm between x_1 and a random choice of x_i. While this latter scheme has noticeable soundness error, in both cases here the prover actually sends no set elements at all. Other strategies are possible to improve soundness in the bounded eavesropping setting. Nevertheless, for schemes of this nature, it seems to always be the case that $t \leq P$.

Our Lower Bound. Our main result is that for eavesdropping security under t transcripts, for any desired polynomial poly:

$$S \geq (1 - P/t - 1/\mathsf{poly}) \times P^{-N} \tag{1}$$

For unbounded transcripts, this shows that the $S = P^{-N}$ of the known group-action-based protocols is essentially tight. It also shows to get non-trivial soundness when the prover sends no elements at all requires the number of elements in the public key to be at least as large as the number of transcripts, matching intuition for such schemes.

Intuition. We now provide the intuition for our lower bound. Consider the collection of set elements seen by the verifier, which we will call V. V includes both set elements in the public key, as well as set elements sent by the prover and any set elements computed by the verifier. Now, consider a group action query by the verifier, such as $g * x$, resulting in output y. The verifier therefore knows the discrete logarithm between x and y. Since the protocol is public coin, this means the discrete logarithm is also revealed by the protocol transcript.

By looking at all such queries, we induce a graph structure on V, where we connect the input and output nodes of any query by the verifier. Since discrete logarithms compose, the verifier knows the discrete logarithm between any two connected nodes.

We can now assume, essentially without loss of generality, that no two public key nodes are in the same connected component. After all, if they were, then the protocol transcript reveals the discrete logarithm between these nodes. If the protocol were zero-knowledge, this would mean the discrete logarithm can be computed from publicly-available information. Even in the eavesdropping setting, it means the discrete logarithm can be computed from the transcripts provided to the adversary. In either case, this means that one of the two nodes was in some sense superfluous. We can make this precise, showing that if the ID protocol is secure even if the adversary sees sufficiently many transcripts, then we can compile the protocol into one where all public key components are in different connected components. This transformation slightly impacts correctness, and results in the P/t term in Eq. 1.

We then give an adversary for any scheme where the public key nodes are in different connected components. Essentially, whenever the adversary is required to send a set element y, it simply guesses which of the public key nodes x that y will be connected to, and generates y such that it knows the discrete logarithm between y and x. We show, essentially, that conditioned on the guess being correct for every node sent by the prover, our adversary can correctly simulate the protocol execution, and convince the verifier. The probability of guessing correctly at every step is exactly P^{-N}, where P is the number of public key elements, and N is the number of elements sent by the prover.

For technical reasons, the above does not quite work perfectly. Essentially, our simulation ensures that the graph seen by the verifier has an edge everywhere it should, but does not guarantee that the graph has no edges where it should not. But we observe that if there is a bad edge in the simulated graph, this connects two nodes that should not be connected. We are able to argue, roughly, that this means we can remove nodes from the graph, somewhat analogous to how we handled public key elements in the same connected component. As in that case, there is still some error in the simulation, though it can be made an arbitrary small polynomial. This results in the 1/poly term in Eq. 1.

Formalizing the above intuition is non-trivial. The main difficulty, analogous to all black box separations, is that the construction and adversary could completely ignore the group action and just run some standard-model short signature scheme such as Schnorr.

Following Impagliazzo-Rudich [19], we block such a construction by giving the adversary unlimited private computation and only bound the number of queries to the group action to a polynomial. This captures constructions whose only source of hardness is the group action.

With unlimited private computation, we can brute force any signature scheme that does not use the group action. The challenge comes in attacking schemes that are a combination of using the group action, but also using standard-model building blocks, as a naive brute force will result in exponentially many queries.

We formalize the above intuition through a sequence of protocol simplification steps, where we gradually restrict the prover and verifier, showing that the simplifications are without loss of generality. Eventually we reach a simplified protocol where we can apply the intuition above and prove our lower bound. See Sect. 3 for details.

Extensions. In Sect. 4, we discuss a couple of extensions to our main lower bound. We first consider a generalized model where it is possible to directly sample set elements, without having to derive them from other elements. While no existing group-action-based signature utilizes such direct sampling, it is supported by elliptic curves and therefore important to consider. We show, with some key modifications to our main proof, that our lower bound applies in this model as well.

We also give a generalization of black box group actions, that we call black box *graph actions*. This captures many of the features of group actions, but eliminates the group structure on the acting set, instead viewing the action as a walk on a graph. This is how isogeny-based signatures tend to work anyway, and by generalizing to a less-structured object, we make our lower bound more general. Our lower bound does not use any particular features of the group structure, and trivially adapts to a graph action.

2   Preliminaries

Notation: We use $\lambda \in \mathbb{Z}$ to denote the security parameter. We use $x \leftarrow y$ to denote the assignment of the value of y to x. We write $x \xleftarrow{\$} S$ to denote sampling an element from the set S independently and uniformly at random. For a randomized algorithm $\mathcal{A}$ we write $y \xleftarrow{\$} \mathcal{A}(x)$ to denote the random variable that is the output of $\mathcal{A}(x)$. We use $[n]$ for the set $\{1, \ldots, n\}$. We denote vectors in bold font: $\mathbf{u} \in \mathbb{Z}_q^m$ is a vector of length m whose elements are each in $\mathbb{Z}_q$.

2.1   Group Actions

A group action consists of a (not necessarily abelian) group G, a set X, and a binary operation $* : G \times X \to X$ satisfying the following properties:

- **Identity:** If $e \in G$ is the identity element, then $e * x = x$ for any $x \in X$.
- **Compatibility:** For all $g, h \in G$ and $x \in X$, $(gh) * X = g * (h * X)$.

For applications to cryptography, we want the group action to have certain computationally intractible problems. A typical minimal hard problem is that of computing "discrete logarithms": computing g from x and $g * x$.

Our Model of Black Box Group Actions. Here, we give our model of a black box group action. Our model is analogous to Maurer's [26] model for generic groups, but adapted to group actions. In our case, we model the group itself as a standard-model object, but then the set elements are only provided via handles. In more detail, the following oracles are provided to all parties:

- $\mathsf{Eq}(\langle x \rangle, \langle y \rangle)$ takes as input two handles for set elements x, y, are returns 1 if $x = y$ and 0 otherwise.
- $\mathsf{Act}(g, \langle x \rangle)$ takes as input a group element g and a handle $\langle x \rangle$ to a set element, and returns a handle $\langle y \rangle$ for the set element $y = g * x$.

Additionally, all parties are provided with a handle $\langle x_0 \rangle$ to a starting set element x_0. Each query incurs unit cost, and all computation outside of queries is zero cost. Algorithms are not allowed any computation on handles, except to pass them to other algorithms or send as inputs to the oracles $\mathsf{Eq}, \mathsf{Act}$. The only handles an algorithm can query to $\mathsf{Eq}, \mathsf{Act}$ are those provided explicitly as input (including $\langle x_0 \rangle$), or provided as output of prior queries to Act. A probabilistic polynomial time algorithm is a probabilistic algorithm in this model whose total cost is bounded by a polynomial.

Remark 2.1. The above model assumes there is a single starting handle $\langle x_0 \rangle$, and the only way to derive additional set elements is to act on this handle. This is how existing isogeny-based identification protocols work. However, isogenies provide a bit more functionality: in particular, it is possible to sample directly into the set elements. This does not give the adversary any more power, since such directly sampled elements will be essentially random and unrelated to any other element. However, such sampling could potentially be used in protocol design.

We will not allow such sampling for the rest of this section, as it allows us to explain our main ideas in a simpler manner. In Sect. 4.1 we extend the black box group action model to capture such a functionality, and show that our impossibility also extends to this model.

Verification Oracle. We can augment our black box group action model with the following oracle:

- $\mathsf{Ver}(g, \langle x \rangle, \langle y \rangle)$ which returns 1 if $g * x = y$ and 0 otherwise.

This oracle can readily be simulated as $\mathsf{Eq}(\mathsf{Act}(g, \langle x \rangle), \langle y \rangle)$, so including Ver does not change the model. However, this oracle will still be convenient for our proofs. Concretely, we will make crucial use of the following lemma:

Lemma 2.2. *Let A be a deterministic algorithm in the black box group action model that may take as input handles $\langle x_1 \rangle, \ldots, \langle x_n \rangle$ and non-handle terms, and outputs k handles $\langle y_1 \rangle, \ldots, \langle y_k \rangle$, as well as non-handle terms. Let q be the number of queries A makes. Then there is another algorithm A' with identical input/output behavior to A. However, A' is restricted in the following way:*

- *It makes no queries to Eq.*
- *It makes at most $O(q)$ queries to Ver, which must all come before any Act query.*
- *After making its queries to Ver, it makes exactly k queries to Act in parallel to produce its handle outputs: $\langle y_1 \rangle = \mathsf{Act}(g_1, \langle x_{i_1} \rangle), \ldots, \langle y_k \rangle = \mathsf{Act}(g_k, \langle x_{i_k} \rangle)$. After making the Act queries, A' is not allowed to make any queries to any oracle.*

Lemma 2.2 allows us to reduce general algorithms to relatively simple forms, which will make analyzing them easier. Note that Lemma 2.2 applies also to randomized algorithms by considering the random coins as an input. Then A' will also get these same random coins. We now prove Lemma 2.2.

Proof. Consider a general algorithm A in the black box group action model, which makes arbitrary queries to Eq and Act. We construct A' as follows. We assume that integers and set elements are encoded such that they are disjoint. A' creates "dummy" handles $\langle 1 \rangle, \ldots, \langle n \rangle$, which it feeds into A along with any non-handle inputs. These dummy handles will be stand-ins for the true handles $\langle x_1 \rangle, \ldots, \langle x_n \rangle$ provided to A'. We will also create a table T containing tuples (j, g, i), which correspond to the dummy handle $\langle j \rangle$ being a stand-in for the real handle $\langle g * x_i \rangle$. Therefore, T is initialized to contain the tuples $(i, \mathbb{1}, i)$ for $i = 1, \ldots, n$. We will maintain that A only ever sees dummy handles.

A' simulates A on the dummy handles $\langle 1 \rangle, \ldots, \langle n \rangle$ as well as any non-handle inputs to A'. However, A' will intercept all the queries A makes. On each query:

- If the query has the form $\mathsf{Act}(g, \langle j \rangle)$ query, A' looks up an entry (j, g', i) in T, which will be guaranteed to exist. It will then add the entry $(j', g \cdot g', i)$ to T, where j' is one more than the number of entries in T so far. A' then replies with the dummy handle $\langle j' \rangle$. Note that the entry $(j, g', i) \in T$ means that $\langle j \rangle$ is a stand-in for $\langle g' * x_i \rangle$. Therefore, A expects the result of the query to be $\langle (g \cdot g') * x_i \rangle$, corresponding exactly to the newly added entry $(j', g \cdot g', i)$.
- If the query has the form $\mathsf{Eq}(\langle j_0 \rangle, \langle j_1 \rangle)$, look up entries $(j_0, g_0, i_0), (j_1, g_1, i_1)$ in T, which are guaranteed to exist. Then it makes a query $b \leftarrow \mathsf{Ver}(g_1^{-1} \cdot g_0, \langle x_{i_0} \rangle, \langle x_{i_1} \rangle)$ and replies with b. Note that since $\langle j_0 \rangle$ is a stand-in for $\langle g_0 * x_{i_0} \rangle$ and $\langle j_1 \rangle$ is a stand-in for $\langle g_1 * x_{i_1} \rangle$, we have equality if any only if $g_0 * x_{i_0} = g_1 * x_{i_1} \Leftrightarrow (g_1^{-1} \cdot g_0) * x_{i_0} = x_{i_1}$, which is exactly the result of the Ver query.

Finally, when it A outputs handles $\langle j_1 \rangle, \ldots, \langle j_k \rangle$, A' will look up entries $(j_t, g_t, i_t) \in T$ for $t = 1, \ldots, k$. It will then make a single round of Act queries $\langle y_t \rangle = \mathsf{Act}(g_t, x_{i_t})$. Observe that $\langle j_t \rangle$ is exactly a stand-in for $\langle g_t * x_{i_t} \rangle = \langle y_t \rangle$. A' will output $\langle y_1 \rangle, \ldots, \langle y_k \rangle$, as well as any non-handle outputs of A.

At every step, we therefore see that A' simply replaces the handles A sees with appropriate stand-ins, but correctly answers the Eq queries and produces the correct output handles and non-handle elements. Thus A' perfectly simulates the outputs of A. □

We then define an abstract model for ID protocols that use a graph action.

2.2 ID Protocols Using a Group Action Oracle

Here, we define the abstract model for an ID protocol using a group action oracle. An ID protocol in the black box group action model consists of the following algorithms:

- Gen(), a probabilistic algorithm which makes a polynomial number of queries, and samples a public key/secret key pair (pk, sk). We will always assume without loss of generality that sk is just the random coins used in Gen(). On the other hand, pk may contain a combination of both (handles to) set elements and non-set element terms.
- $\mathcal{P}$(pk, sk), a probabilistic *interactive* algorithm that makes a polynomial number of queries, which takes as input (pk, sk), and interacts with a verifier through several rounds of interaction. In general, the prover's messages may contain any combination of handles to set elements and also non-set element terms.
- $\mathcal{V}$(pk), a probabilistic interactive algorithm that makes a polynomial number of queries, which takes as input pk, and interacts with the prover. In general, the verifier's messages may contain any combination of handles to set elements and also non-set element terms. At the end of the interaction, $\mathcal{V}$ outputs a bit b.

We denote the interaction of of $\mathcal{P}$ and $\mathcal{V}$ by $b \xleftarrow{\$} \mathcal{V}(\text{pk}) \Longleftrightarrow \mathcal{P}(\text{pk}, \text{sk})$. The *transcript* of the interaction is the list T of all messages sent. As we are in the black box group action model, we bound the number of queries of each algorithm to polynomial, but do not otherwise bound the computation outside of the queries.

Definition 2.3. *A protocol* $\Pi = (\text{Gen}, \mathcal{P}, \mathcal{V})$ *has* completeness C *if*

$$\Pr[1 \xleftarrow{\$} \mathcal{V}(\text{pk}) \Longleftrightarrow \mathcal{P}(\text{pk}, \text{sk})] \geq C \ ,$$

where the probability is over $(\text{pk}, \text{sk}) \xleftarrow{\$} \text{Gen}()$ *and the random coins of* $\mathcal{P}, \mathcal{V}$.

We do not define soundness, but instead define the *opposite* of soundness, since we are interested showing that protocols with too little communication are unsound:

Definition 2.4. *A protocol* $\Pi = (\text{Gen}, \mathcal{P}, \mathcal{V})$ *is* (t, S)-unsound *if there exists an algorithm* $\mathcal{A}$ *making polynomially many queries such that*

$$\Pr[1 \xleftarrow{\$} \mathcal{V}(\text{pk}) \Longleftrightarrow \mathcal{A}(\text{pk}, T_1, \ldots, T_t)] \geq S \ ,$$

where $T_1, \ldots, T_t$ *are* t *transcripts of independent trials of* $\mathcal{V}(\text{pk}) \Longleftrightarrow \mathcal{P}(\text{pk}, \text{sk})$. *Here, the probability is over* $(\text{pk}, \text{sk}) \xleftarrow{\$} \text{Gen}()$, *the randomness of the transcripts* T_i, *and the random coins of* $\mathcal{A}, \mathcal{V}$.

Definition 2.5. *We say a protocol* Π *is* public coin *if* $\mathcal{V}$*'s random coins can be written as* $(c_1, \ldots, c_k)$ *such that the ith message of* $\mathcal{V}$ *is* c_i.

For a public coin protocol, we will equivalently think of $\mathcal{V}$ as just being an algorithm which takes as input the transcript and outputs a bit b. The execution of the protocol itself simply chooses each message from the verifier uniformly at random.

Notation. We will be using the following notation for ID protocols throughout this paper:

C: the correctness probability t: number of transcripts given to the adversary
S: the soundness error P: the number of set elements in the public key
R: the number of rounds N: the number of set elements sent by the prover

We will be considering multiple ID protocols throughout this paper, which we distinguish by subscripts, e.g. $\Pi_1, \Pi_2, \dots$. In such cases, we will use the same subscripts for our notation: e.g. $C_1, C_2, \dots$ for correctness probability, etc.

3   The Lower Bound

This section contains our main theorem, a lower bound on the communication of any secure group-action-based ID protocol.

3.1   The Main Theorem

Theorem 3.1. *If a public coin ID protocol Π in the black box group action model has completeness C, then for any polynomial t, the protocol is (t, S)-unsound, for $S \geq (C - P/t - 1/\mathsf{poly}) \times P^{-N}$, where poly is any polynomial. In particular, if $S \leq 2^{-\lambda}$, $C \geq 0.99$ and $t \geq 2.05P$, then $N \geq (\lambda - 1)/\log_2 P$.*

In other words, if we want λ-bit security, we need the number of set elements sent by the prover to be at least $(\lambda - 1)/\log_2 P$. As each set element itself will generally be at least λ bits, and the number of public key elements is a polymomial, this means λ bits of security requires total prover communication size of $\Omega(\lambda^2/\log \lambda)$. This corresponds to the size of signatures once we apply Fiat-Shamir.

In the remainder of this section, we now prove this theorem using a sequence of protocol simplification steps.

3.2   Normal Form Protocols

Label the set elements of the public key $1, \dots, P$. Given a transcript T, we will then number the set elements in T as $P + 1, \dots, P + N$ in the order they appear in T. Let $V = [P + N]$. We will somewhat abuse notation and refer to $\{1, \dots, P\} \subseteq V$ as public key elements, and $\{P + 1, \dots, P + N\}$ as transcript elements.

Definition 3.2. *A public coin ID protocol is in* normal form *if the following are true:*

- *Verification is deterministic conditioned on the transcript.*
- *Verification only queries* Ver *and not* Act, Eq.

– The final message from the prover contains a list Q, where each entry in Q has the form (g, i, j, b). Here, $i, j \in [P + N]$ index into the combined set elements of the public key and transcript, g is a group element, and b is a bit. Let x_i, x_j be the elements at position i and j, respectively. (g, i, j, b) corresponds to querying $\mathsf{Ver}(g, \langle x_i \rangle, \langle x_j \rangle)$ and receiving outcome b.

– The verifier first makes verification queries corresponding to those in Q: for a tuple (g, i, j, b), it queries $b' \leftarrow \mathsf{Ver}(g, \langle x_i \rangle, \langle x_j \rangle)$. These are the only queries it makes. If any of the query responses are inconsistent with Q, that is if $b \neq b'$, the verifier immediately aborts and rejects.

Assuming all queries are consistent, the verifier is allowed arbitrary subsequent deterministic computation to decide whether to accept or reject, but it can make no additional queries.

Lemma 3.3. *If there is a public coin ID protocol Π in the group action model, then there is also a normal form ID protocol Π_1 such that $t_1 = t, C_1 = C, S_1 = S, N_1 = N, P_1 = P, R_1 = R + 2$.*

Proof. First, observe that we can trivially make any protocol have deterministic verification by adding to the end of the protocol a message from $\mathcal{V}$ to $\mathcal{P}$ containing the random coins of $\mathcal{V}$. We therefore assume deterministic verification. By Lemma 2.2, since verification outputs a bit (and therefore no handles), we can also assume the verifier only makes queries to Ver and not $\mathsf{Eq}, \mathsf{Act}$.

Now that verification is deterministic, let $\mathcal{P}_1$ be the new prover, which runs $\mathcal{P}$. Then, at the end of running $\mathcal{P}$, $\mathcal{P}_1$ runs the verifier for itself, to see exactly what queries the verifier will make, assembling the query list Q.

We now explain how to construct $\mathcal{V}_1$. First, for each $(g, i, j, b) \in Q$, $\mathcal{V}_1$ makes the corresponding query to Ver, obtaining b'. If $b \neq b'$, then $\mathcal{V}_1$ immediately aborts and rejects.

If $b = b'$ for each $(g, i, j, b) \in Q$, then $\mathcal{V}_1$ runs $\mathcal{V}$ on the first $r + 1$ messages of the transcript, except that it has to intercept all of the Ver queries $\mathcal{V}$ makes, which correspond to an entry $(g, i, j, b) \in Q$, and answers the query with b.

It is straightforward that $\mathcal{V}_1 \Longleftrightarrow \mathcal{P}_1$ exactly simulates the behavior of $\mathcal{V} \Longleftrightarrow \mathcal{P}$, and so $C_1 = C$. For soundness, consider an adversary $\mathcal{A}_1$ that convinces $\mathcal{V}_1$ with probability S_1. We construct an adversary $\mathcal{A}$ that convinces $\mathcal{V}$ with probability S. $\mathcal{A}$ runs $\mathcal{A}_1$, and just discards the query list Q that $\mathcal{A}'$ outputs. If $\mathcal{A}_1$ wins, then it must be that all queries $\mathcal{V}_1$ (and hence $\mathcal{V}$) makes are consistent with Q, and also that $\mathcal{V}$ accepts. In other words, $\mathcal{V}$ accepts transcript T whenever $\mathcal{V}_1$ accepts transcript T_1, where T is the same as T' but with the query list Q discarded. Hence $S \geq S_1$. □

3.3 The Transcript Graph

Recall that $V = [P + N]$ indexes the combined set elements of the public key and transcript, with $[P]$ corresponding to the public key elements and $[P + 1, P + N]$ corresponding to the transcript elements.

Consider running the verifier $\mathcal{V}$. Any accepting Ver query by $\mathcal{V}$ corresponds to an edge between nodes in V; call this edge set of accepting queries E. Then

$G_T = (V, E)$ forms an undirected graph. G_T is the *transcript graph* of T. We note that verification may be randomized, yielding different transcript graphs each time. However, we will always assume a normal form protocol with deterministic verification, meaning that G_T is uniquely determined by the protocol transcript.

We say that a transcript graph is *valid* if there is no path between any two distinct public key elements. In other words, each public key element lies in a different connected component. Otherwise, a transcript graph is *invalid*.

3.4   Respecting Verifiers

Definition 3.4. *A* respecting verifier for a normal-form protocol *is one that always rejects transcripts with invalid transcript graphs.*

Lemma 3.5. *If there is a public coin normal form ID protocol Π_1 in the group action model, then there is also a public coin normal form ID protocol Π_2 with a respecting verifier, such that $t_2 = 0, C_2 \geq C_1 - N_1/t_1, S_2 \leq S_1, N_2 = N_1, P_2 \leq P_1, R_2 = R_1$.*

Proof. The intuition is that we use the provided protocol transcripts to compute the discrete logarithms between public key elements, and then use this information to represent certain public key elements in terms of others. This lets us remove such public key elements. If the next protocol run would have likely connected two public key elements together, then the previous runs would have also likely connected them anyway, meaning one of the elements would not have been in the public key in the first place.

In more detail, given $\Pi_1 = (\mathsf{Gen}_1, \mathcal{P}_1, \mathcal{V}_1)$ for a public coin normal form ID protocol, we construct $\Pi_2 = (\mathsf{Gen}_2, \mathcal{P}_2, \mathcal{V}_2)$ as follows.

$\mathsf{Gen}_2()$: First run $(\mathsf{pk}_1, \mathsf{sk}_1) \xleftarrow{\$} \mathsf{Gen}_1()$. Now run $\mathcal{P}_1(\mathsf{pk}_1, \mathsf{sk}_1) \Longleftrightarrow \mathcal{V}_1(\mathsf{pk}_1)$ for t_1 independent trails, collecting transcripts $T_1, \ldots, T_{t_1}$. It then computes the transcript graphs $G_{T_1}, \ldots, G_{T_{t_1}}$. Then for $i = 1, \ldots, P_1$, it does the following:

- If the i-th public key set element $\langle x_i \rangle$ is connected to any previous public key set element $\langle x_j \rangle$ at position $j < i$ through any path of edges in $\cup_{\ell \in [t_1]} G_{T_\ell}$, take the minimal such j. Then use the queries in T_ℓ to determine the group element g such that $x_i = g * x_j$. Delete $\langle x_i \rangle$ from the public key, and replace it with the pair (j, g). If there is no such path, then leave $\langle x_i \rangle$ as is.

Note that since j is minimal, in particular x_j is not connected to any x_ℓ for $\ell < j$. So if $\langle x_i \rangle$ is replaced with (j, g), it must mean that $\langle x_j \rangle$ has not been deleted.

Then $\mathsf{pk}_2 = \mathsf{pk}_1$, except with all the deleted set elements replaced by the appropriate (j, g). $\mathsf{sk}_2 = \mathsf{sk}_1$ [4].

---

[4] Technically, we assumed sk was the random coins of Gen, and so our sk_2 should also include the random coins used to generate the T_i. However, this information will not be needed in the actual protocol, so we can think of sk_2 as being just sk_1.

$\mathcal{P}_2$: $\mathcal{P}_2$ runs $\mathcal{P}_1$, except that any time $\mathcal{P}_2$ would need a deleted $\langle x_i \rangle$ from the public key, $\mathcal{P}_2$ re-computes it as $\langle x_i \rangle = \mathsf{Act}(g, \langle x_j \rangle)$ for the appropriate (j, g).

$\mathcal{V}_2$: $\mathcal{V}_2$ runs $\mathcal{V}_1$, except that any time $\mathcal{V}_1$ would needs a deleted $\langle x_i \rangle$ from the public key, $\mathcal{V}_2$ re-computes it as $\langle x_i \rangle = \mathsf{Act}(g, \langle x_j \rangle)$ for the appropriate (j, g). Moreover, at the end of the protocol $\mathcal{V}_2$ computes the transcript graph G_T, defined over the non-deleted elements in pk_2, and automatically rejects if G_T is invalid.

Security. If $\mathcal{V}_2$ did not check the validity of G_T, then the interaction between $\mathcal{P}_2$ and $\mathcal{V}_2$ is identical to that of $\mathcal{P}_1, \mathcal{V}_1$, since each just re-computes the correct $\langle x_i \rangle$ as needed. Moreover, notice that computing pk_2 from pk_1 can be done by an adversary for $\mathcal{P}_1, \mathcal{V}_1$ using the t_1 transcripts provided to it in the passive security game. Adding a reject condition in $\mathcal{V}_2$ only decreases the adversary's success probability.

Correctness. In order to establish the correctness of the protocol, we just need to bound the probability G_T is invalid. Fix some $(\mathsf{pk}_1, \mathsf{sk}_1)$. For any transcript graph G_T, let G'_T be the induced graph with nodes in $[P_1]$, where there is an edge between two nodes in $[P_1]$ if and only if there is a path between those nodes in G_T. Let n_i be the number of connected components in $G'_i := \cup_{j \leq i} G'_{T_j}$, and $e_i = \mathbb{E}[n_i]$ be the expectation of n_i. Note that $n_0 = P_1$, $n_i \geq 0$ for all i, and $n_{i+1} \leq n_i$. Therefore, these (in)equalities hold in expectation.

Moreover, $i \mapsto e_i$ is convex, meaning $e_i - e_{i+1} \leq e_{i-1} - e_i$ for all i. To see this, let n'_i be the number of connected components in $G'_{T_{i-1}} \cup G'_{T_{i+1}}$. The difference relative to n_i is that we swap out G'_{T_i} for $G'_{T_{i+1}}$. Let $e'_i = \mathbb{E}[n'_i]$. Since G'_{T_i} and $G'_{T_{i+1}}$ come from the same distribution, we must have $e'_i = e_i$. Now let $r_i := n_{i-1} - n_i$ and $r'_i := n_{i-1} - n'_i$. This means $G'_{T_{i+1}}$ connects r_{i+1} pairs of the connected components of G'_i together, and r'_i pairs of connected components of G'_{i-1}. For every connection $G'_{T_{i+1}}$ makes between connected components of G'_i, there are corresponding connected components of G'_{i-1} that it also connects, since the connected components of G'_{i-1} is just a refinement of the connected components of G'_i. Thus $r'_i \geq r_{i+1}$, meaning $\mathbb{E}[r_i] = \mathbb{E}[r'_i] \geq \mathbb{E}[r_{i+1}]$. Hence $e_i - e_{i+1} \leq e_{i-1} - e_i$.

By the triangle inequality, this means $|e_{t_1+1} - e_{t_1}| \leq P_1/t_1$. In particular, $\Pr[n_{t_1+1} < n_{t_1}] < P_1/t_1$. But notice that $n_{t_1+1} = n_{t_1}$ corresponds to the transcript graph of $\mathcal{P}_2 \Longleftrightarrow \mathcal{V}_2$ being valid. This is because pk_2 has exactly n_{t_1} public key elements remaining, one for each connected component in $\cup_{j \in [t_1]} G'_{T_j}$. Then any edge between remaining public key elements in pk_2 would have reduced the number of connected components, implying $n_{t_1+1} < n_{t_1}$.

Therefore, except with probability P_1/t_1, the transcript graph for $\mathcal{P}_2 \Longleftrightarrow \mathcal{V}_2$ is valid. This means $\mathcal{V}_2$ accepts with probability at least $C_2 \geq C_1 - P_1/t_1$. $\square$

3.5   Guessing Provers

A guessing prover has the following structure:

- The prover initially guesses a random partition W of V, such that each set in the partition contains exactly one public key element. In other words, for each transcript element in V, the prover chooses a random public key element to associate the transcript element to. The number of possible W is P^N.
- Recall by Lemma 2.2 that we can always assume the prover only queries Act on input set elements, and immediately outputs the result of the query as an set output. Consider such a query $\langle y \rangle = \mathsf{Act}(g, \langle x \rangle)$. The prover guarantees that for any such query, $\langle y \rangle$ is in the same element of W as is $\langle x \rangle$.
- Let W' be the partition corresponding to the connected components of the final transcript graph G_T. Then if W' is not a refinement of W, the prover aborts and sends $\perp$ for its last message (which the verifier would presumably reject if it were respecting).
- The prover never makes any queries to Eq.

Lemma 3.6. *If there is a public coin normal form ID protocol Π_2 with a respecting verifier in the group action model and $t_2 = 0$, then there is a public coin normal form ID protocol Π_3 with a respecting verifier and guessing prover such that $t_3 = 0, C_3 \geq C_2 \times P_2^{-N_2}, S_3 \leq S_2, N_3 = N_2, P_3 = P_2, R_3 = R_2$. In particular, conditioned on $\mathcal{P}_3$ not sending $\perp$, its correctness probability is at least C_2.*

Proof. Recall that we assume $\mathcal{P}$ is given the random coins used during setup. In particular, $\mathcal{P}$ is able to compute the discrete logs between public key elements. This means it always knows the discrete logs between any group elements, and can therefore answer any Eq query by itself without making the query.

$\mathcal{P}_3$ simply runs $\mathcal{P}_2$, except that it processes each query. Suppose $\mathcal{P}_2$ computes $\langle y \rangle = \mathsf{Act}(g, \langle x_1 \rangle)$ for public key element $\langle x_1 \rangle$, while $\mathcal{P}_3$ needs to compute $\langle y \rangle = \mathsf{Act}(g', \langle x_2 \rangle)$ for some other public key element $\langle x_2 \rangle$. Since $\mathcal{P}_3$ can compute the discrete log h such that $x_1 = h * x_2$, we can simply set $g' = gh$. Thus, $\mathcal{P}_3$ perfectly simulates the messages of $\mathcal{P}_2$, until the last message. Importantly, all the previous messages are independent of W.

Whenever the prover convinces the verifier, since the verifier is respecting, the transcript graph is valid and must therefore have each public key element in a different connecting component. Let W' be the associated partition of the public key elements. Since W' is independent of W, we must have that $W' = W$ with probability $P_2^{-N_2}$. In particular, W' is a refinement of W with probability at least $P_2^{-N_2}$. Hence, the overall correctness probability is at least $C_3 \geq C_2 \times P_2^{-N_2}$. $\square$

3.6   Finishing the Proof of Theorem 3.1

We are now ready to finish the proof of Theorem 3.1, by showing the following

Lemma 3.7. *If there is a public coin normal form ID protocol Π_2 with a respecting verifier in the group action model, then for any polynomial poly, $S_2 \geq (C_2 - 1/\mathsf{poly}) \times P_2^{-N_2}$*

Proof. We first invoke Lemma 3.6 to arrive at a protocol Π_3 with soundness error $S_3 \leq S_2$, and where the guessing prover $\mathcal{P}_3$ has correctness C_2 conditioned on it not sending $\bot$ in the last message, for an overall correctness probability $C_3 \geq C_2 \times P_2^{-N_2}$.

We create a family of malicious provers $\mathcal{A}^{(i)}$, which are only given pk_3, and attempt to simulate $\mathcal{P}_3$. Let aux_3 be the non-set element part of pk_3. $\mathcal{A}^{(i)}$ samples random coins for Gen_3, conditioned on Gen_3 outputting aux_3. By Lemma 2.2, the part of Gen_3 that outputs aux_3 maps bits to bits, and so makes no oracle queries at all. Therefore, sampling the random coins can be done without making any queries. Let $\mathsf{sk}_3^{(1)}$ be the obtained public key.

In the case of $\mathcal{A}^{(1)}$, we now simply run $\mathcal{P}_3(\mathsf{pk}_3, \mathsf{sk}_3^{(1)})$. Let $q^{(1)}$ be the probability of convincing the verifier, conditioned on the final message of $\mathcal{P}_3$ not being $\bot$. When ignoring the set elements, $\mathsf{sk}_3^{(1)}$ is identically distributed to sk_3. Therefore, $\mathcal{P}_3(\mathsf{pk}_3, \mathsf{sk}_3^{(1)})$ is identically distributed to $\mathcal{P}_3(\mathsf{pk}_3, \mathsf{sk}_3)$, unless (1) the $\mathcal{P}_3(\mathsf{pk}_3, \mathsf{sk}_3^{(1)})$ does not send $\bot$, and also (2) there is a query in $(g, i, j, b) \in Q$ where $b \neq \mathsf{Ver}(g, \langle x_i \rangle, \langle x_j \rangle)$. We note that if i, j are in the same part of the partition W, then this is guaranteed to never happen, since all elements within a partition element are generated as in the honest $\mathcal{P}_3$. Also, recall that the verifier is respecting, meaning for i, j in different parts, it rejects if ever $b = 1$.

Therefore, the only "bad" case is when i, j are in different parts of the partition W, $\mathcal{A}^{(1)}$ generates $(g, i, j, b = 0)$, but actually $\mathsf{Ver}(g, \langle x_i \rangle, \langle x_j \rangle) = 1$, meaning $g * x_i = x_j$. But observe that, in this case, the actual Ver query reveals the discrete log between two public key elements, which presumably should be hard. We will use this bad event to create a different adversary with a better success probability.

Concretely, let $\mathcal{A}^{(2)}$, generates $\mathsf{sk}_3^{(1)}$, but then simulates for itself the interaction $\mathcal{V}_3(\mathsf{pk}) \Longleftrightarrow \mathcal{A}^{(1)}(\mathsf{pk}_3, \mathsf{sk}_3^{(1)})$ (choosing its own messages for $\mathcal{V}_3$), but conditioned on the final transcript graph G_T yielding a partition W' that is a refinement of W. Note that since $\mathcal{P}_3$ never makes queries to Eq and the transcript graph G_T does not contain set elements, determining whether the simulation has W' being a refinement of W can be computed without making any oracle queries at all (by Lemma 2.2). So even though this event is exponentially unlikely, conditioning on this event can be done with only a polynomial number of queries (namely the number of queries in the protocol). Let $p^{(1)}$ be the probability a discrete log is revealed. By our conditioning on $\mathcal{P}_3$ not sending $\bot$, we have that $(C_3 - q^{(1)}) \leq p^{(1)}$.

Then $\mathcal{A}^{(2)}$ chooses $\mathsf{sk}_3^{(2)}$ from the same distribution as $\mathsf{sk}_3^{(1)}$, *except* that if any discrete logs $g * x_i = x_j$ are revealed in the first step, it *also* conditions on Gen producing public key elements with these discrete log. As before, this conditional sampling can be done without making any queries. Now $\mathcal{A}^{(2)}$ simply runs $\mathcal{P}_3(\mathsf{pk}_3, \mathsf{sk}_3^{(2)})$. Let $q^{(1)}$ be the probability of convincing the verifier, conditioned on the final output of $\mathcal{P}_3$ not being $\bot$. Now by similar arguments as before, $\mathcal{P}_3(\mathsf{pk}_3, \mathsf{sk}_3^{(2)})$ is identically distributed to $\mathcal{P}_3(\mathsf{pk}_3, \mathsf{sk}_3)$, unless a "bad" case occurs, where Q contains $(g, i, j, b = 0)$ such that $\mathsf{Ver}(g, \langle x_i \rangle, \langle x_j \rangle) = 1$.

Except here, the "bad" case must also reveal a "new" discrete log, meaning $g * x_i = x_j$ could not be derived from any discrete logs revealed in the first step. This is because if $g * x_i = x_j$ could be derived from the discrete logs in the first step, our conditioning on the discrete logs in the first step would have ensured that Q contained the correct value of b. Let $p^{(2)}$ be the probability that a new discrete log is revealed. By our conditioning, we have that $(C_3 - q^{(2)}) \leq p^{(2)}$.

We similarly define $\mathcal{A}^{(3)}, \mathcal{A}^{(4)}, \ldots$. We have that $(C_3 - q^{(i)}) \leq p^{(i)}$.

Now, note that there can only be at most $P_3 - 1$ "new" discrete logs revealed across the various steps. This means that, for any u, $\sum_{i=1}^{u} p^{(i)} \leq P_3 - 1$. This in particular means that, for any u, there must be an $i \in [u]$ such that $p^{(i)} < P_3/u$. So for any desired polynomial error poly, there will be some $i \leq \text{poly} \times P_3$ such that $p^{(i)} < 1/\text{poly}$, in which case $q^{(i)} > C_3 - 1/\text{poly}$. In other words, $\mathcal{A}^{(i)}$, conditioned on not outputting $\perp$ in the final message, convinced the verifier with probability at least $C_3 - 1/\text{poly}$. Then, since $\mathcal{A}^{(i)}$ outputs something other than $\perp$ with probability at least $P_3^{-N_3}$, the overall soundness error of $\mathcal{A}^{(i)}$ is at least $S_3 \geq (C_3 - 1/\text{poly}) \times P_3^{-N_3}$.

It remains to show that $\mathcal{A}^{(i)}$ makes a polynomial number of queries. Indeed, the sampling of the various $\text{sk}_3^{(j)}$ requires no queries, and then $\mathcal{A}^{(i)}$ runs i executions of the protocol, each incurring a polynomial number of queries. Since i itself is polynomial, the total query count is polynomial. □

4 Extensions

Here, we discuss a few possible different models for black box group actions, extending our model from Sect. 3.

4.1 Direct Sampling

We now consider a model which captures the following feature of isogeny-based group actions: the ability to directly sample into the set elements, without having to act on existing elements. Our model is identical to the model from Sect. 2, except that it provides an additional random oracle for sampling elements:

- $\text{Eq}(\langle x \rangle, \langle y \rangle)$ takes as input two handles for set elements x, y, are returns 1 if $x = y$ and 0 otherwise.
- $\text{Act}(g, \langle x \rangle)$ takes as input a group element g and a handle $\langle x \rangle$ to a set element, and returns a handle $\langle y \rangle$ for the set element $y = g * x$.
- $\text{Samp}(s)$ takes as input a string $s \in \{0,1\}^\lambda$ and outputs $\langle L(s) \rangle$ where $L : \{0,1\}^\lambda \to X$ is a uniform random function.

As before, each query incurs unit cost, and all computation outside of queries is zero cost. Algorithms are not allowed any computation on handles, except to pass them to other algorithms or send as inputs to the oracles Eq, Act. The only handles an algorithm can query to Eq, Act are those provided explicitly as input, or provided as output of prior queries to Act or Samp. Note that we do not explicitly provide an $\langle x_0 \rangle$ as it is redundant, given Samp.

We call this model the *extended* black box group action model. We now prove the following:

Theorem 4.1. *If a public coin ID protocol Π in the extended black box group action model has completeness C, then for any polynomial t, the protocol is (t, S)-unsound, for $S \geq (C - P/t - 1/\mathsf{poly}) \times (P+1)^{-N}$, where poly is any polynomial. In particular, if $S \leq 2^{-\lambda}$, $C \geq 0.99$ and $t \geq 2.05P$, then $N \geq (\lambda-1)/\log_2(P+1)$.*

Note that the quantitative theorem statement is almost identical to that of Theorem 3.1, except that P^{-N} is replaced with $(P+1)^{-N}$. This slightly weaker bound is inconsequential for security.

Proof. The proof follows a very similar outline to the proof of Theorem 3.1, with a couple of key changes.

Normal Form Protocols. We first define a normal form protocol similar to Definition 3.2, but with some changes:

- Verification is deterministic conditioned on the transcript. This is identical to Definition 3.2.
- Verification only queries Ver, Samp and not Act, Eq. This is identical to Definition 3.2, except that we allow for Samp queries.
- The final message from the prover contains a list Q, where each entry in Q has either the form (g, i, j, b) or s. Here, (g, i, j, b) represents an Act query as in Definition 3.2. The new part are terms of the form s, which correspond to a query Samp(s).
- The verifier first makes queries corresponding to those in Q. These are the only queries it makes. If any of the query responses are inconsistent with Q, the verifier immediately aborts and rejects.

  Assuming all queries are consistent, the verifier is allowed arbitrary subsequent deterministic computation to decide whether to accept or reject, but it can make no additional queries.

By an essentially identical proof to that of Lemma 3.3, we can conclude the following:

Lemma 4.2. *If there is a public coin ID protocol Π in the group action model, then there is also a normal form ID protocol Π_1 such that $t_1 = t, C_1 = C, S_1 = S, N_1 = N, P_1 = P, R_1 = R + 2$.*

The Transcript Graph. We define the transcript graph similarly to Sect. 3, except that we also include the results of any verifier queries to Samp as nodes in the graph. We connect nodes in this graph via accepting Ver queries as before.

We say that a transcript graph is *valid* if there is no path between any two public key elements, and also no path between a public key element and an Samp element. We include paths of length zero in our notion of paths, so every node has a path to itself. In other words, each public key element lies in a different connected component, and those connected components are distinct from any connected component containing an Samp element. Otherwise, a transcript graph is *invalid*.

Respecting Verifiers. As in Sect. 3, a respecting verifier for a normal-form protocol is one that rejects invalid transcript graphs, except we use our updated notion of invalid transcripts. We now state an updated version of Lemma 3.3 to work with extended group actions, which follows from an essentially identical argument.

Lemma 4.3. *If there is a public coin normal form ID protocol Π_1 in the extended group action model, then there is also a public coin normal form ID protocol Π_2 with a respecting verifier, such that $t_2 = 0, C_2 \geq C_1 - N_1/t_1, S_2 \leq S_1, N_2 = N_1, P_2 \leq P_1, R_2 = R_1$.*

Guessing Provers. A guessing prover has the following structure:

- The prover initially guesses a random partition W of V into $P + 1$ sets, P of which contain exactly one public key element, and the final set containing none. The difference from Sect. 3 is that we allow for this extra set containing no public key elements. The number of possible W is $(P+1)^N$, slightly more than in Sect. 3 owing to the additional set.
- The prover only queries Act on input set elements or the result of a Samp query. It then immediately outputs the result of the Act query as an set output. Moreover, for any such query $\langle y \rangle = \text{Act}(g, \langle x \rangle)$, the prover guarantees that $\langle y \rangle$ and $\langle x \rangle$ are in the same element of W. This is the same as Sect. 3, except we allow the prover to derive its outputs also from Samp queries.
- Let W' be the partition corresponding to the connected components of the final transcript graph G_T. Then if W' is not a refinement of W, the prover aborts and sends $\perp$ for its last message (which the verifier would presumably reject if it were respecting).
- The prover never makes any queries to Eq.

The following is proved via an almost identical proof to Lemma 3.6:

Lemma 4.4. *If there is a public coin normal form ID protocol Π_2 with a respecting verifier in the extended group action model and $t_2 = 0$, then there is a public coin normal form ID protocol Π_3 with a respecting verifier and guessing prover such that $t_3 = 0, C_3 \geq C_2 \times P_2^{-N_2}, S_3 \leq S_2, N_3 = N_2, P_3 = P_2, R_3 = R_2$. In particular, conditioned on $\mathcal{P}_3$ not sending $\perp$, its correctness probability is at least C_2.*

Finishing the Proof. We now give an extension of Lemma 3.7, which finishes the proof of Theorem 4.1:

Lemma 4.5. *If there is a public coin normal form ID protocol Π_2 with a respecting verifier in the group action model, then for any polynomial* poly,
$$S_2 \geq (C_2 - 1/\text{poly}) \times (P_2 + 1)^{-N_2}$$

The proof follows an almost identical argument to that of Lemma 3.7, leveraging Lemma 4.4. Putting Lemmas 4.2, 4.3, and 4.5 together gives Theorem 4.1.

$\square$

4.2   Black Box Graph Actions

Here, we generalize the group structure of the black box group action to what we call a *graph* action. Instead of a group, there is a labelled directed graph $G = (X, E)$ whose nodes are the set X, satisfying the following properties:

- **Reversibility:** If there is an edge $(x, y) \in E$, then $(y, x) \in E$.
- **Composition:** If there is a path p from x to y, then the edge $(x, y) \in E$.
- **Unambiguous labels:** For any node x, all the outgoing edges from x have distinct labels. Likewise, all the incoming edges to x have distinct labels. There may be overlapping edges amongst between the incoming and outgoing edges.
- **Base labels:** There is a set S of labels, such that for every node $x \in X$ and every label $s \in S$, there is an incoming edge and an outgoing edge from x with label s.

In the case of a group action, the edge labels are group elements, and for all nodes x and group elements g, the edge $(x, g * x) \in E$ and has label g. Reversibility, composition, and unambiguous labels follow immediately from the basic properties of group actions.

Now the following oracles are provided to all parties:

- $\mathsf{Eq}(\langle x \rangle, \langle y \rangle)$ takes as input two handles for set elements x, y, are returns 1 if $x = y$ and 0 otherwise.
- $\mathsf{Act}(\ell, \langle x \rangle)$ takes as input a label ℓ and a handle $\langle x \rangle$ to a node. If there is an edge $(x, y) \in E$ with label ℓ, then output $(\ell', \langle y \rangle)$, where ℓ' is the label for $(y, x) \in E$. Otherwise output $\perp$.
- $\mathsf{Inv}(\ell, \langle x \rangle)$ takes as input a label ℓ and a handle $\langle x \rangle$ to a node. If there is an edge $(y, x) \in E$ with label ℓ, then output $(\ell', \langle y \rangle)$, where ℓ' is the label for $(x, y) \in E$. Otherwise output $\perp$.
- $\mathsf{Comp}(\ell_1, \ell_2, \langle x \rangle)$ takes as input labels ℓ_1, ℓ_2 and a handle $\langle x \rangle$ to a node. If there are edges $(x, y) \in E$ and $(y, z) \in E$ with labels ℓ_1, ℓ_2 respectively, then output ℓ_3, the label for the edge (x, z). Otherwise output $\perp$.

Like with the group action model, each query incurs unit cost, and all computation outside of queries is zero cost. Algorithms are not allowed any computation on handles, except to pass them to other algorithms or send as inputs to the oracles $\mathsf{Eq}, \mathsf{Act}, \mathsf{Inv}, \mathsf{Comp}$. A probabilistic polynomial time algorithm is a probabilistic algorithm in this model whose total cost is bounded by a polynomial. We can also consider extending the model to include an Samp which generates handles to random nodes.

By inspecting our proof of Theorem 3.1, we see that our lower bound also holds in the black box graph action model. The limitation of this model, however, is that for many graphs, there is trivially no security. Thus, while our impossibility for short signatures will apply for arbitrary graphs, in many cases the impossibility is uninteresting as there will be more trivial attacks.

In more detail, consider an adversary given a handle $\langle x \rangle$ to a node. The adversary can choose two arbitrary labels ℓ_1, ℓ_2, and compute $\mathsf{Comp}(\ell_1, \ell_2, \langle x \rangle)$, resulting in a label ℓ_3. Observe that ℓ_1, ℓ_2, ℓ_3 are given as *bit-strings*, as opposed to handles.

For a general graph structure, it may be that $\mathsf{Comp}(\ell_1, \ell_2, \langle x \rangle) \neq \mathsf{Comp}(\ell_1, \ell_2, \langle y \rangle)$ for different nodes x, y. Thus, ℓ_3 potentially tells us information about x. If the adversary can generate many such (ℓ_1, ℓ_2) pairs, then after a polynomial number of queries x may be uniquely determined by the list of $\ell_3 = \mathsf{Comp}(\ell_1, \ell_2, \langle x \rangle)$ values. In such a case, the graph action trivially has no security: an adversary can de-reference $\langle x \rangle$ into x by making a polynomial number of queries to get a list of ℓ_3 values, and then brute force search for a node $x \in G$ with the given composition structure. This brute force search may require exponential computation, but since the query count is polynomial this would be considered an adversary in the black box graph action model.

Such a trivial insecurity does not contradict our lower bound, but would render it meaningless.

The obvious way out would be for the graph to have the property that $\mathsf{Comp}(\ell_1, \ell_2, \langle x \rangle) = \mathsf{Comp}(\ell_1, \ell_2, \langle y \rangle)$ for all x, y, or at least for equality to hold with overwhelming probability over random x, y. In other words, for any ℓ_1, ℓ_2, there is a unique ℓ_3 such that $\mathsf{Comp}(\ell_1, \ell_2, \langle x \rangle) = \ell_3$ for most x.

But in this case, if we define $\ell_1 \times \ell_2$ as the unique ℓ_3, this gives us a group structure on the set of labels, and this group acts on the set X. Thus, it appears that to avoid trivial attacks, we actually imposed a group action structure, and thus reduce to the case of Sect. 3.

4.3   A Fully Idealized Graph Action

Here, we present a fully idealized graph action model, which allows for general graphs (not corresponding to group actions) without rendering the graph action model trivially insecure.

The idea is to protect edge labels behind handles, in addition to the nodes. This means that, even though $\mathsf{Comp}(\ell_1, \ell_2, \langle x \rangle) \neq \mathsf{Comp}(\ell_1, \ell_2, \langle y \rangle)$, the actual output of $\mathsf{Comp}(\ell_1, \ell_2, \langle x \rangle)$ is a handle. Attempting to brute force search for x given the list of label handles is no longer possible without making exponentially many queries.

This model is incomparable to the previous graph action model and also the group action model: while it prevents the attacker from making use of the bit representation of edge labels, it also prevents the *construction* from making use of such labels. In much of the group action and isogeny literature, the protocols do not need the bit representation, and would work with such a fully idealized graph action model. But there are construction techniques that would make use of such a bit representation (see [38] for a discussion in the context of generic groups), and our fully idealized model would not allow for such techniques. Thus, while the model extends the graph structure, it limits constructions in other ways.

We now give the model. The graph $G = (X, E)$ is still defined in the same way, but we modify the oracles that are provided to the parties:

- $\mathsf{Eq}(\langle x \rangle, \langle y \rangle)$ takes as input two handles for set elements x, y, are returns 1 if $x = y$ and 0 otherwise.

- Act($\langle \ell \rangle, \langle x \rangle$) takes as input *a handle* $\langle \ell \rangle$ *to* a label and a handle $\langle x \rangle$ to a node. If there is an edge $(x, y) \in E$ with label ℓ, then output $(\langle \ell' \rangle, \langle y \rangle)$, where ℓ' is the label for $(y, x) \in E$. Otherwise output $\perp$.
- Inv($\langle \ell \rangle, \langle x \rangle$) takes as input *a handle* $\langle \ell \rangle$ *to* a label and a handle $\langle x \rangle$ to a node. If there is an edge $(y, x) \in E$ with label ℓ, then output $(\langle \ell' \rangle, \langle y \rangle)$, where ℓ' is the label for $(x, y) \in E$. Otherwise output $\perp$.
- Comp($\langle \ell_1 \rangle, \langle \ell_2 \rangle, \langle x \rangle$) takes as input handles $\langle \ell_1 \rangle, \langle \ell_2 \rangle$ to labels and a handle $\langle x \rangle$ to a node. If there are edges $(x, y) \in E$ and $(y, z) \in E$ with labels ℓ_1, ℓ_2 respectively, then output $\langle \ell_3 \rangle$, the handle to the label for the edge (x, z). Otherwise output $\perp$.

The following is a straightforward extension of Theorem 3.1:

Theorem 4.6. *If a public coin ID protocol Π in the fully idealized black box graph action model has completeness C, then for any polynomial t, the protocol is (t, S)-unsound, for $S \geq (C - P/t - 1/\mathsf{poly}) \times P^{-N}$, where poly is any polynomial. In particular, if $S \leq 2^{-\lambda}$, $C \geq 0.99$ and $t \geq 2.05P$, then $N \geq (\lambda - 1)/\log_2 P$.*

References

1. Alamati, N., De Feo, L., Montgomery, H., Patranabis, S.: Cryptographic group actions and applications. In: Moriai, S., Wang, H. (eds.) ASIACRYPT 2020. LNCS, vol. 12492, pp. 411–439. Springer, Cham (2020). https://doi.org/10.1007/978-3-030-64834-3_14
2. Bellare, M., Rogaway, P.: Random oracles are practical: A paradigm for designing efficient protocols. In: Denning, D.E., Pyle, R., Ganesan, R., Sandhu, R.S., Ashby, V. (eds.) ACM CCS 1993, pp. 62–73. ACM Press (Nov 1993). https://doi.org/10.1145/168588.168596
3. Beullens, W., Kleinjung, T., Vercauteren, F.: CSI-fish: efficient isogeny based signatures through class group computations. In: Galbraith, S.D., Moriai, S. (eds.) ASIACRYPT 2019. LNCS, vol. 11921, pp. 227–247. Springer, Cham (2019). https://doi.org/10.1007/978-3-030-34578-5_9
4. Brassard, G., Yung, M.: One-way group actions. In: Menezes, A.J., Vanstone, S.A. (eds.) CRYPTO 1990. LNCS, vol. 537, pp. 94–107. Springer, Heidelberg (1991). https://doi.org/10.1007/3-540-38424-3_7
5. Castryck, W., Decru, T.: An efficient key recovery attack on SIDH (preliminary version). Cryptology ePrint Archive, Report 2022/975 (2022). https://eprint.iacr.org/2022/975
6. Chen, L., Chen, L., Jordan, S., Liu, Y.K., Moody, D., Peralta, R., Perlner, R., Smith-Tone, D.: Report on post-quantum cryptography, vol. 12. US Department of Commerce, National Institute of Standards and Technology (2016)
7. Couveignes, J.M.: Hard homogeneous spaces. Cryptology ePrint Archive, Report 2006/291 (2006). https://eprint.iacr.org/2006/291
8. Cozzo, D., Smart, N.P.: Sashimi: cutting up CSI-FiSh secret keys to produce an actively secure distributed signing protocol. In: Ding, J., Tillich, J.-P. (eds.) PQCrypto 2020. LNCS, vol. 12100, pp. 169–186. Springer, Cham (2020). https://doi.org/10.1007/978-3-030-44223-1_10

9. De Feo, L., Galbraith, S.D.: SeaSign: compact isogeny signatures from class group actions. In: Ishai, Y., Rijmen, V. (eds.) EUROCRYPT 2019. LNCS, vol. 11478, pp. 759–789. Springer, Cham (2019). https://doi.org/10.1007/978-3-030-17659-4_26

10. De Feo, L., Kohel, D., Leroux, A., Petit, C., Wesolowski, B.: SQISign: compact post-quantum signatures from quaternions and isogenies. In: Moriai, S., Wang, H. (eds.) ASIACRYPT 2020. LNCS, vol. 12491, pp. 64–93. Springer, Cham (2020). https://doi.org/10.1007/978-3-030-64837-4_3

11. De Feo, L., Leroux, A., Wesolowski, B.: New algorithms for the deuring correspondence: SQISign twice as fast. Cryptology ePrint Archive, Report 2022/234 (2022). https://eprint.iacr.org/2022/234

12. Decru, T., Panny, L., Vercauteren, F.: Faster SeaSign signatures through improved rejection sampling. In: Ding, J., Steinwandt, R. (eds.) PQCrypto 2019. LNCS, vol. 11505, pp. 271–285. Springer, Cham (2019). https://doi.org/10.1007/978-3-030-25510-7_15

13. Dodis, Y., Kiltz, E., Pietrzak, K., Wichs, D.: Message authentication, revisited. In: Pointcheval, D., Johansson, T. (eds.) EUROCRYPT 2012. LNCS, vol. 7237, pp. 355–374. Springer, Heidelberg (2012). https://doi.org/10.1007/978-3-642-29011-4_22

14. Don, J., Fehr, S., Majenz, C., Schaffner, C.: Security of the fiat-shamir transformation in the quantum random-oracle model. In: Boldyreva, A., Micciancio, D. (eds.) CRYPTO 2019. LNCS, vol. 11693, pp. 356–383. Springer, Cham (2019). https://doi.org/10.1007/978-3-030-26951-7_13

15. Döttling, N., Hartmann, D., Hofheinz, D., Kiltz, E., Schäge, S., Ursu, B.: On the impossibility of purely algebraic signatures. In: Nissim, K., Waters, B. (eds.) TCC 2021. LNCS, vol. 13044, pp. 317–349. Springer, Cham (2021). https://doi.org/10.1007/978-3-030-90456-2_11

16. El Kaafarani, A., Katsumata, S., Pintore, F.: Lossy CSI-FiSh: efficient signature scheme with tight reduction to decisional CSIDH-512. In: Kiayias, A., Kohlweiss, M., Wallden, P., Zikas, V. (eds.) PKC 2020. LNCS, vol. 12111, pp. 157–186. Springer, Cham (2020). https://doi.org/10.1007/978-3-030-45388-6_6

17. Feo, L.D., Jao, D., Plût, J.: Towards quantum-resistant cryptosystems from supersingular elliptic curve isogenies. J. Math. Cryptol. 8(3), 209–247 (2014)

18. Fiat, A., Shamir, A.: How to prove yourself: practical solutions to identification and signature problems. In: Odlyzko, A.M. (ed.) CRYPTO 1986. LNCS, vol. 263, pp. 186–194. Springer, Heidelberg (1987). https://doi.org/10.1007/3-540-47721-7_12

19. Impagliazzo, R., Rudich, S.: Limits on the provable consequences of one-way permutations. In: 21st ACM STOC, pp. 44–61. ACM Press (May 1989). https://doi.org/10.1145/73007.73012

20. Jao, D., De Feo, L.: Towards quantum-resistant cryptosystems from supersingular elliptic curve isogenies. In: Yang, B.-Y. (ed.) PQCrypto 2011. LNCS, vol. 7071, pp. 19–34. Springer, Heidelberg (2011). https://doi.org/10.1007/978-3-642-25405-5_2

21. Ji, Z., Qiao, Y., Song, F., Yun, A.: General linear group action on tensors: a candidate for post-quantum cryptography. In: Hofheinz, D., Rosen, A. (eds.) TCC 2019. LNCS, vol. 11891, pp. 251–281. Springer, Cham (2019). https://doi.org/10.1007/978-3-030-36030-6_11

22. Kuperberg, G.: A subexponential-time quantum algorithm for the dihedral hidden subgroup problem. SIAM J. Comput. 35(1), 170–188 (2005)

23. Kuperberg, G.: Another subexponential-time quantum algorithm for the dihedral hidden subgroup problem. In: Proceedings of TQC, vol. 22, pp. 20–34 (2013)

24. Liu, Q., Zhandry, M.: Revisiting post-quantum fiat-shamir. In: Boldyreva, A., Micciancio, D. (eds.) CRYPTO 2019. LNCS, vol. 11693, pp. 326–355. Springer, Cham (2019). https://doi.org/10.1007/978-3-030-26951-7_12

25. Maino, L., Martindale, C.: An attack on SIDH with arbitrary starting curve. Cryptology ePrint Archive, Report 2022/1026 (2022). https://eprint.iacr.org/2022/1026

26. Maurer, U.: Abstract models of computation in cryptography. In: Smart, N.P. (ed.) Cryptography and Coding 2005. LNCS, vol. 3796, pp. 1–12. Springer, Heidelberg (2005). https://doi.org/10.1007/11586821_1

27. Merkle, R.C.: A digital signature based on a conventional encryption function. In: Pomerance, C. (ed.) CRYPTO 1987. LNCS, vol. 293, pp. 369–378. Springer, Heidelberg (1988). https://doi.org/10.1007/3-540-48184-2_32

28. Merkle, R.C.: A certified digital signature. In: Brassard, G. (ed.) CRYPTO 1989. LNCS, vol. 435, pp. 218–238. Springer, New York (1990). https://doi.org/10.1007/0-387-34805-0_21

29. Peikert, C.: He gives C-Sieves on the CSIDH. In: Canteaut, A., Ishai, Y. (eds.) EUROCRYPT 2020. LNCS, vol. 12106, pp. 463–492. Springer, Cham (2020). https://doi.org/10.1007/978-3-030-45724-2_16

30. Pointcheval, D., Stern, J.: Provably secure blind signature schemes. In: Kim, K., Matsumoto, T. (eds.) ASIACRYPT 1996. LNCS, vol. 1163, pp. 252–265. Springer, Heidelberg (1996). https://doi.org/10.1007/BFb0034852

31. Regev, O.: A subexponential time algorithm for the dihedral hidden subgroup problem with polynomial space (2004)

32. Reingold, O., Trevisan, L., Vadhan, S.: Notions of reducibility between cryptographic primitives. In: Naor, M. (ed.) TCC 2004. LNCS, vol. 2951, pp. 1–20. Springer, Heidelberg (2004). https://doi.org/10.1007/978-3-540-24638-1_1

33. Rostovtsev, A., Stolbunov, A.: Public-Key Cryptosystem Based On Isogenies. Cryptology ePrint Archive, Report 2006/145 (2006). https://eprint.iacr.org/2006/145

34. Schnorr, C.P.: Efficient identification and signatures for smart cards. In: Brassard, G. (ed.) CRYPTO 1989. LNCS, vol. 435, pp. 239–252. Springer, New York (1990). https://doi.org/10.1007/0-387-34805-0_22

35. Shor, P.W.: Algorithms for quantum computation: Discrete logarithms and factoring. In: 35th FOCS, pp. 124–134. IEEE Computer Society Press (Nov 1994). https://doi.org/10.1109/SFCS.1994.365700

36. Shoup, V.: Lower bounds for discrete logarithms and related problems. In: Fumy, W. (ed.) EUROCRYPT 1997. LNCS, vol. 1233, pp. 256–266. Springer, Heidelberg (1997). https://doi.org/10.1007/3-540-69053-0_18

37. Unruh, D.: Non-interactive zero-knowledge proofs in the quantum random oracle model. In: Oswald, E., Fischlin, M. (eds.) EUROCRYPT 2015. LNCS, vol. 9057, pp. 755–784. Springer, Heidelberg (2015). https://doi.org/10.1007/978-3-662-46803-6_25

38. Zhandry, M.: To label, or not to label (in generic groups). In: Dodis, Y., Shrimpton, T., (eds.) CRYPTO 2022, Part III. LNCS, vol. 13509, pp. 66–96. Springer, Heidelberg (2022). https://doi.org/10.1007/978-3-031-15982-4_3

39. Zhandry, M., Zhang, C.: The relationship between idealized models under computationally bounded adversaries. Cryptology ePrint Archive, Report 2021/240 (2021). https://eprint.iacr.org/2021/240

Short Signatures from Regular Syndrome Decoding in the Head

Eliana Carozza[1], Geoffroy Couteau[2(✉)], and Antoine Joux[3]

[1] IRIF, Université Paris Cité, Paris, France
carozza@irif.fr
[2] CNRS, IRIF, Université Paris Cité, Paris, France
couteau@irif.fr
[3] CISPA Helmholtz Center for Information Security, Saarbrücken, Germany
joux@cispa.de

Abstract. We introduce a new candidate post-quantum digital signature scheme from the regular syndrome decoding (RSD) assumption, an established variant of the syndrome decoding assumption which asserts that it is hard to find w-regular solutions to systems of linear equations over $\mathbb{F}_2$ (a vector is regular if it is a concatenation of w unit vectors). Our signature is obtained by introducing and compiling a new 5-round zero-knowledge proof system constructed using the MPC-in-the-head paradigm. At the heart of our result is an efficient MPC protocol in the preprocessing model that checks correctness of a regular syndrome decoding instance by using a share ring-conversion mechanism.

The analysis of our construction is non-trivial and forms a core technical contribution of our work. It requires careful combinatorial analysis and combines several new ideas, such as analyzing soundness in a relaxed setting where a cheating prover is allowed to use any witness *sufficiently close* to a regular vector. We complement our analysis with an in-depth overview of existing attacks against RSD.

Our signatures are competitive with the best-known code-based signatures, ranging from 12.52 KB (fast setting, with signing time of the order of a few milliseconds on a single core of a standard laptop) to about 9 KB (short setting, with estimated signing time of the order of 15 ms).

1 Introduction

In this work, we introduce a new zero-knowledge proof for proving knowledge of a solution to the regular syndrome decoding problem, using the MPC-in-the-head paradigm. Compiling our zero-knowledge proof into a signature scheme using the Fiat-Shamir paradigm yields a new scheme with plausible post-quantum security and highly competitive performances compared to the state of the art.

Zero-knowledge, Signatures, and Syndrome Decoding. Zero-knowledge proofs of knowledge allow a prover to convince a verifier of his knowledge of

© International Association for Cryptologic Research 2023
C. Hazay and M. Stam (Eds.): EUROCRYPT 2023, LNCS 14008, pp. 532–563, 2023.
https://doi.org/10.1007/978-3-031-30589-4_19

a witness for a NP statement without revealing anything beyond this. Zero-knowledge proofs enjoy countless applications in cryptography. In particular, the Fiat-Shamir transform [23] allows to convert any public-coin zero-knowledge proof system into a signature scheme; this transformation is one of the leading approaches to the construction of efficient signature schemes.

The syndrome decoding problem asks, given a matrix $H \in \mathbb{F}_2^{k \times K}$ and a target vector $y \in \mathbb{F}_2^k$, to find a vector $x \in \mathbb{F}_2^K$ of Hamming weight w such that $H \cdot x = y$. The average-case hardness of the syndrome decoding problem (for random matrices H and appropriate parameters (K, k, w)) is one of the leading candidate post-quantum cryptographic assumptions. The first zero-knowledge proof of knowledge for the syndrome decoding problem was introduced in the seminal work of Stern [35] three decades ago. Unfortunately, Stern's proof has a large *soundness error*: a cheating prover can convince a verifier with probability $2/3$ without knowing a correct solution x. To achieve a low soundness error, e.g. 2^{-128}, the protocol must therefore be repeated τ times, with τ such that $(2/3)^\tau \leq 2^{-128}$. This adds a significant communication overhead, resulting in a large signature size after compilation with Fiat-Shamir.

Code-Based Signatures. Digital signatures form the backbone of authentication on the Internet. However, essentially all deployed constructions will be rendered insecure in the presence of a quantum computer [34]. This motivates the search for alternative constructions of digital signature schemes, that rely on assumptions conjectured to withstand quantum computers. The recent call of the NIST[1] for standardizing post-quantum primitives has boosted the research for efficient post-quantum signatures, particularly code-based signatures.

Among the many candidate code-based signature schemes, the Fiat-Shamir approach, used in the seminal work of Stern, has received careful scrutiny [8, 9, 20, 21, 25]. Indeed, while some alternative approaches such as Wave [18] and Durandal [2] manage to reach smaller signature sizes (under somewhat more exotic but plausible assumptions), they typically require the signer to know a *trapdoor* associated with the code matrix, leading to huge public keys (since the public key must include the full matrix H). In contrast, Fiat-Shamir signatures require no such trapdoor, and the random matrix H can be heuristically compressed to a short seed using a pseudorandom generator, yielding comparatively tiny public keys (in addition to relying on more traditional assumptions). This comes at the expense of slightly larger signature sizes. Nevertheless, the standard efficiency measure (size of the signature + size of the public key) strongly favors the Fiat-Shamir line of work.

The MPC in the Head Paradigm. Several recent works on Fiat-Shamir code-based digital signatures use the *MPC in the head* paradigm, introduced in the seminal work of [27] (MPC stands for *multiparty computation*). At a high level, this paradigm lets the prover run an MPC protocol in his head, where the

---

[1] https://csrc.nist.gov/projects/post-quantum-cryptography.

(virtual) parties are given shares of the witness, and the target function verifies that the witness is correct. Then, the prover commits to the views of all parties, and the verifier asks to see a random subset of the views, checks that they are consistent, and that the output indeed corresponds to the witness being correct. Soundness stems from the fact that a cheating prover (not knowing a valid witness) cannot produce consistent views for all parties, and zero-knowledge follows from the security of the MPC protocol against a honest-but-curious adversary (which gets to see the views of a subset of corrupted parties).

The MPC in the head paradigm reduces the construction of efficient zero-knowledge proofs to the search for suitable MPC protocols with low communication overhead. In recent years, it has led to some of the most competitive candidate post-quantum signature schemes [5,29], and was used in particular in the most efficient Fiat-Shamir code-based signature scheme (and the most efficient code-based signature scheme overall, under the signature + public key size metric) known to date [21].

1.1   Our Contribution

In this work, we introduce a new zero-knowledge proof system for a variant of the syndrome decoding problem, using the MPC in the head paradigm. The variant of the syndrome decoding problem which we consider is the *regular syndrome decoding* (RSD) problem. Given a matrix $H \in \mathbb{F}_2^{k \times K}$ and a syndrome $y \in \mathbb{F}_2^k$, the RSD problem with parameters (k, K, w) asks to find a weight-w *regular* solution $x \in \mathbb{F}_2^K$ to $H \cdot x = y$, where regular means that x is a concatenation of w unit vectors (*i.e.*, x is divided in w equal-length blocks, and has a single 1 per block). The regular syndrome decoding problem is a well-established variant of syndrome decoding: it was introduced in 2003 in [3] as the assumption underlying the FSB candidate to the NIST hash function competition, and was subsequently analyzed in [7,24,30], among others. It has also been used and analyzed in many recent works on secure computation, such as [10–14,16,26,32,36,37].

Brief Overview of Our Approach. While we use the MPC in the head paradigm, as in previous works [9,20,21,25], our choice of the underlying MPC protocol departs significantly from all previous work. Our starting point is the observation that checking $H \cdot x = y$ and checking the structure of x can each be done using linear operations, over $\mathbb{F}_2$ for the former, and over $\mathbb{Z}$ for the latter. In standard MPC protocol, linear operations over a ring $\mathcal{R}$ are usually "for free", provided that the values are shared over $\mathcal{R}$. Therefore, the only component that requires communication is a *share conversion* mechanism, to transform shares over $\mathbb{F}_2$ into shares over a larger integer ring. We introduce a share conversion protocol which exhibit very good performances. However, our protocol works in the preprocessing model, where the parties are initially given correlated random string by a trusted dealer. The use of preprocessing in the MPC in the head paradigm has appeared in previous works [25,29], and handling the preprocessing phase usually incurs a significant communication overhead (due to the need to check that it was correctly emulated by the prover).

Nevertheless, a core technical contribution of our work is a method, tailored to our setting, to handle the preprocessing phase *for free* (*i.e.* without incurring any communication overhead). At a high level, we achieve this by letting the verifier *randomly shuffle* the preprocessing strings, instead of verifying them. A careful and non-trivial combinatorial analysis shows that a cheating prover has very low probability of providing an accepting proof for *any* choice of the initial (pre-permutation) preprocessing strings, over the choice of the verifier permutation. Furthermore, we observe that the cheating probability becomes much lower if we focus on cheating provers using a witness which is *far* from a regular witness (in the sense that it has multiple non-weight-1 blocks). For an appropriate setting of the parameters, the hardness of finding solutions *close* to regular witnesses becomes equivalent to the standard regular syndrome decoding assumption (where the solution must be strictly regular), hence this relaxation of the soundness still yields a signature scheme (after compilation with Fiat-Shamir) whose security reduces to the standard RSD assumption.

To complement our analysis, we also provide an analysis of the RSD assumption. We analyze the relation of RSD to the standard syndrome decoding assumption depending on the parameter regime, and reviewed existing attacks on RSD from the literature, fine-tuning and improving the attacks on several occasions. Eventually, we develop a new "adversary-optimistic" attack against RSD, showing how a linear-time solution to the approximate birthday problem would yield faster algorithms for RSD (in our parameter choices, we assumed that such an algorithm exists for the sake of choosing conservative parameters). We provide a more in-depth overview in the technical overview (Sect. 3).

Performances. While analyzing our approach is relatively involved, the protocol structure is extremely simple. The computation of our zero-knowledge proof is mostly dominated by simple XORs, calls to a length-doubling PRG (which can be instantiated very efficiently from AES over platforms with hardware support for AES) and calls to a hash function. This is in contrast with previous works, which always involved much more complex operations, such as FFTs [21] or compositions of random permutations [9,20]. While we do not yet have an optimized implementation of our new signature scheme (we plan to get such an implementation in a future work), we carefully estimated the runtime of all operations using standard benchmarks, making conservative choices when the exact cost was unclear (we explain our calculations in details in Sect. 5). Our conservative choices likely overestimate the real runtime of these operations. Of course, the runtimes extrapolated this way ignore other costs such as the cost of copying and allocating memory. Nevertheless, in Banquet, another candidate post-quantum signature scheme using the MPC-in-the-head paradigm, the memory costs were estimated to account for 25% of the total runtime. We therefore expect our extrapolated number to be relatively close to real runtimes with a proper implementation. Our numbers indicate that our signature scheme is highly competitive with the state of the art, even if our extrapolated runtimes are off by more than a factor two, which we view as a strong indication that an optimized implementation will achieve competitive runtimes.

For communication, we provide eight sets of parameters. The first four parameters use RSD parameters which guarantee a security reduction to the standard RSD assumption, and we view them as our main candidate parameters. They correspond respectively to a fast signature (rsd-f), two medium signatures (rsd-m1 and rsd-m2) achieving a reasonable speed/size tradeoff, and a short signature (rsd-s). The last four parameters (arsd-f, arsd-m1, arsd-m2, and arsd-s) use a more aggressive setting of the RSD parameters, where security reduce instead to a more exotic assumption, namely, the security of RSD when the adversary is allowed to find an *almost regular* solution (with some fixed number of "faulty blocks" allowed). Since this variant has not yet been thoroughly analyzed, we view these parameters mainly as a motivation for future cryptanalysis of variants of RSD with almost-regular solutions.

We represent in Table 1 the results of our estimations and compare them to the state-of-the-art in code-based signature schemes. Compared to the best-known code-based signature scheme of [21], our conservative scheme (under standard RSD) achieves significantly smaller signature sizes than their scheme based on syndrome decoding over $\mathbb{F}_2$ (12.52 KB for our fast variant versus 17 KB for Var2f, and 9.69 to 8.55 KB for our shorter variants versus 11.8 KB for Var2s). In terms of runtime, our estimates are significantly faster than their reported runtimes (except rsd-s, which is on par with Var2s), hence our runtimes should remain competitive with a proper implementation, even if memory costs turn out to be higher than expected. Their most efficient scheme (variants Var3f and Var3s) relies on the conjectured hardness of syndrome decoding assumption over $\mathbb{F}_{256}$, which has been much less investigated. Yet, our conservative RSD-based schemes remain competitive even with their most efficient scheme: we get slightly larger signatures (12.42 KB versus 11.5 KB, and 9.13 KB versus 8.26 KB), and comparable runtimes. Since the RSD assumption over $\mathbb{F}_2$ has been more investigated, we view our signature scheme as a competitive and viable alternative.

2   Preliminaries

Given an integer $n \in \mathbb{N}$, we denote by $[n]$ the set $\{1, \cdots, n\}$. We use bold lowercase for vectors, and uppercase for matrices. Given a vector $\mathbf{v} \in \mathbb{F}^n$ and a permutation $\pi : [n] \mapsto [n]$, we write $\pi(\mathbf{v})$ to denote the vector $(v_{\pi(1)}, v_{\pi(2)}, \cdots, v_{\pi(n)})$. Given $\mathbf{u}, \mathbf{v} \in \{0,1\}^n$, we write $\mathbf{u} \oplus \mathbf{v}$ for the bitwise-XOR of $\mathbf{u}$ and $\mathbf{v}$, and $\mathbf{u} \odot \mathbf{v}$ for the bitwise-AND (also called Schur product, or Hadamard product) of $\mathbf{u}$ and $\mathbf{v}$, and $\mathsf{HW}(\mathbf{u})$ for the Hamming weight of $\mathbf{u}$ (*i.e.* its number of nonzero entries). Given a set S, we write $s \leftarrow_r S$ to indicate that s is sampled uniformly from S. Given a probabilistic Turing machine $\mathcal{A}$ and an input x, we write $y \leftarrow_r \mathcal{A}(x)$ to indicate that y is sampled by running $\mathcal{A}$ on x with a uniform random tape, or $y \leftarrow \mathcal{A}(x; r)$ when we want to make the random coins explicit. We assume familiarity with some basic cryptographic notions, such as commitment schemes, collision-resistant hash functions, and the random oracle model.

Table 1. Comparison of our signature scheme with other code-based signature schemes from the literature, for 128 bits of security. All timings are in millisecond. Reported timings are those extracted in [21] from the original publications, using a 3.5 Ghz Intel Xeon E3-1240 v5 for Wave, a 2.8 Ghz Intel Core i5-7440HQ for Durandal, and a 3.8 GHz Intel Core i7 for [20, 21]. Our timings are estimated runtimes with the methodology given in Sect. 5.2.

Scheme	|sgn|	|pk|	t_{sgn}	Assumption
Wave	2.07 KB	3.2 MB	300	large-weight SD over $\mathbb{F}_3$, $(U, U + V)$-codes indist.
Durandal - I	3.97 KB	14.9 KB	4	Rank SD over $\mathbb{F}_{2^m}$
Durandal - II	4.90 KB	18.2 KB	5	Rank SD over $\mathbb{F}_{2^m}$
LESS-FM - I	9.77 KB	15.2 KB	–	Linear Code Equivalence
LESS-FM - II	206 KB	5.25 KB	–	Perm. Code Equivalence
LESS-FM - III	11.57 KB	10.39 KB	–	Perm. Code Equivalence
[25] - 256	24.0 KB	0.11 KB	–	SD over $\mathbb{F}_{256}$
[25] - 256	19.8 KB	0.12 KB	–	SD over $\mathbb{F}_{1024}$
[20] (fast)	22.6 KB	0.09 KB	13	SD over $\mathbb{F}_2$
[20] (short)	16.0 KB	0.09 KB	62	SD over $\mathbb{F}_2$
[9] Sig1	23.7 KB	0.1 KB	–	SD over $\mathbb{F}_2$
[9] Sig2	20.6 KB	0.2 KB	–	(QC)SD over $\mathbb{F}_2$
[21] - Var1f	15.6 KB	0.09 KB	–	SD over $\mathbb{F}_2$
[21] - Var1s	10.9 KB	0.09 KB	–	SD over $\mathbb{F}_2$
[21] - Var2f	17.0 KB	0.09 KB	13	SD over $\mathbb{F}_2$
[21] - Var2s	11.8 KB	0.09 KB	64	SD over $\mathbb{F}_2$
[21] - Var3f	11.5 KB	0.14 KB	6	SD over $\mathbb{F}_{256}$
[21] - Var3s	8.26 KB	0.14 KB	30	SD over $\mathbb{F}_{256}$
Our scheme - rsd-f	12.52 KB	0.09 KB	2.8*	RSD over $\mathbb{F}_2$
Our scheme - rsd-m1	9.69 KB	0.09 KB	17*	RSD over $\mathbb{F}_2$
Our scheme - rsd-m2	9.13 KB	0.09 KB	31*	RSD over $\mathbb{F}_2$
Our scheme - rsd-s	8.55 KB	0.09 KB	65*	RSD over $\mathbb{F}_2$
Our scheme - arsd-f	11.25 KB	0.09 KB	2.4*	f-almost-RSD over $\mathbb{F}_2$
Our scheme - arsd-m1	8.76 KB	0.09 KB	15*	f-almost-RSD over $\mathbb{F}_2$
Our scheme - arsd-m2	8.28 KB	0.09 KB	28*	f-almost-RSD over $\mathbb{F}_2$
Our scheme - arsd-s	7.77 KB	0.09 KB	57*	f-almost-RSD over $\mathbb{F}_2$

* Runtimes obtained using conservative upper bounds on the cycle counts of all operations as described in Sect. 5.2, and assuming that the signature is ran on one core of a 3.8 GHz CPU. We stress that these parameters ignore costs such as copying or allocating memory, and should be seen only as a first-order approximation of the real runtimes.

Given a vector $\mathbf{u} \in \mathbb{Z}_T^\ell$ and an integer T, we write $(\mathbf{u_1}, \cdots, \mathbf{u_n}) \leftarrow_r [\![\mathbf{u}]\!]_T$ to indicate that the vectors $\mathbf{u_i}$ (called the *i-th additive share* of $\mathbf{u}$) are sampled uniformly at random over $\mathbb{Z}_T^\ell$ conditioned on $\sum_i \mathbf{u_i} = \mathbf{u}$. We sometime abuse this notation and write $[\![\mathbf{u}]\!]_T$ to denote the tuple $(\mathbf{u_1}, \cdots, \mathbf{u_n})$. For a vector $\mathbf{v} \in \{0,1\}^\ell$, we write $[\![\mathbf{v}]\!]_T$ with $T > 2$ using the natural embedding of $\{0,1\}$ into $\mathbb{Z}_T$.

2.1   Syndrome Decoding Problems

Given a weight parameter w, the syndrome decoding problem asks to find a solution of Hamming weight w (under the promise that it exists) to a random system of linear equations over $\mathbb{F}_2$. Formally, let $\mathcal{S}_w^K$ denote the set of all vectors of Hamming weight w over $\mathbb{F}_2^K$. Then:

Definition 1 (Syndrome Decoding Problem). *Let K, k, w be three integers, with $K > k > w$. The syndrome decoding problem with parameters (K, k, w) is defined as follows:*

- *(Problem generation) Sample $H \leftarrow_r \mathbb{F}_2^{k \times K}$ and $x \leftarrow_r \mathcal{S}_w^K$. Set $y \leftarrow H \cdot x$. Output (H, y)*
- *(Goal) Given (H, y), find $x \in \mathcal{S}_w^K$ such that $H \cdot x = y$.*

A pair (H, y) is called an *instance* of the syndrome decoding problem. In this work, we also consider variants of the syndrome decoding problem, with different restrictions on the solution vector x. In our context, it is useful to rephrase the constraint on x as a linear equation over $\mathbb{N}$: the solution vector x must satisfy the constraint $\langle x, \mathbf{1} \rangle = w$, where $\mathbf{1}$ is the all-1 vector, and the inner product is computed over the integers (note that this view is of course specific to syndrome decoding over $\mathbb{F}_2$). Other standard variants of syndrome decoding from the literature can also be viewed as instances of a more general notion of *syndrome decoding under $\mathbb{N}$-linear constraints*, which we introduce below:

Definition 2 (Syndrome Decoding under $\mathbb{N}$-Linear Constraints). *Let K, k, w, c be four integers, with $K > k > w$ and $k > c$. Let $L \in \mathbb{N}^{c \times K}$ be a matrix and $\mathbf{v} \in \mathbb{N}^c$ be a vector; we call $(L, \mathbf{v})$ the $\mathbb{N}$-linear constraint. We say that $(L, \mathbf{v})$ is a feasible constraint if it is possible to sample a uniformly random element from the set $\{x \in \{0,1\}^K : L \cdot x = \mathbf{v}\}$ in time $\mathsf{poly}(K)$.*

The syndrome decoding problem with parameters (K, k, w) and feasible $\mathbb{N}$-linear constraint $(L, \mathbf{v})$ is defined as follows:

- *(Problem generation) Sample a matrix $H \leftarrow_r \{0,1\}^{k \times K}$ and a vector $x \leftarrow_r \{x \in \{0,1\}^K : L \cdot x = \mathbf{v}\}$. Set $y \leftarrow H \cdot x \bmod 2$. Output (H, y).*
- *(Goal) Given (H, y), find $x \in \{0,1\}^K$ such that*
  - *$H \cdot x = y \bmod 2$ (the $\mathbb{F}_2$-linear constraint), and*
  - *$L \cdot x = \mathbf{v}$ over $\mathbb{N}$ (the $\mathbb{N}$-linear constraint).*

Examples. Setting $c = 1$, $L = (1, \cdots, 1)$, and $\mathbf{v} = w$ corresponds to the constraint "x has Hamming weight w", and is the standard syndrome decoding problem. A common variant in the literature [3,7,10–14,16,24,26,30,32,36,37] is the *regular* syndrome decoding problem, where x is instead required to be a concatenation of w unit vectors, each of length K/w. We recover this variant by setting $c = w$, $\mathbf{v} = (1, \cdots, 1)^{\intercal}$, and defining L as the matrix with rows $L_i = (0 \cdots 0, 1 \cdots 1, 0 \cdots 0)$, where the band of ones is from $(i - 1) \cdot K/w + 1$ to $i \cdot K/w$. Eventually, the d-split syndrome decoding problem from [22], where the vector x is divided into d blocks of weight w/d, is also easily seen to fit in this framework.

2.2 Honest-Verifier Zero-Knowledge Arguments of Knowledge

Given a two-party interactive protocols between PPT algorithms A with input a and B with input b where only B gets an output, we introduce two random variables: $\langle A(a), B(b) \rangle$ denotes the output of the protocol, and $\text{VIEW}(A(a), B(b))$ denotes the transcript of the protocol.

Definition. A honest-verifier zero-knowledge argument of knowledge with soundness error ε for a NP language $\mathcal{L} = \{x \in \{0,1\}^* \ : \ \exists w, (x, w) \in \mathcal{R}_{\mathcal{L}} \wedge |w| = \text{poly}(|x|)\}$ with relation $\mathcal{R}_{\mathcal{L}}$ is a two-party interactive protocol between a prover P and a verifier V which satisfies the following properties:

- **Perfect Completeness:** for every $(x, w) \in \mathcal{R}_{\mathcal{L}}$, the verifier always accept the interaction with a honest prover: $\Pr[\langle \mathsf{P}(x, w), \mathsf{V}(x) \rangle = 1] = 1$.
- **ε-Soundness:** [6] for every PPT algorithm $\tilde{\mathsf{P}}$ such that $\Pr[\langle \tilde{\mathsf{P}}(x), \mathsf{V}(x) \rangle = 1] = \tilde{\varepsilon} > \varepsilon$, there exists an *extractor* algorithm $\mathcal{E}$ which, given rewindable black-box access to $\tilde{\mathsf{P}}$, outputs a valid witness w' for x in time $\text{poly}(\lambda, (\tilde{\varepsilon} - \varepsilon)^{-1})$ with probability at least $1/2$.
- **Honest-Verifier Zero-Knowledge (HVZK):** an argument of knowledge is (computationally, statistically, perfectly) HVZK if there exists a PPT simulator Sim such that for every $(x, w) \in \mathcal{R}_{\mathcal{L}}$, $\text{Sim}(x) \equiv \text{VIEW}(\mathsf{P}(x, w), \mathsf{V}(x))$, where $\equiv$ denotes computational, statistical, or perfect indistinguishability between the distributions.

Gap-HVZK. A *gap* honest-verifier zero-knowledge argument of knowledge [15] with gap $\mathcal{L}'$, where $\mathcal{L}' \supseteq \mathcal{L}$ is an NP language with relation $\mathcal{R}_{\mathcal{L}'}$, is defined as a honest-verifier zero-knowledge argument of knowledge, with the following relaxation of ε-soundness: the extractor $\mathcal{E}$ is only guaranteed to output a witness w' such that $(x, w') \in \mathcal{L}'$. Concretely, in our setting, the witness is a valid solution to the syndrome decoding problem, and the language $\mathcal{L}'$ contains all strings which are *sufficiently close* (in a well-defined sense) to a valid solution. This is similar in spirit to the notion of *soundness slack* often used in the context of lattice-based zero-knowledge proof, where the honest witness is a vector with small entries, and the extracted vector can have significantly larger entries.

2.3   The MPC-in-the-Head Paradigm

The MPC-in-the-head paradigm was introduced in the seminal work of [27]. It provides a compiler which, given an n-party secure computation protocol for computing a function f' in the honest-but-curious model, produces a honest-verifier zero-knowledge argument of knowledge of x such that $f(x) = y$, for some public value y, where f' is a function related to f. In our context, the focus is on zero-knowledge for syndrome decoding problems, for which, for example, a typical choice of f would include a hardcoded description of the matrix H and from a vector x, f would output $f(x) = (H \cdot x, \mathsf{HW}(x))$.

At a high level (and specializing to MPC in the head with all-but-one additive secret sharing – the original compiler is more general), the compiler proceeds by letting the prover additively share the witness x into $(x_1, \cdots, x_n)$ among n virtual parties $(P_1, \cdots, P_n)$, run in his head an MPC protocol for securely computing $f'(x_1, \cdots, x_n) = f(\sum_i x_i)$ (where the sum is over some appropriate ring), and commit to the views of all parties. Then, the verifier queries a random size-$(n-1)$ subset of all views, which the prover opens. The verifier checks that these views are consistent and that the output is correct – for example, equal to (y, w) (when proving knowledge of x such that $H \cdot x = y$ and $\mathsf{HW}(x) = w$). She accepts if all checks succeeded. Soundness follows from the fact that the MPC protocol is correct, hence if the prover does not know a valid x, one of the views must be inconsistent with the output being correct (the soundness error is therefore $1/n$). Honest-verifier zero-knowledge follows from the fact that the MPC protocol is secure against passive corruption of $n-1$ parties (and the fact that $n-1$ shares of x leak no information about x).

3   Technical Overview

In this section, we provide a detailed overview of our zero-knowledge proof, and highlight the technical challenges in constructing an analyzing the proof.

3.1   Our Template Zero-Knowledge Proof

We start with the construction of a zero-knowledge proof of knowledge of a solution to an instance of the syndrome decoding problem, using the MPC-in-the-head paradigm. More generally, our protocol handles naturally any *syndrome decoding under* $\mathbb{N}$-*linear constraints* problem for some $\mathbb{N}$-linear constraint $(L, \mathbf{v})$, see Definition 2. To this end, we construct an n-party protocol Π where the parties have shares of a solution $x \in \{0,1\}^K$ to the syndrome decoding problem, and securely output $H \cdot x \bmod 2$ and $L \cdot x$ over $\mathbb{N}$. Given the output of the MPC protocol, the verifier checks (1) that the execution (in the prover's head) was carried out honestly (by checking a random subset of $n-1$ views of the parties) and (2) that the two outputs are equal to y and $\mathbf{v}$ respectively.

The high level intuition of our approach is the following: in MPC protocols, it is typically the case that linear operations are extremely cheap (or even considered as "free"), because they can be computed directly over secret values shared using a linear secret sharing scheme (such as additive sharing, or Shamir sharing), without communicating. In turn, we observe that several variants of the syndrome decoding problem reduce to finding a solution x that satisfy two types of linear constraints: one linear constraint over $\mathbb{F}_2$ (typically, checking that $H \cdot x = y$ given a syndrome decoding instance (H, y)) and one linear constraint over $\mathbb{N}$ (*e.g.* checking that $\langle x, 1 \rangle = w$, *i.e.* that the Hamming weight of x is w). Now, an appropriate choice of linear secret sharing scheme can make any one of these two constraints *for free* in Π: if x is additively shared over $\mathbb{F}_2$, then verifying $H \cdot x = y$ is for free, while if x is additively shared over a large enough integer ring $\mathcal{R} = \mathbb{Z}_T$ (such that no overflow occurs when computing $L \cdot x$ over $\mathbb{N}$ for any $x \in \{0, 1\}^K$), then verifying $L \cdot x = \mathbf{v}$ is for free.

Share Conversion. By the above observation, the only missing ingredient to construct Π is a *share conversion* mechanism: a protocol where the parties start with $\mathbb{F}_2$-shares $[\![x]\!]_2$ of x, and securely convert them to $\mathcal{R}$-shares $[\![x]\!]_T$ of x. Our next observation is that for any integer ring $\mathbb{Z}_T$, this can be done easily using appropriate *preprocessing material*. Consider the case of a single bit $a \in \{0, 1\}$; the parties initially have $\mathbb{F}_2$-shares $[\![a]\!]_2$ of a. Suppose now that the parties receive the $([\![b]\!]_2, [\![b]\!]_T)$ for a random $b \in \{0, 1\}$ from a trusted dealer. The parties can locally compute $[\![a \oplus b]\!]_2$ and open the bit $c = a \oplus b$ by broadcasting their shares. Now, since $a = c \oplus b = c + b - 2b$ over $\mathbb{N}$, only two cases may arise:

Case 1: $c = 1$. Then $a = 1 - b$ and so $[\![a]\!]_T = [\![1 - b]\!]_T$.
Case 2: $c = 0$. Then $a = b$ and so $[\![a]\!]_T = [\![b]\!]_T$

Therefore, the parties can compute $[\![a]\!]_T$ as $c \cdot [\![1 - b]\!]_T + (1 - c) \cdot [\![b]\!]_T$. This extends directly to an integral solution vector x. Hence, in the protocol Π, prior to the execution, a trusted dealer samples a random vector $r \leftarrow_r \{0, 1\}^K$ and distribute $([\![r]\!]_2, [\![r]\!]_T)$ to the parties, where T is such that no overflow can occur when computing $L \cdot x \bmod T$ (in order to simulate $\mathbb{N}$-linear operations). A similar technique was used previously, in a different context, in [19, 33].

The MPC Protocol. Building on this observation, we introduce an MPC protocol in the preprocessing model, where the trusted dealer picks a random bitstring r, and distributes $([\![r]\!]_2, [\![r]\!]_T)$ to the parties. On input additive shares of the witness x over $\mathbb{F}_2$, the parties can open $z = r + x$. Using the above observation, all parties can reconstruct shares $[\![x]\!]_T$. Then, any linear equation on x over either $\mathbb{F}_2$ or $\mathbb{Z}_T$ can be verified by opening an appropriate linear combination of the $\mathbb{F}_2$-shares or of the $\mathbb{Z}_T$ shares (this last step does not add any communication when compiling the protocol into a zero-knowledge proof).

Handling the Preprocessing Material. At a high level, there are two standard approaches to handle preprocessing material using MPC-in-the-head. The first approach was introduced in [29]. It uses a natural cut-and-choose strategy:

the prover plays the role of the trusted dealer, and executes many instances of the preprocessing, committing to all of them. Afterwards, the verifier asks for openings of a subset of all preprocessings, and checks that all opened strings have been honestly constructed. Eventually, the MPC-in-the-head compiler is applied to the protocol, using the unopened committed instances of the pre-processing phases. This approach is very generic, but induces a large overhead, both computationally and communication-wise. The second approach is tailored to specific types of preprocessing material, such as Beaver triples. It is inspired by the classical sacrificing technique which allows to check the correctness of a batch of Beaver triples, while sacrificing only a few triples. It was used in works such as Banquet [5], or more recently in [21].

Unfortunately, the first approach induces a large overhead, and the second one is tailored to specific types of preprocessing material. In our context, the structure of the preprocessing material makes it unsuitable. Fortunately, we show that, in our setting, the preprocessing material can be handled *essentially for free*.

Our technique works as follows: we let the prover compute (and commit to) the preprocessing material ($[\![\mathbf{r}]\!]_2, [\![\mathbf{r}]\!]_T$) himself, but require that the coordinates of $\mathbf{r}$ are *shuffled using a uniformly random permutation* (chosen by the verifier) before being used in the protocol. Crucially, as we show in our analysis, the verifier *never* needs to check that the preprocessing phase was correctly executed (which would induce some overhead): instead, we demonstrate that a malicious prover (who does not know a valid witness) cannot find *any* (possibly incorrect) preprocessing material that allows him to pass the verification *with the randomly shuffled material* with high probability.

Fundamentally, the intuition is the following: it is easy for the malicious prover to know values x, x' such that $H \cdot x = y \bmod 2$ and $L \cdot x' = \mathbf{v} \bmod T$. To pass the verification test in the protocol, a malicious prover must therefore fine-tune malicious preprocessing strings $(\mathbf{s}, \mathbf{t})$ such that the value $\mathbf{z} \odot (1 - \mathbf{t}) + (1 - \mathbf{z}) \odot \mathbf{t}$, computed from $\mathbf{z} = \mathbf{s} \oplus x$ for some x such that $H \cdot x = y \bmod 2$, is equal to a value x' such that $L \cdot x' = \mathbf{v} \bmod T$ (recall that in the honest protocol, the prover should use $\mathbf{s} = \mathbf{t} = \mathbf{r}$). But doing so requires a careful choice of the entries (s_i, t_i): intuitively, the prover needs $s_i = t_i$ whenever $x_i = x'_i$, and $s_i = 1 - t_i$ otherwise. However, when the coordinates of $(\mathbf{s}, \mathbf{t})$ are randomly shuffled, this is not the case with high probability. While the high-level intuition is clear, we note that formalizing it requires particularly delicate combinatorial arguments.

Full Description of the MPC Protocol. Let (H, y) be an instance of the $\mathbb{N}$-linear syndrome decoding problem with parameters (K, k, w) and feasible $\mathbb{N}$-linear constraint $(L, \mathbf{v})$. Let $x \in \{0, 1\}^K$ denote a solution for this instance. We construct an n-party protocol Π in the preprocessing model, where the parties inputs are additive shares of x over $\mathbb{F}_2$. The protocol Π securely computes $H \cdot x \bmod 2$ and $L \cdot x$ in the honest-but-curious setting, with corruption of up to $n - 1$ parties. Let par $\leftarrow (K, k, w, c, H, L)$. The protocol Π_{par} is represented on Fig. 1.

Parameters: The protocol Π operates with n parties, denoted $(P_1, \cdots, P_n)$. (K, k, w, c) are four integers with $K > k > w$ and $k > c$. $H \in \{0,1\}^{k \times K}$ and $L \in \mathbb{N}^{c \times K}$ are public matrices. Let par $\leftarrow (K, k, w, c, H, L)$, and let $T \leftarrow \|L \cdot \mathbf{1}\|_1$. We view $(\mathbf{x}_1, \cdots, \mathbf{x}_n)$ as forming additive shares $[\![x]\!]_2$ over $\mathbb{F}_2$ of a vector $x \in \{0,1\}^K$.

Inputs: Each party P_i has input $\mathbf{x}_i \in \{0,1\}^K$.

Preprocessing: The trusted dealer samples $\mathbf{r} \leftarrow_r \{0,1\}^K$. He computes $[\![\mathbf{r}]\!]_2 = (\mathbf{s}_1, \cdots, \mathbf{s}_n) \leftarrow_r \mathsf{Share}_2(\mathbf{r})$ and $[\![\mathbf{r}]\!]_T = (\mathbf{t}_1, \cdots, \mathbf{t}_n) \leftarrow_r \mathsf{Share}_T(\mathbf{r})$, viewing bits as elements of the integer ring $\mathbb{Z}_T$ in the natural way. It distributes $(\mathbf{s}_i, \mathbf{t}_i)$ to each party P_i.

Online Phase: The protocol proceeds in broadcast rounds.

- The parties compute $[\![\mathbf{y}']\!]_2 = H \cdot [\![x]\!]_2$ and $[\![\mathbf{z}]\!]_2 = [\![\mathbf{r}]\!]_2 + [\![x]\!]_2$. All parties open $\mathbf{y}'$ and $\mathbf{z}$.
- The parties compute $[\![\mathbf{v}']\!]_T \leftarrow L \cdot (\mathbf{z} \odot [\![1 - \mathbf{r}]\!]_T + (1 - \mathbf{z}) \odot [\![\mathbf{r}]\!]_T)$, viewing $\mathbf{z}$ as a vector over $\mathbb{Z}_T$ in the natural way.
- All parties open $\mathbf{v}'$.

Output. The parties output $(\mathbf{y}', \mathbf{v}')$.

Fig. 1. Protocol Π_{par} for securely computing $H \cdot x \bmod 2$ and $L \cdot x$ in the honest-but-curious up to $n - 1$ corruptions.

A Template Zero-Knowledge Proof. Building upon the above, we describe on Fig. 2 a template zero-knowledge proof. Looking ahead, our final zero-knowledge proof does (1) instantiate this template for a carefully chosen flavor of syndrome decoding with $\mathbb{N}$-linear constraints, and (2) introduce many optimizations to the proof, building both upon existing optimizations from previous works, and new optimizations tailored to our setting.

3.2   Concrete Instantiation for Regular Syndrome Decoding

With the template construction in mind, we can now discuss our concrete choice of syndrome decoding problem with $\mathbb{N}$-linear constraints. Our target is the *regular syndrome decoding problem*, where the linear constraint states that the witness x should be a concatenation of w unit vectors (see Sect. 2.1). The rationale behind this choice stems from the communication complexity of the template zero-knowledge proof from Fig. 2. Intuitively, the communication is dominated by the cost of transmitting the vectors over the ring $\mathbb{Z}_T$ (*i.e.* the $\mathbf{t}_i$ vectors): sending each such vector requires $K \cdot \log T$ bits. Looking ahead, even with proper optimizations, the zero-knowledge proof cannot be competitive with state-of-the-art constructions communication-wise whenever the value of $T = \|L \cdot \mathbf{1}\|_1$ is large.

Typically, for the standard syndrome decoding problem, we have $T = K$, hence the communication involves a $K \cdot \log K$ term, and the overhead is too large (when choosing concrete parameters, K is typically in the thousands, hence $K \log K$ is of the order of a few kilobytes, which becomes a few dozen

Parameters. (K, k, w, c) are four integers with $K > k > w$ and $k > c$. $H \in \{0,1\}^{k \times K}$ and $L \in \mathbb{N}^{c \times K}$ are public matrices. $y \in \{0,1\}^{k}$ and $\mathbf{v} \in \{0,1\}^{c}$ are public vectors. Let $\mathsf{par} \leftarrow (K, k, w, c, H, L)$, and let $T \leftarrow \|\mathbf{v}\|_1$. Let Commit be a non-interactive commitment scheme.

Inputs. The prover and the verifier have common input par and $(y, \mathbf{v})$, which jointly form an instance of the N-linear syndrome decoding problem. The prover additionally holds a witness $x \in \{0,1\}^{K}$ which is a solution of the instance: $H \cdot x = y \bmod 2$ and $L \cdot x = \mathbf{v}(= \mathbf{v} \bmod T)$.

Witness Sharing. The prover samples $(\mathbf{x}_1, \cdots, \mathbf{x}_n) \leftarrow_r \mathsf{Share}_2(x)$. Each share $\mathbf{x}_i$ is the input of the virtual party P_i.

Round 1. The prover runs the trusted dealer of Π_{par} and obtains $((\mathbf{s}_1, \cdots, \mathbf{s}_n), (\mathbf{t}_1, \cdots, \mathbf{t}_n)) = (\llbracket \mathbf{r} \rrbracket_2, \llbracket \mathbf{r} \rrbracket_T)$. He computes and sends $c_i \leftarrow_r \mathsf{Commit}(\mathbf{x}_i, \mathbf{s}_i, \mathbf{t}_i)$ for $i = 1$ to n to the verifier.

Round 2. The verifier picks a uniformly random permutation $\pi \leftarrow_r S_K$ and sends it to the prover.

Round 3. The prover runs the online phase of Π_{par} where the parties $(P_1, \cdots, P_n)$ have inputs $(\mathbf{x}_1, \cdots, \mathbf{x}_n)$, using the shuffled preprocessing material $(\llbracket \pi(\mathbf{r}) \rrbracket_2, \llbracket \pi(\mathbf{r}) \rrbracket_T)$. For each party P_i, let $\mathsf{msg}_i = (\mathbf{y}'_i, \mathbf{z}_i, \mathbf{v}'_i)$ denote the list of all messages sent by P_i during the execution. The prover sends $(\mathsf{msg}_1, \cdots, \mathsf{msg}_n)$ to the verifier.

Round 4. The verifier chooses a challenge $d \in [n]$ and sends it to the prover.

Round 5 The prover opens all commitments c_j for $j \neq d$ to the verifier.

Verification. The verifier checks:

- that all commitments were opened correctly;
- that the output of Π_{par} with transcript $(\mathsf{msg}_1, \cdots, \mathsf{msg}_n)$ is equal to $(y, \mathbf{v})$;
- that the messages msg_j sent by P_j are consistent with $(\mathbf{x}_j, \mathbf{s}_j, \mathbf{t}_j)$.

The verifier accepts if and only if all checks succeed.

Fig. 2. Template 5-round zero-knowledge proof for N-linear syndrome decoding using MPC-in-the-head with the protocol Π_{par}

kilobytes after parallel repetitions). On the other hand, *regular* syndrome decoding appears to minimize this cost: the value of T is only K/w. Hence, by choosing the weight appropriately, we can reduce the value of T.

The regular syndrome decoding problem is also far from new: it was introduced in [3] as the assumption underlying the security of a candidate for the SHA-3 competition, and was subsequently studied in numerous works, including [7,24,30], and more recently in [26]. The hardness of the regular syndrome decoding problem is also the core assumption underlying many recent works in secure computation with silent preprocessing, see *e.g.* [10–14,16,32,36,37] and references therein. It is therefore a well-established assumption.

In the following, we focus on the regular syndrome decoding problem as our primary instantiation of the template. Looking ahead, we seek to minimize the value of $T = K/w$. Concretely, as we show in Sect. 4.1, a standard chinese remainder theorem trick allows to work over the ring $\mathbb{Z}_{T/2}$ instead of $\mathbb{Z}_T$, as long as $\gcd(T/2, 2) = 1$ (*i.e.* $T/2$ is odd; intuitively, this is because the "mod 2 part" of the equation $L \cdot x = \mathbf{v} \bmod T$ can be obtained at no cost from the $\mathbb{F}_2$-sharing of x, hence it only remains to get $L \cdot x \bmod T/2$ and use the CRT to reconstruct $L \cdot x \bmod T$). The smallest possible value of $T/2$ satisfying the above constraint is $T/2 = 3$, implying $T = K/w = 6$. We therefore set $w = K/6$, which is the smallest value of w that sets the bitsize of the vectors $\mathbf{t}_i$ to its minimal value of $K \cdot \log(T/2) = K \cdot \log 3$.

3.3   Combinatorial Analysis

Our discussion so far hinged upon the assumption that when the preprocessing material is randomly shuffled by the verifier, a cheating prover has very low success probability. A core technical contribution of our work is to provide a bound on this success probability. We define (informally) a *combinatorial bound* to be a quantity p that bounds the probability of a cheating prover to find preprocessing material that causes the verifier to accept the interaction.

Definition 3 (Combinatorial bound – informal). *A real $\mathsf{p} \in (0,1)$ is a combinatorial bound for the template zero-knowledge proof if for every incorrect witness x, and every pair $(\mathbf{s}, \mathbf{t})$, the probability, over the random choice of a permutation π, that x satisfies the following equations:*

- $x' = \mathbf{z} \odot (\mathbf{1} - \pi(\mathbf{t})) + (\mathbf{1} - \mathbf{z}) \odot \pi(\mathbf{t})$ *with* $\mathbf{z} = \pi(\mathbf{s}) \oplus x$
- $H \cdot x = y \bmod 2,\ L \cdot x = \mathbf{v} \bmod 2,\ and\ L \cdot x' = \mathbf{v} \bmod T/2$

is upper-bounded by p.

Note that the last two equations stem from the use of the gcd trick, where the "mod 2 part" of the equation $L \cdot x = \mathbf{v} \bmod T$ is verified directly on the original shares of x modulo 2, and the remaining equation is checked modulo $T/2$ (assuming that $\gcd(2, T/2) = 1$). Proving a tight combinatorial bound turns out to be a highly non-trivial task. In this section, we overview the key technical challenges one faces, and outline our solution.

A Balls-and-bins Analysis. A key difficulty in the analysis is that we must handle arbitrary choices of the strings $(\mathbf{s}, \mathbf{t})$ chosen by the prover, but also arbitrary (invalid) witnesses x. In our concrete instantiation, we use the regular syndrome decoding problem, and always enforce $T = K/w = 6$ (this is the choice which maximizes efficiency). Therefore, we focus on this setting in our analysis. In this case, the setting becomes: assume that we are given an incorrect witness x, which is a concatenation of w length-T blocks $x^1, \cdots, x^w$. The equation $L \cdot x = \mathbf{v} \bmod 2$ translates to the condition that each block x^j has odd Hamming weight; since $T = 6$, we have $\mathsf{HW}(x^j) \in \{1, 3, 5\}$ for $j = 1$ to w.

Let us now fix a position $i \leq K$. The pair $(s_{\pi(i)}, t_{\pi(i)}) \in \mathbb{F}_2 \times \mathbb{F}_3$ "transforms" x_i into x'_i as follows: $x'_i = (x_i \oplus s_{\pi(i)}) \cdot (1 - 2t_{\pi(i)}) + t_{\pi(i)}$. In fact, the six elements of $\mathbb{F}_2 \times \mathbb{F}_3$ fall in three categories, depending on their effect on x_i:

- (Identity) $x'_i = x_i$. This happens whenever $s_{\pi(i)} = t_{\pi(i)}$.

- (Flip) $x_i' = 1 \oplus x_i$. This happens whenever $t_{\pi(i)} \in \{0, 1\} \wedge s_{\pi(i)} \neq t_{\pi(i)}$.
- (Constant 2) $x_i' = 2$. This happens whenever $t_{\pi(i)} = 2$.

Therefore, the prover choice of $(\mathbf{s}, \mathbf{t})$ boils down to choosing a sequence of (copy, flip, const2) operators, which are randomly shuffled, and then applied to each bit of the witness x. We formulate the experiment as a balls-into-bins experiment: the witness x is seen as a sequence of K bins, where the i-th bin is labeled by x_i. The prover chooses K balls, where each ball represents an operator (we call type-A, type-B, and type-C the copy, flip, and const2 operators respectively). Then, the balls are randomly thrown into the bins (with exactly one ball per bin), and the label of each bin is changed according to the operator of the ball it receives. The prover wins if, in the end, the sum of the labels in each block of bins is 1 modulo 3 (corresponding to checking that each block of x' has Hamming weight equal to 1 modulo 3).

Our analysis distinguishes two situations, depending on the balls chosen by the prover: either at least 60% of the balls are of the same type (we say that this type *dominates* the balls – the choice of the threshold is somewhat arbitrary), or the types are *well-spread* (no type appears more than 60% of the time). Intuitively, these cases correspond to two different 'failure modes':

- **Dominant Scenario.** Here, the prover's best choice is to pick x 'very close' to a valid witness (say, with a single incorrect block), and to set almost all balls to be type-A balls (type-A is what a honest prover would pick). Then, a few type-B balls are inserted, and the prover hopes that the permutation puts the type-B balls exactly within the incorrect blocks of x (hence correcting them). Alternatively, the prover could also pick x to be close to an 'anti-valid' witness (*i.e.* a valid witness with all its bits flipped) and set almost all balls to be type-B balls, to the same effect. In any case, bounding this scenario is done by bounding the probability that the incorrect blocks of x receive balls of the dominant types.

- **Well-Spread Scenario.** In the well-spread scenario, each bin receive a ball taken randomly from the initial set of balls. Since it is well-spread, this implies that the label of each bin is mapped to an element of $\{0, 1, 2\}$, with a well-spread probability mass on each of the options. For the prover to win, sufficiently many of the labels must be correctly set (so that all blocks have labels summing to 1 mod 3). If the random variables for each label were independent, a Chernoff bound would show that this happens with very low probability. While the labels are not independent from each other, a little bit of work allows to reduce the problem to bounding a hypergeometric distribution, for which strong Chernoff-style bounds exist (see the full version).

To bound the dominant scenario, we use a (slightly involved) counting argument, enumerating the total number of winning configurations for the prover, for each choice of (1) the number of incorrect blocks in x (denoted ℓ), and (2) the number of balls of the dominant type (denoted θ), and divide it by the total number of configurations. For each choice of (ℓ, θ), this provides an explicit (albeit complex) formula for the bound. We conjecture that the best choice of ℓ, θ is to set $\ell = 1$ and $\theta = K - 1$ (*i.e.*, using a witness with a single incorrect block). Though we do not have a proof of this statement, we can still compute a bound explicitly by minimizing the formula over all possible choices of ℓ and θ. When picking concrete parameters, we use a Python script to compute the bound explicitly, given in the full version (we note that the output of the script confirmed the conjecture for all parameters we tried).

In contrast, in the well-spread scenario, our analysis bounds p using a Chernoff-style bound for hypergeometric distribution, which provides directly an explicitly and simple formula for computing p in this case. Due to the exponential decay of the bound, we observe that the well-spread scenario is in fact never advantageous for a malicious prover: the best strategy is always to set $(\mathbf{s}, \mathbf{t})$ so as to be in the dominant scenario.

Allowing Almost-Regular Witnesses. A careful reader might have noticed an apparent issue in our previous analysis: assume that a cheating prover uses an *antiregular* witness x (*i.e.*, a vector such that $x \oplus \mathbf{1}$ is regular), and only type-B balls (*i.e.* the pairs (s_i, t_i) are such that $s_i = 1 - t_i$). Then it passes the verifier checks exacty as an honest prover would: the antiregular vector x still has blocks of odds Hamming weight, and for any choice of π, x' is now equal to $\mathbf{1} \oplus x$: that is, a regular vector. Concretely, this means that our zero-knowledge proof is not a proof of knowledge of a regular solution, but rather a proof of knowledge of either a regular *or an antiregular* solution. Nevertheless, when building a signature scheme, this is not an issue: it simply implies that unforgeability relies instead on the hardness of finding a regular or antiregular solution to an RSD instance. But it is a folklore observation that this variant of RSD does in fact reduce to the standard RSD problem, with only a factor 2 loss in the success probability, hence this does not harm security.

In fact, we push this approach even further. The bound p which we obtain by the previous analysis is essentially tight, but remains relatively high for our purpose. Concretely, fixing a value of $K \approx 1500$ (this is roughly to the range of our parameter choices), we get $\mathsf{p} \approx 1/250$. This bound is met when the prover uses a witness which is regular almost everywhere, with at most one exceptional block, where it has Hamming weight 3 or 5 (or the antiregular version of that). In this case, the prover builds $(\mathbf{s}, \mathbf{t})$ honestly, except on a single position (s_i, t_i), where he sets $s_i = 1 - t_i$. Then, with probability $1/250$, the permutation aligns i with the unique faulty block (there are 250 blocks in total), and the (s_i, t_i) pair "corrects" the faulty block, passing the verifier checks. Even though a $1/250$ bound is not too bad, in our context it largely dominates the soundness error of the proof. This stems from the fact that our protocol has extremely low computational costs, hence we can freely set the number n of virtual parties much higher than in previous works, e.g. $n = 1024$ or $n = 2048$, while still achieving comparable computational costs. In this high-n setting, the hope is to achieve a soundness error close to the best possible value of $1/n$, in order to minimize the number of parallel repetitions (hence reducing communication).

To get around this limitation, we choose to *allow almost-regular witnesses* (or almost-antiregular witnesses). Concretely, we relax the soundness of our zero-knowledge proof to guarantee only that a successful cheating prover must at least know an almost-regular (or almost-antiregular) witness, *i.e.*, a witness whose blocks all have weight 1 except one, which might have weight 1, 3, or 5. This form of zero-knowledge proof with a gap between the language of honest witnesses and the language of extracted witnesses is not uncommon in the literature. In particular, it is similar in spirit to the notion of *soundness slack* in some lattice-based zero-knowledge proofs, where a witness is a vector with small entries, and an extracted witness can have much larger entries [4,17]. By using this relaxation, our bound p improves by (essentially) a quadratic factor: a cheating prover must now cheat on (at least) *two* positions (s_i, t_i), and hope that both align with the (at least) two incorrect blocks of x. Concretely, using $K \approx 1500$, our combinatorial analysis gives $p \approx 3 \cdot 10^{-5}$ in this setting, which becomes a vanishing component of the soundness error (dominated by the $1/n$ term).

When building a signature scheme from this relaxed zero-knowledge proof, we use the Fiat-Shamir transform on a 5-round protocol, and must therefore adjust the number of repetitions to account for the attack of [28]. For a bound of p as above, this severely harms efficiency. Following the strategy of [21], we avoid the problem by making p much smaller. Concretely, denoting τ_{ZK} the smallest integer such that $(1/n + p \cdot (1 - 1/n))^{\tau_{ZK}} \leq 2^{-\lambda}$, the optimal number of repetitions which one can hope for in the signature scheme is $\tau = \tau_{ZK} + 1$. Therefore, denoting f the number of faulty blocks in the witness, we set f to be the smallest value such that the resulting bound p yields $\tau = \tau_{ZK} + 1$, hence achieving the optimal number of repetitions. At this stage, the unforgeability of the signature now reduces to the hardness of finding either an almost-regular or an almost-antiregular solution to an RSD problem (with up to f faulty block), which seems quite exotic (though it remains in itself a plausible assumption). For the sake of relying only on the well-established RSD assumption, we set parameters such that, except with $2^{-\lambda}$ probability, a random RSD instance does not in fact have any almost-regular or almost-antiregular solution (with up to f faulty blocks) on top of the original solution. This implies that, for this choice of parameters, this "f-almost-RSD" assumption is in fact equivalent to the RSD assumption (with essentially no loss in the reduction).

Summing Up. We first describe and construct an optimized zero-knowledge argument of knowledge, following the template outlined in this technical overview. We compile our new zero-knowledge proof into a signature using Fiat-Shamir. We use the combinatorial analysis to identify a bound p on the probability that the verifier picks a *bad permutation*, and formally prove that the zero-knowledge proof achieves ε-soundness, where $\varepsilon = (1/n + p \cdot (1 - 1/n))$ (n being the number of parties in the MPC protocol). To achieve optimal efficiency for the signature scheme, we reduce p by allowing up to f faulty blocks in the witness, and select RSD parameters such that the underlying assumptions remains the standard RSD assumption despite this relaxation of the proof soundness. Due to the page limitations, and although the combinatorial analysis of our construction (the bound p) is a core technical contribution of our work, we had to defer it to the full version, to cover the description of the zero-knowledge proof of the signature scheme in the main body.

3.4 Cryptanalysis of RSD

We complement our analysis by providing an overview of the security of RSD. In particular, we give a precise picture of how RSD relates to the standard syndrome decoding assumption, depending on the parameters (K, k, w). Concretely, we define a "RSD uniqueness bound", analogous to the Gilbert-Varshamov (GV) bound for standard syndrome decoding, and show that (1) above the GV bound, RSD is always easier than SD; (2) below the RSD uniqueness bound, RSD becomes in fact *harder* than SD, and (3) in between the two bounds is a gray zone, where the hardness of the two problems is not directly comparable. Looking ahead, our choice of parameters lies inside this gray zone, and corresponds to a setting where a random RSD instance does not have additional f-almost-regular solutions with high probability, to guarantee a tight reduction to the standard RSD assumption even when allowing such relaxed solutions.

We also overview existing attacks on RSD, and in most cases revisit and improve them to exploit more carefully the structure of the RSD problem, obtaining significant speedups. Eventually, we design a new attack which outperforms all previous attacks. Our attack is not fully explicit: it requires an approximate birthday paradox search (*i.e.*, finding an almost-collision between items of two lists). For the sake of being conservative, when choosing concrete parameters, we assume that this approximate birthday paradox can be solved in time linear in the list size (it is far from clear how to perform such a fast approximate collision search, but it does not seem implausible that it can be done, hence we choose to stay on the safe side. We view finding such an algorithm as an interesting open problem). Due to space limitations, the details on our analysis of the RSD problem are deferred to the full version.

4 Zero-Knowledge Proof for Regular Syndrome Decoding

4.1 Optimizations

We start from the template given in the Technical Overview (Sect. 3), and refine it using various optimizations. Some of these optimizations are standard, used *e.g.* in works such as [5,21,29] (we present them as such when it is the case), and others are new, tailored optimizations.

Using a Collision-Resistant Hash Function. The "hash trick" is a standard approach to reduce the communication of public coin zero-knowledge proofs. It builds upon the following observation: in a zero-knowledge proof, the verification equation on a list of messages $(m_1, \cdots, m_\ell)$ often makes the messages *reverse samplable*: the verifier can use the equation to recover what the value of $(m_1, \cdots, m_\ell)$ should be. Whenever this is the case, the communication can be reduced by sending $h = H(m_1, \cdots, m_\ell)$ instead of $(m_1, \cdots, m_\ell)$, where H denotes collision-resistant hash function. The verification proceeds by reconstructing $(m_1, \cdots, m_\ell)$ and checking that $h = H(m_1, \cdots, m_\ell)$, and security follows from the collision resistance of H. As h can be as small as 2λ-bit long, this significantly reduces communication.

Using Regular Syndrome Decoding in Systematic Form. Without loss of generality, we can set H to be in systematic form, *i.e.* setting $H = [H'|I_k]$, where I_k denotes the identity matrix over $\{0,1\}^{k \times k}$. This strategy was used in the recent code-based signature of [21]. Using H in systematic form, and writing x as $x = (x_1|x_2)$ where $x_1 \in \mathbb{F}_2^{K-k}, x_2 \in \mathbb{F}_2^k$, we have $Hx = H'x_1 + x_2 = y$. Since the instance (H, y) is public, this implies that the prover need not share x entirely over $\mathbb{F}_2$: it suffices for the prover to share x_1, and all parties can reconstruct $[\![x_2]\!]_2 \leftarrow y \oplus H' \cdot [\![x_1]\!]_2$. Additionally, the parties need not opening $\mathbf{z}$ entirely: denoting $\pi(\mathbf{r}) = (r_1|r_2)$, the parties can open instead $[\![z_1]\!]_2 = [\![x_1 \oplus r_1]\!]_2$ and define $z_2 = H'z_1 \oplus y$. This way, they can reconstruct the complete $\mathbf{z}$ as $\mathbf{z} = (z_1|z_2)$. The rest of the protocol proceeds as before. Following the above considerations, and to simplify notations, from now on we refer to the short vector of length $K - k$ in the small field (previously indicated with x_1) simply as x and to the long vector of size K in the large field as $\tilde{x}$ (*i.e.* $\tilde{x} = (x|H'x \oplus y)$).

Exploiting the Regular Structure of x. We further reduce the size of x using an optimization tailored to the RSD setting. Thanks to its regular structure, we can divide x into w blocks each of size $T = K/w$. But since each block has exactly one non-zero entry, given the first $T - 1$ entries $(b_1, \cdots, b_{T-1})$ of any block, the last entry can be recomputed as $b_T = 1 \oplus \bigoplus_{i=1}^{T-1} b_i$. In the zero-knowledge proof, the prover does therefore only share $T - 1$ out of the T bits in each block of x among the virtual parties. Similarly, the size of r_1 and z_1 are reduced by the same factor, since only $T - 1$ bits of each block need to be masked.

Reducing the Size of the Messages. With the above optimizations, the equation $H\tilde{x} = H'x \oplus x_2 = y$ needs not be verified anymore: it now holds by construction, as $\tilde{x}$ is defined as $(x|H'x \oplus y)$. This removes the need to include $\mathbf{y}_i$ in the messages msg_i sent by each party P_i; this is in line with previous works, which also observed that linear operations are for free with proper optimizations. The message of each party becomes simply $\mathsf{msg}_i = (\mathbf{z}_i, \mathbf{v}'_i)$. Note that in this concrete instantiation the entries of $\mathbf{v}'_i$ are computed as $\langle \mathbf{1}, \tilde{\mathbf{x}}_\mathbf{i}^j \rangle$, where the vectors $\tilde{\mathbf{x}}_\mathbf{i}^j$ for $j = 1$ to w are the blocks of P_i's share of the vector $\mathbf{z} \odot (1 - \pi(\mathbf{t})) + (1 - \mathbf{z}) \odot \pi(\mathbf{t})$.

Using the Chinese Remainder Theorem. In the zero-knowledge proof, verifying any linear equation modulo 2 on the witness $\bar{\mathbf{x}}$ is for free communication-wise. Ultimately, the verifier wants to check that $\langle \bar{\mathbf{x}}^j, \mathbf{1} \rangle = 1 \bmod T$. Setting T to be equal to 2 modulo 4 guarantees that T is even, and $\gcd(T/2, 2) = 1$. Hence, it suffices to work over the integer ring $\mathbb{Z}_{T/2}$ instead of $\mathbb{Z}_T$, to let the verifier check the equation $\langle \bar{\mathbf{x}}^j, \mathbf{1} \rangle = 1 \bmod T/2$ for $j = 1$ to w. Indeed, by the Chinese remainder theorem, together with the relations $\langle \bar{\mathbf{x}}^j, \mathbf{1} \rangle = 1 \bmod 2$ (which can be checked for free), this ensures that $\langle \bar{\mathbf{x}}^j, \mathbf{1} \rangle = 1 \bmod T$ for $j = 1$ to w. This reduces the size of the $\mathbf{t}_i$ vectors from $K \cdot \log T$ to $K \cdot \log(T/2)$. As outlined in Sect. 3.2, we actually set $T = 6$ in our concrete instantiation, hence executing the protocol over the integer ring $\mathbb{Z}_3$, the smallest possible ring satisfying the coprimality constraint.

Compressing Share with PRG. Another standard technique from [29] uses a pseudorandom generator to compress all-but-one shares distributed during the input sharing and preprocessing phases. Indeed, writing $[\![\mathbf{x}]\!]_2 = (\mathbf{x}_1, \ldots, \mathbf{x_n})$, then $\mathbf{x_n} = \mathbf{x} - \bigoplus_{i=1}^{n-1} \mathbf{x_i} \bmod 2$. Denoting also $[\![\mathbf{r}]\!]_2 = (\mathbf{s}_1, \ldots, \mathbf{s_n})$ and $[\![\mathbf{r}]\!]_T = (\mathbf{t}_1, \ldots, \mathbf{t_n})$, it holds that $\sum_{i=1}^n \mathbf{t_i} = \bigoplus_{i=1}^n \mathbf{s_i} \bmod T$, which rewrites to $\mathbf{t}_n = \bigoplus_{i=1}^n \mathbf{s_i} - \sum_{i=1}^{n-1} \mathbf{t_i} \bmod T$.

We can compress the description of these shares by giving to each party P_i a λ-bit seed seed_i and letting each of them apply a pseudorandom generator to seed_i in order to obtain (pseudo)random shares $\mathbf{x_i}$, $\mathbf{s_i}$ and $\mathbf{t_i}$. All shares of $\mathbf{s}$ can be compressed this way (since $\mathbf{s}$ need just be a random vector), and all-but-one shares of $[\![\mathbf{x}]\!]_2$ and $\mathbf{t}$. The missing shares can be obtained by letting P_n receive an auxiliary string aux_n defined as:

$$\mathsf{aux}_n \leftarrow \left(\mathbf{x} - \bigoplus_{i=1}^{n-1} \mathbf{x_i} \bmod 2, \bigoplus_{i=1}^{n} \mathbf{s_i} - \sum_{i=1}^{n-1} \mathbf{t_i} \bmod T \right).$$

We refer to the information shared with each party as the *state* of the party. For each P_i for $1 \leq i \leq n - 1$, we therefore have $\mathsf{state}_i = \mathsf{seed}_i$. The last party P_n has $\mathsf{state}_n = (\mathsf{seed}_n | \mathsf{aux}_n)$: in the online phase of the protocol each party seed_n can be used to randomly generate $\mathbf{s_n}$.

Tree-Based Generation of the Seeds. To further reduce the overhead of communicating the seeds, we apply the standard tree-based technique of [29] and generate the seeds as the leaves of a complete binary tree. We introduced a master seed seed^* from which we generate n minor seeds $\mathsf{seed}_1, \cdots, \mathsf{seed}_n$ as the leaves of a binary tree of depth $\log n$, where the two children of each nodes are computed using a length-doubling pseudorandom generators. This way, revealing all seeds except seed_j requires only sending the seeds on the nodes along the co-path from the root to the j-th leaf, which reduces the communication from $\lambda \cdot (n - 1)$ to $\lambda \cdot \log n$. Note that due to this optimization, when compiling the proof into a signature, collisions among seed^* for different signatures are likely to appear after $2^{\lambda/2}$ signatures. To avoid this issue, an additional random salt of length 2λ must be use, see Sect. 5.

Using Deterministic Commitments. As in [29] and other previous works, we observe that all committed values are pseudorandom. Therefore, the commitment scheme does not have to be hiding: in the random oracle model, it suffices to instantiate $\mathsf{Commit}(x; r)$ deterministically as $H(x)$ for zero-knowledge to hold.

Final Zero Knowledge Protocol. We represent on Fig. 3 our final zero-knowledge proof of knowledge for a solution to the regular syndrome decoding problem, taking into account all the optimizations outlined above, except the use of deterministic commitments (using deterministic commitments requires using the ROM, which is otherwise not needed for the zero-knowledge proof. Looking ahead, we still use this optimization when compiling the proof to a signature using Fiat-Shamir, since we use the ROM at this stage anyway).

4.2 Security Analysis

We now turn to the security analysis of the protocol. A crucial component of our analysis is a *combinatorial bound*, which we introduce below. Before, we state some definition.

Definition 4 (f-Strongly invalid candidate witness). *We say that $x \in \mathbb{F}_2^K$ is a f-weakly valid witness if x is almost a regular vector (in the sense that it differs from a regular vector in at most f blocks), or almost an antiregular vector. Formally, let $(x^j)_{j \leq w}$ be the w length-K/w blocks of x. Assume that K/w is even. Then x is an f-weakly valid witness if*

1. *$\forall j \leq w$, $\mathsf{HW}(x^j) = 1 \bmod 2$, and*
2. *$|\{j : \mathsf{HW}(x^j) \neq 1\}| \leq f$ or $|\{j : \mathsf{HW}((1 \oplus x)^j) \neq 1\}| \leq f$,*

where $1 \oplus x$ is the vector obtained by flipping all bits of x. If x is not an f-weakly valid witness, we say that x is an f-strongly invalid candidate witness.

Below, set $T \leftarrow K/w$. We assume for simplicity that the parameters are such that w divides K, and that $T = 2 \bmod 4$. Note that this ensures that a block x^j of the candidate witness x has Hamming weight 1 if and only if $\sum_{i=1}^{K/w} x_i^j = 1 \bmod T/2$ and $\sum_{i=1}^{K/w} x_i^j = 1 \bmod 2$.

Definition 5 (Combinatorial Bound). *Given a vector $u \in \mathbb{N}^K$ divided into w length-K/w blocks u^j, we denote $\mathsf{Succ}(u)$ the event that $\sum_{i=1}^{K/w} u_i^j = 1 \bmod T/2$ for all $j \leq w$. Then, a combinatorial bound for the zero-knowledge proof of Fig. 3 with parameters (K, w) is a real $\mathsf{p} = \mathsf{p}(K, w, f) \in (0, 1)$ such that for any f-strongly invalid candidate witness $x \in \mathbb{F}_2^K$ satisfying $\forall j \leq w$, $\mathsf{HW}(x^j) = 1 \bmod 2$ (i.e. x still satisfies condition 1 of Definition 4), and for any pair of vectors $(s, t) \in \mathbb{F}_2^K \times \mathbb{Z}_{T/2}^K$,*

$$\Pr[\pi \leftarrow_r \mathsf{Perm}_K, x' \leftarrow \pi(t) + (x \oplus \pi(s)) \odot (1 - 2\pi(t)) : \mathsf{Succ}(x')] \leq \mathsf{p}(K, w, f),$$

where Perm_K denotes the set of all permutations of $\{1, \cdots, K\}$.

Informally, the combinatorial bound p is a bound on the probability that a malicious prover passes the verification *without* guessing the subset of views requested by the verifier. The formal notion relax what we mean by a malicious prover, by requesting that they use a witness *sufficiently far* from a honest regular witness. Looking ahead, this feature allows us to obtain much smaller

Inputs: The prover and the verifier have a matrix $H \in \mathbb{F}_2^{k \times K} = [H'|I_k]$ and a vector $y \in \mathbb{F}_2^k$. The prover also knows a regular vector $\tilde{x} = (x|x_2) \in \mathbb{F}_2^K$ with Hamming weight $\mathrm{HW}(\tilde{x}) = w$ and such that $H\tilde{x} = y$.

Parameters and notations. We let n denote number of parties. We let x' denote the vector obtained by deleting the T-th bit in each block of x. We call "expanding" the action of recomputing x from x', *i.e.* adding a T-th bit at the end of each length-$(T-1)$ block, computed as the opposite of the XOR of all bits of the block.

Round 1 The prover emulates the preprocessing phase of Π as follows:

1. Chooses a random seed $seed^*$;
2. Uses $seed^*$ as the root of a depth-$\log n$ full binary tree to produce the leaves $(seed_i, \sigma_i)$ using a length-doubling PRG for each $i \in [n]$;
3. Use $(seed_1, \cdots, seed_{n-1})$ to create pseudorandom shares $(\mathbf{x}'_1, \cdots, \mathbf{x}'_{n-1})$ of x', as well as vectors $(\mathbf{s_i}, \mathbf{t_i}) \in \mathbb{F}_2^{(T-1)\cdot(K-k)/T} \times \mathbb{Z}_{T/2}^K$. Use $seed_n$ to create $\mathbf{s_n}$ as well. Let $\mathbf{x_i}$ denote the vector obtained by "expanding" $\mathbf{x}'_i$ to $K - k$ bits;
4. Let $\mathbf{s}'_i$ denote the value obtained by "expanding" $\mathbf{s_i}$ to a $(K-k)$-bit vector, and let $s' \leftarrow \bigoplus_{i=1}^n \mathbf{s}'_i$. Set $s \leftarrow (s'|H' \cdot s' \oplus y)$. Define
$$\mathsf{aux}_n \leftarrow \left(x' \oplus \bigoplus_{i=1}^{n-1} \mathbf{x_i}, \; s' - \sum_{i=1}^{n-1} \mathbf{t_i} \bmod T/2 \right);$$
5. Sets $\mathsf{state}_i = seed_i$ for $1 \leq i \leq n-1$ and $\mathsf{state}_n = seed_n||\mathsf{aux}_n$;
6. For each $i \in [n]$ computes $\mathsf{com}_i := \mathsf{Commit}(\mathsf{state}_i, \sigma_i)$;
7. Computes $h := H(\mathsf{com}_1, \cdots, \mathsf{com}_n)$ and sends it to the verifier.

Round 2 The verifier chooses a permutation $\pi \in S_{K-k}$ and sends it to the prover.
Round 3 The prover:

1. Simulates the online phase of the n parties protocol Π using the pairs $(\pi(\mathbf{s_i}), \pi(\mathbf{t_i}))$ as the preprocessing material of the i-th party:
   - for each $i \in [n]$ compute $\mathbf{z}'_i = \mathbf{x}'_i \oplus \pi(\mathbf{s_i})$ getting $[\![z_1]\!]_2 = (\mathbf{z_1}, \cdots, \mathbf{z_n})$ by "expanding" the $\mathbf{z}'_i$'s;
   - Define $z_2 = H' \cdot z_1 \oplus y$ and $z = (z_1|z_2)$;
   - Set $[\![\tilde{x}]\!]_{T/2} = (\bar{\mathbf{x}}_1, \ldots, \bar{\mathbf{x}}_n)$ where $\bar{\mathbf{x}}_i = z + (1 - 2z) \odot \pi(\mathbf{t_i}) \bmod T/2$;
   - For each $i \in [n]$ compute:
     - $\bar{\mathbf{w}}_i^j = \mathrm{HW}(\bar{\mathbf{x}}_i{}^j) \bmod T/2$ for all the blocks $1 \leq j \leq w$;
     - $\mathsf{msg}_i = (\mathbf{z_i}, (\bar{\mathbf{w}}_i^j)_{1 \leq j \leq w})$;
2. Compute $h' = H(\mathsf{msg}_1, \cdots, \mathsf{msg}_n)$;
3. Send z_1 and h' to the verifier. // *sending z'_1 actually suffices*

Round 4 The verifier chooses a challenge $d \in [n]$ and sends it to the prover.
Round 5 The prover sends $(\mathsf{state}_i, \sigma_i)_{i \neq d}$ and com_d.
Verification The verifier checks that everything is correct:

1. Recompute $\bar{\mathsf{com}}_j = \mathsf{Commit}(\mathsf{state}_j, \sigma_j)$ for $j \neq d$;
2. Recompute msg_i for all $i \neq d$ using state_i and z_1;
3. Recompute
$$\bar{\mathsf{msg}}_d = \left(z_1 - \sum_{i \neq d} \mathbf{z_i}, \; \left(1 - \sum_{i \neq d} \bar{\mathbf{w}}_i^j \right)_{1 \leq j \leq w} \right);$$
4. Check if $h = H(\bar{\mathsf{com}}_1, \cdots, \mathsf{com}_d, \cdots, \bar{\mathsf{com}}_n)$;
5. Check if $h' = H(\mathsf{msg}_1, \cdots, \bar{\mathsf{msg}}_d, \cdots, \mathsf{msg}_n)$.

Fig. 3. A five-round zero-knowledge proof of knowledge of a solution to the regular syndrome decoding problem

combinatorial bounds for concrete choices of parameters. When building a signature scheme from the zero-knowledge proof, we further prove that finding a "relaxed" witness is at least as hard as solving the standard regular syndrome decoding problem, hence justifying that this relaxation does not harm security.

Theorem 6. *Let* Commit *be a non-interactive commitment scheme, and H be collision-resistant hash function. Let* p *be a combinatorial bound for the protocol of Fig. 3. The protocol given on Fig. 3 is a* gap *honest-verifier zero-knowledge argument of knowledge for the relation $\mathcal{R}$ such that $((H, y), x) \in \mathcal{R}$ if $H \cdot x = y \bmod 2$ and x is a regular vector of weight w. The* gap *relation $\mathcal{R}'$ is such that $((H, y), x) \in \mathcal{R}'$ if $H \cdot x = y \bmod 2$ and x is an f-weakly valid witness. The soundness error of the proof is at most $\varepsilon = \mathsf{p} + 1/n - \mathsf{p}/n$.*

The completeness of the protocol naturally derives from its definition. In the full version, we prove the honest-verifier zero-knowledge and soundness properties.

4.3   Communication

The expected communication of the zero-knowledge argument amounts to:

$$4\lambda + \tau \cdot \left(\lambda(\log n + 1) + \left(\frac{2n-1}{n} \right) \frac{T-1}{T} (K-k) + \left(\frac{n-1}{n} \right) K \log_2 T \right) \text{ bits,}$$

where we assume that hashes are 2λ bits long, and commitments are λ bits long, and where τ denotes the number of parallel repetitions of the proof.

5   A Signature Scheme from Regular Syndrome Decoding

A signature scheme is composed of three algorithms (KeyGen, Sign, Verify). KeyGen, starting with a security parameter λ, returns a key pair (pk, sk) where pk and sk are respectively the public key and the private key. The algorithm Sign on an input a message m and the secret key sk, gives a signature σ. Verify with input a message m, a public key pk and a signature σ, returns 0 or 1 depending on whether the signature σ is verified for m under pk or not. The security property for a signature scheme is the existential unforgeability against chosen message attacks: given a public key pk and an oracle access to Sign(sk, ·) it is hard to obtain a pair (s, m) such that m was not queried to the signing oracle and Verify(pk, s, m) = 1.

In this section, we turn our 5-round protocol into a signature scheme using the Fiat-Shamir transform. The switch from an interactive protocol to a non-interactive protocol is done by calculating the two challenges π and d (corresponding respectively to the challenges chosen by the verifier in rounds 2 and 4 of our 5-round protocol) as follows:

$$h_1 = H(m, \mathsf{salt}, h), \quad \pi \leftarrow \mathsf{PRG}(h_1), \quad h_2 = H(m, \mathsf{salt}, h, h'), \quad d \leftarrow \mathsf{PRG}(h_2)$$

where m is the input message, H is an hash function and h and h' are the Round 1 and Round 3 hash commitments merged for the τ repetitions. As in previous works, we use a salt $\mathsf{salt} \in \{0,1\}^{2\lambda}$ to avoid $2^{\lambda/2}$-query attack resulting from collisions between seeds. We also take into account the forgery attack presented by Kales and Zaverucha [28] against the signature schemes obtained by applying the Fiat-Shamir transform to 5-round protocols. Adapting this attack to our context yields a forgery cost of

$$\mathrm{cost_{forge}} = \min_{\tau_1,\tau_2:\tau_1+\tau_2=\tau} \left\{ \frac{1}{\sum_{i=\tau_1}^{\tau} \binom{\tau}{i}\mathsf{p}^i(1-\mathsf{p})^{\tau-i}} + n^{\tau_2} \right\} \tag{1}$$

5.1   Description of the Signature Scheme

In our signature scheme, the key generation algorithm randomly samples a syndrome decoding instance (H, y) with solution x. We describe it on Fig. 4.

Inputs: A security parameter λ.

1. Randomly chooses a seed $\leftarrow \{0,1\}^{\lambda}$;
2. Using a pseudorandom generator with seed to obtain a regular vector $x \in \mathbb{F}_2^K$ with $\mathsf{HW}(x) = w$ and a matrix H;
3. Compute $y = Hx$;
4. Set $\mathsf{pk} = (H, y)$ and $\mathsf{sk} = (H, y, x)$.

Fig. 4. Key generation algorithm of the signature scheme

For a secret key $\mathsf{sk} = (H, y, x)$ and a message $m \in \{0,1\}^*$, the signing algorithm is described on Fig. 5. Given a public key $\mathsf{pk} = (H, y)$, a message $m \in \{0,1\}^*$ and a signature σ, the verification algorithm is described in Fig. 6.

Theorem 7. *Suppose the PRG used is $(t, \epsilon_{\mathsf{PRG}})$-secure and any adversary running in time t has at most an advantage ϵ_{SD} against the underlying d-split syndrome decoding problem. Model the hash functions H_0, H_1, H_2 as random oracles with output of length 2λ-bit. Then chosen-message adversary against the signature scheme depicted in Fig. 5, running in time t, making q_s signing queries, and making q_0, q_1, q_2 queries, respectively, to the random oracles, succeeds in outputting a valid forgery with probability*

$$\Pr[\mathrm{Forge}] \leq \frac{(q_0 + \tau n_s)^2}{2 \cdot 2^{2\lambda}} + \frac{q_s (q_s + q_0 + q_1 + q_2)}{2^{2\lambda}} + q_s \cdot \tau \cdot \epsilon_{\mathsf{PRG}} + \epsilon_{\mathsf{SD}} + \Pr[X+Y=\tau] \tag{2}$$

where $\epsilon = \mathsf{p} + \frac{1}{n} - \frac{\mathsf{p}}{n}$, with p given in the full version, $X = \max_{\alpha \in Q_1}\{X_\alpha\}$ and $Y = \max_{\beta \in Q_2}\{Y_\beta\}$ with $X_\alpha \sim \mathrm{Binomial}(\tau, \mathsf{p})$ and $Y_\beta \sim \mathrm{Binomial}\left(\tau - X, \frac{1}{n}\right)$ where Q_1 and Q_2 are sets of all queries to oracles H_1 and H_2.

The proof of Theorem 7 follows directly from the standard analysis of Fiat-Shamir-based signatures from 5-round identification protocol. It is identical to the proof of Theorem 5 in [21], and we omit it here.

Inputs: A secret key $\mathsf{sk} = (H, y, x)$ and a message $m \in \{0,1\}^*$.
Sample a random $\mathsf{salt} \in \{0,1\}^{2\lambda}$.
Phase 1 For each iteration $e \in [\tau]$

1. Choose a random seed $\mathsf{seed}_e \leftarrow \{0,1\}^\lambda$;
2. Use seed_e and salt as input of a pseudorandom generator to produce seed_i^e for each $i \in [n]$;
3. Compute aux_n^e;
4. Set $\mathsf{state}_i^e = \mathsf{seed}_i^e$ for $1 \le i \le n-1$ and $\mathsf{state}_n^e = \mathsf{seed}_n^e \| \mathsf{aux}_n^e$;
5. Use all the states to create, through a pseudorandom generator:
   - $[\![x^e]\!]_2 = (\mathbf{x_1^e}, \ldots, \mathbf{x_n^e})$;
   - $s = [\![r_1^e]\!]_2 = (\mathbf{s_1^e}, \ldots, \mathbf{s_n^e})$;
   - $t = [\![r^e]\!]_q = (\mathbf{t_1^e}, \ldots, \mathbf{t_n^e})$;
6. For each $i \in [n]$ computes $\mathsf{com}_i^e := H_0(\mathsf{salt}, i, \mathsf{state}_i^e)$.

Phase 2

1. Compute $h_1 = H_1(m, \mathsf{salt}, \mathsf{com}_1^1, \cdots, \mathsf{com}_n^1, \cdots, \mathsf{com}_1^\tau, \cdots, \mathsf{com}_n^\tau)$;
2. Obtain $\pi_{\{e \in \tau\}}^e \in S_{K-k}$ via a pseudorandom generator using h_1.

Phase 3 For each iteration $e \in [\tau]$

1. Each party P_i computes $\mathbf{z_i^e} = \mathbf{x_i^e} \oplus \pi(\mathbf{s_i^e})$;
2. The parties get $[\![z_1^e]\!]_2 = (\mathbf{z_1^e}, \cdots, \mathbf{z_n^e})$ and set $[\![z_2^e]\!]_2 = H'[\![z_1^e]\!]_2 \oplus y$ and so $z^e = (z_1^e | z_2^e)$;
3. Obtain $[\![\bar{x}^e]\!]_q = (\mathbf{\bar{x}_1^e}, \ldots, \mathbf{\bar{x}_n^e})$ where $\mathbf{\bar{x}_i^e} = z^e + (1 - 2z^e) * \pi(\mathbf{t_i^e})$;
4. For each $j \in [n]$ compute:
   - $\mathbf{\bar{w}_i^{j,e}} = \langle 1, \bar{x}_i^{j,e} \rangle$ for all the blocks $1 \le j \le w$;
   - $\mathsf{msg}_i^e = \left(\mathbf{z_i^e}, \left\{ \mathbf{\bar{w}_i^{j,e}} \right\}_{1 \le j \le w} \right)$.

Phase 4

1. Compute $h_2 = H_2(m, \mathsf{salt}, h_1, \mathsf{msg}_1^1, \cdots, \mathsf{msg}_n^1, \cdots, \mathsf{msg}_1^\tau, \cdots, \mathsf{msg}_n^\tau)$;
2. Obtain $d_{\{e \in \tau\}}^e \in [n]$ via a pseudorandom generator using h_2.

Phase 5 Output the signature

$$\sigma = \mathsf{salt} | h_1 | h_2 | (\mathsf{state}_{i \ne d}^e | \mathsf{com}_{d^e}^e)_{\{e \in \tau\}}.$$

Fig. 5. Signing algorithm of the signature scheme

5.2 Parameters Selection Process

In this section, we explain how to select parameters for the zero-knowledge argument system of Sect. 4.1 and the signature scheme of Sect. 5. Let f be the number of faulty blocks (of Hamming weight 3 or 5) allowed in the witness extracted from a cheating prover. Looking ahead, f is chosen as the smallest value that minimizes τ, the number of repetitions of the underlying zero-knowledge argument, which has a strong impact on the size of the signature. Given a candidate value f, our selection of the parameters (K, k, w) proceeds as outlined below. We remind

---

Inputs: A public key $\mathsf{pk} = (H, y)$, a message $m \in \{0,1\}^*$ and a signature σ.

1. Split the signature as follows

$$\sigma = \mathsf{salt}|h_1|h_2|(\mathsf{state}_{i \neq d}^e|\mathsf{com}_{d^e}^e)_{\{e \in \tau\}};$$

2. Recompute $\pi_{\{e \in \tau\}}^e \in S_{K-k}$ via a pseudorandom generator using h_1;
3. Recompute $d_{\{e \in \tau\}}^e \in [n]$ via a pseudorandom generator using h_2;
4. For each iteration $e \in [\tau]$
    - For each $i \neq d$ recompute $\mathsf{com}_i^e = H_0(\mathsf{salt}, i, \mathsf{state}_i^e)$;
    - Use all the states, except $\mathsf{state}_{d^e}^e$, to simulate the Phase 3 of the signing algorithm for all parties but the d^e−th, obtaining $\mathsf{msg}_{i \neq d^e}^e$;
    - Compute

$$\overline{\mathsf{msg}}_{d^e}^e = \left(z_1^e - \sum_{i \neq d} \mathbf{z_i^e}, \left\{ 1 - \sum_{i \neq d} \overline{\mathbf{w}}_i^{j,e} \right\}_{1 \leq j \leq w} \right);$$

5. Check if $h_1 = H_1(m, \mathsf{salt}, \mathsf{com}_1^1, \cdots, \mathsf{com}_n^1, \cdots, \mathsf{com}_1^\tau, \cdots, \mathsf{com}_n^\tau)$;
6. Check if $h_2 = H_2(m, \mathsf{salt}, h_1, \mathsf{msg}_1^1, \cdots, \mathsf{msg}_n^1, \cdots, \mathsf{msg}_1^\tau, \cdots, \mathsf{msg}_n^\tau)$;
7. Output ACCEPT if both condition are satisfied.

Fig. 6. Verification algorithm of the signature scheme

the reader that we always enforce $w = K/6$ to get a blocksize 6, in order to work over the smallest possible field $\mathbb{F}_3$ in the zero-knowledge proof. We also set the target bit-security to $\lambda = 128$.

Choosing k. As explained in the full version, we set k such that even when allowing $f > 0$ faulty blocks in the zero-knowledge proof, the assumption underlying the unforgeability of the signature remains equivalent to the standard RSD assumption. Concretely, this is achieved by setting k to

$$k \leftarrow \left\lceil \log_2 \left(\sum_{i=0}^{f} 6^{w-i} \cdot \binom{w}{i} \cdot 26^i \right) \right\rceil + b \cdot \lambda,$$

with $b = 1$. We also consider a second choice of parameters, in which we set $b = 0$ in the above equation. This second choice of parameters corresponds to the f-almost-RSD uniqueness bound, the threshold where the number of almost-regular solution becomes close to 1. This setting should intuitively leads to the hardest instance of the almost-RSD problem. However, it does not reduce anymore to the standard RSD problem, since a random RSD instance might have irregular (but almost-regular) solutions. We use this alternative choice as a way to pick more aggressive parameters, under an exotic (albeit plausible) assumption.

Choosing K. Having chosen k (as a function of $w = K/6$), we turn our attention to K. Here, we use the attacks described in the full version, to select the smallest K such that, when setting k as above, we achieve λ bits of security against all attacks. We note that the approximate birthday paradox attack (see full version) is always the most efficient attack, by a significant margin. Yet, it relies upon the assumption that approximate collisions can be found in linear time, and no such linear-time algorithm is known as of today. We view this optimistic evaluation of the attack efficiency as leading to a conservative choice of parameters.

Computing p. Equipped with a candidate instance (K, k, w) for a number f of faulty blocks, we use the formula of a lemma in the full version to compute a bound p on the probability that a malicious prover can use an incorrect witness (with at least $f + 1$ faulty blocks) in the first part of the zero-knowledge proof. More precisely, since computing p exactly using the code given in the full version takes a few hours of computation, we first set p using the value predicted by a conjecture, which is in the full version (which we found to match with all exact calculations we tried with the formula). Then, once we get a final choice of all parameters, we verify that the final bound p obtained was indeed correct, by running the explicit formula (hence running the code only once).

Computing τ. We compute the number of repetitions τ of the zero-knowledge argument, and of the signature scheme. This is where the parameter selection differs in each case:

Zero-Knowledge Argument. For the zero-knowledge argument, τ is computed as the smallest value such that $\varepsilon^\tau \leq 2^{-\lambda}$, where $\varepsilon = 1/n + \mathsf{p} \cdot (1 - 1/n)$, n being the number of parties. Here, there is no optimal choice of f. Instead, f is a tradeoff: choosing $f = 0$ guarantees that the zero-knowledge argument achieves standard soundness (with no gap) but makes ε higher. A larger f reduces p, hence ε, but introduces a gap in soundness. In any case, as soon as $\mathsf{p} \ll 1/n$, we have $\varepsilon \approx 1/n$. In practice, using $f = 1$ already leads to $\mathsf{p} < 5 \cdot 10^{-5}$, which is much smaller than any reasonable value of $1/n$ (since increasing n to such values would blow up computation). Hence, the only reasonable choices are $f = 0$ (for standard soundness) and $f = 1$ (for optimal efficiency).

Signature Scheme. The signature scheme is obtained by compiling the zero-knowledge argument using Fiat-Shamir. Since we are compiling a 5-round zero-knowledge proof, the attack of Kales and Zaverucha [28] applies, and we must choose τ according to Eq. 1. This changes completely the optimal choice, since it is no longer true that any value of $\mathsf{p} \ll 1/n$ already leads to the smallest possible τ. In fact, by the convexity of Eq. 1, the smallest possible τ one can hope for is $\tau_{\mathsf{ZK}} + 1$, where τ_{ZK} is the optimal value of τ for the zero-knowledge argument (*i.e.* the smallest value such that $\varepsilon^{\tau_{\mathsf{ZK}}} \leq 2^{-\lambda}$). Our strategy is therefore the following: we compute τ with Eq. 1 for our candidate choice of f. Then, if $\tau > \tau_{\mathsf{ZK}} + 1$, we increase f by 1, and restart the entire procedure (choosing new parameters K, k, recomputing p, etc.). After a few iterations, the procedure converges and yields the smallest number f of faulty blocks such that the resulting value of τ is minimal.

Choosing n. Eventually, it remains to choose the number of parties n. This choice is orthogonal to the other choices: a larger n always decreases communication (since it lowers the soundness error), but it increases computation (which scales linearly with n). To choose n, we use the same strategy as Banquet [5]: we set n to a power of two, targeting a signing time comparable to that of previous works (on a standard laptop) for fairness of comparison. Then, we compute all parameters (K, k, w, f, τ), and reduce n to the smallest value which still achieves λ bits of security.

Runtime Estimations. Eventually, it remains to estimate the runtime of the signature and verification algorithms of our signature scheme. Unfortunately, we do not yet have a full-fledged implementation of our signature scheme. We plan to write an optimized implementation of our new signature scheme in a future work. In the meantime, we use existing benchmark to conservatively estimate the runtime of our scheme. We consider the following implementation choices:

- The tree-based PRG is implemented with fixed-key AES. This is the standard and most efficient way to implement such PRGs over machines with hardware support for AES [1].
- The commitment scheme is implemented with fixed-key AES when committing to short values (λ bits), and with SHAKE when committing to larger values.
- The hash function is instantiated with SHAKE.

For fixed-key AES operations, the estimated runtime using hardware instructions is 1.3 cycles/byte [31]. For SHAKE, the runtime strongly depends on a machine. However, according to the ECRYPT benchmarkings[2], on one core of a modern laptop, the cost of hashing long messages ranges from 5 to 8 cycles/byte (we used 8 cycles/byte in our estimations, to stay on the conservative side). Eventually, we also counted XOR operations (XORing two 64-bit machine words takes one cycle) and mod-3 operations. The latter are harder to estimate without a concrete implementation at hand. However, the contribution to the overall cost is relatively small: even estimating conservatively up to an order of magnitude of overhead compared to XOR operations has a minor impact on the overall runtime. We assumed an order of magnitude of overhead in our estimations, to remain on the conservative side. Eventually, when converting cycles to runtime, we assumed a 3.8 GHz processor, the same as in the previous work of [21], to facilitate comparison with their work (which is the most relevant to ours).

Of course, the above estimations ignore additional costs such as allocating or copying memory, and should therefore only be seen as a rough approximation of the timings that an optimized implementation could get. For comparison, in the Banquet signature scheme [5], another candidate post-quantum signature scheme based on the MPC-in-the-head paradigm, 25% of the runtime of their optimized implementation was spent on allocating and copying memory, and 75% on the actual (arithmetic and cryptographic) operations.

---

[2] https://bench.cr.yp.to/results-hash.html.

Results. We considered two settings: a conservative setting, where the underlying assumption reduces to the standard RSD assumption, and an aggressive setting, where the parameters rely on the conjectured hardness of the f-almost-RSD assumption. All our numbers are reported on Table 1. We obtained the following parameters:

Conservative Setting (standard RSD). We obtain an optimal choice of number f of faulty blocks equal to $f = 12$. Given this f, we set $K = 1842$, $k = 1017$, and $w = 307$. We targeted 128 bits of security against all known attacks, assuming conservatively that approximate birthday collisions can be found in linear time to estimate the cost of our most efficient attack. In this parameter range, the solution to the random RSD instance is the only 12-almost-regular solution except with probability 2^{-128}, hence 12-almost-RSD reduces to standard RSD. With these parameters, we considered three values of n. Each time, we first set n to a power of two, compute the optimal value of τ, and then reduce n to the smallest value that still works for this value of τ.

- Setting 1 – fast signature (rsd-f): $\tau = 18$, $n = 193$. In this setting, the signature size is 12.52 KB. The runtime estimated with our methodology described above is 2.7 ms.
- Setting 2 – medium signature 1 (rsd-m1): $\tau = 13$, $n = 1723$. In this setting, the signature size is 9.69 KB. The runtime estimated with our methodology described above is 17 ms.
- Setting 3 – medium signature 2 (rsd-m2): $\tau = 12$, $n = 3391$. In this setting, the signature size is 9.13 KB. The runtime estimated with our methodology described above is 31 ms.
- Setting 4 – short signature 2 (rsd-s): $\tau = 11$, $n = 7644$. In this setting, the signature size is 8.55 KB. The runtime estimated with our methodology described above is 65 ms.

Aggressive Setting (f-almost-RSD). In this setting, we set k at the f-almost-RSD uniqueness bound (the threshold above which the number of f-almost-regular solutions approaches 1). In this setting, there might be additional almost-regular solution beyond the regular solution x for a random RSD instance, hence f-almost-RSD does not reduce directly to the standard RSD assumption. We consider this assumption to be plausible but exotic, and investigate how relying on it improves the parameters. We view the conservative parameters as our main choice of parameters. The aggressive parameters yield noticeable improvements in signature size and runtime, which could motivate further cryptanalysis of this exotic variant. We provide four settings of parameters, comparable to our conservative settings, using the optimal value $f = 13$ and the same numbers n of parties as above. In this setting, we have $K = 1530$, $k = 757$, and $w = 255$.

Acknowledgement. This project has received funding from the European Union's Horizon 2020 research and innovation programme under the Marie Skłodowska-Curie grant agreement No 945332.

The first and second author acknowledge the support of the French Agence Nationale de la Recherche (ANR), under grant ANR-20-CE39-0001 (project SCENE). This work was also supported by the France 2030 ANR Project ANR-22-PECY-003 SecureCompute.

The third Author of this work has been supported by the European Union's H2020 Programme under grant agreement number ERC-669891.

References

1. Advanced Encryption Standard (AES). National Institute of Standards and Technology (NIST), FIPS PUB 197, U.S. Department of Commerce (2001)
2. Aragon, N., Blazy, O., Gaborit, P., Hauteville, A., Zémor, G.: Durandal: a rank metric based signature scheme. In: Ishai, Y., Rijmen, V. (eds.) EUROCRYPT 2019. LNCS, vol. 11478, pp. 728–758. Springer, Cham (2019). https://doi.org/10.1007/978-3-030-17659-4_25
3. Augot, D., Finiasz, M., Sendrier, N.: A fast provably secure cryptographic hash function. Cryptology ePrint Archive, Report 2003/230 (2003). https://eprint.iacr.org/2003/230
4. Baum, C., Damgård, I., Larsen, K., Nielsen, M.: How to prove knowledge of small secrets (2016). https://eprint.iacr.org/2016/538
5. Baum, C., de Saint Guilhem, C.D., Kales, D., Orsini, E., Scholl, P., Zaverucha, G.: Banquet: short and fast signatures from AES. In: Garay, J.A. (ed.) PKC 2021. LNCS, vol. 12710, pp. 266–297. Springer, Cham (2021). https://doi.org/10.1007/978-3-030-75245-3_11
6. Bellare, M., Goldreich, O.: On defining proofs of knowledge. In: Brickell, E.F. (ed.) CRYPTO 1992. LNCS, vol. 740, pp. 390–420. Springer, Heidelberg (1993). https://doi.org/10.1007/3-540-48071-4_28
7. Bernstein, D.J., Lange, T., Peters, C., Schwabe, P.: Really fast syndrome-based hashing. In: Nitaj, A., Pointcheval, D. (eds.) AFRICACRYPT 2011. LNCS, vol. 6737, pp. 134–152. Springer, Heidelberg (2011). https://doi.org/10.1007/978-3-642-21969-6_9
8. Beullens, W.: Sigma protocols for MQ, PKP and SIS, and fishy signature schemes. In: Canteaut, A., Ishai, Y. (eds.) EUROCRYPT 2020. LNCS, vol. 12107, pp. 183–211. Springer, Cham (2020). https://doi.org/10.1007/978-3-030-45727-3_7
9. Bidoux, L., Gaborit, P., Kulkarni, M., Mateu, V.: Code-based signatures from new proofs of knowledge for the syndrome decoding problem. arXiv preprint arXiv:2201.05403 (2022)
10. Boyle, E., Couteau, G., Gilboa, N., Ishai, Y.: Compressing vector OLE. In: Lie, D., Mannan, M., Backes, M., Wang, X. (eds.) ACM CCS 2018, pp. 896–912. ACM Press (2018)
11. Boyle, E., et al.: Correlated pseudorandomness from expand-accumulate codes. In: Dodis, Y., Shrimpton, T. (eds.) CRYPTO 2022. LNCS, vol. 13508, pp. 603–633. Springer, Heidelberg (2022). https://doi.org/10.1007/978-3-031-15979-4_21
12. Boyle, E., et al.: Efficient two-round OT extension and silent non-interactive secure computation. In: Cavallaro, L., Kinder, J., Wang, X., Katz, J. (eds.) ACM CCS 2019, pp. 291–308. ACM Press (2019)
13. Boyle, E., Couteau, G., Gilboa, N., Ishai, Y., Kohl, L., Scholl, P.: Efficient pseudorandom correlation generators: silent OT extension and more. In: Boldyreva, A., Micciancio, D. (eds.) CRYPTO 2019. LNCS, vol. 11694, pp. 489–518. Springer, Cham (2019). https://doi.org/10.1007/978-3-030-26954-8_16

14. Boyle, E., Couteau, G., Gilboa, N., Ishai, Y., Kohl, L., Scholl, P.: Efficient pseudo-random correlation generators from ring-LPN. In: Micciancio, D., Ristenpart, T. (eds.) CRYPTO 2020, Part II. LNCS, vol. 12171, pp. 387–416. Springer, Heidelberg (Aug (2020)

15. Camenisch, J., Kiayias, A., Yung, M.: On the portability of generalized schnorr proofs (2009). https://eprint.iacr.org/2009/050

16. Couteau, G., Rindal, P., Raghuraman, S.: Silver: silent VOLE and oblivious transfer from hardness of decoding structured LDPC codes. In: Malkin, T., Peikert, C. (eds.) CRYPTO 2021. LNCS, vol. 12827, pp. 502–534. Springer, Cham (2021). https://doi.org/10.1007/978-3-030-84252-9_17

17. Cramer, R., Damgard, I., Xing, C., Yuan, C.: Amortized complexity of zero-knowledge proofs revisited: achieving linear soundness slack (2016). https://eprint.iacr.org/2016/681

18. Debris-Alazard, T., Sendrier, N., Tillich, J.-P.: Wave: a new family of trapdoor one-way preimage sampleable functions based on codes. In: Galbraith, S.D., Moriai, S. (eds.) ASIACRYPT 2019. LNCS, vol. 11921, pp. 21–51. Springer, Cham (2019). https://doi.org/10.1007/978-3-030-34578-5_2

19. Escudero, D., Ghosh, S., Keller, M., Rachuri, R., Scholl, P.: Improved primitives for MPC over mixed arithmetic-binary circuits. In: Micciancio, D., Ristenpart, T. (eds.) CRYPTO 2020. LNCS, vol. 12171, pp. 823–852. Springer, Cham (2020). https://doi.org/10.1007/978-3-030-56880-1_29

20. Feneuil, T., Joux, A., Rivain, M.: Shared permutation for syndrome decoding: New zero-knowledge protocol and code-based signature. Cryptology ePrint Archive, Report 2021/1576 (2021). https://eprint.iacr.org/2021/1576

21. Feneuil, T., Joux, A., Rivain, M.: Syndrome decoding in the head: Shorter signatures from zero-knowledge proofs. In: Dodis, Y., Shrimpton, T. (eds.) CRYPTO 2022. LNCS, vol. 13508, pp. 541–572. Springer, Heidelberg (2022). https://doi.org/10.1007/978-3-031-15979-4_19

22. Feneuil, T., Joux, A., Rivain, M.: Syndrome decoding in the head: shorter signatures from zero-knowledge proofs. Cryptology ePrint Archive (2022)

23. Fiat, A., Shamir, A.: How to prove yourself: practical solutions to identification and signature problems. In: Odlyzko, A.M. (ed.) CRYPTO 1986. LNCS, vol. 263, pp. 186–194. Springer, Heidelberg (1987). https://doi.org/10.1007/3-540-47721-7_12

24. Finiasz, M., Gaborit, P., Sendrier, N.: Improved fast syndrome based cryptographic hash functions. In: Proceedings of ECRYPT Hash Workshop, vol. 2007, p. 155. Citeseer (2007)

25. Gueron, S., Persichetti, E., Santini, P.: Designing a practical code-based signature scheme from zero-knowledge proofs with trusted setup. Cryptology ePrint Archive, Report 2021/1020 (2021). https://eprint.iacr.org/2021/1020

26. Hazay, C., Orsini, E., Scholl, P., Soria-Vazquez, E.: TinyKeys: a new approach to efficient multi-party computation. In: Shacham, H., Boldyreva, A. (eds.) CRYPTO 2018. LNCS, vol. 10993, pp. 3–33. Springer, Cham (2018). https://doi.org/10.1007/978-3-319-96878-0_1

27. Ishai, Y., Kushilevitz, E., Ostrovsky, R., Sahai, A.: Zero-knowledge from secure multiparty computation. In: Johnson, D.S., Feige, U. (eds.) 39th ACM STOC, pp. 21–30. ACM Press (2007)

28. Kales, D., Zaverucha, G.: An attack on some signature schemes constructed from five-pass identification schemes. In: Krenn, S., Shulman, H., Vaudenay, S. (eds.) CANS 2020. LNCS, vol. 12579, pp. 3–22. Springer, Cham (2020). https://doi.org/10.1007/978-3-030-65411-5_1

29. Katz, J., Kolesnikov, V., Wang, X.: Improved non-interactive zero knowledge with applications to post-quantum signatures. In: Lie, D., Mannan, M., Backes, M., Wang, X. (eds.) ACM CCS 2018, pp. 525–537. ACM Press (2018)

30. Meziani, M., Dagdelen, Ö., Cayrel, P.-L., El Yousfi Alaoui, S.M.: S-FSB: an improved variant of the FSB hash family. In: Kim, T., Adeli, H., Robles, R.J., Balitanas, M. (eds.) ISA 2011. CCIS, vol. 200, pp. 132–145. Springer, Heidelberg (2011). https://doi.org/10.1007/978-3-642-23141-4_13

31. Münch, J.P., Schneider, T., Yalame, H.: VASA: vector AES instructions for security applications. Cryptology ePrint Archive, Report 2021/1493 (2021). https://eprint.iacr.org/2021/1493

32. Rindal, P., Schoppmann, P.: VOLE-PSI: fast OPRF and circuit-PSI from vector-OLE. In: Canteaut, A., Standaert, F.-X. (eds.) EUROCRYPT 2021. LNCS, vol. 12697, pp. 901–930. Springer, Cham (2021). https://doi.org/10.1007/978-3-030-77886-6_31

33. Rotaru, D., Wood, T.: MArBled circuits: mixing arithmetic and boolean circuits with active security. Cryptology ePrint Archive, Report 2019/207 (2019). https://eprint.iacr.org/2019/207

34. Shor, P.W.: Algorithms for quantum computation: discrete logarithms and factoring. In: 35th FOCS, pp. 124–134. IEEE Computer Society Press (1994)

35. Stern, J.: Designing identification schemes with keys of short size. In: Desmedt, Y.G. (ed.) CRYPTO 1994. LNCS, vol. 839, pp. 164–173. Springer, Heidelberg (1994). https://doi.org/10.1007/3-540-48658-5_18

36. Weng, C., Yang, K., Katz, J., Wang, X.: Wolverine: fast, scalable, and communication-efficient zero-knowledge proofs for boolean and arithmetic circuits, pp. 1074–1091. IEEE Computer Society Press (2021)

37. Yang, K., Weng, C., Lan, X., Zhang, J., Wang, X.: Ferret: fast extension for correlated OT with small communication. In: Ligatti, J., Ou, X., Katz, J., Vigna, G. (eds.) ACM CCS 20, pp. 1607–1626. ACM Press (2020)

The Return of the SDitH

Carlos Aguilar-Melchor[1], Nicolas Gama[1], James Howe[1]([✉]),
Andreas Hülsing[2], David Joseph[1], and Dongze Yue[1]

[1] SandboxAQ, Palo Alto, USA
{carlos.aguilar-melchor,nicolas.gama,james.howe,
david.joseph,dongze.yue}@sandboxaq.com
[2] Eindhoven University of Technology, Eindhoven, The Netherlands
andreas@huelsing.net

Abstract. This paper presents a code-based signature scheme based on
the well-known syndrome decoding (SD) problem. The scheme builds
upon a recent line of research which uses the Multi-Party-Computation-
in-the-Head (MPCitH) approach to construct efficient zero-knowledge
proofs, such as Syndrome Decoding in the Head (SDitH), and builds signature schemes from them using the Fiat-Shamir transform.

At the heart of our proposal is a new approach, Hypercube-MPCitH,
to amplify the soundness of any MPC protocol that uses additive secret
sharing. An MPCitH protocol with N parties can be repeated D times
using parallel composition to reach the same soundness as a protocol
run with N^D parties. However, the former comes with D times higher
communication costs, often mainly contributed by the usage of D 'auxiliary' states (which in general have a significantly bigger impact on
size than random states). Instead of that, we begin by generating N^D
shares, arranged into a D-dimensional hypercube of side N containing
only one 'auxiliary' state. We derive from this hypercube D sharings of
size N which are used to run D instances of an N party MPC protocol. Hypercube-MPCitH leads to a protocol with $1/N^D$ soundness error,
requiring N^D offline computation, but with *only* $N \cdot D$ online computation, and *only* 1 'auxiliary'. As the (potentially offline) share generation
phase is generally inexpensive, this leads to trade-offs that are superior
to just using parallel composition.

Our novel method of share generation and aggregation not only
improves certain MPCitH protocols in general but also shows in concrete
improvements of signature schemes. Specifically, we apply it to the work
of Feneuil, Joux, and Rivain (CRYPTO'22) on code-based signatures, and
obtain a new signature scheme that achieves a 8.1x improvement in
global runtime and a 30x improvement in online runtime for their shortest signatures size (8,481 Bytes). It is also possible to leverage the fact
that most computations are offline to define parameter sets leading to
smaller signatures: 6,784 Bytes for 26 ms offline and 5,689 Bytes for 320
ms offline. For NIST security level 1, online signature cost is around 3
million cycles (<1 ms on commodity processors), regardless of signature
size.

A. Hülsing is funded by an NWO VIDI grant (Project No. VI.Vidi.193.066).

© International Association for Cryptologic Research 2023
C. Hazay and M. Stam (Eds.): EUROCRYPT 2023, LNCS 14008, pp. 564–596, 2023.
https://doi.org/10.1007/978-3-031-30589-4_20

1   Introduction

Zero Knowledge (ZK) proofs of knowledge have become a fundamental cryptographic tool for modern privacy-preserving technologies and have many applications which range from authentication to online voting to machine learning.
The idea of ZK proofs is that one party (a prover) can convince another party
(a verifier) of the truth of a statement without revealing any other information
about the statement itself.

A method for constructing efficient ZK proofs is to use the so-called MPC-
in-the-Head (MPCitH) paradigm [IKO+07], in which semi-honest Multi-Party
Computation (MPC) protocols are used as a basis. These protocols do not reveal
any information on the secret used to prove a statement, even if some of the parties internal execution is revealed to an attacker. At a high-level, the MPCitH
protocol has a prover which (i) secretly splits its secret input into *shares*, (ii)
simulates "in their head" parties using said shares for the execution of a MPC
protocol, and (iii) commits to this *execution* and partially reveals the internal
execution of a subset of the parties to a verifier given some challenge. These internal executions can then be checked for consistency by the verifier. To ensure that
the prover has a very low probability to cheat, the verifier runs this protocol multiple times. The zero-knowledge aspect of the overall protocol naturally inherits
from a resilience to semi-honest adversaries of the underlying MPC protocol,
as the verifier will only get to see a subset of the internal executions and the
protocol will not reveal anything other than the correctness of the statement.

A recent proposal by Feneuil, Joux, and Rivain [FJR22] used this MPCitH
idea to improve signature schemes based on the syndrome decoding (SD) problem; we refer to this work as SDitH. Previous proposals to make a signature
scheme based on SD, such as those by Stern [Ste94], suffered from a high soundness error, which aligns to a malicious prover's probability of cheating. Protocols
with a higher soundness error require many more repetitions, compared to a protocol with a smaller soundness error, in order to achieve a target security level.
Utilizing MPCitH in [FJR22] has enabled a low soundness error of $1/N$, for a
party size N, whilst also being able to use a conservative code-based hardness
assumption. At the time of writing, this approach makes the signature scheme
the most performant code-based signature scheme of the common "signature size
+ public key size" metric. Twisting the more traditional permute-and-mask-
the-witness approach using MPCitH has also led to new interesting signature
schemes [BG22] under other metrics (rank-metric) or for other problems (the
Permuted Kernel Problem).

Another reason for this work is the NIST PQC standardization process. None
of the code-based signatures were accepted by NIST into round 2, however, at the
time of writing, we have many promising KEM candidates in the fourth round.
An MPCitH-based signature, Picnic [ZCD+20], was apart of the NIST PQC
process, but NIST ultimately decided to standardize SPHINCS+ due to some
security concerns with Picnic's use of LowMC, but also because "future cryptosystems that evolve out of the multi-party-computation-in-the-head paradigm
may eventually prove significantly superior to the third-round Picnic design".

These two reasons are the motivation for this research; improving and optimizing a promising MPCitH-based signature scheme, which utilizes a well-established and conservative code-based hardness assumption.

1.1 Contributions

- We propose Hypercube-MPCitH, a general geometrical hypercube approach for MPCitH that allows, from a state that was generated and committed for N parties, to obtain the same soundness as in a classical MPC-in-the-head by simulating the work of only $\log_2(N)$ parties instead of N.
- This approach runs multiple linked instances of MPCitH with only one masked auxiliary state, which significantly reduces the communication of the ZK protocol (and thus signature size) with respect to running independent instances of MPCitH with one auxiliary state for each of them.
- Applying these optimizations to SDitH, we observe a reduction of one third in signature size, for similar computational costs and security.
- As for SDitH, the signature resulting from our construction can be split in an offline and an online phase. But, unlike in SDitH, most of the computational cost is associated to the offline phase. Thus the online part of the signature is extremely fast in comparison, even for much smaller signatures.

2 Preliminaries

In this section we describe some standard cryptographic preliminaries which are similar to those in [FJR22]. For the entirety of this paper we will denote $\mathbb{F}$ as a finite field. The Hamming weight of a vector $\mathbf{x} \in \mathbb{F}^m$, denoted as $\mathrm{wt}(\mathbf{x})$, is the number of non-zero coordinates of $\mathbf{x}$. We define the concatenation of two vectors $\mathbf{x}_1 \in \mathbb{F}^{m_1}$ and $\mathbf{x}_2 \in \mathbb{F}^{m_2}$ as $(\mathbf{x}_1|\mathbf{x}_2) \in \mathbb{F}^{m_1+m_2}$. For any $m \in \mathbb{N}_{>0}$, the integer set $\{1, 2, \ldots, m\}$ is denoted as $[m]$. For a probability distribution D, we use the notation $d \leftarrow D$ to denote the value d is sampled from D. For a finite set S, the notation $s \leftarrow S$ denotes that the value s has been uniformly sampled at random from S. For an algorithm $\mathcal{A}$, $out \leftarrow \mathcal{A}(in)$ further means that out is obtained by a call to $\mathcal{A}$ on input in, using uniform random coins whenever $\mathcal{A}$ is probabilistic. We also abbreviate probabilistic polynomial time as PPT.

For ease of reference we provide Table 1 for a complete list of all the parameters and notations used in this work, with some helpful descriptions.

2.1 Basic Cryptographic Definitions and Lemmas

Definition 1 (Indistinguishability). *Two distributions X, Y are (t, ϵ)-indisting-uishable if for an algorithm running in time t, and $D \colon \{0,1\}^m \to \{0,1\}$, $Pr[D(X) = 1] - Pr[D(Y) = 1]| \leq \epsilon(\lambda)$. The distributions are: computationally distinguishable when $t = poly(\lambda)$ and ϵ is a negligible function in λ; and statistically indistinguishable when ϵ is a negligible function in λ for unbounded t.*

Table 1. Descriptions of the notation and parameters used in our scheme.

Indices:	
i	Index of a leaf party, in $[N^D]$
i^*	Index of challenge party, which remains hidden
$(i_1, \ldots, i_D)$	Representation of i on dimension D hypercube with side N
(k, j)	Index of a *main party* in $[D] \times [N]$, where k indexes the hypercube dimension
$\mathbb{F}_{\text{poly}}$	Field extension of $\mathbb{F}_{\text{SD}}$ from which S, Q, P, F coefficients are drawn
$\mathbb{F}_{\text{points}}$	Field from which $\boldsymbol{\alpha}, \boldsymbol{\beta}, \mathbf{v}, r, \epsilon$ are drawn.

Multi-Party Computation:	
Main party	Party using an aggregated share and for which we actually run the MPC protocol
Π	The MPC computation, described in Algorithm 2
a, b, c	Elements of the Beaver triplet such that $a \cdot b = c$
$\boldsymbol{\alpha}, \boldsymbol{\beta}, \mathbf{v}$	Communications output, drawn from $\mathbb{F}_{\text{points}}$
$[\![X]\!]_i$	i^{th} secret share of X
$\{[\![X]\!]\}$	A *full* sharing, such that all shares add up to give X
t	Number of random evaluation points
p	False positive probability.

Syndrome Decoding:	
S, Q, P, F	Polynomials in $\mathbb{F}_{\text{poly}}$ which encode the syndrome decoding proof
aux	Uncompressed secret shares of leaf party $i = N^D$, $[\![S]\!] \| [\![Q]\!] \| [\![P]\!] \| [\![a]\!] \| [\![b]\!] \| [\![c]\!]$
$(state_i, \rho_i)$	State and commitment randomness of a leaf party. For $i \neq N^D$, $state_i$ is a pseudorandom seed, and $state_{N^D} = (seed_{N^D} \| aux)$
q	Syndrome decoding instance
m	Code length
k	Vector dimension
w	Hamming weight bound
d	For the d-splitting variant.

Signature Parameters:	
λ	The security parameter
ϵ	The soundness parameter
D	The dimension of the hypercube
N^D	The number of secret shares
τ	The number of repetitions

Definition 2 (Pseudorandom generation (PRG)). *Let $G : \{0,1\}^* \to \{0,1\}^*$ and let $\ell(\cdot)$ be a polynomial such that for any input $s \in \{0,1\}^\lambda$ we have $G(s) \in \{0,1\}^{\ell(\lambda)}$. Then, G is a (t, ϵ)-secure pseudorandom generator if (i) Expansion: $\ell(\lambda) > \lambda$ and (ii) Pseudorandomness: the distributions $\{G(s) | s \leftarrow \{0,1\}^\lambda\}$ and $\{r | r \leftarrow \{0,1\}^{\ell(\lambda)}\}$ are (t, ϵ)-indistinguishable.*

The standard cryptographic notion of tree PRG (TreePRG), initially proposed by Goldreich, Goldwasser, and Micali [GGM84], is used extensively in our construction. The general idea is to extend a length-doubling PRG and consider it over a tree structure: we start with a master seed (mseed) which is used to label the root node of a tree and expanded using a PRG into N sub-seeds in a structured way. For each node, its label is used as the seed of the PRG function, which generates two seeds that label the two children of the node. By proceeding iteratively at each level, over $\lceil \log_2(N) \rceil$ levels, we construct a binary tree with at least N leaves, labeled with PRG seeds that we denote $(\text{seed}_i)_{i \in [N]}$. For any index i^*, we can get the list of the $N-1$ seeds $(\text{seed}_i)_{i \in [N], i \neq i^*}$ out of the sibling path of seed_{i*}, which contains just $\lceil \log_2(N) \rceil$ seeds. This becomes a key component to efficiently generate the witness shares in Sect. 3.2.

In our security proofs, we make use of the following lemma, which in essence says that a large subset A of a product space $X \times Y$ has many large areas.

Lemma 1 (Splitting Lemma [PS00]). *Let $A \subset X \times Y$, and $Pr[(x,y) \in A] \geq \kappa$. Then for any $\alpha \in [0,1)$, let*

$$B = \{(x,y) \in X \times Y \,|\, Pr_{y' \in Y}[(x,y') \in A] \geq (1-\alpha) \cdot \kappa\}, \tag{1}$$

Then the following are true: $Pr[B] \geq \alpha \cdot \kappa$ and $Pr[B|A] \geq \alpha$.

Lemma 2 (Forking Lemma for 5-pass protocols [DGV+16]). *Let S be an 5-pass signature scheme with security parameter k. Let $\mathcal{A}$ be a PPT algorithm given only the public data as input. Assume that $\mathcal{A}$, after querying the 2 random oracles $\mathcal{O}1, \mathcal{O}2$ polynomially often in k, outputs a valid signature $(\sigma_0, \sigma_1, \sigma_2, h_1, h_2)$ for message m with a non-negligible probability. Let us consider a replay of this machine $\mathcal{A}$ with the same random tape (as a Turing machine), the same response to the query corresponding to $\mathcal{O}1$ but a different output to $\mathcal{O}2$. Then running $\mathcal{A}$ and its reply results in two valid signatures $(\sigma_0, \sigma_1, \sigma_2, h_1, h_2)$ and $(\sigma_0, \sigma_1, \sigma'_2, h_1, h'_2)$ for the same message m and $h_2 \neq h'_2$ with a non-negligible probability.*

While proving equality of polynomials can be inefficient, we can say something about the likelihood that two polynomials are different *and yet* are equal at certain points. This enables us to reduce the checking of polynomial relations to instead checking simple integer arithmetic relations, up to some well defined probabilistic error.

Lemma 3 (Multi-point Schwarz-Zippel lemma). *Let $P \in \mathbb{F}[x]$ be a non zero polynomial in one variable of degree at most d and $S \subseteq \mathbb{F}$ a non empty set of size at least t. For $R \subseteq S$ drawn uniformly from size t subsets of S,*

$$Pr[P(r) = 0, \forall r \in R] \leq \frac{\binom{d}{t}}{\binom{|S|}{t}}. \tag{2}$$

Proof. Let $D \subseteq \mathbb{F}_q$ denote the roots of P. Clearly $|D| \leq d$, since a non-zero polynomial in one variable over a field has at most as many roots as its degree. The lemma follows since R is chosen uniformly from the $\binom{|S|}{t}$ size t subsets of S and there are at most $\binom{d}{t}$ size t subsets of D. $\square$

2.2   Zero-Knowledge Proofs

We define below the required properties for a zero-knowledge proof of knowledge. A proof of knowledge for some language $L \in NP$ is a two-party protocol between prover $\mathcal{P}$ and verifier $\mathcal{V}$, denoted $\langle \mathcal{P}, \mathcal{V} \rangle$ that should satisfy certain properties. The intention is for $\mathcal{P}$ to prove to $\mathcal{V}$ that their common input belongs to the language, i.e. $w \in L$.

Definition 3 ((Perfect) Completeness). *A proof of knowledge $\langle \mathcal{P}, \mathcal{V} \rangle$ is complete if, when both prover and verifier follow the protocol honestly, and the prover has knowledge of a legitimate witness w, then for every witness $w \in L$ the verifier accepts with probability 1:*

$$Pr[\langle \mathcal{P}, \mathcal{V} \rangle(w) = 1] = 1. \tag{3}$$

Definition 4 (Soundness). *A proof of knowledge is sound, with soundness error κ, if for a probabilistic polynomial time adversary, $\mathcal{A}$, with $w \notin L$, the probability of an honest verifier accepting is less than κ:*

$$Pr[\langle \mathcal{A}, \mathcal{V} \rangle(w) = 1] \leq \kappa. \tag{4}$$

Put differently, this means that a prover without a valid witness w cannot convince the verifier to accept with probability greater than κ.

Definition 5 (Honest Verifier Zero-Knowledge (HVZK)). *A proof of knowledge is HVZK if there exists a probabilistic polynomial time simulator $\mathcal{S}$ that, without knowing a witness, outputs transcripts such that its output distribution is computationally indistinguishable from the distribution of transcripts derived from honest executions of the protocol $\langle \mathcal{P}, \mathcal{V} \rangle$.*

This means that running the protocol does not reveal any information about the witness to an honest observer. We use zero-knowledge proof as a shorthand for HVZK proof of knowledge.

The main protocol in this paper is a zero-knowledge proof. This protocol is built with the MPC-in-the-Head construction, which allows to transform a multi-party computation protocol into a zero-knowledge proof. Before introducing the MPC-in-the-Head construction, we will first present some building tools needed for that construction: commitments, and additive secret sharing, a simple but efficient tool to build some MPC protocols.

2.3   Commitments

A commitment scheme is a cryptographic primitive that allows one to publish a value C, called commitment, associated to some other hidden value which can be revealed at a later stage through a procedure called opening using a decommitment value D. Once a party has committed to a hidden value, they should not be able to change the value, and no other party should be able to glean any knowledge of the value that has been committed, until the committing party opens the commitment.

Definition 6 (Commitment scheme). *A commitment scheme consists of two PPT algorithms, **com**, **open**, where*

- ***com**(M) - on input $M \in \{0,1\}^*$ the commitment algorithm outputs $(C, D) \leftarrow$ **com**(M, ρ) where ρ is the commitment randomness.*
- ***open**(C, D) outputs M or $\perp$.*

Definition 7 (Correctness). *If **com**$(M) \to (C, D)$, then **open**$(C, D) \to M$.*

A secure commitment scheme has the following two properties:

Definition 8 (Binding). *A commitment scheme is perfectly binding if, for all probabilistic polynomial time (in security parameter κ) algorithm $\mathcal{A}$, the probability of finding C, D, D' such that **open**$(C, D) = M$, **open**$(C, D') = M'$, and $M \neq M'$ is zero, and computationally binding if the probability is a negligible function in κ.*

Definition 9 (Hiding). *A commitment scheme is perfectly, statistically, or computationally (respectively) hiding if, for any two messages M, M', the distributions $\{C : (C, D) \leftarrow **com**(M)\}_{\kappa \in \mathbb{N}}$, and $\{C : (C, D) \leftarrow **com**(M')\}_{\kappa \in \mathbb{N}}$ are perfectly, statistically, or computationally indistinguishable.*

A commitment scheme cannot be both perfectly hiding and perfectly binding simultaneously. In order to see this, suppose first that the scheme is perfectly binding, and one publishes the commitment $\mathbf{com}^k(open, x)$, therefore no other pair $(open, x)$ outputs $\mathbf{com}^k(open, x)$. Then a computationally unbounded adversary can try inputs $(open', x')$ until they find the correct inputs $(open, x)$, which uniquely give the correct output.

2.4   Additive Secret Sharing and Computing on Shares

In order to perform multi-party computations, it is necessary to break up and then distribute the input data of the function to be evaluated amongst multiple parties. In this work, we use an approach to break and use this data called *additive secret sharing*. It is defined by the following two routines:

- *Share*(**x**): The *Share* routine randomly samples the $(N - 1)$-tuple $([\![\mathbf{x}]\!]_1, [\![\mathbf{x}]\!]_2,..., [\![\mathbf{x}]\!]_{N-1}) \leftarrow (\mathbb{F}^m)^{N-1}$, and then computes $[\![\mathbf{x}]\!]_N \leftarrow \mathbf{x} - \sum_{i=1}^{N-1} [\![\mathbf{x}]\!]_i$. The final output is a tuple of N shares $[\![\mathbf{x}]\!] \leftarrow ([\![\mathbf{x}]\!]_1, [\![\mathbf{x}]\!]_2, \ldots, [\![\mathbf{x}]\!]_N)$.
- *Reconstruct*$([\![\mathbf{x}]\!])$: The *Reconstruct* routine combines all N shares together by summation to obtain the original value $\mathbf{x} \leftarrow \sum_{i=1}^{N} [\![x]\!]_i$.

In practice, one can compress the output of *Share*(**x**) by expanding shares $([\![\mathbf{x}]\!]_1, [\![\mathbf{x}]\!]_2, \ldots, [\![\mathbf{x}]\!]_{N-1})$ from random seeds, however most of the terms in the final share $[\![\mathbf{x}]\!]_N$ must be communicated in full, without compression. We call this final share *aux*, which is defined explicitly in Algorithm 1.

A secret value x can thus be distributed to N parties in a MPC scenario. Each party i in the MPC protocol receives share $[\![\mathbf{x}]\!]_i$. It is important to observe that the parties cannot learn anything of **x** unless they have all N shares. The parties are able to perform the following computations and obtain valid shares of a new secret-shared value:

- *Addition of shares:* Let $[\![\mathbf{x}_A]\!]$, $[\![\mathbf{x}_B]\!]$ be two sets of shares distributed among parties. $[\![\mathbf{x}_A + \mathbf{x}_B]\!]_i := [\![\mathbf{x}_A]\!]_i + [\![\mathbf{x}_B]\!]_i$.
- *Addition with a constant:* $[\![\mathbf{x} + c]\!] := [\![\mathbf{x}]\!]_1 + c, [\![\mathbf{x}]\!]_2, \ldots, [\![\mathbf{x}]\!]_N$.
- *Multiplication with a constant:* $[\![c \cdot \mathbf{x}]\!]_i := c \cdot [\![\mathbf{x}]\!]_i$.
- *Multiplication of shares:* Multiplication is possible using Beaver triples [Bea92] with additional communication between parties (where the parties are given as additional input a secret-shared triplet $[\![a]\!]$, $[\![b]\!]$, $[\![c]\!]$ where a, b are unknown to all players and $c = ab$). This additional triplet is sacrificed in order to validate another triplet, which is defined in the following.

One can evaluate an arbitrary function f over additive shares by decomposing f into an arithmetic circuit using the four types of computation listed above.

2.5 MPC-in-the-Head Paradigm

The MPC-in-the-Head (MPCitH) paradigm originated from the work of Ishai, Kushilevitz, and Ostrovsky [IKO+07] and provides a path towards building ZK proofs for arbitrary circuits from secure multi-party computation (MPC) protocols. In this work, we use a semi-honest MPC protocol with additive shares that evaluates a Boolean decision function. The protocol has the following properties:

- *N-party decision function evaluation:* The N parties $\mathcal{P}_1, \ldots, \mathcal{P}_N$ each possess an additive share $[\![\mathbf{x}]\!]_i$ of the input $\mathbf{x}$. The parties jointly evaluate a decision function $f : \mathbb{Z}^m \to \{0, 1\}$ on $\mathbf{x}$.
- *Semi-honest $(N-1)$-Security:* Assuming the parties adhere to the protocol, the additive shares guarantee that any $N - 1$ parties cannot recover any information about the secret $\mathbf{x}$.

One can efficiently build a ZK proof of knowledge of a secret value $\mathbf{x}$ for which $f(\mathbf{x}) = 1$, for a predicate f that has either a unique solution, or is hard to fulfill. The prover proceeds as follows:

- Generate shares of the secret $[\![\mathbf{x}]\!] \leftarrow Share(\mathbf{x})$ and distribute the shares among N imaginary parties.
- Simulate the decision function evaluation procedure among the N imaginary parties "in the head".
- Commit to the view (initial share, secret random tape, and inbound/outbound communications) of each party and send commitment to the verifier.
- Send the shares of the final computed result $[\![f(\mathbf{x})]\!]$ to the verifier, which should reconstruct to 1.

The verifier performs the following steps to verify the proof:

- Randomly choose $N - 1$ parties, then ask the prover to reveal the views of those parties.

- Upon receiving the views, verify whether the views are consistent with an honest execution of the MPC protocol and agree with the commitments.
- The verifier accepts if the views are consistent and the final shares $[\![f(\mathbf{x})]\!]$ indeed reconstruct to 1.

Some challenge randomness of the decision function f can be provided by the verifier. Therefore, the views of each party (input shares, random tape, initial message from preprocessing phase) prior to the joint function evaluation must be committed before the prover receives the randomness to prevent cheating.

The verifier does not learn any information about the secret value because they only see $N - 1$ shares. The random selection of $N - 1$ parties results in a soundness error of $\frac{1}{N}$ for the MPCitH protocol.

2.6 Syndrome Decoding

The zero-knowledge proof protocol we propose in this paper uses MPC-in-the-Head to prove a solution is known to a syndrome decoding problem. Syndrome decoding (SD) is a problem that is central to many code-based cryptosystems. A syndrome is the result of multiplying a vector with a parity-check matrix, which implies that being a codeword is equivalent to having syndrome $\mathbf{0}$. The Coset Weights flavor of the SD problem [BMT78] can be expressed as follows:

- *Challenge:* Parity-check matrix $\mathbf{H} \leftarrow \mathbb{F}_q^{(m-k) \times m}$, syndrome $\mathbf{y} \in \mathbb{F}_q^{m-k}$.
- *Required Output:* Vector $\mathbf{x} \in \mathbb{F}_q^m$ with $wt(\mathbf{x}) \leq w$ and $\mathbf{H}\mathbf{x} = \mathbf{y}$.

During challenge generation, $\mathbf{H}$ and $\mathbf{x}$ (with $wt(\mathbf{x}) = w$) are drawn uniformly at random, and then $\mathbf{y} = \mathbf{H}\mathbf{x}$ is calculated. For cryptographically relevant parameters, with overwhelming probability there exists only one solution $\mathbf{x}'$ such that $wt(\mathbf{x}') \leq w$, and that is $\mathbf{x}' = \mathbf{x}$ which has weight w.

The two most significant approaches to solving the syndrome decoding problem are information-set decoding and birthday algorithms. In order for a SD-based cryptosystem to achieve security level λ it is necessary to select parameters such that each approach takes more than 2^λ operations to solve the underlying syndrome decoding instance.

2.7 Syndrome Decoding in the Head

In this section we describe the methodology of generating zero-knowledge proofs (ZKP) from MPCitH applied to the syndrome decoding problem, as laid out in [FJR22]. For efficiency, we assume that $\mathbf{H}$ is in standard form $\mathbf{H} = (\mathbf{H}' | I_{m-k})$, where $\mathbf{H}' \in \mathbb{F}_q^{(m-k) \times k}$. This enables us to express

$$\mathbf{y} = \mathbf{H}\mathbf{x} = \mathbf{H}'\mathbf{x_A} + \mathbf{x_B}, \tag{5}$$

so we only need to send $\mathbf{x_A}$ to reveal the solution. The MPC protocol defined divides up $\mathbf{x_A}$ into shares $[\![\mathbf{x_A}]\!]$, from which parties can reconstruct shares of $[\![\mathbf{x}]\!]$. The protocol then verifies that $\mathbf{y} = \mathbf{H}\mathbf{x}$ and that $\mathbf{x}$ has weight less than or equal to w by proving polynomial relations.

2.7.1 Polynomial Construction

Let $\mathbb{F}_{\text{SD}}$ be the finite field over which the syndrome decoding problem is defined. Let $\mathbb{F}_{\text{poly}} \supseteq \mathbb{F}_{\text{SD}}$ with $|\mathbb{F}_{\text{poly}}| > m$. Let $\phi \colon \mathbb{F}_{\text{SD}} \to \mathbb{F}_{\text{poly}}$ define the inclusion of $\mathbb{F}_{\text{SD}}$ in $\mathbb{F}_{\text{poly}}$. We take a bijection, f, between $\{1, \ldots, |\mathbb{F}_{\text{poly}}|\}$ and $\mathbb{F}_{\text{poly}}$ and for ease of notation we denote f_i instead of $f(i)$.

The prover builds three polynomials, $\mathbf{S}$, $\mathbf{Q}$, and $\mathbf{P}$ in order to prove the weight constraint. Polynomial $\mathbf{S} \in \mathbb{F}_{\text{poly}}[X]$ is the interpolation over the point (f_i, x_i), with $\mathbf{S}(f_i) = \phi(x_i)$, $\deg(\mathbf{S}) \leq m - 1$, and $\mathbf{Q}[X] \in \mathbb{F}_{\text{poly}}[X]$ is $\mathbf{Q} = \prod_E (X - f_i)$, where E is a subset of $[m]$ of order $|E| = w$, such that the non-zero coordinates of $\mathbf{x}$ are contained in E. Accordingly, $\mathbf{Q}$ has degree w. Polynomial $\mathbf{P}$ is defined as $\mathbf{P} = \mathbf{S} \cdot \mathbf{Q}/\mathbf{F}$, where $\mathbf{F} = \prod_{[m]} (X - f_i)$. Ultimately, the polynomial relation

$$\mathbf{S} \cdot \mathbf{Q} = \mathbf{P} \cdot \mathbf{F}, \tag{6}$$

must be satisfied in order to prove that $wt(\mathbf{x}) \leq w$. The left-hand side is designed so that $\mathbf{SQ}(f_i) = 0$ for all $f_i \in [m]$. This is because $\mathbf{S}$ is zero everywhere that $\mathbf{x}$ is zero (by construction, as $\mathbf{S}$ is interpolated over $\mathbf{x}$), and $\mathbf{Q}$ is zero everywhere that $\mathbf{x}$ *is not* zero. Polynomial $\mathbf{S}$ has degree $m - 1$ and $\mathbf{Q}$ has degree w.

On the right-hand side, by construction the public polynomial $\mathbf{F}$ is zero over $f_1, f_2, \ldots, f_m$, and polynomial $\mathbf{P}$ is required because $\mathbf{F}$ has degree m, whereas $m < \deg(\mathbf{SQ}) \leq m + w - 1$. If the prover can convince the verifier that they know $\mathbf{P}, \mathbf{Q}$ such that $\mathbf{S} \cdot \mathbf{Q} = \mathbf{P} \cdot \mathbf{F} = 0$ at all points $f_i \in [m]$, then at each point f_i, either $\mathbf{S}(f_i) = \phi(\mathbf{x}_i) = 0$, or $\mathbf{Q}(f_i) = 0$. But since $\mathbf{Q}$ has degree w, it can be zero at at most w points, therefore $\mathbf{S}$ is non-zero in at most w points f_i, and so $\mathbf{x}$ has weight of at most w.

In order to verify the polynomial relation of Eq. 6, the polynomial $\mathbf{S} \cdot \mathbf{Q} - \mathbf{P} \cdot \mathbf{F}$ is evaluated at a series of points to check that it evaluates to zero everywhere. This is because, by the Schwartz-Zippel lemma (Lemma 3), it is unlikely that the relation of Eq. 6 holds true at a random point, if the polynomial relation is not true in general. Picking t points at random to test the relation amplifies this result. Therefore the probability that the relation is satisfied at points $\{r_k\}_{k \in [t]}$ without Eq. 6 being true becomes some sufficiently small probability we call p. This event is referred to as a false positive, which we denote $\mathcal{F}$. False positives affect the soundness of a ZKP, as they represent a way to be accepted by a verifier, but without knowledge of a valid witness. Consequently, the soundness error of an MPCitH protocol based on syndrome decoding would be

$$1 - \left(1 - \frac{1}{N}\right)(1 - p) = \frac{1}{N} + p - \frac{1}{N} \cdot p. \tag{7}$$

2.7.2 Polynomial Relation Proof via MPC-in-the-Head

The shares that are distributed to parties are shares of $\mathbf{x_A} \in \mathbb{F}_{\text{SD}}^k$, the coefficients of $\mathbf{Q} \in \mathbb{F}_{\text{poly}}^w$, and coefficients of $\mathbf{P} \in \mathbb{F}_{\text{poly}}^{w+1}$, as well as the shares of t Beaver triplets $(a_k, b_k, c_k = a_k b_k) \in \mathbb{F}_{\text{points}}^3$. A party's share is denoted with double square brackets and an index, e.g., $[\![\mathbf{x}]\!]_i$. Shares of polynomials are shares of the polynomial's coefficients. For $\mathbf{Q}$, only the last $w - 1$ coefficients are shared due to $\mathbf{Q}$ being monic. Instead of evaluating the full relation of Eq. 6, we validate the relation holds true at t randomly selected points $\mathbf{r} \in \mathbb{F}_{\text{points}}^t$, as explained in the previous section to reduce the probability of $\mathcal{F}$. In order to further reduce p, the points r_i are sampled from a larger space $\mathbb{F}_{\text{points}} \supset \mathbb{F}_{\text{poly}}$ as this makes it more unlikely that an untrue polynomial relation looks correct at a given point r_i. In order to verify the multiplication triple $\mathbf{S}(r_k) \cdot \mathbf{Q}(r_k) = \mathbf{P} \cdot \mathbf{F}(r_k)$, we sacrifice a Beaver triple $a_k \cdot b_k = c_k$. The protocol proceeds as follows:

1. Sample $\mathbf{H} \in \mathbb{F}_q^{(m-k) \times m}$, $\mathbf{x} \in \mathbb{F}_q^m$ uniformly and compute $\mathbf{Hx} = \mathbf{y} \in \mathbb{F}_q^{(m-k)}$.
2. Sample $\mathbf{r}, \boldsymbol{\epsilon} \in \mathbb{F}_{\text{points}}^t \times \mathbb{F}_{\text{points}}^t$ uniformly at random.
3. Construct $[\![\mathbf{x}]\!]$ and express it over $\mathbb{F}_{\text{poly}}$.
4. Interpolate the shares $[\![\mathbf{S}(r_k)]\!]$ and construct $[\![\mathbf{Q}(r_k)]\!]$, and $[\![\mathbf{F} \cdot \mathbf{P}(r_k)]\!]$.
5. Run MPC protocol to verify the triple $([\![\mathbf{S}(r_k)]\!], [\![\mathbf{Q}(r_k)]\!], [\![\mathbf{P} \cdot \mathbf{F}(r_k)]\!])$ with sacrificed triple $([\![a_k]\!], [\![b_k]\!], [\![c_k]\!])$.
   (a) Set $[\![\alpha_k]\!] = \epsilon_k \cdot [\![\mathbf{Q}(r_k)]\!] + [\![a_k]\!]$ and set $[\![\beta_k]\!] = [\![\mathbf{S}(r_k)]\!] + [\![b_k]\!]$.
   (b) Parties open $[\![\alpha_k]\!]$ and $[\![\beta_k]\!]$ on bulletin board to construct α_k and β_k.
   (c) Parties set $[\![v_k]\!] = \epsilon_k \cdot [\![\mathbf{F} \cdot \mathbf{P}(r_k)]\!] - [\![c_k]\!] + \alpha_k \cdot [\![b_k]\!] + \beta_k \cdot [\![a_k]\!] - \alpha_k \cdot \beta_k$.
   (d) Parties open $[\![v_k]\!]$ to obtain v_k and check that it encodes zero.

2.7.3   False-positive Probability

To evaluate the false positive probability, necessary (along with N) to compute the soundness in Eq. 7, consider that at each point r_k, either $\mathbf{S}(r_k) \cdot \mathbf{Q}(r_k) - \mathbf{P} \cdot \mathbf{F}(r_k) = 0$ or is non-zero, so for i of the t challenge points to satisfy the relation (equivalently, to be roots of $\mathbf{S} \cdot \mathbf{Q} - \mathbf{P} \cdot \mathbf{F}$), there are

$$\frac{\max_{l \leq m+w-1} \binom{l}{i} \binom{|\mathbb{F}_{\text{points}}|-l}{t-i}}{\binom{|\mathbb{F}_{\text{points}}|}{t}}, \tag{8}$$

ways this can happen by Lemma 3, since $\mathbf{S} \cdot \mathbf{Q} - \mathbf{P} \cdot \mathbf{F}$ has degree less than $m+w$, thus it has at most $m + w - 1$ roots, from which i of t challenge points could be selected. For the i points being roots of the polynomial, having $c_k = a_k b_k$ makes the MPC protocol pass with probability 1; for the $t - i$ cases where the challenge points are not roots, $\mathbf{S}(r_k) \cdot \mathbf{Q}(r_k) \neq \mathbf{P}(r_k) \cdot \mathbf{F}(r_k)$. In these cases, the MPC protocol will pass if and only if $c_k = a_k \cdot b_k + \epsilon_k(\mathbf{SQ} - \mathbf{PF})(r_k)$, which depends linearly on ϵ_k and thus can only be guessed correctly with probability $1/\mathbb{F}_{\text{points}}$. Since it needs to occur for all non-root positions, this gives a probability $(1/|\mathbb{F}_{\text{points}}|)^{t-i}$. Combining the above reasoning, the probability $\Pr[\mathcal{F}] = p$ of $\mathcal{F}$, is

$$p \leq \sum_{i=0}^{t} \frac{\max_{l \leq m+w-1} \binom{l}{i} \binom{|\mathbb{F}_{\text{points}}|-l}{t-i}}{\binom{|\mathbb{F}_{\text{points}}|}{t}} \cdot \left(\frac{1}{|\mathbb{F}_{\text{points}}|} \right)^{t-i}. \tag{9}$$

A less tight but more intuitive bound can be given by considering that each of the t challenge points is either a root of $\mathbf{S} \cdot \mathbf{Q} - \mathbf{P} \cdot \mathbf{F}$ which occurs with probability $\leq \frac{m+w-1}{|\mathbb{F}_{\text{points}}|}$, else it is not a root, and only satisfies the relation if ϵ_k was guessed correctly, with probability $\leq \frac{1}{|\mathbb{F}_{\text{points}}|}$. Summing these two probabilities (for a given challenge point), and considering that this must happen for all t challenge points, we arrive at the loose bound $p \leq (\frac{m+w}{|\mathbb{F}_{\text{points}}|})^t$. It is necessary that p be comfortably smaller than $1/N$ which is the target soundness error of the MPCitH protocol in order to preserve zero-knowledge for a ZKP.

3   Batch MPCitH on a Hypercube for ZK Proofs

Here we describe how to reduce computational costs while preserving the soundness in MPCitH. We do this by arranging shares onto a hypercube, then performing MPCitH executions on various combinations of the shares. In Sect. 3.1, we introduce a (standalone) parameter, n, for the party size, as this will make comparisons with SDitH (using $n = N$) and our scheme (using $n = N^D$).

3.1   High-Level Description

In the MPCitH setup described in Sect. 2.5, the initial commitment boils down to PRNG expansion from seeds for the first $n - 1$ input shares, subtraction to the plaintext for the last share, and commitments. Using this initial commitment the prover would then, in a traditional MPCitH protocol, simulate the MPC algorithm on each of these n parties to be able to produce the relevant communications. Once the $n - 1$ commitments would be opened, the verifier would also need to replay those $n - 1$ computations for the consistency check. Instead of following that approach, we propose here a geometric method, when $n = 2^D$ is a power of two, using *the same initial commitment*, where the prover and the verifier only need to evaluate $\log_2(n) + 1$ of these evaluations, for the exact same soundness error than the original protocol.

An MPCitH computation based on an additive secret sharing relies on shares of the MPC parties adding up to the witness for which we want a ZK proof. Additive secret sharing correctness does not depend on how these shares are sampled: they can be uniform samples, additions of uniform samples, etc. As long as the shares add up to the witness, the result of the computation is correct. Our hypercube approach proposes a way to re-express one instance of the protocol over $n = N^D$ parties into D instances of N parties, and how to obtain shares for the N parties on each of the D instances. For each of these instances the shares of the N parties add up to the original witness, thus each of these instances will be correct no matter the additive scheme or the functionality computed.

We first explain the construction on a two dimensional toy example, shown in Fig. 1. Let's suppose we consider a traditional 4-party protocol with shares s_1, s_2, s_3, aux that sum up to the witness. If we distribute them in a 2-dimensional hypercube of side 2 (i.e., a two-by-two square) we obtain:

Per construction we have $s_1 + s_2 + s_3 + \text{aux} = \text{Witness}$. The hypercube approach leads to an MPC execution for two parties holding $m_1 = (s_1 + s_2)$ and $m_2 = (s_3 + \text{aux})$ on one side, and an MPC execution for two parties holding $n_1 = (s_1 + s_3)$ and $n_2 = (s_2 + \text{aux})$ on the other side. By associativity and commutativity, in both cases the sum of the shares is equal to the witness, and

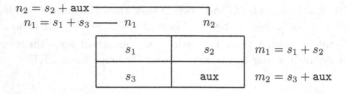

Fig. 1. A simple 2-dimensional example of our hypercube construction.

both MPCitH executions will lead to a correct result. Just as the traditional 4-party protocol would have. The non-trivial part is to prove that by doing this, the soundness error in the presence of a dishonest prover is the same in the hypercube splitting as it is in the original protocol; it will be the target of the next sections.

From a performance standpoint, using a 2-dimensional hypercube of side 2 provides no advantage. In the traditional approach we would: generate 4 states, commit to 4 states, and compute with 4 MPC parties. In our approach we also generate a state, commit, and do an MPC computation $2+2 = 4$ times. However, when the dimension D increases we see an advantage appear. For instance, if an MPCitH protocol does a 256 party protocol, as in SDitH, it requires 256 state generations and commitments. By using an 8-dimensional hypercube of side 2 we will then do only do $2 + 2 + 2 + 2 + 2 + 2 + 2 + 2 = 16$ MPC computations instead of 256, originally. We reveal exactly the same information: we open 255 initial states and give the communications that would have resulted from the unopened state, so we keep the same proof size, but we reduce the MPC cost by a factor of more than 10. For any functionality. As the computational costs become smaller, it is of course also possible to increase the number of parties to compensate, and get smaller proofs.

Finally, an additional benefit of Hypercube-MPCitH is that we can avoid, for most of the D executions, running the MPC protocol for all the parties. Indeed, each of the D executions corresponds to a given aggregation of the same hypercube shares. Thus each secret shared variable that occurs throughout a run of the MPC algorithm corresponds to the same plaintext when the shares are summed up. Therefore the prover only needs to compute these plaintext values once, for instance by evaluating the first N parties, and then, for the remaining $D - 1$ runs, the last share is simply deduced by the difference to the plaintext value. Consequently, only $N - 1$ parties need to be evaluated instead of N per run, $1 + (N - 1)D$ in total. On the previous example of a 256 parties protocol, with this improvement, the prover needs only to do $2+1+1+1+1+1+1+1 = 9$ MPC computations instead of 16 in the last paragraph, and of 256 in the original protocol.

For functionalities for which the MPC computation part is significantly more expensive than the initial state generation and commitment phase (which is in general the case) this allows to balance out the two phases, by increasing n, which only has a logarithmic impact in the amount of dimensions, until both costs are comparable, which can lead for such functionalities to completely unreachable parameters with the traditional approach. The more complex the functionality is, the larger the gap closed, and the hypercube improvement, will be.

For the sake of generality, we will in the next sections consider a general hypercube of side N and dimension D. The $n = N^D$ original parties (also called *leaf-parties*) are indexed on the D dimensions by coordinates $(i_1, \ldots, i_D) \in [1, N]^D$. For each dimension $k \in [1, D]$, we have one MPC run between N *main parties*, and by convention, for each index $j \in [1, N]$, the main party of index (k, j) regroups the contributions of the leaf-party shares whose k-th coordinate is j Hence, for each axis $k \in [1, D]$, the main parties $(k, 1), \ldots, (k, N)$ form a partition of the leaf parties. With this partitioning, whenever we disclose the values of $N^D - 1$ leaf shares and keep a single one hidden, it automatically discloses the value of exactly $N - 1$ out of N main-parties shares on each of the D axes. As in Table 1, we define a *main party* as a party using an aggregated share and for which we actually run the MPC protocol.

3.2 Leaf Witness Share Generation

For SDitH [FJR22] the master seed is expanded into N party seeds. The witness shares for parties $1, \ldots, N - 1$ are then generated by expanding these seeds into random $[\![\mathbf{x}]\!]$, $[\![\mathbf{Q}]\!]$, and $[\![\mathbf{P}]\!]$ in their respective domains. And the shares for party N are defined to be the difference between the sum of the random shares for parties $1, \ldots, N - 1$, and the witness $\mathbf{x}, \mathbf{Q}, \mathbf{P}$.

In our protocol, it is necessary to generate N^D leaf seeds, from which the polynomial shares and other randomness (e.g., Beaver triple shares) are generated. In practice, this part is done identically to in [FJR22], whereby TreePRG is used to recursively expand the master seed until one has N^D leaf seeds.

As depicted in Fig. 2, the master seed is expanded to generate the leaf party seeds, which are then expanded into the leaf witness shares in the canonical way. The leaf parties are indexed by $i' \in [1, \ldots, N^D]$.

3.3 Leaf Witness Shares on a Hypercube

A geometric mapping is necessary in order to manipulate the results in the hypercube setting described in Sect. 3.1. Section 3.2 explained how to output N^D leaf parties and their witness shares. To arrange them on a hypercube, we rewrite the index $i' \in [1, \ldots, N^D]$ equivalently as $i' = (i_1, \ldots i_D)$ where each $i_k \in [1, \ldots, N]$. To reveal the entire hypercube, except for a single leaf party, it is enough to reveal the sibling path of the hidden leaf party. The verifier (who will eventually receive $N^D - 1$ leaf nodes) can reconstruct the hypercube geometry themselves, using the same indexing convention as the signer.

Algorithm 1. ZK proof from Syndrome Decoding on a hypercube in the head

Input: Both parties have $H = (H'|I_{m-k}) \in \mathbb{F}_{SD}^{(m-k) \times m}$ and the syndrome $y \in \mathbb{F}_{SD}^{(m-k)}$.
The prover knows $x \in \mathbb{F}_{SD}^m$ with $y = Hx$ and $\text{wt}(x) \leq w$.

Round 1 (Computation of witness):
1. Choose $E \subset [m]$ such that $|E| = w$ and the non-zero coordinates of x are in E.
2. Compute $Q(X) = \prod_{i \in E}(X - f_i) \in \mathbb{F}_{\text{poly}}(X)$.
3. Compute $S(X) \in \mathbb{F}_{\text{poly}}(X)$ by interpolation over the coordinates of x s.t. $S(f_i) = x_i$.
4. Compute $P(X) = S(X) \cdot Q(X)/F(X)$ with $F(X) \in \mathbb{F}_{\text{poly}}(X)$ s.t. $F(X) = \prod_{i=1}^{m}(X - f_i)$.
5. Sample a root seed: $seed \leftarrow \{0,1\}^\lambda$.
6. Expand root seed $seed_i$ recursively using TreePRG to obtain N^D leafs and $(seed_{i'}, \rho_{i'})$
7. Initialize each main party share to zero: The index of a party is $(k,j) \in [1,\ldots,D] \times [1,\ldots,N]$ and contains all leaf parties whose k-th coordinate is j
for each party $(k,j) \in [1,\ldots,D] \times [1,\ldots,N]$ **do**
    Set $[\![x_A]\!]_{(k,j)}, [\![Q]\!]_{(k,j)}, [\![P]\!]_{(k,j)}, [\![a]\!]_{(k,j)}, [\![b]\!]_{(k,j)}$, and $[\![c]\!]_{(k,j)}$ to zero.
8. Generate polynomial shares (at leaf level):
for each leaf $i' \in [1,\ldots,N^D]$ **do**
    if $i' \neq N^D$ **then**
        $\{[\![a]\!]_{i'}, [\![b]\!]_{i'}, [\![c]\!]_{i'}\} \leftarrow \text{PRG}(seed_{i'}), ([\![x_A]\!]_{i'}, [\![Q]\!]_{i'}, [\![P]\!]_{i'}) \leftarrow \text{PRG}(seed_{i'})$
        $\text{state}_{i'} = seed_{i'}$
    else
        $[\![a]\!]_{N^D}, [\![b]\!]_{N^D} \leftarrow \text{PRG}(seed_{N^D}), [\![c]\!]_{N^D} = \langle a, b \rangle - \sum_{i' \neq N^D}[\![c]\!]_{i'}$
        $[\![x_A]\!]_{N^D} = x_A - \sum_{i' \neq N^D}[\![x_A]\!]_{i'}$
        $[\![Q]\!]_{N^D} = Q - \sum_{i' \neq N^D}[\![Q]\!]_{i'}, [\![P]\!]_{N^D} = P - \sum_{i' \neq N^D}[\![P]\!]_{i'}$,
        $aux = ([\![x_A]\!]_{N^D}, [\![Q]\!]_{N^D}, [\![P]\!]_{N^D}, [\![c]\!]_{N^D})$, and $\text{state}_{N^D} = seed_{N^D}||aux$
   ▷ Add the leaf party's shares to the corresponding main party share and represent
the leaf party by its index on the hypercube $i' = (i_1 \ldots i_D)$, where $i_k \in [1,\ldots,N]$.
    for each main party index p in $\{(1,i_1),(2,i_2),\ldots,(D,i_D)\}$ **do**
        $[\![x_A]\!]_p += [\![x_A]\!]_{i'}, [\![Q]\!]_p += [\![Q]\!]_{i'}$, and $[\![P]\!]_p += [\![P]\!]_{i'}$
        $[\![a]\!]_p += [\![a]\!]_{i'}, [\![b]\!]_p += [\![b]\!]_{i'}$, and $[\![c]\!]_p += [\![c]\!]_{i'}$
9. Leaf parties commit to their state $\text{com}_{i'} = Com(\text{state}_{i'}, \rho_{i'})$.
10. Compute $h = \text{Hash}(\text{com}_1, \ldots, \text{com}_{N^D})$ and send to the verifier

Round 2 (Get evaluation points):
The verifier picks t challenge points, which we denote as vectors $\mathbf{r} \in \mathbb{F}_{\text{points}}^t$ and $\epsilon \in \mathbb{F}_{\text{points}}^t$, and sends $(\mathbf{r}, \epsilon)$ to the prover.

Round 3: For each axis $k \in [1,\ldots,D]$ execute Algorithm 2 between the main parties $(k,1),\ldots,(k,N) \rightarrow ([\![\alpha]\!]_k, [\![\beta]\!]_k, [\![v]\!]_k)$. Prover builds hash $h' = \text{Hash}(H_1,\ldots,H_D)$ where $H_k \leftarrow \text{Algorithm2}([\![x_A]\!], [\![Q]\!], [\![P]\!], [\![a]\!], [\![b]\!], [\![c]\!], \mathbf{r}, \epsilon)$ and sends h' to the verifier.

Round 4: Verifier uniformly picks $(i_1^*,\ldots,i_D^*) \leftarrow [1,\ldots,N]^D$ and sends it to prover.

Round 5: Prover sends $(\text{state}_{i_1,\ldots,i_D}, \rho_{i_1,\ldots,i_D}) \forall (i_1,\ldots,i_D) \neq (i_1^*,\ldots,i_D^*)$, i.e., the sibling path, using TreePRG. Prover also sends $\text{com}_{(i_1^*,\ldots,i_D^*)}, [\![\alpha]\!]_{(i_1^*,\ldots,i_D^*)}, [\![\beta]\!]_{(i_1^*,\ldots,i_D^*)}$

Verification: Verifier accepts if and only if:
1. For each $i' \neq i^*$, expand all states to get leaf party states (they have $D \log N$ seeds in the sibling path, and each of these is expanded down to the leaf party level, giving $N^D - 1$ leaves), and use com_{i^*} provided. Then compute h and verify that it is equal to the one from Step 11, where $h = \text{Hash}(\text{com}_1,\ldots,\text{com}_{i^*},\ldots \text{com}_{N^D})$
2. For $k \in [1,\ldots,D]$: Run Alg. 3 to get $[\![\alpha]\!], [\![\beta]\!], [\![v]\!]$, and each H_k and check that:
    (a) α, β, v is the same for all D runs of Algorithm 3.
    (b) $H = \text{Hash}(H_1,\ldots,H_D)$ agrees with h' provided in Round 3.

Algorithm 2. Execute Π on a full set of parties

Input: $[\![\mathbf{x_A}]\!], [\![\mathbf{Q}]\!], [\![\mathbf{P}]\!], [\![\mathbf{a}]\!], [\![\mathbf{b}]\!], [\![\mathbf{c}]\!], \mathbf{r}, \epsilon$.
Output: $[\![\boldsymbol{\alpha}]\!], [\![\boldsymbol{\beta}]\!], [\![\mathbf{v}]\!], H$

Parties locally set $[\![\mathbf{x_B}]\!] = \mathbf{y} - \mathbf{H}'[\![\mathbf{x_A}]\!]$.
Parties locally compute $[\![\mathbf{S}]\!]$ via interpolation of $[\![\mathbf{x}]\!] = ([\![\mathbf{x_A}]\!] \mid [\![\mathbf{x_B}]\!])$.

// Compute $[\![\boldsymbol{\alpha}]\!], [\![\boldsymbol{\beta}]\!], [\![\mathbf{v}]\!]$ coordinate-wise:
for $l \in [t]$ **do**

Parties locally evaluate $[\![\mathbf{S}(r_l)]\!], [\![\mathbf{Q}(r_l)]\!], [\![\mathbf{P}(r_l)]\!]$.
Parties set $[\![\alpha_l]\!] = \epsilon_l [\![\mathbf{Q}(r_l)]\!] + [\![a_l]\!]$.
Parties set $[\![\beta_l]\!] = [\![\mathbf{S}(r_l)]\!] + [\![b_l]\!]$.
Parties open $[\![\alpha_l]\!]$ and $[\![\beta_l]\!]$ to get α_l, β_l.
Parties locally set

$$[\![v_l]\!] = -[\![c_l]\!] + \langle \epsilon_l F(r_l) \cdot [\![P(r_l)]\!] \rangle + \langle \alpha_l, [\![b_l]\!] \rangle + \langle \beta_l, [\![a_l]\!] \rangle - \langle \alpha_l, \beta_l \rangle.$$

Compute $H = \mathrm{Hash}([\![\boldsymbol{\alpha}]\!], [\![\boldsymbol{\beta}]\!], [\![\mathbf{v}]\!])$

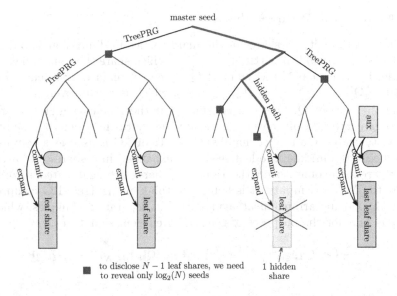

Fig. 2. Witness generation via seed expansion for a depth 3 tree. The N^D leaf party witness shares are derived directly from their seeds, but the $N \cdot D$ main party witness shares are defined as the sum of their leaf party shares. Subsequently, to open all the leaf seeds except one, we reveal only the $\log(N^D)$ sibling nodes along the hidden path (which requires $\log(N^D)$ space).

Algorithm 3. Verify a partition of parties

Input: Secret-shares $[\![\mathbf{x_A}]\!], [\![\mathbf{Q}]\!], [\![\mathbf{P}]\!], [\![\mathbf{a}]\!], [\![\mathbf{b}]\!], [\![\mathbf{c}]\!], \mathbf{r}, \epsilon$. The Party that contains the hidden leaf party i^* (hereafter partially-disclosed Party) uses as shares the partial aggregation from its disclosed leaf parties. The other Parties use fully aggregated shares. Index i^* and communication $\alpha, \beta, \mathbf{v}$ of the hidden leaf party i^*.

Output: $[\![\alpha]\!], [\![\beta]\!], [\![\mathbf{v}]\!], H$

Parties locally set $[\![\mathbf{x_B}]\!] = \mathbf{y} - \mathbf{H}'[\![\mathbf{x_A}]\!]$.

Parties locally compute $[\![\mathbf{S}]\!]$ via interpolation of $[\![\mathbf{x}]\!] = ([\![\mathbf{x_A}]\!] \mid [\![\mathbf{x_B}]\!])$.

for $l \in [t]$ **do**   ▷ Compute $[\![\alpha]\!], [\![\beta]\!], [\![\mathbf{v}]\!]$ coordinate-wise.

  Parties locally evaluate $[\![\mathbf{S}(r_l)]\!], [\![\mathbf{Q}(r_l)]\!], [\![\mathbf{P}(r_l)]\!]$.

  Parties set $[\![\alpha_l]\!] = \epsilon_l[\![\mathbf{Q}(r_l)]\!] + [\![a_l]\!]$. and $[\![\beta_l]\!] = [\![\mathbf{S}(r_l)]\!] + [\![b_l]\!]$.

  The Partially-disclosed Party adds i^* communications to $[\![\alpha_l]\!]$ and $[\![\beta_l]\!]$.

  Parties open $[\![\alpha_l]\!]$ and $[\![\beta_l]\!]$ to get α_l, β_l.

  All Parties but the partially-disclosed one locally set

  $$[\![v_l]\!] = -[\![c_l]\!] + \langle \epsilon_l F(r_l) \cdot [\![P(r_l)]\!]\rangle + \langle \alpha_l, [\![b_l]\!]\rangle + \langle \beta_l, [\![a_l]\!]\rangle - \langle \alpha_l, \beta_l\rangle.$$

  The local share $[\![v_l]\!]$ of the partially-disclosed Party is set so that $v_l = 0$

Compute $H = \text{Hash}([\![\alpha]\!], [\![\beta]\!], [\![\mathbf{v}]\!])$

3.4   Main Party Witness Shares

To construct the witness shares of the main parties in dimension k, one aggregates the shares of all leaf parties $(i_1, \ldots, i_D)$ which share the same index i_k. For example, in dimension 1, the share of $\mathbf{Q}$ of the jth main party, denoted $(1, j)$, would be $[\![\mathbf{Q}]\!]_{(1,j)} = \sum_{i'_2, \ldots, i'_D} [\![\mathbf{Q}]\!]_{(j, i'_2, \ldots, i'_D)}$, which is a sum over N^{D-1} of the leaf party shares of $\mathbf{Q}$. One can consider that the following high-level flow is used to generate and ultimately aggregate the shares in order to generate the main party shares. On the left hand side the TreePRG is used as a compression technique; in the middle, the leaf seeds are expanded into shares and arranged in a hypercube geometry; on the right the shares are aggregated in order to provide the MPCitH inputs. It is helpful to think of the TreePRG compression and the hypercube arrangement/aggregation as separate techniques, which are combined here for the purposes of generating efficient signatures.

$$seed \xrightarrow{\text{TreePRG}} \{seed_{i'}\}_{i' \in [N^D]} \xrightarrow{\text{PRG}} \{[\![\mathbf{x}]\!]_{i'}, [\![\mathbf{P}]\!]_{i'}, [\![\mathbf{Q}]\!]_{i'}\}_{i' \in [N^D]} \xrightarrow{\Sigma} [\![\mathbf{x}]\!]_k, [\![\mathbf{P}]\!]_k, [\![\mathbf{Q}]\!]_k,$$

3.5   Proofs of Security

The proofs in this section closely follow [FJR22] due to similarities in underlying hardness assumptions. Protocol 1 implicitly defines the interaction between an *honest prover* executing the odd rounds 1, 3, 5 and an *honest verifier* executing the even rounds 2, 4. Throughout the security proof, a general prover, not necessarily knowing the secret, is a party that reads and produces the same type of messages as the honest prover, without necessarily following the algorithm.

We first show that an honest prover is accepted with certainty, and conversely, any prover who commits to a bad witness that does not encode the SD secret in the first round has probability lower than $\epsilon \approx 1/N^D$ of being accepted. Consequently, any prover that has a higher rate of acceptance necessarily knows the secret. Then, we prove that the protocol is zero knowledge, since its transcript distribution can be simulated without the secret.

Theorem 1 ((Perfect) Completeness). *Protocol 1 is perfectly complete. That is to say, a prover with knowledge of a witness w (contained in sk) who performs $\mathcal{P}(sk)$ correctly, will be accepted by a verifier $\mathcal{V}(pk)$ with probability 1.*

Proof Proof of Theorem 1 For any choice of randomness for $\mathcal{P}, \mathcal{V}$, the computations of $\mathcal{P}$ pass all of the the verification checks of $\mathcal{V}$ by construction.   □

Lemma 4. *A prover $\tilde{\mathcal{P}}$ that commits to a bad witness s.t. $\mathbf{S} \cdot \mathbf{Q} \neq \mathbf{P} \cdot \mathbf{F}$ in Round 1 of Protocol 1 and is unable to find a commitment/hash collision has probability $\leq \epsilon = (p + (1-p)/N^D)$ of being accepted by an honest verifier $\mathcal{V}$.*

Proof. For $\mathcal{V}$ to accept, given $\mathbf{S} \cdot \mathbf{Q} \neq \mathbf{P} \cdot \mathbf{F}$, one of two scenarios must occur:

1. the random value $[\![\mathbf{v}]\!]$ encodes is zero with probability p, or otherwise,
2. $\tilde{\mathcal{P}}$ must cheat on the communications they send, which correspond to the MPCitH protocols on the main parties, so that it *appears* that the resulting $\mathbf{v}$ is the zero vector.

After the initial commitment, $\mathcal{V}$ sends the challenge points $\mathbf{r}, \epsilon$. In the first scenario, with probability p, the plaintext vector $\mathbf{v}$ generated by the MPC protocol is the zero vector (i.e., on all t points, it happens to be the case that $\delta = (\mathbf{S} \cdot \mathbf{Q} - \mathbf{P} \cdot \mathbf{F})(\mathbf{r})$ is zero, and/or that the beaver triplets committed in round 1 satisfy $\mathbf{c} - \mathbf{ab} = \epsilon\delta$.)

However, with probability $(1 - p)$, at *at least* one of the challenge points, $\mathbf{S} \cdot \mathbf{Q}(r_i) \neq \mathbf{P} \cdot \mathbf{F}(r_i)$, meaning at least one of the coordinates of $\mathbf{v} = \mathbf{c} - \mathbf{ab} - \epsilon\delta$ is non zero. In this case, the communications $[\![\alpha]\!], [\![\beta]\!], [\![\mathbf{v}]\!]$ resulting from an honest execution will not be accepted therefore $\tilde{\mathcal{P}}$ must alter some communications so that the resultant $\mathbf{v}$ is the zero vector.

In Round 3, $\tilde{\mathcal{P}}$ commits to his communications to D independent SDitH runs (one for each dimension on the hypercube). Let us assume that he needs to cheat on the communications of a single run (out of D), and without loss of generality, this can be cheating on the shares of α (cheating on β or $\mathbf{v}$) are equally valid).

The $[\![\alpha]\!]$ in this dimension consists of N main party shares $[\![\alpha]\!]_i$. So $\tilde{\mathcal{P}}$ must pick one to cheat on, having $1/N$ chance of success. Each of the main party shares consists of the sum of $N^{(D-1)}$ leaf shares in that particular slice, and all but one of the leaf shares will be opened. Therefore $\tilde{\mathcal{P}}$ must cheat on the share $[\![\alpha]\!]$ of a single leaf party s, shifting its value by $\delta \neq 0$. Cheating on more than one leaf party means certain detection as all but one leaf parties are opened, and cheating on none means that $\mathbf{v}$ is not the zero vector so won't be accepted.

However, leaf party s belongs to a single main share for each run of SDitH (one for each dimension of the hypercube). In each of these other main shares, their value for $[\![\alpha]\!]$ must be shifted by the same δ, as they cannot offset this value using other leaf parties, as all but one leaf party is revealed in Round 5 so this would mean certain detection. Thus each main share to which s belongs must cheat in their respective SDitH. No other cheating pattern is possible, because all leaf parties bar one are revealed in Round 5, so only one leaf party can cheat by δ, and this is exhibited in one main party for each dimension.

The only way to avoid detection using this method, is if the (uniformly random) challenge i^* in Round 4 gives the exact coordinates of s, as this means the main party to which s belongs in each dimension is the one that remains hidden. This has probability $(1/N)^D$, and is equivalent to the challenge leaving hidden the exact leaf party s out of N^D leaf parties. Hence, in a non-false positive scenario, $\tilde{\mathcal{P}}$ has $\leq 1/N^D$ chance of cheating. This yields the bound $p+(1-p)/N^D$ for the prover to be accepted using a bad witness in round 1. $\qquad\square$

Theorem 2 (Soundness). *If an efficient prover $\tilde{\mathcal{P}}$ with knowledge of only $(\boldsymbol{H}, \boldsymbol{y})$ can convince verifier $\mathcal{V}$ with probability*

$$\tilde{\epsilon} = Pr[\langle\tilde{\mathcal{P}}, \mathcal{V}\rangle \to 1] > \epsilon = (p + (1-p)\frac{1}{N^D}), \qquad (10)$$

where p is bounded in Eq. 9, then there exists an extraction function E that produces a commitment collision, or a good witness $\mathbf{x}'$ such that $\mathbf{Hx}' = \mathbf{y}$ and $wt(\mathbf{x}') < w$ by making an average number of calls to $\tilde{\mathcal{P}}$ is bounded from above:

$$\frac{4}{\tilde{\epsilon} - \epsilon} \cdot \left(1 + \frac{2\tilde{\epsilon}\ln 2}{\tilde{\epsilon} - \epsilon}\right) \qquad (11)$$

Should a prover $\tilde{\mathcal{P}}$ cheat with probability $p \leq \epsilon$ then this is not an issue, as it corresponds to ordinary vanilla cheating, i.e. cheating on a particular node, hoping that node does not have to be revealed at challenge time, or by hoping to guess some polynomials $\mathbf{S}, \mathbf{Q}, \mathbf{P}, \mathbf{F}$ which do not satisfy $\mathbf{S} \cdot \mathbf{Q} = \mathbf{P} \cdot \mathbf{F}$ in general, but which are equal at the challenge points which are subsequently selected.

Sketch of the proof of Theorem 2: The proof largely follows the soundness proof for the original SDitH [FJR22] scheme. The main difference lies in the details of witness extraction. More specifically, in the argument why we can extract. In our case, we are running D instances of SDitH in parallel. For each instance, the state of each party is secret shared. These secret shares are arranged in a hypercube, so every share is used as a secret share of D different instances. The first message contains a commitment to each of these secret shares.

Regarding extraction we prove (as for SDitH) that we can extract a candidate witness (an $\mathbf{x}$ s.t. $\mathbf{Hx} = \mathbf{y}$) as soon as we see two accepting transcripts that agree on the commitments, i.e., the first message, but disagree on the second challenge. As we always open all but one commitment, and this second challenge that decides which commitment not to open differs for the two transcripts, we learn the openings of all commitments (assuming that the commitment scheme is binding). It remains to argue that this is sufficient for extraction.

The soundness proof for the original SDitH protocol also shows that a candidate witness can be extracted from two accepting transcripts that share the same commitments but differ in the second challenge. This does not immediately imply extraction in our case as we committed to secret shares of the state and communications of the parties. However, we can rephrase the extraction condition shown for SDitH as the following; extraction is possible given the opened state and communication for *all* parties, so long as each party is verified in at least one accepting transcript. As only one commitment is not opened per transcript, there is the state and communication of exactly one party per SDitH proof that is not verified in each transcript. As the second challenges differ between the two transcripts per assumption, there has to be *at least* one dimension, in which the unopened leaf party secret shares belong to different main parties. In this dimension, we have obtained the openings of all main parties. Furthermore, in this dimension, the state and communication of each main party was verified during the verification of at least one of the transcripts. Therefore, we can apply the extraction argument of the original SDitH protocol. Equivalently, one now has knowledge of all leaf parties which together represent a complete sharing of the witness, and by the argument above, all leaf parties have been verified in at least one transcript. It remains to show that the candidate witness is a good witness, i.e., has $wt(\mathbf{x}) < w$. This follows the same argument from SDitH proof.

Proof. Assume the commitment scheme is perfectly binding (as opposed to computationally binding), as per Definition 8. For two sets of transcripts with the same initial commitment $h = \text{Hash}(\mathbf{com}_1, \ldots \mathbf{com}_{N^D})$, but different challenge leaf parties $i^* \neq j^*$, either:

- $[\![\mathbf{x}]\!], [\![\mathbf{Q}]\!], [\![\mathbf{P}]\!]$ differ and one finds a collision in the commitment hash, or
- the openings are equal in both transcripts, and therefore the shares $[\![\mathbf{x}]\!], [\![\mathbf{Q}]\!]$, and $[\![\mathbf{P}]\!]$ are also equal in both transcripts.

In the second case, the witness can be recovered from two transcripts with $i^* \neq j^*$ where $i^*, j^* \in [1, \ldots N^D]$ are the challenge indices in the first and second transcripts respectively. This is because in the first case the verifier receives the $N^D - 1$ leaf parties which are not i^*, and in the second transcript they receive the $N^D - 1$ leaf parties which are not j^*. Thus with both transcripts, the verifier knows the full set of witness shares and so can reconstruct the full witness by summing all of the N^D leaf party shares.

Now we explain why this means the extractor function is able to learn a good witness. Consider the hypercube geometry: $i^* \neq j^*$ means that their coordinates in the hypercube are not equal in *at least* one position $(i_1^*, \ldots, i_D^*) \neq (j_1^*, \ldots, j_D^*)$. Let the first coordinate in which they differ be $i_k^* \neq j_k^*$. Then for the MPCitH protocol for dimension k, one has two transcripts with different hidden (main) parties, where the sum of witness shares for both runs has been successfully verified. This scenario almost identically resembles the protocol of [FJR22], thus the remainder of the proof of soundness proceeds in the same manner.

In the following we demonstrate that to generate two such accepted transcripts with the same initial commitment but different challenge points, the witness must be good. Call $[\![\mathbf{x}]\!], [\![\mathbf{Q}]\!]$, and $[\![\mathbf{P}]\!]$ a good witness if $\mathbf{S} \cdot \mathbf{Q} = \mathbf{F} \cdot \mathbf{P}$.

R_h is the random variable for the randomness used to generate the initial commitment, with r_h being a given value of R_h.

The extractor works by simple application of the Forking lemma, Lemma 2: $\tilde{\mathcal{P}}$ is run with honest $\mathcal{V}$ until successful transcript T_1 is found, having second challenge i^*. Then rewind $\tilde{\mathcal{P}}$, using the same randomness r_h as in T_1 until one gets a successful transcript T_2 with different second challenge j^*. Then extract the witness. If the witness is bad, start over.

Next we estimate how many calls to $\tilde{\mathcal{P}}$ the extractor E makes. Let $\alpha \in (0, 1)$ such that $(1 - \alpha) \cdot \tilde{\epsilon} > \epsilon$. We say r_h is 'good' if $\Pr[succ_{\tilde{p}} | r_h] \geq (1 - \alpha) \cdot \tilde{\epsilon}$. By the splitting lemma (Lemma 1), $\Pr[r_h \text{ is good} | succ_{\tilde{p}}] \geq \alpha$, which implies that a good randomness can be found after gathering roughly $1/\alpha$ successful transcripts. Also, by (the converse of) Lemma 4, when r_h is good, since the probability $(1 - \alpha)\tilde{\epsilon} > \epsilon$, then the initial commitment provided by the transcript necessarily encodes a good witness, that can be extracted from any other successful transcript that starts from r_h.

Given a good transcript T_1 (i.e. a success in the outer loop) we now provide a lower bound on the number of iterations of the inner loop in order to find another good transcript T_2 with the same randomness r_h such that $i^* \neq j^*$.

$$\Pr[succ_{\tilde{p}} \cap i^* \neq j^* | r_h \text{ good}] = \Pr[succ_{\tilde{p}} | r_h \text{ good}] - \Pr[succ_{\tilde{p}} \cap i^* = j^* | r_h \text{ good}]$$

$$\geq \Pr[succ_{\tilde{p}} | r_h \text{ good}] - \frac{1}{N^D}$$

$$\geq (1 - \alpha)\tilde{\epsilon} - \frac{1}{N^D}$$

$$\geq (1 - \alpha)\tilde{\epsilon} - \epsilon. \tag{12}$$

Then by running $\tilde{\mathcal{P}}$ for L repetitions one has a probability greater than $1/2$ of obtaining a second transcript T_2 with a different challenge leaf party to T_1, where both T_1 and T_2 are generated using the same (good) randomness r_h, where

$$L > \frac{\ln 2}{\ln \frac{1}{1 - ((1-\alpha)\tilde{\epsilon} - \epsilon)}} \simeq \frac{\ln 2}{(1 - \alpha)\tilde{\epsilon} - \epsilon}. \tag{13}$$

Denote the expected number of calls to $\tilde{\mathcal{P}}$ as $\mathbb{E}(\tilde{\mathcal{P}})$. Then $\mathbb{E}(\tilde{\mathcal{P}})$ can be written as a recursive formula; as a function of firstly the probability of succeeding in the outer loop to obtain T_1, and secondly the probability of obtaining T_2 with L calls once one has found a successful transcript T_1. Step by step, this is

1. Make an initial call to $\tilde{\mathcal{P}}$.
2. If we do not find T_1, with probability $(1 - \Pr[succ_{\tilde{p}}]))$, then repeat the procedure from Step 1.
3. If we find a successful T_1, then r_h is good with probability α by the splitting lemma (Lemma 1). Then make L calls to $\tilde{\mathcal{P}}$, after which there is probability above $1/2$ of success. If successful, terminate, else return to Step 1.
4. The probability that r_h is bad is $1 - \alpha$. Thus, there is no guarantee on the probability of finding T_2. Make L calls to $\tilde{\mathcal{P}}$ (because we do not yet know that r_h is bad), then when unsuccessful, return to Step 1.

Consequently, if a call in Step 1 to $\tilde{\mathcal{P}}$ does not yield T_1, then repeat Step 1. If Step 1 is successful, giving T_1, then we perform L further calls seeking to obtain T_2, because we do not know a priori whether r_h is good or bad. If r_h is good (with probability α), then there is $1/2$ probability that we find T_2 and the algorithm terminates. With r_h good, there is also $1/2$ probability that we do not find T_2. If r_h is bad (with probability $(1-\alpha)$, there is no guarantee about finding T_2 so to provide an upper bound for the number of calls to $\tilde{\mathcal{P}}$ we say that this part is always unsuccessful at finding T_2. Thus

$$\Pr[\text{no } T_2 | succ_{\tilde{p}}] = \Pr[\text{no } T_2 | r_h \text{ good}] + \Pr[\text{no } T_2 | r_h \text{ bad}] = \alpha/2 + (1-\alpha),$$

and in this case return to Step 1. So the expression for $\mathbb{E}(\tilde{\mathcal{P}})$ can be written

$$\mathbb{E}(\tilde{\mathcal{P}}) \leq 1 + \underbrace{(1 - \Pr[succ_{\tilde{p}}])\mathbb{E}(\tilde{\mathcal{P}})}_{\text{Do not find } T_1} + \underbrace{\Pr[succ_{\tilde{p}}]\left(L + \left(1 - \frac{\alpha}{2}\right)\mathbb{E}(\tilde{\mathcal{P}})\right)}_{\text{Find } T_1}, \qquad (14)$$

which reduces to

$$\mathbb{E}(\tilde{\mathcal{P}}) \leq \frac{2}{\alpha\tilde{\epsilon}}\left(1 + \tilde{\epsilon}L\right) = \frac{2}{\alpha\tilde{\epsilon}}\left(1 + \frac{\tilde{\epsilon}\ln 2}{(1-\alpha)\tilde{\epsilon} - \epsilon}\right). \qquad (15)$$

Define $(1-\alpha)\tilde{\epsilon} = \frac{1}{2}(\epsilon + \tilde{\epsilon})$, i.e., halfway between ϵ and $\tilde{\epsilon}$ in order to obtain a formula in terms of just ϵ and $\tilde{\epsilon}$. Then we arrive at the upper bound

$$\mathbb{E}(\tilde{\mathcal{P}}) \leq \frac{4}{\tilde{\epsilon} - \epsilon}\left(1 + \frac{2\tilde{\epsilon}\ln 2}{\tilde{\epsilon} - \epsilon}\right). \qquad (16)$$

$\square$

We now prove that the protocol is zero-knowledge. The main intuition is that any prover who learns the challenge points $\mathbf{r}, \epsilon$ from Round 2 challenge before committing to the state on Round 1 can update c in the aux to force a false positive. Similarly any prover who learns the challenge coordinates i^* from Round 4 before committing to the MPC communications on Round 3 can alter the communication of the hidden party such that $\mathbf{v}$ becomes the zero vector. The following simulator exploits the second option.

Theorem 3 (Honest-Verifier Zero Knowledge (HVZK)). *If the PRG of Algorithm 1 and commitment Com are indistinguishable from the uniform random distribution, then Algorithm 1 is Honest-Verifier Zero Knowledge.*

Proof. To prove the HVZK property, we construct a simulator $\mathcal{S}$ which outputs transcripts of Algorithm 1 which are computationally indistinguishable from real transcripts. For this we assume that the PRG of Algorithm 1 is $(t, \epsilon_{\text{PRG}})$-secure and the commitment Com is $(t, \epsilon_{\text{Com}})$-hiding. For ease of reading, in the following, we sometimes denote general leaf party indices $(i_{k_1}, \ldots, i_{k_D})$ by i', and the challenge party index $(i_1^*, \ldots, i_D^*)$ as simply i^*. First consider a simulator, $\mathcal{S}$, described in Algorithm 4 which produces the transcript responses

Algorithm 4. HVZK Simulator

Sample seed $\leftarrow_\$ \{0,1\}^\lambda$.

Generate $(\text{seed}_{i'}, \rho_{i'})$ for all leaf parties via TreePRG(seed).

Step 1 (Sample Challenges):

Where $\text{CH1} = \{\mathbf{r}, \epsilon\} \leftarrow \mathbb{F}_{\text{points}}^t \times \mathbb{F}_{\text{points}}^t$ and $\text{CH2} = i^* \leftarrow [1, \dots, N^D]$

Step 2 (Generate N^D Leaf Party States):

Expand root seed_i recursively via TreePRG to get N^D leaf states and $(\text{seed}_{i'}, \rho_{i'})$

Step 3 (Generate Leaf Party Commitments and Witness Shares):

for $i' \neq i^*$ do

    Compute $\mathbf{com}_{i'} = \text{Hash}(\text{state}_{i'}, \rho_{i'})$

    if $i' \neq N^D$ then

        Expand the leaf party seeds into witness shares

    else

        Generate aux for the last leaf party, $i' = N^D$, randomly draw $[\![\mathbf{x}_A]\!]_{N^D}$, $[\![\mathbf{Q}]\!]_{N^D}$, $[\![\mathbf{P}]\!]_{N^D}$, and $[\![\mathbf{c}]\!]_{N^D}$.

for $i' = i^*$ do

    Draw $\mathbf{com}_{i^*}$ at random

Compute initial commitment $\text{COM} = \text{Hash}(\mathbf{com}_1, \dots, \mathbf{com}_{i^*}, \dots, \mathbf{com}_{N^D})$

Step 4 (Generate Party Communications):

Draw $[\![\boldsymbol{\alpha}]\!]_{i^*}$ and $[\![\boldsymbol{\beta}]\!]_{i^*}$ uniformly at random from their respective domains.

for $k \in [1, \dots, D]$ do

    if $i_k \neq i_k^*$ then

        Get communications $\{[\![\boldsymbol{\alpha}]\!]_{i_k}, [\![\boldsymbol{\beta}]\!]_{i_k}, [\![\mathbf{v}]\!]_{i_k}\}$ as stated in Algorithms 1, 2

    if i_k^* then

        Compute party communication shares $[\![\boldsymbol{\alpha}]\!]_{i_k^*}, [\![\boldsymbol{\beta}]\!]_{i_k^*}, [\![\mathbf{v}]\!]_{i_k^*}$ by running Π on the sum of the witnesses of the $N - 1$ *revealed* leaf parties in their respective slices, as described in Algorithm 1, then add on $[\![\boldsymbol{\alpha}]\!]_{i^*}$ and $[\![\boldsymbol{\beta}]\!]_{i^*}$

        Set $[\![\mathbf{v}]\!]_{i^*} = -\sum_{i' \neq i^*} [\![\mathbf{v}]\!]$.

Step 5 (Output transcript):

$\text{RSP}_1 = h' = \text{Hash}(H_1, \dots, H_D)$ where $H_k \leftarrow \text{Alg. 2}([\![\mathbf{x}_A]\!], [\![\mathbf{Q}]\!], [\![\mathbf{P}]\!], [\![\mathbf{a}]\!], [\![\mathbf{b}]\!], [\![\mathbf{c}]\!], \mathbf{r}, \epsilon)$

$\text{RSP}_2 = \mathbf{com}_{i^*}, [\![\boldsymbol{\alpha}]\!]_{i^*}, [\![\boldsymbol{\beta}]\!]_{i^*}, \{(\text{state}_{i_1, \dots, i_D}, \rho_{i_1, \dots, i_D}) \forall (i_1, \dots, i_D) \neq (i_1^*, \dots, i_D^*)\}$.

Output $(\text{COM}, \text{CH}_1, \text{RSP}_1, \text{CH}_2, \text{RSP}_2)$

$(\text{COM}, \text{CH}_1, \text{RSP}_1, \text{CH}_2, \text{RSP}_2)$. Next we demonstrate that this simulator produces indistinguishable transcripts from the distribution of real transcripts by starting with a simulator that produces 'true' transcripts, and altering the outputs section-by-section until arriving at $\mathcal{S}$ defined above. At each simulator alteration we argue why the distribution remains unchanged.

True transcripts (v0): This takes as input a witness $\mathbf{x}_A$ as well as the honest verifier's challenges $(\mathbf{r}, \epsilon, i^*)$. It then executes Algorithm 1 correctly, hence its output distribution is the 'correct' distribution.

Simulator v1: In this simulator, the only difference versus v0 is that randomness in leaf party i^* is replaced with true randomness. If $i^* = (N, \dots, N)$ then $[\![\mathbf{x}_A]\!]_{N^D}, [\![\mathbf{Q}]\!]_{N^D}$, and $[\![\mathbf{P}]\!]_{N^D}$ are generated in the usual way. So the witness shares of all leaf parties still sum to give the input witness (and by extension, all parties for each MPCitH run in $[1, \dots, D]$), therefore only $[\![\mathbf{a}]\!]_{N^D}$ and

$[\![\mathbf{b}]\!]_{N^D}$ are random (and by extension, so are the shares $[\![\mathbf{a}]\!], [\![\mathbf{b}]\!]$ for the D parties $[(1, N), \ldots, (D, N)]$ which contain challenge leaf party $i^* = N^D$). We can see that the difficulty in distinguishing the output of Simulator v1 from the real distribution is equal to distinguishing ϵ_{PRG} from true randomness.

Simulator v2: Replace $[\![\mathbf{x}_A]\!]_{N^D}, [\![\mathbf{Q}]\!]_{N^D}, [\![\mathbf{P}]\!]_{N^D}$, and $[\![\mathbf{c}]\!]_{N^D}$ with true randomness (i.e. sample these shares randomly, and not via the protocol). This means that $[\![\mathbf{x}_A]\!], [\![\mathbf{Q}]\!]$, and $[\![\mathbf{P}]\!]$ are now independent of input witness, so the inputs to $\mathcal{S}$ are reduced to the challenges $(\mathrm{ch}_1, \mathrm{ch}_2)$.

For $i^* = N^D$ this means that only $[\![\boldsymbol{\alpha}]\!]_{i^*}, [\![\boldsymbol{\beta}]\!]_{i^*}$ are affected because in this scenario aux is not sent in RSP_2. These shares do not change in distribution from Simulator v1 to Simulator v2 because we already have in Simulator v1 the $[\![\boldsymbol{\alpha}]\!]_{i^*}$ and $[\![\boldsymbol{\beta}]\!]_{i^*}$ which appear to be uniformly distributed and are unaffected by the other parties, and $[\![\mathbf{v}]\!]_{i^*} = -\sum_{i \neq i^*} [\![\mathbf{v}]\!]_i$.

For $i^* \neq N^D$ only aux is affected in the transcript. In Simulator v1, aux is computed via the sum of true uniform randomness of leaf party i^*, and every other leaf party's pseudo-randomness, also generating aux via true uniform randomness does not alter the distribution between Simulators v1 and v2.

Simulator v3: Here, $[\![\boldsymbol{\alpha}]\!]_{i^*}, [\![\boldsymbol{\beta}]\!]_{i^*}$ are also drawn via true randomness (affecting communications of party i^*). But these already appear to be uniformly distributed in Simulator v2, thus the output distribution does not change between Simulator v2 and v3. The outputs of Simulator v3 $(\mathrm{RSP}_1, \mathrm{RSP}_2)$ are thus indistinguishable from those of an honest execution of Algorithm 1. To obtain a global HVZK simulator we take the simulator described in Algorithm 4, apply the hiding property of $\mathbf{com}_{i^*}$, with the final simulator performing as follows:

1. Generate random challenges $\mathrm{ch}_1, \mathrm{ch}_2$.
2. Run Simulator v3 to get $\mathrm{RSP}_1, \mathrm{RSP}_2$.
3. For initial leaf party commitments $i' \neq i^*$ compute $\mathbf{com}_{i'} = \mathrm{Com}(\mathrm{state}_{i'}, \rho_{i'})$.
4. For leaf party i^*, draw $\mathbf{com}_{i^*}$ at random.
5. Set initial commitment to $\mathrm{Com} = \mathrm{Hash}(\mathbf{com}_1, \ldots, \mathbf{com}_{N^D})$.

The output of the global HVZK simulator is $(t, \epsilon_{\mathrm{PRG}} + \epsilon_{\mathrm{Com}})$-indistinguishable from the real distribution. □

4   A Signature Scheme Based on Syndrome Decoding with Hypercube-MPCitH

In order to transform our ZK proof into a signature we use a classical Fiat-Shamir transform [FS87]. Both the transform and the associated proof closely follow the proof provided in the original SDitH proposal [FJR22], which in turn is similar in nature to the Picnic proof [ZCD+20]. For this section, the reader is referred to the full version of this paper [AMGH+22, Section 4].

5   Performance and Analysis

In this section we analyse the protocol with respect to the communication cost. We provide costs for the ZK protocol, in order to compare with the others using syndrome decoding, and then provide parameters and costs for the signature scheme. In the original SDitH work, the authors present a variant of the underlying SD problem known as the d−split problem, and explain how their signature scheme can be adapted to be based on this variant of the SD problem. We do not present the same adaptations to this problem for our signature scheme. However, the difference presented by the d−split problem affects only the underlying hardness assumptions, and so it is still instructive to present parameter sets for the d−split variants for comparison with the previous signature schemes.

There are a few points in the protocol which we do not include as their impact is arbitrarily small compared to the main communication cost, these being the challenges from the verifier. The communication cost is then calculated from:

- Com: the hash, h, of the N^D commitments.
- Res$_1$: the hash, h', of the D hashes output from the MPC simulation.
- Res$_2$: the $(\text{state}_{i_1,\ldots,i_D}, \rho_{i_1,\ldots,i_D}) \,\forall\, (i_1,\ldots,i_D) \neq (i_1^*,\ldots,i_D^*)$, $\mathbf{com}_{(i_1^*,\ldots i_D^*)}$, $[\![\boldsymbol{\alpha}]\!]_{(i_1^*,\ldots,i_D^*)}, [\![\boldsymbol{\beta}]\!]_{(i_1^*,\ldots,i_D^*)}$.

If we consider each leaf $(i' = (i_1,\cdots,i_D) \in \{1,\cdots,N^D\})$ of the hypercube, for all but the final leaf $(i' \neq N^D)$ the cost of each state$_{i'}$ is the size of a seed of λ bits. For the case of the final leaf $(i' = N^D)$, the state$_{i'}$ consists of seed$_{N^D}$ and the auxiliary which consists of (i) the plaintext share $[\![\mathbf{x_A}]\!]_{N^D}$, (ii) the shares $[\![\mathbf{Q}]\!]_{N^D}$, $[\![\mathbf{P}]\!]_{N^D}$ being two polynomials of degree $w-1$, and (iii) the shares $[\![\mathbf{c}]\!]_{N^D}$ of the t points of $\mathbb{F}_{\text{points}}$.

The only parts within the commitment and responses that are affected by the hypercube component, D, is the number of, and thus size of, the seed and commitment randomness. This in essence becomes a sibling path, of length D, from $(\text{state}_{i_1^*,\ldots,i_D^*}, \rho_{i_1^*,\ldots,i_D^*})$ to the tree root, which will cost at most $D\cdot\lambda\cdot\log_2(N)$ bits. For the remaining costs, we have the commitment $\mathbf{com}_{(i_1^*,\ldots i_D^*)}$ of 2λ bits and $[\![\boldsymbol{\alpha}]\!]_{(i_1^*,\ldots,i_D^*)}, [\![\boldsymbol{\beta}]\!]_{(i_1^*,\ldots,i_D^*)}$ are elements of $\mathbb{F}_{\text{points}}$. We then calculate the size of the communication cost (in bits) of a single round of the protocol as:

Total Size $= 4\lambda$	size of h and h'.
$+\, k \cdot \log_2(|\mathbb{F}_{\text{SD}}|)$	size of $[\![\mathbf{x_A}]\!]_{N^D}$.
$+\, 2w \cdot \log_2(|\mathbb{F}_{\text{poly}}|)$	sizes of $[\![\mathbf{Q}]\!]_{N^D}$ and $[\![\mathbf{P}]\!]_{N^D}$.
$+\, (2 \cdot d + 1) \cdot t \cdot \log_2(|\mathbb{F}_{\text{points}}|)$	sizes of $[\![\boldsymbol{\alpha}]\!]_{(i_1^*,\ldots,i_D^*)}, [\![\boldsymbol{\beta}]\!]_{(i_1^*,\ldots,i_D^*)}, [\![\mathbf{c}]\!]_{N^D}$.
$+\, D \cdot \lambda \cdot \log_2(N)$	size of the seeds.
$+\, 2\lambda$	size of $\mathbf{com}_{(i_1^*,\ldots i_D^*)}$.

In order to achieve the target security level and soundness, $2^{-\lambda}$, we perform τ parallel repetitions. Using the definition of the forgery cost in Eq. 17 in [AMGH+22] and predefined values for false positivity, we find the minimum number of repetitions, τ, that satisfies Eq. 17. Also, we do not need to repeat this process for the entire communication costs, the values for h and h' can be merged for each τ. Thus, the total communication cost (in bits) of the scheme with τ repetitions is:

$$\text{Size} = 4\lambda + \tau \cdot (k \cdot \log_2(|\mathbb{F}_{\text{SD}}|) + 2w \cdot \log_2(|\mathbb{F}_{\text{poly}}|)$$
$$+ (2d+1) \cdot t \cdot \log_2(|\mathbb{F}_{\text{points}}|) + D \cdot \lambda \cdot \log_2(N) + 2\lambda).$$

Using Eq. 10 we have the obtained soundness error as $(p + (1-p)\frac{1}{N^D})^\tau$.

5.1 Comparing Code-Based Zero-Knowledge Protocols

The SDitH protocol is not the first proposal for a zero-knowledge protocol using syndrome decoding. There have been other proposals for identity schemes and signature schemes, we can compare these protocols on different instances of syndrome decoding for 128-bit security. Table 2 shows this comparison which is also given in [FJR22], which also provides further calculation costs and parameters. Each scheme in Table 2 utilizes the same parameters (m, k, w); either Instance 1 [FJR21] which is SD on $\mathbb{F}_2$ for $(1280, 640, 132)$ or Instance 2 [CVE11] which is SD on $\mathbb{F}_{2^8}$ for $(208, 104, 78)$, for the given communication costs.

In order to directly compare with [FJR22], we utilize the same parameters for $(N, \tau, |\mathbb{F}_{\text{poly}}|, |\mathbb{F}_{\text{points}}|, t)$, which only differ in (N, τ), in which our protocol optimizes. Our protocol also differs slightly in the calculation of the soundness error, ε, which affects the security level being attained; with SDitH using $(p + \frac{1}{N} - p \cdot \frac{1}{N})$ whereas we use $(p + \frac{1}{N^D} - p \cdot \frac{1}{N^D})$.

SDitH ZKP parameters:	Our ZKP parameters:
Instance 1:	Instance 1:
Short: $(256, 16, 2^{11}, 2^{22}, 2)$; $\varepsilon^\tau = 2^{-128}$	**Shorter:** $(2^{12}, 11, 2^{11}, 2^{22}, 2)$; $\varepsilon^\tau = 2^{-132}$
Fast: $(32, 26, 2^{11}, 2^{22}, 1)$; $\varepsilon^\tau = 2^{-129.6}$	**Shortest:** $(2^{16}, 8, 2^{11}, 2^{22}, 2)$; $\varepsilon^\tau = 2^{-128}$
Instance 2:	Instance 2:
Short: $(256, 16, 2^8, 2^{24}, 2)$; $\varepsilon^\tau = 2^{-128}$	**Shorter:** $(2^{12}, 11, 2^8, 2^{24}, 2)$; $\varepsilon^\tau = 2^{-132}$
Fast: $(32, 26, 2^8, 2^{24}, 1)$; $\varepsilon^\tau = 2^{-130.0}$	**Shortest:** $(2^{16}, 8, 2^8, 2^{24}, 2)$; $\varepsilon^\tau = 2^{-128}$

For Instance 1 and Instance 2, and using a target soundness of 2^{-128}, Table 2 provides the corresponding communication costs for the different ZK protocols using syndrome decoding. We reuse the parameters used in SDitH for the Fast and Short variants, thus we achieve similar costs for these. We also extended these parameters for a large number of simulated parties to achieve Shorter and Shortest variants. This means the Fast parameters for SDitH are also the fastest parameters for our scheme, with the speed monotonically decreasing as go from Short, Shorter, and Shortest. Details on the communication costs for the other protocols can be found in the full version of [FJR22, Appendix B]. Also, it is worth noting that there are some differences between the proved statements; i.e. either proving the equality or inequality for the Hamming weight of w.

Table 2. Communication sizes of ZK protocols using syndrome decoding.

Scheme	Year	Instance 1	Instance 2	Proved Statement
Stern [Ste94]	1993	37.4 KB	46.1 KB	$y = Hx, \mathrm{wt}(x) = w$
Véron [Vér97]	1997	31.7 KB	38.7 KB	*message decoding*
CVE11 [CVE11]	2010	–	37.4 KB	$y = Hx, \mathrm{wt}(x) = w$
AGS11 [AGS11]	2011	24.8 KB	–	$y = Hx, \mathrm{wt}(x) = w$
GPS22 [GPS22] (Short)	2021	–	15.2 KB	$y = Hx, \mathrm{wt}(x) = w$
GPS22 [GPS22] (Fast)	2021	–	19.9 KB	$y = Hx, \mathrm{wt}(x) = w$
FJR21 [FJR21] (Short)	2021	12.9 KB	15.6 KB	$y = Hx, \mathrm{wt}(x) = w$
FJR21 [FJR21] (Fast)	2021	20.0 KB	24.7 KB	$y = Hx, \mathrm{wt}(x) = w$
SDitH [FJR22] (Short)	2022	9.7 KB	6.9 KB	$y = Hx, \mathrm{wt}(x) \leq w$
SDitH [FJR22] (Fast)	2022	14.4 KB	9.7 KB	$y = Hx, \mathrm{wt}(x) \leq w$
Ours (shortest)	2022	6.0 KB	4.5 KB	$y = Hx, \mathrm{wt}(x) \leq w$
Ours (shorter)	2022	7.5 KB	5.5 KB	$y = Hx, \mathrm{wt}(x) \leq w$
Ours (short)	2022	9.7 KB	6.9 KB	$y = Hx, \mathrm{wt}(x) \leq w$
Ours (fast)	2022	14.4 KB	9.7 KB	$y = Hx, \mathrm{wt}(x) \leq w$

5.2 Parameter Selection

Here we derive the parameters we use for our proposed signature scheme. Due to similarities with SDitH we utilize the same values for many of the parameters; this also makes it simpler to compare the two protocols in terms of efficiency and communication costs. As with SDitH, the parameters chosen are for attaining at least 128 bits of security, equivalent to the NIST Level 1 security level.

5.2.1 Syndrome Decoding and MPC Parameters

To estimate the security of cryptographic schemes based on the hardness of solving a syndrome decoding instance for a random linear code over $\mathbb{F}_2$ we use algorithms which perform the best practical attacks. Currently this is a version of the Information-Set Decoding (ISD) algorithm [MMT11], based on previous work by Finiasz and Sendrier [FS09]. Recently an argument was made that the lower bound cost of the attack can be calculated by considering the cost of its topmost recursion step [FJR21]. The details of the algorithm will be omitted since the SD parameters will be reused from [FJR22], but we provide a description of each parameter set (or variant) and their differences below. Each variant listed will have associated parameters for (q, m, k, w, d) which define its hardness.

- Variant 1: based on the standard binary syndrome decoding problem with some parameters used from [FJR21].
- Variant 2: based on the d-split binary syndrome decoding problem, where d is chosen such that $m/d \leq 2^8$, meaning that $\mathbb{F}_{\mathrm{poly}} = \mathbb{F}_{2^8}$.
- Variant 3: based on the syndrome decoding problem defined over $\mathbb{F}_{2^8}$ with some parameters used from [CVE11].

Table 3. The SD and MPC parameters for our protocol, originally from [FJR22].

Scheme	SD Parameters					MPC Parameters			
	q	m	k	w	d	$|\mathbb{F}_{\text{poly}}|$	$|\mathbb{F}_{\text{points}}|$	t	p
Variant 1	2	1280	640	132	1	2^{11}	2^{22}	6	$\approx 2^{-69}$
Variant 2	2	1536	888	120	6	2^8	2^{24}	5	$\approx 2^{-79}$
Variant 3	2^8	256	128	80	1	2^8	2^{24}	5	$\approx 2^{-78}$

Table 4. SDitH [FJR22] parameters with key and signature sizes for $\lambda = 128$.

Scheme	Aim	Parameters		Sizes (in bytes)		
		N	τ	pk	sk	Sign (Max)
Variant 1	Fast	32	27	96	16	16 422
	Short	256	17	96	16	11 193
Variant 2	Fast	32	27	97	16	17 866
	Short	256	17	97	16	12 102
Variant 3	Fast	32	27	144	16	12 115
	Short	256	17	144	16	8 481

The MPC parameters (which follow from [FJR22]) are chosen so the resulting communication cost is small, thus the smallest possible field for $\mathbb{F}_{\text{poly}}$ is used as the communication includes polynomials in this field. The SD and MPC parameters for the three variants are provided in Table 3.

5.2.2 Signature Scheme Parameters

With SD and MPC parameters we can propose parameters for our signature scheme and provide costs. The signature parameters that primarily contribute to the communication cost are $(N, D, \tau, |\mathbb{F}_{\text{poly}}|, |\mathbb{F}_{\text{points}}|, t)$. We fix many of these parameters for comparison, these being those shown in Table 3.

Table 4 shows the parameters proposed for SDitH. The parameters are derived using the three different variations, as well as having two different values for the party size, N, with the aim of producing a fast computation version, for $N = 32$, and a short communication cost version, for $N = 256$. Once the party size is defined, the number of repetitions, τ can thus be calculated such that they gain the target security level, which in this work is at least 128 bits of security.

The parameters in which our protocol primarily optimizes over SDitH are the party size, being N or in our case N^D, and the resulting repetitions required, τ. A large part of the signature scheme in SDitH is the auxiliary, being made up of $([\![\mathbf{x_A}]\!]_N, [\![\mathbf{Q}]\!]_N, [\![\mathbf{P}]\!]_N, [\![\mathbf{c}]\!]_N)$, which is then repeated for each τ. Being able to significantly reduce τ means we drastically reduce this cost. In Fig. 3, we show the relationship between τ and D and how this affects the size of the signature.

In our parameter selection, we fix the value for $N = 2$ and adapt for different dimension sizes, D. It is possible for parameters to become equivalent, e.g., ($N = 2^{16}, \tau = 9$) produces the same communication costs and computations as ($N = 256^2, \tau = 9$), however the former parameters require significantly less (potentially expensive) MPC computations and in turn require (probably less expensive) hash calculations. This quality in the flexibility we gain with parameters is particularly coveted when its applications on a variety of hardware is considered; which range from CPUs with dedicated instructions for field arithmetic, to mid-range devices with AES-NI and SHA extension support, to low-end constrained devices with limited ISA support for cryptographic operations.

A list of our scheme's parameters are given in Table 5. Similarly to SDitH we provide parameters for the three SD and MPC variants, and those parameters with the aim of having short communication costs (for $N = 2^{16}$ and $N = 2^{12}$) and fast computations ($N = 2^8$ and $N = 2^5$). The associated public-key and secret-key values are unchanged compared to SDitH, the major differences are seen in the signature sizes and computation costs. We use similar nomenclature to SDitH, but due to the savings we make in performance, we 'upgrade' their previous parameters from Fast and Short, to Faster and Fast, respectively. The latter parameters we propose increase the dimension size, thus the party size in the MPC protocol, which finally results in Short and Shorter parameters.

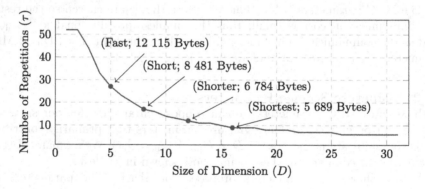

Fig. 3. The relationship between the dimension, D, and the repetitions rate, τ, using $N = 2$. Parameters and signature sizes provided for Variant 3.

Table 6 provides a comparison between SDitH and our scheme, with an overview of their similarities and differences. The major differences are in the online costs of the signature schemes, which is also the most computationally expensive part of SDitH and is thus the reason we see these significant improvements. In SDitH, there is one MPC computation per secret share, meaning N MPC computations are required. However, in our proposal, by placing the secret shares onto a hypercube, we only need MPC computations for all-but-the-final row ($N-1$) per dimension (D), with an additional computation for the auxiliary; thus requiring $(N-1) \cdot D + 1$ MPC computations in total. This is achieved while

Table 5. Our parameters with key and signature sizes in bytes for $\lambda = 128$.

Scheme	Aim	Parameters			Sizes (in bytes)		
		N	D	τ	pk	sk	Sign (Max)
Variant 1	Fast	2	5	27	96	16	16 422
	Short	2	8	17	96	16	11 193
	Shorter	2	12	12	96	16	8 698
	Shortest	2	16	9	96	16	7 125
Variant 2	Fast	2	5	27	97	16	17 866
	Short	2	8	17	97	16	12 102
	Shorter	2	12	12	97	16	9 340
	Shortest	2	16	9	97	16	7 606
Variant 3	Fast	2	5	27	144	16	12 115
	Short	2	8	17	144	16	8 481
	Shorter	2	12	12	144	16	6 784
	Shortest	2	16	9	144	16	5 689

maintaining the same number of secret shares in both signature schemes; thus for equivalent signature sizes we achieve a much faster signature runtime, and conversely for similar runtimes (i.e., 5.96 vs 7.17 ms) we achieve a much smaller signature size. We also see the similarities between the two schemes in Table 6, those being specifically their offline costs.

5.3 Implementation

We focus on the implementation of Variant 3 parameters, since these are the most interesting as they provide the fastest and smallest signatures. The Hypercube-MPCitH approach does not affect key generation; the secret and public keys are identical, both seeded and expanded. We provide benchmarks for signature and verification runtimes of our scheme compared to SDitH in Table 7. For fair comparison, the same processor is used, and the SDitH authors kindly shared their code for the benchmarks. We also ran the SDitH implementation for the Shorter parameter set, however the Shortest parameters gave issues and have thus been omitted.

In both implementations, the offline phase uses the AES native instructions for seed expansion and SHAKE for hash and commitments purposes. Both implementations also rely on a fast gf256 library[1], which utilizes AVX2 instructions. Our processor does not support the newer Galois Field New Instructions (GFNI)

---

[1] https://github.com/catid/gf256.

Table 6. Variant 3 signature generation costs for SDitH vs our scheme. Our MPC computation costs are calculated as $(N-1)\cdot D+1$ for signing, $(N-1)\cdot D$ for verifying. Thus, (i) for equivalent signature sizes our scheme is significantly faster, (ii) for similar runtimes (i.e., 2.87 vs 5.96 ms) are signatures are significantly smaller. Both ran on a single CPU core of a 3.1 GHz Intel Core i9-9990K.

Scheme	Secret Shares	Offline Costs		Online Costs	Signature Costs	
		State Gen.	Commits	MPC Comps	Size (Bytes)	Time (ms)
Ours ($N=2, D=5$)	32	32	32	6	12 115	1.30
SDitH ($N=32$)	32	32	32	32	12 115	5.96
Ours ($N=2, D=8$)	256	256	256	9	8 481	2.87
SDitH ($N=256$)	256	256	256	256	8 481	23.56
Ours ($N=2, D=12$)	4096	4096	4096	12	6 784	26.43
SDitH ($N=2^{12}$)	4096	4096	4096	4096	6 784	313.70

Table 7. Reference implementation benchmarks of SDitH [FJR22] vs our scheme for $\lambda = 128$. Both ran on a single CPU core of a 3.1 GHz Intel Core i9-9990K.

Scheme	Aim	Signature Size	Parameters			Sign Time (in ms)			Verify Time
			N	D	τ	Offline	Online	Total	(in ms) Total
SDitH	Fast	12 115	32	–	27	0.87	5.03	5.96	4.74
[FJR22]	Short	8 481	256	–	17	4.33	18.95	23.56	20.80
(Variant 3)	Shorter	6 784	2^{12}	–	12	59.24	251.14	313.70	244.30
	Shortest	5 689	2^{16}	–	9	–	–	–	–
Ours (Variant 3)	Fast	12 115	2	5	27	0.47	0.83	1.30	0.98
	Short	8 481	2	8	17	2.26	0.61	2.87	2.59
	Shorter	6 784	2	12	12	25.93	0.50	26.43	25.79
	Shortest	5 689	2	16	9	320.24	0.42	320.66	312.67

opcodes. For the same number of leaf shares, N for SDitH and N^D for our protocol, the performance of both signature schemes in the offline phase are more or less the same as the one in their implementation, which confirms our expectations, and highlights that both software implementations are equivalent in performance, the performance differences observed come from the protocol differences. Our online phase however is largely accelerated compared to the reference implementation, which confirms the expected $N^D \to N \cdot D$ algorithmic speedup. Again, we can verify that the gain is roughly $N \cdot D/N^D$ as we would expect from comparable implementations. In fact, our online costs are more-or-less constant for a given security level as they are in $N \cdot D \cdot \tau$ and the security is roughly in $\log_2 N \cdot D \cdot \tau$ (and N is constant). Besides being roughly constant, they are also very small, less than 1 ms, and can probably be further optimized.

Acknowledgements. We would like to thank Thibauld Feneuil, Antoine Joux, and Matthieu Rivain for their input and feedback on an earlier version of this paper, as well as dharing their source code with us. We also thank Adrien Guinet for his help on improving the performance of our implementation. We would also like to thank the anonymous reviewers of EUROCRYPT 2023 for their constructive feedback which helped improved the quality of the paper.

References

[AGS11] Aguilar, C., Gaborit, P., Schrek, J.: A new zero-knowledge code based identification scheme with reduced communication. In: 2011 IEEE Information Theory Workshop, pp. 648–652. IEEE (2011)

[AMGH+22] Aguilar-Melchor, C., Gama, N., Howe, J., Hülsing, A., Joseph, D., Yue, D.: The return of the SDitH. Cryptology ePrint Archive, Report 2022/1645 (2022). https://eprint.iacr.org/2022/1645

[Bea92] Beaver, D.: Efficient multiparty protocols using circuit randomization. In: Feigenbaum, J. (ed.) CRYPTO 1991. LNCS, vol. 576, pp. 420–432. Springer, Heidelberg (1992). https://doi.org/10.1007/3-540-46766-1_34

[BG22] Bidoux, L., Gaborit, P.: Compact post-quantum signatures from proofs of knowledge leveraging structure for the PKP, SD and RSD Problems (2022)

[BMT78] Berlekamp, E., McEliece, R., Tilborg, H.V.: On the inherent intractability of certain coding problems (corresp.) IEEE Trans. Inf. Theory **3**, 384–386 (1978)

[CVE11] Cayrel, P.-L., Véron, P., El Yousfi Alaoui, S.M.: A zero-knowledge identification scheme based on the q-ary syndrome decoding problem. In: Biryukov, A., Gong, G., Stinson, D.R. (eds.) SAC 2010. LNCS, vol. 6544, pp. 171–186. Springer, Heidelberg (2011). https://doi.org/10.1007/978-3-642-19574-7_12

[DGV+16] Dagdelen, Ö., Galindo, D., Véron, P., El Yousfi Alaoui, S.M., Cayrel, P.-L.: Extended security arguments for signature schemes. Designs Codes Crypt. **2**, 441–461 (2016)

[FJR21] Feneuil, T., Joux, A., Rivain, M.: Shared permutation for syndrome decoding: new zero-knowledge protocol and code-based signature. Cryptology ePrint Archive, Report 2021/1576 (2021). https://eprint.iacr.org/2021/1576

[FJR22] Feneuil, T., Joux, A., Rivain, M.: Syndrome decoding in the head: shorter signatures from zero-knowledge proofs. Cryptology ePrint Archive, Report 2022/188 (2022). https://eprint.iacr.org/2022/188

[FS09] Finiasz, M., Sendrier, N.: Security bounds for the design of code-based cryptosystems. In: Matsui, M. (ed.) ASIACRYPT 2009. LNCS, vol. 5912, pp. 88–105. Springer, Heidelberg (2009). https://doi.org/10.1007/978-3-642-10366-7_6

[FS87] Fiat, A., Shamir, A.: How to prove yourself: practical solutions to identification and signature problems. In: Odlyzko, A.M. (ed.) CRYPTO 1986. LNCS, vol. 263, pp. 186–194. Springer, Heidelberg (1987). https://doi.org/10.1007/3-540-47721-7_12

[GGM84] Goldreich, O., Goldwasser, S., Micali, S.: How to construct random functions (extended abstract). In: 25th FOCS, pp. 464–479. IEEE Computer Society Press (1984). https://doi.org/10.1109/SFCS.1984.715949

[GPS22] Gueron, S., Persichetti, E., Santini, P.: Designing a practical code-based signature scheme from zero-knowledge proofs with trusted setup. Cryptography **1**, 5 (2022)

[IKO+07] Ishai, Y., Kushilevitz, E., Ostrovsky, R., Sahai, A.: Zero-knowledge from secure multiparty computation. In: Johnson, D.S., Feige, U. (eds.) 39th ACM STOC, pp. 21–30. ACM Press (2007). https://doi.org/10.1145/1250790.1250794

[MMT11] May, A., Meurer, A., Thomae, E.: Decoding random linear codes in $\tilde{O}(2^{0.054n})$. In: Lee, D.H., Wang, X. (eds.) ASIACRYPT 2011. LNCS, vol. 7073, pp. 107–124. Springer, Heidelberg (2011). https://doi.org/10.1007/978-3-642-25385-0_6

[PS00] Pointcheval, D., Stern, J.: Security arguments for digital signatures and blind signatures. J. Cryptol. **3**, 361–396 (2000). https://doi.org/10.1007/s001450010003

[Ste94] Stern, J.: Designing identification schemes with keys of short size. In: Desmedt, Y.G. (ed.) CRYPTO 1994. LNCS, vol. 839, pp. 164–173. Springer, Heidelberg (1994). https://doi.org/10.1007/3-540-48658-5_18

[Vér97] Véron, P.: Improved identification schemes based on error-correcting codes. Appl. Algebra Eng. Commun. Comput. **1**, 57–69 (1997)

[ZCD+20] Zaverucha, G., et al.: Technical report, National Institute of Standards and Technology (2020). https://csrc.nist.gov/projects/post-quantum-cryptography/post-quantum-cryptography-standardization/round-3-submissions

Chopsticks: Fork-Free Two-Round Multi-signatures from Non-interactive Assumptions

Jiaxin Pan[1] and Benedikt Wagner[2,3(✉)]

[1] NTNU – Norwegian University of Science and Technology, Trondheim, Norway
jiaxin.pan@ntnu.no
[2] CISPA Helmholtz Center for Information Security, Saarbrücken, Germany
benedikt.wagner@cispa.de
[3] Saarland University, Saarbrücken, Germany

Abstract. Multi-signatures have been drawing lots of attention in recent years, due to their applications in cryptocurrencies. Most early constructions require three-round signing, and recent constructions have managed to reduce the round complexity to two. However, their security proofs are mostly based on non-standard, interactive assumptions (e.g. one-more assumptions) and come with a huge security loss, due to multiple uses of rewinding (aka the Forking Lemma). This renders the quantitative guarantees given by the security proof useless.

In this work, we improve the state of the art by proposing two efficient two-round multi-signature schemes from the (standard, non-interactive) Decisional Diffie-Hellman (DDH) assumption. Both schemes are proven secure in the random oracle model without rewinding. We do not require any pairing either. Our first scheme supports key aggregation but has a security loss linear in the number of signing queries, and our second scheme is the *first* tightly secure construction.

A key ingredient in our constructions is a new homomorphic dual-mode commitment scheme for group elements, that allows to equivocate for messages of a certain structure. The definition and efficient construction of this commitment scheme is of independent interest.

Keywords: Multi-Signatures · Tightness · Forking Lemma · Commitment Scheme · Round Complexity

1 Introduction

A multi-signature scheme [5,24] allows N parties to jointly sign a message, where each party i holds an independent key pair $(\mathsf{pk}_i, \mathsf{sk}_i)$. Recently, multi-signature

J. Pan—Supported by the Research Council of Norway under Project No. 324235.

C. Hazay and M. Stam (Eds.): EUROCRYPT 2023, LNCS 14008, pp. 597–627, 2023.
https://doi.org/10.1007/978-3-031-30589-4_21

schemes have been drawing new attention due to their applications in cryptocurrencies. In this setting, multiple parties share ownership of funds, and can use multi-signatures to sign transactions spending these funds. For details, we refer to [8]. A trivial construction is that each signer i computes a signature σ_i using sk_i, and the final signature is $(\sigma_1, \ldots, \sigma_N)$. Yet, this trivial approach leads to large signature size. Motivated by this, cryptographers are proposing more sophisticated multi-signature schemes with interactive signing protocols to compress the signature size. In this work, we focus on concrete security of two-round multi-signature schemes.

Security Models. There are different models in which multi-signatures have been proposed and analyzed. Namely, schemes may require interactive key generation [31], or require that keys are verified and include a proof of possesion of the secret key [11,14]. Other schemes require to use a knowledge of secret key assumption [7,29]. Besides these models, the widely accepted model for multi-signatures nowadays is the so called *plain public key model*, introduced by Bellare and Neven in their seminal work [5]. In this model, each signer generates her key pair independently, and no knowledge assumption or proof of possession is needed. In this paper, we are interested in the plain public key model.

Concrete Security and Tightness. Cryptographic schemes are proven secure using reductions. To prove security of a scheme S, we transform any adversary $\mathcal{A}_\mathsf{S}$ against the security of S with success probability ϵ_S into a solver $\mathcal{A}_\Pi$ for some underlying hard problem Π with success probability ϵ_Π. Thereby, we establish a bound $\epsilon_\mathsf{S} \leq L \cdot \epsilon_\Pi$. We call L the *security loss*. Ideally, we want the underlying hardness assumption to be as standard as possible, since a more standard assumption gives us more confidence on the scheme's security. We also want the security loss as small as possible, since it relates the concrete security of our scheme to the hardness of the underlying computational problem. This is reflected when we use the security proof as a quantitative statement to derive concrete parameters for scheme S based on cryptanalytic results for the well-studied problem Π. Roughly speaking, to get κ bits of security for S, we have to guarantee $\kappa + \log L$ bits of security for Π. If L is large, or depends on choices of the adversary unknown at deployment time, instantiating the scheme in this way leads to prohibitively large parameters, or is not even possible. This motivates striving for a *tight reduction*, i.e. a reduction where L is a small constant. Tightness has been studied for many primitives, including standard digital signatures and related primitives, e.g., [6,22,26,28]. Unfortunately, most of existing multi-signature schemes are non-tight. Even worse, existing two-round multi-signature schemes have only non-tight reductions based on strong, non-standard assumptions.

Limitations of Existing Constructions. An overview of existing schemes (based on assumptions in cyclic groups) and their properties and security loss can be found in Table 1. In the plain public key model, Bellare and Neven [5] constructed a three-round multi-signature scheme (BN) based on the Discrete Logarithm

Assumption (DLOG). Proving the security of this scheme relies on rewinding and uses the (general) Forking Lemma [5], which leads to a highly non-tight security bound. To improve this, Bellare and Neven introduced a second three-round construction (BN+) tightly based on the Decisional Diffie-Hellman (DDH) Assumption. Further works focus on key aggregation [8,16,30]. This feature allows to publicly compute a single aggregated key from a given list of public keys, which can later be used for verification. The key aggregation property saves bandwidth and is desirable in many applications. Notably, the three-round scheme Musig [8,30] can be seen as a variant of BN that supports key aggregation. The scheme is based on DLOG and a double forking technique is introduced for its analysis. This leads to a security bound of the form $\epsilon_S^4 \leq L \cdot \epsilon_\Pi$, which is useless in terms of concrete security. Using the Decisional Diffie-Hellman (DDH) assumption, a tightly secure variant Musig+ of Musig has been proposed in [16].

To further reduce round complexity, recent works focused on two-round constructions [2,4,11,13,32]. However, while achieving certain desirable properties (e.g. deterministic signing [33]) the proposed schemes have their drawbacks in terms of assumptions and concrete security. The scheme [33] makes use of heavy cryptographic machinery and is not comparable with others in terms of efficiency. Further, even in the more idealized models such as the algebraic group model, security proofs of most two-round schemes rely on non-standard interactive assumptions [2,4,11,32]. The only exceptions are [4,9,13]. A second drawback is the apparent need for (double) rewinding in the random oracle model [4,9,13,14,32]. While such security proofs show the absence of major structural attacks, concrete parameters are not supported by cryptanalytic evidence.

Our Goal. Motivated by the state of the art, we study whether interactive assumptions and rewinding techniques are necessary for two-round multi-signatures. If not, we want to construct a scheme without either of them. Ideally, our scheme comes with additional features such as key aggregation or a fully tight security proof. We summarize our central question as follows, which is of both practical and theoretical interest.

Can we construct two-round multi-signatures
from non-interactive pairing-free assumptions without the use of rewinding?

1.1 Our Contribution

Our work answers the above question in the affirmative. Our contributions are the *first* two multi-signature schemes that are two-round from a non-interactive assumption without using the Forking Lemma. Both of our schemes are proven secure in the random oracle model based on the DDH assumption. Concretely, we construct

1. a two-round multi-signature scheme with a security loss $O(Q_S)$ and key aggregation, where Q_S is the number of signing queries, and
2. the first two-round multi-signature scheme with a fully tight security proof

We compare our schemes with existing schemes in Table 1[1]. For roughly 128 bit security, our second scheme can be instantiated with standardized 128 bit secure curves, in contrast to all previous two-round schemes. For our first scheme, its proof is non-tight, but it does not rely on rewinding and has tighter security based on standard, non-interactive assumptions than other non-tight schemes (such as HBMS and Musig2). Hence, as long as the number of signing queries Q_S is less than $2^{192-128} = 2^{64}$, we can implement our first scheme with a standardized 192-bit secure curve to achieve 128-bit security, while this is not the case for HBMS and Musig2. We note that our schemes do not have some additional beneficial properties (e.g. having Schnorr-compatible signatures or supporting preprocessing) as in Musig2 [32]. We leave achieving these properties without rewinding as an interesting open problem.

Table 1. Comparison of existing multi-signature schemes (top) in the random oracle model with our schemes (bottom). Here, Q_H, Q_S denote the number of random oracle and signing queries, respectively, ϵ denotes the advantage of an adversary against the scheme. The algebraic one-more discrete logarithm (AOMDL) assumption is a (stronger) interactive variant of DLOG.

Scheme	Assumption	Rounds	Key Aggregation	Loss
BN [5]	DLOG	3	✗	$O(Q_H/\epsilon)$
BN+ [5]	DDH	3	✗	$O(1)$
Musig [8,30]	DLOG	3	✓	$O(Q_H^3/\epsilon^3)$
Musig+ [16]	DDH	3	✓	$O(1)$
Musig2 [32]	AOMDL	2	✓	$O(Q_H^3/\epsilon^3)$
HBMS [4]	DLOG	2	✓	$O(Q_S^4 Q_H^3/\epsilon^3)$
Ours (Sect. 3.2)	DDH	2	✓	$O(Q_S)$
Ours (Sect. 3.3)	DDH	2	✗	$O(1)$

A crucial building block for our construction is a special kind of DDH-based commitment scheme without pairings. Concretely, our commitment scheme has the following properties.

- It commits to pairs of group elements in a homomorphic way.
- It has a dual-mode property, i.e. indistinguishable keys in statistically hiding and statistically binding mode, with tight multi-key indistinguishability.
- The hiding mode offers a special form of equivocation trapdoor, which allows to open commitments to group elements output by the Honest-Verifier Zero-Knowledge (HVZK) simulator of Schnorr-like identification protocols.

Such a commitment scheme can be useful to construct other interactive signature variants, and we believe that this is of independent interest. In this paper,

---
[1] We do not consider proofs in the (idealized) algebraic group model and do not list schemes that are not in the plain public key model.

we construct the first commitment scheme satisfying the above properties simultaneously without using pairings. Our commitment scheme can be seen as an extension of the commitment scheme in [3][2]. Contrary to our scheme, the commitment scheme in [3] commits to single group elements and no statistically binding mode is shown, which makes it less desirable for our multi-signature constructions. Other previous commitment schemes either have no trapdoor property [19,20], or homomorphically commit to ring or field elements [21,35]. To the best of our knowledge, there is only a solution using pairings [18].

1.2 Concurrent Work

In a concurrent work (also at Eurocrypt 2023), Tessaro and Zhu [37] also presented (among other contributions) a new two-round multi-signature scheme. Both our work and theirs focus on avoiding interactive assumptions. However, while we additionally remove the security loss, Tessaro and Zhu concentrate on having a partially non-interactive scheme. That is, the first round of the signing protocol is independent of the message being signed. In a nutshell, they generalize Musig2 to linear function families. Then, under a suitable instantiation, the interactive assumption for Musig2 can be avoided. Similar to Musig2, the resulting scheme is partially non-interactive. Still, their scheme inherits the security loss of Musig2 due to (double) rewinding.

1.3 Technical Overview

We give an intuitive overview of our constructions and the challenges we solve.

Schnorr-Based Multi-Signatures. We start by recalling the basic template for multi-signatures based on the Schnorr identification scheme [36]. Let $\mathbb{G}$ be a group of prime order p with generator g. We explain the template using the vector space homomorphism $\mathsf{F} : x \mapsto g^x$ mapping from $\mathbb{Z}_p$ to $\mathbb{G}$, and write both domain and range additively. In a first approach to get a multi-signature scheme, we let each signer i with secret key sk_i sample a random $r_i \in \mathbb{Z}_p$, and send $R_i := \mathsf{F}(r_i)$ to all other signers. Then, an aggregated R is computed as $R = \sum_i R_i$. From this R, signers derive challenges c_i using a random oracle. Then, each signer computes a response $s_i = c_i \mathsf{sk}_i + r_i$ and sends this response. Finally, the signature contains R and the aggregated response $s = \sum_i s_i$. Verification is very similar to the verification of Schnorr signatures. As each signer in this simple two-round scheme is almost identical to the prover algorithm of the Schnorr identification scheme, one may hope that this scheme is secure. However, early works already noted that it is not [5].

While there are concrete attacks against the scheme, for our purposes it is more important to understand where the security proof fails. The proof fails when we try to simulate honest signer without knowing its secret key sk_1. Following

---

[2] Drijvers et al. [14] showed a flaw in the proof of the multi-signature scheme presented in [3], but it does not affect their commitment scheme.

Schnorr signatures and identification, this would be done by sampling $R_1 :=$ $F(s_1) - c_1 pk_1$ for random c_1 an s_1, and then programming the random oracle accordingly at position R. The problem in the multi-signature setting is that we first have to output R_1, and then the adversary can output the remaining R_i, such that he has full control over the aggregate R. Thus, the random oracle may already be defined. Previous works [5, 8, 30] solve this issue by introducing an additional round, in which all signers commit to their R_i using a random oracle. This allows us to extract all R_i from these commitments in the reduction, and therefore R has enough entropy to program the random oracle.

A second problem that we encounter in the above approach is the extraction of a solution from the forgery. Namely, to extract a discrete logarithm of pk_1, we need to rely on rewinding. Some of the well-known schemes [8, 30] even use rewinding multiple times. This leads to security bounds with essentially no useful quantitative guarantee for concrete security.

Towards a Scheme without Rewinding. To avoid rewinding, our first idea is to rely on a different homomorphism F. Namely, we borrow techniques from lossy identification [1, 26, 27] and use $F : x \mapsto (g^x, h^x)$ for a second generator $h \in \mathbb{G}$. We can then give a non-rewinding security proof for the three-round schemes in [5, 8, 30]. Concretely, we first switch pk_1 from the range of F to a random element in $\mathbb{G}^2$, using the DDH assumption. Then, we can argue that a forgery is hard to compute using a statistical argument. We note that this idea is (implicitly) already present in [5, 16]. As we will see, combining it with techniques to avoid the extra round is challenging.

Towards Two-Round Schemes. To go from a three-round scheme as above to a two-round scheme, our goal is to avoid the first round. Recall that this round was needed to simulate R_1 using random oracle programming. Our idea to tackle the simulation problem is a bit different. Namely, going back to the (insecure) two-round scheme, our goal is to send R_1 *after* we learn c_1. If we manage to do that, we can simulate by setting it as $R_1 := F(s_1) - c_1 pk_1$ for random s_1. Of course, just sending R_1 after learning c_1 should only be possible for the reduction. Following Damgård [12], this high-level strategy can be implemented using a trapdoor commitment scheme Com, and sending $com_1 = \text{Com}(ck, R_1)$ as the first message. The challenges c_i are then derived from an aggregated commitment com using the random oracle. Later, the reduction can open this commitment to $F(s_1) - c_1 pk_1$ using the trapdoor for commitment key ck. To support aggregation, the commitment scheme should have homomorphic properties. Note that this approach has been used in the lattice setting in a recent work [13]. However, implementing such a commitment scheme for (pairs of) group elements is highly non-trivial, as we will see. Also, as already pointed out in [13], it is hard to make this two-round approach work while avoiding rewinding at the same time. The reason is that a trapdoor commitment scheme can not be statistically binding. But if we want to make use of the statistical argument from lossy identification discussed above, we need that R is fixed before the c_i are sampled, which requires statistical binding. With a computationally binding commitment scheme, we end up in a rewinding reduction (to binding) again. Our first technical main contribution is to overcome this issue.

Chopstick One: Our Scheme Without Rewinding. Our idea to overcome the above problem is to demand a dual-mode property from the commitment scheme Com. Namely, there should be an indistinguishable second way to set up the commitment key ck, such that for such a key the scheme is statistically binding. This does not solve the problem yet, because we require ck to be in trapdoor mode for simulation, and in binding mode for the final forgery. The solution is to sample ck in a message-dependent way using another random oracle, which is (for other reasons) already done in earlier works [13,14]. In this way, we can embed a binding commitment key in some randomly guessed random oracle queries, and a trapdoor key in others. Note that this requires a tight multi-key indistinguishability of the commitment scheme. Assuming we have such a commitment scheme, we end up with our first construction, which is presented formally in Sect. 3.2. Of course, this strategy still has a security loss linear in the number of signing queries due to the guessing argument, but it avoids rewinding, leading to an acceptable security bound. In addition, we can implement the approach in a way that supports key aggregation.

Chopstick Two: Our Fully Tight Scheme. The security loss in our first scheme results from partitioning random oracle queries into two classes, namely queries returning binding keys, and queries returning trapdoor keys. To do such a partitioning in a tight way, we may try to use a Katz-Wang random bit approach [17]. This simple approach can be used in standard digital signatures. However, it turns out that it does not work for our case. To see this, recall that following this approach, we would compute two message-dependent commitment keys

$$\mathsf{ck}_0 := \mathsf{H}(0, \mathsf{m}), \quad \mathsf{ck}_1 := \mathsf{H}(1, \mathsf{m}).$$

Then, for each message, we would embed a binding key in one branch, and a trapdoor key in the other branch, e.g. ck_0 binding and ck_1 with trapdoor. In the signing protocol, we would abort one of the branches pseudorandomly based on the message. Then we could use the trapdoor branch in the signing, and hope that the forgery uses the binding branch. However, this strategy crucially relies on the fact that the aborting happens in a way that is pseudorandom to the adversary. Otherwise the adversary could always choose the trapdoor branch for his forgery. While we can implement this in a signature scheme, in our multi-signature scheme this fails, because all signers must use the *same commitment key* to make aggregation possible. At the same time, the aborted branch must depend on secret data of the simulated signer to remain pseudorandom.

To solve this problem, we observe that the above approach uses a pseudorandom "branch selection" and aborts the other branch. Our solution can be phrased as a pseudorandom "branch-to-key matching". Namely, we give each signer two public keys $(\mathsf{pk}_{i,0}, \mathsf{pk}_{i,1})$. The signing protocol is run in two instances in parallel. One instance uses ck_0, and one uses ck_1 as above. More precisely, we commit to R_0 via ck_0 and to R_1 via ck_1. Then we aggregate and determine the challenges $c_{i,0}$ and $c_{i,1}$. However, before sending the response $s_i = (s_{i,0}, s_{i,1})$, *each signer separately* determines which key to use in which instance, i.e. it computes

$$s_{i,0} = c_{i,0} \cdot x_{i,b_i} + r_{i,0}, \quad s_{i,1} = c_{i,1} \cdot x_{i,1-b_i} + r_{i,1},$$

where b_i is a pseudorandom bit that each signer i computes *independently*, and that will be included in the final signature to make verification possible. This decouples the public key that is used from the commitment key that is used. Now we are ready to discuss the implication of this change. Namely, our reduction chooses $\mathsf{pk}_{1,0}$ honestly and $\mathsf{pk}_{1,1}$ as a lossy key, i.e. random instead of in the range of F. Then, in each signing interaction, the reduction can match the honest public key with the binding commitment key and the lossy public key with the trapdoor commitment key by setting b_1 accordingly. In this way, we can simulate one branch using the actual secret key, and the other branch using the commitment trapdoor. For the forgery, we hope that the matching is the other way around, such that binding commitment key and lossy public key match, which makes the statistical argument from lossy identification possible. Overall, this approach leads to our fully tight scheme, presented in Sect. 3.3.

The Challenge of Instantiating the Commitment. One may observe that we shifted a lot of the challenges that we encountered into properties of the underlying commitment scheme. This naturally raises the question if such a commitment scheme can be found. In fact, constructing this commitment scheme can be understood as our second technical main contribution.

Let us first explain why it is non-trivial to construct such a scheme. The main barrier results from the algebraic structure that we demand. Namely, we need to commit to group elements[3] $R \in \mathbb{G}$. A naive idea would be to use any trapdoor commitment scheme, e.g. Pedersen commitments, by first encoding R in the appropriate message space. However, this would destroy all homomorphic properties that we need, and we should not forget that we need a dual-mode property. This brings us to Groth-Sahai commitments [20], which can commit to group elements. Indeed, these commitments are homomorphic, and have (indistinguishable from) random keys, such that we can sample them using a random oracle. They are also dual-mode based on DDH, which allows us to use the random self-reducibility of DDH to show tight multi-key indistinguishability. However, the trapdoor property turns out to be the main challenge. To see why this is problematic, note that the opening information of these commitments typically contains elements from $\mathbb{Z}_p$ that are somehow used as exponents. There are exceptions to this rule, like [18], but they use pairings and the DLIN assumption, which we aim to avoid. This means that the trapdoor should allow us to sample exponents, given a group element R to which we want to open the commitment. This naturally corresponds to having a trapdoor for the discrete logarithm problem, which we do not have.

---

[3] In the actual construction, we need to commit to pairs of group elements, but we consider the simpler setting of one group element in this overview.

Our Solution: Weakly Equivocable Commitments. Our starting point is the commitment scheme for group elements given in [20]. Namely, commitment keys correspond to matrices $\boldsymbol{A} = (A_{i,j})_{i,j} \in \mathbb{G}^{2\times2}$, and to commit to a message $R = g^r \in \mathbb{G}$ with randomness $(\alpha, \beta) \in \mathbb{Z}_p$, one computes

$$\mathsf{com} := (C_0, C_1)^t := \left(A_{1,1}^\alpha \cdot A_{1,2}^\beta, R \cdot A_{2,1}^\alpha \cdot A_{2,2}^\beta \right)^t.$$

That is, setting $\boldsymbol{E} = (E_{i,j})_{i,j} \in \mathbb{Z}_p$ such that $g^{E_{i,j}} = A_{i,j}$, we can write the discrete logarithm of com as $(0, r)^t + \boldsymbol{E} \cdot (\alpha, \beta)^t$. In binding mode, matrix $\boldsymbol{E}$ is a matrix of rank 1, while $\boldsymbol{E}$ has full rank in hiding mode. It is easy to see that this commitment scheme to group elements is homomorphic. However, we stress that there is no simple solution to implement a trapdoor for equivocation. To see this, note that if we want to open a commitment com to a message $R' \in \mathbb{G}$, we need to output a suitable tuple (α, β). If we knew the discrete logarithm of com, then we still would need to know the discrete logarithm of R' to find such a tuple. The key insight of our trapdoor construction is that we do not need to be able to open com to any message R'. Instead, it will be sufficient if we can open it to messages of the form $R' = g^s \cdot \mathsf{pk}^c$, where we do not know c when we fix the commitment com, but *we know* pk *when setting up* $\boldsymbol{A}$. To explain why this helps, assume we want to find a valid opening (α, β) in this case. Then we need to satisfy

$$\mathsf{com} = \binom{C_0}{C_1} = \binom{0}{g^s \mathsf{pk}^c} \cdot g^{\boldsymbol{E} \cdot (\alpha, \beta)^t}.$$

It seems like we did not make progress, because even if we know the discrete logarithms of C_0, C_1, the term pk^c is not known in the exponent. Now, our key idea to solve this is to write and generate $\boldsymbol{A}$ with respect to basis pk in the second row. Namely, we generate $\boldsymbol{A}$ as

$$\boldsymbol{A} = \begin{pmatrix} A_{1,1} & A_{1,2} \\ A_{2,1} & A_{2,2} \end{pmatrix} := \begin{pmatrix} g^{d_{1,1}} & g^{d_{1,2}} \\ \mathsf{pk}^{d_{2,1}} & \mathsf{pk}^{d_{2,2}} \end{pmatrix}.$$

In this way, the equation that we need to satisfy becomes

$$\binom{C_0}{C_1} = \binom{g^{d_{1,1}\alpha + d_{1,2}\beta}}{g^s \mathsf{pk}^{c + d_{2,1}\alpha + d_{2,2}\beta}}.$$

Next, we get rid of the term g^s by shifting C_1 accordingly. Namely, recall that we can sample s at random long before we learn c. Setting $C_0 = g^\tau$ and $C_1 = g^s \mathsf{pk}^\rho$ for random τ, ρ, we obtain the equation

$$\binom{g^\tau}{\mathsf{pk}^\rho} = \binom{g^{d_{1,1}\alpha + d_{1,2}\beta}}{\mathsf{pk}^{c + d_{2,1}\alpha + d_{2,2}\beta}}.$$

Given the trapdoor $\boldsymbol{D} = (d_{i,j})_{i,j}$, this can easily be solved for (α, β) by solving $(\tau, \rho - c)^t = \boldsymbol{D} \cdot (\alpha, \beta)^t$. We are confident that such a weak and structured equivocation property can be used in other applications as well, and formally define this type of commitment scheme in Sect. 3.1.

2   Preliminaries

We denote the security parameter by $\lambda \in \mathbb{N}$, and all algorithms get 1^λ implicitly as input. We write $x \xleftarrow{\$} S$ if x is sampled uniformly at random from a finite set S, and we write $x \leftarrow \mathcal{D}$ if x is sampled according to a distribution $\mathcal{D}$. We write $y \leftarrow \mathcal{A}(x)$, if y is output from (probabilistic) algorithm $\mathcal{A}$ on input x with uniform coins. To make the coins explicit, we use the notation $y = \mathcal{A}(x; \rho)$. The notation $y \in \mathcal{A}(x)$ indicates that y is a possible output of $\mathcal{A}(x)$. We use standard asymptotic notation, and the notions of negligible functions, and PPT algorithms. If $\mathbf{G}$ is a security game, we write $\mathbf{G} \Rightarrow b$ to state that $\mathbf{G}$ outputs b. In all our games, numerical variables are implicitly initialized with 0, and lists and sets are initialized with $\emptyset$. We define $[K] := \{1, \dots, K\}$, and denote the Bernoulli distribution with parameter $\gamma \in [0, 1]$ by $\mathcal{B}_\gamma$.

Multi-signatures. We introduce syntax and security for multi-signatures, following the established security notions in the plain public key model [5]. We will assume that there is an canonical ordering of given multi-sets, e.g. lexicographically, that allows us to uniquely encode multi-sets $\mathcal{P} = \{\mathsf{pk}_1, \dots, \mathsf{pk}_N\}$. For this encoding, we write $\langle \mathcal{P} \rangle$ throughout the paper. Further, for simplicity of notation, we assume that the honest public key in our security definition is the entry pk_1 in this multi-set.

Alg $\mathsf{MS.Exec}(\mathcal{P}, \mathcal{S}, \mathsf{m})$
01 **let** $\mathcal{P} = \{\mathsf{pk}_1, \dots, \mathsf{pk}_N\}$, $\mathcal{S} = \{\mathsf{sk}_1, \dots, \mathsf{sk}_N\}$
02 **for** $i \in [N] : (\mathsf{pm}_{1,i}, St_{1,i}) \leftarrow \mathsf{Sig}_0(\mathcal{P}, \mathsf{sk}, \mathsf{m})$
03 $\mathcal{M}_1 := (\mathsf{pm}_{1,1}, \dots, \mathsf{pm}_{1,N})$
04 **for** $i \in [N] : (\mathsf{pm}_{2,i}, St_{2,i}) \leftarrow \mathsf{Sig}_1(St_{1,i}, \mathcal{M}_1)$
05 $\mathcal{M}_2 := (\mathsf{pm}_{2,1}, \dots, \mathsf{pm}_{2,N})$
06 **for** $i \in [N] : \sigma_i \leftarrow \mathsf{Sig}_2(St_{2,i}, \mathcal{M}_2)$
07 **if** $\exists i \neq j \in [N]$ s.t. $\sigma_i \neq \sigma_j : \textbf{return } \bot$
08 **return** $\sigma := \sigma_1$

Fig. 1. The algorithm $\mathsf{MS.Exec}$ for a (two-round) multi-signature scheme $\mathsf{MS} = (\mathsf{Setup}, \mathsf{Gen}, \mathsf{Sig}, \mathsf{Ver})$, representing an honest execution of the signing protocol Sig.

Definition 1 (Multi-signature Scheme). *A (two-round) multi-signature scheme is a tuple of PPT algorithms* $\mathsf{MS} = (\mathsf{Setup}, \mathsf{Gen}, \mathsf{Sig}, \mathsf{Ver})$ *with the following syntax:*

- $\mathsf{Setup}(1^\lambda) \to \mathsf{par}$ *takes as input the security parameter 1^λ and outputs global system parameters* par. *We assume that* par *implicitly defines sets of public keys, secret keys, messages and signatures, respectively. All algorithms related to* SIG *take at least implicitly* par *as input.*
- $\mathsf{Gen}(\mathsf{par}) \to (\mathsf{pk}, \mathsf{sk})$ *takes as input system parameters* par, *and outputs a public key* pk *and a secret key* sk.

- Sig = $(\text{Sig}_0, \text{Sig}_1, \text{Sig}_2)$ *is split into three algorithms:*
  - $\text{Sig}_0(\mathcal{P}, \text{sk}, \text{m}) \rightarrow (\text{pm}_1, St_1)$ *takes as input a multi-set* $\mathcal{P} = \{\text{pk}_1, \ldots, \text{pk}_N\}$ *of public keys, a secret key* sk*, and a message* m*, and outputs a protocol message* pm_1 *and a state* St_1*.*
  - $\text{Sig}_1(St_1, \mathcal{M}_1) \rightarrow (\text{pm}_2, St_2)$ *takes as input a state* St_1 *and a tuple* $\mathcal{M}_1 = (\text{pm}_{1,1}, \ldots, \text{pm}_{1,N})$ *of protocol messages, and outputs a protocol message* pm_2 *and a state* St_2*.*
  - $\text{Sig}_2(St_2, \mathcal{M}_2) \rightarrow \sigma_i$ *takes as input a state* St_2 *and a tuple* $\mathcal{M}_2 = (\text{pm}_{2,1}, \ldots, \text{pm}_{2,N})$ *of protocol messages, and outputs a signature* σ*.*
- $\text{Ver}(\mathcal{P}, \text{m}, \sigma) \rightarrow b$ *is deterministic, takes as input a multi-set* $\mathcal{P} = \{\text{pk}_1, \ldots, \text{pk}_N\}$ *of public keys, a message* m*, and a signature* σ*, and outputs a bit* $b \in \{0, 1\}$*.*

We require that MS *is complete, i.e. for all* $\text{par} \in \text{Setup}(1^\lambda)$*, all* $N = \text{poly}(\lambda)$*, all* $(\text{pk}_j, \text{sk}_j) \in \text{Gen}(\text{par})$ *for* $j \in [N]$*, and all messages* m*, we have*

$$\Pr\left[\text{Ver}(\mathcal{P}, \text{m}, \sigma) = 1 \;\middle|\; \begin{array}{l} \mathcal{P} = \{\text{pk}_1, \ldots, \text{pk}_N\}, \mathcal{S} = \{\text{sk}_1, \ldots, \text{sk}_N\}, \\ \sigma \leftarrow \text{MS.Exec}(\mathcal{P}, \mathcal{S}, \text{m}) \end{array}\right] = 1,$$

where algorithm MS.Exec *is defined in Fig. 1.*

Definition 2 (Key Aggregation). *A multi-signature scheme* MS = (Setup, Gen, Sig, Ver) *is said to support key aggregation, if the algorithm* Ver *can be split into two deterministic polynomial time algorithms* Agg, VerAgg *with the following syntax:*

- $\text{Agg}(\mathcal{P}) \rightarrow \tilde{\text{pk}}$ *takes as input a multi-set* $\mathcal{P} = \{\text{pk}_1, \ldots, \text{pk}_N\}$ *of public keys and outputs an aggregated key* $\tilde{\text{pk}}$*.*
- $\text{VerAgg}(\tilde{\text{pk}}, \text{m}, \sigma) \rightarrow b$ *is deterministic, takes as input an aggregated key* $\tilde{\text{pk}}$*, a message* m*, and a signature* σ*, and outputs a bit* $b \in \{0, 1\}$*.*

Precisely, algorithm $\text{Ver}(\mathcal{P}, \text{m}, \sigma)$ *can be written as* $\text{VerAgg}(\text{Agg}(\mathcal{P}), \text{m}, \sigma)$*.*

Definition 3 (MS-EUF-CMASecurity). *Let* MS = (Setup, Gen, Sig, Ver) *be a multi-signature scheme and consider the game* **MS-EUF-CMA** *defined in Fig. 2. We say that* MS *is* MS-EUF-CMA*secure, if for all PPT adversaries* $\mathcal{A}$*, the following advantage is negligible:*

$$\text{Adv}_{\mathcal{A}, \text{MS}}^{\text{MS-EUF-CMA}}(\lambda) := \Pr\left[\textbf{MS-EUF-CMA}_{\text{MS}}^{\mathcal{A}}(\lambda) \Rightarrow 1\right].$$

Linear Function Families. To present our constructions in a modular way, we make use of the abstraction of linear function families. Our definition is close to previous definitions [10,23,25]. As it is not needed for our instantiations, we restrict our setting to vector spaces instead of pseudo modules.

Definition 4 (Linear Function Family). *A linear function family (LFF) is a tuple of PPT algorithms* LF = (Gen, F) *with the following syntax:*

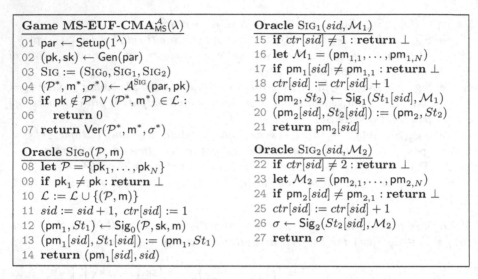

Fig. 2. The game **MS-EUF-CMA** for a (two-round) multi-signature scheme MS and an adversary $\mathcal{A}$. For simplicity of exposition, we assume that the canonical ordering of multi-sets is chosen such that pk is always at the first position if it is included.

- Gen(1^λ) $\to$ par *takes as input the security parameter* 1^λ *and outputs parameters* par. *We assume that* par *implicitly defines the following sets:*
  - *A set of scalars* $\mathcal{S}_{\mathsf{par}}$, *which forms a field.*
  - *A domain* $\mathcal{D}_{\mathsf{par}}$, *which forms a vector space over* $\mathcal{S}_{\mathsf{par}}$.
  - *A range* $\mathcal{R}_{\mathsf{par}}$, *which forms vector space over* $\mathcal{S}_{\mathsf{par}}$.
  We omit the subscript par *if it is clear from the context, and naturally denote the operations of these fields and vector spaces by* $+$ *and* $\cdot$.
- F(par, x) $\to$ X *is deterministic, takes as input parameters* par, *an element* $x \in \mathcal{D}$, *and outputs an element* $X \in \mathcal{R}$. *For all parameters* par, F(par, $\cdot$) *realizes a homomorphism, i.e.*

$$\forall s \in \mathcal{S}, x, y \in \mathcal{D} : \quad \mathsf{F}(\mathsf{par}, s \cdot x + y) = s \cdot \mathsf{F}(\mathsf{par}, x) + \mathsf{F}(\mathsf{par}, y).$$

We omit the input par *if it is clear from the context.*

We formalize necessary conditions under which a linear function family can be used to construct so called lossy identification [1]. Our constructions will rely on such linear function families. We also give a similar definition that captures a similar property in the context of key aggregation.

Definition 5 (Lossiness Admitting LFF). *We say that a linear function family* LF = (Gen, F) *is* ε_l-*lossiness admitting, if the following properties hold:*

- **Key Indistinguishability.** *For any PPT algorithm* $\mathcal{A}$, *the following advantage is negligible:*

$$\mathsf{Adv}^{\mathsf{keydist}}_{\mathcal{A},\mathsf{LF}}(\lambda) := |\Pr\left[\mathcal{A}(\mathsf{par}, X) = 1 \,\big|\, \mathsf{par} \leftarrow \mathsf{Gen}(1^\lambda), \ x \xleftarrow{\$} \mathcal{D}, \ X := \mathsf{F}(x)\right]$$
$$- \Pr\left[\mathcal{A}(\mathsf{par}, X) = 1 \,\big|\, \mathsf{par} \leftarrow \mathsf{Gen}(1^\lambda), \ X \xleftarrow{\$} \mathcal{R}\right]|.$$

- **Lossy Soundness.** *For any unbounded algorithm $\mathcal{A}$, the following probability is at most ε_l:*

$$\Pr\left[F(s) - c \cdot X = R \; \middle| \; \begin{array}{l} \mathsf{par} \leftarrow \mathsf{Gen}(1^\lambda), \; X \xleftarrow{\$} \mathcal{R}, \\ (St, R) \leftarrow \mathcal{A}(\mathsf{par}, X), \\ c \xleftarrow{\$} \mathcal{S}, \; s \leftarrow \mathcal{A}(St, c) \end{array}\right].$$

Definition 6 (Aggregation Lossy Soundness). *We say that a linear function family* $\mathsf{LF} = (\mathsf{Gen}, \mathsf{F})$ *satisfies* ε_al-*aggregation lossy soundness, if for any unbounded algorithm $\mathcal{A}$, the following probability is at most ε_al:*

$$\Pr\left[F(s) - c \cdot \sum_{i=1}^{N} a_i X_i = R \; \middle| \; \begin{array}{l} \mathsf{par} \leftarrow \mathsf{Gen}(1^\lambda), \; X_1 \xleftarrow{\$} \mathcal{R}, \\ (St, (X_2, a_2), \ldots, (X_N, a_N)) \leftarrow \mathcal{A}(\mathsf{par}, X_1), \\ a_1 \xleftarrow{\$} \mathcal{S}, \; (St', R) \leftarrow \mathcal{A}(St, a_1), \\ c \xleftarrow{\$} \mathcal{S}, \; s \leftarrow \mathcal{A}(St', c) \end{array}\right].$$

Assumptions. We recall the computational assumptions that we need.

Definition 7 (DDH Assumption). *Let* GGen *be an algorithm that on input 1^λ outputs the description of a prime order group $\mathbb{G}$ of order p with generator g. We say that the DDH assumption holds relative to GGen, if for all PPT algorithms $\mathcal{A}$, the following advantage is negligible:*

$$\mathsf{Adv}^{\mathsf{DDH}}_{\mathcal{A},\mathsf{GGen}}(\lambda) := |\Pr\left[\mathcal{A}(\mathbb{G}, p, g, h, g^a, h^a) = 1 \; \middle| \; \begin{array}{l} (\mathbb{G}, g, p) \leftarrow \mathsf{GGen}(1^\lambda), \\ h \xleftarrow{\$} \mathbb{G}, a \xleftarrow{\$} \mathbb{Z}_p \end{array}\right]$$

$$- \Pr\left[\mathcal{A}(\mathbb{G}, p, g, h, g^a, g^b) = 1 \; \middle| \; \begin{array}{l} (\mathbb{G}, g, p) \leftarrow \mathsf{GGen}(1^\lambda), \\ h \xleftarrow{\$} \mathbb{G}, a, b \xleftarrow{\$} \mathbb{Z}_p \end{array}\right]|.$$

In the following, we define an equivalent variant of the DDH assumption, uDDH3. uDDH3 is the 2-fold $\mathcal{U}_{3,1}$-Matrix-DDH (MDDH) assumption (with terminology in [15]). By its random self-reducibility [15, Lemma 1], the 2-fold $\mathcal{U}_{3,1}$-Matrix-DDH (MDDH) assumption (namely, the uDDH3 assumption) is tightly equivalent to the $\mathcal{U}_{3,1}$-MDDH assumption. By Lemma 1 in [28], $\mathcal{U}_{3,1}$-MDDH is tightly equivalent to $\mathcal{U}_1$-MDDH that is the DDH assumption. Hence, the DDH and uDDH3 assumptions are tightly equivalent.

Definition 8 (uDDH3 Assumption). *Let* GGen *be an algorithm that on input 1^λ outputs the description of a prime order group $\mathbb{G}$ of order p with generator g. We say that the uDDH3 assumption holds relative to GGen, if for all PPT algorithms $\mathcal{A}$, the following advantage is negligible:*

$$\mathsf{Adv}^{\mathsf{uDDH3}}_{\mathcal{A},\mathsf{GGen}}(\lambda) := |\Pr\left[\mathcal{A}(\mathbb{G}, p, g, (h_{i,j})_{i,j \in [3]}) = 1 \; \middle| \; \begin{array}{l} (\mathbb{G}, g, p) \leftarrow \mathsf{GGen}(1^\lambda), \\ a, b \xleftarrow{\$} \mathbb{Z}_p, \\ h_{1,1}, h_{2,1}, h_{3,1} \xleftarrow{\$} \mathbb{G} \\ h_{1,2} := h_{1,1}^a, h_{1,3} := h_{1,1}^b \\ h_{2,2} := h_{2,1}^a, h_{2,3} := h_{2,1}^b \\ h_{3,2} := h_{3,1}^a, h_{3,3} := h_{3,1}^b \end{array}\right]$$

$$- \Pr\left[\mathcal{A}(\mathbb{G}, p, g, (h_{i,j})_{i,j \in [3]}) = 1 \; \middle| \; \begin{array}{l} (\mathbb{G}, g, p) \leftarrow \mathsf{GGen}(1^\lambda), \\ \forall (i,j) \in [3] \times [3] : h_{i,j} \xleftarrow{\$} \mathbb{G} \end{array}\right]|.$$

3 Constructions

In this section, we present our construction of two-round multi-signatures. First, we give a definition of a special commitment scheme that will be used in both constructions. Then, we present the constructions in an abstract way. For the instantiation, we refer to Sect. 4.

3.1 Preparation: Special Commitments

In this section we define a special kind of commitment scheme. We will make use of such a scheme in our constructions of multi-signatures. Before we give the definition, we explain the desired properties at a high level. First of all, we want to be able to commit to elements $R \in \mathcal{R}$ in the range of a given linear function family. Second, we need the commitment scheme to be homomorphic in both messages and randomness, allowing us to aggregate commitments during the signing protocol. Third, we need a certain dual mode property, ensuring that we can set up keys either in a perfectly hiding or in a perfectly binding mode. This will allow us to make the commitment key for the forgery binding, while associating a equivocation trapdoor to the keys used to answer signing queries. We emphasize that we do not need a full-fledged equivocation feature. This is because we already know parts of the structure of messages to which we want to open the commitment. Looking ahead, this is the reason we can instantiate the commitment in the DDH setting.

Game $Q\text{-}\mathbf{KEYDIST}^{\mathcal{A}}_{0,\mathsf{CMT}}(\lambda)$	Game $Q\text{-}\mathbf{KEYDIST}^{\mathcal{A}}_{1,\mathsf{CMT}}(\lambda)$
01 par $\leftarrow$ LF.Gen(1^λ), $x \xleftarrow{\$} \mathcal{D}$	06 par $\leftarrow$ LF.Gen(1^λ), $x \xleftarrow{\$} \mathcal{D}$
02 **if** (par, x) $\notin$ Good : **return** 0	07 **if** (par, x) $\notin$ Good : **return** 0
03 **for** $i \in [Q]$: $\mathsf{ck}_i \leftarrow$ BGen(par)	08 **for** $i \in [Q]$: $\mathsf{ck}_i \xleftarrow{\$} \mathcal{K}_{\mathsf{par}}$
04 $\beta \leftarrow \mathcal{A}(\mathsf{par}, x, (\mathsf{ck}_i)_{i \in [Q]})$	09 $\beta \leftarrow \mathcal{A}(\mathsf{par}, x, (\mathsf{ck}_i)_{i \in [Q]})$
05 **return** β	10 **return** β

Fig. 3. The games $\mathbf{KEYDIST}_0, \mathbf{KEYDIST}_1$ for a special commitment scheme CMT and an adversary $\mathcal{A}$.

Definition 9 (Special Commitment Scheme). *Let* LF $=$ (LF.Gen, F) *be a linear function family and* $\mathcal{G} = \{\mathcal{G}_{\mathsf{par}}\}, \mathcal{H} = \{\mathcal{H}_{\mathsf{par}}\}$ *be families of subsets of abelian groups with efficiently computable group operations* $\oplus$ *and* $\otimes$, *respectively. Let* $\mathcal{K} = \{\mathcal{K}_{\mathsf{par}}\}$ *be a family of sets. An* $(\varepsilon_\mathsf{b}, \varepsilon_\mathsf{g}, \varepsilon_\mathsf{t})$*-special commitment scheme for* LF *with key space* $\mathcal{K}$, *randomness space* $\mathcal{G}$ *and commitment space* $\mathcal{H}$ *is a tuple of PPT algorithms* CMT $=$ (BGen, TGen, Com, TCom, TCol) *with the following syntax:*

- BGen(par) $\rightarrow$ ck *takes as input parameters* par, *and outputs a key* ck $\in \mathcal{K}_{\mathsf{par}}$.

- $\mathsf{TGen}(\mathsf{par}, X) \to (\mathsf{ck}, \mathsf{td})$ *takes as input parameters* par, *and an element* $X \in \mathcal{R}$, *and outputs a key* $\mathsf{ck} \in \mathcal{K}_{\mathsf{par}}$ *and a trapdoor* td.
- $\mathsf{Com}(\mathsf{ck}, R; \varphi) \to \mathsf{com}$ *takes as input a key* ck, *an element* $R \in \mathcal{R}$, *and a randomness* $\varphi \in \mathcal{G}_{\mathsf{par}}$, *and outputs a commitment* $\mathsf{com} \in \mathcal{H}_{\mathsf{par}}$.
- $\mathsf{TCom}(\mathsf{ck}, \mathsf{td}) \to (\mathsf{com}, St)$ *takes as input a key* ck *and a trapdoor* td, *and outputs a commitment* $\mathsf{com} \in \mathcal{H}_{\mathsf{par}}$ *and a state* St.
- $\mathsf{TCol}(St, c) \to (\varphi, R, s)$ *takes as input a state* St, *and an element* $c \in \mathcal{S}$, *and outputs randomness* $\varphi \in \mathcal{G}_{\mathsf{par}}$, *and elements* $R \in \mathcal{R}, s \in \mathcal{D}$.

We omit the subscript par *if it is clear from the context.*

Further, the algorithms are required to satisfy the following properties:

- **Homomorphism.** *For all* $\mathsf{par} \in \mathsf{LF.Gen}(1^\lambda), \mathsf{ck} \in \mathcal{K}_{\mathsf{par}}, R_0, R_1 \in \mathcal{R}$ *and* $\varphi_0, \varphi_1 \in \mathcal{G}$, *the following holds:*

$$\mathsf{Com}(\mathsf{ck}, R_0; \varphi_0) \otimes \mathsf{Com}(\mathsf{ck}, R_1; \varphi_1) = \mathsf{Com}(\mathsf{ck}, R_0 + R_1; \varphi_0 \oplus \varphi_1).$$

- **Good Parameters.** *There is a set* Good, *such that membership to* Good *can be decided in polynomial time, and*

$$\Pr\left[(\mathsf{par}, x) \notin \mathsf{Good} \mid \mathsf{par} \leftarrow \mathsf{LF.Gen}(1^\lambda),\ x \xleftarrow{\$} \mathcal{D}\right] \leq \varepsilon_{\mathsf{g}},$$

- **Uniform Keys.** *For all* $(\mathsf{par}, x) \in \mathsf{Good}$, *the following distributions are identical:*

$$\{(\mathsf{par}, x, \mathsf{ck}) \mid \mathsf{ck} \xleftarrow{\$} \mathcal{K}_{\mathsf{par}}\}\ and\ \{(\mathsf{par}, x, \mathsf{ck}) \mid (\mathsf{ck}, \mathsf{td}) \leftarrow \mathsf{TGen}(\mathsf{par}, X)\}.$$

- **Special Trapdoor Property.** *For all* $(\mathsf{par}, x) \in \mathsf{Good}$, *and all* $c \xleftarrow{\$} \mathcal{S}$, *the following distributions* $\mathcal{T}_0$ *and* $\mathcal{T}_1$ *have statistical distance at most* ε_{t}:

$$\mathcal{T}_0 := \left\{ (\mathsf{par}, \mathsf{ck}, \mathsf{td}, x, c, \mathsf{com}, \mathsf{tr}) \;\middle|\; \begin{array}{l} (\mathsf{ck}, \mathsf{td}) \leftarrow \mathsf{TGen}(\mathsf{par}, \mathsf{F}(x)) \\ (\mathsf{com}, St) \leftarrow \mathsf{TCom}(\mathsf{ck}, \mathsf{td}), \\ \mathsf{tr} \leftarrow \mathsf{TCol}(St, c) \end{array} \right\}$$

$$\mathcal{T}_1 := \left\{ (\mathsf{par}, \mathsf{ck}, \mathsf{td}, x, c, \mathsf{com}, \mathsf{tr}) \;\middle|\; \begin{array}{l} (\mathsf{ck}, \mathsf{td}) \leftarrow \mathsf{TGen}(\mathsf{par}, \mathsf{F}(x)) \\ r \xleftarrow{\$} \mathcal{D},\ R := \mathsf{F}(r),\ \varphi \xleftarrow{\$} \mathcal{G}, \\ \mathsf{com} := \mathsf{Com}(\mathsf{ck}, R; \varphi), \\ s := c \cdot x + r,\ \mathsf{tr} := (\varphi, R, s) \end{array} \right\}$$

- **Multi-Key Indistinguishability.** *For every* $Q = \mathsf{poly}(\lambda)$ *and any PPT algorithm* $\mathcal{A}$, *the following advantage is negligible:*

$$\mathsf{Adv}^{Q\text{-keydist}}_{\mathcal{A},\mathsf{CMT}}(\lambda) := \big|\Pr\left[Q\text{-}\mathbf{KEYDIST}^{\mathcal{A}}_{0,\mathsf{CMT}}(\lambda) \Rightarrow 1\right]$$
$$- \Pr\left[Q\text{-}\mathbf{KEYDIST}^{\mathcal{A}}_{1,\mathsf{CMT}}(\lambda) \Rightarrow 1\right]\big|,$$

where games $\mathbf{KEYDIST}_0, \mathbf{KEYDIST}_1$ *are defined in Fig. 3.*

- **Statistically Binding.** *There exists some (unbounded) algorithm* Ext, *such that for every (unbounded) algorithm* $\mathcal{A}$ *the following probability is at most* ε_{b}:

$$\Pr\left[\begin{array}{c} \mathsf{Com}(\mathsf{ck}, R'; \varphi') = \mathsf{com} \\ \wedge\ R \neq R' \end{array} \;\middle|\; \begin{array}{l} \mathsf{par} \leftarrow \mathsf{LF.Gen}(1^\lambda), \\ \mathsf{ck} \leftarrow \mathsf{BGen}(\mathsf{par}),\ (\mathsf{com}, St) \leftarrow \mathcal{A}(\mathsf{ck}), \\ R \leftarrow \mathsf{Ext}(\mathsf{ck}, \mathsf{com}),\ (R', \varphi') \leftarrow \mathcal{A}(St) \end{array} \right\}.$$

3.2   Our Construction with Key Aggregation

In this section, we construct a two-round multi-signature scheme with key aggregation. Although the scheme will not be tight, the security proof will not use rewinding, leading to an acceptable security loss. For our scheme, we need a lossiness admitting linear function family $\mathsf{LF} = (\mathsf{LF.Gen}, \mathsf{F})$. It should also satisfy aggregation lossy soundness. Further, let $\mathsf{CMT} = (\mathsf{BGen}, \mathsf{TGen}, \mathsf{Com}, \mathsf{TCom}, \mathsf{TCol})$ be an $(\varepsilon_b, \varepsilon_g, \varepsilon_t)$-special commitment scheme for LF with key space $\mathcal{K}$ randomness space $\mathcal{G}$ and commitment space $\mathcal{H}$. We make use of random oracles $\mathsf{H} \colon \{0,1\}^* \to \mathcal{K}$, $\mathsf{H}_a \colon \{0,1\}^* \to \mathcal{S}$, and $\mathsf{H}_c \colon \{0,1\}^* \to \mathcal{S}$. We give a verbal description of our scheme $\mathsf{MS}_a[\mathsf{LF}, \mathsf{CMT}]$.

Setup and Key Generation. The public parameters of the scheme are $\mathsf{par} \leftarrow \mathsf{LF.Gen}(1^\lambda)$ defining the linear function $\mathsf{F} = \mathsf{F}(\mathsf{par}, \cdot)$. To generate a key (algorithm Gen), a user samples $\mathsf{sk} := x \xleftarrow{\$} \mathcal{D}$. The public key is $\mathsf{pk} := X := \mathsf{F}(x)$.

Key Aggregation. For N users with public keys $\mathcal{P} = \{\mathsf{pk}_1, \ldots, \mathsf{pk}_N\}$, the aggregated public key $\tilde{\mathsf{pk}}$ is computed (by algorithm Agg) as

$$\tilde{\mathsf{pk}} := \tilde{X} := \sum_{i=1}^N a_i \cdot X_i,$$

where $\mathsf{pk}_i = X_i$ and $a_i := \mathsf{H}_a(\langle \mathcal{P} \rangle, \mathsf{pk}_i)$ for each $i \in [N]$.

Signing Protocol. Suppose N users with public keys $\mathcal{P} = \{\mathsf{pk}_1, \ldots, \mathsf{pk}_N\}$ want to sign a message $\mathsf{m} \in \{0,1\}^*$. We describe the signing protocol (algorithms $\mathsf{Sig}_0, \mathsf{Sig}_1, \mathsf{Sig}_2$) from the perspective of the first user, which holds a secret key $\mathsf{sk}_1 = x_1$ for public key $\mathsf{pk}_1 = X_1$.

1. *Commitment Phase.* The user derives the aggregated public key $\tilde{\mathsf{pk}}$ as described above. Then, it derives a commitment key $\mathsf{ck} := \mathsf{H}(\tilde{\mathsf{pk}}, \mathsf{m})$ depending on the message. The user samples an element $r_1 \xleftarrow{\$} \mathcal{D}$ and sets $R_1 := \mathsf{F}(r_1)$. Next, it commits to R_1 by sampling $\varphi_1 \xleftarrow{\$} \mathcal{G}$ and setting $\mathsf{com}_1 := \mathsf{Com}(\mathsf{ck}, R_1; \varphi_1)$. Finally, it sends $\mathsf{pm}_{1,1} := \mathsf{com}_1$ to all users.
2. *Response Phase.* Let $\mathcal{M}_1 = (\mathsf{pm}_{1,1}, \ldots, \mathsf{pm}_{1,N})$ be the list of messages output in the commitment phase. Here, message $\mathsf{pm}_{1,i}$ is sent by user i and has the form $\mathsf{pm}_{1,i} = \mathsf{com}_i$. With this notation, the user aggregates the commitments via $\mathsf{com} := \bigotimes_{i \in [N]} \mathsf{com}_i$. It computes the challenge c and coefficient a_1 via $c := \mathsf{H}_c(\tilde{\mathsf{pk}}, \mathsf{com}, \mathsf{m})$ and $a_1 := \mathsf{H}_a(\langle \mathcal{P} \rangle, \mathsf{pk}_1)$. Then, it computes the response s_1 as $s_1 := c \cdot a_1 \cdot x_1 + r_1$.
   Finally, the user sends $\mathsf{pm}_{2,1} := (s_1, \varphi_1)$ to all users.
3. *Aggregation Phase.* Let $\mathcal{M}_2 = (\mathsf{pm}_{2,1}, \ldots, \mathsf{pm}_{2,N})$ be the list of messages output in the response phase. Here, message $\mathsf{pm}_{2,i}$ is sent by user i and has the form $\mathsf{pm}_{2,i} = (s_i, \varphi_i)$. To compute the final signature, users aggregate the responses and commitment randomness as follows:

$$s := \sum_{i \in [N]} s_i, \quad \varphi := \bigoplus_{i \in [N]} \varphi_i.$$

They output the final signature $\sigma := (\mathsf{com}, s, \varphi)$.

Verification. For verification (algorithm Ver), let $\mathcal{P} = \{\mathsf{pk}_1, \ldots, \mathsf{pk}_N\}$ be a multi-set of public keys, $\mathsf{m} \in \{0,1\}^*$ be a message, and $\sigma = (\mathsf{com}, s, \varphi)$ be a signature. To verify σ, we determine the aggregated public key $\tilde{\mathsf{pk}} = \tilde{X}$ as above. We reconstruct the commitment key $\mathsf{ck} := \mathsf{H}(\tilde{\mathsf{pk}}, \mathsf{m})$, and the challenge $c := \mathsf{H}_c(\tilde{\mathsf{pk}}, \mathsf{com}, \mathsf{m})$. Then, we output 1 if and only if the following equation holds:

$$\mathsf{com} = \mathsf{Com}\left(\mathsf{ck}, \mathsf{F}(s) - c \cdot \tilde{X}; \varphi\right).$$

Completeness easily follows from the homomorphic properties of CMT and F. For a similar calculation, we refer to the proof of Lemma 2.

Lemma 1. *Let* LF *be a linear function family. Let* CMT *be a* $(\varepsilon_b, \varepsilon_g, \varepsilon_t)$*-special commitment scheme for* LF*. Then* $\mathsf{MS}_a[\mathsf{LF}, \mathsf{CMT}]$ *is complete.*

Theorem 1. *Let* LF *be a* ε_l*-lossiness admitting linear function family with* ε_{al}*-aggregation lossy soundness. Let* CMT *be a* $(\varepsilon_b, \varepsilon_g, \varepsilon_t)$*-special commitment scheme for* LF*. Further, let* $\mathsf{H}: \{0,1\}^* \to \mathcal{K}, \mathsf{H}_a: \{0,1\}^* \to \mathcal{S}$, *and* $\mathsf{H}_c: \{0,1\}^* \to \mathcal{S}$ *be random oracles. Then* $\mathsf{MS}_a[\mathsf{LF}, \mathsf{CMT}]$ *is* MS-EUF-CMA*secure.*

Concretely, for any PPT algorithm $\mathcal{A}$ *that makes at most* $Q_\mathsf{H}, Q_{\mathsf{H}_a}, Q_{\mathsf{H}_c}, Q_S$ *queries to oracles* $\mathsf{H}, \mathsf{H}_a, \mathsf{H}_c, \mathrm{SIG}_0$, *respectively, there are PPT algorithms* $\mathcal{B}, \mathcal{B}'$ *with* $\mathbf{T}(\mathcal{B}) \approx \mathbf{T}(\mathcal{A}), \mathbf{T}(\mathcal{B}') \approx \mathbf{T}(\mathcal{A})$ *and*

$$\mathsf{Adv}^{\mathsf{MS\text{-}EUF\text{-}CMA}}_{\mathcal{A},\mathsf{MS}_a[\mathsf{LF},\mathsf{CMT}]}(\lambda) \leq \varepsilon_g + 4Q_S^2 \varepsilon_t + 4Q_S \varepsilon_g + 4Q_S Q_\mathsf{H} Q_{\mathsf{H}_c} \varepsilon_b$$
$$+ \frac{4Q_S}{|\mathcal{R}|} + \frac{4Q_S Q_{\mathsf{H}_a} Q_{\mathsf{H}_c}}{|\mathcal{S}|} + 4Q_S Q_{\mathsf{H}_a} Q_{\mathsf{H}_c} \varepsilon_{al}$$
$$+ 4Q_S \left(\mathsf{Adv}^{Q_\mathsf{H}\text{-keydist}}_{\mathcal{B},\mathsf{CMT}}(\lambda) + \mathsf{Adv}^{\mathsf{keydist}}_{\mathcal{B}',\mathsf{LF}}(\lambda)\right).$$

We postpone the proof to the full version [34].

3.3 Our Tight Construction

In this section, we present a tightly secure two-round multi-signature scheme $\mathsf{MS}_t[\mathsf{LF}, \mathsf{CMT}] = (\mathsf{Setup}, \mathsf{Gen}, \mathsf{Sig}, \mathsf{Ver})$. Let us first describe the building blocks that we need. We make use of a lossiness admitting linear function family $\mathsf{LF} = (\mathsf{LF.Gen}, \mathsf{F})$. Also, let $\mathsf{CMT} = (\mathsf{BGen}, \mathsf{TGen}, \mathsf{Com}, \mathsf{TCom}, \mathsf{TCol})$ be an $(\varepsilon_b, \varepsilon_g, \varepsilon_t)$-special commitment scheme for LF with key space $\mathcal{K}$ randomness space $\mathcal{G}$ and commitment space $\mathcal{H}$. We make use of random oracles $\mathsf{H}: \{0,1\}^* \to \mathcal{K}$, $\mathsf{H}_b: \{0,1\}^* \to \{0,1\}$, and $\mathsf{H}_c: \{0,1\}^* \to \mathcal{S}$. We give a verbal description of the scheme.

Setup and Key Generation. The public parameters of the scheme are $\mathsf{par} \leftarrow \mathsf{LF.Gen}(1^\lambda)$. They define the linear function $\mathsf{F} = \mathsf{F}(\mathsf{par}, \cdot)$. To generate a key (algorithm Gen), a user samples $x_0, x_1 \xleftarrow{\$} \mathcal{D}$ and a seed $\mathsf{seed} \xleftarrow{\$} \{0,1\}^\lambda$. Then, it sets

$$\mathsf{sk} := (x_0, x_1, \mathsf{seed}), \quad \mathsf{pk} := (X_0, X_1) := (\mathsf{F}(x_0), \mathsf{F}(x_1)).$$

Signing Protocol. Suppose N users with public keys $\mathcal{P} = \{\mathsf{pk}_1, \ldots, \mathsf{pk}_N\}$ want to sign a message $\mathsf{m} \in \{0,1\}^*$. We describe the signing protocol (algorithms $\mathsf{Sig}_0, \mathsf{Sig}_1, \mathsf{Sig}_2$) from the perspective of the first user, which holds a secret key $\mathsf{sk}_1 = (x_{1,0}, x_{1,1}, \mathsf{seed}_1)$ for public key $\mathsf{pk}_1 = (X_{1,0}, X_{1,1})$.

1. *Commitment Phase.* The user derives commitment keys $\mathsf{ck}_0 := \mathsf{H}(0, \langle \mathcal{P} \rangle, \mathsf{m})$, $\mathsf{ck}_1 := \mathsf{H}(1, \langle \mathcal{P} \rangle, \mathsf{m})$ depending on the message. Then, the user computes a bit $b_1 := \mathsf{H}_b(\mathsf{seed}_1, \langle \mathcal{P} \rangle, \mathsf{m})$. It samples two elements $r_{1,0}, r_{1,1} \xleftarrow{\$} \mathcal{D}$ and sets

$$R_{1,0} := \mathsf{F}(r_{1,0}), \quad R_{1,1} := \mathsf{F}(r_{1,1}).$$

Next, it commits to the resulting elements by sampling $\varphi_{1,0}, \varphi_{1,1} \xleftarrow{\$} \mathcal{G}$ and setting

$$\mathsf{com}_{1,0} := \mathsf{Com}(\mathsf{ck}_0, R_{1,0}; \varphi_{1,0}), \quad \mathsf{com}_{1,1} := \mathsf{Com}(\mathsf{ck}_1, R_{1,1}; \varphi_{1,1}).$$

Finally, it sends $\mathsf{pm}_{1,1} := (b_1, \mathsf{com}_{1,0}, \mathsf{com}_{1,1})$ to all users.

2. *Response Phase.* Let $\mathcal{M}_1 = (\mathsf{pm}_{1,1}, \ldots, \mathsf{pm}_{1,N})$ be the list of messages output in the commitment phase. Here, message $\mathsf{pm}_{1,i}$ is sent by user i and has the form $\mathsf{pm}_{1,i} = (b_i, \mathsf{com}_{i,0}, \mathsf{com}_{i,1})$. With this notation, the user sets $B := b_1 \ldots b_N \in \{0,1\}^N$. Then, it aggregates the commitments via

$$\mathsf{com}_0 := \bigotimes_{i \in [N]} \mathsf{com}_{i,0}, \quad \mathsf{com}_1 := \bigotimes_{i \in [N]} \mathsf{com}_{i,1}.$$

It computes user specific challenges via

$$c_{1,0} := \mathsf{H}_c(\mathsf{pk}_1, \mathsf{com}_0, \mathsf{m}, \langle \mathcal{P} \rangle, B, 0), \quad c_{1,1} := \mathsf{H}_c(\mathsf{pk}_1, \mathsf{com}_1, \mathsf{m}, \langle \mathcal{P} \rangle, B, 1),$$

and the responses as

$$s_{1,0} := c_{1,0} \cdot x_{1,b_1} + r_{1,0}, \quad s_{1,1} := c_{1,1} \cdot x_{1,1-b_1} + r_{1,1}.$$

Observe that the bit b_1 determines the link between the responses, challenges, and public keys. Finally, the user sends $\mathsf{pm}_{2,1} := (s_{1,0}, s_{1,1}, \varphi_{1,0}, \varphi_{1,1})$ to all users.

3. *Aggregation Phase.* Let $\mathcal{M}_2 = (\mathsf{pm}_{2,1}, \ldots, \mathsf{pm}_{2,N})$ be the list of messages output in the response phase. Here, message $\mathsf{pm}_{2,i}$ is sent by user i and has the form $\mathsf{pm}_{2,i} = (s_{i,0}, s_{i,1}, \varphi_{i,0}, \varphi_{i,1})$. To compute the final signature, users aggregate the responses and commitment randomness as follows:

$$s_0 := \sum_{i \in [N]} s_{i,0}, \quad s_1 := \sum_{i \in [N]} s_{i,1}, \quad \varphi_0 := \bigoplus_{i \in [N]} \varphi_{i,0}, \quad \varphi_1 := \bigoplus_{i \in [N]} \varphi_{i,1}.$$

They define $\sigma_0 := (\mathsf{com}_0, \varphi_0, s_0), \sigma_1 := (\mathsf{com}_1, \varphi_1, s_1)$ and output the final signature $\sigma := (\sigma_0, \sigma_1, B)$.

Verification. For verification (algorithm Ver), let $\mathcal{P} = \{\mathsf{pk}_1, \ldots, \mathsf{pk}_N\}$ be a multi-set of public keys, $\mathsf{m} \in \{0,1\}^*$ be a message, and $\sigma = (\sigma_0, \sigma_1, B)$ be a signature. To verify σ, we write $B = b_1 \ldots b_N, \sigma_0 = (\mathsf{com}_0, \varphi_0, s_0)$ and $\sigma_1 = (\mathsf{com}_1, \varphi_1, s_1)$. Further, we write the public keys pk_i as $\mathsf{pk}_i = (X_{i,0}, X_{i,1})$. We reconstruct the commitment keys $\mathsf{ck}_0 := \mathsf{H}(0, \langle \mathcal{P} \rangle, \mathsf{m}), \mathsf{ck}_1 := \mathsf{H}(1, \langle \mathcal{P} \rangle, \mathsf{m})$, and the user specific challenges

$$c_{i,0} := \mathsf{H}_c(\mathsf{pk}_i, \mathsf{com}_0, \mathsf{m}, \langle \mathcal{P} \rangle, B, 0), \quad c_{i,1} := \mathsf{H}_c(\mathsf{pk}_i, \mathsf{com}_1, \mathsf{m}, \langle \mathcal{P} \rangle, B, 1).$$

Then, we output 1 if and only if the following two equations hold:

$$\mathsf{com}_0 = \mathsf{Com}\left(\mathsf{ck}_0, \mathsf{F}(s_0) - \sum_{i=1}^{N} c_{i,0} \cdot X_{i,b_i}; \varphi_0\right)$$

$$\mathsf{com}_1 = \mathsf{Com}\left(\mathsf{ck}_1, \mathsf{F}(s_1) - \sum_{i=1}^{N} c_{i,1} \cdot X_{i,1-b_i}; \varphi_1\right).$$

Lemma 2. *Let* LF *be a linear function family. Let* CMT *be a* $(\varepsilon_\mathsf{b}, \varepsilon_\mathsf{g}, \varepsilon_\mathsf{t})$-*special commitment scheme for* LF. *Then* $\mathsf{MS}_t[\mathsf{LF}, \mathsf{CMT}]$ *is complete.*

The proof is an easy calculation and is given in the full version [34].

Theorem 2. *Let* LF *be a* ε_l-*lossiness admitting linear function family. Let* CMT *be a* $(\varepsilon_\mathsf{b}, \varepsilon_\mathsf{g}, \varepsilon_\mathsf{t})$-*special commitment scheme for* LF. *Further, let* $\mathsf{H}: \{0,1\}^* \to \mathcal{K}$, $\mathsf{H}_b: \{0,1\}^* \to \{0,1\}, \mathsf{H}_c: \{0,1\}^* \to \mathcal{S}$ *be random oracles. Then* $\mathsf{MS}_t[\mathsf{LF}, \mathsf{CMT}]$ *is* MS-EUF-CMA*secure.*

Concretely, for any PPT algorithm $\mathcal{A}$ *that makes at most* $Q_\mathsf{H}, Q_{\mathsf{H}_b}, Q_{\mathsf{H}_c}, Q_S$ *queries to oracles* $\mathsf{H}, \mathsf{H}_b, \mathsf{H}_c, \mathrm{SIG}_0$, *respectively, there are PPT algorithms* $\mathcal{B}, \mathcal{B}'$ *with* $\mathbf{T}(\mathcal{B}) \approx \mathbf{T}(\mathcal{A}), \mathbf{T}(\mathcal{B}') \approx \mathbf{T}(\mathcal{A})$ *and*

$$\mathsf{Adv}^{\text{MS-EUF-CMA}}_{\mathcal{A}, \mathsf{MS}_t[\mathsf{LF}, \mathsf{CMT}]}(\lambda) \leq \frac{Q_{\mathsf{H}_b}}{2^\lambda} + 4\varepsilon_\mathsf{g} + 2Q_S\varepsilon_\mathsf{t} + 2Q_\mathsf{H}Q_{\mathsf{H}_c}\varepsilon_\mathsf{b} + 2Q_{\mathsf{H}_c}\varepsilon_\mathsf{l}$$

$$+ 2 \cdot \mathsf{Adv}^{Q_\mathsf{H}\text{-keydist}}_{\mathcal{B}, \mathsf{CMT}}(\lambda) + 2 \cdot \mathsf{Adv}^{\text{keydist}}_{\mathcal{B}', \mathsf{LF}}(\lambda).$$

Proof. Set $\mathsf{MS} := \mathsf{MS}_t[\mathsf{LF}, \mathsf{CMT}]$. Let $\mathcal{A}$ be a PPT algorithm as in the statement. We prove the claim via a sequence of games $\mathbf{G}_0$-$\mathbf{G}_8$. For each game $\mathbf{G}_i, i \in [8]$, we define

$$\mathsf{Adv}_i := \Pr[\mathbf{G}_i \Rightarrow 1].$$

Game $\mathbf{G}_0$: We define $\mathbf{G}_0$ to be exactly as $\text{MS-EUF-CMA}^{\mathcal{A}}_{\mathsf{MS}}$, with the following modification: The adversary $\mathcal{A}$ does not get access to oracle SIG_2. Note that in MS, algorithm Sig_2 does not make any use of the secret key or a secret state and can be publicly run using the messages output in Sig_0 and Sig_1. Therefore, for any adversary in the original game, there is an adversary in game $\mathbf{G}_0$ that simulates oracle SIG_2 and has the same advantage.

Before we proceed, let us describe game $\mathbf{G}_0$ in more detail to fix some notation. In the beginning, the game samples parameters $\mathsf{par} \leftarrow \mathsf{LF}.\mathsf{Gen}(1^\lambda)$. It also samples a public key $\mathsf{pk}^* = (X_{1,0}, X_{1,1}) = (\mathsf{F}(x_{1,0}), \mathsf{F}(x_{1,1}))$ for a secret key $\mathsf{sk}^* = (x_{1,0}, x_{1,1}, \mathsf{seed}_1)$ with $x_{1,0}, x_{1,1} \xleftarrow{\$} \mathcal{D}, \mathsf{seed}_1 \xleftarrow{\$} \{0,1\}^\lambda$. Then, it runs $\mathcal{A}$ on input $\mathsf{par}, \mathsf{pk}^*$ with access to the following oracles:

- Signing oracles $\mathrm{SIG}_0, \mathrm{SIG}_1$: The oracles simulate algorithms Sig_0 and Sig_1 on secret key sk^*, respectively. Here, $\mathcal{A}$ can submit a query $\mathrm{SIG}_0(\mathcal{P}, \mathsf{m})$ to start a new interaction in which message m is signed for public keys $\mathcal{P} = \{\mathsf{pk}_1, \ldots, \mathsf{pk}_N\}$. We assume that $\mathsf{pk}^* = \mathsf{pk}_1$, and the oracle adds $(\mathcal{P}, \mathsf{m})$ to a list $\mathcal{L}$.
- Random oracles $\mathsf{H}, \mathsf{H}_b, \mathsf{H}_c$: The random oracles H, H_c are simulated honestly via lazy sampling. To this end, the game holds maps h, h_c that map the inputs of the respective random oracles to their outputs. Random oracle H_b, however, is simulated by forwarding the query to an internal oracle $\bar{\mathsf{H}}_b$ with the same interface. This oracle holds a similar map $\hat{h}_b$, is kept internally by the game, and is not provided to the adversary. Looking ahead, this indirection allows us to distinguish queries to H_b that some of the following games issue from the queries that the adversary issues.

In the end, $\mathcal{A}$ outputs a forgery $(\mathcal{P}^*, \mathsf{m}^*, \sigma^*)$. The game outputs 1 if and only if $\mathsf{pk}^* \in \mathcal{P}^*, (\mathcal{P}^*, \mathsf{m}^*) \notin \mathcal{L}$, and $\mathsf{Ver}(\mathcal{P}^*, \mathsf{m}^*, \sigma^*) = 1$. Without loss of generality, we assume that the public key pk^* is equal to pk_1 for $\mathcal{P}^* = \{\mathsf{pk}_1, \ldots, \mathsf{pk}_N\}$. To fix notation, write $\sigma^* = (\sigma_0^*, \sigma_1^*, B^*)$, $B^* = b_1^* \ldots b_N^*$ and $\sigma_0^* = (\mathsf{com}_0^*, \varphi_0^*, s_0^*), \sigma_1^* = (\mathsf{com}_1^*, \varphi_1^*, s_1^*)$. Clearly, we have

$$\mathsf{Adv}_0 = \mathsf{Adv}^{\mathsf{MS\text{-}EUF\text{-}CMA}}_{\mathcal{A}, \mathsf{MS}_t[\mathsf{LF}, \mathsf{CMT}]}(\lambda).$$

Game $\mathbf{G}_1$: In game $\mathbf{G}_1$, we add an abort. Namely, the game sets $\mathsf{bad} := 1$, and aborts, if the adversary makes a random oracle query $\mathsf{H}_b(\mathsf{seed}_1, \cdot)$. Note that this does not include the queries that are made by the game itself, as these are done using oracle $\bar{\mathsf{H}}_b$ directly. As the only information about seed_1 that $\mathcal{A}$ gets are the values of $\mathsf{H}_b(\mathsf{seed}_1, \cdot)$, and seed_1 is sampled uniformly at random from $\{0,1\}^\lambda$, we can upper bound the probability of bad by $Q_{\mathsf{H}_b}/2^\lambda$. Therefore, we have

$$|\mathsf{Adv}_0 - \mathsf{Adv}_1| \leq \Pr[\mathsf{bad}] \leq \frac{Q_{\mathsf{H}_b}}{2^\lambda}.$$

Game $\mathbf{G}_2$: In game $\mathbf{G}_2$, we restrict the winning condition. Namely, the game outputs 0, if the forgery $(\mathcal{P}^*, \mathsf{m}^*, \sigma^*)$ output by $\mathcal{A}$ satisfies $b_1^* \neq 1 - \bar{\mathsf{H}}_b(\mathsf{seed}_1, \langle \mathcal{P}^* \rangle, \mathsf{m}^*)$. Recall that b_1^* is the bit related to $\mathsf{pk}_1 = \mathsf{pk}^*$ that is included in the signature σ^*. Assuming $\mathbf{G}_1$ outputs 1, we know that $(\mathcal{P}^*, \mathsf{m}^*) \notin \mathcal{L}$. Therefore, $\mathcal{A}$ can only get information about the bit $\bar{\mathsf{H}}_b(\mathsf{seed}_1, \langle \mathcal{P}^* \rangle, \mathsf{m}^*)$, if it queries the wrapper random oracle H_b at this position. However, in this case $\mathbf{G}_1$ would set $\mathsf{bad} := 1$ and abort. Thus, the view of $\mathcal{A}$ is independent of bit $\bar{\mathsf{H}}_b(\mathsf{seed}_1, \langle \mathcal{P}^* \rangle, \mathsf{m}^*)$. We obtain

$$\mathsf{Adv}_2 = \Pr[\mathbf{G}_2 \Rightarrow 1] = \Pr[\mathbf{G}_1 \Rightarrow 1 \wedge b_1^* = 1 - \bar{\mathsf{H}}_b(\mathsf{seed}_1, \langle \mathcal{P}^* \rangle, \mathsf{m}^*)] = \frac{1}{2}\mathsf{Adv}_1.$$

Game G_3: In game G_3, the game aborts if $(\mathsf{par}, x_{1,1}) \notin \mathsf{Good}$, where Good is as in the definition of a special commitment scheme. It is clear that

$$|\mathsf{Adv}_2 - \mathsf{Adv}_3| \leq \Pr\left[(\mathsf{par}, x_{1,1}) \notin \mathsf{Good}\right] \leq \varepsilon_g.$$

Game G_4: In game G_4, we change the behavior of random oracle H. Recall that before, to answer a query $\mathsf{H}(b, \langle \mathcal{P} \rangle, \mathsf{m})$ for which the hash value has not been defined, a key $\mathsf{ck} \xleftarrow{\$} \mathcal{K}$ was sampled and returned. In this game, the oracle instead distinguishes two cases. In the first case, if $b = 1 - \bar{\mathsf{H}}_b(\mathsf{seed}_1, \langle \mathcal{P} \rangle, \mathsf{m})$, the game samples $(\mathsf{ck}, \mathsf{td}) \leftarrow \mathsf{TGen}(\mathsf{par}, X_{1,1})$. It also stores $tr[\langle \mathcal{P} \rangle, \mathsf{m}] := \mathsf{td}$, where tr is a map. In the second case, if $b = \bar{\mathsf{H}}_b(\mathsf{seed}_1, \langle \mathcal{P} \rangle, \mathsf{m})$, it samples $\mathsf{ck} \leftarrow \mathsf{BGen}(\mathsf{par})$. In both cases, ck is returned as before. To see that G_3 and G_4 are indistinguishable, we first note that for the first case, the distribution of ck stays the same. This is because we can assume $(\mathsf{par}, x_{1,1}) \in \mathsf{Good}$ due to the previous change. The keys returned in the second case are indistinguishable by the multi-key indistinguishability of CMT. More precisely, we give a reduction $\mathcal{B}$ against the multi-key indistinguishability of CMT that interpolates between G_3 and G_4. The reduction gets as input $\mathsf{par}, x_{1,1}$ and Q_H commitment keys $\mathsf{ck}_1, \ldots, \mathsf{ck}_{Q_\mathsf{H}}$. It simulates G_3 for $\mathcal{A}$ with par while embedding the commitment keys in random oracle responses for queries $\mathsf{H}(b, \langle \mathcal{P} \rangle, \mathsf{m})$ with $b = 1 - \bar{\mathsf{H}}_b(\mathsf{seed}_1, \langle \mathcal{P} \rangle, \mathsf{m})$. In the end, it outputs whatever the game outputs[4] . We have

$$|\mathsf{Adv}_3 - \mathsf{Adv}_4| \leq \mathsf{Adv}_{\mathcal{B},\mathsf{CMT}}^{Q_\mathsf{H}\text{-keydist}}(\lambda).$$

Game G_5: In game G_5, we change the signing oracles $\mathrm{SIG}_0, \mathrm{SIG}_1$. Our goal is to eliminate the use of the secret key component $x_{1,1}$. Recall that in previous games, oracle SIG_0 derived a bit $b_1 := \bar{\mathsf{H}}_b(\mathsf{seed}_1, \langle \mathcal{P} \rangle, \mathsf{m})$ and sampled random $r_{1,0}, r_{1,1}$ and $\varphi_{1,0}, \varphi_{1,1}$. Then, these were used with to compute commitments $\mathsf{com}_{1,0}, \mathsf{com}_{1,1}$, which where then output together with b_1. Then, in oracle SIG_1 the values $s_{1,0}, s_{1,1}$ were computed using the secret keys $x_{1,b_1}, x_{1,1-b_1}$, respectively.

In this game, we change how the commitment $\varphi_{1,1-b_1}$ and the value $s_{1,1-b_1}$ is computed to eliminate the dependency on $x_{1,1}$. Namely, in oracle SIG_0, we do not compute $r_{1,1-b_1}, \varphi_{1,1-b_1}$ and $R_{1,1-b_1}$ anymore. Instead, we compute the commitment $\mathsf{com}_{1,1-b_1}$ via

$$\mathsf{td} := tr[\langle \mathcal{P} \rangle, , \mathsf{m}], \quad (\mathsf{com}_{1,1-b_1}, St) \leftarrow \mathsf{TCom}(\mathsf{ck}_{1-b_1}, \mathsf{td}).$$

Note that $\mathsf{ck}_{1-b_1} = \mathsf{H}(1-b_1, \langle \mathcal{P} \rangle, \mathsf{m})$, and therefore ck_{1-b_1} and td were generated using $\mathsf{TGen}(\mathsf{par}, X_{1,1})$ due to the change in G_4. Later, in oracle SIG_1, we derive

$$(\varphi_{1,1-b_1}, R_{1-b_1}, s_{1,1-b_1}) \leftarrow \mathsf{TCol}(St, c_{1,1-b_1}).$$

Then, message $\mathsf{pm}_{2,1} := (s_{1,0}, s_{1,1}, \varphi_{1,0}, \varphi_{1,1})$ is output as before.

---

[4] Note that at this point, it was important that we introduced the oracle $\bar{\mathsf{H}}_b$. This is because otherwise, if we queried $\mathsf{H}_b(\mathsf{seed}_1, \cdot)$ in oracle H, game G_3 would always output 0 and the games would not be indistinguishable.

We can easily argue indistinguishability by using the special trapdoor property of CMT Q_{S_0} many times and get

$$|\mathsf{Adv}_4 - \mathsf{Adv}_5| \le Q_S \varepsilon_t.$$

Game $\mathbf{G}_6$: Here we do not abort if $(\mathsf{par}, x_{1,1}) \notin \mathsf{Good}$ anymore. That is, we revert the change introduced in $\mathbf{G}_3$. It is clear that

$$|\mathsf{Adv}_5 - \mathsf{Adv}_6| \le \Pr\left[(\mathsf{par}, x_{1,1}) \notin \mathsf{Good}\right] \le \varepsilon_{\mathsf{g}}.$$

Game $\mathbf{G}_7$: In game $\mathbf{G}_7$, we change how the public key component $X_{1,1}$ is computed. Recall that before, $X_{1,1}$ is computed as $X_{1,1} := \mathsf{F}(x_{1,1})$ for $x_{1,1} \xleftarrow{\$} x_{1,1} \xleftarrow{\$} \mathcal{D}$. Also, note that due to the previous changes, the value $x_{1,1}$ is not used anymore. In $\mathbf{G}_7$, we sample $X_{1,1} \xleftarrow{\$} \mathcal{R}$. A direct reduction $\mathcal{B}'$ against the key indistinguishability of the lossiness admitting linear function family LF shows indistinguishability of $\mathbf{G}_6$ and $\mathbf{G}_7$. Concretely, $\mathcal{B}'$ gets par and $X_{1,1}$ as input, and simulates $\mathbf{G}_6$ for $\mathcal{A}$. In the end, it outputs whatever the game outputs. We have

$$|\mathsf{Adv}_6 - \mathsf{Adv}_7| \le \mathsf{Adv}_{\mathcal{B}',\mathsf{LF}}^{\mathsf{keydist}}(\lambda).$$

Game $\mathbf{G}_8$: Ins game $\mathbf{G}_8$, we change how H_c is executed. Concretely, consider a query $\mathsf{H}_c(\mathsf{pk}, \mathsf{com}, \mathsf{m}, \langle\mathcal{P}\rangle, B, b)$ with $\mathsf{pk} = \mathsf{pk}^*$ and $b = \bar{\mathsf{H}}_b(\mathsf{seed}_1, \langle\mathcal{P}\rangle, \mathsf{m})$. For these queries, the game now runs $R \leftarrow \mathsf{Ext}(\mathsf{H}(b, \langle\mathcal{P}\rangle, \mathsf{m}), \mathsf{com})$ and stores $r[\mathsf{com}, \mathsf{m}, \langle\mathcal{P}\rangle, B] := R$, where r is another map. Here, Ext is the (unbounded) extractor for the statistical binding property of CMT. The rest of the oracle docs not change. Note that for b of this form, the value $\mathsf{ck} = \mathsf{H}(b, \langle\mathcal{P}\rangle, \mathsf{m})$ is sampled as $\mathsf{ck} \leftarrow \mathsf{BGen}(\mathsf{par})$ (cf. $\mathbf{G}_4$). We also slightly change the winning condition of the game. Namely, in $\mathbf{G}_8$, consider the forgery $(\mathcal{P}^*, \mathsf{m}^*, \sigma^*)$ with $\sigma^* = (\sigma_0^*, \sigma_1^*, B^*)$, $B^* = b_1^* \ldots b_N^*$, and let $R_0^*, R_1^* \in \mathcal{R}$ be the values that are computed during the execution of $\mathsf{Ver}(\mathcal{P}^*, \mathsf{m}^*, \sigma^*)$. The game returns 0 if $R_{1-b_1^*}^* \ne r[\mathsf{com}_{1-b_1^*}^*, \mathsf{m}^*, \langle\mathcal{P}^*\rangle, B^*]$.

We claim that indistinguishability of $\mathbf{G}_7$ and $\mathbf{G}_8$ can be argued using the statistical binding property of CMT. To see this, assume that $\mathbf{G}_7$ outputs 1. Then, due to the change in $\mathbf{G}_2$, we know that $1 - b_1^* = \bar{\mathsf{H}}_b(\mathsf{seed}_1, \langle\mathcal{P}^*\rangle, \mathsf{m}^*)$. Therefore, in the corresponding query $\mathsf{H}_c(\mathsf{pk}_1, \mathsf{com}_{1-b_1^*}^*, \mathsf{m}^*, \langle\mathcal{P}^*\rangle, B^*, 1-b_1^*)$ algorithm Ext was run and the value $r[\mathsf{com}_{1-b_1^*}^*, \mathsf{m}^*, \langle\mathcal{P}^*\rangle, B^*]$ is defined. Next, by definition of Ver, we have $\mathsf{Com}(\mathsf{ck}_{1-b_1^*}, R_{1-b_1^*}^*; \varphi_{1-b_1^*}^*) = \mathsf{com}_{1-b_1^*}^*$. Therefore, if $R_{1-b_1^*}^* \ne r[\mathsf{com}_{1-b_1^*}^*, \mathsf{m}^*, \langle\mathcal{P}^*\rangle, B^*]$, we have a contradiction to the statistical binding property of CMT. More precisely, we sketch an (unbounded) reduction from the statistical binding property. Namely, this reduction gets as input par and a commitment key ck^*. Then, the reduction guesses $i_\mathsf{H} \xleftarrow{\$} [Q_\mathsf{H}]$ and $i_{\mathsf{H}_c} \xleftarrow{\$} [Q_{\mathsf{H}_c}]$. It simulates game $\mathbf{G}_8$ honestly, except for query i_H to random oracle H and query i_{H_c} to random oracle H_c. If it had to sample a $\mathsf{ck} \leftarrow \mathsf{BGen}(\mathsf{par})$ in the former query, it instead responds with ck^*. Similarly, if it had to run Ext in the latter query, it outputs com to the binding experiment. If these queries are the queries of interest (i.e. query i_H was used to derive $\mathsf{ck}_{1-b_1^*}$ and query i_{H_c} was used to derive $c_{1,1-b_1^*}^*$) for the forgery, and $R_{1-b_1^*}^* \ne r[\mathsf{com}_{1-b_1^*}^*, \mathsf{m}^*, \langle\mathcal{P}^*\rangle, B^*]$, then the reduction outputs $R^*_{1-b^*_1}; \varphi^*_{1-b^*_1}$. Otherwise, it outputs $\bot$. It is easy to see that if the reduction guesses the correct queries and the bad event separating $\mathbf{G}_7$ and $\mathbf{G}_8$ occurs, then it breaks the statistical binding property. As the view of $\mathcal{A}$ is as in $\mathbf{G}_8$, and independent of $(i_{\mathsf{H}}, i_{\mathsf{H}_c})$, we obtain

$$|\mathsf{Adv}_7 - \mathsf{Adv}_8| \leq Q_{\mathsf{H}} Q_{\mathsf{H}_c} \varepsilon_{\mathsf{b}}.$$

Finally, we use lossy soundness of LF to bound the probability that $\mathbf{G}_8$ outputs 1. To do that, we give an unbounded reduction from the lossy soundness experiment, which is as follows.

- The reduction gets par, $X_{1,1}$ as input. It samples $\hat{i} \xleftarrow{\$} [Q_{\mathsf{H}_c}]$. Then, it simulates $\mathbf{G}_8$ honestly until $\mathcal{A}$ outputs a forgery, except for query $\hat{i}$ to oracle H_c.
- Consider this query $\mathsf{H}_c(\mathsf{pk}, \mathsf{com}, \mathsf{m}, \langle\mathcal{P}\rangle, B, b)$. The reduction aborts its execution, if the hash value for this query is already defined, or if $\mathsf{pk} \neq \mathsf{pk}^* \vee b \neq \bar{\mathsf{H}}_b(\mathsf{seed}_1, \langle\mathcal{P}\rangle, \mathsf{m})$. Otherwise, it runs $\hat{R} \leftarrow \mathsf{Ext}(\mathsf{H}(b, \langle\mathcal{P}\rangle, \mathsf{m}), \mathsf{com})$ as in $\mathbf{G}_8$. Then, it parses $\mathcal{P} = \{\mathsf{pk}_1, \ldots, \mathsf{pk}_N\}$ and $B = b_1 \ldots b_N$. It parses $\mathsf{pk}_i = (X_{i,0}, X_{i,1})$ for each $i \in [N]$, and it sets $c_{i,b} = \mathsf{H}_c(\mathsf{pk}_i, \mathsf{com}, \mathsf{m}, \langle\mathcal{P}\rangle, B, b)$ for each $i \in [N] \setminus \{1\}$. Next, it defines

$$R := \hat{R} + \sum_{i=2}^{N} c_{i,b} \cdot X_{i,\hat{b}_i},$$

where $\hat{b}_i := (b + b_i) \mod 2$. It outputs R to the lossy soundness game and obtains a value c in return. Then, it sets $h_c[\mathsf{pk}, \mathsf{com}, \mathsf{m}, \langle\mathcal{P}\rangle, B, b] := c$ and continues the simulation as in $\mathbf{G}_8$.
- When the reduction gets the forgery $(\mathcal{P}^*, \mathsf{m}^*, \sigma^*)$ from $\mathcal{A}$, it runs all the verification steps in $\mathbf{G}_8$. Additionally, it checks if the value $\mathsf{H}_c(\mathsf{pk}_1, \mathsf{com}^*_{1-b^*_1}, \mathsf{m}^*, \langle\mathcal{P}^*\rangle, B^*, 1 - b^*_1)$ was defined during query $\hat{i}$ to H_c. If this is not the case, it aborts its execution. Otherwise, it returns $s := s^*_{1-b^*_1}$ to the lossy soundness game.

It is clear that the view of $\mathcal{A}$ is independent of the index $\hat{i}$ until a potential abort of the reduction. Also, if the reduction does not abort its execution, it perfectly simulates game $\mathbf{G}_8$ for $\mathcal{A}$. Thus, it remains to show that if $\mathbf{G}_8$ outputs 1, then the values output by the reduction satisfy $\mathsf{F}(s) - c \cdot X_{1,1} = R$. Once we have shown this, it follows that

$$\mathsf{Adv}_8 \leq Q_{\mathsf{H}_c} \varepsilon_{\mathsf{l}}.$$

To show the desired property, assume that the reduction does not abort and $\mathbf{G}_8$ outputs 1. Then, define $\hat{b}^*_i = (1 - b^*_1 + b_i) \mod 2$ for all $i \in [N]$. Note that $\hat{b}^*_i = 1$. Due to the change in $\mathbf{G}_2$, we have

$$b = 1 - b^*_1 = \bar{\mathsf{H}}_b(\mathsf{seed}_1, \langle\mathcal{P}^*\rangle, \mathsf{m}^*).$$

As the reduction guessed the right query and does not abort, we have

$$c^*_{1,1-b^*_1} = \mathsf{H}_c(\mathsf{pk}_1, \mathsf{com}^*_{1-b^*_1}, \mathsf{m}^*, \langle\mathcal{P}^*\rangle, B^*, 1 - b^*_1) = c.$$

620   J. Pan and B. Wagner

Due to the change in $\mathbf{G}_8$, we have

$$F(s^*_{1-b^*_1}) - \sum_{i=1}^{N} c^*_{i,1-b^*_i} \cdot X_{i,\hat{b}^*_i} = R^*_{1-b^*_1} = \hat{R}.$$

Therefore, we have

$$F(s) - c \cdot X_{1,1} = F(s^*_{1-b^*_1}) - c^*_{1,1-b^*_1} \cdot X_{1,1}$$

$$= F(s^*_{1-b^*_1}) - \sum_{i=1}^{N} c^*_{i,1-b^*_1} \cdot X_{i,\hat{b}^*_i} + \sum_{i=2}^{N} c^*_{i,1-b^*_1} \cdot X_{i,\hat{b}^*_i}$$

$$= \hat{R} + \sum_{i=2}^{N} c^*_{i,1-b^*_1} \cdot X_{i,\hat{b}^*_i} = R.$$

Concluded.   □

4   Instantiation

In this section, we show how to instantiate the building blocks that are needed for our constructions in the previous section. Concretely, we give a linear function family and a commitment scheme based on the DDH assumption. Then, we also discuss the efficiency of the resulting multi-signature schemes.

4.1   Linear Function Family

We make use of the well-known [27] linear function family $\mathsf{LF_{DDH}} = (\mathsf{Gen}, \mathsf{F})$ based on the DDH assumption. Precisely, let GGen be an algorithm that on input 1^λ outputs the description of a prime order group $\mathbb{G}$ of order p with generator g. Then, Gen runs GGen and outputs[5] $\mathsf{par} := (g, h) \in \mathbb{G}^2$ for $h \xleftarrow{\$} \mathbb{G}$. Then, the set of scalars, domain, range, and function $\mathsf{F}(\mathsf{par}, \cdot)$ are given as follows:

$$\mathcal{S} := \mathbb{Z}_p, \quad \mathcal{D} := \mathbb{Z}_p, \quad \mathcal{R} := \mathbb{G} \times \mathbb{G}, \quad \mathsf{F}(\mathsf{par}, x) := (g^x, h^x).$$

It is easily verified that this constitutes a linear function family. Due to space limitation, the proofs of the following two lemmas are postponed to the full version [34].

Lemma 3. *Assuming that the* DDH *assumption holds relative to* GGen, *the linear function family* $\mathsf{LF_{DDH}}$ *is* ε_l-lossiness admitting, with $\varepsilon_l \leq 3/p$. *Concretely, for any PPT algorithm* $\mathcal{A}$ *there is a PPT algorithm* $\mathcal{B}$ *with* $\mathbf{T}(\mathcal{B}) \approx \mathbf{T}(\mathcal{A})$ *and*

$$\mathsf{Adv}^{\mathsf{keydist}}_{\mathcal{A},\mathsf{LF_{DDH}}}(\lambda) \leq \mathsf{Adv}^{\mathsf{DDH}}_{\mathcal{B},\mathsf{GGen}}(\lambda).$$

Lemma 4. *Linear function family* $\mathsf{LF_{DDH}}$ *satisfies* $\varepsilon_{\mathsf{al}}$-aggregation lossy soundness with $\varepsilon_{\mathsf{al}} \leq 4/p$.

---
[5] We omit the description of $\mathbb{G}$ from par to make the presentation concise.

4.2   Commitment Scheme

We give a special trapdoor commitment scheme $\mathsf{CMT_{DDH}} = (\mathsf{BGen}, \mathsf{TGen}, \mathsf{Com},$
$\mathsf{TCom}, \mathsf{TCol})$ for the linear function family $\mathsf{LF_{DDH}}$. For given parameters of
$\mathsf{LF_{DDH}}$, the commitment scheme has key space $\mathcal{K} := \mathbb{G}^{3\times3}$ and message space
$\mathcal{D} = \mathbb{G} \times \mathbb{G}$. It has randomness space $\mathcal{G} = \mathbb{Z}_p^3$ and commitment space $\mathcal{H} = \mathbb{G}^3$.
Both are associated with the natural componentwise group operations. We
describe the algorithms of the scheme verbally.

- $\mathsf{BGen}(\mathsf{par}) \to \mathsf{ck}$: Sample $g_1, g_2, g_3 \xleftarrow{\$} \mathbb{G}$, and $a, b \xleftarrow{\$} \mathbb{Z}_p$, and set

$$\mathsf{ck} := A := \begin{pmatrix} A_{1,1} & A_{1,2} & A_{1,3} \\ A_{2,1} & A_{2,2} & A_{2,3} \\ A_{3,1} & A_{3,2} & A_{3,3} \end{pmatrix} := \begin{pmatrix} g_1 & g_1^a & g_1^b \\ g_2 & g_2^a & g_2^b \\ g_3 & g_3^a & g_3^b \end{pmatrix} \in \mathbb{G}^{3\times3}.$$

- $\mathsf{TGen}(\mathsf{par}, X = (X_1, X_2)) \to (\mathsf{ck}, \mathsf{td})$: Sample $d_{i,j} \xleftarrow{\$} \mathbb{Z}_p$ for all $(i, j) \in [3] \times [3]$
  and set

$$\mathsf{ck} := A := \begin{pmatrix} A_{1,1} & A_{1,2} & A_{1,3} \\ A_{2,1} & A_{2,2} & A_{2,3} \\ A_{3,1} & A_{3,2} & A_{3,3} \end{pmatrix} := \begin{pmatrix} g^{d_{1,1}} & g^{d_{1,2}} & g^{d_{1,3}} \\ X_1^{d_{2,1}} & X_1^{d_{2,2}} & X_1^{d_{2,3}} \\ X_2^{d_{3,1}} & X_2^{d_{3,2}} & X_2^{d_{3,3}} \end{pmatrix} \in \mathbb{G}^{3\times3}.$$

Next, set

$$\mathsf{td} := (D, X_1, X_2), \text{ for } D := \begin{pmatrix} d_{1,1} & d_{1,2} & d_{1,3} \\ d_{2,1} & d_{2,2} & d_{2,3} \\ d_{3,1} & d_{3,2} & d_{3,3} \end{pmatrix} \in \mathbb{Z}_p^{3\times3}.$$

- $\mathsf{Com}(\mathsf{ck}, R = (R_1, R_2); \varphi) \to \mathsf{com}$: Let $\varphi = (\alpha, \beta, \gamma) \in \mathbb{Z}_p^3$. Compute

$$\mathsf{com} := (C_0, C_1, C_2), \text{ for } \begin{pmatrix} C_0 \\ C_1 \\ C_2 \end{pmatrix} := \begin{pmatrix} A_{1,1}^\alpha \cdot A_{1,2}^\beta \cdot A_{1,3}^\gamma \\ R_1 \cdot A_{2,1}^\alpha \cdot A_{2,2}^\beta \cdot A_{2,3}^\gamma \\ R_2 \cdot A_{3,1}^\alpha \cdot A_{3,2}^\beta \cdot A_{3,3}^\gamma \end{pmatrix}.$$

- $\mathsf{TCom}(\mathsf{ck}, \mathsf{td}) \to (\mathsf{com}, St)$: Sample $\tau, \rho_1, \rho_2, s \xleftarrow{\$} \mathbb{Z}_p$. Set $St := (\mathsf{td}, \tau, \rho_1, \rho_2, s)$
  and compute

$$\mathsf{com} := (C_0, C_1, C_2), \text{ for } \begin{pmatrix} C_0 \\ C_1 \\ C_2 \end{pmatrix} := \begin{pmatrix} g^\tau \\ X_1^{\rho_1} \cdot g^s \\ X_2^{\rho_2} \cdot h^s \end{pmatrix}.$$

- $\mathsf{TCol}(St, c) \to (\varphi, R, s)$: Set $R := (R_1, R_2) := (g^s \cdot X_1^{-c}, h^s \cdot X_2^{-c})$. Then, if
  D is not invertible, return $\bot$. Otherwise, compute

$$\varphi := (\alpha, \beta, \gamma), \text{ for } \begin{pmatrix} \alpha \\ \beta \\ \gamma \end{pmatrix} = D^{-1} \cdot \begin{pmatrix} \tau \\ \rho_1 + c \\ \rho_2 + c \end{pmatrix}.$$

Theorem 3. *If the* DDH *assumption holds relative to* GGen, *then* $\mathsf{CMT_{DDH}}$ *is a* $(\varepsilon_\mathsf{b}, \varepsilon_\mathsf{g}, \varepsilon_\mathsf{t})$-*special commitment scheme for* $\mathsf{LF_{DDH}}$, *with*

$$\varepsilon_\mathsf{b} \leq 1/p, \quad \varepsilon_\mathsf{g} \leq 2/p, \quad \varepsilon_\mathsf{t} \leq 6/p.$$

Concretely, for any PPT algorithm $\mathcal{A}$, *there is a PPT algorithm* $\mathcal{B}$ *with* $\mathbf{T}(\mathcal{B}) \approx \mathbf{T}(\mathcal{A})$ *and*

$$\mathsf{Adv}_{\mathcal{A},\mathsf{CMT_{DDH}}}^{Q\text{-keydist}}(\lambda) \leq \mathsf{Adv}_{\mathcal{B},\mathsf{GGen}}^{\mathsf{uDDH3}}(\lambda) + \frac{6}{p}.$$

The homomorphism property is trivial to check. Next, we define the set Good as in the definition of a special commitment scheme. Namely, we define

$$\mathsf{Good} = \{((g,h),x) \in \mathbb{G}^2 \times \mathbb{Z}_p \mid (g,h) \in \mathsf{LF.Gen}(1^\lambda) \wedge h \neq g^0 \wedge x \neq 0\}.$$

Clearly, for $(g,h) \leftarrow \mathsf{LF.Gen}(1^\lambda)$ and $x \overset{\$}{\leftarrow} \mathbb{Z}_p$, the probability that $((g,h),x) \notin \mathsf{Good}$ is at most $2/p$. Therefore, $\varepsilon_\mathsf{g} \leq 2/p$. In the following we also need the following observation: If $((g,h),x) \in \mathsf{Good}$, then the elements g, h, g^x, h^x are all generators of $\mathbb{G}$. The rest of proof of the theorem is given in separate lemmas.

Lemma 5. $\mathsf{CMT_{DDH}}$ *satisfies the uniform keys property of an* $(\varepsilon_\mathsf{b}, \varepsilon_\mathsf{g}, \varepsilon_\mathsf{t})$-*special commitment scheme for* $\mathsf{LF_{DDH}}$.

Proof. Let $(\mathsf{par}, x) \in \mathsf{Good}$ for $\mathsf{par} = (g, h)$. Let $(X_1, X_2) = \mathsf{F}(x) = (g^x, h^x)$. Consider the distribution of ck for $(\mathsf{ck}, \mathsf{td}) \leftarrow \mathsf{TGen}(\mathsf{par}, (X_1, X_2))$. Then ck has the form

$$\begin{pmatrix} g^{d_{1,1}} & g^{d_{1,2}} & g^{d_{1,3}} \\ X_1^{d_{2,1}} & X_1^{d_{2,2}} & X_1^{d_{2,3}} \\ X_2^{d_{3,1}} & X_2^{d_{3,2}} & X_2^{d_{3,3}} \end{pmatrix} \in \mathbb{G}^{3\times 3}$$

for uniformly random and independent exponents $d_{i,j} \in \mathbb{Z}_p$ $(i, j \in [3])$. As g, X_1, X_2 are generators, we see that ck is uniform over $\mathbb{G}^{3\times 3}$, proving the claim.

$\square$

Lemma 6. $\mathsf{CMT_{DDH}}$ *satisfies the special trapdoor property of an* $(\varepsilon_\mathsf{b}, \varepsilon_\mathsf{g}, \varepsilon_\mathsf{t})$-*special commitment scheme for* $\mathsf{LF_{DDH}}$, *where* $\varepsilon_\mathsf{t} \leq 6/p$.

Proof. Let $((g,h),x) \in \mathsf{Good}$ and $c \in \mathbb{Z}_p$. Set $(X_1, X_2) := (g^x, h^x)$. We have to show that the distributions $\mathcal{T}_0$ and $\mathcal{T}_1$ of tuples

$$((g,h), \boldsymbol{A}, \boldsymbol{D}, X_1, X_2, x, c, (C_0, C_1, C_2), \alpha, \beta, \gamma, R_1, R_2, s)$$

are identical. Here, we have $(\boldsymbol{A}, \boldsymbol{D}, X_1, X_2) \leftarrow \mathsf{TGen}(\mathsf{par}, (X_1, X_2))$. The remaining components in $\mathcal{T}_0$ are generated via

$$((C_0, C_1, C_2), St) \leftarrow \mathsf{TCom}(\mathsf{ck}, \mathsf{td}), \quad ((\alpha, \beta, \gamma), (R_1, R_2), s) \leftarrow \mathsf{TCol}(St, c),$$

and in $\mathcal{T}_1$ via

$$r \overset{\$}{\leftarrow} \mathbb{Z}_p, \; R_1 := g^r, \; R_2 := h^r, \; s := c \cdot x + r$$
$$\alpha, \beta, \gamma \overset{\$}{\leftarrow} \mathbb{Z}_p, \; (C_0, C_1, C_2) := \mathsf{Com}(\boldsymbol{A}, (R_1, R_2); (\alpha, \beta, \gamma)).$$

First, we make the assumption that in both distributions, the matrix D has full rank. The probability that this does not hold can easily be bounded by $3/p$.

We can equivalently[6] write T_1 as

$$s \overset{\$}{\leftarrow} \mathbb{Z}_p, \; R_1 := g^s \cdot X_1^{-c}, \; R_2 := h^s \cdot X_2^{-c},$$
$$\alpha, \beta, \gamma \overset{\$}{\leftarrow} \mathbb{Z}_p, \; (C_0, C_1, C_2) := \mathsf{Com}(A, (R_1, R_2); (\alpha, \beta, \gamma)).$$

Using that D is full rank and g, X_1, X_2 are generators of $\mathbb{G}$, we see that in this distribution, (C_0, C_1, C_2) is uniform over $\mathbb{G}^3$. Therefore, this is identically distributed to the distribution that we get from

$$s \overset{\$}{\leftarrow} \mathbb{Z}_p, \; R_1 := g^s \cdot X_1^{-c}, \; R_2 := h^s \cdot X_2^{-c},$$
$$\tau, \rho_1, \rho_2 \overset{\$}{\leftarrow} \mathbb{Z}_p, \; (C_0, C_1, C_2) := (g^\tau, X_1^{\rho_1} g^s, X_2^{\rho_2} h^s),$$

and then finding the unique values (α, β, γ) that satisfy $(C_0, C_1, C_2) = \mathsf{Com}(A, (R_1, R_2); (\alpha, \beta, \gamma))$. We claim that this can be done using $(\alpha, \beta, \gamma)^t := D^{-1}(\tau, \rho_1 + c, \rho_2 + c)^t$, which is equivalent to distribution T_0.

To see this, note that $(C_0, C_1, C_2) = \mathsf{Com}(A, (R_1, R_2); (\alpha, \beta, \gamma))$ is equivalent to

$$\begin{pmatrix} C_0 \\ C_1 \\ C_2 \end{pmatrix} = \begin{pmatrix} A_{1,1}^\alpha \cdot A_{1,2}^\beta \cdot A_{1,3}^\gamma \\ R_1 \cdot A_{2,1}^\alpha \cdot A_{2,2}^\beta \cdot A_{2,3}^\gamma \\ R_1 \cdot A_{3,1}^\alpha \cdot A_{3,2}^\beta \cdot A_{3,3}^\gamma \end{pmatrix} = \begin{pmatrix} g^{d_{1,1}\alpha} \cdot g^{d_{1,2}\beta} \cdot g^{d_{1,3}\gamma} \\ g^s \cdot X_1^{-c} \cdot X_1^{d_{2,1}\alpha} \cdot X_1^{d_{2,2}\beta} \cdot X_1^{d_{2,3}\gamma} \\ h^s \cdot X_2^{-c} \cdot X_2^{d_{3,1}\alpha} \cdot X_2^{d_{3,2}\beta} \cdot X_2^{d_{3,3}\gamma} \end{pmatrix}.$$

Using the way we generate (C_0, C_1, C_2), we see that the g^s and h^s terms cancel out, and this is equivalent to

$$\begin{pmatrix} g^\tau \\ X_1^{\rho_1} \\ X_2^{\rho_2} \end{pmatrix} = \begin{pmatrix} g^{d_{1,1}\alpha} \cdot g^{d_{1,2}\beta} \cdot g^{d_{1,3}\gamma} \\ X_1^{d_{2,1}\alpha} \cdot X_1^{d_{2,2}\beta} \cdot X_1^{d_{2,3}\gamma} \\ X_2^{d_{3,1}\alpha} \cdot X_2^{d_{3,2}\beta} \cdot X_2^{d_{3,3}\gamma} \end{pmatrix} \iff \begin{pmatrix} \tau \\ \rho_1 + c \\ \rho_2 + c \end{pmatrix} = D \cdot \begin{pmatrix} \alpha \\ \beta \\ \gamma \end{pmatrix}.$$

This concludes the proof. □

Lemma 7. $\mathsf{CMT}_{\mathsf{DDH}}$ *satisfies the statistically binding property of an* $(\varepsilon_b, \varepsilon_g, \varepsilon_t)$-*special commitment scheme for* $\mathsf{LF}_{\mathsf{DDH}}$, *with* $\varepsilon_b \leq 1/p$.

Proof. We describe an unbounded algorithm Ext, that takes as input a commitment key $\mathsf{ck} = A = (A_{i,j})_{i,j} \in \mathbb{G}^{3\times 3}$, and a commitment $\mathsf{com} = (C_0, C_1, C_2) \in \mathbb{G}^3$, and outputs a tuple $R = (R_1, R_2) \in \mathbb{G} \times \mathbb{G}$. It is given as follows:

1. Extract discrete logarithms $c = (c_0, c_1, c_2)^t \in \mathbb{Z}_p^3$ and $a = (a_0, a_1, a_2)^t \in \mathbb{Z}_p^3$ such that

$$\begin{pmatrix} C_0 \\ C_1 \\ C_2 \end{pmatrix} = \begin{pmatrix} g^{c_0} \\ g^{c_1} \\ g^{c_2} \end{pmatrix} \quad \text{and} \quad \begin{pmatrix} A_{1,1} \\ A_{2,1} \\ A_{3,1} \end{pmatrix} = \begin{pmatrix} g^{a_0} \\ g^{a_1} \\ g^{a_2} \end{pmatrix}.$$

---

[6] This corresponds to the HVZK property of linear identification protocols.

2. If $a_0 = 0$, return $\perp$. Otherwise, let $e_2 = (0, 1, 0)^t$ and $e_3 = (0, 0, 1)^t$. Note that a, e_2, e_3 form a basis of $\mathbb{Z}_p^3$.
3. Write c as $c = ta + r_1 e_2 + r_2 e_3$ for $t, r_1, r_2 \in \mathbb{Z}_p$, and return $(R_1, R_2) := (g^{r_1}, g^{r_2})$.

To finish the proof, let $\mathcal{A}$ be any algorithm. We have to bound the probability

$$
\Pr\left[
\begin{array}{c|c}
\begin{array}{c}
\mathsf{Com}(\boldsymbol{A}, (R_1', R_2'); \varphi') = (C_0, C_1, C_2) \\
\wedge \ (R_1, R_2) \neq (R_1', R_2')
\end{array}
&
\begin{array}{l}
(g, h) \leftarrow \mathsf{LF.Gen}(1^\lambda), \\
\boldsymbol{A} \leftarrow \mathsf{BGen}(\mathsf{par}), \\
((C_0, C_1, C_2), St) \leftarrow \mathcal{A}(\boldsymbol{A}), \\
(R_1, R_2) \leftarrow \mathsf{Ext}(\boldsymbol{A}, (C_0, C_1, C_2)), \\
(R_1, R_2', \varphi') \leftarrow \mathcal{A}(St)
\end{array}
\end{array}
\right].
$$

Note that the probability that Ext outputs $\perp$ in this experiment is $1/p$, as $A_{1,1}$ is uniform in $\mathbb{G}$. We assume that Ext does not output $\perp$, and want to show that the above probability conditioned on this event is zero. First, it is easy to see that we have $\mathsf{Com}(\boldsymbol{A}, (R_1, R_2); (t, 0, 0)) = (C_0, C_1, C_2)$. Further, assume that $\mathcal{A}$ outputs $(R_1', R_2') = (g^{r_1'}, g^{r_2'})$ and $\varphi' = (\alpha, \beta, \gamma)$ such that

$$
\mathsf{Com}(\boldsymbol{A}, (R_1', R_2'); \varphi') = (C_0, C_1, C_2) = \mathsf{Com}(\boldsymbol{A}, (R_1, R_2); (t, 0, 0)).
$$

Using the definition of Com and BGen, we see that this implies the vector $(0, r_1 - r_1', r_2 - r_2')^t$ is in the span of a. As $a_0 \neq 0$ this implies that it is the zero vector, showing that $R_1 = R_1'$ and $R_2 = R_2'$. $\square$

Lemma 8. *For any PPT algorithm $\mathcal{A}$, there is a PPT algorithm $\mathcal{B}$ with $\mathbf{T}(\mathcal{B}) \approx \mathbf{T}(\mathcal{A})$ and*

$$
\mathsf{Adv}_{\mathcal{A}, \mathsf{CMT}_{\mathsf{DDH}}}^{Q\text{-keydist}}(\lambda) \leq \mathsf{Adv}_{\mathcal{B}, \mathsf{GGen}}^{\mathsf{uDDH3}}(\lambda) + \frac{6}{p}.
$$

The lemma is proven by a simple reduction. Looking at one fixed commitment key $\boldsymbol{A}_i$, indistinguishability would directly follow from the uDDH3 assumption. To give a tight reduction for any $Q = \mathsf{poly}(\lambda)$, we use the random self-reducibility of uDDH3. We postpone it to the full version [34].

4.3   Efficiency

In our full version [34], we discuss the efficiency of our schemes both asymptotically, as well as in terms of concrete parameters.

Acknowledgments. We thank the anonymous reviewers from Eurocrypt 2023 for their useful feedback and suggestions. In particular, it was pointed out the similarity between the commitment scheme of Bagherzandi, Cheon, and Jarecki in [3] and ours.

References

1. Abdalla, M., Fouque, P.-A., Lyubashevsky, V., Tibouchi, M.: Tightly-secure signatures from lossy identification schemes. In: Pointcheval, D., Johansson, T. (eds.) EUROCRYPT 2012. LNCS, vol. 7237, pp. 572–590. Springer, Heidelberg (2012). https://doi.org/10.1007/978-3-642-29011-4_34

2. Kılınç Alper, H., Burdges, J.: Two-round trip schnorr multi-signatures via delinearized witnesses. In: Malkin, T., Peikert, C. (eds.) CRYPTO 2021. LNCS, vol. 12825, pp. 157–188. Springer, Cham (2021). https://doi.org/10.1007/978-3-030-84242-0_7

3. Bagherzandi, A., Cheon, J.H., Jarecki, S.: Multisignatures secure under the discrete logarithm assumption and a generalized forking lemma. In: Ning, P., Syverson, P.F., Jha, S. (eds.) ACM CCS 2008, pp. 449–458. ACM Press (2008). https://doi.org/10.1145/1455770.1455827

4. Bellare, M., Dai, W.: Chain reductions for multi-signatures and the HBMS scheme. In: Tibouchi, M., Wang, H. (eds.) ASIACRYPT 2021. LNCS, vol. 13093, pp. 650–678. Springer, Cham (2021). https://doi.org/10.1007/978-3-030-92068-5_22

5. Bellare, M., Neven, G.: Multi-signatures in the plain public-key model and a general forking lemma. In: Juels, A., Wright, R.N., De Capitani di Vimercati, S. (eds.) ACM CCS 2006, pp. 390–399. ACM Press (2006). https://doi.org/10.1145/1180405.1180453

6. Blazy, O., Kiltz, E., Pan, J.: (Hierarchical) identity-based encryption from affine message authentication. In: Garay, J.A., Gennaro, R. (eds.) CRYPTO 2014. LNCS, vol. 8616, pp. 408–425. Springer, Heidelberg (2014). https://doi.org/10.1007/978-3-662-44371-2_23

7. Boldyreva, A.: Threshold signatures, multisignatures and blind signatures based on the gap-diffie-hellman-group signature scheme. In: Desmedt, Y.G. (ed.) PKC 2003. LNCS, vol. 2567, pp. 31–46. Springer, Heidelberg (2003). https://doi.org/10.1007/3-540-36288-6_3

8. Boneh, D., Drijvers, M., Neven, G.: Compact multi-signatures for smaller blockchains. In: Peyrin, T., Galbraith, S. (eds.) ASIACRYPT 2018. LNCS, vol. 11273, pp. 435–464. Springer, Cham (2018). https://doi.org/10.1007/978-3-030-03329-3_15

9. Boschini, C., Takahashi, A., Tibouchi, M.: MuSig-L: lattice-based multi-signature with single-round online phase. In: Dodis, Y., Shrimpton, T. (eds.) CRYPTO 2022, Part II. LNCS, vol. 13508, pp. 276–305. Springer, Heidelberg (2022). https://doi.org/10.1007/978-3-031-15979-4_10

10. Chairattana-Apirom, R., Hanzlik, L., Loss, J., Lysyanskaya, A., Wagner, B.: PI-cut-choo and friends: Compact blind signatures via parallel instance cut-and-choose and more. In: Dodis, Y., Shrimpton, T. (eds.) CRYPTO 2022, Part III. LNCS, vol. 13509, pp. 3–31. Springer, Heidelberg (2022). https://doi.org/10.1007/978-3-031-15982-4_1

11. Crites, E., Komlo, C., Maller, M.: How to prove schnorr assuming schnorr: security of multi- and threshold signatures. Cryptology ePrint Archive, Report 2021/1375 (2021). https://eprint.iacr.org/2021/1375

12. Damgård, I.: Efficient concurrent zero-knowledge in the auxiliary string model. In: Preneel, B. (ed.) EUROCRYPT 2000. LNCS, vol. 1807, pp. 418–430. Springer, Heidelberg (2000). https://doi.org/10.1007/3-540-45539-6_30

13. Damgård, I., Orlandi, C., Takahashi, A., Tibouchi, M.: Two-round n-out-of-n and multi-signatures and trapdoor commitment from lattices. In: Garay, J.A. (ed.) PKC 2021. LNCS, vol. 12710, pp. 99–130. Springer, Cham (2021). https://doi.org/10.1007/978-3-030-75245-3_5

14. Drijvers, M., et al.: On the security of two-round multi-signatures. In: 2019 IEEE Symposium on Security and Privacy, pp. 1084–1101. IEEE Computer Society Press (2019). https://doi.org/10.1109/SP.2019.00050

15. Escala, A., Herold, G., Kiltz, E., Ràfols, C., Villar, J.: An algebraic framework for diffie-hellman assumptions. In: Canetti, R., Garay, J.A. (eds.) CRYPTO 2013. LNCS, vol. 8043, pp. 129–147. Springer, Heidelberg (2013). https://doi.org/10.1007/978-3-642-40084-1_8

16. Fukumitsu, M., Hasegawa, S.: A tightly secure ddh-based multisignature with public-key aggregation. Int. J. Netw. Comput. **11**(2), 319–337 (2021). http://www.ijnc.org/index.php/ijnc/article/view/257

17. Goh, E.-J., Jarecki, S., Katz, J., Wang, N.: Efficient signature schemes with tight reductions to the diffie-hellman problems. J. Cryptol. **20**(4), 493–514 (2007). https://doi.org/10.1007/s00145-007-0549-3

18. Groth, J.: Homomorphic trapdoor commitments to group elements. Cryptology ePrint Archive, Report 2009/007 (2009). https://eprint.iacr.org/2009/007

19. Groth, J., Ostrovsky, R., Sahai, A.: Non-interactive zaps and new techniques for NIZK. In: Dwork, C. (ed.) CRYPTO 2006. LNCS, vol. 4117, pp. 97–111. Springer, Heidelberg (2006). https://doi.org/10.1007/11818175_6

20. Groth, J., Sahai, A.: Efficient non-interactive proof systems for bilinear groups. In: Smart, N. (ed.) EUROCRYPT 2008. LNCS, vol. 4965, pp. 415–432. Springer, Heidelberg (2008). https://doi.org/10.1007/978-3-540-78967-3_24

21. Guillou, L.C., Quisquater, J.-J.: A practical zero-knowledge protocol fitted to security microprocessor minimizing both transmission and memory. In: Barstow, D., et al. (eds.) EUROCRYPT 1988. LNCS, vol. 330, pp. 123–128. Springer, Heidelberg (1988). https://doi.org/10.1007/3-540-45961-8_11

22. Han, S., et al.: Authenticated key exchange and signatures with tight security in the standard model. In: Malkin, T., Peikert, C. (eds.) CRYPTO 2021. LNCS, vol. 12828, pp. 670–700. Springer, Cham (2021). https://doi.org/10.1007/978-3-030-84259-8_23

23. Hauck, E., Kiltz, E., Loss, J.: A modular treatment of blind signatures from identification schemes. In: Ishai, Y., Rijmen, V. (eds.) EUROCRYPT 2019. LNCS, vol. 11478, pp. 345–375. Springer, Cham (2019). https://doi.org/10.1007/978-3-030-17659-4_12

24. Itakura, K., Nakamura, K.: A public-key cryptosystem suitable for digital multisignatures. NEC Res. Dev. **71**, 1–8 (1983)

25. Katz, J., Loss, J., Rosenberg, M.: Boosting the security of blind signature schemes. In: Tibouchi, M., Wang, H. (eds.) ASIACRYPT 2021. LNCS, vol. 13093, pp. 468–492. Springer, Cham (2021). https://doi.org/10.1007/978-3-030-92068-5_16

26. Katz, J., Wang, N.: Efficiency improvements for signature schemes with tight security reductions. In: Jajodia, S., Atluri, V., Jaeger, T. (eds.) ACM CCS 2003, pp. 155–164. ACM Press (2003). https://doi.org/10.1145/948109.948132

27. Kiltz, E., Masny, D., Pan, J.: Optimal security proofs for signatures from identification schemes. In: Robshaw, M., Katz, J. (eds.) CRYPTO 2016. LNCS, vol. 9815, pp. 33–61. Springer, Heidelberg (2016). https://doi.org/10.1007/978-3-662-53008-5_2

28. Langrehr, R., Pan, J.: Unbounded HIBE with tight security. In: Moriai, S., Wang, H. (eds.) ASIACRYPT 2020. LNCS, vol. 12492, pp. 129–159. Springer, Cham (2020). https://doi.org/10.1007/978-3-030-64834-3_5

29. Lu, S., Ostrovsky, R., Sahai, A., Shacham, H., Waters, B.: Sequential aggregate signatures and multisignatures without random oracles. In: Vaudenay, S. (ed.) EUROCRYPT 2006. LNCS, vol. 4004, pp. 465–485. Springer, Heidelberg (2006). https://doi.org/10.1007/11761679_28

30. Maxwell, G., Poelstra, A., Seurin, Y., Wuille, P.: Simple Schnorr multi-signatures with applications to Bitcoin. Des. Codes Cryptogr. **87**(9), 2139–2164 (2019). https://doi.org/10.1007/s10623-019-00608-x

31. Micali, S., Ohta, K., Reyzin, L.: Accountable-subgroup multisignatures: extended abstract. In: Reiter, M.K., Samarati, P. (eds.) ACM CCS 2001, pp. 245–254. ACM Press (2001). https://doi.org/10.1145/501983.502017

32. Nick, J., Ruffing, T., Seurin, Y.: MuSig2: simple two-round schnorr multi-signatures. In: Malkin, T., Peikert, C. (eds.) CRYPTO 2021. LNCS, vol. 12825, pp. 189–221. Springer, Cham (2021). https://doi.org/10.1007/978-3-030-84242-0_8

33. Nick, J., Ruffing, T., Seurin, Y., Wuille, P.: MuSig-DN: schnorr multi-signatures with verifiably deterministic nonces. In: Ligatti, J., Ou, X., Katz, J., Vigna, G. (eds.) ACM CCS 2020, pp. 1717–1731. ACM Press (2020). https://doi.org/10.1145/3372297.3417236

34. Pan, J., Wagner, B.: Chopsticks: fork-free two-round multi-signatures from non-interactive assumptions. Cryptology ePrint Archive, Paper 2023/198 (2023). https://eprint.iacr.org/2023/198, https://eprint.iacr.org/2023/198

35. Pedersen, T.P.: Non-interactive and information-theoretic secure verifiable secret sharing. In: Feigenbaum, J. (ed.) CRYPTO 1991. LNCS, vol. 576, pp. 129–140. Springer, Heidelberg (1992). https://doi.org/10.1007/3-540-46766-1_9

36. Schnorr, C.P.: Efficient signature generation by smart cards. J. Cryptol. **4**(3), 161–174 (1991). https://doi.org/10.1007/BF00196725

37. Tessaro, S., Zhu, C.: Threshold and multi-signature schemes from linear hash functions. In: Eurocrypt 2023, LNCS (to appear). Springer, Heidelberg (2023)

Threshold and Multi-signature Schemes from Linear Hash Functions

Stefano Tessaro[iD] and Chenzhi Zhu[✉][iD]

Paul G. Allen School of Computer Science & Engineering,
University of Washington, Seattle, USA
{tessaro,zhucz20}@cs.washington.edu

Abstract. This paper gives new constructions of two-round multi-signatures and threshold signatures for which security relies solely on either the hardness of the (plain) discrete logarithm problem or the hardness of RSA, in addition to assuming random oracles. Their signing protocol is partially non-interactive, i.e., the first round of the signing protocol is independent of the message being signed.

We obtain our constructions by generalizing the most efficient discrete-logarithm based schemes, MuSig2 (Nick, Ruffing, and Seurin, CRYPTO '21) and FROST (Komlo and Goldberg, SAC '20), to work with suitably defined linear hash functions. While the original schemes rely on the stronger and more controversial one-more discrete logarithm assumption, we show that suitable instantiations of the hash functions enable security to be based on either the plain discrete logarithm assumption or on RSA. The signatures produced by our schemes are equivalent to those obtained from Okamoto's identification schemes (CRYPTO '92).

More abstractly, our results suggest a general framework to transform schemes secure under OMDL into ones secure under the plain DL assumption and, with some restrictions, under RSA.

1 Introduction

Many novel applications, such as digital wallets [25], are re-energizing a multi-decade agenda aimed at developing new efficient multi-signatures [33] and threshold signatures [18,19] from a variety of assumptions. Threshold signatures are also at the center of standardization efforts by NIST [42] and IETF [15]. Both signature types are relatively straightforward to obtain from pairings (using, e.g., BLS [13,14]); however, specific implementation constraints make pairing-free schemes, which are based on either variants of the discrete logarithm or RSA problems, appealing in several contexts.

This paper aims to build the best possible pairing-free multi-signatures and threshold signatures under the weakest possible assumptions. As our main contribution, we develop new two-round protocols that are secure under the (1) discrete logarithm assumption and (2) the RSA assumption. In both cases, we also assume the random oracle model (ROM) [10]. Our RSA multi-signatures require a trusted setup to produce a public RSA modulus with unknown factorization. The signatures produced by both schemes resemble those proposed by

© International Association for Cryptologic Research 2023
C. Hazay and M. Stam (Eds.): EUROCRYPT 2023, LNCS 14008, pp. 628–658, 2023.
https://doi.org/10.1007/978-3-031-30589-4_22

Okamoto [46]. Furthermore, our signing protocols are partially non-interactive, i.e., the first round messages do not depend on the message being signed, which is a desirable property in practice.

SIGNIFICANCE. Our DL-based schemes are the first partially non-interactive 2-round schemes based solely on the hardness of the discrete logarithm assumption. For threshold signatures, in particular, no two-round scheme is known from only the discrete logarithm assumption. For RSA, the landscape is more complex, and our main contribution is to provide a viable multi-signature scheme, as all prior solutions impose restrictions.

OUR APPROACH. Our schemes are the outcome of the same paradigm applied to the two most efficient DL-based schemes, FROST [6,37] and MuSig2 [43]. It is not known how to prove the security of either scheme under the plain discrete logarithm assumption, and they are instead proved secure under the (stronger) *one-more discrete logarithm assumption* (OMDL) [8], an assumption that has been the subject of criticism [35,36]. As we explain next, our paradigm can be seen as a general recipe to remove the OMDL assumption from these schemes.

The main ingredient of our approach are *linear hash functions*, which have also been used in recent works [3,30,31] to abstract identification schemes from which signature variants are derived. Here, we observe that both FROST ad MuSig2 can naturally be generalized by replacing the exponentiation map $x \mapsto g^x$ with a linear hash function $F : \mathcal{D} \to \mathcal{R}$, where $\mathcal{D}, \mathcal{R}$ are $\mathcal{S}$-modules for a field $\mathcal{S}$. We generically refer to these instantiations as FROST-H and MuSig2-H. (In fact, we present two variants for FROST-H but make no distinction in the introduction.) In particular, we require that:

- F is an epimorphism of $\mathcal{S}$-modules from $\mathcal{D}$ to $\mathcal{R}$, i.e., F is a surjection from $\mathcal{D}$ to $\mathcal{R}$ such that for any $r \in \mathcal{S}$ and $x, y \in \mathcal{D}$, $F(x + r \cdot y) = F(x) + r \cdot F(y)$.
- F is *not a monomorphism*, which is equivalent to postulating that there exists $z^* \in \mathcal{D}$ such that $z^* \neq 0$ and $F(z^*) = 0$.

We then define a natural analogue of the OMDL assumption, which we refer to as the *Algebraic One-More Preimage Resistance* (AOMPR). Roughly speaking, the corresponding security game allows the attacker to obtain multiple *challenges* $X_i = F(x_i)$ for a random element $x_i \leftarrow_\$ \mathcal{D}$, and the attacker also gets access to an *inversion oracle* which, on input $X \in \mathcal{R}$, returns a element in the preimage set of X under F. The restriction here, and hence the term *algebraic*, is that X must be an affine combination of previously obtained X_i's, and this affine combination is given to the inversion oracle, along with X. (This makes the assumption falsifiable since the oracle can efficiently answer such inversion queries.) To win the game, the attacker is then asked to invert $q + 1$ challenges after querying the inversion oracle at most q times.

Our results then follow from the combination of the following two theorems, which we state here informally:

Theorem (informal). The security of FROST-H and MuSig2-H follows from the AOMPR assumption on the underlying linear hash function.

Theorem (informal). If F is collision-resistant, then the AOMPR assumption holds with respect to F.

The proof of the first theorem is, on its own, not particularly surprising and mostly generalizes the prior proofs in the literature, in particular those of [43] and [6]. Our main contribution here is to notice that these proofs, and the resulting schemes, can be abstracted in terms of linear hash functions. In particular, for threshold signatures, as in [6], we consider an abstract setting with an ideal distributed key generation, and we target the security notions of TS-SUF-2 and TS-SUF-3, which were shown to be achieved by two variants of FROST, both of which we model here abstractly. Since we are targeting feasibility, we are less concerned with the concrete round complexity of distributed key generation and could use any secure multi-party computation protocol for this task.

In contrast, the rough intuition behind a proof of the latter theorem is that for any execution of a (wlog deterministic) adversary $\mathcal{A}$ playing the AOMPR game with challenges $\boldsymbol{X} = \mathsf{F}(\boldsymbol{x})$, since F is not a monomorphism, there exists another execution with challenges $\boldsymbol{X} = \mathsf{F}(\boldsymbol{x}')$ such that $\boldsymbol{x} \neq \boldsymbol{x}'$, but the views of $\mathcal{A}$ are identical in the two executions. Then, if $\mathcal{A}$ wins the game given $\boldsymbol{x}$ by outputting $\boldsymbol{y}$ such that $\mathsf{F}(\boldsymbol{y}) = \boldsymbol{X}$, $\mathcal{A}$ also wins the game given $\boldsymbol{x}'$ by outputting $\boldsymbol{y}$. Therefore, we have $\mathsf{F}(\boldsymbol{x}) = \mathsf{F}(\boldsymbol{y}) = \mathsf{F}(\boldsymbol{x}') \wedge (\boldsymbol{x} \neq \boldsymbol{y} \vee \boldsymbol{x}' \neq \boldsymbol{y})$, which implies that we can find a collision in at least one of the executions. Indeed, special cases of this technique already underlie several works, including Okamoto's [46], but our main challenges are to prove the concrete mapping of $\boldsymbol{x}'$ from $\boldsymbol{x}$ and to package this in terms of the AOMPR abstraction.

1.1 DL-Based Instantiations

To obtain an instantiation of FROST-H and MuSig2-H based on the hardness of the discrete logarithm (DL) problem, we can use the Pedersen linear hash function [49]

$$\mathsf{F}(x_1, x_2) = g^{x_1} Z^{x_2} \ ,$$

which is well known to be collision-resistant under the hardness of DL whenever g, Z are generators of a group with prime size p. While MuSig2 and FROST produce valid Schnorr signatures [52], the signatures produced by our DL-based instantiations of FROST-H and MuSig2-H are slightly less efficient, and effectively compatible with Okamoto's signatures [46]. Here, as in Schnorr signatures, the secret signing key is $x \in \mathbb{Z}_p$, and the public verification key $\mathsf{pk} = g^x$, and a signature for a message $m \in \{0,1\}^*$ has format

$$\sigma = (R = g^a Z^b, a + \mathsf{H}(\mathsf{pk}, m, R) \cdot x, b) \ ,$$

where H is a hash function that is modeled as a random oracle in our proofs. To verify a signature (R, a, b), we check that $g^a Z^b = R \cdot \mathsf{pk}^{\mathsf{H}(\mathsf{pk}, M, R)}$. The only difference from Okamoto's scheme [46] is that the latter uses a secret key $(x_1, x_2) \in \mathbb{Z}_p^2$, and a signature has form $(R = g^a Z^b, a + c \cdot x_1, b + c \cdot x_2)$, where $c = \mathsf{H}(\mathsf{pk}, m, R)$, i.e., here, we restrict the scheme to the case where $(x_1, x_2) = (x, 0)$. This optimization is generic and could have been applied to Okamoto's scheme directly; however, it is particularly advantageous for threshold signatures since it lets us leverage any distributed key generation protocol for Schnorr signatures. Here, we need a trusted setup to generate Z as a random group element independent of g, but we note that this is a minimal setup since it can be made transparent, e.g., g, Z can be generated as outputs of a hash function.

RELATED WORK (DL). Our DL-based threshold signatures are the first two-round scheme with security proved based solely on the discrete logarithm assumption in the ROM. The most efficient protocol is FROST [6, 37], which is slightly more efficient than our scheme since it generates plain Schnorr signatures; however, FROST relies on the stronger OMDL assumption. Though schemes based solely on the discrete logarithm assumption exist [28, 39, 55], they use more rounds. We stress that not all schemes achieve the same security goals, and here we target the notions of [6], whereas Lindell [39] targets UC security.

Our DL-based scheme gives the first partially non-interactive two-round multi-signatures based on plain DL and the ROM. It is almost as efficient as MuSig2 [43], which is based on OMDL. Drijvers et al. [21] proposed a less efficient two-round scheme, called mBCJ, based on DL and ROM only, and it repairs a prior scheme by Bagherzandi, Cheon, and Jarecki [4]. mBCJ signatures, less efficient than ours, consist of two group elements and three scalars, and public keys also consist of one group element and two scalars. Moreover, mBCJ is not partially non-interactive (i.e., the first round does depend on the message being signed). Another option is the MuSig-DN scheme [44], but it relies on heavy machinery from zero-knowledge proofs.

A more efficient DL-based alternative is the HBMS scheme by Bellare and Dai [7], but HBMS is not partially non-interactive. Further, our security reduction is tighter than that of HBMS. Most relevant to us, Lee and Kim [38] gave a multi-signature scheme based on Okamoto signatures that, however, is proved secure only in the AGM [24]; their signing is also not partially non-interactive.

More recently, Pan and Wagner [47] proposed a two-round multi-signature scheme based only on the Decisional Diffie-Hellman (DDH) assumption with a tight reduction, but their scheme is also not partially non-interactive.

Finally, the work of Drijvers et al. [21], as well as recent ROS attacks [12], also surfaced several security issues in earlier DL-based proposals that we do not discuss here.

1.2 RSA-Based Instantiation

The situation with RSA is slightly more complex since the above framework, as is, does not appear to support an RSA instantiation directly: no natural RSA-based linear hash function realizes an appropriate $\mathcal{S}$-module where $\mathcal{S}$ is a field, which is of critical importance for our constructions and proofs of theorems. However, we show that the framework can be adapted to support the RSA-based linear hash function

$$\mathsf{F}(x_1, x_2) = x_1^e w^{x_2} \ ,$$

based on public parameters $par = (N, e, w)$, where N is an RSA modulus, $e \in \mathbb{Z}_N^*$ is a prime such that $\gcd(e, \phi(N)) = 1$ and $w \in \mathbb{Z}_N^*$. We refer to this linear hash function as RLHF. Here, it is important to note that the supported scalar space is set to $\mathcal{S} := \mathbb{Z}$, which is only a ring. (We refer to such hash functions as *weak* linear hash functions.)

RSA-SPECIFIC CHALLENGES. We now describe the problems caused by the lack of inversion in $\mathcal{S}$, and briefly explain how we fix them for the specific case of RLHF. We stress that these fixes are very ad-hoc for RSA, and *do not work* in general for weak linear hash functions.

- FROST-H generates signing keys using Shamir secret sharing [53], which requires the scalar space to be a field in order to compute the Lagrange coefficients. This is a common problem for RSA-based threshold schemes [16, 54], and we address it via the standard trick of multiplying the Lagrange coefficients with a large number to make them integers.
- One place in the proof of our first informal theorem above (reducing the security of MuSig2-H and FROST-H to AOMPR) where the scalar space needs to be a field is to invert challenges $\boldsymbol{X} \in \mathcal{R}^n$, given a linear equation $A\boldsymbol{X} = \mathsf{F}(\boldsymbol{b})$, where A in $\mathcal{S}^{n \times n}$, $\boldsymbol{X}$ in $\mathcal{R}^n$, and $\boldsymbol{b}$ in $\mathcal{D}^n$. Since $\mathcal{S}$ is a field in our original proof, we show that A has full rank; thus, one can compute $\boldsymbol{x}$ such that $\boldsymbol{X} = \mathsf{F}(\boldsymbol{x})$ by multiplying the inverse of A on both sides of the equation. Clearly, this fails if $\mathcal{S}$ is not a field. Fortunately, to instantiate RLHF, we find that this equation can be solved efficiently whenever A has full rank modulo e (which, recall, is a prime), and we show this condition holds whenever we need to solve the equation in the proof for the special case of RLHF. In addition, for MuSig2-H, we require one of the prime factors of N to be a safe prime in order to make the reduction go through. We also show how to remove this safe-prime requirement by minimally modifying the key aggregation algorithm.
- For our second informal theorem (reducing AOMPR to the collision-resistance of the linear hash function), we need the scalar space to be a field upon showing that, for any matrix $B \in \mathcal{S}^{\ell \times q}$ for $\ell < q$, there exists $\boldsymbol{u} \in \mathcal{S}^q$ such that
    1. $B\boldsymbol{u} = 0$;
    2. $u_i z^* \neq 0$ for some $i \in [q]$, where z^* is an a prior fixed non-zero element in $\mathcal{D}$ such that $\mathsf{F}(z^*) = 0$.

  Again, if $\mathcal{S}$ is a ring, such an $\boldsymbol{u}$ might not exist. However, for the RSA-based linear hash function, since $\mathcal{S} = \mathbb{Z}$, we can always find a non-zero $\boldsymbol{u} \in \mathbb{Z}^q$ such that $B\boldsymbol{u} = 0$. Showing the second condition involves some technical details of RLHF, but roughly, we need to show that there exists $i \in [q]$ such that $u_i \not\equiv 0 \bmod e$.

RESULTING SCHEMES. Our RSA-based instantiations of FROST-H and MuSig2-H produce signatures that also resemble the RSA-based signatures by Okamoto [46]. Given public parameters $par = (N, e, w)$, where $e \in \mathbb{Z}_N^*$ is a prime such that $\gcd(e, \phi(N)) = 1$ and $w \in \mathbb{Z}_N^*$, the secret signing key is $x \in \mathbb{Z}_N^*$, and the public verification key $\mathsf{pk} = x^e$, and a signature for a message $m \in \{0, 1\}^*$ has format

$$\sigma = (R = a^e w^b, a \cdot x^{\mathsf{H}(\mathsf{pk}, m, R)}, b) .$$

To verify a signature (R, s, b), one checks whether $s^e w^b = R \cdot \mathsf{pk}^{\mathsf{H}(\mathsf{pk}, m, R)}$. We give a simpler scheme that assumes that N is the product of safe primes, but we then drop this restriction in a slightly less efficient scheme.

We note that this scheme's drawback is that the public parameters *par* must be generated honestly. In the multi-signature case, this requires a trusted setup, whereas in the threshold signature case, *par* could be generated as part of the distributed key generation process. An important open question is whether we can remove a trusted setup, but we note that no better construction without a trusted setup is known, as we discuss next. Another unusual aspect of our use of the RSA assumption is that we require e to be large and prime, but this does not appear to weaken the assumption in any way.

RELATED WORK (RSA). Threshold signatures based on RSA go back to the work of Shoup [54], whose scheme is more efficient than ours since it is round optimal. Shoup's basic scheme guarantees only the inability to come up with a signature for messages for which no party has issued a signature share. A stronger notion would require that the only way to issue a valid signature is for sufficiently many honest parties to contribute, i.e., if k signature shares are needed for a valid signature to be created, and t parties can be corrupted, no valid signature should be generated *unless* at least $k-t$ parties create shares. (This notion is referred to as TS-UF-1 in [6,11].) To achieve this stronger notion, Shoup [54] modifies the scheme and relies on a variant of the DDH assumption, which we do not need here. All previous works on RSA-based threshold signatures [2,16,17,22,23,26, 27,51] do not consider this stronger security goal, although some of these works consider properties such as proactivity [2,51], robustness [23,27,51], removing trusted dealers [16,22], and adaptive-security [2], which we do not consider.

Our RSA-based instantiation of MuSig2-H improves upon the state-of-the-art even further. Indeed, only a few works on RSA multi-signatures, e.g., [1,20], support fully non-interactive signing, but they all assume a trusted third party that distributes *all* signing keys and that the number of signers is fixed. Others [29,32,34,40,41,45,46,48,50] support only sequential signing, i.e., all signers engage in the signing process one by one. Another relevant line of works addresses identity-based multi-signatures [5,9] (IBMS). IBMS can be viewed as multi-signature schemes where each ID plays the role of the public key for each signer. However, if used as a multi-signature scheme, these schemes require a trusted dealer to generate the keys for each signer. Also, they do not support key aggregation, which our scheme supports.

2 Preliminaries

2.1 Notations

For any positive integers $k < n$, $[n]$ denotes $\{1, \ldots, n\}$, and $[k..n]$ denotes $\{k, \ldots, n\}$. We use κ to denote the security parameter. For a finite set S, $|S|$ denotes the size of S, and $x \leftarrow\!\!\!{}_{\$}\, S$ denotes sampling an element uniformly from S and assigning it to x.

2.2 Basic Algebra

MODULES. For any ring R with multiplicative identity 1 and any abelian group $(M, +)$, we say M is an R-module if there exists an operation $\cdot : R \times M \to M$ such that for any $a, b \in R$ and any $x, y \in M$, (i) $a \cdot (x + y) = a \cdot x + a \cdot y$, (ii) $(a + b) \cdot x = a \cdot x + b \cdot x$, (iii) $(ab) \cdot x = a \cdot (b \cdot x)$, (iv) $1 \cdot x = x$. Also, we use 0 to denote the identity of M.

MODULE HOMOMORPHISMS. For any R-modules M and N, a map $f : M \to N$ is a homomorphism of R-modules if for any $r \in R$ and $x, y \in M$, $f(x + r \cdot y) = f(x) + r \cdot f(y)$. We say a homomorphism f is an epimorphism if f is a surjection. We say a homomorphism f is a monomorphism if f is an injection.

CHARACTERISTIC OF A FIELD. For any field $\mathbb{F}$, the characteristic of $\mathbb{F}$, denoted by $\mathrm{char}(\mathbb{F})$, is the smallest positive number k such that $k \cdot \mathbf{1} = \sum_{i=1}^{k} \mathbf{1} = \mathbf{0}$, where $\mathbf{1}$ denotes the multiplicative identity of $\mathbb{F}$ and $\mathbf{0}$ denotes the additive identity of $\mathbb{F}$. If k does not exist, we say the characteristic of F is 0.

3 Algebraic One-More Preimage Resistance

In this section, we first give the definition of linear hash functions, then define collision resistance and algebraic one-more preimage resistance (AOMPR) of a linear hash function family, and finally show AOMPR is implied by collision resistance.

3.1 Linear Hash Functions

The notion of linear hash functions is introduced in [30,31], which is in turn adapted from [3]. We adapt the definition from [30] by additionally requiring the scalar set $\mathcal{S}$ to be a field and $\mathcal{D}$ and $\mathcal{R}$ to be $\mathcal{S}$-modules, which is necessary for the reduction from collision resistance to AOMPR and for our constructions in Sect. 4 to work.

Definition 1. *A linear hash function family* LHF *is a pair of algorithms* (PGen, F) *such that*

a) PGen *is a randomized algorithm that takes as input the security parameter* 1^κ *and returns the system parameter par that defines three sets* $\mathcal{S} = \mathcal{S}(par), \mathcal{D} = \mathcal{D}(par)$ *and* $\mathcal{R} = \mathcal{R}(par)$, *where* $\mathcal{S}$ *is a field, and* $\mathcal{D}$ *and* $\mathcal{R}$ *are* $\mathcal{S}$-modules. *Moreover, we require* $|\mathcal{S}| \geqslant 2^\kappa, |\mathcal{D}| \geqslant 2^\kappa$, *and* $|\mathcal{R}| \geqslant 2^\kappa$.
b) F *is a deterministic function that takes as input the system parameter par and an element* $x \in \mathcal{D}$ *and returns an element in* $\mathcal{R}$ *such that* $\mathsf{F}(par, \cdot) : \mathcal{D} \to \mathcal{R}$ *is a epimorphism of* $\mathcal{S}$-modules. *Moreover,* F *is not a monomorphism, which is equivalent to there exists* $z^* \in \mathcal{D}$ *such that* $z^* \neq 0$ *and* $\mathsf{F}(par, z^*) = 0$. *For simplicity, we omit par from the input of* F *from now on.*

$$
\begin{array}{|l|}
\hline
\text{Game } \mathrm{CR}^{\mathcal{A}}_{\mathsf{LHF}}(\kappa): \\
\hline
par \leftarrow \mathsf{PGen}(1^{\kappa}) \\
(x_1, x_2) \leftarrow_\$ \mathcal{A}(par) \\
\text{If } x_1 \neq x_2 \text{ and } \mathsf{F}(x_1) = \mathsf{F}(x_2) \text{ then} \\
\quad \text{Return } 1 \\
\text{Return } 0 \\
\hline
\end{array}
$$

Fig. 1. The CR security game for a linear hash family $\mathsf{LHF} = (\mathsf{PGen}, \mathsf{F})$.

Game $\mathrm{AOMPR}^{\mathcal{A}}_{\mathsf{LHF}}(\kappa)$:	Oracle $\mathrm{CHAL}()$:
$par \leftarrow_\$ \mathsf{PGen}(1^{\kappa})$	$\mathrm{cid} \leftarrow \mathrm{cid} + 1$
$\mathrm{cid} \leftarrow 0 \; ; \; \ell \leftarrow 0$	$x_{\mathrm{cid}} \leftarrow_\$ \mathcal{D} \; ; \; X_{\mathrm{cid}} \leftarrow \mathsf{F}(x_{\mathrm{cid}})$
$\{y_i\}_{i \in [\mathrm{cid}]} \leftarrow \mathcal{A}^{\mathrm{CHAL},\mathrm{PI}}(par)$	Return X_{cid}
If $\ell \geqslant \mathrm{cid}$ then return 0	
If $\forall i \in [\mathrm{cid}] \; \mathsf{F}(y_i) = X_i$ then	Oracle $\mathrm{PI}(Y, \alpha, \{\beta_i\}_{i \in [\mathrm{cid}]})$:
$\quad$ Return 1	Require: $Y = \mathsf{F}(\alpha) + \sum_{i \in [\mathrm{cid}]} \beta_i X_i$
Return 0	$\ell \leftarrow \ell + 1$
	Return $\alpha + \sum_{i \in [\mathrm{cid}]} \beta_i x_i$

Fig. 2. The AOMPR game for a linear hash function family $\mathsf{LHF} = (\mathsf{PGen}, \mathsf{F})$. For the inputs of PI, X is in $\mathcal{R}$, α is in $\mathcal{D}$, and each β_i is in $\mathcal{S}$.

COLLISION RESISTANCE. Collision resistance of linear hash functions is analogous to collision resistance of cryptographic hash functions, which ensures that it is hard to find two distinct inputs that map to the same output. The $\mathrm{CR}^{\mathcal{A}}_{\mathsf{LHF}}$ game is defined in Fig. 1. The corresponding advantage of $\mathcal{A}$ is defined as $\mathsf{Adv}^{\mathrm{cr}}_{\mathsf{LHF}}(\mathcal{A}, \kappa) := \Pr\left[\mathrm{CR}^{\mathcal{A}}_{\mathsf{LHF}} = 1\right]$.

3.2 Algebraic One-More Preimage Resistance

We introduce the notion of algebraic one-more preimage resistance (AOMPR) for linear hash functions, which is formally defined via the game $\mathrm{AOMPR}^{\mathcal{A}}_{\mathsf{LHF}}$, as described in Fig. 2. It guarantees that any adversary given a description of a linear hash function $(\mathcal{S}, \mathcal{D}, \mathcal{R}, \mathsf{F})$ cannot invert $q + 1$ challenges $X_1, \ldots, X_{q+1}$, where $X_i = \mathsf{F}(x_i)$ for $x_i \leftarrow_\$ \mathcal{D}$, by making at most q queries to the PI oracle that, on any input $Y \in \mathcal{R}$ that is an affine combination of the challenges, outputs an element in the preimage of Y. It is syntactically analogous to the algebraic one-more discrete logarithm (AOMDL) problem [43], where the adversary wants to compute the discrete logarithms of $q + 1$ random challenges in $\mathbb{G}$ by making at most q queries to the DLOG oracle, which outputs the discrete logarithm of the input Y only when Y is an affine combination of the challenges and the combination is known to the adversary.

The following theorem, our main result on AOMPR, shows that AOMPR of a linear hash function family is implied by its collision resistance.

Theorem 1. *For any linear hash function family* LHF *and any AOMPR adversary* $\mathcal{A}$ *making at most* q *queries to* CHAL, *there exists an adversary* $\mathcal{B}$ *for the* CR^{LHF} *game running in a similar running time as* $\mathcal{A}$ *such that* $\mathsf{Adv}_{\mathsf{LHF}}^{\mathrm{aompr}}(\mathcal{A}, \kappa) \leqslant 2\mathsf{Adv}_{\mathsf{LHF}}^{\mathrm{cr}}(\mathcal{B}, \kappa)$.

Proof. (of Theorem 1). Given an adversary $\mathcal{A}$ for the AOMPR^{LHF} game, without loss of generality, we assume that $\mathcal{A}$ is deterministic, queries CHAL exactly q times, and queries PI exactly $q - 1$ times. The construction of $\mathcal{B}$ is straightforward. After receiving *par* from the CR^{LHF} game, $\mathcal{B}$ runs $\mathcal{A}$ on input *par* by simulating the oracles CHAL and PI exactly the same as in the AOMPR^{LHF} game. After $\mathcal{A}$ outputs $\{y_i\}_{i\in[q]}$, if

$$\exists\, i \in [q] \text{ such that } \mathsf{F}(y_i) = X_i \text{ and } y_i \neq x_i, \tag{1}$$

where x_i and X_i are generated in the oracle CHAL, then $\mathcal{B}$ outputs (x_i, y_i). Otherwise, $\mathcal{B}$ aborts.

ANALYSIS OF $\mathcal{B}$. Denote the event $\mathsf{WIN}_{\mathcal{B}}$ as after $\mathcal{A}$ returns, the condition (1) holds. If $\mathsf{WIN}_{\mathcal{B}}$ occurs, $\mathcal{B}$ wins the CR^{LHF} game since $\mathsf{F}(x_i) = X_i = \mathsf{F}(y_i)$, which implies $\mathsf{Adv}_{\mathsf{LHF}}^{\mathrm{cr}}(\mathcal{B}, \kappa) = \Pr\left[\mathsf{WIN}_{\mathcal{B}}\right]$.

It is left to show that $\Pr\left[\mathsf{WIN}_{\mathcal{B}}\right] \geqslant \frac{1}{2}\mathsf{Adv}_{\mathsf{LHF}}^{\mathrm{aompr}}(\mathcal{A}, \kappa)$. Since $\mathcal{A}$ is deterministic, the execution of $\mathcal{A}$ is fixed given the pair $(par, \boldsymbol{x})$, where $\boldsymbol{x} \in \mathcal{D}^q$ denotes the randomness generated in the oracle CHAL. Denote the event $\mathsf{WIN}_{\mathcal{A}}$ as $\mathcal{A}$ wins the AOMPR^{LHF} game simulated by $\mathcal{B}$. Since $\mathcal{B}$ simulate the game perfectly, we know $\Pr[\mathsf{WIN}_{\mathcal{A}}] = \mathsf{Adv}_{\mathsf{LHF}}^{\mathrm{aompr}}(\mathcal{A}, \kappa)$. For each *par*, denote

$$\mathcal{W}_{\mathcal{A}} := \{\boldsymbol{x} \mid \mathsf{WIN}_{\mathcal{A}} \text{ occurs given } (par, \boldsymbol{x})\}\,,$$

$$\mathcal{W}_{\mathcal{B}} := \{\boldsymbol{x} \mid \mathsf{WIN}_{\mathcal{B}} \text{ occurs given } (par, \boldsymbol{x})\}\,.$$

Claim 1. *For each par, there exists a bijection* $\varPhi : \mathcal{W}_{\mathcal{A}} \to \mathcal{W}_{\mathcal{A}}$ *such that for any* $\boldsymbol{x} \in \mathcal{W}_{\mathcal{A}}$, *we have* $\boldsymbol{x} \in \mathcal{W}_{\mathcal{B}} \vee \varPhi(\boldsymbol{x}) \in \mathcal{W}_{\mathcal{B}}$.

From the above claim, we can conclude the proof since $\Pr\left[\mathsf{WIN}_{\mathcal{B}}\right] = \Pr[\boldsymbol{x} \in \mathcal{W}_{\mathcal{B}}] = \frac{1}{2}\left(\Pr[\boldsymbol{x} \in \mathcal{W}_{\mathcal{B}}] + \Pr[\varPhi(\boldsymbol{x}) \in \mathcal{W}_{\mathcal{B}}]\right) \geqslant \frac{1}{2}\Pr[\boldsymbol{x} \in \mathcal{W}_{\mathcal{B}} \vee \varPhi(\boldsymbol{x}) \in \mathcal{W}_{\mathcal{B}}] \geqslant \frac{1}{2}\Pr[\boldsymbol{x} \in \mathcal{W}_{\mathcal{A}}] = \frac{1}{2}\Pr[\mathsf{WIN}_{\mathcal{A}}] = \frac{1}{2}\mathsf{Adv}_{\mathsf{LHF}}^{\mathrm{aompr}}(\mathcal{A}, \kappa)$. $\qquad\square$

Proof. (of Claim 1). We construct $\varPhi$ as follows. For each $\boldsymbol{x} \in \mathcal{W}_{\mathcal{A}}$, consider the execution of $\mathcal{A}$ given $(par, \boldsymbol{x})$. Denote $B \in \mathcal{S}^{(q-1)\times q}$ as the query matrix of the execution, which is defined as follows.

Definition 2. *Given an execution of an adversary* $\mathcal{A}$ *for the AOMPR game, where* $\mathcal{A}$ *makes* q *queries to* CHAL *and* ℓ *queries to* PI, *define the* query matrix *of the execution as* $B \in \mathcal{S}^{\ell\times q}$ *such that* $B_{i,j} = \beta_i^{(j)}$ *for* $i \in [\mathrm{cid}^{(j)}]$ *and* $B_{i,j} = 0$ *otherwise, where* $\beta_i^{(j)}$ *and* $\mathrm{cid}^{(j)}$ *are the values of* β_i *and* cid *when* $\mathcal{A}$ *makes the* j-*th query to* PI.

We now define
$$\Phi(x) := x + u^{(B)}z^* ,$$
where $z^* \in \mathcal{D}$ and $u^{(B)} \in \mathcal{S}^q$ are defined in the following claim.

Claim 2. *There exists $z^* \in \mathcal{D}$ such that $\mathsf{F}(z^*) = 0$ and for any matrix $A \in \mathcal{S}^{\ell \times q}$ where $0 < \ell < q$, there exists a vector $u^{(A)} \in \mathcal{S}^q$ and $i \in [q]$ such that*

$$Au^{(A)} = 0 \ \wedge \ \exists i \in [q] \ : \ u_i^{(A)} z^* \neq 0 . \tag{2}$$

Proof (of Claim 2). Since F is not a monomorphism from $\mathcal{D}$ to $\mathcal{R}$, there exists a non-zero element $z^* \in \mathcal{D}$ such that $\mathsf{F}(z^*) = 0$. Since $\mathcal{S}$ is a field and A has rank at most $\ell < q$, there exists a non-zero vector $u^{(A)} \in \mathcal{S}^q$ such that $Au^{(A)} = 0$. Also, since $u^{(A)}$ is non-zero, there exists $i \in [q]$ such that $u_i^{(A)} \neq 0$, and since $\mathcal{S}$ is a field and $z^* \neq 0$, we have $u_i^{(A)} z^* \neq 0$.

ANALYSIS OF Φ. For simplicity, we use u to denote $u^{(B)}$ in the following analysis. We first show that the executions of $\mathcal{A}$ given (par, x) and given $(par, \Phi(x))$ are identical. Since $\mathsf{F}(\Phi(x)) = \mathsf{F}(x) + u \cdot \mathsf{F}(z^*) = \mathsf{F}(x) + u \cdot 0 = \mathsf{F}(x)$, the challenges output by CHAL are the same in the two executions. For the j-th query to PI, suppose the prior views of $\mathcal{A}$ are identical. Then, $\mathcal{A}$ must make the same query $\left(X^{(j)}, \alpha^{(j)}, \{\beta_i^{(j)}\}_{i \in [\mathrm{cid}^{(j)}]} \right)$ in both executions. Since $Bu = 0$, we have $\alpha^{(j)} + \sum_{i \in [\mathrm{cid}^{(j)}]} \beta_i^{(j)} x_i = \alpha^{(j)} + \left(\beta^{(j)} \right)^T x = \alpha^{(j)} + \left(\beta^{(j)} \right)^T (x + uz^*) = \alpha^{(j)} + \sum_{i \in [\mathrm{cid}^{(j)}]} \beta_i^{(j)} (\Phi(x))_i$, where $\beta^{(j)}$ denotes the j-th row of B. Therefore, $\mathcal{A}$ receives the same value from PI in both executions. By induction, the views of $\mathcal{A}$ are identical in both executions and thus $\mathcal{A}$ outputs the same values in both executions, which implies $\Phi(x) \in \mathcal{W}_{\mathcal{A}}$ and thus Φ is a map from $\mathcal{W}_{\mathcal{A}}$ to $\mathcal{W}_{\mathcal{A}}$.

Then, it is not hard to see that $x \in \mathcal{W}_{\mathcal{B}} \ \vee \ \Phi(x) \in \mathcal{W}_{\mathcal{B}}$. Since the executions of $\mathcal{A}$ given x and $\Phi(x)$ are identical, the outputs $y_1, \ldots, y_q$ of $\mathcal{A}$ are also identical in the two executions. Since there exists $i \in [q]$ such that $u_i z^* \neq 0$, we have either $y_i \neq x_i$ or $y_i \neq x_i + u_i \cdot z^*$, which means WIN$_{\mathcal{B}}$ occurs either in the execution given x or $\Phi(x)$.

It is left to show that Φ is a bijection. Since both the domain and range of Φ are $\mathcal{W}_{\mathcal{A}}$, which is a finite set, it is enough to show that Φ is an injection. For any $x_1, x_2 \in \mathcal{W}_{\mathcal{A}}$ such that $\Phi(x_1) = \Phi(x_2)$, since the execution of $\mathcal{A}$ given x_1 is identical to that given $\Phi(x_1)$ and the execution of $\mathcal{A}$ given x_2 is identical to that given $\Phi(x_2)$, we know the executions of $\mathcal{A}$ given x_1 and x_2 are identical, which implies the query matrix B in the two executions are identical. Therefore, we have $\Phi(x_1) = x_1 + uz^*$ and $\Phi(x_2) = x_2 + uz^*$ for the same $u \in \mathcal{S}^q$, which implies $x_1 = x_2$. This shows that Φ is an injection. $\square$

4   Schemes Based on Linear Hash Functions

For a cyclic group $\mathbb{G}$ with prime size p and generator g, we can view the description of a linear hash function with description $(\mathcal{S}, \mathcal{D}, \mathcal{R}, \mathsf{F})$ as an analogue to

$(\mathbb{G}, p, g)$, where $\mathcal{R}$ corresponds to the group $\mathbb{G}$, the preimage under the function F corresponds to the discrete logarithm to base g, and $\mathcal{S}$ corresponds to the field of scalar $\mathbb{Z}_p$. Also, the AOMPR game is analogous to the AOMDL game. This suggests a general way of transforming any scheme that is secure under the AOMDL assumption into a scheme that is constructed from linear hash functions and is secure under the AOMPR assumption. In this section, we discuss how this idea is applied to two specific examples: MuSig2 [43], a multi-signature scheme, and FROST [37], a threshold signature scheme.

4.1   Multi-signatures

MuSig2 [43] is a two-round multi-signature scheme with key aggregation. Moreover, the first signing round is message-independent. We first give the syntax and security definition of two-round multi-signatures following [43], then present a new scheme MuSig2-H based on LHF that is transformed from MuSig2, and finally show the security of the new scheme under the AOMPR assumption.

SYNTAX. A two-round multi-signature scheme with key aggregation is a tuple of efficient (randomized) algorithms MS = (Setup, KeyGen, KeyAgg, PreSign, PreAgg, Sign, SignAgg, Ver) that behave as follows. The setup algorithm $\mathsf{Setup}(1^\kappa)$ returns a system parameter par, and we assume par is given to all other algorithms implicitly. The key generation algorithm KeyGen() returns a pair of secret and public keys $(\mathsf{sk}, \mathsf{pk})$. The (deterministic) key aggregation algorithm KeyAgg takes as input a multiset of public keys L with size at most 2^κ and returns an aggregate public key apk. For n signers, where the i-th signer has key-pair $(\mathsf{sk}_i, \mathsf{pk}_i)$, the signing protocol between them and an aggregator node to sign a message $m \in \{0, 1\}^*$ is defined by the following experiment:

$$
\begin{aligned}
&(pp_i, \mathsf{st}_i) \leftarrow \mathsf{PreSign}() \,, \text{ for each } i \in SS \,, \\
&app \leftarrow \mathsf{PreAgg}(\{pp_1, \ldots, pp_n\}) \,, \\
&(out_i, \mathsf{st}_i) \leftarrow \mathsf{Sign}(\mathsf{st}_i, app, \mathsf{sk}_i, \mathsf{pk}_i, m, \{\mathsf{pk}_j\}_{j \in [n] \setminus \{i\}}) \,, \text{ for each } i \in SS \,, \\
&\sigma \leftarrow \mathsf{SignAgg}(\{out_1, \ldots, out_n\}) \,,
\end{aligned}
\tag{3}
$$

where each signer runs the algorithms PreSign and Sign; the aggregator node runs the algorithms PreAgg and SignAgg and outputs the signature σ. The aggregator node can be one of the signers and is untrusted in our security model. The (deterministic) verification algorithm $\mathsf{Ver}(\mathsf{apk}, m, \sigma)$ outputs a bit that indicates whether or not σ is valid for apk and m or not. We say that MS is (perfectly) correct if, for any $m \in \{0, 1\}^*$, $\Pr[\mathsf{Ver}(\mathsf{KeyAgg}(\{\mathsf{pk}_1, \ldots, \mathsf{pk}_n\}), m, \sigma)] = 1$, where σ is generated in the experiment in (3) and the probability is taken over the sampling of the system parameter par, all key-pairs $\{(\mathsf{sk}_i, \mathsf{pk}_i)\}_{i \in [n]}$.

SECURITY. The security notion of multi-signatures considered in the prior work [43] is referred to as MS-UF-CMA, which guarantees that it is not possible to forge a valid multi-signature that involves at least one honest party. The MS-UF-CMA game for a multi-signature scheme MS is defined in Fig. 3, where MS.HF denotes the space of the hash functions used in MS from which

Game MS-UF-CMA$_{\mathsf{MS}}^{\mathcal{A}}(\kappa)$:	Oracle PRESIGN() :
$par \leftarrow \mathsf{Setup}(1^{\kappa})$	$\mathrm{sid} \leftarrow \mathrm{sid} + 1$; $S \leftarrow S \cup \{\mathrm{sid}\}$
$\mathsf{H} \leftarrow_{\$} \mathsf{MS.HF}$	$(pp, \mathsf{st}^{(\mathrm{sid})}) \leftarrow \mathsf{PreSign}()$
$(\mathsf{sk}, \mathsf{pk}) \leftarrow_{\$} \mathsf{KeyGen}()$	Return pp
$\mathrm{sid} \leftarrow 0$	
$S \leftarrow \varnothing$; $S' \leftarrow \varnothing$; $Q \leftarrow \varnothing$	Oracle SIGN(k, app, m, L) :
$(L, m, \sigma) \leftarrow \mathcal{A}^{\mathrm{SIGN,SIGN',RO}}(par, \mathsf{pk})$	If $k \notin S$ then return $\bot$
If $\mathsf{pk} \notin L \wedge (L, m) \notin Q$	$out \leftarrow \mathsf{Sign}(\mathsf{st}^{(k)}, app, \mathsf{sk}, m, L)$
$\wedge \mathsf{Ver}(\mathsf{KeyAgg}(L), m, \sigma) = 1$ then	$L \leftarrow L \cup \{\mathsf{pk}\}$
Return 1	$Q \leftarrow Q \cup \{(L, m)\}$
Return 0	$S \leftarrow S \backslash \{k\}$; $S' \leftarrow S' \cup \{k\}$
	Return out
	Oracle RO(x) :
	Return $\mathsf{H}(x)$

Fig. 3. The MS-UF-CMA game for a mutil signature scheme MS.

the random oracle is drawn. In the game, we assume the adversary corrupts the aggregator node and all signers except one and can engage in any number of (concurrent) signing sessions with the honest party. The corresponding advantage of $\mathcal{A}$ is defined as $\mathsf{Adv}_{\mathsf{MS}}^{\mathrm{ms\text{-}uf\text{-}cma}}(\mathcal{A}, \kappa) := \Pr\left[\mathsf{MS\text{-}UF\text{-}CMA}_{\mathsf{MS}}^{\mathcal{A}}(\kappa) = 1\right]$.

OUR SCHEME. Figure 4 shows the scheme MuSig2-H, which is transformed from MuSig2 [43] with the parameter $\nu = 4$, where ν denotes the number of nonces generated in the first round of the signing protocol. In addition to the general transformation, we do two optimizations to MuSig2-H. First, in KeyGen(), the secret key sk is not sampled from $\mathcal{D}$ but from a subset $\mathcal{D}_{\mathsf{key}} \subseteq \mathcal{D}$ such that F is a bijection from $\mathcal{D}_{\mathsf{key}}$ to $\mathcal{R}$. It can reduce the size of the secret key to the size of the public key. Also, the range of each hash function is set to $\mathcal{S}_{\mathsf{hash}}$ instead of $\mathcal{S}$, where $\mathcal{S}_{\mathsf{hash}}$ is an arbitrary subset of $\mathcal{S}$ with size at least 2^{κ}. Further, we require the characteristic of the field $\mathcal{S}$ to be at least 2^{κ}.

The original paper shows the unforgeability of MuSig2 under the AOMDL assumption. Analogous to that, the following theorem shows that the security of MuSig2-H[LHF] is implied by AOMPR of the underlying linear hash function family LHF in the random oracle model.

Theorem 2. *For any* MS-UF-CMA *adversary* $\mathcal{A}$ *making at most* q_s *queries to* PRESIGN *and* q_h *queries to* RO, *there exists an* AOMPR *adversary* $\mathcal{B}$ *making at most* $4\mathsf{q}_s + 1$ *queries to* CHAL *running in time roughly four times that of* $\mathcal{A}$ *such that*

$$\mathsf{Adv}_{\mathsf{MuSig2\text{-}H[LHF]}}^{\mathrm{ms\text{-}uf\text{-}cma}}(\mathcal{A}, \kappa) \leqslant \sqrt[4]{\mathsf{q}^3 \cdot \mathsf{Adv}_{\mathsf{LHF}}^{\mathrm{aompr}}(\mathcal{B}, \kappa) + (16\mathsf{q}^2 + 15)/2^{\kappa}} \,,$$

where $\mathsf{q} = \mathsf{q}_h + \mathsf{q}_s + 1$.

Setup(1^κ) :

$par \leftarrow \mathsf{PGen}(1^\kappa)$
Return par

KeyGen() :

$\mathsf{sk} \leftarrow_\$ \mathcal{D}_{\mathrm{key}}$; $\mathsf{pk} \leftarrow \mathsf{F}(sk)$
Return $(\mathsf{sk}, \mathsf{pk})$

KeyAgg(L) :

$\{\mathsf{pk}_1, \ldots, \mathsf{pk}_n\} \leftarrow L$
For $i \in [n]$ do
  $a_i \leftarrow \mathrm{H}_{\mathrm{agg}}(L, \mathsf{pk}_i)$
Return $\mathsf{apk} \leftarrow \sum_{i \in [n]} a_i \mathsf{pk}_i$

Ver(apk, m, σ) :

$c \leftarrow \mathrm{H}_{\mathrm{sig}}(\mathsf{apk}, R, m)$; $(R, s) \leftarrow \sigma$
If $\mathsf{F}(s) = R + c\mathsf{apk}$ then return 1
Return 0

PreSign() :

For $j \in [4]$ do
  $r_j \leftarrow_\$ \mathcal{D}$; $R_j \leftarrow \mathsf{F}(r_j)$
$pp \leftarrow (R_1, \ldots, R_4)$
$\mathsf{st} \leftarrow (r_1, \ldots, r_4)$
Return (pp, st)

PreAgg($\{pp_1, \ldots, pp_n\}$) :

For $i \in [n]$ do
  $(R_{i,1}, \ldots, R_{i,4}) \leftarrow pp_i$
For $j \in [4]$ do
  $R_j \leftarrow \sum_{i \in [n]} R_{i,j}$
Return $app \leftarrow (R_1, \ldots, R_4)$

Sign($\mathsf{st}, app, \mathsf{sk}, \mathsf{pk}, m, L$) :

$(r_1, \ldots, r_4) \leftarrow \mathsf{st}$
$L \leftarrow L \cup \{\mathsf{pk}\}$
$\mathsf{apk} \leftarrow \mathsf{KeyAgg}(L)$
$a \leftarrow \mathrm{H}_{\mathrm{agg}}(L, \mathsf{pk})$
$(R_1, \ldots, R_4) \leftarrow app$
$b \leftarrow \mathrm{H}_{\mathrm{non}}(\mathsf{apk}, (R_1, \ldots, R_4), m)$
$R \leftarrow \sum_{j \in [4]} b^{j-1} R_j$
$c \leftarrow \mathrm{H}_{\mathrm{sig}}(\mathsf{apk}, R, m)$
$s \leftarrow \sum_{j \in [4]} b^{j-1} r_j + ca \cdot \mathsf{sk}$
Return $out \leftarrow (R, s)$

SignAgg($\{out_1, \ldots, out_n\}$) :

$(R, s) \leftarrow out_1$
For $i \in [2..n]$ do
  $(R_i, s_i) \leftarrow out_i$
  If $R_i \neq R$ then return $\bot$
  $s \leftarrow s + s_i$
Return $\sigma \leftarrow (R, s)$

Fig. 4. The multi-signature scheme MuSig2-H[LHF], where LHF $=$ (PGen, F) is a linear hash function family. We assume $n \leqslant 2^\kappa$ and $|L| \leqslant 2^\kappa$. $\mathcal{D}_{\mathrm{key}}$ is a subset of $\mathcal{D}$ such that F is a bijection from $\mathcal{D}_{\mathrm{key}}$ to $\mathcal{R}$. Further, $\mathrm{H}_{\mathrm{agg}}(\cdot) := \mathrm{H}(1, \cdot)$, $\mathrm{H}_{\mathrm{non}}(\cdot) := \mathrm{H}(2, \cdot)$, $\mathrm{H}_{\mathrm{sig}}(\cdot) := \mathrm{H}(3, \cdot)$, where $\mathrm{H} : \{0,1\}^* \to \mathcal{S}_{\mathrm{hash}}$, $\mathcal{S}_{\mathrm{hash}} \subseteq \mathcal{S}$, and $|\mathcal{S}_{\mathrm{hash}}| \geqslant 2^\kappa$. Moreover, we require $\mathrm{char}(\mathcal{S}) \geqslant 2^\kappa$.

We prove the above theorem using the same techniques as used in the security proof of MuSig2 [43] to construct $\mathcal{B}$ given an adversary $\mathcal{A}$. Here, we briefly highlight the differences:

- We need to show that $\mathcal{B}$ simulates the MS-UF-CMA$^{\mathsf{MuSig2\text{-}H[LHF]}}$ game perfectly when no bad event occurs and that the bad events occur with a negligible probability (Claim 3 and Lemma 2) when the secret key is sampled from $\mathcal{D}_{\mathrm{key}}$ instead of $\mathbb{Z}_p$, and the randomness r_j is sampled from $\mathcal{D}$ instead of $\mathbb{Z}_p$.
- We need to show that $\mathcal{B}$ can compute a preimage for each challenge (Claim 4 and Claim 5) instead of the discrete logarithm to the base element. More precisely, the problem can be described as follows. Denote the challenges by $U_1, \ldots, U_\ell \in \mathcal{R}$. After the interaction with $\mathcal{A}$, $\mathcal{B}$ computes a matrix $A \in \mathcal{S}^{\ell \times \ell}$

$\mathsf{Fork}^{\mathcal{A}}(x, v_1, v_1', \dots, v_{q'}, v_{q'}')$:

Pick the random coin ρ of $\mathcal{A}$ at random
$h_1, h_1', \dots, h_q, h_q' \leftarrow H$
$(I, J, \mathrm{Out}) \leftarrow \mathcal{A}(x, h_1, \dots, h_q, v_1, \dots, v_{q'}; \rho)$
If $I = \bot$ or $J = \bot$ then return $\bot$
$(I', J', \mathrm{Out}') \leftarrow \mathcal{A}(x, h_1, \dots, h_{I-1}, h_I', \dots, h_q', v_1 \dots, v_{J-1}, v_J', \dots, v_{q'}'; \rho)$
If $I \neq I'$ or $h_I = h_I'$ then return $\bot$
Return $(I, \mathrm{Out}, \mathrm{Out}')$

Fig. 5. The forking algorithm built from $\mathcal{A}$ for Lemma 1.

and a vector $\boldsymbol{b} \in \mathcal{D}^\ell$ such that $A \cdot \boldsymbol{U} = \mathsf{F}(\boldsymbol{b})$, we need to show that A has full rank and thus $\mathcal{B}$ can compute a vector $\boldsymbol{u} = A^{-1}\boldsymbol{b}$ such that $\mathsf{F}(\boldsymbol{u}) = \boldsymbol{U}$.

Before turning to the proof, we first recall the following variant of the forking lemma from [43] that will be used in the proof.

Lemma 1. *Let $q, q' \geqslant 1$ be integers and H, V be two sets. Let $\mathcal{A}$ be a randomized algorithm that, on input $x, h_1, \dots, h_q, v_1, \dots, v_{q'}$, outputs a tuple (I, J, Out), where $I \in \{\bot\} \cup [q]$, $J \in \{\bot\} \cup [q'+1]$ and Out is a side output. Let IG be a randomized algorithm that generates x. The accepting probability of $\mathcal{A}$ is defined as $\mathrm{acc}(\mathcal{A}) = \Pr[(I, J, \mathrm{Out}) \leftarrow_\$ \mathcal{A}(x, h_1, \dots, h_q, v_1, \dots, v_{q'}) : I \neq \bot \wedge J \neq \bot]$, where the probability is over $x \leftarrow_\$ \mathsf{IG}, h_1, \dots, h_q \leftarrow_\$ H, v_1, \dots, v_{q'} \leftarrow_\$ V$ and the random coins of $\mathcal{A}$. Consider algorithm $\mathsf{Fork}^{\mathcal{A}}$ described in Fig. 5. The accepting probability of $\mathsf{Fork}^{\mathcal{A}}$ is defined as*

$$\mathrm{acc}(\mathsf{Fork}^{\mathcal{A}}) = \Pr[\alpha \leftarrow_\$ \mathsf{Fork}^{\mathcal{A}}(x, v_1, v_1', \dots, v_{q'}, v_{q'}') : \alpha \neq \bot],$$

where the probability is over $x \leftarrow_\$ \mathsf{IG}, v_1, v_1', \dots, v_{q'}, v_{q'}' \leftarrow_\$ V$. Then, $\mathrm{acc}(\mathsf{Fork}^{\mathcal{A}}) \geqslant \mathrm{acc}(\mathcal{A}) \left(\frac{\mathrm{acc}(\mathcal{A})}{q} - \frac{1}{H} \right).$

Proof. (of Theorem 2). Let $\mathcal{A}$ be an adversary as described in the theorem. Denote the output message-signature pair of $\mathcal{A}$ as $(L^*, m^*, \sigma^* = (R^*, z^*))$. Without loss of generality, we assume $\mathcal{A}$ always queries RO on $\mathsf{H}_{\mathrm{sig}}(\mathsf{apk}^*, m^*, R^*)$ before $\mathcal{A}$ returns, where $\mathsf{apk}^* = \mathsf{KeyAgg}(L^*)$, and always queries RO on $\mathsf{H}_{\mathrm{non}}(\mathsf{apk}, (R_1, \dots, R_4), m)$ prior to each $\mathrm{SIGN}(k, (R_1, \dots, R_4), m, L)$ query, where $\mathsf{apk} = \mathsf{KeyAgg}(L)$. (This adds up to $\mathsf{q}_s + 1$ additional RO queries, and we let $\mathsf{q} = \mathsf{q}_h + \mathsf{q}_s + 1$.)

We first construct an algorithm $\mathcal{C}$ compatible with the syntax in Lemma 1, then construct an algorithm $\mathcal{C}'$ from $\mathsf{Fork}^{\mathcal{C}}$, and finally construct $\mathcal{B}$ from $\mathsf{Fork}^{\mathcal{C}'}$.

THE ADVERSARY $\mathcal{C}$. The input of $\mathcal{C}$ consists of *par*, which defines a linear hash function $(\mathcal{S}, \mathcal{D}, \mathcal{R}, \mathsf{F})$, and uniformly random elements $h_1^{(\mathrm{agg})}, \dots, h_{\mathsf{q}}^{(\mathrm{agg})}, h_1^{(\mathrm{sig})}$, $\dots, h_{\mathsf{q}}^{(\mathrm{sig})}, h_1^{(\mathrm{non})}, \dots, h_{\mathsf{q}}^{(\mathrm{non})} \in \mathcal{S}_{\mathrm{hash}}$. Also, $\mathcal{C}$ can access oracles CHAL and PI, defined the same way as those in the AOMPR^{LHF} game. (We can think of this oracle as part of $\mathcal{C}$ in the context of the Forking Lemma.) For simplicity, when

$\mathcal{C}$ makes a query $(X, \alpha, \{\beta_i\})$ to PI, we omit the coefficients $\alpha, \{\beta_i\}$ whenever they are clear from the context.

To start with, $\mathcal{C}$ makes $4q_s + 1$ queries to CHAL and denotes the challenges as $X, U_1, \ldots, U_{4q_s} \in \mathcal{D}$. Then, $\mathcal{C}$ initializes H to an empty table. In addition, it initializes counters $\mathrm{ctr}_s, \mathrm{ctr}_{\mathrm{agg}}, \mathrm{ctr}_{\mathrm{sig}}, \mathrm{ctr}_{\mathrm{non}}$ to 0 and a function dt to an empty table, which are used to record the PI query related to each U_j.

We also use a flag BadKey, initially set to false, to denote whether a bad event occurs. Then, $\mathcal{C}$ sets pk $\leftarrow X$ and runs $\mathcal{A}(par, \mathsf{pk})$ with access to the oracles $\widetilde{\mathrm{PreSign}}, \widetilde{\mathrm{Sign}}, \widetilde{\mathrm{RO}}$, which are simulated as follows.

$\widetilde{\mathrm{RO}}$ **query** $\mathrm{H}_{\mathrm{agg}}(x)$: If $\mathrm{H}_{\mathrm{agg}}(x) \neq \perp$, $\mathcal{C}$ returns $\mathrm{H}_{\mathrm{agg}}(x)$. Otherwise, parse x as $(L, \widetilde{\mathsf{pk}})$. If the parsing fails, or $X \notin L$, $\mathcal{C}$ sets $\mathrm{H}_{\mathrm{agg}}(x) \leftarrow^\$ \mathcal{S}_{\mathrm{hash}}$ and returns $\mathrm{H}_{\mathrm{agg}}(x)$. Otherwise, $\mathcal{C}$ increases $\mathrm{ctr}_{\mathrm{agg}}$ by 1, sets $\mathrm{H}_{\mathrm{agg}}(L, X) \leftarrow h_{\mathrm{ctr}_{\mathrm{agg}}}^{(\mathrm{agg})}$ and $\mathrm{H}_{\mathrm{agg}}(L, \mathsf{pk}') \leftarrow^\$ \mathcal{S}_{\mathrm{hash}}$ for each $\mathsf{pk}' \in L$ and $\mathsf{pk}' \neq X$. Let apk $\leftarrow \mathsf{KeyAgg}(L)$. If apk $\in K$, $\mathcal{B}$ sets BadKey $\leftarrow$ true. Otherwise, $\mathcal{C}$ sets $K \leftarrow K \cup \{\mathsf{apk}\}$ and returns $\mathrm{H}_{\mathrm{agg}}(x)$.

$\widetilde{\mathrm{RO}}$ **query** $\mathrm{H}_{\mathrm{non}}(x)$: If $\mathrm{H}_{\mathrm{non}}(x) \neq \perp$, $\mathcal{C}$ returns $\mathrm{H}_{\mathrm{non}}(x)$. Otherwise, parse x as $(\widetilde{\mathsf{apk}}, (R_1, \ldots, R_4), m)$. If the parsing fails, $\mathcal{C}$ sets $\mathrm{H}_{\mathrm{non}}(x) \leftarrow^\$ \mathcal{S}_{\mathrm{hash}}$ and returns $\mathrm{H}_{\mathrm{non}}(x)$. Otherwise, $\mathcal{C}$ increases $\mathrm{ctr}_{\mathrm{non}}$ by 1 and sets $\mathrm{H}_{\mathrm{non}}(x) \leftarrow h_{\mathrm{ctr}_{\mathrm{non}}}^{(\mathrm{non})}$. Also, $\mathcal{C}$ computes $R \leftarrow \sum_{i \in [4]} (h_{\mathrm{ctr}_{\mathrm{non}}}^{(\mathrm{non})})^{j-1} R_j$. If $\mathrm{H}_{\mathrm{sig}}(\widetilde{\mathsf{apk}}, R, m) = \perp$, $\mathcal{C}$ increases $\mathrm{ctr}_{\mathrm{sig}}$ by 1 and sets $\mathrm{H}_{\mathrm{sig}}(\widetilde{\mathsf{apk}}, R, m) = h_{\mathrm{ctr}_{\mathrm{sig}}}^{(\mathrm{sig})}$. Finally, $\mathcal{C}$ returns $\mathrm{H}_{\mathrm{non}}(x)$.

$\widetilde{\mathrm{RO}}$ **query** $\mathrm{H}_{\mathrm{sig}}(x)$: If $\mathrm{H}_{\mathrm{sig}}(x) \neq \perp$, $\mathcal{C}$ returns $\mathrm{H}_{\mathrm{sig}}(x)$. Otherwise, parse x as $(\widetilde{\mathsf{apk}}, m, R)$. If the parsing fails, $\mathcal{C}$ sets $\mathrm{H}_{\mathrm{sig}}(x) \leftarrow^\$ \mathcal{S}_{\mathrm{hash}}$ and returns $\mathrm{H}_{\mathrm{sig}}(x)$. Otherwise, $\mathcal{C}$ increases $\mathrm{ctr}_{\mathrm{sig}}$ by 1 and sets $\mathrm{H}_{\mathrm{sig}}(x) \leftarrow h_{\mathrm{ctr}_{\mathrm{sig}}}^{(\mathrm{sig})}$. Finally, $\mathcal{C}$ sets $K \leftarrow K \cup \{\widetilde{\mathsf{apk}}\}$ and returns $\mathrm{H}_{\mathrm{sig}}(x)$.

$\widetilde{\mathrm{PreSign}}(i)$ **query:** Same as in the game MS-UF-CMA$^{\mathsf{MuSig2\text{-}H}}$, except in the simulation of algorithm Sign, $\mathcal{C}$ first increases ctr_s by 1 and sets $R_{1,i} \leftarrow U_{i+4(\mathrm{ctr}_s-1)}$ for $i \in [4]$.

$\widetilde{\mathrm{Sign}}(k, app, m, L)$ **query:** Same as in the game MS-UF-CMA$^{\mathsf{MuSig2\text{-}H}}$, except in the simulation of algorithm Sign', $\mathcal{C}$ sets $s \leftarrow \mathrm{PI}(\sum_{j \in [4]} b^{j-1} U_{i+4(k-1)} + ca \cdot \mathsf{pk})$, and sets $\mathsf{dt}(k) \leftarrow (b, c, a, s)$.

After receiving the output $(L^*, m^*, \sigma^* = (R^*, s^*))$ from $\mathcal{A}$, $\mathcal{C}$ returns $\perp$ if BadKey = true or $\mathcal{A}$ does not win the game. Otherwise, $\mathcal{C}$ computes $\mathsf{apk}^* \leftarrow \mathsf{KeyAgg}(L^*)$ and:

- I_{sig} as the index such that $\mathrm{H}_{\mathrm{sig}}(\mathsf{apk}^*, m^*, R^*)$ is set to $h_{I_{\mathrm{sig}}}^{(\mathrm{sig})}$;
- J_{sig} as the value of $\mathrm{ctr}_{\mathrm{non}}$ when $\mathrm{H}_{\mathrm{sig}}(\mathsf{apk}^*, m^*, R^*)$ is assigned;
- I_{agg} as the index such that $\mathrm{H}_{\mathrm{agg}}(L^*, X)$ is set to $h_{I_{\mathrm{agg}}}^{(\mathrm{agg})}$;
- J_{agg} as the value of $\mathrm{ctr}_{\mathrm{non}}$ when $\mathrm{H}_{\mathrm{agg}}(\mathsf{apk}^*, m^*, R^*)$ is assigned.

Since $\mathcal{A}$ wins the game by our simulation, we know such I_{agg} and I_{sig} must exist. Then, $\mathcal{C}$ returns $(I_{\mathrm{sig}}, J_{\mathrm{sig}}, \mathrm{Out})$, where Out consists of all variables received or generated by $\mathcal{C}$.

ANALYSIS OF $\mathcal{C}$. To use Lemma 1, we define IG as the algorithm that sets $par \leftarrow_\$$ PGen(1^κ), uniformly samples $h_1^{(\mathrm{agg})}, \ldots, h_{\mathsf{q}}^{(\mathrm{agg})} \in \mathcal{S}_{\mathrm{hash}}$, and returns $(par, h_1^{(\mathrm{agg})}, \ldots, h_{\mathsf{q}}^{(\mathrm{agg})})$. Also, $(h_1^{(\mathrm{sig})}, \ldots, h_{\mathsf{q}}^{(\mathrm{sig})})$ plays the role of $(h_1, \ldots, h_q)$, and $(h_1^{(\mathrm{non})}, \ldots, h_{\mathsf{q}}^{(\mathrm{non})})$ plays the role of $(v_1, \ldots, v_{q'})$.

We now show that $\mathcal{C}$ simulates the game MS-UF-CMA perfectly. In the real game, sk is uniformly sampled from $\mathcal{D}_{\mathrm{key}}$, and, since F is a bijection from $\mathcal{D}_{\mathrm{key}}$ to $\mathcal{S}$, pk is uniformly distributed over $\mathcal{S}$, which is identical to the simulation. Also, it is clear that the output distributions of each $\widetilde{\mathrm{RO}}$ query and each $\widetilde{\mathrm{PRESIGN}}$ query are identical to those of the real game. For the simulation of $\widetilde{\mathrm{SIGN}}$, from the MS-UF-CMA game, we know that $\mathcal{C}$ makes at most one query to PI for each session k. Therefore, from the AOMPR game, we know s_1 is uniformly distributed over the preimage of $\sum_{j \in [4]} b^{j-1} U_{i+4(k-1)} + ca_1 \cdot \mathsf{pk}$ given the view of the adversary, which is identical to the real game.

Therefore, since $\mathcal{C}$ simulates the game MS-UF-CMA perfectly, $\mathrm{acc}(\mathcal{C}) \geqslant \mathrm{Adv}_{\mathrm{MuSig2\text{-}H[LHF]}}^{\mathrm{ms\text{-}uf\text{-}cma}}(\mathcal{A}) - \Pr[\mathsf{BadKey}]$, where $\Pr[\mathsf{BadKey}]$ is the probability that $\mathsf{BadKey} = \mathtt{true}$ at the end of $\mathcal{C}$'s execution. By the following claim and Lemma 1,

$$\mathrm{acc}(\mathrm{Fork}^{\mathcal{C}}) \geqslant \left(\mathrm{Adv}_{\mathrm{MuSig2\text{-}H[LHF]}}^{\mathrm{ms\text{-}uf\text{-}cma}}(\mathcal{A}) - (2q^2+1)/2^\kappa\right)^2 / q - \frac{1}{|\mathcal{S}_{\mathrm{hash}}|}$$

$$\geqslant \frac{(\mathrm{Adv}_{\mathrm{MuSig2\text{-}H[LHF]}}^{\mathrm{ms\text{-}uf\text{-}cma}}(\mathcal{A}))^2}{q} - \frac{4q+3}{2^\kappa}. \tag{4}$$

Claim 3. $\Pr[\mathsf{BadKey}] \leqslant \frac{2q^2+1}{2^\kappa}$.

Proof (of Claim 3). Consider a $\widetilde{\mathrm{RO}}$ query $\mathrm{H}_{\mathrm{agg}}(L, \widetilde{\mathsf{pk}})$ from $\mathcal{A}$ such that $X \in L$ and $\mathrm{H}_{\mathrm{agg}}(L, X)$ is not assigned prior to the query. The aggregated key from L can be represented as $\mathsf{apk} = (X)^{t \cdot h_{\mathrm{ctr_{agg}}}^{(\mathrm{agg})}} Z$, where t is the number of times X appears in L and $Z := \sum_{\mathsf{pk} \in L, \mathsf{pk} \neq X} \mathsf{pk}^{\mathrm{H}_{\mathrm{agg}}(L, \mathsf{pk})}$, which is independent of $h_{\mathrm{ctr_{agg}}}^{(\mathrm{agg})}$. BadKey is set to true if and only if $\mathsf{apk} \in K$. We use the following lemma, which we show later, to bound the probability that $\mathsf{apk} \in K$.

Lemma 2. *For any $X \in \mathcal{R}$ and any integer t, denote $C(t, X) := \{(ts) \cdot X \mid s \in \mathcal{S}_{\mathrm{hash}}\}$. We say X is Good if and only if $|C(t, X)| = |\mathcal{S}_{\mathrm{hash}}|$ for any $1 \leqslant t \leqslant 2^\kappa$. Then, we have $\Pr_{X \leftarrow_\$ \mathcal{R}}[X \text{ is not Good}] \leqslant 1/2^\kappa$.*

Suppose X is Good. Given Z, since $t \leqslant 2^\kappa$, we have that apk is uniformly distributed over the set $\{YZ \mid Y \in C(t, X)\}$, which has size $|\mathcal{S}_{\mathrm{hash}}|$. Also, from the execution, we have that $|K| \leqslant \mathsf{q} + \mathsf{q}_s \leqslant 2q$, and thus the probability that BadKey is set to true after the query is at most $|K| / |\mathcal{S}_{\mathrm{hash}}| \leqslant 2q/2^\kappa$. Since there are at most q RO queries, the probability that BadKey is set to true during the simulation is at most $2q^2/2^\kappa$. Therefore, we have that $\Pr[\mathsf{BadKey}] \leqslant \Pr[X \text{ is not Good}] + \Pr[\mathsf{BadKey} \wedge X \text{ is Good}] \leqslant \frac{2q^2+1}{2^\kappa}$. $\square$

Proof (of Lemma 2). For any $1 \leqslant t \leqslant 2^\kappa$, $s_1, s_2 \in \mathcal{S}$, and $X \in \mathcal{R}$ such that $s_1 \neq s_2$ and $X \neq 0$, since $\mathrm{char}(\mathcal{S}) \geqslant 2^\kappa$, we know that $t \cdot (s_1 - s_2) \neq 0$ and thus $t \cdot (s_1 - s_2) \cdot X \neq 0$, which implies $ts_1 \cdot X \neq ts_2 \cdot X$. Therefore, $|C(t, X)| = |\mathcal{S}_{\mathrm{hash}}|$, which means that X is Good. Thus, we have that $\Pr_{X \leftarrow \mathcal{R}}[X \text{ is not Good}] \leqslant \Pr_{X \leftarrow \mathcal{R}}[X = 0] = \frac{1}{|\mathcal{R}|} \leqslant 1/2^\kappa$.   □

CONSTRUCT $\mathcal{C}'$ FROM $\mathsf{Fork}^{\mathcal{C}}$. The input of $\mathcal{C}'$ consists of par, which defines a linear hash function $(\mathcal{S}, \mathcal{D}, \mathcal{R}, \mathsf{F})$ and uniformly random elements $h_1^{(\mathrm{agg})}, \ldots, h_{\mathsf{q}}^{(\mathrm{agg})}$ $h_1^{(\mathrm{non})}, h_1^{(\mathrm{non})'}, \ldots, h_{\mathsf{q}}^{(\mathrm{non})}, h_{\mathsf{q}}^{(\mathrm{non})'} \in \mathcal{S}_{\mathrm{hash}}$. Also, $\mathcal{C}'$ can access oracles CHAL and PI defined the same way as those in the AOMPR game. To begin, $\mathcal{C}'$ runs $\mathsf{Fork}^{\mathcal{C}}(par, h_1^{(\mathrm{agg})}, \ldots, h_{\mathsf{q}}^{(\mathrm{agg})}, h_1^{(\mathrm{non})}, h_1^{(\mathrm{non})'}, \ldots, h_{\mathsf{q}}^{(\mathrm{non})}, h_{\mathsf{q}}^{(\mathrm{non})'})$. All queries to oracle CHAL from the first execution of $\mathcal{C}'$ are relayed by $\mathcal{B}$ to its own CHAL oracle, and for all CHAL queries from the second execution of $\mathcal{C}'$, $\mathcal{B}$ answers them with the same challenges as in the first execution. All PI queries from $\mathsf{Fork}^{\mathcal{C}'}$ are relayed by $\mathcal{B}$ to its own PI oracle.

After $\mathsf{Fork}^{\mathcal{C}}$ returns $(I_{\mathrm{sig}}, J_{\mathrm{sig}}, \mathsf{Out}, \mathsf{Out}')$, by the following claim, $\mathcal{C}'$ computes $\widetilde{x}$ such that $\mathsf{F}(\widetilde{x}) = \mathsf{apk}^*$ and returns $(I_{\mathrm{agg}}, J_{\mathrm{agg}}, (\widetilde{x}, \mathsf{Out}, \mathsf{Out}'))$, where $I_{\mathrm{agg}}, J_{\mathrm{agg}}$, and apk^* are from Out.

Claim 4. *If $\mathsf{Fork}^{\mathcal{C}}$ returns $(I_{\mathrm{sig}}, J_{\mathrm{sig}}, \mathsf{Out}, \mathsf{Out}')$, $\mathcal{C}'$ can compute $\widetilde{x}$ such that $\mathsf{F}(\widetilde{x}) = \mathsf{apk}^*$, where apk^* is from Out.*

Proof (of Claim 4). We directly use the notations in the description of $\mathcal{C}$ to denote the variables in Out and use $(\cdot)'$ to denote the variables in Out'. Since $\mathsf{Fork}^{\mathcal{C}}$ does not return $\bot$, we have $\mathsf{H}_{\mathrm{sig}}(\mathsf{apk}^*, m^*, R^*) = h_I \neq h_I' = \mathsf{H}_{\mathrm{sig}}'(\mathsf{apk}^*, m^*, R^*)$. Since the two executions of $\mathcal{C}$ are identical before $\mathsf{H}_{\mathrm{sig}}(\mathsf{apk}^*, m^*, R^*)$ is assigned h_I, we know $(\mathsf{apk}^*, m^*, R^*) = (\mathsf{apk}^{*\prime}, m^{*\prime}, R^{*\prime})$. Therefore, we have $\mathsf{F}(s^*) = R^* + h_I \mathsf{apk}^*$ and $\mathsf{F}(s^{*\prime}) = R^* + h_I' \mathsf{apk}^*$, and $\mathcal{C}'$ computes $\widetilde{x} \leftarrow \frac{s^* - s^{*\prime}}{h_I - h_I'}$.   □

ANALYSIS OF $\mathcal{C}'$. To use Lemma 1, we define IG as the algorithm that sets $par \leftarrow_{\$} \mathsf{PGen}(1^\kappa)$ and returns par. Also, $(h_1^{(\mathrm{agg})}, \ldots, h_{\mathsf{q}}^{(\mathrm{agg})})$ plays the role of $(h_1, \ldots, h_q)$, and $((h_1^{(\mathrm{non})}, h_1^{(\mathrm{non})'}), \ldots, (h_{\mathsf{q}}^{(\mathrm{non})}, h_{\mathsf{q}}^{(\mathrm{non})'}))$ plays the role of $(v_1, \ldots, v_{q'})$. It is clear that $\mathsf{acc}(\mathcal{C}') = \mathsf{acc}(\mathsf{Fork}^{\mathcal{C}})$. Therefore, by Lemma 1 and (4), $\mathsf{acc}(\mathsf{Fork}^{\mathcal{C}'}) \geqslant (\mathsf{acc}(\mathsf{Fork}^{\mathcal{C}}))^2/q - \frac{1}{|\mathcal{S}_{\mathrm{hash}}|} \geqslant (\mathsf{Adv}_{\mathsf{MuSig2\text{-}H[LHF]}}^{\mathrm{ms\text{-}uf\text{-}cma}}(\mathcal{A}))^4/q^3 - \frac{15}{2^\kappa}$.

CONSTRUCT $\mathcal{B}$ FROM $\mathsf{Fork}^{\mathcal{C}'}$. We now give a construct of the AOMPR adversary $\mathcal{B}$ using $\mathsf{Fork}^{\mathcal{C}'}$ and the available CHAL and PI oracles. To start with, $\mathcal{B}$ receives par from the AOMPR^{LHF} game and uniformly samples $h_1^{(\mathrm{non})}, h_1^{(\mathrm{non})'}$, $h_1^{(\mathrm{non})''}, h_1^{(\mathrm{non})'''}, \ldots, h_{\mathsf{q}}^{(\mathrm{non})}, h_{\mathsf{q}}^{(\mathrm{non})'}, h_{\mathsf{q}}^{(\mathrm{non})''}, h_{\mathsf{q}}^{(\mathrm{non})'''} \in \mathcal{S}_{\mathrm{hash}}$. Then, $\mathcal{B}$ runs $\mathsf{Fork}^{\mathcal{C}'}$ on input par, $(h_1^{(\mathrm{non})}, h_1^{(\mathrm{non})'})$, $(h_1^{(\mathrm{non})''}, h_1^{(\mathrm{non})'''}), \ldots, (h_{\mathsf{q}}^{(\mathrm{non})}, h_{\mathsf{q}}^{(\mathrm{non})'}), (h_{\mathsf{q}}^{(\mathrm{non})''},$ $h_{\mathsf{q}}^{(\mathrm{non})'''})$, where $(h_i^{(\mathrm{non})}, h_i^{(\mathrm{non})'})$ plays the role of v_i and $(h_i^{(\mathrm{non})''}, h_i^{(\mathrm{non})'''})$ plays the role of v_i'. All CHAL queries from the first execution of $\mathcal{C}'$ are relayed by $\mathcal{B}$ to its own CHAL oracle, and, for all CHAL queries from the second execution of $\mathcal{C}'$, $\mathcal{B}$ answers them with the same challenges as the first execution. All PI queries from $\mathsf{Fork}^{\mathcal{C}'}$ are relayed by $\mathcal{B}$ to its own PI oracle. Without loss of generality, we can assume all challenges are different since otherwise $\mathcal{B}$ can solve them trivially. Denote the event BadHash as any two of the scalars $h_1^{(non)}$, $h_1^{(non)'}$, $h_1^{(non)''}$, $h_1^{(non)'''}$, ..., $h_q^{(non)}$, $h_q^{(non)'}$, $h_q^{(non)''}$, $h_q^{(non)'''}$ are same. Since they are sampled uniformly from $\mathcal{S}_{hash}$, we know $\Pr[\mathsf{BadHash}] \leqslant (4q)^2/|\mathcal{S}_{hash}| \leqslant \frac{16q^2}{2^\kappa}$. Then, we can conclude the proof with the following claim, which implies $\mathsf{Adv}_{\mathsf{LHF}}^{\mathsf{aompr}}(\mathcal{B}) \geqslant \mathsf{acc}(\mathsf{Fork}^{\mathcal{C}}) - \Pr[\mathsf{BadHash}] \geqslant (\mathsf{Adv}_{\mathsf{MuSig2-H[LHF]}}^{\mathsf{ms-uf-cma}}(\mathcal{A}))^4/q^3 - \frac{16q^2+15}{2^\kappa}$.

Claim 5. *If* $\mathsf{Fork}^{\mathcal{C}'}$ *returns* $(I_{agg}, J_{agg}, \mathsf{Out}, \mathsf{Out}')$ *and* BadHash *does not occur,* $\mathcal{B}$ *can win the game* $\mathsf{AOMPR}_{\mathsf{LHF}}$.

□

Proof (proof of Claim 5). Denote $(\widetilde{x}, \mathsf{Out}^{(1)}, \mathsf{Out}^{(2)}) \leftarrow \mathsf{Out}$ and $(\widetilde{x}', \mathsf{Out}^{(3)}, \mathsf{Out}^{(4)}) \leftarrow \mathsf{Out}'$, and we use $(\cdot)^{(i)}$ to denote the variables in $\mathsf{Out}^{(i)}$. The total number of CHAL queries is $4q_s + 1$, and the corresponding challenges are $X, U_1, \ldots, U_{4q_s}$.

We first show how to compute x^* such that $\mathsf{F}(x^*) = X$. Since $\mathsf{Fork}^{\mathcal{C}'}$ returns I_{agg}, we have $\mathsf{H}_{agg}^{(1)}(L^{*(1)}, X) = h_{I_{agg}}^{(agg)} \neq h_{I_{agg}}^{(agg)'} = \mathsf{H}_{agg}^{(3)}(L^{*(3)}, X)$. Since the two executions of $\mathcal{C}$ are identical before H_{sig} is assigned $h_{I_{agg}}^{(agg)}$, we have $L^{*(1)} = L^{*(3)}$ (we denote $L^{*(1)}$ as L^* from here forward) and $\mathsf{H}_{agg}^{(1)}(L^*, \mathsf{pk}') = \mathsf{H}_{agg}^{(3)}(L^*, \mathsf{pk}')$ for any $\mathsf{pk}' \in L^*$ and $\mathsf{pk}' \neq X$. Therefore, the aggregated keys from L^* in the two execution can be represented as $\mathsf{apk}^{*(1)} = t \cdot h_{I_{agg}}^{(agg)} \cdot X + Z$, $\mathsf{apk}^{*(3)} = t \cdot h_{I_{agg}}^{(agg)'} \cdot X + Z$, where t is the number of times X appears in L^* and $Z := \sum_{\mathsf{pk}' \in L^*, \mathsf{pk}' \neq X} \mathsf{H}_{agg}^{(1)}(L^*, \mathsf{pk}) \cdot \mathsf{pk}'$. By Claim 4, $\mathsf{F}(\widetilde{x}) = \mathsf{apk}^{*(1)}$ and $\mathsf{F}(\widetilde{x}') = \mathsf{apk}^{*(3)}$. Therefore, $\mathcal{B}$ computes $x^* = \frac{\widetilde{x} - \widetilde{x}'}{t(h_{I_{agg}}^{(agg)} - h_{I_{agg}}^{(agg)'})}$.

We now show how to compute $u_1, \ldots, u_{4q_s}$ such that $\mathsf{F}(u_i) = U_i$. For $k \in [q_s]$, $\mathsf{dt}^{(i)}(k) = (b, c, a, s) \neq \bot$ if and only if $\mathcal{C}$ queries PI on $\sum_{j \in [4]} b^{j-1} U_{i+4(k-1)} + ca \cdot X$. Define a set $T := \{(b, c \cdot a, s) \; : \; i \in [4], \mathsf{dt}^{(i)}(k) = (b, c, a, s)\}$. The total number of PI queries for simulating those PI queries from $\mathcal{C}$ is equal to $|T|$. From the execution of $\mathcal{B}$, we know for any $i_1, i_2 \in [4]$ and $i_1 \neq i_2$, where $(b, c, a, s) = \mathsf{dt}^{(i_1)}(k)$ and $(b', c', a', s') = \mathsf{dt}^{(i_2)}(k)$, if $b = b'$, then we have $(b, c, a, s) = (b', c', a', s')$. Therefore, we know for any distinct $(b, v, s), (b', v', s') \in T$, it holds that $b \neq b'$. Also, we have $|T| \leqslant 4$. If $|T| < 4$, $\mathcal{B}$ picks an arbitrary $b' \in \mathcal{S}_{hash} \backslash \{b \; : \; (b, v, s) \in T\}$ and sets $s' \leftarrow \mathsf{PI}\left(\sum_{j \in [4]} b'^{j-1} U_{i+(4-1)k}\right)$. Then, $\mathcal{B}$ adds $(b', 0, s')$ to T and repeats this until T has size 4. Denote the elements in T as $(b_1, v_1, s_1), \ldots, (b_4, v_4, s_4)$, and we have $AU = \mathsf{F}(s)$, where

$$A = \begin{pmatrix} 1 & b_1 & b_1^2 & b_1^3 \\ \vdots & \vdots & \vdots & \vdots \\ 1 & b_4 & b_4^2 & b_4^3 \end{pmatrix} , \quad U = \begin{pmatrix} U_{1+4(k-1)} \\ \vdots \\ U_{4k} \end{pmatrix} , \quad s = \begin{pmatrix} s_1 - v_1 x^* \\ \vdots \\ s_4 - v_4 x^* \end{pmatrix} .$$

Since A is a Vandermonde matrix over the field $\mathcal{S}$, A has full rank. Therefore, $\mathcal{B}$ can compute $(u_{1+(k-1)4}, \ldots, u_{k4})^T = A^{-1}s$. Also, the number of PI queries for simulating the PI queries from $\mathcal{C}$ and computing T is equal to 4. Therefore, the total number of PI queries made by $\mathcal{B}$ is $4\mathsf{q}_s$, which implies $\mathcal{B}$ wins the game $\mathsf{AOMPR}^{\mathsf{LHF}}$. □

4.2   Threshold Signatures

FROST1 [37] and a more efficient version FROST2 [6] of FROST1 are (partially) non-interactive threshold signature schemes as formalized in [6]. We first give the syntax and security definitions of non-interactive threshold signature schemes following [6], then present new schemes based on LHF that are transformed from FROST1/2, and finally show the security of the new schemes under the AOMPR assumption.

SYNTAX. A (partially) non-interactive threshold signature schemes for n signers and threshold t is a tuple of efficient (randomized) algorithms $\mathsf{TS} = (\mathsf{Setup}, \mathsf{KeyGen}, \mathsf{SPP}, \mathsf{LPP}, \mathsf{LR}, \mathsf{PS}, \mathsf{Agg}, \mathsf{Vf})$ that behave as follows. Parties involved are a leader and n signers. The setup algorithm $\mathsf{Setup}(1^\kappa)$ initializes the state st_i for each signer $i \in [n]$ and st_0 for the leader and returns a system parameter par. We assume par is given to all other algorithms implicitly. The key generation algorithm $\mathsf{KeyGen}()$ returns a public verification key pk, public auxiliary information aux, and a secret key sk_i for each signer i.

The signing protocol consists of two rounds: a message-independent pre-processing round and a signing round. In the pre-processing round, any signer i can run $\mathsf{SPP}(\mathsf{st}_i)$ to generate a pre-processing token pp, which is sent to the leader, and the leader runs $\mathsf{LPP}(i, pp, \mathsf{st}_0)$ to update its state st_0 to incorporate token pp. In a signing round, for any signer set $SS \subseteq [n]$ with size t and message $m \in \{0,1\}^*$, the leader runs $\mathsf{LR}(m, SS, \mathsf{st}_0)$ to generate a leader request lr with $lr.\mathsf{msg} = m$ and $lr.\mathsf{SS} = SS$ and sends lr to each signer $i \in SS$. Then, each signer i runs $\mathsf{PS}(lr, i, \mathsf{st}_i)$ to generate its partial signature $psig_i$. Finally, the leader computes a signature σ for m by running $\mathsf{Agg}(\{psig_i\}_{i \in SS})$. In summary, the signing protocol between signers in SS and the leader to sign a message $m \in \{0,1\}^*$ is represented by the following experiment:

$$
\begin{aligned}
&(pp_i, \mathsf{st}_i) \leftarrow \mathsf{SPP}() \,, \ \mathsf{st}_0 \leftarrow \mathsf{LPP}(i, pp_i, \mathsf{st}_0) \,, \ \text{for each } i \in SS \,, \\
&(lr, \mathsf{st}_0) \leftarrow \mathsf{LR}(m, SS, \mathsf{st}_0) \,, \\
&(psig_i, \mathsf{st}_i) \leftarrow \mathsf{PS}(lr, i, \mathsf{st}_i) \,, \ \text{for each } i \in SS \,, \\
&\sigma \leftarrow \mathsf{Agg}(\{psig_i\}_{i \in SS}) \,.
\end{aligned}
\tag{5}
$$

The (deterministic) verification algorithm $\mathsf{Vf}(\mathsf{pk}, m, \sigma)$ outputs a bit that indicates whether or not σ is valid for pk and m or not. We say that TS is (perfectly) *correct* if for any $SS \subseteq [n]$ and any $m \in \{0,1\}^*$, $\Pr[\mathsf{Vf}(\mathsf{pk}, m, \sigma)] = 1$, where σ is output from the experiment in (5) and the probability is taken over the sampling of the system parameter par and the randomness of KeyGen.

SECURITY. A hierarchy for security notions of threshold signatures is proposed in [6]. Here, we focus on two of them, TS-SUF-2 and TS-SUF-3, which are achieved by FROST2 and FROST1, respectively. TS-SUF-2 and TS-SUF-3 require that there exists an efficient strong verification algorithm SVf that takes as input a public key pk, a leader request lr, and a signature σ and outputs a bit that indicates whether σ is obtained legitimately for lr. SVf satisfies that for each (pk, lr), there exists at most one signature σ such that $\mathsf{SVf}(pk, lr, \sigma) = 1$ and for any $SS \subseteq [n]$ and any $m \in \{0, 1\}^*$, $\Pr[\mathsf{SVf}(pk, lr, \sigma)] = 1$, where lr and σ are generated in the experiment in (5) and the probability is taken over the sampling of the system parameter par and the randomness of KeyGen. TS-SUF-2 guarantees that an adversary can generate a valid signature σ for m only if it receives partial signatures from at least $t - |CS|$ honest parties for the same leader request lr such that $lr.\mathsf{msg} = m$ and $\mathsf{SVf}(pk, lr, \sigma) = 1$, where CS denotes the set of corrupted signers.

TS-SUF-3 is defined only for schemes where lr additionally specifies a function $lr.\mathsf{PP}$ that maps each $i \in lr.\mathsf{SS}$ to a pre-processing token generated by signer i. TS-SUF-3 guarantees that an adversary can generate a valid signature σ for m only if, in addition to the condition of TS-SUF-2, it receives partial signatures from each honest signer i such that $lr.\mathsf{PP}(i)$ is honestly generated by signer i for lr. Formally, the TS-SUF-2 game and the TS-SUF-3 game are defined in Fig. 6, where TS.HF denotes the space of the hash functions used in TS from which the random oracle is drawn. The advantage of $\mathcal{A}$ for the TS-SUF-X game is defined as $\mathsf{Adv}_{\mathsf{TS}}^{\mathsf{ts\text{-}suf\text{-}X}}(\mathcal{A}, \kappa) := \Pr\left[\text{TS-SUF-X}_{\mathsf{TS}}^{\mathcal{A}}(\kappa) = 1\right]$ for $\mathsf{X} \in \{2, 3\}$.

Our Schemes. Figure 7 shows the protocols FROST1-H and FROST2-H that are transformed from FROST1 and FROST2, respectively. In addition to the general transformation, we need to pick an injection $\mathsf{x}_{(\cdot)} : [n] \to \mathcal{S}$. The choice of $\mathsf{x}_{(\cdot)}$ can be arbitrary, and the corresponding Lagrange coefficient for a set of index $S \subseteq [n]$ and $i \in S$ is defined as $\lambda_i^S := \prod_{j \in S \setminus \{i\}} \frac{\mathsf{x}_j}{\mathsf{x}_i - \mathsf{x}_j}$. We analyse the correctness of the scheme in the full version of this paper. Also, similar to the multi-signature case, we optimize the schemes by sampling key shares from $\mathcal{D}_{\mathsf{key}} \subseteq \mathcal{D}$ and setting the hash range to be $\mathcal{S}_{\mathsf{hash}} \subseteq \mathcal{S}$.

The following theorems show that, under the AOMPR assumption, FROST2-H is TS-SUF-2-secure and FROST1-H is TS-SUF-3-secure in the random oracle model. We prove the theorems in the full version of this paper.

Theorem 3. *For any* TS-SUF-2 *adversary* $\mathcal{A}$ *game making at most* q_s *queries to* PPO *and* q_h *queries to* RO, *there exists an* AOMPR *adversary* $\mathcal{B}$ *making at most* $2\mathsf{q}_s + t$ *queries to* CHAL *running in time roughly equal two times that of* $\mathcal{A}$ *such that* $\mathsf{Adv}_{\mathsf{FROST2\text{-}H[LHF]}}^{\mathsf{ts\text{-}suf\text{-}2}}(\mathcal{A}, \kappa) \leqslant \sqrt{\mathsf{q} \cdot (\mathsf{Adv}_{\mathsf{LHF}}^{\mathsf{aompr}}(\mathcal{B}, \kappa) + (3\mathsf{q}^2)/2^\kappa)}$, *where* $\mathsf{q} = \mathsf{q}_h + \mathsf{q}_s + 1$.

Theorem 4. *For any* TS-SUF-3 *adversary* $\mathcal{A}$ *making at most* q_s *queries to* PPO *and* q_h *queries to* RO, *there exists an* AOMPR *adversary* $\mathcal{B}$ *making at most* $2\mathsf{q}_s + t$ *queries to* CHAL *running in time roughly equal two times that of* $\mathcal{A}$ *such that* $\mathsf{Adv}_{\mathsf{FROST1\text{-}H[LHF]}}^{\mathsf{ts\text{-}suf\text{-}3}}(\mathcal{A}, \kappa) \leqslant 4n \cdot \mathsf{q} \cdot \sqrt{(\mathsf{Adv}_{\mathsf{LHF}}^{\mathsf{aompr}}(\mathcal{B}, \kappa) + 6\mathsf{q}/2^\kappa)}$, *where* $\mathsf{q} = \mathsf{q}_h + \mathsf{q}_s + 1$.

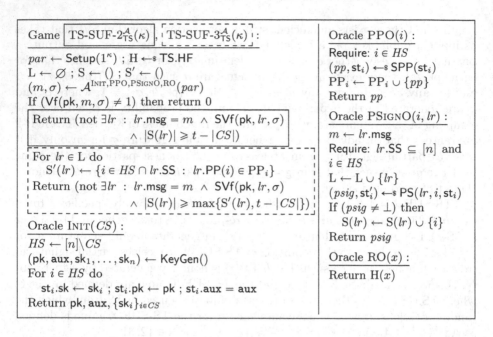

Fig. 6. The TS-SUF-2 game and the TS-SUF-3 game for a threshold signature scheme TS. The TS-SUF-2 game contains all but the dashed box, and the TS-SUF-3 game contains all but the solid box.

5   Instantiations

5.1   Instantiations from the Discrete Logarithm Problem

DISCRETE LOGARITHM PROBLEM. The discrete logarithm problem is formalized by the DLog game defined in the left side of Fig. 8. The group generation algorithm $\mathsf{GGen}(1^\kappa)$ outputs $(\mathbb{G}, p, g)$, where $\mathbb{G}$ is a cyclic group with prime size $p \geqslant 2^\kappa$ and generator g. The corresponding advantage of $\mathcal{A}$ is defined as $\mathsf{Adv}^{\mathrm{dlog}}_{\mathsf{GGen}}(\mathcal{A}, \kappa) := \Pr\left[\mathrm{DLog}^{\mathcal{A}}_{\mathsf{GGen}} = 1\right]$.

INSTANTIATION. Following the instantiation from [30], a linear hash function family GLHF is instantiated from a group generation algorithm GGen as follows.

- On input 1^κ, PGen runs $\mathsf{GGen}(1^\kappa)$ and receives a group description $(\mathbb{G}, p, g)$. Then, PGen uniformly samples $Z \in \mathbb{G}$ and returns $\kappa \leftarrow (\mathbb{G}, p, g, Z)$.
- Given $\kappa = (\mathbb{G}, p, g, Z)$, define $\mathcal{S} := \mathbb{Z}_p$, $\mathcal{D} := \mathbb{Z}_p^2$, $\mathcal{R} := \mathbb{G}$. Also, for any $(x_1, x_2) \in \mathbb{Z}_p^2$, define $\mathsf{F}(x_1, x_2) := g^{x_1} Z^{x_2}$.
- The operation over $\mathcal{D}$ is defined as follows. For any $(x_1, y_1), (x_2, y_2) \in \mathcal{D}$ and $s \in \mathcal{S}$, $(x_1, y_1) + (x_2, y_2) = (x_1 + x_2, y_1 + y_2)$ and $s \cdot (x_1, y_1) = (sx_1, sy_1)$.
- The operation over $\mathcal{R}$ is defined as follows. For any $x_1, x_2 \in \mathcal{R}$ and $s \in \mathcal{S}$, $x_1 + x_2 = x_1 x_2$, $s \cdot x_1 = x_1^s$, where $x_1 x_2$ and x_1^s are the group operations of $\mathbb{G}$.

$\underline{\mathsf{Setup}(1^\kappa):}$
$par \leftarrow_\$ \mathsf{PGen}(1^\kappa)$
For $i \in [n]$ do
$\quad \mathsf{st}_0.\mathsf{curPP}_i \leftarrow \varnothing$
$\quad \mathsf{st}_i.\mathsf{mapPP} \leftarrow ()$
Return par

$\underline{\mathsf{KeyGen}():}$
For $i \in [0..t-1]$ do
$\quad a_i \leftarrow_\$ \mathcal{D}_{\mathsf{key}}$
For $i \in [n]$ do
$\quad \mathsf{sk}_i \leftarrow_\$ \sum_{j=0}^{t-1} a_j \cdot \mathsf{x}_i^j \ ; \ \mathsf{pk}_i \leftarrow \mathsf{F}(\mathsf{sk}_i)$
$\mathsf{pk} \leftarrow \mathsf{F}(a_0)$
$\mathsf{aux} \leftarrow (\mathsf{pk}_1, \ldots, \mathsf{pk}_n)$
Return $\mathsf{pk}, \mathsf{aux}, \{\mathsf{sk}_i\}_{i\in[1..n]}$

$\underline{\mathsf{SPP}(\mathsf{st}_i):}$
$r \leftarrow_\$ \mathcal{D} \ ; \ s \leftarrow_\$ \mathcal{D}$
$pp \leftarrow (\mathsf{F}(r), \mathsf{F}(s))$
$\mathsf{st}_i.\mathsf{mapPP}(pp) \leftarrow (r, s)$
Return (pp, st_i)

$\underline{\mathsf{LPP}(i, pp, \mathsf{st}_0):}$
$\mathsf{st}_0.\mathsf{curPP}_i \leftarrow \mathsf{st}_0.\mathsf{curPP}_i \cup \{pp\}$
Return st_0

$\underline{\mathsf{LR}(M, SS, \mathsf{st}_0):}$
If $\exists\, i \in SS : \mathsf{st}_0.\mathsf{curPP}_i = \varnothing$ then
$\quad$ Return $\bot$
$lr.\mathsf{msg} \leftarrow M \ ; \ lr.\mathsf{SS} \leftarrow SS$
For $i \in SS$ do
$\quad$ Pick pp_i from $\mathsf{st}_0.\mathsf{curPP}_i$
$\quad lr.\mathsf{PP}(i) \leftarrow pp_i$
$\quad \mathsf{st}_0.\mathsf{curPP}_i \leftarrow \mathsf{st}_0.\mathsf{curPP}_i \backslash \{pp_i\}$
Return (lr, st_0)

$\underline{\mathsf{Vf}(\mathsf{pk}, m, \sigma):}$
$(R, s) \leftarrow \sigma$
$c \leftarrow \mathsf{H}_2(\mathsf{pk}, m, R)$
Return $(\mathsf{F}(s) = R + c \cdot \mathsf{pk})$

$\underline{\mathsf{CompPar}(\mathsf{pk}, lr):}$
$m \leftarrow lr.\mathsf{msg} \ ; \ (R^*, s^*) \leftarrow \sigma$
For $i \in lr.\mathsf{SS}$ do
$\quad \boxed{d_i \leftarrow \mathsf{H}_1(\mathsf{pk}, lr, i)}$
$\quad \dashbox{d_i \leftarrow \mathsf{H}_1(\mathsf{pk}, lr)}$
$\quad (R_i, S_i) \leftarrow lr.\mathsf{PP}(i)$
$R \leftarrow \sum_{i\in lr.\mathsf{SS}}(R_i + d_i S_i)$
$c \leftarrow \mathsf{H}_2(\mathsf{pk}, M, R)$
Return $(R, c, \{d_i\}_{i\in lr.\mathsf{SS}})$

$\underline{\mathsf{PS}(lr, i, \mathsf{st}_i):}$
$pp_i \leftarrow lr.\mathsf{PP}(i)$
If $\mathsf{st}_i.\mathsf{mapPP}(pp_i) = \bot$ then
$\quad$ Return $(\bot, \mathsf{st}_i)$
$(r_i, s_i) \leftarrow \mathsf{st}_i.\mathsf{mapPP}(pp_i)$
$\mathsf{st}_i.\mathsf{mapPP}(pp_i) \leftarrow \bot$
$(R, c, \{d_j\}_{j\in lr.\mathsf{SS}})$
$\quad \leftarrow \mathsf{CompPar}(\mathsf{st}_i.\mathsf{pk}, lr)$
$z_i \leftarrow r_i + d_i \cdot s_i + c \cdot \lambda_i^{lr.\mathsf{SS}} \cdot$
$\mathsf{st}_i.\mathsf{sk}$
Return $((R, z_i), \mathsf{st}_i)$

$\underline{\mathsf{Agg}(\mathsf{PS}, \mathsf{st}_0):}$
$R \leftarrow \bot \ ; \ z \leftarrow 0$
For $(R', z') \in \mathsf{PS}$ do
$\quad$ If $R = \bot$ then $R \leftarrow R'$
$\quad$ If $R \neq R'$ then return
$\quad (\bot, \mathsf{st}_0)$
$\quad z \leftarrow z + z'$
Return $((R, z), \mathsf{st}_0)$

$\underline{\mathsf{SVf}(\mathsf{pk}, lr, \sigma):}$
$(R^*, z^*) \leftarrow \sigma$
$(R, c, \{d_j\}_{j\in lr.\mathsf{SS}})$
$\quad \leftarrow \mathsf{CompPar}(\mathsf{st}_i.\mathsf{pk}, lr)$
Return $(R = R^*) \wedge$
$(\mathsf{F}(z^*) = R + c \cdot \mathsf{pk})$

Fig. 7. The protocol FROST1-H[LHF] and FROST1-H[LHF], where LHF = (PGen, F) is a linear hash function family. The protocol FROST1-H contains all but the dashed box, and the protocol FROST2-H contains all but the solid box. Further, n is the number of parties, and t is the threshold of the schemes. $\mathsf{x}_{(\cdot)}$ is an injection from $[n]$ to $\mathcal{S}$ and $\lambda_i^{lr.\mathsf{SS}}$ denotes the Lagrange coefficient which is computed as $\lambda_i^{lr.\mathsf{SS}} := \prod_{j\in\mathcal{S}\backslash\{i\}} \frac{\mathsf{x}_j}{\mathsf{x}_j - \mathsf{x}_i}$. $\mathcal{D}_{\mathsf{key}}$ is a subset of $\mathcal{D}$ such that F is a bijection between $\mathcal{D}_{\mathsf{key}}$ and $\mathcal{S}$. The function $\mathsf{H}_i(\cdot)$ is computed as $\mathsf{H}(i, \cdot)$ for $i = 1, 2$, where $\mathsf{H} : \{0,1\}^* \to \mathcal{S}$.

Game $\mathrm{DLog}_{\mathsf{GGen}}^{\mathcal{A}}(\kappa)$:	Game $\mathrm{RSA}_{\mathsf{RGen}}^{\mathcal{A}}(\kappa)$:
$(\mathbb{G}, p, g) \leftarrow_{\$} \mathsf{GGen}(1^{\kappa})$	$(N, e) \leftarrow_{\$} \mathsf{RGen}(1^{\kappa})$
$Z \leftarrow_{\$} \mathbb{G}$	$w \leftarrow_{\$} \mathbb{Z}_N^*$
$z \leftarrow_{\$} \mathcal{A}(\mathbb{G}, p, g, Z)$	$u \leftarrow_{\$} \mathcal{A}(N, e, w)$
If $g^z = Z$ then	If $u^e = w$ then
Return 1	Return 1
Return 0	Return 0

Fig. 8. The DLog game and the RSA game.

The following theorem shows that GLHF is a linear hash function family and collision resistance of GLHF is implied by the discrete logarithm assumption. [30] shows similar statements, and we also give the proof in the full version of this paper.

Lemma 3. *For any group generation algorithm* GGen, GLHF[GGen] *is a linear hash function family (Definition 1). Moreover, for any adversary $\mathcal{A}$ for the* $\mathrm{CR}^{\mathsf{GLHF[GGen]}}$ *game, there exists an adversary $\mathcal{B}$ for the* $\mathrm{DLog}^{\mathsf{GGen}}$ *game such that* $\mathrm{Adv}_{\mathsf{GLHF[GGen]}}^{\mathrm{cr}}(\mathcal{A}, \kappa) \leqslant \mathrm{Adv}_{\mathsf{GGen}}^{\mathrm{dlog}}(\mathcal{B}, \kappa).$

To instantiate MuSig2-H, FROST1-H, and FROST2-H, we set $\mathcal{D}_{\mathsf{key}} := \{(x, 0) : x \in \mathbb{Z}\}$ and $\mathcal{S}_{\mathsf{hash}} := \mathcal{S}$. It is clear that $\mathrm{char}(\mathcal{S}) = p \geqslant 2^{\kappa}$, F is a bijection from $\mathcal{D}_{\mathsf{key}}$ to $\mathcal{R}$, and $|\mathcal{S}_{\mathsf{hash}}| = |\mathcal{S}| \geqslant 2^{\kappa}$. Also, for instantiating FROST1-H and FROST2-H, we set $\mathsf{x}_i := i$.

By combining Theorem 1 and Lemma 3 with the theorems in Sect. 4, we show the security of MuSig2-H, FROST1-H, and FROST2-H instantiated from GLHF under the discrete logarithm assumption in the random oracle model.

5.2   Instantiations from the RSA Problem

RSA PROBLEM. The RSA problem we use here is formalized by the RSA game defined on the right side of Fig. 8. The RSA parameter generation algorithm $\mathsf{RGen}(1^{\kappa})$ outputs (N, e), where $N = P \cdot Q$ for two primes P and Q and e is a prime such that $\gcd(N, e) = \gcd(\phi(N), e) = 1$ such that $\phi(N) \geqslant 2^{\kappa}$ and $e \geqslant 2^{\kappa}$.[1] The corresponding advantage of $\mathcal{A}$ is defined as $\mathrm{Adv}_{\mathsf{RGen}}^{\mathrm{rsa}}(\mathcal{A}, \kappa) := \Pr\left[\mathrm{RSA}_{\mathsf{RGen}}^{\mathcal{A}} = 1\right]$.

INSTANTIATION. To instantiate linear hash function families from the RSA problem, we have to use a weaker notion, referred to as *weak linear hash functions*, which are the same as linear hash functions except that $\mathcal{S}$ is only required to be a ring instead of a field. Formally, we construct a weak linear hash function family, RLHF, from an RSA parameter generation algorithm RGen as follows.

---

[1] Comparing this to the plain RSA problem, here we additionally require that e is prime such that $\gcd(N, e) = 1$ and $e \geqslant 2^{\kappa}$.

- On input 1^κ, PGen runs RGen(1^κ) and receives (N, e). Then, PGen uniformly samples $w \in \mathbb{Z}_N^*$ and returns $par \leftarrow (N, e, w)$.
- Given $par = (N, e, w)$, define $\mathcal{S} := \mathbb{Z}$, $\mathcal{D} := \mathbb{Z}_e \times \mathbb{Z}_N^*$, $\mathcal{R} := \mathbb{Z}_N^*$. Also, for any $(a, x) \in \mathbb{Z}_e \times \mathbb{Z}_N^*$, define $\mathsf{F}(a, x) := w^a x^e \in \mathbb{Z}_N^*$.
- The operations of $\mathcal{D}$ are defined as follows. For any $(a_1, x_1), (a_2, x_2) \in \mathcal{D}$ and $s \in \mathcal{S}$, $(a_1, x_1) + (a_2, x_2) = (a_1 + a_2, x_1 x_2 w^{\lfloor (a_1 + a_2)/e \rfloor})$ and $s \cdot (a_1, x_1) = (sa_1, x_1^s w^{\lfloor sa_1/e \rfloor})$, where $a_1 + a_2$ and sa_1 are computed over $\mathbb{Z}_e$.
- The operations of $\mathcal{R}$ are defined as follows. For any $x_1, x_2 \in \mathcal{R}$ and $s \in \mathcal{S}$, $x_1 + x_2 = x_1 x_2$, $s \cdot x_1 = x_1^s$, where $x_1 x_2$ is the multiplicative operation over $\mathbb{Z}_N^*$ and x_1^s is the exponential operation over $\mathbb{Z}_N^*$. Note here and also in the following discussion, we use "+" to denote the group operation of $\mathcal{R}$ instead of the additive operation over $\mathbb{Z}$ and "·" to denote the scalar multiplicative operation of $\mathcal{R}$ instead of the multiplicative operation over $\mathbb{Z}$.

The preceding instantiation is similar to the one from [30]. The only difference is that we set $\mathcal{S}$ to $\mathbb{Z}$ in order to make both $\mathcal{D}$ and $\mathcal{R}$ to be $\mathcal{S}$-modules. The following theorem shows that RLHF is a weak linear hash function family and collision resistance of RLHF is implied by the RSA assumption. We give the proof in the full version of this paper.

Lemma 4. *For any RSA parameter generation algorithm* RGen, *RLHF[RGen] is a weak linear hash function family. Moreover, for any adversary $\mathcal{A}$ for the* $\mathrm{CR}^{\mathsf{RLHF[RGen]}}$ *game, there exists an adversary $\mathcal{B}$ for the* $\mathrm{RSA}^{\mathsf{RGen}}$ *game such that* $\mathsf{Adv}^{\mathrm{cr}}_{\mathsf{RLHF[RGen]}}(\mathcal{A}, \kappa) \leqslant \mathsf{Adv}^{\mathrm{rsa}}_{\mathsf{RGen}}(\mathcal{B}, \kappa)$.

REDUCTION FROM CR TO AOMPR. Unfortunately, Theorem 1 does not hold for weak linear hash functions: in the proof of Claim 1, if $\mathcal{S}$ is not a field, it is possible that there does not exist u satisfying the condition in (2). Nonetheless, we can show for RLHF that the reduction still works. Formally, we have the following theorem.

Theorem 5. *For any adversary $\mathcal{A}$ for the* $\mathrm{AOMPR}^{\mathsf{RLHF}}$ *game, there exists an adversary $\mathcal{B}$ for the* $\mathrm{CR}^{\mathsf{RLHF}}$ *game running in a similar running time as $\mathcal{A}$ such that* $\mathsf{Adv}^{\mathrm{aompr}}_{\mathsf{RLHF}}(\mathcal{A}, \kappa) \leqslant 2\mathsf{Adv}^{\mathrm{cr}}_{\mathsf{RLHF}}(\mathcal{B}, \kappa)$.

Proof (of Theorem 5). We prove the above theorem following the proof of Theorem 1, where the only difference is that in the proof of Claim 1, we need to show the following fact:

There exists $z^* \in \mathcal{D}$ such that $\mathsf{F}(z^*) = 0$, and, for any matrix $B \in \mathcal{S}^{\ell \times q}$ with $\ell < q$, there exists a vector $u \in \mathcal{S}^q$ and $i \in [q]$ such that $Bu = 0$ and $u_i z^* \neq 0$, where 0 denotes the identity of $\mathcal{D}$ and $\mathcal{R}$ and the additive identity of $\mathcal{S}$.

We prove the above fact for RLHF as follows. Given the parameter (N, e, w) that defines $(\mathcal{S}, \mathcal{D}, \mathcal{R}, \mathsf{F})$, the identity of $\mathcal{D}$ is $(0, 1)$, and the identity of $\mathcal{R}$ is 1. We first set $z^* = (e - 1, w^{1-1/e})$, where $1/e$ denotes the multiplicative inverse of e over $\mathbb{Z}_{\phi(N)}$. $1/e$ exists since $\gcd(\phi(N), e) = 1$. We can verify that $\mathsf{F}(z^*) =$

$w^{e-1+e(1-1/e)} = 1$. Since $\ell < q$, we can always find a non-zero vector $\boldsymbol{v} \in \mathbb{Z}$ such that $B\boldsymbol{v} = 0$ using Gaussian eliminations. Denote $k := \gcd(\{v_i\}_{i \in [q]})$. Let $\boldsymbol{u} = \boldsymbol{v}/k$, and we have $\gcd(\{u_i\}_{i \in [q]}) = 1$. Therefore, there exists $i \in [q]$ such that $u_i \not\equiv 0 \bmod e$ and thus $u_i z^* \neq (0,1)$. Since $B\boldsymbol{u} \cdot k = B\boldsymbol{v} = 0$ and $k \neq 0$, we know $B\boldsymbol{u} = 0$. $\qquad\square$

SOLVING LINEAR EQUATIONS. Another issue with weak linear hash functions is that it is unclear how to invert challenges $\boldsymbol{X} \in \mathcal{R}$ given $A\boldsymbol{X} = \mathsf{F}(\boldsymbol{b})$, where $A \in \mathcal{S}^{n \times n}$ and $\boldsymbol{b} \in \mathcal{D}^n$, which is a common problem we encounter in the security proofs in Sect. 4. In these proofs, to solve this problem, we show A has full rank and then, since $\mathcal{S}$ is a field, we can compute $\boldsymbol{x} \in \mathcal{D}^n$ such that $\mathsf{F}(\boldsymbol{x}) = \boldsymbol{X}$ by multiplying the inverse of A on both sides of the equation. However, in the case of weak linear hash functions, A might not have an inverse.

Fortunately, for RLHF, we show that such linear equations can be solved efficiently if A has full rank modulo e, which is formally stated in the following lemma.

Lemma 5. *For any integer $n \geqslant 1$ and any parameter $par = (N, e, w)$ for* RLHF, *which defines $(\mathcal{S}, \mathcal{D}, \mathcal{R}, \mathsf{F})$, given $A \in \mathcal{S}^{n \times n}$, $\boldsymbol{X} \in \mathcal{R}^n$, and $\boldsymbol{b} \in \mathcal{D}^n$ such that A has full rank modulo e and $A\boldsymbol{X} = \mathsf{F}(\boldsymbol{b})$, there exists an efficient algorithm with input $(A, \boldsymbol{X}, \boldsymbol{b})$ that outputs $\boldsymbol{x} \in \mathcal{D}^n$ such that $\mathsf{F}(x_i) = X_i$.*

Proof. We compute $\boldsymbol{x}$ as follows.

1. Since A has full rank modulo e and e is a prime, we can efficiently compute the inverse of A modulo e as A'.
2. Set $C \leftarrow A'A$. Since A' is the inverse of A modulo e, we know for any $i, j \in [n]$,
$$C_{i,j} \equiv \begin{cases} 1 \bmod e, & \text{for } i = j \\ 0 \bmod e, & o.w. \end{cases}.$$
3. Set $\boldsymbol{b}' \leftarrow A'\boldsymbol{b}$ and $x_i \leftarrow b_i' - \sum_{j \in [n]} \lfloor C_{i,j}/e \rfloor \cdot (0, X_j)$ for each $i \in [n]$.

Since $A\boldsymbol{X} = \mathsf{F}(\boldsymbol{b})$, we have $C\boldsymbol{X} = A'A\boldsymbol{X} = A'\mathsf{F}(\boldsymbol{b}) = \mathsf{F}(A'\boldsymbol{b}) = \mathsf{F}(\boldsymbol{b}')$, which implies $\mathsf{F}(b_i') = \sum_{j \in [n]} C_{i,j} X_j = \prod_{j \in [n]} X_j^{C_{i,j}}$. Therefore, due to the above property of C, for $i \in [n]$, $\mathsf{F}(x_i) = \mathsf{F}(b_i') - \sum_{j \in [n]} X_j^{e\lfloor C_{i,j}/e \rfloor} = \prod_{j \in [n]} X_j^{C_{i,j} - e\lfloor C_{i,j}/e \rfloor} = X_i$. $\qquad\square$

$\mathcal{D}_{\text{key}}$ AND $\mathcal{S}_{\text{hash}}$. For instantiating MuSig2-H, FROST1-H, and FROST2-H from RLHF, we set $\mathcal{D}_{\text{key}} := \{(0, x) \mid x \in \mathbb{Z}_N^*\}$ and $\mathcal{S}_{\text{hash}} := \mathbb{Z}_{2^\kappa}$. It is clear that F is bijection from $\mathcal{D}_{\text{key}}$ to $\mathcal{R}$ and $|\mathcal{S}_{\text{hash}}| \geqslant 2^\kappa$.

5.3   Multi-signatures from RSA

To instantiate MuSig2-H from RLHF, we additionally require that for $N = P \cdot Q$, P is a safe prime and $P > 2^{\kappa+1}$ for the security proof to go through. We discuss how to remove this requirement later in this section. To show the security, we prove Theorem 2 holds if LHF is replaced by RLHF. Combining it with Theorem 5 and Lemma 4 shows the security of RLHF-based MuSig2-H under the RSA assumption in the random oracle model.

We now show the proof of Theorem 2 for the case LHF = RLHF by discussing only those places that differ from the original proof of Theorem 2.

Proof (of Theorem 2 for RLHF*).* We follow the original proof of Theorem 2 to construct the adversary $\mathcal{B}$. Then, we just need to show that Claim 3, Claim 4, and Claim 5 hold.

Proof (of Claim 3 for RLHF*).* We only need to show that Lemma 2 holds for RLHF, and the rest is the same as the original proof of Claim 3. Denote $r \in \mathbb{Z}_P^*$ as the primitive root of $\mathbb{Z}_P^*$. For any $X \in \mathbb{Z}_N^* = \mathcal{R}$, there exists $k \in \mathbb{Z}_{P-1}^*$ such that $X \equiv r^k \mod P$. Suppose $k \neq P'$. For any $1 \leqslant t, s \leqslant 2^\kappa < P'$ and any $1 \leqslant s < P'$, we have $(X)^{ts} \equiv r^{kts} \not\equiv r^0 \mod P$, which implies $(X^*)^{t \cdot s_1} \neq (X^*)^{t \cdot s_2}$ for any distinct $s_1, s_2 \in \mathbb{Z}_{2^\kappa} = \mathcal{S}_{\text{hash}}$. Therefore, we have $|C(t, X)| = |\mathcal{S}_{\text{hash}}|$. Therefore, X is Good if $X \not\equiv r^{P'} \mod P$. Therefore, we have $\Pr_{X \twoheadleftarrow \mathcal{R}}[X \text{ is not Good}] \leqslant \Pr_{X \twoheadleftarrow \mathbb{Z}_N^*}[X \equiv r^{P'} \mod P] \leqslant 1/(P-1) \leqslant 1/2^\kappa$.   □

Proof (of Claim 4 for RLHF*).* Following the original proof of Claim 4, we have $\mathsf{F}(s^*) = R^* + h_I \cdot \mathsf{apk}^*$ and $\mathsf{F}(s^{*\prime}) = R^* + h_I' \mathsf{apk}^*$, which implies $(h_I - h_I') \cdot \mathsf{apk}^* = \mathsf{F}(s^* - s^{*\prime})$. Assume $h_I' < h_I$ without loss of generality. Since $h_I, h_I' \in \mathcal{S}_{\text{hash}} = \mathbb{Z}_{2^\kappa} \subseteq \mathbb{Z}_e$, we have $1 \leqslant h_I - h_I' < e$. Therefore, $\mathcal{C}'$ computes $\widetilde{x}$ using Lemma 5 for the case $n = 1$.   □

Proof (of Claim 5 for RLHF*).* The total number of CHAL queries made by $\mathcal{B}$ is $4\mathsf{q}_s + 1$ and the corresponding challenges are $X, U_1, \ldots, U_{4\mathsf{q}_s}$. We follow the original proof to show how $\mathcal{B}$ computes $x^*, u_1, \ldots, u_{4\mathsf{q}_s}$ such that $\mathsf{F}(x^*) = X$ and $\mathsf{F}(u_i) = U_i$ for $i \in [4\mathsf{q}_s]$.

To compute x^*, following the original proof, we have $\mathsf{F}(\widetilde{x}) = t \cdot h_{I_{\text{agg}}}^{(\text{agg})} \cdot X + Z$, $\mathsf{F}(\widetilde{x}') = t \cdot h_{I_{\text{agg}}}^{(\text{agg})\prime} \cdot X + Z$, where $h_{I_{\text{agg}}}^{(\text{agg})} \neq h_{I_{\text{agg}}}^{(\text{agg})\prime} \in \mathcal{S}_{\text{hash}} = \mathbb{Z}_{2^\kappa}$, $1 \leqslant t \leqslant 2^\kappa$, and $Z \in \mathcal{R}$. Therefore, $t(h_{I_{\text{agg}}}^{(\text{agg})} - h_{I_{\text{agg}}}^{(\text{agg})\prime}) \cdot X = \mathsf{F}(\widetilde{x} - \widetilde{x}')$. Assume $h_{I_{\text{agg}}}^{(\text{agg})\prime} < h_{I_{\text{agg}}}^{(\text{agg})}$ without loss of generality. We have $1 \leqslant t \leqslant 2^\kappa < e$ and $1 \leqslant (h_{I_{\text{agg}}}^{(\text{agg})} - h_{I_{\text{agg}}}^{(\text{agg})\prime}) \leqslant 2^\kappa < e$, which implies $t(h_{I_{\text{agg}}}^{(\text{agg})} - h_{I_{\text{agg}}}^{(\text{agg})\prime}) \not\equiv 0 \mod e$. Therefore, $\mathcal{B}$ computes x^* using Lemma 5 for the case $n = 1$.

For each $k \in [\mathsf{q}_s]$, to compute $u_{1+4(k-1)}, \ldots, u_{4k}$, following the original proof, we have $AU = \mathsf{F}(s)$, where

$$A = \begin{pmatrix} 1 & b_1 & b_1^2 & b_1^3 \\ \vdots & \vdots & \vdots & \vdots \\ 1 & b_4 & b_4^2 & b_4^3 \end{pmatrix}, \quad U = \begin{pmatrix} U_{1+4(k-1)} \\ \vdots \\ U_{4k} \end{pmatrix}, \quad s = \begin{pmatrix} s_1 \\ \vdots \\ s_4 \end{pmatrix}. \tag{6}$$

Also, $b_i \in \mathcal{S}_{\text{hash}} = \mathbb{Z}_{2^\kappa} \subseteq \mathbb{Z}_e$ for $i \in [4]$, and $b_1, \ldots, b_4$ differ from each other. Therefore, A is a Vandermonde matrix modulo e, which implies A has full rank modulo e. Therefore, $\mathcal{B}$ can compute $u_{1+4(k-1)}, \ldots, u_{4k}$ using Lemma 5 for the case $n = 4$. Then, the rest follows from the original proof.   □

REMOVING THE SAFE-PRIME REQUIREMENT. We briefly mention how to remove the safe-prime requirement by slightly modifying MuSig2-H as follows. Denote the modified schemes as MuSig2-HR. MuSig2-HR is identical to MuSig2-H except:

- In algorithm $\mathsf{KeyAgg}(L)$, it additionally computes $a_0 \leftarrow \mathrm{H}'(L)$, where $\mathrm{H}'(L) : \{0,1\}^* \rightarrow \mathcal{D}_{\mathsf{key}}$, and sets $\mathsf{apk} \leftarrow \mathsf{F}(a_0) + \sum_{i \in [n]} a_i \mathsf{pk}_i$.
- In algorithm Sign, after s is assigned, it additionally computes $a_0 \leftarrow c \cdot \mathrm{H}'(L)$ and returns (R, a_0, s).
- In algorithm $\mathsf{SignAgg}(\{(R^{(1)}, a_0^{(1)}, s^{(1)}), \ldots, (R^{(n)}, a_0^{(n)}, s^{(n)})\})$, it checks if $(R^{(1)}, a_0^{(1)}), \ldots, (R^{(n)}, a_0^{(n)})$ are all the same. If not, it aborts. Otherwise, it returns $\sigma \leftarrow (R^{(1)}, a_0^{(1)} + \sum_{i \in [n]} s^{(i)})$.

We can show the security of MuSig2-HR following the proof of Theorem 2 for RLHF. The only difference is the proof of Claim 3, which is also the only place where we need the safe-prime condition. Claim 3 essentially shows that for any new RO query $\mathrm{H}_{\mathsf{agg}}(L, \widetilde{\mathsf{pk}})$, the probability that $\mathsf{apk} \leftarrow \mathsf{KeyAgg}(L)$ collides with the set K of existing aggregated keys is small. We can easily show it for MuSig2-HR since, for any new L in the random oracle model, $\mathrm{H}'(L)$ is uniformly random over $\mathcal{D}_{\mathsf{key}}$; thus, $\mathsf{apk} \leftarrow \mathsf{KeyAgg}(L)$ is uniformly random over $\mathcal{R}$ even given previous queries, which implies the collision probability is small.

5.4   Threshold Signatures from RSA

To instantiate FROST1-H and FROST2-H from RLHF, the only difficulty is that the Lagrange coefficient λ_i^S might not be defined in $\mathcal{S} = \mathbb{Z}$ for $S \subseteq [n]$. To fix this, we set $\mathsf{x}_i = i$ for $i \in [n]$ and modify the schemes as follows.

Denote the modified schemes as FROST1-HR and FROST2-HR. Define $\widetilde{\lambda}_i^S := r\Delta \cdot \lambda_i^{lr.\mathsf{SS}}$, where $\Delta = n!$ and $r \in \mathbb{Z}_e^*$ is the multiplicative inverse of Δ modulo e. FROST1-HR/FROST2-HR is identical to FROST1-H/ FROST2-H except:

- In algorithm PS, the Lagrange coefficient λ_i^S is replaced by $\widetilde{\lambda}_i^S$, and (R, c, z_i) is returned as a partial signature.
- In algorithm Agg, we additionally set $\widetilde{z} \leftarrow z - (ck) \cdot (0, \mathsf{pk})$, where $k = \lfloor r\Delta/e \rfloor$, and return $(R, \widetilde{z})$ as the signature.

It is not hard to show the correctness of the schemes. Since the denominator of λ_i^S, which is equal to $\prod_{j \in S}(i - j)$, divides $i!(n - i)!$ and thus divides Δ, we know $\widetilde{\lambda}_i^S \in \mathbb{Z}$. Also, for a leader request lr, if each signer i in $lr.\mathsf{SS}$ follows the protocol to compute the partial signature (R, c, z_i), we have $\mathsf{F}(z) = R + (cr\Delta) \cdot \mathsf{pk}$, where $z = \sum_{i \in lr.\mathsf{SS}} z_i$. Since r is the multiplicative inverse of Δ modulo e, we have $r\Delta = ke + 1$. Since $\mathsf{F}(0, \mathsf{pk}) = \mathsf{pk}^e$, we have $\mathsf{F}(\widetilde{z}) = R + c \cdot \mathsf{pk}$, which implies $(R, \widetilde{z})$ is a valid signature.

We show the security of FROST2-HR and FROST1-HR under the RSA assumption in the random oracle model by showing Theorem 3 and Theorem 4 hold for RLHF and combining them with Theorem 5 and Lemma 4. We give a more detailed analysis in the full version of this paper.

Acknowledgments. We thank the EUROCRYPT 2023 reviewers for their useful comments and feedback. This research was partially supported by NSF grants CNS-2026774, CNS-2154174, a JP Morgan Faculty Award, a CISCO Faculty Award, and a gift from Microsoft.

References

1. Aboud, S.J., Al-Fayoumi, M.A.: Two efficient RSA digital multisignature and blind multisignature schemes. In: Hamza, M.H. (ed.) IASTED International Conference on Computational Intelligence, Calgary, Alberta, Canada, 4–6 July 2005, pp. 359–362. IASTED/ACTA Press (2005)
2. Almansa, J.F., Damgård, I., Nielsen, J.B.: Simplified threshold RSA with adaptive and proactive security. In: Vaudenay, S. (ed.) EUROCRYPT 2006. LNCS, vol. 4004, pp. 593–611. Springer, Heidelberg (2006). https://doi.org/10.1007/11761679_35
3. Backendal, M., Bellare, M., Sorrell, J., Sun, J.: The Fiat-Shamir Zoo: relating the security of different signature variants. In: Gruschka, N. (ed.) NordSec 2018. LNCS, vol. 11252, pp. 154–170. Springer, Cham (2018). https://doi.org/10.1007/978-3-030-03638-6_10
4. Bagherzandi, A., Cheon, J.H., Jarecki, S.: Multisignatures secure under the discrete logarithm assumption and a generalized forking lemma. In: Ning, P., Syverson, P.F., Jha, S. (eds.) ACM CCS 2008, pp. 449–458. ACM Press (Oct 2008). https://doi.org/10.1145/1455770.1455827
5. Bagherzandi, A., Jarecki, S.: Identity-based aggregate and multi-signature schemes based on RSA. In: Nguyen, P.Q., Pointcheval, D. (eds.) PKC 2010. LNCS, vol. 6056, pp. 480–498. Springer, Heidelberg (2010). https://doi.org/10.1007/978-3-642-13013-7_28
6. Bellare, M., Crites, E.C., Komlo, C., Maller, M., Tessaro, S., Zhu, C.: Better than advertised security for non-interactive threshold signatures. In: Dodis, Y., Shrimpton, T. (eds.) CRYPTO 2022, Part IV. LNCS, vol. 13510, pp. 517–550. Springer, Heidelberg (2022). https://doi.org/10.1007/978-3-031-15985-5_18
7. Bellare, M., Dai, W.: chain reductions for multi-signatures and the HBMS scheme. In: Tibouchi, M., Wang, H. (eds.) ASIACRYPT 2021. LNCS, vol. 13093, pp. 650–678. Springer, Cham (2021). https://doi.org/10.1007/978-3-030-92068-5_22
8. Bellare, M., Namprempre, C., Pointcheval, D., Semanko, M.: The one-more-RSA-inversion problems and the security of Chaum's blind signature scheme. J. Cryptol. **16**(3), 185–215 (2003). https://doi.org/10.1007/s00145-002-0120-1
9. Bellare, M., Neven, G.: Identity-based multi-signatures from RSA. In: Abe, M. (ed.) CT-RSA 2007. LNCS, vol. 4377, pp. 145–162. Springer, Heidelberg (2006). https://doi.org/10.1007/11967668_10
10. Bellare, M., Rogaway, P.: Random oracles are practical: A paradigm for designing efficient protocols. In: Denning, D.E., Pyle, R., Ganesan, R., Sandhu, R.S., Ashby, V. (eds.) ACM CCS 1993, pp. 62–73. ACM Press (Nov 1993). https://doi.org/10.1145/168588.168596
11. Bellare, M., Tessaro, S., Zhu, C.: Stronger security for non-interactive threshold signatures: Bls and frost. Cryptology ePrint Archive (2022)
12. Benhamouda, F., Lepoint, T., Loss, J., Orrù, M., Raykova, M.: On the (in)security of ROS. In: Canteaut, A., Standaert, F.-X. (eds.) EUROCRYPT 2021. LNCS, vol. 12696, pp. 33–53. Springer, Cham (2021). https://doi.org/10.1007/978-3-030-77870-5_2

13. Boldyreva, A.: Threshold signatures, multisignatures and blind signatures based on the gap-diffie-hellman-group signature scheme. In: Desmedt, Y.G. (ed.) PKC 2003. LNCS, vol. 2567, pp. 31–46. Springer, Heidelberg (2003). https://doi.org/10.1007/3-540-36288-6_3

14. Boneh, D., Lynn, B., Shacham, H.: Short signatures from the weil pairing. In: Boyd, C. (ed.) ASIACRYPT 2001. LNCS, vol. 2248, pp. 514–532. Springer, Heidelberg (2001). https://doi.org/10.1007/3-540-45682-1_30

15. Connolly, D., Komlo, C., Goldberg, I., Wood, C.A.: Two-Round Threshold Schnorr Signatures with FROST. Internet-Draft draft-irtf-cfrg-frost-10, Internet Engineering Task Force (Sep 2022). https://datatracker.ietf.org/doc/draft-irtf-cfrg-frost/10/, work in Progress

16. Damgård, I., Koprowski, M.: Practical threshold RSA signatures without a trusted dealer. In: Pfitzmann, B. (ed.) EUROCRYPT 2001. LNCS, vol. 2045, pp. 152–165. Springer, Heidelberg (2001). https://doi.org/10.1007/3-540-44987-6_10

17. De Santis, A., Desmedt, Y., Frankel, Y., Yung, M.: How to share a function securely. In: 26th ACM STOC, pp. 522–533. ACM Press (May 1994). https://doi.org/10.1145/195058.195405

18. Desmedt, Y.: Society and group oriented cryptography: a new concept. In: Pomerance, C. (ed.) CRYPTO 1987. LNCS, vol. 293, pp. 120–127. Springer, Heidelberg (1988). https://doi.org/10.1007/3-540-48184-2_8

19. Desmedt, Y., Frankel, Y.: Threshold cryptosystems. In: Brassard, G. (ed.) CRYPTO 1989. LNCS, vol. 435, pp. 307–315. Springer, New York (1990). https://doi.org/10.1007/0-387-34805-0_28

20. Desmedt, Y., Frankel, Y.: Shared generation of authenticators and signatures. In: Feigenbaum, J. (ed.) CRYPTO 1991. LNCS, vol. 576, pp. 457–469. Springer, Heidelberg (1992). https://doi.org/10.1007/3-540-46766-1_37

21. Drijvers, M., et al.: On the security of two-round multi-signatures. In: 2019 IEEE Symposium on Security and Privacy, pp. 1084–1101. IEEE Computer Society Press (May 2019). https://doi.org/10.1109/SP.2019.00050

22. Fouque, P.-A., Stern, J.: Fully distributed threshold RSA under standard assumptions. In: Boyd, C. (ed.) ASIACRYPT 2001. LNCS, vol. 2248, pp. 310–330. Springer, Heidelberg (2001). https://doi.org/10.1007/3-540-45682-1_19

23. Frankel, Y., MacKenzie, P.D., Yung, M.: Robust efficient distributed RSA-key generation. In: Coan, B.A., Afek, Y. (eds.) 17th ACM PODC, p. 320. ACM (Jun/Jul 1998). https://doi.org/10.1145/277697.277779

24. Fuchsbauer, G., Kiltz, E., Loss, J.: The algebraic group model and its applications. In: Shacham, H., Boldyreva, A. (eds.) CRYPTO 2018. LNCS, vol. 10992, pp. 33–62. Springer, Cham (2018). https://doi.org/10.1007/978-3-319-96881-0_2

25. Gennaro, R., Goldfeder, S., Narayanan, A.: Threshold-optimal DSA/ECDSA signatures and an application to bitcoin wallet security. In: Manulis, M., Sadeghi, A.-R., Schneider, S. (eds.) ACNS 2016. LNCS, vol. 9696, pp. 156–174. Springer, Cham (2016). https://doi.org/10.1007/978-3-319-39555-5_9

26. Gennaro, R., Halevi, S., Krawczyk, H., Rabin, T.: Threshold RSA for dynamic and Ad-Hoc Groups. In: Smart, N. (ed.) EUROCRYPT 2008. LNCS, vol. 4965, pp. 88–107. Springer, Heidelberg (2008). https://doi.org/10.1007/978-3-540-78967-3_6

27. Gennaro, R., Jarecki, S., Krawczyk, H., Rabin, T.: Robust and efficient sharing of RSA functions. In: Koblitz, N. (ed.) CRYPTO 1996. LNCS, vol. 1109, pp. 157–172. Springer, Heidelberg (1996). https://doi.org/10.1007/3-540-68697-5_13

28. Gennaro, R., Jarecki, S., Krawczyk, H., Rabin, T.: Secure distributed key generation for discrete-log based cryptosystems. J. Cryptol. **20**(1), 51–83 (2006). https://doi.org/10.1007/s00145-006-0347-3

29. Harn, L., Kiesler, T.: New scheme for digital multisignatures. Electron. Lett. **25**(15), 1002–1003 (1989)
30. Hauck, E., Kiltz, E., Loss, J.: A modular treatment of blind signatures from identification schemes. In: Ishai, Y., Rijmen, V. (eds.) EUROCRYPT 2019. LNCS, vol. 11478, pp. 345–375. Springer, Cham (2019). https://doi.org/10.1007/978-3-030-17659-4_12
31. Hauck, E., Kiltz, E., Loss, J., Nguyen, N.K.: Lattice-based blind signatures, revisited. In: Micciancio, D., Ristenpart, T. (eds.) CRYPTO 2020. LNCS, vol. 12171, pp. 500–529. Springer, Cham (2020). https://doi.org/10.1007/978-3-030-56880-1_18
32. Itakura, K.: A public-key cryptosystem suitable for digital multisignatures (1983)
33. Itakura, K; Nakamura, K.: A public-key cryptosystem suitable for digital multisignatures. NEC research & development (1983)
34. Kiesler, T., Harn, L.: Rsa blocking and multisignature schemes with no bit expansion. Electron. Lett. **18**(26), 1490–1491 (1990)
35. Koblitz, N., Menezes, A.: Another look at non-standard discrete log and diffie-hellman problems. J. Math. Cryptol. **2**(4), 311–326 (2008). https://doi.org/10.1515/JMC.2008.014, https://doi.org/10.1515/JMC.2008.014
36. Koblitz, N., Menezes, A.J.: Another look at "provable security". J. Cryptol. **20**(1), 3–37 (2007). https://doi.org/10.1007/s00145-005-0432-z
37. Komlo, C., Goldberg, I.: FROST: flexible round-optimized schnorr threshold signatures. In: Dunkelman, O., Jacobson, Jr., M.J., O'Flynn, C. (eds.) SAC 2020. LNCS, vol. 12804, pp. 34–65. Springer, Cham (2021). https://doi.org/10.1007/978-3-030-81652-0_2
38. Lee, K., Kim, H.: Two-round multi-signatures from okamoto signatures. Cryptology ePrint Archive, Report 2022/1117 (2022). https://eprint.iacr.org/2022/1117
39. Lindell, Y.: Simple three-round multiparty schnorr signing with full simulatability. Cryptology ePrint Archive, Paper 2022/374 (2022).https://eprint.iacr.org/2022/374
40. Mambo, M., Okamoto, E., et al.: On the security of the rsa-based multisignature scheme for various group structures. In: Australasian Conference on Information Security and Privacy, pp. 352–367. Springer (2000)
41. Mitomi, S., Miyaji, A.: A Multisignature Scheme with Message Flexibility, Order Flexibility and Order Verifiability. In: Dawson, E.P., Clark, A., Boyd, C. (eds.) ACISP 2000. LNCS, vol. 1841, pp. 298–312. Springer, Heidelberg (2000). https://doi.org/10.1007/10718964_25
42. National Institute of Standards and Technology: Multi-Party Threshold Cryptography (2018-Present). https://csrc.nist.gov/Projects/threshold-cryptography
43. Nick, J., Ruffing, T., Seurin, Y.: MuSig2: simple two-round schnorr multi-signatures. In: Malkin, T., Peikert, C. (eds.) CRYPTO 2021. LNCS, vol. 12825, pp. 189–221. Springer, Cham (2021). https://doi.org/10.1007/978-3-030-84242-0_8
44. Nick, J., Ruffing, T., Seurin, Y., Wuille, P.: MuSig-DN: Schnorr multi-signatures with verifiably deterministic nonces. In: Ligatti, J., Ou, X., Katz, J., Vigna, G. (eds.) ACM CCS 2020, pp. 1717–1731. ACM Press (Nov 2020). https://doi.org/10.1145/3372297.3417236
45. Okamoto, T.: A digital multisignature scheme using bijective public-key cryptosystems. ACM Trans. Comput. Syst. (TOCS) **6**(4), 432–441 (1988)
46. Okamoto, T.: Provably secure and practical identification schemes and corresponding signature schemes. In: Brickell, E.F. (ed.) CRYPTO 1992. LNCS, vol. 740, pp. 31–53. Springer, Heidelberg (1993). https://doi.org/10.1007/3-540-48071-4_3
47. Pan, J., Wagner, B.: Chopsticks: Fork-free two-round multi-signatures from non-interactive assumptions. In: EUROCRYPT 2023 (2023)

48. Park, S., Park, S., Kim, K., Won, D.: Two efficient RSA multisignature schemes. In: Han, Y., Okamoto, T., Qing, S. (eds.) ICICS 1997. LNCS, vol. 1334, pp. 217–222. Springer, Heidelberg (1997). https://doi.org/10.1007/BFb0028477

49. Pedersen, T.P.: Non-interactive and information-theoretic secure verifiable secret sharing. In: Feigenbaum, J. (ed.) CRYPTO 1991. LNCS, vol. 576, pp. 129–140. Springer, Heidelberg (1992). https://doi.org/10.1007/3-540-46766-1_9

50. Pon, S.F., Lu, E.H., Lee, J.Y.: Dynamic reblocking rsa-based multisignatures scheme for computer and communication networks. IEEE Commun. Lett. 6(1), 43–44 (2002)

51. Rabin, T.: A simplified approach to threshold and proactive RSA. In: Krawczyk, H. (ed.) CRYPTO 1998. LNCS, vol. 1462, pp. 89–104. Springer, Heidelberg (1998). https://doi.org/10.1007/BFb0055722

52. Schnorr, C.P.: Efficient identification and signatures for smart cards. In: Brassard, G. (ed.) CRYPTO 1989. LNCS, vol. 435, pp. 239–252. Springer, New York (1990). https://doi.org/10.1007/0-387-34805-0_22

53. Shamir, A.: How to share a secret. Commun. Assoc. Comput. Mach. 22(11), 612–613 (1979)

54. Shoup, V.: Practical threshold signatures. In: Preneel, B. (ed.) EUROCRYPT 2000. LNCS, vol. 1807, pp. 207–220. Springer, Heidelberg (2000). https://doi.org/10.1007/3-540-45539-6_15

55. Stinson, D.R., Strobl, R.: Provably secure distributed Schnorr signatures and a (t, n) threshold scheme for implicit certificates. In: Varadharajan, V., Mu, Y. (eds.) ACISP 2001. LNCS, vol. 2119, pp. 417–434. Springer, Heidelberg (2001). https://doi.org/10.1007/3-540-47719-5_33

New Algorithms for the Deuring Correspondence
Towards Practical and Secure SQISign Signatures

Luca De Feo[1]([⊠])(iD), Antonin Leroux[2,3,4,5], Patrick Longa[6],
and Benjamin Wesolowski[7,8,9](iD)

[1] IBM Research Europe, Zürich, Switzerland
eurocrypt23@defeo.lu
[2] DGA-MI, Bruz, France
antonin.leroux@polytechnique.org
[3] IRMAR, Université de Rennes, Rennes, France
[4] LIX, CNRS, Ecole Polytechnique, Institut Polytechnique de Paris,
Palaiseau, France
[5] INRIA, Saclay, France
[6] Microsoft Research, Redmond, USA
plonga@microsoft.com
[7] Univ. Bordeaux, CNRS, Bordeaux INP, IMB, UMR 5251, 33400 Talence, France
benjamin.wesolowski@math.u-bordeaux.fr
[8] INRIA, IMB, UMR 5251, 33400 Talence, France
[9] ENS de Lyon, CNRS, UMPA, UMR 5669, Lyon, France

Abstract. The Deuring correspondence defines a bijection between isogenies of supersingular elliptic curves and ideals of maximal orders in a quaternion algebra. We present a new algorithm to translate ideals of prime-power norm to their corresponding isogenies — a central task of the effective Deuring correspondence. The new method improves upon the algorithm introduced in 2021 by De Feo, Kohel, Leroux, Petit and Wesolowski as a building-block of the SQISign signature scheme. SQISign is the most compact post-quantum signature scheme currently known, but is several orders of magnitude slower than competitors, the main bottleneck of the computation being the ideal-to-isogeny translation. We implement the new algorithm and apply it to SQISign, achieving a more than two-fold speedup in key generation and signing with a new choice of parameter. Moreover, after adapting the state-of-the-art $\mathbb{F}_{p^2}$ multiplication algorithms by Longa to implement SQISign's underlying extension field arithmetic and adding various improvements, we push the total speedups to over three times for signing and four times for verification.

In a second part of the article, we advance cryptanalysis by showing a very simple distinguisher against one of the assumptions used in SQISign. We present a way to impede the distinguisher through a few changes to the generic KLPT algorithm. We formulate a new assumption capturing these changes, and provide an analysis together with experimental evidence for its validity.

This research was funded in part by the Agence Nationale de la Recherche under grant ANR-20-CE40-0013 MELODIA, and the France 2030 program under grant ANR-22-PETQ-0008 PQ-TLS

© International Association for Cryptologic Research 2023
C. Hazay and M. Stam (Eds.): EUROCRYPT 2023, LNCS 14008, pp. 659–690, 2023.
https://doi.org/10.1007/978-3-031-30589-4_23

Keywords: Post-quantum cryptography · Isogenies · Group actions

1   Introduction

Isogeny-based cryptography is one of the active areas of post-quantum cryptography. Protocols constructed from isogenies between supersingular curves are generally very compact (in particular with respect to key sizes) but less efficient than other families of schemes. A good illustration of this situation is the recent signature scheme SQISign of De Feo, Kohel, Leroux, Petit and Wesolowski [8,9]. It is, by a decent margin, the most compact post-quantum signature scheme, but signing takes a couple of seconds, which is several orders of magnitude slower than other solutions. In a way reminiscent of Galbraith, Petit and Silva [14], SQISign makes a constructive use of the Deuring correspondence, a mathematical equivalence between supersingular elliptic curves (and isogenies connecting them) and maximal orders in a quaternion algebra (and ideals connecting them). This correspondence was first introduced to isogeny-based cryptography for cryptanalytic ends [10,12,16,26], but it has since revealed its potential as a constructive tool: for signatures [8,14], for encryption schemes [7], and for key exchange [17]. These applications exploit the following idea: certain problems involving elliptic curves and isogenies are hard to solve, but their quaternion counterparts are easy. A trapdoor can be used to translate between both worlds, letting the secret holder solve problems that would otherwise be hard. Note that SQISign's security is not affected by the recent attacks against SIDH [3,20,21].

Better algorithms for the Deuring correspondence therefore have both constructive and destructive applications. The main technical contribution of [8] is a pair of algorithms to solve two of the major tasks of the computational Deuring correspondence: *translating ideals to isogenies*, and finding *quaternion ℓ-isogeny paths*. The efficiency of SQISign is mostly governed by the ideal-to-isogeny translation, while its security strongly depends on properties of the quaternion-path-finding algorithm. In this work, we improve both.

Translating Ideals to Isogenies. Polynomial time algorithms to translate ideals to isogenies have been known since at least 2016 [12,14], however these were hardly practical, and certainly too slow for cryptographic purposes. One of the main contributions in SQISign [8] is the design and implementation of a new practical algorithm for this task. Despite this considerable improvement, the ideal-to-isogeny translation remains the main bottleneck in SQISign.

Our first contribution is a new algorithm to translate ideals to isogenies when the norm of the ideal is a power of a small prime ℓ (IdealToIsogenyEichler, Algorithm 5). The new algorithm proves to be more efficient than the one in [8], as we demonstrate by applying it to SQISign.

One important building block here is an algorithm to solve norm equations inside any maximal order (SpecialEichlerNorm, Algorithm 3), which may be of independent interest.

Security of SQISign. In [8], SQISign was proven existentially unforgeable under several computational assumptions, among which there is an *ad hoc* assumption on the distribution of the outputs of the quaternion-path-finding algorithm. We show that this assumption does not hold, by presenting a simple and efficient distinguisher. Although we are unable to derive a complete attack, this shows that the security of SQISign relies on an easy problem.

We explain how to modify the path-finding algorithm so that our distinguisher does not work anymore. We formulate a computational assumption for the modified algorithm, and analyze it via the study of ideals and isogenies derived from solutions of norm equations over maximal orders.

Plan. This article is organized as follows. After a brief technical overview, we introduce in Sect. 2 the fundamental mathematical notions and notations. In Sect. 3 we focus on solving norm equations inside unforgettable orders and introduce our new algorithm SpecialEichlerNorm. In Sect. 4, we present in full detail our new ideal-to-isogeny algorithm. The application of our method to SQISign and the associated C implementation are discussed in Sect. 5. This section also reports our results after adapting the efficient multiplication algorithms over $\mathbb{F}_{p^2}$ proposed by Longa [18] to our proposed parameters for SQISign. Finally, in Sect. 6, we study the security of SQISign.

1.1 Technical Overview

We now give a succinct outline of our technical contributions.

Translating Ideals to Isogenies. The main bottleneck in SQISign is the following task: given a maximal order $\mathcal{O}$ corresponding to the endomorphism ring of some curve E defined over a finite field $\mathbb{F}_{p^2}$, given an ideal I of norm a prime power ℓ^e corresponding to an isogeny $\varphi_I : E \to E'$ of the same degree ℓ^e, compute an ℓ-*isogeny walk* for φ_I (i.e., a sequence of isogenies of degree ℓ whose composition is φ_I).

Following [12,14], this is achieved by decomposing the isogeny $\varphi_I = \varphi_m \circ \cdots \circ \varphi_1$ into isogenies $\varphi_i : E_i \to E_{i+1}$ of smaller degree ℓ^f, where f is a system parameter depending on p. Such decomposition requires computing the endomorphism rings $\mathcal{O}_i$ of each intermediate curve E_i, a task for which SQISign (see [9, Algorithm 9]) employs a variant of the KLPT algorithm [16]. Our main technical contribution consists in replacing the full endomorphism ring $\mathcal{O}_i$ by a single well-chosen endomorphism ω_i, computed by SpecialEichlerNorm (Algorithm 3), a new algorithm to solve norm equations inside any maximal order.

SpecialEichlerNorm is not, *per se*, faster than KLPT: the true performance gain happens further down the line. Indeed, KLPT produces a representation of $\mathcal{O}_i$ by using an isogeny of degree T coprime to ℓ, where $T \approx p^{3/2}$ is another fixed system parameter. In contrast, the degree of the endomorphism ω_i output by SpecialEichlerNorm is only $T \approx p^{5/4}$. These endomorphisms then need to be evaluated on the torsion subgroup $E_i[\ell^f]$, something that can only be done efficiently when T is a smooth integer and $E_i[T]$ is defined over a small degree extension of $\mathbb{F}_{p^2}$.

All these facts combined create a strong constraint $\ell^f T | (p^{2d} - 1)$ for some small integer d, and in fact SQISign even forces $d = 1$, for maximum efficiency. Primes p such that $p^2 - 1$ has such a large smooth factor are extremely difficult to find, and thus the overall efficiency of SQISign comes from a balancing act between f, the smoothness of T, and the computational resources available to search for p. In this light, it is clear that moving from $T \approx p^{3/2}$ to $T \approx p^{5/4}$ constitutes a big improvement as one may hope to find better "SQISign-friendly" primes, as we do here. In fact, even using the same prime p as in [8], our new algorithm leads to a (smaller) improvement because we can ignore some factors of T and use a smaller endomorphism degree $T' | T$.

Security of SQISign. The SQISign signature scheme is obtained by applying the Fiat–Shamir transform [13] to an interactive identification scheme. While it is straightforward to prove that the identification scheme is a 2-special sound proof of knowledge of an endomorphism (a statement closely related to the knowledge of the endomorphism ring [1,25]), proving zero-knowledge turns out to be much more difficult.

Indeed, De Feo *et al.* could not construct a statistically indistinguishable simulator, and had to resort instead to a computational assumption [9, Problem 2] stating that the ideals in output of the quaternion-path-finding algorithm SigningKLPT [9, Algorithm 5] are indistinguishable from uniformly random ideals of the same norm. They provided evidence for the assumption by showing that the output of SigningKLPT is uniformly distributed in an exponentially large set whose size does not depend on the secret.

We show that their assumption does not hold by proving that the first step of the 2-isogeny walk constituting the response isogeny is not distributed uniformly among the possible first steps. Indeed, we show that the ideal I output by Signing-KLPT is contained in an ideal of norm 2 that is not uniformly distributed. This condition can be easily checked, immediately implying that SQISign signatures can be distinguished with non-negligible advantage from random 2-isogeny walks of fixed length.

This bias is due to the fact that RepresentInteger a sub-algorithm of Signing-KLPT, solves norm equations inside a suborder of a *special maximal order* $\mathcal{O}_0$ (see definition in Sect. 2.1). We present in Sect. 3.1 a variant of RepresentInteger fixing the bias, then we provide both heuristic and empirical evidence that the newly defined distribution cannot be distinguished by considering the first k-steps of the response for some small k.

2   Preliminaries

Throughout this work, p is a prime number and $\mathbb{F}_{p^2}$ is a finite field of size p^2.

A negligible function $f : \mathbb{Z}_{>0} \to \mathbb{R}_{>0}$ is a function whose growth is bounded by $O(x^{-n})$ for all $n > 0$. In the analysis of a probabilistic algorithm, we say that an event happens with *overwhelming probability* if its probability of failure is a negligible function of the length of the input.

We say that a distinguishing problem is hard when any probabilistic polynomial-time distinguisher has a negligible advantage with respect to the length of the instance. Two distributions are computationally indistinguishable if their associated distinguishing problem is hard.

2.1   Mathematical Background on the Deuring Correspondence

We now briefly present mathematical notions used in this article.

Elliptic Curves, Isogenies and Endomorphisms. Elliptic curves are abelian varieties of dimension 1, and isogenies are non-constant morphisms between them. The degree of an isogeny is its degree as a rational map. An isogeny is *separable* if its degree is equal to the size of its kernel. Let E be an elliptic curve. To any finite subgroup G of E, one can associate a separable isogeny $\varphi : E \to E/G$ with kernel $\ker \varphi = G$, and this isogeny is unique up to an isomorphism of the target. Isogenies can be computed from their kernels with Vélu's formula [23]. An isogeny from a curve E to itself is an endomorphism of E; together with the constant zero-map they form a ring, denoted by $\mathrm{End}(E)$. In positive characteristic, $\mathrm{End}(E)$ is isomorphic either to an order in a quadratic imaginary field or a maximal order in a quaternion algebra. In the first case, the curve is said to be *ordinary* and otherwise it is *supersingular*. We focus on the supersingular case in this article. Silverman's book [22] is a good reference for more details on elliptic curves and isogenies.

Supersingular elliptic curves over $\overline{\mathbb{F}}_p$ always have a model defined over $\mathbb{F}_{p^2}$. Furthermore, this model can always be chosen so that all its endomorphisms are also defined over $\mathbb{F}_{p^2}$. This property is preserved by the $\mathbb{F}_{p^2}$-isogeny class, and in this article, we work in one such class.

Quaternion Algebras, Orders and Ideals. The endomorphism rings of supersingular elliptic curves over $\mathbb{F}_{p^2}$ are isomorphic to maximal orders of $B_{p,\infty}$, the quaternion algebra ramified at p and ∞. We fix a basis $1, i, j, k$ of $B_{p,\infty}$, satisfying $i^2 = -q$, $j^2 = -p$ and $k = ij = -ji$ for some positive integer q. The canonical involution of conjugation sends an element $\alpha = a + ib + jc + kd$ to $\overline{\alpha} = a - (ib + jc + kd)$. A *fractional ideal* I is a $\mathbb{Z}$-lattice of rank four inside $B_{p,\infty}$. We denote by $n(I)$ the *norm* of I as the largest rational number such that $n(\alpha) \in n(I)\mathbb{Z}$ for any $\alpha \in I$. Given fractional ideals I and J, if $J \subseteq I$ then the index $[I : J]$ is defined to be the order of the finite quotient group I/J. We define the ideal conjugate $\overline{I} = \{\overline{\alpha}, \alpha \in I\}$. An order $\mathcal{O}$ is a subring of $B_{p,\infty}$ that is also a fractional ideal. An order is called *maximal* when it is not contained in any other larger order. The left order of a fractional ideal is defined as $\mathcal{O}_L(I) = \{\alpha \in B_{p,\infty} \mid \alpha I \subset I\}$ and similarly for the right order $\mathcal{O}_R(I)$. Then I is said to be an $(\mathcal{O}_L(I), \mathcal{O}_R(I))$-ideal or a left $\mathcal{O}_L(I)$-ideal. A fractional ideal is *integral* if it is contained in its left order, or equivalently in its right order; we refer to integral ideals hereafter as ideals. An ideal can be written as $I = \mathcal{O}_L(I)\alpha + \mathcal{O}_L(I)n(I) = \mathcal{O}_L(I)\langle\alpha, n(I)\rangle$ for some $\alpha \in \mathcal{O}_L(I)$. Two left $\mathcal{O}$-ideals I and J are equivalent if there exists $\beta \in B_{p,\infty}^\times$, such that $I = J\beta$. For a given $\mathcal{O}$, this defines equivalences classes of left $\mathcal{O}$-ideals, and we denote the set of such classes by $\mathrm{Cl}(\mathcal{O})$. We will reuse the following notation from [8]: for any ideal K and any $\alpha \in B_{p,\infty}^{\times}$, we write $\chi_K(\alpha) = K\bar{\alpha}/n(K)$. Ideals equivalent to K are precisely the ideals $\chi_K(\alpha)$ with $\alpha \in K \setminus \{0\}$. An Eichler order is the intersection of two maximal orders.

The Deuring Correspondence. In [11], Deuring made the link between elliptic curves and quaternion algebras over $\mathbb{Q}$ by showing that the endomorphism ring of a supersingular elliptic curve E defined over $\mathbb{F}_{p^2}$ is isomorphic to a maximal order in $B_{p,\infty}$. Fix a supersingular elliptic curve E_0, and an order $\mathcal{O}_0 \simeq \mathrm{End}(E_0)$. The curve/order correspondence allows one to associate each outgoing isogeny $\varphi : E_0 \to E_1$ to an integral left $\mathcal{O}_0$-ideal, and every such ideal arises in this way (see [15] for instance). Through this correspondence, the ring $\mathrm{End}(E_1)$ is isomorphic to the right order of this ideal. This isogeny/ideal correspondence is defined in [24], and in the separable case, it is explicitly given as follows.

Definition 1. *Given I an integral left $\mathcal{O}_0$-ideal coprime to p, we define the I-torsion $E_0[I] = \{P \in E_0(\overline{\mathbb{F}}_{p^2}) : \alpha(P) = 0 \text{ for all } \alpha \in I\}$. To I, we associate the separable isogeny φ_I of kernel $E_0[I]$. Conversely given an isogeny φ, the corresponding ideal is defined as $I_\varphi = \{\alpha \in \mathcal{O}_0 : \alpha(P) = 0 \text{ for all } P \in \ker(\varphi)\}$.*

We summarize properties of the Deuring correspondence in Table 1, borrowed from [8].

Table 1. The Deuring correspondence, a summary [8].

Supersingular j-invariants over $\mathbb{F}_{p^2}$ $j(E)$ (up to Galois conjugacy)	Maximal orders in $B_{p,\infty}$ $\mathcal{O} \cong \mathrm{End}(E)$ (up to isomorpshim)
(E_1, φ) with $\varphi : E \to E_1$	I_φ integral left $\mathcal{O}$-ideal and right $\mathcal{O}_1$-ideal
$\theta \in \mathrm{End}(E_0)$	Principal ideal $\mathcal{O}\theta$
$\deg(\varphi)$	$n(I_\varphi)$
$\hat{\varphi}$	$\overline{I_\varphi}$
$\varphi : E \to E_1, \psi : E \to E_1$	Equivalent ideals $I_\varphi \sim I_\psi$
Supersingular j-invariants over $\mathbb{F}_{p^2}$	$\mathrm{Cl}(\mathcal{O})$
$\tau \circ \rho : E \to E_1 \to E_2$	$I_{\tau \circ \rho} = I_\rho \cdot I_\tau$
N-isogenies (up to isomorphism)	$\mathrm{Cl}(\mathfrak{O})$, with Eichler order $\mathfrak{O}$ of level N

Special Extremal Order. A *special extremal order* is an order $\mathcal{O}_0$ in $B_{p,\infty}$ which contains a suborder of the form $R + jR$, where $R = \mathbb{Z}[\omega] \subset \mathbb{Q}(i)$ is a quadratic order and ω has minimal discriminant. When $p \equiv 3 \bmod 4$, we have the special extremal order $\mathcal{O}_0 = \langle 1, i, \frac{i+j}{2}, \frac{1+k}{2} \rangle$, with $i^2 = -1$, $j^2 = -p$ and $k = ij$. It is isomorphic to the endomorphism ring $\mathrm{End}(E_0)$ of the elliptic curve of j-invariant 1728. For the rest of the paper, we fix this special extremal order $\mathcal{O}_0$, with subring $\mathbb{Z}[\omega]$, and the corresponding elliptic curve E_0.

2.2 The SQISign Protocol

We now present SQISign [8], the main target for applying the present work. The signature scheme is based on an interactive identification protocol, made non-interactive through the classic Fiat–Shamir transform. The initial setup and key generation are as follows.

setup : $\lambda \mapsto$ param] Pick a prime number p and a supersingular elliptic curve E_0 defined over $\mathbb{F}_{p^2}$, with known special extremal endomorphism ring $\mathcal{O}_0$. Select an odd smooth number D_c of λ bits and $D = 2^e$ where e is larger than the diameter of the supersingular 2-isogeny graph.

keygen : param $\mapsto$ (pk $= E_A$, sk $= \tau$)] Pick a random isogeny walk $\tau : E_0 \to E_A$, leading to a random elliptic curve E_A. The public key is E_A, and the secret key is the isogeny τ.

The goal of the prover is to prove knowledge of the secret τ (or equivalently End(E_A)). Intuitively, the prover will reach that goal by finding a path between two vertices of the isogeny graph, a task notoriously hard without the knowledge of the endomorphism ring. Concretely, the prover engages in the following Σ-protocol with the verifier.

Commitment. The prover generates a random (secret) isogeny walk $\psi : E_0 \to E_1$, and sends E_1 to the verifier.

Challenge. The verifier sends the description of a cyclic isogeny $\varphi : E_1 \to E_2$ of degree D_c to the prover.

Response. From the isogeny $\varphi \circ \psi \circ \hat{\tau} : E_A \to E_2$, the prover constructs a new isogeny $\sigma : E_A \to E_2$ of degree D such that $\hat{\varphi} \circ \sigma$ is cyclic, and sends σ to the verifier.

Verification. The verifier accepts if σ is an isogeny of degree D from E_A to E_2 and $\hat{\varphi} \circ \sigma$ is cyclic. They reject otherwise.

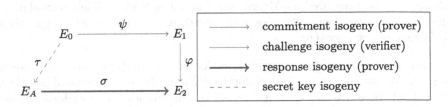

Fig. 1. A picture of the identification protocol

The main algorithmic challenge in this Σ-protocol is the response computation and this is the task that we try to improve throughout this work. It is made of two parts: a computation over the quaternions called SigningKLPT that gives an ideal, and a translation of this ideal into the corresponding response isogeny σ. In [8], this translation is achieved with IdealToIsogeny [9, Algorithm 9] and we present our new variant IdealToIsogenyEichler as Algorithm 5.

2.3 Algorithms from Previous Works

We will rely upon or mention several algorithms existing in the literature. In the interest of conciseness, we will use the algorithms below without describing them. The interested reader will find pseudo-code for most of them in [8,9], the others are standard:

- Cornacchia(M): either find x, y such that $x^2 + y^2 = M$ or output $\perp$.
- RepresentInteger(M), given $M \in \mathbb{N}$ with $M > p$, finds $\gamma \in \mathcal{O}_0$ of norm dividing M.
- EquivalentPrimeIdeal(I), given a left $\mathcal{O}_0$-ideal I, finds the smallest equivalent left $\mathcal{O}_0$-ideal of prime norm.
- EquivalentRandomEichlerIdeal(I, N), given a left $\mathcal{O}_0$-ideal I and an integer N, finds a random equivalent left $\mathcal{O}_0$-ideal of norm coprime to N.
- IdealModConstraint(I, γ), given a left $\mathcal{O}_0$-ideal I of norm N, and $\gamma \in \mathcal{O}_0$ of norm Nn, finds $(C_0 : D_0) \in \mathbb{P}^1(\mathbb{Z}/N\mathbb{Z})$ such that $\gamma j(C_0 + \omega D_0) \in I$.
- EichlerModConstraint(I, γ, δ), given a left $\mathcal{O}_0$-ideal I of norm N, and $\gamma, \delta \in \mathcal{O}_0$ of norms coprime with N, finds $(C_0 : D_0) \in \mathbb{P}^1(\mathbb{Z}/N\mathbb{Z})$ such that $\gamma j(C_0 + \omega D_0)\delta \in \mathbb{Z} + I$.
- StrongApproximation(N, C_0, D_0), given a prime N and $C_0, D_0 \in \mathbb{Z}$, and a subset $\mathcal{N} \subset \mathbb{N}$, finds $\mu = \lambda\mu_0 + N\mu_1 \in \mathcal{O}_0$ of norm in $\mathcal{N}$ (striving for the smallest possible), with $\mu_0 = j(C_0 + \omega D_0)$ and $\mu_1 \in \mathcal{O}_0$. When $\mathcal{N} = \{d \in \mathbb{N}, d | D\}$ for some $D \in \mathbb{N}$, we simply write StrongApproximation. We will also use the notation $\ell^\bullet = \{\ell^e, e \in \mathbb{N}\}$.

Remark 2. Variants of RepresentInteger and StrongApproximation (denoted as FullXxx) will be presented as Algorithms 1 and 2 in Sect. 3. Their formulations differ only slightly from the ones introduced in [8], but we will argue these modifications are necessary.

Remark 3. The algorithm EquivalentPrimeIdeal above finds the smallest possible solution. We sometimes use its randomized version (written RandomEquivalent-PrimeIdeal) where we choose a random output among a set of solutions of small norm.

3 Solving Norm Equations Inside Maximal Orders

In this section, we consider the following problem: given a maximal order $\mathcal{O}$ of $B_{p,\infty}$, and a set of integers $\mathcal{N}$, find an element $\beta \in \mathcal{O}$ with $n(\beta) \in \mathcal{N}$. The relevant case for our application is the following: we fix an integer T, and $\mathcal{N}$ is the set of divisors of T^2. Algorithms to solve this task are presented in [9, Section 5.1], but they find solutions that are not well distributed in $\mathcal{O}$: they always fall in a particular sublattice, inducing a bias that affects both the efficiency and security of its applications. We explain how to eliminate this bias.

For ease of exposition, we fix $p \equiv 3 \mod 4$, and the special extremal order $\mathcal{O}_0 = \langle 1, i, \frac{i+j}{2}, \frac{1+k}{2} \rangle$ (see page 6), where we set $\omega = i$. Most of what follows remains true for other primes and special extremal orders under small adjustments.

The method underlying Algorithm 3 follows the blueprint introduced in [9, Section 5.1]: find an Eichler order of small prime level embedded inside both $\mathcal{O}$ and the special extremal order $\mathcal{O}_0$ (considered as an implicit parameter of the algorithm below) and solve the norm equation inside this Eichler order. As a first step, we study in Sect. 3.1 the problem of solving norm equations in the full maximal order $\mathcal{O}_0$ (rather than the convenient suborder $\mathbb{Z}[i,j]$ as in [8,16]). This study, and the resulting new algorithms, will prove useful for Algorithm 3 (as pointed out in Remark 7) and also prevents a simple distinguisher against a problem relating to the zero-knowledge property of SQISign; the latter point is further investigated in Sect. 6.

3.1 Special Extremal Order Case: Exploiting the Full Order

We first deal with norm equations in the special extremal order $\mathcal{O}_0$. In this case, algorithms from [8,16] only find solutions in the suborder $\mathbb{Z}[i,j]$, exploiting the orthogonal basis $\langle 1, i, j, k \rangle$. This suborder has index 4 inside $\mathcal{O}_0$, so many potential solutions are excluded, a source of complications for some applications. In this section, we describe how to heuristically obtain well-distributed solutions in $\mathcal{O}_0$.

The norm form of $\langle 1, i, j, k \rangle$ is $f : (x, y, z, t) \mapsto x^2 + y^2 + p(z^2 + t^2)$ and the usual way to find a representation of a given integer M (a method common to both RepresentInteger and StrongApproximation) is to choose z, t (possibly with some additional conditions) until $M - p(z^2 + t^2)$ is a prime represented by $x^2 + y^2$, then use Cornacchia's algorithm [4] to solve $x^2 + y^2 = M - p(z^2 + t^2)$. Solutions in the full order $\mathcal{O}_0$ can be found from solutions in $\mathbb{Z}[i,j]$ thanks to Lemma 4. Let $g : (x, y, z, t) \mapsto (x + t/2)^2 + (y + z/2)^2 + p((z/2)^2 + (t/2)^2)$ be the norm form of $\mathcal{O}_0 = \langle 1, i, \frac{i+j}{2}, \frac{1+k}{2} \rangle$.

Lemma 4. *An integer M is represented by g if and only if $4M$ is represented by f with $x = t \mod 2$ and $y = z \mod 2$.*

Proof. If we have $M = (x + t/2)^2 + (y + z/2)^2 + p((z/2)^2 + (t/2)^2)$, we have that $4M = (2x + t)^2 + (2y + z)^2 + p(z^2 + t^2)$. Thus, an integer M is represented by g (with solution (x, y, z, t)) if and only if $4M$ is represented by f with a solution $(x', y', z', t') = (2x + t, 2y + z, z, t)$ satisfying $x' = t' \mod 2$ and $y' = z' \mod 2$. □

From Lemma 4 and the algorithm RepresentInteger from [16], we derive FullRepresentInteger in Algorithm 1. It has exactly the same specifications as RepresentInteger (and the same goes for StrongApproximation and FullStrong-Approximation). Just as RepresentInteger is heuristically believed to return well-distributed solutions in $\mathbb{Z}[i,j]$, the variant FullRepresentInteger is believed to

---

Algorithm 1. FullRepresentInteger(M)

Input: $M \in \mathbb{Z}$ such that $M > p$
Output: $\gamma = x + yi + z\frac{i+j}{2} + t\frac{1+k}{2}$ with $n(\gamma) = M$.

1: Set $m' = \lfloor \sqrt{\frac{4M}{p}} \rfloor$ and sample a random integer $z' \in [-m', m']$.
2: Set $m'' = \lfloor \sqrt{\frac{4M}{p} - z'^2} \rfloor$ and take a random t' inside $[-m'', m'']$. Set $M' = 4M - p((z')^2 + (t')^2)$.
3: If Cornacchia(M') = $\perp$ go back to Step 1. Otherwise set $x', y' = $ Cornacchia(M').
4: If $x' \neq t' \mod 2$ or $z' \neq y' \mod 2$ then go back to Step 1.
5: Set $\gamma = (x' + iy' + jz' + kt')/2$.
6: **return** γ.

---

return well-distributed solutions in $\mathcal{O}_0$. This distribution depends on the factorization pattern of the inputs to the Cornacchia subroutine. This question is further investigated in Sect. 6, with heuristic and experimental evidence.

The running time of FullRepresentInteger is the same as the running time of RepresentInteger, divided by the success probability of the condition in Step 4. Heuristically, this constant is $2/3$: the solutions $(x', y', z', t') \mod 2$ of the equation $x'^2 + y'^2 + p(z'^2 + t'^2) = 0 \mod 4$ are $(0,0,0,0)$, $(1,1,1,1)$, $(1,0,0,1)$, $(0,1,1,0)$, $(1,0,1,0)$, and $(0,1,0,1)$. Among these 6, there are 2 that do not lead to $\gamma/2 \in \mathcal{O}_0$: the solutions $(1,0,1,0)$ and $(0,1,0,1)$.

Remark 5. One might wonder why we do not propose to swap x' and y' when the constraint modulo 2 is not satisfied. Undeniably, this would be a good way to ensure that each set of values x', y', z', t' leads to a solution. However, this introduces a distinguishable bias, precisely of the kind investigated in Sect. 6.

The StrongApproximation algorithm can also be modified to find solutions in the full order $\mathcal{O}_0$ with Lemma 4. In Algorithm 2, we present FullStrongApproximation as a generic reduction to StrongApproximation. Thanks to Lemma 4, properties of the distribution of the output of FullStrongApproximation directly follow from properties of the distribution of StrongApproximation. As in the case of FullRepresentInteger, we expect the running time of FullStrongApproximation to be equal to the running time of StrongApproximation multiplied by $3/2$.

Algorithm 2. FullStrongApproximation

Input: A prime number N, two values $C, D \in \mathbb{Z}$.
Output: $\mu \in \mathcal{O}_0$ such that $2\mu = \lambda\mu_0 + N\mu_1$ with $\mu_0 = j(C + \omega D)$, $\mu_1 \in \mathcal{O}_0$, and $n(\mu) \in \mathcal{N}$.

1: Let $4\mathcal{N} = \{4n \mid n \in \mathcal{N}\}$.
2: Set $\mu' = $ StrongApproximation(N, C, D).
3: If $\mu' \notin 2\mathcal{O}_0$, go back to Step 2.
4: **return** $\mu = \mu'/2$.

3.2   Norm Equations in Generic Maximal Orders: The Algorithm

We are now ready to describe an algorithm to solve equations inside generic maximal orders. For simplicity, we restrict the description to the case that will be useful for our new variant of *ideal to isogeny translation* (see Sect. 4). Thus, we require that the algorithm outputs elements of norm dividing T^2 for some parameter T and that the solution β satisfies the following constraint: given the additional input K, a left $\mathcal{O}$-ideal of norm ℓ coprime to T, we need that $\beta \notin \mathbb{Z} + K$ (see Step 5 in Algorithm 3). A justification for this constraint is provided in Sect. 4.1.

Algorithm 3. SpecialEichlerNorm$(\mathcal{O}, K)$

Input: $\mathcal{O}$ a maximal order and K a left $\mathcal{O}$-ideal of norm ℓ.
Output: $\beta \in \mathcal{O} \smallsetminus (\mathbb{Z} + K)$ of norm dividing T^2.
  1: Compute $I = I(\mathcal{O}_0, \mathcal{O})$, the ideal connecting $\mathcal{O}_0$ to $\mathcal{O}$.
  2: Set $L = $ RandomEquivalentPrimeIdeal(I), $N = n(L)$ and compute α s.t $L = I\alpha$.
  3: Compute $K' = \alpha^{-1}K\alpha$
  4: Compute $(C : D) = $ EichlerModConstraint$(L, 1, 1)$.
  5: Enumerate all possible solutions of $\mu = $ FullStrongApproximation(N, C, D) until $\mu \notin \mathbb{Z} + K'$. If it fails go back to Step 2.
  6: **return** $\beta = \alpha\mu\alpha^{-1}$.

Proposition 6. *Under plausible heuristics, the algorithm* SpecialEichlerNorm *is correct and terminates with constant probability when $T > p^{5/4}$.*

Proof. Under the heuristics from [16], we know that the value $N = n(L)$ has size approximately $p^{1/2}$ when L is the output of RandomEquivalentPrimeIdeal. Then, it was proven in [8] that EichlerModConstraint is correct and terminates. We argued correctness and termination with constant probability for FullStrong-Approximation in Sect. 3.1. Now, we introduce the following heuristic assumption: the output μ of FullStrongApproximation satisfies $\mu \notin \mathbb{Z} + K'$ with probability approximately $[\mathcal{O}_0 : \mathbb{Z} + K']^{-1}$ (which is the probability one would get if $\mu \in \mathcal{O}_0$ were drawn uniformly in a large enough ball). Even though the precise distribution of μ appears difficult to analyse, this heuristic is plausible since the algorithm FullStrongApproximation seems to constrain possible values of μ only locally at N and T, both coprime with ℓ. The proof is concluded by the fact that FullStrongApproximation$(N, \cdot)$ finds at least one solution with constant probability when $T^2 > pN^3 \approx p^{5/2}$ (see [9, Section 5.3]). Thus, we have proven heuristic termination. For correctness, it is easy to see that $n(\mu) = n(\beta)$ and so the correctness of FullStrongApproximation proves that $n(\beta)|T^2$. Since $\mu \in \mathbb{Z} + L = \mathcal{O}_0 \cap \mathcal{O}_R(L)$ where $L = I\alpha$, and since $\mathcal{O} = \alpha\mathcal{O}_R(L)\alpha^{-1}$, we have that $\beta \in \mathcal{O}$. Since $\mu \notin \mathbb{Z} + K'$, then $\alpha\mu\alpha^{-1} \notin \mathbb{Z} + \alpha K'\alpha^{-1} = \mathbb{Z} + K$. $\qquad\blacksquare$

Remark 7. Note that the new heuristic introduced in the proof of Proposition 6 would not have held if we had used the StrongApproximation from [16]. Indeed, the solutions of StrongApproximation lie in $\mathbb{Z}\langle 1, i, j, k\rangle$ which is contained in the Eichler order $(\mathbb{Z}+\mathcal{O}_0\langle 1+i, 2\rangle)$. Thus, when $K \cap L = \mathcal{O}_0\langle 1+i, 2\rangle \cap L$, the condition $\mu \notin \mathbb{Z} + K$ can never be satisfied. This is why it is important to use our new variant FullStrongApproximation.

Failures. Algorithm 3 may fail when the heuristics used in the proof of Proposition 6 are not accurate. In particular, the problematic case is when the size of the output of RandomEquivalentPrimeIdeal(I) is bigger than expected. This situation occurs when there exists a representative in the ideal class of I with norm considerably smaller than $p^{1/2}$ (see the bounds on the norm of elements in a Minkowski-reduced basis of a lattice from [16, §3.1]). There are only a negligible number of problematic maximal orders but we still need to handle those few bad cases. The simplest solution to avoid that problem altogether is to increase the size of T. We have the absolute bound $N < p$ and so we can ensure termination by taking $T > p^2$. However, we want the bound of T to be as tight as possible and so this is not a suitable solution for us. There is a way to handle the bad cases without increasing T but it does not always work. Let us assume for the rest of this paragraph that there exists $J \sim I$ with $n(J) \ll p^{1/2}$. FullStrongApproximation($M, \cdot$) does not strictly require its input M to be prime (see [9, §6.3]) and so FullStrongApproximation can be modified to work with $n(J)$ in input instead of N. We can also run EichlerModConstraint with J instead of L if we accept possible failures due to non-invertible elements mod $n(J)$. Since $n(J) \ll p^{1/2}$ it should be possible to complete the computation when $T \approx p^{5/4}$. However, we may be in trouble with the additional condition $\mu \notin \mathbb{Z} + K$. Indeed, if $J \subset K$, this constraint will never be satisfied because $\mu \in \mathbb{Z} + J$. If $n(J)$ is coprime with ℓ, this will not happen but it can occur when $\ell | n(J)$.

In summary, SpecialEichlerNorm cannot terminate on input $\mathcal{O}, K$ with $T \approx p^{5/4}$ when $\mathcal{O}$ is connected to $\mathcal{O}_0$ with an ideal of small norm included in K. We will explain in Sect. 4.3 how to overcome this obstacle.

4   A New Algorithm for Ideal to Isogeny Translation

The goal of this section is to introduce our new algorithm to perform the *ideal-to-isogeny translation* required in computations of the effective Deuring correspondence. We start with an informal overview of how our new method manages to be more efficient than previous ones. A more detailed cost analysis tailored to SQISign will be provided in Sect. 5.1.

The goal is, given as input an $\mathcal{O}$-ideal I of norm D and a curve E with End(E) $\cong \mathcal{O}$, to compute the kernel of the D-isogeny $\varphi_I : E \to E/E[I]$. We assume for simplicity that this isogeny is cyclic (this is the important case for us). For this task, SQISign introduces [9, Algorithm 9] a generalization of [14, Algorithm 2]. Its principle is the following: evaluate the endomorphisms corresponding to elements of I on a basis of the D-torsion, then solve a discrete logarithm to find a generator of ker φ_I.

For this algorithm to be efficient, it is necessary that the evaluation points are defined over an extension of $\mathbb{F}_p$ of small degree. In [9], this is solved by decomposing the ideal I as a chain of ideals I_i of smaller norm D_i: small enough that the D_i-torsion is defined over $\mathbb{F}_{p^2}$. The idea is then to apply the technique introduced in [14], enhanced with several tricks, to translate each I_i.

It is not obvious, however, how to evaluate endomorphisms of all the I_i at arbitrary points. This task is easy in special cases: for example, the explicit correspondence between the maximal order $\mathcal{O}_0 = \langle 1, i, (i+j)/2, (1+ij)/2 \rangle$ and the endomorphism ring of $E_0 : y^2 = x^3 + x$ was leveraged in [14]. Instead, for ideals I_i of a generic order $\mathcal{O}$, the ideal-to-isogeny translation of [9] first computes an isogeny walk ϕ_K of degree T, coprime to D_i, from a special curve E_0 to E (see [9, Algorithm 7]), then evaluates it at the points of order D_i. The repeated evaluation of such isogenies of large degree is the bottleneck of the computation, consequently the size and smoothness of T greatly affect performance. In SQISign, ϕ_K is computed using a variant of the KLPT algorithm [16], and thus it is required to have $T > p^{3/2}$.

Here, in Sect. 4.1 we introduce IdealToIsogenyEichler, a new variant of IdealToIsogeny that only requires one well-chosen endomorphism of $\text{End}(E)$ to perform the translation above. The endomorphism is computed by SpecialEichlerNorm and translated to an isogeny from E to itself. We will show in Lemma 8 that the kernel of φ_I can be found via a single evaluation at a point of order D. Like in [9], we will use T-isogenies, with T coprime to D, and, thanks to Proposition 6, we need $T \approx p^{5/4}$. This reduction in size affords us a lot more flexibility in the choice of p. Several tradeoffs can be made on the size and smoothness of T and D_i; in any case, our new method speeds up SQISign key generation and signing, as we will demonstrate in Sect. 5.3.

4.1 Ideal to Isogeny Translation

Below, we introduce the new IdealToIsogenyEichler algorithm. We remind the reader that the goal of this algorithm in SQISign is to derive the response isogeny. It takes an ideal computed with SigningKLPT as input and outputs the response isogeny.

The specifications are exactly the same as those of [9, Algorithm 9] and we follow the same idea to apply sequentially a sub-algorithm that performs the translation for ideals of small norm. In our case, this sub-algorithm is called IdealToIsogenyEichler, we introduce it below as Algorithm 4, and it works for ideals of norms ℓ^f (it is analogous to [9, Algorithms 7 and 8]). Overall, our algorithm IdealToIsogenyEichler builds upon three sub-routines: IdealToIsogeny that is [14, Algorithm 2] (performing the ideal-to-isogeny translation on $\mathcal{O}_0$-ideals by performing operations on the D-torsion), SpecialEichlerNorm presented in Algorithm 3 (that replaces KLPT) and IdealToIsogenyEichler. For the rest of this section, we fix the prime p and we take f as the largest exponent such that $\ell^f | (p^2 - 1)/2$. We also fix a parameter T coprime with ℓ dividing $p^2 - 1$ and assume that $T > p^{5/4}$.

The Sub-algorithm. IdealTolsogenyEichler describes a way to translate $\mathcal{O}$-ideals of norm ℓ^f into ℓ^f-isogenies of domain E where $\mathcal{O} \cong \text{End}(E)$, using one evaluation of an element of $\text{End}(E)$. Intuitively, the idea is to choose an endomorphism θ such that $P, \theta(P)$ constitutes a basis of the ℓ^f-torsion for some point P given in input. We now present Lemma 8 to explain how the generator of the kernel of the desired isogeny can be obtained as a linear combination of $P, \theta(P)$.

Lemma 8. *Let E be a supersingular curve and $\mathcal{O} \cong \text{End}(E)$ be a maximal order. Let K and I be two $\mathcal{O}$-ideals of norm ℓ^f not contained in $\ell\mathcal{O}$. Let $\theta \in \mathcal{O} \setminus (\mathbb{Z} + K + \ell\mathcal{O})$ have norm coprime to ℓ. Let $E[K] = \langle P \rangle$, then $E[I] = \langle [C]P + [D]\theta(P) \rangle$ iff $\gcd(C, D, \ell) = 1$ and $\alpha \circ (C + D\theta) \in K$ for any α s.t $I = \mathcal{O}\langle \alpha, \ell^f \rangle$.*

Proof. Let us take $Q = [C]P + [D]\theta(P)$ and assume that $E[I] = \langle Q \rangle$. Since Q has order ℓ^f, it is clear that $\gcd(C, D, \ell) = 1$. Let us take $\alpha \in I$ such that $I = \mathcal{O}\langle \alpha, \ell^f \rangle$. This condition is equivalent to $\ker \alpha \cap E[\ell^f] = E[I]$. We want to show that $\alpha \circ (C + D\theta) \in K$ i.e. that $\alpha \circ (C + D\theta)(P) = 0$ which is straightforward since $E[I] = \langle [C]P + [D]\theta(P) \rangle$. Conversely, let us assume that $\gcd(C, D, \ell) = 1$ and $\alpha \circ (C + D\theta) \in K$ for any α s.t $I = \mathcal{O}\langle \alpha, \ell^f \rangle$. Taking such an α we get that $\alpha \circ (C + D\theta)(P) = 0$ which must imply that $[C]P + [D]\theta(P) = \lambda Q$ for some $\lambda \in \mathbb{Z}$ and Q such that $E[I] = \langle Q \rangle$. If we show that $\gcd(\lambda, \ell^f) = 1$ then we will have shown our result as P and $\theta(P)$ have order ℓ^f. Let us assume this is not the case. We have $\gcd(\lambda, \ell^f) = \ell^{e_0}$ for $e_0 > 0$. Then the point $P_0 = [\ell^{f-e_0}]P$ of order ℓ^{e_0} satisfies $[D]\theta(P_0) = [-C]P_0$. Since $\gcd(C, D, \ell) = 1$, we must have $\gcd(D, \ell) = 1$ and so $\theta(P_0) = [\mu]P_0$ where $\mu = -C/D \mod \ell^{e_0}$. This proves that we have $\theta \in \mathbb{Z} + K + \ell^{e_0}\mathcal{O} \subset \mathbb{Z} + K + \ell\mathcal{O}$ which contradicts our initial assumption. Hence, $\gcd(\lambda, \ell^f) = 1$ and we have proven the result.

Let us go back to IdealTolsogenyEichler. The correct endomorphism θ is computed during Step 2, then the computation of α, C, D as in Lemma 8 is performed during Steps 3 and 4. The representation of $\text{End}(E)$ that we use to compute θ is based on an isogeny $\varphi_J : E_0 \to E$ of norm in $\ell^\bullet$. The ideal J and the corresponding isogeny φ_J are included in the inputs, and we use them during Step 6 to compute the isogenies φ_1, φ_2 that compose the endomorphism θ; in this step, $[J]^*H$ denotes the *pullback* of H by J and $\varphi = [\varphi]_*\psi$ the *pushforward* of ψ by φ (see [9, Section 4.1]). After that, we evaluate θ on the point P during Step 7 and then, we apply Lemma 8 during Step 8 to compute the kernel of φ_I. In the execution of IdealTolsogenyEichler during IdealTolsogenyEichler, φ_J will be composed of all the ℓ^f isogenies computed during the previous iterations. The point P will then be a generator of the kernel of the dual of the isogeny computed in the previous step. For efficiency, we will take θ of norm dividing T^2 so we can represent θ using two isogenies φ_1, φ_2 of degree n_1, n_2 dividing T such that $\theta = \varphi_2 \circ \hat{\varphi}_1$.

Proposition 9. *Under plausible heuristics, IdealTolsogenyEichler is correct and terminates with overwhelming probability.*

Algorithm 4. IdealToIsogenyEichler($\mathcal{O}, I, J, \varphi_J, P$)

Input: I a left $\mathcal{O}$-ideal of norm ℓ^f, an $(\mathcal{O}_0, \mathcal{O})$-ideal J of norm $\ell^{\bullet}$ and $\varphi_J : E_0 \to E$ the corresponding isogeny, a generator P of $E[\ell^f] \cap \ker(\hat{\varphi}_J)$.
Output: φ_I of degree ℓ^f
1: Set $K = \bar{J} + \mathcal{O}\ell^f$.
2: Compute $\theta = \mathsf{SpecialEichlerNorm}(\mathcal{O}, K + \mathcal{O}\ell)$ of norm dividing T^2.
3: Select $\alpha \in I$ s.t $I = \mathcal{O}\langle \alpha, \ell^f \rangle$.
4: Compute C, D s.t. $\alpha \cdot (C + D\theta) \in K$ and $\gcd(C, D, \ell) = 1$ using linear algebra.
5: Take any $n_1 | T$ and $n_2 | T$ s.t $n_1 n_2 = n(\theta)$. Compute $H_1 = \mathcal{O}\langle \theta, n_1 \rangle$ and $H_2 = \mathcal{O}\langle \bar{\theta}, n_2 \rangle$.
6: Compute $L_i = [J]^* H_i$, and $\varphi_i = [\varphi_J]_* \mathsf{IdealToIsogeny}(L_i)$ for $i \in \{1, 2\}$.
7: Compute $Q = \hat{\varphi}_2 \circ \varphi_1(P)$.
8: Compute φ_I of kernel $\langle [C]P + [D]Q \rangle$.
9: **return** φ_I.

Proof. By Proposition 6, we have that $\mathsf{SpecialEichlerNorm}$ is correct and terminates with overwhelming probability under plausible heuristics. Apart from the execution of $\mathsf{SpecialEichlerNorm}$, the only step that neeeds justification is Step 4. First, it is not clear that such a solution must always exist. In fact, the existence of such C, D follows from $\theta \notin \mathbb{Z} + (K + \ell\mathcal{O})$. This condition implies that $P, \theta(P)$ form a basis of $E[\ell^f]$, for otherwise we would have $[\ell^{f-1}]P = [\ell^{f-1}]\theta(P)$ and so $\theta \in \mathbb{Z} + (K + \ell\mathcal{O})$, since $E[K] = \langle P \rangle$. When it exists, a solution C, D can easily be found using linear algebra in a similar fashion to $\mathsf{EichlerModConstraint}$.

Correctness follows from Lemma 8. When we identify the endomorphisms α and $[C] + [D]\theta$ in $\mathrm{End}(E)$ with their image through the isomorphism between $\mathrm{End}(E)$ and $\mathcal{O}$, we get that the composition $\alpha \circ (C + D\theta)$ becomes the multiplication of the quaternion elements $\alpha \cdot (C + D\theta)$. Thus, by Lemma 8, the values C, D computed at Step 4 are such that $\ker \varphi_I = \langle [C] + [D]\theta(P) \rangle$. By definition of H_1, H_2, we have that $\theta = \hat{\varphi}_2 \circ \varphi_1$ and this concludes the proof that the output isogeny is indeed the one corresponding to I through the Deuring Correspondence. $\qquad\square$

The Full Algorithm. Now we are ready for our full algorithm. For simplicity, we assume in Algorithm 5 that the ideal input to $\mathsf{IdealToIsogenyEichler}$ has norm ℓ^e, where $e = fg$ for some $g \in \mathbb{N}$. The general case is easily derived.

Proposition 10. *Under plausible heuristics,* $\mathsf{IdealToIsogenyEichler}$ *is correct and terminates with overwhelming probability.*

Proof. It is easily verified that the $\mathcal{O}_i, I_i, J_i, \varphi_J \circ \varphi_I, P_i$ are correct inputs to $\mathsf{IdealToIsogenyEichler}$. Thus, the result follows from Proposition 9. $\qquad\square$

Below, we explain more precisely how to perform Step 7 of $\mathsf{IdealToIsogeny}$-Eichler. The technical details were left out of the description in Algorithm 4 to clarify the explanations but they are important for an efficient implementation. Throughout this entire section, we have avoided the issues of potential failures of

---

Algorithm 5. IdealToIsogenyEichler(I, J, φ_J)

Input: I a left $\mathcal{O}$-ideal of norm ℓ^e with $e = fg$, an $(\mathcal{O}_0, \mathcal{O})$-ideal J of norm $\ell^\bullet$ and $\varphi_J : E_0 \to E$ the corresponding isogeny

Output: φ_I of degree ℓ^e.

1: Set $J_i = J$, $I_i = I + \ell^f \mathcal{O}$, $I'_i = I_i^{-1} I$, $\mathcal{O}_i = \mathcal{O}$.
2: Set φ_i of degree ℓ^f as the isogeny such that $\hat{\varphi}_J = \varphi' \circ \varphi_i$
3: Set $\varphi_I = [1]_E$ and $E_i = E$.
4: **for** $i \in [1, g]$ **do**
5:     Compute $P_i \in E_i[\ell^f]$ s.t ker $\varphi_i = \langle P_i \rangle$.
6:     Compute $\varphi_{I_i} = \mathsf{IdealToIsogenyEichler}(\mathcal{O}_i, I_i, J_i, \varphi_I \circ \varphi_J, P_i)$.
7:     Set $\varphi_i = \hat{\varphi}_{I_i}$, $\varphi_I = \varphi_{I_i} \circ \varphi_I$ and E_i is the codomain of φ_{I_i}.
8:     Set $J_i = J_i \cdot I_i$, $\mathcal{O}_i = \mathcal{O}_L(I'_i)$, $I_i = I'_i + \ell^f \mathcal{O}_i$ and $I'_i = I_i^{-1} I'_i$.
9: **end for**
10: **return** φ_I.

SpecialEichlerNorm that were mentioned at the end of Sect. 3.2. We will discuss in Sect. 4.3 how to perform the computation in this eventuality.

4.2 A Detailed Description of the Ideal Translation Algorithm.

Endomorphism Evaluation. In Step 7 of IdealToIsogenyEichler we need to evaluate the endomorphisms $\theta = \hat{\varphi}_2 \circ \varphi_1$ after the two isogenies φ_1, φ_2 have been computed. One might assume that it suffices to push P through φ_1 and then do the same through $\hat{\varphi}_2$. This apparently simple algorithm is not so easy to implement. The first problem lies with signs. Efficient isogeny algorithms are using x-only arithmetic which imply that we can only evaluate isogenies up to signs. This is problematic as the ultimate goal is to compute $[C]P + [D]\theta(P)$. Solving this issue requires to evaluate several other points through φ_1, φ_2 and there does not seem to be another easy way to remove the ambiguity. The second issue is with the dual computation in itself. For an isogeny φ of degree T and kernel $\langle P \rangle$, computing $\hat{\varphi}(R)$ for some point R would first require to compute $\varphi(Q)$ where Q is of order T and orthogonal to P to get ker $\hat{\varphi}$, before using this kernel to compute $\hat{\varphi}(R)$. In the context of SQISign where T-isogenies have kernel made of two points, this is already 2 T-isogeny computations and 3 evaluations (see Sect. 5.1 for a more detailed account on operation estimates). Together with the computation of $\varphi_1(P)$, we have a total of 3 T-isogeny computations and 4 evaluations and this is without whatever would be required to lift the sign ambiguity.

Targeting the application to IdealToIsogenyEichler, we present in Algorithm 6 a method to compute the kernel of φ_I in Step 8 of Algorithm 4, without computing the intermediate value Q in Step 7. This method evaluates an endomorphism of the form $C + D\theta$, where $\theta = \hat{\varphi}_2 \circ \varphi_1$, at an arbitrary point P; it requires only 2 T-isogeny computations and 5 evaluations, plus a few discrete logarithms, which are efficient as long as P has smooth order.

Here is a sketch of how the method works, using x-only arithmetic. Let (P, Q) be a basis of the ℓ^f-torsion. The main principle is to express $\varphi_1(P)$ as a linear combination of $\varphi_2(P), \varphi_2(Q)$ and see that $\hat{\varphi}_2 \circ \varphi_1(P)$ is a multiple of the linear combination of P, Q with the same coefficients. When dealing with x-only arithmetic we need also to compute $\varphi_2(P + Q)$ to perform the discrete log computations. Finally, to lift the ambiguity (the linear combination that we obtain is only up to sign) we use the trace of $\theta = \hat{\varphi}_2 \circ \varphi_1$ (which can be computed by expressing θ in the basis $\langle 1, i, j, k \rangle$). In the basis P, Q, the action of θ can be seen as a matrix of $\mathbb{M}_2(\mathbb{Z}/\ell^f \mathbb{Z})$. This matrix is essentially the one we obtain with the coefficient of the two discrete logarithms and so it suffices to check the value of the trace to lift any sign ambiguity.

In Algorithm 6 we call to a function $\mathsf{xBIDIM}(x(R), x(P), x(Q), x(P + Q))$, which computes the two-dimensional discrete logarithm of R to base (P, Q), i.e. a pair of scalars a, b such that $x(R) = x([a]P + [b]Q)$. Assuming R, P, Q have order ℓ^f, it has complexity $O(f)$.

Algorithm 6. EndomorphismEvaluation$(\varphi_1, \varphi_2, C, D, t, P)$

Input: Two isogenies $\varphi_1, \varphi_2 : E \to E'$, scalars C, D, the trace $t = \operatorname{tr}(\hat{\varphi}_2 \circ \varphi_1)$ and a point P of order ℓ^f

Output: $[C]P + [D]\hat{\varphi}_2 \circ \varphi_1(P)$

1: Compute Q such that P, Q is a basis of $E[\ell^f]$ and compute $P + Q$.
2: Compute $x(\varphi_1(P)), x(\varphi_1(Q)), x(\varphi_2(P)), x(\varphi_2(Q)), x(\varphi_2(P + Q))$.
3: Compute $x_1, x_2 = \mathsf{xBIDIM}(x(\varphi_1(P)), x(\varphi_2(P)), x(\varphi_2(Q)), x(\varphi_2(P + Q)))$ and $x_3, x_4 = \mathsf{xBIDIM}(x(\varphi_1(Q)), x(\varphi_2(P)), x(\varphi_2(Q)), x(\varphi_2(P + Q)))$.
4: Change the signs of $(x_1, x_2), (x_3, x_4)$ until $(x_1 + x_4) \deg \varphi_2 = t \mod \ell^f$.
5: Set $a = C + x_1 D$ and $b = x_2 D$.
6: Compute $R = [a]P + [b]Q$.
7: **return** R.

Remark 11. For the signature, one needs to compute a canonical representation of the output of IdealToIsogenyEichler. The method from [9, Section 8.5] is to compute a deterministic basis at each intermediate curve E_i and represent the kernel of the next step as a linear combination of this basis. The first point of the basis can be taken as the kernel of the previous isogeny, so it suffices to pick one other point. Typically, this would be done in Step 1 of EndomorphismEvaluation in the choice of Q.

On T-isogenies Computation. The computation of T-isogenies during Step 6 is an important part of IdealToIsogenyEichler. The optimization we describe next was already used in the code implementing [9], but no explanation was given. We simply fill this void. The task at hand can be divided in two parts: the IdealToIsogeny and the push-forward through φ_J. Since IdealToIsogeny is always performed on the special order $\mathcal{O}_0$, the action of a basis of $\operatorname{End}(E_0) \cong \mathcal{O}_0$ on a basis of the T-torsion can be precomputed (and stored as matrices). Then, for an ideal given in input, it suffices to decompose the elements of this ideal on the basis of $\mathcal{O}_0$ and use the precomputed matrices to get the action of these elements on the T-torsion basis before doing some linear algebra to find the linear combination of the basis that will generate the kernel of the desired isogeny. After the execution of IdealToIsogeny, it suffices to push the generators of the kernels through φ_J. For a given execution, we do not know how to do better than what is described above. However IdealToIsogenyEichler is executed sequentially with an isogeny φ_J of increasing size, thus, if we do it naively, we will end up evaluating the first isogenies many times. To avoid this extra computation, it suffices to push the basis of the T-torsion through each φ_I and store it. If the basis is the same as the one used to precompute the action of $\mathrm{End}(E_0)$, it suffices to apply the linear combination obtained from IdealToIsogeny to the pushed basis to obtain directly the generator of the kernel. Over the course of the entire execution, this will save a non-negligible amount of ℓ^f-isogeny computations.

4.3   Handling Special Failure Cases

In the analysis proposed at the end of Sect. 3.2, we explained that there are some inputs $\mathcal{O}, K$ for which the computation of SpecialEichlerNorm$(\mathcal{O}, K)$ will fail if $T \approx p^{5/4}$. In rare occasions, we will encounter an order $\mathcal{O}_i$ that is one of those bad orders, causing the execution of IdealToIsogenyEichler at the i-th iteration in IdealToIsogenyEichler to fail. Since we cannot afford to increase the size of T, we can handle this issue in two manners: revert to the method of [8] to perform the translation, or use a special extremal order other than $\mathcal{O}_0$ with SpecialEichlerNorm.

Applying the IdealToIsogeny$_{\ell^f}$ from [8]. At first glance going back to the old method might seem like an odd thing to do. However, the failure cases for SpecialEichlerNorm are actually good cases for the method from [8] because there is an ideal of norm $M \ll p^{1/2}$ connecting $\mathcal{O}_0$ and $\mathcal{O}$. As we explained, this is only a bad thing for SpecialEichlerNorm because we have an additional constraint with the ideal K but IdealToIsogeny does not suffer from the same limitation. Ideal-ToIsogeny relies on the KLPT algorithm that will succeed in finding an element of norm T^2 if $T \approx pM$. Hence, when $M < p^{1/4}$, we can hope to make it work with $T \approx p^{5/4}$. However, there is an obvious range of degrees $p^{1/4} \ll M \ll p^{1/2}$ where this solution will not work. This is why in practice, we will use the second method described below.

Using Another Special Extremal Order. The bad property depends on the special extremal order $\mathcal{O}_0$ that we use. In practice, when $p = 3 \mod 4$, it is standard in the literature to use the maximal extremal order $\langle 1, i, \frac{1+k}{2}, \frac{i+j}{2} \rangle$, but this canonical example is not the only maximal order matching the definition of extremal orders given in [16]. We recall that a maximal order in $B_{p,\infty}$ containing a given quadratic order $\mathfrak{O}$ exists when p is an inert prime in the quadratic imaginary field associated to $\mathfrak{O}$. Even if other quadratic orders will not be as efficient as $\mathbb{Z}[i] \subset \mathcal{O}_0$, the complexity of SpecialEichlerNorm is logarithmic in disc $\mathfrak{O}$ and so we can expand the range of choices without affecting the performance too much. Thus, we can gather a small list of good candidates for $\mathcal{O}_0$ and enumerate through that list until we find one that does not have the bad property. To prove that this idea works, we need to make sure that a maximal order $\mathcal{O}$ will not have the bad property with all the extremal orders. Unfortunately, we do not have a definitive proof of this fact and are reduced to make it a heuristic assumption. Boneh and Love [19] showed that maximal quaternion orders admitting embeddings of small quadratic orders are far apart in the isogeny graph. While this conveys the right idea, their bound in [19, Proposition 4.5] is too loose to help us. In practice, switching to another maximal order seems to work well enough in our implementation.

5 Parameters and Implementation for SQISign

We now present our methodology to set parameters for SQISign using our new ideal-to-isogeny algorithm, and report on our implementation. We start with a method to give a rough estimate of the relative efficiency of two parameter choices. Based on these estimates, we report on our search for new primes better suited to our new algorithm. Finally, we benchmark our implementation, including the improvements provided by the state-of-the-art algorithms for the arithmetic over $\mathbb{F}_{p^2}$ [18], and compare it to the original SQISign implementation.

For the rest of this section we let p be a prime such that $\ell^f T \mid (p^2 - 1)$, where T is smooth and coprime with ℓ. Following [8], we will take $\ell = 2$, as this leads to the fastest verification and simplest implementation overall. It is an interesting question whether other choices for ℓ could lead to useful compromises. With the choice of $\ell = 2$, the authors from [8] advised to take a σ of degree 2^{1000}.

5.1 Cost Estimate

It was already observed in [8] that algebraic operations over $\mathbb{F}_{p^2}$ make up for most of the cost of SQISign: up to $\approx 90\%$ in our experiments. It is thus reasonable to ignore computations over the quaternions and linear algebra, and focus on these. Ideally, we would count the number of $\mathbb{F}_{p^2}$-operations performed for each choice of parameters, however this is already difficult given the complexity of the algorithms. Instead, we will use a much coarser metric based on four indicators.

We are only going to compare [9, Algorithm 9] and Algorithm 5. Both algorithms decompose an ideal of norm ℓ^e into ideals of smaller norm. The former decomposes into ideals of norm $\ell^{2f+\Delta}$ for some constant Δ, which are then translated to isogenies by [9, Algorithm 8]. The latter decomposes into ideals of norm ℓ^f, which are translated by Algorithm 4. Both sub-algorithms consist mostly of isogeny computations of degree T and ℓ^f. For each of them, we will count:

(T_c) How many isogenies of degree T are *computed*;
(T_e) On how many points the isogenies of degree T are *evaluated*;
(ℓ_c) How many isogenies of degree ℓ^f are computed/evaluated;

(Δ_c) How many meet-in-the-middle searches for isogenies of degree ℓ^Δ are performed (this is exclusive to [9, Algorithm 8]).

The costs of T_c and T_e depend on the factorization of T. Instead of using the full factorization, we will only base our estimate on a bound B such that all prime factors of T are $< B$. Using [2], the costs of computing and evaluating an isogeny of prime degree n grow as $\sqrt{n}$ (ignoring logarithmic factors), we will thus multiply T_c and T_e by $\sqrt{B}$. Since ℓ is small, the cost of computing and evaluating an isogeny of degree ℓ^f grows as $f\log(f)$ (ignoring the dependency in ℓ), we shall thus multiply ℓ_c by this factor. Finally, the meet-in-the-middle requires to compute all $\sqrt{\ell^\Delta}$ isogenies, so we multiply Δ_c by $\sqrt{\ell^\Delta}$.

Given an ideal of norm ℓ^e, SQISign will call [9, Algorithm 8] $\approx e/(2f+\Delta)$ times, whereas our new method will call Algorithm 5 $\approx e/f$ times. For this reason, we shall divide all counts by $2f+\Delta$ and f, respectively.

Summarizing, for [9, Algorithm 8] we will use the following 4-valued estimator:

$$(T_c\sqrt{B}, T_e\sqrt{B}, \ell_c f\log(f), \sqrt{\ell^\Delta}\Delta_c)/(2f+\Delta), \qquad (1)$$

where the division is applied component-wise. For Algorithm 5, given that it does not use a meet-in-the-middle search, we will instead use

$$(T_c\sqrt{B}/f, T_e\sqrt{B}/f, \ell_c\log(f)). \qquad (2)$$

Original method. For convenience, Algorithm 7 reproduces [9, Algorithm 8] without modifications. Some of the steps therein are quite vague, so we also refer to the code at https://github.com/SQISign/sqisign.

The operation count for Algorithm 7 goes as follows: Step 3 is $2\,T_e$ (push ker φ_1 through φ_J) and $1\,\ell_c$ (compute φ_1), Step 8 is $1\,T_c$ (compute ψ_1), Step 9 is $1\,T_e$, $1\,T_c$ (compute ψ_2 and ker ρ_2) and $1\,\ell_c$ (compute φ_2), Step 10 is $1\,\Delta_c$, Step 11 is $2\,T_e$ (compute ker $\hat\psi_1$), $2\,\ell_c$ (push ker $\hat\psi_1$ through $\rho_2\circ\eta$), $1\,T_c$ and $1\,T_e$ (compute ψ_1' and ker $\hat\rho_2$), $1\,\ell_c$ (compute φ_2) and $1\,\Delta_c$ (compute θ). Thus a total of $3\,T_c$, $6\,T_e$, $2\,\Delta_c$ and $5\,\ell_c$.

New Method. Step 7 requires to solve a DLP instance over the ℓ^f-torsion and we overestimate the complexity by saying that this is equivalent to $1\,\ell_c$ operation (asymptotically it is the same cost but the DLP is faster in practice). We obtain the following count: $2\,T_c$ for Step 6, $5\,T_e$ and $1\,\ell_c$ for Step 7 (see Algorithm 6), Step 8 is $1\,\ell_c$. Overall, we get $2\,T_c$, $5\,T_e$ and $2\,\ell_c$.

5.2   New Prime Search

Recall that the main advantage of our new ideal-to-isogeny algorithm is to decrease T from $\sim p^{3/2}$ to $\sim p^{5/4}$. Primes p such that $\ell^f T \mid (p^2-1)$ for such large

Algorithm 7. IdealToIsogeny($I, J, K, \varphi_J, \varphi_K$) [9, Algorithm 8]

Input: I a left $\mathcal{O}_0$-ideal of norm dividing $T^2 \ell^{2f+\Delta}$, an $\mathcal{O}_0$-ideal in J containing I of norm dividing T^2, and an ideal $K \sim J$ of norm a power of ℓ, as well as φ_J and φ_K.
Output: $\varphi = \varphi_2 \circ \theta \circ \varphi_1 : E_1 \to E_2$ of degree $\ell^{2f+\Delta}$ such that $\varphi_I = \varphi \circ \varphi_J$, $L \sim I$ of norm dividing T^2 and φ_L.
0: Write $\varphi_J, \varphi_K : E_0 \to E_1$.
1: Let $I_1 = I + \ell^f \mathcal{O}_0$.
2: Let $\varphi_1' = $ IdealToIsogeny(I_1).
3: Let $\varphi_1 = [\varphi_J]_* \varphi_1' : E_1 \to E_3$.
4: Let $L = $ KLPT(I).
5: Let $\alpha \in K$ such that $J = \chi_K(\alpha)$.
6: Let $\beta \in I$ such that $L = \chi_I(\beta)$.
7: Let $\gamma = \beta\alpha/n(J)$. We have $\gamma \in K$, $\bar{\gamma} \in L$, and $n(\gamma) = T^2 \ell^{2f+\Delta} n(K)$.
8: Let $H_1 = \langle \gamma, n(K)\ell^f T \rangle$. We have $\varphi_{H_1} = \psi_1 \circ \varphi_1 \circ \varphi_K : E_0 \to E_5$, where ψ_1 has degree T.
9: Let $H_2 = \langle \bar{\gamma}, \ell^f T \rangle$. We have $\varphi_{H_2} = \rho_2 \circ \psi_2 : E_0 \to E_6$, where ψ_2 has degree T and ρ_2 has degree ℓ^f.
10: Find $\eta : E_5 \to E_6$ of degree ℓ^Δ with meet-in-the-middle.
11: Let $\varphi_2 \circ \theta = [\hat{\psi}_1]_* \hat{\rho}_2 \circ \eta : E_3 \to E_2$ and $\psi_1' = [\hat{\varphi}_2 \circ \eta]_* \hat{\psi}_1$
12: **return** $\varphi = \varphi_2 \circ \theta \circ \varphi_1$, L and $\psi_1' \circ \psi_2$.

T are rare, and thus a search must be performed in order to instantiate SQISign. Following [8], we focus on primes of ≈ 256 bits, which offer ≈ 128 bits of classical security. In [8], the prime p with

$$p + 1 = 2^{33} \cdot 5^{21} \cdot 7^2 \cdot 11 \cdot 31 \cdot 83 \cdot 107 \cdot 137 \cdot 751 \cdot 827 \cdot 3691 \cdot 4019 \cdot 6983$$
$$\cdot\, 517434778561 \cdot 26602537156291 \,,$$

$$p - 1 = 2 \cdot 3^{53} \cdot 43 \cdot 103^2 \cdot 109 \cdot 199 \cdot 227 \cdot 419 \cdot 491 \cdot 569 \cdot 631 \cdot 677 \cdot 857 \cdot 859$$
$$\cdot\, 883 \cdot 1019 \cdot 1171 \cdot 1879 \cdot 2713 \cdot 4283$$

is recommended, giving $f = 33$ and a $T > 2^{393}$ that is 2^{13}-smooth. We shall call it p_{6983}, after the largest factor in T. This prime can be used both for the old and the new method, however in our new method we can discard some of the largest factors of T, getting down to a $T' > 2^{333}$ that is 2^{11}-smooth. Knowing that $\Delta = 14$ in [8], we can already use our estimator to compare the two methods. The values are reported in Table 4. Based on this metric, it appears that the new method could be slightly faster than the old one.

However, a less stringent requirement on T makes the search for p considerably easier, it is thus natural to look for a new one that is better adapted to our method. The prime p_{6983} was found using an XGCD-based method described in [9, Appendix C], which we used to find more primes. In the meantime, more algorithms to find primes such that $p^2 - 1$ is smooth were introduced in [5,6]. Unfortunately, only the sieve of [5], when looking for primes of the form $p = 2x^n - 1$, adapts well to the requirement of having $2^f \mid (p^2 - 1)$ for some moderately large f. Indeed, we can modify this method by forcing $2^{\lceil f/n \rceil} \mid x$. Trying to do the same in the sieve of [6] leads to a search space too small to yield any primes.

Regardless of the method we use, given that we look for a smaller T, we can choose to either increase f or decrease the smoothness bound B on T. Looking at estimator (2), it appears that we can divide the first two entries by 2 in one of two ways: multiplying f by 2, or dividing B by 4. We experimented with both. We used the method of [5] to look for primes $p = 2^{61}x^4 - 1$, sieving the whole interval $x \in [2^{47}, 2^{49}[$ in approximately 360 cpu-days. We found 398 integers such that $p^2 - 1$ has a 2^{11}-smooth odd factor of more than 330 bits, of which 15 were prime (see Table 2); none of them has a large enough 2^{10}-smooth factor.

Table 2. List of integers $x \in [2^{47}, 2^{49}[$ such that $2^{61}x^4 - 1$ is prime and $x^4(2^{15}x - 1)(2^{15}x + 1)(2^{30}x^2 + 1)$ contains a 2^{11}-factor $> 2^{330}$.

143189100303149	369428710635531	391443251922757	411099446409699
424067696488337	431716591494287	491224940548057	491531434028942
512391149388477	512583833108361	514414280000642	515727186701509
548396183941255	550470785518701	562456538440551	

Using the XGCD method of [9], we found out that we could obtain primes with $f \approx 64$ and $B = 2^{12}$ at a reasonable cost. The best candidate we found, which we name p_{3923}, has 254 bits and

$$p + 1 = 2^{65} \cdot 5^2 \cdot 7 \cdot 11 \cdot 19 \cdot 29^2 \cdot 37^2 \cdot 47 \cdot 197 \cdot 263 \cdot 281 \cdot 461 \cdot 521$$
$$\cdot 3923 \cdot 62731 \cdot 96362257 \cdot 3924006112952623 \,,$$
$$p - 1 = 2 \cdot 3^{65} \cdot 13 \cdot 17 \cdot 43 \cdot 79 \cdot 157 \cdot 239 \cdot 271 \cdot 283 \cdot 307 \cdot 563 \cdot 599$$
$$\cdot 607 \cdot 619 \cdot 743 \cdot 827 \cdot 941 \cdot 2357 \cdot 10069 \,.$$

Despite the slightly larger smoothness bound, we found that p_{3923} performs better in practice than primes of the form $2^{61}x^4 - 1$, probably owing to the large power of 3, which contributes favorably to T-isogeny computations. Moreover, the fact that $p' = -p^{-1} \bmod 2^w \equiv 1$ for standard computer wordlengths like $w = 32, 64$ bits enables the use of variants of [18, Alg. 5] to implement the multiplication over $\mathbb{F}_{p^2}$ (in contrast, primes like p_{6983} are limited to use the slightly more complex [18, Alg. 2]; see §5). Finally, practical implementations of the underlying field arithmetic can also benefit from the extra room at the word boundary that the 254-bit length provides.

Reporting the estimator values for p_{3923} in Table 3, we see that applying our new algorithm to the new prime yields a significant gain during T-isogeny computations and meet-in-the-middle at the cost of a modest loss during ℓ^f-isogeny computations. Since the former tends to affect performance much more than the latter, in practice, we expect our new method to compare favorably to the old one. We will see in the next section that, in practice, the gain is even larger than predicted by our rough estimator. Finding more accurate estimators to guide the prime search in SQISign is an interesting problem for future research.

Table 3. Operation estimates for several variants of *ideal-to-isogeny* translation. B is the smoothness bound of T.

algorithm	p	$\log(p)$	f	B	T_c	T_e	ℓ_c	Δ_c	estimator
Old	p_{6983}	256	33	2^{13}	3	6	5	2	$(3.4, 6.8, 10.4, 3.2)$
New	p_{6983}	256	33	2^{11}	2	5	2	–	$(2.7, 6.9, 10.1)$
New	p_{3923}	254	65	2^{12}	2	5	2	–	$(2.0, 4.9, 12.0)$

Other Changes. Having a smaller T forces some other changes to SQISign's challenge and commitment steps. To get λ bits of security, the commitment must have degree $T' \geq 2^{2\lambda}$, while the challenge must have degree $D_c \geq 2^{\lambda}$ coprime to T'. The authors of [8] could take $T'D_c = T \approx p^{3/2} \approx 2^{3\lambda}$. To optimize verification, they chose D_c to be as smooth as possible, i.e., $D_c = 3^{53}5^{21}$.

However, with a smaller T, we can no longer have $T = T'D_c$. Instead, we incorporate some powers of ℓ in D_c; incidentally, this happens to increase verification speed. For p_{3923}, we take $D_c = 2^{65}3^{40}$, which is a marked improvement over $D_c = 3^{53}5^{21}$. Of course, one could also incorporate powers of 2 to D_c with p_{6983}. But $p_{6983} + 1$ only contains a factor 2^{33}, so verification with p_{3923} still beats p_{6983}.

In fact, at the cost of increasing the signer's work, it is possible to take D_c as a power of ℓ, which could further decrease verification time. The concrete gain for the instantiation with p_{3923} will be the difference between a 2^{64}-isogeny computation and a 3^{40}-isogeny computation. This is a marginal gain compared to the cost for the signer (at least several additional executions of IdealToIsogenyEichler), so we chose not to pursue this idea further.

5.3   C Implementation

We took the official SQISign implementation[1] and incorporated our new ideal-to-isogeny algorithm plus some other minor improvements. In particular, we implemented the compression method described in [9, §8.5] for verification, which, along with the use of powers of 2 in the challenge degree D_c, explains the faster verification. In addition, we fully rewrote the hand-optimized assembly implementation of the $\mathbb{F}_{p^2}$ arithmetic layer and, more importantly, adapted to our primes the faster multiplication algorithms over $\mathbb{F}_{p^2}$ from [18] (specifically, we use Algorithm 2 for p_{6983} and adapted Algorithm 5 to p_{3923}).

Our code is available at https://github.com/SQISign/sqisign-ec23. We ran benchmarks on two platforms: a 3.4GHz Intel Core i7-6700 (Skylake) processor, and a 3.2GHz Intel Core i7-8700 (Coffee Lake) processor. As is standard practice, Turbo Boost was deactivated during the tests. The results are summarized in Table 4. With all our improvements, and moving from p_{6983} to p_{3923}, we observe a more than 4× speedup in key generation and verification, while signing is sped up by more than 3×. For instance, we report signing computations averaging

---

[1] https://github.com/SQISign/sqisign.

Table 4. Performance comparison between the original implementation of SQISign [8] and our implementations using the proposed optimizations. Results are shown in millions of cycles (rounded to the nearest 10^6), and correspond to the average counts of 100 runs for key generation and signature, and of 250 runs for verification. The columns "Std." correspond to results using standard implementations for the arithmetic over $\mathbb{F}_{p^2}$, while the columns "Opt." report results using the optimized $\mathbb{F}_{p^2}$ algorithms from [18]. The cost reductions obtained for each operation, relative to the results from [8], are shown in the columns "%".

	SQISign [8]	New/p_{6983}				New/p_{3923}			
	p_{6983}	Std.	%	Opt.	%	Std.	%	Opt.	%
3.4GHz Intel Core i7-6700 (Skylake)									
Keygen	1,828	2,792	−53%	2,243	−23%	670	63%	**421**	77%
Sign	7,020	6,074	13%	4,178	40%	3,311	53%	**1,987**	72%
Verify	143	87	39%	52	64%	66	54%	**30**	79%
3.2GHz Intel Core i7-8700 (Coffee Lake)									
Keygen	1,242	1,916	−54%	1,529	−19%	463	63%	**286**	77%
Sign	4,811	4,086	15%	2,850	41%	2,274	53%	**1,354**	72%
Verify	99	60	39%	37	63%	46	54%	**21**	79%

424 msec. on a 3.2GHz Intel machine, well below the over a second computation reported in [8]. Meanwhile, verification times average 6.7 msec. on the same machine, which is $\sim 4.6\times$ faster than the mark obtained by [8].

We note that the proposed prime p_{3923} gets an additional boost in performance because of its synergy with the techniques from [18]. Indeed, this prime facilitates the use of a variant of [18, Alg. 5] by exploiting the fact that $p' = -p^{-1} \bmod 2^w \equiv 1$ for a computer wordlength of $w = 64$ bits, in contrast to p_{6983} which is limited to use the somewhat slower [18, Alg. 2].

6   Cryptanalysis

In this section, we present a distinguisher against one of the computational assumptions underlying the security of SQISign. This distinguisher does not lead to an attack on the signature scheme but it invalidates the claimed hardness of the problem. We present a fix to protect the scheme against the distinguisher and propose further theoretical analysis and experimental results to argue that a modified assumption holds.

More concretely, we show in Sect. 6.1 that the set $\mathcal{P}_{N_\tau}$ involved in the formulation of Problem 14 has a problematic property that leads to a distinguisher. Fortunately, a slight change of SigningKLPT, explained in Sect. 6.1, seems to be enough to remove the problem. In Sect. 6.2, we analyse the new assumption more precisely, to argue that it does not suffer from a similar weakness.

Before getting to our contributions, we give a quick summary of some of the relevant content from [8] regarding the zero-knowledge property of the underlying identification scheme. We start in Algorithm 8 with the description of the Signing-KLPT algorithm from [8].

Algorithm 8. SigningKLPT(I, I_τ)

Input: I_τ a left $\mathcal{O}_0$-ideal and right $\mathcal{O}$-ideal of norm N_τ, and I, a left $\mathcal{O}$-ideal.
Output: $J \sim I$ of norm ℓ^e, where e is fixed.
1: Compute $K = \mathsf{EquivalentRandomEichlerIdeal}(I, N_\tau)$
2: Compute $K' = [I_\tau]^* K$ and set $L = \mathsf{EquivalentPrimeIdeal}(K')$, $L = \chi_{K'}(\delta)$ for $\delta \in K'$
   with $N = n(L)$. Set $e_0 = e_0(N)$ and $e_1 = e - e_0$.
3: Compute $\gamma = \mathsf{RepresentInteger}(N\ell^{e_0})$.
4: Compute $(C_0 : D_0) = \mathsf{IdealModConstraint}(L, \gamma)$.
5: Compute $(C_1 : D_1) = \mathsf{EichlerModConstraint}(\mathbb{Z} + I_\tau, \gamma, \delta)$.
6: Compute $C = \mathsf{CRT}_{N_\tau, N}(C_0, C_1)$ and $D = \mathsf{CRT}_{N_\tau, N}(D_0, D_1)$. If $\ell^e p(C^2 + D^2)$ is not
   a quadratic residue, go back to Step 3.
7: Compute $\mu = \mathsf{StrongApproximation}(NN_\tau, C, D)$ of norm ℓ^{e_1}
8: Set $\beta = \gamma\mu$.
9: **return** $J = [I_\tau]_* \chi_L(\beta)$.

In SQISign, the output J of SigningKLPT is converted into the corresponding isogeny σ, and the signature is a representation of this isogeny. The zero-knowledge property is proved assuming the hardness of Problem 14, described below. This assumption formalises that σ is indistinguishable from a random isogeny of the same degree.

The structure of this isogeny is analysed in [8], with more details in [9, Lemma 13] reproduced here as Lemma 12 for the reader's convenience.

Lemma 12. *Let $L \subset \mathcal{O}$ and $\beta \in L$ be as in steps 2, 8 respectively of Algorithm 8. The isogeny σ corresponding to the output J of Algorithm 8 is equal to $\sigma = [\tau]_* \iota$, where ι is an isogeny of degree ℓ^e verifying $\beta = \hat{\iota} \circ \varphi_L$.*

Before giving a precise statement of the distinguishing problem, we need to recall some notation from [8]. For what follows, we keep the notation introduced in Lemma 12 and Algorithm 8. For a given ideal L of norm N, we consider $\mathcal{U}_{L,N_\tau}$ as the set of all isogenies ι computed as in Lemma 12 from elements $\beta = \gamma\mu \in L$ where γ is any possible output of the non-deterministic function $\mathsf{RepresentInteger}(N\ell^{e_0(N)})$, and μ is computed as in Algorithm 8.

For an equivalence class $\mathcal{C}$ in $\mathrm{Cl}(\mathcal{O}_0)$ we write $\mathcal{U}_{\mathcal{C},N_\tau}$ for $\mathcal{U}_{L,N_\tau}$ where $L = \mathsf{EquivalentPrimeIdeal}(\mathcal{C})$ (recall that EquivalentPrimeIdeal is deterministic).

Definition 13. $\mathcal{P}_{N_\tau} = \bigcup_{\mathcal{C} \in \mathrm{Cl}(\mathcal{O}_0)} \mathcal{U}_{\mathcal{C},N_\tau}$

For $D \in \mathbb{N}$ and a supersingular curve E, we define $\mathrm{Iso}_{D,j(E)}$ as the set of cyclic isogenies of degree D, whose domain is a curve inside the isomorphism class of E. When $\mathcal{P}$ is a subset of $\mathrm{Iso}_{D,j(E)}$ and $\tau : E \to E'$ is an isogeny with $\gcd(\deg \tau, D) = 1$, we write $[\tau]_* \mathcal{P}$ for the subset $\{[\tau]_* \varphi \mid \varphi \in \mathcal{P}\}$ of $\mathrm{Iso}_{D,j(E')}$. Finally, we denote by $\mathcal{K}$ a probability distribution on the set of cyclic isogenies whose domain is E_0, representing the distribution of SQISign private keys. With these notations, we define the following computational problem:

Problem 14. Let p be a prime, and D a smooth integer. Let $\tau : E_0 \rightarrow E_A$ be a random isogeny drawn from $\mathcal{K}$, and let N_τ be its degree. Let $\mathcal{P}_{N_\tau} \subset \mathrm{Iso}_{D,j_0}$ as in Definition 13, and let O_τ be an oracle sampling random elements in $[\tau]_* \mathcal{P}_{N_\tau}$. Let $\sigma : E_A \rightarrow \star$ of degree D where either

1. σ is uniformly random in $\mathrm{Iso}_{D,j(E_A)}$;
2. σ is uniformly random in $[\tau]_* \mathcal{P}_{N_\tau}$.

The problem is, given $p, D, \mathcal{K}, E_A, \sigma$, to distinguish between the two cases with a polynomial number of queries to O_τ.

6.1 An Attack on SQISign's Zero-Knowledge Assumption

Our distinguisher for Problem 14 is a consequence of the limitations pointed out in Sect. 3.1 and it occurs specifically when $\ell = 2$ (which is the value used in [8] and in our implementation), so for the rest of this section and the next we take $D = 2^e$. Lemma 15 and the resulting Proposition 16 links the observations of Sect. 3.1 to a property on the set $[\tau]_* \mathcal{P}_{N_\tau}$.

Lemma 15. *Let L be an $\mathcal{O}_0$-ideal of norm N and let γ be an element in $\mathcal{O}_0$ of norm $N\ell^e$ for some prime N. Let us take $\mu \in \mathcal{O}_0$ such that $\beta = \gamma\mu \in L$. If $\gamma \in \langle 1, i, j, k \rangle$, then $\chi_L(\beta) \subset \mathcal{O}_0 \langle 1 + i, 2 \rangle$.*

Proof. We have $\gamma \in \langle 1, i, j, k \rangle \subset \mathcal{O}_0 \langle 1 + i, 2 \rangle$. Now, $\chi_L(\beta) = \mathcal{O}_0 \langle \overline{\mu\gamma}, 2^e \rangle$, hence $\overline{\mu\gamma} \in \mathcal{O}_0 \overline{\gamma} \subseteq \mathcal{O}_0 \langle 1 + \overline{i}, 2 \rangle = \mathcal{O}_0 \langle 1 + i, 2 \rangle$, which proves the proposition.

Proposition 16. *Let $D = 2^e$ and τ, N_τ be as in Problem 14 and let the set $\mathcal{P}_{N_\tau}$ be defined from Algorithm 8. There exists an isogeny $\iota_0 \in \mathrm{Iso}_{2,j(E_0)}$ such that every $\iota \in \mathcal{P}_{N_\tau}$ can be decomposed as $\iota = \iota_1 \circ \iota_0$ where ι_1 is an isogeny of degree 2^{e-1}.*

Proof. Let J be the ideal corresponding to $\sigma \in [\tau]_* \mathcal{P}_{N_\tau}$. By definition of $\mathcal{P}_{N_\tau}$, ι corresponds to the ideal $\chi_L(\gamma\mu)$. It is easily verified that L, γ, μ satisfy the requirements of Lemma 15 and that $\gamma \in \langle 1, i, j, k \rangle$ since it is a possible output of RepresentInteger. Thus, we can apply Lemma 15 and we get that $\chi_L(\beta) \subset \mathcal{O}_0 \langle 1 + i, 2 \rangle$. This proves the result by taking ι_0 to be the isogeny corresponding to the ideal $\mathcal{O}_0 \langle 1 + i, 2 \rangle$.

Thus, Proposition 16 implies that, when defined as in Definition 13, the family $\mathcal{P}_{N_\tau}$ satisfies one of the special properties introduced in [9, Appendix B.2]. Indeed, we obtain that $I_\tau^1 = \{\iota_1 \text{ of degree } 2, \text{s.t } \exists \iota_2, \ \iota_2 \circ \iota_1 \in \mathcal{P}_{N_\tau}\}$ has size 1 (instead of 3), and so a trivial distinguisher can be built against Problem 14 simply by looking at the distribution of the first step of σ.

A fix against the attack. To block the distinguisher, it suffices to use the Full-RepresentInteger variant that we described in Algorithm 1 during Step 3 of Algorithm 8, instead of RepresentInteger. This alternate version of the algorithm was designed specifically to produce solutions γ that were not necessarily contained in $\langle 1, i, j, k \rangle$. If $\gamma = (x' + y'i + z'j + t'k)/2$ it is easy to see that $\gamma \notin \langle 1, i, j, k \rangle$ as soon as $(x', y', z', t') \neq (0, 0, 0, 0) \mod 2$. Our analysis at the end of Sect. 3.1 showed that there were 4 possible configurations for $(x', y', z', t') \mod 2$ and each can be obtained when the value of m' is bigger than 1 (which we may assume). The reasoning above justifies that $\#I_\tau^1 > 1$ but not that it reaches the desired value of 3. Let us write I_1, I_2 the two other $\mathcal{O}_0$ ideals of norm 2. It can be verified that $I_1 = I_2 i$. Since $(x' + y'i + z'j + t'k)i = -y' + x'i + t'j - z'k$, it is easy to see that if some outputs of FullRepresentInteger are contained in I_1, then the same must be true for I_2 (and conversely). This proves that $\#I_\tau^1 = 3$, i.e., all three first steps are possible. Yet, there could still be a bias in the distribution of that step, which would still give rise to an attack on Problem 14. We argue in the next section that there is no such exploitable bias. Note that with the modifications we just described, the set $\mathcal{P}_{N_\tau}$ must be updated accordingly to obtain security under the hardness of Problem 14.

6.2   Further Analysis on the First Steps of σ

We continue the analysis by looking at what happens beyond the first 2-isogeny of the elements $\iota \in \mathcal{P}_{N_\tau}$. Henceforth, we will consider the set $\mathcal{P}_{N_\tau}$ associated to a modified version of SigningKLPT. First, we replace RepresentInteger by FullRepresentInteger as suggested in Sect. 6.1. Second, we modify the computation of the exponent e_0. Instead of setting a unique value $e_0(N)$ and then taking $e_0 = e_0(N)$, we propose to take $e_0(N)$ as a range of values from which e_0 will be sampled. The rationale behind this last modification is to cover more γ's (and expand the size of I_τ^k as a result) and it will play a role in the proof of Proposition 20. The proposed range for $e_0(N)$ will be given precisely below.

For any $k \in \mathbb{N}$ smaller than e, let us define $\pi_k : \iota \mapsto \iota_k$ where ι_k is the unique isogeny of degree 2^k such that $\iota = \iota' \circ \iota_k$. We will study the sets $I_\tau^k = \pi_k(\mathcal{P}_{N_\tau})$. We will start by trying to estimate $\#I_\tau^k$ for values of $k \approx 1/2 \log(p)$. Our analysis culminates in Proposition 20, which we prove under several plausible assumptions. Even though it does not prove that Problem 14 is hard, showing that $\#I_\tau^k$ is exponential in the security parameter rules out attacks similar to the one outlined in Sect. 6.1.

A truly meaningful result would be to show that the distribution $\mathcal{D}_\tau^k$ of the $\pi_k(\iota)$ when ι is uniformly random in $\mathcal{P}_{N_\tau}$ is indistinguishable from the uniform distribution on the isogenies of degree 2^k. In the end of this section, we will try to argue that the $\mathcal{D}_\tau^k$ are not biased for small values of k. The result we obtain are not very formal but we back them up with experimental results.

The size of I_τ^k. Our goal is to show that I_τ^k contains a good portion of the isogenies of degree 2^k for values of $k \approx p^{1/2}$. Our final result is stated in Proposition 20 and basically follows from the fact that the isogenies of I_τ^k only depend on the quaternion element γ of norm $N\ell^{e_0}$ when $k \leq e_0$ (this fact follows from the analysis underlying Lemma 12). We recall that in the definition of $\mathcal{P}_{N_\tau}$, γ is a possible output of FullRepresentInteger such that the end of the computation in Algorithm 8 terminates. Thus, one of the main ingredients of our proof is a result (stated as Proposition 17) on the number of γ of norm M that can be obtained as output of FullRepresentInteger. We use the notation Γ_M for the set of primitive $\gamma \in \mathcal{O}_0$ of norm M.

For Proposition 17, we assume that the algorithm Cornacchia outputs $\perp$ on input M' when M' is not a near-prime (the multiple of a prime by a smooth factor) or if M' is a near-prime but cannot be represented by the quadratic form $x^2 + y^2$. Otherwise, the algorithm outputs any of the possible solutions to the quadratic equation.

Proposition 17. *Let $M > p$. Under plausible heuristics, there exists a constant $c_1 > 0$ such that the number of $\gamma \in \Gamma_M$ that are possible outputs of FullRepresent-Integer on input M is larger than $\#\Gamma_M c_1 / \log(M)$.*

Proof. Let $2\gamma = x' + iy' + jz' + kt'$ and $M' = 4M - p(f(z', t'))$. Given our assumption on Cornacchia, γ is going to be an admissible output if and only if M' is a near-prime and the pair z', t' can be sampled during the first two steps of Algorithm 3. For z', t' it is easy to verify that this is the case. Indeed, the value of $|z'|$ must be smaller than $2m$. Thus, there is a possibility that this value is picked. After that, we know that the correct value of $|t'|$ must be smaller than m' and so there is also a possibility that the correct value is picked. Then, under the assumption that the M' behave as normal integers of the same size, we get that there exists a constant c_1 such that a fraction $c_1 / \log(M)$ of all the M' are near-primes. Thus, the same fraction of γ are going to be possible outputs of FullRepresentInteger and this concludes the proof.

Before proceeding to the last part of the proof, we will need some of the estimates used in [9, Section 6.4]. We give without proof a reformulation of [9, Lemmas 9 and 10] as Lemmas 18 and 19.

Lemma 18. *There exists $\varepsilon = O(\log\log(p))$ such that for a random class $\mathcal{C} \in \mathrm{Cl}(\mathcal{O}_0)$, the norm N of EquivalentPrimeIdeal($\mathcal{C}$) verifies $\log(p)/2 - \varepsilon < \log(N) < \log(p)/2 + \varepsilon$ with overwhelming probability.*

Lemma 19. *For any $\kappa \in \mathbb{N}$, there exists $\eta_0 = O(\log\log(p) + \log(\kappa))$ such that for any $e_0 \geq \log(p) - \log(N) + \varepsilon + \eta_0$, the probability that there exists a solution $\gamma = $ FullRepresentInteger($N\ell^{e_0}$) that will lead to a correct execution of SigningKLPT is higher than $1 - 2^{-\kappa}$.*

We recall that we study $\mathcal{P}_{N_\tau}$ for a modified version of SigningKLPT (the full list of changes is given in the beginning of this section) that samples the exponent e_0 inside a range that we denote by $e_0(N)$. We define $e_0(N) = [\log_2(p) - \log_2(N) + \varepsilon + \eta_0, \log_2(p) - \log_2(N) + \varepsilon + \eta_0 + \delta]$, where ε, η_0 are defined as in Lemmas 18 and 19 (these results tells us that the execution of SigningKLPT succeeds with overwhelming probability when $e_0 \in e_0(N)$). We also introduce the variable parameter δ upon which the statement of Proposition 20 will depend. If we want that SigningKLPT terminates with overwhelming probability we need to have $\delta = O(\log \log(p))$ so that $e_1 = e - e_0$ remains in the range prescribed by [9, Lemma 11].

Proposition 20. *Let δ be a positive value and ε, η_0 be as defined for Lemmas 18 and 19. If $k \in [\frac{\log_\ell(p)}{2} + \eta_0, \frac{\log_\ell(p)}{2} + 2\varepsilon + \eta_0 + \delta]$, then under plausible heuristics there exists a constant $c > 0$ such that*

$$\#I_\tau^k \geq c \cdot 2 \cdot 3^{k-1}/(\log(p) + \delta).$$

Proof. Let φ be an isogeny of degree 2^k. We write I_φ for the corresponding ideal and $L_\varphi = \mathsf{EquivalentPrimeIdeal}(I_\varphi)$, $N_\varphi = n(L_\varphi)$. There exists a quaternion element γ_φ of norm $N_\varphi 2^k$ such that $\mathcal{O}_0 \gamma_\varphi = I_\varphi \cdot \overline{L}_\varphi$. It can be easily verified that $\varphi \in I_\tau^k$ if and only γ_φ is in the set of possible γ involved in the definition of $\mathcal{P}_{N_\tau}$. We write this set Γ_τ. For γ_φ to be in Γ_τ, we need to verify the following things: $k \in e_0(N_\varphi)$, γ_φ is a possible output of $\mathsf{FullRepresentInteger}$ on input $N_\varphi 2^k$ and the rest of the computation of SigningKLPT (Step 4 to Step 7) must succeed from γ_φ.

Lemmas 18 and 19 and the definition of $e_0(N)$ and k ensures that only a negligible number of isogenies φ would have $k \notin e_0(N_\varphi)$. After that, if we assume that γ_φ is distributed correctly in the $\Gamma_{N_\varphi 2^k}$, Proposition 17 tells us there exists a constant $c_2 > 0$ such that more than a fraction $c_2/(\log(p) + \delta)$ of the γ_φ will be possible outputs of $\mathsf{FullRepresentInteger}$. Finally, we can make the assumption that a constant fraction of those γ_φ will satisfy the last requirement (see the analysis led in [8] to justify this assumption). Thus, we obtain that there exists some constant $c > 0$ such that a fraction bigger than $c/(\log(p) + \delta)$ of all the γ_φ are contained in Γ_τ, and we can conclude the proof.

Proposition 20 does not fully rule out a simple distinguisher. Proposition 20 proves that I_τ^k is large, which is necessary for security. To rule out the distinguisher, one needs to understand the distribution, which is the matter of the following paragraph.

The distribution $\mathcal{D}_\tau^k$ is another matter of importance. Biased distributions, especially for small values of k, can be easily detected which would break Problem 14. Once again, our analysis focuses on the quaternion element γ and on the distribution $\mathcal{O}_0\langle\gamma, \ell^k\rangle$ among the ideals of norm 2^k. If $2\gamma = x + yi + zj + tk$ for $x, y, z, t \in \mathbb{Z}$, it can be shown that $\mathcal{O}_0\langle\gamma, \ell^k\rangle$ will depend on the values of (x, y, z, t) mod $(2\ell^k)$. It is easy to argue that the values of z, t are sampled without any bias mod $(2\ell^k)$ when m', m'' are big enough compared to ℓ^k (which we may assume since we look at small values of k). After that, we can only argue informally that the near-primality condition on $M - pf(z, t)$ should not introduce any bias on the value of $z, t \mod 2 \cdot \ell^k$. It also seems plausible that the output of Cornacchia on random near-prime inputs of a given size should not skew the distribution of x, y but we cannot really prove it.

The formulation of our new algorithm FullRepresentInteger avoids several pitfalls that would have lead to noticeable bias in the distribution of $x, y, z, t \mod 2$. This is for instance the explanation behind Remark 5.

Experimental evidence. We present below in Fig. 2 the result of an experiment to study the distributions $\mathcal{D}_\tau^k$ for small values of k. The results are consistent with our informal analysis.

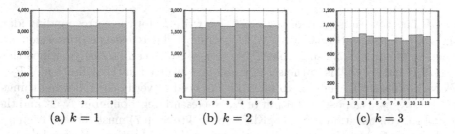

(a) $k = 1$ (b) $k = 2$ (c) $k = 3$

Fig. 2. Distribution of the k-first steps of σ for 10 SQISign keys and random ideal in input over 1000 attempts.

7   Open Problems

Arguably, the contributions presented in this work bring off solid progress towards the development of practical and secure SQISign signatures. Nevertheless, a number of questions remains open. The first one is about efficiency. In particular, we need finer cost metrics to improve our understanding of our algorithm's behavior. This is important for both optimization and parameter selection. The second one is about further improvements of the ideal-to-isogeny procedure. Our new algorithm simplifies and improves upon the method from [8], yet it is still slow and the algorithm remains convoluted. Short of any radically new ideas, one might try to improve what we already have. The impact of improving the quality of the outputs of KLPT has been argued in [8], and the same is true for SpecialEichlerNorm. In general, any improvement in solving norm equations inside the lattices of $B_{p,\infty}$ could have a positive impact on our scheme. Finally, cryptanalysis of SQISign still needs maturity. We provided some heuristic evidence that our proposed fixes prevent distinguishing attacks. However, future work should try to come up with a formal proof, even based on heuristics, that distributions of simulated transcripts are statistically close to real ones.

References

1. Arpin, S., Chen, M., Lauter, K.E., Scheidler, R., Stange, K.E., Tran, H.T.N.: Orienteering with one endomorphism. Cryptology ePrint Archive, Report 2022/098 (2022), https://eprint.iacr.org/2022/098

2. Bernstein, D.J., De Feo, L., Leroux, A., Smith, B.: Faster computation of isogenies of large prime degree. Open Book Series **4**(1), 39–55 (2020). https://doi.org/10.2140/obs.2020.4.39

3. Castryck, W., Decru, T.: An efficient key recovery attack on SIDH (preliminary version). Cryptology ePrint Archive, Report 2022/975 (2022), https://eprint.iacr.org/2022/975

4. Cornacchia, G.: Su di un metodo per la risoluzione in numeri interi dell'equazione $\sum_{h=0}^{n} c_h x^{n-h} y^h = p$. Giornale di Matematiche di Battaglini **46**, 33–90 (1908)

5. Costello, C.: B-SIDH: supersingular isogeny diffie-hellman using twisted torsion. In: Moriai, S., Wang, H. (eds.) ASIACRYPT 2020. LNCS, vol. 12492, pp. 440–463. Springer, Cham (2020). https://doi.org/10.1007/978-3-030-64834-3_15

6. Costello, C., Meyer, M., Naehrig, M.: Sieving for twin smooth integers with solutions to the prouhet-tarry-escott problem. In: Canteaut, A., Standaert, F.-X. (eds.) EUROCRYPT 2021. LNCS, vol. 12696, pp. 272–301. Springer, Cham (2021). https://doi.org/10.1007/978-3-030-77870-5_10

7. De Feo, L., et al.: Séta: supersingular encryption from torsion attacks. In: Tibouchi, M., Wang, H. (eds.) ASIACRYPT 2021. LNCS, vol. 13093, pp. 249–278. Springer, Cham (2021). https://doi.org/10.1007/978-3-030-92068-5_9

8. De Feo, L., Kohel, D., Leroux, A., Petit, C., Wesolowski, B.: SQISign: compact postquantum signatures from quaternions and isogenies. In: Moriai, S., Wang, H. (eds.) ASIACRYPT 2020. LNCS, vol. 12491, pp. 64–93. Springer, Cham (2020). https://doi.org/10.1007/978-3-030-64837-4_3

9. De Feo, L., Kohel, D., Leroux, A., Petit, C., Wesolowski, B.: SQISign: compact postquantum signatures from quaternions and isogenies. Cryptology ePrint Archive, Report 2020/1240 (2020), https://eprint.iacr.org/2020/1240

10. De Feo, L., Masson, S., Petit, C., Sanso, A.: Verifiable delay functions from supersingular isogenies and pairings. In: Galbraith, S.D., Moriai, S. (eds.) ASIACRYPT 2019. LNCS, vol. 11921, pp. 248–277. Springer, Cham (2019). https://doi.org/10.1007/978-3-030-34578-5_10

11. Deuring, M.: Die Typen der Multiplikatorenringe elliptischer Funktionenkörper. Abhandlungen aus dem Mathematischen Seminar der Universität Hamburg **14**(1), 197–272 (1941)

12. Eisenträger, K., Hallgren, S., Lauter, K., Morrison, T., Petit, C.: Supersingular isogeny graphs and endomorphism rings: reductions and solutions. In: Nielsen, J.B., Rijmen, V. (eds.) EUROCRYPT 2018. LNCS, vol. 10822, pp. 329–368. Springer, Cham (2018). https://doi.org/10.1007/978-3-319-78372-7_11

13. Fiat, A., Shamir, A.: How to prove yourself: practical solutions to identification and signature problems. In: Odlyzko, A.M. (ed.) CRYPTO 1986. LNCS, vol. 263, pp. 186–194. Springer, Heidelberg (1987). https://doi.org/10.1007/3-540-47721-7_12

14. Galbraith, S.D., Petit, C., Silva, J.: Identification protocols and signature schemes based on supersingular isogeny problems. J. Cryptol. **33**(1), 130–175 (2019). https://doi.org/10.1007/s00145-019-09316-0

15. Kohel, D.: Endomorphism rings of elliptic curves over finite fields. Ph.D. thesis, University of California at Berkley (1996), http://www.i2m.univ-amu.fr/perso/david.kohel/pub/thesis.pdf

16. Kohel, D.R., Lauter, K., Petit, C., Tignol, J.P.: On the quaternion ℓ-isogeny path problem. LMS J. Comput. Math. **17**(A), 418–432 (2014). https://doi.org/10.1112/S1461157014000151

17. Leroux, A.: A new isogeny representation and applications to cryptography. In: Agrawal, S., Lin, D. (eds.) ASIACRYPT 2022, Part II. LNCS, vol. 13792, pp. 3–35. Springer, Heidelberg (Dec 2022). https://doi.org/10.1007/978-3-031-22966-4_1

18. Longa, P.: Efficient algorithms for large prime characteristic fields and their application to bilinear pairings and supersingular isogeny-based protocols. Cryptology ePrint Archive, Report 2022/367 (2022), https://eprint.iacr.org/2022/367
19. Love, J., Boneh, D.: Supersingular curves with small noninteger endomorphisms. Open Book Series 4(1), 7–22 (2020). https://doi.org/10.2140/obs.2020.4.7
20. Maino, L., Martindale, C.: An attack on SIDH with arbitrary starting curve. Cryptology ePrint Archive, Report 2022/1026 (2022), https://eprint.iacr.org/2022/1026
21. Robert, D.: Breaking SIDH in polynomial time. Cryptology ePrint Archive, Report 2022/1038 (2022), https://eprint.iacr.org/2022/1038
22. Silverman, J.H.: The Arithmetic of Elliptic Curves, Gradute Texts in Mathematics, vol. 106. Springer-Verlag (1986)
23. Vélu, J.: Isogénies entre courbes elliptiques. Comptes rendus de l'Académie des Sciences, Séries A-B **273**, A238–A241 (1971)
24. Waterhouse, W.C.: Abelian varieties over finite fields. Annales scientifiques de l'École Normale Supérieure **2**(4), 521–560 (1969)
25. Wesolowski, B.: Orientations and the supersingular endomorphism ring problem. In: Dunkelman, O., Dziembowski, S. (eds.) EUROCRYPT 2022, Part III. LNCS, vol. 13277, pp. 345–371. Springer, Heidelberg (May / Jun 2022). https://doi.org/10.1007/978-3-031-07082-2_13
26. Wesolowski, B.: The supersingular isogeny path and endomorphism ring problems are equivalent. In: 2021 IEEE 62nd Annual Symposium on Foundations of Computer Science (FOCS), pp. 1100–1111 (2022). https://doi.org/10.1109/FOCS52979.2021.00109

Revisiting BBS Signatures

Stefano Tessaro and Chenzhi Zhu[✉]

Paul G. Allen School of Computer Science & Engineering, University of Washington,
Seattle, USA
{tessaro,zhucz20}@cs.washington.edu

Abstract. BBS signatures were implicitly proposed by Boneh, Boyen,
and Shacham (CRYPTO '04) as part of their group signature scheme,
and explicitly cast as stand-alone signatures by Camenisch and Lysyanskaya (CRYPTO '04). A provably secure version, called BBS+, was then
devised by Au, Susilo, and Mu (SCN '06), and is currently the object
of a standardization effort which has led to a recent RFC draft. BBS+
signatures are suitable for use within anonymous credential and DAA
systems, as their algebraic structure enables efficient proofs of knowledge of message-signature pairs that support partial disclosure.

BBS+ signatures consist of one group element and two scalars. As our
first contribution, we prove that a variant of BBS+ producing shorter
signatures, consisting only of one group element and one scalar, is also
secure. The resulting scheme is essentially the original BBS proposal,
which was lacking a proof of security. Here we show it satisfies, under
the q-SDH assumption, the same provable security guarantees as BBS+.
We also provide a complementary tight analysis in the algebraic group
model, which heuristically justifies instantiations with potentially shorter
signatures.

Furthermore, we devise simplified and shorter zero-knowledge proofs
of knowledge of a BBS message-signature pair that support partial disclosure of the message. Over the BLS12-381 curve, our proofs are 896 bits
shorter than the prior proposal by Camenisch, Drijvers, and Lehmann
(TRUST '16), which is also adopted by the RFC draft.

Finally, we show that BBS satisfies one-more unforgeability in the
algebraic group model in a scenario, arising in the context of credentials,
where the signer can be asked to sign arbitrary group elements, meant
to be commitments, without seeing their openings.

1 Introduction

The seminal works of Camenisch and Lysyanskaya [16,17] highlighted how certain digital signature schemes with suitable algebraic structures are amenable
to applications such as anonymous credentials, direct anonymous attestation
(DAA), and group signatures. These schemes easily enable the signing of a *commitment*, typically by being algebraically compatible with a Pedersen commitment [31], and support very efficient zero-knowledge proofs of knowledge of a
valid message-signature pair.

© International Association for Cryptologic Research 2023
C. Hazay and M. Stam (Eds.): EUROCRYPT 2023, LNCS 14008, pp. 691–721, 2023.
https://doi.org/10.1007/978-3-031-30589-4_24

This paper revisits and improves BBS signatures [6,10,15], one of the most efficient pairing-based schemes with these properties, which has recently been in the midst of renewed interest in the context of decentralized identity. This has led to reference implementations [1,2], to a standardization effort by the W3C Verifiable Credentials Working group, and to an RFC draft [28]. BBS is also a building block for DAA [12,15,18], and is used by Intel SGX's EPID protocol [13]. Furthermore, BBS signatures are theoretically interesting, due to their simplicity and efficiency. Most applications, and the RFC draft, consider the provably-secure version of BBS referred to as BBS+ [6,15], whose signatures consist of *one* group element in $\mathbb{G}_1$ and *two* scalars in $\mathbb{Z}_p$, where p is the group order.

OUR CONTRIBUTIONS, IN A NUTSHELL. As our first main contribution, we prove the strong unforgeability of a variant of BBS+ which produces shorter signatures only consisting of one group element and one scalar. The resulting scheme is in fact the original BBS signature scheme by Boneh, Boyen, and Shacham [10] as stated by Camenisch and Lysyanskaya [17], for which however no proof of security was known. Our new proof gives us a more efficient version of the scheme that can replace BBS+ in applications and standards with no loss, and re-affirms the security of prior works (e.g., [12,18]) which already used this optimized version but relied on an incorrect proof.

Furthermore, we provide a tighter security proof in the Algebraic Group Model [23], which also supports potentially shorter signatures. We also optimize the associated proofs of knowledge of BBS signatures, achieving substantial savings over the current state-of-the-art [28]. Finally, we study the security of BBS in contexts where group elements are signed, and show that the scheme satisfies, in the AGM, a security property which is a natural weakening of what is achieved by structure-preserving signatures [5].

BBS+. The BBS+ scheme was proposed by Au, Susilo, and Mu [6], based on ideas by [10,17], and proved secure under the q-SDH assumption. The proof was then adapted to type-3 pairings by Camenisch, Drijvers, and Lehmann [15]. It signs vectors $\boldsymbol{m} \in \mathbb{Z}_p^\ell$. To do so, the public parameters consist of $\ell+2$ generators $g_1, h_0, h_1, \ldots, h_\ell \in \mathbb{G}_1$, and a signature has the format (A, e, s), where $s, e \in \mathbb{Z}_p$ are randomly chosen, and

$$A = \left(g_1 h_0^s \prod_{i=1}^{\ell} h_i^{m[i]} \right)^{\frac{1}{x+e}} .$$

Here, $x \in \mathbb{Z}_p$ is the secret key, and given the public key $X_2 = g_2^x \in \mathbb{G}_2$, and a pairing, it is easy to verify a valid BBS+ signature.

SECURITY FOR BBS SIGNATURES. The only difference between BBS and BBS+ is the additional term h_0^s in the latter, which mandates the inclusion of s in the signature. A natural question is whether this term is necessary, or instead an artifact of the proofs [6,15]. Indeed, no attack seems to affect plain BBS, without the term h_0^s, but prior proof attempts (e.g., [12]) contained fundamental errors.

We prove that (plain) BBS signatures are indeed secure under the q-SDH assumption. The concrete security guarantees are essentially identical to those established for BBS+, and this suggests a more efficient drop-in replacement for BBS+ in existing applications. Our techniques close in particular gaps left by incorrect proofs, and can be used to prove exculpability of the original BBS group signature scheme [10].

TIGHT AGM BOUNDS. Our new proof, not unlike the prior proofs for BBS+, is not tight, i.e., it incurs a multiplicative loss equal to the number of signing queries q. As a strong hint that this loss may be artificial, we give a tight proof for BBS signatures in the Algebraic Group Model [23].

Our AGM analysis also addresses a different artificial aspect of the standard-model analysis, namely the random choice of e values from $\mathbb{Z}_p$. Instead, our AGM analysis merely asks that these values are unlikely to collide, and their collision probability becomes a term (meant to be negligible) in the security bound. This allows for more flexibility, in that the e values could be generated from a counter or (assuming random oracles) as a hash of the message. It also suggests a BBS variant, which we call *truncated BBS*, where e is chosen from $\mathbb{Z}_{2^{2\lambda}}$, where λ is the desired security level (typically, $\lambda = 128$). On BLS12-381, this does not have any benefit. However, as in all schemes based on q-SDH, one may want to assess the potential impact of attacks such as those by Brown and Gallant [14] and Cheon [20] and choose an even bigger curve—in that case, truncation of the scalar may become effective.

SIGNING COMMITMENTS. An important question is to which extent BBS can be thought as a signature scheme signing a user-supplied group element, i.e., an element $C \in \mathbb{G}_1$ is signed as $(C^{\frac{1}{x+e}}, e)$. Indeed, in the context of blind issuance of credentials, one can think of $C = g_1 h_1^{m_1} \cdots h_\ell^{m_\ell}$ as a commitment sent from the user to the signer, and the signer's response $(C^{1/(x+e)}, e)$ is a valid BBS signature on $\boldsymbol{m} = (m_1, \ldots, m_\ell)$. It is not hard to see that this form of BBS does not yield a secure signature scheme over group elements as e.g., a signature on C can easily be transformed, by squaring it, into a signature on C^2. However, we show that, in the AGM, BBS satisfies a form of one-more unforgeability, where obtaining signatures of q group elements does not enable the attacker to produce valid BBS signatures (e.g., by "opening" these group elements as commitments) on more than q messages. This is sufficient in the context of blind issuance.

ZERO-KNOWLEDGE PoKs. We also revisit the problem of proving knowledge of a BBS message-signature pair with new zero-knowledge proofs of knowledge which are shorter than state-of-the art solutions adopted in the RFC draft [28] and initially proposed in [15]. To prove knowledge of a BBS message-signature pair $(\boldsymbol{m}, \sigma)$, without revealing k out of the ℓ components of $\boldsymbol{m}$, our proof (when compiled as a NIZK via the Fiat-Shamir transform) consists of 2 elements in $\mathbb{G}_1$, as well as $k + 3$ scalars in $\mathbb{Z}_p$. The proof adopted in the RFC draft, in contrast, consists of 3 elements in $\mathbb{G}_1$, and $k + 5$ scalars. While a reduction by one scalar is possible due to our removal of the random value s from a signature, the remaining optimizations are the result of a different approach.

RELATED SCHEMES. We note that when signing individual elements of $\mathbb{Z}_p$, the simpler Boneh-Boyen signatures [9] would typically outperform BBS. The closest scheme to BBS is the one by Pointcheval-Sanders (PS) [32]. PS signatures consist of two group elements, and are comparably efficient to the short version of BBS from this paper. However, both the public and the secret keys grow linearly with ℓ, the length of the message vector to be signed, whereas in BBS they consist of a single element. (The group generators in BBS can be generated as the output of a hash function, and they should not be part of the key materials.) PS signatures feature properties which BBS does not possess, including re-randomizability and aggregability. The latter property is essential for their use in the recent Coconut system [33], for which BBS does not appear suitable.

OUTLINE. Our new proof for BBS is given in Sect. 3, followed by our AGM analysis in Sect. 4. Our new zero-knowledge proofs are given in Sect. 5, and our analysis of BBS as a signature scheme on group elements is in Sect. 6. We give a technical overview next.

1.1   Technical Overview

NEW BBS PROOF. It is instructive to first review existing proofs [6,15] for BBS+. To this end, we consider the special case where we sign a *single* scalar $m \in \mathbb{Z}_p$, i.e., a signature under secret key $x \in \mathbb{Z}_p$ takes form, for random $s, e \in \mathbb{Z}_p$,

$$\sigma = (A, s, e) , \quad \text{where } A = (g_1 h_0^s h_1^m)^{\frac{1}{x+e}} .$$

If an attacker obtains q adaptively chosen signatures (A_i, s_i, e_i) for message $m_i \in \mathbb{Z}_p$ and finally produces a valid forgery (A^*, e^*, s^*) for a message $m^* \in \mathbb{Z}_p$, we can identify three cases, which are to be addressed differently:

(1) There exists an $i \in [q]$ such that $A_i = A^*$ and $e_i = e^*$
(2) There exists an $i \in [q]$ such that $A_i \neq A^*$ and $e_i = e^*$
(3) $e^* \notin \{e_1, \ldots, e_q\}$.

The most challenging case is **(2)**. Indeed, **(1)** implies that $g_1 h_0^{s_i} h_1^{m_i} = g_1 h_0^{s^*} h_1^{m^*}$, while $(s_i, m_i) \neq (s^*, m^*)$, which in turn implies a break of the discrete logarithm assumption in $\mathbb{G}_1$. For **(3)**, instead, one resorts to a by-now classical technique by Boneh and Boyen [9]. The key point here is that to break q-SDH, given $g_1, g_1^x, \ldots, g_1^{x^q} \in \mathbb{G}_1$, along with g_2, g_2^x in $\mathbb{G}_2$, it is enough to compute $g_1^{p(x)/(x+e)}$, for a polynomial $p(\mathsf{X})$ which is not divisible by $\mathsf{X} + e$. This indeed allows us to recover $g_1^{1/(x+e)}$, which gives us a valid q-SDH solution.

To do so, the reduction picks $e_1, \ldots, e_q$ ahead of time. It uses g_2^x as the public key, but uses new generators $\overline{g}_1 = g_1^{\theta p(x)}$, $h_0 = g_1^{\alpha p(x)}$ and $h_1 = g_1^{\beta p(x)}$ for $\mathbb{G}_1$, where $p(\mathsf{X}) = \prod_{i=1}^q (\mathsf{X} + e_i)$ and $\alpha, \beta, \theta \leftarrow_\$ \mathbb{Z}_p$. Note that $\overline{g}_1, h_0, h_1$ can easily be computed from $g_1^{x^i}$ for $i \in [q]$, since $p(\mathsf{X})$ has degree q, and that for any m, s, and $i \in [q]$, the reduction can always simulate a signature $(\overline{g}_1 h_0^s h_1^m)^{\frac{1}{x+e_i}}$, since $p(\mathsf{X})$ is divisible by $\mathsf{X} + e_i$. Moreover, a forgery for $e^* \notin \{e_1, \ldots, e_q\}$, allows us to compute $(e^*, g_1^{\frac{1}{x+e^*}})$, and break q-SDH.

HANDLING CASE (2). The value s was crucial in [6,15] to deal with (2). To see how it was used, let us assume that we can actually guess the index i for which (2) occurs. Then, with $p'(\mathsf{X}) = \prod_{j \neq i}(\mathsf{X} + e_j)$, the reduction can set

$$\overline{g}_1 = g_1^{\theta p'(x)}, \quad h_0 = \overline{g}_1^{\frac{(x+e_i)\delta - 1}{\alpha}}, \quad h_1 = h_0^\beta.$$

Queries for $j \neq i$ can be answered as above for any (s, m), since $p'(\mathsf{X})$ is divisible by $\mathsf{X} + e_i$. In contrast, for the i-th query, on message m_i, the reduction can only answer for the specific choice of $s_i = \alpha - \beta \cdot m_i$, since

$$A_i = (\overline{g}_1 h_0^{s_i} h_1^{m_i})^{\frac{1}{x+e_i}} = \left(\overline{g}_1^{(x+e_i)\delta}\right)^{\frac{1}{x+e_i}} = \overline{g}_1^\delta.$$

Despite the fact that s_i depends on m_i, one can show that its distribution is uniform. If the attacker now produces a forgery with $e^* = e_i$, it means that we have

$$A^* = \left(\overline{g}_1 h_0^{s^*} h_1^{m^*}\right)^{\frac{1}{x+e_i}} = \overline{g}_1^{\frac{1}{x+e_i}\left(1 + \frac{(x+e_i)\delta - 1}{\alpha}(s^* + \beta m^*)\right)}$$

and the reduction can solve q-SDH because $1 + \frac{(\mathsf{X}+e_i)\delta - 1}{\alpha}(s^* + \beta m^*)$ is not divisible by $\mathsf{X} + e_i$.

OUR IMPROVEMENT. The reduction for BBS+ programs s in a message-dependent way to handle (2). Our main idea here is to let e play this role instead, thus dispensing with the use of s, and in fact obtaining a slightly simpler reduction. Concretely, for BBS, we drop h_0, as it is not needed any more, and we set up

$$\overline{g}_1 = g_1^{\alpha p'(x)(x+\varepsilon_i)}, \quad h_1 = g_1^{\beta p'(x)}.$$

Here, $p'(\mathsf{X})$ is as above, and $\alpha, \beta, \varepsilon_i$ are random, and, most importantly, ε_i will not necessarily equal e_i. Now, every query $j \neq i$ can be answered as before. To answer the i-th query, however, we first observe that

$$C_i = \overline{g}_1 h_1^{m_i} = g_1^{\alpha p'(x)(x+\varepsilon_i)} \cdot g_1^{\beta p'(x) m_i} = g_1^{\alpha p'(x)(x+\varepsilon_i+\frac{\beta}{\alpha}m_i)}.$$

We are going to show that if we set $e_i = \varepsilon_i + \frac{\beta}{\alpha}m_i$, not only we can compute $A_i = C_i^{\frac{1}{x+e_i}}$, but also, this e_i has the right distribution. This last argument is somewhat involved. For example, it turns out that if message m_i is such that $x + \varepsilon_i + \frac{\beta}{\alpha}m_i = 0$, the distribution of e_i is not correct. Luckily, however, this is the only case, and moreover, if this indeed happened, this would mean $x = -\varepsilon_i - \frac{\beta}{\alpha}m_i$, and we could break q-SDH directly. If we then obtain a forgery (A^*, e^*) with $e^* = e_i$ for a message m^*, we note that the discrete logarithm of A^* is

$$\mathrm{DL}_{g_1}(A^*) = \frac{\alpha p'(x)(x + \varepsilon_i + \frac{\beta}{\alpha}m^*)}{x + \varepsilon_i + \frac{\beta}{\alpha}m_i}.$$

However, one can show that $\mathsf{X} + \varepsilon_i + \frac{\beta}{\alpha}m_i$ does not divide $\alpha p'(\mathsf{X})(\mathsf{X} + \varepsilon_i + \frac{\beta}{\alpha}m^*)$ if $m_i \neq m^*$.

AGM SECURITY. In the AGM, we restrict our focus to algebraic adversaries, and in the case of BBS, this means that the adversary outputs a forgery A^* and its representation in terms of $g_1, h_1, \ldots, h_\ell$, as well as the $\mathbb{G}_1$-part the prior signatures $A_1, \ldots, A_q$. We note that the discrete logarithm of each A_i equals $\varphi^{\boldsymbol{y}}_{\boldsymbol{m}_i, e_i}(x)$, where x is the secret key, $\boldsymbol{y}$ is the vectors of discrete logarithms of h_1 relative to g_1, and

$$\varphi^{\boldsymbol{y}}_{\boldsymbol{m}_i, e_i}(\mathsf{X}) = \frac{1 + \langle \boldsymbol{y}, \boldsymbol{m}_i \rangle}{\mathsf{X} + e_i}.$$

Analogously, the discrete logarithm of A^* for a forgery A^*, e^* for a message $\boldsymbol{m}^*$ equals $\varphi^{\boldsymbol{y}}_{\boldsymbol{m}^*, e^*}(x)$. Further, the algebraic adversary gives us a representation of $\varphi^{\boldsymbol{y}}_{\boldsymbol{m}^*, e^*}(x)$ as an affine combination of the $\varphi^{\boldsymbol{y}}_{\boldsymbol{m}_i, e_i}(x)$'s. Our key observation is that unless some very specific properties are satisfied by $\boldsymbol{y}$, the *function* $\varphi^{\boldsymbol{y}}_{\boldsymbol{m}^*, e^*}(\mathsf{X})$, as opposed to its evaluation at x, *cannot* be expressed as an affine combination of the functions $\varphi^{\boldsymbol{y}}_{\boldsymbol{m}_i, e_i}(\mathsf{X})$. Therefore, x must be a zero to a (known) polynomial of degree at most q, and it can be recovered by factoring this polynomial. It also turns out that whenever the choice of $\boldsymbol{y}$ does not allow this argument to go through, we are going to be able to recover a non-trivial discrete-logarithm relation, and break the discrete logarithm problem directly.

BBS SIGNATURES OF COMMITTED VALUES. Our AGM proof will enable us to also study the scenario where the adversary can query an oracle on an arbitrary $C \in \mathbb{G}_1$ and obtain $C^{\frac{1}{x+e}}$ for a random e. We show that in the AGM it is impossible, except with negligible probability, to come up with $q + 1$ valid BBS signatures upon querying this oracle q times. The main difficulty is that an AGM adversary here can query this oracle with group elements which are combinations of the outputs of previous queries. However, we are going to show how an algebraic adversary making q oracle queries can be simulated by one making queries to the actual BBS signing oracle. To do this, we rely on a property of our AGM proof above, namely that the statement holds even if the values $e_1, e_2, \ldots$ are known to the adversary beforehand, and we use this to give an inductive argument which shows how to build these signing queries in order to emulate the oracle signing a group element instead.

NEW PROOFS OF KNOWLEDGE. We give new Σ-protocols to prove knowledge of a message-signature pair for BBS, given, possibly, partial knowledge of the message. Our basic observation is that valid signature (A, e) for $\boldsymbol{m}$ satisfies $\mathsf{e}(A, X_2) = \mathsf{e}(B, g_2)$, where $B = C(\boldsymbol{m})A^{-e}$, and $C(\boldsymbol{m}) = g_1 \prod_{i=1}^{\ell} h_i^{\boldsymbol{m}[i]}$. For the case where $\boldsymbol{m}$ is fully known to the verifier, for example, our prover commits to a randomized version of A, B, namely $\overline{A} = A^r$ and $\overline{B} = B^r = C(\boldsymbol{m})^r \overline{A}^{-e}$. Then, the prover engages in a homomorphism proof [29] to show knowledge of a representation (r, e) of $\overline{B}$ to the base $C(\boldsymbol{m})$ and $\overline{A}$.

2   Preliminaries

NOTATION. We will use the shorthand $[n] = \{1, \ldots, n\}$. We will denote formal variables in polynomials with sans-serif letters $\mathsf{X}, \mathsf{Y}, \ldots$, and for any modulus p, we let $\mathbb{Z}_p[\mathsf{X}]$ be the ring of formal polynomials $a(\mathsf{X}) = \sum_{i=0}^{d} a_i \mathsf{X}^i$ with coefficients in $\mathbb{Z}_p$. As usual, d is the *degree* of $a(\mathsf{X})$.

Throughout the paper, we adopt as far as possible the concrete security and efficiency approach, and avoid qualitative statements. We refer to "efficient" informally to stress that an algorithm is meant to be as efficient as possible, but make theorems precise by giving explicit reductions in their proofs.

GROUPS AND PAIRINGS. We work with prime-order groups. For such a group $\mathbb{G}$, we denote by $1_\mathbb{G}$ the identity element, and let $\mathbb{G}^* = \mathbb{G} \setminus \{1_\mathbb{G}\}$ be the set of $p-1$ generators. We use multiplicative notation, and generally denote group elements with upper case letters, scalars with lower case ones, with the exception of generators. For a generator $g \in \mathbb{G}^*$ and a group element $X \in \mathbb{G}$, we also let $\mathrm{DL}_g(X)$ be the discrete logarithm $x \in \mathbb{Z}_p$ of X to the base g, i.e., $g^x = X$.

For prime-order groups $\mathbb{G}_1, \mathbb{G}_2, \mathbb{G}_T$, a *bilinear map* is an efficiently computable function $\mathsf{e} : \mathbb{G}_1 \times \mathbb{G}_2 \to \mathbb{G}_T$ which satisfies both (1) *bi-linearity*, i.e., $\mathsf{e}(A^x, B^y) = \mathsf{e}(A, B)^{xy}$ for all $A \in \mathbb{G}_1$, $B \in \mathbb{G}_2$, and $x, y \in \mathbb{Z}_p$, and (2) *non-triviality*, i.e., $\mathsf{e}(g_1, g_2) \in \mathbb{G}_T^*$ for all generators $g_1 \in \mathbb{G}_1^*$ and $g_2 \in \mathbb{G}_2^*$. We normally consider a *group parameters generation algorithm* GGen such that $\mathsf{GGen}(1^\lambda)$ outputs a description $(p, \mathbb{G}_1, \mathbb{G}_2, \mathbb{G}_T, \mathsf{e})$ such that $\mathbb{G}_1, \mathbb{G}_2, \mathbb{G}_T$ are groups of order p, $\mathsf{e} : \mathbb{G}_1 \times \mathbb{G}_2 \to \mathbb{G}_T$ is a bilinear map, and p is a λ-bit prime.

Our treatment is compatible with type-3 pairings (cf. e.g. [24]) like BLS curves [7] which allow for some of the most efficient implementations, e.g., using BLS12-381 [11]. The most relevant property is that $\mathbb{G}_1 \neq \mathbb{G}_2$ and no efficiently computable homomorphism $\mathbb{G}_2 \to \mathbb{G}_1$ exists.

SIGNATURE SCHEMES. A *signature scheme* SS consists of a setup algorithm SS.Setup, a *key generation algorithm* SS.KG, a (possibly randomized) *signing algorithm* SS.Sign, and a deterministic *verification algorithm* SS.Ver, satisfying the usual syntax and correctness requirement. In particular, SS.Setup outputs parameters par, upon which all algorithms depend. We also let the message space SS.M = SS.M(par) depend on par. (We implicitly assume that the signing algorithm returns an error symbol $\perp$, which is not a valid signature, if the message is not in the message space.) We target *strong unforgeability*, which is defined by Game $\mathsf{SUF}_{\mathsf{SS}}^{\mathcal{A}}(\lambda)$ in Fig. 1. The corresponding advantage metric is

$$\mathsf{Adv}_{\mathsf{SS}}^{\mathsf{suf}}(\mathcal{A}, \lambda) = \Pr\left[\mathsf{SUF}_{\mathsf{SS}}^{\mathcal{A}}(\lambda)\right] .$$

THE SECURITY ASSUMPTIONS. We will use the following variant of the q-*Strong Diffie-Hellman* (q-SDH) assumption, as defined by Boneh and Boyen [9] in a format meant to support type-3 pairings. It is formalized by Game $q\text{-}\mathsf{SDH}_{\mathsf{GGen}}^{\mathcal{A}}(\lambda)$ on the left of Fig. 2. We also consider the related q-*Discrete Logarithm* (q-DL) assumption, as formulated on the right of Fig. 2 by Game $q\text{-}\mathsf{DL}_{\mathsf{GGen}}^{\mathcal{A}}(\lambda)$, which only differs in the winning condition. We associate with these games the corresponding advantage metrics

$$\mathsf{Adv}_{\mathsf{GGen}}^{q\text{-}\mathsf{sdh}}(\mathcal{A}, \lambda) = \Pr\left[q\text{-}\mathsf{SDH}_{\mathsf{GGen}}^{\mathcal{A}}(\lambda)\right] , \quad \mathsf{Adv}_{\mathsf{GGen}}^{q\text{-}\mathsf{dl}}(\mathcal{A}, \lambda) = \Pr\left[q\text{-}\mathsf{DL}_{\mathsf{GGen}}^{\mathcal{A}}(\lambda)\right] . \quad (1)$$

Game $\mathsf{SUF}_{\mathsf{SS}}^{\mathcal{A}}(\lambda)$:	Oracle $\text{SIGN}(M)$:
$\mathsf{S} \leftarrow \emptyset$, par $\leftarrow_\$ \mathsf{SS}.\mathsf{Setup}(1^\lambda)$	$\sigma \leftarrow_\$ \mathsf{SS}.\mathsf{Sign}(\mathsf{par}, \mathsf{sk}, M)$
$(\mathsf{vk}, \mathsf{sk}) \leftarrow_\$ \mathsf{SS}.\mathsf{KG}(\mathsf{par})$	If $\sigma \neq \perp$ then $\mathsf{S} \overset{\cup}{\leftarrow} \{(M, \sigma)\}$
$(M^*, \sigma^*) \leftarrow_\$ \mathcal{A}^{\text{SIGN}}(\mathsf{par}, \mathsf{vk})$	Return σ
If $(M^*, \sigma^*) \notin \mathsf{S} \wedge \mathsf{SS}.\mathsf{Ver}(\mathsf{par}, \mathsf{vk}, M^*, \sigma^*)$ then	
Return **true**	
Return **false**	

Fig. 1. Strong unforgeability.

Game $q\text{-}\mathsf{SDH}_{\mathsf{GGen}}^{\mathcal{A}}(\lambda)$:	Game $q\text{-}\mathsf{DL}_{\mathsf{GGen}}^{\mathcal{A}}(\lambda)$:
$\mathsf{par} = (p, \mathbb{G}_1, \mathbb{G}_2, \mathbb{G}_T, \mathsf{e}) \leftarrow \mathsf{GGen}(1^\lambda)$	$\mathsf{par} = (p, \mathbb{G}_1, \mathbb{G}_2, \mathbb{G}_T, \mathsf{e}) \leftarrow \mathsf{GGen}(1^\lambda)$
$g_1 \leftarrow_\$ \mathbb{G}_1^*$, $g_2 \leftarrow_\$ \mathbb{G}_2^*$	$g_1 \leftarrow_\$ \mathbb{G}_1^*$, $g_2 \leftarrow_\$ \mathbb{G}_2^*$
$x \leftarrow_\$ \mathbb{Z}_p$	$x \leftarrow_\$ \mathbb{Z}_p$
$(c, Z) \leftarrow_\$ \mathcal{A}(\mathsf{par}, g_1, (g_1^{x^i})_{i \in [q]}, g_2, g_2^x)$	$x' \leftarrow_\$ \mathcal{A}(\mathsf{par}, g_1, (g_1^{x^i})_{i \in [q]}, g_2, g_2^x)$
Return $Z = g_1^{1/(x+c)}$	Return $x' = x$

Fig. 2. Assumptions. The assumptions could also be defined with respect to fixed generators, but this would invalidate some of our security proofs.

We note that the q-SDH assumption implies the q-DL assumption for any q, as finding x implies finding $g_1^{1/(x+c)}$ for any c. The converse is not known to be true *in general*, but it is true for algebraic adversaries [8]. Notation-wise, we drop q whenever it equals one, and refer to the resulting assumption as the *Discrete Logarithm* (DL) assumption.

Remark 1. Our security proofs will repeatedly rely on the observation (due to Boneh and Boyen [9]) that, given $g_1, g_1^x, g_1^{x^2}, \ldots, g_1^{x^q}$, computing $A = g_1^{p(x)/(x-e)}$, for any known non-zero polynomial $p(\mathsf{X}) \in \mathbb{Z}_p[X]$ with degree at most q such that $p(e) \neq 0$, leads to a break q-SDH. This is because, by the polynomial remainder theorem, we can write $p(\mathsf{X}) = d(\mathsf{X})(X - e) + r$, where the remainder $r = p(e) \in \mathbb{Z}_p$ is a non-zero integer mod p, whereas $d(\mathsf{X})$ has degree at most $q - 1$. Therefore, $A = g_1^{d(x)+r/(x-e)}$, and also,

$$(Ag_1^{-d(x)})^{1/r} = g_1^{\frac{1}{x-e}}$$

can be efficiently computed, and $(-e, g_1^{1/(x-e)})$ is a q-SDH solution.

3   New Proof for (Short) BBS Signatures

3.1   Description and Implementation Details

Figure 3 describes a version of BBS with shorter signatures than BBS+ [6]. We refer formally to this scheme as BBS = BBS[GGen, $\mathcal{D}_e$, ℓ], where GGen is a group parameter generator, $\mathcal{D}_e$ is a distribution over $\mathbb{Z}_p$, and $\ell \geq 1$ a parameter. We

Algorithm BBS.Setup(1^λ) :	Algorithm BBS.Sign(sk $= x, \boldsymbol{m}$) :
$(p, \mathbb{G}_1, \mathbb{G}_2, \mathbb{G}_T, e) \leftarrow \mathsf{GGen}(1^\lambda)$	$C \leftarrow g_1 \prod_i h_1[i]^{m[i]}$
$g_1 \leftarrow\!\!{\scriptstyle\$}\ \mathbb{G}_1^*,\ \boldsymbol{h}_1 \leftarrow\!\!{\scriptstyle\$}\ \mathbb{G}_1^\ell,\ g_2 \leftarrow\!\!{\scriptstyle\$}\ \mathbb{G}_2^*$	$e \leftarrow\!\!{\scriptstyle\$}\ \mathcal{D}_e$
par $\leftarrow (p, g_1, \boldsymbol{h}_1, g_2, \mathbb{G}_1, \mathbb{G}_2, \mathbb{G}_T, e)$	$A \leftarrow C^{\frac{1}{x+e}}$
Return *par*	Return $\sigma = (A, e)$
Algorithm BBS.KG(*par*) :	Algorithm BBS.Ver(vk, $\boldsymbol{m}, \sigma = (A, e)$) :
$(p, g_1, \boldsymbol{h}_1, g_2, \mathbb{G}_1, \mathbb{G}_2, \mathbb{G}_T, e) \leftarrow par$	$C \leftarrow g_1 \prod_i h_1[i]^{m[i]}$
$x \leftarrow\!\!{\scriptstyle\$}\ \mathbb{Z}_p;\ X_2 \leftarrow g_2^x$	Return $e(A, g_2^e \mathsf{vk}) = e(C, g_2)$
sk $\leftarrow x$; vk $\leftarrow X_2$	
Return (sk, vk)	

Fig. 3. BBS signature. The scheme is parameterized by GGen, $\mathcal{D}_e$, and the message length $\ell = \ell(\lambda) \geqslant 1$. Here, group operations are in the groups $\mathbb{G}_1$ and $\mathbb{G}_2$ determined by the parameters.

omit $\mathcal{D}_e$ whenever it is understood to be the uniform distribution over $\mathbb{Z}_p$, and ℓ whenever it is clear from the context. Here, the message space is BBS.M $= \mathbb{Z}_p^\ell$, and it depends on the parameters in that the modulus p is determined by GGen via BBS.Setup. There is an unlikely event that the inversion to compute $1/(x+e)$ during signature issuance fails because $x + e = 0$—for ease of syntax, we use the convention that $1/0 = 0$. The BBS$^+$ scheme is a special case where each signed message $\boldsymbol{m}$ is such that its first component, $\boldsymbol{m}[1]$, is randomly chosen. (And, therefore, needs to be made part of the signature.)

MODELING CHOICES. Our modeling is similar to that of [6,10,15], in that in particular we fix the message length via ℓ. One can easily accommodate unbounded-length messages, as in practice, the generators in $\boldsymbol{h}_1$ do not need to be fixed beforehand, and $\boldsymbol{h}_1[i]$ can be the output of a hash function (modeled as a random oracle) on some input that depends on i. This allows us to also sign messages in $\mathbb{Z}_p^+$, given a suitable encoding. (The RFC draft [28] suggests hashing a length-dependent set of parameters into the first message block, although more efficient encodings certainly exist.)

We also model BBS as randomized, as this feature may be useful in some contexts, but we can de-randomize the scheme by applying a PRF to $\boldsymbol{m}$, or (more efficiently) to C, to derive e.

3.2   Security Analysis

We show security of BBS in the standard model, under the q-SDH assumption, for the setting where $\mathcal{D}_e$ is the uniform distribution over $\mathbb{Z}_p$. Here, q is the number of signing queries issued by the signer. Note that this theorem *also* implies security of BBS+, as it corresponds to a special case of BBS where the first block of each signed message is randomly chosen, and included in the signature.

Theorem 1 (Security of BBS). *Let* GGen *be a group parameter generator, producing groups of order* $p = p(\lambda)$*. For every SUF adversary* $\mathcal{A}$ *issuing at most*

$q = q(\lambda)$ *signing queries, there exist adversaries* $\mathcal{B}_1$, $\mathcal{B}_2$, *and* $\mathcal{B}_3$ *such that*

$$\mathsf{Adv}^{\mathsf{suf}}_{\mathsf{BBS}[\mathsf{GGen}]}(\mathcal{A}, \lambda) \leqslant q \cdot \mathsf{Adv}^{q\text{-sdh}}_{\mathsf{GGen}}(\mathcal{B}_1, \lambda) + \mathsf{Adv}^{\mathsf{dl}}_{\mathsf{GGen}}(\mathcal{B}_2, \lambda)$$

$$+ \mathsf{Adv}^{q\text{-sdh}}_{\mathsf{GGen}}(\mathcal{B}_3, \lambda) + \frac{q^2}{2p} + \frac{q+2}{p} .$$

The adversaries $\mathcal{B}_1$, $\mathcal{B}_2$ *and* $\mathcal{B}_3$ *are given explicitly in the proof, and run in time roughly comparable to that of* $\mathcal{A}$.

The proof of the theorem is given in Sect. 3.3 below. The concrete bound is essentially the same as prior analyses of BBS+ [6,15], and we incur a factor q loss in the reduction. Below, in Theorem 2, we give a tight reduction to q-DL in the algebraic group model, which suggests this loss may be artificial.

DISCUSSION OF CONCRETE PARAMETERS. Even assuming the tight bound as the correct one, the reliance on q-SDH raises the question of the extent to which parameters should accommodate for Cheon's attack [20] on q-SDH/q-DL, which achieves complexity (roughly) $O(\sqrt{p/q})$ for certain choices of q. The RFC [28] suggests the use of BLS12-381 [11], which gives (roughly) a 256-bit group order. We could accommodate for roughly $q = 2^{36}$, for example, while still having 110-bit security. (This type of reasoning was for example adopted to justify BLS12-381 in zkSNARKs [4].) But even then, we observe that the only way we know to *actually* break BBS via Cheon's attack is the reduction by Jao and Yoshida [27], which requires all signatures to be on the same message, with different e-values.[1] Not only this situation is unlikely to arise, but it *does not* occur if we de-randomize BBS, which is the choice the RFC also adopted for BBS+. It is an excellent question to see whether a similar attack exists even for de-randomized BBS.

3.3   Proof of Theorem 1

Let us consider an interaction of the adversary $\mathcal{A}$ in the SUF game, where the adversary finally outputs a forgery $(\boldsymbol{m}^*, \sigma^*)$, where $\sigma^* = (A^*, e^*)$. We define three events, depending on the specific format of the forgery:

- Forge$_1$: This is the event where σ^* is a valid forgery, and a prior SIGN query has output a signature $\sigma_i = (A_i, e_i)$ for $A_i \neq A^*$, $e_i = e_i^*$, and some message $\boldsymbol{m}_i \neq \boldsymbol{m}^*$.
- Forge$_2$: This is the event where σ^* is a valid forgery, and a prior SIGN query output the *same* signature $\sigma_i = \sigma^*$ for a message $\boldsymbol{m}_i \neq \boldsymbol{m}^*$, or the forgery A^* equals $1_{\mathbb{G}_1}$.
- Forge$_3$: This is the event where σ^* is a valid forgery and completely fresh, i.e., neither of Forge$_1$ or Forge$_2$ occurs.

---

[1] Roughly, their attack considers the setting where $g^{\frac{1}{x+e_i}}$ is obtained for multiple e_i's.

As the union of these three events equal the event that $(\boldsymbol{m}^*, \sigma^*)$ is a valid forgery, the union bound yields

$$\mathsf{Adv}^{\mathsf{suf}}_{\mathsf{BBS}}(\mathcal{A}, \lambda) \leqslant \Pr\left[\mathsf{Forge}_1\right] + \Pr\left[\mathsf{Forge}_2\right] + \Pr\left[\mathsf{Forge}_3\right] .$$

We will proceed in upper bounding these three probabilities via separate reductions. The hardest case is the analysis of Forge_1, and this is where out proof differs from prior work. The analyses of Forge_2 and Forge_3 are essentially the same as in the original analysis of BBS+. The theorem statement then follows by combining Lemmas 1, 2, and 3, which we state next. The proof of Lemma 1 is given below in Sect. 3.4, whereas the proofs of Lemmas 2 and 3, which are more standard, are deferred to the full version.

Lemma 1 (Analysis of Forge_1). *There exists a q-sdh adversary $\mathcal{B}_1$ such that*

$$\Pr\left[\mathsf{Forge}_1\right] \leqslant q \cdot \mathsf{Adv}^{q\text{-sdh}}_{\mathsf{GGen}}(\mathcal{B}_1, \lambda) + \frac{q^2}{2p} + \frac{1}{p} .$$

Lemma 2 (Analysis of Forge_2). *There exists a dl adversary $\mathcal{B}_2$ such that*

$$\Pr\left[\mathsf{Forge}_2\right] \leqslant \mathsf{Adv}^{\mathsf{dl}}_{\mathsf{GGen}}(\mathcal{B}_2, \lambda) + \frac{1}{p} .$$

Lemma 3 (Analysis of Forge_3). *There exists a q-sdh adversary $\mathcal{B}_3$ such that*

$$\Pr\left[\mathsf{Forge}_3\right] \leqslant \mathsf{Adv}^{q\text{-sdh}}_{\mathsf{GGen}}(\mathcal{B}_3, \lambda) + \frac{q}{p} .$$

3.4 Proof of Lemma 1

We give an overview of the adversary $\mathcal{B}_1$ that underlies the reduction to q-SDH for Forge_1. The formal pseudocode description is in Fig. 4, although we omit there some lengthier and tedious descriptions of how to compute certain elements, and give them here in the text instead. Recall that q is a bound on the number of generated signatures, i.e., the number of queries to SIGN issued by the adversary $\mathcal{A}$. We assume here that exactly q queries are made, without loss of generality.

Given the q-SDH setup $g_1, X_{1,1} = g_1^x, \ldots, X_{1,q} = g_1^{x^q}, g_2, X_2 = g_2^x$, the adversary $\mathcal{B}_1$ first generates a suitable setup to run $\mathcal{A}$. In particular, it picks random values $\varepsilon_1, \ldots, \varepsilon_q \leftarrow_{\$} \mathbb{Z}_p$, as well as randomizers $\alpha \leftarrow_{\$} \mathbb{Z}_q^*$ and $\beta_1, \ldots, \beta_q \leftarrow_{\$} \mathbb{Z}_q$. Then, the generators $\bar{g}_1 \in \mathbb{G}_1^*$ and $\boldsymbol{h}_1 \in \mathbb{G}_1^\ell$ are set to

$$\bar{g}_1 = g_1^{\alpha \cdot p(x) \cdot (x + \varepsilon_{i^*})} , \quad \boldsymbol{h}_1[i] \leftarrow g_1^{\beta_i \cdot p(x)} \text{ for all } i \in [\ell],$$

where $i^* \leftarrow_{\$} [q]$ and

$$p(\mathsf{X}) = \prod_{i \in [q] \setminus \{i^*\}} (\mathsf{X} + \varepsilon_i) .$$

Adversary $\mathcal{B}_1(\mathrm{par}, g_1, (X_{1,i})_{i\in[q]}, g_2, X_{2,1})$:	Oracle $\mathrm{SIGN}(\boldsymbol{m})$:
$(p, \mathbb{G}_1, \mathbb{G}_2, \mathbb{G}_T, e) \leftarrow \mathrm{par}$	$\mathrm{cnt} \leftarrow \mathrm{cnt} + 1,\ \boldsymbol{m}_{\mathrm{cnt}} \leftarrow \boldsymbol{m}$

Adversary $\mathcal{B}_1(\mathrm{par}, g_1, (X_{1,i})_{i\in[q]}, g_2, X_{2,1})$:

$(p, \mathbb{G}_1, \mathbb{G}_2, \mathbb{G}_T, e) \leftarrow \mathrm{par}$

$i^* \leftarrow\!\!\$\ [q];\ \mathrm{cnt} \leftarrow 0;\ \mathrm{Sigs} \leftarrow \emptyset;\ x^* \leftarrow \bot$

$\varepsilon_1, \ldots, \varepsilon_q \leftarrow\!\!\$\ \mathbb{Z}_p$

$\alpha \leftarrow\!\!\$\ \mathbb{Z}_p^*;\ \beta_1, \beta_2, \ldots, \beta_\ell \leftarrow\!\!\$\ \mathbb{Z}_p$

$\overline{g}_1 \leftarrow g_1^{\alpha \cdot p(x) \cdot (x + \varepsilon_{i^*})}$

For $i = 1$ to ℓ do $\boldsymbol{h}_1[i] \leftarrow g_1^{\beta_i \cdot p(x)}$

$X_2 \leftarrow X_{2,1};\ \overline{\mathrm{par}} \leftarrow (p, \overline{g}_1, \boldsymbol{h}_1, g_2, \mathbb{G}_1, \mathbb{G}_2, \mathbb{G}_T, e)$

$(\boldsymbol{m}^*, A^*, e^*) \leftarrow\!\!\$\ \mathcal{A}^{\mathrm{SIGN}}(\overline{\mathrm{par}}, X_2)$

$C^* \leftarrow \overline{g}_1 \prod_{i=1}^q \boldsymbol{h}_1[i]^{\boldsymbol{m}^*[i]}$

If $e_{i^*} = e^* \wedge e(A^*, X_2 g_2^{e^*}) = e(C^*, g_2) \wedge$
$\qquad\qquad (A^*, e^*) \notin \mathrm{Sigs}$ then

$\quad$ If $x^* \neq \bot$ then

$\qquad$ Return $(0, g_1^{1/x^*})$ $\qquad$ // direct break

$\quad$ If $e_{i^*} \notin \{e_i\}_{i\in[q]\setminus\{i^*\}}$ then

$\qquad \gamma \leftarrow \sum_{i=1}^\ell \beta_i(\boldsymbol{m}^*[i] - \boldsymbol{m}_{i^*}[i])$

$\qquad$ Return $(e_{i^*}, [A^* \cdot (A_{i^*}^{-1})]^{\frac{1}{\gamma}})$

Oracle $\mathrm{SIGN}(\boldsymbol{m})$:

$\mathrm{cnt} \leftarrow \mathrm{cnt} + 1,\ \boldsymbol{m}_{\mathrm{cnt}} \leftarrow \boldsymbol{m}$

$C_{\mathrm{cnt}} \leftarrow \overline{g}_1 \prod_{i=1}^q \boldsymbol{h}_1[i]^{\boldsymbol{m}[i]}$

If $\mathrm{cnt} \neq i^*$ then

$\quad e_{\mathrm{cnt}} \leftarrow \varepsilon_{\mathrm{cnt}}$

Else

$\quad e_{\mathrm{cnt}} \leftarrow \varepsilon_{i^*} + \sum_{i=1}^\ell \frac{\beta_i}{\alpha} \boldsymbol{m}[i]$

$\quad$ If $C_{\mathrm{cnt}} = 1_{\mathbb{G}_1}$ then

$\qquad x^* \leftarrow \{x' \in \{-e_{\mathrm{cnt}}\} \cup$
$\qquad \{\varepsilon_i\}_{i\neq i^*} \mid g_1^{x'} = X_{1,1}\}$

$\quad e_{\mathrm{cnt}} \leftarrow \varepsilon_{\mathrm{cnt}}$

$A_{\mathrm{cnt}} \leftarrow C_{\mathrm{cnt}}^{\frac{1}{x + e_{\mathrm{cnt}}}}$

$\sigma_{\mathrm{cnt}} \leftarrow (A_{\mathrm{cnt}}, e_{\mathrm{cnt}})$

$\mathrm{Sigs} \overset{\cup}{\leftarrow} \{\sigma_{\mathrm{cnt}}\}$

Return σ_{cnt}

Fig. 4. Adversary $\mathcal{B}_1$ in the proof of Lemma 1. Recall that once $\varepsilon_1, \ldots, \varepsilon_q$ are fixed and understood from the context, we use the shorthand $p(\mathsf{X}) = \prod_{i\in[q]\setminus\{i^*\}}(\mathsf{X} + \varepsilon_i)$ for convenience. In the pseudo-code, we omit the explicit computations of $\overline{g}, \boldsymbol{h}_1$, and A_{cnt} from C_{cnt}, which are detailed in the text.

It is not hard to see that $\overline{g}_1$ and $\boldsymbol{h}_1$ can be computed efficiently from part of the q-SDH setup $g_1, X_{1,1}, \ldots, X_{1,q}$. Moreover, at least informally, it should be clear that as long as $x \notin \{-\varepsilon_1, \ldots, -\varepsilon_q\}$, the distributions of $\overline{g}_1$ and $\boldsymbol{h}_1$ are correct, i.e., they are uniform in $\mathbb{G}_1^*$ and $\mathbb{G}_1^\ell$, respectively, since $g_1 \in \mathbb{G}_1^*$. (The formal argument about the correctness of distributions is given below, and this is only meant to serve as some intuition.) We stress that our simulation will not be correct if $x \in \{-\varepsilon_1, \ldots, -\varepsilon_q\}$, so it is easiest to assume that this is not the case to understand the rest of the reduction.

HANDLING SIGNING QUERIES. The oracle SIGN then simulates the correct signing oracle, keeping a query counter cnt. Whenever $\mathrm{cnt} \neq i^*$, it is not hard to see that SIGN can easily answer the query using $e_{\mathrm{cnt}} = \varepsilon_{\mathrm{cnt}}$. Indeed, if $x + \varepsilon_{\mathrm{cnt}} \neq 0$, on input $\boldsymbol{m}$, the simulate SIGN can compute

$$A_{\mathrm{cnt}} = \left(\overline{g}_1 \prod_{i=1}^\ell \boldsymbol{h}_1[i]^{\boldsymbol{m}[i]}\right)^{\frac{1}{x+\varepsilon_{\mathrm{cnt}}}} = g_1^{p_i(x)[\alpha(x+\varepsilon_{i^*}) + \sum_{i=1}^\ell \beta_i \boldsymbol{m}[i]]},$$

where $p_i(x) = \prod_{i\notin\{\mathrm{cnt}, i^*\}}(x + \varepsilon_i)$. It is easy to detect $x + \varepsilon_{\mathrm{cnt}} = 0$, and in that case, $A_{\mathrm{cnt}} = 1_{\mathbb{G}_1}$ by definition.

Crucially, when cnt $= i^*$ the adversary $\mathcal{B}_1$ answers the signing query differently. We observe first that, with $C_{\mathrm{cnt}} \leftarrow \overline{g}_1 \prod_{i=1}^{q} h_1[i]^{m[i]}$,

$$
\begin{aligned}
\mathrm{DL}_{g_1}(C_{\mathrm{cnt}}) &= \alpha \cdot p(x) \cdot (x + \varepsilon_{i^*}) + \sum_{i=1}^{\ell} \beta_i m[i] p(x) \\
&= \alpha \cdot p(x) \left(x + \varepsilon_{i^*} + \sum_{i=1}^{\ell} \frac{\beta_i}{\alpha} m[i] \right) .
\end{aligned}
\tag{2}
$$

Here, there are two cases. Either $C_{\mathrm{cnt}} = 1_{\mathbb{G}_1}$, and then we return $A_{\mathrm{cnt}} = 1_{\mathbb{G}_1}$, along with a $e_{\mathrm{cnt}} = \varepsilon_{\mathrm{cnt}}$. Alternatively, and more interestingly, if $C_{\mathrm{cnt}} \neq 1_{\mathbb{G}_1}$, we set $e_{i^*} = \varepsilon_{i^*} + \sum_{i=1}^{\ell} \frac{\beta_i}{\alpha} m[i]$, and

$$
A_{i^*} = C_{i^*}^{\frac{1}{x + e_{i^*}}} = g_1^{\alpha \cdot p(x)} ,
$$

which can be efficiently computed. The bulk of our analysis below will show that if $C_{i^*} \neq 1_{\mathbb{G}_1}$, then we indeed generate a random e_{i^*} in this way.

Note that by equation (2) if $C_{i^*} = 1_{\mathbb{G}_1}$, then $x = -\varepsilon_{i^*} - \sum_{i=1}^{\ell} \frac{\beta_i}{\alpha} m[i]$ or $x \in \{\varepsilon_i\}_{i \neq i^*}$, and hence we can directly break of q-SDH. (The variable x^* here stores the recovered discrete logarithm.) To simplify the analysis below, in this case, it is convenient for the reduction $\mathcal{B}_1$ to defer breaking q-SDH to end, and return the signature $(1_{\mathbb{G}_1}, \varepsilon_{i^*})$ instead.

EXTRACTING A SOLUTION. Assume now that $\mathcal{A}$ outputs a valid forgery m^*, σ^*, where $\sigma^* = (A^*, e^*)$, $e^* = e_{i^*}$, and $A^* \neq A_{i^*}$. Further, assume that $C_{i^*} \neq 1_{\mathbb{G}_1}$, which implies that $x + e_{i^*} \neq 0$ and $p(x) \neq 0$. (If this was not true, as highlighted above, we would have extracted x already.) Then,

$$
\begin{aligned}
\mathrm{DL}_{g_1}(A^*) &= \alpha p(x) \frac{x + \varepsilon_{i^*} + \sum_{i=1}^{\ell} \frac{\beta_i}{\alpha} m^*[i]}{x + \varepsilon_{i^*} + \sum_{i=1}^{\ell} \frac{\beta_i}{\alpha} m[i]} \\
&= \alpha \cdot p(x) + p(x) \frac{\sum_{i=1}^{\ell} \beta_i(m^*[i] - m[i])}{x + e_{i^*}} .
\end{aligned}
$$

Further, because $A_{i^*} \neq A^*$ but $e^* = e_{i^*}$, we also have $\gamma = \sum_{i=1}^{\ell} \beta_i(m^*[i] - m[i]) \neq 0$, and then

$$
\left[A^* \cdot (A_{i^*}^{-1}) \right]^{\frac{1}{\gamma}} = g_1^{\frac{p(x)}{x + e_{i^*}}} .
$$

If $e_{i^*} \notin \{e_i\}_{i \in [q] \setminus \{i^*\}}$, $\mathsf{X} + e_{i^*}$ does not divide $p(\mathsf{X})$. We can then compute $g_1^{\frac{1}{x + e_{i^*}}}$ using Remark 1 and break q-SDH.

FORMAL ANALYSIS. We now proceed with a formal analysis to show that the probability guarantees for $\mathcal{B}_1$ as stated in the lemma indeed hold. To this end, we use $\mathrm{Pr}_0[\cdot]$ to denote probabilities in the experiment $\mathrm{SUF}^{\mathcal{A}}_{\mathsf{BBS}}(\lambda)$, where $\mathcal{A}$ plays the SUF game against BBS. Similarly, we use $\mathrm{Pr}_1[\cdot]$ to denote probabilities in the simulated experiment where $\mathcal{A}$ is run within $\mathcal{B}_1$ in Game q-$\mathrm{SDH}^{\mathcal{B}_1}_{\mathsf{GGen}}(\lambda)$.

In both experiments, we can define the event Forge_1, as it only depends on the output of the adversary and the property of this output relative to its earlier signing query. Moreover, let $\mathsf{Forge}_1^{(i)}$ for $i \in [q]$ be the event that Forge_1 happens and the i-th query is the first signing query that satisfies the condition for Forge_1 to happen. Let GoodE be the event that all e_i's are distinct. Note that $\mathcal{B}_1$ is guaranteed to output a q-SDH solution if $\mathsf{Forge}_1^{(i)}$ happens and $i = i^*$ and, moreover, GoodE also occurs. Also, note that the probability that GoodE and $\mathsf{Forge}_1^{(i)}$ occurs is independent of whether $i = i^*$ or not, and therefore

$$\mathsf{Adv}_{\mathsf{GGen}}^{q\text{-sdh}}(\mathcal{B}_1, \lambda) \geq \sum_{i=1}^{q} \Pr_1\left[\mathsf{GoodE} \wedge \mathsf{Forge}_1^{(i)}\right] \cdot \Pr_1[i^* = i]$$

$$= \frac{1}{q} \cdot \sum_{i=1}^{q} \Pr_1\left[\mathsf{GoodE} \wedge \mathsf{Forge}_1^{(i)}\right] = \frac{1}{q} \cdot \Pr_1[\mathsf{GoodE} \wedge \mathsf{Forge}_1] .$$

We rely on the following central lemma, which in particular shows that the simulation of $\mathcal{A}$'s execution within $\mathcal{B}$ is nearly correct. While the intuition has been given above, the formal proof is rather subtle and we rely on the H-coefficient method [19,30] to prove the following.

Lemma 4. $\Pr_0[\mathsf{GoodE} \wedge \mathsf{Forge}_1] - \Pr_1[\mathsf{GoodE} \wedge \mathsf{Forge}_1] \leq \frac{q}{p}$.

Before turning to a proof of the lemma in Sect. 3.5 below, we observe that plugging the inequality of the lemma into the above yields

$$\mathsf{Adv}_{\mathsf{GGen}}^{q\text{-sdh}}(\mathcal{B}_1, \lambda) \geq \frac{1}{q} \cdot \Pr_0[\mathsf{GoodE} \wedge \mathsf{Forge}_1] - \frac{1}{p}$$

$$\geq \frac{1}{q}\left(\Pr_0[\mathsf{Forge}_1] - \Pr_0[\overline{\mathsf{GoodE}}]\right) - \frac{1}{p} .$$

On the other hand, $\Pr_0[\overline{\mathsf{GoodE}}] \leq \binom{q}{2}\frac{1}{p} \leq \frac{q^2}{2p}$, and thus we obtain the bound in Lemma 1 by re-arranging terms.

3.5 Proof of Lemma 4

We assume $\mathcal{A}$ to be deterministic without loss of generality. We describe the transcripts of the interaction of $\mathcal{A}$ in the SUF and within $\mathcal{B}_1$ as part of the q-SDH experiment, respectively, via the following two random variables

$$T_0 = (g_1, g_2, \boldsymbol{h}_1, x, i^*, (\boldsymbol{m}_1, e_1), \ldots, (\boldsymbol{m}_q, e_q)) ,$$
$$T_1 = (\overline{g}_1, g_2, \boldsymbol{h}_1, x, i^*, (\boldsymbol{m}_1, e_1), \ldots, (\boldsymbol{m}_q, e_q))$$

where in T_0, i^* is sampled uniformly from $[q]$, independently of everything else. We do not include X_2, as $X_2 = g_2^x$ in both experiments. Moreover, in both experiments, the first component $A_1, A_2, \ldots$ of the the answer to each signature query is removed, as it is also a deterministic function of the rest of the transcript.

Similarly, the final forgery (A^*, e^*) is also a function of T_0/T_1. For this reason, we note that that the event $\mathsf{GoodE} \wedge \mathsf{Forge}_1$ is deterministically determined from T_0 and T_1, in their respective experiments, i.e., there exists a Boolean function ϕ such that $\phi(T_b) = 1$ if and only if the event happens in the corresponding experiment. Therefore,

$$\Pr_0 [\mathsf{GoodE} \wedge \mathsf{Forge}_1] - \Pr_1 [\mathsf{GoodE} \wedge \mathsf{Forge}_1] \leqslant \mathsf{SD}(T_0, T_1) ,$$

where $\mathsf{SD}(T_0, T_1) = \frac{1}{2} \sum_\tau |\Pr [T_0 = \tau] - \Pr [T_1 = \tau]|$ is the total variation distance, which we upper bound by a special case of Patarin's H-coefficient method [30], which we introduce on the way. (We use the formalism from [26] here.)

INTERPOLATION PROBABILITIES. Concretely, for any potential value τ of T_b for $b \in \{0, 1\}$, which we denote as

$$\tau = (\underline{g}_1, \underline{g}_2, \underline{h}_1, \underline{x}, \underline{i}^*, (\underline{m}_1, \underline{e}_1), \dots, (\underline{m}_q, \underline{e}_q)) ,$$

we let $\mathsf{p}_0(\tau)$ and $\mathsf{p}_1(\tau)$ be its interpolation probabilities, i.e., the probabilities that we pick randomness in the respective experiment that would lead to transcript τ if queries $\underline{m}_1, \dots, \underline{m}_q$ are fixed ahead of time. (These probabilities are independent of $\mathcal{A}$, and only depend on τ and the randomness of the experiment.) We want to isolate the following type of good transcript.

Definition 1 (Good transcript). *We call* τ *good if* $\underline{x} \notin \{-\underline{e}_1, \dots, -\underline{e}_q\}$. *Otherwise,* τ *is bad.*

We are then going to prove that for all good transcripts τ, $\mathsf{p}_0(\tau) = \mathsf{p}_1(\tau)$. This is enough to conclude the proof, as it implies that

$$\mathsf{SD}(T_0, T_1) \leqslant \Pr [T_0 \text{ is bad}] = \Pr_0 [x \in \{-e_1, \dots, -e_q\}] \leqslant \frac{q}{p} .$$

To compute $\mathsf{p}_1(\tau)$ for a good transcript τ, we assume that the generator g_1 given to $\mathcal{B}_1$ is fixed. (Of course, it is actually sampled randomly from $\mathbb{G}_1^*$ as part of the q-SDH instance, but the interpolation probability is the same conditioned on any particular choice, and thus we fix it.) The randomness then consists of $i^* \leftarrow_{\$} [q]$, $x \leftarrow_{\$} \mathbb{Z}_p$, $\alpha \leftarrow_{\$} \mathbb{Z}_p^*$, $\varepsilon_1, \dots, \varepsilon_q \leftarrow_{\$} \mathbb{Z}_p$, and $g_2 \leftarrow_{\$} \mathbb{G}_2^*$. To generate the transcript τ, we need in particular

$$i^* = \underline{i}^*, \quad g_2 = \underline{g}_2, \quad x = \underline{x}, \quad (\varepsilon_i)_{i \in [q] \setminus \{\underline{i}^*\}} = (\underline{e}_i)_{i \in [q] \setminus \{\underline{i}^*\}}$$

and as these values are chosen independently, this is true with probability

$$\frac{1}{q} \cdot \frac{1}{p-1} \cdot \frac{1}{p} \cdot \frac{1}{p^{q-1}} = \frac{1}{q(p-1)p^q}$$

over the choice of $i^*, g_2, x, \{\varepsilon_i\}_{i \in [q] \setminus \{\underline{i}^*\}}$. Let us assume this initial part of the transcript is consistent. We also need $\beta_1, \dots, \beta_\ell$ to ensure $h_1 = \underline{h}_1$, which, conditioned on $x = \overline{x}$, is equivalent to the fact that

$$p(\underline{x}) \cdot \beta_i = \mathrm{DL}_{g_1}(\underline{h}_1[i]) \quad \text{for all } i \in [\ell].$$

Because τ is good, $p(\underline{x}) \neq 0$, and therefore the ℓ equalities hold with probability $1/p^\ell$ over the choice of $\beta_1, \ldots, \beta_\ell$.

Finally, conditioned on $i^*, g_2, x, \{\varepsilon_i\}_{i \in [q] \setminus \{i^*\}}, \{\beta\}_{i \in [\ell]}$ satisfying all above constraints, we need $\varepsilon_{\underline{i}^*}$ and α to ensure that

$$\overline{g}_1 = g_1^{\alpha p(\underline{x})(\underline{x} + \varepsilon_{\underline{i}^*})} = \underline{g}_1 \,, \quad e_{\underline{i}^*} = \underline{e}_{\underline{i}^*} \,.$$

There are two cases here, depending on $\underline{m} = \underline{m}_{\underline{i}^*}$ and the associated value

$$\underline{C} = \underline{g}_1 \prod_{i=1}^{\ell} \underline{h}_1[i]^{\underline{m}[i]} \,.$$

Case 1: $\underline{C} = 1_{\mathbb{G}_1}$. Then, in this case, $\mathcal{B}_1$ ensures $e_{\underline{i}^*} = \varepsilon_{\underline{i}^*}$, and this value, which is uniform, equals $\underline{e}_{\underline{i}^*}$ with probability $1/p$. Conditioned on this,

$$p(\underline{x})(\underline{x} + \varepsilon_{\underline{i}^*}) = p(\underline{x})(\underline{x} + \underline{e}_{\underline{i}^*}) \neq 0$$

because τ is good. Thus $\underline{g}_1 = g_1^{\alpha p(\underline{x})(\underline{x} + \varepsilon_{\underline{i}^*})}$ holds with probability $1/(p-1)$ over the choice of α from $\mathbb{Z}_p^*$.

Case 2: $\underline{C} \neq 1_{\mathbb{G}_1}$. For convenience, we write $\underline{e} = \underline{e}_{\underline{i}^*}$, $\varepsilon = \varepsilon_{\underline{i}^*}$, $\underline{a} = \mathrm{DL}_{g_1}(\underline{g}_1)$, and $\underline{y} = \sum_i \beta_i \underline{m}[i]$. Here, $\alpha \leftarrow_{\!s} \mathbb{Z}_p^*$ and $\varepsilon \leftarrow_{\!s} \mathbb{Z}_p$ need to satisfy

$$\alpha p(\underline{x})(\underline{x} + \varepsilon) = \underline{a}$$

$$\varepsilon + \frac{1}{\alpha} \underline{y} = \underline{e}$$

The second equation directly implies that

$$\varepsilon = \underline{e} - \frac{1}{\alpha} \cdot \underline{y} \,. \tag{3}$$

Substituting this into the first equation yields

$$\alpha \cdot p(\underline{x}) \left(\underline{x} + \underline{e} - \frac{1}{\alpha} \cdot \underline{y} \right) = p(\underline{x})(\alpha(\underline{x} + \underline{e}) - \underline{y}) = \underline{a} \,.$$

Re-arranging terms we get

$$\alpha = \frac{\underline{a}/p(\underline{x}) + \underline{y}}{\underline{x} + \underline{e}} \,. \tag{4}$$

This is indeed a value in $\mathbb{Z}_p^*$ for two reasons. First off, $\underline{x} + \underline{e} \neq 0$ as τ is good. Second, $\underline{a}/p(\underline{x}) + \underline{y} \neq 0$. Indeed, if instead $\underline{a}/p(\underline{x}) + \underline{y} = 0$ were true, we would have

$$\underline{C} = \underline{g}_1 \prod_{i=1}^{\ell} \underline{h}_1[i]^{\underline{m}[i]} = g_1^{\underline{a}} \prod_{i=1}^{\ell} g_1^{p(\underline{x}) \cdot \beta_i \cdot \underline{m}[i]} = g_1^{\underline{a} + p(\underline{x})\underline{y}} = g_1^0 = 1_{\mathbb{G}_1} \,,$$

a contradiction with the fact that we are in Case 2. Therefore, the probability over the choice of α, ε that (3) and (4) are both satisfied is $\frac{1}{p(p-1)}$.

Game $\mathsf{SUF+}^{\mathcal{A}}_{\mathsf{GGen,eG,eS}}(\lambda)$:	Oracle $\mathrm{SIGN}(\boldsymbol{m})$:
$\mathsf{Sigs} \leftarrow \emptyset;\ \mathrm{cnt} \leftarrow 0$	$\mathrm{cnt} \leftarrow \mathrm{cnt} + 1$
$(p, \mathbb{G}_1, \mathbb{G}_2, \mathbb{G}_T, e) \leftarrow_\$ \mathsf{GGen}(1^\lambda)$	$e_{\mathrm{cnt}} \leftarrow \mathsf{eS}(\mathsf{st}_e, \mathrm{cnt})$
$g_1 \leftarrow_\$ \mathbb{G}_1^*,\ \boldsymbol{h}_1 \leftarrow_\$ \mathbb{G}_1,\ g_2 \leftarrow_\$ \mathbb{G}_2^*$	$C_{\mathrm{cnt}} \leftarrow g_1 \prod_{i=1}^{\ell} \boldsymbol{h}_1[i]^{\boldsymbol{m}[i]}$
$\mathrm{par} \leftarrow (p, g_1, \boldsymbol{h}_1, g_2, \mathbb{G}_1, \mathbb{G}_2, \mathbb{G}_T, e)$	$A_{\mathrm{cnt}} \leftarrow C_{\mathrm{cnt}}^{1/(x+e_{\mathrm{cnt}})}$
$\mathsf{st}_e \leftarrow \mathsf{eG}(p, \mathbb{G}_1, \mathbb{G}_2, \mathbb{G}_T, e)$	$\mathsf{Sigs} \overset{\cup}{\leftarrow} \{(\boldsymbol{m}, (A_{\mathrm{cnt}}, e_{\mathrm{cnt}}))\}$
$x \leftarrow_\$ \mathbb{Z}_p;\ X_2 \leftarrow g_2^x;\ \mathsf{sk} \leftarrow x;\ \mathsf{vk} \leftarrow X_2$	Return A_{cnt}
$(\boldsymbol{m}^*, (A^*, e^*)) \leftarrow_\$ \mathcal{A}^{\mathrm{SIGN}}(\mathrm{par}, \mathsf{st}_e, \mathsf{vk})$	
If $(\boldsymbol{m}^*, (A^*, e^*)) \notin \mathsf{Sigs}$ then	
$\quad C^* \leftarrow_\$ g_1 \prod_{i=1}^{\ell} \boldsymbol{h}_1[i]^{\boldsymbol{m}^*[i]}$	
$\quad$ If $e\left(A^*, X_2 g_2^{e^*}\right) = e(C^*, g_2)$ then return	
true	
Return false	

Fig. 5. Stronger security for BBS. Stronger ad-hoc unforgeability achieved by BBS in the AGM, where the e_i's are sampled deterministically from an algorithm that uses an initially generated state st_e, known to the adversary.

Therefore, in summary, we have

$$\mathsf{p}_1(\tau) = \frac{1}{q(p-1)p^q} \cdot \frac{1}{p^\ell} \cdot \frac{1}{p(p-1)} = \frac{1}{q(p-1)^2 p^{q+\ell+1}}.$$

It is not hard to observe that we also have

$$\mathsf{p}_0(\tau) = \frac{1}{p^{q+\ell+1}(p-1)^2 q},$$

because g_1, g_2 are uniform over $\mathbb{G}_1^*$, $\overline{h}_1$ is uniform over $\mathbb{G}_1^\ell$, and $x, e_1, \ldots, e_q$ are uniform in in $\mathbb{Z}_p$, and i^* is uniform in $[q]$.

4 Tighter Proofs for BBS in the AGM

This section complements the above standard-model analysis with a tight analysis of BBS in the *algebraic group model* (AGM) [23]. In addition, we prove here that security holds even if the attacker is given the values $e_1, e_2, \ldots$ *ahead of time*, and we allow these values to be sampled from a more general distribution. The former fact will be helpful later in Sect. 6. The latter fact will allow for instantiations of BBS with shorter signatures in some contexts, as we explain further below.

STRONGER SECURITY. We formalize our security goal in terms of Game SUF+ in Fig. 5. This is *not* a generic security game, as it is specific to BBS, but clearly, it does imply its strong unforgeability in a number of settings when the scheme instantiation corresponds to a particular pick to eG and eS. The ad-hoc feature is that we allow part of the signature (namely, the e value in a pair (A, e)) to be generated initially. To model this, in addition to the group parameter generator GGen, the game is parameterized by a pair of algorithms, eG and eS, where eG, on input the group parameters, outputs a state st_e, and then $\mathsf{eS}(\mathsf{st}_e, i)$ (deterministically) outputs the value e_i used for the i-th signature. The initial state st_e is given to the adversary, who can run eS to pre-compute the e_i's. It will be convenient to define the collision probability

$$\delta_{\mathsf{eG},\mathsf{eS}}(q, \lambda) = \Pr\left[\begin{matrix} \mathsf{par} \leftarrow_{\$} \mathsf{GGen}(1^\lambda) \\ \mathsf{st}_e \leftarrow_{\$} \mathsf{eG}(\mathsf{par}) \end{matrix} : \exists 1 \leqslant i < j \leq q : \mathsf{eS}(\mathsf{st}_e, i) = \mathsf{eS}(\mathsf{st}_e, j)\right].$$

We also define the advantage metric

$$\mathsf{Adv}^{\mathsf{suf}+}_{\mathsf{GGen},\mathsf{eG},\mathsf{eS}}(\mathcal{A}, \lambda) = \Pr\left[\mathsf{SUF}+^{\mathcal{A}}_{\mathsf{GGen},\mathsf{eG},\mathsf{eS}}(\lambda)\right].$$

ALGEBRAIC SECURITY. We are now ready to state our main theorem, which is proved below in Sect. 4.1. We dispense with a full formalization of the AGM [23], as its use is relatively straightforward here. Namely, we consider *algebraic adversaries* that provide an explanation of the element $A^* \in \mathbb{G}_1$ contained in the forgery in terms of all previously seen group elements in $\mathbb{G}_1$, which include the generators g_1, h_1, as well as the issued signatures. (Because we consider type-3 pairings, we do not include $\mathbb{G}_2$ elements in these representations.) We also give our reduction here to q-DL, as opposed to q-SDH as in the case of Theorem 1, but note that the assumptions are equivalent in the AGM.

Theorem 2 (AGM Security of BBS). *Let GGen be a group parameter generator, producing groups of order $p(\lambda)$, and let eG, eS as above. For every algebraic SUF+ adversary $\mathcal{A}$ issuing at most q signing queries, there exist adversaries $\mathcal{B}_1$ and $\mathcal{B}_2$ such that*

$$\mathsf{Adv}^{\mathsf{suf}+}_{\mathsf{GGen},\mathsf{eG},\mathsf{eS}}(\mathcal{A}, \lambda) \leqslant \mathsf{Adv}^{q\text{-dl}}_{\mathsf{GGen}}(\mathcal{B}_1, \lambda) + \mathsf{Adv}^{\mathsf{dl}}_{\mathsf{GGen}}(\mathcal{B}_2, \lambda) + \delta_{\mathsf{eG},\mathsf{eS}}(q, \lambda) + \frac{1}{p(\lambda)}.$$

The adversaries $\mathcal{B}_1$ and $\mathcal{B}_2$ are given explicitly in the proof, and have running times comparable to that of $\mathcal{A}$. The adversary $\mathcal{B}_1$ need to additionally factor a polynomial of degree (at most) q.

The only property required from eG and eS is that $\delta_{\mathsf{eG},\mathsf{eS}}(q, \lambda)$ is small. We note that the lack of collisions is a necessary condition. Indeed, if we generate two signatures (A, e), (A', e) for messages $\boldsymbol{m}$ and $\boldsymbol{m}'$, respectively, it is easy to verify that $((A \cdot A')^{\frac{1}{2}}, e)$ is a signature for $\frac{1}{2}(\boldsymbol{m} + \boldsymbol{m}')$, where $\frac{1}{2}$ is the inverse of 2 mod p.

The above theorem supports the security (in the AGM) of some interesting and natural instantiations of BBS with shorter signatures, which we discuss next.

COUNTER BBS. One natural instantiation, which we refer to as *Counter BBS*, generates the e_i's from a counter, i.e., $\mathsf{eS}(\mathsf{st}_e, i) = i$. This can be advantageous if the signer can reliably maintain such a counter. Signatures then would consist of a group element in $\mathbb{G}_1$ and then $\log q$ additional bits, where q is an upper bound on the number of issued signatures. In particular, one could safely set $q = 2^{50}$ in many applications, leading to very short signatures.

TRUNCATED BBS. A different application scenario considers a conservative instantiation that uses a 384-bit group $\mathbb{G}_1$ to prevents Cheon's attack [20]. Then, the above bound allows us to choose the e_i's from $\mathbb{Z}_{2^{256}}$, as opposed to $\mathbb{Z}_p$ for a 384-bit prime p, hence saving 128-bit of signature length. We refer to the resulting scheme as *Truncated BBS*. While we need to rely on the AGM to trust this optimization, we do note that the uniformity of the e_i's needed by Theorem 1 appears to be an artifact of the proof, and does not appear to prevent actual attacks.

4.1 Proof of Theorem 2

Before we turn to the construction of the adversaries $\mathcal{B}_1$ and $\mathcal{B}_2$, and their formal analysis, we introduce the algebraic framework that will guide their construction.

ALGEBRAIC FRAMEWORK. To start with, in an execution of $\mathsf{SUF+}_{\mathsf{GGen,eG,eS}}^{\mathcal{A}}(\lambda)$, it is convenient to associate the discrete logarithms of group elements in $\mathbb{G}_1$ with formal rational functions (which are then evaluated in the actual execution to obtain the discrete logarithm). In particular, let us denote the discrete logarithms of $\boldsymbol{h}_1$ to the base g_1 by the vector $\boldsymbol{y} \in \mathbb{Z}_p^{\ell}$. Then, the i-th SIGN query for $\boldsymbol{m} \in \mathbb{Z}_p^{\ell}$, where $e_i = e$, returns a value with discrete logarithm $\varphi_{\boldsymbol{m},e}^{\boldsymbol{y}}(x)$, where

$$\varphi_{\boldsymbol{m},e}^{\boldsymbol{y}}(\mathsf{X}) = \frac{1 + \langle \boldsymbol{y}, \boldsymbol{m} \rangle}{\mathsf{X} + e_i} .$$

Here, $\langle \boldsymbol{x}, \boldsymbol{y} \rangle$ denotes inner product in $\mathbb{Z}_p$. It turns out that these functions are essentially linearly independent, except for some unfortunate configurations for $\boldsymbol{y}$. This is captured by the following central lemma.

Lemma 5. *Let* $e_1, \ldots, e_q \in \mathbb{Z}_p$ *be distinct, let* $\boldsymbol{y} \in \mathbb{Z}_p^{\ell}$, *and let* $\boldsymbol{m}_1, \ldots, \boldsymbol{m}_q \in \mathbb{Z}_p^{\ell}$. *Further, let* $(\boldsymbol{m}^*, e^*) \notin \{(\boldsymbol{m}_i, e_i)\}_{i \in [q]}$. *Then, assume that there exist* $\lambda_1, \ldots, \lambda_q, \gamma \in \mathbb{Z}_p$ *such that*

$$\varphi_{\boldsymbol{m}^*,e^*}^{\boldsymbol{y}}(\mathsf{X}) = \sum_{i=1}^{q} \lambda_i \cdot \varphi_{\boldsymbol{m}_i,e_i}^{\boldsymbol{y}}(\mathsf{X}) + \gamma . \tag{5}$$

Then, one of the following two conditions must be true:

(i) There exists $i \in [q]$ *such that* $e^* = e_i$ *and* $1 - \lambda_i + \langle \boldsymbol{y}, \boldsymbol{m}^* - \lambda_i \cdot \boldsymbol{m}_i \rangle = 0$.
(ii) We have $e^* \notin \{e_1, \ldots, e_q\}$, *but* $1 + \langle \boldsymbol{y}, \boldsymbol{m}^* \rangle = 0$.

Proof. To verify (i), assume indeed that $e^* \in \{e_1, \ldots, e_q\}$, and wlog, let $e^* = e_1$. We multiply both sides of (5) by $p(\mathsf{X}) = \prod_{i=1}^{\ell}(\mathsf{X} + e_i)$, and after re-arranging terms, we get

$$(1 - \lambda_1 + \langle \boldsymbol{y}, \boldsymbol{m}^* - \lambda_1 \cdot \boldsymbol{m}_1 \rangle) \cdot p_1(\mathsf{X}) = \gamma \cdot p(\mathsf{X}) + \sum_{i=2}^{q} \lambda_i \cdot \varphi_{\boldsymbol{m}_i,e_i}^{\boldsymbol{y}}(\mathsf{X}) \cdot p_i(\mathsf{X}) , \tag{6}$$

where we have used the shorthand $p_i(\mathsf{X}) = \prod_{j \in [q] \setminus \{i\}}(\mathsf{X} + e_j) = p(\mathsf{X})/(\mathsf{X} + e_i)$. We claim that the LHS and RHS of (6) cannot be identical functions, unless

$1 - \lambda_1 + \langle \boldsymbol{y}, \boldsymbol{m}^* - \lambda_1 \cdot \boldsymbol{m}_1 \rangle = 0$. Indeed, the RHS is always divisible by $\mathsf{X} + e_1$, because either $\lambda_2, \ldots, \lambda_q$ are all 0, in which case this is vacuously true, or $p(\mathsf{X})$ and $p_i(\mathsf{X})$ for $i \geqslant 2$ are divisible by $(\mathsf{X} + e_1)$. In contrast, if $1 - \lambda_1 + \langle \boldsymbol{y}, \boldsymbol{m}^* - \lambda_1 \cdot \boldsymbol{m}_1 \rangle \neq 0$, then the RHS is not divisible by $\mathsf{X} + e_1$ because $p_1(e_1) \neq 0$.

Let us consider instead the case $e^* \notin \{e_1, \ldots, e_q\}$. For notational convenience, we let $e_{q+1} = e^*$, $p'(\mathsf{X}) = \prod_{i \in [q+1]}(\mathsf{X}+e_i)$, and $p'_k(\mathsf{X}) = \prod_{i \in [q+1] \setminus \{k\}}(\mathsf{X}+e_i)$. Then, multiplying both sides of (5) by $p'(\mathsf{X})$ yields

$$(1 + \langle \boldsymbol{y}, \boldsymbol{m}^* \rangle) \cdot p'_{q+1}(\mathsf{X}) = \gamma \cdot p'(\mathsf{X}) + \sum_{i=2}^{q} \lambda_i \cdot \varphi^{\boldsymbol{y}}_{\boldsymbol{m}_i, e_i}(\mathsf{X}) \cdot p'_i(\mathsf{X}) .$$

We notice that if $1 + \langle \boldsymbol{y}, \boldsymbol{m}^* \rangle \neq 0$ the LHS is non-zero, and not divisible by $\mathsf{X} + e_{q+1}$, as $p'_{q+1}(e_{q+1}) \neq 0$. In contrast, the RHS is always divisible by $\mathsf{X} + e_{q+1}$. A contradiction. $\qquad\square$

OVERVIEW OF THE REDUCTION. Let $\mathcal{A}$ be an algebraic adversary in Game $\mathsf{SUF+}^{\mathcal{A}}_{\mathsf{GGen}, \mathsf{eG}, \mathsf{eS}}(\lambda)$. It initially receives group elements $g_1 \in \mathbb{G}_1$, $\boldsymbol{h}_1 \in \mathbb{G}_1^\ell$, along with $\mathbb{G}_2$ elements $g_2, X_2 = g_2^x$. For each signing query, she also gets $A_i \in \mathbb{G}_1$. Finally, when producing a forgery $(\boldsymbol{m}^*, (A^*, e^*))$, by virtue of being algebraic, the adversary $\mathcal{A}$ also provides a representation $(\gamma_0, \gamma_1, \ldots, \gamma_\ell, \lambda_1, \ldots, \lambda_q) \in \mathbb{Z}_p^{q+\ell+1}$ of A^* such that

$$A^* = g_1^{\gamma_0} \prod_{i=1}^{\ell} \boldsymbol{h}_1[i]^{\gamma_i} \prod_{i=1}^{q} A_i^{\lambda_i} = (C^*)^{\frac{1}{x+e^*}} = g_1^{\varphi^{\boldsymbol{y}}_{\boldsymbol{m}^*, e^*}(x)} ,$$

where $\boldsymbol{y}[i] = \mathsf{DL}_{g_1}(\boldsymbol{h}_1[i])$ for all $i \in [\ell]$. Further, we have $A_i = g_1^{\varphi^{\boldsymbol{y}}_{\boldsymbol{m}_i, e_i}(x)}$. Therefore, setting $\gamma = \gamma_0 + \sum_{i \in [\ell]} \gamma_i \cdot \boldsymbol{y}[i]$, this implies in particular that

$$\gamma + \sum_{i=1}^{q} \lambda_i \cdot \varphi^{\boldsymbol{y}}_{\boldsymbol{m}_i, e_i}(x) - \varphi^{\boldsymbol{y}}_{\boldsymbol{m}^*, e^*}(x) = 0 .$$

Let us now assume that the two conditions in Lemma 5 do not hold, and that $e_1, \ldots, e_q$ are distinct. Then, Lemma 5 implies that

$$\rho(\mathsf{X}) = \gamma + \sum_{i=1}^{q} \lambda_i \cdot \varphi^{\boldsymbol{y}}_{\boldsymbol{m}_i, e_i}(\mathsf{X}) - \varphi^{\boldsymbol{y}}_{\boldsymbol{m}^*, e^*}(\mathsf{X}) \neq 0 ,$$

and therefore x is one of its zeros. Assuming that $x \notin \{-e_1, \ldots, -e_q, -e^*\}$, such zeros can be obtained by factoring the non-zero polynomial

$$q(\mathsf{X}) = \rho(\mathsf{X}) \cdot \prod_{e \in \{e_1, \ldots, e_q, e^*\}} (\mathsf{X} + e) ,$$

which has degree at most $q + 1$. One of the zeros has to equal x.

We still need to handle the case where either $1 + \langle \boldsymbol{y}, \boldsymbol{m}^* \rangle = 0$ or $1 - \lambda_i + \langle \boldsymbol{y}, \boldsymbol{m}^* - \lambda_i \cdot \boldsymbol{m}_i \rangle = 0$. It is however not hard to see that this gives us non-trivial discrete logarithm relation, and we can use this to compute the discrete logarithm directly.

FORMAL REDUCTION. To formalize the above analysis, we consider three events during the execution of Game $\text{SUF+}^{\mathcal{A}}_{\text{GGen,eG,eS}}(\lambda)$:

- Forge: This is the event that $\mathcal{A}$ outputs a successful forgery and wins the game.
- Rel: This is the event that the forgery is for a message $\boldsymbol{m}^*$ such that either Condition (i) or (ii) of Lemma 5 holds.
- Col: Is the event that there exist distinct $i, j \in [q]$ with $e_i = e_j$.

Then, by the law of total probability,

$$
\begin{aligned}
\text{Adv}^{\text{suf+}}_{\text{GGen,eG,eS}}(\mathcal{A}, \lambda) &= \Pr\left[\text{Forge} \wedge \overline{\text{Rel}}\right] + \Pr\left[\text{Forge} \wedge \text{Rel}\right] \\
&\leq \Pr\left[\text{Forge} \wedge \overline{\text{Rel}} \wedge \text{Col}\right] + \Pr\left[\text{Forge} \wedge \overline{\text{Rel}} \wedge \overline{\text{Col}}\right] + \Pr\left[\text{Rel}\right] \\
&\leq \Pr\left[\text{Col}\right] + \Pr\left[\text{Forge} \wedge \overline{\text{Rel}} \wedge \overline{\text{Col}}\right] + \Pr\left[\text{Rel}\right] .
\end{aligned}
$$

By definition, we know that $\Pr\left[\text{Col}\right] = \delta_{\text{eG,eS}}(q, \lambda)$. We now give adversaries $\mathcal{B}_1$ and $\mathcal{B}_2$ such that

$$
\Pr\left[\text{Forge} \wedge \overline{\text{Rel}} \wedge \overline{\text{Col}}\right] \leq \text{Adv}^{q\text{-dl}}_{\text{GGen}}(\mathcal{B}_1) , \quad \Pr\left[\text{Rel}\right] \leq \text{Adv}^{\text{dl}}_{\text{GGen}}(\mathcal{B}_2) + \frac{1}{p} .
$$

THE ADVERSARY $\mathcal{B}_1$. If $x \notin \{-e_1, \dots, -e_q\}$ (which can be checked right away, and gives x), the reduction simulates the original generator g_1 as $\overline{g}_1 = g_1^{\alpha p(x)}$, where $p(x) = \prod_{i \in [q]} (x + e_i)$. (This can be computed given the inputs $X_{1,i} = g^{x^i}$ for $i \in [q]$.) Since $\alpha \in \mathbb{Z}_p^*$ and $p(x) \neq 0$, the simulation is perfect. Also, we can easily compute the answers to SIGN queries due to our choice of $\overline{g}_1$. The adversary then checks that $q(X)$ is non-zero (which is implied by $\overline{\text{Rel}}$), and if so, proceeds to compute its zeros. It is easy to verify that the adversary succeeds with probability at least $\Pr\left[\text{Forge} \wedge \overline{\text{Rel}} \wedge \overline{\text{Col}}\right]$.

THE ADVERSARY $\mathcal{B}_2$. The construction is somewhat standard. Let us assume one of the two conditions leading to Rel occurs in Game $\text{SUF+}^{\mathcal{A}}_{\text{GGen,eG,eS}}(\lambda)$. First, if (i) occurs for some $i \in [q]$, then

$$
g_1^{1-\lambda_i} \prod_{j=1}^{\ell} \boldsymbol{h}_1^{\boldsymbol{m}^*[j] - \lambda_i \boldsymbol{m}_i[j]} = 1_{\mathbb{G}_1} . \tag{7}
$$

In contrast, if (ii) occurs, then

$$
g_1 \prod_{j=1}^{\ell} \boldsymbol{h}_1^{\boldsymbol{m}_i[j]} = 1_{\mathbb{G}_1} . \tag{8}
$$

Therefore, in both cases, we obtain a non-zero vector $(a, \boldsymbol{b}) \in \mathbb{Z}_p^{\ell+1}$ such that $g_1^a \prod_{i \in [\ell]} \boldsymbol{h}_1[i]^{\boldsymbol{b}[i]} = 1_{\mathbb{G}_1}$. Given the DL instance $X_{1,1} = g_1^x \in \mathbb{G}_1$, the adversary $\mathcal{B}_2$ simulates the generator by picking $\alpha_i, \beta_i \leftarrow_\$ \mathbb{Z}_p$ for $i \in [\ell]$, and lets

$$
\overline{g}_1 = X_{1,1} = g_1^x , \quad \boldsymbol{h}_1[i] = X_{1,1}^{\alpha_i} g_1^{-\beta_i} = g_1^{\alpha_i x - \beta_i} \quad \text{for } i \in [\ell] .
$$

This simulates the right distribution if $X_{1,1} \neq 1_{\mathbb{G}_1}$, which is ensured beforehand. Then, as outlined above, the adversary simulates a correct execution with $\mathcal{A}$, and checks if we obtain a non-trivial relation as above. If so, we are given a non-zero $(a, \boldsymbol{b}) \in \mathbb{Z}_p^{\ell+1}$ such that

$$ ax + \sum_{i=1}^{\ell} \boldsymbol{b}[i] \cdot (\alpha_i x - \beta_i) = 0 \, , $$

and, in turn, we get

$$ x = \frac{\sum_{i=1}^{\ell} \beta_i \boldsymbol{b}[i]}{a + \sum_{i=1}^{\ell} \alpha_i \boldsymbol{b}[i]} \, . $$

Note that this is well defined, unless $a + \sum_{i=1}^{\ell} \alpha_i \boldsymbol{b}[i] = 0$. However, because $(a, \boldsymbol{b}) \neq \boldsymbol{0}$, and the fact that the α_i's are uniform and independent given the adversary's view, this happens with probability at most $1/p$. This concludes the proof.   □

5   Efficient Proofs of Knowledge for BBS Signatures

We discuss zero-knowledge proofs of knowledge (zkPoK) of a BBS message-signature pair $(\boldsymbol{m}, \sigma)$ that are shorter than those from [15] adopted by the RFC draft [28]. If we do not want to reveal k of the components of $\boldsymbol{m}$, our proof (when compiled as a NIZK via the Fiat-Shamir transform) consists of 2 elements in $\mathbb{G}_1$, as well as $k+3$ scalars in $\mathbb{Z}_p$. The prior proof, in contrast, consists of 3 elements in $\mathbb{G}_1$, and $k+5$ scalars. The benefit of our new proofs is also computational: We save 4 group exponentiations in $\mathbb{G}_1$ and 3 scalar multiplications for the prover, and save 3 group exponentiations in $\mathbb{G}_1$ for the verifier. We note that the CDL proofs are tailored at BBS+, but even for the latter scheme, we can achieve savings, as we can think of a BBS+ signature for $\boldsymbol{m}$ as a BBS signature for $(s, \boldsymbol{m})$, for a secret s, and merely increase k by one.

5.1   Proofs of Knowledge for Signatures

We consider zkPoKs associated with a signature scheme SS with message space $\mathsf{SS.M(par)} = \mathcal{M}(\mathrm{par})^\ell$ for some set $\mathcal{M}$ that can depend on the public parameters par, and some understood vector length $\ell = \ell(\lambda)$. We give proofs of knowledge of a signature consistent with a partial message vector $\boldsymbol{m} \in (\mathcal{M} \cup \{\star\})^\ell$. For any two such partial messages $\boldsymbol{m}, \boldsymbol{m}'$, we denote $\boldsymbol{m} \subseteq \boldsymbol{m}'$ if for all $i \in [\ell]$, $\boldsymbol{m}[i] \neq \star$ implies $\boldsymbol{m}[i] = \boldsymbol{m}'[i]$.

We only consider three-move public-coin protocols between a *prover* and a *verifier*, described by a tuple $\mathsf{PoK} = (\mathsf{PoK.P_1}, \mathsf{PoK.P_2}, \mathsf{PoK.C}, \mathsf{PoK.V})$. Informally, we think of running the protocol in settings where the parameters for SS are available, i.e., $\mathrm{par} \leftarrow_{\$} \mathsf{SS.Setup}(1^\lambda)$, $(\mathsf{sk}, \mathsf{vk}) \leftarrow_{\$} \mathsf{SS.KG(par)}$, and the protocol is run as follows, on private input $(\boldsymbol{m}, \sigma)$, where $\boldsymbol{m} \in \mathcal{M}^\ell$, and public input $\boldsymbol{m}' \in (\mathcal{M} \cup \{\star\})^\ell$:

Distribution $\mathsf{Real}^{\mathcal{A}}_{\mathsf{PoK,SS}}(\lambda)$:	Distribution $\mathsf{Ideal}^{\mathcal{A},\mathcal{S},\mathcal{L}}_{\mathsf{PoK,SS}}(\lambda)$:
$\mathsf{par} \leftarrow\!\!\!{}^{\$} \ \mathsf{SS.Setup}(1^\lambda)$	$\mathsf{par} \leftarrow\!\!\!{}^{\$} \ \mathsf{SS.Setup}(1^\lambda)$
$(\mathsf{sk},\mathsf{vk}) \leftarrow\!\!\!{}^{\$} \ \mathsf{SS.KG}(\mathsf{par})$	$(\mathsf{sk},\mathsf{vk}) \leftarrow\!\!\!{}^{\$} \ \mathsf{SS.KG}(\mathsf{par})$
$(m',m,\sigma) \leftarrow\!\!\!{}^{\$} \ \mathcal{A}(\mathsf{par},\mathsf{sk},\mathsf{vk})$	$(m',m,\sigma) \leftarrow\!\!\!{}^{\$} \ \mathcal{A}(\mathsf{par},\mathsf{sk},\mathsf{vk})$
If $m' \subseteq m \land \mathsf{SS.Ver}(\mathsf{par},\mathsf{vk},(m,\sigma))$ then	If $m' \subseteq m \land \mathsf{SS.Ver}(\mathsf{par},\mathsf{vk},(m,\sigma))$
$\quad (a,\mathsf{st_P}) \leftarrow\!\!\!{}^{\$} \ \mathsf{PoK.P_1}(\mathsf{par},\mathsf{vk},m',(m,\sigma))$	then
$\quad c \leftarrow\!\!\!{}^{\$} \ \mathsf{PoK.C}(\mathsf{par},\mathsf{vk})$	$\quad z \leftarrow\!\!\!{}^{\$} \ \mathcal{L}(\mathsf{par},\mathsf{sk})$
$\quad s \leftarrow\!\!\!{}^{\$} \ \mathsf{PoK.P_2}(\mathsf{st_P},c)$	$\quad (a,c,s) \leftarrow\!\!\!{}^{\$} \ \mathcal{S}(\mathsf{par},\mathsf{vk},m',z)$
$\quad$ Return $(\mathsf{sk},\mathsf{vk},m',(a,c,s))$	$\quad$ Return $(\mathsf{sk},\mathsf{vk},m',(a,c,s))$
Return $\bot$	Return $\bot$

Fig. 6. Distributions for the definition of HVZK

(1) The prover initially takes inputs par, vk, and a candidate signature-message pair (m,σ), and outputs $(a,\mathsf{st_P}) \leftarrow\!\!\!{}^{\$} \ \mathsf{PoK.P_1}(\mathsf{par},\mathsf{vk},m', (m,\sigma))$. The message a is sent to the verifier.

(2) The verifier outputs $c \leftarrow\!\!\!{}^{\$} \ \mathsf{PoK.C}(\mathsf{par},\mathsf{vk})$, and the *challenge* c is sent to the prover.

(3) The prover outputs $s \leftarrow\!\!\!{}^{\$} \ \mathsf{PoK.P_2}(\mathsf{st_P},c)$, and sends s to the verifier.

(4) Finally, the verifier outputs a Boolean value $\mathsf{PoK.V}(\mathsf{par},\mathsf{vk},m',a,c,s) \in \{\mathtt{true},\mathtt{false}\}$.

We say that PoK is correct if, whenever $\mathsf{SS.Ver}(\mathsf{par},\mathsf{vk},(m,\sigma)) = \mathtt{true}$ and $m' \subseteq m$, then the verifier also outputs $\mathtt{true}$.

SPECIAL SOUNDNESS. We target *special soundness*. To this end, we say that $(\mathsf{par},\mathsf{vk},m',a,c,s)$ is an *accepting* transcript if par is a valid output of $\mathsf{SS.Setup}$, vk is a valid output of $\mathsf{SS.KG}(\mathsf{par})$, c is a valid output of $\mathsf{PoK.C}(\mathsf{par},\mathsf{vk})$, and $\mathsf{PoK.V}(\mathsf{par},\mathsf{vk},m',a,c,s)$ is $\mathtt{true}$.

Definition 2. *We say that* PoK *as above is* special-sound *if there exists an efficient algorithm* $\mathsf{Extract}$ *which, given any two valid transcripts* $(\mathsf{par},\mathsf{vk},m',a,c,s)$, $(\mathsf{par},\mathsf{vk},m',a,c',s')$ *such that* $c \neq c'$, *then* $(m,\sigma) \leftarrow \mathsf{Extract}(\mathsf{par},\mathsf{vk},a, (c,s),(c',s'))$ *is such that* $\mathsf{SS.Ver}(\mathsf{par},\mathsf{vk},(m,\sigma)) = \mathtt{true}$ *and* $m' \subseteq m$.

We do not specify more general soundness goals further, as the use of special soundness will largely depend on the concrete security game modeling the security of the system using the PoK.

HONEST-VERIFIER ZERO-KNOWLEDGE. The protocols we give will be shown to be honest-verifier zero-knowledge, which suffices for their use as NIZKs via the Fiat-Shamir transform. We will in fact weaken the notion to allow for some *leakage* of the parameters given to the simulator. In particular, we model such leakage as a (possibly randomized) function $\mathcal{L}(\mathsf{par},\mathsf{sk})$ taking as input the parameters and the signing key.

Definition 3 (HVZK). *The protocol* PoK *for* SS *as above is perfectly* $\mathcal{L}$-*honest-verifier zero-knowledge* ($\mathcal{L}$-*HVZK*) *if there exists an efficient simulator* $\mathcal{S}$ *such* *that for all $\mathcal{A}$ and $\lambda \in \mathbb{N}$, the distributions* $\mathsf{Real}_{\mathsf{PoK},\mathsf{SS}}^{\mathcal{A}}(\lambda)$ *and* $\mathsf{Ideal}_{\mathsf{PoK},\mathsf{SS}}^{\mathcal{A},\mathcal{S},\mathcal{L}}(\lambda)$ *given in Fig. 6 are identical.*

5.2   Protocols

FULL DISCLOSURE. We start with the protocol for the case $m = m'$, i.e., the full-disclosure case. Recall that a BBS signature for a message $m \in \mathbb{Z}_p^{\ell}$ takes form $\sigma = (A = C(m)^{1/(x+e)}, e)$, where $C(m) = g_1 \prod_{i=1}^{\ell} h_1[i]^{m[i]}$. We assume from now on that $A \neq 1_{\mathbb{G}_1}$, and this assumption is almost without loss of generality, as a valid signature with $A = 1_{\mathbb{G}_1}$ implies finding a non-trivial DLOG relation, as $C(m) = 1_{\mathbb{G}_1}$ would be true as well. Recall that the signature is valid if

$$e(A, g_2^e X_2) = e(C(m), g_2) \,,$$

where $X_2 = g_2^x$ is the verification key. However, by bilinearity,

$$e(A, g_2^e X_2) = e(A, g_2^e) \cdot e(A, X_2) = e(A^e, g_2) \cdot e(A, X_2) \,.$$

And therefore, one can equivalently check that

$$e(A, X_2) = e(C(m) \cdot A^{-e}, g_2) \,. \tag{9}$$

The main idea is to provide suitably randomized versions of A and $B = C(m) \cdot A^{-e}$, which can be computed from a signature (A, e), and extend this with a proof of correctness attesting to the format of these values. In particular, we use $\overline{A} = A^r$ and $\overline{B} = (C(m) \cdot A^{-e})^r$, for which we still have $e(\overline{A}, X_2) = e(\overline{B}, g_2)$.

PROTOCOL DESCRIPTION. Concretely, we consider the following Σ-protocol:

- Given a signature (A, e) for the message m with $A \neq 1_{\mathbb{G}_1}$, the prover picks $r \leftarrow \mathbb{Z}_p^*$, and computes

$$\overline{A} \leftarrow A^r \,, \quad \overline{B} \leftarrow (C(m)A^{-e})^r = C(m)^r \overline{A}^{-e} \,.$$

  It also picks $\alpha, \beta \leftarrow_\$ \mathbb{Z}_p$, and computes $U \leftarrow C(m)^\alpha \overline{A}^\beta$. It sends $(\overline{A}, \overline{B}, U)$ to the verifier.
- The verifier picks a random challenge $c \leftarrow_\$ \mathbb{Z}_p$, and sends it to the prover
- The prover responds with (s, t), where

$$s \leftarrow \alpha + r \cdot c \,, \quad t \leftarrow \beta - e \cdot c \,.$$

- The verifier accepts if and only if

$$e(\overline{A}, X_2) = e(\overline{B}, g_2) \,, \quad U \cdot \overline{B}^c = C(m)^s \overline{A}^t \,.$$

SPECIAL-SOUNDNESS. It is not hard to see that the protocol is special sound. Indeed, given $\overline{A}, \overline{B}, U$, as well as $c_1 \neq c_2$, and (s_1, s_1, t_1, t_2) such that

$$e(\overline{A}, X_2) = e(\overline{B}, g_2), \quad U \cdot \overline{B}^{c_i} = C(m)^{t_i} \overline{A}^{s_i} \quad \text{for } i = 1, 2,$$

we can first extract r and e such that $\overline{B} = C(m)^r \overline{A}^{-e}$, because

$$\overline{B}^{c_1 - c_2} = C(m)^{t_1 - t_2} \overline{A}^{s_1 - s_2},$$

and thus we can set $r = (t_1 - t_2)/(c_1 - c_2)$ and $e = (s_2 - s_1)/(c_1 - c_2)$. If $r \neq 0$, then $(A = \overline{A}^{r^{-1}}, e)$ is a valid signature on m, because $e(\overline{A}, X_2) = e(\overline{B}, g_2)$ implies that $e(\overline{A}^{r^{-1}}, X_2) = e(\overline{B}^{r^{-1}}, g_2)$, and $\overline{B}^{r^{-1}} = C(m)A^{-e}$. If $r = 0$, then $e(\overline{A}, X_2) = e(\overline{A}^{-e}, g_2)$, which means $x = -e$, and this gives us a signature on m.

ZERO-KNOWLEDGE. The protocol is $\mathcal{L}$-HVZK, for $\mathcal{L}$ which, on input g_1, x, outputs (g_1^r, g_1^{rx}) for $r \leftarrow_{\$} \mathbb{Z}_p^*$, i.e., a random pair of form (U, U^x). The simulator then computes $\overline{A} \leftarrow_{\$} \mathbb{G}_1^*$, and set $\overline{C} = \overline{A}^x \in \mathbb{G}_1$ – this can be done by re-randomizing the leakage (U, U^x). Then, the simulator picks a random challenge $c \leftarrow_{\$} \mathbb{Z}_p$, as well as random $s, t \leftarrow_{\$} \mathbb{Z}_p$, and sets $U = C(m)^s \overline{A}^t \overline{B}^{-c}$.

The fact that the simulator needs a sample (U, U^x), and cannot simulate solely given the parameters and the verification key $X_2 = g_2^x$ is a technical oddity inherited from the use of type-3 pairings, and was also present in prior protocols [15]. Indeed, it is hard to compute g_1^x from the verification key g_2^x. However, this additional leakage is not really harmful. For example, *any* signature (A, e) on a message m already satisfies $A^x = C(m) \cdot A^{-e}$, and thus the protocol leaks no more than *any* valid message-signature pair. In particular, BBS remains secure given such leakage.

PARTIAL DISCLOSURE. For the case $m' \subsetneq m$, the components $m[i]$ for which $m'[i] = \star$ become parts of the witness. We let $I := \{i \in [\ell] : m[i] = \star\}$ and $J := [n] \setminus I$. We also let $C_J(m) = g_1 \prod_{i \in J} h_1[i]^{m[i]}$, and note that $C_J(m)$ can be computed from the public input m' by the verifier.

- Given a signature (A, e) for the message m with $A \neq 1_{\mathbb{G}_1}$, the prover picks $r \leftarrow \mathbb{Z}_p^*$, and computes

$$\overline{A} \leftarrow A^r, \quad \overline{B} \leftarrow (C(m)A^{-e})^r = C_J(m)^r \cdot \left(\prod_{i \in I} h_1[i]^{m[i]} \right)^r \cdot \overline{A}^{-e}.$$

It also picks $\alpha, \beta \leftarrow_{\$} \mathbb{Z}_p$, and also $\delta_i \leftarrow_{\$} \mathbb{Z}_p$ for every $i \in I$ and computes

$$U \leftarrow C_J(m)^\alpha \cdot \overline{A}^\beta \cdot \prod_{i \in I} h_1[i]^{\delta_i}$$

It sends $(\overline{A}, \overline{B}, U)$ to the verifier.
- The verifier picks a random challenge $c \leftarrow_{\$} \mathbb{Z}_p$, and sends it to the prover

– The prover responds with $(s, t, (u_i)_{i \in I})$, where

$$s \leftarrow \alpha + r \cdot c, \quad t \leftarrow \beta - e \cdot c, \quad u_i \leftarrow \delta_i + r \cdot m[i] \cdot c \; \forall i \in I.$$

– The verifier accepts if and only if

$$e(\overline{A}, X_2) = e(\overline{B}, g_2), \quad U \cdot \overline{B}^c = C_J(m)^s \overline{A}^t \prod_{i \in I} h_1[i]^{u_i}.$$

One can easily adapt the arguments for the above protocols for full disclosure to show special soundness and $\mathcal{L}$-HVZK.

NIZKs. Our protocols can be transformed into NIZKs in the random oracle model via the Fiat-Shamir transform [21] or Fischlin's transform [22]. For the Fiat-Shamir version, the prover computes $\overline{A}, \overline{B}, U$ as above, then lets $c \leftarrow H(m', \overline{A}, \overline{B}, U)$, and finally computes $s, t, (u_i)_{i \in I}$ as above. The final proof is

$$\pi = (\overline{A}, \overline{B}, c, s, t, (u_i)_{i \in I}).$$

Verification checks that $e(\overline{A}, X_2) = e(\overline{B}, g_2)$ and that $c = H(m', \overline{A}, \overline{B}, U)$ with

$$U \leftarrow \overline{B}^{-c} C_J(m)^s \overline{A}^t \prod_{i \in I} h_1[i]^{u_i}.$$

Note that we could include U instead of c, but this leads to longer proofs for curves like BLS12-381, where elements in $\mathbb{G}_1$ have longer descriptions than scalars.

6 Signatures for Group Elements and Blind Issuance

One central property of BBS is its support of *blind issuance*, the setting where a user sends a commitment $C \in \mathbb{G}_1$ to the signer to obtain a pair $\sigma = (A, e)$ with $A = C^{\frac{1}{x+e}}$—if $C = g_1 \prod_{i=1}^{\ell} h_1[i]^{m[i]}$ for a message m, then σ is a valid signature on m, but crucially, the signer never learns m. In fact, the user could make $m[1]$ uniform, turning C into a perfectly-hiding (generalized) Pedersen commitment [31]. This approach is particularly important when σ acts as a credential, and we want to hide the actual attributes from the issuer. Blind issuance of BBS signatures is also part of an unofficial draft [3], which also requires the addition of a proof of knowledge for a representation of C, which consists of $O(\ell)$ scalars and can be expensive when ℓ is large. Here, we show that in the AGM the scheme is already sufficiently secure without such a proof. A suitable proof of knowledge is however still necessary if the user needs to reveal part of the attributes to the issuer, to prove these are consistent with the commitment. However, we note that this aspect would be orthogonal to our analysis below.

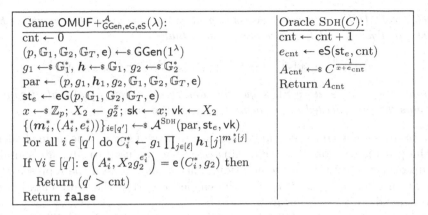

Fig. 7. One-more unforgeability of BBS. This game captures the one-more unforgeability of BBS when given an SDH oracle which returns $C^{1/(x+e_i)}$ for its i-th query, where e_i is generated via eS. We assume here that $\mathcal{A}$ returns a set of q' distinct forgery attempts (i.e., no double entry are present in the list returned by $\mathcal{A}$.)

ONE-MORE UNFORGEABILITY. BBS can be thought as a signature scheme signing a group element $C \in \mathbb{G}_1$ as $\sigma = (A = C^{\frac{1}{x+e}}, e)$. However, it does not achieve unforgeability when signing group elements (as in the case of *structure-preserving signatures* (SPS) [5]). Indeed, the attacker, given $\sigma = (A, e)$, directly obtains other valid signatures, such as $\sigma' = (A^2, e)$, which is a valid signature for $C^2 \neq C$. Nonetheless, if $C = g_1 \prod_{i=1}^{\ell} h_1[i]^{m[i]}$, it is very unlikely that the attacker can exhibit a message m' such that $C^2 = g_1 \prod_{i=1}^{\ell} h_1[i]^{m'[i]}$, i.e., such that (A^2, e) is valid for m'.

We formalize this by showing BBS satisfies *one-more unforgeability* (OMUF), where given access q times to an oracle SDH that signs group elements as above— i.e., on input $C \in \mathbb{G}_1$ it returns $\sigma = (A, e)$ with $A = C^{\frac{1}{x+e}}$—it is impossible for the attacker to come up with $q + 1$ valid BBS signatures. This property is defined via Game $\mathsf{OMUF}+^{\mathcal{A}}_{\mathsf{GGen},\mathsf{eG},\mathsf{eS}}(\lambda)$ in Fig. 7. Similar to Sect. 4, the game is parameterized by the group generator GGen and by a pair of algorithms eG, eS used to generate the e_i's ahead of time. We also define

$$\mathsf{Adv}^{\mathsf{omuf}+}_{\mathsf{GGen},\mathsf{eG},\mathsf{eS}}(\mathcal{A}, \lambda) = \Pr\left[\mathsf{OMUF}+^{\mathcal{A}}_{\mathsf{GGen},\mathsf{eG},\mathsf{eS}}(\lambda)\right] .$$

We stress that we *could* define a general notion of signatures on commitment values, and require that upon obtaining q signatures on arbitrary elements from the commitment space, the attacker cannot come up with $q + 1$ valid signatures on commitments, along with their openings. However, we prefer the rather straightforward BBS-specific game as a better illustration of this property.

MAIN RESULT. We prove now that BBS satisfies one-more unforgeability in the AGM, and we do so via a reduction to its SUF+ security as defined in Sect. 4.

Theorem 3 (One-more unforgeability). *Let* GGen *be a group parameter generator, producing groups of order* $p(\lambda)$, *and let* eG, eS *as above. For every* *algebraic OMUF+ adversary $\mathcal{A}$ issuing at most $q = q(\lambda)$ SDH queries, there exists an algebraic SUF+ adversary $\mathcal{B}$ such that*

$$\mathsf{Adv}^{\mathsf{omuf+}}_{\mathsf{GGen,eG,eS}}(\mathcal{A}, \lambda) \leqslant \mathsf{Adv}^{\mathsf{suf+}}_{\mathsf{GGen,eG,eS}}(\mathcal{B}, \lambda) + \delta_{\mathsf{eG,eS}}(q, \lambda) \, .$$

The adversary $\mathcal{B}$ issues q SIGN queries, and runs in time equal that of running $\mathcal{A}$, plus the time needed to perform $O(q^3)$ operations in $\mathbb{Z}_p$.

The proof is deferred to the full version due to lack of space. The main challenge in the proof is to show how the signing oracle can be used to simulate signing a group element, given its representation. This is easy to do if the representation is only in terms of g_1 and h_1, but the challenge is that the representation can also depend on prior signatures.

Theorem 3 yields the following corollary when combined with Theorem 2.

Corollary 1 (One-more unforgeability). *Let GGen be a group parameter generator, producing groups of order $p(\lambda)$, and let eG, eS as above. For every algebraic OMUF+ adversary $\mathcal{A}$ issuing at most q SDH queries, there exists a q-DL adversary $\mathcal{C}_1$ and a DL adversary $\mathcal{C}_2$ such that*

$$\mathsf{Adv}^{\mathsf{omuf+}}_{\mathsf{GGen,eG,eS}}(\mathcal{A}, \lambda) \leqslant \mathsf{Adv}^{q\text{-dl}}_{\mathsf{GGen}}(\mathcal{C}_1, \lambda) + \mathsf{Adv}^{\mathsf{dl}}_{\mathsf{GGen}}(\mathcal{C}_2, \lambda) + 2\delta_{\mathsf{eG,eS}}(q, \lambda) + \frac{1}{p(\lambda)} \, .$$

The adversaries $\mathcal{C}_1$ and $\mathcal{C}_2$ are obtained by using $\mathcal{B}$ from Theorem 3 within the adversaries of Theorem 2.

APPLICATIONS. As mentioned above, a typical application of BBS signatures is in the context of credentials. The above result validates the security of the canonical solution where the user obtains a credential for a vector of attributes m by sending $C = g_1 \prod_{i=1}^{\ell} h_1[i]^{m[i]}$ to the authority, which in turn responds with the actual credential $(C^{\frac{1}{x+e}}, e)$ for a random e. The OMUF security from Theorem 3 and Corollary 1 implies that a malicious user (or any set of multiple such users) can only obtain q credentials by interacting with the authority q times. The user can then show the credential multiple times in an unlinkable way by using the zk-PoKs from Sect. 5, typically compiled via the Fiat-Shamir transform. These showings are then consistent with at most q attribute vectors. When issuing a credential, the user does not need to send any proof of knowledge along with C, unless the credential issuing needs to enforce some format on the values contained by C, in which case extra proofs need to be sent along.

We note that analyzing the security of the entire credential system is non-trivial, especially if we want to resort to PoKs compiled via the Fiat-Shamir transform, which are not online extractable. We believe that a security analysis of variants of this system is however possible, albeit very tedious, in the AGM, where one can resort to the online-extractability of the proposed PoKs from Sect. 5 in the AGM, along the lines of [25]. This goes however beyond the scope of this paper.

Acknowledgments. We wish to thank Christian Paquin and Greg Zaverucha for extensive discussions around BBS and for providing feedback throughout this project. We also thank the EUROCRYPT 2023 reviewers for their excellent comments and suggestions. This research was partially supported by NSF grants CNS-2026774, CNS-2154174, a JP Morgan Faculty Award, a CISCO Faculty Award, and a gift from Microsoft.

References

1. BBS+ implementation. https://github.com/mattrglobal/bbs-signatures, Accessed 10 Apr 2022
2. BBS+ implementation. https://github.com/microsoft/bbs-node-referenceAccessed 10 Apr 2022
3. Blind signatures extension of the BBS signature scheme. https://identity.foundation/bbs-signature/draft-blind-bbs-signatures.txt Accessed 10 Apr 2022
4. Cheon's attack and its effect on the security of big trusted setups. https://ethresear.ch/t/cheons-attack-and-its-effect-on-the-security-of-big-trusted-setups/6692 Accessed 10 Apr 2022
5. Abe, M., Fuchsbauer, G., Groth, J., Haralambiev, K., Ohkubo, M.: Structure-preserving signatures and commitments to group elements. In: Rabin, T. (ed.) CRYPTO 2010. LNCS, vol. 6223, pp. 209–236. Springer, Heidelberg (2010). https://doi.org/10.1007/978-3-642-14623-7_12
6. Au, M.H., Susilo, W., Mu, Y.: Constant-size dynamic k-TAA. In: De Prisco, R., Yung, M. (eds.) SCN 2006. LNCS, vol. 4116, pp. 111–125. Springer, Heidelberg (2006). https://doi.org/10.1007/11832072_8
7. Barreto, P.S.L.M., Lynn, B., Scott, M.: Constructing elliptic curves with prescribed embedding degrees. In: Cimato, S., Persiano, G., Galdi, C. (eds.) SCN 2002. LNCS, vol. 2576, pp. 257–267. Springer, Heidelberg (2003). https://doi.org/10.1007/3-540-36413-7_19
8. Bauer, B., Fuchsbauer, G., Loss, J.: A classification of computational assumptions in the algebraic group model. In: Micciancio, D., Ristenpart, T. (eds.) CRYPTO 2020. LNCS, vol. 12171, pp. 121–151. Springer, Cham (2020). https://doi.org/10.1007/978-3-030-56880-1_5
9. Boneh, D., Boyen, X.: Short signatures without random oracles and the SDH assumption in bilinear groups. J. Cryptol. **21**(2), 149–177 (2007). https://doi.org/10.1007/s00145-007-9005-7
10. Boneh, D., Boyen, X., Shacham, H.: Short group signatures. In: Franklin, M. (ed.) CRYPTO 2004. LNCS, vol. 3152, pp. 41–55. Springer, Heidelberg (2004). https://doi.org/10.1007/978-3-540-28628-8_3
11. Bowe, S.: BLS12-381: New zk-SNARK elliptic curve construction. https://electriccoin.co/blog/new-snark-curve/ (2017)
12. Brickell, E., Li, J.: A pairing-based DAA scheme further reducing TPM resources. In: Acquisti, A., Smith, S.W., Sadeghi, A.-R. (eds.) Trust 2010. LNCS, vol. 6101, pp. 181–195. Springer, Heidelberg (2010). https://doi.org/10.1007/978-3-642-13869-0_12
13. Brickell, E., Li, J.: Enhanced privacy ID from bilinear pairing for hardware authentication and attestation. Int. J. Inf. Priv. Secur. Integr. **1**(1), 3–33 (2011). https://doi.org/10.1504/IJIPSI.2011.043729, https://doi.org/10.1504/IJIPSI.2011.043729
14. Brown, D.R.L., Gallant, R.P.: The static Diffie-Hellman problem. Cryptology ePrint Archive, Report 2004/306 (2004), https://eprint.iacr.org/2004/306

15. Camenisch, J., Drijvers, M., Lehmann, A.: Anonymous attestation using the strong diffie hellman assumption revisited. In: Franz, M., Papadimitratos, P. (eds.) Trust 2016. LNCS, vol. 9824, pp. 1–20. Springer, Cham (2016). https://doi.org/10.1007/978-3-319-45572-3_1

16. Camenisch, J., Lysyanskaya, A.: A Signature Scheme with Efficient Protocols. In: Cimato, S., Persiano, G., Galdi, C. (eds.) SCN 2002. LNCS, vol. 2576, pp. 268–289. Springer, Heidelberg (2003). https://doi.org/10.1007/3-540-36413-7_20

17. Camenisch, J., Lysyanskaya, A.: Signature schemes and anonymous credentials from bilinear maps. In: Franklin, M. (ed.) CRYPTO 2004. LNCS, vol. 3152, pp. 56–72. Springer, Heidelberg (2004). https://doi.org/10.1007/978-3-540-28628-8_4

18. Chen, L.: A DAA scheme requiring less TPM resources. In: Bao, F., Yung, M., Lin, D., Jing, J. (eds.) Inscrypt 2009. LNCS, vol. 6151, pp. 350–365. Springer, Heidelberg (2010). https://doi.org/10.1007/978-3-642-16342-5_26

19. Chen, S., Steinberger, J.: Tight security bounds for key-alternating ciphers. In: Nguyen, P.Q., Oswald, E. (eds.) EUROCRYPT 2014. LNCS, vol. 8441, pp. 327–350. Springer, Heidelberg (2014). https://doi.org/10.1007/978-3-642-55220-5_19

20. Cheon, J.H.: Security analysis of the strong diffie-hellman problem. In: Vaudenay, S. (ed.) EUROCRYPT 2006. LNCS, vol. 4004, pp. 1–11. Springer, Heidelberg (2006). https://doi.org/10.1007/11761679_1

21. Fiat, A., Shamir, A.: How to prove yourself: practical solutions to identification and signature problems. In: Odlyzko, A.M. (ed.) CRYPTO 1986. LNCS, vol. 263, pp. 186–194. Springer, Heidelberg (1987). https://doi.org/10.1007/3-540-47721-7_12

22. Fischlin, M.: Communication-efficient non-interactive proofs of knowledge with online extractors. In: Shoup, V. (ed.) CRYPTO 2005. LNCS, vol. 3621, pp. 152–168. Springer, Heidelberg (2005). https://doi.org/10.1007/11535218_10

23. Fuchsbauer, G., Kiltz, E., Loss, J.: The algebraic group model and its applications. In: Shacham, H., Boldyreva, A. (eds.) CRYPTO 2018. LNCS, vol. 10992, pp. 33–62. Springer, Cham (2018). https://doi.org/10.1007/978-3-319-96881-0_2

24. Galbraith, S., Paterson, K., Smart, N.: Pairings for cryptographers. Cryptology ePrint Archive, Report 2006/165 (2006), https://eprint.iacr.org/2006/165

25. Ghoshal, A., Tessaro, S.: Tight state-restoration soundness in the algebraic group model. In: Malkin, T., Peikert, C. (eds.) CRYPTO 2021. LNCS, vol. 12827, pp. 64–93. Springer, Cham (2021). https://doi.org/10.1007/978-3-030-84252-9_3

26. Hoang, V.T., Tessaro, S.: Key-alternating ciphers and key-length extension: exact bounds and multi-user security. In: Robshaw, M., Katz, J. (eds.) CRYPTO 2016. LNCS, vol. 9814, pp. 3–32. Springer, Heidelberg (2016). https://doi.org/10.1007/978-3-662-53018-4_1

27. Jao, D., Yoshida, K.: Boneh-Boyen signatures and the strong Diffie-Hellman problem. In: Shacham, H., Waters, B. (eds.) Pairing 2009. LNCS, vol. 5671, pp. 1–16. Springer, Heidelberg (2009). https://doi.org/10.1007/978-3-642-03298-1_1

28. Looker, T., Kalos, V., Whitehead, A., Lodder, M.: The BBS Signature Scheme. Internet-Draft draft-irtf-cfrg-bbs-signatures-01, Internet Engineering Task Force (Oct 2022), https://datatracker.ietf.org/doc/draft-irtf-cfrg-bbs-signatures/01/, work in Progress

29. Maurer, U.: Unifying zero-knowledge proofs of knowledge. In: Preneel, B. (ed.) AFRICACRYPT 2009. LNCS, vol. 5580, pp. 272–286. Springer, Heidelberg (2009). https://doi.org/10.1007/978-3-642-02384-2_17

30. Patarin, J.: A proof of security in $O(2^n)$ for the Benes scheme. In: Vaudenay, S. (ed.) AFRICACRYPT 08. LNCS, vol. 5023, pp. 209–220. Springer, Heidelberg (Jun (2008)

31. Pedersen, T.P.: Non-interactive and information-theoretic secure verifiable secret sharing. In: Feigenbaum, J. (ed.) CRYPTO 1991. LNCS, vol. 576, pp. 129–140. Springer, Heidelberg (1992). https://doi.org/10.1007/3-540-46766-1_9

32. Pointcheval, D., Sanders, O.: Short randomizable signatures. In: Sako, K. (ed.) CT-RSA 2016. LNCS, vol. 9610, pp. 111–126. Springer, Cham (2016). https://doi.org/10.1007/978-3-319-29485-8_7

33. Sonnino, A., Al-Bassam, M., Bano, S., Meiklejohn, S., Danezis, G.: Coconut: Threshold issuance selective disclosure credentials with applications to distributed ledgers. In: NDSS 2019. The Internet Society (Feb 2019)

Non-interactive Blind Signatures
for Random Messages

Lucjan Hanzlik[✉]

CISPA Helmholtz Center for Information Security, Saarbrücken, Germany
hanzlik@cispa.de

Abstract. Blind signatures allow a signer to issue signatures on messages chosen by the signature recipient. The main property is that the recipient's message is hidden from the signer. There are many applications, including Chaum's e-cash system and Privacy Pass, where no special distribution of the signed message is required, and the message can be random. Interestingly, existing notions do not consider this practical use case separately. In this paper, we show that constraining the recipient's choice over the message distribution spawns a surprising new primitive that improves the well-established state-of-the-art. We formalize this concept by introducing the notion of non-interactive blind signatures (NIBS). Informally, the signer can create a presignature with a specific recipient in mind, identifiable via a public key. The recipient can use her secret key to finalize it and receive a blind signature on a random message determined by the finalization process. The key idea is that online interaction between the signer and recipient is unnecessary. We show an efficient instantiation of NIBS in the random oracle model from signatures on equivalence classes. The exciting part is that, in this case, for the recipient's public key, we can use preexisting keys for Schnorr, ECDSA signatures, El-Gamal encryption scheme or even the Diffie-Hellman key exchange. Reusing preexisting public keys allows us to distribute anonymous tokens similarly to cryptocurrency airdropping. Additional contributions include tagged non-interactive blind signatures (TNIBS) and their efficient instantiation. A generic construction in the random oracle or common reference string model based on verifiable random functions, standard signatures, and non-interactive proof systems.

Keywords: Blind Signatures · Non-Interactive Scheme · Random Oracle Model · Signatures on Equivalence Classes

1 Introduction

Blind signatures are a cryptographic primitive introduced by David Chaum [16]. Contrary to standard digital signature schemes, the signing process is an interactive protocol between two parties: the signer and the user (also called the recipient). The main property of blind signature schemes is like the name suggests *blindness*. It ensures that the signer does not 'see' the signed message. Blind

© International Association for Cryptologic Research 2023
C. Hazay and M. Stam (Eds.): EUROCRYPT 2023, LNCS 14008, pp. 722–752, 2023.
https://doi.org/10.1007/978-3-031-30589-4_25

signatures also require *one-more unforgeability*, where an adversary has access to a signing oracle and must return one-more message-signature pair than the number of queries made.

Blind signature schemes find many applications. In Chaum's seminal work [16], it was shown how to use a blind signature for electronic cash (or e-cash), the forerunner of modern cryptocurrencies. The design of e-cash inspired many follow-up work [4,12,21,37]. The idea is elegant but simple. The bank issues e-cash as signatures on random identifiers chosen by users. To spend, the user shows the identifier (i.e., message) and the corresponding signature to the merchant, who can collect the amount from the bank. The bank keeps a list of 'used' identifiers to prevent double-spending. To make transactions unlinkable, the bank uses a blind signature to create the signature together with the user.

E-cash implements the idea of a single-use unlinkable electronic coins (e-coins), coupons or tokens. This interpretation inspired recent advances. Tumblebit [31] is a cryptographic tumbler that uses blind signatures as a building block. It introduces an intermediary party that issues a single-use coupon in exchange for cryptocurrency. The payer can send this coupon to another user who can redeem it for cryptocurrency. To ensure unlinkability, the intermediary issues several coupons in a given interval, creating an anonymity set. Blindness provides the property that any combination of sender/recipient is equally likely for the given anonymity set. This idea was also used in Privacy Pass [17], which relies on single-use coupons to make web browsing using anonymous networks more user-friendly. One of the use cases of Privacy Pass allows users to redeem coupons while omitting the increased number of CAPTCHAs that service providers challenge when using anonymous networks. Privacy Pass was recently extended with a rate-limiting version [32] also called Private Access Tokens. One of the main changes is that the coupon is not created on a random message but rather on a challenge created by the server. The challenge is to ensure that malicious users do not hoard coupons to circumvent daily limits. Blind signatures are used differently in voting schemes [14] and anonymous credentials (AC) [6,23]. Voters can get a signed receipt without revealing their vote. In AC, blind signatures provide means for issuing unlinkable credentials. Contrary to the e-cash application, the signed message in those applications is not a random identifier.

We observe that the user can randomly choose the blindly signed message in many applications, and the selected message does not need to be from a specific distribution. Following this, we consider the following research question.

Can we use this observation to move research on blind signatures forward?

Prior Work on Blind Signatures

In his seminal work [16], David Chaum introduced the idea of blind signatures. He defined a signing function s that commutes with a function c. The user can now send $c(m)$ to the signer, who signs this blinded message and returns $s(c(m))$. Because of the commutativeness property, the user can extract $s(m)$ using the inverse function c^{-1} without the signer learning anything about the signed message m. It is worth noting that the user can always pick what gets

Table 1. Comparison between two-move blind signatures, Privacy Pass, and our NIBS and TNIBS. n denotes the number of signatures/tokens issued concurrently. All results are given in bits and refer to a 3072-bit RSA modulus, BLS12-381 [11] parameters for pairing-based schemes and a standard 256-bit elliptic curve for Privacy Pass. We assume that messages/nonces are 128-bit long. We indicate if the first message of user U can be reused by signer S to issue new tokens.

Scheme	Communication complexity		$|m| + |sig|$	$|pk|$	Reusable 1st msg.	Security
	U → S	S → U				
Blind BLS [10]	$n \times 382$	$n \times 382$	510	3072	✗	ROM
Privacy Pass [17]	$n \times 257$	$n \times 257 + 512$	385	257	✗	ROM
RSA (PAT) [16,35]	$n \times 3072$	$n \times 3072$	3200	3072	✗	ROM
NIBS	$382^\dagger$	$n \times 1655$	1909	1526	✓	ROM+GGM
TNIBS	$382^\dagger$	$n \times 2546$	2800	1526	✓	ROM+GGM
Our Generic	$O(1)^\dagger$	$O(n)$			✓	ROM or CRS

†– The recipient's public key must be sent to the signer. There is no cost if a PKI is available.

signed. The main security properties defined by Chaum are that the inverse function s^{-1} does not leak anything about s, and $c(x)$ does not leak anything about x. Those intuitions for unforgeability and blindness were more formally captured in follow-up work.

Pointcheval and Stern [40,41] defined unforgeability using a so-called one more forgery. Instead of defining it as the inability to extract the secret key s from the public key s^{-1}, they introduced a security experiment where the adversary is given oracle access to the signer. The winning condition is to output $k+1$ message-signature pairs while only making k queries to the oracle. Juels, Luby, and Ostrovsky [33] introduced a formal experiment defining the notion of blindness, where the adversary must guess the order in which it issues two messages (m_0, m_1) of its choosing. This definition considers the signing keys to be *honestly* generated by the experiment and given to the adversary. Contrary to that, the adversary outputs the public key in the *maliciously* generated key model [18]. The adversary is not required to execute the key generation algorithm or even to know the corresponding secret key. At the end of the blindness experiment, the adversary also receives the corresponding signatures (σ_0, σ_1). If one of the signatures was incorrect or the user algorithm aborted, the adversary gets $(\perp, \perp)$ instead information about which interaction failed. Camenisch, Neven, and Shelat introduced blindness under selective failure [13], which considers this additional information. Fischlin and Schröder later showed [19] how to turn every blind signature scheme into a selective-failure blind one.

Chaum's definition considers what we call today a two-move blind signature scheme with one message from the user and one from the signer. While follow-up work considers the interaction between the user and signer as an interactive protocol with multiple rounds, two-move blind signatures are considered round-optimal and provide concurrent security. Many round-optimal schemes were proposed [18,22,34], including the practical blind BLS scheme [10] with concise signature size. Interestingly, in his work Pass [38], calls two-move blind signatures non-interactive. Notably, interaction is inherent since the user must keep an internal state to de-blind the signer's response. Three-move blind signatures were also explicitly defined [29] since they can be generically constructed from linear identification schemes in the random oracle model. Constructing such schemes from standard assumptions without the random oracle or common reference string model seems hard [20]. We can build blind signatures from various assumptions, including post-quantum secure ones [3,30]. Recently, Chairattana-Apirom et al. [15] showed how to build concurrent secure blind signature schemes from discrete logarithm and RSA-type assumptions.

Paraphrasing the research question stated above. Can we use the observation that in many applications, the user can randomly choose the message to design something new that was not considered in prior work and opens a new chapter in the blind signature literature?

Our Contribution

In the case of two-move blind signatures, the user/recipient sends the requested message in the blinded form to the signer and later uses the interactions state to unblind the response. Our main idea is that since the recipient does not require any specific distribution or structure of the message, the message can be an output of the unblinding step. In other words, *there is no need for interaction.*

We capture this by defining a new cryptographic primitive called non-interactive blind signatures for random messages or NIBS for short. As it turned out, defining meaningful notation for such signatures is not simple, and the following strawman approach *does not work*. Since no interaction is required, the signer can create a presignature psig on some random message/nonce and share it. The recipient can then finalize the presignature to a signature on a random message. As already mentioned, such a notion does not work and cannot provide meaningful security properties. The problem with defining non-interactive blind signatures in that way is that the recipient can repeat the process and get a new message-signature pair. The returned pair must be a signature on a new message. Otherwise, the signer could link the issuing process to the final signature. Fortunately, our notion of NIBS does not have the same problems as the strawman approach.

What is needed is some secret input from the recipient. The natural idea is to use the recipient's public key. The signer must include the recipient's public key as input to the signing process. The returned presignature can be finalized using the recipient's secret key and the signer's nonce. Later, we will show a scheme where we can use, for example, the recipient's PKI public key or ephemeral keys from TLS connections. Using the preexisting public key of the recipient, we can use NIBS in various applications where we cannot use standard blind signatures.

The main contribution of this paper is the formal definition of NIBS and an appropriate security model. The intuition behind NIBS can be easily explained using an analogous notion to the one used by Chaum [16]. The signer computes a presignature $s(\mathsf{nonce}, c)$ using issuing function s, a nonce of its choosing, and the recipient's function c. The recipient can finalize the presignature using $c^{-1}(\text{nonce}, s(\text{nonce}, c)) = (m, s(m))$, i.e., use the corresponding secret key c^{-1} to its public key c. We require that m and $s(m)$ not leak any information about c and the used nonce. We capture those properties using two definitions called *recipient blindness* and *nonce blindness*. The former captures the property that m and $s(m)$ do not leak information about c while the latter property that they do not leak any information about nonce. We formally define recipient blindness via an experiment where the adversary is explicitly given two honestly generated public keys of recipients and outputs two presignatures finalized by the experiment to (m_0, sig_0) and (m_1, sig_1). Finally, the adversary is given (m_0, sig_0) and (m_1, sig_1) in random order. For nonce blindness, the adversary is given just one recipient public key. In both cases, we do not consider aborts, i.e., if one of the signatures cannot be finalized, we give $(\perp, \perp)$ to the adversary. Our blindness definitions are defined in the malicious key model, where the adversary generates the signing key. We also define an honest key model notion. For unforgeability, we consider the standard one-more definition. The adversary gets access to an oracle returning presignatures for the adversary-specified nonce and public key. In the end, the adversary must return more valid signatures than queries, similar to one-more unforgeability of standard blind signatures.

NIBS are distinct from two-move blind signatures [38] and standard blind signatures in general. The former supports recipient-specified messages, while in NIBS, the message is an output of the unblinding process and is unpredictable for the recipient and the signer. NIBS can be issued without interaction, given the recipient's public key. Standard blind signatures are inherently interactive and require the recipient to keep a state to unblind the signer's response successfully. There are two ways of using NIBS. The first way is to use an existing PKI for recipients' public keys. A signer can issue presignatures to a set of users without interacting with them and publish the corresponding presignatures. Recipient blindness ensures that a given final message-signature pair cannot be linked to any particular recipient in the set. Nonce blindness allows the signer to repeat the process and issue more than one presignature per user. Alternatively, NIBS can be part of a two-move protocol. The first message is a freshly generated recipient public key, and the signer's response is the presignature. The result is not a standard two-move blind signature since the recipient will receive a signature under a random message. However, as we already discussed, this is acceptable in many applications. The main advantage compared to standard blind signature is that we can reuse the first message of the two-move protocol with NIBS in consecutive runs. The same is not possible for standard blind signatures. Nonce blindness ensures that reusing the recipient's public key does not allow an adversary to link final message-signature pairs to a recipient.

The main disadvantage of non-interactive blind signatures is that there is no simple way of including information about the freshness of the signature. Consider the following scenario. The user must provide a fresh signature that she adheres to the service's policies to access it, which might include a per-day limit. The signature is implemented via a blind signature scheme to protect the user's privacy. Of course, the user can hoard signatures and reuse them later. So the service requires that a challenge be signed instead of a random message, and NIBS cannot be used here. However, note that we already know how to date blind signatures [2] using partial blindness. We can formalize a similar definition in the non-interactive setting. Our next contribution is the definition of tagged non-interactive blind signatures TNIBS.

Definitions themself are not attractive if one cannot instantiate them with existing cryptography. Therefore we show how to build NIBS and TNIBS efficiently in the random oracle model. The central primitive we use are signatures on equivalence classes (SPS-EQ) [24, 27] and their tagged version (TBEQ) [28]. Interestingly, both schemes support recipient public keys in the form of standard discrete logarithm public keys $\mathsf{pk} = g^{\mathsf{sk}}$. Thus, our construction supports keys from various schemes like El-Gamal encryption, Diffie-Hellman key exchange, Schnorr, and DSA/ECDSA signatures. One caveat is that the underlying group (generated by g) must be a source group for which an admissible bilinear pairing function exists. Fortunately, we know how to construct such pairing-friendly groups [9] and use them to support the above algorithms. As our last contribution, we propose a generic construction of NIBS and TNIBS, which we can construct by generalizing ideas from the equivalence class construction. Both generic constructions are setup-free but rely on the random oracle model. We targetted a setup-free setting since it, by definition, allows to reuse recipients keys from different schemes, i.e., the recipients are not required to use a common reference string (CRS) to generate their keys. However, one can easily translate both schemes to work with a CRS instead of the random oracle model. For completeness, we will now summarize our contribution. In this paper, we improved the state-of-the-art of blind signatures as follows.

1. We introduce the notion and security model for (tagged) non-interactive blind signatures.
2. We show a very efficient construction in the random oracle model from signatures on equivalence classes that works well with preexisting public keys.
3. We provide a generic construction of NIBS and TNIBS in the random oracle model using verifiable random functions, digital signatures, and non-interactive proofs. Depending on the requirements, one can easily replace the random oracle model with the common reference string model.

Our Techniques

One of the main contributions of our paper is the efficient instantiation of non-interactive blind signatures in the random oracle model. Our construction is based on signature on equivalence classes that were already used as a building block to construct round-optimal blind signatures [22, 23]. A SPS-EQ signature on (g, g^x) can be transformed to a signature under (g^r, g^{rx}) without the secret signing key. Moreover, the transformed signature on (g^r, g^{rx}) is indistinguishable from a fresh signature on this message. This property is called the perfect adaptation of signatures. Together with the fact that messages (g, g^x) and (g^r, g^{rx})

are indistinguishable, under the decisional Diffie-Hellman assumption, form the main privacy property used in the design of [22,23].

The idea of our construction is as follows. The signer uses the SPS-EQ scheme to sign $(g^{\mathsf{sk}_R}, \mathsf{H}(\mathsf{nonce}))$, where g^{sk_R} is the recipients public key. It is worth noting that this key can be a preexisting public key of the recipient, as already mentioned in the introduction. The equivalence class signature is the NIBS presignature the user receives from the signer. The user can easily check the presignature using the SPS-EQ verification function. The interesting part follows. The actual NIBS signature is a SPS-EQ signature on the message $(g, \mathsf{H}(\mathsf{nonce})^{\mathsf{sk}_R^{-1}})$, also called the canonical representative of the equivalence class [5]. Note that we fix the first component of the message vector to g for the user to be able to compute exactly one blind signature from a presignature.

The unforgeability of the scheme directly follows from the unforgeability of the SPS-EQ scheme and the canonical representative notion. A "fresh" blind signature implies a signature on a class that was not signed already, which constitutes a valid forgery for the SPS-EQ scheme. On the other hand, blindness follows from the perfect adaptation of the SPS-EQ scheme and the inverse and strong decisional Diffie-Hellman assumptions. The idea is that anyone but the recipient cannot distinguish $\mathsf{H}(\mathsf{nonce})$ from $\mathsf{H}(\mathsf{nonce})^{\mathsf{sk}_R^{-1}}$. Thanks to careful random oracle programming, we show that the blindness of our construction relies on those assumptions.

We can easily modify this construction to support tags. In other words, with small changes, we can construct a TNIBS scheme using the same ideas. Hanzlik and Slamanig [28] introduced the notion of tag-based equivalence class signatures TBEQ. Contrary to SPS-EQ, they allow the signer to specify a tag τ that remains unchanged even after the user transforms the signature to a different representative of the same class. The idea of our TNIBS scheme is simple. We replace the SPS-EQ scheme in the NIBS construction above with a TBEQ scheme. The resulting construction is a tag-based, non-interactive blind signature scheme. Blindness follows from the same assumptions. The main difference is the unforgeability, which is now based on the unforgeability of the TBEQ scheme.

Surprisingly this construction follows a blueprint that we describe in the form of our generic construction. Firstly, we notice that the message in the construction is $\mathsf{H}(\mathsf{nonce})^{\mathsf{sk}_R^{-1}}$. The key property we use is that this value is unpredictable for the signer. Otherwise, the blindness property cannot hold. Looking at this value more closely, we notice that it can be interpreted as an evaluation of a pseudo-random function (PRF) on input nonce with key sk_R. In other words, the presignature defines the input to the PRF and its key. The blind signature is a signature on the evaluation of the PRF. Note that rather than a PRF, we have to consider a verifiable random function (VRF) since it provides a verification key that can be used as a public key. Finally, we observe that the SPS-EQ signature ensures that the recipient can only receive a valid blind signature if she correctly evaluates the VRF. Thus, the signature on equivalence classes actually acts as a proof system that binds the recipient and ensures correct evaluation of the random function.

Equipped with all those observations, we define our generic construction as follows. The signer creates the presignature by signing the recipient's VRF verification key pk_R and a nonce nonce. Since the presignature is a standard digital signature, it can be easily verified. The random blind signature message m is the evaluation of the VRF on nonce. The signature is a non-interactive proof that the recipient knows a signature on pk_R and nonce and that m is a proper evaluation of a VRF with key pk_R on input nonce. We can also use this blueprint to construct TNIBS generically. The only difference is that the presignature is additionally a signature under the tag τ. The statement of the proof system also changes a bit and now must include τ as part of the statement.

Applications

Privacy Pass. Privacy Pass [17] is a system designed to make life easier for anonymous network users who frequently solve CAPTCHAs. The idea is to let users first get a single-use token from an issuer via a non-anonymous network connection and let them redeem those tokens instead of solving CAPTCHAs. This provides a more user-friendly experience when using an anonymous network like TOR or a VPN connection. A Privacy-pass token is composed of the input and output of an oblivious pseudo-random function, where the issuer holds the function's secret key. During the issuing process, the user's platform (e.g., browser extension) requests an evaluation of the PRF on a chosen random input, similar to the e-cash scenario. It is worth noting that an oblivious PRF can be seen as a designated-verifier blind signature.

Recently, a rate-limiting version of Privacy Pass [32] called Private Access Token (PAT) was introduced. In this new variant, the number of tokens a user can get depend on a policy enforced by a trusted mediator. Moreover, the RSA blind signature scheme is used instead of the oblivious PRF, and the signed message is chosen as part of the service's challenge. This new version was recently introduced into iOS 16 and is supported by Apple[1]. In this setting, iCloud plays the role of the mediator and enforces the service's access policy. If the policy applies to the user, the issuer finalizes an RSA blind signature query made by the user. For a formal analysis of the RSA blind signature scheme used in PAT, see [35]. In both versions, the user and issuer must repeat the protocol several times to create multiple tokens at once, i.e., batch issuing. Although both parties can execute the protocol concurrently, the user is always required to participate. The same problem arises in the case of issuing more tokens after some time. We can improve this using (tagged) non-interactive blind signatures (see Table 1).

As we mentioned multiple times in the e-cash scenario, we are not always interested in the structure of the signed message and only care about the freshness of the token. This is also the case for the standard version of Privacy Pass, where the user chooses the input of the oblivious PRF. Replacing the oblivious

---

[1] https://developer.apple.com/videos/play/wwdc2022/10077/.

PRF with NIBS would improve the communication complexity in the case of multi-token issuance. In such a case, the user sends her public key to the issuer and reives n presignatures, which can be finalized into n unique tokens. The communication complexity from the user to the issuer is independent of n. The issuer can also afterward decide on the number of issued tokens. The exciting part is that to create more tokens, the issuer does not need to interact with the user and can make fresh presignatures using the user's public key. This design allows the issuer to issue new tokens periodically without interaction. Users can then later download them at their convenience. It is worth noting that this is impossible with an oblivious PRF or standard blind signatures, which inherently require interaction between both parties.

Unfortunately, standard NIBS cannot replace the RSA blind signature scheme in Private Access Token since the service and not the user chooses the signed message. PAT was introduced to enforce an access policy and only issue tokens for users adhering to the policy. Because the service chooses the blindly signed message, it knows that the user must conform to the latest policy, and the proof is fresh. Otherwise, a malicious user could hoard and use tokens during a given period breaking any per-day (or other) time policies. It is worth noting that the service gains no additional properties by picking a non-random message since it is hidden from both the mediator and the issuer. To get around this, instead of using NIBS, we can use the tagged version TNIBS. The tag remains unchanged after the user transforms the presignature into the final signature. This way, the service can date signatures. Using TNIBS instead of the RSA blind signature would have the same benefits as using NIBS in the case of the standard Privacy Pass. Moreover, our TNIBS solution is DLP based, which would be an alternative to the required RSA assumption.

Whistleblowing System. Ring signatures [42] were introduced as a way for whistleblowers to leak trusted intel without revealing their identity. According to a recent EU directive [1], big companies must implement a whistleblowing system for their employees to leak information anonymously about any misconduct of the employer. Ring signatures would be an ideal candidate to support such a system. The whistleblower combines the public keys of all employees and creates the ring signature. This solution does not work in case no PKI is implemented at the company. An alternative approach would be to build a system supporting Privacy Pass. A company or third-party supported service would issue single-use tokens to verified employees, who can later redeem the token with the intel. Unfortunately, this solution is inherently not private. Employees must first request a token, making them a target, i.e., whistleblowers hide inside the anonymity set of token owners and not in the set of all employees.

Implementing a whistleblowing system using NIBS would mitigate some of those problems. Assuming the recipient's public key is the ephemeral Diffie-Hellman key used for establishing a TLS connection, the system could look as follows. Every time an employee connects to some internal system of the company, she gets a token for the whistleblowing system. To redeem the token, the employee must install a plugin that retains the ephemeral TLS credential and later uses them to finalize the NIBS. It is worth noting that in this design, the company is oblivious to who installed the plugin, and potentially all employees could be the owner of a token showing up in the whistleblowing system. This application shows the power of our non-interactive blind signatures. We can use NIBS in systems where all recipients are potential users and can either use the presignature or just ignore it without the signer knowing about their choice.

Airdropping e-coins. Airdropping is a mechanism that allows sending cryptocurrency to users. This technique is frequently used to bootstrap interest in a currency by gifting cryptocurrency to users. An ideal scheme preserves the privacy of the recipient [43] once she redeems her coins. An airdropping system must also provide means for public accountability so that users can check that the airdropping mechanism will only produce a limited number of unique tokens.

Tublebit [31] is a protocol for anonymous cryptocurrency payments. At its core, the protocol implements the e-cash scenario. A designated party called the tumbler issues blind signatures for cryptocurrency payments. Blind signatures can later be redeemed to finalize the payment. Non-interactive blind signatures can add the airdropping functionality to the tumbler, introducing potential ways to attract new users. The key property of NIBS that allows this is non-interactives. The tumbler can look for publicly available public keys/addresses (e.g., on the blockchain or Github) and blindly drop NIBS to their owners.

Lottery System. NIBS can also be used to implement a fair lottery system. Users can register their public key for a given round by paying the lottery fee. What each user receives from the service is a NIBS presignature. The lottery winner is the user with a valid signature under the smallest/biggest message. This approach requires the service to replace the signing key with each lottery round. However, if we use the tagged version, the service can easily tag each signature with the round for which it was created. The lottery is fair, and the service cannot predict the outcome of the lottery because of the blindness property. On the other hand, because of one-more unforgeability, only users that pay can receive the prize.

Open Problems and Relation to Impossibility Results

The main open problem is to design an efficient NIBS scheme without pairings. Although one can instantiate our generic construction without using them, it will probably not be efficient due to the general-purpose use of proof systems. Efficient instantiations of NIBS from post-quantum assumptions are also desired. Another interesting problem is instantiating NIBS from standard assumptions without the CRS or random oracle model. Fischlin and Schröder [20] showed that constructing a statistical blind three-move blind signature from standard falsifiable assumptions without relying on the random oracle model or the common reference string model is impossible. The results carry over to two-move schemes and computational blind schemes with certain additional constraints.

Fortunately, there exist ways to circumvent those impossibility results, e.g., using complexity leveraging [25].

As already mentioned, one way of using NIBS is to run a two-move protocol. One would think this means that impossibility results also apply to NIBS. However, this is unclear and requires further investigation. Recall that a two-move protocol from NIBS is not a standard blind signature. In the latter, the recipient can arbitrarily choose the message, whereas, in the former protocol, the message depends on the nonce selected by the signer and the recipient's secret key. In other words, despite the NIBS two-move protocol being useful in similar applications as standard blind signatures, the notion is different.

We leave two open questions here. The first would be to verify if one can extend the impossibility results to blind signature schemes, where the message is not chosen by the recipient but is an output of the signing protocol. Note that the two-move protocol based on NIBS is an instantiation of such blind signatures. A positive answer to this question would mean that NIBS cannot be instantiated from standard falsifiable assumptions without ROM or a trusted setup phase. Alternatively, one could try to construct such a NIBS scheme, implying that the impossibility results from [20] do not hold if the message is not chosen by the recipient but as part of the protocol.

2   Preliminaries

2.1   Notation, Bilinear Groups and Assumptions

We denote by $y \leftarrow \mathcal{A}(x)$ the execution of algorithm $\mathcal{A}$ on input x and with output y. By $r \leftarrow_\$ S$ we mean that r is chosen uniformly at random over the set S. We will use $1_{\mathbb{G}}$ to denote the identity element in group $\mathbb{G}$ and $[n]$ to denote the set $\{1, \ldots, n\}$. Throughout the paper we will use the multiplicative notation and by $\mathcal{A}^{\mathcal{O}}$ we denote an algorithm $\mathcal{A}$ that has access to oracle $\mathcal{O}$.

Definition 1 (Bilinear Groups). *Let us consider cyclic groups $\mathbb{G}_1$, $\mathbb{G}_2$, $\mathbb{G}_T$ of prime order p. Let g_1, g_2 be generators of respectively $\mathbb{G}_1$ and $\mathbb{G}_2$. We call $e : \mathbb{G}_1 \times \mathbb{G}_2 \to \mathbb{G}_T$ a bilinear map (pairing) if it is efficiently computable and the following holds: 1) Bilinearity: $\forall (S,T) \in \mathbb{G}_1 \times \mathbb{G}_2$, $\forall a, b \in \mathbb{Z}_p$, we have $e(S^a, T^b) = e(S,T)^{a \cdot b}$, 2) Non-degeneracy: $e(g_1, g_2) \neq 1$ is a generator of group $\mathbb{G}_T$. We will consider Type-3 pairings, i.e., there is no efficiently computable isomorphism between $\mathbb{G}_1$ and $\mathbb{G}_2$.*

Definition 2 (Inverse Decisional Diffie-Hellman Assumption in $\mathbb{G}_1$ [7]). *For all PPT adversaries $\mathcal{A}$ given elements $(g_1^\alpha, g_1^\beta) \in \mathbb{G}_1^2$ it is hard to decide whether $\beta = \alpha^{-1} \bmod p$ or $\beta \leftarrow_\$ \mathbb{Z}_p^*$. We will use $\mathbf{Adv}_{\mathrm{invDDH}}(\mathcal{A})$ to denote the advantage of the adversary $\mathcal{A}$ in solving this problem.*

Definition 3 (Strong Decisional Diffie-Hellman Assumption in $\mathbb{G}_1$ [39]). *For all PPT adversaries $\mathcal{A}$ given elements $(g_1^\alpha, g_1^\beta, g_1^{\beta^{-1}}, g_1^\gamma) \in \mathbb{G}_1^4$ it is hard to decide whether $\gamma = \alpha \cdot \beta \bmod p$ or $\gamma \leftarrow_\$ \mathbb{Z}_p^*$. We will use $\mathbf{Adv}_{\mathrm{sDDH}}(\mathcal{A})$ to denote the advantage of the adversary $\mathcal{A}$ in solving this problem.*

2.2   Signature Schemes

Definition 4. *A signature scheme* SIG *consists of three PPT algorithms* (KeyGen, Sign, Verify) *with the following syntax.*

KeyGen(λ): *On input a security parameter λ, it outputs a public and secret signing key* (pk, sk).

Sign(sk, m): *On input a key* sk *and a message* m, *it outputs a signature* σ.

Verify(pk, m, σ): *On input a public key* pk, *a message* m *and a signature* σ, *it outputs either* 0 *or* 1.

We require the following properties of a signature scheme.

Correctness: *For every security parameter $\lambda \in \mathbb{N}$ and every message* m *given that* (pk, sk) $\leftarrow$ SIG.KeyGen(λ), sig $\leftarrow$ SIG.Sign(sk, m) *it holds that*

$$\text{SIG.Verify(pk, m, sig)} = 1.$$

Existential Unforgeability under Chosen Message Attacks: *Every PPT adversary $\mathcal{A}$ has at most negligible advantage in the following experiment.*

$\text{EUF-CMA}_{\mathcal{A},\text{SIG}}(\lambda)$	$\mathcal{O}_1(\text{sk}, \text{m})$
$Q := \emptyset$	$\sigma \leftarrow$ SIG.Sign(sk, m)
(sk, pk) $\leftarrow$ SIG.KeyGen(λ)	$Q := Q \cup \{\text{m}\}$
$(\text{m}^*, \sigma^*) \leftarrow \mathcal{A}^{\mathcal{O}_1(\text{sk},\cdot)}(\text{pk})$	**return** σ
return $\text{m}^* \neq \text{m} \ \forall \text{m} \in Q \ \wedge$	
$\qquad$ SIG.Verify(pk, $\text{m}^*, \sigma^*) = 1$	

The advantage of $\mathcal{A}$ is defined by $\mathbf{Adv}_{\text{SIG}}(\mathcal{A}) = \Pr[\text{EUF-CMA}_{\mathcal{A},\text{SIG}}(\lambda) = 1]$.

2.3   Dual-Mode Witness Indistinguishable Proofs

In our generic construction, we will use non-interactive proofs. To this end, we will use the dual-mode non-interactive witness indistinguishable proof system proposed by Groth-Sahai (GS) [26]. The main property of this system is that there exists a common reference string (crs) that can be either in the "binding" or "hiding" modes. Depending on the type, the system satisfies perfect soundness and extractability or perfect witness indistinguishability.

An interesting property of GS proofs [26] is that crs is composed of group elements that depending on the mode, fulfill a specific relation, e.g., a DDH tuple can be used as in the binding mode, and a non-DDH tuple in the hiding mode. Thus, instead of generating the common string by a trusted party, we can use the random oracle to output it. The idea is that with high probability, we will end up with a string in the hiding mode by querying the random oracle $\text{H}_{\text{crs}}(1)$, which outputs values of the form of reference strings. On the other hand, the reduction in the proof can program oracle H_{crs} to output a string in binding mode.

Definition 5 (Dual-Mode Witness Indistinguishable Proofs). *A dual-mode witness indistinguishable proof system for language $\mathcal{L_R}$ consists of algorithms* DMWI = (Setup, Prove, Verify, Extract) *with the following syntax.*

Setup(λ, binding): *On input of security parameter, it outputs a common reference string* crs *which we call binding. It additionally outputs a trapdoor* td_{Ext}.

Setup(λ, hiding): *On input of security parameter, it outputs a common reference string* crs, *which we call a hiding reference string.*

Prove(crs, x, w): *On input a common reference string* crs, *a statement* x *and a witness* w, *it outputs a proof* π.

Verify(crs, x, π): *On input the common reference string* crs, *a statement* x, *a proof* π, *it outputs either* 0 *or* 1.

Extract(td_{Ext}, x, π): *On input the extraction trapdoor* td_{Ext}, *a statement* x *and a proof* π, *it outputs a witness* w.

We require that DMWI *meets the following properties.*

Mode Indistinguishability: *For all λ we define the advantage of $\mathcal{A}$ against mode indistinguishability as follows:* $\mathbf{Adv}_{modeIND,\mathcal{A}}(\lambda) =$

$$\left| \Pr \left[\text{mode} = \text{mode}^* : \begin{array}{c} \text{mode} \leftarrow_\$ \{\text{binding, hiding}\}; \\ (\text{crs}) \leftarrow \text{Setup}(\lambda, \text{mode}); \\ \text{mode}^* \leftarrow \mathcal{A}(\lambda, \text{crs}) \end{array} \right] - \frac{1}{2} \right|,$$

where the probability is taken over the random choice of mode *and the random coins of* Setup. *We say that the proof system is mode indistinguishable if for all PPT adversaries, $\mathcal{A}$ the advantage is negligible.*

Perfect Completeness in both Modes: *For all security parameters $\lambda \in \mathbb{N}$, all statements $x \in \mathcal{L_R}$ and all witnesses w for which $\mathcal{R}(x, w) = 1$,* crs $\leftarrow$ Setup(λ, binding), *and* $\pi \leftarrow$ Prove(crs, x, w) *it holds that* Verify(crs, x, π) = 1. *The same holds for* crs $\leftarrow$ Setup(λ, hiding).

Perfect Soundness in Binding Mode: *For all adversaries $\mathcal{A}$ we have*

$$\Pr \left[\begin{array}{c} (\text{crs}, td_{Ext}) \leftarrow \text{Setup}(\lambda, \text{binding}) \\ (x, \pi) \leftarrow \mathcal{A}(\text{crs}) \end{array} : \begin{array}{c} \text{Verify}(\text{crs}, x, \pi) = 1 \\ \wedge\ x \notin \mathcal{L_R} \end{array} \right] = 0$$

Extractability in Binding Mode: *For any* (x, π), *it holds:*

$$\Pr \left[\begin{array}{c} (\text{crs}, td_{Ext}) \leftarrow \text{Setup}(\lambda, \text{binding}) \\ w \leftarrow \text{Extract}(td_{Ext}, x, \pi) \end{array} : \begin{array}{c} \text{Verify}(\text{crs}, x, \pi) = 1 \\ \implies \mathcal{R}(x, w) = 1 \end{array} \right] = 1$$

Perfect Witness-Indistinguishability in Hiding Mode: *We say that proof system for language $\mathcal{L_R}$ is perfectly witness indistinguishable if all adversaries $\mathcal{A}$ the following is* 0:

$$\left| \Pr \left[\begin{array}{c} \text{crs} \leftarrow \text{Setup}(\lambda, \text{hiding}) \\ (x, w_0, w_1) \leftarrow \mathcal{A}(\text{crs}) \\ b \leftarrow_\$ \{0, 1\} \\ \pi^* \leftarrow \text{Prove}(\text{crs}, x, w_b) \end{array} : \hat{b} \leftarrow \mathcal{A}(\text{crs}, \pi^*) \right] - \frac{1}{2} \right|,$$

where $\mathcal{A}$ is restricted to outputs such that $\mathcal{R}(x, w_0) = \mathcal{R}(x, w_1) = 1$.

2.4 Verifiable Random Function [36]

Definition 6 (Verifiable Random Function VRF). *A verifiable random function* $\mathsf{VRF} = (\mathsf{Gen}, \mathsf{Eval}, \mathsf{P}, \mathsf{V})$ *with input length* $n(\lambda)$ *and output length* $m(\lambda)$ *consists of the following PPT algorithms:*

$\mathsf{Gen}(\lambda)$**:** *On input of security parameter, outputs secret key* $\mathsf{sk}_{\mathsf{VRF}}$ *and public verification key* $\mathsf{pk}_{\mathsf{VRF}}$.

$\mathsf{Eval}(\mathsf{sk}_{\mathsf{VRF}}, x)$**:** *On input a secret key* $\mathsf{sk}_{\mathsf{VRF}}$ *and input value* $x \in \{0,1\}^{n(\lambda)}$ *it returns the output value* $y \in \{0,1\}^{m(\lambda)}$

$\mathsf{P}(\mathsf{sk}_{\mathsf{VRF}}, x)$**:** *On input a secret key* $\mathsf{sk}_{\mathsf{VRF}}$ *and* x *this prover algorithm outputs a proof* π_{VRF} *that* y *is consistent with the verification key* $\mathsf{pk}_{\mathsf{VRF}}$.

$\mathsf{V}(\mathsf{pk}_{\mathsf{VRF}}, \pi_{\mathsf{VRF}}, x, y)$**:** *On input a verification key* $\mathsf{pk}_{\mathsf{VRF}}$, *proof* π_{VRF}, x, y *this algorithm outputs 1 or 0.*

We require that VRF *meets the following properties.*

Completness: *For every security parameter* λ *and input* $x \in \{0,1\}^{n(\lambda)}$

$$\Pr\left[\begin{array}{l} (\mathsf{sk}_{\mathsf{VRF}}, \mathsf{pk}_{\mathsf{VRF}}) \leftarrow \mathsf{Gen}(\lambda) \\ y \leftarrow \mathsf{Eval}(\mathsf{sk}_{\mathsf{VRF}}, x) \\ \pi_{\mathsf{VRF}} \leftarrow \mathsf{P}(\mathsf{sk}_{\mathsf{VRF}}, x) \end{array} : \mathsf{V}(\mathsf{pk}_{\mathsf{VRF}}, \pi_{\mathsf{VRF}}, x, y) = 1\right] = 1.$$

Uniqueness: *For every security parameter* λ *and input* $x \in \{0,1\}^{n(\lambda)}$, *arbitrary verification key* $\mathsf{pk}_{\mathsf{VRF}}$, *there exists at most a single* $y \in \{0,1\}^{m(\lambda)}$ *for which there exists an accepting proof* π_{VRF}. *That is, if*

$$\mathsf{V}(\mathsf{pk}_{\mathsf{VRF}}, \pi_{\mathsf{VRF}}, x, y) = \mathsf{V}(\mathsf{pk}_{\mathsf{VRF}}, \pi'_{\mathsf{VRF}}, x, y') = 1$$

then $y = y'$.

Adaptive Indistinguishability: *Every PPT adversary* $\mathcal{A}$ *has at most negligible advantage in the following experiment.*

$\mathsf{Exp}_{\mathcal{A}, \mathsf{VRF}}(\lambda)$	$\mathcal{O}_1(\mathsf{sk}_{\mathsf{VRF}}, x)$
$Q := \emptyset$	$y \leftarrow \mathsf{Eval}(\mathsf{sk}_{\mathsf{VRF}}, x)$
$b \leftarrow_{\$} \{0,1\}$	$\pi_{\mathsf{VRF}} \leftarrow \mathsf{P}(\mathsf{sk}_{\mathsf{VRF}}, x)$
$(\mathsf{sk}_{\mathsf{VRF}}, \mathsf{pk}_{\mathsf{VRF}}) \leftarrow \mathsf{Gen}(\lambda)$	$Q := Q \cup \{x\}$
$(\mathsf{st}, x^*) \leftarrow \mathcal{A}^{\mathcal{O}_1(\mathsf{sk}_{\mathsf{VRF}}, \cdot)}(\mathsf{pk}_{\mathsf{VRF}})$	**return** (y, π_{VRF})
$y_0 \leftarrow \mathsf{Eval}(\mathsf{sk}_{\mathsf{VRF}}, x^*)$	
$y_1 \leftarrow_{\$} \{0,1\}^{m(\lambda)}$	
$\bar{b} \leftarrow \mathcal{A}^{\mathcal{O}_1(\mathsf{sk}_{\mathsf{VRF}}, \cdot)}(\mathsf{st}, y_b)$	
return $b = \bar{b} \wedge x^* \notin Q$	

The advantage of $\mathcal{A}$ *is defined by* $\mathbf{Adv}_{\mathsf{VRF}}(\mathcal{A}) = \Pr[\mathsf{Exp}_{\mathcal{A}, \mathsf{VRF}}(\lambda) = 1]$.

2.5   Structure-Preserving Signatures of Equivalence Classes

Structure-preserving signatures on equivalence classes (SPS-EQ) [24,27] can be used to sign equivalence classes $[M]$ of vectors $M \in (\mathbb{G}_i^*)^\ell$ for $\ell > 1$ and with equivalence relation: $M, N \in \mathbb{G}_i^\ell : M \sim_{\mathcal{R}} N \Leftrightarrow \exists s \in \mathbb{Z}_p^* : M = N^s$.

Definition 7 (SPS-EQ). *An SPS-EQ scheme* SPS-EQ *on message space* $(\mathbb{G}_i^*)$ *for* $i \in \{1,2\}$ *consists of the following PPT algorithms.*

$\mathsf{KeyGen}_{\mathsf{EQ}}(\lambda, \ell)$: *On input of security parameter* λ *and input message vector length* $\ell > 1$, *it outputs a key pair* $(\mathsf{sk}_{\mathsf{EQ}}, \mathsf{pk}_{\mathsf{EQ}})$.
$\mathsf{Sign}_{\mathsf{EQ}}(\mathsf{sk}_{\mathsf{EQ}}, M)$: *On input of input a secret key* $\mathsf{sk}_{\mathsf{EQ}}$ *and representative* $M \in (\mathbb{G}_i^*)^\ell$, *outputs a signature* σ_{EQ} *for equivalence class* $[M]$.
$\mathsf{ChgRep}_{\mathsf{EQ}}(M, \sigma_{\mathsf{EQ}}, \mu, \mathsf{pk})$: *On input of input representative* $M \in (\mathbb{G}_i^*)^\ell$ *of equivalence class* $[M]$, *a signature* σ_{EQ} *on* M, *a value* μ *and a public key* $\mathsf{pk}_{\mathsf{EQ}}$, *returns an updated message-signature pair* (M', σ'), *where the new representative is* $M' = M^\mu$ *and* σ'_{EQ} *its corresponding (or, updated) signature.*
$\mathsf{Verify}_{\mathsf{EQ}}(\mathsf{pk}_{\mathsf{EQ}}, M, \sigma_{\mathsf{EQ}})$: *On input of a public key* $\mathsf{pk}_{\mathsf{EQ}}$, *a representative* $M \in (\mathbb{G}_i^*)^\ell$, *and a signature* σ_{EQ} *it deterministically outputs a bit* $b \in \{0,1\}$.
$\mathsf{VKey}_{\mathsf{EQ}}(\mathsf{sk}_{\mathsf{EQ}}, \mathsf{pk}_{\mathsf{EQ}})$: *On input of secret key* $\mathsf{sk}_{\mathsf{EQ}}$ *and a public key* $\mathsf{pk}_{\mathsf{EQ}}$, *it deterministically checks if it represents a valid key pair and outputs a bit* b.

Definition 8 (Correctness). *An SPS-EQ scheme on* $(\mathbb{G}_i^*)^\ell$ *is called correct if for all security parameters* $\lambda \in \mathbb{N}$, $\ell > 1$, $(\mathsf{sk}_{\mathsf{EQ}}, \mathsf{pk}_{\mathsf{EQ}}) \leftarrow \mathsf{KeyGen}_{\mathsf{EQ}}(\lambda, \ell)$, $M \in (\mathbb{G}_i^*)^\ell$ *and* $\mu \in \mathbb{Z}_p^*$:

$$\mathsf{VKey}_{\mathsf{EQ}}(\mathsf{sk}_{\mathsf{EQ}}, \mathsf{pk}_{\mathsf{EQ}}) = 1 \ \wedge \ \Pr\left[\mathsf{Verify}_{\mathsf{EQ}}(M, \mathsf{Sign}_{\mathsf{EQ}}(M, \mathsf{sk}_{\mathsf{EQ}}), \mathsf{pk}_{\mathsf{EQ}}) = 1\right] = 1$$
$$\wedge \Pr\left[\mathsf{Verify}_{\mathsf{EQ}}(\mathsf{ChgRep}_{\mathsf{EQ}}(M, \mathsf{Sign}_{\mathsf{EQ}}(M, \mathsf{sk}_{\mathsf{EQ}}), \mu, \mathsf{pk}_{\mathsf{EQ}}), \mathsf{pk}_{\mathsf{EQ}}) = 1\right] = 1.$$

Definition 9 (EUF-CMA). *For scheme* SPS-EQ *and adversary* $\mathcal{A}$ *we define the following experiment:*

EUF-CMA$_{\mathcal{A},\mathsf{SPS\text{-}EQ}}(\lambda, \ell)$	$\mathcal{O}_1(\mathsf{sk}_{\mathsf{EQ}}, M)$
$Q := \emptyset$	$\sigma \leftarrow \mathsf{Sign}_{\mathsf{EQ}}(\mathsf{sk}_{\mathsf{EQ}}, M)$
$(\mathsf{sk}_{\mathsf{EQ}}, \mathsf{pk}_{\mathsf{EQ}}) \leftarrow \mathsf{KeyGen}_{\mathsf{EQ}}(\lambda, \ell)$	$Q := Q \cup \{M\}$
$(M^*, \sigma_{\mathsf{EQ}}^*) \leftarrow \mathcal{A}^{\mathcal{O}_1(\mathsf{sk}_{\mathsf{EQ}}, \cdot)}(\mathsf{pk}_{\mathsf{EQ}})$	**return** σ_{EQ}
return $[M^*] \neq [M] \ \forall M \in Q \ \wedge$	
$\mathsf{Verify}_{\mathsf{EQ}}(\mathsf{pk}, M^*, \sigma_{\mathsf{EQ}}^*) = 1$	

A SPS-EQ *over* $(\mathbb{G}_i^*)^\ell$ *is unforgeable if for all PPT adversaries* $\mathcal{A}$, *their advantage defined as* $\mathbf{Adv}_{\mathsf{SPS\text{-}EQ}}(\mathcal{A}) = \Pr[\text{EUF-CMA}_{\mathcal{A},\mathsf{SPS\text{-}EQ}}(\lambda, \ell) = 1]$ *is negligible.*

Definition 10 (Perfect adaption of signatures under malicious keys [23]). *Let* $\ell > 1$. *A* SPS-EQ *scheme on* $(\mathbb{G}_i^*)^\ell$ *perfectly adapts signatures under malicious keys if for all tuples* $(\mathsf{pk}_{\mathsf{EQ}}, M, \sigma_{\mathsf{EQ}}, \mu)$ *with*

$$M \in (\mathbb{G}_i^*)^\ell \ \wedge \ \mathsf{Verify}_{\mathsf{EQ}}(M, \sigma_{\mathsf{EQ}}, \mathsf{pk}_{\mathsf{EQ}}) = 1 \ \wedge \ \mu \in \mathbb{Z}_p^*$$

we have that the output of $\mathsf{ChgRep}_{\mathsf{EQ}}(M, \sigma_{\mathsf{EQ}}, \mu, \mathsf{pk}_{\mathsf{EQ}})$ *is a uniformly random element in the space of signatures, conditioned on* $\mathsf{Verify}_{\mathsf{EQ}}(M^\mu, \sigma'_{\mathsf{EQ}}, \mathsf{pk}_{\mathsf{EQ}}) = 1$.

In this work, we will use the scheme presented by Fuchsbauer, Hanser, and Slamanig in [24]. A signature on a message $(M_1, \ldots, M_\ell) \in (\mathbb{G}_1^*)^\ell$ is of the form (Z, Y_1, Y_2) where $Z = \left(\prod_{i=1}^\ell (M_i)^{x_i} \right)^y$, $Y_1 = g_1^{1/y}$, $Y_2 = g_2^{1/y}$ and $x_1, \ldots, x_\ell$ is the secret key of the signer. The signatures can be adapted to a signature on message $(M_1^b, \ldots, M_\ell^b)$ using random coins $r, b \leftarrow \mathbb{Z}_p^*$ and computing $(Z^{r \cdot b}, Y_1^{1/r}, Y_2^{1/r})$.

2.6 Tag-Based Equivalence Class Signatures

Hanzlik and Slamanig [28] introduced the notion of tag-based equivalence class signatures (TBEQ). Additionally, to the message M being a representative of class $[M]$, the signature scheme support an auxiliary tag $\tau \in \{0,1\}^*$. The key idea is that the tag remains the same for a given signature and does not change with the change of the representation. They also propose an efficient instantiation of their scheme, which is an adaptation of scheme from [24] with an additional component $H(\tau)^{\frac{1}{y}}$ in σ_{EQ}. We define TBEQ more formally below.

Definition 11 (TBEQ). *Tag-Based Equivalence Class Signature* TBEQ *consists of the following PPT algorithms.*

$\mathsf{KeyGen}_{\mathsf{TEQ}}(\lambda, \ell)$: *On input of security parameters λ and message vector length $\ell > 1$, it outputs a key pair $(\mathsf{sk}_{\mathsf{TEQ}}, \mathsf{pk}_{\mathsf{TEQ}})$.*

$\mathsf{Sign}_{\mathsf{TEQ}}(\mathsf{sk}_{\mathsf{TEQ}}, M, \tau)$: *On input of a secret key $\mathsf{sk}_{\mathsf{TEQ}}$, representative $M \in (\mathbb{G}_i^*)^\ell$, and tag $\tau \in \{0,1\}^*$, outputs a signature σ_{TEQ} for equivalence class $[M]$.*

$\mathsf{ChgRep}_{\mathsf{TEQ}}(M, \sigma_{\mathsf{TEQ}}, \mu, \mathsf{pk})$: *On input of representative $M \in (\mathbb{G}_i^*)^\ell$ of equivalence class $[M]$, a signature σ_{TEQ} on M, a value μ and a public key $\mathsf{pk}_{\mathsf{TEQ}}$, returns an updated message-signature pair (M', σ'), where the new representative is $M' = M^\mu$ and σ'_{TEQ} its corresponding (or, updated) signature.*

$\mathsf{Verify}_{\mathsf{TEQ}}(\mathsf{pk}_{\mathsf{TEQ}}, M, \tau, \sigma_{\mathsf{TEQ}})$: *On input of a public key $\mathsf{pk}_{\mathsf{TEQ}}$, a representative $M \in (\mathbb{G}_i^*)^\ell$, tag $\tau \in \{0,1\}^*$ and a signature σ_{TEQ} it deterministically outputs a bit $b \in \{0,1\}$.*

$\mathsf{VKey}_{\mathsf{TEQ}}(\mathsf{sk}_{\mathsf{TEQ}}, \mathsf{pk}_{\mathsf{TEQ}})$: *On input secret key $\mathsf{sk}_{\mathsf{TEQ}}$ and a public key $\mathsf{pk}_{\mathsf{TEQ}}$, it deterministically checks if it is a valid key pair and outputs a bit $b \in \{0,1\}$.*

Definition 12 (EUF-CMA). *For scheme* TBEQ *and adversary $\mathcal{A}$ we define the following experiment:*

$\mathsf{EUF\text{-}CMA}_{\mathcal{A}, \mathsf{TBEQ}}(\lambda, \ell)$	$\mathcal{O}_1(\mathsf{sk}, M, \tau)$
$Q := \emptyset$	$\sigma \leftarrow \mathsf{Sign}(\mathsf{sk}, M, \tau)$
$(\mathsf{sk}_{\mathsf{TEQ}}, \mathsf{pk}_{\mathsf{TEQ}}) \leftarrow \mathsf{KeyGen}(\lambda, \ell)$	$Q := Q \cup \{(M, \tau)\}$
$(M^*, \sigma^*_{\mathsf{TEQ}}, \tau^*) \leftarrow \mathcal{A}^{\mathcal{O}_1(\mathsf{sk}_{\mathsf{TEQ}}, \cdot, \cdot)}(\mathsf{pk}_{\mathsf{TEQ}})$	**return** σ
return $\mathsf{Verify}(\mathsf{pk}_{\mathsf{TEQ}}, M^*, \tau^*, \sigma^*_{\mathsf{TEQ}}) = 1 \wedge$	
$\quad ([M^*], \tau^*) \neq ([M], \tau) \;\; \forall (M, \tau) \in Q$	

A TBEQ *is EUF-CMA, secure if for all PPT adversaries $\mathcal{A}$, their advantage defined as $\mathbf{Adv}_{\mathsf{TBEQ}}(\mathcal{A}) = \Pr[\mathsf{EUF\text{-}CMA}_{\mathcal{A}, \mathsf{TBEQ}}(\lambda, \ell) = 1]$ is negligible.*

3   Non-interactive Blind Signatures (NIBS)

We will now discuss the syntax and security of non-interactive blind signatures NIBS. The signer uses the recipient's public key pk_R to generate a presignature psig. To do so, the signer first creates a signing keypair (sk, pk) using the KeyGen algorithm. The idea is for the recipient's public key to be a key for a scheme that is independent of NIBS. However, to model the security definition, we need to introduce a key generation algorithm RKeyGen that outputs a keypair (sk_R, pk_R).

To issue a presignature, the signer uses the Issue algorithm that takes as input the secret key sk, the recipient's public key pk_R, and a nonce. The nonce allows the signer to issue multiple signatures for the same public key. We made the nonce an explicit parameter to model what we call *nonce blindness* that captures the unlinkability of NIBS issued to the same public key. After receiving a presignature the user can execute the Obtain algorithm and compute the final signature or output $\perp$ in case the presignature is invalid (e.g., issued for a different public key or nonce). We provide the syntax more formally in Definition 13.

Definition 13 (Non-interactive Blind Signature). *A non-interactive blind signature NIBS scheme consists of the following PPT algorithms.*

KeyGen(λ): *On input security parameter λ, outputs a key pair* (sk, pk).
RKeyGen(λ): *On input security parameter λ, outputs a key pair* (sk_R, pk_R).
Issue(sk, pk_R, nonce): *On input a secret key* sk, *user public key* pk_R *and nonce* nonce $\in \mathcal{N}$, *outputs a pre-signature* psig.
Obtain(sk_R, pk, psig, nonce): *On input a user secret key* sk_R, *signer's public key* pk, *pre-signature* psig *and nonce* nonce $\in N$, *outputs a message-signature pair* (m, sig) *or* $\perp$.
Verify(pk, (m, sig)): *On input a public key* pk, *a message-signature pair* (m, σ) *deterministically outputs a bit* $b \in \{0, 1\}$.

Similar to standard blind signatures, one can define NIBS with respect to a common reference string. In such a case, we would define a $crs_{NIBS} \leftarrow_\$ Setup(\lambda)$ *setup algorithm, where* crs_{NIBS} *becomes an implicit input to all other algorithms.*

Definition 14 (Correctness). *A NIBS scheme is called correct if for all security parameters λ,* (sk, pk) $\leftarrow$ KeyGen(λ), $(sk_R, pk_R) \leftarrow$ RKeyGen(λ), *nonce:*

$$\Pr\left[\text{Verify}(pk, \text{Obtain}(sk_R, pk, \text{Issue}(sk, pk_R, nonce), nonce)) = 1\right] = 1.$$

We model unforgeability using a standard one-more definition. The adversary is allowed to make any number k of signing queries but, in the end, must return at least $\ell = k + 1$ valid message-signature pairs for unique messages. The main difference in our definition is that we allow the adversary to specify the recipient's public key and the nonce. We discuss one-more unforgeability more formally in Definition 15.

Definition 15 (One-More Unforgeability). *For scheme NIBS and adversary $\mathcal{A}$ we define the following experiment:*

$\text{OM-UNF}_{\mathcal{A},\text{NIBS}}(\lambda)$	$\mathcal{O}_1(\text{sk}, \text{pk}_R, \text{nonce})$
$(\text{sk}, \text{pk}) \leftarrow \text{KeyGen}(\lambda)$	**if** k *not initialized* **then**
$((\text{m}_1, \text{sig}_1), \ldots, (\text{m}_\ell, \text{sig}_\ell)) \leftarrow \mathcal{A}^{\mathcal{O}_1(\text{sk},\cdot,\cdot)}(\text{pk})$	$\quad k := 0$
return $\text{m}_i \neq \text{m}_j$ *for* $1 \leq i < j \leq \ell \wedge$	$\text{psig} \leftarrow \text{Issue}(\text{sk}, \text{pk}_R, \text{nonce})$
$\quad \text{Verify}(\text{pk}, \text{m}_i, \text{sig}_i) = 1$ *for* $1 \leq i \leq \ell \wedge$	$k := k + 1$
$\quad k < \ell$	**return** psig

A NIBS *scheme is one-more unforgeable, if for all PPT adversaries* $\mathcal{A}$*, their advantage defined as* $\mathbf{Adv}^{\text{OM-UNF}}_{\mathcal{A},\text{NIBS}} = \Pr[\text{OM-UNF}_{\mathcal{A},\text{NIBS}}(\lambda) = 1]$ *is negligible.*

We will now discuss the blindness properties of our non-interactive blind signatures. On a high level, we want presignatures and signatures to be unlinkable for the signer, independent of which public keys and nonces were used. We introduce two security definitions, recipient blindness and nonce blindness, which capture this intuition formally. We will also use the notion of *full blindness* to define a non-interactive blind signature scheme that is recipient and nonce blind.

In the case of nonce blindness, we consider the scenario of a malicious signer trying to distinguish who was the original recipient of a signature it sees. To do so formally, we create an experiment where the adversary is given two unique public keys and issues two presignatures (psig_0 and psig_1) for potentially different nonces and a public key that it can choose maliciously. We will also consider a variant called the honest key model, where the adversary must additionally return the secret signing key that matches the returned public key. In the experiment, the challenger finalizes both presignatures and gives the finalized signatures ($\text{sig}_b, \text{sig}_{1-b}$) to the adversary. The order of the signatures provided to the adversary depends on a bit b, which the adversary must guess. If the Obtain algorithm outputs $\perp$ for one of the presignatures, the challenger sends $(\perp, \perp)$ to omit simple distinguishing attacks. The experiment is defined more formally in Fig. 1 and recipient blindness in Definition 23.

Recipient blindness considers only single signatures issued to a particular public key. To create more signatures for the same public key, we introduced the explicit parameter nonce. We will now look at a scenario where the signer issues several presignatures to the same public key under different nonces and later wants to link the presignatures to the final signatures. We formalize it with the notion of nonce blindness. We create an experiment similar to the above one. The adversary is given one public key and issues two presignatures for two unique nonces. Again, the challenger finalizes both presignatures and gives signatures ($\text{sig}_b, \text{sig}_{1-b}$) to the adversary. The adversary must guess bit b. The experiment is defined more formally in Fig. 1 and nonce blindness in Definition 24

Finally, we define full blindness as the combination of both definitions. In other words, if a scheme is recipient and nonce blind, then it is fully blind. The intuition behind that follows from a hybrid argument. Recipient blindness ensures that signatures issued to different public keys are unlinkable, independent of the nonce used. On the other hand, nonce blindness ensures that multiple signatures for the same public key are unlinkable.

$\mathsf{RBnd}_{\mathcal{A},\mathsf{NIBS}}(\lambda)$	$\mathsf{NBnd}_{\mathcal{A},\mathsf{NIBS}}(\lambda)$
$(\mathsf{sk}_{R_0},\mathsf{pk}_{R_0}) \leftarrow \mathsf{RKeyGen}(\lambda)$	$(\mathsf{sk}_R,\mathsf{pk}_R) \leftarrow \mathsf{RKeyGen}(\lambda)$
$(\mathsf{sk}_{R_1},\mathsf{pk}_{R_1}) \leftarrow \mathsf{RKeyGen}(\lambda)$	$(\mathsf{psig}_0,\mathsf{nonce}_0,\mathsf{psig}_1,\mathsf{nonce}_1,\mathsf{pk}) \leftarrow \mathcal{A}(\mathsf{pk}_R)$
$(\mathsf{psig}_0,\mathsf{nonce}_0,\mathsf{psig}_1,\mathsf{nonce}_1,\mathsf{pk}) \leftarrow \mathcal{A}(\mathsf{pk}_{R_0},\mathsf{pk}_{R_1})$	$(m_0,\mathsf{sig}_0) \leftarrow \mathsf{Obtain}(\mathsf{sk}_R,\mathsf{pk},\mathsf{psig}_0,\mathsf{nonce}_0)$
$(m_0,\mathsf{sig}_0) \leftarrow \mathsf{Obtain}(\mathsf{sk}_{R_0},\mathsf{pk},\mathsf{psig}_0,\mathsf{nonce}_0)$	$(m_1,\mathsf{sig}_1) \leftarrow \mathsf{Obtain}(\mathsf{sk}_R,\mathsf{pk},\mathsf{psig}_1,\mathsf{nonce}_1)$
$(m_1,\mathsf{sig}_1) \leftarrow \mathsf{Obtain}(\mathsf{sk}_{R_1},\mathsf{pk},\mathsf{psig}_1,\mathsf{nonce}_1)$	if $\mathsf{sig}_0 = \bot$ or $\mathsf{sig}_1 = \bot$ then
if $\mathsf{sig}_0 = \bot$ or $\mathsf{sig}_1 = \bot$ then	$\quad (m_0,\mathsf{sig}_0) := \bot; (m_1,\mathsf{sig}_1) := \bot$
$\quad (m_0,\mathsf{sig}_0) := \bot; (m_1,\mathsf{sig}_1) := \bot$	$b \leftarrow_{\$} \{0,1\}$
$b \leftarrow_{\$} \{0,1\}$	$\hat{b} \leftarrow \mathcal{A}((m_b,\mathsf{sig}_b),(m_{1-b},\mathsf{sig}_{1-b}))$
$\hat{b} \leftarrow \mathcal{A}((m_b,\mathsf{sig}_b),(m_{1-b},\mathsf{sig}_{1-b}))$	return $b = \hat{b}$
return $b = \hat{b}$	

Fig. 1. Blindness Experiments for Non-interactive Blind Signatures

Definition 16 (Recipient Blindness). *A* NIBS *scheme is recipeint blind, if for all PPT adversaries* $\mathcal{A}$, *their advantage is negligible:*

$$\mathbf{Adv}_{\mathcal{A},\mathsf{NIBS}}^{\mathsf{RBnd}} = |\Pr[\mathsf{RBnd}_{\mathcal{A},\mathsf{NIBS}}(\lambda) = 1] - 1/2|.$$

Definition 17 (Nonce Blindness). *A* NIBS *scheme is nonce blind, if for all PPT adversaries* $\mathcal{A}$, *their advantage is negligible:*

$$\mathbf{Adv}_{\mathcal{A},\mathsf{NIBS}}^{\mathsf{NBnd}} = |\Pr[\mathsf{NBnd}_{\mathcal{A},\mathsf{NIBS}}(\lambda) = 1] - 1/2|.$$

Definition 18 (Full Blindness). *A* NIBS *scheme is fully blind if it is recipient and nonce blind.*

In both cases, we define blindness in a way that the adversary returns just the public key pk. The definitions do not assume any particular structure of the public key. Moreover, they allow the adversary to choose the public key so that a corresponding secret key sk might not even exist. We call this notion *malicious key model*. We will define a weaker version of blindness, where we will require the adversary to output sk additionally. This notion is called *honest key model* and is known for the case of standard blind signatures. Below we will define it more formally.

Definition 19 (Honest Key Model). *A* NIBS *scheme is recipient blind in the honest key model, respectively nonce blind in the honest key model if the adversary outputs* $(\mathsf{psig}_0,\mathsf{nonce}_0,\mathsf{psig}_1,\mathsf{nonce}_1,\mathsf{sk},\mathsf{pk}) \leftarrow \mathcal{A}(\mathsf{pk}_{R_0},\mathsf{pk}_{R_1})$ *in experiment* $\mathsf{RBnd}_{\mathcal{A},\mathsf{NIBS}}$, *respectively outputs* $(\mathsf{psig}_0,\mathsf{nonce}_0,\mathsf{psig}_1,\mathsf{nonce}_1,\mathsf{sk},\mathsf{pk})$ *in experiment* $\mathsf{NBnd}_{\mathcal{A},\mathsf{NIBS}}$

Remark 1. Any honest key can be transformed into a malicious key blind non-interactive blind signature using a zero-knowledge proof of knowledge of the secret key sk. In this transformation, the pubic key pk′ for the malicious key blind scheme is composed of the old public key pk and the proof of possession of the secret key sk in the form of a proof of knowledge. The security reduction follows by extracting the secret key from the adversary's proof of possession and running the reduction for honest key blindness.

4 Tagged NIBS

Partially blind signatures [2] allow the signer and recipient to agree on some common information that is included as part of the signed message. The signer knows that the user cannot change this information. At the same time, the recipient is assured that blindness holds with respect to this information. Since both parties agree on the message, partially blind signatures are, in some sense, interactive by definition.

We will show how to adapt the partially blind notion to the non-interactive case. The common information will be only chosen by the signer, which might limit the application compared to partially blind signatures. However, we show that this is enough for protocols that require some kind of freshness nonce to be included in the signature. To distinguish that in case of NIBS only the signer chooses the common information, we will call our primitive tagged NIBS. The main changes in the syntax in comparison to standard NIBS are that the Issue, Obtain, and Verify take an additional input in the form of the tag τ.

Definition 20 (Tagged Non-interactive Blind Signature). *A tagged non-interactive blind signature scheme* TNIBS *consists of the following PPT algorithms.*

KeyGen(λ): *On input security parameter* λ, *outputs a key pair* (sk, pk).
RKeyGen(λ): *On input security parameter* λ, *outputs a key pair* (sk$_R$, pk$_R$).
Issue(sk, pk$_R$, nonce, τ): *On input a secret key* sk, *user public key* pk$_R$, *nonce* nonce $\in \mathcal{N}$, *and tag* $\tau \in \mathcal{T}$, *outputs a pre-signature* psig.
Obtain(sk$_R$, pk, psig, nonce, τ): *On input a user secret key* sk$_R$, *signer's public key* pk, *pre-signature* psig , *nonce* nonce $\in \mathcal{N}$ *and tag* $\tau \in \mathcal{T}$, *outputs the tuple* (m, τ, sig) *or* $\perp$.
Verify(pk, (m, τ, sig)): *On input a public key* pk, *a message* m, *tag* $\tau \in \mathcal{T}$ *and signature* σ *deterministically outputs a bit* $b \in \{0, 1\}$.

Definition 21 (Correctness). *A* TNIBS *scheme on is called correct if for all security parameters* λ, (sk, pk) $\leftarrow$ KeyGen(λ), (sk$_R$, pk$_R$) $\leftarrow$ RKeyGen(λ), nonce $\in \mathcal{N}$, $\tau \in \mathcal{T}$:

$$\Pr\left[\text{Verify}(\text{pk}, \text{Obtain}(\text{sk}_R, \text{pk}, \text{Issue}(\text{sk}, \text{pk}_R, \text{nonce}, \tau), \text{nonce}, \tau)) = 1\right] = 1.$$

To define one-more unforgeability for our tagged NIBS we need to change the signing oracle. We now allow the adversary to query it with the recipient's public key pk$_R$, a nonce nonce, and a tag τ. We say that an adversary succeeded in breaking unforgeability if it returns at least $\ell = k_\tau + 1$ valid signatures on unique messages and only queried the signing oracle k_τ times for a given tag τ. More details are given in Definition 22.

Definition 22 (One-More Unforgeability). *For scheme tagged* TNIBS *and adversary* $\mathcal{A}$ *we define the following experiment:*

OM-UNF$_{\mathcal{A},\text{TNIBS}}(\lambda)$

$(\text{sk}, \text{pk}) \leftarrow \text{KeyGen}(\lambda)$

$(\tau, (m_1, \text{sig}_1), \ldots, (m_\ell, \text{sig}_\ell)) \leftarrow \mathcal{A}^{\mathcal{O}_1(\text{sk}, \cdot, \cdot, \cdot)}(\text{pk})$

return $m_i \neq m_j$ for $1 \leq i < j \leq \ell \wedge$

$\quad\quad \text{Verify}(\text{pk}, (m_i, \tau, \text{sig}_i)) = 1$ *for* $1 \leq i \leq \ell \wedge$

$\quad\quad k_\tau < \ell$

$\mathcal{O}_1(\text{sk}, \text{pk}_R, \text{nonce}, \tau)$

if k_τ *not initialized* **then**

$\quad k_\tau := 0$

$\text{psig} \leftarrow \text{Issue}(\text{sk}, \text{pk}_R, \text{nonce}, \tau)$

$k_\tau := k_\tau + 1$

return psig

A TNIBS *scheme is one-more unforgeable, if for all PPT adversaries* $\mathcal{A}$, *their advantage defined as* $\mathbf{Adv}_{\mathcal{A},\text{TNIBS}}^{\text{OM-UNF}} = \Pr[\text{OM-UNF}_{\mathcal{A},\text{TNIBS}}(\lambda) = 1]$ *is negligible.*

We will now move our attention to the blindness definitions of tagged non-interactive blind signatures. As we already mentioned, blindness can only hold with respect to the same tag. Since the tag is chosen by the signer and cannot be changed, it is additional information that can be used to distinguish if two signatures were signed under the same tag or not. The experiments for the blindness definitions are defined formally in Fig. 2.

RBnd$_{\mathcal{A},\text{TNIBS}}(\lambda)$

$(\text{sk}_{R_0}, \text{pk}_{R_0}) \leftarrow \text{RKeyGen}(\lambda)$

$(\text{sk}_{R_1}, \text{pk}_{R_1}) \leftarrow \text{RKeyGen}(\lambda)$

$(\text{psig}_0, \text{nonce}_0, \text{psig}_1, \text{nonce}_1, \text{pk}, \tau) \leftarrow \mathcal{A}(\text{pk}_{R_0}, \text{pk}_{R_1})$

$(m_0, \text{sig}_0) \leftarrow \text{Obtain}(\text{sk}_{R_0}, \text{pk}, \text{psig}_0, \text{nonce}_0, \tau)$

$(m_1, \text{sig}_1) \leftarrow \text{Obtain}(\text{sk}_{R_1}, \text{pk}, \text{psig}_1, \text{nonce}_1, \tau)$

if $\text{sig}_0 = \bot$ or $\text{sig}_1 = \bot$ **then**

$\quad (m_0, \text{sig}_0) := \bot; (m_1, \text{sig}_1) := \bot$

$b \leftarrow_\$ \{0,1\}$

$\hat{b} \leftarrow \mathcal{A}((m_b, \text{sig}_b), (m_{1-b}, \text{sig}_{1-b}))$

return $b = \hat{b}$

NBnd$_{\mathcal{A},\text{TNIBS}}(\lambda)$

$(\text{sk}_R, \text{pk}_R) \leftarrow \text{RKeyGen}(\lambda)$

$(\text{psig}_0, \text{nonce}_0, \text{psig}_1, \text{nonce}_1, \text{pk}, \tau) \leftarrow \mathcal{A}(\text{pk}_R)$

$(m_0, \text{sig}_0) \leftarrow \text{Obtain}(\text{sk}_R, \text{pk}, \text{psig}_0, \text{nonce}_0, \tau)$

$(m_1, \text{sig}_1) \leftarrow \text{Obtain}(\text{sk}_R, \text{pk}, \text{psig}_1, \text{nonce}_1, \tau)$

if $\text{sig}_0 = \bot$ or $\text{sig}_1 = \bot$ **then**

$\quad (m_0, \text{sig}_0) := \bot; (m_1, \text{sig}_1) := \bot$

$b \leftarrow_\$ \{0,1\}$

$\hat{b} \leftarrow \mathcal{A}((m_b, \text{sig}_b), (m_{1-b}, \text{sig}_{1-b}))$

return $b = \hat{b}$

Fig. 2. Blindness Experiments for Tagged Non-interactive Blind Signatures

Definition 23 (Recipient Blindness). *A* TNIBS *scheme is recipeint blind, if for all PPT adversaries* $\mathcal{A}$, *their advantage is negligible:*

$$\mathbf{Adv}_{\mathcal{A},\text{TNIBS}}^{\text{RBnd}} = |\Pr[\text{RBnd}_{\mathcal{A},\text{TNIBS}}(\lambda) = 1] - 1/2|.$$

Definition 24 (Nonce Blindness). *A* TNIBS *scheme is nonce blind, if for all PPT adversaries* $\mathcal{A}$, *their advantage is negligible:*

$$\mathbf{Adv}^{\mathsf{NBnd}}_{\mathcal{A},\mathsf{TNIBS}} = |\Pr[\mathsf{NBnd}_{\mathcal{A},\mathsf{TNIBS}}(\lambda) = 1] - 1/2|.$$

Definition 25 (Full Blindness). *A* TNIBS *scheme is fully blind if it is recipient and nonce blind.*

5 SPS-EQ Construction of NIBS

In this section, we present an efficient construction of non-interactive blind signatures from signatures on equivalence classes. The main advantage of our solution is that it admits recipients' public keys of the form used by many discrete logarithm schemes. The idea of the construction is as follows. The signer uses a signature on equivalence classes to create a presignature psig on the vector $(\mathsf{pk}_R = g_1^{\mathsf{sk}_R}, \mathsf{H}(\mathsf{nonce}))$, where H is a hash function modeled as a random oracle. The recipient knowing the secret key sk_R can change the presignatures representation to a SPS-EQ signature on the vector $(g_1, \mathsf{H}(\mathsf{nonce})^{\mathsf{sk}_R^{-1}})$ which is returned as the final signature sig. In the end, a valid blind signature is SPS-EQ on a vector of messages where the first element is g_1 and the second element is $\mathsf{H}(\mathsf{nonce})^{\mathsf{sk}_R^{-1}}$. Full blindness of the construction relies on the fact that the value $\mathsf{H}(\mathsf{nonce})^{\mathsf{sk}_R^{-1}}$ is indistinguishable from a random element under the inverse decisional Diffie-Hellman assumption. One more unforgeability follows directly from the unforgeability of SPS-EQ. The construction is presented in detail in Scheme 1. Note that the scheme is only blind in the honest key model since we rely on the perfect adaptation of signatures, i.e., to prove security, the reduction will use the SPS-EQ signing key to resign messages. We could use the DMWI proof system and its extraction property, which, based on Remark 1, would allow us to transform the scheme into one secure in the malicious key model. We opted to present it this way because of two reasons. Firstly, it simplifies the presentation and shows the essence of our construction. Secondly, we want an efficient scheme, and using a proof system for NP languages would be impractical. We will later show in the discussion section that for the SPS-EQ from [24], proof of knowledge of the signing key can be done via ℓ proofs of knowledge of discrete logarithms in $\mathbb{G}_2$. Note that in our scheme $\ell = 2$, which shows that our instantiation can be easily transformed into the malicious key model.

Security

Theorem 1 (One-more Unforgeability). *Scheme 1 is one-more unforgeable in the random oracle model assuming the SPS-EQ scheme is existentially unforgeable under adaptively chosen-message attacks.*

Proof (Sketch). The proof follows by a straightforward reduction to the security of the SPS-EQ. The reduction uses the provided signing oracle to generate

---

KeyGen(λ): generate SPS-EQ keypair $(\mathsf{pk_{EQ}}, \mathsf{sk_{EQ}}) \leftarrow \mathsf{KeyGen_{EQ}}(\lambda, 2)$ and set $(\mathsf{sk}, \mathsf{pk}) := (\mathsf{sk_{EQ}}, \mathsf{pk_{EQ}})$.

RKeyGen(λ): choose $x \leftarrow_\$ \mathbb{Z}_p^*$. Set $\mathsf{sk}_R := x$ and $\mathsf{pk}_R := g_1^x$.

Issue($\mathsf{sk}, \mathsf{pk}_R, \mathsf{nonce}$): generate SPS-EQ signature $\mathsf{psig} \leftarrow \mathsf{Sign_{EQ}}(\mathsf{sk}, (\mathsf{pk}_R, \mathsf{H(nonce)}))$.

Obtain($\mathsf{sk}_R, \mathsf{pk}, \mathsf{psig}, \mathsf{nonce}$): output $\bot$ if $\mathsf{Verify_{EQ}}(\mathsf{pk}, (\mathsf{pk}_R, \mathsf{H(nonce)}), \mathsf{psig}) = 0$, otherwise adapt presignature $\mathsf{sig} \leftarrow \mathsf{ChgRep_{EQ}}((\mathsf{pk}_R, \mathsf{H(nonce)}), \mathsf{psig}, \mathsf{sk}_R^{-1}, \mathsf{pk})$ output message-signature pair $(\mathsf{m} = \mathsf{H(nonce)}^{\mathsf{sk}_R^{-1}}, \mathsf{sig})$.

Verify($\mathsf{pk}, (\mathsf{m}, \mathsf{sig})$): output $\mathsf{Verify_{EQ}}(\mathsf{pk}, (g_1, \mathsf{m}), \mathsf{sig})$.

Scheme 1: SPS-EQ Construction of NIBS

presignatures for the adversary's $\mathcal{A}$ queries. Finally, the adversary outputs ℓ valid message-signature pairs for the NIBS scheme, simultaneously making only q_s signing queries. Without loss of generality, we can assume that $\ell = q_s + 1$ (otherwise, the reduction omits the additional message-signature pairs). Note that since all ℓ pairs are signatures under unique messages, it follows that they also belong to separate equivalence classes due to the notion of canonical representative. Thus, the adversary returned SPS-EQ message-signature pair for ℓ different classes, while the reduction only queries the SPS-EQ signing oracle $\ell - 1$ times. However, because of the hiding property, the reduction cannot guess the class for which it did not query the SPS-EQ signing oracle, i.e., the forgery. So the only way to win the unforgeability experiment is for the reduction to choose one message-signature pair at random. With probability $1/\ell$, this guess will be correct, and the pair will be a valid forgery against the SPS-EQ scheme. The complete proof can be found in the full version of the paper.

Theorem 2 (Recipient Blindness). *Scheme 1 is recipient blind (in the honest key model) in the random oracle model assuming the inverse decision Diffie-Hellman assumption holds in $\mathbb{G}_1$ and that the SPS-EQ scheme perfectly adapts signatures under a malicious signer.*

Proof (Sketch). The idea behind the proof is to make the challenged messages $\mathsf{m}_0, \mathsf{m}_1$ and corresponding signatures $\mathsf{sig}_0, \mathsf{sig}_1$ independent of the public keys $\mathsf{pk}_{R_0}, \mathsf{pk}_{R_1}$. We achieve this by making indistinguishable changes to how the recipient blindness experiment generates them. Firstly, the reduction program the random oracle H so that for all queried nonces nonce the reductions know r_nonce, such that $\mathsf{H(nonce)} = g_1^{r_\mathsf{nonce}}$. It replaces the public key of one of the recipients with g_1^α, where (g_1^α, g_1^β) is an instance of the inverse decisional Diffie-Hellman problem. Thanks to the programming of the oracle, the reduction can compute the messages as $(g_1, (g_1^\beta)^{r_\mathsf{nonce}})$, without knowing the recipient's secret key. The reduction uses the known SPS-EQ signing key and perfect adaptation of signatures to resign the presignature. If (g_1^α, g_1^β) is an inverse decisional Diffie-Hellman tuple, then the reductions simulation is perfect. This way, the reduction can change the messages signed by the challenged signatures $\mathsf{sig}_0, \mathsf{sig}_1$ to be independent of the public keys $\mathsf{pk}_{R_0}, \mathsf{pk}_{R_1}$. Thus, the best an adversary can do is to guess the bit b in the experiment. The complete proof can be found in the full version of the paper.

Theorem 3 (Nonce Blindness). *Scheme 1 is nonce blind (in the honest key model) in the random oracle model assuming the strong decision Diffie-Hellman assumption holds in $\mathbb{G}_1$ and that the SPS-EQ scheme perfectly adapts signatures under a malicious signer.*

Proof (Sketch). The proof follows a blueprint similar to the above one. The main difference is that now given a strong decisional Diffie-Hellman instance $(g_1^\alpha, g_1^\beta, g_1^{\beta^{-1}}, g_1^\gamma)$, we set the recipient's public key to $g_1^{\beta^{-1}}$. The reduction programs the oracle H similarly but tries to guess the query $\mathsf{H}(\mathsf{nonce}_0)$ to program it to g_1^α. The programming allows the reduction to compute the message m_0 as (g_1, g_1^γ). Note that if $\gamma = \alpha \cdot \beta$, the simulation is perfect, and the reduction can use an adversary noticing that m_0 is computed incorrectly to solve the strong decisional Diffie-Hellman problem. The reduction can make message m_0 and signature sig_0 independent of nonce_0. It can use the same strategy to make m_1 and sig_1 independent of nonce_1. Finally, the adversary is given only messages and signatures independent of $\mathsf{nonce}_0, \mathsf{nonce}_1$. The best it can do is guess the bit $\bar{b}$. The complete proof can be found in the full version of the paper.

5.1   Tagged NIBS from TBEQ

Scheme 1 can be easily transformed into a TNIBS. The only change is to replace the standard structure-preserving signature scheme with the tagged version TBEQ. For completeness, we present Scheme 2.

Security

All proofs follow the same strategy as the corresponding ones for Scheme 1. The complete proofs can be found in the full version of the paper.

Theorem 4 (One-more Unforgeability). *Scheme 2 is one-more unforgeable in the random oracle model assuming the TBEQ scheme is existentially unforgeable under adaptively chosen-message attacks.*

Theorem 5 (Recipient Blindness). *Scheme 2 is recipient blind (in the honest key model) in the random oracle model assuming the inverse decision Diffie-Hellman assumption holds in $\mathbb{G}_1$ and that the SPS-EQ scheme perfectly adapts signatures under a malicious signer.*

Theorem 6 (Nonce Blindness). *Scheme 2 is nonce blind (in the honest key model) in the random oracle model assuming the strong decision Diffie-Hellman assumption holds in $\mathbb{G}_1$ and that the SPS-EQ scheme perfectly adapts signatures under a malicious signer.*

KeyGen(λ): generate TBEQ keypair $(\mathsf{pk_{TEQ}}, \mathsf{sk_{TEQ}}) \leftarrow \mathsf{KeyGen_{TEQ}}(\lambda, 2)$ and set $(\mathsf{sk}, \mathsf{pk}) := (\mathsf{sk_{TEQ}}, \mathsf{pk_{TEQ}})$.

RKeyGen(λ): choose $x \leftarrow_{\$} \mathbb{Z}_p^*$. Set $\mathsf{sk}_R := x$ and $\mathsf{pk}_R := g_1^x$.

Issue($\mathsf{sk}, \mathsf{pk}_R, \mathsf{nonce}, \tau$): return presignature $\mathsf{psig} \leftarrow \mathsf{Sign_{TEQ}}(\mathsf{sk}, (\mathsf{pk}_R, \mathsf{H}(\mathsf{nonce})), \tau)$.

Obtain($\mathsf{sk}_R, \mathsf{pk}, \mathsf{psig}, \mathsf{nonce}, \tau$): output $\perp$ if $\mathsf{Verify_{TEQ}}(\mathsf{pk}, (\mathsf{pk}_R, \mathsf{H}(\mathsf{nonce})), \tau, \mathsf{psig}) = 0$, otherwise adapt pre-signature $\mathsf{sig} \leftarrow \mathsf{ChgRep_{TEQ}}((\mathsf{pk}_R, \mathsf{H}(\mathsf{nonce})), \mathsf{psig}, \mathsf{sk}_R^{-1}, \mathsf{pk})$ output message-signature pair $(\mathsf{m} = \mathsf{H}(\mathsf{nonce})^{x^{-1}}, \mathsf{sig})$.

Verify($\mathsf{pk}, (\mathsf{m}, \mathsf{sig})$): output $\mathsf{Verify_{TEQ}}(\mathsf{pk}, (g_1, \mathsf{m}), \tau, \mathsf{sig})$.

Scheme 2: TBEQ Construction of TNIBS

5.2   Discussion

Instantiating NIBS *and* TNIBS. We already mentioned at the beginning of this section that depending on how the SPS-EQ scheme is instantiated in our construction, we can end up with schemes with different properties. An efficient instantiation follows if we use the SPS-EQ scheme from [24]. The used equivalence class signature requires type 3 pairings groups. Barreto, Lynn, and Scott [8] introduced the BLS family of pairing-friendly groups that can be used in this case. We instantiate it with the popular BLS12-381 parameters [11]. In this setting the groups are defines as $\mathbb{G}_1 = E(\mathbb{F}_q)$, $\mathbb{G}_2 = E'(\mathbb{F}_{q^2})$ and $\mathbb{G}_T = \mathbb{F}_{q^{12}}$ for a 381-bit prime q. Consequently, the recipient's public key and the message space are in $\mathbb{G}_1$. The blind signature comprises two elements in $\mathbb{G}_1$ and one in $\mathbb{G}_2$. The signer's public key is two group elements in $\mathbb{G}_2$. Assuming we use the BLS12-381 groups, this constitutes a *signature size of* 1527-*bits*, where the message is an element of $\mathbb{G}_1$ and size 382-bit.

Recipient Public Key. With the above instantiation, the recipient's public key space is set to $\mathbb{G}_1$, where $\mathbb{G}_1$ is a standard elliptic curve. Thus, preexisting public keys for other schemes can be used as the recipient's public key. In particular, we can use public keys for the ECDSA, Schnorr signature scheme, ephemeral keys for the Diffie-Hellman protocol, and keys for the El-Gamal encryption scheme defined over the group $\mathbb{G}_1$ in our instantiation.

Composing the above schemes with NIBS does not seem to introduce security issues. Still, it will require providing proof for a composed primitive. We leave the formal proofs for future work. However, we can reduce the security of those schemes to the strong decisional Diffie-Hellman assumption, allowing the security of NIBS to hold independent of the use of the secret key in the other scheme.

Interestingly, we cannot use a BLS signature scheme public key. Recall that for BLS (for type-3 pairings), the public key g_1^x is in $\mathbb{G}_1$, then signatures are in $\mathbb{G}_2$ and of the form $\mathsf{H}_{\mathbb{G}_2}(m)^x$. The message in our construction for such a public key would be $\mathsf{m} = \mathsf{H}(\mathsf{nonce})^{x^{-1}}$. A malicious signer could then compute $e(\mathsf{m}, \mathsf{H}_{\mathbb{G}_2}(m)^x)$, for some known BLS signature of the recipient under m, and compare it with $e(\mathsf{H}(\mathsf{nonce}), \mathsf{H}(m))$. How the BLS signature scheme uses the recipient's secret key breaks the blindness properties of NIBS. The intuition is that the assumption used in unforgeability proof of BLS signatures cannot hold simultaneously with the strong decisional Diffie-Hellman assumption.

6   Generic Construction

In the previous section, we presented one NIBS and one TNIBS scheme that can efficiently be instantiated using signatures on equivalence classes and its variant. An interesting observation we make here is that the resulting random message in both of those schemes is $\mathsf{H}(\mathsf{m})^{\mathsf{sk}^{-1}}$. Blindness then follows from the inverse and strong decisional Diffie-Hellman assumptions. However, looking at it more closely, we notice that this is actually a valid evaluation of a pseudo-random function with key sk. Note that $\mathsf{PRF}_{\mathsf{sk}}(\mathsf{m}) := \mathsf{H}(\mathsf{m})^{\mathsf{sk}^{-1}}$ is a known construction. This observation is key to why blindness holds for those schemes. Even though the signer is choosing the input to the function, its evaluation is indistinguishable from random. Let us use this intuition to derive a generic construction.

The main problem is ensuring that given a presignature on the input to the function, the recipient will evaluate it correctly and preserve the signer's signature. In Schemes 1 and 2, this was possible because the relation defined by the equivalence class signatures worked well with the PRF. We can achieve something similar using non-interactive proofs and a verifiable random function VRF. Unfortunately, we will require proofs for NP languages. Additionally, we will use a trapdoor witness that will allow us to simulate this proof, i.e., we will allow for a trapdoor witness that we will be able to use in the proof by programming the random oracle $\mathsf{H}_{\mathsf{crs}}$. Alternatively, instead of using a trapdoor witness to simulate proofs, we can use a DMWI proof system with a trusted setup. Thus, this allows us to rely on the common reference string instead of the random oracle model. The idea of the scheme is as follows. The presignature is a standard digital signature psig on the recipients VRF public key $\mathsf{pk}_{\mathsf{VRF}}$ and the nonce. To obtain a valid signature, the recipient first evaluates the VRF on input nonce to receive message m. Later the recipient creates proof that it knows a signature psig under a key $\mathsf{pk}_{\mathsf{VRF}}$ and nonce nonce and that m is the result of the VRF's evaluation. The actual non-interactive blind signature is then this proof. More details are given in Scheme 3.

Remark 2 (Generic TNIBS). We can easily transform Scheme 3 to a tagged version. To make it work, the signer must include the tag τ as the message in the presignature, i.e., we replace $\mathsf{psig} \leftarrow \mathsf{SIG.Sign}(\mathsf{sk}, (\mathsf{nonce}, \mathsf{pk}_R))$ with $\mathsf{psig} \leftarrow \mathsf{SIG.Sign}(\mathsf{sk}, (\mathsf{nonce}, \mathsf{pk}_R, \tau))$ and modify relation $\mathcal{R}$ accordingly. In the generic TNIBS version, the tag τ is part of the statement x.

Let $\mathsf{VRF} = (\mathsf{Gen}, \mathsf{Eval}, \mathsf{P}, \mathsf{V})$ be a verifiable random function, $\mathsf{DMWI} = (\mathsf{Setup}, \mathsf{Prove}, \mathsf{Verify}, \mathsf{Extract})$ be a dual-mode witness indistinguishable proof system for the language $\mathcal{L}_\mathcal{R}$ and $\mathsf{SIG} = (\mathsf{KeyGen}, \mathsf{Sign}, \mathsf{Verify})$ be a standard digital signature scheme. Moreover, let $\mathsf{H_{crs}}$ be a random oracle that, on inputs from $\{0,1\}^*$, outputs elements from the space of reference strings for the DMWI system. Finally, let us define the following relation $\mathcal{R}$:

$$((\mathsf{m}, \mathsf{pk}), (\mathsf{nonce}, \mathsf{psig}, \mathsf{pk}_R, \pi_{\mathsf{VRF}}, r)) \in \mathcal{R} \iff$$
$$\mathsf{H_{crs}}(1) = \mathsf{DMWI.Setup}(\lambda, \mathsf{binding}; r) \ \vee$$
$$\mathsf{VRF.V}(\mathsf{pk}_R, \pi_{\mathsf{VRF}}, \mathsf{nonce}, \mathsf{m}) = 1 \ \wedge$$
$$\mathsf{SIG.Verify}(\mathsf{pk}, (\mathsf{pk}_R, \mathsf{nonce}), \mathsf{psig}) = 1$$

KeyGen(λ): generate keypair $(\mathsf{sk}, \mathsf{pk}) \leftarrow \mathsf{SIG.KeyGen}(\lambda)$.

RKeyGen(λ): generate keypair $(\mathsf{sk}_R, \mathsf{pk}_R) \leftarrow \mathsf{VRF.Gen}(\lambda)$.

Issue($\mathsf{sk}, \mathsf{pk}_R, \mathsf{nonce}$): create presignature $\mathsf{psig} \leftarrow \mathsf{SIG.Sign}(\mathsf{sk}, (\mathsf{nonce}, \mathsf{pk}_R))$.

Obtain($\mathsf{sk}_R, \mathsf{pk}, \mathsf{psig}, \mathsf{nonce}$): output $\bot$ if $\mathsf{SIG.Verify}(\mathsf{pk}, (\mathsf{nonce}, \mathsf{pk}_R)), \mathsf{psig}) = 0$, otherwise compute $\mathsf{m} \leftarrow \mathsf{VRF.Eval}(\mathsf{sk}_R, \mathsf{nonce})$, compute $\pi_{\mathsf{VRF}} \leftarrow \mathsf{VRF.P}(\mathsf{sk}_R, \mathsf{nonce})$, set statement $x = (\mathsf{m}, \mathsf{pk})$ and witness $w = (\mathsf{nonce}, \mathsf{psig}, \mathsf{pk}_R, \pi_{\mathsf{VRF}}, \cdot)$. Compute blind signature $\mathsf{sig} \leftarrow \mathsf{DMWI.Prove}(\mathsf{H_{crs}}(0), x, w)$. Output message-signature pair $(\mathsf{m}, \mathsf{sig})$.

Verify($\mathsf{pk}, (\mathsf{m}, \mathsf{sig})$): Set statement $x = (\mathsf{m}, \mathsf{pk})$ and output $\mathsf{DMWI.Verify}(\mathsf{H_{crs}}(0), x, \mathsf{sig})$.

Scheme 3: Generic Construction of NIBS

Security

Theorem 7 (One-more Unforgeability). *Scheme 3 is one-more unforgeable in the random oracle model assuming the signature scheme* SIG *is existentially unforgeable under adaptively chosen-message attacks, the dual-mode proof system* DMWI *is mode indistinguishable and extractable in binding mode, and the* VRF *meets the uniqueness property.*

Proof (Sketch). The proof works as follows. We first program the random oracle $\mathsf{H_{crs}}$ in a way that we can extract the witness used by the adversary, i.e., we set $\mathsf{H_{crs}}(0)$ to output a string in binding mode. Additionally, we program the oracle so the adversary cannot use the trapdoor witness for $\mathsf{H_{crs}}(1)$, i.e., we set $\mathsf{H_{crs}}(1)$ to output a string in hiding mode. Now a reduction can extract ℓ valid digital signatures for the SIG scheme while at the same time only querying $\ell - 1$ time. Moreover, the adversary can easily identify the $(\mathsf{pk}^*, \mathsf{nonce}^*, \mathsf{psig}^*)$ which is valid $\mathsf{SIG.Verify}(\mathsf{pk}, (\mathsf{pk}^*, \mathsf{nonce}^*), \mathsf{psig}^*) = 1$ while at the same time was not queried to the signing oracle of the signature scheme SIG. It is possible thanks to the uniqueness property of the VRF and the fact that the adversary must output distinct messages. Thus, $(\mathsf{pk}^*, \mathsf{nonce}^*, \mathsf{psig}^*)$ is a valid forgery for the SIG unforgeability experiment. The complete proof can be found in the full version of the paper.

Theorem 8 (Recipient Blindness). *Scheme 3 is recipient blind in the random oracle model assuming* DMWI *is mode indistinguishable and perfect witness indistinguishable in the hiding mode, and the* VRF *is indistinguishable.*

Proof (Sketch). The proof works as follows. The reduction programs the random oracle H_{crs} in a way that it can simulate the DMWI proof using the trapdoor witness $(\cdot, \cdot, \cdot, \cdot, r)$, where $H_{crs}(1) = crs$ and $(crs, \cdot) \leftarrow Setup(\lambda, binding; r)$. Now the reduction does not need the VRF to generate signatures. Thus, we can replace the messages m_0, m_1 with random values. Since we do not query for proofs of correct evaluation, this follows from the indistinguishability of the VRF. The complete proof can be found in the full version of the paper.

Theorem 9 (Nonce Blindness). *Scheme 3 is nonce blind in the random oracle model assuming* DMWI *is mode indistinguishable and perfect witness indistinguishable in the hiding mode, and the* VRF *is indistinguishable.*

Proof (Sketch). The proof sketch follows the same strategy as above. The complete proof can be found in the full version of the paper.

7 Conclusions

In this paper, we looked at blind signatures from a practical perspective. We noticed that in many use cases, the distribution of the signed message does not have to be chosen by the recipient. In other words, the application will work even if the message is random but eventually known. By formalizing this idea, we introduced the notion of non-interactive blind signatures for random messages. The key property is that no online interaction between the signer and the recipient is required. It allows us to use blind signature in new applications, including distributing e-coins similarly to cryptocurrency airdropping. We also showed two constructions. One is efficient and admits preexisting public keys from other schemes. The other scheme generically captures the concept of NIBS and is constructed from well-known primitives. We also show how to date non-interactive signatures by introducing the notion of tagged NIBS. We also proposed open problems.

References

1. Abazi, V.: The European union whistleblower directive: a 'Game Changer' for whistleblowing protection? Ind. Law J. **49**(4), 640–656 (2020). https://doi.org/10.1093/indlaw/dwaa023
2. Abe, M., Fujisaki, E.: How to date blind signatures. In: Kim, K., Matsumoto, T. (eds.) ASIACRYPT 1996. LNCS, vol. 1163, pp. 244–251. Springer, Heidelberg (1996). https://doi.org/10.1007/BFb0034851

3. Agrawal, S., Kirshanova, E., Stehlé, D., Yadav, A.: Practical, round-optimal lattice-based blind signatures. In: Yin, H., Stavrou, A., Cremers, C., Shi, E. (eds.) ACM CCS 2022, pp. 39–53. ACM Press (2022). https://doi.org/10.1145/3548606.3560650

4. Au, M.H., Susilo, W., Mu, Y.: Practical compact E-cash. In: Pieprzyk, J., Ghodosi, H., Dawson, E. (eds.) ACISP 2007. LNCS, vol. 4586, pp. 431–445. Springer, Heidelberg (2007). https://doi.org/10.1007/978-3-540-73458-1_31

5. Backes, M., Hanzlik, L., Schneider-Bensch, J.: Membership privacy for fully dynamic group signatures. In: Cavallaro, L., Kinder, J., Wang, X., Katz, J. (eds.) ACM CCS 2019, pp. 2181–2198. ACM Press (2019). https://doi.org/10.1145/3319535.3354257

6. Baldimtsi, F., Lysyanskaya, A.: Anonymous credentials light. In: Sadeghi, A.R., Gligor, V.D., Yung, M. (eds.) ACM CCS 2013, pp. 1087–1098. ACM Press (2013). https://doi.org/10.1145/2508859.2516687

7. Bao, F., Deng, R.H., Zhu, H.F.: Variations of Diffie-Hellman problem. In: Qing, S., Gollmann, D., Zhou, J. (eds.) ICICS 2003. LNCS, vol. 2836, pp. 301–312. Springer, Heidelberg (2003). https://doi.org/10.1007/978-3-540-39927-8_28

8. Barreto, P.S.L.M., Lynn, B., Scott, M.: Constructing elliptic curves with prescribed embedding degrees. In: Cimato, S., Persiano, G., Galdi, C. (eds.) SCN 2002. LNCS, vol. 2576, pp. 257–267. Springer, Heidelberg (2003). https://doi.org/10.1007/3-540-36413-7_19

9. Barreto, P.S.L.M., Naehrig, M.: Pairing-friendly elliptic curves of prime order. In: Preneel, B., Tavares, S. (eds.) SAC 2005. LNCS, vol. 3897, pp. 319–331. Springer, Heidelberg (2006). https://doi.org/10.1007/11693383_22

10. Boldyreva, A.: Threshold signatures, multisignatures and blind signatures based on the Gap-Diffie-Hellman-Group signature scheme. In: Desmedt, Y.G. (ed.) PKC 2003. LNCS, vol. 2567, pp. 31–46. Springer, Heidelberg (2003). https://doi.org/10.1007/3-540-36288-6_3

11. Bowe, S.: BLS12-381: New zk-SNARK elliptic curve construction (2017). https://electriccoin.co/blog/new-snark-curve/

12. Camenisch, J., Hohenberger, S., Lysyanskaya, A.: Compact E-cash. In: Cramer, R. (ed.) EUROCRYPT 2005. LNCS, vol. 3494, pp. 302–321. Springer, Heidelberg (2005). https://doi.org/10.1007/11426639_18

13. Camenisch, J., Neven, G., shelat: Simulatable adaptive oblivious transfer. In: Naor, M. (ed.) EUROCRYPT 2007. LNCS, vol. 4515, pp. 573–590. Springer, Heidelberg (2007). https://doi.org/10.1007/978-3-540-72540-4_33

14. Canard, S., Gaud, M., Traoré, J.: Defeating malicious servers in a blind signatures based voting system. In: Di Crescenzo, G., Rubin, A. (eds.) FC 2006. LNCS, vol. 4107, pp. 148–153. Springer, Heidelberg (2006). https://doi.org/10.1007/11889663_11

15. Chairattana-Apirom, R., Hanzlik, L., Loss, J., Lysyanskaya, A., Wagner, B.: PI-Cut-Choo and friends: compact blind signatures via parallel instance cut-and-choose and more. In: Dodis, Y., Shrimpton, T. (eds.) CRYPTO 2022, Part III. LNCS, vol. 13509, pp. 3–31. Springer, Heidelberg (2022). https://doi.org/10.1007/978-3-031-15982-4_1

16. Chaum, D.: Blind signatures for untraceable payments. In: Chaum, D., Rivest, R.L., Sherman, A.T. (eds.) Advances in Cryptology, pp. 199–203. Springer, Boston (1983). https://doi.org/10.1007/978-1-4757-0602-4_18

17. Davidson, A., Goldberg, I., Sullivan, N., Tankersley, G., Valsorda, F.: Privacy pass: bypassing internet challenges anonymously. PoPETs **2018**(3), 164–180 (2018). https://doi.org/10.1515/popets-2018-0026

18. Fischlin, M.: Round-optimal composable blind signatures in the common reference string model. In: Dwork, C. (ed.) CRYPTO 2006. LNCS, vol. 4117, pp. 60–77. Springer, Heidelberg (2006). https://doi.org/10.1007/11818175_4

19. Fischlin, M., Schröder, D.: Security of blind signatures under aborts. In: Jarecki, S., Tsudik, G. (eds.) PKC 2009. LNCS, vol. 5443, pp. 297–316. Springer, Heidelberg (2009). https://doi.org/10.1007/978-3-642-00468-1_17

20. Fischlin, M., Schröder, D.: On the impossibility of three-move blind signature schemes. In: Gilbert, H. (ed.) EUROCRYPT 2010. LNCS, vol. 6110, pp. 197–215. Springer, Heidelberg (2010). https://doi.org/10.1007/978-3-642-13190-5_10

21. Frankel, Y., Tsiounis, Y., Yung, M.: Fair off-line E-cash made easy. In: Ohta, K., Pei, D. (eds.) ASIACRYPT 1998. LNCS, vol. 1514, pp. 257–270. Springer, Heidelberg (1998). https://doi.org/10.1007/3-540-49649-1_21

22. Fuchsbauer, G., Hanser, C., Kamath, C., Slamanig, D.: Practical round-optimal blind signatures in the standard model from weaker assumptions. In: Zikas, V., De Prisco, R. (eds.) SCN 2016. LNCS, vol. 9841, pp. 391–408. Springer, Cham (2016). https://doi.org/10.1007/978-3-319-44618-9_21

23. Fuchsbauer, G., Hanser, C., Slamanig, D.: Practical round-optimal blind signatures in the standard model. In: Gennaro, R., Robshaw, M. (eds.) CRYPTO 2015. LNCS, vol. 9216, pp. 233–253. Springer, Heidelberg (2015). https://doi.org/10.1007/978-3-662-48000-7_12

24. Fuchsbauer, G., Hanser, C., Slamanig, D.: Structure-preserving signatures on equivalence classes and constant-size anonymous credentials. J. Cryptol. 32(2), 498–546 (2018). https://doi.org/10.1007/s00145-018-9281-4

25. Garg, S., Gupta, D.: Efficient round optimal blind signatures. In: Nguyen, P.Q., Oswald, E. (eds.) EUROCRYPT 2014. LNCS, vol. 8441, pp. 477–495. Springer, Heidelberg (2014). https://doi.org/10.1007/978-3-642-55220-5_27

26. Groth, J., Sahai, A.: Efficient non-interactive proof systems for bilinear groups. In: Smart, N. (ed.) EUROCRYPT 2008. LNCS, vol. 4965, pp. 415–432. Springer, Heidelberg (2008). https://doi.org/10.1007/978-3-540-78967-3_24

27. Hanser, C., Slamanig, D.: Structure-preserving signatures on equivalence classes and their application to anonymous credentials. In: Sarkar, P., Iwata, T. (eds.) ASIACRYPT 2014. LNCS, vol. 8873, pp. 491–511. Springer, Heidelberg (2014). https://doi.org/10.1007/978-3-662-45611-8_26

28. Hanzlik, L., Slamanig, D.: With a little help from my friends: constructing practical anonymous credentials. In: Vigna, G., Shi, E. (eds.) ACM CCS 2021, pp. 2004–2023. ACM Press (2021). https://doi.org/10.1145/3460120.3484582

29. Hauck, E., Kiltz, E., Loss, J.: A modular treatment of blind signatures from identification schemes. In: Ishai, Y., Rijmen, V. (eds.) EUROCRYPT 2019. LNCS, vol. 11478, p. 375. Springer, Cham (2019). https://doi.org/10.1007/978-3-030-17659-4_12

30. Hauck, E., Kiltz, E., Loss, J., Nguyen, N.K.: Lattice-based blind signatures, revisited. In: Micciancio, D., Ristenpart, T. (eds.) CRYPTO 2020. LNCS, vol. 12171, pp. 500–529. Springer, Cham (2020). https://doi.org/10.1007/978-3-030-56880-1_18

31. Heilman, E., Alshenibr, L., Baldimtsi, F., Scafuro, A., Goldberg, S.: TumbleBit: an untrusted bitcoin-compatible anonymous payment hub. In: NDSS 2017. The Internet Society (2017)

32. Hendrickson, S., Iyengar, J., Pauly, T., Valdez, S., Wood, C.A.: Rate-limited token issuance protocol. Internet-Draft draft-privacypass-rate-limit-tokens-03, IETF Secretariat (2022)

33. Juels, A., Luby, M., Ostrovsky, R.: Security of blind digital signatures. In: Kaliski, B.S. (ed.) CRYPTO 1997. LNCS, vol. 1294, pp. 150–164. Springer, Heidelberg (1997). https://doi.org/10.1007/BFb0052233

34. Katsumata, S., Nishimaki, R., Yamada, S., Yamakawa, T.: Round-optimal blind signatures in the plain model from classical and quantum standard assumptions. In: Canteaut, A., Standaert, F.-X. (eds.) EUROCRYPT 2021. LNCS, vol. 12696, pp. 404–434. Springer, Cham (2021). https://doi.org/10.1007/978-3-030-77870-5_15

35. Lysyanskaya, A.: Security analysis of RSA-BSSA. Cryptology ePrint Archive, Report 2022/895 (2022). https://eprint.iacr.org/2022/895

36. Micali, S., Rabin, M.O., Vadhan, S.P.: Verifiable random functions. In: 40th FOCS, pp. 120–130. IEEE Computer Society Press (1999). https://doi.org/10.1109/SFFCS.1999.814584

37. Miyazaki, S., Sakurai, K.: A more efficient untraceable e-cash system with partially blind signatures based on the discrete logarithm problem. In: Hirchfeld, R. (ed.) FC 1998. LNCS, vol. 1465, pp. 296–308. Springer, Heidelberg (1998). https://doi.org/10.1007/BFb0055490

38. Pass, R.: Limits of provable security from standard assumptions. In: Fortnow, L., Vadhan, S.P. (eds.) 43rd ACM STOC, pp. 109–118. ACM Press (2011). https://doi.org/10.1145/1993636.1993652

39. Pfitzmann, B.P., Sadeghi, A.-R.: Anonymous fingerprinting with direct non-repudiation. In: Okamoto, T. (ed.) ASIACRYPT 2000. LNCS, vol. 1976, pp. 401–414. Springer, Heidelberg (2000). https://doi.org/10.1007/3-540-44448-3_31

40. Pointcheval, D., Stern, J.: Provably secure blind signature schemes. In: Kim, K., Matsumoto, T. (eds.) ASIACRYPT 1996. LNCS, vol. 1163, pp. 252–265. Springer, Heidelberg (1996). https://doi.org/10.1007/BFb0034852

41. Pointcheval, D., Stern, J.: Security arguments for digital signatures and blind signatures. J. Cryptol. 13(3), 361–396 (2000). https://doi.org/10.1007/s001450010003

42. Rivest, R.L., Shamir, A., Tauman, Y.: How to leak a secret. In: Boyd, C. (ed.) ASIACRYPT 2001. LNCS, vol. 2248, pp. 552–565. Springer, Heidelberg (2001). https://doi.org/10.1007/3-540-45682-1_32

43. Wahby, R.S., Boneh, D., Jeffrey, C., Poon, J.: An airdrop that preserves recipient privacy. In: Bonneau, J., Heninger, N. (eds.) FC 2020. LNCS, vol. 12059, pp. 444–463. Springer, Cham (2020). https://doi.org/10.1007/978-3-030-51280-4_24

Rai-Choo! Evolving Blind Signatures to the Next Level

Lucjan Hanzlik[1], Julian Loss[1] (ID), and Benedikt Wagner[1,2](✉) (ID)

[1] CISPA Helmholtz Center for Information Security, Saarbrücken, Germany
{hanzlik,loss,benedikt.wagner}@cispa.de
[2] Saarland University, Saarbrücken, Germany

Abstract. Blind signatures are a fundamental tool for privacy-preserving applications. Known constructions of concurrently secure blind signature schemes either are prohibitively inefficient or rely on non-standard assumptions, even in the random oracle model. A recent line of work (ASIACRYPT '21, CRYPTO '22) initiated the study of concretely efficient schemes based on well-understood assumptions in the random oracle model. However, these schemes still have several major drawbacks: 1) The signer is required to keep state; 2) The computation grows linearly with the number of signing interactions, making the schemes impractical; 3) The schemes require at least five moves of interaction.

In this paper, we introduce a blind signature scheme that eliminates *all* of the above drawbacks at the same time. Namely, we show a round-optimal, concretely efficient, concurrently secure, and stateless blind signature scheme in which communication and computation are independent of the number of signing interactions. Our construction also naturally generalizes to the partially blind signature setting.

Our scheme is based on the CDH assumption in the asymmetric pairing setting and can be instantiated using a standard BLS curve. We obtain signature and communication sizes of 9 KB and 36 KB, respectively. To further improve the efficiency of our scheme, we show how to obtain a scheme with better amortized communication efficiency. Our approach *batches* the issuing of signatures for multiple messages.

Keywords: Blind Signatures · Standard Assumptions · Random Oracle Model · Cut-and-Choose · Computation Complexity · Round Complexity

1 Introduction

Blind signatures, introduced by David Chaum in 1982 [15] are an interactive type of signature scheme with special privacy features. Informally, in a blind signature scheme, a Signer, holding a secret key sk, and a User, holding a corresponding public key pk and a message m, engage in a two-party protocol. At the end of the interaction, the user obtains a signature on m that can be verified using pk. *Blindness* ensures that the Signer learns no information about

© International Association for Cryptologic Research 2023
C. Hazay and M. Stam (Eds.): EUROCRYPT 2023, LNCS 14008, pp. 753–783, 2023.
https://doi.org/10.1007/978-3-031-30589-4_26

m. On the other hand, *unforgeabillity* guarantees that the User cannot obtain valid signatures without interacting with the Signer. These properties make blind signatures a useful building block for privacy-sensitive applications, e.g. e-cash [15,36], anonymous credentials [10,11], e-voting [25], and blockchain-based systems [29].

Unfortunately, even in the random oracle model, existing constructions of blind signatures either rely on non-standard assumptions [5,7,19], or have parameters (e.g. communication and signature sizes) that grow linearly in the number of concurrent signing interactions [27,33,39]. Very recently, Chairattana-Apirom et al. [13] gave the first blind signature schemes from standard assumptions in the random oracle model that are simultaneously size and communication efficient. Even so, their schemes cannot be considered practical. For one, they require many rounds of interaction, which may be problematic if network conditions are poor. Second, they still require computation that grows linearly in the number of signatures that the server has already issued. This can become a heavy burden as the number of signatures grows large, say 2^{30}. In this work, we propose a novel construction of a blind signature scheme that overcomes *all* of these limitations. Concretely, our scheme has the following properties:

- Our scheme can be instantiated from the (co)-CDH assumption in type-3 pairings in the random oracle model (to get a proof from plain CDH, we can easily use type-2 or type-1 pairings).
- It has compact signatures and communication complexity.
- Signing and verifying are computationally efficient and require only a few hundred hash and group operations per signature; we provide a prototypical implementation to demonstrate practicality.
- Our scheme is round-optimal, i.e., it requires only a single message from both the signer and the user.

1.1   Background and Limitations of Existing Constructions

A long line of work [1,2,27,28,39] has explored constructions of blind signatures from witness indistinguishable linear identification schemes such as the Okamoto-Schnorr and Okamoto-Guillou-Quisquater schemes [34]. The resulting blind signature schemes are secure under well-understood assumptions, such as RSA, factoring, or discrete logarithm. On the downside, some these schemes admit an efficient attack [6,40,43] if the number of (concurrent) singing interactions ever exceeds a polylogarithmic bound.

Inspired by an early work by Pointcheval [38], Katz, Loss, and Rosenberg [33] recently introduced a boosting transform that turns linear blind signature schemes into fully secure ones (i.e., admitting a polynomial number of concurrent signing interactions). Applying their transform, one obtains schemes that rely on well-studied assumptions and have short signatures. Unfortunately, the resulting communication and computational complexity renders them impractical. This is because in the Nth interaction between Signer and User, the communication and computation depend *linearly on N*. To ameliorate some of these drawbacks, Chairattana-Apirom et al. [13] introduced a more compact version of Katz et al.'s generic transform in which the communication only depends *logarithmically on N*. Their work also presents two more optimized blind signature schemes which do not follow from their transform generically. We focus here on their BLS-based [7,8] construction (called 'PI-Cut-Choo') which can be instantiated from CDH.

We briefly highlight the remaining drawbacks of PI-Cut-Choo. The idea of the boosting transform fundamentally relies on a 1-of-N cut-and-choose where N, the number of signing interactions, grows over time. This requires to execute N copies of the base scheme and has the following implications:

- The Signer is stateful, as it has to keep track of the current value of N.
- The computation grows linearly in N for both the Signer and the User. To issue $N \approx 2^{30}$ signatures, this would require prohibitive computational effort (roughly $\sum_{i=1}^{2^{30}} i \approx 2^{59}$ operations).
- Issuing a signature requires five moves of interaction between Signer and User which is a far cry from the theoretical one-round limit achieved by some schemes [7].

Thus, even though PI-Cut-Choo significantly improves over prior schemes, it can still not be considered useful for practical deployment.

1.2   Our Contribution

In this work, we eliminate *all* of the aforementioned drawbacks.

Our Scheme. We construct a practical blind signature scheme using a new variant of the cut-and-choose technique, that is polynomially secure and does not require the signer to keep a state. This eliminates the dependency on a counter N as in [13,33] entirely, thereby also significantly reducing the computational complexity, see Table 1. Additionally, in contrast to schemes in [13,33], our scheme is round-optimal. Our scheme is statistically blind against malicious signers. We show one-more unforgeability based on the (co)-CDH assumption in asymmetric pairing groups. One-more unforgeability holds for any (a priori unbounded) polynomial number of signing interactions. We obtain several parameter settings for our scheme. This leads to a trade-off between signature and communication size, see Table 2. For example, we can instantiate parameters to obtain 9 KB signature size and 36 KB communication complexity. To demonstrate that our scheme is computationally efficient, we implemented a prototype over the BLS12-381 curve. Our experiments show that signing takes less than 0.2 s, see Table 2.

Partial Blindness and Batching. We show that our scheme naturally generalizes to the setting of partially blind signatures. Additionally, we show how we can *batch* multiple signing interactions to improve communication complexity (see also Table 2), and provide the first formal model and analysis for that. Batching has been used in many other contexts as well, e.g. in oblivious transfer [9,30].

Table 1. Comparison of number of moves, communication and computation for the line of work [13,33] and our work in the Nth signing interaction. The security parameter is denoted by λ. Communication is given in bits, and computation is given by treating pairings, group and field operations, and hash evaluations as one unit.

	Boosting [33]	Compact Boosting [13]		Our Work
Moves	7	7	5	2
Communication	$\Theta(\lambda N)$	$\Theta(\lambda \log N)$	$\Theta(\lambda \log N + \lambda^2)$	$\Theta(\lambda^2)$
Computation	$\Theta(N)$	$\Theta(N \log N)$	$\Theta(\lambda N)$	$\Theta(\lambda)$

Table 2. Efficiency of different parameter settings of our scheme. Sizes and times are given in kilobytes and milliseconds, respectively. Communication is amortized per message. Details can be found in Sect. 5.

	|pk|	|σ|	Communication with batch size L				Running Time	
			$L = 1$	$L = 4$	$L = 16$	$L = 256$	Sign	Verify
(I)	0.14	13.98	33.20	16.98	12.92	11.65	163	54
(II)	0.14	9.41	36.21	20.11	16.08	14.82	169	36
(III)	0.14	5.71	72.79	43.97	36.77	34.52	333	22

We believe that batching blind signatures has a lot of natural use-cases. As an example, consider an e-cash scenario. Here, parties withdraw coins from a bank by getting blind signature for a random message. Later, the coin can be deposited by presenting the message-signature pair. Blindness ensures that the process of withdrawal is not linkable to the process of depositing. This approach is also used to do enhance the anonymity in electronic payment systems [29]. We remark that it is crucial that all issued coins are of equal amount to guarantee a large anonymity set. Therefore, any user that wants to retrieve more than one coin has to interact with the bank multiple times to get multiple coins (i.e. signatures). Using batch blind signatures, these interactions can all happen in parallel, leading to improved communication and computational efficiency, as well as reduced overhead to initiate interactions.

Remark on Assumptions. In our construction, we use the asymmetric type-3 pairing setting, as standard in practical pairing-based schemes. This also means that we need to use the standard variant of CDH in this setting, sometimes called co-CDH [14]. We emphasize that this variant is even needed to prove unforgeability of standard BLS signatures in the asymmetric type-3 setting [8]. On the other hand, it is straight-forward to instantiate our scheme in the symmetric pairing setting, or the asymmetric type-2 pairing setting based on plain CDH. We refer to Sect. 5 for more details.

1.3   Technical Overview

We give an intuitive overview of our techniques. For full formal details, we refer to the main body.

Boosting and PI-Cut-Choo. We start this overview by recalling the boosting transform [33] and its parallel instance variant [13]. Let BS be a blind signature scheme which is secure against an adversary that queries the signer for a small number of signatures (we will give a suitable definition of "small" below). The boosting transform results in a new scheme which is secure for any number of signing interactions between signer and adversary. In the Nth signing interaction, the User and the Signer behave as follows.

1. The user commits to its message m using randomness φ_j, $j \in [N]$, thereby obtaining N commitments μ_j. It also samples random coins ρ_j, $j \in [N]$ for the user algorithm of BS. Then, it commits to each pair (μ_j, ρ_j) using a random oracle, and sends the resulting commitments $,_j$ to the Signer.
2. Signer and User run the underlying scheme BS N times in parallel. We refer to these N parallel runs as *sessions*. More precisely, the Signer uses its secret key sk, and the User uses the public key pk, μ_i as the message, and ρ_j as the random coins in the jth session, for $j \in [N]$.
3. Before the final messages s_j, $j \in [N]$ are sent from the Signer to the User, the Signer selects a random session $J \in [N]$. The user now has to open all the commitments $,_j$ for $j \in [N] \setminus \{J\}$ by sending (μ_j, ρ_j). The Signer can now verify that the User behaved honestly for all but the Jth session. In case the User behaved dishonestly in one session, the Signer aborts.
4. The Signer completes the Jth session by sending the final message s_J. Finally, the User derives a signature σ_J from that session as in BS, and outputs $\sigma = (\sigma_J, \varphi_J)$ as its final signature.

Katz, Loss, and Rosenberg [33] show that the above scheme is secure for polynomially many signing interactions, given that the underlying scheme BS is secure for logarithmically many signing interactions. In more detail, they provide a reduction that simulates a signer oracle for the new scheme, given a logarithmic number of queries to the signer oracle for BS. Their reduction distinguishes the following cases for the Nth signing interaction.

1. If the adversary (i.e. the User) is dishonest in at least two sessions, then the adversary is caught. Hence, no response has to be provided and no secret key is needed.
2. If the adversary is honest in all sessions, the reduction can extract all (μ_j, ρ_j) by inspecting random oracle queries. Using a special property of the underlying scheme BS, this allows the reduction to simulate the response, e.g. by programming the random oracle.
3. If the adversary is dishonest in exactly one session j^*, then either $J \neq j^*$ and the reduction works as in the previous case, or $J = j^*$, and the reduction has to use the signer oracle of BS to provide the response s_J. In this case, we say that there is a *successful cheat*.

It is clear that the probability of a successful cheat is at most $1/N$ in the Nth signing interaction. Therefore, the expected number of successful cheats over q signing interactions is at most $\sum_{N=2}^{q+1} 1/N \leq O(\log q)$. Using an appropriate concentration bound, it therefore can be argued that the underlying signer oracle for BS is called logarithmically many times.

Unfortunately, the above transform yields impractical parameter sizes for the resulting signature scheme, which results from a relatively loose reduction to BS. To overcome these issues, recent work introduced a parallel instance version of the boosting transform (hereafter PI-Cut-Choo) [13]. The primary goal of this version is to work for key-only secure schemes BS, i.e. such that the reduction can simulate signing queries in the transformed scheme entirely without accessing the signing oracle of BS. First, N is scaled by some constant, such that the expected number of successful cheats is less than 1^1. Thus, in expectation, the reduction does not need access to a signer oracle for BS. To ensure that this is true with overwhelming probability, the entire boosting transform is repeated with $K = \Theta(\lambda)$ *instances* in parallel. These instances use independent public keys $\mathsf{pk}_1, \dots, \mathsf{pk}_K$ and independent random coins[2]. This implies that with overwhelming probability, there will be an instance $i^* \in [K]$, such that there is no successful cheat in instance i^* over the entire runtime of the reduction. The reduction can now guess i^* and embed the target public key of BS in pk_{i^*}. If the guess was correct, the reduction to key-only security of BS goes through.

The above discussion highlights the importance of growing the parameter N as a function of the number of signing interactions over time. In summary, it allows to bound the expected number of successful cheats, which is the central idea of prior work [13,33]. Thus, keeping N fixed presents several technical challenges that we discuss in the next paragraph.

Strawman One: Fixed Cut-and-Choose. We are now ready to describe our central ideas to avoid a growing cut-and-choose parameter N. As explained above, the key idea of PI-Cut-Choo is to ensure that for one of the parallel instances i^*, the adversary *never cheats* in any of its interactions with the signer. This argument fails if we set N to be constant, e.g. $N = 2$. However, by keeping the number of parallel instances K the same, we can still argue that with overwhelming probability *in each signing interaction*, there is a non-cheating instance i^*. We highlight the reversed role of quantifiers: The non-cheating instance i^* could now be different for every signing interaction. Unfortunately, the reduction approach presented in PI-Cut-Choo only allows to embed the target public key of the underlying scheme BS in a *fixed key* among the keys $\mathsf{pk}_1, \dots, \mathsf{pk}_K$ corresponding to the K parallel instances. Once this key is fixed, the reduction fails if ever there is a successful cheat with respect to this instance.

---

[1] This assumes an upper known bound on the number of signing interactions, which is a minor limitation. Alternatively, one could instead increase N as N^2 to achieve an expected constant number of successful cheats.

[2] In PI-Cut-Choo, this parallel repetition comes almost for free due to a lot of optimizations that we do not cover in this overview.

Strawman Two: Dynamic Key Structure (Naively). The above discussion shows that we have to support a *dynamic embedding* of the target public key into one of the keys $pk_1, \ldots, pk_K$. The first (naive) idea would be to use a fresh set of public keys $pk_1, \ldots, pk_K$ and secret keys $sk_1, \ldots, sk_K$ in each interaction. Observe that in PI-Cut-Choo, the base scheme BS is a two-move scheme, in which the first message c (challenge) sent from user to signer does not depend on the public key. Thus, our reduction for the resulting scheme can identify the non-cheating instance i^* *after* seeing the commitments $,_{i,j}$ and the challenges $c_{i,j}$. Using this observation, we could let the Signer send the (fresh) public keys $pk_1, \ldots, pk_K$ that will be used in the current signing interaction after receiving commitments and challenges. This way, the reduction knows in which key pk_{i^*} to embed the target public key in each signing interaction. To do so, the reduction first identifies the non-cheating instance i^*, and then samples (pk_i, sk_i) for $i \neq i^*$ honestly, while setting pk_{i^*} to (a rerandomization of) the target public key. Finally, the reduction can use sk_i to simulate all instances except i^*, while using random oracle programming in instance i^*.

We can use random-self reducibility of the underlying signature scheme to ensure blindness of this construction. Namely, the User re-randomizes the keys and signatures it receives from the user. (Otherwise, it would be trivial to link signatures to signing interactions). The final signature then contains the rerandomized set of keys and signatures. Fortunately, the BLS scheme [7], which serves as the basis of PI-Cut-Choo, has such a property.

However, the above scheme is insecure. Since a fresh set of keys $pk_1, \ldots, pk_K$ is used in every interaction, there is nothing tying signatures to the Signer's actual public and secret key. In particular, there is no way from preventing the adversary from (trivially) creating a forgery containing a set of keys of its own choice. In the security proof, the reduction can not extract a forgery for BS with respect to the target public key in this scenario.

Our Solution: PI-Cut-Choo evolves to Rai-Choo. To overcome the remaining issues of the above strawman approach, we fix one public key pk and one secret key sk for our scheme. Instead of using independent public keys $pk_1, \ldots, pk_K$ for each interaction, we instead use a sharing

$$(pk_1, sk_1), \ldots, (pk_K, sk_K) \text{ such that } \sum_i sk_i = sk \text{ and } \prod_i pk_i = pk.$$

By setting pk to be the target public key of the underlying scheme BS and carefully working out the details, our reduction is now able to extract a forgery as required. It remains to sketch why the simulation of the signing oracle is still possible with this new structure of the $pk_1, \ldots, pk_K$. Note that the reduction can define the $pk_1, \ldots, pk_K$ in a way that allows it to know all but one sk_i. Concretely, after identifying the non-cheating instance i^* in an interaction with the adversary, the reduction first samples (pk_i, sk_i) for all $i \in [K] \setminus \{i^*\}$, and then sets $pk_{i^*} := pk \cdot \prod_{i \neq i^*} pk_i^{-1}$. This is identically distributed to the real sharing.

In summary, we have successfully transformed a key-only secure scheme BS into a fully secure one, while using a constant cut-and-choose parameter N. We can further optimize the scheme using many minor tricks, some of them similar to [13]. In the process we also manage to reduce the number of moves to two, which is optimal. This is because in our new scheme, we can make the cut-and-choose step completely non-interactive using a random oracle, and the signer does not need to send N anymore, as it is fixed.

1.4   More on Related Work

We discuss related work in more detail.

There are several impossibility results about the construction of blind signatures in the standard model [4,18,37]. Fischlin and Schröder showed that statistically blind three-move schemes can not be constructed from non-interactive assumptions under certain conditions [18]. Pass showed that unique round-optimal blind signatures can not be based on a class of interactive assumptions [37]. Baldimtsi and Lysyanskaya showed that schemes with a unique secret key and a specific structure can not be proven secure, even under interactive assumptions [4].

In terms of unforgeability, one distinguishes concurrent and sequential security. For sequential security, the adversary has to finish one interaction with the signer before initiating the following interaction. In contrast, concurrent security allows the adversary to interact with the signer in an arbitrarily interleaved way. In practice, restricting communication with the signer to sequential access opens a door for denial of service attacks. Therefore, concurrent security is the widely accepted notion.

One can build blind signatures generically from standard signatures and secure two-party computation (2PC), as shown by Juels, Luby and Ostrovsky [31]. Unfortunately, this construction only achieves sequential security. Contrary to that, Fischlin [17] gave a (round-optimal) generic construction that is secure even in the universal composability framework [12]. However, it turns out that instantiating these generic constructions efficiently is highly non-trivial. For example, instantiating Fischlin's construction requires to prove statements in zero-knowledge about a combination of commitment and signature scheme. If we instantiate the signature scheme efficiently in the random oracle model, we end up treating the random oracle as a circuit. This leads to unclear implications in terms of security. Additionally, schemes based on Fischlin's construction inherently require strong decisional assumptions due to the use of zero-knowledge proofs and encryption. The recent work by Katsumata and del Pino [16] makes significant progress in this direction. By carefully choosing building blocks and slightly tweaking the construction, they give an instantiation of Fischlin's paradigm in the lattice setting. However, the communication complexity of their protocol is still far from being practical.

In addition to the generic constructions mentioned above, there are direct constructions of blind signatures. While some constructions make use of complexity leveraging [22,23], others are proven secure under non-standard q-type or interactive assumptions [19,23,24,35]. Notably, there are efficient and round-optimal schemes based on the full-domain-hash paradigm [3,5,7]. For example,

Boldyreva [7] introduces a blinded version of the BLS signature scheme [8]. To prove security, one relies on the non-standard one-more variant of the underlying assumption (e.g. one-more CDH for BLS).

In addition to the works in the standard and random oracle model mentioned before, there are also constructions [21,32,42] that are proven secure in more idealized models, such as the algebraic or generic group model [20,41]. While it leads to efficient schemes, we want to avoid using such a model, as it is non-standard.

2 Preliminaries

We denote the security parameter by $\lambda \in \mathbb{N}$, and assume that all algorithms get 1^λ implicitly as input. Let S be a finite set and $\mathcal{D}$ be a distribution. We write $x \leftarrow_\$ S$ to indicate that x is sampled uniformly at random from S. We write $x \leftarrow \mathcal{D}$ if x is sampled according to $\mathcal{D}$. Let $\mathcal{A}$ be a (probabilistic) algorithm. We write $y \leftarrow \mathcal{A}(x)$, if y is output from $\mathcal{A}$ on input x with uniformly sampled random coins. To make these random coins ρ explicit, we write $y = \mathcal{A}(x; \rho)$ The notation $y \in \mathcal{A}(x)$ means that y is a possible output of $\mathcal{A}(x)$. As always, an algorithm is said to be PPT if its running time $\mathbf{T}(\mathcal{A})$ is bounded by a polynomial in its input size. A function $f : \mathbb{N} \to \mathbb{R}_+$ is negligible in its input λ, if $f \in \lambda^{-\omega(1)}$. Let $\mathbf{G}$ be a security game. We write $\mathbf{G} \Rightarrow b$ to indicate that $\mathbf{G}$ outputs b. The first K natural numbers are denoted by $[K] := \{1, \ldots, K\}$. Next, we define the cryptographic primitive of interest and the computational assumption that we use.

Definition 1 (Blind Signature Scheme). *A blind signature scheme is a quadruple of PPT algorithms* $\mathsf{BS} = (\mathsf{Gen}, \mathsf{S}, \mathsf{U}, \mathsf{Ver})$ *with the following syntax:*

- $\mathsf{Gen}(1^\lambda) \to (\mathsf{pk}, \mathsf{sk})$ *takes as input the security parameter* 1^λ *and outputs a pair of keys* $(\mathsf{pk}, \mathsf{sk})$. *We assume that the public key* pk *defines a message space* $\mathcal{M} = \mathcal{M}_{\mathsf{pk}}$ *implicitly.*
- S *and* U *are interactive algorithms, where* S *takes as input a secret key* sk *and* U *takes as input a key* pk *and a message* $\mathsf{m} \in \mathcal{M}$. *After the execution,* U *returns a signature* σ *and we write* $(\perp, \sigma) \leftarrow \langle \mathsf{S}(\mathsf{sk}), \mathsf{U}(\mathsf{pk}, \mathsf{m}) \rangle$.
- $\mathsf{Ver}(\mathsf{pk}, \mathsf{m}, \sigma) \to b$ *is deterministic and takes as input public key* pk, *message* $\mathsf{m} \in \mathcal{M}$, *and a signature* σ, *and returns* $b \in \{0, 1\}$.

We require that BS *is complete in the following sense. For all* $(\mathsf{pk}, \mathsf{sk}) \in \mathsf{Gen}(1^\lambda)$ *and all* $\mathsf{m} \in \mathcal{M}_{\mathsf{pk}}$ *it holds that*

$$\Pr\left[\mathsf{Ver}(\mathsf{pk}, \mathsf{m}, \sigma) = 1 \mid (\perp, \sigma) \leftarrow \langle \mathsf{S}(\mathsf{sk}), \mathsf{U}(\mathsf{pk}, \mathsf{m}) \rangle\right] = 1.$$

Definition 2 (One-More Unforgeability). *Let* $\mathsf{BS} = (\mathsf{Gen}, \mathsf{S}, \mathsf{U}, \mathsf{Ver})$ *be a blind signature scheme and* $\ell \colon \mathbb{N} \to \mathbb{N}$. *For an algorithm* $\mathcal{A}$, *we consider the following game* $\ell\text{-}\mathbf{OMUF}_{\mathsf{BS}}^{\mathcal{A}}(\lambda)$:

1. Sample keys $(\mathsf{pk}, \mathsf{sk}) \leftarrow \mathsf{Gen}(1^\lambda)$.

2. *Let* O *be an interactive oracle simulating* S(sk). *Run*

$$((m_1, \sigma_1), \ldots, (m_k, \sigma_k)) \leftarrow \mathcal{A}^O(\mathsf{pk}),$$

where $\mathcal{A}$ *can query* O *in an arbitrarily interleaved way and complete at most* $\ell = \ell(\lambda)$ *of the interactions with* O.

3. *Output 1 if and only if all* $m_i, i \in [k]$ *are distinct,* $\mathcal{A}$ *completed at most* $k - 1$ *interactions with* O *and for each* $i \in [k]$ *it holds that* $\mathsf{Ver}(\mathsf{pk}, m_i, \sigma_i) = 1$.

We say that BS *is* ℓ*-one-more unforgeable (*ℓ*-OMUF), if for every PPT algorithm* $\mathcal{A}$ *the following advantage is negligible:*

$$\mathsf{Adv}_{\mathcal{A},\mathsf{BS}}^{\ell\text{-OMUF}}(\lambda) := \Pr\left[\ell\text{-}\mathbf{OMUF}_{\mathsf{BS}}^{\mathcal{A}}(\lambda) \Rightarrow 1\right].$$

We say that BS *is one-more unforgeable (OMUF), if it is* ℓ*-OMUF for all polynomial* ℓ.

Definition 3 (Blindness). *Consider a blind signature scheme* BS = (Gen, S, U, Ver). *For an algorithm* $\mathcal{A}$ *and bit* $b \in \{0, 1\}$, *consider the following game* $\mathbf{BLIND}_{b,\mathsf{BS}}^{\mathcal{A}}(\lambda)$:

1. *Run* $(\mathsf{pk}, m_0, m_1, St) \leftarrow \mathcal{A}(1^\lambda)$.
2. *Let* O_0 *be an interactive oracle simulating* $\mathsf{U}(\mathsf{pk}, m_b)$ *and* O_1 *be an interactive oracle simulating* $\mathsf{U}(\mathsf{pk}, m_{1-b})$. *Run* $\mathcal{A}$ *on input* St *with arbitrary interleaved one-time access to each of these oracles, i.e.* $St' \leftarrow \mathcal{A}^{O_0, O_1}(St)$.
3. *Let* σ_b, σ_{1-b} *be the local outputs of* O_0, O_1, *respectively. If* $\sigma_0 = \perp$ *or* $\sigma_1 = \perp$, *then run* $b' \leftarrow \mathcal{A}(St', \perp, \perp)$. *Else, obtain a bit* b' *from* $\mathcal{A}$ *on input* σ_0, σ_1, *i.e. run* $b' \leftarrow \mathcal{A}(St', \sigma_0, \sigma_1)$.
4. *Output* b'.

We say that BS *satisfies malicious signer blindness, if for every PPT algorithm* $\mathcal{A}$ *the following advantage is negligible:*

$$\mathsf{Adv}_{\mathcal{A},\mathsf{BS}}^{\mathsf{blind}}(\lambda) := \left|\Pr\left[\mathbf{BLIND}_{0,\mathsf{BS}}^{\mathcal{A}}(\lambda) \Rightarrow 1\right] - \Pr\left[\mathbf{BLIND}_{1,\mathsf{BS}}^{\mathcal{A}}(\lambda) \Rightarrow 1\right]\right|.$$

We make use of the natural variant of the CDH assumption in the asymmetric pairing setting [14].

Definition 4 (CDHAssumption). *Let* $\mathsf{PGGen}(1^\lambda)$ *be a bilinear group generation algorithm that outputs cyclic groups* $\mathbb{G}_1, \mathbb{G}_2$ *of prime order* p *with generators* $g_1 \in \mathbb{G}_1, g_2 \in \mathbb{G}_2$, *and a non-degenerate*[3] *pairing* $e : \mathbb{G}_1 \times \mathbb{G}_2 \to \mathbb{G}_T$ *into some target group* $\mathbb{G}_T$. *We say that the* CDH *assumption holds relative to* PGGen, *if for all PPT algorithms* $\mathcal{A}$, *the following advantage is negligible:*

$$\mathsf{Adv}_{\mathcal{A},\mathsf{PGGen}}^{\mathsf{CDH}}(\lambda) := \Pr\left[z = xy \left| \begin{array}{l} (\mathbb{G}_1, \mathbb{G}_2, g_1, g_2, p, e) \leftarrow \mathsf{PGGen}(1^\lambda), \\ x, y \leftarrow_{\$} \mathbb{Z}_p, X_1 := g_1^x, X_2 := g_2^x, Y := g_1^y \\ g_1^z \leftarrow \mathcal{A}(\mathbb{G}_1, \mathbb{G}_2, g_1, g_2, p, e, X_1, Y, X_2) \end{array} \right.\right]$$

---

[3] Non-degenerate means that $e(g_1, g_2)$ is a generator of the group $\mathbb{G}_T$.

3   Our Blind Signature Scheme

In this section, we present our blind signature scheme.

3.1   Construction

Let $\mathsf{PGGen}(1^\lambda)$ be a bilinear group generation algorithm that outputs cyclic groups $\mathbb{G}_1, \mathbb{G}_2$ of prime order p with generators $g_1 \in \mathbb{G}_1, g_2 \in \mathbb{G}_2$, and a non-degenerate pairing $e : \mathbb{G}_1 \times \mathbb{G}_2 \to \mathbb{G}_T$ into some target group $\mathbb{G}_T$. We assume that these system parameters are known to all algorithms. Note that their correctness can be verified efficiently. Our scheme $\mathsf{BS}_R = (\mathsf{Gen}, \mathsf{S}, \mathsf{U}, \mathsf{Ver})$ is parameterized by integers $K = K(\lambda), N(\lambda) \in \mathbb{N}$. These do not depend on the number of previous interactions. We only need that N^{-K} is negligible in λ. Our scheme does not require the signer to hold a state. The scheme makes use of random oracles $\mathsf{H}_r, \mathsf{H}_\mu : \{0,1\}^* \to \{0,1\}^\lambda, \mathsf{H}_\alpha : \{0,1\}^* \to \mathbb{Z}_p, \mathsf{H}_{cc} : \{0,1\}^* \to [N]^K$, and $\mathsf{H} : \{0,1\}^* \to \mathbb{G}_1$.

Key Rerandomization. Our scheme makes use of an algorithm ReRa, that takes as input tuples $(\mathsf{pk}_i, h_i)_{i \in [K]}$ and an element $\bar\sigma \in \mathbb{G}_1$, where $\mathsf{pk}_i = (\mathsf{pk}_{i,1}, \mathsf{pk}_{i,2}) \in \mathbb{G}_1 \times \mathbb{G}_2$, and $h_i \in \mathbb{G}_1$ for all $i \in [K]$. The algorithm is as follows:

1. Choose $r_1, \dots, r_{K-1} \leftarrow_\$ \mathbb{Z}_p$ and set $r_K := -\sum_{i=1}^{K-1} r_i$.
2. For all $i \in [K]$, set $\mathsf{pk}_i' := (\mathsf{pk}_{i,1}', \mathsf{pk}_{i,2}') := \left(\mathsf{pk}_{i,1} \cdot g_1^{r_i}, \mathsf{pk}_{i,2} \cdot g_2^{r_i}\right)$.
3. Set $\bar\sigma' := \bar\sigma \cdot \prod_{i=1}^K h_i^{r_i}$ and return $((\mathsf{pk}_i')_{i \in [K]}, \bar\sigma')$.

It is easy to see that $\prod_{i \in K} \mathsf{pk}_{i,j} = \prod_{i \in K} \mathsf{pk}_{i,j}'$ for both $j \in \{1, 2\}$. Further, if we assume that the inputs satisfy $e(\bar\sigma, g_2) = \prod_{i=1}^K e(h_i, \mathsf{pk}_{i,2})$ and $e(\mathsf{pk}_{i,1}, g_2) = e(g_1, \mathsf{pk}_{i,2})$ for all $i \in [K]$, then the outputs satisfy $e(\bar\sigma', g) = \prod_{i=1}^K e(h_i, \mathsf{pk}_{i,2}')$ and $e(\mathsf{pk}_{i,1}', g_2) = e(g_1, \mathsf{pk}_{i,2}')$ for all $i \in [K]$. Additionally, the output does not reveal anything about the input, except what is already revealed by these properties. We will make this more formal in Lemma 1 when we analyze the blindness property of our scheme.

Key Generation. To generate keys algorithm $\mathsf{Gen}(1^\lambda)$ does the following:

1. Sample $\mathsf{sk} \leftarrow_\$ \mathbb{Z}_p$, set $\mathsf{pk}_1 := g_1^{\mathsf{sk}}$ and $\mathsf{pk}_2 := g_2^{\mathsf{sk}}$.
2. Return public key $\mathsf{pk} = (\mathsf{pk}_1, \mathsf{pk}_2)$ and secret key sk.

Signature Issuing. The algorithms S, U and their interaction are formally given in Figs. 1 and 2.

Verification. The resulting signature $\sigma := ((\mathsf{pk}_i, \varphi_i)_{i=1}^{K-1}), \varphi_K, \bar\sigma)$ for a message m is verified by algorithm $\mathsf{Ver}(\mathsf{pk}, \mathsf{m}, \sigma)$ as follows:

1. Write $\mathsf{pk}_i = (\mathsf{pk}_{i,1}, \mathsf{pk}_{i,2})$ for each $i \in [K-1]$.
2. Compute $\mathsf{pk}_{K,1} := \mathsf{pk}_1 \cdot \prod_{i=1}^{K-1} \mathsf{pk}_{i,1}^{-1}$ and $\mathsf{pk}_{K,2} := \mathsf{pk}_2 \cdot \prod_{i=1}^{K-1} \mathsf{pk}_{i,2}^{-1}$.

3. If there is an $i \in [K]$ with $e\left(\mathsf{pk}_{i,1}, g_2\right) \neq e\left(g_1, \mathsf{pk}_{i,2}\right)$, return 0.
4. For each instance $i \in [K]$, compute $\mu_i := \mathsf{H}_\mu(\mathsf{m}, \varphi_i)$.
5. Return 1 if and only if

$$e\left(\bar{\sigma}, g_2\right) = \prod_{i=1}^{K} e\left(\mathsf{H}(\mu_i), \mathsf{pk}_{i,2}\right).$$

3.2 Security Analysis

Completeness of the scheme follows by inspection. We show blindness and one-more unforgeability. Before we give the proof of blindness, we first show a lemma that is needed. Intuitively, it states that algorithm ReRa perfectly rerandomizes the key shares.

Lemma 1. *For any* $\mathsf{pk}_1 \in \mathbb{G}_1$ *and* $\mathsf{pk}_{i,1} \in \mathbb{G}_1, i \in [K]$ *such that* $\prod_{i=1}^{K} \mathsf{pk}_{i,1} = \mathsf{pk}$, *the following distributions* $\mathcal{D}_1$ *and* $\mathcal{D}_2$ *are identical:*

$$\mathcal{D}_1 := \left\{ \left(\mathsf{pk}_1, (\mathsf{pk}_{i,1})_{i \in [K]}, (\mathsf{pk}'_{i,1})_{i \in [K]}\right) \;\middle|\; \begin{array}{l} r_1, \ldots, r_{K-1} \leftarrow_s \mathbb{Z}_p, \; r_K := -\sum_{i=1}^{K-1} r_i \\ \forall i \in [K] : \mathsf{pk}'_{i,1} := \mathsf{pk}_{i,1} \cdot g_1^{r_i} \end{array} \right\}$$

$$\mathcal{D}_2 := \left\{ \left(\mathsf{pk}_1, (\mathsf{pk}_{i,1})_{i \in [K]}, (\mathsf{pk}'_{i,1})_{i \in [K]}\right) \;\middle|\; \begin{array}{l} \forall i \in [K] : \mathsf{pk}'_{i,1} \leftarrow_s \mathbb{G} \\ \mathsf{pk}'_{K,1} := \mathsf{pk}_1 \cdot \prod_{i=1}^{K-1} \mathsf{pk}'^{-1}_{i,1} \end{array} \right\}$$

We give a formal proof of the lemma in our full version [26].

Theorem 1. *Let* $\mathsf{H}_r, \mathsf{H}_\mu \colon \{0,1\}^* \to \{0,1\}^\lambda$ *and* $\mathsf{H}_\alpha \colon \{0,1\}^* \to \mathbb{Z}_p$ *be random oracles. Then* BS_R *satisfies malicious signer blindness.*

Concretely, for any algorithm $\mathcal{A}$ that makes at most $Q_{\mathsf{H}_r}, Q_{\mathsf{H}_\mu}, Q_{\mathsf{H}_\alpha}$ queries to $\mathsf{H}_r, \mathsf{H}_\mu, \mathsf{H}_\alpha$ respectively, we have

$$\mathsf{Adv}^{\mathsf{blind}}_{\mathcal{A},\mathsf{BS}}(\lambda) \leq \frac{KNQ_{\mathsf{H}_\mu}}{2^{\lambda-2}} + \frac{KQ_{\mathsf{H}_r}}{2^{\lambda-2}} + \frac{KQ_{\mathsf{H}_\alpha}}{2^{\lambda-2}}.$$

Proof. We set $\mathsf{BS} := \mathsf{BS}_R$ and let $\mathcal{A}$ be an adversary against the blindness of BS. Our proof is presented as a sequence of games $\mathbf{G}_{i,b}$ for $i \in [8]$ and $b \in \{0,1\}$. We set $\mathbf{G}_{0,b} := \mathbf{BLIND}^{\mathcal{A}}_{b,\mathsf{BS}}(\lambda)$. Then, our goal is bound the distinguishing advantage

$$\mathsf{Adv}^{\mathsf{blind}}_{\mathcal{A},\mathsf{BS}}(\lambda) = |\Pr\left[\mathbf{G}_{0,0} \Rightarrow 1\right] - \Pr\left[\mathbf{G}_{0,1} \Rightarrow 1\right]|.$$

To do that, we will change our game to end up at a game $\mathbf{G}_{8,b}$ for which we have

$$\Pr\left[\mathbf{G}_{8,0} \Rightarrow 1\right] = \Pr\left[\mathbf{G}_{8,1} \Rightarrow 1\right].$$

Game $\mathbf{G}_{0,b}$: Game $\mathbf{G}_{0,b}$ is defined as $\mathbf{G}_{0,b} := \mathbf{BLIND}^{\mathcal{A}}_{b,\mathsf{BS}}(\lambda)$. We recall this game to fix some notation. First, $\mathcal{A}$ outputs a public key pk and two messages

$\underline{\mathsf{S}(\mathsf{sk})}$ | $\underline{\mathsf{U}(\mathsf{pk}, m)}$

S(sk)

for $i \in [K-1]$:

$\quad \mathsf{sk}_i \leftarrow_\$ \mathbb{Z}_p$

$\mathsf{sk}_K := \mathsf{sk} - \sum_{i=1}^{K-1} \mathsf{sk}_i$

for $i \in [K]$:

$\quad \mathsf{pk}_{i,1} = g_1^{\mathsf{sk}_i}$

$\quad \mathsf{pk}_{i,2} = g_2^{\mathsf{sk}_i}$

$\quad \mathsf{pk}_i := (\mathsf{pk}_{i,1}, \mathsf{pk}_{i,2})$

if $\mathsf{Check}(\mathsf{open}) = 0$: $\xleftarrow{\quad \mathsf{open} \quad}$

$\quad$ **abort**

for $i \in [K]$: $s_i := c_{i,\mathbf{J}_i}^{\mathsf{sk}_i}$

$\bar{s} := \prod_{i=1}^{K} s_i$ $\xrightarrow{\quad (\mathsf{pk}_i)_{i=1}^{K-1}, \bar{s} \quad}$

U(pk, m)

for $(i,j) \in [K] \times [N]$:

$\quad \varphi_{i,j} \leftarrow_\$ \{0,1\}^\lambda, \ \mu_{i,j} := \mathsf{H}_\mu(m, \varphi_{i,j})$

$\quad \gamma_{i,j} \leftarrow_\$ \{0,1\}^\lambda, \ \alpha_{i,j} := \mathsf{H}_\alpha(\gamma_{i,j})$

$\quad r_{i,j} := (\mu_{i,j}, \gamma_{i,j}), \ ,_{i,j} := \mathsf{H}_r(r_{i,j})$

$\quad c_{i,j} := \mathsf{H}(\mu_{i,j}) \cdot g_1^{\alpha_{i,j}}$

$, := (,_{1,1}, \ldots, ,_{K,N})$

$c := (c_{1,1}, \ldots, c_{K,N})$

$\mathbf{J} := \mathsf{H}_{cc}(,, c)$

$\mathsf{open} := \left(\mathbf{J}, \left((r_{i,j})_{j \neq \mathbf{J}_i}, c_{i,\mathbf{J}_i}, ,_{i,\mathbf{J}_i} \right)_{i \in [K]} \right)$

$\mathsf{pk}_{K,1} := \mathsf{pk}_1 \cdot \prod_{i=1}^{K-1} \mathsf{pk}_{i,1}^{-1}$

$\mathsf{pk}_{K,2} := \mathsf{pk}_2 \cdot \prod_{i=1}^{K-1} \mathsf{pk}_{i,2}^{-1}$

$\mathsf{pk}_K := (\mathsf{pk}_{K,1}, \mathsf{pk}_{K,2})$

for $i \in [K]$:

$\quad$ **if** $e\left(\mathsf{pk}_{i,1}, g_2\right) \neq e\left(g_1, \mathsf{pk}_{i,2}\right)$: **abort**

if $e(\bar{s}, g_2) \neq \prod_{i=1}^{K} e\left(c_{i,\mathbf{J}_i}, \mathsf{pk}_{i,2}\right)$: **abort**

$\bar{\sigma} := \bar{s} \cdot \prod_{i=1}^{K} \mathsf{pk}_{i,1}^{-\alpha_{i,\mathbf{J}_i}}$

$((\mathsf{pk}'_i)_i, \bar{\sigma}') \leftarrow \mathsf{ReRa}((\mathsf{pk}_i, \mathsf{H}(\mu_{i,\mathbf{J}_i}))_i, \bar{\sigma})$

return $\sigma := ((\mathsf{pk}'_i, \varphi_{i,\mathbf{J}_i})_{i=1}^{K-1}, \varphi_{K,\mathbf{J}_K}, \bar{\sigma}')$

Fig. 1. Signature issuing protocol of the blind signature scheme BS_R, where algorithm Check is defined in Fig. 2.

$$\mathbf{Alg}\ \mathsf{Check}\left(\mathsf{open} = \left(\mathbf{J}, \left((\mathsf{r}_{i,j})_{j \neq \mathbf{J}_i}, c_{i,\mathbf{J}_i}, ,_{i,\mathbf{J}_i}\right)_{i \in [K]}\right)\right)$$

01 **for** $i \in [K]$:
02   **for** $j \in [N] \setminus \{\mathbf{J}_i\}$:
03   **parse** $\mathsf{r}_{i,j} = (\mu_{i,j}, \gamma_{i,j}) \in \{0,1\}^\lambda \times \{0,1\}^\lambda$
04      $\alpha_{i,j} := \mathsf{H}_\alpha(\gamma_{i,j}), \quad c_{i,j} := \mathsf{H}(\mu_{i,j}) \cdot g_1^{\alpha_{i,j}}, \quad ,_{i,j} := \mathsf{H}_\mathsf{r}(\mathsf{r}_{i,j})$
05    $, := (,_{1,1}, \ldots, ,_{K,N}), \quad c := (c_{1,1}, \ldots, c_{K,N})$
06 **if** $\mathbf{J} \neq \mathsf{H}_{cc}(, , c)$: **return** 0
07 **return** 1

Fig. 2. The algorithm Check used in the signature issuing protocol of blind signature scheme BS_R.

$\mathsf{m}_0, \mathsf{m}_1$. Second, $\mathcal{A}$ is run with access to two interactive oracles O_0 and O_1. These simulate $\mathsf{U}(\mathsf{pk}, \mathsf{m}_b)$ and $\mathsf{U}(\mathsf{pk}, \mathsf{m}_{1-b})$, respectively. To distinguish variables used in the two oracles, we use superscripts L and R. That is, variables with superscript L (resp. R) are part of the interaction between $\mathcal{A}$ and O_0 (resp. O_1). For example, $\mathbf{J}^L := \mathsf{H}_{cc}(,^L, c^L)$ denotes the cut-and-choose vector that O_0 computes, and open^R denotes the first message that O_1 sends to $\mathcal{A}$. For descriptions with variables without a superscript, the reader should understand them as applying to both oracles.

Game $\mathbf{G}_{1,b}$: This game is as $\mathbf{G}_{0,b}$, but we let the game abort on a certain event. Namely, the game aborts if $\mathcal{A}$ ever makes a query of the form $\mathsf{H}_\mu(\cdot, \varphi_{i,j})$ for some $i \in [K]$ and $j \in [N] \setminus \{\mathbf{J}_i\}$. Note that for these values (i,j), $\mathcal{A}$ obtains no information about $\varphi_{i,j}$ throughout the entire game. Thus, the probability that a query is of this form is at most $1/2^\lambda$. A union bound over all such (i,j), the two oracles, and the random oracle queries leads to

$$|\Pr[\mathbf{G}_{0,b} \Rightarrow 1] - \Pr[\mathbf{G}_{1,b} \Rightarrow 1]| \leq \frac{KNQ_{\mathsf{H}_\mu}}{2^{\lambda-1}}.$$

Game $\mathbf{G}_{2,b}$: This game is as $\mathbf{G}_{1,b}$, but with another abort event. Concretely, the game aborts if $\mathcal{A}$ ever makes a query $\mathsf{H}_\mathsf{r}(\mathsf{r}_{i,\mathbf{J}_i})$, or a query $\mathsf{H}_\alpha(\gamma_{i,\mathbf{J}_i})$ for some $i \in [K]$. Note that $\mathsf{r}_{i,\mathbf{J}_i}$ has the form $\mathsf{r}_{i,\mathbf{J}_i} = (\mu_{i,\mathbf{J}_i}, \gamma_{i,\mathbf{J}_i})$, where $\gamma_{i,\mathbf{J}_i}$ is sampled uniformly at random from $\{0,1\}^\lambda$. Further, $\mathcal{A}$ obtains no information about $\gamma_{i,\mathbf{J}_i}$ throughout the entire game. Therefore, taking a union bound over all instances $i \in [K]$, the two user oracles, and the random oracle queries for both random oracles H_r and H_α, we get

$$|\Pr[\mathbf{G}_{1,b} \Rightarrow 1] - \Pr[\mathbf{G}_{2,b} \Rightarrow 1]| \leq \frac{KQ_{\mathsf{H}_\mathsf{r}}}{2^{\lambda-1}} + \frac{KQ_{\mathsf{H}_\alpha}}{2^{\lambda-1}}.$$

Game $\mathbf{G}_{3,b}$: In this game, we change how the final signatures are computed. Specifically, suppose that the user oracle does not abort due to the condition $e(\bar{s}, g_2) \neq \prod_{i=1}^{K} e(c_{i,\mathbf{J}_i}, \mathsf{pk}_{i,2})$ and does not abort due to condition $e(\mathsf{pk}_{i,1}, g_2) \neq e(g_1, \mathsf{pk}_{i,2})$ for any $i \in [K]$. Then, in previous games, the user oracle first computed $\bar{\sigma}$, and then executed $((\mathsf{pk}'_i)_i, \bar{\sigma}') \leftarrow \mathsf{ReRa}((\mathsf{pk}_i, \mathsf{H}(\mu_{i,\mathbf{J}_i}))_i, \bar{\sigma})$.

The value $\bar{\sigma}'$ is part of the final signature. In game $\mathbf{G}_{3,b}$, we instead let the user oracle run a brute-force search to compute the unique $\bar{\sigma}''$ such that $e\left(\bar{\sigma}'', g_2\right) = \prod_{i=1}^{K} e\left(\mathsf{H}(\mu_{i,\mathbf{J}_i}), \mathsf{pk}'_{i,2}\right)$. Then, we include $\bar{\sigma}''$ in the final signature instead of $\bar{\sigma}'$. We claim that this does not change the view of $\mathcal{A}$. To see this, first note that we did not change any verification or abort condition of the user oracles. Therefore, we can first consider the case where one of the user oracles locally outputs $\bot$. In this case, $\mathcal{A}$ gets $\bot, \bot$ as its final input in both $\mathbf{G}_{2,b}$ and $\mathbf{G}_{3,b}$. It remains to analyze the case where both user oracles do not abort. We claim that $\bar{\sigma}'$ and $\bar{\sigma}''$ are the same. To see this, assume $e\left(\bar{s}, g_2\right) = \prod_{i=1}^{K} e\left(c_{i,\mathbf{J}_i}, \mathsf{pk}_{i,2}\right)$, and multiply both sides by $\prod_{i=1}^{K} e\left(\mathsf{pk}_{i,1}^{-\alpha_{i,\mathbf{J}_i}}, g_2\right)$. We obtain

$$e\left(\bar{s}, g_2\right) \cdot \prod_{i=1}^{K} e\left(\mathsf{pk}_{i,1}^{-\alpha_{i,\mathbf{J}_i}}, g_2\right) = \prod_{i=1}^{K} e\left(c_{i,\mathbf{J}_i}, \mathsf{pk}_{i,2}\right) \cdot \prod_{i=1}^{K} e\left(\mathsf{pk}_{i,1}^{-\alpha_{i,\mathbf{J}_i}}, g_2\right)$$

$$\implies e\left(\bar{s} \cdot \prod_{i=1}^{K} \mathsf{pk}_{i,1}^{-\alpha_{i,\mathbf{J}_i}}, g_2\right) = \prod_{i=1}^{K} e\left(c_{i,\mathbf{J}_i}, \mathsf{pk}_{i,2}\right) \cdot e\left(g_1^{-\alpha_{i,\mathbf{J}_i}}, \mathsf{pk}_{i,2}\right)$$

$$\implies e\left(\bar{\sigma}, g_2\right) = \prod_{i=1}^{K} e\left(\mathsf{H}(\mu_{i,\mathbf{J}_i}), \mathsf{pk}_{i,2}\right),$$

where we used $e\left(\mathsf{pk}_{i,1}, g_2\right) = e\left(g_1, \mathsf{pk}_{i,2}\right)$ for all $i \in [K]$ on the right-hand side. Using the definition of algorithm ReRa, it is easy to see that this implies

$$e\left(\bar{\sigma}', g_2\right) = \prod_{i=1}^{K} e\left(\mathsf{H}(\mu_{i,\mathbf{J}_i}), \mathsf{pk}'_{i,2}\right).$$

By definition, $\bar{\sigma}''$ satisfies the same equation. As their is a unique solution to this equation for given $\mathsf{pk}'_{i,2}$ and $\mu_{i,\mathbf{J}_i}, i \in [K]$, we see that $\bar{\sigma}' = \bar{\sigma}''$. We have

$$\Pr\left[\mathbf{G}_{2,b} \Rightarrow 1\right] = \Pr\left[\mathbf{G}_{3,b} \Rightarrow 1\right].$$

Game $\mathbf{G}_{4,b}$: We make another change to the computation of the final signatures. Again, suppose that the user oracle does not abort. In this game $\mathbf{G}_{4,b}$, we no longer run algorithm ReRa in this case. Instead, we compute the $\mathsf{pk}'_i = (\mathsf{pk}'_{i,1}, \mathsf{pk}'_{i,2})$ as a fresh sharing via

$$\mathsf{sk}'_i \leftarrow_\$ \mathbb{Z}_p, \quad \mathsf{pk}'_{i,1} := g_1^{\mathsf{sk}_i}, \quad \mathsf{pk}'_{i,2} := g_2^{\mathsf{sk}_i} \text{ for } i \in [K-1],$$

$$\mathsf{pk}'_{K,1} := \mathsf{pk}_1 \cdot \prod_{i=1}^{K-1} \mathsf{pk}'^{-1}_{i,1}, \quad \mathsf{pk}'_{K,2} := \mathsf{pk}_2 \cdot \prod_{i=1}^{K-1} \mathsf{pk}'^{-1}_{i,2}.$$

Note that the other output $\bar{\sigma}'$ of algorithm ReRa is no longer needed due to the previous change. To analyze this change, we first argue that the $\mathsf{pk}'_{i,2}$ are uniquely determined by the $\mathsf{pk}'_{i,1}$. Namely, if the user oracle does not abort, we know that $e\left(\mathsf{pk}_{i,1}, g_2\right) = e\left(g_1, \mathsf{pk}_{i,2}\right)$ for all $i \in [K]$, and $e\left(\mathsf{pk}_1, g_2\right) = e\left(g_1, \mathsf{pk}_2\right)$. It is easy to see that property is preserved by algorithm ReRa, i.e. $e\left(\mathsf{pk}_{i,1}', g_2\right) = e\left(g_1, \mathsf{pk}_{i,2}'\right)$ for all $i \in [K]$. One can verify that our new definiton of the $\mathsf{pk}_{i,1}', \mathsf{pk}_{i,2}'$ also satisfies this. It remains to analyze the distribution of the $\mathsf{pk}_{i,1}'$. By Lemma 1 the distribution of the $\mathsf{pk}_{i,1}'$ stays the same. This implies that

$$\Pr\left[\mathbf{G}_{3,b} \Rightarrow 1\right] = \Pr\left[\mathbf{G}_{4,b} \Rightarrow 1\right].$$

Game $\mathbf{G}_{5,b}$: In game $\mathbf{G}_{5,b}$, we first sample random vectors $\hat{\mathbf{J}}^L \leftarrow_{\$} [N]^K$ and $\hat{\mathbf{J}}^R \leftarrow_{\$} [N]^K$. Then, we let the game abort, if later we do not have $\hat{\mathbf{J}}^L = \mathbf{J}^L$ and $\hat{\mathbf{J}}^R = \mathbf{J}^R$. As the view of $\mathcal{A}$ is independent of $\hat{\mathbf{J}}^L, \hat{\mathbf{J}}^R$ until a potential abort, we have

$$\Pr\left[\mathbf{G}_{5,b} \Rightarrow 1\right] = \frac{1}{N^{2K}} \cdot \Pr\left[\mathbf{G}_{4,b} \Rightarrow 1\right].$$

Game $\mathbf{G}_{6,b}$: In game $\mathbf{G}_{6,b}$, we change how the values $\mu_{i,j}$ for $i \in [K]$ and $j \in [N] \setminus \{\hat{\mathbf{J}}_i\}$ are computed. Recall that before, they were computed as $\mu_{i,j} = \mathsf{H}_\mu(\mathsf{m}, \varphi_{i,j})$. In $\mathbf{G}_{6,b}$, we sample $\mu_{i,j} \leftarrow_{\$} \{0,1\}^\lambda$ for $i \in [K]$ and $j \in [N] \setminus \{\hat{\mathbf{J}}_i\}$ instead. We highlight that the game still samples the values $\varphi_{i,j}$ to determine when it has to abort according to $\mathbf{G}_{1,b}$. Due to the changes introduced in $\mathbf{G}_{1,b}$ and $\mathbf{G}_{5,b}$, we can assume that $\hat{\mathbf{J}} = \mathbf{J}$ and $\mathcal{A}$ never queries $\mathsf{H}_\mu(\mathsf{m}, \varphi_{i,j})$, and therefore this change does not influence the view of $\mathcal{A}$. We have

$$\Pr\left[\mathbf{G}_{5,b} \Rightarrow 1\right] = \Pr\left[\mathbf{G}_{6,b} \Rightarrow 1\right].$$

Game $\mathbf{G}_{7,b}$: In game $\mathbf{G}_{7,b}$, we change how the values $\alpha_{i,\hat{\mathbf{J}}_i}$ and $_{i,\hat{\mathbf{J}}_i}$ are computed for all $i \in [K]$. Concretely, in this game, $\alpha_{i,\hat{\mathbf{J}}_i}$ is sampled uniformly at random as $\alpha_{i,\hat{\mathbf{J}}_i} \leftarrow_{\$} \mathbb{Z}_p$. Further, $_{i,\hat{\mathbf{J}}_i} \leftarrow_{\$} \{0,1\}^\lambda$ is sampled uniformly at random. Assuming that the game does not abort, we argue that the view of $\mathcal{A}$ does not change. This follows directly from the changes in $\mathbf{G}_{5,b}$ and $\mathbf{G}_{2,b}$. Namely, we can assume that $\hat{\mathbf{J}} = \mathbf{J}$ and that $\mathcal{A}$ never makes a query $\mathsf{H}_r(r_{i,\hat{\mathbf{J}}_i})$. We have

$$\Pr\left[\mathbf{G}_{6,b} \Rightarrow 1\right] = \Pr\left[\mathbf{G}_{7,b} \Rightarrow 1\right].$$

Game $\mathbf{G}_{8,b}$: In game $\mathbf{G}_{8,b}$, we change how the values $c_{i,\hat{\mathbf{J}}_i}$ for $i \in [K]$ are computed. First, recall that in the previous games, these are computed as $c_{i,\hat{\mathbf{J}}_i} = \mathsf{H}(\mu_{i,\hat{\mathbf{J}}_i}) \cdot g_1^{\alpha_{i,\hat{\mathbf{J}}_i}}$. Now, we sample it at random using $c_{i,\hat{\mathbf{J}}_i} \leftarrow_{\$} \mathbb{G}_1$. We argue indistinguishability as follows. Due to the change introduced in $\mathbf{G}_{5,b}$, we can assume that $\hat{\mathbf{J}} = \mathbf{J}$. Then, we know that in this case $\alpha_{i,\hat{\mathbf{J}}_i}$ is only used to define $c_{i,\hat{\mathbf{J}}_i}$ and nowhere else. In particular, it is not used to derive the final signatures from the interaction, due to the change introduced in $\mathbf{G}_{3,b}$, and it is not used to define $_{i,\hat{\mathbf{J}}_i}$ due to the change in $\mathbf{G}_{7,b}$. As $\alpha_{i,\hat{\mathbf{J}}_i}$ is sampled uniformly at random due to the change in $\mathbf{G}_{7,b}$, we know that $c_{i,\hat{\mathbf{J}}_i}$ is distributed uniformly at random in $\mathbf{G}_{7,b}$. This shows that

$$\Pr\left[\mathbf{G}_{7,b} \Rightarrow 1\right] = \Pr\left[\mathbf{G}_{8,b} \Rightarrow 1\right].$$

Finally, it can be observed that the view of $\mathcal{A}$ does not depend on the bit b anymore. This is because the messages m_0, m_1 are not used in the user oracles. Instead, the user oracles use random $\mu_{i,j}$, independent of the messages, for all opened sessions $j \neq \mathbf{J}_i$, and the final signatures σ_0, σ_1 that $\mathcal{A}$ gets are computed using brute-force independent of the interactions, assuming that both interactions accept. This shows that

$$\Pr[\mathbf{G}_{8,0} \Rightarrow 1] = \Pr[\mathbf{G}_{8,1} \Rightarrow 1].$$

To conclude, we upper bound $\mathsf{Adv}^{\mathsf{blind}}_{\mathcal{A},\mathsf{BS}}(\lambda) = |\Pr[\mathbf{G}_{0,0} \Rightarrow 1] - \Pr[\mathbf{G}_{0,1} \Rightarrow 1]|$ by

$$|\Pr[\mathbf{G}_{4,0} \Rightarrow 1] - \Pr[\mathbf{G}_{4,1} \Rightarrow 1]| + 2\left(\frac{KNQ_{\mathsf{H}_\mu}}{2^{\lambda-1}} + \frac{KQ_{\mathsf{H}_r}}{2^{\lambda-1}} + \frac{KQ_{\mathsf{H}_\alpha}}{2^{\lambda-1}}\right)$$

$$= N^{2K}|\Pr[\mathbf{G}_{5,0} \Rightarrow 1] - \Pr[\mathbf{G}_{5,1} \Rightarrow 1]| + \frac{KNQ_{\mathsf{H}_\mu}}{2^{\lambda-2}} + \frac{KQ_{\mathsf{H}_r}}{2^{\lambda-2}} + \frac{KQ_{\mathsf{H}_\alpha}}{2^{\lambda-2}}$$

$$= N^{2K}|\Pr[\mathbf{G}_{8,0} \Rightarrow 1] - \Pr[\mathbf{G}_{8,1} \Rightarrow 1]| + \frac{KNQ_{\mathsf{H}_\mu}}{2^{\lambda-2}} + \frac{KQ_{\mathsf{H}_r}}{2^{\lambda-2}} + \frac{KQ_{\mathsf{H}_\alpha}}{2^{\lambda-2}}$$

$$= \frac{KNQ_{\mathsf{H}_\mu}}{2^{\lambda-2}} + \frac{KQ_{\mathsf{H}_r}}{2^{\lambda-2}} + \frac{KQ_{\mathsf{H}_\alpha}}{2^{\lambda-2}}.$$

$\square$

Theorem 2. *Let* $\mathsf{H}_r, \mathsf{H}_\mu \colon \{0,1\}^* \to \{0,1\}^\lambda$, *and* $\mathsf{H}_{cc} \colon \{0,1\}^* \to [N]^K$, *and* $\mathsf{H} \colon \{0,1\}^* \to \mathbb{G}$ *be random oracles. If* CDH *assumption holds relative to* PGGen, *then* BS_R *is one-more unforgeable.*

Concretely, for any polynomial ℓ and any PPT algorithm $\mathcal{A}$ that makes at most $Q_{\mathsf{H}_{cc}}, Q_{\mathsf{H}_r}, Q_{\mathsf{H}_\mu}, Q_{\mathsf{H}}$ queries to $\mathsf{H}_{cc}, \mathsf{H}_r, \mathsf{H}_\mu, \mathsf{H}$ respectively, there is a PPT algorithm $\mathcal{B}$ with $\mathbf{T}(\mathcal{B}) \approx \mathbf{T}(\mathcal{A})$ and

$$\mathsf{Adv}^{\ell\text{-OMUF}}_{\mathcal{A},\mathsf{BS}_R}(\lambda) \leq \frac{Q^2_{\mathsf{H}_\mu} + Q^2_{\mathsf{H}_r} + Q_{\mathsf{H}}Q_{\mathsf{H}_{cc}} + Q_{\mathsf{H}}Q_{\mathsf{H}_\mu}}{2^\lambda} + \frac{\ell}{N^K}$$
$$+ 4\ell \cdot \mathsf{Adv}^{\mathsf{CDH}}_{\mathcal{B},\mathsf{PGGen}}(\lambda).$$

Proof. We set $\mathsf{BS} := \mathsf{BS}_R$ and let $\mathcal{A}$ be an adversary against the one-more unforgeability of BS. We show the statement by presenting a sequence of games. Before we go into detail, we explain the overall strategy of the proof. In our final step, we give a reduction that breaks the CDH assumption. This reduction works similar to the reduction for the BLS signature scheme [8]. Namely, it embeds one part of the CDH instance in the public key, and one part in some of the random oracle queries for oracle H. In the first part of our proof, we prepare simulation of the signer oracle without using the secret key. Here, the strategy is to extract the users randomness using the cut-and-choose technique. With overwhelming probability, in a fixed interaction, we can extract the randomness for one of the K instances, say instance i^*. Then, we compute the public key shares pk_i in a way that allows us to know all corresponding secret keys except sk_{i^*}. For instance

i^*, we can simulate the signing oracle by programming random oracle H. In the second part of our proof, we prepare the extraction of the CDH solution from the forgery that $\mathcal{A}$ returns. Here, it is essential that the scheme uses random oracle H_μ to compute commitments $\mu_{i,j}$. This allows us to embed the part of the CDH input in H in a consistent way. We will now proceed more formally.

Game G_0: Game G_0 is the real one-more unforgeability game, i.e. $G_0 := \ell\text{-}\mathbf{OMUF}_{BS}^{\mathcal{A}}$. Let us recall this game. First, the game samples $(\mathsf{pk}, \mathsf{sk}) \leftarrow \mathsf{Gen}(1^\lambda)$. Then, $\mathcal{A}$ is executed on input pk, and gets concurrent access to signer oracle O, simulating $S(\mathsf{sk})$. Additionally, $\mathcal{A}$ gets access to random oracles H, H_μ, H_r, H_{cc}. These are simulated by the game in the standard lazy way. Finally, $\mathcal{A}$ outputs pairs $(m_1, \sigma_1), \ldots, (m_k, \sigma_k)$. Denote the number of completed interactions (i.e. interactions in which O sent $\bar{s}$ to $\mathcal{A}$) by ℓ. If all m_i are distinct, all σ_i are valid signatures for m_i with respect to pk, and $k > \ell$, the game outputs 1. By definition, we have

$$\mathsf{Adv}_{\mathcal{A},BS}^{\ell\text{-}\mathsf{OMUF}}(\lambda) = \Pr[G_0 \Rightarrow 1].$$

Game G_1: Game G_1 is as G_0, but it aborts if a collision for one of the random oracles H_r, H_μ occurs. More precisely, let $* \in \{r, \mu\}$ and consider a query $H_*(x)$ for which the hash value is not yet defined. The game samples $H_*(x)$ as in game G_0. Then, the game aborts if there is another $x' \neq x$ such that $H_*(x')$ is already defined and $H_*(x) = H_*(x')$. As the outputs of H_* are sampled uniformly from $\{0,1\}^\lambda$, we can use a union bound over all pairs of queries and get

$$|\Pr[G_0 \Rightarrow 1] - \Pr[G_1 \Rightarrow 1]| \leq \frac{Q_{H_\mu}^2}{2^\lambda} + \frac{Q_{H_r}^2}{2^\lambda}.$$

Game G_2: Game G_2 is as game G_1, but we introduce a bad event and let the game abort if this bad event occurs. Concretely, consider any fixed query to oracle H_{cc} of the form $H_{cc}(,,c) = \mathbf{J}$ for $, = (,_{1,1}, \ldots, _{K,N})$ and $c = (c_{1,1}, \ldots, c_{K,N})$. For such queries and all $(i,j) \in [K] \times [N]$, the game now tries to extract values $\bar{r}_{i,j}$ such that $,_{i,j} = H_r(\bar{r}_{i,j})$. To do that, it searches through the random oracle queries for random oracle H_r. For those (i,j) for which such a value can not be extracted, we write $\bar{r}_{i,j} = \bot$. Due to the change introduced in G_1, there can be at most one extracted value for each (i,j). The game now aborts, if in such a query, there is some $(i,j) \in [K] \times [N]$ such that $\bar{r}_{i,j} = \bot$, but later oracle H_r is queried and returns $,_{i,j}$. Clearly, for a fixed pair of queries to H_{cc} and H_r, respectively, this bad event can only with probability $1/2^\lambda$. By a union bound we get

$$|\Pr[G_1 \Rightarrow 1] - \Pr[G_2 \Rightarrow 1]| \leq \frac{Q_{H_r} Q_{H_{cc}}}{2^\lambda}.$$

Before we continue, we summarize what we established so far and introduce some terminology. For that, we fix an interaction between $\mathcal{A}$ and the signer oracle O. Consider the first message

$$\mathsf{open} = \left(\mathbf{J}, \left((r_{i,j})_{j \neq \mathbf{J}_i}, c_{i,\mathbf{J}_i}, ,_{i,\mathbf{J}_i} \right)_{i \in [K]} \right)$$

that is sent by $\mathcal{A}$. Recall that after receiving this message, algorithm Check uses open to compute values $, = (,_{1,1}, \ldots, ,_{K,N})$ and $c = (c_{1,1}, \ldots, c_{K,N})$. Then, it also checks if $\mathbf{J} = \mathsf{H}_{cc}(,,c)$. Also, consider the values $\bar{r}_{i,j}$ related to the query $\mathsf{H}_{cc}(,,c)$, as defined in $\mathbf{G}_2$. Assuming Check outputs 1 (i.e. $\mathbf{J} = \mathsf{H}_{cc}(,,c)$), we make two observations for any instance $i \in [K]$.

1. If for some $j \in [N]$ we have $\bar{r}_{i,j} = \bot$, then $j = \mathbf{J}_i$. This is due to the bad event introduced in $\mathbf{G}_2$.
2. If for some $j \in [N]$ we have $\bar{r}_{i,j} = (\mu, \gamma) \neq \bot$ but $c_{i,j} \neq \mathsf{H}(\mu) \cdot g_1^\alpha$ for $\alpha := \mathsf{H}_\alpha(\gamma)$, then $\mathbf{J}_i = j$. This is because we ruled out collisions for H_r in $\mathbf{G}_1$. Namely, as there are no collisions, we know that $\bar{r}_{i,j} = r_{i,j}$ for all $j \neq \mathbf{J}_i$. Therefore, $c_{i,j} = \mathsf{H}(\mu) \cdot g_1^\alpha$ by definition of Check.

If one of these two events occur for some i, we say that there is a *successful cheat in instance i*. Note that the game can efficiently check if there is a successful cheat in an instance once it received open. Also note that the values $\bar{r}_{i,j}$ are fixed in the moment $\mathcal{A}$ queries $\mathsf{H}_{cc}(,,c)$ for the first time. In particular, they are fixed before $\mathcal{A}$ obtains any information about the uniformly random $\mathbf{J} = \mathsf{H}_{cc}(,,c)$. Therefore, using the two observations above, the probability of a successful cheat in instance i is at most $1/N$. Further, as the components of $\mathbf{J}$ are sampled independently, the probability that there is a successful cheat in all K instances (in this fixed interaction) is at most $1/N^K$.

Game $\mathbf{G}_3$: In game $\mathbf{G}_3$, we introduce another abort. Namely, the game aborts, if in some interaction between $\mathcal{A}$ and the signer oracle O, there is a successful cheat in every instance $i \in [K]$, and that interaction is completed. By the discussion above, we have

$$|\Pr[\mathbf{G}_2 \Rightarrow 1] - \Pr[\mathbf{G}_3 \Rightarrow 1]| \leq \frac{\ell}{N^K}.$$

Game $\mathbf{G}_4$: In game $\mathbf{G}_4$, we change the way the signer oracle computes the shares sk_i. Recall that before, these were computed as

$$\mathsf{sk}_i \leftarrow_\$ \mathbb{Z}_p \text{ for } i \in [K-1], \quad \mathsf{sk}_K := \mathsf{sk} - \sum_{i=1}^{K-1} \mathsf{sk}_i.$$

Then, the corresponding public key shares were computed as $\mathsf{pk}_i = (g_1^{\mathsf{sk}_i}, g_2^{\mathsf{sk}_i})$ for all $i \in [K]$. In game $\mathbf{G}_4$, the game instead defines the sk_i after it received the first message open from $\mathcal{A}$ in the following way. If Check outputs 0 or there is a successful cheat in every instance, the game behaves as before (i.e. it aborts the interaction, or the entire execution). Otherwise, let $i^* \in [K]$ be the first instance in which there is no successful cheat. Then, the game computes

$$\mathsf{sk}_i \leftarrow_\$ \mathbb{Z}_p \text{ for } i \in [K] \setminus \{i^*\}, \quad \mathsf{sk}_{i^*} := \mathsf{sk} - \sum_{i \in [K] \setminus \{i^*\}} \mathsf{sk}_i.$$

The game defines pk_i for all $i \in [K]$ as before. It is clear that this change is only conceptual, as a uniformly random additive sharing of sk is computed in both $\mathbf{G}_3$ and $\mathbf{G}_4$. Therefore, we have

$$\Pr[\mathbf{G}_3 \Rightarrow 1] = \Pr[\mathbf{G}_4 \Rightarrow 1].$$

Game G_5: In game G_5, we introduce an abort related to the random oracles H and H_μ. Namely, the game aborts if the following occurs. The adversary $\mathcal{A}$ first queries $H(\mu)$ for some $\mu \in \{0,1\}^*$, and after that a hash value $H_\mu(x)$ is defined for some $x \in \{0,1\}^*$, and we have $H_\mu(x) = \mu$. Clearly, once μ is fixed, the probability that a previously undefined hash value $H_\mu(x)$ is equal to μ is at most $1/2^\lambda$. Therefore, we can use a union bound over the random oracle queries and get

$$|\Pr[G_4 \Rightarrow 1] - \Pr[G_5 \Rightarrow 1]| \leq \frac{Q_H Q_{H_\mu}}{2^\lambda}.$$

Game G_6: In this game, we introduce a purely conceptual change. To do that, we introduce maps $b[\cdot]$ and $\hat{b}[\cdot]$. Then, on a query $H_\mu(m, \varphi)$ for which the hash value is not yet defined, the game samples bit $\hat{b}[m] \in \{0,1\}$ from a Bernoulli distribution, such that the probability that $\hat{b}[m] = 1$ is $1/(\ell + 1)$. Additionally, on a query $H(\mu)$ for which the hash value is not yet defined, the game first searches for a previous query (m_μ, φ) to H_μ such that $H_\mu(m_\mu, \varphi) = \mu$. Then, it sets $b[\mu] := \hat{b}[m_\mu]$. If no such query can be found, it sets $b[\mu] := 0$. Note that due to the change in G_1, the game can find at most one such query and m_μ is well defined. The view of $\mathcal{A}$ does not change, and we have

$$\Pr[G_5 \Rightarrow 1] = \Pr[G_6 \Rightarrow 1].$$

Game G_7: In this game, we introduce an initially empty set $\mathcal{L}$ and an abort related to it. In each interaction between $\mathcal{A}$ and the signer oracle O, the game simulates the oracle as in G_6. Additionally, if the game has to provide the final message $(pk_i)_{i=1}^{K-1}, \bar{s}$, then we know that Check output 1 and the game did not abort. Therefore, there is at least one instance $i^* \in [K]$ such that $\mathcal{A}$ did not cheat successfully in instance i^*. Fix the first such instance. This means that the game could extract $\bar{r}_{i^*, J_{i^*}} = (\mu, \gamma)$ before (see the discussion after G_2). In game G_7, the game tries to extract m_μ as defined in G_6 from μ using H_μ, and inserts (μ, m_μ) into set $\mathcal{L}$ if it could extract. Also, the game aborts if $b[\mu] = 1$. Otherwise, it computes and sends $(pk_i)_{i=1}^{K-1}, \bar{s}$ as before. We highlight that the size of $\mathcal{L}$ is at most the number of completed interactions ℓ.

Next, consider the final output $(m_1, \sigma_1), \ldots, (m_k, \sigma_k)$ of $\mathcal{A}$, write $\sigma_r = ((pk_{r,i}, \varphi_{r,i})_{i=1}^{K-1}), \varphi_{r,K}, \bar{\sigma}_r)$, and set $\mu_{r,i} := H_\mu(m_r, \varphi_{r,i})$ for all $r \in [k], i \in [K]$. If $\mathcal{A}$ is successful, we know that $k > \ell$. Therefore, by the pigeonhole principle, there is at least one $(\tilde{r}, \tilde{i}) \in [k] \times [K]$ such that $(\mu_{\tilde{r}, \tilde{i}}, m_{\tilde{r}}) \notin \mathcal{L}$. Game G_7 finds the first such $\mu_{\tilde{r}, \tilde{i}}$, sets $\mu^* := \mu_{\tilde{r}, \tilde{i}}$ and aborts if $b[\mu^*] = 0$. Note that we can assume that $b[\mu^*]$ is defined, as verification of $\mathcal{A}$'s output involves computing $H(\mu^*)$. For the sake of analysis, G_7 also appends further entries of the form (μ, m_μ) to $\mathcal{L}$ such that $|\mathcal{L}| = \ell$ and all entries in $\mathcal{L} \cup \{\mu^*\}$ have distinct components m_μ. It queries $H(\mu)$ for all $(\mu, m_\mu) \in \mathcal{L}$. Then, it aborts if for some $(\mu, m_\mu) \in \mathcal{L}$ it holds that $b[\mu] = 1$.

To analyze the change we introduced, note that G_6 and G_7 only differ if $b[\mu^*] = 0$ or $b[\mu] = 1$ for some $(\mu, m_\mu) \in \mathcal{L}$. This is because if the game could not extract m_μ in some interaction, then due to the changes in G_5 and G_6, we know that $b[\mu] = 0$. The view of $\mathcal{A}$ is independent of these bits until a potential abort occurs. This implies that

$$\Pr\left[\mathbf{G}_7 \Rightarrow 1\right] = \Pr\left[\mathbf{G}_6 \Rightarrow 1\right] \cdot \Pr\left[b[\mu^*] = 1 \wedge \forall (\mu, \mathsf{m}_\mu) \in \mathcal{L} : b[\mu] = 0\right].$$

By definition of the bits $b[\cdot]$, and the change in $\mathbf{G}_5$, we can rewrite the latter term in the product as

$$\Pr\left[\hat{b}[\mathsf{m}_{\tilde{r}}] = 1 \wedge \forall (\mu, \mathsf{m}_\mu) \in \mathcal{L} : \hat{b}[\mathsf{m}_\mu] = 0\right] = \frac{1}{\ell + 1}\left(1 - \frac{1}{\ell + 1}\right)^\ell$$

$$= \frac{1}{\ell}\left(1 - \frac{1}{\ell + 1}\right)^{\ell + 1} \geq \frac{1}{4\ell},$$

where we used the fact $(1 - 1/x)^x \geq 1/4$ for all $x \geq 2$, and that all bits $\hat{b}[\cdot]$ are independent. Thus, we have

$$\Pr\left[\mathbf{G}_7 \Rightarrow 1\right] \geq \frac{1}{4\ell} \cdot \Pr\left[\mathbf{G}_6 \Rightarrow 1\right].$$

Game $\mathbf{G}_8$: In this game, we change how random oracle H is simulated. Namely, in the beginning of the game, the game samples $Y \leftarrow_\$ \mathbb{G}_1$ and initiates a map $t[\cdot]$. Then, on a query $\mathsf{H}(\mu)$ for which the hash value is not yet defined, the game first determines bit $b[\mu]$ as before. Then, it samples $t[\mu] \leftarrow_\$ \mathbb{Z}_p$ and sets $\mathsf{H}(\mu) := Y^{b[\mu]} \cdot g_1^{t[\mu]}$. Clearly, all hash values are still uniformly random and independent. Therefore, we have

$$\Pr\left[\mathbf{G}_7 \Rightarrow 1\right] = \Pr\left[\mathbf{G}_8 \Rightarrow 1\right].$$

Game $\mathbf{G}_9$: In this game, we change how the signing oracle computes public keys $(\mathsf{pk}_i)_i$ and the values $s_i, i \in [K]$ used to compute the final message $(\mathsf{pk}_i)_{i=1}^{K-1}, \bar{s}$. Consider an interaction between $\mathcal{A}$ and the signer oracle and recall the definition of the instance i^* as in game $\mathbf{G}_4$. This is the first instance for which there is no successful cheat in this interaction, i.e. $\bar{r}_{i^*, \mathsf{J}_{i^*}} = (\mu, \gamma) \neq \perp$ could be extracted and $c_{i^*, \mathsf{J}_{i^*}} = \mathsf{H}(\mu) \cdot g_1^\alpha$ for $\alpha := \mathsf{H}_\alpha(\gamma)$. In $\mathbf{G}_9$, the public keys $\mathsf{pk}_i = (\mathsf{pk}_{i,1}, \mathsf{pk}_{i,2})$ are computed via

$$\mathsf{pk}_{i,1} = g_1^{\mathsf{sk}_i} \text{ for } i \in [K] \setminus \{i^*\}, \quad \mathsf{pk}_{i^*,1} := \mathsf{pk}_1 \cdot \prod_{i \in [K] \setminus \{i^*\}} \mathsf{pk}_{i,1}^{-1},$$

$$\mathsf{pk}_{i,2} = g_2^{\mathsf{sk}_i} \text{ for } i \in [K] \setminus \{i^*\}, \quad \mathsf{pk}_{i^*,2} := \mathsf{pk}_2 \cdot \prod_{i \in [K] \setminus \{i^*\}} \mathsf{pk}_{i,2}^{-1}.$$

Further, due to the aborts introduced in previous games, we know that the game only has to send $(\mathsf{pk}_i)_{i=1}^{K-1}, \bar{s}$ if i^* is defined and $b[\mu] = 0$, where μ is as above. In this case, game $\mathbf{G}_8$ would compute

$$s_{i^*} = c_{i^*, \mathsf{J}_{i^*}}^{\mathsf{sk}_{i^*}} = \mathsf{H}(\mu)^{\mathsf{sk}_{i^*}} \cdot g_1^{\alpha \cdot \mathsf{sk}_{i^*}} = \left(Y^{b[\mu]} \cdot g_1^{t[\mu]}\right)^{\mathsf{sk}_{i^*}} \cdot \mathsf{pk}_{i^*,1}^\alpha = \mathsf{pk}_{i^*,1}^{\alpha + t[\mu]}.$$

Game $\mathbf{G}_9$ computes s_{i^*} directly as $\mathsf{pk}_{i^*,1}^{\alpha+t[\mu]}$, and all other s_i, $i \neq i^*$ as before using sk_i. Both changes are only conceptual and allow the game to provide the signer oracle without using the secret key sk at all. We have

$$\Pr\left[\mathbf{G}_8 \Rightarrow 1\right] = \Pr\left[\mathbf{G}_9 \Rightarrow 1\right].$$

Finally, we give a reduction $\mathcal{B}$ against the CDH assumption that is successful if $\mathbf{G}_9$ outputs 1. We argue that

$$\Pr\left[\mathbf{G}_9 \Rightarrow 1\right] \leq \mathsf{Adv}_{\mathcal{B},\mathsf{PGGen}}^{\mathsf{CDH}}(\lambda).$$

The reduction $\mathcal{B}$ is as follows.

- Reduction $\mathcal{B}$ gets as input g_1, g_2, e, p, $X_1, Y \in \mathbb{G}_1$, and $X_2 \in \mathbb{G}_2$. It sets $\mathsf{pk}_1 := X_1, \mathsf{pk}_2 := X_2$ and uses Y as explained in $\mathbf{G}_8$.
- Reduction $\mathcal{B}$ simulates $\mathbf{G}_9$ for $\mathcal{A}$. Note that it can do that efficiently, as sk is not needed.
- When $\mathcal{A}$ terminates with its final output $(\mathsf{m}_1, \sigma_1), \ldots, (\mathsf{m}_k, \sigma_k)$, the reduction $\mathcal{B}$ writes $\sigma_r = ((\mathsf{pk}_{r,i}, \varphi_{r,i})_{i=1}^{K-1}), \varphi_{r,K}, \bar{\sigma}_r)$, $\mathsf{pk}_{r,i} = (\mathsf{pk}_{r,i,1}, \mathsf{pk}_{r,i,2})$, sets $\mu_{r,i} := \mathsf{H}_\mu(\mathsf{m}_r, \varphi_{r,i})$ for all $r \in [k], i \in [K]$ and $\mathsf{pk}_{r,K,1} := \mathsf{pk}_1 \cdot \prod_{i=1}^{K-1} \mathsf{pk}_{r,i,1}^{-1}$ and $\mathsf{pk}_{r,K,2} := \mathsf{pk}_2 \cdot \prod_{i=1}^{K-1} \mathsf{pk}_{r,i,2}^{-1}$ for all $r \in [k]$. It performs all checks as in $\mathbf{G}_9$. If $\mathbf{G}_9$ outputs 1, we know that $\mathcal{B}$ defined $\mu^* := \mu_{\tilde{r},\tilde{i}}$ as $\mathbf{G}_9$ does. Then, $\mathcal{B}$ outputs

$$Z := \bar{\sigma}_{\tilde{r}} \cdot \prod_{i=1}^{K} \mathsf{pk}_{\tilde{r},i,1}^{-t[\mu_{\tilde{r},i}]}.$$

It is clear that $\mathcal{B}$ perfectly simulates $\mathbf{G}_9$ and the running time of $\mathcal{B}$ is dominated by the running time of $\mathcal{A}$. Thus, it remains to argue that if $\mathbf{G}_9$ outputs 1, the Z is a valid CDH solution. To this end, assume that $\mathbf{G}_9$ outputs 1. It is sufficient to show that $e(Y, X_2) = e(Z, g_2)$.

First, note that due to the abort that we introduced in $\mathbf{G}_5$, we know that for all $i \in [K]$, the query $\mathsf{H}_\mu(\mathsf{m}_{\tilde{r}}, \varphi_{\tilde{r},i})$ was made before bit $b[\mu_{\tilde{r},i}]$ was defined. Therefore, due to the change in $\mathbf{G}_6$, we obtain for all $i \in [K]$

$$b[\mu_{\tilde{r},i}] = \hat{b}[\mathsf{m}_{\tilde{r}}] = b[\mu_{\tilde{r},\tilde{r}}] = b[\mu^*] = 1.$$

Second, we know that we have $\prod_{i=1}^{K} \mathsf{pk}_{\tilde{r},i,2} = X_2$, and by definition of the verification algorithm we have

$$e(\bar{\sigma}_{\tilde{r}}, g_2) = \prod_{i=1}^{K} e\left(\mathsf{H}(\mu_{r,i}), \mathsf{pk}_{\tilde{r},i,2}\right) = \prod_{i=1}^{K} e\left(Y \cdot g^{t[\mu_{\tilde{r},i}]}, \mathsf{pk}_{\tilde{r},i,2}\right)$$

$$= \prod_{i=1}^{K} e\left(Y, \mathsf{pk}_{\tilde{r},i,2}\right) \cdot e\left(\mathsf{pk}_{\tilde{r},i,1}^{t[\mu_{\tilde{r},i}]}, g_2\right) = e(Y, X_2) \cdot e\left(\prod_{i=1}^{K} \mathsf{pk}_{\tilde{r},i,1}^{t[\mu_{\tilde{r},i}]}, g_2\right).$$

In the third equation we used $e\left(\mathsf{pk}_{\tilde{r},i,1},g_2\right) = e\left(g_1,\mathsf{pk}_{\tilde{r},i,2}\right)$ for all $i \in [K]$. This implies that

$$e\left(Z,g_2\right) = e\left(\bar{\sigma}_{\tilde{r}} \cdot \prod_{i=1}^{K} \mathsf{pk}_{\tilde{r},i,1}^{-t[\mu_{\tilde{r},i}]},g_2\right) = e\left(Y,X_2\right).$$

□

4 Extension: Partial Blindness and Batching

In this section, we present a batching technique for our blind signature scheme, which leads to a significant efficiency improvement in terms of communication. At the same time, we show how to make our scheme partially blind. We first give an informal overview. In the second part of the section, we present the formal model for batching (partially) blind signatures. Then, we present our scheme and its analysis.

4.1 Overview

We give an overview of the extensions we present in this section. These cover partial blindness, and batching to further improve the communication complexity.

Partially Blind Signatures. Recall that a partially blind signature scheme allows to sign messages with respect to some public information string info, that the signer knows. This string acts as a form of domain separator. Namely, one-more unforgeability now guarantees that the user can output at most ℓ valid message signature pairs with respect to any public information string info, for which it interacted at most ℓ times with the signer oracle. It turns out that we can extend our blind signature scheme into a partially blind signature scheme, by changing the definition of the values $c_{i,j}$ from $c_{i,j} = \mathsf{H}(\mu_{i,j}) \cdot g_1^{\alpha_{i,j}}$ to $c_{i,j} = \mathsf{H}(\mathsf{info},\mu_{i,j}) \cdot g_1^{\alpha_{i,j}}$. Intuitively, the cut-and-choose technique now ensures that the user uses the correct info to compute the $c_{i,j}$'s.

Batching. We show how we can batch multiple signing interactions. Namely, we observe that if we sign multiple messages in one interaction, the (amortized) communication complexity decreases. Batching has been subject of study for other primitives, e.g. in oblivious transfer [9,30]. Let us briefly sketch how we can apply batching to our blind signature scheme. For that, consider one signing interaction in which a batch $m_1,\ldots,m_L$ of L messages should be signed. Recall that in our scheme, cut-and-choose ensured that there is an instance $i^* \in [K]$, such that the user does not cheat successfully in instance i^*. Then, the purpose of sending a fresh public key sharing $\mathsf{pk}_1,\ldots,\mathsf{pk}_K$ was to dynamically embed the unknown share of the secret key in instance i^*. For this strategy, it is not relevant that we cover one message per instance. Therefore we can use the same public key sharing $\mathsf{pk}_1,\ldots,\mathsf{pk}_K$, and the same cut-and-choose index for every instance, leading to our batched scheme.

4.2   Model for Batched (Partially) Blind Signatures

In this section, we sketch the definition of batched (partially) blind signatures and their security. For formal definitions, we refer to the full version [26]. The reader should observe that batched partially blind signatures imply partially blind signatures by fixing the batch size $L = 1$. Further, the partial blindness can be lifted to standard blindness by fixing a default public information string. We start with the syntax of batched partially blind signatures. Recall that in partially blind signatures, the signer gets the public information string info, while the user gets info and the message m. Here, we generalize the syntax of partially blind signatures to the setting, where both user and signer get the batch size L as input, and multiple pairs $(info_l, m_l)$ are signed. This models that the batch size is not fixed, but instead it can be chosen dynamically. More precisely, while the syntax of key generation and verification is as for partially blind signatures, an interaction between S and U can now be described as

$$(\perp, (\sigma_1, \dots, \sigma_L)) \leftarrow \langle S(sk, L, (info_l)_{l \in [L]}), U(pk, L, (m_l, info_l)_{l \in [L]} \rangle.$$

Completeness requires that for all $l \in [L]$, it holds that $Ver(pk, info_l, m_l, \sigma_l) = 1$.

In terms of security, we require the same security guarantees, as if we just run a normal (partially) blind signature scheme L times in parallel. We let the adversary determine the batch size in each interaction separately. This leads to a natural definition of batch one-more unforgeability.

As for unforgeability, blindness should give the same guarantees as if we just run a normal (partially) blind signature scheme L times in parallel. Especially, it should not be possible to tell if two signatures result from the same interaction or not. In our security game, we let the malicious signer choose two batches of (potentially different) sizes L_0 and L_1. The signer also points to one element for each batch. Then, the game either swaps these two elements, or not, and the signer has to distinguish these two cases. Via a hybrid argument, this implies that the signer does not know which message is signed in which interaction.

4.3   Construction

As for BS_R, we let $PGGen(1^\lambda)$ be a bilinear group generation algorithm that outputs cyclic groups $\mathbb{G}_1, \mathbb{G}_2$ of prime order p with generators $g_1 \in \mathbb{G}_1, g_2 \in \mathbb{G}_2$, and a non-degenerate pairing $e : \mathbb{G}_1 \times \mathbb{G}_2 \to \mathbb{G}_T$ into some target group $\mathbb{G}_T$. Again, we assume that these system parameters are known to all algorithms and note that their correctness can be verified efficiently. Our scheme $BPBS_R = (Gen, S, U, Ver)$ is parameterized by integers $K = K(\lambda), N(\lambda) \in \mathbb{N}$, where we need that N^{-K} is negligible in λ. We assume that the space $\mathcal{I}$ contains bitstrings of bounded length[4]. The scheme makes use of random oracles $H_r, H_\mu : \{0,1\}^* \to \{0,1\}^\lambda, H_\alpha : \{0,1\}^* \to \mathbb{Z}_p, H_{cc} : \{0,1\}^* \to [N]^K$, and $H : \{0,1\}^* \to \mathbb{G}_1$.

We verbally describe the signature issuing protocol (S, U) and verification of scheme $BPBS_R$. Key generation (algorithm Gen) is exactly as in BS_R.

---

[4] This is without loss of generality, using a collision-resistant hash function.

Signature Issuing. The interactive signature issuing protocol between algorithms $S(sk, L, (info_l)_{l \in [L]})$ and $U(pk, L, (m_l, info_l)_{l \in [L]})$ is given as follows.

1. User U does the following.
   (a) *Preparation.* First, for each instance $i \in [K]$ and session $j \in [N]$, U commits to all L messages via

   $$\varphi_{i,j,l} \leftarrow_\$ \{0,1\}^\lambda, \quad \mu_{i,j,l} := H_\mu(m_l, \varphi_{i,j,l}) \text{ for all } (i,j,l) \in [K] \times [N] \times [L].$$

   (b) *Commitments.* Next, for each instance $i \in [K]$ and session $j \in [N]$, U samples a seed $\gamma_{i,j} \leftarrow_\$ \{0,1\}^\lambda$. It then defines

   $$r_{i,j} := (\gamma_{i,j}, \mu_{i,j,1}, \dots, \mu_{i,j,L}), \quad \text{,}_{i,j} := H_r(r_{i,j}) \text{ for all } (i,j) \in [K] \times [N].$$

   Then, U sets $\text{,} := (\text{,}_{1,1}, \dots, \text{,}_{K,N})$.
   (c) *Challenges.* Now, U derives randomness $\alpha_{i,j,l}$ and computes challenges $c_{i,j,l}$ via $\alpha_{i,j,l} := H_\alpha(\gamma_{i,j}, l)$ and

   $$c_{i,j,l} := H(info_l, \mu_{i,j,l}) \cdot g_1^{\alpha_{i,j,l}} \text{ for all } (i,j,l) \in [K] \times [N] \times [L].$$

   Then, U sets $c := (c_{1,1,1}, \dots, c_{K,N,L})$.
   (d) *Cut-and-Choose.* Next, U derives a cut-and-choose vector $\mathbf{J} \in [N]^K$ as $\mathbf{J} := H_{cc}(\text{,}, c)$. It then defines an opening

   $$\text{open} := \left(\mathbf{J}, \left((r_{i,j})_{j \neq \mathbf{J}_i}, (c_{i,\mathbf{J}_i,l})_{l \in [L]}, \text{,}_{i,\mathbf{J}_i}\right)_{i \in [K]}\right).$$

   Finally, U sends open to S.
2. Signer S does the following.
   (a) *Key Sharing.* First, S samples $sk_i \leftarrow_\$ \mathbb{Z}_p$ for $i \in [K-1]$. It computes $sk_K := sk - \sum_{i=1}^{K-1} sk_i$ and $pk_i := (pk_{i,1}, pk_{i,2}) := (g_1^{sk_i}, g_2^{sk_i})$ for all $i \in [K]$.
   (b) *Cut-and-Choose Verification.* To verify the opening, S runs algorithm $\mathsf{Check}(L, (info_l)_{l \in [L]}, \text{open})$ (see Fig. 3). If this algorithm returns 0, S aborts the interaction.
   (c) *Responses.* For each instance $i \in [K]$ and each $l \in [L]$, S computes responses $s_{i,l} := c_{i,\mathbf{J}_i,l}^{sk_i}$. Then, it aggregates them for each $l \in [L]$ by computing $\bar{s}_l := \prod_{i=1}^K s_{i,l}$. Finally, S sends $(pk_i)_{i=1}^{K-1}, \bar{s}_1, \dots, \bar{s}_L$ to U.
3. User U does the following.
   (a) *Key Sharing Verification.* First, U recomputes key pk_K as $pk_K := (pk_{K,1}, pk_{K,2})$ for $pk_{K,1} := pk_1 \cdot \prod_{i=1}^{K-1} pk_{i,1}^{-1}$ and $pk_{K,2} := pk_2 \cdot \prod_{i=1}^{K-1} pk_{i,2}^{-1}$. Next, U checks validity of the pk_i by checking if

   $$e(pk_{i,1}, g_2) = e(g_1, pk_{i,2}) \text{ for all } i \in [K].$$

   If any of these equations does not hold, U aborts the interaction.

(b) *Response Verification.* Then, U verifies the responses $\bar{s}_l$ by checking

$$e\left(\bar{s}_l, g_2\right) = \prod_{i=1}^{K} e\left(c_{i,\mathsf{J}_i,l}, \mathsf{pk}_{i,2}\right) \text{ for all } l \in [L].$$

If any of these equations does not hold, U aborts the interaction. Otherwise, it computes

$$\bar{\sigma}_l := \bar{s}_l \cdot \prod_{i=1}^{K} \mathsf{pk}_{i,1}^{-\alpha_{i,\mathsf{J}_i,l}} \text{ for all } l \in [L].$$

(c) *Key Rerandomization.* Next, U computes rerandomized key sharings via

$$((\mathsf{pk}'_{i,l})_i, \bar{\sigma}'_l) \leftarrow \mathsf{ReRa}((\mathsf{pk}_i, \mathsf{H}(\mathsf{info}_l, \mu_{i,\mathsf{J}_i,l}))_i, \bar{\sigma}_l) \text{ for all } l \in [L].$$

It then defines signatures

$$\sigma_l := ((\mathsf{pk}'_{i,l}, \varphi_{i,\mathsf{J}_i,l})_{i=1}^{K-1}, \varphi_{K,\mathsf{J}_K,l}, \bar{\sigma}'_l) \text{ for all } l \in [L].$$

(d) Finally, U outputs the signatures $\sigma_1, \ldots, \sigma_L$.

Verification. The resulting signature $\sigma := ((\mathsf{pk}_i, \varphi_i)_{i=1}^{K-1}), \varphi_K, \bar{\sigma})$ for a message m and string info is verified by algorithm $\mathsf{Ver}(\mathsf{pk}, \mathsf{info}, \mathsf{m}, \sigma)$ as follows:

1. Write $\mathsf{pk}_i = (\mathsf{pk}_{i,1}, \mathsf{pk}_{i,2})$ for each $i \in [K-1]$.
2. Compute $\mathsf{pk}_{K,1} := \mathsf{pk}_1 \cdot \prod_{i=1}^{K-1} \mathsf{pk}_{i,1}^{-1}$ and $\mathsf{pk}_{K,2} := \mathsf{pk}_2 \cdot \prod_{i=1}^{K-1} \mathsf{pk}_{i,2}^{-1}$.
3. If there is an $i \in [K]$ with $e\left(\mathsf{pk}_{i,1}, g_2\right) \neq e\left(g_1, \mathsf{pk}_{i,2}\right)$, return 0.
4. For each instance $i \in [K]$, compute $\mu_i := \mathsf{H}_\mu(\mathsf{m}, \varphi_i)$.
5. Return 1 if and only if

$$e\left(\bar{\sigma}, g_2\right) = \prod_{i=1}^{K} e\left(\mathsf{H}(\mathsf{info}, \mu_i), \mathsf{pk}_{i,2}\right).$$

4.4   Security Analysis

Completeness of the scheme follows by inspection. The proofs and concrete security bounds for blindness and one-more unforgeability are almost identical to the proofs of the corresponding theorems in Sect. 3. Due to space limitation, we postpone the formal analysis to the full version [26].

5   Concrete Parameters and Efficiency

In this section, we discuss concrete parameters and efficiency of our scheme.

$$\textbf{Alg Check}\left(L, (\text{info}_l)_{l\in[L]}, \text{open} = \left(\mathbf{J}, \left((r_{i,j})_{j\neq\mathbf{J}_i}, (c_{i,\mathbf{J}_i,l})_{l\in[L]}, ,_{i,\mathbf{J}_i}\right)_{i\in[K]}\right)\right)$$

```
01  for i ∈ [K] :
02    for j ∈ [N] \ {Jᵢ} :
03      ,ᵢ,ⱼ := Hᵣ(rᵢ,ⱼ)
04      parse rᵢ,ⱼ = (γᵢ,ⱼ, μᵢ,ⱼ,₁, ..., μᵢ,ⱼ,L) ∈ ({0,1}^λ)^{L+1}
05      for l ∈ [L] :  αᵢ,ⱼ,ₗ := Hₐ(γᵢ,ⱼ, l),  cᵢ,ⱼ,ₗ := H(infoₗ, μᵢ,ⱼ,ₗ) · g₁^{αᵢ,ⱼ,ₗ}
06  , := (,₁,₁, ..., ,K,N),  c := (c₁,₁,₁, ..., cK,N,L)
07  if J ≠ H_cc(, , c) : return 0
08  return 1
```

Fig. 3. The algorithm Check used in the signature issuing protocol of batched blind signature scheme BPBS$_R$.

Instantiating Parameters. We instantiate our scheme over the BLS12-381 curve, using SHA-256 as a hash function. It remains to determine appropriate choices for parameters K and N. To do that, we first fix some choice of N and a bit security level $\kappa = 128$. Then, we assume a maximum number of $\ell = 2^{30}$ signing interactions with the same key. Following the security bound, we can now set $K := \lceil (\kappa + \log \ell)/\log N \rceil + 1$. This approach leads to the instantiations

(I) $K = 80$, $N = 4$, (II) $K = 54$, $N = 8$, (III) $K = 33$, $N = 32$.

For these, we compute the sizes of signatures and communication in a Python script (see the full version [26]). Our results are presented in Table 2.

Implementation. To demonstrate computational practicality, we prototypically implemented our scheme in C++ using above parameter settings. Our implementation uses the MCL library[5] and can be found at

https://github.com/b-wagn/Raichoo

Although our scheme is highly parallelizable, we did not implement any parallelization. To evaluate the efficiency of our implementation, we determined the average running time over 100 runs of the signing interaction (i.e. running U_1, then S, then U_2), and the verification algorithm. For our tests, we used a Intel Core i5-7200U processor @2,5 GHz with 4 cores and 8 GB of RAM, running Ubuntu 20.04.4 LTS 64-bit. Our results are presented in Table 2. In general, the table shows a tradeoff between signature size, communication complexity, and computational efficiency.

Concrete Bit Security. In contrast to [13], we compute our parameters using standardized curves and hash functions instead of estimating parameters based on the security loss. The reason for this is twofold. First, we want our numbers be consistent with our implementation and therefore have to rely on standardized

---

[5] See https://github.com/herumi/mcl.

components. Second, the estimations in [13] assume a generic mapping from the bit security of CDH to the size of an appropriate group. This is not always given. To discuss the effect of the security loss, we now assume all components are roughly 128 bit secure. Then, the guaranteed security for our scheme is roughly $128 - \log \ell = 98$ bit. This is the same for the PI-Cut-Choo scheme [13], and the standard BLS signature scheme [8].

References

1. Abe, M.: A secure three-move blind signature scheme for polynomially many signatures. In: Pfitzmann, B. (ed.) EUROCRYPT 2001. LNCS, vol. 2045, pp. 136–151. Springer, Heidelberg (2001). https://doi.org/10.1007/3-540-44987-6_9
2. Abe, M., Okamoto, T.: Provably secure partially blind signatures. In: Bellare, M. (ed.) CRYPTO 2000. LNCS, vol. 1880, pp. 271–286. Springer, Heidelberg (2000). https://doi.org/10.1007/3-540-44598-6_17
3. Agrawal, S., Kirshanova, E., Stehle, D., Yadav, A.: Can round-optimal lattice-based blind signatures be practical? Cryptology ePrint Archive, Report 2021/1565 (2021). https://eprint.iacr.org/2021/1565
4. Baldimtsi, F., Lysyanskaya, A.: On the security of one-witness blind signature schemes. In: Sako, K., Sarkar, P. (eds.) ASIACRYPT 2013. LNCS, vol. 8270, pp. 82–99. Springer, Heidelberg (2013). https://doi.org/10.1007/978-3-642-42045-0_5
5. Bellare, M., Namprempre, C., Pointcheval, D., Semanko, M.: The one-more-RSA-inversion problems and the security of Chaum's blind signature scheme. J. Cryptol. **16**(3), 185–215 (2003). https://doi.org/10.1007/s00145-002-0120-1
6. Benhamouda, F., Lepoint, T., Loss, J., Orrù, M., Raykova, M.: On the (in)security of ROS. In: Canteaut, A., Standaert, F.-X. (eds.) EUROCRYPT 2021. LNCS, vol. 12696, pp. 33–53. Springer, Cham (2021). https://doi.org/10.1007/978-3-030-77870-5_2
7. Boldyreva, A.: Threshold signatures, multisignatures and blind signatures based on the gap-diffie-hellman-group signature scheme. In: Desmedt, Y.G. (ed.) PKC 2003. LNCS, vol. 2567, pp. 31–46. Springer, Heidelberg (2003). https://doi.org/10.1007/3-540-36288-6_3
8. Boneh, D., Lynn, B., Shacham, H.: Short signatures from the weil pairing. In: Boyd, C. (ed.) ASIACRYPT 2001. LNCS, vol. 2248, pp. 514–532. Springer, Heidelberg (2001). https://doi.org/10.1007/3-540-45682-1_30
9. Brakerski, Z., Branco, P., Döttling, N., Pu, S.: Batch-OT with optimal rate. In: Dunkelman, O., Dziembowski, S. (eds.) EUROCRYPT 2022, Part II. LNCS, vol. 13276, pp. 157–186. Springer, Heidelberg (2022). https://doi.org/10.1007/978-3-031-07085-3_6
10. Camenisch, J., Groß, T.: Efficient attributes for anonymous credentials. In: Ning, P., Syverson, P.F., Jha, S. (eds.) ACM CCS 2008, pp. 345–356. ACM Press (2008). https://doi.org/10.1145/1455770.1455814
11. Camenisch, J., Lysyanskaya, A.: An efficient system for non-transferable anonymous credentials with optional anonymity revocation. In: Pfitzmann, B. (ed.) EUROCRYPT 2001. LNCS, vol. 2045, pp. 93–118. Springer, Heidelberg (2001). https://doi.org/10.1007/3-540-44987-6_7
12. Canetti, R.: Security and composition of multiparty cryptographic protocols. J. Cryptol. **13**(1), 143–202 (2000). https://doi.org/10.1007/s001459910006

13. Chairattana-Apirom, R., Hanzlik, L., Loss, J., Lysyanskaya, A., Wagner, B.: PI-cut-choo and friends: Compact blind signatures via parallel instance cut-and-choose and more. In: Dodis, Y., Shrimpton, T. (eds.) CRYPTO 2022, Part III. LNCS, vol. 13509, pp. 3–31. Springer, Heidelberg (2022). https://doi.org/10.1007/978-3-031-15982-4_1

14. Chatterjee, S., Hankerson, D., Knapp, E., Menezes, A.: Comparing two pairing-based aggregate signature schemes. Cryptology ePrint Archive, Report 2009/060 (2009). https://eprint.iacr.org/2009/060

15. Chaum, D.: Blind signatures for untraceable payments. In: Chaum, D., Rivest, R.L., Sherman, A.T. (eds.) Advances in Cryptology, pp. 199–203. Springer, Boston (1983). https://doi.org/10.1007/978-1-4757-0602-4_18

16. del Pino, R., Katsumata, S.: A new framework for more efficient round-optimal lattice-based (partially) blind signature via trapdoor sampling. In: Dodis, Y., Shrimpton, T. (eds.) CRYPTO 2022, Part II. LNCS, vol. 13508, pp. 306–336. Springer, Heidelberg (2022). https://doi.org/10.1007/978-3-031-15979-4_11

17. Fischlin, M.: Round-optimal composable blind signatures in the common reference string model. In: Dwork, C. (ed.) CRYPTO 2006. LNCS, vol. 4117, pp. 60–77. Springer, Heidelberg (2006). https://doi.org/10.1007/11818175_4

18. Fischlin, M., Schröder, D.: On the impossibility of three-move blind signature schemes. In: Gilbert, H. (ed.) EUROCRYPT 2010. LNCS, vol. 6110, pp. 197–215. Springer, Heidelberg (2010). https://doi.org/10.1007/978-3-642-13190-5_10

19. Fuchsbauer, G., Hanser, C., Slamanig, D.: Practical round-optimal blind signatures in the standard model. In: Gennaro, R., Robshaw, M. (eds.) CRYPTO 2015. LNCS, vol. 9216, pp. 233–253. Springer, Heidelberg (2015). https://doi.org/10.1007/978-3-662-48000-7_12

20. Fuchsbauer, G., Kiltz, E., Loss, J.: The algebraic group model and its applications. In: Shacham, H., Boldyreva, A. (eds.) CRYPTO 2018. LNCS, vol. 10992, pp. 33–62. Springer, Cham (2018). https://doi.org/10.1007/978-3-319-96881-0_2

21. Fuchsbauer, G., Plouviez, A., Seurin, Y.: Blind schnorr signatures and signed ElGamal encryption in the algebraic group model. In: Canteaut, A., Ishai, Y. (eds.) EUROCRYPT 2020. LNCS, vol. 12106, pp. 63–95. Springer, Cham (2020). https://doi.org/10.1007/978-3-030-45724-2_3

22. Garg, S., Gupta, D.: Efficient round optimal blind signatures. In: Nguyen, P.Q., Oswald, E. (eds.) EUROCRYPT 2014. LNCS, vol. 8441, pp. 477–495. Springer, Heidelberg (2014). https://doi.org/10.1007/978-3-642-55220-5_27

23. Garg, S., Rao, V., Sahai, A., Schröder, D., Unruh, D.: Round optimal blind signatures. In: Rogaway, P. (ed.) CRYPTO 2011. LNCS, vol. 6841, pp. 630–648. Springer, Heidelberg (2011). https://doi.org/10.1007/978-3-642-22792-9_36

24. Ghadafi, E.: Efficient round-optimal blind signatures in the standard model. In: Kiayias, A. (ed.) FC 2017. LNCS, vol. 10322, pp. 455–473. Springer, Cham (2017). https://doi.org/10.1007/978-3-319-70972-7_26

25. Grontas, P., Pagourtzis, A., Zacharakis, A., Zhang, B.: Towards everlasting privacy and efficient coercion resistance in remote electronic voting. In: Zohar, A., Eyal, I., Teague, V., Clark, J., Bracciali, A., Pintore, F., Sala, M. (eds.) FC 2018. LNCS, vol. 10958, pp. 210–231. Springer, Heidelberg (2019). https://doi.org/10.1007/978-3-662-58820-8_15

26. Hanzlik, L., Loss, J., Wagner, B.: Rai-choo! Evolving blind signatures to the next level. Cryptology ePrint Archive, Report 2022/1350 (2022). https://eprint.iacr.org/2022/1350

27. Hauck, E., Kiltz, E., Loss, J.: A modular treatment of blind signatures from identification schemes. In: Ishai, Y., Rijmen, V. (eds.) EUROCRYPT 2019. LNCS, vol. 11478, pp. 345–375. Springer, Cham (2019). https://doi.org/10.1007/978-3-030-17659-4_12

28. Hauck, E., Kiltz, E., Loss, J., Nguyen, N.K.: Lattice-based blind signatures, revisited. In: Micciancio, D., Ristenpart, T. (eds.) CRYPTO 2020. LNCS, vol. 12171, pp. 500–529. Springer, Cham (2020). https://doi.org/10.1007/978-3-030-56880-1_18

29. Heilman, E., Baldimtsi, F., Goldberg, S.: Blindly signed contracts: anonymous on-blockchain and off-blockchain bitcoin transactions. In: Clark, J., Meiklejohn, S., Ryan, P.Y.A., Wallach, D., Brenner, M., Rohloff, K. (eds.) FC 2016. LNCS, vol. 9604, pp. 43–60. Springer, Heidelberg (2016). https://doi.org/10.1007/978-3-662-53357-4_4

30. Ishai, Y., Kilian, J., Nissim, K., Petrank, E.: Extending oblivious transfers efficiently. In: Boneh, D. (ed.) CRYPTO 2003. LNCS, vol. 2729, pp. 145–161. Springer, Heidelberg (2003). https://doi.org/10.1007/978-3-540-45146-4_9

31. Juels, A., Luby, M., Ostrovsky, R.: Security of blind digital signatures. In: Kaliski, B.S. (ed.) CRYPTO 1997. LNCS, vol. 1294, pp. 150–164. Springer, Heidelberg (1997). https://doi.org/10.1007/BFb0052233

32. Kastner, J., Loss, J., Xu, J.: On pairing-free blind signature schemes in the algebraic group model. In: Hanaoka, G., Shikata, J., Watanabe, Y. (eds.) PKC 2022, Part II. LNCS, vol. 13178, pp. 468–497. Springer, Heidelberg (2022). https://doi.org/10.1007/978-3-030-97131-1_16

33. Katz, J., Loss, J., Rosenberg, M.: Boosting the security of blind signature schemes. In: Tibouchi, M., Wang, H. (eds.) ASIACRYPT 2021. LNCS, vol. 13093, pp. 468–492. Springer, Cham (2021). https://doi.org/10.1007/978-3-030-92068-5_16

34. Okamoto, T.: Provably secure and practical identification schemes and corresponding signature schemes. In: Brickell, E.F. (ed.) CRYPTO 1992. LNCS, vol. 740, pp. 31–53. Springer, Heidelberg (1993). https://doi.org/10.1007/3-540-48071-4_3

35. Okamoto, T.: Efficient blind and partially blind signatures without random oracles. In: Halevi, S., Rabin, T. (eds.) TCC 2006. LNCS, vol. 3876, pp. 80–99. Springer, Heidelberg (2006). https://doi.org/10.1007/11681878_5

36. Okamoto, T., Ohta, K.: Universal electronic cash. In: Feigenbaum, J. (ed.) CRYPTO 1991. LNCS, vol. 576, pp. 324–337. Springer, Heidelberg (1992). https://doi.org/10.1007/3-540-46766-1_27

37. Pass, R.: Limits of provable security from standard assumptions. In: Fortnow, L., Vadhan, S.P. (eds.) 43rd ACM STOC, pp. 109–118. ACM Press (2011). https://doi.org/10.1145/1993636.1993652

38. Pointcheval, D.: Strengthened security for blind signatures. In: Nyberg, K. (ed.) EUROCRYPT 1998. LNCS, vol. 1403, pp. 391–405. Springer, Heidelberg (1998). https://doi.org/10.1007/BFb0054141

39. Pointcheval, D., Stern, J.: Security arguments for digital signatures and blind signatures. J. Cryptol. 13(3), 361–396 (2000). https://doi.org/10.1007/s001450010003

40. Schnorr, C.P.: Security of blind discrete log signatures against interactive attacks. In: Qing, S., Okamoto, T., Zhou, J. (eds.) ICICS 2001. LNCS, vol. 2229, pp. 1–12. Springer, Heidelberg (2001). https://doi.org/10.1007/3-540-45600-7_1

41. Shoup, V.: Lower bounds for discrete logarithms and related problems. In: Fumy, W. (ed.) EUROCRYPT 1997. LNCS, vol. 1233, pp. 256–266. Springer, Heidelberg (1997). https://doi.org/10.1007/3-540-69053-0_18

42. Tessaro, S., Zhu, C.: Short pairing-free blind signatures with exponential security. In: Dunkelman, O., Dziembowski, S. (eds.) EUROCRYPT 2022, Part II. LNCS, vol. 13276, pp. 782–811. Springer, Heidelberg (2022). https://doi.org/10.1007/978-3-031-07085-3_27

43. Wagner, D.: A generalized birthday problem. In: Yung, M. (ed.) CRYPTO 2002. LNCS, vol. 2442, pp. 288–304. Springer, Heidelberg (2002). https://doi.org/10.1007/3-540-45708-9_19

Author Index

© International Association for Cryptologic Research 2023
C. Hazay and M. Stam (Eds.): EUROCRYPT 2023, LNCS 14008, pp. 785–786, 2023.
https://doi.org/10.1007/978-3-031-30589-4

Printed in the United States
by Baker & Taylor Publisher Services